# AAOS
### AMERICAN ACADEMY OF ORTHOPAEDIC SURGEONS

OKU

Orthopaedic Knowledge Update:

# Shoulder and Elbow

## 3

Edited by
Leesa M. Galatz, MD

*Developed by the*
**American Shoulder and Elbow Surgeons**

Published 2008 by the
American Academy of Orthopaedic Surgeons
6300 North River Road
Rosemont, IL 60018

The material presented in *Orthopaedic Knowledge Update: Shoulder and Elbow 3* has been made available by the American Academy of Orthopaedic Surgeons for educational purposes only. This material is not intended to present the only, or necessarily best, methods or procedures for the medical situations discussed, but rather is intended to represent an approach, view, statement, or opinion of the author(s) or producer(s), which may be helpful to others who face similar situations.

Some drugs or medical devices demonstrated in Academy courses or described in Academy print or electronic publications have not been cleared by the Food and Drug Administration (FDA) or have been cleared for specific uses only. The FDA has stated that it is the responsibility of the physician to determine the FDA clearance status of each drug or device he or she wishes to use in clinical practice.

Furthermore, any statements about commercial products are solely the opinion(s) of the author(s) and do not represent an Academy endorsement or evaluation of these products. These statements may not be used in advertising or for any commercial purpose.

Some of the authors or the departments with which they are affiliated have received something of value from a commercial or other party related directly or indirectly to the subject of their chapter.

Third Edition
Copyright 2008
by the American Academy of Orthopaedic Surgeons

ISBN 10: 0-89203-409-2
ISBN 13: 978-0-89203-409-3

Printed in the USA
Library of Congress Cataloging-in-Publication Data

# Acknowledgments

## Editorial Board

### Orthopaedic Knowledge Update: Shoulder and Elbow 3

Leesa M. Galatz, MD
Associate Professor of Orthopedic Surgery
Shoulder and Elbow Service
Department of Orthopedic Surgery
Washington University School of Medicine
Barnes-Jewish Hospital
St. Louis, Missouri

Jeffrey S. Abrams, MD
Attending Surgeon
University Medical Center at Princeton
Medical Director
Princeton Orthopaedic and Rehabilitative Associates
Princeton, New Jersey

Thay Q. Lee, PhD
Research Career Scientist
Orthopaedic Biomechanics Laboratory
VA Long Beach Healthcare System
Professor and Vice Chairman for Research,
  Department of Orthopaedic Surgery
Professor, Department of Biomedical Engineering
University of California Irvine
Long Beach, California

Peter J. Millett, MD
Director of Shoulder Surgery
Shoulder, Knee, Elbow, Sports Medicine
Orthopaedic Surgery
Steadman Hawkins Clinic
Vail, Colorado

Michael Pearl, MD
Shoulder and Elbow Surgery
Assistant Clinical Professor
University of Southern California
Kaiser Permanente, Los Angeles
Los Angeles, California

Matthew L. Ramsey, MD
Associate Professor of Orthopaedic Surgery
Thomas Jefferson University
Rothman Institute
Philadelphia, Pennsylvania

Herbert Resch, MD
Professor
Department of Traumatology and Sports Injuries
Paracelsus Medical University
Salzburg, Austria

Benjamin Shaffer, MD
Chief, DC Sports Medicine Institute
Department of Orthopaedics
Sibley Memorial Hospital
Washington, DC

John W. Sperling, MD
Associate Professor
Department of Orthopaedic Surgery
Mayo Clinic
Rochester, Minnesota

## American Shoulder and Elbow Surgeons

### Executive Committee

Christopher M. Jobe, MD, *President*
Evan L. Flatow, MD, *President-Elect*
W.Z. (Buz) Burkhead, Jr, MD, *Immediate Past President*
Joseph P. Iannotti, MD, PhD, *Past President*
Gerald R. Williams, Jr, MD, *Secretary-Treasurer*
Richard J. Friedman, MD, FRCS(C), *Member-at-Large*
Jonathan B. Ticker, MD, *Member-at-Large*

# Contributors

Jeffrey S. Abrams, MD
Attending Surgeon
University Medical Center at Princeton
Medical Director
Princeton Orthopaedic and Rehabilitative Associates
Princeton, New Jersey

Kenneth J. Accousti, MD
Fredericksburg Orthopaedic Associates
Fredericksburg, Virginia

Christopher S. Ahmad, MD
Assistant Professor of Orthopaedic Surgery
Center for Shoulder, Elbow, and Sports Medicine
Columbia University
New York, New York

Kimberly K. Amrami, MD
Associate Professor of Radiology
Chair, Division of Body Magnetic Resonance Imaging
Department of Radiology
Mayo Clinic
Rochester, Minnesota

James R. Andrews, MD
Orthopaedic Surgeon
Andrews Sports Medicine and Orthopaedic Center
Birmingham, Alabama

Richard L. Angelo, MD
Clinical Professor
Department of Orthopaedics
University of Washington
Seattle, Washington

Robert A. Arciero, MD
Professor, Orthopaedic Surgery
Department of Orthopaedics
University of Connecticut Health Center
Farmington, Connecticut

April D. Armstrong, MD, BSc(PT), MSc, FRCSC
Assistant Professor
Orthopaedics and Rehabilitation
Penn State Milton S. Hershey Medical Center
Hershey, Pennsylvania

F. Alan Barber, MD
Fellowship Codirector
Plano Orthopaedic and Sports Medicine Center
Plano, Texas

Allen T. Bishop, MD
Chair, Division of Hand Surgery
Mayo Clinic
Professor of Orthopaedic Surgery
Mayo Clinic College of Medicine
Rochester, MN

Theodore A. Blaine, MD
Assistant Professor of Orthopaedic Surgery
Columbia University
New York, New York

Pascal Boileau, MD
Professor
Department of Orthopaedic Surgery and
 Sports Traumatology
L'Archet 2 Hospital
Nice, France

James P. Bradley, MD
Clinical Professor
University of Pittsburgh Medical Center
Head Team Physician, Pittsburgh Steelers
Pittsburgh, Pennsylvania

Gabriel Brown, MD
Senior Resident
Orthopaedic Surgery
Columbia University Medical Center
New York, New York

Kelton M. Burbank, MD
Orthopaedic Surgeon
Department of Orthopaedic Surgery
UMass Memorial Health Care
Health Alliance Campus
Leominster, Massachusetts

Wayne Z. Burkhead, MD
Attending Orthopaedic Surgeon
Shoulder and Elbow Service
The Carrell Clinic
Dallas, Texas

Brian D. Busconi, MD
Associate Professor
Chief of Sports Medicine
Orthopaedic and Physical Rehabilitation
UMass Memorial Medical Center
Worcester, Massachusetts

Mark S. Cohen, MD
Professor
Director, Hand and Elbow Section
Director, Orthopaedic Education
Department of Orthopaedic Surgery
Rush University Medical Center
Chicago, Illinois

John G. Costouros, MD
Chief, Center for Shoulder Disorders
Department of Orthopaedic Surgery
Kaiser Permanente – Santa Teresa
San Jose, California

Alan S. Curtis, MD
Clinical Instructor
Director, Bioskills Laboratory
Department of Orthopaedic Surgery
New England Baptist Hospital
Boston, Massachusetts

Nicola A. DeAngelis, MD
Assistant Professor
University of Massachusetts Medical School
Department of Orthopaedics
Division of Sports Medicine
UMass Memorial Health Care
Worcester, Massachusetts

Richard E. Debski, PhD
Associate Professor
Department of Bioengineering
University of Pittsburgh
Pittsburgh, Pennsylvania

Kathleen A. Derwin, PhD
Assistant Staff Scientist
Biomedical Engineering
Cleveland Clinic
Cleveland, Ohio

Jeffrey R. Dugas, MD
Fellowship Director
Orthopaedic Surgery and Sports Medicine
American Sports Medicine Institute
Birmingham, Alabama

Sara Edwards, MD
Oakland Bone and Joint Specialists
Oakland, California

Larry D. Field, MD
Upper Extremity Service
Mississippi Sports Medicine and Orthopaedic Center
Jackson, Mississippi

Evan L. Flatow, MD
Laslor Professor and Chairman
Leni and Peter May Department of
  Orthopaedic Surgery
Mount Sinai Medical Center
New York, New York

Christian Gerber, MD
Professor
Chief, Department of Orthopaedic Surgery
University of Zurich, Balgrist
Zurich, Switzerland

Charles L. Getz, MD
Assistant Professor
Thomas Jefferson Medical School
Rothman Institute
Philadelphia, Pennsylvania

Gregory D. Gramstad, MD
Rebound Orthopaedics
Vancouver, Washington

Andrew Green, MD
Chief, Division of Shoulder and Elbow Surgery
Associate Professor
Orthopaedic Surgery
Brown Medical School
Providence, Rhode Island

Andreas Hartmann, MD
Department of Traumatology and Sports Injuries
Paracelsus Medical University
Salzburg, Austria

Samer S. Hasan, MD, PhD
Associate Director
Cincinnati Sports Medicine and Orthopaedic Center
Cincinnati, Ohio

George F. Hatch III, MD
Assistant Professor of Orthopaedic Surgery
Department of Orthopaedic Surgery
University of Southern California Keck School
  of Medicine
Los Angeles, California

Terese T. Horlocker, MD
Professor of Anesthesiology and Orthopaedics
Department of Anesthesiology
Mayo Clinic College of Medicine
Rochester, Minnesota

Michael J. Huang, MD
Steadman Hawkins Clinic
Vail, Colorado

G. Russell Huffman, MD
Assistant Professor
Sports, Shoulder, and Elbow
University of Pennsylvania
Philadelphia, Pennsylvania

Joseph P. Iannotti, MD, PhD
Maynard Madden Professor and Chairman
Department of Orthopaedic Surgery
The Cleveland Clinic Foundation
Cleveland, Ohio

John M. Itamura, MD
Associate Professor of Orthopaedic Surgery
Department of Orthopaedic Surgery
University of Southern California Keck School
  of Medicine
Los Angeles, California

Bernhard Jost, MD
Department of Orthopaedic Surgery
University of Zurich, Balgrist
Zurich, Switzerland

Jeffrey I. Kauffman, MD
Sacramento Knee and Sports Medicine
Sacramento, California

Jay D. Keener, MD
Assistant Professor
Shoulder and Elbow Service
Department of Orthopaedic Surgery
Washington University
St. Louis, Missouri

Graham J.W. King, MD, MSc, FRCSC
Professor
Department of Surgery
University of Western Ontario
Hand and Upper Limb Centre
St. Joseph's Health Centre
London, Ontario, Canada

Raymond A. Klug, MD
Fellow
Department of Orthopaedic Surgery
Mount Sinai Medical Center
New York, New York

Sumant G. Krishnan, MD
Attending Orthopaedic Surgeon
Shoulder and Elbow Service
The Carrell Clinic
Dallas, Texas

William N. Levine, MD
Vice Chairman and Professor
Orthopaedic Surgery
Columbia University Medical Center
New York, New York

Orr Limpisvasti, MD
Orthopaedic Surgeon
Kerlan-Jobe Orthopaedic Clinic
Los Angeles, California

Kenneth C. Lin, MD
Fellow
Shoulder and Elbow Service
The Carrell Clinic
Dallas, Texas

Ian K.Y. Lo, MD, FRCSC
Orthopaedic Surgeon
Department of Surgery
University of Calgary
Calgary, Alberta, Canada

Robert G. Marx, MD
Orthopaedic Surgery
Hospital for Special Surgery
New York, New York

Augustus D. Mazzocca, MD
Assistant Professor
Department of Orthopaedic Surgery
University of Connecticut
Farmington, Connecticut

Jesse McCarron, MD
Clinical Associate
Department of Orthopaedic Surgery
The Cleveland Clinic Foundation
Cleveland, Ohio

Patrick J. McMahon, MD
McMahon Orthopaedics and Rehabilitation
Adjunct Associate Professor, University of Pittsburgh
Pittsburgh, Pennsylvania

Dominik C. Meyer, MD
Department of Orthopaedic Surgery
University of Zurich, Balgrist
Zurich, Switzerland

Peter J. Millett, MD
Director of Shoulder Surgery
Shoulder, Knee, Elbow, Sports Medicine
Orthopaedic Surgery
Steadman Hawkins Clinic
Vail, Colorado

Daniel Molé, MD
Professor and Chairman
Clinique de Traumatologie et d'Orthopédie
Nancy, France

Lionel Neyton, MD
Centre Médical Santy
Lyon, France

Gregory P. Nicholson, MD
Assistant Professor
Department of Orthopaedic Surgery
Rush University Medical Center
Chicago, Illinois

Jan Nowak, MD, PhD
Shoulder Unit
Department of Orthopedics
University Hospital
Uppsala, Sweden

Carol A. Parise, PhD
Research Scientist
Sutter Institute for Medical Research
Sacramento, California

Maxwell C. Park, MD
Southern California Permanente Medical Group
Department of Orthopaedic Surgery
Woodland Hills Medical Center
Los Angeles, California

Bradford O. Parsons, MD
Assistant Professor
Department of Orthopaedic Surgery
Mount Sinai Medical Center
New York, New York

Michael Pearl, MD
Shoulder and Elbow Surgery
Assistant Clinical Professor
University of Southern California
Kaiser Permanente, Los Angeles
Los Angeles, California

Kevin E. Peltier, MD
Northern Virginia Orthopaedic Specialists
Prince William Hospital System
Manassas, Virginia

Brent Ponce, MD
Assistant Professor
Orthopaedic Surgery
University of Alabama at Birmingham
Birmingham, Alabama

James Randall Ramsey, MD
Upper Extremity Service
Mississippi Sports Medicine and Orthopaedic Center
Jackson, Mississippi

Matthew L. Ramsey, MD
Associate Professor of Orthopaedic Surgery
Thomas Jefferson University
Rothman Institute
Philadelphia, Pennsylvania

Michael M. Reinold, PT, DPT, ATC, CSCS
Rehabilitation Coordinator and
  Assistant Athletic Trainer
Boston Red Sox Baseball Club
Coordinator of Rehabilitation Research
  and Education
Department of Orthopaedic Surgery
  Division of Sports Medicine
Massachusetts General Hospital
Boston, Massachusetts

Herbert Resch, MD
Professor
Department of Traumatology and Sports Injuries
Paracelsus Medical University
Salzburg, Austria

David Ring, MD, PhD
Medical Director and Director of Research
Orthopaedic Hand and Upper Extremity Service
Massachusetts General Hospital
Boston, Massachusetts

Mark W. Rodosky, MD
Chief, Division of Shoulder Surgery and
  Sports Medicine
University of Pittsburgh
Pittsburgh, Pennsylvania

P.M. Rommens, MD, PhD
Professor and Director
Department of Trauma Surgery
University Hospitals of the Johannes Gutenberg
  University
Mainz, Germany

Richard K.N. Ryu, MD
Private Practice
Santa Barbara, California

Joaquin Sanchez-Sotelo, MD, PhD
Senior Associate Consultant and Assistant Professor
Department of Orthopaedic Surgery
Mayo Clinic
Rochester, Minnesota

Felix H. Savoie III, MD
Professor
Department of Orthopaedic Surgery
Tulane University School of Medicine
New Orleans, Louisiana

Benjamin Shaffer, MD
Chief, DC Sports Medicine Institute
Department of Orthopaedics
Sibley Memorial Hospital
Washington, DC

Seth L. Sherman, MD
Orthopaedic Surgery
Hospital for Special Surgery
New York, New York

Alexander Y. Shin, MD
Professor of Orthopaedic Surgery
Consultant, Department of Orthopaedic Surgery
Mayo Clinic
Rochester, Minnesota

François Sirveaux, MD, PhD
Clinique de Traumatologie et d'Orthopédie
Nancy, France

Adam M. Smith, MD
West Tennessee Bone and Joint Clinic
Jackson, Tennessee

Stephen Sohmer, MD, FRCSC
Orthopaedic Surgery
Campbell River and District Hospital
Campbell River, British Columbia, Canada

John W. Sperling, MD
Associate Professor
Department of Orthopaedic Surgery
Mayo Clinic
Rochester, Minnesota

Robert J. Spinner, MD
Professor
Departments of Neurosurgery, Orthopaedics,
 and Anatomy
Peripheral Nerve Surgery
Mayo Clinic
Rochester, Minnesota

Robert Z. Tashjian, MD
Assistant Professor
Department of Orthopaedics
University of Utah School of Medicine
Salt Lake City, Utah

Stavros Thomopoulos, PhD
Assistant Professor
Orthopaedic Surgery and Biomedical Engineering
Washington University
St. Louis, Missouri

Fotios P. Tjoumakaris, MD
Attending Physician
Cape Orthopaedics
Cape Regional Medical Center
Cape May Court House, New Jersey

John M. Tokish, MD
Chief of Sports Medicine
Head Team Physician
Orthopaedic Surgery
US Air Force Academy
Colorado Springs, Colorado

Robert G. Turner, MB, BCh, FRCS
Clinical Fellow
Hand and Upper Limb Centre
St. Joseph's Health Centre
London, Ontario, Canada

Jon J.P. Warner, MD
Chief, The Harvard Shoulder Service
Professor of Orthopaedic Surgery
Massachusetts General Department of
 Orthopaedic Surgery
Harvard Medical School
Boston, Massachusetts

Stephen C. Weber, MD
Sacramento Knee and Sports Medicine
Sacramento, California

Kevin E. Wilk, PT, DPT
Clinical Director
Vice President of Education, Physiotherapy
Champion Sports Medicine
Birmingham, Alabama

Gerald R. Williams Jr, MD
Professor of Orthopaedic Surgery
Thomas Jefferson University
Rothman Institute
Philadelphia, Pennsylvania

Ken Yamaguchi, MD
Sam and Marilyn Fox Distinguished Professor of
 Orthopaedic Surgery
Chief, Shoulder and Elbow Surgery
Department of Orthopaedic Surgery
Washington University School of Medicine
St. Louis, Missouri

# Preface

The field of shoulder and elbow surgery continues to evolve and expand. The last several years have witnessed a multitude of developments in all aspects of shoulder surgery and basic science. The amount of new information is increasingly difficult to keep up with, as the number of new published articles increases each year, not only in our own journals but also in journals of sports medicine, arthroscopy, trauma, and arthroplasty. This book is written to update general orthopaedic surgeons and shoulder specialists, as well as residents and fellows in training, as to the latest published information in shoulder and elbow surgery, in a concise and easily readable fashion.

Several additions and changes from the preceding edition reflect the current trends in the field. The section on basic science has a new chapter on the rotator cuff, as there has been a recent explosion of interest in the area of tendon healing. The other chapters contain the newest developments in other areas of shoulder biology and biomechanics. The instability section contains additional consideration of athletic injuries. The rotator cuff section has a new chapter on biologic augmentation of rotator cuff healing, with an in-depth, unbiased discussion of the science behind currently marketed devices and the direction in which this field of study is headed. The separate arthroscopy section was retained. Surgical techniques have changed dramatically, and new procedures have evolved. This section allows a more in-depth, practical approach to this knowledge. The arthroplasty section contains the latest information on glenoid resurfacing and reverse shoulder arthroplasty, as well as the complicated topic of arthroplasty for fracture. These new developments over the past few years have revolutionized arthroplasty in the shoulder. The strong international influence in the trauma section gives an extraordinary modern perspective on these challenging problems. The elbow section encompasses the rapidly increasing body of knowledge available on biomechanics and treatment options. The section on miscellaneous shoulder topics has been revised and reorganized to include important new subjects. The authors of several chapters in this section offer a multidisciplinary perspective.

I would like to thank all of the authors for their time and effort throughout the production of this book. Their efforts are truly greatly appreciated. The section editors comprise a strong team, and I am grateful for their coordinating and editing efforts. In addition, I would like to thank the publications staff of the American Academy of Orthopaedic Surgeons for their tireless work throughout the editing and production of this volume. Specifically, I would like to acknowledge Deborah Williams, Lisa Moore, and Marilyn Fox, PhD. I am honored to have been chosen by the Executive Committee of the American Shoulder and Elbow Surgeons to edit this book and am grateful to have been afforded the opportunity to work on this important contribution on behalf of the ASES and AAOS. Lastly, I would like to express my gratitude to my husband and son. Their patience, love, and support throughout this process made it all worthwhile. I know that this book will be a useful resource for many students at all levels in the study of the shoulder and elbow.

*Leesa M. Galatz, MD*
*Editor*

# Table of Contents

WITHDRAWN

## Section 3 The Rotator Cuff

**Section Editor:** Leesa M. Galatz, MD

## Section 4 Arthroscopy

**Section Editors:** Jeffrey S. Abrams, MD
Benjamin Shaffer, MD

## Section 5 Arthritis and Arthroplasty

**Section Editor:** Michael Pearl, MD

## Section 6 Trauma and Fractures

**Section Editor:** Herbert Resch, MD

**American Academy of Orthopaedic Surgeons**

## Section 7 Elbow Trauma, Fracture, and Reconstruction
Section Editor: Matthew L. Ramsey, MD

## Section 8: Miscellaneous Shoulder Topics
Section Editor: John W. Sperling, MD

# Section 1

# Basic Science

Section Editor
Thay Q. Lee, PhD

# Chapter 1

# Anatomy and Function of the Shoulder Structures

Maxwell C. Park, MD

## Introduction

The shoulder can be described as a set of active and passive stabilizers surrounding an osseous scaffold. The structures that generate glenohumeral shoulder motion represent a complex balance of activity, stability, and synchronicity. Much is still not understood, and the potential for advancement in shoulder surgery is great. This chapter addresses human shoulder anatomy, especially recently acquired knowledge, pertaining to diagnoses and treatments frequently encountered by the shoulder surgeon.

## Osseous Anatomy

### Proximal Humerus

The proximal humerus consists of an ellipsoidal humeral head covered with hyaline articular cartilage. The anatomic neck is marked by a bony transition from cartilage to capsular attachment and tendinous insertion. The tuberosities are lateral to the anatomic neck. The lesser tuberosity contains the subscapularis insertion, or footprint, and the greater tuberosity delimits the supraspinatus, infraspinatus, and teres minor insertions. The greater tuberosity has superior, middle, and inferior facets.[1] The insertions on these tuberosities create an interconnected cuff of tendons that surrounds the humeral head. The transition to the humeral shaft, just distal to the tuberosities, marks the surgical neck. The bicipital groove is flanked by both tuberosities and provides a stabilizing path for the long head of the biceps tendon (LHBT). The soft tissues surrounding the proximal humerus consist of active and passive stabilizers that coordinate glenohumeral balance.

The morphologic measurements of the proximal humerus vary greatly and are primarily related to a person's overall size. One study used three-dimensional computer analysis to assess the intramedullary and extramedullary morphology of 30 pairs of proximal humeri.[2] Head retroversion averaged 19° (range, 9° to 31°); head inclination, or neck-shaft angle, 41° (34° to 47°); head radius, 23 mm (17 mm to 28 mm); head thickness, 19 mm (15 mm to 24 mm); medial head center off-

set, 7 mm (4 mm to 12 mm); and posterior head center offset, 2 mm (–1 mm to 8 mm). These findings underscore the importance of individualizing the restoration of anatomy during humeral head arthroplasty. Because of the extreme variation in proximal humeral anatomy, general guidelines have only limited use.

During reconstructive procedures, it is important for the surgeon to recognize the anatomic geometry of the proximal humerus. For example, restoring the correct prosthetic anatomy during arthroplasty has significant clinical implications for range of motion, kinematics, and impingement.[3] Inferior malpositioning of more than 4 mm can create increased subacromial contact, and an offset of 8 mm in any direction compromises passive range of motion. Minimizing subacromial contact and maximizing glenohumeral motion after humeral head replacement can be achieved with anatomic reconstruction of the humeral head–humeral shaft offset to within 4 mm.[3]

The bicipital groove is commonly used during surgery as a bony landmark of the proximal humerus[4,5] (Figure 1). In a CT analysis of embalmed cadavers, the bicipital groove was measured at both the anatomic and surgical necks relative to the transepicondylar axis at the elbow.[4] As the bicipital groove coursed distally, it was found to internally rotate; the mean change in rotation was 15.9° (SD ± 6.8°; range, 4° to 32°). A similar study found a 9.3° difference (range, –3° to 22.5°) between the bicipital groove at the anatomic neck and the surgical neck.[5] The shoulder surgeon must appreciate this variability whenever the bicipital groove is used as a landmark in humeral head replacement. It is a particularly relevant factor during humeral head replacement involving a three-part or four-part fracture, when the proximal bicipital groove often cannot be used as a reliable landmark. Placing the lateral fin of the prosthesis either 9 mm or 12 mm posterior to the bicipital groove at the anatomic neck has been recommended.[6,7] Using the bicipital groove at the surgical neck as a landmark may create excessive retroversion of the humeral head. Therefore, bicipital groove anatomy is a potential guide when individualizing anatomic restoration during arthroplasty.

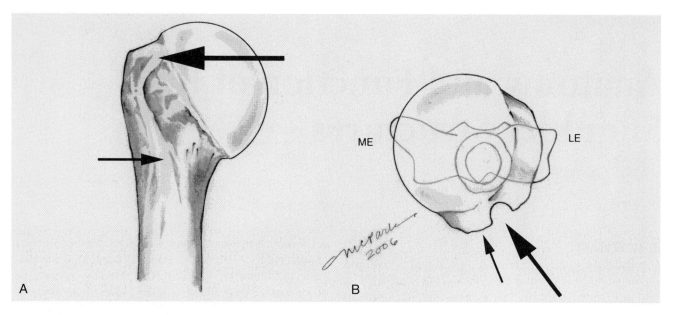

**Figure 1** Coronal and axial views of the proximal humerus. **A,** Coronal view, showing the internal rotation of the bicipital groove as it courses distally from the anatomic neck (*large arrow*) to the surgical neck (*small arrow*). **B,** Axial view, showing the overlapping humeral head, shaft, and epicondyles. LE = lateral epicondyle, ME = medial epicondyle. (*Courtesy of Maxwell C. Park, MD, Los Angeles, CA.*)

Although the bicipital groove stabilizes the LHBT, the tuberosities that flank the groove determine the rotator cuff length and tension relationships and, therefore, shoulder function. The importance of restoring tuberosity anatomy has been highlighted by biomechanical studies. Medial-to-lateral tuberosity displacement in a four-part fracture model altered kinematics and increased the torque necessary to externally rotate the humerus 50°.[8] This finding is relevant to the use of the bicipital groove as a landmark for prosthesis placement, because after the prosthesis orientation is determined, the tuberosity position is obligatory. In another four-part fracture model, 10 mm of inferior tuberosity placement resulted in significantly more superior glenohumeral force displacement, which suggests a compromise in the mechanical advantage of abduction.[9] These studies provide a biomechanical rationale for optimizing the restoration of proximal humeral anatomy during arthroplasty, which can be difficult with a four-part fracture.

The extreme variability of the osseous proximal humerus anatomy is an important reason for using modular components in humeral head arthroplasty. In addition, individualized anatomic bony restoration creates the most favorable environment for soft-tissue function.

### Glenoid

The glenoid functions as the socket of the glenohumeral joint. It projects laterally from the scapular body, to which it is attached. The glenoid is pear shaped, with a wider inferior half. The average superior-inferior dimension of the glenoid was found to be 39 mm (±3.7 mm; range, 30 mm to 48 mm); the anteroposterior dimension of the lower half of the glenoid, 29 mm (±3.1 mm; 21 mm to 35 mm); and the anteroposterior dimension of the upper half at its midpoint, 23 mm (±2.7 mm; 18 mm to 30 mm). The ratio of the anteroposterior dimension of the lower half of the glenoid to that of the upper half was 1:0.8 (±0.01).[10] Recognition of the normal pear shape of the glenoid can be useful in analyzing bony glenohumeral instability. In a study of 344 scapulae (patient age, 20 to 30 years), the glenoid had an average inclination of approximately 4.2° (range, −7° to 15.8°; a positive value denotes a superior inclination, and a negative value, an inferior inclination).[11] The glenoid was retroverted an average of 1.23° (±3.5°; range, 9.5° anteverted to 10.5° retroverted). Like proximal humerus anatomy, glenoid anatomy varies greatly among individuals.

The complex and variable anatomy of the glenoid presents a challenge in the face of pathologic bone loss. The effect of glenoid malpositioning on humeral head stability was biomechanically tested in eight normal cadaver shoulders.[12] The glenoid component was retroverted 15° to simulate the posterior glenoid bone loss often seen with osteoarthritis, and modular components were used to test the proximal humeral stem in anatomic and 15°-anteverted versions. Three humeral rotation positions were tested with a servohydraulic testing system, and energy and peak load were analyzed to assess joint stability. The study found that an anteverted humeral component could not stabilize the shoulder or compensate for a severely retroverted glenoid, and, therefore, that reaming the glenoid to neutral version might be preferable to altering humeral version. It is unknown whether these findings would be altered by the

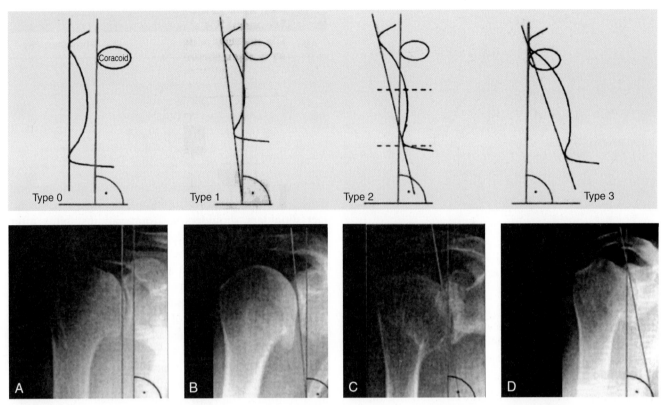

**Figure 2** Pathoanatomy of glenoid wear in the coronal plane, using the classification of glenoid inclination. **A,** Type 0: The coracoid base line and glenoid line are parallel, orthogonal to the inferior border of the radiograph. **B,** Type 1: The coracoid base line and glenoid line intersect below the glenoid. **C,** Type 2: The coracoid base line and glenoid line intersect between the inferior glenoid rim and middle glenoid. **D,** Type 3: The coracoid base line and glenoid line intersect above the coracoid base. *(Reproduced with permission from Habermeyer P, Magosch P, Luz V, Lichtenberg S: Three-dimensional glenoid deformity in patients with osteoarthritis: A radiographic analysis. J Bone Joint Surg Am 2006;88:1301-1307).*

presence of a patulous posterior capsule, which is often encountered in conjunction with posterior glenoid bone loss. A study using a three-dimensional finite element model of the shoulder found that glenoid retroversion greater than 10° can lead to major biomechanical alterations and possibly increase the risk of loosening.[13] The surgeon should consider forgoing glenoid resurfacing if retroversion cannot be corrected below 10°.

The pathoanatomy of osteoarthritis can lead to posteroinferior glenoid erosion and wear. Posterior glenoid wear, as shown on transverse-plane imaging, is a recognized measure of pathoanatomy that must be considered when performing arthroplasty.[14,15] Glenoid inclination, as seen in the coronal plane, is another useful tool for surgical decision making. Standard radiographs of 100 consecutive patients with primary osteoarthritis were compared with radiographs of 100 otherwise healthy patients with shoulder pain. Inferior glenoid erosion was classified by the degree of inclination to represent increasing inferior glenoid wear (Figure 2). In type 0, the mean angle of inclination was 1.7° (range, −7° to 7°); in type I, −7.1° (−16° to −2°); in type II, −16° (−32° to −5°); and in type III, −17.7° (−28° to −12°). The authors recommended normalizing type II and type III glenoid inclination, as well as retroversion of more than

15°, for glenoid replacement, for the purpose of improving uneven stress distributions across the implant.[16] However, excessive medialization should be avoided.

## Labral and Ligament Anatomy
### Inferior Glenohumeral Ligament Complex
The inferior glenohumeral ligament complex (IGHLC) is attached to the glenoid in the 7-o'clock to 9-o'clock and 3-o'clock to 5-o'clock positions, in a right shoulder. The collagen fibers are directly affixed to the rigid fibrocartilaginous labrum and more medially to the periosteum along the glenoid neck. An anterior thickening, called the superior or anterior band, is present. A posterior capsular thickening or band was found in 63% of specimens.[17,18]

Dissection of the IGHLC attachment on the humeral side in 12 cadaver shoulders revealed two attachment geometries: the split type (58%) and the broad type (42%).[19] Both extend inferiorly 2 cm from the articular surface at approximately the 4 o'clock and 8 o'clock positions. The split type is a capsular bifurcation having internal and external folds with an interposed loose connective tissue. The broad type does not have separate folds (Figure 3). Failure to release the external fold may tether the capsular pouch in a patient with multidirectional instability. Releasing the entire capsule

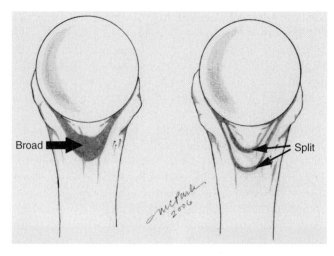

**Figure 3** Broad and split types of humeral attachment to the inferior glenohumeral ligament complex. *(Courtesy of Maxwell C. Park, MD, Los Angeles, CA.)*

**Table 1 | Types of Biceps Tendon Origin**

| Type | Origin | Frequency (%) |
|---|---|---|
| I | Posterosuperior labrum | 22 |
| II | Anterosuperior and posterosuperior labrum (primarily posterior) | 33 |
| III | Anterior and posterior labrum (equally) | 37 |
| IV | Superior labrum (primarily anterior) | 8 |

from the humeral attachment, particularly posteriorly, may be necessary during a capsulorrhaphy.

The tissue between the anterior and posterior capsular thickenings has been likened to a hammock, with the glenoid labrum and humerus acting as posts that swing or rotate with humeral rotation to provide static stability with reciprocal load sharing. During abduction and external rotation, such as in overhead throwing, the anterior complex resists anterior translation; during abduction and internal rotation, the posterior complex resists posterior translation.

The biomechanical parameters of the three IGHLC anatomic regions (superior band, anterior axillary pouch, and posterior axillary pouch) were characterized by testing bone-ligament-bone segments at relatively low strain rates. This study highlighted the significance of permanent stretching of the capsule.[20] An isolated Bankart lesion caused only minor humeral head translation,[21] suggesting that IGHLC plastic deformations are required to create pathologic recurrent instability. Another study found unrecoverable IGHLC strain as a result of cyclic loading and thereby supported the hypothesis that repeated subfailure strain, such as from an overuse injury, can lead to irreversible stretching of the IGHLC and contribute to the development of acquired shoulder instability.[22] Testing of specimens in the apprehension position (abduction and external rotation) with higher strain rates revealed that unrecoverable capsular elongation was greatest in the ligament midsubstance (mean, 0.53 mm) and smallest at the humeral insertion (mean, 0.04 mm).[23] The low absolute strain values suggest that only slight plication of the anteroinferior capsulolabral structures may be necessary to restore capsular anatomy after a primary instability injury.

In a study of six cadaver shoulders, glenohumeral translation and external rotation were measured in intact shoulders, shoulders with anterior instability after capsular stretching, and shoulders after 10-mm anteroinferior arthroscopic suture plication.[24] Arthroscopic plication, which involved doubling the effective bumper height of the labrum, was found to effectively reduce anterior translation and external rotation while shifting the glenohumeral center of rotation posteriorly and inferiorly. This finding suggests that arthroscopic techniques have the potential to restore functional IGHLC anatomy. Additional studies are required to increase understanding of surgical restoration of anatomic tension after traumatic injury or overuse.

The IGHLC, with its variable anatomy, provides a static restraint to excessive humeral head translation. Its function is determined by arm position. Biomechanical findings with respect to IGHLC pathoanatomy suggest that midsubstance deformations should be addressed. Arthroscopic techniques have the potential to restore normal static stability, and a deeper understanding of the pathoanatomy may improve the ability to restore normal function using individualized surgical techniques.

### Superior Labrum

The labrum is a triangular rim of fibrocartilaginous tissue surrounding the glenoid. The labrum deepens the socket by 9 mm in the superior-inferior dimension and by 5 mm in the anterior-posterior plane, which represents as much as 50% of the glenoid socket depth.[25] The labrum probably provides some static translational stability to the humeral head. Superiorly, the LHBT shares its origin with labral tissue and the supraglenoid tubercle.

Appreciation of anatomic labral variation is important in discerning true pathoanatomy that may require surgical repair.[26] A cordlike middle glenohumeral ligament with an associated sublabral foramen is an anatomic variant that does not require repair, as is an isolated sublabral foramen. A meniscoid labrum is another normal anatomic variant. Four anatomic variants of the biceps tendon origin have been described in relation to the superior labrum[27] (Table 1).

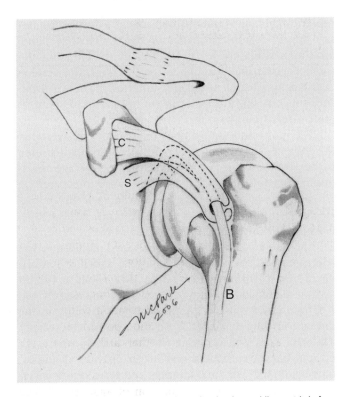

**Figure 4** The coracohumeral ligament and superior glenohumeral ligament help form a sling for the proximal long head of the biceps tendon. At the level of the bicipital groove, the CHL and SGHL have converged. B = long head of the biceps tendon, C = coracohumeral ligament, S = superior glenohumeral ligament. (*Courtesy of Maxwell C. Park, MD, Los Angeles, CA.*)

A laboratory study found that a type II superior labrum anterior and posterior (SLAP) tear can create statistically significant glenohumeral translation and increased range of motion.[28] Six cadaver shoulders underwent arthroscopic superior labrum–biceps tendon release. Rotational and translational glenohumeral motions were measured before and after type II SLAP tear simulation, as well as after arthroscopic repair of the lesion. Creation of a SLAP lesion resulted in significant increases in total range of motion, external rotation, internal rotation, anteroposterior translation, and inferior translation ($P < 0.05$). Translation and rotation were found to increase only slightly using a static loading model. Arthroscopic repair using two suture anchors on either side of the biceps origin was found to restore glenohumeral stability to approximately the pretear state.[28]

## Rotator Interval

The rotator interval is a triangular space within the glenohumeral joint capsule. It is bordered by the coracoid at its base and by the supraspinatus and subscapularis muscles, which converge to an apex laterally. The coracoid separates the subscapularis from the supraspinatus medial to the glenohumeral joint. These muscles insert laterally, converging over the intertubercular sulcus. The rotator interval consists of the coracohumeral ligament (CHL)

superficially and the superior glenohumeral ligament (SGHL) in a deeper layer. The LHBT traverses this space intra-articularly from the supraglenoid tubercle, exiting the intertubercular groove distally. In an examination of 32 cadaver shoulders, the area of the rotator interval triangle was found to be significantly larger in male than in female specimens. The dimensions changed with rotation, becoming smaller with internal rotation.[29]

It is recommended that rotator interval closure be performed with the arm externally rotated because imbricating the rotator interval with the arm internally rotated may lead to overtightening, with loss of external rotation. In addition, the medial aspect of the rotator interval was shown to control humeral head inferior translation in the adducted arm.[30] In clinical practice, a sulcus sign with an adducted externally rotated arm suggests rotator interval insufficiency. Rotator interval imbrication should be considered in a patient with multidirectional instability.

The rotator interval is important for LHBT stability.[30-32] The CHL, SGHL, supraspinatus, and subscapularis are laterally interdigitated, contributing to a sling that supports the LHBT within its groove. The CHL is attached proximally at the coracoid and fans out distally over the tuberosities, converging with the supraspinatus and subscapularis insertions. A deep layer of fibers from the CHL is primarily attached to the greater tuberosity, although a lesser component is attached to the lesser tuberosity, forming an anterior band that covers the LHBT.[30] The SGHL is attached proximally to the superior labrum and supraglenoid tubercle and is attached distally to the lesser tuberosity, forming an indissociable structure with the CHL (Figure 4). The CHL forms a roof over the LHBT, and the SGHL forms a floor; the anterior convergence of the CHL and SGHL forms a reflection pulley for the LHBT, which is also in contact with the subscapularis.[32] This anatomy is critical to appreciate with respect to "hidden" lesions where the LHBT subluxates or dislocates deep to the subscapularis, invisible from the bursal side. A histoanatomic study performed on 13 cadaver specimens indicated that, based on collagen fiber orientation, the SGHL contributes to most of the fibrous sling that stabilizes the intra-articular portion of the LHBT.[31]

The most distal aspect of the rotator interval has been described as a convergence and interdigitation of subscapularis and supraspinatus tendon fibers over the biceps tendon.[33,34] A recent study questioned the presence of a transverse humeral ligament at the area of this interdigitation.[34] In 14 cadaver shoulders, MRI analysis followed by gross and histologic examination revealed that tissue covering the bicipital groove formed a sling primarily of subscapularis tendon fibers, with less important contributions from the supraspinatus tendon and CHL. The subscapularis tendon fibers were found to divide and form a sling around the biceps tendon where it leaves the glenohumeral joint at the proximal part of the bicipital groove. This finding indicates that an isolated deep rupture of the subscapularis tendon can explain a hidden LHBT lesion and that a concomitant subscapularis tendon tear should be ruled out when an LHBT lesion is encountered.

Arthroscopic techniques have been developed to tension the rotator interval in patients with instability. Studies to quantify the effect of capsulorrhaphy found that external rotation can be significantly reduced with rotator interval imbrication. One study found that interval closure with the arm externally rotated 30° significantly decreased flexion (mean, 6°), external rotation (mean, 10°), and anterior translation (mean, 3 mm) in the adducted shoulder.[35] In another study, anterosuperior capsular plication performed with the humerus in neutral rotation significantly decreased external rotation by 30° with the arm adducted.[36] Further study is required to understand the effect of rotator interval imbrication on specific pathoanatomies.

In an anatomic study to assess arthroscopic release of the rotator interval and CHL, 15 cadaver specimens were dissected and studied.[37] The rotator interval was found to be 3 mm to 4 mm away from the coracoacromial ligament, with glenohumeral joint distention to 40 mm Hg. The coracoacromial ligament served as a useful landmark for complete release of the CHL. Release from the supraspinatus to the subscapularis resulted in complete resection of the CHL in all specimens. Intraarticular arthroscopic release of the rotator interval was found to safely and completely release the CHL, if the dissection was taken superficially to the level of the coracoacromial ligament. Release of the CHL is particularly relevant during capsular release for adhesive capsulitis.

The anatomy of the rotator interval is complex. Increased understanding should lead to reliable, reproducible capsulorrhaphy techniques for patients with instability and help the surgeon appreciate hidden lesions and treat them appropriately. In addition, this area can be safely released arthroscopically in patients with adhesive capsulitis.

## Muscle and Tendon Anatomy
### Rotator Cuff
The rotator cuff consists of four muscles that surround and dynamically compress the humeral head into the glenoid socket. The subscapularis muscle originates on the anterior scapula and inserts into the lesser tuberosity of the proximal humerus. The supraspinatus originates within the fossa superior to the scapular spine, the infraspinatus originates from the fossa inferior to the scapular spine, and the teres minor originates from the dorsal surface of the axillary scapular border; these three muscles all insert into the greater tuberosity.

The anatomy and histology of the posterior rotator interval have implications for release during rotator cuff

repair.[38] The supraspinatus consists of a fusiform anterior muscle region that has a physiologic cross-sectional area approximately 2.5 times greater than that of the smaller posterior straplike muscle region; the tendon cross-sectional area is smaller anteriorly. This relationship suggests that the anterior supraspinatus encounters more stress than the posterior region.[39]

The insertional footprint of the rotator cuff has been the subject of recent attention. This footprint is the area to be restored during a surgical repair. Average maximum insertion lengths and widths were measured in 20 cadaver specimens for the subscapularis (40 mm × 20 mm), supraspinatus (23 mm × 16 mm), infraspinatus (29 mm × 19 mm), and teres minor (29 mm × 21 mm).[40] In other studies, the anterior-posterior dimension of the supraspinatus insertion averaged 22.5 mm (±3.1 mm)[1] or 25 mm.[41] The medial-to-lateral dimension of the insertion averaged 12.7 mm (±6.3 mm) in one study[42] and 12.3 mm (±0.4 mm) in another.[43] The variability in the dimensions largely depends on the size of the patient. The supraspinatus footprint ends posteriorly where the normal bare area begins, and it can provide an important landmark. The infraspinatus and teres minor insertions mark the lateral extent of the bare area.[40] The greater tuberosity has three facets (superior, middle, and inferior) on which the rotator cuff inserts.[1] The supraspinatus shares its footprint with the infraspinatus on the anterior aspect of the middle facet; therefore, repair of the supraspinatus may involve an obligatory repair of the infraspinatus. A "transosseous-equivalent" rotator cuff repair technique was shown to restore greater anatomic footprint contact and provide greater ultimate strength, compared with a double-row repair technique.[44] A follow-up study using a dynamic 30° external rotation arc found a significantly higher yield strength for the transosseous-equivalent repair than for the double-row repair technique.[45]

Analysis of rotator cuff origins and insertions highlights their lines of action and helps predict their function. The subscapularis internally rotates the humeral head in relation to the scapula, and the infraspinatus and teres minor externally rotate the proximal humerus. The primary function of the supraspinatus is to initiate the first 30° of forward elevation and assist the deltoid in the first 90° of abduction. The supraspinatus also plays a role in rotation; the center of rotation relative to the supraspinatus changes depending on the initial position of the humerus. With a starting position of neutral or external rotation, the supraspinatus externally rotates the humerus; in internal rotation, the supraspinatus internally rotates the humeral head.[46,47] Dynamic rotational effects on rotator cuff repair have not been studied in most biomechanical studies; instead, load testing has been performed with the humerus fixed.

A comparison of six matched pairs of cadaver shoulders elucidated the effect of dynamic external rotation

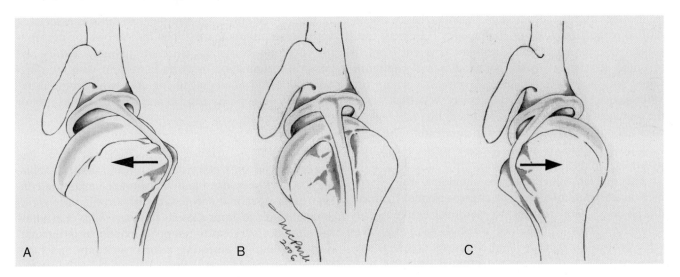

**Figure 5** The LHBT at the extremes of humeral rotation, providing a centering force vector (*arrows*) for the humeral head on the glenoid. **A,** External rotation. **B,** Neutral rotation. **C,** Internal rotation. (*Courtesy of Maxwell C. Park, MD, Los Angeles, CA.*)

on a supraspinatus single-row repair, using two suture anchors and four simple suture configurations.[48] Based on electromyographic data, a relatively low load for cyclic testing (60 N) was used to simulate actual loads that may be encountered during postsurgical exercises.[49,50] The anterior supraspinatus tendon was found to undergo significantly more strain and gap formation with external rotation (at yield strength, 1.95 mm [±0.74 mm]) than with the humerus fixed (1.06 mm [±0.54 mm], $P = 0.0083$).[48] The small gap formation confirms that a single-row repair can withstand the relatively low loads expected during rehabilitation after surgery. Approximately 2 mm of gap formation could represent one sixth (17%) of the footprint in the medial-lateral dimension, which may be significant.[42,43] The posterior tendon underwent negative strain (compression) with external rotation. For tested repairs allowing external rotation, gap formation and tendon strain were significantly greater in the anterior tendon than in the posterior tendon at both 30° external rotation and yield load ($P < 0.05$). No such differences appeared in the specimens tested with the humerus fixed.[48] This comparison suggests better load sharing between anterior and posterior tendon regions during load sharing with the humerus fixed. Strain and gap formation differences should be considered as new repair constructs are developed to restore normal anatomy. A study using a rat model found that repair tension (strain) has adverse effects on rotator cuff tendon-to-bone healing.[51]

### Long Head of the Biceps Tendon

The LHBT originates on the supraglenoid tubercle and has an intimate association with the superior labrum. The LHBT exits the glenohumeral joint via the bicipital groove. The small head originates at the coracoid, and the muscle belly from each origin converges to form the biceps muscle proper. The insertion of the biceps is ultimately attached to the proximal radius on its tuberosity. Because the LHBT is associated with a muscle that acts across both the glenohumeral and ulnohumeral joints, it has been difficult to isolate its dynamic functional role in the shoulder.

Six cadaver shoulders were tested before and during biceps tendon release and after repair of a simulated type II SLAP tear.[52] The tear was created by releasing the biceps anchor 8 mm anterior and 8 mm posterior to the biceps origin, with a 10 mm lateral-to-medial depth of release. Rotational and translational changes were recorded, as was the path of glenohumeral articulation at maximal internal rotation, 30°, 60°, 90° and maximal external rotation. Sequential loading of the LHBT with 0 N, 11 N, and 22 N revealed significant decreases in external rotation, internal rotation, and total range of motion with 22-N loading. Glenohumeral translation in the anterior, posterior, superior, and inferior directions was significantly decreased with 22-N loading. The humeral head shifted posteriorly with biceps loading at maximal internal rotation and 30° and 60° of external rotation ($P < 0.05$). At maximal external rotation, biceps loading shifted the humeral head anterior and superior compared with unloaded shoulders ($P < 0.05$). These findings support the belief that at least one functional role of the LHBT may be to act as a ligament to center the humeral head on the glenoid during the end ranges of rotational motion (Figure 5).

### Coracoacromial Arch Anatomy
#### Coracoacromial Ligament

The coracoacromial ligament bridges the anterolateral acromion and coracoid, creating an arch that helps contain the humeral head from excessive superior translation. The coracoacromial ligament has been described as quadrangular or Y shaped.[53,54] In most individuals, the coracoacromial ligament fans out from its acromial attachment to the coracoid in a V configuration. An accessory band is present in a few individuals.[53-55] A lateral extension of soft tissue from the coracoacromial ligament, termed the falx, blends with the conjoined tendon on the coracoid.[56] The coracoid process projects from the anterior scapular neck with variable inclination.

Fifty-six embalmed cadaver shoulders were examined in an anatomic study of coracoacromial ligament morphology with respect to acromial enthesopathy (spur formation).[53] Nineteen dimensional parameters were defined for measurement. The most common anatomic structures of the coracoacromial ligament were an anterolateral band and a posteromedial band. The anterolateral band covered the entire anterior acromial undersurface; in 75% of the shoulders it extended to blend with the conjoined tendon, forming a coracoacromial falx. In 25%, there was no clear ligamentous differentiation. Spur formation was found to be correlated with a coracoacromial ligament that was relatively narrow, short, thick, and less divergent. Whether this morphology causes impingement or is a result of impingement could not be determined.

### Acromioclavicular Joint

The acromioclavicular joint is stabilized by the acromioclavicular joint capsule ligaments and conoid and trapezoid coracoclavicular ligaments. The conoid and trapezoid ligaments are attached from the distal clavicle inferiorly to the coracoid process superiorly. The acromioclavicular ligaments help stabilize anterior and posterior horizontal translations. The coracoclavicular ligaments prevent excessive superior translation across the acromioclavicular joint. The stability provided by each of these ligaments is believed to be critical in restoring the anatomy after a destabilizing acromioclavicular dislocation. The coracoclavicular ligaments provide vertical stability but not necessarily horizontal stability.[57] Recent reports describe anatomic reconstructions of both the acromioclavicular and coracoclavicular ligaments.[58,59]

### Coracoid Process

The coracoid process projects anteriorly and laterally from the scapular neck. It serves as a medial boundary to the subacromial space and rotator interval. Coracoid impingement against the subscapularis tendon and bursa can lead to anterior shoulder pain. Coracohumeral distance can be measured by examining axial shoulder images, usually on MRI; the measurement from the cortical margin of the coracoid to the cortical margin of the humeral head is approximately 3 mm to 11 mm. On average, a 5-mm measurement is associated with subscapularis tearing. The indications for performing coracoplasty are not clear; the patient's history and physical examination must be consistent with the diagnosis of coracoid impingement. An arthroscopic intra-articular coracoplasty can be performed via the rotator interval.[60]

## Summary

A complex orchestration of passive and active stabilizers leads to shoulder function. Shoulder anatomy consists of osseous and soft-tissue structures, and it varies among patients. Appreciating this variability can allow the shoulder surgeon to adapt to individual pathoanatomy and help in restoring normal anatomy and function.

## Annotated References

1. Minagawa H, Itoi E, Konno N, et al: Humeral attachment of the supraspinatus and infraspinatus tendons: An anatomic study. *Arthroscopy* 1998;14:302-306.

2. Robertson DD, Yuan J, Bigliani LU, Flatow EL, Yamaguchi K: Three-dimensional analysis of the proximal part of the humerus: Relevance to arthroplasty. *J Bone Joint Surg Am* 2000;82:1594-1602.

3. Iannotti JP, Spencer EE, Winter U, Deffenbaugh D, Williams G: Prosthetic positioning in total shoulder arthroplasty. *J Shoulder Elbow Surg* 2005;14:111S-121S.

   The effects of humeral and glenoid malpositioning are reviewed, using cadaver and finite-element modeling. Inferior humeral malpositioning greater than 4 mm can lead to increased subacromial contact, and humeral offset of 8 mm in any direction significantly decreases passive range of motion. Compensation of glenoid retroversion with humeral anteversion is ineffective in improving humeral stability.

4. Itamura J, Dietrick T, Roidis N, Shean C, Chen F, Tibone JE: Analysis of the bicipital groove as a landmark for humeral head replacement. *J Shoulder Elbow Surg* 2002;11:322-326.

   The course of the bicipital groove was evaluated as it moves distally along the humerus, and a significant amount of internal rotation was found. This finding has clinical implications when the bicipital groove is used as a landmark for humeral head replacement in fractures of the proximal humerus.

5. Balg F, Boulianne M, Boileau P: Bicipital groove orientation: Consideration for the retroversion of a prosthesis in fractures of the proximal humerus. *J Shoulder Elbow Surg* 2006;15:195-198.

   Forty cadaveric humeri were analyzed using CT. The bicipital groove was found to internally rotate as it courses distally from the anatomic neck to the surgical neck. This

factor may be significant during arthroplasty when the anatomic neck is distorted.

6. Doyle AJ, Burks RT: Comparison of humeral head retroversion with the humeral axis/biceps groove relationship: A study in live subjects and cadavers. *J Shoulder Elbow Surg* 1998;7:453-457.

7. Tillett E, Smith M, Fulcher M, Shankin J: Anatomic determination of humeral head retroversion: The relationship of the central axis of the humeral head to the bicipital groove. *J Shoulder Elbow Surg* 1993;5: 255-256.

8. Frankle MA, Greenwald DP, Markee BA, Ondrovic LE, Lee WE III: Biomechanical effects of malposition of tuberosity fragments on the humeral prosthetic reconstruction for four-part proximal humerus fractures. *J Shoulder Elbow Surg* 2001;10:321-326.

    To compare the effects of anatomic and nonanatomic tuberosity placement, external rotation torque was tested in five cadaver shoulders. The findings underscore the importance of rotational alignment of tuberosities during reconstruction.

9. Huffman GR, Itamura JM, McGarry MH, Tibone JE, Gililland J, Lee TQ: Biomechanical assessment of inferior tuberosity placement during hemiarthroplasty for 4-part proximal humerus fractures. *J Shoulder Elbow Surg*. 2007;16(2);e50-e51.

    Eight cadaver shoulders were tested to assess the biomechanical effects of inferior tuberosity position, by 10 mm and 20 mm, on glenohumeral joint forces and kinematics after hemiarthroplasty. Inferior tuberosity malpositioning led to significant alterations in glenohumeral joint forces, particularly in the superior direction, and may explain diminished motion and function observed after surgery.

10. Iannotti JP, Gabriel JP, Schneck SL, Evans BG, Misra S: The normal glenohumeral relationships: An anatomical study of one hundred and forty shoulders. *J Bone Joint Surg Am* 1992;74:491-500.

11. Churchill RS, Brems JJ, Kotschi H: Glenoid size, inclination, and version: An anatomic study. *J Shoulder Elbow Surg* 2001;10:327-332.

    Glenoid height, width, inclination, and version were measured in cadaver scapular bones of four groups: black and white men and women, mean age 25.6 years at time of death. Significant differences were found in glenoid version based on race.

12. Spencer EE, Valdevit A, Kambic H, Brems JJ, Iannotti JP: The effect of humeral component anteversion on shoulder stability with glenoid component retroversion. *J Bone Joint Surg Am* 2005;87:808-814.

    Total shoulder arthroplasty was performed in eight cadaver specimens with the glenoid component retroverted. Biomechanical analyses revealed that anteverting the humeral component to compensate for a retroverted glenoid does not increase stability.

13. Farron A, Terrier A, Buchler P: Risks of loosening of a prosthetic glenoid implanted in retroversion. *J Shoulder Elbow Surg* 2006;15:521-526.

    A three-dimensional finite element model was employed using data from an intact cadaver shoulder. Excessive glenoid retroversion (above 10°) was found to increase stress and micromotion and should be corrected during arthroplasty. If correction is impossible, consideration should be given to forgoing glenoid replacement.

14. Walch G, Badet R, Boulahia A, Khoury A: Morphologic study of the glenoid in primary glenohumeral osteoarthritis. *J Arthroplasty* 1999;14:756-760.

15. Levine WN, Djurasovic M, Glasson JM, Pollock RG, Flatow EL, Bigliani LU: Hemiarthroplasty for glenohumeral osteoarthritis: Results correlated to degree of glenoid wear. *J Shoulder Elbow Surg* 1997;6:449-454.

16. Habermeyer P, Magosch P, Luz V, Lichtenberg S: Three-dimensional glenoid deformity in patients with osteoarthritis: A radiographic analysis. *J Bone Joint Surg Am* 2006;88:1301-1307.

    A radiographic classification system for osteoarthritis was created to highlight glenoid deformity in the superior-inferior direction. Addressing glenoid version in both the axial and coronal planes may be useful to reduce eccentric loading.

17. Ticker JB, Bigliani LU, Soslowsky LJ, et al: Viscoelastic and geometric properties of the inferior glenohumeral ligament. *Orthop Trans* 1992;16:304-305.

18. Gohlke F, Essigkrug B, Schmitz F: The pattern of the collagen fiber bundles of the capsule of the glenohumeral joint. *J Shoulder Elbow Surg* 1994;3:111-128.

19. Sugalski MT, Wiater JM, Levine WN, Bigliani LU: An anatomic study of the humeral insertion of the inferior glenohumeral capsule. *J Shoulder Elbow Surg* 2005;14:91-95.

    Twelve cadaver humeri were dissected to characterize the inferior capsule attachment. Broad and split attachments were identified. Recognition of these variations may facilitate capsular shifting by ensuring adequate release of attachments.

20. Bigliani LU, Pollock RG, Soslowsky LJ, Flatow EL, Pawluk RJ: Tensile properties of the inferior glenohumeral ligament. *J Orthop Res* 1992;10:187-197.

21. Speer KP, Deng X, Borrero S, Torzilli PA, Altchek DW, Warren RF: Biomechanical evaluation of a simulated Bankart lesion. *J Bone Joint Surg Am* 1994;76:1819-1826.

22. Pollock RG, Wang VM, Bucchieri JS, et al: Effects of repetitive subfailure strains on the mechanical behavior of the inferior glenohumeral ligament. *J Shoulder Elbow Surg* 2000;9:427-435.

23. McMahon PJ, Dettling JR, Sandusky MD, Lee TQ: Deformation and strain characteristics along the length of the anterior band of the inferior glenohumeral ligament. *J Shoulder Elbow Surg* 2001;10: 482-488.

Twelve cadaver glenoid–soft-tissue–humerus complexes were tested to evaluate the amount and location of nonrecoverable stretching. Nonrecoverable deformation differed along the length of the anterior band but was slight in all locations. Rupture of the anterior band resulted in little nonrecoverable stretching.

24. Alberta FG, ElAttrache NS, Mihata T, McGarry MH, Tibone JE, Lee TQ: Arthroscopic anteroinferior suture plication resulting in decreased glenohumeral translation and external rotation: Study of a cadaver model. *J Bone Joint Surg Am* 2006;88:179-187.

Six cadaver shoulders were tested using an anterior instability model. The intact, stretched, and retensioned states were analyzed. Arthroscopic plication effectively reduced anterior translation and external rotation.

25. Howell SM, Galinat BJ: The glenoid-labral socket: A constrained articular surface. *Clin Orthop Relat Res* 1989;243:122-125.

26. Rao AG, Kim TK, Chronopoulous E, MacFarland EG: Anatomical variants in the anterosuperior aspect of the glenoid labrum: A statistical analysis of seventy-three cases. *J Bone Joint Surg Am* 2003;85: 653-659.

Three distinct variations of the anterosuperior aspect of the labrum were found in 13.4% of 546 patients: a sublabral foramen only in 3.3%, a sublabral foramen with a cordlike middle glenohumeral ligament in 8.6%, and an absence of anterosuperior labral tissue with a cordlike middle glenohumeral ligament in 1.5%.

27. Vangsness CT, Jorgenson SS, Watson T, et al: The origin of the long head of the biceps from the scapula and glenoid labrum. *J Bone Joint Surg Br* 1994;76: 951-954.

28. Panossian VR, Mihata T, Tibone JE, Fitzpatrick MJ, McGarry MH, Lee TQ: Biomechanical analysis of isolated type II SLAP lesions and repair. *J Shoulder Elbow Surg* 2005;14:529-534.

Six cadaver shoulders were tested in intact, type II SLAP lesion, and arthroscopically repaired conditions. Type II SLAP lesions created significant increases in total motion and anteroposterior and inferior translations. Arthroscopic repair techniques have the potential to restore native anatomy.

29. Plancher KD, Johnston JC, Peterson RK, Hawkins RJ: The dimensions of the rotator interval. *J Shoulder Elbow Surg* 2005;14:620-625.

Thirty-two specimens were dissected, and the anterior rotator interval dimensions were measured. The dimensions changed with glenohumeral motion, closing with internal rotation. Imbrication in this position may lead to overtightening, with loss of external rotation.

30. Jost B, Koch PP, Gerber C: Anatomy and functional aspects of the rotator interval. *J Shoulder Elbow Surg* 2000;9:336-341.

31. Werner A, Mueller T, Boehm D, Gohlke F: The stabilizing sling for the long head of the biceps tendon in the rotator cuff interval: A histoanatomic study. *Am J Sports Med* 2000;28:28-31.

32. Walch G, Nove-Josserand L, Levigne C, Renaud E: Tears of the supraspinatus tendon associated with "hidden" lesions of the rotator interval. *J Shoulder Elbow Surg* 1994;3-6:353-360.

33. Boon JM, deBeer MA, Botha D, Maritz NGJ, Fouche AA: The anatomy of the subscapularis tendon insertion as applied to rotator cuff repair. *J Shoulder Elbow Surg* 2004;13:165-169.

Forty-three cadaver specimens were dissected 1 cm below the superior ridge of the greater tuberosity at the bicipital groove. A continuous band of interdigitating, collagen-dense tissue consisting of the supraspinatus and subscapularis muscles was found both macroscopically and microscopically.

34. Gleason PD, Beall DP, Sanders TG, et al: The transverse humeral ligament: A separate anatomical structure or a continuation of the osseous attachment of the rotator cuff? *Am J Sports Med* 2006;34:72-77.

No identifiable transverse humeral ligament was found in dissection of 14 cadaver shoulders. Fibers covering the intertubercular groove were composed of a sling derived from the subscapularis and supraspinatus tendons and the coracohumeral ligament. Biceps tendon dislocation can disrupt the deep portions of the subscapularis tendon.

35. Plausinis D, Bravman JT, Heywood C, Kummer FJ, Kwon YW, Jazrawi LM: Arthroscopic rotator interval closure: Effect of sutures on glenohumeral motion and anterior-posterior translation. *Am J Sports Med* 2006;34:1656-1661.

Arthroscopic interval closure produced significant decreases in range of motion and anterior-posterior translation in cadaver shoulders. The effects of single lateral or medial suture sutures were similar those of two sutures.

36. Gerber C, Werner CML, Macy JC, Jacob HAC, Nyffeler RW: Effect of selective capsulorrhaphy on the passive range of motion of the glenohumeral joint. *J Bone Joint Surg Am* 2003;85:48-55.

The effect of rotator interval closure was measured in a cadaver study. Flexion, external rotation, and anterior-posterior translation were significantly decreased. Using one and two sutures had similar effects. Normal capsules were used, and inferior translations were not measured.

37. Tetro AM, Bauer G, Hollstein SB, Yamaguchi K: Arthroscopic release of the rotator interval and coraco-

humeral ligament: An anatomic study in cadavers. *Arthroscopy* 2002;18:145-150.

A study of 15 cadaver specimens confirmed that intra-articularly directed arthroscopic release of the rotator interval can safely lead to complete release of the coracohumeral ligament, if dissection is taken superficially to the level of the coracoacromial ligament.

38. Miller SL, Gladstone JN, Cleeman E, Klein MJ, Chiang AS, Flatow EL: Anatomy of the posterior rotator interval: Implications for cuff mobilization. *Clin Orthop Relat Res* 2003;408:152-156.

Ten cadaver shoulders were dissected to expose the region between the infraspinatus and supraspinatus from the spinoglenoid notch to the greater tuberosity, and measurements were taken.

39. Roh MS, Wang VM, April EW, Pollock RG, Bigliani LU, Flatow EL: Anterior and posterior musculotendinous anatomy of the supraspinatus. *J Shoulder Elbow Surg* 2000;9:436-440.

40. Curtis AS, Burbank KM, Tierney JJ, Scheller AD, Curran AR: The insertional footprint of the rotator cuff: An anatomic study. *Arthroscopy* 2006;22:609.

Twenty fresh-frozen specimens were dissected. Rotator cuff tendon insertion dimensions were measured, and landmarks were noted. Appreciating insertion anatomy may facilitate grading and repairing of rotator cuff tears.

41. Ruotolo C, Fow JE, Nottage WM: The supraspinatus footprint: An anatomic study of the supraspinatus insertion. *Arthroscopy* 2004;20:246-249.

Forty-eight cadaver shoulders were dissected, and supraspinatus insertion dimensions were measured. Footprint dimensions may help in estimating tear depth and provide treatment guidelines.

42. Dugas JR, Campbell DA, Warren RF, Robie BH, Millett PJ: Anatomy and dimensions of rotator cuff insertions. *J Shoulder Elbow Surg* 2002;11:498-503.

The area and dimensions of the rotator cuff tendon insertions and their distance from the articular surface were measured in 20 cadaver upper extremity specimens.

43. Kim DH, ElAttrache NS, Tibone JE, et al: Biomechanical comparison of a single-row versus double-row suture anchor technique for rotator cuff repair. *Am J Sports Med* 2006;34:407-414.

Nine matched pairs of repaired rotator cuffs were biomechanically tested. Double-row rotator cuff repairs had improved biomechanical parameters compared with single-row repairs, with respect to gap formation, strain, and ultimate strength. Supraspinatus footprint dimensions were also measured.

44. Park MC, ElAttrache NS, Tibone JE, et al: Part I: Footprint contact characteristics for an arthroscopic transosseous-equivalent rotator cuff repair technique compared with a double row technique. *J Shoulder Elbow Surg* 2007;16;461-468.

A cadaver study tested footprint contact using pressure-sensitive film at the tendon-footprint interface. A transosseous-equivalent rotator cuff repair technique using tendon-bridging sutures improved contact area and pressure, compared with a double-row technique.

45. Park MC, ElAttrache NS, Idjadi JA, Tibone JE, McGarry MH, Lee TQ: Biomechanical analyses for the effect of physiological rotation at a repaired rotator cuff footprint comparing "transosseous-equivalent" and double-row techniques. *Annual Meeting Proceedings*. Rosemont, IL, American Orthopaedic Society for Sports Medicine, 2007, p. 217.

Six matched pairs of cadaver shoulders comparing transosseous-equivalent and double row repairs were load tested allowing for 30° external rotation and using relatively low loads, as may be experienced postsurgically. The transosseous-equivalent repair had a higher yield load, and there were no differences with respect to gap formation.

46. Ihashi K, Matsushita N, Yagi R, Handa Y: Rotational action of the supraspinatus muscle on the shoulder joint. *J Electromyogr Kinesiol* 1998;8:337-346.

47. Langenderfer JE, Patthanacharoenphon C, Carpenter JE, Hughes RE: Variation in external rotation moment arms among subregions of supraspinatus, infraspinatus, and teres minor muscles. *J Orthop Res* 2006;24:1737-1744.

Rotation moment arms for rotator cuff muscles were determined in 10 specimens. Moment arms across subregions of the infraspinatus and supraspinatus were significantly different. Interaction between cuff regions may explain why some patients retain strength after partial rotator cuff tears.

48. Park MC, Jun BJ, Park CJ, ElAttrache NS, Ahmad CS, Lee TQ: The biomechanical effects of dynamic external rotation on rotator cuff repair compared to testing with the humerus fixed. *Am J Sports Med* 2007;37: 1931-1939.

In six matched pairs of cadaver shoulders after rotator cuff repair, dynamic humeral external rotation to 30° created significantly more anterior tendon strain and gap formation than load testing with the humerus fixed. Appreciating the effect of rotation on repair may provide a framework from which to prescribe postsurgical rehabilitation guidelines.

49. Dockery ML, Wright TW, LaStayo PC: Electromyography of the shoulder: An analysis of passive modes of exercise. *Orthopedics* 1998;21:1181-1184.

50. Ballantyne BT, O'Hare SJ, Paschall JL, et al: Electromyographic activity of selected shoulder muscles in commonly used therapeutic exercises. *Phys Ther* 1993;73:668-681.

51. Gimbel JA, Van Kleunen JP, Lake SP, Williams GR, Soslowsky LJ: The role of repair tension on tendon to bone healing in an animal model of chronic rotator cuff tears. *J Biomech* 2007;40:561-568.

Using a rat model of chronic rotator cuff repair, supraspinatus tendons were surgically detached and repaired immediately and at intervals to 16 weeks after detachment. Older tears placed more tension on the repair, which was related to a decrease in failure properties.

52. Youm T, Tibone JE, ElAttrache NS, McGarry MH, Lee TQ: Loading the long head of the biceps affects glenohumeral kinematics. *Trans Orthop Res Soc* 2006;31:286.

Six cadaver shoulders with a type II SLAP lesion were tested before and after repair. Various loads were applied, and kinematic measurements were analyzed. The biceps tendon was found to have a humeral head–centering function at the extremes of rotational motion.

53. Fealy S, April EW, Khazzam M, Armengol-Barallat J, Bigliani LU: The coracoacromial ligament: Morphology and study of acromial enthesopathy. *J Shoulder Elbow Surg* 2005;14:542-548.

Fifty-six cadaver shoulders were dissected, and the coracoacromial ligament was studied. The two most common variations in morphology were distinct anterolateral and posteromedial bands. Recognizing this anatomy may facilitate adequate subacromial decompression.

54. Holt EM, Allibone RO: Anatomic variants of the coracoacromial ligament. *J Shoulder Elbow Surg* 1995;4:370-375.

55. Pieper HG, Radas CB, Krahl H, Blank M: Anatomic variation of the coracoacromial ligament: A macroscopic and microscopic cadaveric study. *J Shoulder Elbow Surg* 1997;6:291-296.

56. Renoux S, Monet J, Pupin P, et al: Preliminary note on biometric data relating to the human coracoacromial arch. *Surg Radiol Anat* 1986;8:189-195.

57. Debski RE, Parsons IM IV, Woo SL, Fu FH: Effect of capsular injury on acromioclavicular joint mechanics. *J Bone Joint Surg Am* 2001;83:1344-1351.

Cadaver shoulders were tested in their intact state and after transection of the acromioclavicular joint capsule using a robotic universal force–moment sensor system.

58. Mazzocca AD, Santangelo SA, Johnson ST, Rios CG, Dumonski ML, Arciero RA: A biomechanical evaluation of an anatomical coracoclavicular ligament reconstruction. *Am J Sports Med* 2006;34:236-246.

Forty-two cadaver shoulders were biomechanically tested with three different acromioclavicular reconstructions: arthroscopic, anatomic coracoclavicular, and modified Weaver-Dunn. Anatomic reconstruction using a free tendon graft more closely restored the intact state, restoring function of the acromioclavicular and coracoclavicular ligaments.

59. Grutter PW, Petersen SA: Anatomical acromioclavicular ligament reconstruction: A biomechanical comparison of reconstructive techniques of the acromioclavicular joint. *Am J Sports Med* 2005;33:1723-1728.

Six cadaver shoulders were biomechanically tested with three different acromioclavicular reconstructions. Anatomic reconstruction with a flexor carpi radialis tendon graft restored the tensile strength of the native acromioclavicular joint and was superior to a modified Weaver-Dunn repair.

60. Lo IKY, Burkhart SS: Technical note: Arthroscopic coracoplasty through the rotator interval. *Arthroscopy* 2003;19:667-671.

An intra-articular method of coracoplasty though the rotator interval is described. It is easier to execute than a subacromial approach and allows appropriate orientation of the coracoplasty in the plane of the subscapularis tendon.

# Chapter 2

# The Basic Science of Shoulder Instability

Orr Limpisvasti, MD

## Introduction

The recent research on the basic science and clinical implications of shoulder instability has focused on both the functional anatomy of the glenohumeral joint and the thrower's shoulder. Studies defining pathologic changes in the shoulder have allowed instability to be specifically addressed and normal shoulder function to be restored. Clinical studies of the developmental and pathologic changes in the thrower's shoulder may lead to the creation of appropriate cadaver models.

## Functional Anatomy of the Glenohumeral Joint

### Normal Glenohumeral Structure and Function

The structures contributing to glenohumeral stability have passive and active components. The passive components include the osseous morphology of the glenohumeral joint, the glenoid labrum, and the capsuloligamentous structures. The active components are the muscles that exert a stabilizing force on the glenohumeral joint through concavity-compression. Recent cadaver studies of glenohumeral stability have examined the interaction of the passive and active components, as well as the role of joint position and rotation.

The glenoid labrum is an important passive component of glenohumeral stability. By deepening the relatively shallow glenoid, it enhances the compression of the humeral head into the glenolabral concavity. A cadaver study investigated the contributions of the glenoid labrum, joint compression force, and abduction angle to glenohumeral stability and found that the average contribution of the labrum through concavity-compression is approximately 10%.[1] Measurement of the stability ratio (the peak translational force divided by the applied compression force) in multiple directions revealed that the glenohumeral joint is least stable in the anterior direction, regardless of whether the labrum is intact. The adducted hanging-arm position had the highest average stability ratio in all directions, compared with the abducted shoulder. These findings corroborate clinical experience of increased anterior instability in the ab-

ducted shoulder. The study also found that increasing the joint compression loads decreased glenohumeral stability. This finding suggests that only moderate joint compression forces are necessary to produce concavity-compression.

The glenoid labrum serves as an attachment for the glenohumeral ligaments, which confer joint stability where concavity-compression alone is insufficient. The biomechanical properties of the glenohumeral ligaments influence glenohumeral instability injury patterns and treatment decisions. Patient age is one factor affecting the biomechanical properties of the labroligamentous complex. A cadaver study of the complex formed by the glenoid, the inferior glenohumeral ligament complex (IGHLC), and the humerus found age-related differences in biomechanical properties and mode of failure.[2] Older shoulder specimens (mean age, 74.8 years) failed under lower loads, and they tended to fail in the midsubstance. In contrast, younger specimens (mean age, 38.5 years), were more likely to fail at the soft-tissue insertion into the glenoid or humerus. These findings suggest a need for stronger ligamentous restraint in younger shoulders and, possibly, stronger repair to achieve glenohumeral stability.

The exact role of the glenohumeral capsule and ligaments is still being elucidated, particularly with reference to glenohumeral position and rotation. In a study of the role of various passive and active stabilizers in limiting external rotation of the shoulder, the entire IGHLC and coracohumeral ligament (CHL) were found to limit external rotation more than the anterior band of the IGHLC or the superior and middle glenohumeral ligaments combined, when the shoulder was in a neutral position (15° of abduction).[3] The IGHLC limited external rotation in the abducted position (60° of abduction) more than the other ligaments. Therefore, the entire IGHLC is the most important restraint to external rotation in either the neutral or abducted position. The role of several ligaments in providing independent resistance to external rotation supports the belief that the glenohumeral joint capsule functions more like a continuous cylinder than a collection of isolated ligamentous

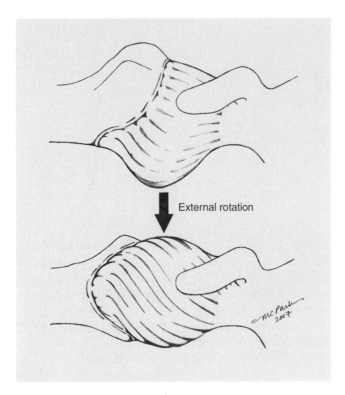

**Figure 1** The glenohumeral capsule behaves like a cylinder, undergoing strain in multiple areas during rotation and translation. (*Courtesy of Maxwell C. Park, MD, Los Angeles, CA.*)

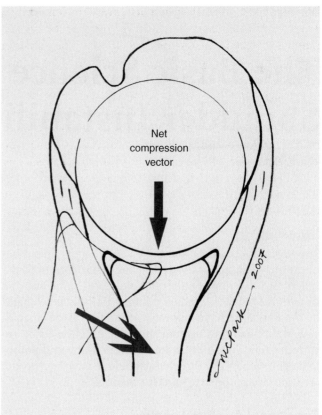

**Figure 2** Scapulothoracic motion can assist in concavity-compression by positioning the glenoid to receive the net compression vector of the humeral head. (*Courtesy of Maxwell C. Park, MD, Los Angeles, CA.*)

structures (Figure 1). This understanding contrasts with earlier studies that proposed isolated ligaments as the primary restraint against translational and rotational instability in different glenohumeral positions. Corroborating earlier research, the study also found that the CHL is a significant restraint to external rotation, particularly in a neutral adducted position.[3] The connection of the CHL to the coracoacromial (CA) ligament may also contribute to shoulder stability. A cadaver study found that release of the CA ligament increased anterior and inferior glenohumeral translation in relatively low abduction (0° and 30°).[4] The authors explained this finding by documenting a consistent structural connectivity between the CHL and the CA ligament, called the falx. The falx is a proximal thickening of the clavipectoral fascia connecting the conjoint tendon, the CA ligament, and the CHL. The authors concluded that the CA ligament supports the CHL and that release of the CA ligament can compromise the stabilizing function of the CHL on the glenohumeral joint. Caution is therefore required when performing CA ligament release in a patient with instability and concomitant subacromial symptoms.

The passive restraints to glenohumeral instability do not work in isolation from the active components, which include the rotator cuff and scapular positioners. The rotator cuff produces concavity-compression of the glenohumeral joint by creating a net-force vector that directs

the humeral head into a relatively shallow glenoid surface. The glenoid is not a fixed platform for the humeral head, and the scapular positioners can position the glenoid to receive the compression vector of the humeral head (Figure 2). The positioning of the glenoid through scapulothoracic motion can also affect the passive components of glenohumeral stability. A cadaver study revealed that a scapular protraction of only 10° can significantly increase the strain on the anterior band of the IGHLC during anterior translation of the humeral head.[5] Scapular protraction increases the strain and tension on the IGHLC, thereby decreasing the anterior translation of the glenohumeral joint. The relationship between scapular position and glenohumeral capsular strain may partially explain capsular laxity and intra-articular pathology in overhead throwing athletes with poor scapulothoracic mechanics.

Many studies have documented the importance of active stabilization of the glenohumeral joint through the rotator cuff, biceps, and scapular positioners. Recent research evaluated the role of the deltoid muscle in glenohumeral stability. A cadaver study found that loading the deltoid provides stability and decreases anterior translation of the glenohumeral joint in the apprehension position.[6] The stabilizing effect was most prominent if a simulated Bankart lesion was present. This finding supports deltoid strengthening in the treatment of glenohumeral instability. Conversely, active muscle function was implicated in glenohumeral instability. In cadaver and computational models, pectoral muscle forces were shown to increase anteriorly directed forces on the glenohumeral joint in the apprehension position.[7] This finding suggests that all of the muscles exerting force across the glenohumeral joint, including humerothoracic muscles such as the pectoralis major and latissimus dorsi, should be included in the concept of active shoulder stability. The effect of these muscles is likely to be position dependent, as it is in the rotator cuff, and further active instability models must be developed to assess the relationship of joint position and active muscle function.

### The Clinical Pathology of Instability

The glenoid labrum is commonly repaired surgically to treat traumatic anterior instability, as well as superior labral and biceps anchor lesions in overhead athletes. The morphology of the anterosuperior quadrant of the glenoid labrum and the attached capsuloligamentous structures varies significantly among individuals. A recent study of more than 500 patients undergoing diagnostic arthroscopy for various diagnoses found that 13% of the shoulders had anatomic variants in the anterosuperior aspect of the glenoid labrum, including a sublabral foramen, a cordlike middle glenohumeral ligament, and the complete absence of labral tissue in different combinations.[8] The surgeon must be aware that normal variations exist when performing labral repairs in or near the anterosuperior quadrant, so as to avoid restricting the patient's motion by repairing normal labral tissue and restraining attached capsuloligamentous structures, such as the superior or middle glenohumeral ligament.

The possible presence of a concomitant osseous glenoid injury must also be considered in an anterior labral repair to correct recurrent anterior or anteroinferior instability. Performing an isolated labral repair in the presence of osseous glenohumeral insufficiency may increase the risk of recurrence. Recent studies evaluated the prevalence and morphology of glenoid defects in shoulders with recurrent anterior glenohumeral instability. A CT and arthroscopic evaluation of 100 consecutive shoulders with recurrent unilateral anterior instability found a Bankart lesion in 97 and an osseous glenoid fragment in 50.[9] Most of the osseous fragments were small (<5% of the glenoid fossa) or medium sized (<20% of the glenoid fossa). In the 50 remaining shoulders, 40 had blunting or erosion of the normal osseous contour of the anterior glenoid. These findings suggest that osseous glenoid insufficiency is common, although no correlation was established between defect size and severity of instability or number of instability episodes.

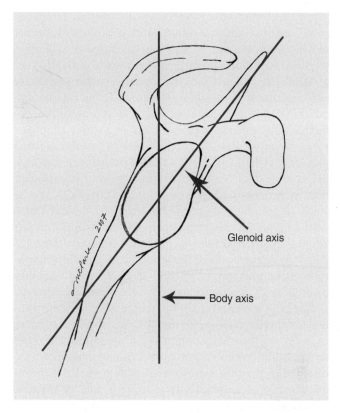

**Figure 3** In a normal shoulder, the superior-inferior axis of the glenoid is tilted anteriorly approximately 40° in relation to the body because of the inclination of the glenoid on the scapula and the position of the scapula on the thoracic cage. (*Courtesy of Maxwell C. Park, MD, Los Angeles, CA.*)

The exact location of glenoid defects in traumatic anterior instability was defined using three-dimensional CT. Imaging of 123 shoulders with a recurrent anterior dislocation and osseous glenoid defects found that more than 80% of the glenoid defects were located between the 2:30 and 4:20 clock-face positions (mean position, 3 o'clock).[10] The direction represents an anterior rather than an anteroinferior pathology. This difference in direction can be explained by both the inclination of the glenoid on the scapula (study average, 18.4°) and the tilt of the scapula on the thoracic cage (estimated at 20°). The surgeon may find that the humeral head is dislocated in an anteroinferior direction in relation to the body but in an anterior direction in relation to the superior-inferior axis of the glenoid (Figure 3). Understanding this discrepancy is important in laboratory modeling of instability, as well as clinical treatment.

The clinical pathology of glenohumeral instability is not confined to the glenohumeral joint. Active stabilization of the scapular and humeral positioners is significantly affected by glenohumeral instability. An electromyographic study of shoulders with anterior glenohumeral instability found significant impairment of reflexive muscle activation.[11] In the apprehension position, shoulders with recurrent anterior instability had suppressed pectoralis and biceps activation, increased peak rotator cuff activation, and decreased subscapularis-supraspinatus coactivation in response to perturbation. These findings suggest that muscle activation alterations in patients with recurrent anterior instability can contribute to instability episodes. Rehabilitative exercises and other modalities may restore the normal reflexive muscle-firing patterns found in a stable shoulder. In an unstable shoulder, the alterations in muscle-firing pattern may be secondary to altered proprioception. Earlier studies documented alterations in joint proprioception in patients with glenohumeral instability. A recent study of patients with recurrent anterior shoulder dislocation found that this impairment of joint proprioception could be corrected following surgical Bankart lesion repair.[12] Surgical repair of the labrum and capsuloligamentous structures may restore glenohumeral stability through both neuromuscular and structural alterations.

Interest is increasing in the scapulothoracic contribution to shoulder biomechanics and instability. Exercises to improve concavity-compression by addressing the strength and coordination of the rotator cuff musculature are commonly used to treat glenohumeral instability. Control of scapulothoracic motion may be equally important in addressing glenohumeral instability. An MRI study of patients with atraumatic shoulder instability found that glenohumeral motion increased more than scapular motion in unstable shoulders.[13] The study also found increased scapular internal rotation and malcentering of the glenohumeral articulation. Although rotator cuff function was not addressed, the findings suggest that a clinically unstable shoulder can result from poor scapulothoracic positioning, even in the absence of a structural injury. Therapy for glenohumeral instability should include strengthening and coordination of both humeral and scapular positioners.

### Injury Models and the Effects of Surgical Restoration

Cadaver studies have improved the understanding of glenohumeral instability and the effects of surgical restoration. A recent study to evaluate the effect of surgically created superior labrum anterior and posterior (SLAP) tears on glenohumeral motion and translation found that external rotation, internal rotation, anterior-posterior translation, and inferior translation all were increased.[14] Surgical repair using two suture anchors restored preinjury rotation and translation. Another study found that anterior translation increased after creation of a SLAP lesion; the severity of the injury affected the degree of instability.[15] Elevation of the superior labrum and the biceps anchor caused less instability than complete detachment of the superior labrum and the entire biceps anchor. This study corroborated the finding of earlier studies that the long head of the biceps tendon is an important contributor to glenohumeral stability. Al-

though the origin of in vivo SLAP tears is not well understood, this study and others suggest the pathology involves more than the labral lesion alone. Future studies are needed to evaluate the interplay between the superior labrum, the long head of the biceps tendon, and the superior glenohumeral ligament in the etiology of SLAP lesions and to create appropriate injury models.

Technical advances allow more precise soft-tissue manipulation during arthroscopic treatment of glenohumeral joint instability. Although the goal is usually to restore normal anatomy, the amount of tissue that should be repaired or plicated has not been determined. Recent studies attempted to quantify the effect of different soft-tissue procedures on glenohumeral motion and biomechanics. One study evaluated a capsulolabral augmentation procedure using suture plication of the posteroinferior quadrant of the capsule to the glenoid labrum.[16] The authors found that a 1-cm plication increased glenolabral depth, as well as resistance to humeral head translation (the stability ratio), but it also restricted internal rotation. This study is consistent with earlier findings that a 1-cm capsular plication resulted in an approximately 20° loss of rotation. Therefore, surgeons should be cautious about routine capsular plication in patients with primary labral pathology because of the risk of motion loss. A study using an external rotation stretch model found a decrease in external rotation and anterior translation following capsulolabral plication using suture anchors in the anteroinferior quadrant.[17] Anteroinferior plication restored some, but not all, of the rotation arc following the external rotation stretch. The glenohumeral center of rotation was shifted in the posteroinferior direction after plication. These findings suggest that capsulolabral plication can significantly alter joint kinematics and decrease glenohumeral translation and rotation. Earlier clinical studies documented the detrimental effects of overconstraining the glenohumeral joint during stabilization procedures. Therefore, until the exact effect of capsular plication on the glenohumeral joint is better defined, the surgeon should take care during these procedures to avoid unnecessary restriction of joint motion and altered kinematics.

Recent studies using glenohumeral instability injury models focused on the effect of osseous glenoid defects in patients with recurrent anterior instability. A cadaver study evaluated the effect on glenohumeral stability of a glenoid defect and subsequent bone grafting.[18] The authors found that the presence of a defect that was approximately 21% of the glenoid face length led to a 50% decrease in anteroinferior stability. Subsequent bone grafting restored stability, and a contoured graft was best able to restore normal ball-and-socket contact. This study did not evaluate the soft-tissue contributions of the labrum and capsuloligamentous structures. Another cadaver study using intact soft tissues evaluated the progressive effect of increasing anteroinferior glenoid defects. The authors found that in abduction-external rotation (the apprehension position), a Bankart repair alone restored stability to the shoulder, regardless of the size of the osseous lesion.[19] However, Bankart repair of a shoulder with a glenoid loss of more than 20% limited external rotation. Pretensioning of the capsule in external rotation occurred because the repair closed the gap between the truncated glenoid rim and the detached capsule. The surgeon should keep this effect in mind when repairing anterior instability in a shoulder that has lost its normal glenoid morphology. The presence of significant glenoid bone loss may require both an osseous and a soft-tissue procedure to restore stability and external rotation.

The use of novel cadaver instability models has yielded information on the relationship between glenohumeral rotation and instability. A study using a model created with progressive external rotation stretching found that a 30% stretch beyond maximum external rotation led to a significant increase in the length of the IGHLC anterior band and increased anterior and inferior glenohumeral translations.[20] This study suggested that rotational and translational instabilities are related. Understanding the effect of rotation on the capsuloligamentous structures may be important to the treatment of glenohumeral instability. A study of the effect of glenohumeral rotation on a surgically created Bankart lesion found increasing contact pressure between the separated labrum and the glenoid as external rotation was increased.[21] Although increasing contact pressure may influence the healing of soft tissue to bone, surgically created Bankart lesions did not reproduce the capsuloligamentous injury that occurs with anterior glenohumeral dislocation. In the future, injury models that better replicate true clinical pathology must be used to define the relationship of glenohumeral rotation and instability.

## The Thrower's Shoulder
### Developmental Changes

The act of throwing, and particularly pitching, exerts significant stress on the upper extremity, and the cumulative effect often leads to pathologic changes in the thrower's shoulder. Skeletally immature throwers can develop physeal injuries, and older throwers, particularly those at the elite level, often develop soft-tissue injuries of the labrum or rotator cuff. Understanding developmental changes in the thrower's shoulder and their progression to pathology can lead to better methods of preventing and treating injuries.

Developmental shoulder changes arise from the significant rotational forces generated during throwing. A cross-sectional study of asymptomatic young baseball players (ages 8 to 16 years) found that the total arc of

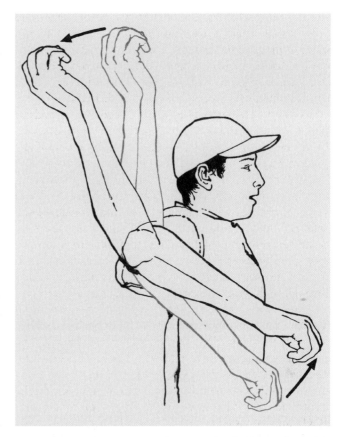

**Figure 4** In the thrower's shoulder, the arc of rotation shifts into external rotation because of developmental osseous changes such as humeral retroversion. External rotation is increased and internal rotation is decreased, but the total arc of rotation is maintained. *(Reproduced with permission from Limpisvasti O, ElAttrache NS, Jobe FW: Understanding shoulder and elbow injuries in baseball. J Am Acad Orthop Surg 2007; 15:139-147.)*

rotation in the throwing shoulder decreases and shifts into external rotation before and during adolescence.[22] The most significant decrease occurs between ages 13 and 14 years, during a period of significant skeletal development. These findings suggest that the increased external rotation and decreased internal rotation commonly seen in skeletally mature throwers begin during a period of skeletal growth, sometimes without symptoms. Although the shift in the rotation arc of a thrower's shoulder is often attributed to soft-tissue changes, several studies suggest that in an asymptomatic thrower it occurs through developmental osseous changes[23-25] (Figure 4). In a group of collegiate baseball players, both shoulders were studied to clinically document glenohumeral rotation and radiographically document humeral retroversion.[23] The total arc of motion did not differ between the dominant and the nondominant shoulders, but in the dominant shoulder the arc was shifted into approximately 10° of external rotation. The dominant arm also had a 10° greater humeral retroversion. Other studies clinically measured a similar shift in rotation arc in collegiate baseball players and

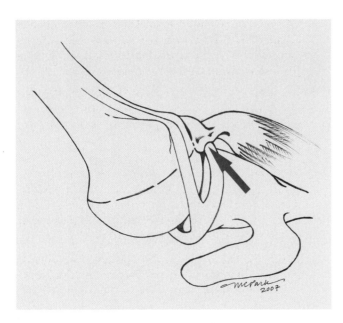

**Figure 5** Internal impingement occurs during the late cocking phase of pitching, when extreme horizontal abduction and external rotation create contact between the undersurface of the rotator cuff and the posterosuperior glenoid. (*Courtesy of Maxwell C. Park, MD, Los Angeles, CA.*)

professional baseball pitchers.[24,25] These findings conflict with the belief that repetitive external rotation stretching of the soft-tissue glenohumeral capsule alone is responsible for the shift in the rotation arc of a thrower's shoulder.

The effect of repetitive throwing on the glenohumeral capsule also has been evaluated. A quantitative assessment measured glenohumeral translation in collegiate and professional baseball players using an electromagnetic sensor system.[26] Pitchers were found to have significantly more anterior-posterior translation in the dominant shoulder than in the nondominant shoulder. These developmental changes will provide a reference point for study of the mechanism of injury, which is unknown. In clinical practice, the surgeon needs to be aware of both osseous and soft-tissue changes to properly evaluate an injured thrower's shoulder.

### Internal Impingement and Cadaver Models of the Thrower's Shoulder

An injured thrower often reports primary posterior and posterosuperior shoulder pain that peaks in the late cocking phase of pitching. Decreased ball velocity and control also are commonly reported. The clinical diagnosis is typically internal impingement or posterosuperior glenoid impingement, as determined through clinical examination and imaging. Throwers diagnosed with internal impingement often have positive labral signs, such as positive relocation and active compression tests, as well as posterior shoulder tightness, which manifests

itself as decreased internal rotation with the glenohumeral joint in abduction.[27] Arthroscopic evaluation and MRI typically reveal superior and posterosuperior labral injuries along with articular-sided injuries of the posterior supraspinatus. Although the intra-articular pathology of internal impingement is common and can be reproducibly diagnosed in injured throwers, controversy exists about its etiology and pathomechanics. It is difficult to confirm the pathomechanics of internal impingement because the in vivo glenohumeral kinematics are still poorly understood. A common hypothesis is that the posterosuperior glenoid and the articular surface of the rotator cuff may impinge as the glenohumeral joint reaches maximum horizontal abduction and external rotation in the late cocking phase (Figure 5).

Modeling the thrower's shoulder is difficult because of the complexity of the developmental changes. Recent attempts to study the thrower's shoulder using cadaver models focused on the etiology of the SLAP lesion. One study modeled the pathologic thrower's shoulder using alterations in the glenohumeral capsule to reproduce an external rotation shift in the arc of motion.[28] The capsule was stretched in external rotation, and the posterior capsule was subsequently plicated. At maximum external rotation (the late cocking position) of intact, stretched, and plicated specimens, the humeral head translated posteroinferiorly. Posterior capsular plication caused no statistically significant superior migration. Although this study did not assess posterosuperior glenohumeral contact, it suggested that external rotation stretching of the capsule and posterior capsular tightness can alter glenohumeral kinematics. To evaluate the effect of biceps loading in creating a SLAP lesion, the biceps anchor was loaded both posteriorly (to reproduce the late cocking phase) and in line with the biceps anchor.[29] Posterior loading led to lower ultimate strength and SLAP lesion creation; in-line loading led to higher ultimate strength and tendon failure. These findings suggest that in a thrower's shoulder the posterior vector of the biceps tendon during the late cocking phase may also contribute to superior labral pathology.

### Summary

The clinical treatment of glenohumeral instability will evolve as understanding of the in vivo pathology of shoulder instability increases. Functional anatomy studies have led to improvements in the ability to model this pathology and assess surgical repairs. Clinical studies are improving the understanding of the complex developmental and pathologic changes in the thrower's shoulder. As the understanding of the in vivo glenohumeral kinematics of pitching improves, it will be possible to more appropriately model the pathologic thrower's shoulder.

## Annotated References

1. Halder AM, Kuhl SG, Zobitz ME, Larson D, An KN: Effects of the glenoid labrum and glenohumeral abduction on stability of the shoulder joint through concavity-compression. *J Bone Joint Surg Am* 2001; 83:1062-1069.

    The effects of joint position on glenohumeral stability through concavity-compression were tested in 10 cadaver shoulders. Stability was greater in the hanging-arm position than in glenohumeral abduction. The average contribution of the labrum was 10%. Stability decreased with higher compressive loads.

2. Lee TQ, Dettling J, Sandusky MD, McMahon PJ: Age related biomechanical properties of the glenoid-anterior band of the inferior glenohumeral ligament-humerus complex. *Clin Biomech (Bristol, Avon)* 1999;14:471-476.

3. Kuhn JE, Huston LJ, Soslowsky LJ, Shyr Y, Blasier RB: External rotation of the glenohumeral joint: Ligament restraints and muscle effects in the neutral and abducted positions. *J Shoulder Elbow Surg* 2005;14: 39S-48S.

    This cadaver study tested the role of the ligament restraints to external rotation. Multiple areas of the glenohumeral capsule were found to contribute to resisting of external rotation, suggesting that the capsule functions as a cylinder.

4. Lee TQ, Black AD, Tibone JE, McMahon PJ: Release of the coracoacromial ligament can lead to glenohumeral laxity: A biomechanical study. *J Shoulder Elbow Surg* 2001;10:68-72.

    The change in glenohumeral joint translation after release of the CA ligament was studied in six cadaver shoulders. The findings suggest that the CA ligament provides a suspension function in the joint and may restrain anterior and inferior translation through interaction with the CHL.

5. Weiser WM, Lee TQ, McMaster WC, McMahon PJ: Effects of simulated scapular protraction on anterior glenohumeral stability. *Am J Sports Med* 1999;27: 801-805.

6. Kido T, Itoi E, Lee S, Neale PG, An KN: Dynamic stabilizing function of the deltoid muscle in shoulders with anterior instability. *Am J Sports Med* 2003;31: 399-403.

    In a study of nine cadaver shoulders, the deltoid muscle was found to be an anterior stabilizer of the glenohumeral joint with the arm in the abduction and external rotation. This function becomes more important as the shoulder becomes unstable.

7. Labriola JE, Lee TQ, Debski RE, McMahon PJ: Stability and instability of the glenohumeral joint: The role of shoulder muscles. *J Shoulder Elbow Surg* 2005;14:32S-38S.

    Computational and experimental models were used to quantify contributions of muscle forces on glenohumeral joint stability. Based on these findings, a cadaver model of glenohumeral dislocation was developed.

8. Rao AG, Kim TK, Chronopoulous E, MacFarland EG: Anatomical variants in the anterosuperior aspect of the glenoid labrum. *J Bone Joint Surg Am* 2003;85:653-659.

    Prospective evaluation for anatomic variations in the anterosuperior aspect of the labrum in 546 patients was followed by intrasurgical evaluation and analysis. Seventy-three patients had one of three variations, which did not in themselves appear to contribute to instability but may predispose the shoulder to other abnormalities.

9. Sugaya H, Moriishi J, Dohi M, Kon Y, Tsuchiya A: Glenoid rim morphology in recurrent anterior glenohumeral instability. *J Bone Joint Surg Am* 2003;85: 878-884.

    The morphology of the glenoid rim was studied using CT three-dimensional reconstruction and arthroscopy in 100 consecutive shoulders with anterior instability.

10. Saito H, Itoi E, Sugaya H, Minagawa H, Yamamoto N, Tuoheti Y: Location of the glenoid defect in shoulders with recurrent anterior dislocations. *Am J Sports Med* 2005;33:889-893.

    Three-dimensional CT was used to evaluate a glenoid defect in 123 patients with recurrent anterior dislocation. The mean orientation of the defect was at the 3 o'clock position on the glenoid. Level of evidence: II.

11. Myers JB, Ju Y, Hwang J, McMahon PJ, Rodosky MW, Lephart SM: Reflexive muscle activations in shoulders with anterior glenohumeral instability. *Am J Sports Med* 2004;32:1013-1021.

    Electromyography was used to characterize reflex muscle activation in 11 patients diagnosed with anterior glenohumeral instability. Compared with control subjects, patients with instability had suppressed pectoralis and biceps brachii mean activation; increased peak activation of the subscapularis, supraspinatus, and infraspinatus; and slower biceps brachii reflex latency.

12. Potzl W, Thorwesten L, Gotze C, Garmann S, Steinbeck J: Proprioception of the shoulder joint after surgical repair for instability. *Am J Sports Med* 2004;32: 425-429.

    Joint position sense was assessed in 14 patients before and at least 5 years after surgical repair for instability. Postsurgical measurements confirmed that proprioception improved in abduction, flexion, and rotation, compared with presurgical measurements.

13. Von Eisenhart-Rothe R, Matsen FA, Eckstein F, Vogl T, Graichen H: Pathomechanics in atraumatic shoulder instability. *Clin Orthop Relat Res* 2005;433:82-89.

    Scapular positioning and glenohumeral centering were evaluated in patients with atraumatic instability and in control subjects, using MRI. A correlation was found between scapular positioning and glenohumeral centering.

14. Panossian VR, Mihata T, Tibone JE, Fitzpatrick MJ, McGarry MH, Lee TQ: Biomechanical analysis of isolated type II SLAP lesions and repair. *J Shoulder Elbow Surg* 2005;14:529-534.

    A SLAP lesion was surgically created in six cadaver shoulders to assess its effect on range of motion (ROM) and stability. Rotational ROM and instability increased following creation of the SLAP lesion, which was corrected with labral repair.

15. McMahon PJ, Burkart A, Musahl V, Debski RE: Glenohumeral translations are increased after a type II superior labrum anterior-posterior lesion: A cadaveric study of severity of passive stabilizer injury. *J Shoulder Elbow Surg* 2004;13:39-44.

    This cadaver study evaluated the effect on glenohumeral joint translations of two different superior labral lesions of increasing severity. Glenohumeral translations increased following creation of both types of labral lesions.

16. Metcalf MH, Pond JD, Harryman DT, Loutzenheiser T, Sidles JA: Capsulolabral augmentation increases glenohumeral stability in the cadaver shoulder. *J Shoulder Elbow Surg* 2001;10:532-538.

    Glenohumeral depth and stability, as well as the effect of diminished capsular laxity on motion, were examined before and after labral augmentation. Humeral head stability within the glenolabral fossa is increased by local capsular augmentation. A simultaneous reduction on capsular laxity limits glenohumeral motion.

17. Alberta FG, ElAttrache NS, Mihata T, McGarry MH, Tibone JE, Lee TQ: Arthroscopic anteroinferior suture plication resulting in decreased glenohumeral translation and external rotation. *J Bone Joint Surg Am* 2006;88:179-187.

    Glenohumeral rotation and translation were tested in cadaver shoulders following anterior capsular stretching and subsequent anteroinferior suture plication. Capsular stretching caused increased external rotation, which decreased following plication. Suture plication also increased the height of the capsulolabral bumper, possibly explaining the decreased anterior translation following suture plication.

18. Montgomery WH, Wahl M, Hettrich C, Itoi E, Lippitt SB, Matsen FA: Anteroinferior bone-grafting can restore stability in osseous glenoid defects. *J Bone Joint Surg Am* 2005;87:1972-1976.

    This cadaver study measured the effect of anteroinferior glenoid defects on glenohumeral instability. An approximate 21% defect of the glenoid face created a 50% decrease in stability. Bone grafting restored the stability of the joint, particularly with use of a contoured graft.

19. Itoi E, Lee S, Berglund LJ, Berge LL, An KN: The effect of a glenoid defect on anteroinferior stability of the shoulder after Bankart repair. *J Bone Joint Surg Am* 2000;82:35-46.

20. Mihata T, Lee Y, McGarry MH, Abe M, Lee TQ: Excessive humeral external rotation results in increased shoulder laxity. *Am J Sports Med* 2004;32:1278-1285.

    Seven cadaver shoulders were tested for rotational ROM, glenohumeral translations, and length of the IGHLC before and after nondestructive external rotation stretching. A 30% stretch resulted in a significant increase in the length of the IGHLC, as well as increased glenohumeral translation in the anterior, inferior, and anterior-posterior direction.

21. Miller BS, Sonnabend DH, Hatrick C, et al: Should acute anterior dislocations of the shoulder be immobilized in external rotation? A cadaveric study. *J Shoulder Elbow Surg* 2004;13:589-592.

    Surgically created Bankart lesions were used in this cadaver study to evaluate the effect of external rotation on glenolabral contact pressure within a Bankart lesion. External rotation increased the contact pressure between the labrum and the glenoid from 0 to a mean of 83.5 g.

22. Meister K, Day T, Horodyski M, Kaminski TW, Wasik MP, Tillman S: Rotational motion changes in the glenohumeral joint of the adolescent/Little League Baseball player. *Am J Sports Med* 2005;33:693-698.

    This cross-sectional study of Little League and adolescent baseball players measured the elevation and rotation of the shoulder in dominant and nondominant shoulders. Elevation and total ROM decreased with age, particularly in those age 13 or 14 years.

23. Reagan KM, Meister K, Horodyski MB, Werner DW, Carruthers C, Wilk KE: Humeral retroversion and its relationship to glenohumeral rotation in the shoulder of college baseball players. *Am J Sports Med* 2002;30:354-360.

    In 54 collegiate baseball players, glenohumeral range of motion was measured and humeral retroversion was determined radiologically. A pattern of increased external rotation and decreased internal rotation in the dominant extremity was significantly correlated with an increase in humeral retroversion.

24. Osbahr DC, Cannon DL, Speer KP: Retroversion of the humerus in the throwing shoulder of college baseball pitchers. *Am J Sports Med* 2002;30:347-353.

    Both shoulders of 19 male collegiate baseball pitchers were evaluated, and retroversion of the humerus was calculated. Rotational changes in the throwing shoulder were found to result from both bony and soft-tissue changes.

25. Crockett HC, Gross LB, Wilk KE, et al: Osseous adaptation and range of motion at the glenohumeral joint in professional baseball pitchers. *Am J Sports Med* 2002;30:20-26.

    Glenohumeral range of motion and laxity along the humeral head and glenoid version were studied in 25 professional pitchers and 25 nonthrowers. External rotation at 90° and humeral head retroversion were significantly greater in the pitchers.

26. Sethi PM, Tibone JE, Lee TQ: Quantitative assessment of glenohumeral translation in baseball players: A comparison of pitchers and nonpitching athletes. *Am J Sports Med* 2004;32:1711-1715.

   Glenohumeral translation was quantified in baseball players using electromagnetic position sensors. Pitchers, but not position players, had a significant increase in external rotation and anteroposterior translation in the dominant arm, compared with the nondominant arm.

27. Myers JB, Laudner KG, Pasquale MR, Bradley JP, Lephart SM: Glenohumeral range of motion deficits and posterior shoulder tightness in throwers with pathologic internal impingement. *Am J Sports Med* 2006;34:385-391.

   Eleven throwing athletes with clinically diagnosed internal impingement were compared with demographically matched control-subject throwing athletes. The athletes with internal impingement had a greater glenohumeral internal rotation deficit and posterior shoulder tightness.

28. Grossman MG, Tibone JE, McGarry MH, Schneider DJ, Veneziani S, Lee TQ: A cadaveric model of the throwing shoulder: A possible etiology of superior labrum anterior-to-posterior lesions. *J Bone Joint Surg Am* 2005;87:824-831.

   A cadaver thrower's shoulder model was created through external rotation stretching of the glenohumeral joint, followed by a posterior capsular plication. At maximum external rotation, the humeral head translated posteroinferiorly in the intact, stretched, and plicated state. External rotation stretching increased anterior translation of the joint. Posterior capsular plication decreased internal rotation of the shoulder.

29. Shepard MF, Dugas JR, Zeng N, Andrews JR: Differences in the ultimate strength of the biceps anchor and the generation of type II superior labral anterior posterior lesions in a cadaveric model. *Am J Sports Med* 2004;32:1197-1201.

   To reproduce the late cocking phase of throwing, the biceps anchor was loaded to failure in cadaver shoulders, with the biceps tendon in line with the anchor and posteriorly. Posterior loading of the biceps tendon led to a lower ultimate strength and creation of a superior labral tear. In-line loading led to a higher ultimate strength and tendon failure.

# Chapter 3

# Basic Science Considerations in the Rotator Cuff

Stavros Thomopoulos, PhD

## Introduction

The muscles of the rotator cuff provide stability and motion at the glenohumeral joint. Early studies of the rotator cuff focused first on the gross anatomy and histologic appearance of the rotator cuff muscles and tendons and later on the biochemical makeup of the tendons, as well as joint kinematics. The etiology, pathogenesis, and healing capacity of the rotator cuff have only recently been studied from the basic science perspective. Cadaver tissues are being used to research rotator cuff injury mechanisms and the biomechanics of torn and repaired rotator cuff tendons. Animal models have been developed to test the mechanisms leading to rotator cuff pathology and the healing characteristics of the repaired cuff. The healing of tendon to bone is of particular interest because most rotator cuff injuries require repair of the tendons to their humeral head insertions. Innovations in molecular biology allow researchers to study the biologic changes that occur during rotator cuff degeneration, as well as genetic expression patterns during healing. Several novel treatments have been proposed to improve the healing of rotator cuff tendons, including the use of growth factors (directly or through gene transfection), biologically active scaffolds, and specific rehabilitation protocols.

## Anatomy, Composition, and Structure

The rotator cuff is composed of the supraspinatus, infraspinatus, subscapularis, and teres minor muscles and their tendons.[1] Collagen bundles from the tendons are interdigitated to form a hood that inserts around the humeral head.[2] Any of the four rotator cuff tendons can be affected by injury or disease. The supraspinatus tendon is most frequently affected, at least partly because it passes through the coracoacromial arch during normal shoulder motion; impingement of the tendon by the bony arch can lead to tendon deterioration. The acromion may play a particularly significant role in bursal-side cuff tears.[1,3,4]

Rotator cuff tendons differ from other tendons in composition and structure. Type I collagen makes up approximately 85% of their dry weight, and a small amount of type III collagen is also present. The levels of type III collagen increase with tendon degeneration, age, and tearing.[5] The rotator cuff tendons contain a surprisingly high level of glycosaminoglycan (GAG) compared with purely tensional tendons. For example, the supraspinatus tendon has 2.5 times more GAG than the distal end of the biceps tendon (the GAG is primarily hyaluronic acid).[5] The rotator cuff probably has a high level of GAG because of the multiaxial stresses to which it is subjected. The compressive loads applied by impingement of the coracoacromial arch on the cuff tendons may promote expression of extracellular matrix proteins that are normally found only in articular cartilage and fibrocartilage. This composition may be an adaptation to prevent degeneration caused by compression or friction loads.[6]

The tendons of the rotator cuff are inserted into the humeral head across a specialized fibrocartilaginous tissue called the enthesis (Figure 1). The structure and composition of the supraspinatus enthesis minimize the stress concentrations that would otherwise arise between tendon and bone.[7] The composition, structure, and biomechanics of the enthesis vary dramatically from tendon to bone to effectively transfer stresses between the two materials, which have dramatically different mechanical properties.[8] The tendon enthesis is categorized into four zones, although changes in the tissue are gradual and continuous.[9] The first zone consists of the tendon proper and has properties similar to those of the tendon midsubstance. It contains well-aligned type I collagen fibers with small amounts of the proteoglycan decorin. The second zone is fibrocartilage composed of types II and III collagen, with small amounts of types I, IX, and X collagen and the proteoglycans aggrecan and decorin. It marks the beginning of the transition from tendinous to bony material.[8,10] The third zone contains mineralized fibrocartilage, predominantly composed of type II collagen, as well as significant amounts of type X collagen and aggrecan.[8,10] The fourth zone consists of bone, predominantly composed of type I collagen with a high mineral content.

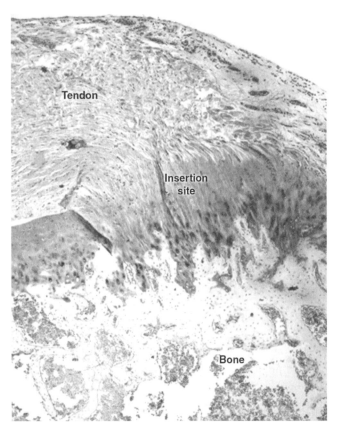

**Figure 1** The supraspinatus enthesis. The supraspinatus tendon inserts into bone across a fibrocartilaginous transition zone (the insertion site). The tendon enthesis effectively minimizes stress concentrations that would otherwise arise at the interface between tendon and bone. *(Reproduced with permission from Thomopoulos S, Williams GR, Gimbel JA, Favata M, Soslowsky LJ: Variation of biomechanical, structural, and compositional properties along the tendon to bone insertion site. J Orthop Res 2003;21:414-419.)*

Effective healing of the tendon enthesis is difficult because of its complex composition, structure, and biomechanics. This specialized tissue is not regenerated during tendon-to-bone healing. The repaired tissue may therefore be subjected to stress concentrations leading to recurrent tears, which occur after 68% to 94% of rotator cuff surgical repairs.[11,12]

## Biomechanics

The primary functions of the rotator cuff are to mechanically stabilize the glenohumeral joint and aid in shoulder motion. The deltoid muscles provide most of the force needed to create upper arm motion, but the rotator cuff muscles are necessary to maintain the proper position of the humeral head relative to the glenoid.[1] Rotator cuff function and the effects of tendon tearing, decreased muscle force, tissue pathology, and surgical repair have been studied extensively using experimental models. The use of computer simulations and human cadaver joints allows researchers to simulate the action of one or more rotator cuff muscles and determine the effect on shoulder biomechanics.

The Delft Shoulder and Elbow Model is a large-scale musculoskeletal computer model incorporating all 31 muscles and all bones, tendons, and ligaments relevant to the shoulder.[13] It is useful for studying shoulder motion and predicting the consequences of an injury or surgical intervention. Recently, it has been used to analyze scapular neck malunion,[14] shoulder muscle activation patterns,[15] the load transfer across the scapula during humeral abduction,[16] tendon transfers to repair massive rotator cuff tears,[17,18] and mechanical loads at the glenohumeral joint.[19] To simulate joint motion, each morphologic structure is represented by an appropriate finite element or series of elements: bones are represented as rigid bodies; joints, as hinges; muscles, as force generators; and tendons and ligaments, as passive springs (Figure 2). Geometric parameters (such as the joint rotation center), muscle parameters (such as the pennation angle), and joint kinematics are determined from cadaver measurements. The model calculates the muscle forces required to achieve the measured kinematics, with the solution constrained by two rules: stability must be achieved in the glenohumeral joint, and the external moments must be balanced by the muscle forces.

### Tendon Deformation

Researchers are using noninvasive imaging to examine tendon deformation, and these techniques have potential for use in clinical measurement. One series of studies used MRI to examine intratendinous strain.[20,21] Earlier theories on the etiology of rotator cuff tears stipulated a relationship between tears and tissue deformation in which variations in intratendinous strains at different joint positions affect tendon tears. MRI was used to examine the supraspinatus tendon in cadaver specimens at different joint positions under neutral and physiologically relevant loads, and texture correlation imaging was used to map the strain field within the tendon. The strain did not differ through the thickness of the tendon (from the bursal to the articular surface), although it dramatically increased as the joint angle increased. This finding suggests that joint position plays a critical role in rotator cuff mechanics. A simulated articular surface tear resulted in a significant increase in strain in all joint positions except 15° and on the bursal and middle regions of the tendon. This finding indicates that, at almost all joint positions, a small articular-side tendon tear puts the rest of the tendon at risk of failure.

A study of isolated supraspinatus tendons also found that the mechanical behavior of the tissue is not homogeneous.[22] Strains were typically higher near the tendon-to-bone insertion, compared with the tendon midsubstance, and on the articular surface, compared with the bursal surface. Tendon strain also varied from anterior to posterior locations. This complex mechanical

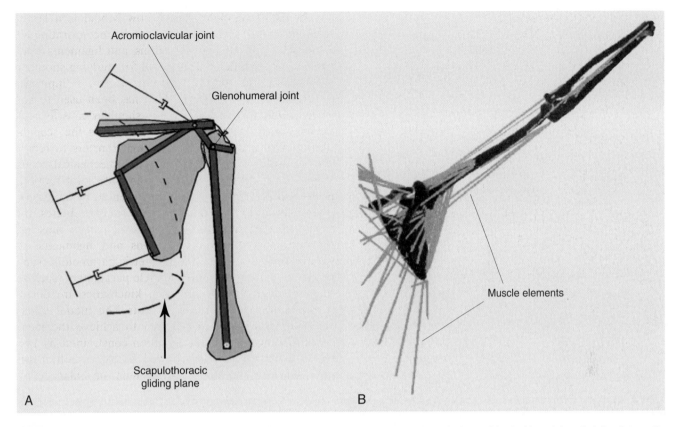

**Figure 2** Schematic representations of the Delft Shoulder and Elbow Model. **A,** The beam structures approximate the bones of the shoulder and the articulations between the bones. **B,** The muscle elements used in the model are indicated by the lines. *(Reproduced with permission from Kirsch RF, Acosta AM, van der Helm FC, Rotteveel RJ, Cash LA: Model-based development of neuroprostheses for restoring proximal arm function. J Rehabil Res Dev 2001;38:619-626.)*

behavior suggests a propensity for tears to begin on the articular tendinous surface.

### Kinematics

Shoulder kinematic studies using cadaver specimens have provided valuable information on rotator cuff functioning. Loads are applied using weights, and motion is applied using a mechanical testing frame or robotic arm. The innovative use of robotic arms has allowed investigators to study the role of each structure through the principle of superposition.[23] In a typical study, a cadaver humerus is moved through a physiologic range of motion using the robotic arm, and the forces are recorded. One shoulder structure, such as the infraspinatus tendon, is then cut. The robotic arm is used to precisely repeat the three-dimensional motion, and the forces are again recorded. The difference in the measured forces can be directly attributed to the function of the structure that was cut.

Cadaver models also have been used extensively to study rotator cuff pathology. One study measured the variation in external rotational moment arms among subregions of rotator cuff tendons after simulated rotator cuff tears.[24] The findings indicate that rotator cuff tendons increase their effective moment arms through

connections to other subregions, but the advantage is lost after a rotator cuff tear. The study data suggest that a partial rotator cuff repair is worthwhile if a complete repair is not possible.

The stability of the glenohumeral joint was studied using cadaver specimens.[25,26] Asymmetric contact between the glenoid and the humerus occurred in normal shoulders when overhead activity was simulated; it appears that excessive or repetitive asymmetric loads may eventually lead to the posterior glenoid erosion often seen in clinical practice. Full-thickness rotator cuff tears resulted in changes in the glenoid's position relative to the humerus and changes in contact pressure. Tendon repair restored most, but not all, of the normal biomechanics.

Cadaver studies cannot completely duplicate the joint motions, muscle forces, and other complex motions found in dynamic in vivo movement. A recent study used a model-based tracking technique that produces high-resolution dynamic kinematic data by combining CT (which offers high spatial resolution) and biplane fluoroscopy (which offers high temporal resolution).[27] To track the three-dimensional motion of the glenohumeral joint, digitally reconstructed radiographs were generated by projection through a three-dimensional

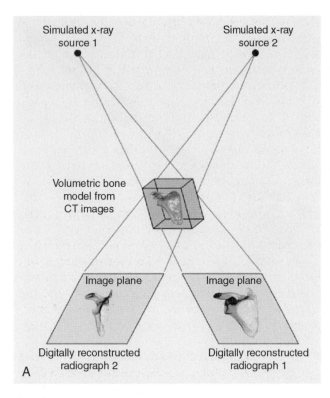
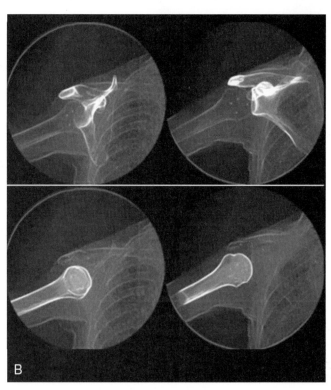

**Figure 3**   Noninvasive in vivo measurement of bone motion. **A,** A schematic representation of radiographs digitally reconstructed from a CT bone model using simulated biplane radiographic images. **B,** Radiographs digitally reconstructed by superimposing images (the highlighted bones) over the biplane radiographic images. *(Reproduced with permission from Bey MJ, Zauel R, Brock SK, Tashman S: Validation of a new model-based tracking technique for measuring three-dimensional, in vivo glenohumeral joint kinematics. J Biomech Eng 2006;128:604-609.)*

CT bone model and matched to biplane radiographic images to determine the in vivo position and orientation of the bone being studied (Figure 3). Validation of the technique using cadaver specimens found accuracy levels superior to those of earlier noninvasive methods of measuring dynamic in vivo glenohumeral motion. This method can be used in future studies to analyze shoulder motion under different conditions, such as pitching and rehabilitation, and to evaluate the effect of treatment.

## Animal Models for Studying Disease

Earlier studies of the rotator cuff emphasized the extrinsic or intrinsic mechanism of injury. In the extrinsic mechanism, tendon damage is caused by compression of the tendon against a surrounding structure, usually the coracoacromial arch. In the intrinsic mechanism, the tendon injury originates within the tendon, as from direct tendon overload or degeneration. Overuse also has been implicated as an important cause of injury. In clinical practice, dominance of the extrinsic or intrinsic mechanism in a patient's injury affects the approach to treatment and prevention of rotator cuff disease.

To address the inherent limitations of human in vivo and cadaver studies, several animal models have been developed to study rotator cuff etiology, injury, and healing. The nonprimate considered most appropriate for the study of the rotator cuff is the rat. The rat's prominent supraspinatus tendon is inserted onto the greater tuberosity of the humeral head under a bony arch composed of the coracoid, clavicle, and acromion.[28] However, larger animals, such as dogs and sheep, must be used to evaluate surgical techniques and test treatments requiring US Food and Drug Administration approval. Although surgical repair in larger animals better approximates clinical practice than repair in small animals, larger animals lack a coracoacromial arch through which the tendons must pass. The rabbit subscapularis tendon was recently found to be a good model of the human supraspinatus tendon in terms of soft tissue and bony anatomy, and it may serve as a useful compromise between extablished small (rodent) and large (canine and sheep) animal models.[29]

### Tendinosis Models

Rats have been used to model the extrinsic, intrinsic, and overuse mechanisms of rotator cuff pathogenesis.[28,30-33] In the first attempt to simulate extrinsic impingement, an Achilles tendon allograft was wrapped around the acromion to effectively reduce the space within the coracoacromial arch.[30,31] The model involved soft-tissue rather than bony impingement, and a subsequent study avoided this limitation by using allografts secured to the inferior surface of the acromion.[33] The intrinsic mechanism of injury has been modeled through the use of collagenase, which promotes matrix degeneration and thereby re-creates the degeneration that occurs with tendinosis.[30,31] The overuse mechanism of injury has been modeled in rats by treadmill activity.[30-32,34,35] Overuse led to decreased mechanical properties as well as a histologic appearance similar to that seen in rotator cuff tendinosis. Another study showed that inflammatory factors are upregulated over time because of overuse; the implication is that nonsteroidal anti-inflammatory drugs may be effective in the treatment of overuse injuries.[34] Angiogenesis factors also were upregulated; this finding indicates that new blood vessels are formed throughout the period of overuse. Another study found that nitrous oxide synthases were upregulated as a result of overuse activity.[35] Nitrous oxide, a free radical produced by nitrous oxide synthases, has a role in tendon degeneration and healing. A small increase in nitrous oxide may have the beneficial effect of stimulating blood flow or matrix synthesis, but the large increase in nitrous oxide produced during overuse probably has significant detrimental effects, such as increases in the level of apoptosis and production of metalloproteinases.

### Tendon Tear Models

Acute injury models of the rat and rabbit supraspinatus tendons,[36-49] rabbit subscapularis tendon,[29] and sheep, dog, and goat infraspinatus tendons[50-55] have been developed to study rotator cuff tendon healing. In these studies, the tendon is sharply detached at its bony insertion and then surgically repaired to its anatomic location to approximate the surgical presentation of acute rotator cuff injuries, which typically require tendon-to-bone healing.

### Chronic Degeneration Models

Modeling of acute injury and repair is useful in studying the healing of rotator cuff tendons, but it has limited relevance to clinical rotator cuff pathology. Rotator cuff tears typically occur after years of chronic tendon degeneration. The causes of degeneration are unclear and may involve the extrinsic, intrinsic, and overuse mechanisms. The effect of degeneration on tissue quality is well defined: chronically degenerated rotator cuff muscles have a high fat content,[56] retracted tendons are stiffer than normal tendons, and the levels of type III collagen (a type associated with scarring) and hyaluronic acid (a GAG typically associated with cartilage) are higher.[57,58]

Several investigators have attempted to develop a clinically relevant model by reproducing human chronic rotator cuff pathology in animal models. To study the healing process, the infraspinatus tendon was released in a sheep model and repaired immediately or after a 6-week or 18-week delay.[51,52,59] The tendons in the delayed-repair groups were wrapped in a dura substitute to prevent adhesion formation. The study found that in vivo muscle force contraction decreased significantly in the delayed-repair groups. Intramuscular fat concentration increased twelvefold, although the concentration was partially reversed after the tendon was repaired. The modulus of elasticity was increased in the detached tendons; this change was also partially reversed after tendon repair. In a second sheep model, the infraspinatus tendon was released and encased in a silicone tube, then allowed to retract for 40 weeks.[52] Muscle atrophy developed, and the amount of intramuscular fat increased. After a canine infraspinatus tendon was detached and wrapped in polyvinylidene fluoride to prevent adhesion formation between the tendon and the surrounding structures, muscle stiffness increased, muscle volume decreased, and intramuscular fat content increased[54] (Figure 4).

In a rabbit model used to study muscle atrophy and fatty infiltration in rotator cuff degeneration and healing, supraspinatus tendons were detached and either repaired after a delay of 12 weeks or reattached after 6 weeks and examined at 12 weeks.[44,46,47,49] Significant muscle atrophy and fatty infiltration appeared in both groups and were not reversed by reattachment.[46] After being detached, another group of tendons was wrapped in a polyvinylidene fluoride membrane for 12 weeks; the membrane was removed, and the tendon was inserted into a bony trough.[47] Fat accumulation was significantly increased on the muscle surface, between the muscle fascicles, and occasionally in the sarcoplasm. Surgical reattachment of the tendon did not reverse atrophy or fat accumulation.

Chronic degeneration was simulated in a rat model by cutting the supraspinatus tendon and allowing it to retract for an extended period.[40,60] Tendon detachment resulted in a rapid loss of muscle mass, an increase in the proportion of fast-twitch muscle fibers, and an increase in the fibrotic content of the muscle bed. To allow formation of adhesions between the retracted tendon and the surrounding structures, the tendons were not wrapped in a membrane. The muscle morphology had returned to its normal state 16 weeks after detachment, presumably because of the new attachments. The mechanical and collagen organization properties of the tendon also rapidly deteriorated after detachment, but after 16 weeks they had regained their normal state. In this model, the degeneration of the measured structural, biomechanical, and morphologic properties was temporary.

No current animal model fully reproduces clinical rotator cuff pathology, and the findings of animal studies differ with regard to the potential for the recovery of

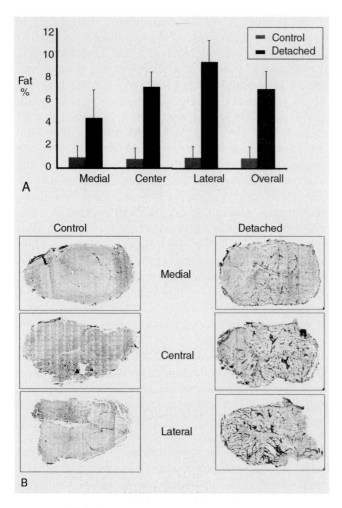

**Figure 4** A study of chronically detached infraspinatus muscles using an animal model. **A,** Graph showing the percentage of fat in control and study muscles at 12 weeks, as determined from histologic sections stained with osmium tetroxide. **B,** Representative cross-sections of control and study muscles at 12 weeks; the black stain represents fat. *(Reproduced with permission from Safran O, Derwin KA, Powell K, Iannotti JP: Changes in rotator cuff muscle volume, fat content, and passive mechanics after chronic detachment in a canine model. J Bone Joint Surg Am 2005;87: 2662-2670.)*

muscle and tendon properties after repair of chronic rotator cuff degeneration. In the rat model, muscle and tendon properties returned to their normal state or were enhanced by 16 weeks of tendon detachment. Fatty infiltration, a critical component of human chronic rotator cuff degeneration, did not appear in the rat model. In large animal models, fatty infiltration developed only if synthetic tendon sheaths were used to prevent adhesion formation.

### Brachial Plexus Birth Injury Models

Approximately 1 of every 1,000 neonates experiences shoulder paralysis caused by a brachial plexus injury.[61] Most neonatal brachial plexus injuries result from a difficult childbirth, frequently involving shoulder dystocia.[62] The shoulder muscles are fully active in utero, and unilateral paralysis occurs at birth. A brachial plexus in-

jury can lead to glenoid dysplasia, posterior shoulder subluxation, humeral head flattening, or shoulder dislocation,[63,64] primarily resulting from an imbalance in muscle forces. In a recent study, one shoulder of a mouse was injected with botulinum toxin A to paralyze the rotator cuff muscles at birth.[65] The contralateral shoulder was injected with saline to serve as a paired internal control. Paralysis of the cuff muscles led to significantly smaller supraspinatus muscle volume and therefore to a reduction of load across the shoulder joint, which delayed postnatal development by impeding the accumulation of mineralized bone and preventing fibrocartilage formation (Figure 5). Humeral head deformities developed, as they do in humans.

### Tendon Healing

The healing of a rotator cuff tendon after acute injury and repair is similar to the healing of other tendons.[66] An inflammatory phase lasting a few days is followed by a proliferative phase lasting several weeks, during which fibroblasts multiply and begin to produce type III collagen. A study using a rat model found that after injury and repair, rapid proliferation reached a peak at 10 days[38] (Figure 6). The expression of matrix genes, especially collagen genes, increased rapidly.[38,43] The expression of two proteoglycans that play a role in collagen fibrillogenesis dramatically changed after injury and repair; decorin expression decreased and biglycan expression increased, indicating an increase in collagen fibrillogenesis. The proliferative phase is followed by the remodeling phase, in which significant amounts of extracellular matrix are produced and the existing scar matrix is reorganized. Disorganized scar laid down during the proliferative phase is remodeled.[43]

The expression of matrix genes is mediated by cytokine and growth factor expression, which follows a finely controlled temporal pattern during early healing. Studies using a rabbit model found that the levels of basic fibroblast growth factor peaked at 7 days; insulin-like growth factor 1, at 5 days; and platelet-derived growth factor, between 7 days and 14 days. Transforming growth factor β (TGF-β) was constant throughout the early healing period.[67] Factors associated with shoulder pain, such as interleukin-1β and cyclooxygenase, were also highly elevated in the early period after injury; they decline to normal levels over time.[68]

In the rat model, collagen organization was found to improve as the scar tissue was remodeled over time, although it never returned to a normal state.[43] Biomechanical properties improved during all phases of healing, although never returning to normal.[38,43] The suture-grasping strength of the surgical repair provided the initial strength of the structure; as the tendon healed against its bony insertion, surgical repair strength was augmented by new collagen fibers anchored into the humeral head.

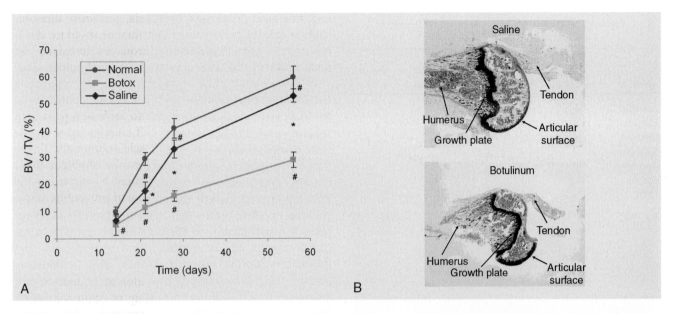

**Figure 5** A mouse model of neonatal brachial plexus palsy, in which the supraspinatus tendon was paralyzed at birth. **A,** Graph of humeral head bone volume over time, as measured using micro CT and deformities in humeral head shape. * = significant difference between saline-treated and botulinum toxin (Botox®)-treated tendons, # = significant difference between saline-treated or botulinum toxin–treated tendons and normal tendons. BV = bone volume, TV = total volume. **B,** Histologic sections show a delay in enthesis maturation in the botulinum-treated group and a deformity in humeral head shape.

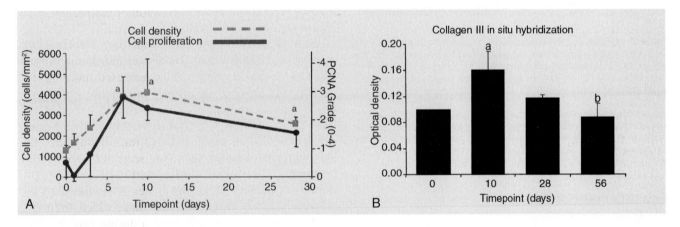

**Figure 6** Graphic representations of rotator cuff healing. **A,** Cell density and cell proliferation peak approximately 10 days after injury and repair and then decrease over time. PCNA = proliferating cell nuclear antigen. **B,** Collagen III mRNA peaks approximately 10 days after injury and then decreases over time, indicating a scar-mediated healing response. a = significant difference compared with day 0 ($P < 0.05$), b = significant difference compared with day 10 ($P < 0.05$). *(Reproduced with permission from Galatz LM, Sandell LJ, Rothermich SY, et al: Characteristics of the rat supraspinatus tendon during tendon-to-bone healing after acute injury. J Orthop Res 2006;24:541-550.)*

Two studies using a rat model found that the healing of tendons after a chronic rotator cuff injury differs from healing after an acute injury. One study found that the tension required to repair the supraspinatus tendon increases rapidly after injury.[40] A delay between injury and repair therefore results in significantly greater tension on the healing interface. Increased repair site tension could be detrimental to healing; increased tension at the time of repair led to a decrease in failure properties and stiffness and an increase in cross-sectional area.[41] The findings of a study of mechanical properties and cross-sectional area were similar.[37] In addition, the study found that a delay between injury and repair led to dramatic

losses of bone mineral density in the humeral head. These studies indicate that in the clinical setting both repair site tension and the time between injury and repair should be minimized. However, in a study using a rabbit model,[44] a delay of as much as 12 weeks between injury and repair did not affect the formation of a fibrocartilaginous enthesis between the healing tendon and bone; progressive enthesis formation occurred regardless of delay. Ordered chondrocytes and well-aligned collagen were seen in all animals after 8 to 12 weeks of healing. These conflicting results highlight the need for the development of a reliable, clinically relevant model of chronic rotator cuff degeneration.

**A**   Expression of Connective Tissue Markers in Ectopic Tissues Induced by BMP-12 and BMP-2

| Marker | T/L embryonic | T/L Ad | BMP-12 3 d | BMP-12 10 d | BMP-2 10 d | Control 10 d |
|---|---|---|---|---|---|---|
| Six 1/Six 2 | + | + | ± | ± | - | - |
| Elastin | + | + | + | + | - | - |
| Decorin | + | + | + | + | + | + |
| Collagen I | + | + | + | + | + | + |
| Aggrecan | ± | + | + | ± | - | - |
| Alphos | - | - | - | - | - | - |
| OCN | - | - | - | - | + | - |

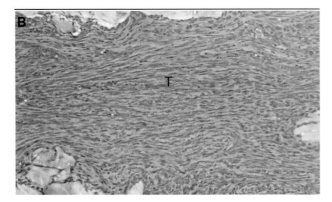

**Figure 7**   **A,** Levels of mRNA expression found in developing tendons (Six 1 and Six 2), adult tendon (elastin, decorin, and collagen I), cartilage (aggrecan), and bone (alphos [alkaline phosphatase] and osteocalcin [OCN]), compared with levels in tissues induced using BMP-12, BMP-2 (a growth factor that stimulates bone formation), or the carrier matrix only (control). T/L = tendon or ligament, Ad = adult, d = days postimplantation. **B,** Subcutaneous implantation of BMP-12 (25 mg) resulted in tissue with a highly organized linear arrangement of cells and deposition of large amounts of extracellular matrix. T = neotendon-ligament tissue. *(Reproduced with permission from Wolfman NM, Hattersley G, Cox K, et al: Ectopic induction of tendon and ligament in rats by growth and differentiation factors 5, 6, and 7, members of the TGF-β gene family. J Clin Invest 1997;100:321-330.)*

## Enhancement of Healing

### The Mechanical Environment

Investigators have studied mechanical, biologic, and tissue-engineering approaches to enhancing rotator cuff healing. Musculoskeletal tissues are highly sensitive to their mechanical environment, and immobilization of healthy joints leads to rapid deterioration of tendon and ligament mechanical properties.[69] The compression of healthy tendons (most notably in the hand) leads to the production of matrix proteins normally found in cartilage.[6] Because of research on uninjured tissues, the trend in postsurgical rehabilitation is to encourage early mobilization and joint loading. However, the results of a recent study indicate that the response of healing rotator cuff tendons to loading may be different from that of uninjured tissues. In a rat model, increased activity levels after rotator cuff injury and repair were detrimental to the healing tissue, compared with unrestricted activity or immobilization.[43] Immobilization of the repaired shoulder led to formation of the best mechanical

and structural properties. Therefore, protective immobilization may benefit rotator cuff healing after repair. It has not yet been determined how soon after repair the patient should begin rehabilitation and increase loading.

### The Biologic Environment

Biologic factors can be used to stimulate healing. Unlike rehabilitation, biologic stimuli are not dependent on patient compliance, and they can be administered at the time of surgical repair. A number of growth factors for tendon and ligament repair have been studied.[70] Platelet-derived growth factor can stimulate fibroblast proliferation and matrix synthesis and therefore can accelerate early healing.[70] Basic fibroblast growth factor can stimulate matrix synthesis and angiogenesis and therefore improve healing during the remodeling phase.[70] TGF-β is active in every phase of rotator cuff healing.[38] The TGF-β3 isoform is normally found during fetal development and healing and may lead to a regenerative healing response;[71,72] the TGF-β1 isoform is normally expressed during adult healing and may promote a scar-mediated healing response.[38,71,72] In the future, these TGF-β isoforms may be used to improve the healing response through substitution of regenerative healing for scar-mediated healing.[73,74]

Several growth and differentiation factors show promise in tendon repair. Bone morphogenetic protein 12 (BMP-12), also called cartilage-derived morphogenic protein 3 (CDMP-3) or growth differentiation factor 7 (GDF-7), and the genetically similar factors BMP-13 (also called CDMP-2 or GDF-6) and BMP-14 (also called CDMP-1 or GDF-5) have been identified in developing tendons and ligaments as well as their bony insertions.[75-80] BMP-12, BMP-13, and BMP-14 are important regulatory molecules in synovial joint morphogenesis. Recombinant BMP-12 induced new tendon formation at ectopic sites in vivo; BMP-13 and BMP-14 were less effective[79] (Figure 7). BMP-12, BMP-13, and BMP-14 were localized to the developing insertion site of a periodontal ligament and thus implicated in the formation of the dental attachment apparatus.[80] Two studies using a mouse knockout model found that the absence of BMP-14 leads to detrimental changes in the properties of the Achilles tendon and delayed tendon healing.[81,82] The acute application of the three BMP factors[76,77] or delivery of BMP-12 through gene transfer[78] improved the properties of healing tendon in two animal models. Although these growth factors have not yet been evaluated in rotator cuff healing, they hold great promise.

### Tissue Engineering

Tissue engineering is the regeneration of injured tissue through the merging of signaling biofactors, such as growth factors; responding cells, such as fibroblasts; and matrix microenvironments, such as the collagen scaffold. The scaffold can serve as a delivery system for biofactors, an environment to attract or immobilize cells, or a mechanical stabilizer. Responding cells can be seeded onto the scaffold before implantation, or they can infiltrate the acellular scaffold after implantation. The biofactors can be released by the scaffold during a short or a long period of time.

Several investigators have attempted to improve rotator cuff healing through tissue-engineering approaches. In one series of studies using xenogeneic scaffolds to promote an enhanced biologic response,[83-86] porcine small intestine submucosa was isolated, processed, and sterilized, and it was then tested in sheep,[84] rat,[85] and canine[86] rotator cuff models. The scaffold was found to provide a biologic stimulus to accelerate the repair process. In all three animal models, the histologic appearance and mechanical properties of the rotator cuff tendons improved after treatment with small intestine submucosa. Based on these results, a similar test was conducted with human subjects.[83] Surprisingly, augmentation of the surgical repair of large rotator cuff tears with porcine small intestine submucosa did not improve the rate of healing or clinical outcome scores. Instead, the small intestine submucosa may have been detrimental to the repair process, possibly because of an inflammatory reaction to porcine DNA not removed from the submucosa during processing.[87]

Polymer-based scaffolds have also been used to promote rotator cuff regeneration. These scaffolds are attractive because their mechanical properties and degradation rates are controllable. A chitosan-based scaffold was successfully used to enhance the biologic and mechanical properties of healing tendons.[88,89] Acellular as well as cell-seeded constructs were used to repair the infraspinatus tendons of rabbits; the mechanical properties were improved because of the engineered scaffold and were further improved when cells were added. The scaffold material also enhanced the production of type I collagen. In a separate study, poly-L-lactic acid felt was used to reconstruct the rotator cuffs of rabbits and dogs.[90] The mechanical properties of the treated tendons were significantly better than those of untreated tendons; histologic evaluation revealed that fibroblasts had infiltrated the scaffold and were degrading the felt fibers.

## Summary

The rotator cuff is critical to shoulder stability and motion, and its anatomy and kinematics have been studied extensively. Recent biomechanical studies have used powerful computer simulations and high-resolution noninvasive techniques to measure tendon strain and bone motion. Recent studies also have resulted in the development of animal models with which to study the etiology and pathogenesis of rotator cuff disease and

tear healing. Investigators now can focus on improving the healing response using mechanical, biologic, and tissue-engineering approaches.

## Annotated References

1. Soslowsky LJ, Carpenter JE, Bucchieri JS, Flatow EL: Biomechanics of the rotator cuff. *Orthop Clin North Am* 1997;28:17-30.

2. Clark JM, Harryman DT II: Tendons, ligaments, and capsule of the rotator cuff: Gross and microscopic anatomy. *J Bone Joint Surg Am* 1992;74:713-725.

3. Neer CS II: Impingement lesions. *Clin Orthop Relat Res* 1983;173:70-77.

4. Ozaki J, Fujimoto S, Nakagawa Y, Masuhara K, Tamai S: Tears of the rotator cuff of the shoulder associated with pathological changes in the acromion: A study in cadavera. *J Bone Joint Surg Am* 1988;70:1224-1230.

5. Blevins FT, Djurasovic M, Flatow EL, Vogel KG: Biology of the rotator cuff tendon. *Orthop Clin North Am* 1997;28:1-16.

6. Vogel KG, Koob TJ: Structural specialization in tendons under compression. *Int Rev Cytol* 1989;115:267-293.

7. Thomopoulos S, Marquez JP, Weinberger B, Birman V, Genin GM: Collagen fiber orientation at the tendon to bone insertion and its influence on stress concentrations. *J Biomech* 2006;39:1842-1851.

   The stress transfer between the supraspinatus tendon and its humeral insertion was modeled. The collagen microstructure of the natural enthesis was found to minimize stress concentrations that otherwise would arise between the two mechanically dissimilar materials.

8. Thomopoulos S, Williams GR, Gimbel JA, Favata M, Soslowsky LJ: Variation of biomechanical, structural, and compositional properties along the tendon to bone insertion site. *J Orthop Res* 2003;21:413-419.

   The viscoelastic properties, collagen structure, and extracellular matrix composition of the tendon-to-bone insertion site was found to vary dramatically along its length.

9. Benjamin M, Kumai T, Milz S, Boszczyk BM, Boszczyk AA, Ralphs JR: The skeletal attachment of tendons: Tendon "entheses." *Comp Biochem Physiol A Mol Integr Physiol* 2002;133:931-945.

   Tendon entheses are classified by the tissue present at the skeletal attachment site as fibrous or fibrocartilaginous. Additional fibrocartilaginous specialization in the tendon or bone next to the enthesis creates an "enthesis organ" that reduces wear and tear.

10. Kumagai J, Sarkar K, Uhthoff HK, Okawara Y, Ooshima A: Immunohistochemical distribution of type I, II and III collagens in the rabbit supraspinatus tendon insertion. *J Anat* 1994;185:279-284.

11. Galatz LM, Ball CM, Teefey SA, Middleton WD, Yamaguchi K: The outcome and repair integrity of completely arthroscopically repaired large and massive rotator cuff tears. *J Bone Joint Surg Am* 2004;86-A:219-224.

Repairs of large and massive rotator cuff tears led to a high percentage of recurrent defects. Evaluation of pain relief and ability to perform daily activities found high levels of patient satisfaction, despite the high rate of recurrent defects. Level of evidence:IV.

12. Harryman DT II, Mack LA, Wang KY, Jackins SE, Richardson ML, Matsen FA III: Repairs of the rotator cuff: Correlation of functional results with integrity of the cuff. *J Bone Joint Surg Am* 1991;73:982-989.

13. van der Helm FC: Analysis of the kinematic and dynamic behavior of the shoulder mechanism. *J Biomech* 1994;27:527-550.

14. Chadwick EK, van Noort A, van der Helm FC: Biomechanical analysis of scapular neck malunion: A simulation study. *Clin Biomech (Bristol, Avon)* 2004; 19:906-912.

In this biomechanical modeling study, loss of rotator cuff muscle force and other changes in muscle activation led to loss of arm function in patients with scapular neck malunion.

15. de Groot JH, Rozendaal LA, Meskers CG, Arwert HJ: Isometric shoulder muscle activation patterns for 3-D planar forces: A methodology for musculoskeletal model validation. *Clin Biomech (Bristol, Avon)* 2004;19:790-800.

A methodology is presented for validation of a shoulder model simulation by means of experimentally obtained electromyography.

16. Gupta S, van der Helm FC: Load transfer across the scapula during humeral abduction. *J Biomech* 2004; 37:1001-1009.

The stress distribution in the scapula and the function of the coracoacromial ligament were determined. Force transfer takes place through the bony ridges, whereas the fossa acts as a muscle attachment site. During humeral abduction the coracoacromial ligament is under tension.

17. Magermans DJ, Chadwick EK, Veeger HE, Rozing PM, van der Helm FC: Effectiveness of tendon transfers for massive rotator cuff tears: A simulation study. *Clin Biomech (Bristol, Avon)* 2004;19:116-122.

According to the computer simulation procedure used in the study, a tendon transfer of teres major and latissimus dorsi or teres major alone to the supraspinatus insertion is the most effective procedure for repair of a dysfunctional rotator cuff.

18. Magermans DJ, Chadwick EK, Veeger HE, van der Helm FC, Rozing PM: Biomechanical analysis of tendon transfers for massive rotator cuff tears. *Clin Biomech (Bristol, Avon)* 2004;19:350-357.

Based on a biomechanical model, the study concluded that a tendon transfer of the teres major to the supraspinatus insertion produces the best functional outcome in the treatment of massive rotator cuff tears.

19. Praagman M, Stokdijk M, Veeger HE, Visser B: Predicting mechanical load of the glenohumeral joint, using net joint moments. *Clin Biomech (Bristol, Avon)* 2000;15:315-321.

20. Bey MJ, Song HK, Wehrli FW, Soslowsky LJ: Intratendinous strain fields of the intact supraspinatus tendon: The effect of glenohumeral joint position and tendon region. *J Orthop Res* 2002;20:869-874.

Intratendinous strain in the rotator cuff was quantified using MRI in cadaver specimens at 15°, 30°, 45°, and 60° of glenohumeral abduction in the scapular plane. Few differences were found in intratendinous strain across tendon regions, but increasing joint angle markedly increased intratendinous strain.

21. Bey MJ, Song HK, Wehrli FW, Soslowsky LJ: A noncontact, nondestructive method for quantifying intratissue deformations and strains. *J Biomech Eng* 2002;124:253-258.

Intratendinous strain can be quantified by applying texture correlation analysis to MRI studies. The accuracy and reproducibility of this approach are assessed

22. Huang CY, Wang VM, Pawluk RJ, et al: Inhomogeneous mechanical behavior of the human supraspinatus tendon under uniaxial loading. *J Orthop Res* 2005;23:924-930.

Strains were higher at the tendon insertion site than at the midtendon. The existence of nonhomogeneous strains in the intact supraspinatus tendon showed that intratendinous shear occurs within the tendon. The greater strain on the articular side of the tendon suggested a tendency for tears to originate in the articular tendinous zone.

23. Woo SL, Debski RE, Wong EK, Yagi M, Tarinelli D: Use of robotic technology for diathrodial joint research. *J Sci Med Sport* 1999;2:283-297.

24. Langenderfer JE, Patthanacharoenphon C, Carpenter JE, Hughes RE: Variation in external rotation moment arms among subregions of supraspinatus, infraspinatus, and teres minor muscles. *J Orthop Res* 2006;24:1737-1744.

This study determined rotation moment arms for the rotator cuff muscles. The data have the potential to help surgeons identify cuff tears that would benefit from repair.

25. Gupta R, Lee TQ: Positional-dependent changes in glenohumeral joint contact pressure and force: Possible biomechanical etiology of posterior glenoid wear. *J Shoulder Elbow Surg* 2005;14:105S-110S.

A cadaver model was used to study glenohumeral contact pressures. The contribution of the humerothoracic muscles is significant and should be considered in restoration of glenohumeral joint biomechanics. Asymmetric loading with excessive or repetitive overhead activities may lead to posterior glenoid erosion.

26. Yu J, McGarry MH, Lee YS, Duong LV, Lee TQ: Biomechanical effects of supraspinatus repair on the glenohumeral joint. *J Shoulder Elbow Surg* 2005;14: 65S-71S.

    This study examined whether repair of a supraspinatus tear will result in a change in joint forces, contact pressures and area, and position of the humerus. The data showed greater concavity-compression in pathologic tears, implying that repair may provide a biomechanical benefit.

27. Bey MJ, Zauel R, Brock SK, Tashman S: Validation of a new model-based tracking technique for measuring three-dimensional, in vivo glenohumeral joint kinematics. *J Biomech Eng* 2006;128:604-609.

    A new model-based tracking approach was developed for noninvasive measurement of dynamic glenohumeral joint motion under in vivo conditions. The technique achieved accuracy levels that surpassed that of all previously reported noninvasive techniques.

28. Soslowsky LJ, Carpenter JE, DeBano CM, Banerji I, Moalli MR: Development and use of an animal model for investigations on rotator cuff disease. *J Shoulder Elbow Surg* 1996;5:383-392.

29. Gupta R, Lee TQ: Contributions of the different rabbit models to our understanding of rotator cuff pathology. *J Shoulder Elbow Surg* 2007;16(suppl 5): S149-S157.

    Using data from earlier studies, the rabbit subscapularis tendon is described as a model for the human supraspinatus tendon.

30. Carpenter JE, Flanagan CL, Thomopoulos S, Yian EH, Soslowsky LJ: The effects of overuse combined with intrinsic or extrinsic alterations in an animal model of rotator cuff tendinosis. *Am J Sports Med* 1998;26:801-807.

31. Soslowsky LJ, Thomopoulos S, Esmail A, et al: Rotator cuff tendinosis in an animal model: Role of extrinsic and overuse factors. *Ann Biomed Eng* 2002;30: 1057-1063.

    A rat shoulder model was used to study the roles of extrinsic compression and overuse, individually and in combination, on the development of rotator cuff tendinosis. Overuse plus extrinsic compression was found to create greater injury than either factor alone, particularly when important biomechanical variables are considered.

32. Soslowsky LJ, Thomopoulos S, Tun S, et al: Overuse activity injures the supraspinatus tendon in an animal model: A histologic and biomechanical study. *J Shoulder Elbow Surg* 2000;9:79-84.

33. Schneeberger AG, Nyffeler RW, Gerber C: Structural changes of the rotator cuff caused by experimental subacromial impingement in the rat. *J Shoulder Elbow Surg* 1998;7:375-380.

34. Perry SM, McIlhenny SE, Hoffman MC, Soslowsky LJ: Inflammatory and angiogenic mRNA levels are altered in a supraspinatus tendon overuse animal model. *J Shoulder Elbow Surg* 2005;14:79S-83S.

    Levels of inflammatory and angiogenic markers increased in a rat model of supraspinatus tendon overuse injury.

35. Szomor ZL, Appleyard RC, Murrell GA: Overexpression of nitric oxide synthases in tendon overuse. *J Orthop Res* 2006;24:80-86.

    Nitrous oxide synthases were upregulated in a rat supraspinatus tendon overuse injury model.

36. Barton ER, Gimbel JA, Williams GR, Soslowsky LJ: Rat supraspinatus muscle atrophy after tendon detachment. *J Orthop Res* 2005;23:259-265.

    Tendon detachment resulted in a rapid loss of muscle mass, an increase in fast-muscle fibers, and an increase in fibrotic content. By 16 weeks after detachment, muscle mass and fiber properties had returned to normal levels.

37. Galatz LM, Rothermich SY, Zaegel M, Silva MJ, Havlioglu N, Thomopoulos S: Delayed repair of tendon to bone injuries leads to decreased biomechanical properties and bone loss. *J Orthop Res* 2005;23:1441-1447.

    A delay between injury and repair in a rat supraspinatus tendon tear model led to bone loss in the humeral head.

38. Galatz LM, Sandell LJ, Rothermich SY, et al: Characteristics of the rat supraspinatus tendon during tendon-to-bone healing after acute injury. *J Orthop Res* 2006;24:541-550.

    Rotator cuff healing in a rat model is presented with regard to cell proliferation, collagen expression, and TGF-β expression. Repair tension increased with time following detachment and was related to a decrease in the failure properties of the insertion site. The authors recommend that repair tension be minimized in the clinical setting.

39. Galatz LM, Silva MJ, Rothermich SY, Zaegel MA, Havlioglu N, Thomopoulos S: Nicotine delays tendon-to-bone healing in a rat shoulder model. *J Bone Joint Surg Am* 2006;88:2027-2034.

    Nicotine caused a delay in tendon-to-bone healing in a rat rotator cuff model.

40. Gimbel JA, Mehta S, Van Kleunen JP, Williams GR, Soslowsky LJ: The tension required at repair to reappose the supraspinatus tendon to bone rapidly increases after injury. *Clin Orthop Relat Res* 2004;426: 258-265.

    The tension needed to repair a torn supraspinatus tendon increased rapidly after the tear in a rat rotator cuff model. The findings suggest that in the clinical setting rotator cuff tears should be repaired quickly.

41. Gimbel JA, Van Kleunen JP, Lake SP, Williams GR, Soslowsky LJ: The role of repair tension on tendon to bone healing in an animal model of chronic rotator cuff tears. *J Biomech* 2007;40:561-568.

Increased tension at the time of repair in a rat rotator cuff tear model led to a decrease in mechanical properties.

42. Thomopoulos S, Hattersley G, Rosen V, et al: The localized expression of extracellular matrix components in healing tendon insertion sites: An in situ hybridization study. *J Orthop Res* 2002;20:454-463.

The localized expression of extracellular matrix genes was evaluated over time in a rat rotator cuff injury model. The supraspinatus tendon was ineffective in re-creating the original insertion site in the absence of biological or biomechanical enhancements.

43. Thomopoulos S, Williams GR, Soslowsky LJ: Tendon to bone healing: Differences in biomechanical, structural, and compositional properties due to a range of activity levels. *J Biomech Eng* 2003;125:106-113.

Rat shoulder tendons were surgically detached and repaired, then immobilized, allowed cage activity, or exercised. Contrary to expectations, the immobilized shoulders had superior structural, compositional, and quasilinear viscoelastic properties than the exercised shoulders.

44. Koike Y, Trudel G, Curran D, Uhthoff HK: Delay of supraspinatus repair by up to 12 weeks does not impair enthesis formation: A quantitative histologic study in rabbits. *J Orthop Res* 2006;24:202-210.

A delay in the time from injury to repair did not affect the formation of a fibrocartilaginous enthesis between the healing tendon and bone in a rabbit rotator cuff tear model.

45. Koike Y, Trudel G, Uhthoff HK: Formation of a new enthesis after attachment of the supraspinatus tendon: A quantitative histologic study in rabbits. *J Orthop Res* 2005;23:1433-1440.

A fibrocartilaginous enthesis formed between tendon and bone in a rabbit rotator cuff injury and repair model. Formation of an enthesis was not complete by 24 weeks. This finding suggests that an early and aggressive rehabilitation program is not advisable.

46. Uhthoff HK, Matsumoto F, Trudel G, Himori K: Early reattachment does not reverse atrophy and fat accumulation of the supraspinatus: An experimental study in rabbits. *J Orthop Res* 2003;21:386-392.

In a rabbit model, supraspinatus tendon reattachment 6 weeks after detachment did not reverse muscle atrophy or fat accumulation but did prevent an increase in fat accumulation compared with reattachment at 12 weeks. The later reattachment did not lead to an increase in muscle atrophy.

47. Matsumoto F, Uhthoff HK, Trudel G, Loehr JF: Delayed tendon reattachment does not reverse atrophy and fat accumulation of the supraspinatus: An experimental study in rabbits. *J Orthop Res* 2002;20:357-363.

In a rabbit model, one group of supraspinatus tendons was wrapped in a polyvinylidine flouride membrane after detachment. Neither atrophy nor fat accumulation was reversed by surgical reattachment of the supraspinatus tendon.

48. Choi HR, Kondo S, Hirose K, Ishiguro N, Hasegawa Y, Iwata H: Expression and enzymatic activity of MMP-2 during healing process of the acute supraspinatus tendon tear in rabbits. *J Orthop Res* 2002; 20:927-933.

The spontaneous healing process of a surgically created tendon tear was investigated in rabbits. The results suggest that matrix metalloproteinaise-2 is expressed and activated during healing and can play an important role in the remodeling process.

49. Uhthoff HK, Sano H, Trudel G, Ishii H: Early reactions after reimplantation of the tendon of supraspinatus into bone: A study in rabbits. *J Bone Joint Surg Br* 2000;82:1072-1076.

50. Gerber C, Schneeberger AG, Beck M, Schlegel U: Mechanical strength of repairs of the rotator cuff. *J Bone Joint Surg Br* 1994;76:371-380.

51. Coleman SH, Fealy S, Ehteshami JR, et al: Chronic rotator cuff injury and repair model in sheep. *J Bone Joint Surg Am* 2003;85-A:2391-2402.

A chronic rotator cuff injury model was developed in sheep. Earlier repair of the tendon was found to result in a more rapid recovery of muscle function and tendon elasticity than a delayed repair.

52. Gerber C, Meyer DC, Schneeberger AG, Hoppeler H, von Rechenberg B: Effect of tendon release and delayed repair on the structure of the muscles of the rotator cuff: An experimental study in sheep. *J Bone Joint Surg Am* 2004;86-A:1973-1982.

Musculotendinous retraction induced by tendon release was associated with profound changes in the structure and function of the affected muscle in a sheep model. Muscle atrophy, infiltration by fat cells, and an increase of interstitial connective tissue led to impairment of the physiologic properties of the muscle.

53. Aoki M, Oguma H, Fukushima S, Ishii S, Ohtani S, Murakami G: Fibrous connection to bone after immediate repair of the canine infraspinatus: The most effective bony surface for tendon attachment. *J Shoulder Elbow Surg* 2001;10:123-128.

This histologic study of the canine infraspinatus concluded that ruptured tendon ends should be attached to the remaining distal tendon end or to a cancellous surface, not to a calcified fibrocartilage layer.

54. Safran O, Derwin KA, Powell K, Iannotti JP: Changes in rotator cuff muscle volume, fat content, and pas-

sive mechanics after chronic detachment in a canine model. *J Bone Joint Surg Am* 2005;87:2662-2670.

The chronically detached infraspinatus muscle became stiffer, and the passive loads required to repair it became excessive in a canine model. A significant reduction in muscle volume occurred within weeks. Nonuniformity of muscle fat changes suggests that fat content should be used cautiously as an indicator of muscle quality.

55. MacGillivray JD, Fealy S, Terry MA, Koh JL, Nixon AJ, Warren RF: Biomechanical evaluation of a rotator cuff defect model augmented with a bioresorbable scaffold in goats. *J Shoulder Elbow Surg* 2006;15: 639-644.

A bioresorbable patch was used in an attempt to augment rotator cuff repair in an animal model. No significant difference in load to failure was found between groups.

56. Nakagaki K, Ozaki J, Tomita Y, Tamai S: Fatty degeneration in the supraspinatus muscle after rotator cuff tear. *J Shoulder Elbow Surg* 1996;5:194-200.

57. Riley GP, Harrall RL, Constant CR, Chard MD, Cawston TE, Hazleman BL: Glycosaminoglycans of human rotator cuff tendons: Changes with age and in chronic rotator cuff tendinitis. *Ann Rheum Dis* 1994; 53:367-376.

58. Riley GP, Harrall RL, Constant CR, Chard MD, Cawston TE, Hazleman BL: Tendon degeneration and chronic shoulder pain: Changes in the collagen composition of the human rotator cuff tendons in rotator cuff tendinitis. *Ann Rheum Dis* 1994;53:359-366.

59. Gerber C, Schneeberger AG, Perren SM, Nyffeler RW: Experimental rotator cuff repair: A preliminary study. *J Bone Joint Surg Am* 1999;81:1281-1290.

60. Gimbel JA, Van Kleunen JP, Mehta S, Perry SM, Williams GR, Soslowsky LJ: Supraspinatus tendon organizational and mechanical properties in a chronic rotator cuff tear animal model. *J Biomech* 2004;37: 739-749.

Tendon detachment led to loss of muscle mass and a decrease in mechanical properties in a rat rotator cuff model. These properties returned to normal within 16 weeks, presumably because of attachments that formed between the tendon and the surrounding tissues.

61. Birch R: Obstetric brachial plexus palsy. *J Hand Surg Br* 2002;27:3-8.

62. Mehta SH, Blackwell SC, Bujold E, Sokol RJ: What factors are associated with neonatal injury following shoulder dystocia? *J Perinatol* 2006;26:85-88.

Maternal obesity was associated with an increased risk of neonatal injury after shoulder dystocia, and a short second stage of labor was associated with a lower rate of neonatal injury.

63. Waters PM, Smith GR, Jaramillo D: Glenohumeral deformity secondary to brachial plexus birth palsy. *J Bone Joint Surg Am* 1998;80:668-677.

64. Moukoko D, Ezaki M, Wilkes D, Carter P: Posterior shoulder dislocation in infants with neonatal brachial plexus palsy. *J Bone Joint Surg Am* 2004;86-A:787-793.

Posterior shoulder dislocation may occur before age 1 year in infants with neonatal brachial plexus palsy. Following diagnosis, attention should be focused on improving the stability and congruency of the shoulder joint.

65. Thomopoulos S, Kim HM, Rothermich SY, Biederstadt C, Das R, Galatz LM: Decreased muscle loading delays maturation of the tendon enthesis during post-natal development. *J Orthop Res* 2007;25:1154-1163.

Decreased muscle loading during postnatal development led to a delay in bone formation and enthesis maturation in a mouse neonatal brachial plexus model.

66. Lin TW, Cardenas L, Soslowsky LJ: Biomechanics of tendon injury and repair. *J Biomech* 2004;37:865-877.

The biomechanics of tendon injury and repair are reviewed.

67. Kobayashi M, Itoi E, Minagawa H, et al: Expression of growth factors in the early phase of supraspinatus tendon healing in rabbits. *J Shoulder Elbow Surg* 2006;15:371-377.

The levels of basic fibroblast growth factor, insulin-like growth factor, platelet-derived growth factor BB, and TGF-β were evaluated during healing in a rabbit rotator cuff model.

68. Koshima H, Kondo S, Mishima S, et al: Expression of interleukin-1beta, cyclooxygenase-2, and prostaglandin E2 in a rotator cuff tear in rabbits. *J Orthop Res* 2007;25:92-97.

When the rotator cuff is torn in a rabbit model, interleukin-1β is produced by the tendon, stimulating cyclooxygenase-2 production in the torn tendon and the articular cartilage. Cyclooxygenase-2 in turn produces prostaglandin E2, which mediates shoulder pain.

69. Woo SL, Gomez MA, Woo YK, Akeson WH: Mechanical properties of tendons and ligaments: Part II. The relationships of immobilization and exercise on tissue remodeling. *Biorheology* 1982;19:397-408.

70. Molloy T, Wang Y, Murrell G: The roles of growth factors in tendon and ligament healing. *Sports Med* 2003; 33:381-394.

This review covers some recent investigations into the roles of five growth factors involved in tendon healing, as well their use as therapeutic agents to increase the efficacy and efficiency of tendon and ligament healing.

71. Beredjiklian PK, Favata M, Cartmell JS, Flanagan CL, Crombleholme TM, Soslowsky LJ: Regenerative versus reparative healing in tendon: A study of

biomechanical and histological properties in fetal sheep. *Ann Biomed Eng* 2003;31:1143-1152.

The healing properties of adult and fetal sheep tendons were compared. TGF-β1 expression was low in the fetal but upregulated in the adult wounds. Regenerative healing properties were identified in the fetal tendon; the adult tendon healed with scar formation.

72. Ferguson MW, O'Kane S: Scar-free healing: From embryonic mechanisms to adult therapeutic intervention. *Philos Trans R Soc Lond B Biol Sci* 2004;359: 839-850.

Scar-free embryonic healing is reviewed.

73. Shah M, Foreman DM, Ferguson MW: Neutralisation of TGF-beta 1 and TGF-beta 2 or exogenous addition of TGF-beta 3 to cutaneous rat wounds reduces scarring. *J Cell Sci* 1995;108:985-1002.

74. Chang J, Thunder R, Most D, Longaker MT, Lineaweaver WC: Studies in flexor tendon wound healing: Neutralizing antibody to TGF-beta1 increases postoperative range of motion. *Plast Reconstr Surg* 2000;105:148-155.

75. Forslund C, Aspenberg P: CDMP-2 induces bone or tendon-like tissue depending on mechanical stimulation. *J Orthop Res* 2002;20:1170-1174.

The response to CDMP-2 implants at different sites and under different loading condition was analyzed in a rat model. The findings suggest that the response to CDMP-2 is dependent o the mechanical situation at the site where it is applied.

76. Forslund C, Rueger D, Aspenberg P: A comparative dose-response study of cartilage-derived morphogenetic protein (CDMP)-1, -2 and -3 for tendon healing in rats. *J Orthop Res* 2003;21:617-621.

The influence on tendon healing of CDMPs at four different dosages was investigated in a rat model. There was a significant dosage-related increase in strength and stiffness with all three CDMPs, but no difference between them was found.

77. Aspenberg P, Forslund C: Enhanced tendon healing with GDF 5 and 6. *Acta Orthop Scand* 1999;70: 51-54.

78. Lou J, Tu Y, Burns M, Silva MJ, Manske P: BMP-12 gene transfer augmentation of lacerated tendon repair. *J Orthop Res* 2001;19:1199-1202.

An investigation into the effect of BMP-12 gene transfer on tendon cells found an increase in type I collagen synthesis. A twofold increase in tensile strength and stiffness of repaired tendons also was found.

79. Wolfman NM, Hattersley G, Cox K, et al: Ectopic induction of tendon and ligament in rats by growth and differentiation factors 5, 6, and 7, members of the TGF-beta gene family. *J Clin Invest* 1997;100: 321-330.

80. Sena K, Morotome Y, Baba O, Terashima T, Takano Y, Ishikawa I: Gene expression of growth differentiation factors in the developing periodontium of rat molars. *J Dent Res* 2003;82:166-171.

GDF-5, -6, and -7 appear to be involved in the formation of the dental attachment apparatus.

81. Chhabra A, Tsou D, Clark RT, Gaschen V, Hunziker EB, Mikic B: GDF-5 deficiency in mice delays Achilles tendon healing. *J Orthop Res* 2003;21: 826-835.

Histologic, biochemical, and ultrastructural analyses found that GDF-5 may have an important role in modulating tendon repair, consistent with its previously posited roles in cell recruitment, migration-adhesion, differentiation, proliferation, and angiogenesis.

82. Mikic B, Schalet BJ, Clark RT, Gaschen V, Hunziker EB: GDF-5 deficiency in mice alters the ultrastructure, mechanical properties and composition of the Achilles tendon. *J Orthop Res* 2001;19:365-371.

A mouse model was used to study GDF-5/CDMP-1 genetic mutations in acromesomelic dysplasia of the Hunter-Thompson and Grebe types. The findings suggest that increased tendon and ligament laxity may be the cause of joint dislocations seen in patients, rather than developmental abnormalities in the joints.

83. Iannotti JP, Codsi MJ, Kwon YW, Derwin K, Ciccone J, Brems JJ: Porcine small intestine submucosa augmentation of surgical repair of chronic two-tendon rotator cuff tears: A randomized, controlled trial. *J Bone Joint Surg Am* 2006;88:1238-1244.

Surgical repair and augmentation of large, massive chronic rotator cuff tears with porcine small intestine submucosa did not improve tendon healing rate or clinical outcome scores. It is not recommended for use with the described surgical and postsurgical procedures. Level of evidence: II.

84. Schlegel TF, Hawkins RJ, Lewis CW, Motta T, Turner AS: The effects of augmentation with swine small intestine submucosa on tendon healing under tension: Histologic and mechanical evaluations in sheep. *Am J Sports Med* 2006;34:275-280.

Augmentation of sheep infraspinatus tendon repairs using porcine small intestine submucosa improved early healing characteristics in sheep.

85. Zalavras CG, Gardocki R, Huang E, Stevanovic M, Hedman T, Tibone J: Reconstruction of large rotator cuff tendon defects with porcine small intestinal submucosa in an animal model. *J Shoulder Elbow Surg* 2006;15:224-231.

Porcine small intestine submucosa grafts served as scaffolds promoting host tissue ingrowth in a rat model. Use of these grafts appeared promising for the management of large rotator cuff defects in humans.

86.  Dejardin LM, Arnoczky SP, Ewers BJ, Haut RC, Clarke RB: Tissue-engineered rotator cuff tendon using porcine small intestine submucosa: Histologic and mechanical evaluation in dogs. *Am J Sports Med* 2001;29:175-184.

To determine its efficacy in stimulating regeneration of a rotator cuff tendon, porcine small intestinal submucosa was used to replace the infraspinatus tendon in adult dogs. Ultimate strength was less than that of native infraspinatus tendons but similar to that of reimplanted tendons at 3 and 6 months.

87.  Zheng MH, Chen J, Kirilak Y, Willers C, Xu J, Wood D: Porcine small intestine submucosa (SIS) is not an acellular collagenous matrix and contains porcine DNA: Possible implications in human implantation. *J Biomed Mater Res B Appl Biomater* 2005;73:61-67.

Porcine small intestine submucosa can cause an inflammatory reaction if the porcine DNA is not completely removed from the submucosa before implantation.

88.  Funakoshi T, Majima T, Iwasaki N, et al: Application of tissue engineering techniques for rotator cuff regeneration using a chitosan-based hyaluronan hybrid fiber scaffold. *Am J Sports Med* 2005;33:1193-1201.

A chitosan-based scaffold material enhanced the production of type I collagen and led to improved mechanical strength in a rabbit rotator cuff model.

89.  Funakoshi T, Majima T, Suenaga N, Iwasaki N, Yamane S, Minami A: Rotator cuff regeneration using chitin fabric as an acellular matrix. *J Shoulder Elbow Surg* 2006;15:112-118.

A chitosan-based scaffold was used to enhance the biologic and mechanical properties of the healing rabbit infraspinatus tendon.

90.  Aoki M, Miyamoto S, Okamura K, Yamashita T, Ikada Y, Matsuda S: Tensile properties and biological response of poly(L-lactic acid) felt graft: An experimental trial for rotator-cuff reconstruction. *J Biomed Mater Res B Appl Biomater* 2004;71:252-259.

A poly-L-lactic acid scaffold was used to enhance the mechanical properties of healing rabbit and canine rotator cuffs.

# Chapter 4

# Kinematics and Kinesiology of the Shoulder

Patrick J. McMahon, MD

Richard E. Debski, PhD

## Introduction

Kinematics is the study of joint motion and stability, including rotation and translation. In the shoulder, the activity of numerous muscles must be coordinated at four separate articulations to yield motion and joint stability. Kinesiology is the study of muscles and their neural system control. It includes the sensory, motor, and central integration and processing components of the central nervous system as they are involved in motion and joint stability. Recent study of shoulder kinematics and kinesiology has improved knowledge of shoulder functioning and its integration with the functioning of other areas of the body.

## Kinematics

Normal shoulder motion requires coordinated action of the sternoclavicular, acromioclavicular, glenohumeral, and scapulothoracic joints (Figure 1), as well as the complex interaction of 30 muscles and the upper thorax, humerus, clavicle, and scapula. In a normal shoulder, motion is composed of large angular rotations and small glenohumeral translations.[1,2] Small linear movements between the articular surfaces of the humeral head and the glenoid are called translations; large, symptomatic translations constitute glenohumeral joint instability. The three possible translations can be defined as anterior-posterior, superior-inferior, and medial-lateral. The three rotations are internal-external, adduction-abduction in the scapular plane, and adduction-abduction in the horizontal plane (Figure 2).

Laxity is defined as normal motion of the joint and is often called joint play. In contrast, instability is defined as abnormal motion of the joint. Instability in some joints can be precisely defined. For example, in the knee, a Lachman test finding of more than 5 mm of translation, compared with the contralateral side, is widely accepted as associated with anterior cruciate ligament rupture resulting in instability. Instability in the shoulder is more poorly defined as translation that results in symptoms. In addition, a shoulder is considered hyperlax if the examiner can easily elicit humeral head subluxation from the glenoid in the anterior, posterior, and inferior directions, without producing symptoms. Distinguishing between shoulder laxity and instability is sometimes difficult, because of the wide variability in normal joint laxity and the absence of biomechanical studies to delineate laxity.

### Sternoclavicular Joint Kinematics

The sternoclavicular joint connects the upper extremity and the axial skeleton and is the only true synovial joint. It is stabilized by four ligaments and the intra-articular disk. The interclavicular ligament restrains superior joint motion and is taut when the shoulder is at the body's side.[3] The anterior and posterior capsular structures prevent anterior and posterior motion; the anterior structures also resist superior motion.[4] The costoclavicular ligaments run obliquely and laterally from the first rib to the inferior surface of the clavicle to provide additional joint stability. The intra-articular disk protects the clavicle from medial displacement (Figure 3).

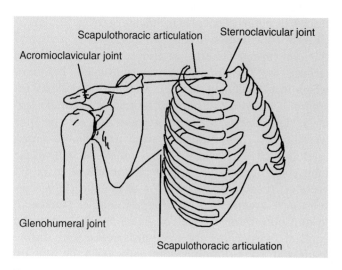

**Figure 1** Normal shoulder function requires coordination of the sternoclavicular, acromioclavicular, glenohumeral, and scapulothoracic joints.

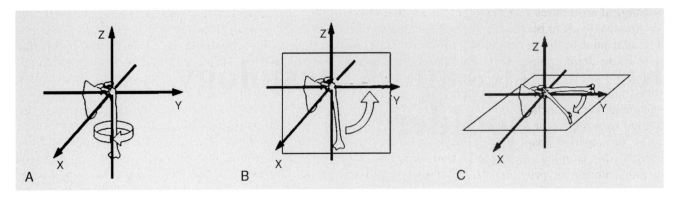

**Figure 2** Only three axes are needed to describe the rotation of the shoulder: internal-external **(A)**, adduction-abduction in the scapular plane **(B)**, and adduction-abduction in the horizontal plane **(C)**.

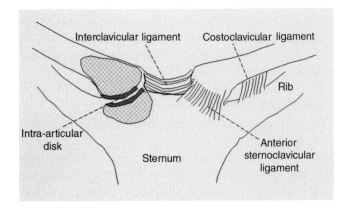

**Figure 3** The sternoclavicular joint is stabilized by the interclavicular ligament, the anterior and posterior capsular structures, the costoclavicular ligaments, and the intra-articular disk.

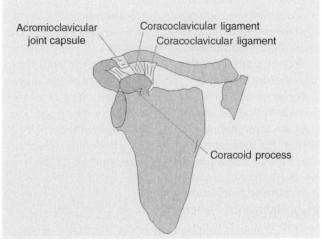

**Figure 4** The conoid and trapezoid coracoclavicular ligaments and the joint capsule stabilize the acromioclavicular joint.

## Acromioclavicular Joint Kinematics

The acromioclavicular joint is inclined between 20° and 50° in the coronal plane;[5,6] this incline may affect joint stability. The acromioclavicular joint is stabilized by structures other than the joint capsule. The conoid and trapezoid coracoclavicular ligaments stabilize the clavicle's superior motion at the acromioclavicular joint, and the joint capsule restrains anterior and posterior motion (Figure 4). The inferior acromioclavicular ligament, which is a thickening of the capsule, is the primary restraint to anterior translation. The trapezoid coracoclavicular ligament is the primary restraint to posterior translation.[7] These functions were determined during joint motion and change, based on acromioclavicular joint constraints.[8] During joint motion allowing six degrees of freedom, the translation of the clavicle was almost 50% greater than was found in earlier studies allowing only three degrees of freedom. The kinematic constraints placed on the acromioclavicular joint during loading affect the resulting joint motion (in the primary direction of loading), the magnitude and direction of force of each ligament, and the coupled motions.

Motion at the acromioclavicular joint also changes as a result of joint pathology and surgical procedures. When shoulders with acromioclavicular joint capsule injury were subjected to three loading conditions, differences were found between the force in the trapezoid and the force in the conoid.[9] This finding suggests that these ligaments should not be surgically treated as one structure. During anterior-posterior loading, the coracoclavicular ligaments could not compensate for the loss of capsular function, as occurs after acromioclavicular joint injury. In a study of the effect of acromioplasty and distal clavicle resection on joint kinematics and in situ forces in response to external loads, acromioplasty alone did not significantly affect acromioclavicular joint motion or the in situ forces on each ligament.[10] However, distal clavicle resection significantly affected the motion of the acromioclavicular joint in response to posterior loading. Some of these changes in joint motion and in situ forces may increase the likelihood of further degeneration at the distal clavicle and lead to loss of function.

Surgical procedures also can affect the ability of high compressive loads to be transmitted across the acromioclavicular joint to the axial skeleton during activities of daily living. Joint compression was shown to decrease posterior translation in response to a posterior load.[11] The application of joint compression to a capsule-transected acromioclavicular joint decreased the amount of posterior or superior translation during posterior or superior loading, respectively, while it increased the coupled translations (anterior-posterior, superior-inferior, or proximal-distal). The joint contact force also increased. Some common surgical techniques, such as distal clavicle resection, initially reduce painful joint contact but require unusually high loads to be supported by the soft-tissue structures at the acromioclavicular joint. In addition, the compressive loads transmitted across a capsule-transected acromioclavicular joint may be concentrated in a smaller area because of the increased coupled motions and joint contact force.

Reports differ on the movement of the clavicle during shoulder motion.[3,12] During the past decade, the in vivo kinematics of the acromioclavicular joint and clavicle during arm elevation have been examined using three-dimensional MRI and electromagnetic tracking devices. Vertically open MRI of 14 shoulders during arm elevation revealed that posterior translation of the clavicle occurred (−1.9 mm ± 1.3 mm) at 90° of abduction and anterior translation (1.6 mm ± 2.7 mm), at maximum abduction.[13] There was slight translation of the clavicle in the superior direction (0.9 mm ± 1.9 mm). The scapula rotated 34.9° (±8.4°) during arm elevation, around an axis passing through the middle of the acromioclavicular joint and the insertion site of the coracoclavicular ligaments on the coracoid process. Clavicular motion with respect to the thorax was found to include elevation (range, 11° to 15°), retraction (range, 15° to 29°), and posterior long-axis rotation (range, 15° to 31°), regardless of the presence of shoulder pathology, with variability among subjects and planes of motion during arm elevation.[14]

## Scapulothoracic Kinematics

Motion between the scapula and the thorax, called the scapulothoracic articulation, is an integral part of normal shoulder function. The scapula is supported only by muscular attachments, the acromioclavicular joint, and the coracoclavicular ligaments. It is mobile in many directions because of its unique articulation. The scapulothoracic muscles include the trapezius (upper, middle, and lower portions), levator scapulae, serratus anterior, pectoralis minor, and rhomboids, all of which act during shoulder motion to position the scapula on the thoracic cage. The levator scapulae and the upper trapezius provide postural support. The middle trapezius and rhomboids retract the scapula, and the serratus anterior protracts the scapula. The trapezius and serratus anterior rotate the lateral part of the scapula upward. The upper trapezius and levator scapulae elevate the scapula. This positioning of the scapula provides maximum stability at the glenohumeral joint while maintaining an extensive range of motion.

The motion that takes place between the thorax, the scapula, and the humerus is extremely complex. Basic science studies have focused on isolated motions at the glenohumeral joint, with the scapula fixed. Only in vivo kinematic studies of the shoulder, including studies of glenohumeral and scapulothoracic motion, should be performed until sufficient information is available to allow simulation of the complex motions in cadaver studies.

The relative motion of the glenohumeral joint and the scapulothoracic articulation during abduction is called the scapulothoracic rhythm. During the first 30° of abduction, glenohumeral motion is much greater than scapulothoracic motion; the reported ratios range from 4:1 to 7:1.[2,15] At greater degrees of abduction, both joints have approximately the same amount of motion.[2,15] Studies of three-dimensional motion at the scapulothoracic articulation found that three rotations (upward-downward rotation, external-internal rotation, and posterior-anterior tilting) describe the orientation of the scapula on the thorax.[16-18] The scapula has been shown to undergo upward rotation, external rotation, and posterior tilt during arm elevation in asymptomatic individuals under static and dynamic conditions.[16,18,19]

In an assessment of the effect of numerous factors on scapulothoracic motion, including fatigue, pectoral muscle length, impingement syndrome, and growth and development, differences appeared between adults and children with normal shoulder function during elevation of the arm in the scapular plane.[20] In children, the contribution of the scapulothoracic joint was greater, most notably during upward rotation. In adults, scapular rotation differed in active and passive arm elevation. Increased upward rotation and external rotation of the scapula was observed during active arm elevation.[21] These findings suggest that the upper and lower trapezius and serratus anterior muscles have an important role during arm elevation and that the glenohumeral capsule and passive muscle tension both contribute to arm elevation.

Fatigue caused by external rotation was found to alter the resting position of the scapula and posterior tilt during the early range of arm elevation in the scapular plane.[22] These kinematic changes may affect the subacromial space and cause impingement of the humerus on the acromion. No changes in scapular kinematics were found after a 6-week rehabilitation program for patients with shoulder impingement, even though the range of motion increased.[23] This finding indicates that scapular kinematics were not responsible for the improvement in function in these patients. The resting length of the pectoralis major was shown to alter scapular kinematics during arm elevation.[24] The scapular kinematics of subjects with a short pectoralis minor were similar to those of subjects with shoulder impingement in earlier studies. These results suggest that a short pectoralis minor may be a mechanism for subacromial impingement.

Subjects with symptoms of shoulder impingement were found to have a different scapulothoracic motion.[17] Decreased scapular upward rotation, increased anterior tipping, and increased scapular medial rotation were typical and therefore must be considered during rehabilitation of patients with symptoms of shoulder impingement related to overhead work. When 45 subjects with impingement syndrome and 45 subjects without known pathology or impairment were matched by age, sex, and hand dominance, the impingement group demonstrated slightly greater scapular upward rotation during flexion and slightly greater scapular posterior tilt during scapular plane elevation.[25] These variant scapular kinematics in subjects with impingement syndrome may represent strategies to compensate for glenohumeral weakness or motion loss.

### Glenohumeral Joint Kinematics

Three types of motion are possible at the glenohumeral joint: spinning, sliding, and rolling. Spinning is simple rotation of the humeral head on the articular surface of the glenoid. Sliding is pure translation of the humeral head on the articular surface of the glenoid; at the extremes of motion and in an unstable joint, glenohumeral translation occurs. Rolling is a combination of translation and rotation of the humerus with respect to the glenoid. Some believe that all of these motions take place at the glenohumeral joint.[26]

The normal glenohumeral joint is lax in all directions. Passive glenohumeral translation in cadaver shoulders is approximately 12 mm in the anterior and posterior directions.[27] In patients with normal shoulder function, passive humeral translation was found to be 8 mm anteriorly, 9 mm posteriorly, and 11 mm inferiorly. However, each of these measurements can be as great as 20 mm in individuals who do not have symptoms of instability. These measurements represent normal laxity, not in vivo kinematics occurring when muscle force is present and creates joint compression.

The amount of anterior-posterior translation observed during loading experiments using a robotic testing system supports the common description of the glenohumeral joint capsule as restricting motion of the humerus at the limits of motion, rather than in the mid range.[27-31] Translations under maximum loading were smaller at 0° and 90° of abduction than at 30° and 60° of abduction. However, posterior translation was restricted in some subjects by contact between the acromion and humerus, and anterior translation was limited by contact with the coracoid at all abduction angles.

Because six degrees of freedom is commonly used in kinematic clinical tests to diagnose shoulder injuries, it is important to understand glenohumeral joint translation during simulated simple translation tests.[32] At 60° of glenohumeral abduction and 0° of flexion or extension, a clinician applied anterior and posterior loads to the humerus at 0°, 30°, and 60° of external rotation until a manual maximum was achieved. Before each test, the reference position of the humerus shifted posteriorly 1.8 mm (±2.0 mm) or 4.1 mm (±3.8 mm) at 30° or 60° of external rotation, respectively. Anterior translation decreased significantly, from 18.2 mm (±5.3 mm) at 0° of external rotation to 15.5 mm (±5.1 mm) or 9.9 mm (±5.5 mm) at 30° or 60°, respectively. Coupled translations at 0°, 30°, and 60° of external rotation occurred in the inferior direction. These findings indicate that a simulated simple translation test should result in coupled inferior translations and anterior translations that are a function of external rotation.

Glenohumeral translation also has been assessed in vivo using electromagnetic sensors and instrumented shoulder arthrometers. An electromagnetic position sensor was used to compare anteroposterior laxity of the shoulders in 43 female swimmers and soccer players.[33] At 90° of abduction and neutral rotation, the glenohumeral translation in the soccer players was 9.6 mm in the dominant shoulder and 10.7 mm in the nondominant shoulder. The translations in the swimmers were significantly greater, at 12.4 mm in the dominant shoulder and 13.8 mm in the nondominant shoulder. These results suggest either that athletic activity influences joint laxity or that joint laxity influences an individual's selection of activity. In vivo glenohumeral joint laxity was analyzed using an instrumented shoulder arthrometer to compare the right and left shoulders of 51 recreational athletes with no history of shoulder injury. No differences in glenohumeral joint laxity were found.[34] However, the amount of glenohumeral joint translation as a function of the force needed to reach a capsular end point was found to differ with loading direction.[35] Anterior-directed translation required more applied force than inferior-directed translation to reach the capsular end point, although there was no difference in the magnitude of translation.

Much less glenohumeral translation occurs during arm elevation and rotation than during drawer or laxity testing.[27] In cadaver shoulders with a rigidly fixed scapula, passive forward elevation of the humerus to 55° and passive extension to 35° in the sagittal plane was correlated with ball-and-socket motion; there was no glenohumeral translation. However, translation began to occur beyond 55° of flexion or 35° of extension. Ball-and-socket motion also was produced by humeral elevation to 90° in the scapular plane and by cables attached to the deltoid and rotator cuff tendons to simulate muscle forces.[36] The findings of other studies, using different internal-external humeral rotations, were similar.[37]

Radiographic analysis found that precise centering of the humeral head on the glenoid is normally maintained in all positions in the horizontal plane, except that 4 mm of posterior translation occurs when the arm is in maximum horizontal extension and external rotation.[1] Analyses of active elevation in the scapular plane, as well as cadaver studies with simulated muscle forces, found only 1 mm of translation in the superior direction throughout the range of motion[36,38] and support the belief that the glenohumeral joint acts as a ball-and-socket joint.

In vivo three-dimensional kinematic studies of the shoulder joint during active abduction assessed the effects of joint pathology. Three rotations (internal-external rotation, abduction-adduction, and flexion-extension) were examined in 25 patients who had symptoms of impingement syndrome of more than 18 months' duration but did not have a full-thickness rotator cuff tear. Abduction did not differ from that of the control subjects, and translation occurred in both groups in the medial, proximal, and anterior directions. However, proximal translation was greater in the patients with shoulder symptoms.[39] Because rotator cuff tears are usually associated with excessive superior translation in the glenohumeral joint, in vivo translations in the glenohumeral joint were analyzed using open MRI during active shoulder abduction, with and without infraspinatus and supraspinatus muscle paralysis.[40] The humeral head invariably remained centered in the glenoid fossa during active abduction. This finding suggests that a structurally intact muscle-tendon-bone unit can prevent superior translation, even if the muscles are not functioning properly. The in vivo analysis was supported by cadaver experiments to simulate active abduction of the upper extremity.[38]

Internal rotation and external rotation of the humerus are important to shoulder motion and are often related to instability and injury at the glenohumeral joint. The rotational range of motion at 45° of abduction with an applied 4-N·m moment about the long axis of the humerus was found to be 139° (±41°) in subjects without shoulder pathology.[41] The neutral-zone laxity was 78° (±46°). These values could be used to assess normal joint laxity or outcomes following surgery or rehabilitation.

## Kinesiology

Everyday activities require coordinated functioning of the numerous shoulder components, including bones, joints, muscles, and the sensorimotor system. Injury that can cause structural damage also affects shoulder motion, muscles, and neural system control. The first com-

prehensive biomechanical analysis of shoulder function, in 1944, used anatomic, radiographic, and electromyographic analysis to discover how the muscles move and stabilize the shoulder.[12] The finding that the supraspinatus and deltoid muscles act as a single unit throughout elevation contradicted the conventional belief that the supraspinatus acts only to initiate elevation. The sensorimotor control of the shoulder is now studied during complex sporting activities and after injury, and the study of joint proprioception has increased the understanding of protective shoulder mechanisms.[42-53]

### Shoulder Muscle Function in the Overhead Pitcher

The phases of a baseball pitch are described in Table 1 and illustrated in Figures 5 and 6. The buildup of energy begins in the lower extremity. The energy is transmitted through the trunk and up to the arm. If the mechanics are faulty early in the process, shoulder pathology may result.

### Reflexive Shoulder Muscle Activity

A normal reflexive arc exists between the capsule and shoulder muscles. In the feline glenohumeral joint, electrical stimulation of the joint capsule was used to show a spinal reflex between the joint capsule and the musculature surrounding the joint.[54-56] A similar reflex arc was found to exist in humans between the shoulder capsule and the deltoid, trapezius, pectoralis major, and rotator cuff muscles.[57,58] Stimulation of the shoulder capsule during arthroscopic examination was found to be transmitted by way of the dorsal columns of the spinal cord and to have a direct effect on the $\alpha$ motor neurons that innervate the shoulder musculature.[59]

In a study of electromyographic activity, latency resulting from an anterior translation force, joint perturbation was used to simulate the occurrence of an instability injury in normal shoulders.[60] The anterior shoulder muscles fired first and were followed by the posterior muscles. The shortest latency was approximately 110 ms. The authors concluded that the reflexive responses were too slow to protect the joint from a traumatic event. In this study, reflex latencies were assessed while the muscles were in a relaxed state. A later study found that the induction of muscle contraction significantly diminished muscle reflex latency.[42] Diminished muscle reflex latency may occur when underlying muscle contraction increases the muscle spindles' sensitivity to intramuscular length changes and thus quickens the reflexive response of the muscle.[61-63] Coactivation of the gamma motor neuron may innervate the muscle spindle and, with the capsule's effect on the $\alpha$ motor neuron, partially explain the mechanism by which athletes can sustain severe blows without suffering injury.[64-66] Questions remain as to whether the reflex actions are sufficiently fast to protect the joint.

| Table 1 | Phases of a Baseball Pitch (Right-Handed Pitcher) | |
|---|---|---|
| **Phase** | **Description** | **Comments** |
| Windup | The hands are together holding the ball. The body is aligned in good balance. The pitcher takes a small, comfortable step back with the left leg, in line with home plate. The right foot is then positioned parallel to the rubber. (Some coaches have the pitcher wedge the foot so that the lateral half is on top of the rubber.) The left lower extremity is picked up in a controlled, active fashion, and the hips remain level while pointing toward home plate. As the hips begin to move forward, a V is formed in which the hips are the apex and the torso and right leg form the two sides. The hips point toward the batter. The right hand comes out of the glove holding the ball. | These are the components of all successful pitches, although a pitcher's windup phase has individual stylistic adaptations that raise the center of gravity. The shoulders are relatively uninvolved. They move slowly, the hands are together, and the muscle activity is low. |
| Early Cocking | The hand stays on top of the ball as it comes out of the glove. The shoulder is then elevated approximately 100° in the scapular plane and is externally rotated to approximately 45°. The V becomes more pronounced as the hips continue to move forward toward home plate. The hips stay level; rotation of the hips is delayed as long as possible. The ball is hidden from the batter, who cannot yet determine the type of pitch to be delivered. The left leg slowly, easily, and comfortably comes down until the foot reaches the mound. | The initial position of the hand helps the shoulder stay in internal rotation, which is a safer position for the glenohumeral joint. The deltoid and supraspinatus act together to abduct the humerus. The other rotator cuff muscles are not active. |
| Late Cocking | The left foot makes contact with the mound, landing within the width of the right foot and pointing toward home plate. The pitcher's center of gravity has been lowered, releasing energy. The pitcher's weight is evenly distributed between the two legs, and the legs are firm. The torso is balanced between the legs in an upright position. The pitcher delays trunk rotation as long as possible. | The goal is to move the humerus into maximum external rotation. The humerus maintains its level of elevation in the scapular plane and externally rotates from 46° to 170°. Deltoid and supraspinatus activity diminishes, but the other rotator cuff muscles' activity increases for joint stability. The middle portion of the trapezius, rhomboids, levator scapulae, and serratus anterior muscles are active so the scapula can provide an effective base for the humeral head. |
| Acceleration | The acceleration phase is initiated when the humerus begins to internally rotate. In approximately 1/20th of a second, the ball is released from the hand at a speed as high as 100 miles per hour. Both feet are on the mound. The acceleration of the arm coincides with the deceleration of the rest of the body, producing efficient transfer of energy to the upper extremity and ball. | The motion occurs on the very firm base provided by the lower extremities. Synchronous muscular contraction about the glenohumeral joint and scapulothoracic articulation provides both stability and rapid motion of the upper extremity. |
| Deceleration | The right hip is brought up and over the left leg after the ball is released. The right foot disengages from the mound, and the body goes into a controlled forward fall. | The kinetic energy not transferred to the ball is dissipated by large muscle activity, beginning with the arm. |
| Follow Through | The arm is brought down. | The forces affecting the arm decrease. |

*(Adapted with permission from McMahon PJ, Tibone JE, Pink MM: Functional anatomy and biomechanics of the shoulder, in Delee JC, Drez D Jr, Miller MD (eds), Delee and Drez's Orthopaedic Sports Medicine: Principles and Practice, ed 2. Philadelphia, PA, Saunders, 2003, p. 850.)*

## Shoulder Injury

The effect of shoulder muscle dysfunction can be dramatic. In a person with anterior shoulder instability, the activity of the supraspinatus and serratus anterior muscles is decreased during simple activities such as shoulder elevation,[43] and anterior and middle deltoid activity is decreased with shoulder flexion and shoulder abduction.[44]

The mean activation magnitude of the pectoralis major and biceps brachii and the peak activation magnitude of the rotator cuff muscles are increased, and biceps brachii reflex latency and supraspinatus-subscapularis activation are suppressed.[45] Shoulder instability also results in abnormal muscle function during complex shoulder activities such as baseball pitching. Increased supraspinatus

| Windup | Early Cocking | Late Cocking | Acceleration | Deceleration | Follow Through |

**Figure 5** Phases of the baseball pitch.

**Figure 6** In the early cocking phase of the baseball pitch, the V initiated during windup becomes more pronounced, as the hips advance toward home plate, and the foot is wedged into the rubber. *(Reproduced with permission from McMahon PJ, Tibone JE, Pink MM: Functional anatomy and biomechanics of the shoulder, in Delee JC, Drez D Jr, Miller MD (eds), Delee and Drez's Orthopaedic Sports Medicine: Principles and Practice, ed 2. Philadelphia, PA, WB Saunders, 2003, p. 850.)*

and biceps brachii muscle activity was found during pitching, probably to accommodate for glenohumeral instability.[46] Decreased subscapularis, pectoralis major, latissimus dorsi, and serratus anterior muscle activity was found during the late cocking phase in pitchers with shoulder instability.[46]

Abnormal muscle activity may alter the shoulder's normal force couples, such as that between the deltoid and rotator cuff muscles, as well as the coordinated movements of the shoulder, such as the scapulothoracic rhythm. This alteration inhibits optimal performance and can lead to further injury.

## Shoulder Proprioception

Conscious and unconscious awareness of body position is called proprioception. Sensory information, including proprioception, travels through afferent pathways to the central nervous system, where it is integrated with information from other levels of the nervous system to elicit the efferent motor responses vital to coordinated movement and joint stability. Shoulder function depends on proprioceptive input from the glenohumeral capsule, musculotendinous structures, and cutaneous structures.[54,56,67] Clinicians must be aware not only that injury can alter the mechanical function of the shoulder but also that corresponding sensorimotor deficits occur.

Shoulder proprioception has been most studied in the glenohumeral joint, in both normal and injured shoulders. Defects have been found to occur with fatigue, pain, and joint injury.[47-50] Glenohumeral stability depends primarily on the glenoid and humeral articular surfaces, muscle activity, and the capsule. Dislocation may result in a Bankart lesion (tearing of the anteroinferior labrum and capsule from the glenoid bone). The mechanical restraint is lost, as well as the proprioceptive information normally transmitted from mechanoreceptors embedded within the capsule. The coordinated motor patterns, reflex activity, and joint stiffness that enhance stability are also altered.

Studies of injured shoulders found that normal proprioception may return after surgical repair and rehabilitation to restore neuromuscular control.[51,52] Rehabilitation can also enhance proprioception in a normal shoulder.[53]

## Summary

Recent research on the kinematics and kinesiology of the shoulder has revealed that the shoulder, although a complex structure, is similar to other joints and that findings related to the shoulder are applicable to other joints. Although knowledge of shoulder anatomy, patho-anatomy, biomechanics, and neural control has increased, many patients still have difficulty in returning to their preinjury state. Research is needed to better understand shoulder function, as well as to diagnose and classify shoulder injuries.

The study of kinesiology has helped clinicians in evaluating the shoulder in relation to the function of the rest of the body. Additional in vitro and in vivo study of the shoulder will improve the understanding of human joint function and advance the treatment of joint injury.

## Annotated References

1. Howell SM, Galinat BJ, Renzi AJ, Marone PJ: Normal and abnormal mechanics of the glenohumeral joint in the horizontal plane. *J Bone Joint Surg Am* 1988;70:227-232.

2. Poppen NK, Walker PS: Normal and abnormal motion of the shoulder. *J Bone Joint Surg Am* 1976;58: 195-201.

3. Rockwood C, Green D: *Fractures in Adults*, ed 2. Philadelphia, PA, JB Lippincott, 1984.

4. Bearn JG: Direct observations on the function of the capsule of the sternoclavicular joint in clavicular support. *J Anat* 1967;101:159-170.

5. DePalma A: *Surgery of the Shoulder*. Philadelphia, PA, JB Lippincott, 1983.

6. Williams PL, Warrick R: *Gray's Anatomy*, ed 36. Baltimore, MD, Williams and Wilkins, 1980.

7. Lee KW, Debski RE, Chen CH, Woo SL-Y, Fu FH: Functional evaluation of the ligaments at the acromioclavicular joint during anteroposterior and superoinferior translation. *Am J Sports Med* 1997;25:858-862.

8. Debski RE, Parsons IM III, Fenwick J, Vangura A: Ligament mechanics during three degree-of-freedom motion at the acromioclavicular joint. *Ann Biomed Eng* 2000;28:612-618.

9. Debski RE: Parsons IM IV, Woo SL, Fu FH: Effect of capsular injury on acromioclavicular joint mechanics. *J Bone Joint Surg Am* 2001;83-A:1344-1351.

    In 11 cadaver shoulders tested using a robotic and universal force and moment sensor system, large differences were found in the change of force in the conoid and trapezoid ligaments. This finding suggests that they should not be considered as one structure for surgical treatment.

10. Debski RE, Fenwick JA, Vangura A Jr, Fu FH, Woo SL, Rodosky MW: Effect of arthroscopic procedures on the acromioclavicular joint. *Clin Orthop Relat Res* 2003;406:89-96.

    In 10 cadaver shoulders tested using a robotic and universal force and moment sensor system, translations in response to posterior load increased 30% after combined acromioplasty and distal clavicle resection, compared with intact and acromioplasty conditions.

11. Costic RS, Jari R, Rodosky MW, Debski RE: Joint compression alters the kinematics and loading patterns of the intact and capsule-transected AC joint. *J Orthop Res* 2003;21:379-385.

    Twelve cadaver shoulders were tested using a robotic and universal force and moment sensor system. The findings suggest that distal clavicle resection may cause unusually high loads to be supported by soft-tissue structures at the acromioclavicular joint and that compressive loads transmitted across a capsule-transected acromioclavicular joint could be concentrated over a smaller area because of the increased coupled motion and joint contact force.

12. Inman V, Saunders M, Abbott L: Observations on the function of the shoulder joint. *J Bone Joint Surg Am* 1944;27:1-30.

13. Sahara W, Sugamoto K, Murai M, Tanaka H, Yoshikawa H: 3D kinematic analysis of the acromioclavicular joint during arm abduction using vertically open MRI. *J Orthop Res* 2006;24:1823-1831.

    Fourteen shoulders were examined in seven static positions, using three-dimensional MRI to analyze the kinematics of the acromioclavicular joint during arm abduction. The scapula rotated about a specific screw axis passing through the acromioclavicular joint and the insertion of the coracoclavicular ligaments on the coracoid process. The average rotation was 34.9° (±8.4°).

14. Ludewig PM, Behrens SA, Meyer SM, Spoden SM, Wilson LA: Three-dimensional clavicular motion during arm elevation: Reliability and descriptive data. *J Orthop Sports Phys Ther* 2004;34:140-149.

    Clavicle rotation was studied during shoulder flexion and abduction in 30 asymptomatic individuals and 9 with shoulder pathology. During elevation, the clavicle elevates 11° to 15° maximum with respect to the thorax, retracts 15° to 29° maximum, and undergoes posterior long-axis rotation (15° to 31° maximum).

15. Doody SG, Freedman L, Waterland JC: Shoulder movements during abduction in the scapular plane. *Arch Phys Med Rehabil* 1970;51:595-604.

16. Karduna AR, McClure PW, Michener LA, Sennett B: Dynamic measurements of three-dimensional scapular kinematics: A validation study. *J Biomech Eng* 2001;123:184-190.

    Two methods using a magnetic tracking device were used to measure the dynamic three-dimensional kinematics of the human scapula, and both were found to offer reasonably accurate representation of scapular motion.

17. Ludewig PM, Cook TM: Alterations in shoulder kinematics and associated muscle activity in people with symptoms of shoulder impingement. *Phys Ther* 2000; 80:276-291.

18. McClure PW, Michener LA, Sennett BJ, Karduna AR: Direct 3-dimensional measurement of scapular kinematics during dynamic movements in vivo. *J Shoulder Elbow Surg* 2001;10:269-277.

    Three-dimensional scapular motion patterns were studied during dynamic shoulder movement using a direct technique. Normal scapular motion consists of substantial rotations around three axes, not simply upward rotation.

19. Ludewig PM, Cook TM, Nawoczenski DA: Three-dimensional scapular orientation and muscle activity at selected positions of humeral elevation. *J Orthop Sports Phys Ther* 1996;24:57-65.

20. Dayanidhi S, Orlin M, Kozin S, Duff S, Karduna A: Scapular kinematics during humeral elevation in adults and children. *Clin Biomech (Bristol, Avon)* 2005;20:600-606.

    Fifteen healthy adults and 14 normally developing children elevated the arm in the scapular plane in three trials. The children had greater upward rotation than the adults.

21. Ebaugh DD, McClure PW, Karduna AR: Three-dimensional scapulothoracic motion during active and passive arm elevation. *Clin Biomech (Bristol, Avon)* 2005;20:700-709.

    Comparison of three-dimensional scapulothoracic motion and muscle activity during active and passive arm elevation in 20 individuals with normal shoulders found more scapular upward rotation and external rotation and more clavicular retraction and elevation during active elevation.

22. Tsai NT, McClure PW, Karduna AR: Effects of muscle fatigue on 3-dimensional scapular kinematics. *Arch Phys Med Rehabil* 2003;84:1000-1005.

    Three-dimensional scapular kinematics were recorded in 30 healthy individuals during arm elevation in the scapular plane. Fatigue in external rotation altered the scapular resting position and the movement of posterior tilting in the early range.

23. McClure PW, Bialker J, Neff N, Williams G, Karduna A: Shoulder function and 3-dimensional kinematics in people with shoulder impingement syndrome before and after a 6-week exercise program. *Phys Ther* 2004;84:832-848.

    After rehabilitation, 39 patients with shoulder impingement syndrome had increased passive range of motion in external and internal rotation but not elevation. Abduction and external and internal rotation force increased. Scapular kinematics did not differ. Pain, satisfaction, and shoulder function improved.

24. Borstad JD, Ludewig PM: The effect of long versus short pectoralis minor resting length on scapular kinematics in healthy individuals. *J Orthop Sports Phys Ther* 2005;35:227-238.

    Individuals without shoulder pain were grouped by pectoralis minor resting length (long or short) and compared for three-dimensional scapular orientation relative to the trunk at different arm elevation angles. Scapular kinematics of the two groups differed significantly.

25. McClure PW, Michener LA, Karduna AR: Shoulder function and 3-dimensional scapular kinematics in people with and without shoulder impingement syndrome. *Phys Ther* 2006;86:1075-1090.

    Three-dimensional scapular kinematics, shoulder range of motion, muscle force, and posture were compared in 90 individuals, half of whom had impingement syndrome. The impingement group had greater scapular upward rotation and clavicular elevation during flexion and slightly greater scapular posterior tilt and clavicular retraction during scapular plane elevation.

26. Morrey BM, Itoi E, An K-N: Biomechanics of the shoulder, in Rockwood CA, Matsen FA (eds): *The Shoulder*, ed 2. Philadelphia, PA, WB Saunders, 1998, pp 233-276.

27. Harryman DT II, Sidles JA, Clark JM, McQuade KJ, Gibb TD, Matsen FA III: Translation of the humeral head on the glenoid with passive glenohumeral motion. *J Bone Joint Surg Am* 1990;72:1334-1343.

28. Debski RE, Wong EK, Woo SL, Sakane M, Fu FH, Warner JJ: In situ force distribution in the glenohumeral joint capsule during anterior-posterior loading. *J Orthop Res* 1999;17:769-776.

29. Harryman DT II, Sidles JA, Harris SL, Matsen FA III: The role of the rotator interval capsule in passive motion and stability of the shoulder. *J Bone Joint Surg Am* 1992;74:53-66.

30. Howell SM, Galinat BJ, Renzi AJ, Marone PJ: Normal and abnormal mechanics of the glenohumeral joint in the horizontal plane. *J Bone Joint Surg Am* 1988;70:227-232.

31. Turkel SJ, Panio MW, Marshall JL, Girgis FG: Stabilizing mechanisms preventing anterior dislocation of the glenohumeral joint. *J Bone Joint Surg Am* 1981;63:1208-1217.

32. Moore SM, Musahl V, McMahon PJ, Debski RE: Multidirectional kinematics of the glenohumeral joint during simulated simple translation tests: Impact on clinical diagnoses. *J Orthop Res* 2004;22:889-894.

    In eight cadaver glenohumeral joints, a simulated simple translation test revealed coupled anterior and inferior translations that were a function of external rotation. Compared with the neutral position, the reference position of the humerus shifted posteriorly, at 30° and 60° of external rotation, respectively.

33. Tibone JE, Lee TQ, Csintalan RP, Dettling J, McMahon PJ: Quantitative assessment of glenohumeral translation. *Clin Orthop Relat Res* 2002;400:93-97.

    Cutaneous electromagnetic position sensors were used to quantify anterior-posterior laxity of the shoulder in both shoulders of 43 female athletes with no shoulder disorders.

34. Sauers EL, Borsa PA, Herling DE, Stanley RD: Instrumented measurement of glenohumeral joint laxity and its relationship to passive range of motion and generalized joint laxity. *Am J Sports Med* 2001;29: 143-150.

In vivo glenohumeral joint laxity was characterized using an instrumented shoulder arthrometer in 51 recreational athletes. The data confirmed the presence of a wide spectrum of symmetric laxity that is not strongly correlated with passive range of motion or generalized joint laxity.

35. Borsa PA, Sauers EL, Herling DE, Manzour WF: In vivo quantification of capsular end-point in the non-impaired glenohumeral joint using an instrumented measurement system. *J Orthop Sports Phys Ther* 2001;31:419-426.

An arthrometric technique was used to measure anterior, posterior, and inferior glenohumeral translation in 20 unimpaired shoulders. The magnitude of applied force required to reach capsular end point differed significantly among directions of translation.

36. McMahon PJ, Debski RE, Thompson WO, Warner JJ, Fu FH, Woo SL: Shoulder muscle forces and tendon excursions during glenohumeral abduction in the scapular plane. *J Shoulder Elbow Surg* 1995;4:199-208.

37. Kelkar R, Wang VM, Flatow EL, et al: Glenohumeral mechanics: A study of articular geometry, contact, and kinematics. *J Shoulder Elbow Surg* 2001;10:73-84.

Stereophotogrammetry was used to investigate the functional relation of articular surface geometry, contact patterns, and kinematics of the glenohumeral joint in nine normal shoulder specimens. Small translation of the humeral head center occurred in neutral and starting rotation.

38. Thompson WO, Debski DE, Boardman ND, et al: A biomechanical analysis of rotator cuff deficiency in a cadaveric model. *Am J Sports Med* 1996;24:286-292.

39. Hallstrom E, Karrholm J: Shoulder kinematics in 25 patients with impingement and 12 controls. *Clin Orthop Relat Res* 2006;448:22-27.

The presence of impingement syndrome was associated with increased proximal translation of the humeral head center, which occurred in the early phase of the arc of motion. Level of evidence: I.

40. Werner CM, Weishaupt D, Blumenthal S, Curt A, Favre P, Gerber C: Effect of experimental suprascapular nerve block on active glenohumeral translations in vivo. *J Orthop Res* 2006;24:491-500.

In glenohumeral translations measured during active shoulder abduction, the humeral head was found to remain centered in the glenoid. Therefore, static or dynamic superior humeral head displacement is not prevented by active supraspinatus or infraspinatus muscle function when the muscle-tendon-bone unit is structurally intact.

41. Novotny JE, Woolley CT, Nichols CE III, Beynnon BD: In vivo technique to quantify the internal-external rotation kinematics of the human glenohumeral joint. *J Orthop Res* 2000;18:190-194.

42. Myers JB, Riemann BL, Ju Y-Y, Hwang J-H, McMahon PJ, Lephart SM: Shoulder muscle reflex latencies under various levels of muscle contraction. *Clin Orthop Relat Res* 2003;407:92-101.

Shoulder muscle reflex latencies were assessed under different levels of muscle contraction in 17 healthy individuals. In general, introducing muscle contraction was found to significantly quicken muscle reflex latencies.

43. McMahon PJ, Jobe F, Pink M, Brault J, Perry J: Comparative electromyographic analysis of shoulder muscles during planar motions: Anterior glenohumeral instability versus normal. *J Shoulder Elbow Surg* 1996;5:118-123.

44. Kronberg M, Brostreom LA, Naemeth G: Differences in shoulder muscle activity between patients with generalized joint laxity and normal controls. *Clin Orthop Relat Res* 1991;269:181-192.

45. Myers JB, Ju YY, Hwang JH, McMahon PJ, Rodosky MW, Lephart SM: Reflexive muscle activation alterations in shoulders with anterior glenohumeral instability. *Am J Sports Med* 2004;32:1013-1021.

Eleven patients with anterior glenohumeral instability and 11 control subjects received external humeral rotation apprehension perturbation while reflexive muscle activation characteristics were measured using electromyography. Those with instability had suppressed pectoralis major and biceps brachii mean activation; increased peak activation of the subscapularis, supraspinatus, and infraspinatus; significantly slower biceps brachii reflex latency; and significantly suppressed supraspinatus-subscapularis coactivation.

46. Glousman R, Jobe F, Tibone J, Moynes D, Antonelli D, Perry J: Dynamic electromyographic analysis of the throwing shoulder with glenohumeral instability. *J Bone Joint Surg Am* 1988;70:220-226.

47. Lephart SM, Warner JP, Borsa PA, Fu FH: Proprioception of the shoulder in normal, unstable and surgical individuals. *J Shoulder Elbow Surg* 1994;3:371-381.

48. Myers JB, Guskiewicz KM, Schneider RA, Prenrice WC: Proprioception and neuromuscular control of the shoulder after muscle fatigue. *J Athl Train* 1999; 34:362-367.

49. Safran MR, Borsa PA, Lephart SM, Fu FH, Warner JJ: Shoulder proprioception in baseball pitchers. *J Shoulder Elbow Surg* 2001;10:438-444.

A proprioceptive testing device was used to measure kinesthesia and joint position sense in both shoulders of 21 collegiate baseball pitchers with no history of shoulder instability. Training, exercise-induced laxity, and increased external rotation did not affect proprioception, although shoulder pain was associated with reduced kinesthetic sensation.

50. Warner JJ, Lephart S, Fu FH: Role of proprioception in pathoetiology of shoulder instability. *Clin Orthop Relat Res* 1996;330:35-39.

51. Borsa PA, Lephart SM, Kocher MS, Lephart SP: Functional assessment and rehabilitation of shoulder proprioception for glenohumeral instability. *J Sport Rehab* 1994;3:84-104.

52. Lephart SM, Pincivero DM, Giraldo JL, Fu FH: The role of proprioception in the management and rehabilitation of athletic injuries. *Am J Sports Med* 1997; 25:130-137.

53. Swanik KA, Lephart SM, Swanik CB, Lephart SP, Stone DA, Fu FH: The effects of shoulder plyometric training on proprioception and selected muscle performance characteristics. *J Shoulder Elbow Surg* 2002;11:579-586.

    The effect of plyometric training of the shoulder internal rotators on proprioception, kinesthesia, and muscle performance was studied in 24 female collegiate swimmers. Plyometric exercises were found to offer significant neuromuscular benefit in shoulder rehabilitation programs.

54. Guanche C, Knatt T, Solomonow M, Lu T, Baratta R: The synergistic action of the capsule and the shoulder muscles. *Am J Sports Med* 1995;23:301-306.

55. Knatt T, Guanche C, Solomonow M, Baratta R, Lu Y: The glenohumeral-biceps reflex. *Clin Orthop Relat Res* 1995;314:247-252.

56. Solomonow M, Guanche C, Wink C, Knatt T, Baratta RV, Lu Y: Shoulder capsule reflex arc in the feline shoulder. *J Shoulder Elbow Surg* 1996;5:139-146.

57. Jerosch J, Moersler M, Castro WH: The function of passive stabilizers of the glenohumeral joint: A biomechanical study. *Z Orthop Ihre Grenzgeb* 1990;128: 206-212.

58. Jerosch J, Steinbeck J, Schrode M, Westhues M: Intraoperative EMG-ableitungbein reizug de gleno-

humeralin glenehkapsel. *Unfallchirurg* 1995;98:580-585.

59. Tibone JE, Fechter J, Kao JT: Evaluation of a proprioception pathway in patients with stable and unstable shoulders with somatosensory cortical evoked potentials. *J Shoulder Elbow Surg* 1997;6: 440-443.

60. Latimer HA, Tibone JE, Berger K, Pink M: Shoulder reaction time and muscle firing patterns in response to an anterior translation force. *J Shoulder Elbow Surg* 1998;7:610-615.

61. Allum JHJ, Maurits KH: Compensation for intrinsic muscle stiffness by short-latency reflexes in human triceps surae muscles. *J Neurophysiol* 1984;52:797-818.

62. Nichols TR: The organization of heterogenic reflexes among muscles crossing the ankle joint in the decerebrate cat. *J Physiol* 1989;410:463-477.

63. Sinkjaer T, Toft E, Andreassen S, Hornemann B: Muscle stiffness in human ankle dorsiflexors: Intrinsic and reflex components. *J Neurophysiol* 1988;60:1110-1121.

64. Johansson H, Sjolander P, Sojka P: A sensory role for the cruciate ligaments. *Clin Orthop Relat Res* 1991; 268:161-178.

65. Johansson H, Sjolander P, Sojka P, Wadell I: Reflex actions on the gamma muscle spindle systems of muscle activity at the knee joint elicited by stretch of the posterior cruciate ligament. *Neuro Orthop* 1989;8: 9-21.

66. Johansson H, Sojka P: Action on gamma motoneurones elicited by electrical stimulation of cutaneous afferent fibres in the hind limb of the cat. *J Physiol* 1985;366:343-363.

67. Vangness CT, Ennis M, Taylor JG, Atkinson R: Neural anatomy of the glenohumeral ligaments, labrum, and subacromial bursa. *J Arthosc Relat Res* 1995;11:180-184.

# Chapter 5

# Basic Science Considerations in Proximal Humerus Fractures

G. Russell Huffman, MD

## Introduction

Proximal humerus fractures are common, especially among postmenopausal women, and the incidence is increasing as the population ages. Both women and men who sustain fractures of the proximal humerus tend to have medical comorbidities. They are at risk of subsequent fracture and increased age-related mortality.

Most proximal humerus fractures can be treated nonsurgically. After surgical treatment with fixation or prosthetic replacement, satisfactory pain relief has been reported more consistently than satisfactory functional outcome.[1] Achieving the optimal results after surgical intervention for a proximal humerus fracture requires the surgeon to understand and apply basic science principles.

## Epidemiology

Proximal humerus fractures usually result from high-energy trauma or poor bone quality. Isolated greater tuberosity fractures are associated with younger patients and those who have a dislocation of the glenohumeral joint. Patients with other types of proximal humerus fractures are likely to be older and female;[2] one study of people older than 60 years found an incidence of 105 fractures per 100,000 persons, and the incidence was 2.5 times greater in women than in men.[3] These patients are likely to have significant medical comorbidities. Compared with people of similar age who do not have an osteoporotic fracture, patients with a proximal humerus fracture have a higher incidence of diabetes and other chronic diseases such as hypothyroidism, hyperthyroidism, stroke, and psychiatric disorders.[4] The incidence of proximal humerus fractures from low-energy trauma has increased during the past 35 years.

Hormone replacement therapy was found to be statistically associated with a decreased risk of proximal humerus fractures in postmenopausal women.[5] The risk of osteoporotic fracture is directly correlated with the T scores derived from dual x-ray absorptiometry scans of the hip and spine. Each unit decrease in hip and spine T scores, compared with age- and population-matched predictions, is associated with a 30% increase in the fracture risk.[6] Osteoporosis by itself may not predict the risk of a proximal humerus fracture in women; a longitudinal study of 6,900 women found that both osteoporosis and an increased risk of falling (assessed from a history of falling, low physical activity, impaired balance, and pain in a lower extremity) were necessary to establish an increased risk of proximal humerus fracture.[7]

A proximal humerus fracture is significantly related to the risk of subsequent fracture of the spine or upper or lower extremity.[8] The risk of an insufficiency fracture is highest in the immediate postfracture period,[9] and mortality is highest during the first year after an insufficiency fracture.[10,11] Older patients and patients with fracture displacement or medical comorbidities have worse long-term general health than other patients with a proximal humerus fracture.[12] However, osteoporotic postmenopausal women who sustained a proximal humerus fracture returned to baseline health-related quality of life within 2 years, as measured by the Medical Outcomes Study Short Form-36 Heath Survey. A similar return to baseline health-related quality of life did not occur after hip or spine insufficiency fractures.[13]

The risks associated with proximal humerus fractures justify efforts to identify those at risk. Patients who have sustained a proximal humerus fracture should be screened for osteoporosis and referred for treatment, as necessary.

## Classification and Anatomy
### Classification Systems

The Neer classification system is commonly used to define proximal humerus fractures. In the Neer system, each of the four components of the proximal humerus (humeral shaft, humeral head proximal to the surgical neck, greater tuberosity, and lesser tuberosity) is defined as fractured if 1 cm of displacement or 45° of angulation is present.[14,15] The less commonly used AO-ASIF fracture classification system is designed to predict the risk of vascular compromise in the humeral head. Type A is an extra-articular, metaphyseal (surgical neck), or greater tuberosity fracture; type B is an extra-articular

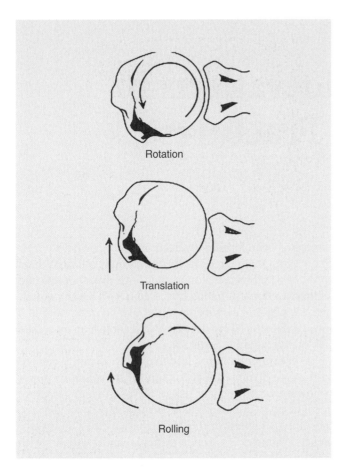

**Figure 1** Glenohumeral motion is defined by rotation, translation, and rolling. During active shoulder motion with intact anatomic relationships and normal kinematics, glenohumeral translation is minimal. (*Reproduced with permission from the Mayo Foundation.*)

(surgical neck) fracture with or without tuberosity fracture or glenohumeral dislocation; and type C is a fracture extending into the humeral head with an associated tuberosity fragment or anatomic neck fracture. Osteonecrosis of the humeral head is associated with the severity of fracture. In the AO-ASIF system, a type C fracture carries the highest risk of osteonecrosis. A Neer type IV fracture (a displaced fracture of the surgical neck and greater and lesser tuberosities), with the exception of a valgus-impacted four-part fracture, is associated with an increased incidence of osteonecrosis.[15,16]

The Neer and AO-ASIF classification systems are based on radiographic findings, and both have poor interobserver reliability.[17,18] Neither system accounts for fractures that have subcapital fragments recognized at the time of surgery.[19] The presence of subcapital fragments increases the risk of osteonecrosis and makes secure fixation of humeral head fragments more difficult. The basic trauma radiographic series should include an AP view in the plane of the scapula, a scapular Y lateral view, and an axillary lateral view. The axillary lateral view is particularly important, because it significantly

contributes to accurate fracture classification using the Neer system.[20]

## Anatomic Considerations

The vascular supply to the humeral head is derived from the anterior lateral branch of the anterior humeral circumflex artery.[21,22] This branch ascends the lateral aspect of the bicipital groove and becomes the arcuate artery to the humeral head. Preservation of the anterior lateral branch is critical during internal fixation of a proximal humerus fracture because the tuberosities contribute only poor collateral circulation to the articular segment. Rigid internal fixation that does not take this factor into account can lead to osteonecrosis. Partly because of concern about osteonecrosis, the treatment of three-part and four-part proximal humerus fractures is controversial. Good results were reported after open reduction and internal fixation using a T plate and cerclage wire. The rate of osteonecrosis was 37%, although 85% of the patients were satisfied with the result.[23] Other studies found that the results were inferior if osteonecrosis occurred, and the risk of osteonecrosis was correlated with nonanatomic fracture reduction.[24] Function was shown to be correlated with anatomic fracture reduction[25] although subsequent osteonecrosis led to a poor outcome, even if anatomic reduction was achieved during surgical treatment.[26]

## Biomechanical Factors
### Kinematics

Normal glenohumeral motion is characterized as rolling, translation, or rotation (Figure 1). In rolling, the point of rotation is continually changing on both the humerus and the glenoid. In translation, the humeral articular point is fixed and the glenoid articular point is changing. In rotation, the humeral articular point is changing and the glenoid articular point is fixed.

In normal glenohumeral kinematics, only 1 mm of superior glenohumeral translation occurs during initiation of elevation from 0° to 30°, and less than 1 mm of additional translation occurs during elevation from 30° to 180°. Indirect evidence suggests that excessive humeral translation can lead to glenohumeral degenerative changes.[27] A cadaver study of proximal humerus reconstruction examined the effects of tuberosity malpositioning and found no kinematic alteration at the point of humeral articulation on the glenoid, through a wide range of motion. However, significant glenohumeral force alterations were observed.[28] Specifically, an increase in the vertical glenohumeral joint reactive force appeared with increasing malreduction of the tuberosities. This finding explains the poor motion observed in patients who have undergone hemiarthroplasty for a four-part proximal humerus fracture with surgical neck comminution, in which tuberosity

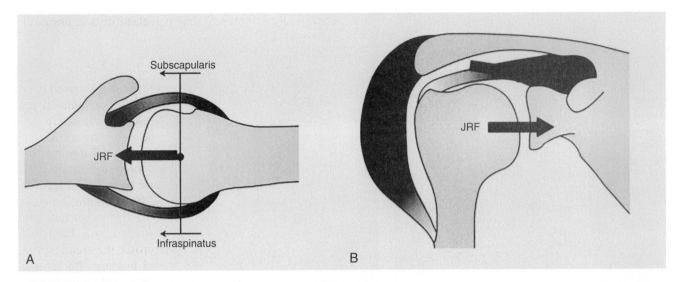

**Figure 2**   Transverse **(A)** and coronal **(B)** plane force couples. Force is proportional to the cross-sectional area and the working length of each muscle. JRF = joint reactive force.

malposition is necessary to achieve osseous union. The coronal and transverse glenohumeral force couples must remain intact to maintain or restore normal kinematics and biomechanics after a proximal humerus fracture (Figure 2).

Failure to restore proximal humerus anatomy and motion can lead to altered glenohumeral contact forces and kinematics. A study of functional losses after hemiarthroplasty to treat four-part proximal humerus fractures found that decreased shoulder strength in the scapular plane results from decreased glenohumeral motion and compensatory increased scapulothoracic motion, rather than from a true decrease in measured strength.[29] After nonsurgical treatment of nondisplaced proximal humerus fractures, the functional outcome was poor in as many as 23% of patients. Early motion and physical therapy were correlated with satisfactory outcomes.[1]

The nonsurgical treatment of a nondisplaced proximal humerus fracture should include a brief period of sling immobilization followed by early passive motion. A displaced fracture that is amenable to surgical fixation should be treated with rigid anatomic fixation and early motion. For an irreparable displaced four-part fracture, the current standard of care is secure tuberosity fixation and anatomic tuberosity reduction in conjunction with a cemented hemiarthroplasty, followed by early postsurgical range-of-motion exercises. Regardless of treatment type, arthroscopic capsular release may be necessary after osseous union to correct refractory stiffness[30,31] (Figure 3).

### Vertical and Transverse Force Couples

Disruption of the normal force couples about the shoulder has been associated with adverse functional outcomes (Figure 4). The normal distance from the greater tuberosity to the superior portion of the articular surface of the humeral head is 7 to 8 mm, according to anatomic and radiographic studies.[32,33] During hemiarthroplasty performed by experienced surgeons to repair four-part proximal humerus fractures, intrasurgical vertical plane malpositioning of the tuberosities occurred in as many of 18% of patients, and horizontal plane malreduction occurred in as many as 23%.[34] Inferior malpositioning of the greater tuberosity 2 cm or more below the superior articular surface of the implant led to relatively poor clinical and functional outcomes.[35] Other studies found an association between unsatisfactory results and inferior tuberosity positioning and healing.[36]

Cadaver biomechanical studies have helped to explain the variable functional results in patients treated for a displaced proximal humerus fracture. A 10-mm inferior tuberosity malpositioning in hemiarthroplasty for proximal humerus fracture led to an increase in superiorly directed glenohumeral contact forces with glenohumeral abduction angles as low as 30°.[28] The maximum abduction angle obtained with elevation of the humeral implant diminished with changes in height as small as 5 mm.[37] These studies together established that more energy is required to achieve a functional range of motion after an inferior displacement of the tuberosities relative to the humeral articular segment. Similarly, superior malpositioning of isolated greater tuberosity fractures in a nonprosthetic model, with displacement as small as 5 mm, caused not only subacromial impingement but also the need for greater force to achieve humeral abduction in the scapular plane.[38]

Alterations in the transverse force couple also result in measurable changes in glenohumeral biomechanics. In a cadaver model of hemiarthroplasty to reconstruct a four-part proximal humerus fracture, nonanatomic tuberosity reconstruction led to significant impairment in

**American Academy of Orthopaedic Surgeons**

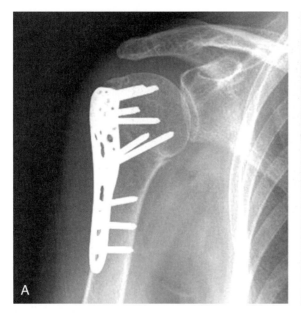 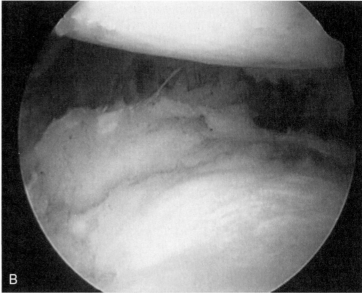

**Figure 3**   **A,** Plain radiograph showing a three-part proximal humerus fracture treated with locked-plate combined suture fixation. Despite early patient motion, posttraumatic adhesive capsulitis developed. **B,** Arthroscopic view of capsular release.

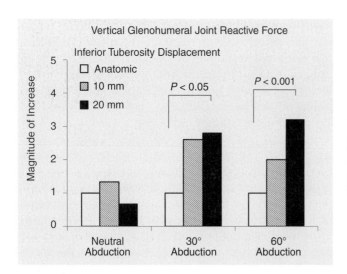

**Figure 4**   Inferior displacement of the tuberosities during hemiarthroplasty reconstruction for a four-part proximal humerus fracture significantly increases the vertical component of the glenohumeral joint reactive force. The magnitude of the displacement increases as much as three times with greater glenohumeral abduction after 10 or 20 mm of inferior tuberosity displacement.

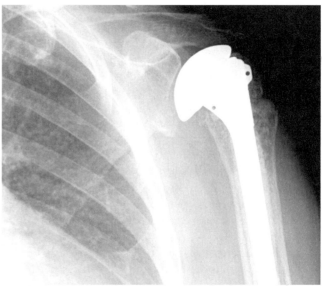

**Figure 5**   Plain radiograph showing restoration of the tuberosity position in the vertical plane, without overreduction or inferior malpositioning, after a hemiarthroplasty for a four-part proximal humerus fracture. Anatomic tuberosity positioning is possible with a proximally porous-coated fracture implant that allows secure suture fixation of the tuberosities to the humeral shaft and implant.

external rotation kinematics and an eightfold increase in torque requirement, possibly as a result of slight malpositioning of tuberosity fragments in the horizontal plane.[39] The current recommendation is to fix tuberosity fragments if displacement of 5 mm or more is present. The surgeon should also pay attention to tuberosity position during prosthetic proximal humerus replacement. Appropriate tuberosity height can be achieved using implants that are medially offset, proximally porous coated, and specifically designed for anatomic tuberosity fixation (Figures 5 and 6). In treating a four-part

fracture with a hemiarthroplasty, the prosthetic humeral implant should be cemented to prevent the rotational instability associated with the surgical neck. The reconstruction should be augmented by suturing the rotator cuff so as to secure the tuberosities to each other as well as to the humeral implant and humeral shaft. Adding a cerclage around the medial aspect of the implant and the tuberosities significantly decreases interfragmentary motion and strain.[40]

Clear recommendations are not available for glenoid resurfacing during prosthetic reconstruction. Hemiarthroplasty remains the standard of care because of the kinematic and biomechanical alterations that occur with relatively small amounts of proximal humeral malpositioning and the potential for glenoid component loosening.

## Surgical Fixation

### Implant Choice

Regardless of the type of implant used in surgical fixation of a displaced proximal humerus fracture, achieving optimal results requires rigid and secure fixation, attention to the vascular supply of the articular segment, and early postsurgical motion. The anterosuperior region of the humeral head has a lower trabecular bone mineral density than other regions of the proximal humerus, as well as an inferior pullout strength for cancellous screws.[41,42] Therefore, screw and implant placement is important in obtaining both a secure initial fixation and an optimal functional outcome. In a cadaver model of a three-part fracture, the use of calcium phosphate cement immediately and significantly improved the mechanical performance of a fixation using smooth wires, cloverleaf plates, or a fixed-angle blade plate. Interfragmentary motion was significantly decreased, and both torque to failure and torsional stiffness were significantly increased.[43]

A study using historical controls found that valgus-impacted proximal humerus fractures are better treated surgically than nonsurgically and are more successfully treated with open reduction and internal fixation than with prosthetic replacement.[16,44] Both rigid internal fixation and transosseous suture techniques have been recommended for treating four-part valgus-impacted fractures. Good clinical results have been reported, although most available studies were case series.[45] To stabilize three-part and four-part valgus-impacted proximal humerus fractures, sutures are minimally invasive and use the relative strength of the rotator cuff tendon. Suture use avoids the risk of fixation failure in osteoporotic tuberosity segments, as well as possible hardware complications. With attention to the vascular supply to the humeral head, suture use also avoids the risk of osteonecrosis associated with rigid osteosynthesis.[45-47] The disadvantage is that tension band techniques provide relatively low rigidity in torsion and bending, compared with fixed-angle constructs such as locking plates.

Biomechanical studies have compared the strength of commonly used implants and techniques in the fixation of displaced proximal humerus fractures. Locked or unlocked plating provided greater interfragmentary stability than wire fixation alone in abduction and cyclic loading in external rotation.[43] Under cyclic loading of cadaver surgical neck fractures, locked plate designs offered significantly more rigidity of fixation than un-

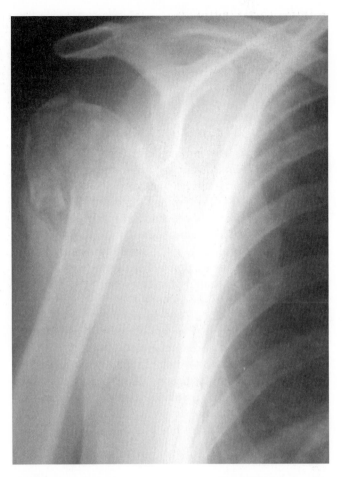

**Figure 6**　Plain radiograph showing malunion of a four-part proximal humerus fracture. Treatment with a reverse prosthesis is best able to restore function.

locked plate designs,[48] as well as greater torsional strength and equal bending strength compared with blade plate designs.[49] In a simulated comminuted surgical neck fracture of the proximal humerus, a locked 3.5-mm plate provided significantly more torsional and varus angular stiffness than a proximal humeral nail.[50] Locked proximal humeral plates provide the most rigid fixation of displaced surgical neck fractures. The currently available plates have eyelets to allow suture fixation to rotator cuff tendons in appropriate two-part, three-part, and four-part proximal humerus fractures. Regardless of other considerations, the choice of fixation technique ultimately is based on the fracture pattern, the surgeon's experience, and the patient's comorbidities.

### Humeral Prosthetic Reconstruction

Prosthetic treatment of comminuted proximal humerus fractures reliably achieves relief of pain; 73% to 97% of patients reported good or excellent pain relief.[51] However, the reported functional results are more varied; rates as high as 25% have been reported for common complications, including intrasurgical tuberosity and implant malpositioning.[51] The functional results are compromised by a failure to properly address every principle of prosthetic treatment, including anatomic tuberosity height, immediate stability of the tuberosity fragments, proper implant retroversion, and proper humeral implant height.

### Timing of Surgery

Proximal humeral anatomy restoration, tuberosity healing, and restoration of motion depend on prompt surgical treatment, if hemiarthroplasty is chosen as appropriate treatment of the fracture. The results of hemiarthroplasty and tuberosity osteotomy for malpositioning performed more than 2 to 3 weeks after injury were poorer than the results of the same treatment performed within 2 to 3 weeks after injury.[36,52-54] Similarly, osteosynthesis or prosthetic reconstruction is better performed as the primary treatment than as a later treatment to correct a malunited fracture. Late treatment of malunion with a shoulder prosthesis led to less predictable functional outcomes,[52] particularly after osteotomy of a malunited greater tuberosity[55] or a tuberosity osteotomy.[56] The results after reconstruction of a malunited proximal humerus fracture using a nonconstrained prosthesis were superior when all soft-tissue and osseous abnormalities were corrected.[57] However, in a significant tuberosity malunion requiring osteotomy at the time of reconstruction, the use of a reverse prosthesis led to better and more predictable functional results[58] (Figure 6).

### Proper Implant Version

Restoring glenohumeral anatomy and biomechanics is essential to restoring function in humeral prosthetic reconstruction. Postsurgical CT of both arms of patients after hemiarthroplasty for fracture reconstruction revealed better clinical results if the retroversion achieved was within 10° of that of the uninjured arm and the working humeral length was within 14 mm.[59] Malrotation of the humeral implant or malpositioning of the tuberosities in the horizontal plane led to a significant increase in the work required to achieve external rotation.[39] In anatomic glenohumeral reconstruction to correct a degenerative condition, the bicipital groove can be used as a consistent anatomic guide for proper humeral component retroversion.[60] However, use of the bicipital groove as a landmark can lead to excessive implant retroversion if the surgical neck is comminuted. CT of 21 cadaver humeri showed that the bicipital groove rotates internally from proximal to distal on the transepicondylar axis. Routine reliance on measurements using the transepicondylar axis may be inadequate because humeral retrotorsion varies widely. However, the average side-to-side difference in individuals is less than 2° and can be reliably measured using CT of the contralateral humerus.[61] This method is not practical in many health care settings. Instead, a standard fracture

jig with set retroversion can be used to consistently obtain a satisfactory implant position.[34,62,63]

### Implant Height

Improper implant height is associated with inferior clinical results. Proper humeral implant height is difficult to achieve if the surgical neck is comminuted, as it commonly is in a four-part proximal humerus fracture. Limited abduction has been observed with increased implant elevation;[36] superior malpositioning of a humeral implant of as little as 5 to 10 mm limits the maximum possible abduction angle.[37] The mean distance between the pectoralis major tendon and the top of the humeral articular surface was found to be 5.6 cm (±0.5 cm, 95% confidence interval) and is a useful anatomic landmark for restoring humeral height in complex fractures of the proximal humerus requiring prosthetic reconstruction.[64]

### Tuberosity Nonunion

Proper anatomic tuberosity positioning during prosthetic reconstruction is critical to a good functional outcome, and stable tuberosity fixation is critical to healing without displacement, as well as pain relief and functional recovery. Tuberosity migration and nonunion lead to measurably poorer clinical results.[65] Tuberosity healing is related to patient outcome, revision rates, and patient satisfaction.[66,67] Tuberosity fixation requires secure fixation to the implant, humeral shaft, and each tuberosity. The goal is to achieve sufficient stability to allow early passive shoulder motion. However, in one study prolonged immobilization was promoted to allow healing, with subsequent arthroscopic capsular release.[31]

Failure of tuberosity healing is associated with several factors. Tuberosity migration has been reported in as many as 23% of patients, and nonunion rates as high as 17% have been reported.[51] Failure of tuberosity healing is associated with poor initial humeral implant position (either excessive implant height or excessive retroversion), poor initial greater tuberosity position, and poor bone quality.[34] Immediate tuberosity stability is enhanced by securing the tuberosities to the humeral shaft, the humeral implant, and each other. Failure to perform this step can allow tuberosity migration and angular deformity.[68] Immediate tuberosity stability is enhanced by incorporating a circumferential cerclage around the medial aspect of the prosthesis and the tuberosities to diminish interfragmentary strain.[40]

## Summary

Proximal humerus fractures occur in patients who sustain a high-energy trauma or have osteoporosis, and the incidence is increasing as the population ages. Most proximal humerus fractures can be nonsurgically treated. For fractures requiring surgery, the principles of fixation and prosthetic reconstruction include restoration of the proximal humeral anatomy and secure fixation of fracture segments to allow an early range of motion. Adherence to these principles is associated with better functional results and predictably better outcomes.

## Annotated References

1. Goldman RT, Koval KJ, Cuomo F, Gallagher MA, Zuckerman JD: Functional outcome after humeral head replacement for acute three- and four-part proximal humeral fractures. *J Shoulder Elbow Surg* 1995;4:81-86.

2. Kim E, Shin HK, Kim CH: Characteristics of an isolated greater tuberosity fracture of the humerus. *J Orthop Sci* 2005;10:441-444.

    Patients with an isolated greater tuberosity fracture are more likely to be male, relatively young, and have fewer medical comorbidities than patients with any other type of proximal humerus fracture. Isolated greater tuberosity fractures are more likely to be associated with glenohumeral dislocation.

3. Palvanen M, Kannus P, Niemi S, Parkkari J: Update in the epidemiology of proximal humeral fractures. *Clin Orthop Relat Res* 2006;442:87-92.

    An epidemiologic study from Finland assessed low-energy proximal humerus fractures that occurred from 1970 to 2002. During this period, the overall and age-adjusted incidence of these injuries more than doubled. Level of evidence: IV.

4. Ahmed LA, Schirmer H, Berntsen GK, Fonnebo V, Joakimsen RM: Self-reported diseases and the risk of non-vertebral fractures: The Tromso study. *Osteoporos Int* 2006;17:46-53.

    Self-reported diabetes mellitus, stroke, asthma, hypothyroidism, hyperthyroidism, and psychiatric disorders were associated with an increased risk of nonvertebral fractures, including proximal humerus fractures.

5. Keegan TH, Gopalakrishnan G, Sidney S, Quesenberry CP Jr, Kelsey JL: Hormone replacement therapy and risk for foot, distal forearm, proximal humerus, and pelvis fractures. *Osteoporos Int* 2003;14:469-475.

    This case-control study examined the relationship between hormone replacement therapy and the risk of fractures in women age 45 years or older. The risk of proximal humerus fracture was reduced in women who were taking or had taken hormone replacement therapy, compared with those who had never taken hormone replacement therapy. Level of evidence: III.

6. Abrahamsen B, Vestergaard P, Rud B, et al: Ten-year absolute risk of osteoporotic fractures according to BMD T score at menopause: The Danish Osteoporosis Prevention Study. *J Bone Miner Res* 2006;21:796-800.

    Postmenopausal women who were not being treated with hormone replacement therapy, bisphosphonates, or raloxifene were prospectively assessed for the risk of fracture of the spine, hip, proximal humerus, or wrist. The risk of fracture increased significantly with each unit decrease from baseline in femoral neck and lumbar spine T scores.

7. Lee SH, Dargent-Molina P, Breart G: Risk factors for fractures of the proximal humerus: Results from the EPIDOS prospective study. *J Bone Miner Res* 2002; 17:817-825.

    Women who had osteoporosis or were at risk of a fall (determined from a history of falling, a low level of physical activity, impaired balance, and lower extremity pain) were at increased risk of proximal humerus fracture. If both risk factors were present, the risk was doubled. Level of evidence: II.

8. Olsson C, Nordqvist A, Petersson CJ: Increased fragility in patients with fracture of the proximal humerus: A case control study. *Bone* 2004;34:1072-1077.

    In this case-control study, a fracture of the proximal humerus was associated with both an earlier fracture and a twofold increase in the risk of a future fracture of the spine or extremities.

9. Johnell O, Kanis JA, Oden A, et al: Fracture risk following an osteoporotic fracture. *Osteoporos Int* 2004; 15:175-179.

    In patients with an insufficiency fracture of the spine, shoulder, or hip, the immediate risk of subsequent fracture was found to be higher than in the general population. The incidence of further fractures of the shoulder, spine, or hip diminished over time.

10. Johnell O, Kanis JA, Oden A, et al: Mortality after osteoporotic fractures. *Osteoporos Int* 2004;15:38-42.

    In both men and women, patient mortality after a hip, shoulder, or spine insufficiency fracture was significantly higher in the year after the fracture than mortality in the general population.

11. Olsson C, Petersson CJ: Clinical importance of comorbidity in patients with a proximal humerus fracture. *Clin Orthop Relat Res* 2006;442:93-99.

    Patients with significant comorbidities at the time of proximal humerus fracture had an increased risk of mortality in the year after the fracture. The long-term symptoms in survivors were correlated with the amount of initial fracture displacement. Level of evidence: II.

12. Olsson C, Nordquist A, Petersson CJ: Long-term outcome of a proximal humerus fracture predicted after 1 year: A 13-year prospective population-based follow-up study of 47 patients. *Acta Orthopaedica* 2005:76:397-402.

    After a proximal humerus fracture, patients with a displaced fracture or a chronic disease had significantly worse long-term results than patients with a nondisplaced fracture or no history of chronic disease. Examination results at 1 year predicted long-term shoulder dysfunction. The mortality rate was greater than that of an age-matched population.

13. Hallberg I, Rosenqvist AM, Kartous L, Lofman O, Wahlstrom O, Toss G: Health-related quality of life after osteoporotic fractures. *Osteoporos Int* 2004;15: 834-841.

    Patients with a proximal humerus fracture reported a return to normal health-related quality of life 2 years after injury. This result contrasts with that of patients with hip and spine fractures, who reported persistent deficits.

14. Neer CS II: Displaced proximal humeral fractures: Part I. Classification and evaluation. *J Bone Joint Surg Am* 1970;52:1077-1089.

15. Neer CS II: Displaced proximal humerus fractures: Part II. Treatment of three-part and four-part displacement. *J Bone Joint Surg Am* 1970;52:1090-1103.

16. Jakob RP, Miniaci A, Anson PS, Jaberg H, Osterwalder A, Ganz R: Four-part valgus impacted fractures of the proximal humerus. *J Bone Joint Surg Br* 1991;73:295-298.

17. Siebenrock KA, Gerber C: The reproducibility of classification of fractures of the proximal end of the humerus. *J Bone Joint Surg Am* 1993;75:1751-1755.

18. Bernstein J, Adler LM, Blank JE, Dalsey RM, Williams GR, Iannotti JP: Evaluation of the Neer system of classification of proximal humeral fractures with computerized tomographic scans and plain radiographs. *J Bone Joint Surg Am* 1996;78:1371-1375.

19. Tamai K, Hamada J, Ohno W, Saotome K: Surgical anatomy of multipart fractures of the proximal humerus. *J Shoulder Elbow Surg* 2002;11:421-427.

    Three- and four-part proximal humerus fractures were assessed after surgical treatment by comparing presurgical radiographic classification using the Neer and AO systems. Neither system predicted more than 30% of the fractures. The authors concluded that accounting for displacement of the articular portion of the humeral head fragment would increase accuracy.

20. Sidor ML, Zuckerman JD, Lyon T, Koval K, Cuomo F, Schoenberg N: The Neer classification system for proximal humeral fractures: An assessment of interobserver reliability and intraobserver reproducibility. *J Bone Joint Surg Am* 1993;75:1745-1750.

21. Gerber C, Schneeberger AG, Vinh TS: The arterial vascularization of the humeral head: An anatomical study. *J Bone Joint Surg Am* 1990;72:1486-1494.

22. Laing PG: The arterial supply to the adult humerus. *J Bone Joint Surg Am* 1956;38:1105-1116.

23. Wijgman AJ, Roolker W, Patt TW, Raaymakers EL, Marti RK: Open reduction and internal fixation of three and four-part fractures of the proximal part of the humerus. *J Bone Joint Surg Am* 2002;84:1919-1925.

    Of 60 patients who underwent open reduction and internal fixation of a three- or four-part fracture using a T plate and cerclage wire, 37% developed osteonecrosis. However, 87% had a favorable result, as measured using Constant and visual analog pain scores; 77% of the patients with osteonecrosis had a favorable result.

24. Gerber C, Hersche O, Berberat C: The clinical relevance of posttraumatic avascular necrosis of the humeral head. *J Shoulder Elbow Surg* 1998;7:586-590.

25. Resch H, Povacz P, Frohlich R, Wambacher M: Percutaneous fixation of three- and four-part fractures of the proximal humerus. *J Bone Joint Surg Br* 1997;79: 295-300.

26. Gerber C, Werner CM, Vienne P: Internal fixation of complex fractures of the proximal humerus. *J Bone Joint Surg Br* 2004;86:848-855.

    Patients who developed osteonecrosis had significantly worse shoulder function than other patients, as measured by the Constant Shoulder Score, despite anatomic reduction of the injuries.

27. Marx RG, McCarty EC, Montemurno TD, Altchek DW, Craig EV, Warren RF: Development of arthrosis following dislocation of the shoulder: A case-control study. *J Shoulder Elbow Surg* 2002;11:1-5.

    A significant association was found between a history of traumatic shoulder instability and the development of glenohumeral degenerative joint disease.

28. Huffman GR, Itamura J, McGarry MH, Tibone JE, Gililland J, Lee TQ: Biomechanical assessment of inferior tuberosity placement during hemiarthroplasty for four-part proximal humerus fractures. *J Shoulder Elbow Surg* 2007;16(2):e50-e51.

    In a cadaver study, inferior tuberosity malpositioning did not change the humeral center of articulation on the glenoid surface. However, as little as 10 mm of inferior tuberosity displacement significantly increased the superior glenohumeral joint forces within a functional range of motion.

29. Becker R, Pap G, Machner A, Neumann WH: Strength and motion after hemiarthroplasty in displaced four-fragment fracture of the proximal humerus: 27 patients followed for 1-6 years. *Acta Orthop Scand* 2002;73:44-49.

    Isometric muscle strength was relatively well preserved after hemiarthroplasty for four-part proximal humerus fracture. Range of motion was less predictable and was inversely related to poor functional scores. Patients who underwent early hemiarthroplasty had improved function compared with those who underwent delayed treatment.

30. Holloway GB, Schenk T, Williams GR, Ramsey ML, Iannotti JP: Arthroscopic capsular release for the treatment of refractory postoperative or post-

fracture shoulder stiffness. *J Bone Joint Surg Am* 2001;83:1682-1687.

Patients underwent arthroscopic capsular release to treat idiopathic adhesive capsulitis, posttraumatic stiffness, or postsurgical stiffness. Release for adhesive capsulitis or posttraumatic stiffness was successful in relieving pain and restoring function. Patients with postsurgical stiffness had less improvement.

31.  Barth JR, Burkhart SS: Arthroscopic capsular release after hemiarthroplasty of the shoulder for fracture: A new treatment paradigm. *Arthroscopy* 2005; 21:1150.

Complete immobilization after prosthetic reconstruction is promoted, until the tuberosities have healed. In this paradigm, all patients undergo subsequent arthroscopic capsular release.

32.  Iannotti JP, Gabriel JP, Schneck SL, Evans BG, Misra S: The normal glenohumeral relationships: An anatomical study of one hundred and forty shoulders. *J Bone Joint Surg Am* 1992;74:491-500.

33.  Takase K, Imakiire A, Burkhead WZ Jr: Radiographic study of the anatomic relationships of the greater tuberosity. *J Shoulder Elbow Surg* 2002;11: 557-561.

Radiographs of 519 shoulders without osseous lesions were reviewed to determine the normal relationships between the neck-shaft angle and the tuberosity-to-head distance. The tuberosity-to-head distance averaged 7 mm and was significantly correlated with the neck-shaft angle in both men and women.

34.  Boileau P, Krishnan SG, Tinsi L, Walch G, Coste JS, Mole D: Tuberosity malposition and migration: Reasons for poor outcomes after hemiarthroplasty for displaced fractures of the proximal humerus. *J Shoulder Elbow Surg* 2002;11:401-412.

A review of 66 shoulder hemiarthroplasties performed for proximal humerus fracture revealed that initial tuberosity malposition was present in 27% of shoulders and tuberosity detachment and migration were present in 23%, leading to final tuberosity malpositioning in 50%. This result was significantly correlated with an unsatisfactory clinical result.

35.  Mighell MA, Kolm GP, Collinge CA, Frankle MA: Outcomes of hemiarthroplasty for fractures of the proximal humerus. *J Shoulder Elbow Surg* 2003;12: 569-577.

A review of 60 shoulder replacements for proximal humerus fracture found that tuberosity complications occurred in 16 shoulders. Malunion of the greater tuberosity was the most common complication. Healing of the greater tuberosity more than 2 cm below the humeral head was correlated with a poor functional result.

36.  Demirhan M, Kilicoglu O, Altinel L, Eralp L, Akalin Y: Prognostic factors in prosthetic replacement for acute proximal humerus fractures. *J Orthop Trauma* 2003;17:181-188.

Outcome after prosthetic replacement for proximal humerus fracture is improved if surgery is performed within 14 days of injury, with proper implant positioning. Tuberosity malposition and nonunion were the most common complications (50%) and had a significant adverse effect on patient outcome.

37.  Nyffeler RW, Sheikh R, Jacob HA, Gerber C: Influence of humeral prosthesis height on biomechanics of glenohumeral abduction: An in vitro study. *J Bone Joint Surg Am* 2004;86:575-580.

This cadaver study assessed the biomechanics of superior placement of the humeral prosthesis. Elevation of the implant 5 mm above the anatomic position led to a significant decrease in both maximum glenohumeral abduction and moment arms of the infraspinatus and subscapularis.

38.  Bono CM, Renard R, Levine RG, Levy AS: Effect of displacement of fractures of the greater tuberosity on the mechanics of the shoulder. *J Bone Joint Surg Br* 2001;83:1056-1062.

In a biomechanical assessment of the abduction force required after greater tuberosity malpositioning of 0.5 cm and 1 cm vertically, the abduction force required for glenohumeral abduction from 0° to 90° was found to be significantly increased with as little as 0.5 cm of displacement.

39.  Frankle MA, Greenwald DP, Markee BA, Ondrovic LE, Lee WE III: Biomechanical effects of malposition of tuberosity fragments on the humeral prosthetic reconstruction for four-part proximal humerus fractures. *J Shoulder Elbow Surg* 2001;10:321-326.

Anatomic and nonanatomic reduction of the tuberosities was biomechanically tested in a cadaver model of hemiarthroplasty for four-part fracture. Nonanatomic tuberosity reconstruction led to significant impairment in external rotation kinematics and an eightfold increase in torque requirement (*P* = 0.001). In contrast, anatomic reconstruction produced results indistinguishable from a normal shoulder.

40.  Frankle MA, Ondrovic LE, Markee BA, Harris ML, Lee WE III: Stability of tuberosity reattachment in proximal humeral hemiarthroplasty. *J Shoulder Elbow Surg* 2002;11:413-420.

Cadaver shoulders with a four-part fracture were biomechanically tested using a hemiarthroplasty with five techniques for fixation of the tuberosities. Incorporation of a circumferential medial cerclage was found to decrease interfragmentary motion and strain, maximizing fracture stability. This technique should facilitate early postsurgical rehabilitation.

41.  Fankhauser F, Schippinger G, Weber K, et al: Cadaveric-biomechanical evaluation of bone-implant construct of proximal humerus fractures (Neer type 3). *J Trauma* 2003;55:345-349.

The optimal position of screws in the fixation of surgical neck fractures is described in this biomechanical cadaver study. The data may be useful in determining the optimal placement of other percutaneous fixation devices.

42. Tingart MJ, Lehtinen J, Zurakowski D, Warner JJ, Apreleva M: Proximal humeral fractures: Regional differences in bone mineral density of the humeral head affect the fixation strength of cancellous screws. *J Shoulder Elbow Surg* 2006;15:620-624.

    This cadaver study found that trabecular bone mineral density and screw pullout strength are significantly correlated in the proximal humerus. The greatest bone density was found in the central region of the humeral head.

43. Kwon BK, Goertzen DJ, O'Brien PJ, Broekhuyse HM, Oxland TR: Biomechanical evaluation of proximal humeral fracture fixation supplemented with calcium phosphate cement. *J Bone Joint Surg Am* 2002;84:951-961.

    A cadaver model of a three-part proximal humerus fracture was used to test fixation using a cloverleaf plate, blade plate, or wires. Wires used alone were found to be biomechanically inferior. The addition of calcium phosphate cement significantly improved the mechanical performance of all three forms of internal fixation, as demonstrated by a significant decrease in interfragmentary motion and a significant increase in torque to failure and torsional stiffness.

44. Robinson CM, Page RS: Severely impacted valgus proximal humeral fractures. *J Bone Joint Surg Am* 2004;86(suppl 1):143-155.

    No patients with a valgus-impacted proximal humerus fracture who were treated with rigid internal fixation and bone cement augmentation developed osteonecrosis. These patients had better clinical results than those of historical control subjects who were treated nonsurgically.

45. Panagopoulos AM, Dimakopoulos P, Tyllianakis M, et al: Valgus impacted proximal humeral fractures and their blood supply after transosseous suturing. *Int Orthop* 2004;28:333-337.

    In 16 patients with a displaced, valgus-impacted four-part fracture fixed with transosseous suture alone, osteonecrosis was measured using digital segmentation angiography and was found in 1 patient. Outcomes were favorable, as measured using the Constant-Murley Shoulder Outcome Score.

46. Hockings M, Haines JF: Least possible fixation of fractures of the proximal humerus. *Injury* 2003;34:443-447.

    An absorbable suture was used between the rotator cuff tendons, without other hardware or bone grafting, to reliably achieve satisfactory union.

47. Park MC, Murthi AM, Roth NS, Blaine TA, Levine WN, Bigliani LU: Two-part and three-part fractures of the proximal humerus treated with suture fixation. *J Orthop Trauma* 2003;17:319-325.

    Reduction and treatment of proximal humerus fractures with suture-only fixation, using heavy polyester nonabsorbable suture, was found to be successful and unlikely to disrupt the vascular supply to the humeral head in two- and three-part fractures. In 86% of patients, near-anatomic reduction and healing were achieved.

48. Chudik SC, Weinhold P, Dahners LE: Fixed-angle plate fixation in simulated fractures of the proximal humerus: A biomechanical study of a new device. *J Shoulder Elbow Surg* 2003;12:578-588.

    This biomechanical study of matched cadaver humeri found superior load to failure and stiffness with a locked proximal humeral plate design, compared with an unlocked proximal humerus T plate, in both comminuted and noncomminuted surgical neck fractures.

49. Siffri PC, Peindl RD, Coley ER, Norton J, Connor PM, Kellam JF: Biomechanical analysis of blade plate versus locking plate fixation for a proximal humerus fracture: Comparison using cadaveric and synthetic humeri. *J Orthop Trauma* 2006;20:547-554.

    Cyclic loading was performed on a cadaver surgical neck fracture model after fixation using a 3.5-mm cannulated blade plate or a 3.5-mm proximal humerus locking plate. The torsional stability of the locking plates was significantly greater than that of the blade plates, and the bending stability was similar.

50. Edwards SL, Wilson NA, Zhang LQ, Flores S, Merk BR: Two-part surgical neck fractures of the proximal part of the humerus: A biomechanical evaluation of two fixation techniques. *J Bone Joint Surg Am* 2006;88:2258-2264.

    Cadaver specimens were matched based on bone mineral density, and a comminuted surgical neck fracture model was created. A proximal humeral nail construct had a high failure rate with cyclic loading in torsion, compared with a 3.5-mm humeral locking plate.

51. Plausinis D, Kwon YW, Zuckerman JD: Complications of humeral head replacement for proximal humeral fractures. *Instr Course Lect* 2005;54:371-380.

    The complications of humeral head replacement in the setting of proximal humerus fractures are outlined.

52. Antuna SA, Sperling JW, Sanchez-Sotelo J, Cofield RH: Shoulder arthroplasty for proximal humeral malunions: Long-term results. *J Shoulder Elbow Surg* 2002;11:122-129.

    Fifty patients underwent hemiarthroplasty or total shoulder arthroplasty for malunion of a three- or four-part fracture. Those who had undergone initial surgical fracture treatment or who required tuberosity osteotomy had a significantly poorer result with respect to postsurgical motion and overall function.

53. Antuna SA, Sperling JW, Sanchez-Sotelo J, Cofield RH: Shoulder arthroplasty for proximal humeral nonunions. *J Shoulder Elbow Surg* 2002;11:114-121.

Twenty-seven patients underwent hemiarthroplasty or total shoulder arthroplasty for nonunion of a two- or three-part proximal humerus fracture. Although function was not completely restored, pain relief and high levels of subjective satisfaction were achieved.

54. Norris TR, Green A, McGuigan FX: Late prosthetic shoulder arthroplasty for displaced proximal humerus fractures. *J Shoulder Elbow Surg* 1995;4:271-280.

55. Mansat P, Guity MR, Bellumore Y, Mansat M: Shoulder arthroplasty for late sequelae of proximal humeral fractures. *J Shoulder Elbow Surg* 2004;13: 305-312.

    The data from this case series suggest that malunion of the greater tuberosity can be tolerated if it does not compromise acceptable positioning of the humeral component. An osteotomy must be performed if there is a malunion of the greater tuberosity with major displacement, but the results are inferior.

56. Boileau P, Trojani C, Walch G, Krishnan SG, Romeo A, Sinnerton R: Shoulder arthroplasty for the treatment of the sequelae of fractures of the proximal humerus. *J Shoulder Elbow Surg* 2001;10:299-308.

    In a multicenter case study of shoulder arthroplasty after nonunion of proximal humerus fracture, four types of nonunion are described. Type I is humeral head collapse or necrosis with minimal tuberosity malunion; type II, locked dislocation or fracture-dislocation; type III, nonunion of the surgical neck; and type IV, severe malunion of the tuberosities. The most significant factor related to poor outcome was osteotomy of the greater tuberosity, which is necessary in some type III and IV nonunions.

57. Beredjiklian PK, Iannotti JP, Norris TR, Williams GR: Operative treatment of malunion of a fracture of the proximal aspect of the humerus. *J Bone Joint Surg Am* 1998;80:1484-1497.

58. Boileau P, Chuinard C, Le Huec JC, Walch G, Trojani C: Proximal humerus fracture sequelae: Impact of a new radiographic classification on arthroplasty. *Clin Orthop Relat Res* 2006;442:121-130.

    The sequelae of proximal humerus fractures are classified. For fractures with surgical neck nonunion or severe tuberosity malunion, the use of a nonconstrained shoulder prosthesis yielded inferior results. For tuberosity malunions requiring osteotomy, a reverse prosthesis is recommended. Level of evidence: IV.

59. Christoforakis JJ, Kontakis GM, Katonis PG, et al: Relevance of the restoration of humeral length and retroversion in hemiarthroplasty for humeral head fractures. *Acta Orthop Belg* 2003;69:226-232.

    CT scans of intact and reconstructed humeri were taken at least 20 months after hemiarthroplasty reconstruction of proximal humerus fractures. A successful outcome, as measured by the Constant Shoulder Score, was achieved in patients with a less-than-10° difference in retroversion and a less-than-14-mm difference in length between the fractured and intact humeri. The mean difference in retroversion was 8.7°, and the mean difference in length between the fractured and intact humeri was 0.65 cm.

60. Tillet E, Smith M, Fulcher M, Shanklin J: Anatomic determination of humeral head retroversion: The relationship of the central axis of the humeral head to the bicipital groove. *J Shoulder Elbow Surg* 1993;2: 255-263.

61. Hernigou P, Duparc F, Hernigou A: Determining humeral retroversion with computed tomography. *J Bone Joint Surg Am* 2002;84:1753-1762.

    CT scans of cadaver humeri were compared with retroversion measurements taken using the transepicondylar axis. Despite a wide variation in the humeral torsion angle among the specimens, two normal humeri of the same individual had a similar angle (mean side-to-side difference, 2.1°). CT scans of the contralateral humerus had excellent reliability in determining proper retroversion.

62. Itamura J, Dietrick T, Roidis N, Shean C, Chen F, Tibone J: Analysis of the bicipital groove as a landmark for humeral head replacement. *J Shoulder Elbow Surg* 2002;11:322-326.

    CT scans of 21 cadaver humeri were evaluated to determine the reliability of the distal bicipital groove in determining implant retroversion during hemiarthroplasty for four-part proximal humerus fracture. The bicipital groove was seen to internally rotate 12° to 19° as it courses distally and therefore is unreliable for use with fracture comminution.

63. Balg F, Boulianne M, Boileau P: Bicipital groove orientation: Considerations for the retroversion of a prosthesis in fractures of the proximal humerus. *J Shoulder Elbow Surg* 2006;15:195-198.

    Based on observations of the variability of bicipital groove orientation, the authors caution surgeons about using the bicipital groove as a landmark in shoulder replacement for fractures and recommend a fracture jig with standard retroversion.

64. Murachovsky J, Ikemoto RY, Nascimento LG, Fujiki EN, Milani C, Warner JJ: Pectoralis major tendon reference (PMT): A new method for accurate restoration of humeral length with hemiarthroplasty for fracture. *J Shoulder Elbow Surg* 2006;15:675-678.

    The pectoralis major tendon was evaluated in 40 cadaver shoulders as a reliable reference in restoring humeral length during hemiarthroplasty for four-part proximal humerus fractures. The mean distance between the top of the pectoralis tendon and the superior portion of the humeral head was 5.6 cm.

65. Boileau P, Caligaris-Cordero B, Payeur F, Tinsi L, Argenson C: Prognostic factors during rehabilitation after shoulder prostheses for fracture [in French]. *Rev Chir Orthop Reparatrice Appar Mot* 1999;85:106-116.

66. Hasan SS, Leith JM, Campbell B, Kapil R, Smith KL, Matsen FA III: Characteristics of unsatisfactory shoulder arthroplasties. *J Shoulder Elbow Surg* 2001; 11:431-441.

A review of 139 patients who were dissatisfied with the result of their shoulder arthroplasty found that many did not meet the established criteria for failure. Greater attention to achieving proper component position, postsurgical motion, and tuberosity fixation may increase patient satisfaction after shoulder arthroplasaty.

67. Loew M, Heitkemper S, Parsch D, Schneider S, Rickert M: Influence of the design of the prosthesis on the outcome after hemiarthroplasty of the shoulder in displaced fractures of the head of the humerus. *J Bone Joint Surg Br* 2006;88:345-350.

No differences in outcome were found in a comparison of functional results and rate of tuberosity healing using an anatomic humeral prosthesis and a prosthesis designed specifically for proximal humerus fractures. The healing of the tuberosities was significantly related to improved function and ultimate outcome.

68. Abu-Rajab RB, Stansfield BW, Nunn T, Nicol AC, Kelly IG: Re-attachment of the tuberosities of the humerus following hemiarthroplasty for four-part fracture. *J Bone Joint Surg Br* 2006;88:1539-1544.

In a biomechanical assessment of tuberosity fixation using a sawbones model of hemiarthroplasty for four-part fracture, angular movement and tuberosity migration were significantly decreased by secure suture fixation of the greater and lesser tuberosities to each other, the implant, and the humeral shaft.

# Section 2

# Instability and Athletic Injuries

Section Editor
Peter J. Millett, MD

# Chapter 6

# Classification, Clinical Assessment, and Imaging of Glenohumeral Instability

John G. Costouros, MD

Jon J.P. Warner, MD

## Introduction

The treatment of glenohumeral instability has evolved rapidly because of advancements in the understanding of shoulder biomechanics and pathophysiology, imaging technology, and surgical techniques. Current approaches in the treatment of shoulder instability focus on restoring normal anatomy and biomechanics, rather than restricting or creating barriers to physiologic motion.

Proper classification of glenohumeral instability is critical to successful treatment. Instability, which is a subjective phenomenon resulting in pathologic pain and dysfunction, must be distinguished from laxity, which is an objective clinical finding of the degree of passive glenohumeral translation. Although laxity is not inherently pathologic, it can be a risk factor for the development of instability.[1] Laxity can be affected by patient age, gender, congenital factors, and arm position.

## Pathophysiology

The glenohumeral joint is minimally constrained to allow a wide range of motion. Stability is maintained through a complex interplay of osseous and soft-tissue architecture that involves both static constraints (osteochondral articulation, ligaments, and tendons) and dynamic constraints (active muscular contraction.)[2-6] Static and dynamic constraints are listed in Table 1.

### Static Constraints

Static constraint begins with the inherently unstable articulation between the proximal humerus and the glenoid, which is a function of osseous architecture and capsuloligamentous anatomy. The humeral head has a disproportionately large surface and small radius of curvature relative to the glenoid. The average neck-shaft angle of the humerus is between 130° and 140°, and the retroversion is 30° relative to the distal humeral epicondylar axis. In most individuals, the glenoid is in 7° of retroversion, with an average superior tilt of 5°. When the arm is in adduction, the scapula is tilted anteriorly 30° relative to the chest wall, upward 3° relative to the

transverse plane, and forward 20° relative to the sagittal plane.[7]

The glenoid labrum functions as an extension of the glenoid articular surface by increasing the width and depth of the glenoid socket, providing an anchor for capsuloligamentous structures, and facilitating the concavity-compression mechanism when the humeral head is compressed into the glenoid during rotator cuff contraction (Figures 1 and 2). In any position of rotation, only 25% to 30% of the humeral head is in contact with the glenoid surface.[8] (The position resembles that of a golf ball on a tee.) Thus, the integrity of the glenoid labrum is critical to stability.

| Table 1 | Static and Dynamic Constraints to Joint Instability | |
|---|---|
| **Type** | **Subtypes** |
| **Static** | |
| Osteochondral | Proximal humerus: articular surface (Hill-Sachs lesion, posttraumatic defect, osteonecrosis), abnormal humeral version |
| | Glenoid: articular surface; bony defect, fracture, or erosion; abnormal morphology (dysplasia); abnormal glenoid version |
| Capsulolabral complex | Glenoid labrum |
| | Glenohumeral ligaments |
| | Coracohumeral ligament |
| Coracoacromial ligament | |
| Negative intra-articular pressure | |
| Synovial fluid adhesion-cohesion | |
| Rotator cuff | |
| **Dynamic** | |
| Rotator cuff | |
| Long head of biceps | |
| Scapulothoracic rhythm | |
| Concavity-compression | |
| Proprioception | |

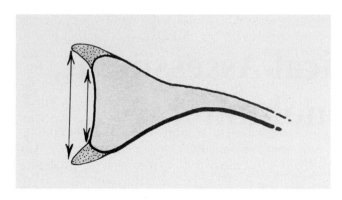

**Figure 1**  The glenoid labrum functions to increase the depth of the glenoid articular surface.

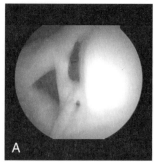 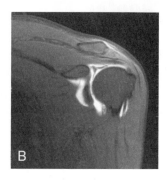

**Figure 3**  **A,** The Buford complex seen in an intrasurgical photograph. **B,** The Buford complex seen in a coronal MRI enhanced with intra-articular gadolinium.

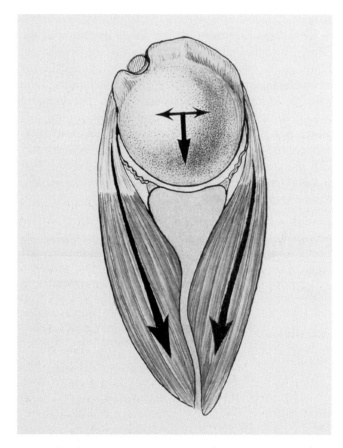

**Figure 2**  Rotator cuff contraction contributes to the dynamic stability of the glenohumeral joint and concavity-compression. Muscular contraction of the rotator cuff (large arrows) contributes to concavity-compression at the glenohumeral joint (small arrows). Improved concavity-compression prevents anterior or posterior instability.

A Bankart lesion represents the dissociation of the glenoid labrum and the middle and inferior glenohumeral ligaments from the anterior glenoid rim.[9] Loss of the labrum can result in a 50% decrease in glenoid depth and a 20% reduction in the translational force required for dislocation.[6,10] The relatively uncommon posterior, or reverse, Bankart lesion involves disruption of the posterior band of the inferior glenohumeral ligament complex (IGHLC) and its associated labrum from the posterior glenoid rim. Either type of Bankart lesion can occur alone or in conjunction with fracture or erosion of the glenoid. The Bankart lesion should not be confused with normal anatomic variants of the glenohumeral joint, such as the Buford complex or a loosely attached superior labrum and associated sublabral foramen[11] (Figure 3).

In cadaver studies to assess the importance of the superior portion of the labrum to glenohumeral stability, an isolated anterosuperior labral lesion did not affect glenohumeral translation. However, a complete superior lesion associated with destabilization of the long head of the biceps resulted in significant increases in anterior-posterior and superior-inferior translation of the humerus on the glenoid in the lower ranges of elevation.[12]

Glenohumeral stability is augmented by negative intra-articular pressure, which limits glenohumeral translation. Because of high osmotic pressure in the interstitial tissues, water and synovial fluid are drawn out of the sealed glenohumeral joint. A relative vacuum is thereby created, and it increases as the articular surfaces are pulled apart.[13] In addition, the viscous and hydrodynamic forces in synovial fluid create adhesion and cohesion between the humeral head and glenoid articulation, which permit translation but limit separation. This process is analogous to the manipulation of two glass plates separated by a thin film of water: the plates slide easily against each other, but separating them requires significant force.

The glenohumeral ligaments primarily stabilize the shoulder joint at the extremes of motion. Each ligament functions based on its anatomic position in the capsule, the position of the arm, and the degree and direction of load being applied to the proximal humerus. The superior glenohumeral ligament and coracohumeral ligament are constituents of the rotator interval.[14] Although the function of the coracohumeral ligament is controversial, it may prevent excessive inferior translation of the adducted upper extremity and provide stability to the long head of the biceps.[15] Selective sectioning studies indicated that the superior glenohumeral ligament limits both anterior translation and combined inferior translation and external rotation of the adducted arm,[16] and it may limit posterior translation when the shoulder is in forward flexion, adduction, and internal rotation.[16]

The middle glenohumeral ligament has the greatest structural and morphologic variability of the glenohumeral ligaments. It functions as a passive restraint to anterior-posterior translation of the humeral head when the arm is in 60° to 90° of abduction and external rotation, and it limits inferior translation of the humerus in adduction.[5]

The IGHLC consists of both anterior and posterior bands. It restrains external rotation of the arm in both neutral rotation and abduction;[17] in abduction, it also limits inferior translation. The IGHLC has been described as a hammock underneath the humeral head, having both selective posterior movement in internal rotation (to limit posterior translation of the humerus) and selective anterior movement in external rotation (to limit anterior translation of the humerus).[18] With the arm in 90° of abduction, the IGHLC is the primary restraint to anterior translation of the humerus.[19] Studies found that injury to the IGHLC, in association with anteroinferior labral injury, is integral to the development of recurrent anterior instability.[18,19]

The posterior capsule is much less robust than the anterior capsule. It acts as a passive restraint to posterior translation of the humerus in forward flexion, adduction, and internal rotation. Lesions of the posterior capsulolabral complex, such as a posterior Bankart lesion, contribute to posterior instability.[20]

### Dynamic Constraints

Dynamic constraint to glenohumeral instability is provided by active muscular contraction and is affected by the muscles' level of conditioning and strength.[21,22] In the middle range of motion, stability is maintained by dynamic action of the rotator cuff and the long head of the biceps, which provide compression of the humeral head into the glenoid and a fixed fulcrum for rotation.[23] Coordinated scapulothoracic and glenohumeral motion provide additional dynamic stability. Proper scapulothoracic rhythm provides a platform onto which the humeral head can rotate, thereby maintaining the position of the glenoid underneath the humeral head.[24]

Both static and dynamic constraints maintain stability during concavity-compression.[6] Contraction of the rotator cuff and long head of the biceps compresses the convex humeral head into a matching concavity of the glenoid-labrum complex. Elimination of tension provided by the subscapularis may result in static or dynamic anterior instability and subluxation, especially at the extremes of motion.[21] Combined tears of the supraspinatus and infraspinatus can result in static and dy-

namic superior subluxation and instability, especially if the coracoacromial arch is deficient.[25] Furthermore, in patients older than 45 years, rotator cuff tears are commonly associated with traumatic instability.

The specific role of the long head of the biceps as a dynamic stabilizer is controversial. Studies have described the long head of the biceps as limiting anterior translation and external rotation and limiting anterior-posterior translation of the humerus during the late cocking phase of throwing.[23] Glenohumeral stability is further augmented by proprioceptive nerve endings in the joint capsule and tendons, which provide afferent feedback to modulate muscular contraction and thereby prevent excessive glenohumeral translation during overhead motion.[26]

## Pathoanatomy

Several pathologic entities can contribute to glenohumeral instability. A single, violent traumatic event can create a deficiency of a specific anatomic region, such as a Bankart lesion, glenoid fracture, or capsular rupture. Voluntary instability or repetitive microtrauma usually results in plastic deformation or attenuation of the soft tissues that contribute to shoulder stability.

### Bankart Lesions

Bankart lesions are the most common pathologic lesions leading to recurrent anterior subluxation or dislocation of the shoulder.[9] They involve detachment of the anteroinferior labrum from the glenoid rim, along with the anterior band of the IGHLC and the middle glenohumeral ligament (Figure 4). Arthroscopy reveals an isolated Bankart lesion in as many as 97% of patients with a first traumatic anterior dislocation.[27] A reverse Bankart lesion involves disruption of the posteroinferior glenoid labrum, along with the posterior band of the IGHLC, in a patient with posterior instability (Figure 5). A superficial tear between the posteroinferior labrum and the glenoid, with no detachment of the labrum, was recently named a Kim lesion.[28] Plastic deformation of the associated capsule and glenohumeral ligaments occurs with either an acute or chronic Kim lesion and is believed to be a necessary component of recurrent dislocation.[29]

In the presence of either anterior or posterior instability, capsulolabral detachment can occur as an avulsion fracture or bony Bankart lesion. In chronic instability, the detachment can become malunited along the scapular neck. Routine CT of a suspected bony Bankart lesion is useful to determine bone loss in the glenoid and humerus and guide surgical intervention (Figure 6).

### Capsular Lesions

Traumatic injury to the capsule and glenohumeral ligaments commonly occurs in a dislocation. Depending on

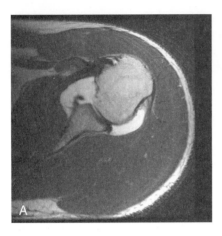
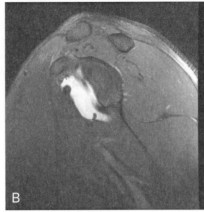
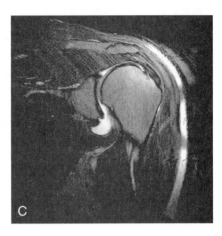

**Figure 4**   MRIs showing a Bankart lesion in a patient with anterior instability. **A,** Axial view. **B,** Sagittal oblique view. **C,** Coronal view.

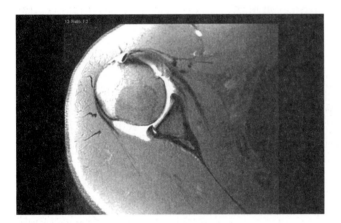

**Figure 5**   Axial MRI showing a posterior or reverse Bankart lesion in a patient with isolated posterior instability.

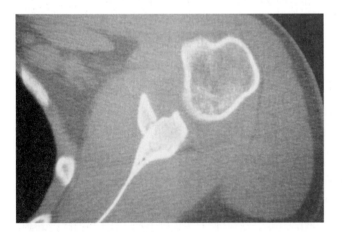

**Figure 6**   CT in the axial plane showing an anterior glenoid fracture in a patient with anterior instability.

the magnitude of the force, the injury can cause plastic intrasubstance deformation or complete rupture. Plastic deformation can be difficult to diagnose clinically or arthroscopically.

Forceful abduction can cause humeral avulsion of the capsule or glenohumeral ligaments (HAGL).[30,31] HAGL lesions are thickened or rolled edges of capsule, typically in the inferior recess. They are rare but can occur with recurrent instability, if glenohumeral bone loss or a Bankart lesion is not present.[32] Bony HAGL lesions also occur. HAGL and bony HAGL lesions can be difficult to diagnose; they are visible on radiographs in only 20% of patients.[33] However, recognition of these rare lesions is critical because they require open or arthroscopic surgical repair.

Recent studies on the effect of selective capsular plication have increased understanding of the role of the glenohumeral joint capsule and associated structures in obligate motion. In a biomechanical study of the effect of selective capsular tightening on humeral head translation at the end ranges of motion, selective anterior capsular plication increased or decreased translation during flexion, external rotation, and internal rotation; posterior plication had little or no effect on translation.[34]

Congenital disorders of collagen, such as Ehlers-Danlos syndrome, can cause structural collagen alterations that affect capsular biomechanics. The clinical manifestations of Ehlers-Danlos syndrome include joint laxity aberrations, vascular anomalies, and pathologic wound healing.[35] Most patients have a multidirectional instability pattern that frequently recurs after surgical intervention.

## Superior Labral Lesions

Lesions of the superior labrum are associated with glenohumeral instability, especially if the biceps anchor is destabilized or the entire anteroposterior extent of the superior labrum is detached. Cadaver studies found that these lesions cause significant increases in anterior-posterior and superior-inferior translation of the humerus on the glenoid in the lower ranges of elevation.[12]

## Rotator Interval Lesions

The biomechanical role of the rotator interval in glenohumeral stability is being intensely studied. Cadaver research has found that sectioning the rotator interval increases glenohumeral translation in all planes and is most pronounced in inferior translation and external rotation. Sectioning of the rotator interval led to dislocation in 50% of specimens positioned in 60° of abduction and external rotation.[36] In general, rotator interval lesions are present in patients who have anteroinferior, posterior, or multidirectional instability, and closure is warranted if an abnormal rotator interval is found during surgery.[36]

## Humeral Deficiencies

Isolated or recurrent anterior instability can create an impression fracture, called a Hill-Sachs lesion, on the posterolateral articular margin of the humerus, as the humerus dislocates over the anterior glenoid (Figures 7 and 8). A reverse Hill-Sachs lesion occurs on the anterolateral articular margin of the humerus as a consequence of posterior instability.[37] The extent of the impression fracture must be assessed because a relatively large lesion can disrupt articulation of the glenohumeral joint and contribute to instability. Hill-Sachs lesions are always present with recurrent anterior instability. They also occur in 90% of anterior dislocations and 25% of anterior subluxations.[38] The defects are usually small, and they rarely contribute to instability. However, surgical treatment may be advisable if the lesion includes more than 30% of the articular surface (determined using CT) and is associated with instability.[39] Abnormalities in humeral version leading to symptomatic instability are extremely rare and can be treated with proximal humeral osteotomy.[40]

## Glenoid Deficiencies

A deficiency of the glenoid articular surface or an abnormality of glenoid version is rarely a cause of recurrent instability but often leads to treatment failure (Figure 9). CT is used to determine the amount of bone loss that leads to clinically relevant instability.[1] If the length of the glenoid defect exceeds the radius of the glenoid at its maximum diameter, the force necessary for dislocation to occur is decreased by 30% (Figure 10). The normal pear-shaped glenoid takes on an inverted pear configuration in the presence of a glenoid deficiency.[41] Bony reconstruction is preferable to routine capsulolabral repair if the glenoid surface deficiency is greater than 25%.[42,43]

In addition to osteoarticular bone loss affecting the glenoid, alterations in glenoid morphology and excessive retroversion can contribute to posterior instability.[44] Excessive retroversion or glenoid erosion usually develops from recurrent posterior instability and eccen-

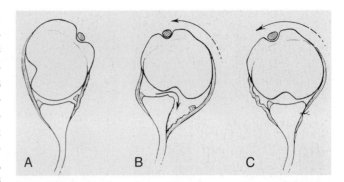

**Figure 7** Drawings of an impression fracture of the posterolateral humeral head (Hill-Sachs lesion) in a patient with anterior instability. **A,** Anterior labral injury with anterior capsular laxity. **B,** Anterior subluxation-dislocation, creating a Hill-Sachs deformity and progression of the capsulolabral defect. **C,** Surgical repair of the capsulolabral (Bankart) lesion; the Hill-Sachs lesion is not addressed.

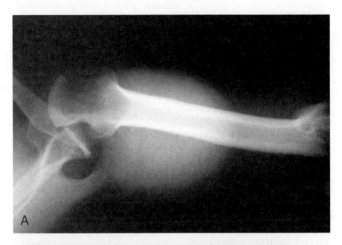

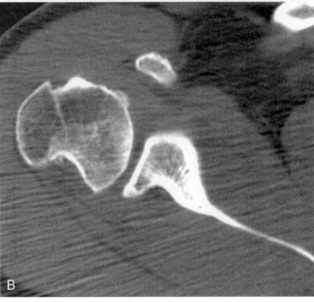

**Figure 8** An engaging Hill-Sachs lesion. **A,** Axillary lateral plain radiograph. **B,** Axial CT study.

tric glenoid wear. Posterior bone grafting is suggested to treat severe eccentric wear, in addition to capsular

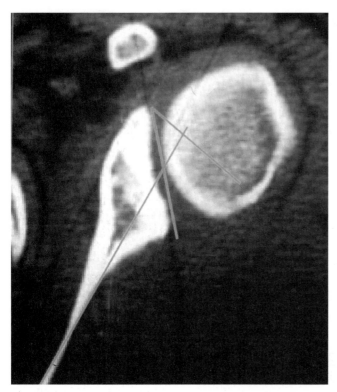

**Figure 9** CT in the axial plane showing excessive retroversion as a result of congenital dysplasia.

**Table 2 | Classification of Glenohumeral Instability**

| Criterion | Type of Instability |
|---|---|
| Direction | Unidirectional |
| |   Anterior |
| |   Posterior |
| |   Inferior |
| | Bidirectional |
| |   Anteroinferior |
| |   Posteroinferior |
| | Multidirectional |
| Etiology | Traumatic (macrotraumatic) |
| | Atraumatic |
| |   Voluntary |
| |   Involuntary |
| | Acquired (microtraumatic) |
| | Congenital |
| | Neuromuscular |
| Frequency | Acute (primary) |
| | Chronic |
| |   Recurrent |
| |   Fixed |
| Degree | Dislocation |
| | Subluxation |
| | Microinstability |

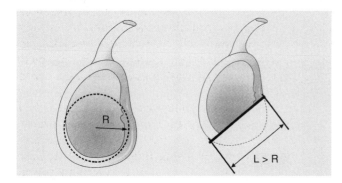

**Figure 10** Drawing showing the biomechanical impact of anteroinferior glenoid deficiency. If the length of the glenoid defect (L) is greater than the radius of the glenoid at its maximum diameter (R), the force required for anterior dislocation is reduced by 30%, compared with a normal glenohumeral joint. *(Adapted with permission from Gerber C, Nyffeler RW: Classification of glenohumeral joint instability. Clin Orthop 2002; 400:65.)*

repair.[45] Glenoid dysplasia is congenital and can be treated with a glenoid opening-wedge osteotomy.[46] The specific contribution of alterations in glenoid and humeral version to glenohumeral instability is under investigation.

### Neurologic Imbalance

Instability can result from an imbalance in the neuromuscular forces acting on the glenohumeral joint. Seizure disorders and electric shock are associated with posterior dis-

location;[37] an imbalance in muscle forces occurs as the sustained contraction of the subscapularis (the largest rotator cuff muscle) overwhelms the anterior stabilizing structures and weak external rotators, driving the humeral head posteriorly in internal rotation.

## Classification

The key elements of any classification system are reproducibility, intraobserver and interobserver reliability, and consistent usefulness in directing treatment. Several systems have been proposed to classify glenohumeral joint instability, based on the direction, etiology, or mechanism of instability.[1,47-51] Historically, instability was classified only on the basis of direction, because it was understood as anteriorly or posteriorly unidirectional.[52-55] Neer and Foster introduced the term multidirectional instability (defined as progressive anteroposterior instability leading to inferior laxity and a sulcus sign) to include patients with multiplanar instability, presumably caused by repetitive microtrauma or congenital hyperlaxity of the joint capsule.[56] A sulcus sign is a hallmark clinical finding in patients with multidirectional stability. Static, dynamic, and voluntary instability also have been classified[1,49,51]

The classification system outlined in Table 2 is based on four criteria: direction, etiology, frequency, and degree.

## Direction

The direction of instability can be anterior, posterior, inferior, or a combination. Thus, unidirectional instability is anterior, posterior, or inferior. Anterior instability is unidirectional. Bidirectional instability is anterior-posterior, anterior-inferior, or posterior-inferior. Multidirectional instability occurs in three planes: anterior, posterior, and inferior.

## Etiology

Most glenohumeral instability requiring treatment is categorized as traumatic.[57] Traumatic instability is created when the force of a single high-velocity event overwhelms the normal barriers to excessive glenohumeral translation and causes a deficiency in a specific anatomic region, such as a Bankart lesion in anterior instability. In atraumatic voluntary instability, dislocation or subluxation of the joint results from the patient's selective muscular contraction and relaxation, often in the absence of pain.[1] In atraumatic involuntary instability, destabilization of the joint often results from inadvertent placement of the arm in a position of risk, as may occur during sleep; it is usually associated with pain. Repetitive microtrauma or recurrent atraumatic instability usually results in plastic deformation or attenuation of the soft tissues, which contributes to shoulder instability.[1] A congenital cause of instability most often is associated with chronic instability.[58] Glenoid dysplasia and excessive glenoid retroversion can contribute to posterior instability, and a collagen disorder such as Ehlers-Danlos syndrome can contribute to multidirectional instability. Finally, the neuromuscular causes of instability usually are associated with a developmental or acquired condition, such as a seizure disorder, stroke, or cerebral palsy, that results in muscular imbalance and loss of coordinated movement.

## Frequency

Instability is categorized as acute or chronic. Acute instability represents a single episode, typically occurring within the preceding 24 hours. The instability may spontaneously resolve itself and not require closed reduction. Two types of chronic instability exist: a fixed, locked dislocation that cannot be reduced; or several episodes of acute instability occurring during a period of time. Most commonly, a chronic fixed dislocation is a posterior dislocation that has been neglected for a long period of time. Chronic recurrent instability involves multiple acute episodes.

## Degree

Complete disarticulation between the humerus and glenoid is referred to as dislocation, and incomplete disarticulation is referred to as subluxation. Reduction of a dislocation may be required to restore normal joint alignment. A more subtle instability pattern that lacks objective signs of laxity but may manifest itself as pain with overhead motion is referred to as microinstability or pathologic laxity.[59]

## Clinical Evaluation

### History

The clinical evaluation begins with a thorough history that includes the patient's age, occupation, hand dominance, and mechanism of injury, as well as any additional medical problems. The direction, etiology, frequency, and degree of instability are determined. Frequently, the history elicits clues as to the pathology of the instability. If a young participant in contact sports describes an anteriorly directed blow to the posterior shoulder while it was abducted and externally rotated, the examiner can conclude that the instability probably is a traumatic anterior dislocation. If the patient has had a seizure or electric shock or is a chronic alcohol abuser, posterior subluxation or dislocation is likely. Voluntary multidirectional instability should be suspected in a patient whose self-description includes "loose jointed" or "able to pop my shoulder out."[56]

Determining the arm position that elicits pain or dysfunction provides valuable information, especially if the instability is unidirectional. A patient with anterior instability often reports pain or becomes apprehensive when reaching behind the back in external rotation or attempting an overhead throwing motion. A patient with posterior instability often reports dull discomfort in the posterior shoulder when reaching across the body with the arm in internal rotation or attempting a bench press or push-up.

The patient's surgical history should be researched in detail because the surgical report may suggest areas of potential recurrence. For example, subscapularis and axillary nerve functioning should be investigated if the patient has had an open anterior stabilization procedure.[60] The patient should also be questioned about all possible causes of shoulder pain.

### Physical Examination

A systematic physical examination includes a general inspection, palpation of pertinent structures and painful areas, assessment of range of motion, and specialized tests to detect instability. The contralateral shoulder is always examined first to provide a basis for comparing physiologic laxity in the affected shoulder. Furthermore, the cervical spine must be examined as a possible source of pain or weakness referred to the shoulder.

The inspection begins with the osseous and muscular contour of the shoulder, with special attention to the contour of the deltoid muscle and the relationship of the humerus to the acromion. A neurologic examination follows, to rule out underlying injury to the axillary

**Table 3 | Clinical Tests for Instability**

| Type of Instability | Test |
|---|---|
| Anterior | Apprehension |
| | Anterior drawer |
| | Relocation |
| | Hyperabduction |
| | Anterior load and shift |
| Posterior | Posterior drawer |
| | Posterior load and shift |
| | Jerk |
| | Posterior stress |
| Inferior | Inferior drawer |
| |   Adduction and neutral rotation |
| |   Adduction and maximum external rotation |
| Multidirectional | Generalized laxity |
| |   Metacarpophalangeal hyperextension |
| |   Elbow hyperextension |
| |   Patellar instability |
| |   Thumb to forearm |

nerve or a spinocerebellar disorder.[61] In a patient with chronic posterior dislocation, the humeral head may be prominent posteriorly and held in adduction and internal rotation. Scapular motion should be inspected during active shoulder elevation to exclude medial (long thoracic) or lateral (cranial nerve 11) neuropathic winging as a cause of instability.[62,63]

The patient's range of motion should be documented in forward elevation, abduction, internal rotation, and external rotation. Active and passive range of motion should be generally equivalent, unless a rotator cuff tear is present. Rotator cuff strength should be assessed; in patients with traumatic instability who are older than 45 years, rotator cuff tearing is often present and alters the course of treatment. If the patient has anterior instability, it is especially important to assess the functioning of the subscapularis using the lift-off, modified lift-off, and belly-press tests. Patients with a subscapularis injury have increased passive external rotation with the arm in adduction, compared with the unaffected side.[64]

## Tests for Instability
Specialized provocative tests are available to refine a diagnosis of anterior, posterior, inferior, or multidirectional instability, as outlined in Table 3.

### Anterior Instability
The apprehension test is performed by placing the affected extremity into abduction and external rotation. Discomfort or apprehension suggests incompetence of the anteroinferior labrum and IGHLC. Apprehension with

maximum external rotation in adduction implies injury to the anterosuperior labrum or rotator interval.[56]

The anterior drawer test is performed with the patient sitting and the arm in slight abduction; an anteriorly directed force is applied to the posterior humeral head. This maneuver is used to quantify anterior translation by assessing the degree of anterior humeral displacement (0 = no translation; +1 = translation to glenoid rim; +2 = translation over glenoid rim, which is reduced when the force is removed; +3 = complete dislocation and locking over glenoid rim).[65]

The Jobe relocation test is performed with the patient supine and the arm in abduction and external rotation. A posteriorly directed force is applied to the proximal humerus to relocate the humeral head and eliminate a sense of apprehension.[66]

The Gagey hyperabduction test assesses the laxity of the IGHLC and is performed by bringing the arm into maximum abduction and internal rotation, then comparing it with the contralateral arm.[67] If the abduction of the affected arm is more than 10° greater than that of the contralateral arm, incompetence of the IGHLC may be indicated.

The anterior load-and-shift test is used to measure the degree of translation and is performed with the patient sitting. A compressive force is applied laterally through the humeral head while an anterior force is applied to the proximal humerus.

### Posterior Instability
The posterior drawer and posterior load-and-shift tests are similar to the tests for anterior instability, with the force applied in the posterior direction. The jerk test is performed by placing the patient's arm into 90° of flexion, adduction, and internal rotation while palpating the posterior aspect of the humerus and applying a posterior force along the axis of the humerus.[68] The test is positive if the maneuver elicits pain, apprehension, or a palpable shift as the humeral head subluxates posteriorly. The posterior stress test is performed with the patient supine. A posterior force is applied through the humerus, and the test is positive if there is palpable crepitus or subluxation.[69]

### Inferior Instability
To determine the degree of inferior shift, the sulcus sign is elicited by applying inferior traction to the arm in adduction.[56] An asymmetric sulcus with pain indicates inferior instability. A persistent sulcus sign with the arm in maximum external rotation, adduction, and inferior traction implies incompetence of the rotator interval.

### Multidirectional Instability
In many patients with multidirectional instability, symmetric signs of generalized ligament laxity can be found in multiple joints. The signs include metacarpopha-

langeal hyperextension of more than 90°, genu recurvatum, elbow hyperextension of more than 10°, patellar instability, and the ability of the thumb to bend back to the forearm. Patients with multidirectional instability have signs of anterior or posterior instability leading to inferior instability, in varying severity.

In some patients, multidirectional instability is caused by a connective tissue disorder such as Marfan syndrome or Ehlers-Danlos syndrome. If a patient's subluxation or dislocation appears to be voluntary, an underlying psychiatric disorder or secondary gain issue may be present. Surgical intervention is usually not successful for these patients.[70]

# Imaging
## Plain Radiography

Three plain radiographic views, including the axillary lateral view and Grashey (true AP) views in internal and external rotation, are sufficient for determining the direction of dislocation and the presence of a fracture or other osseous lesion.

To obtain a true AP view, the x-ray beam is directed at a 45° angle relative to the sagittal plane of the body. This projection allows the glenohumeral joint space to be seen and allows calculation of the acromiohumeral distance (the perpendicular distance between the apex of the humeral head and the undersurface of the acromion in neutral rotation).[71] In normal shoulders, the average acromiohumeral distance is 10.5 mm; in shoulders with a full-thickness rotator cuff tear, it is 7 mm or less.[72] The acromiohumeral distance is calculated from a radiograph using the Grashey view and corrected for scale; it cannot be reliably calculated using MRI.[73] A Hill-Sachs or reverse Hill-Sachs defect can be seen with the shoulder in internal or external rotation, respectively, on a Grashey view.[71]

The axillary lateral view is important for determining anterior or posterior dislocation. If pain interferes with the ability to obtain an axillary lateral view, a modified axillary projection that does not require arm abduction, such as the Velpeau view, may be substituted.[74] In the Velpeau view, the arm remains in a sling, and the patient leans back 30° over the film cassette while the x-ray beam is directed perpendicularly through the shoulder from superior to inferior. The supraspinatus outlet (Y scapular) view can also show the position of the humeral head relative to the glenoid but is not as accurate as the axillary lateral view.[74]

Other specialized views, including the West Point and Stryker notch views, can further delineate any osseous injury or deformity contributing to the instability.[74] The West Point view best shows the anteroinferior glenoid rim in patients with an osseous Bankart lesion. The patient is positioned prone, with the shoulder and elbow abducted 90° over the end of the table; the film cassette is positioned superior to the shoulder, and the x-ray beam is directed inferomedially to the acromioclavicular joint through the axilla, at a 25° angle to the cassette. The Stryker notch view reveals the posterolateral humeral head and any Hill-Sachs defect.[74] The patient is positioned supine and asked to place his or her hand on the top of the head. With the cassette placed behind the scapula, the x-ray beam is directed 45° cephalad while centered on the axillary fold.

## Computed Tomography

CT is the best modality for studying bone and should be obtained if glenoid dysplasia, congenital version anomaly, acquired version abnormality from erosion, glenoid rim fracture, or a large humeral head defect is suspected or if revision surgery is being considered. CT is more accurate than plain radiography in showing and quantifying an osseous injury. Its three-dimensional imaging aids in diagnosis and decision making. Labral lesions can be detected, and the quality and integrity of the joint capsule can be assessed using intra-articular contrast, although MRI is superior to CT arthrography for these purposes.[71,75-77]

CT arthrography of the shoulder has reported sensitivity and specificity as high as 100% for loose bodies, glenoid fracture, and posterior labral defects; for anterior labral defects, the sensitivity and specificity are as high as 90% and 73%, respectively.[71] Although MRI is superior for the diagnosis of rotator cuff tears, biceps pathology, and capsulolabral defects, CT arthrography can be used if MRI is contraindicated, such as for a patient who has undergone stabilization or rotator cuff repair using metallic anchors (Figure 11).

CT assessment can be used to accurately calculate glenoid version;[78] the use of plain radiography or MRI may result in an incorrect calculation. CT is also used to determine static subluxation of the glenohumeral joint with the arm in neutral rotation; external rotation can lead to static anterior subluxation, and internal rotation can lead to static posterior subluxation (Figure 12).[79] Glenoid morphology can be classified based on erosion, dysplasia, and retroversion[44] (Figure 13).

## Magnetic Resonance Imaging

MRI is a sensitive and noninvasive method of evaluating glenohumeral instability. Its advantages, compared with plain radiography or CT, include lack of exposure to ionizing radiation and superior soft-tissue resolution and detail.[77,80] In a standard protocol, three orthogonal planes are used: spin-echo coronal oblique, sagittal oblique, and axial sequence. The first two sequences are ideal for evaluating the rotator cuff; the third is ideal for assessing the glenoid labrum, bicipital groove, biceps, and subscapularis tendon.[77,81-83] The T1-weighted and proton-density sequences provide excellent anatomic

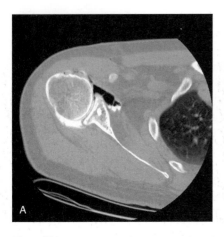
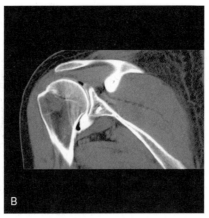
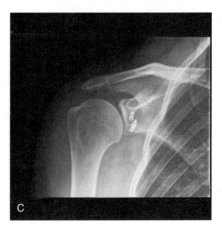

**Figure 11** CT arthrography of the shoulder of a patient with recurrent anterior instability in the axial **(A)** and coronal **(B)** planes, showing failure of an earlier open Bankart repair. **C,** AP radiograph showing well-seated metallic anchors in the anteroinferior glenoid labrum of the same patient.

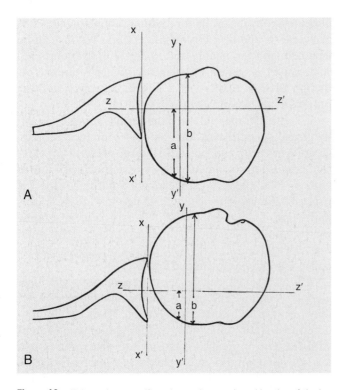

**Figure 12** CT is used to quantify static anterior-posterior subluxation of the humerus. The subluxation index is defined by a/b × 100%. An index of 45% to 65% is normal, an index of less than 45% indicates anterior subluxation, and an index of more than 65% indicates static posterior subluxation. **A,** Static posterior subluxation. **B,** Static anterior subluxation. *(Adapted with permission from Walch G, Boulahia A, Boileau J, Kempf JF, and Aequalis Group. Primary glenohumeral osteoarthritis: Clinical and radiographic classification. Acta Orthop Belg 1998;64[suppl 2]:48.)*

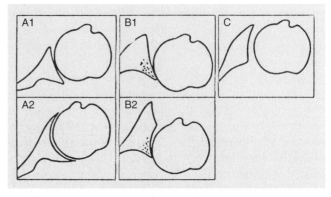

**Figure 13** Classification of glenoid morphology in primary glenohumeral osteoarthritis. Type A, erosion (A1, minor; A2, major), type B, dysplasia (B1, posterior subluxation; B2, biconcavity), type C, retroversion. *(Adapted with permission from Walch G, Boulahia A, Boileau J, Kempf JF, and Aequalis Group. Primary glenohumeral osteoarthritis: Clinical and radiographic classification. Acta Orthop Belg 1998;64[suppl 2]:50.)*

detail, and the T2-weighted sequences indicate fluid location.[82,83]

MRI is superior to other imaging modalities for diagnosing capsulolabral, ligamentous, or rotator cuff lesions.[77] The addition of intra-articular contrast, specifically the rare-earth element gadolinium, enhances the sensitivity and specificity of MRI in diagnosing labral lesions and distinguishing partial-thickness from full-thickness rotator cuff tears.[81,84,85] Magnetic resonance arthrography (MRA) has reported sensitivity and specificity of 88% and 91%, respectively, in the diagnosis of labroligamentous lesions.[82,83] In labral pathology diagnosis, MRA was found to possess sensitivity and specificity (87% and 88%, respectively) superior to that of CT arthrography (33% and 75%, respectively).[80]

Because lesions of the glenoid labrum account for most instability that requires surgery, it is important to distinguish the appearance of pathologic glenoid labrum tissue on MRI from that of normal tissue. On the axial sequences, the labrum is normally triangular and low signal, although it can be rounded and have clefts. The anterior labrum and capsule are larger and more developed than the posterior capsule. Intra-articular contrast can be used to identify labral tears or a patulous capsule. An insertion of the capsule into the glenoid more than 1 cm proximal to the tip of the labrum is associated with instability.[82]

## Summary

The ability to distinguish shoulder laxity from instability is critical in determining whether a patient requires further treatment. Recent studies have enhanced the understanding of normal and pathologic glenohumeral motion, as well as the key static and dynamic elements contributing to glenohumeral stability and function. Accurate classification based on direction, etiology, frequency, and degree of instability can direct treatment. Before surgical intervention is considered, MRI or CT should be selectively used to define and quantify the abnormal anatomy contributing to instability.

## Annotated References

1. Gerber C, Nyffeler RW: Classification of glenohumeral joint instability. *Clin Orthop Relat Res* 2002; 400:65-76.

    The authors describe a classification system that distinguishes static from dynamic glenohumeral instability and from voluntary instability. A biomechanical rationale is introduced for the degree of glenoid bone loss seen on CT that leads to a high risk of recurrent instability. Level of evidence: V.

2. Harryman DT II, Sidles JA, Harris SL, Matsen FA III: The role of the rotator interval capsule in passive motion and stability of the shoulder. *J Bone Joint Surg Am* 1992;74:53-66.

3. Debski RE, Sakone M, Woo SL, Wong EK, Fu FH, Warner JJ: Contributions of the passive properties of the rotator cuff to glenohumeral stability during anterior-posterior loading. *J Shoulder Elbow Surg* 1999;8:324-329.

4. Warner JJ, McMahon PJ: The role of the long head of the biceps brachii in superior stability of the glenohumeral joint. *J Bone Joint Surg Am* 1995;77: 366-372.

5. Warner JJ, Deng X, Warren RF, Torzilli PA: Static capsuloligamentous restraints to superior-inferior translation of the glenohumeral joint. *Am J Sports Med* 1992;20:675-685.

6. Lippitt SB, Vanderhooft J, Harris SL, Sidles J, Harryman DT, Matsen F III: Glenohumeral stability from concavity-compression: A quantitative analysis. *J Shoulder Elbow Surg* 1993;2:27-34.

7. Saha AK: Dynamic stability of the glenohumeral joint. *Acta Orthop Scand* 1971;42:491-505.

8. O'Brien SJ, Arnoczsky SP, Warren RF, Rozbruch SR: Developmental anatomy of the shoulder and anatomy of the glenohumeral joint, in Matsen F, Rockwood C (eds): *The Shoulder.* Philadelphia, PA, Saunders, 1990, pp 1-33.

9. Bankart A: Pathology and treatment of recurrent dislocation of shoulder-joint. *Br J Surg* 1938;26:23-29.

10. Itoi E, Hsu HC, An KN: Biomechanical investigation of the glenohumeral joint. *J Shoulder Elbow Surg* 1996;5:407-424.

11. Williams MM, Snyder SJ, Buford D Jr: The Buford complex: The "cord-like" middle glenohumeral ligament and absent anterosuperior labrum complex. A normal anatomic capsulolabral variant. *Arthroscopy* 1994;10:241-247.

12. Pagnani MJ, Deng XH, Warren RF, Torzilli PA, Altchek DW: Effects of lesions of the superior portion of the glenoid labrum on glenohumeral translation. *J Bone Joint Surg Am* 1995;77:1003-1010.

13. Itoi E, Motzkin NE, Browne AO, Hoffmeyer P, Morrey BF, An KN: Intraarticular pressure of the shoulder. *Arthroscopy* 1993;9:406-413.

14. Hunt SA, Kwon YW, Zuckerman JD: The rotator interval: Anatomy, pathology, and strategies for treatment. *J Am Acad Orthop Surg* 2007;15:218-227.

    This excellent review of the rotator interval includes pathophysiology and current treatment options.

15. Neer CS II, Satterlee CC, Dalsey RM, Flatow EL: The anatomy and potential effects of contracture of the coracohumeral ligament. *Clin Orthop Relat Res* 1992; 280:182-185.

16. Burkart AC, Debski RE: Anatomy and function of the glenohumeral ligaments in anterior shoulder instability. *Clin Orthop Relat Res* 2002;400:32-39.

    This is a detailed overview of the anatomy and function of the glenohumeral ligaments and capsule.

17. Kuhn JE, Huston LJ, Soslowsky LJ, Shyr Y, Blasier RB: External rotation of the glenohumeral joint: Ligament restraints and muscle effects in the neutral and abducted positions. *J Shoulder Elbow Surg* 2005; 14(suppl 1):39S-48S.

    A cadaver biomechanical study of the ligamentous restraints and muscle effects limiting external rotation of the glenohumeral joint found that the long head of the biceps is a dynamic restraint to external rotation in the abducted shoulder.

18. O'Brien SJ, Neves MC, Arnoczky SP, et al: The anatomy and histology of the inferior glenohumeral ligament complex of the shoulder. *Am J Sports Med* 1990; 18:449-456.

19. O'Brien SJ, Schwartz RS, Warren RF, Torzilli PA: Capsular restraints to anterior-posterior motion of the abducted shoulder: A biomechanical study. *J Shoulder Elbow Surg* 1995;4:298-308.

20. Costouros JG, Clavert P, Warner JJ. Trans-cuff portal for arthroscopic posterior capsulorrhaphy. *Arthroscopy* 2006;22:1138.

    Posterior capsulolabral pathology is discussed as a source of recurrent instability, and a novel portal for arthroscopic treatment is described.

21. Labriola JE, Lee TQ, Debski RE, McMahon PJ: Stability and instability of the glenohumeral joint: The role of shoulder muscles. *J Shoulder Elbow Surg* 2005;14(suppl 1):32S-38S.

Computational and experimental cadaver models of shoulder instability were used to determine the specific role of the shoulder girdle musculature in active and passive motion toward glenohumeral stability.

22. Warner JJ, Micheli LJ, Arslanian LE, Kennedy J, Kennedy R: Patterns of flexibility, laxity, and strength in normal shoulders and shoulders with instability and impingement. *Am J Sports Med* 1990;18:366-375.

23. Itoi E, Kuechle DK, Newman SR, Morrey BF, An KN: Stabilising function of the biceps in stable and unstable shoulders. *J Bone Joint Surg Br* 1993;75:546-550.

24. Warner JJ, Micheli LJ, Arslanian LE, Kennedy J, Kennedy R: Scapulothoracic motion in normal shoulders and shoulders with glenohumeral instability and impingement syndrome: A study using Moire topographic analysis. *Clin Orthop Relat Res* 1992;285:191-199.

25. Saupe N, Pfirrmann CW, Schmid MR, Jost B, Werner CM, Zanetti M: Association between rotator cuff abnormalities and reduced acromiohumeral distance. *AJR Am J Roentgenol* 2006;187:376-382.

An acromiohumeral distance less than or equal to 7 mm, as measured on standardized plain radiographs, is associated with high rates of full-thickness supraspinatus tears (90%) and infraspinatus tears (67%), as well as increased fatty degeneration of the rotator cuff musculature based on MRA. Level of evidence: IV.

26. Lephart S, Warner JP, Borsa PA, Fu FH: Proprioception of the shoulder in normal, unstable and surgical individuals. *J Shoulder Elbow Surg* 1994;3:371-381.

27. Taylor DC, Arciero RA: Arthroscopic and physical examination findings in first-time, traumatic anterior dislocations. *Am J Sports Med* 1997;25:306-311.

28. Kim SH, Ha KI, Yoo JC, Noh KC: Kim's lesion: An incomplete and concealed avulsion of the posteroinferior labrum in posterior or multidirectional posteroinferior instability of the shoulder. *Arthroscopy* 2004;20:712-720.

In a report of a case series, an incomplete and concealed avulsion of the posteroinferior labrum was found to contribute to posterior and multidirectional instability. Level of evidence: IV.

29. Speer KP, Deng X, Borrero S, Torzilli PA, Altchek DA, Warren RF: Biomechanical evaluation of a simulated Bankart lesion. *J Bone Joint Surg Am* 1994;76:1819-1826.

30. Nicola T: Recurrent dislocation of the shoulder. *Am J Surg* 1953;86:85-91.

31. Wolf EM, Cheng JC, Dickson K: Humeral avulsion of glenohumeral ligaments as a cause of anterior shoulder instability. *Arthroscopy* 1995;11:600-607.

32. Bokor DJ, Conboy VB, Olson C: Anterior instability of the glenohumeral joint with humeral avulsion of the glenohumeral ligaments: A review of 41 cases. *J Bone Joint Surg Br* 1999;81:93-96.

33. Bach BR, Warren RF, Fronek J: Disruption of the lateral capsule of the shoulder: A cause of recurrent dislocation. *J Bone Joint Surg Br* 1988;70:274-276.

34. Werner CM, Nyffeler RW, Jacob HA, Gerber C: The effect of capsular tightening on humeral head translations. *J Orthop Res* 2004;22:194-201.

Selective capsular plication was performed in eight cadaver shoulders, and the shoulder kinematics were analyzed. Selective anterior plication reproducibly altered obligate humeral head translation at the end ranges of passive shoulder motion. Posterior plication had little effect on humeral head translation.

35. Stanitski DF, Nadjarian R, Stanitski CL, Bawle E, Tsipouras P: Orthopaedic manifestations of Ehlers-Danlos syndrome. *Clin Orthop Relat Res* 2000;376:213-221.

36. Fitzpatrick MJ, Powell SE, Tibone JE, Warren RF: The anatomy, pathology, and definitive treatment of rotator interval lesions: Current concepts. *Arthroscopy* 2003;19(suppl 1):70-79.

The pathoanatomy of rotator interval lesions and currently accepted methods of treatment are reveiwed.

37. Robinson CM, Akhtar A, Mitchell M, Beavis C: Complex posterior fracture-dislocation of the shoulder: Epidemiology, injury patterns, and results of operative treatment. *J Bone Joint Surg Am* 2007;89:1454-1466.

Twenty-eight consecutive patients with a Neer two-, three-, or four-part fracture associated with posterior dislocation were treated with open reduction and internal fixation, with bone grafting of the reverse Hill-Sachs lesion if there was persistent instability. At 2-year follow-up, the median Constant and Disability of Arm, Shoulder and Hand Questionnaire scores were 83.5 and 17.5, respectively. Level of evidence: IV.

38. Calandra JJ, Baker CL, Uribe J: The incidence of Hill-Sachs lesions in initial anterior shoulder dislocations. *Arthroscopy* 1989;5:254-257.

39. Gerber C, Lambert SM: Allograft reconstruction of segmental defects in the humeral head for the treatment of chronic locked posterior dislocation of the shoulder. *J Bone Joint Surg Am* 1996;78:376-382.

40. Kronberg M, Brostrom LA: Rotational osteotomy of the proximal humerus to stabilise the shoulder: Five years' experience. *J Bone Joint Surg Br* 1995;77:924-927.

41. Burkhart SS, De Beer JF: Traumatic glenohumeral bone defects and their relationship to failure of arthroscopic Bankart repairs: Significance of the inverted-pear glenoid and the humeral engaging Hill-Sachs lesion. *Arthroscopy* 2000;16:677-694.

42. Bigliani LU, Newton PM, Steinmann SP, Connor PM, McLlveen SJ: Glenoid rim lesions associated with recurrent anterior dislocation of the shoulder. *Am J Sports Med* 1998;26:41-45.

43. Warner JJ, Gill TJ, O'Hollerhan JD, Pathare N, Millett PJ: Anatomical glenoid reconstruction for recurrent anterior glenohumeral instability with glenoid deficiency using an autogenous tricortical iliac crest bone graft. *Am J Sports Med* 2006;34:205-212.

    In 11 patients with traumatic anterior instability and significant glenoid bone loss evident on CT scan, the length of the anterior glenoid defect exceeded the maximum anteroposterior glenoid radius. Patients were treated with a tricortical iliac crest bone graft contoured to reestablish the concavity and width of the glenoid. At 33-month follow-up, the mean American Shoulder and Elbow Surgeons Shoulder Index score improved from 65 to 94, and the mean University of California Los Angeles Shoulder Scale score improved from 18 to 33. Level of evidence: IV.

44. Walch G, Badet R, Boulahia A, Khoury A: Morphological study of the glenoid in primary glenohumeral osteoarthritis. *J Arthroplasty* 1999;14:756-760.

45. Sirveaux F, Leroux J, Roche O, Gosselin O, DeGasperi M, Mole D: Surgical treatment of posterior instability of the shoulder joint using an iliac bone block or an acromial pediculated bone block: Outcome in eighteen patients. *Rev Chir Orthop Reparatrice Appar Mot* 2004;90:411-419.

    This is a retrospective review of 18 patients with involuntary posterior instability who were treated using iliac crest bone graft or the Kouvalchouk technique. At a mean 13.5-year follow-up of the first group and a mean 3.5-year follow-up of the second group, Duplay scores had improved to 70 and 86, respectively. Level of evidence: IV.

46. Hawkins RH: Glenoid osteotomy for recurrent posterior subluxation of the shoulder: Assessment by computed axial tomography. *J Shoulder Elbow Surg* 1996;5:393-400.

47. Hatch GF, Costouros JG, Millett PJ, Warner JJ: Shoulder labral tears and instability, in Johnson DH, Pedowitz RA (eds): *Practical Orthopaedic Sports Medicine and Arthroscopy*. Philadelphia, PA, Lippincott Williams & Wilkins, 2006, pp 171-200.

48. Maruyama K, Sano S, Saito K, Yamaguchi Y: Trauma-instability-voluntarism classification for glenohumeral instability. *J Shoulder Elbow Surg* 1995;4: 194-198.

49. Lippitt S, Matsen F: Mechanisms of glenohumeral joint stability. *Clin Orthop Relat Res* 1993;291:20-28.

50. Mallon WJ, Speer KP: Multidirectional instability: Current concepts. *J Shoulder Elbow Surg* 1995;4: 54-64.

51. Rowe CR, Pierce DS, Clark JG: Voluntary dislocation of the shoulder: A preliminary report on a clinical, electromyographic, and psychiatric study of twenty-six patients. *J Bone Joint Surg Am* 1973;55: 445-460.

52. McLaughlin HL: Posterior dislocation of the shoulder. *J Bone Joint Surg Am* 1952;34:584-590.

53. Bankart A: Recurrent or habitual dislocation of the shoulder joint. *BMJ* 1923;2:1132-1133.

54. Dubousset J: Luxation postérieure de l'épaule. *Rev Chir Orthop Reparatrice Appar Mot* 1967;53: 65-85.

55. Noble W: Posterior traumatic dislocation of the shoulder. *J Bone Joint Surg Am* 1962;44:523-524.

56. Neer CS II, Foster CR: Inferior capsular shift for involuntary inferior and multidirectional instability of the shoulder: A preliminary report. *J Bone Joint Surg Am* 1980;62:897-908.

57. Mohtadi NG, Bitar IJ, Sasyniuk TM, Hollinshead RM, Harper WP: Arthroscopic versus open repair for traumatic anterior shoulder instability: A meta-analysis. *Arthroscopy* 2005;21:652-658.

    A meta-analysis of 11 studies comparing outcomes and recurrence in open and arthroscopic anterior stabilization found that pooled Mantel-Haenszel odds ratios for recurrent instability and return to activity were 2.04 and 2.85 in favor of open repair. Level of evidence: III.

58. Itoi E: Pathophysiology and treatment of atraumatic instability of the shoulder. *J Orthop Sci* 2004;9: 208-213.

    Atraumatic instability is effectively treated nonsurgically with appropriate muscular strengthening exercises, if glenoid morphology is normal. Congenital hypoplasia of the glenoid with atraumatic instability may require glenoid osteotomy.

59. Burkhart SS, Morgan CD, Kibler WB: The disabled throwing shoulder: Spectrum of pathology. Part 1: Pathoanatomy and biomechanics. *Arthroscopy* 2003; 19:404-420.

    This is the first in a detailed three-part examination of the pathophysiology inherent in the disabled throwing shoulder. The superior labrum anterior and posterior lesion, internal impingement, posteroinferior capsular contracture, and peel-back phenomenon are discussed.

60. Lazarus MD, Harryman DT: Complications of open anterior stabilization of the shoulder. *J Am Acad Orthop Surg* 2000;8:122-132.

61. Visser CP, Coene LN, Brand R, Tavy DL: The incidence of nerve injury in anterior dislocation of the shoulder and its influence on functional recovery: A

prospective clinical and EMC study. *J Bone Joint Surg Br* 1999;81:679-685.

62. Wiater JM, Flatow EL: Long thoracic nerve injury. *Clin Orthop Relat Res* 1999;368:17-27.

63. Wiater JM, Bigliani LU: Spinal accessory nerve injury. *Clin Orthop Relat Res* 1999;368:5-16.

64. Gerber C, Hersche O, Farron A: Isolated rupture of the subscapularis tendon. *J Bone Joint Surg Am* 1996; 78:1015-1023.

65. Gerber C, Ganz R: Clinical assessment of instability of the shoulder: With special reference to anterior and posterior drawer tests. *J Bone Joint Surg Br* 1984; 66:551-553.

66. Kvitne RS, Jobe FW: The diagnosis and treatment of anterior instability in the throwing athlete. *Clin Orthop Relat Res* 1993;291:107-110.

67. Gagey OJ, Gagey N: The hyperabduction test. *J Bone Joint Surg Br* 2001;83:69-74.

    In an anatomic study of 100 human cadaver shoulders, the average range of passive abduction was defined. Values in excess of 105° indicate lengthening and laxity of the inferior glenohumeral ligament.

68. Lerat JL, Chotel F, Besse JL: Dynamic anterior jerk of the shoulder: A new clinical test for shoulder instability: A preliminary study. *Rev Chir Orthop Reparatrice Appar Mot* 1994;80:461-462.

69. Millett PJ, Clavert P, Hatch GF, Warner JJ: Recurrent posterior shoulder instability. *J Am Acad Orthop Surg* 2006;14:464-476.

    This review of the pathophysiology and treatment of posterior instability includes unidirectional posterior instability, multidirectional instability, and locked posterior dislocation.

70. Fuchs B, Jost B, Gerber C: Posterior-inferior capsular shift for the treatment of recurrent, voluntary posterior subluxation of the shoulder. *J Bone Joint Surg Am* 2000;82:16-25.

71. Callaghan JJ, McNiesh LM, DeHaven JP, Savory CG, Polly DWJ: A prospective comparison study of double contrast computed tomography (CT) arthrography and arthroscopy of the shoulder. *Am J Sports Med* 1988;16:13-20.

72. Cotty P, Proust F, Bertrand P, et al: Rupure de la coiffe des rotateurs: Quantification des signes indirects en radiologie standard et manoeuvre de leclerq. *J Radiol* 1988;69:633-638.

73. van de Sande MA, Rozing PM: Proximal migration can be measured accurately on standardized anteroposterior shoulder radiographs. *Clin Orthop Relat Res* 2006;443:260-265.

    Accuracy in measuring proximal migration of the humerus was compared in 43 shoulders using CT and standardized AP plain radiography. Plain radiographs accurately measured the acromiohumeral interval if controlled for patient position, scaling, and individual differences by using the upward migration index. Level of evidence: I.

74. Warner JJP, Gerber C: Fractures of the proximal humerus, in Bucholz RW, Heckman JD, Court-Brown C, Tornetta P, Koval KJ, Wirth M (eds): *Rockwood and Green's Fractures in Adults,* ed 6. Philadelphia, PA, Lippincott Williams & Wilkins, 2005.

75. Osinski T, Malfair D, Steinbach L: Magnetic resonance arthrography. *Orthop Clin North Am* 2006;37: 299-319.

    A review of the development of direct and indirect MRA since 1987 is presented.

76. Tuite MJ, Rubin D: CT and MR arthrography of the glenoid labroligamentous complex. *Semin Musculoskelet Radiol* 1998;2:363-376.

77. Jahnke AHJ, Petersen SA, Neumann C, Steinbach LS, Morgan F: A prospective comparison of computed arthrotomography and magnetic resonance imaging of the glenohumeral joint. *Am J Sports Med* 1992; 20:695-700.

78. Friedman RJ, Hawthorne KB, Genez BM: The use of computerized tomography in the measurement of glenoid version. *J Bone Joint Surg Am* 1992;74:1032-1037.

79. Badet R, Boulahia A, Walch G: CT scan measurement of the humeral head subluxation in a sagittal plane method and application in primary glenohumeral osteoarthritis without humeral head elevation. *Rev Chir Orthop Reparatrice Appar Mot* 1998;84:508-514.

80. Sano H, Kato Y, Haga K, Iroi E, Tabata S: Magnetic resonance arthrography in the assessment of anterior instability of the shoulder: Comparison with double-contrast computed tomography arthrography. *J Shoulder Elbow Surg* 1996;5:280-285.

81. Flannigan B, Kursunoglu-Brahme S, Snyder S, Karzel R, Del Pizzo W, Resnick D: MR arthrography of the shoulder: Comparison with conventional MR imaging. *AJR Am J Roentgenol* 1990;155:829-832.

82. Waldt S, Burkart A, Imhoff AB, Bruegel M, Rummeny EJ, Woertler K: Anterior shoulder instability: Accuracy of MR arthrography in the classification of anteroinferior labroligamentous injuries. *Radiology* 2005;237:578-583.

    A retrospective study compared the accuracy of MRA and diagnostic arthroscopy in the diagnosis of anteroinferior labral injuries in 104 patients with labral injury and 101 patients with an intact labroligamentous complex. Labroligamentous lesions were detected and properly classified with high sensitivity, specificity, and accuracy.

83. Iannotti JP, Zlatkin MB, Esterhai JL, Kressel HY, Dalinka MK, Spindler KP: Magnetic resonance im-

aging of the shoulder: Sensitivity, specificity, and predictive value. *J Bone Joint Surg Am* 1991;73:17-29.

84. Dinauer PA, Flemming DJ, Murphy KP, Doukas WC: Diagnosis of superior labral lesions: Comparison of noncontrast MRI with indirect MR arthrography in unexercised shoulders. *Skeletal Radiol* 2007;36: 195-202.

   A prospective, blinded comparison of routine and contrast MRI in 104 patients with labral pathology with arthroscopic findings found that MRA is more sensitive in the diagnosis of superior labral pathology. Level of evidence: III.

85. Applegate GR, Hewitt M, Snyder S, Watson EM, Kwak SD, Resnick D: Chronic labral tears: Value of magnetic resonance arthrography in evaluating the glenoid labrum and labral-bicipital complex. *Arthroscopy* 2004;20:959-963.

   In a consecutive series of 36 patients with chronic labral tears, diagnosis using noncontrast MRI was correlated with arthroscopic findings. MRA was found to be accurate for assessing the glenoid labrum in chronic tears. Level of evidence: I.

# Chapter 7

# Acute and Chronic Shoulder Dislocations

*Andrew Green, MD

## Introduction

The glenohumeral joint is the most commonly dislocated large joint. Adults 18 to 70 years of age were reported to have a 1.7% incidence of shoulder dislocation.[1] Although shoulder dislocation is commonly considered to be an injury of young athletes, the distribution is approximately even among patients younger and older than 45 years. Dislocation is more common in males. Anterior dislocation is more common than posterior dislocation, which accounts for only 2% of all glenohumeral dislocations.[2]

Although the shoulder's unique anatomy allows a tremendous range of motion, it predisposes the glenohumeral joint to instability. Normal glenohumeral kinematics, described as a balance between mobility and stability, depends on complex interaction of the intrinsically unstable skeletal anatomy of the humeral head and glenoid, the static restraints of the labrum and capsule, and the dynamic action of the rotator cuff.

Recent clinical and basic orthopaedic research has focused on evaluation and management of recurrent glenohumeral instability. Treatment-related issues in acute and chronic shoulder dislocation are different from those in recurrent instability. Concomitant traumatic injuries must be considered, as well as different approaches to treatment.

## Anterior Glenohumeral Dislocation

Most acute anterior glenohumeral dislocations are traumatic. Almost all are subcoracoid, unless the coracoid is fractured. The diagnosis of acute traumatic anterior glenohumeral dislocation is usually not difficult, although in some patients a spontaneous reduction of the shoulder can present a diagnostic challenge.

### Pathology and Associated Injury

The patient's age is the most important factor determining the anatomic pathology, possible complications, and

prognosis of an acute anterior glenohumeral dislocation. A younger patient is likely to have a ligamentous injury involving the labrum and capsule. In a patient who is older than approximately 40 years, the rotator cuff, proximal humerus, and surrounding neurovascular structures are at risk of associated injury.

### Capsulolabral Injury

Arthroscopic examination after acute anterior dislocation has identified several types of capsulolabral injury, including anterior labral tear, superior labral tear, anterior capsule insufficiency, and humeral avulsion of the glenohumeral ligaments. One study identified three patterns of injury, based on pathology and degree of instability: A capsular tear with no labral lesion (found in 13% of patients) was considered stable, a capsular tear with partial labral detachment (in 24%) was considered mildly unstable, and a capsular tear with complete labral detachment (in 62%) was considered grossly unstable[3] (Figure 1).

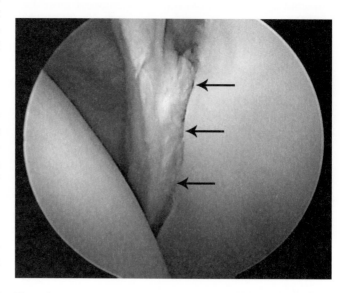

**Figure 1** Arthroscopic view from the posterior portal showing anterior labral detachment (*arrows*) in a patient with recurrent anterior-inferior glenohumeral dislocation.

---

*Andrew Green, MD is a consultant or employee for Tornier, Inc.*

In vitro biomechanical studies found that an isolated anteroinferior labral detachment does not result in glenohumeral dislocation. A study of 50 cadaver shoulders found that a Bankart lesion does not result in an anterior-inferior dislocation of the humeral head. Extension of the detachment to the superoposterior labrum was required for the tensioning mechanism in external rotation and abduction to fail sufficiently to cause dislocation.[4] This finding suggests that surgeons should carefully search for other lesions during surgical repair.

Dislocation rarely occurs as the result of minor trauma. When it does occur, the typical patient is relatively young and has underlying glenohumeral hyperlaxity and an intact labrum.

### Rotator Cuff Injury

The posterior mechanism of anterior glenohumeral dislocation involves avulsion of the posterosuperior rotator cuff.[5] Less commonly, the subscapularis tendon is disrupted. The true incidence of acute rotator cuff tearing associated with anterior dislocation is difficult to determine because tears are found even in asymptomatic shoulders.

Rotator cuff injury becomes more common with advancing age. In a patient older than 40 years, the rotator cuff should be carefully evaluated during physical examination. External rotation weakness and an external rotation lag sign suggest a relatively large rotator cuff tear, and internal rotation weakness and a positive belly-press sign suggest subscapularis tendon tearing.

### Fracture

A fracture of the glenoid, proximal humerus, or coracoid can occur with a glenohumeral dislocation. Coracoid fractures are rare and usually involve the tip of the coracoid process. Glenoid rim fractures occur more frequently, usually as a bony avulsion of the anteroinferior capsulolabral structures. Glenoid fractures with large bony fragments can also occur with glenohumeral dislocation, although they are less common. Greater tuberosity fractures occur in as many as one third of anterior glenohumeral dislocations and become more common with advancing patient age. Hill-Sachs lesions have long been recognized in association with anterior glenohumeral dislocation, although their clinical relevance is debatable and surgical treatment is rarely required to address the humeral head defect. Nevertheless, Hill-Sachs lesions seen on initial radiography have a statistically significant association with recurrent dislocation. An acute anterior glenohumeral dislocation resulting from a seizure is often associated with a large bony lesion such as a Hill-Sachs lesion or glenoid fracture.

### Neurologic Injury

Neurologic injury is usually considered to be relatively rare in acute anterior glenohumeral dislocation. However-er, nerve injuries were identified in 32% to 65% of patients with dislocation. Nerve injuries were more common in older patients and patients with an associated fracture.[6,7] A greater tuberosity fracture-dislocation is most commonly associated with an axillary nerve injury.[8] The axillary nerve is at risk of injury because of its anatomy and course; it is tethered anterior and posterior to the glenohumeral joint and has limited excursion as it branches from the posterior cord and passes through the quadrilateral space to innervate the deltoid muscle. In a younger patient, an axillary nerve injury may not be initially evident. If the rotator cuff is strong and intact, weakness of shoulder elevation can be difficult to detect, and careful examination of the deltoid is essential. The devastating combination of an axillary nerve injury and a rotator cuff tear should always be considered.

A patient with nerve injury is relatively likely to have limited motion and significant symptoms at follow-up evaluation. The prognosis is worse for an older patient with a nerve injury than for a younger patient.

### Treatment
### Closed Reduction

A closed reduction of an acute anterior glenohumeral dislocation should be as atraumatic as possible; it is essential to provide adequate relaxation and analgesia. Several methods of closed reduction are available. The Kocher method involves external rotation of the humerus and elevation of the elbow; after reduction, the hand is brought to the opposite shoulder. Although it is a successful method of reduction, the Kocher maneuver is associated with neurovascular complications and humeral fractures and therefore is not usually recommended. The traction-countertraction maneuver is commonly used and effective: With the patient supine, a sheet is placed around the chest to apply countertraction and the arm is carefully pulled in the direction of the deformity; gentle rotation of the arm helps disengage the humeral head from the glenoid to achieve the reduction. In the Stimson technique, the patient is positioned prone with the arm hanging down; the reduction is achieved with traction and rotation of the humerus. In the Milch technique, the physician places one hand in the axilla of the dislocated shoulder while the other hand is used to hold the patient's hand. The patient's arm is gently abducted, and pressure is applied to the humeral head. When the arm is fully abducted, it is externally rotated, and gentle traction is applied to reduce the humeral head. In scapular manipulation, which is the least traumatic technique, the glenoid is internally rotated to disengage the humeral head. The patient is placed prone, and 5 to 15 lb of traction is applied to the arm. With the patient relaxed, the inferior angle of the scapula is raised and rotated medially and the superior aspect is rotated laterally to reduce the humeral head.

The difficulty of reduction is in part determined by the elapsed time from dislocation to treatment. The goals of every attempt at reduction are to relocate the shoulder as soon as possible and to avoid additional injury. Parenteral narcotics and sedatives are the most commonly used medications; intra-articular local anesthetic injections also are effective. The use of intra-articular lidocaine avoids the risk of common complications associated with intravenous medication, including oversedation, nausea, and vomiting, and it significantly shortens the length of time until the patient can be discharged. Occasionally, the patient requires additional anesthesia. An interscalene block does not have the risks and adverse effects of general anesthesia. If a chronic dislocation is to be reduced or if a nondisplaced proximal humeral fracture is suspected, use of an interscalene block or general anesthesia should be considered to avoid the possibility of iatrogenic fracture displacement. If the injury is a greater tuberosity fracture-dislocation, the possibility of an associated surgical neck fracture should be investigated. If one is found, closed reduction with adequate anesthesia or open reduction of the shoulder should be strongly considered.

An external rotation reduction method was found to be effective, rapid, and relatively painless; in 29 of 40 patients, reduction was achieved without premedication.[9] Another study evaluated the Milch technique; all 76 shoulders were reduced on the first attempt, and the patients did not require anesthesia. In two thirds of the patients, anatomic reduction of the greater tuberosity was achieved when the glenohumeral joint was reduced.[10]

Little evidence is available to determine the best method of management following a closed reduction of an acute anterior dislocation of the shoulder. For many years, immobilization of the shoulder in a sling in internal rotation has been the accepted method after a first acute anterior glenohumeral dislocation. Several studies found that the duration of immobilization, especially in younger patients, is a factor in the incidence of recurrence, but other studies refuted this claim. Immobilization of the arm in external rotation was recently investigated. In 10 human cadaver shoulders with a simulated Bankart lesion, there was no contact force between the glenoid labrum and the glenoid when the arm was in internal rotation. The contact force increased as the arm passed through neutral rotation and reached a maximum of 45° of external rotation.[11] An arthroscopic evaluation of 25 patients, performed to determine the effect of shoulder position on reduction of the labrum, found that the best reduction was obtained when the arm was in 30° of abduction and 60° of external reduction. The authors concluded that the standard immobilization of the shoulder with the arm in internal rotation contributes to the incidence of recurrent instability.[12] In a prospective, randomized study of 40 patients, immobilization was compared in external and internal rotation. At

a mean 15.5-month follow-up, there was no recurrence in the external rotation group; the internal rotation group had a 30% recurrence rate. The difference between the groups was even greater among those younger than 30 years.[13] However, subsequent analysis did not fully support these findings.[14]

The timing of a patient's return to activity after an acute anterior dislocation depends on several factors. A study of the risk of rapid return to sports activity found that 26 of 30 young athletes injured during the playing season were able to return to their sport in 10 days, on average; 10 of the 26 athletes had a sports-related recurrent instability episode.[15]

### Primary Surgical Repair
The traditional practice is to treat acute anterior glenohumeral dislocation nonsurgically. However, interest in early surgical treatment has recently increased, primarily because of high recurrence rates in younger patients and the improved success of arthroscopic repairs. In a survey of British trauma clinicians, 19% recommended an immediate arthroscopic stabilization in a young, fit patient with a first anterior glenohumeral dislocation.[16] Evidence is available to support primary surgical treatment of young adults who engage in highly demanding physical activity.[17] A prospective, nonrandomized study of rugby players found that 95% of nonsurgically treated patients had a recurrent dislocation within 18 months; in contrast, only 5% of patients treated with arthroscopic repair had a recurrent dislocation.[18] A small prospective, randomized study of young military patients also compared nonsurgical and acute arthroscopic repair, finding that at an average 36-month follow-up, 75% of the nonsurgically treated patients and only 12% of the arthroscopically treated patients had recurrent instability.[19]

### Chronic Anterior Glenohumeral Dislocation
Chronic anterior glenohumeral dislocation is rare. Although the definition is inexact, most experts agree that a dislocation lasting more than 3 weeks is chronic. Many patients are elderly and have osteopenia, which increases the likelihood of a more severe glenoid fracture or a larger Hill-Sachs lesion. An anterior dislocation is less likely to be detected in a patient who is elderly or obese or who abuses alcohol. A patient with a chronic anterior glenohumeral dislocation usually has limited motion and some degree of pain. The patient may have a less severe internal rotation contracture and be better able to reach away from the body than a patient with a chronic posterior dislocation. An elderly patient may have shoulder deformity and pain but no clear history of trauma. If a glenoid fracture is present, an axial CT should be obtained to determine the extent of injury.

A closed reduction of a chronic dislocation is risky and usually avoided; the likelihood it will be successful or even possible decreases as the length of time since the dislocation increases. If the duration of the dislocation is unclear, the surgeon should assume it is chronic. For a subacute dislocation (duration of less than 1 week), a gentle closed reduction can be attempted. Closed reduction should never be forced, and the surgeon should be ready to proceed with an open reduction. A closed reduction should be performed using general anesthesia with paralysis or an interscalene nerve block. It is acceptable to perform no treatment for some patients, especially elderly, lower demand patients or those with a long-standing chronic dislocation and minimal pain.

Before reduction, evaluation and preparation for shoulder reconstruction are required. The specific surgical treatment depends on the extent of the skeletal injury. A glenoid fracture must be repaired or reconstructed to restore stability. A large Hill-Sachs lesion may require reconstruction using an osteochondral allograft, humeral head resurfacing, or humeral head replacement. If a large Hill-Sachs lesion is present in addition to a deficient anterior glenoid, the shoulder can be reconstructed with a humeral head replacement and a glenoid bone graft that uses the patient's humeral head (Figure 2).

In five patients with a chronic anterior dislocation (mean duration, 14 months) who were treated with anterior capsulolabral repair, stability and function were restored to satisfactory levels.[20] Another study followed 31 chronic anterior glenohumeral dislocations; treatment was not attempted in 10, and 20 underwent open reduction, which was successful in 10.[21]

## Posterior Glenohumeral Dislocation

Posterior glenohumeral dislocation is much less common than anterior dislocation. Physicians' lack of familiarity with the condition frequently leads to a missed diagnosis and development of a chronic injury. If acute posterior glenohumeral dislocations were routinely identified, it is likely that chronic posterior dislocations would become as rare as chronic anterior dislocations.

Posterior dislocation usually results from an adduction and axial load force to the shoulder or a direct blow to the anterior aspect of the shoulder. As many as 50% are reported to occur during a seizure.[22] Most posterior dislocations are locked; the impact of the anterior aspect of the humeral head against the posterior glenoid creates a reverse Hill-Sachs lesion. A concomitant surgical neck fracture is sometimes found. More complex posterior fracture-dislocations, such as four-part fractures, are rare.

Physical examination findings characteristic of a posterior dislocation include posterior shoulder prominence, flattening of the anterior shoulder, prominence of the coracoid process, limited glenohumeral elevation, and inability to externally rotate the arm. The diagnosis

can be confirmed using axillary lateral plain radiography or CT. MRI is not as useful as CT in showing bone pathology.

### Treatment
#### Closed Reduction
The treatment chosen for a posterior dislocation depends on the timeliness of the diagnosis and the size of the anterior impression fracture in the humeral head. The posterior capsule is invariably stretched by the injury, and the dislocation is usually accompanied by a humeral head impression fracture. Closed reduction is most likely to be stable and successful if the humeral articular injury is less than 20%. Closed reduction can be attempted if the head impression fracture is between 20% and 40%, but the likelihood of redislocation is greater. A more severe humeral articular injury often requires surgical treatment for maximum functional restoration.

To achieve reduction and avoid additional iatrogenic fracture, it is essential to minimize muscular resistance. Closed reduction may require local anesthesia, intravenous sedation, regional nerve block, or general anesthesia. The arm is flexed forward, internally rotated, and adducted to disengage the head from the posterior glenoid rim. Reduction is achieved by applying longitudinal traction and anterior pressure on the humeral head from behind. The arm is externally rotated, lowered to the side, and then immobilized for 4 to 6 weeks in a position of 15° extension and 15° external rotation, using a light fiberglass cast or prefabricated brace. This position relaxes the posterior capsule and allows initial healing in a shortened position.

Closed reduction is contraindicated for a fixed dislocation that is not easily reducible or an associated fracture at the surgical neck or greater tuberosity. If the glenohumeral joint is unstable after closed reduction, temporary percutaneous fixation can be considered.[23] This procedure is more reliable if the articular segment injury involves 20% or less of the articular surface, but it can be considered if as much as 40% is involved and more extensive surgical treatment is contraindicated. Fixation from the acromion into the humeral head is preferable to transarticular glenohumeral fixation. The pins should be buried to avoid the risk of pin tract infection, and they should be removed 4 to 6 weeks later.

#### Primary Surgical Repair
Open reduction is used if the humeral head defect is relatively large. The most common contraindications to open reduction of a chronic posterior glenohumeral dislocation are the presence of a long-standing chronic injury, medical comorbidities that preclude surgical intervention, and the inability of the patient to undergo postsurgical rehabilitation. Open reduction is usually

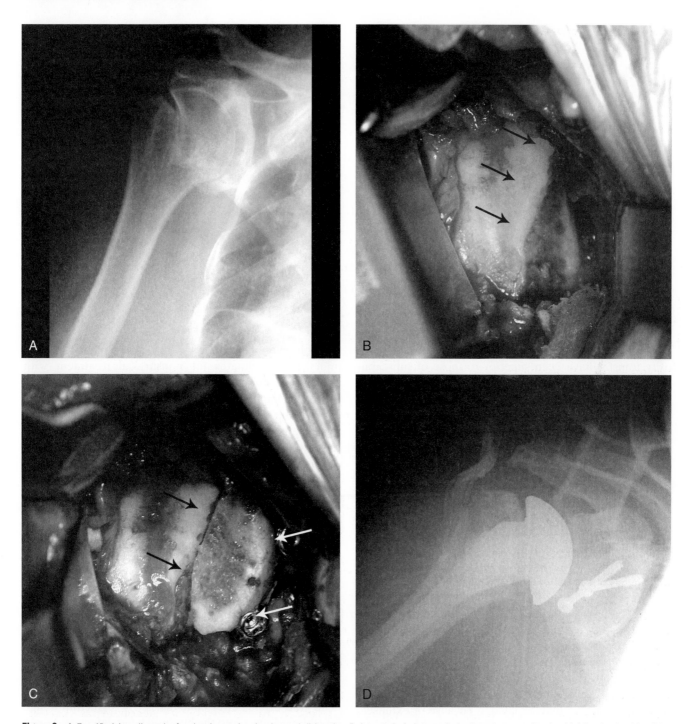

**Figure 2** **A,** True AP plain radiograph of a chronic anterior glenohumeral dislocation. **B,** Intrasurgical photograph showing a large anterior glenoid defect (to the right of the arrows). **C,** Intrasurgical photograph showing a bone graft harvested from the humeral head and fixed to the anterior glenoid with two compression screws. (The arrows surround the bone graft). **D,** Postsurgical AP plain radiograph showing a humeral head replacement, with the glenohumeral joint reduced.

performed using an anterior deltopectoral approach, which permits evaluation of the anterior impression fracture. The humeral head is carefully disengaged from the posterior aspect of the glenoid using a wide, flat elevator. A superior deltoid-splitting approach also can be used; it requires incising the supraspinatus tendon for access to the glenohumeral joint.

Several alternatives are available for reconstructing the anterior humeral head impression defect to restore glenohumeral stability and shoulder function. In rare patients, the impacted articular surface of the humeral head can be disimpacted. A bone graft is packed underneath the reduced articular surface to support it and prevent collapse. Transfer of the lesser tuberosity or

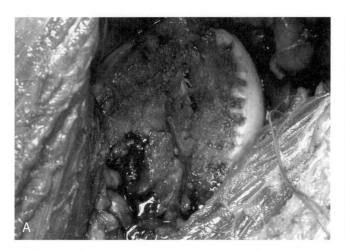 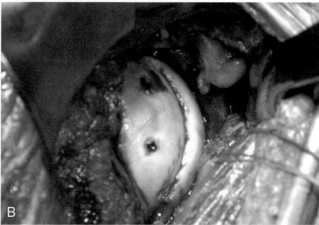

**Figure 3** **A,** A large reverse Hill-Sachs lesion in the right shoulder of a patient with an acute posterior fracture-dislocation. **B,** Reconstruction of the reverse Hill-Sachs lesion with a segmental humeral allograft.

subscapularis tendon into the impression defect is effective in restoring articular congruity. The results of tuberosity transfer have been superior to those of subscapularis transfer.[24]

Femoral head or humeral head allograft can be used to reconstruct a large humeral head defect. Femoral head allograft offers better bone quality. If the humeral head defect is large or a greater-than-40% degeneration of the articular surface has occurred, humeral or femoral head allograft can be used to avoid the longer term risk of allograft collapse (Figure 3).

### Chronic Posterior Glenohumeral Dislocation

Although a number of published reports have highlighted errors in diagnosis, posterior fracture-dislocation frequently appears as a chronic injury. The patient often complains of limited shoulder motion and functional difficulties, as well as mild or more severe pain. The choice of treatment is determined by whether a stable closed reduction is possible and the extent of degenerative change in the intact humeral and glenoid articular surfaces. Closed reduction is rarely possible. An alternative to open reduction and subscapularis or lesser tuberosity transfer may be needed because of extensive injury to the articular segment of the humeral head.

Open reduction of a chronic posterior dislocation with an impression fracture that involves more than 40% of the articular surface usually requires restoration of the articular surface, achieved using a prosthetic humeral head replacement, segmental humeral head resurfacing, or a segmental osteoarticular allograft. Glenohumeral arthrodesis can be considered for a patient with a long-standing posterior fracture-dislocation and significant shoulder pain. Although arthrodesis does not improve shoulder motion, the pain reduction achieved may improve the patient's functioning.

Very elderly patients with significant comorbidities and some younger patients with a long-standing chronic injury are candidates for nonsurgical treatment with skillful neglect. A neglected locked posterior dislocation results in functional limitation because of limited shoulder motion. Nonetheless, some patients remain relatively pain free. Patients with a long-standing posterior fracture-dislocation who do not have significant pain should not be treated with surgery.

The use of a prosthetic replacement is relatively likely to be necessary because of degeneration of the articular surface, osteopenia of the articular segment, and articular cartilage degeneration. Studies of prosthetic replacement in chronic posterior fracture-dislocation found results inferior to those of arthroplasty for glenohumeral osteoarthritis. A recent report of long-term follow-up in 12 patients found significant pain relief and functional improvement (1 excellent, 6 satisfactory, and 5 unsatisfactory).[25] Articular reconstruction with segmental osteoarticular allograft has also been described.[26] It is ideally used in the acute setting, before the intact humeral articular segment becomes osteopenic and degenerative. A humeral head or femoral head graft can be used; femoral head graft offers better bone density. A segmental wedge is fashioned, inset into the humeral head defect, and fixed with countersunk screws. The longevity of allograft reconstruction in partial humeral head reconstruction is uncertain and is a concern because of resorption, degeneration, and collapse of osteoarticular allograft in other types of reconstruction.

### Summary

Acute and chronic shoulder dislocations present vastly different clinical problems. Acute glenohumeral dislocation, whether anterior or posterior, often can be successfully treated with closed reduction. Recent biomechanical, anatomic, and clinical studies have focused on methods of closed reduction and postreduction management, as well as primary arthroscopic treatment of acute anterior dislocations. In some circumstances, surgical treatment is selected or required to optimize the functional outcome. Chronic dislocations are substantially more difficult to treat, and surgical treatment is usually required to restore shoulder function.

## Annotated References

1. Hovelius L: Incidence of shoulder dislocation in Sweden. *Clin Orthop Relat Res* 1982;166:127-131.

2. Rowe CR: Prognosis in dislocations of the shoulder. *J Bone Joint Surg Am* 1956;38:957-977.

3. Baker CL, Uribe JW, Whitman C: Arthroscopic evaluation of acute initial anterior shoulder dislocations. *Am J Sports Med* 1990;18:25-28.

4. Pouliart N, Marmor S, Gagey O: Simulated capsulolabral lesion in cadavers: Dislocation does not result from a Bankart lesion only. *Arthroscopy* 2006;22: 748-754.

   A cadaver model was used to determine the effect of the extent of labral detachment on anteroinferior glenohumeral stability. In the presence of an isolated Bankart lesion, the humeral head did not become dislocated. Dislocation in the anteroposterior position of apprehension required superoposterior extension of the labral detachment. This finding is consistent with other in vitro study findings that additional injury to the capsule, glenohumeral ligaments, and labrum is important in anteroinferior glenohumeral instability.

5. Craig EV: The posterior mechanism of acute anterior shoulder dislocations. *Clin Orthop Relat Res* 1984; 190:212-216.

6. Blom S, Dahlback LO: Nerve injuries in dislocations of the shoulder joint and fractures of the neck of the humerus. *Acta Chir Scand* 1970;136:461-466.

7. deLaat EA, Visser CPJ, Coene LN, Pahlplatz PV, Tavy DL: Nerve lesions in primary shoulder dislocations and humeral neck fractures. *J Bone Joint Surg Br* 1994;76:381-383.

8. Toolanen G, Hildingsson C, Hedlund T, et al: Early complications after anterior dislocation of the shoulder in patients over 40 years: An ultrasonographic and electromyographic study. *Acta Orthop Scand* 1993;64:549-552.

9. Eachempati KK, Dua A, Malhotra R, Bhan S, Bera JR: The external rotation method for reduction of acute anterior dislocations and fracture-dislocations of the shoulder. *J Bone Joint Surg Am* 2004;86:2431-2434.

   Closed reduction of an acute anterior shoulder dislocation was successfully performed in an emergency depart-ment using the external rotation method and with minimal premedication in 29 of 40 patients. This approach could allow a faster reduction than is possible using conscious sedation and avoid the complications and resource requirements of conscious sedation.

10. O'Connor DR, Schwarze D, Fragomen AT, Perdomo M: Painless reduction of acute anterior shoulder dislocations without anesthesia. *Orthopedics* 2006; 29:528-532.

    Use of the Milch technique resulted in successful reduction of an acute anterior shoulder dislocation in 100% of patients, without anesthesia. The Milch technique involves shoulder abduction and external rotation and is gentle and relatively painless. Reduction of an acute anterior glenohumeral dislocation does not routinely require anesthesia.

11. Miller BS, Sonnabend DH, Hatrick C, et al: Should acute anterior dislocations of the shoulder be immobilized in external rotation? A cadaveric study. *J Shoulder Elbow Surg* 2004;13:589-592.

    A cadaver shoulder model of a Bankart lesion was used to assess the effect of humeral rotational position on the contact force between the anteroinferior labrum and the glenoid. No contact force was detectable when the arm was in neutral rotation. The contact force reached a maximum at 45° of external rotation. The external rotation position might improve the healing of a Bankart lesion after closed reduction of an anterior glenohumeral dislocation.

12. Hart WJ, Kelly CP: Arthroscopic observation of capsulolabral reduction after shoulder dislocation. *J Shoulder Elbow Surg* 2005;14:134-137.

    In 25 patients with an acute traumatic anterior shoulder dislocation who underwent arthroscopic evaluation at a mean 10 days after injury, reduction of the labrum onto the glenoid was improved in 22 patients (92%). Reduction of the inferior labrum was further improved with arm abduction. The best reduction was consistently found when the arm was in 30° of abduction and approximately 60° of external rotation.

13. Itoi E, Hatakeyama Y, Kido T, et al: A new method of immobilization after traumatic anterior dislocation of the shoulder: A preliminary study. *J Shoulder Elbow Surg* 2003;12:413-415.

    Immobilization of an acute anterior glenohumeral dislocation in external rotation is compared with conventional sling immobilization. At a mean 15-month follow-up, 5 of the 11 patients younger than 30 years who were treated with internal rotation had a recurrent dislocation, compared with none of the 11 treated with external rotation ($P = 0.008$).

14. Handoll HH, Hanchard NC, Goodchild L, Feary J: Conservative management following closed reduction of traumatic anterior dislocation of the shoulder. *Cochrane Database Syst Rev* 2006;25:CD004962.

Only one quasirandomized controlled study of conservative treatment after traumatic anterior shoulder dislocation (Itoi et al, 2003) was identified in this meta-analysis. In contrast to that study, this analysis concluded that there is no statistically significant difference in rates of recurrent instability between patients treated with external or internal rotation immobilization. No difference was found in athletes' return to preinjury sport. However, recent study findings have not yet been published.

15. Lynch GP, Meyer CP, Huber SM, Freehill MQ: Nonoperative management for in-season athletes with anterior shoulder instability. *Am J Sports Med* 2004; 32:1430-1433.

Thirty in-season athletes who sustained a traumatic anterior dislocation or subluxation were treated with physical therapy and, in some patients, bracing. Twenty-six were able to return to their sport to complete the season, 10 had additional sports-related instability episodes, and 16 underwent surgical repair during the subsequent off-season. Level of evidence: IV.

16. Chong M, Karataglis D, Learmonth D: Survey of the management of acute traumatic first-time anterior shoulder dislocation among trauma clinicians in the UK. *Ann R Coll Surg Engl* 2006;88:454-458.

A survey of emergency physicians' management of first-time traumatic anterior shoulder dislocation found that 78% did not have a specific protocol for reduction. Conscious sedation was preferred by 68%, 9% used intra-articular local anesthetic injection, and 93% used sling immobilization in internal rotation. Many did not standardize treatment or apply scientifically obtained information to their practice.

17. Handoll HH, Almaiyah MA, Rangan A: Surgical versus non-surgical treatment for acute anterior shoulder dislocation. *Cochrane Database Syst Rev* 2004;1: CD004325.

A meta-analysis of five studies comparing surgical and nonsurgical treatment of acute anterior shoulder dislocation reported results from 239 patients. Surgical treatment led to significantly lower rates of recurrent instability and dislocation or subluxation. Insufficient evidence was available to determine whether nonsurgical treatment should remain the primary treatment for other patients, especially those at lower risk of activity-limiting recurrence.

18. Larrain MV, Botto GJ, Montenegro HJ, Mauas DM: Arthroscopic repair of acute traumatic anterior shoulder dislocation in young athletes. *Arthroscopy* 2001;17:373-377.

In a prospective, nonrandomized comparison of arthroscopic and nonsurgical treatment of acute traumatic anterior shoulder dislocations, 36 of the 46 patients were rugby players (mean age, 21 years; range, 17 to 27 years). In the nonsurgical group, 94.5% had a redislocation within

18 months of the original injury. In the surgical group, 96% had an excellent result, with only one recurrent dislocation.

19. Bottoni CR, Wilckens JH, DeBerardino TM, et al: A prospective, randomized evaluation of arthroscopic stabilization versus nonoperative treatment in patients with acute, traumatic, first-time shoulder dislocations. *Am J Sports Med* 2002;30:576-580.

A relatively small prospective, randomized study compared arthroscopic shoulder stabilization and nonsurgical treatment of first-time acute traumatic anterior shoulder dislocations. One of the nine surgically treated patients had a recurrent dislocation; 9 of 12 nonsurgically treated patients developed recurrent instability. Level of evidence:I.

20. Mansat P, Guity MR, Mansat M, Bellumore Y, Rongieres M, Bonnevialle P: Chronic anterior shoulder dislocation treated by open reduction sparing the humeral head [in French]. *Rev Chir Orthop Reparatrice Appar Mot* 2003;89:19-26.

Five patients (mean age 39 years) underwent a joint-saving procedure for chronic anterior shoulder dislocation. At an average 25-month follow-up, the outcome was excellent in one patient, good in three, and poor in one, as measured using the Rowe and Zarins criteria.

21. Goga IE: Chronic shoulder dislocations. *J Shoulder Elbow Surg* 2003;12:446-450.

In the largest reported chronic anterior glenohumeral dislocation series, 10 of the 30 patients were treated with skillful neglect and 20 were treated with open reduction. Fifteen patients (10 surgical, 5 nonsurgical) were followed for more than 2 years. The surgically treated patients were determined to have better results, based on Rowe and Zarins criteria.

22. Hawkins RJ, Neer CS II, Pianta RM, Mendoza FX: Locked posterior dislocation of the shoulder. *J Bone Joint Surg Am* 1987;69:9-18.

23. Aparicio G, Calvo E, Bonilla L, Espejo L, Box R: Neglected traumatic posterior dislocations of the shoulder: Controversies on indications for treatment and new CT scan findings. *J Orthop Sci* 2000;5: 37-42.

24. Finkelstein JA, Waddell JP, O'Driscoll SW, Vincent G: Acute posterior fracture dislocations of the shoulder treated with the Neer modification of the McLaughlin procedure. *J Orthop Trauma* 1995;9: 190-193.

25. Sperling JW, Pring M, Antuna SA, Cofield RH: Shoulder arthroplasty for locked posterior dislocation of the shoulder. *J Shoulder Elbow Surg* 2004;13: 522-527.

Arthroplasty in 12 patients with locked posterior dislocation of the shoulder resulted in statistically significant longer term improvement in pain and external rotation. The results were rated better than unsatisfactory in only 7 patients (58%) and were inferior to reported results of arthroplasty for primary glenohumeral osteoarthritis.

26. Gerber C, Lambert SM: Allograft reconstruction of segmental defects of the humeral head for the treatment of chronic locked posterior dislocation of the shoulder. *J Bone Joint Surg Am* 1996;78:376-382.

# Chapter 8

# Recurrent Anterior Shoulder Instability

Nicola A. DeAngelis, MD

*Brian D. Busconi, MD

*Augustus D. Mazzocca, MD

*Robert A. Arciero, MD

## Introduction

The glenohumeral joint is one of the least constrained joints in the body, having few bony restraints and only a small area of articular contact. Stability depends on the surrounding soft tissues and a balance of static and dynamic restraints to motion. Because of this delicate balance, instability is more common in the glenohumeral joint than in other joints. The instability ranges from frank dislocation with associated bony and soft-tissue disruption, to subluxation with abnormal glenohumeral translation but no true dislocation, to microinstability with subtle symptoms such as functional impairment or pain. When shoulder subluxation or dislocation occurs repeatedly and is unresponsive to measures such as immobilization, strengthening, and activity modification, surgical intervention is indicated. The principles of treatment for recurrent traumatic anterior instability, as described here, apply to an array of other shoulder instability patterns.

## Clinical Evaluation

### History

A thorough history is crucial in defining the etiology of instability and planning the treatment. The patient may have experienced either a traumatic event or general laxity and repetitive microtrauma. Loss of sensation during contact, abduction, and external rotation, which is called dead arm syndrome, is associated with transient subluxation. The position of the arm during instability and the location of pain in the shoulder also are important in determining the pathology and direction of instability.

*Brian D. Busconi, MD or the department with which he is affiliated has received research or institutional support from DePuy, Johnson and Johnson, and Mitek. Augustus D. Mazzocca, MD or the department with which he is affiliated has received research or institutional support from Arthrex. Robert A. Arciero, MD or the department with which he is affiliated has received research or institutional support from Arthrex, Smith & Nephew, and Mitek.

The patient should be asked about the magnitude of a traumatic event, any reduction required after the event, the elapsed time between the event and the onset of instability, the number of episodes of instability, and any activities or arm positions that must be avoided. The patient's answers can help the surgeon determine whether the primary etiology of the instability is generalized laxity or a true traumatic episode with capsulolabral disruption. In addition, the answers can suggest the direction of instability and the presence of a bone deficiency. The patient's age, activity level, and arm dominance should be recorded, as well as the direction and frequency of dislocation. A patient younger than 25 years who is treated nonsurgically is at risk of developing recurrent dislocation.[1] High rates of recurrence have been observed among participants in collision and contact sports, but the exact correlation has not been defined. If the patient has undergone rehabilitation, it is important to learn its effect in controlling the instability.[1,2]

### Physical Examination

A complete shoulder examination should include passive and active range of motion, strength testing, and neurovascular status. The required testing includes the sulcus sign, the anterior and posterior load-and-shift test, and general laxity tests (thumb to forearm, elbow recurvatum, knee hyperextension). Provocative tests, especially the apprehension and relocation tests, are used to specifically assess for anterior instability.

### Imaging

The standard shoulder trauma radiographic series includes a true AP view, with the beam aimed 30° from the sagittal plane; a scapular Y view; and an axillary lateral view, which is useful in assessing the humeral head location on the glenoid surface and discovering any bony glenoid deficiency.[3] West Point and Stryker notch views may also be useful. In the West Point view, the patient is prone, the arm is abducted 90°, and the beam is aimed 25° medial from inferior and 25° from the horizontal. This view allows a bony Bankart lesion to be

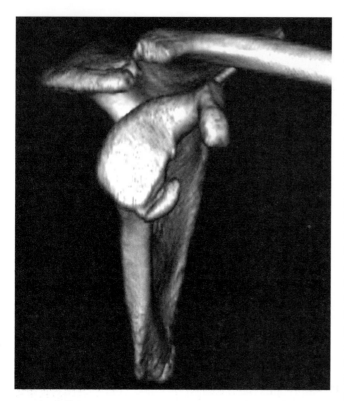

**Figure 1** Three-dimensional CT reconstruction of an acute anterior rim glenoid fracture in a patient with a traumatic subluxation.

seen. In the Stryker notch view, the patient is supine, the arm is forward elevated 90° (the hand on the head), and the beam is directed 10° cephalad and centered over the coracoid. This view allows a Hill-Sachs lesion on the humerus to be seen.

MRI, with or without arthrography, can be used to further define soft-tissue pathology, including a labral injury, rotator cuff tear, or lateral or humeral avulsion of the glenohumeral ligament. CT, particularly with three-dimensional reconstruction, can be useful in further defining and measuring bony deformities, especially the extent and location of a glenoid deficiency or humeral (Hill-Sachs) lesion[4] (Figure 1). Sophisticated CT images are helpful in evaluating bone deficiency.

## Pathophysiology
### Bony Deficiency
A patient with repeated instability or instability with the arm in a relatively low degree of abduction and external rotation may have significant bone loss. Instability during sleep or a seizure or after an earlier stabilization procedure also may indicate the presence of a bone defect. A physical examination finding of significant apprehension with the arm in relatively little abduction and external rotation suggests bone loss. Imaging studies can be important in selecting a surgical procedure and determining whether bone grafting or transfer is required.

### Capsulolabral Lesions
The inferior glenohumeral ligament complex (IGHLC) is the primary restraint to anterior translation of the humeral head in abduction and external rotation. The IGHLC can be described as a set of anterior and posterior bands connected by a capsular pouch; it is attached to the glenoid and confluent with the labrum (a fibrocartilaginous ring that deepens the glenoid and provides a buttress against anterior translation of the humeral head). The Bankart lesion (a detachment of the anteroinferior labrum and IGHLC from the glenoid) is associated with a high rate of recurrent instability, and repairing it is considered essential. Recurrent instability is characterized by both labral pathology and plastic, stretching deformation of the IGHLC. Successful surgical intervention must include restoration of labral anatomy and retensioning of the IGHLC. In a patient with chronic instability, the labrum may have healed in a medial position on the glenoid neck. The result is a loss of the bumper effect and a lack of tension in the IGHLC, called an anterior labroligamentous periosteal sleeve avulsion (ALPSA). A patient with recurrent dislocation may also have a superior extension of the labral pathology, leading to a type II superior labrum anterior and posterior (SLAP) lesion. An anteroinferior labral lesion that occurred simultaneously with a superior labral lesion may be observed in a high-demand patient or as the result of a significant trauma.[5]

### Ligamentous Injury
Recurrent dislocation can result in plastic deformation of the capsuloligamentous complex. MRI has been used to document increased capsular stretching caused by repeated instability.[6] The ligamentous laxity must be addressed, in addition to the labral repair on the glenoid rim, if surgical intervention is to be successful. The insertion of the glenohumeral ligaments on the humerus can also fail and must be repaired to restore the appropriate tension to the IGHLC. This humeral avulsion of the glenohumeral ligaments (HAGL lesion) is much less common than injury at the glenoid rim (Figure 2).

### Rotator Cuff Injury
A rotator cuff tear after a traumatic anterior dislocation is uncommon in a patient younger than 40 years, but it should be suspected if pain and weakness persist 3 or 4 weeks after the injury. Early redislocation was observed in patients with a rotator cuff tear who were older than 50 years and had a bone defect.[7]

## Nonsurgical Treatment
Most patients with recurrent traumatic anterior shoulder instability require surgical intervention. Rehabilitation is not routinely successful in treating these patients. However, surgery may not be the preferred treatment

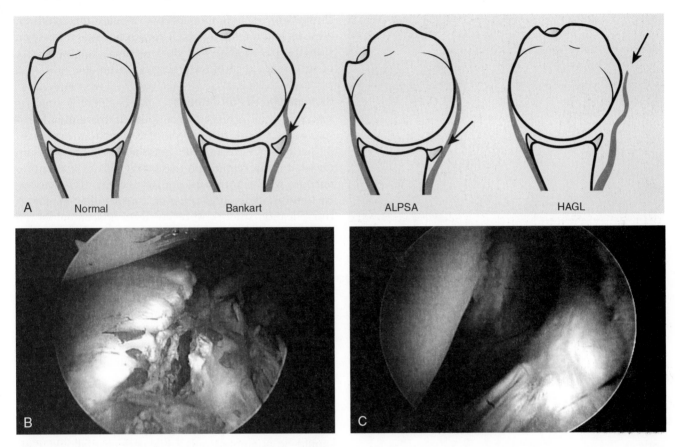

**Figure 2** **A,** Schematic drawing showing the normal labral attachment, a Bankart lesion, an ALPSA lesion, and a HAGL lesion in the inferior glenohumeral ligament. **B,** ALPSA lesion in the left shoulder, seen from the anterosuperior portal. Note the medial position of the avulsed capsulolabral complex. **C,** Humeral-sided avulsion of the inferior glenohumeral ligament in the left shoulder, seen from the posterior portal.

for a patient who is elderly; has low physical demands, has significant medical comorbidity; has a poorly managed seizure disorder; or will be unable to complete postsurgical rehabilitation.

Nonsurgical protocols should focus on dynamic rotator cuff and periscapular strengthening after immobilization for 3 to 6 weeks.[8] In a patient with acute primary anterior dislocation, a period of immobilization in external rotation may decrease the risk of recurrent anterior dislocation.[9-11] In cadaver, MRI, and clinical studies, arm positioning in external rotation had the effect of reducing the Bankart lesion. Compared with arm positioning in internal rotation, the recurrence rates were lower.

Athletes who are injured during the playing season have unique needs. A recent study suggested that many athletes are able to return to play and finish the season after a dislocation; the athletes returned to play in less than 2 weeks, on average, after a brief immobilization, early range-of-motion exercises, and cuff strengthening.[12] A brace or harness was used to limit external rotation after return to play. However, almost 40% of patients had episodes of subluxation or dislocation before the season ended, and more than half underwent surgical stabilization at the end of the season.

## Surgical Treatment

The goals of surgical treatment for recurrent anterior shoulder instability are to repair the Bankart lesion by restoring the bumper effect of the anteroinferior glenoid labrum and retension the anterior capsulolabral complex by performing an adequate capsulorrhaphy.

With the patient's muscles relaxed under general or regional anesthesia, a stability assessment should compare the injured and contralateral shoulders. The load-and-shift test is used to quantify anterior instability. A posterior force applied to the adducted and forward-flexed arm determines posterior stability. The sulcus sign is used to evaluate the rotator interval and generalized capsular laxity. For some surgeons, a persistent sulcus sign with the arm in external rotation is an indication to close or imbricate the rotator interval.

As surgeons have gained experience with arthroscopic stabilization and implants and as techniques continue to improve, the failure rates for arthroscopic stabilization have decreased. They now approach the rates for open stabilization. The use of suture anchors has allowed surgeons to perform an inferior-to-superior capsular shift while reestablishing the correct labral position on the glenoid rim. In several studies, the results

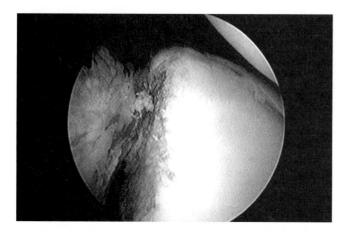

**Figure 3** Arthroscopic view of the inverted pear configuration in a right shoulder.

of open and arthroscopic anterior stabilization were found to be equivalent.[14-16] The rate of recurrent instability after arthroscopic anterior stabilization is now less than 10%, although the rate may be higher among high-demand athletes, particularly those participating in collision sports.[17,18] As techniques improve, arthroscopic repair is being performed with good results for patients who would formerly have received open stabilization, including collision athletes,[19] patients with small glenoid rim fractures,[20] and patients undergoing revision surgery.

Bone deficiency remains the primary indication for open stabilization procedures, including coracoid transfer and bone grafting. In patients with bone loss, arthroscopic stabilization performed by skilled arthroscopic surgeons had a 67% failure rate; in patients without significant bone loss, the results were comparable to those of open stabilization.[13] Open stabilization is indicated in the presence of a measured bony defect of the glenoid of at least 20% or a humeral head defect that engages easily in external rotation[13,21]

Open surgery also may be preferable for patients who require revision surgery, have a HAGL lesion or capsular deficiency, or are collision athletes. The open Bankart repair procedure with capsulorrhaphy has been extremely reliable. Studies of young athletes, including football players, found excellent outcomes and rates of recurrent dislocation lower than 5%.[22-24] Other studies that included collision athletes found arthroscopy results comparable to those of open surgery.[14,17,19] One recent study suggested that postsurgical subscapularis function is critical in determining the patient's perception of success.[25] (Open surgery involves an incision into the subscapularis muscle.) However, two recent meta-analyses suggested that the results of open stabilization procedures may be superior to those of arthroscopic procedures.[26,27] A 29-year follow-up study found that the open procedure had excellent results in the control of instability, but 40% of patients had a dislocation ar-

thropathy.[24] The finding of two studies that collision athletes had a relatively high recurrence rate after open stabilization suggests that these patients may be at risk of recurrence regardless of surgical technique.[28,29]

### Bankart and ALPSA Lesions

Some authors promote placing posterior capsular sutures, and rotator interval closure is also an option. In 85 patients with recurrent anterior instability who underwent arthroscopic anterior labral repair using suture anchors with a transsubscapularis portal, 10% had recurrent instability at a minimum 2-year follow-up. Posterior plication stitches were not used. Placement of the anchors onto the glenoid face and as low as possible was emphasized.[17] In another study, 71 patients with recurrent anterior instability underwent arthroscopic anterior labral repair using suture anchors; posterior plication was used in 54% of patients. At an average 33-month follow-up, 7% had recurrent instability. Anchor placement on the glenoid face was emphasized. The decision to place posterior plication stitches was based on subjective intrasurgical assessment of capsulolabral laxity.[18]

### HAGL Lesions

HAGL lesions are technically difficult to manage. Suture anchor techniques using accessory anterior portals should be attempted only by experienced shoulder arthroscopic surgeons.[30,31] A mini-open subscapularis tendon-sparing approach to repairing HAGL lesions was recently described.[32]

### Bone Loss and Bony Lesions

Glenoid bone loss has been reported in as many as 22% of initial dislocations and 73% of recurrent dislocations; Hill-Sachs lesions have been reported in as many as 80% of initial dislocations and 100% of recurrent dislocations.[33-35] The choice of treatment should be based on the size, orientation, and functional involvement of the glenoid and humeral bone loss. Axillary lateral radiography and CT, with or without reconstruction, can be used to quantify the amount of bone loss.[4,36] A bony lesion of less than 20% of the glenoid or humeral surface can usually be successfully treated with a soft-tissue stabilization procedure (capsulolabral repair with or without capsular shift).

#### Glenoid Deficiency

Glenoid bony deficiency results from traumatic injury to the glenoid rim or, in fewer than 2% of patients, from dysplasia. Traumatic bone loss may occur after a singular event or repeated erosive events. Bone loss in the anteroinferior region of the glenoid can result in the inverted pear glenoid configuration, which is associated with a recurrence rate as high as 67% (Figure 3). In contrast, the recurrence rate is as low as 4% in patients who do not have this defect.[13,37] Soft-tissue repair failed in more than 80% of those who had the inverted pear morphology.[13] Loss of glenoid bone stock leads to a loss of glenohumeral contact area and a resulting increase in contact stress, with loss of the buttressing normally provided by the glenoid rim and capsulolabral complex.[36,38] Soft-tissue Bankart repairs performed on cadaver specimens with significant bone loss found that only a low force is required for dislocation.[4,21] To optimize the results of surgical intervention, both soft-tissue and large bony defects should be addressed.

Bone loss greater than 30% that is contributing to instability requires augmentation of the glenoid surface area. The results of iliac crest bone grafting for structural bone stock to re-create the functional arc of the glenoid have been good to excellent.[36,39] A coracoid transfer can provide static bony support without the morbidity associated with iliac crest harvesting. In the Bristow procedure, only the tip of the coracoid is transferred. In the Latarjet procedure, the coracoid is removed at its base and transferred with a portion of coracoacromial ligament, which can be sutured to the capsular tissue to provide additional soft-tissue support[40] (Figure 4). Coracoid transfer fails to re-create normal anatomy but usually provides good stabilization, with reported recurrence rates lower than 6%.[41,42]

### Humeral Head Lesions

A defect in the articular surface of the humeral head (a Hill-Sachs lesion) is found in more than 80% of traumatic dislocations. The lesions are usually small and have little effect on function. If the lesion is smaller than 20% of the articular surface, nonsurgical treatment and standard soft-tissue capsulolabral repair are usually successful. A Hill-Sachs lesion is more problematic if a glenoid defect is present or the lesion engages the glenoid rim. In an engaging Hill-Sachs lesion, the humeral head defect is aligned with the glenoid rim and rides over the anterior edge when the arm is in abduction and external rotation. These lesions contribute to recurrence and may grow larger with subsequent dislocation. A nonengaging lesion does not align with the angle of the glenoid and is much less clinically significant.[40,43]

Symptomatic humeral head defects require surgical treatment using allograft reconstruction or subchondral impaction grafting. Concurrent augmentation of the anterior glenoid rim may be necessary to correct the instability[40,44,45] (Figure 5). Management of these lesions has not been studied in controlled series; the surgical

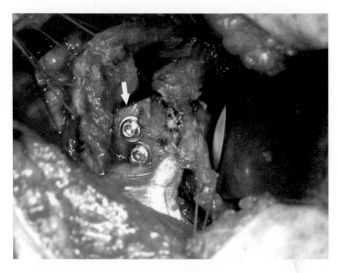

**Figure 4**  Intrasurgical photograph of a transferred coracoid process during a Laterjet procedure. Note the coracoid secured in an extracapsular location immediately adjacent to the Bankart repair *(arrow)*.

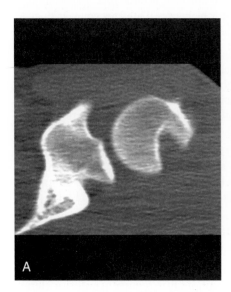  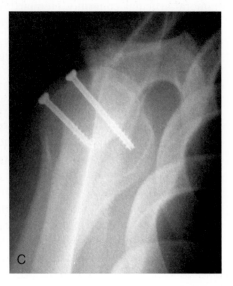

**Figure 5**  **A,** CT scan showing a large humeral head defect. **B,** Intrasurgical photograph showing provisional fixation of a humeral head allograft segment filling a Hill-Sachs lesion. **C,** Postsurgical radiograph showing the final fixation of the allograft in the posterolateral humeral head.

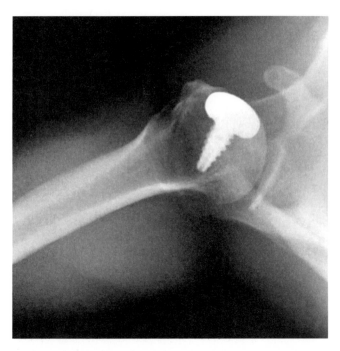

**Figure 6** Radiograph showing focal arthroplasty to treat an engaging Hill-Sachs lesion in an older patient with recurrent anterior instability and a large bone defect.

recommendations are based on case reports and biomechanical cadaver studies. For defects that are 30% or more of the glenoid surface, rotational osteotomy, a humeral head resurfacing prosthesis, total resurfacing arthroplasty, and half or total joint arthroplasty can be considered (Figure 6). Humeral rotational osteotomy was found to be successful in patients younger than 40 years who had a large defect and were not candidates for prosthetic replacement.[46] In this procedure, the humeral defect is rotated away from the glenoid surface through a transverse osteotomy to improve glenohumeral articular congruity. Hemiarthroplasty and total shoulder arthroplasty (if significant glenoid degeneration was present) were found to have a good to excellent result in patients older than 50 years who had a large defect.[47]

## Capsular Deficiency

Capsular deficiency is a rare cause of recurrent anterior shoulder instability. It is most often the result of multiple earlier surgical procedures or thermal capsulorrhaphy. The tissue must be reconstructed using other local tissue or an allograft. Capsular reconstruction using hamstring autograft, iliotibial band, and Achilles autograft and allograft have been described. In three patients, semitendinosus and gracilis allograft were used in reconstruction of severe anterior capsular deficiency, with good results.[48] A pectoralis major transfer may restore dynamic stability in a muscle-deficient shoulder with a subscapularis tear or attenuation.[40]

## Thermal Capsulorrhaphy

Thermal capsulorrhaphy has generally fallen out of favor because of high failure rates. The complications include axillary nerve palsies, capsular ablation, and chondrolysis. In some patients, capsular insufficiency has resulted.[49-53] A recent study comparing arthroscopic Bankart repair performed with and without thermal capsulorrhaphy found that the use of thermal energy did not improve the outcome.[49] The use of modern instrumentation is making arthroscopic suture plication more effective, and this procedure is beginning to replace thermal capsulorrhaphy.

## Summary

Recurrent anterior shoulder instability most commonly occurs in people who are younger than 25 years. Assessment is important to determine the exact cause of the individual patient's recurrent instability. The surgical success rate is approximately 90% if the procedure is technically correct and the appropriate pathology is addressed.

## Annotated References

1. Kirkley A, Werstine R, Ratjek A, Griffin S: Prospective randomized clinical trial comparing the effectiveness of immediate arthroscopic stabilization versus immobilization and rehabilitation in first traumatic anterior dislocations of the shoulder: Long-term evaluation. *Arthroscopy* 2005;21:55-63.

   Forty subjects younger than 30 years with a first traumatic anterior shoulder dislocation randomly received immediate anterior stabilization and rehabilitation or immobilization followed by rehabilitation. At an average 75-month follow-up, the difference in the rate of redislocation was significant. Immediate arthroscopic stabilization is recommended for higher level athletes younger than 30 years. Level of evidence: II.

2. Kirkley A, Griffin S, Richards C: Prospective randomized clinical trial comparing the effectiveness of immediate arthroscopic stabilization versus immobilization and rehabilitation in first traumatic anterior dislocations of the shoulder. *Arthroscopy* 1999;15: 507-514.

3. Itoi E, Lee SB, Amrami KK, Wenger DE, An KN: Quantitative assessment of classic anteroinferior bony Bankart lesions by radiography and computed tomography. *Am J Sports Med* 2003;31:112-118.

   Precise glenoid defects were created in a cadaver study. CT and radiographs using the modified axillary and West Point views reliably estimated bone loss.

4. Sugaya H, Moriishi J, Dohi M, Kon Y, Tsuchiya A: Glenoid rim morphology in recurrent anterior glenohumeral instability. *J Bone Joint Surg Am* 2003;85-A: 878-884.

Three-dimensional CT of shoulders with recurrent anteroinferior instability and normal shoulders were used to determine glenoid morphology, and the unstable shoulders were examined arthroscopically. Fifty percent of shoulders with recurrent instability had an osseous Bankart lesion, and another 40% had loss of normal glenoid contour consistent with erosion or compression of the glenoid rim.

5. Kim TK, Queale WS, Cosgarea AJ, McFarland EG: Clinical features of the different types of SLAP lesions: An analysis of one hundred and thirty-nine cases. Superior labrum anterior posterior. *J Bone Joint Surg Am* 2003;85-A:66-71.

SLAP lesions were categorized through arthroscopy in 139 patients: 74% were Snyder type I; 21%, type II, 1%, type III; and 4%, type IV. Type II lesions in patients younger than 40 years were associated with a Bankart lesion. In patients older than 40 years, type II lesions were associated with a supraspinatus tear and osteoarthritis.

6. Urayama M, Itoi E, Sashi R, Minagawa H, Sato K: Capsular elongation in shoulders with recurrent anterior dislocation: Quantitative assessment with magnetic resonance arthrography. *Am J Sports Med* 2003;31:64-67.

In an MRI evaluation of the anterior capsule in 12 patients with recurrent anterior shoulder instability, the anteroinferior and inferior capsule was found to be elongated in 19%.

7. Robinson CM, Kelly M, Wakefield AE: Redislocation of the shoulder during the first six weeks after a primary anterior dislocation: Risk factors and results of treatment. *J Bone Joint Surg Am* 2002;84-A:1552-1559.

Seventeen of 538 patients (3.2%) sustained a redislocation within 1 week of the original dislocation. Patients at increased risk included those with a high energy injury, neurologic deficit, large rotator cuff tear, fracture of the glenoid rim, or fracture of the glenoid rim and greater tuberosity.

8. Bottoni CR, Wilckens JH, DeBerardino TM, et al: A prospective randomized evaluation of arthroscopic stabilization versus nonoperative treatment in patients with acute, traumatic, first-time shoulder dislocations. *Am J Sports Med* 2002;30:576-580.

Two groups of young patients with traumatic anterior shoulder instability were treated nonsurgically or with labral repair using tacks. At 36-month follow-up, the recurrence rate was 75% in the nonsurgically treated patients and 11% in the surgically treated patients.

9. Itoi E, Hatakeyama Y, Kido T, Sato T, Minagawa H: A new method of immobilization after traumatic anterior dislocation of the shoulder: A preliminary study. *J Shoulder Elbow Surg* 2003;12:413-415.

This preliminary study of emergency department patients of all ages who had an anterior shoulder dislocation

immobilized in external rotation suggests a decrease in recurrent instability compared with historical controls.

10. Itoi E, Hatakeyama Y, Urayama M: Position of immobilization after dislocation of the shoulder: A cadaveric study. *J Bone Joint Surg Am* 1999;81:385-390.

11. Itoi E, Sashi R, Minagawa H, Shimiuziu T: Position of immobilization after dislocation of the glenohumeral joint: A study with the use of MRI. *J Bone Joint Surg Am* 2001;83:661-667.

An MRI study found that in shoulders with a Bankart lesion, immobilization in external rotation positions the anterior labrum in a more anatomic position than immobilization in internal rotation.

12. Buss DD, Lynch GP, Meyer CP, Huber SM, Freehill MQ: Non-operative management of in-season athletes with anterior shoulder instability. *Am J Sports Med* 2004;32:1430-1433.

Thirty in-season athletes who had sustained anterior shoulder dislocations returned to play, on average, in less than 2 weeks. More than 80% were able to finish the season, although 40% had a recurrent episode of subluxation or dislocation during the season.

13. Burkhart SS, DeBeer JF: Traumatic glenohumeral bone defects and their relationship to failure of arthroscopic Bankart repairs: Significance of the "inverted pear" glenoid and the humeral engaging Hill-Sachs lesion. *Arthroscopy* 2000;16:677-694.

14. Bottoni CR, Smith EL, Berkowitz MJ, Towle RB, Moore JH: Arthroscopic versus open shoulder stabilization for recurrent anterior instability: A prospective randomized clinical trial. *Am J Sports Med* 2006;34:1730-1737.

Sixty-four patients with anterior shoulder instability randomly received arthroscopic or open repair. At an average 32-month follow-up, the results were comparable.

15. Fabbriciani C, Milano G, Demontis A, Fadda S, Zirano F, Mulas PD: Arthroscopic versus open treatment of Bankart lesions of the shoulder: A prospective randomized study. *Arthroscopy* 2004;20:456-462.

In a randomized prospective study, 60 patients received open or arthroscopic repair. Neither group had repeat dislocations at 2-year follow-up, and the Constant and Rowe scores were similar. Level of evidence: I.

16. Tjoumakaris FP, Abboud JA, Hasan SA, Ramsey ML, Williams GR: Arthroscopic and open Bankart repairs provide similar outcomes. *Clin Orthop Relat Res* 2006;446:227-232.

A comparison of open and arthroscopic stabilization procedures found the outcomes to be similar. Level of evidence: III.

17. Carreira DS, Mazzocca AD, Oryhon J, Romeo AA: A prospective outcome evaluation of arthroscopic Bankart repairs: Minimum 2 year follow-up. *Am J Sports Med* 2006;34:771-777.

Eighty-five patients with Bankart lesions were treated arthroscopically using suture anchors, and 72 were evaluated at a minimum 2-year follow-up. The incidence of recurrent instability was 10%. Level of evidence: IV.

18. Westerheide KJ, Dopirak RM, Snyder SJ: Arthroscopic anterior stabilization and posterior capsular plication for anterior gleno-humeral instability: A report of 71 cases. *Arthroscopy* 2006;22:539-547.

    Recurrence rates were less than 10% in 71 patients treated with arthroscopic Bankart repair and posterior capsular plication. Level of evidence: IV.

19. Mazzocca AD, Brown FM, Carreira DS, Hayden J, Romeo AA: Arthroscopic stabilization of the shoulder in collision and contact athletes. *Am J Sports Med* 2005;33:52-60.

    Thirteen collision athletes and five contact athletes with Bankart lesions were treated arthroscopically with suture anchors and capsular plication. Two patients (11%) had recurrent dislocations at an average 37-month follow-up.

20. Sugaya H, Moriishi J, Kanisawa I, Tsuchrya A: Arthroscopic osseous Bankart repair for chronic recurrent anterior glenohumeral instability. *J Bone Joint Surg Am* 2005;87:1752-1760.

    Forty-one patients with glenoid rim fractures and recurrent anterior instability underwent arthroscopic repair using suture anchors. At an average 34-month follow-up, 39 patients had good or excellent results.

21. Itoi E, Lee SB, Berglund LJ, Berge LL, An KN: The effect of a glenoid defect on anteroinferior stability of the shoulder after Bankart repair: A cadaveric study. *J Bone Joint Surg Am* 2000;82:35-46.

22. Gill TJ, Zarins B: Open repairs for the treatment of anterior shoulder instability. *Am J Sports Med* 2003;31:142-153.

    Open stabilization is described as the standard, especially for a revision procedure, a patient with a severe instability, or an athlete in a contact sport. Open surgical techniques used for the treatment of anterior instability of the shoulder are reviewed.

23. Pagnani MJ, Dome DC: Surgical treatment of traumatic anterior shoulder instability in American football players. *J Bone Joint Surg Am* 2002;84:711-715.

    The results of open surgical treatment of shoulder instability in football players are described. In 58 patients, there were no recurrent dislocations and two subluxations. The average Rowe score was 93.6 points, and the American Shoulder and Elbow Surgeons Index score was 97 points.

24. Pelet S, Jolles BM, Farron A: Bankart repair for recurrent anterior glenohumeral instability: Results at twenty-nine years' follow-up. *J Shoulder Elbow Surg* 2006;15:203-207.

    At a 29-year follow-up of 30 patients, 10% had recurrent dislocation. The global rate of osteoarthritis was 40%, with 5 patients needing total shoulder arthroplasty. Compared with a normal shoulder, the average Rowe and Constant scores were 20 points and 13 points lower, respectively.

25. Sachs RA, Williams B, Stone ML, Paxton L, Kuney M: Open Bankart repair: Correlation of results with postoperative subscapularis function. *Am J Sports Med* 2005;33:1458-1462.

    Postsurgical results after open Bankart repair were found to be correlated with subscapularis function. Only the integrity and strength of the subscapularis muscle were correlated with overall patient satisfaction and outcomes score, using a validated instability index.

26. Freedman KB, Smith AP, Romeo AA, Cole BJ, Bach BR: Open Bankart versus arthroscopic repair with transglenoid sutures or bioabsorbable tacks for recurrent anterior instability of the shoulder: A meta-analysis. *Am J Sports Med* 2004;32:1520-1527.

    Six studies met the meta-analysis inclusion criteria. The authors concluded that arthroscopic Bankart repair using transglenoid sutures or bioabsorbable tacks results in a higher incidence of recurrent instability than open repair.

27. Mohtadi NG, Bitar JJ, Sasyniuk TM, Hollinshead RM, Harper WB: Arthroscopic versus open repair for traumatic anterior shoulder instability: A meta-analysis. *Arthroscopy* 2005;21:652-658.

    In a meta-analysis of 11 studies from 1966 to 2003, the authors concluded that open repair has a more favorable outcome with respect to recurrence and return to activity.

28. Magnusson L, Kartus J, Ejerhed L, Hultenheim I, Sernert N, Karlsson J: Revisiting the open Bankart experience: A four- to nine-year follow-up. *Am J Sports Med* 2002;30:778-782.

    A 6-year review of open Bankart procedures found an overall recurrence rate of 17%, despite the average Rowe score of 90 and Constant score of 88.5.

29. Uhorchak JM, Arciero RA, Huggard D, Taylor DC: Recurrent shoulder instability after open reconstruction in athletes involved in collision and contact sports. *Am J Sports Med* 2000;28:794-799.

30. Kon Y, Shiozaki H, Sugaya H: Arthroscopic repair of a humeral avulsion of the glenohumeral ligament lesion. *Arthroscopy* 2005;21:632.

    All-arthroscopic repair of a HAGL lesion is reported in three patients.

31. Spang JT, Karas SG: The HAGL lesion: An arthroscopic technique for repair of humeral avulsion of the glenohumeral ligaments. *Arthroscopy* 2005;21:498-502.

    A technique for all-arthroscopic repair of a HAGL lesion is described.

32. Arciero RA, Mazzocca AD: Mini open repair technique of HAGL (humeral avulsion of the glenohumeral ligament) lesion. *Arthroscopy* 2005;21:1152.

An open technique for HAGL lesion repair to spare the superior portion of the subscapularis is described.

33. Calandra JJ, Baker CL, Uribe J: The incidence of Hill-Sachs lesions in initial anterior shoulder dislocations. *Arthroscopy* 1989;5:254-257.

34. Hovelius L, Augustini BG, Fredin H, Johansson O, Norlin R, Thorling J: Primary anterior dislocation of the shoulder in young patients: A ten year prospective study. *J Bone Joint Surg Am* 1996;78:1677-1684.

35. Taylor DC, Arciero RA: Pathologic changes associated with shoulder dislocations. *Am J Sports Med* 1997; 25:306-311.

36. Chen AL, Hunt SA, Hawkins RJ, Zuckerman JD: Management of bone loss associated with recurrent anterior glenohumeral instability. *Am J Sports Med* 2005;33:912-925.

    The authors provide a comprehensive review of treatment options, indications, and techniques for addressing anterior instability resulting from osseous deficiencies. A detailed treatment algorithm puts recent and historical reconstructive procedures into context for maximizing stability and functional recovery.

37. Burkhart SS, Debeer JF, Tehrany AM, Parten PM: Quantifying glenoid bone loss arthroscopically in shoulder instability. *Arthroscopy* 2002;18:488-491.

    The location of the glenoid bare spot was arthroscopically measured and found to be a consistent reference because of its location at the center of a circle defined by the inferior glenoid rim. The bare spot can be used as a clinical reference in determining whether bone grafting is necessary to restore stability in a bone-deficient glenoid.

38. Greis PE, Scuderi MG, Mohr A, Backus KN, Burks RT: Glenohumeral contact areas and pressures following labral and osseous injury to the anteroinferior quadrant of the glenoid. *J Shoulder Elbow Surg* 2002; 11:442-451.

    The effect of progressive labral and bone loss on articular contact area and pressure was determined under compressive loads of 220 N and 440 N. The loss of labrum decreased the contact area by 7% to 15% and increased pressure by 8% to 20%. Anteroinferior bone loss of 30% resulted in a decrease in contact area of 41% and an increase in contact pressure of nearly 100%, increasing to between 300% and 400% when the anteroinferior quadrant was analyzed alone.

39. Montgomery WH, Wahl M, Hettrich C, Ito E, Lippitt SB, Matsen FA: Anteroinferior bone-grafting can restore stability in osseous glenoid defects. *J Bone Joint Surg Am* 2005;87:1972-1977.

    Anteroinferior stability before and after bone grafting procedures was studied in cadaver glenoids with and without standardized defects. A significant decrease in anteroinferior stability appeared with glenoid bone loss. Stability was restored with bone-grafting procedures, particularly contoured grafts 6 to 8 mm in height.

40. Millett PJ, Clavert P, Warner JJ: Open operative treatment for anterior shoulder instability: When and why? *J Bone Joint Surg Am* 2005;87:419-432.

    The indications, techniques, and complications of open surgical treatment are reviewed, with specific situations in which open surgery remains the preferred treatment; these include extensive bone loss, soft-tissue deficiency, and revision surgery.

41. Allain J, Goutallier D, Glorion C: Long-term results of the Latarjet procedure for the treatment of anterior instability of the shoulder. *J Bone Joint Surg Am* 1998;80:841-852.

42. Levigne C: [Long-term results of anterior coracoid abutments: Apropos of 52 cases with homogenous 12-year follow-up]. *Rev Chir Orthop Reparatrice Appar Mot* 2000;86(suppl 1):114-121.

43. Ito H, Takayama A, Shirai Y: Radiographic evaluation of the Hill-Sachs lesion in patients with recurrent anterior shoulder instability. *J Shoulder Elbow Surg* 2000;9:495-497.

44. Gerber C, Lambert SM: Allograft reconstruction of segmental defects of the humeral head for the treatment of chronic locked posterior dislocation of the shoulder. *J Bone Joint Surg Am* 1996;78:376-382.

45. Kazel MD, Sekiya JK, Greene JA, Bruker CT: Percutaneous correction (humeroplasty) of humeral head defects (Hill-Sachs) associated with anterior shoulder instability: A cadaveric study. *Arthroscopy* 2005; 21:1473-1478.

    A cadaver study investigated the feasibility of using a curved bone tamp to correct Hill-Sachs lesions.

46. Weber BG, Simpson LA, Hardegger F: Rotational humeral osteotomy for recurrent anterior dislocation of the shoulder associated with a large Hill-Sachs lesion. *J Bone Joint Surg Am* 1984;66:1443-1450.

47. Flatow E, Miller SR, Neer CS: Chronic anterior dislocation of the shoulder. *J Shoulder Elbow Surg* 1993; 2:2-10.

48. Warner JJ, Venegas AA, Lehtinen JJ, Macy JJ: Management of capsular deficiency of the shoulder: A report of three cases. *J Bone Joint Surg Am* 2002;84: 1668-1671.

49. Chen S, Haen PS, Walton J, Murrell GA: The effects of thermal capsular shrinkage on the outcomes of arthroscopic stabilization for primary anterior shoulder instability. *Am J Sports Med* 2005;33:705-711.

    A comparison of arthroscopic Bankart repair using bioabsorbable tack and arthroscopic tack repair plus thermal capsulorrhaphy found no difference in outcomes or recurrence rates. The addition of thermal shrinkage did not affect the results.

50. D'Alessandro DF, Bradley JP, Fleischli JE, Connor PM: Prospective evaluation of thermal capsulorrhaphy for shoulder instability: Indications and results, two- to five-year follow-up. *Am J Sports Med* 2004;32: 21-33.

Thermal capsulorrhaphy was used to treat patients with traumatic dislocation, recurrent anterior shoulder instability, or multidirectional instability; 37% had an unsatisfactory result.

51. Levine WN, Clark AM Jr, D'Alessandro DF, Yamaguchi K: Chondrolysis following arthroscopic thermal capsulorrhaphy to treat shoulder instability: A report of two cases. *J Bone Joint Surg Am* 2005;87: 616-621.

Two patients, ages 19 and 20 years, developed chondrolysis following thermal capsulorrhaphy for shoulder instability.

52. Miniaci A, Codsi MJ: Thermal capsulorrhaphy for the treatment of shoulder instability. *Am J Sports Med* 2006;34:1356-1363.

The updated role of thermal capsulorrhaphy for the treatment of shoulder instability is discussed with regard to clinical sports medicine.

53. Wong KL, Williams GR: Complications of thermal capsulorrhaphy of the shoulder. *J Bone Joint Surg Am* 2001;83-A(suppl 2, pt 2):151-155.

A survey of 379 surgeons found low rates of recurrent shoulder instability after the use of thermal energy. When recurrent instability occurred, capsular insufficiency was often present.

# Chapter 9

# Multidirectional and Posterior Shoulder Instability

Michael J. Huang, MD

*Peter J. Millett, MD

## Multidirectional Instability

Neer and Foster first described the diagnosis and management of multidirectional instability (MDI), based on their study of patients with inferior subluxation or dislocation and associated anterior-posterior subluxation or dislocation.[1] They identified three types of MDI: anterior-inferior dislocation and posterior subluxation, posterior-inferior dislocation and anterior subluxation, and dislocation in all three directions. Neer and Foster distinguished MDI from the more commonly recognized unidirectional anteroposterior instability, emphasizing the often-subtle presentation of MDI and the pitfalls of treating it with a traditional unidirectional repair. They proposed using an inferior capsular shift, and this procedure has had good intermediate-term results.

### Definition and Classification

Despite progress in shoulder instability research, the understanding of MDI is still incomplete. There is no standard definition in the literature, and patient symptoms are variable. Therefore, research outcomes must be carefully interpreted with regard to the study's definition of MDI.

Instability is defined either as pathologic joint translation that causes symptoms or as an inability to keep the humeral head centered within the glenoid cavity during active motion. The term is reserved for symptomatic shoulders and specifically for those in which the sensation of the humeral head translating on the glenoid is present. Instability is frequently associated with pain or discomfort. Laxity is defined as translation in a particular direction or rotation. A person who has significant laxity may have no symptoms. MDI can be defined as shoulder laxity that is global (anterior, posterior, and inferior) and concurrently produces symptoms inferiorly and in at least one other direction. The symptoms are usually experienced in the end ranges of glenohumeral motion and may limit the patient's activities of daily living. Extremes of motion are avoided because of significant apprehension.

### Etiology

MDI can have a congenital or acquired etiology. Congenital, or primary, MDI occurs in patients with an inherited ligamentous laxity; some of these patients have a collagen disorder such as Ehlers-Danlos syndrome or Marfan syndrome. These patients tend to develop MDI at a relatively young age and are less likely to be successfully treated with surgery. Frequently they have a positive family history. In contrast, acquired, or secondary, MDI results from repetitive microtrauma to the shoulder. It is commonly seen in swimmers, weight lifters, gymnasts, and athletes who participate in throwing or racquet sports. These patients may have some underlying hyperlaxity. A previously asymptomatic individual may become symptomatic after a single traumatic event, which can be relatively minor.

The etiology of MDI is believed to be multifactorial, and the current theories focus on anatomic, biochemical, and neuromuscular abnormalities. In a normal shoulder, glenohumeral stability is maintained by an intricate balance of static and dynamic mechanisms. The capsuloligamentous restraints in the shoulder function as checkreins to impart stability at the extremes of motion. In the midrange of glenohumeral motion, the precise centering of the humeral head on the glenoid is enhanced by the rotator cuff muscles through a mechanism known as concavity-compression. Labral detachment can compromise concavity-compression because the labrum normally deepens the glenoid by 50% and contributes 20% of the stability ratio in the inferior and posteroinferior directions.[2] Recurrent instability can lead to muscle imbalance of the dynamic stabilizers, which can also compromise effective concavity-compression.

A deficiency of the rotator interval tissue and a redundant inferior capsular pouch are the two anatomic

---

*Peter J. Millett, MD or the department with which he is affiliated has received royalties from Arthrex and is a consultant or employee for Arthrex.

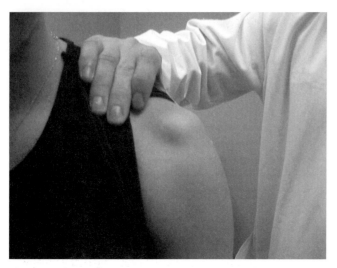

**Figure 1** Squaring of the shoulder, indicating the presence of inferior instability.

lesions associated with MDI. Cadaver studies have demonstrated the importance of the rotator interval and inferior capsular pouch in resisting inferior-posterior displacement of the humeral head. In MDI patients, the rotator interval tissue was found to have a cleft or to be insubstantial.[3,4] Defects in the interval can disrupt the normal negative intra-articular pressure and thereby contribute to instability.[5] The superior glenohumeral ligament is the primary restraint to inferior subluxation when the arm is in adduction.[6] The inferior glenohumeral ligament is the primary restraint to inferior translation when the arm is progressively abducted; during humeral rotation, it also imparts anteroposterior stability. Thus, a capacious inferior pouch can contribute to instability in the inferior, anterior, and posterior directions. The inferior glenohumeral ligament, a hammock-like structure with anchors on both sides of the glenoid, contributes to the stability of the glenohumeral joint.

Basic science studies have examined the type and quantity of collagen in patients with MDI. Collagen fibril diameter and cross-linking are directly related to tensile strength. Capsular tissue from patients with MDI or unidirectional instability was found to have more stable and reducible collagen cross-links, greater mean collagen fibril diameter, higher cysteine concentration, and higher density of elastin, compared with tissue from unaffected individuals.[7] It is unknown whether these differences represent a predisposition to laxity or a response to repetitive stretching injuries. Skin samples from patients with MDI were found to have a significantly smaller mean collagen fibril diameter than samples from patients with unidirectional instability.[7] This finding suggests the presence of an underlying connective tissue abnormality.

Neuromuscular abnormalities have been investigated as a factor in MDI. The theory that MDI has an underlying neuromuscular cause is supported by several research findings. Many patients have equal or greater laxity in the contralateral, asymptomatic shoulder.[8] Symptoms occur in the midrange of glenohumeral motion, in which capsuloligamentous restraints remain lax.[9] Patients have altered glenohumeral and scapulothoracic rhythm.[9] Mechanoreceptors were identified in the shoulder joint capsule of patients with MDI, as well as proprioceptive deficits that can be reversed by surgical stabilization.[10,11] In patients with MDI and laxity, electromyography revealed abnormalities in the deltoid muscle, rather than in the rotator cuff muscles.[12] Another study found significant differences between the activation parameters of the supraspinatus, infraspinatus, posterior deltoid, and pectoralis major muscles of patients with MDI and those of control subjects.[13]

## Clinical Evaluation
### History
A patient with MDI may have a variety of symptoms, such as pain, instability, weakness, paresthesias, fatigue, popping, clicking, grinding, dead arm syndrome, and difficulty in throwing, lifting, or sleeping. The patient should be asked about the positions that provoke symptoms because this information can help in defining the primary direction of instability. Discomfort and traction paresthesias are usually associated with inferior instability. A patient with anterior instability will report difficulty in reaching overhead or sleeping with the arms overhead. MDI should be differentiated from traumatic anterior instability, which has a poor prognosis with nonsurgical treatment. Symptoms that occur with shoulder forward flexion can indicate posterior instability. In addition, patients should be asked whether the subluxation or dislocation has a voluntary component.

The incidence of MDI is greatest in the second and third decades of life, and most patients are younger than 35 years. There is apparently no gender difference. Preadolescent patients are more likely to have voluntary subluxation; they usually do not have pain.[8] Surgical intervention is probably not advisable for a preadolescent patient because MDI in this age group has a favorable natural history.

### Physical Examination
A complete shoulder examination should be performed, including an evaluation of the cervical spine and the scapulothoracic articulation. The shoulder should be visually inspected for asymmetry, scapular winging, atrophy, and the presence of previous incisions. Squaring of the shoulder is a common finding in inferior instability because the normally round contour of the deltoid is lost as the humeral head is inferiorly subluxated (Figure 1). The acromioclavicular, sternoclavicular, and scapulothoracic joints are often overlooked as possible

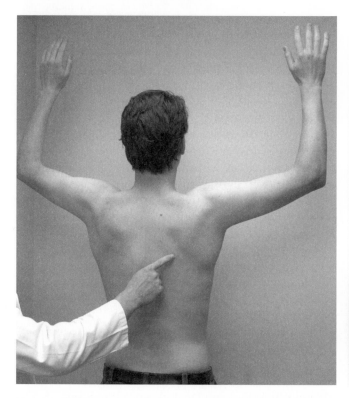

**Figure 2** Scapulohumeral examination, showing the normal position of the scapula.

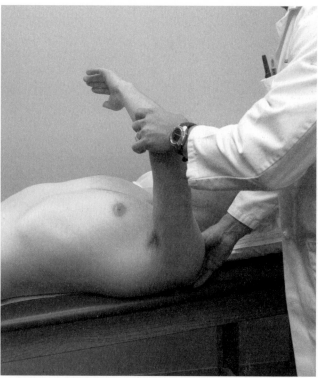

**Figure 3** The posterior stress test.

sources of the patient's symptoms. These joints can generate mechanical symptoms that may be misinterpreted as originating from the glenohumeral joint.

Generalized ligamentous laxity should be assessed by evaluating the contralateral shoulder, the elbows, and the knees and by testing the patient's ability to oppose the thumb to the forearm. Signs of generalized ligamentous laxity have been reported in 45% to 75% of patients undergoing surgery for MDI.[1,9,14] Sulcus testing should be performed and quantified as the distance from the greater tuberosity to the acromion. A value greater than 2 cm is considered pathognomonic for MDI, although pain and symptoms of inferior instability must also be present for the diagnosis to be conclusive. If the sulcus distance does not decrease as the arm is externally rotated, the shoulder should be considered to have a pathologic defect in the rotator interval.

To exclude the possibility of scapular winging, which can be confused with posterior instability, scapulohumeral rhythm and scapulothoracic mechanics should be assessed (Figure 2). Compensatory scapular winging can occur; it dynamically increases bony stability by anteverting the glenoid. A thorough neurologic examination and appropriate neurologic testing should be performed.

Most patients with MDI have increased passive range of motion in the shoulder joint, which is not considered pathologic unless accompanied by symptoms. The redundancy of the inferior capsule can be assessed by holding the arm in 90° of abduction, with the forearm in neutral rotation and with a downward force applied to the lateral brachium. In the hyperabduction test, passive range of abduction greater than 105° is associated with laxity in the inferior glenohumeral ligament.[15] Anteroposterior instability can be assessed using the load-and-shift test and the modified load-and-shift test. The apprehension, relocation, posterior stress, and jerk tests can be used to further isolate anteroposterior instability.[16] Impingement tests are commonly positive in patients with MDI. A distinction should be made between maneuvers that cause pain and those that cause apprehension.

The posterior stress, jerk, load-and-shift, and modified load-and-shift tests are performed specifically to identify posterior instability. The posterior stress test is performed with the patient supine. The arm is flexed to 90° and internally rotated. An axial load is applied to the humerus with one hand, with the other hand applied to the back of the shoulder (Figure 3). A positive test results in palpable or observable subluxation of the humeral head over the glenoid rim.

The jerk test is performed with the patient sitting upright; the arm is flexed 90° and internally rotated, and the elbow is flexed 90°. An axial load is applied to the arm, with the other arm supporting the posterior shoulder, and the arm is then extended. If the test is positive, the glenohumeral joint will be reduced from a posteriorly subluxated or dislocated position with a jerk.

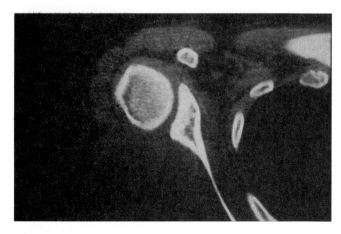

**Figure 4** MRI showing glenoid dysplasia.

The load-and-shift test is performed with the patient sitting upright, with the arm at the side. The humeral head and proximal humerus are grasped and compressed into the glenoid fossa; anteroposterior stress is applied, and the degree of translation is graded. A 50% displacement of the humeral head is considered the upper limit of the normal range.

The modified load-and-shift test is performed with the patient supine and the affected shoulder positioned at the edge of the examination table. The shoulder is placed in neutral rotation in the scapular plane. Axial force is applied at the elbow to concentrically reduce the humeral head in the glenoid fossa. Anteroposterior force is applied to the proximal humerus in varying degrees of rotation and elevation, and the degree of translation is graded. The load-and-shift and modified load-and-shift tests are typically graded as follows: grade 0, minimal translation; grade 1, translation of the humeral head to the glenoid rim; grade 2, translation of the humeral head over the glenoid rim, with spontaneous reduction; and grade 3, translation of the humeral head over the glenoid rim, without spontaneous reduction.

The load-and-shift, sulcus, and provocative tests were found to be reliable in detecting instability,[17] and positive sulcus sign and load-and-shift tests were found to have a high positive predictive value for MDI.[18]

### Imaging Studies

Plain radiography is required for any patient suspected of having shoulder instability. The standard series includes the AP, true AP, and axillary or West Point views. Osseous pathology is occasionally present, and therefore it is important to look for a humeral head defect (Hill-Sachs or reverse Hill-Sachs lesion), traumatic glenoid change (bony Bankart lesion, erosion, or rounding), or an inherent bony abnormality such as glenoid dysplasia or retroversion (Figure 4). CT should be used if examination of plain radiographs suggests the presence of a bony abnormality. CT arthrography can accu-

rately assess capsulolabral detachment. In many centers, MRI is used rather than CT, although it does not provide as much bony detail. The use of CT or MRI may not be warranted in the absence of a suspected bony abnormality or traumatic history.

### Nonsurgical Treatment

MDI should first be treated using nonsurgical methods. Physical therapy programs for shoulder rehabilitation focus on strengthening and retraining the rotator cuff muscles, as well as strengthening the periscapular musculature. The goal is to restore effective concavity-compression and normal muscle-firing patterns and to improve proprioceptive function. In most patients, positive results appear within the first 3 months. An 80% success rate was found after nonsurgical treatment of patients with MDI.[14] In 57 patients at an average 8-year follow-up after rehabilitation for MDI, 19 (33%) had a poor result.[19]

### Surgical Treatment

Surgical treatment should be considered for a patient whose MDI has not responded to nonsurgical treatment. The open inferior capsular shift procedure is intended to reduce capsular volume and thicken and overlap the capsule on the side of greatest instability. This procedure can be performed through an anterior, posterior, or combined surgical approach. In using a posterior approach, it is important to recognize that the posterior capsule is thin and pliable in comparison with the robust anterior capsule. The capsular shift can be humeral or glenoid based, according to the surgeon's preference. At an average 8.3-year follow-up of 34 shoulders, the inferior capsular shift procedure was found to have a satisfactory outcome in 88% of shoulders, with recurrent instability in 26%; radiographs revealed a posterolateral defect in the humeral head in 9 of 14 shoulders treated with a posterior or combined surgical approach.[20] A cadaver study found decreased joint volume after inferior capsular shift.[21]

As shoulder arthroscopy has evolved during the past decade, the frequency of arthroscopic treatment of MDI has also increased. High rates of failure were initially reported, but recent studies have found results equal to or better than those of open procedures. In current arthroscopic techniques, multiple portals and suture anchors are used to reduce capsular volume and re-create the capsulolabral construct.[22] Twenty-five patients having no history of earlier shoulder surgery were treated for MDI with an arthroscopic capsular shift using a transglenoid technique; 88% had a satisfactory result (using the Neer rating) at an average 5-year follow-up.[23] Another study found a successful result in 44 of 47 patients (94%) at 2- to 5-year follow-up after an arthroscopic capsular shift using suture anchors; 85% had returned to their desired level of sports activity.[24]

Thermal capsulorrhaphy was briefly popular for treating MDI and capsular laxity. The procedure is easy to perform and was based on valid basic science findings. However, there was no solid clinical evidence to support its popularity. The most popular thermal capsulorrhaphy techniques used laser or radiofrequency heat technology. Collagen shrinkage was found to occur at temperatures between 65°C and 75°C. The amount of shrinkage depended on the length of exposure and the cross-linking of the exposed tissue.[25] Cell death begins when the temperature of the tissue reaches 45°C and concludes at 55°C to 60°C. The biologic response to this injury varies but is characterized by fibroplasia and angiogenesis. In some in vitro studies, anteroposterior laxity increased after thermal treatment;[26] other studies found decreased capsular volume and glenohumeral translation.[27] The clinical results of thermal capsulorrhaphy for MDI were comparable to the results of cadaver studies. Success rates from 40% to 100% were reported. At 2-year follow-up, thermal capsulorrhaphy had failed in 9 of 19 shoulders with MDI (47%); during revision surgery, 3 patients (33%) were found to have a capsular deficiency.[28] Another study found that 37% of patients with recurrent anterior dislocation or MDI had an unsatisfactory result at 2- to 5-year follow-up after thermal capsulorrhaphy.[29]

Although the role of thermal capsulorrhaphy in the treatment of MDI has yet to be determined, it is important to note that this technique is not recommended because of its high failure rate and the risk of complications, such as thermal necrosis and axillary neuritis.

## Posterior Instability

Posterior instability is an uncommon condition, affecting only 2% to 5% of all patients with shoulder instability. It can occur in isolation or as a component of MDI; unidirectional posterior instability is more common than posterior instability associated with MDI. Trauma is believed to be the underlying cause in approximately half of the patients with posterior instability. Most patients are athletes who participate in activities that cause repetitive stress to the posterior capsule.

### Definition and Classification

Posterior shoulder instability can be classified by direction, degree, cause, or volition. The distinction between posterior laxity and posterior instability is important. Patients with posterior instability frequently have pain. The degree of instability can range from mild subluxation to frank dislocation, although recurrent posterior subluxation is the most common form.

Posterior instability is most commonly caused by acquired trauma, which can be a single traumatic event that occurs when the shoulder is in an at-risk position (flexion, adduction, or internal rotation) or as the culmi-

nation of multiple smaller traumatic episodes.[16] The presence of posterior instability without trauma should alert the physician to the possibility of an underlying collagen disease or bony abnormality. Surgical intervention for such patients should be approached with caution.

Determining the volitional aspect of posterior instability is important. Involuntary posterior instability typically results from a traumatic event and most commonly is manifested as mild subluxation. The patient cannot control the symptoms. Voluntary posterior instability occurs when the patient is able to willfully dislocate or subluxate the shoulder. These patients have voluntary muscular and positional patterns, as well as an underlying muscular imbalance that allows posterior subluxation or dislocation. A patient with voluntary posterior instability is usually considered a poor surgical candidate, although a patient with voluntary positional posterior instability and no underlying psychiatric or secondary gain issues may respond well to surgical intervention. Such a patient has instability when the arm is flexed and adducted. Although able to voluntarily produce the instability, the patient prefers to avoid doing so.

### Clinical Evaluation
#### History
A fall or blow to the arm in an at-risk position can result in a posterior labral detachment (reverse Bankart lesion). Repetitive stress on the posterior capsule during sports or another activity can lead to acquired posterior subluxation. Patients commonly report pain and weakness, and other instability symptoms may also be present. Overhead athletes often describe insidious pain occurring late in their sports activity, when muscle fatigue and dynamic stability are compromised. Direction, frequency, severity, mechanical symptoms, and volition should be investigated as part of the patient history.

#### Physical Examination
Physical examination findings are often more subtle in a patient with posterior instability than in a patient with anterior instability or MDI. The active and passive ranges of motion are usually normal and symmetric. Posterior joint line tenderness may be present with palpation, and crepitus may occur as the arm is internally rotated. Strength testing usually reveals symmetry, although rare patients have a posterior rotator cuff deficiency or nerve injury with external rotation weakness. Atrophy of the posterior rotator cuff musculature may be apparent. Skin dimpling along the posteromedial border of the deltoid also has been associated with recurrent posterior shoulder dislocation.[30]

Generalized ligamentous laxity should be assessed by evaluating the contralateral shoulder, the elbows, and the knees and by testing the patient's ability to oppose the thumb to the forearm. The evaluation of a patient with suspected posterior instability should include sulcus testing, assessment of scapulohumeral rhythm and compensatory scapular winging, and a thorough neurologic examination. Specific posterior instability tests include the posterior stress test, jerk test, load-and-shift test, and modified load-and-shift test.

### Imaging Studies

Standard plain radiographs of the shoulder should be obtained. CT or MRI can be used in assessing glenoid morphology and version. CT arthrography provides the most useful information for assessing bony anatomy and articular orientation.

### Nonsurgical Treatment

Patients with posterior instability had a 63% to 91% success rate after nonsurgical treatment, with no limitations in activities of daily living and only moderate limitations in sports activities.[31,32] The goal of physical therapy is to strengthen the dynamic muscular stabilizers to compensate for damaged or deficient static stabilizers. The exercises should focus on strengthening the posterior deltoid, the external rotators, and the periscapular muscles, and they should be augmented with activity modification and biofeedback.

### Surgical Treatment

The open posteroinferior capsular shift procedure is often used to address soft-tissue abnormalities resulting in posterior instability. The joint can be inspected, any posterior labral injury can be repaired, and the capsular shift and repair can be performed through a posterior approach.[31,33] An 85% success rate was reported at an average 7-year follow-up after open posterior capsulorrhaphy.[33] An 80% success rate was reported at an average 5-year follow-up, and the success rate increased to 96% when revision procedures were excluded.[34] In 44 shoulders (41 patients) treated with primary shoulder stabilization using an open posterior capsular shift, 8 shoulders (19%) had a recurrence of posterior instability at 1.8-year to 22.5-year follow-up; 84% of patients were satisfied with the current status of their shoulder.[35] However, satisfaction and outcome scores were significantly poorer in shoulders found to have a chondral defect at the time of stabilization and in patients older than 37 years at the time of surgery.

A patient with a posterior Bankart lesion is an ideal candidate for either an open posteroinferior capsular shift or arthroscopic treatment. The relative contraindications for an arthroscopic procedure include an unsuccessful earlier arthroscopic stabilization, humeral avulsion of the glenohumeral ligament, or gross bidirectional instability or MDI from generalized laxity caused by a condition such as Ehlers-Danlos syndrome

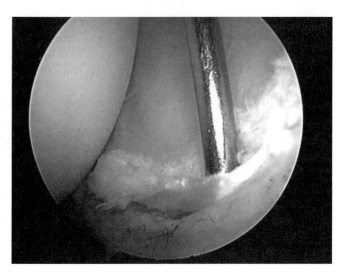

**Figure 5** Arthroscopic view of a posterior Bankart lesion.

or Marfan syndrome. However, patients with multidirectional laxity that is symptomatic only in a posterior direction respond well to arthroscopic stabilization. Glenoid erosion and excessive glenoid retroversion are absolute contraindications for an arthroscopic procedure. Arthroscopic treatment can successfully address capsulolabral injury and capsular redundancy, and rotator interval closure can provide additional inferior stability. With the patient in the beach chair position, an accessory portal placed through the midportion of the rotator cuff allows easy and complete viewing of the posterior glenohumeral joint and does not require traction.[36] This portal provides a superior-to-inferior view of the posterior glenoid rim and capsule and allows the use of standard anterior and posterior portals for posterior Bankart repair (Figure 5).

The posteroinferior labral lesion associated with posterior instability has recently received increased attention. Four types have been identified: type I, an incomplete detachment; type II, a marginal crack (Kim lesion); type III, a chondrolabral erosion; and type IV, a flap tear.[37-39]

Arthroscopic posterior capsular plication for unidirectional posterior instability was successful in 16 of 17 patients; 11 returned to their preinjury level of function.[40] After arthroscopic posteroinferior capsulolabral augmentation, 35 of 41 patients noted improvement.[41] The success rate was 92% in 27 shoulders repaired arthroscopically; 55% of the patients were American football players.[42] After arthroscopic stabilization, 26 of 27 patients who had recurrent posterior instability were able to return to their sport with little or no limitation. Of 33 patients who underwent successful arthroscopic treatment of posterior shoulder instability, those with voluntary dislocation and earlier surgery had poorer outcomes.[43] At a minimum 2-year follow-up of

100 shoulders, the mean American Shoulder and Elbow Surgeons (ASES) Shoulder Index score improved from 50.36 to 85.66 ($P < 0.001$); stability, pain, and function significantly improved based on standardized subjective scales ($P < 0.001$).[44] Contact athletes did not have significantly different outcomes from the entire group on any measure. Overall, 89% of patients were able to return to their sport, and 67% were able to return to their earlier level of function.

Thermal shrinkage was formerly used to decrease a patulous posterior capsule. The clinical result was unpredictable, and the reported failure rates were unacceptably high, ranging from 4% to 60%.[29,45] In addition, capsular necrosis and rupture were reported.[46] For these reasons, the technique is not recommended.

## Summary

Posterior instability and MDI are diagnosed based on the patient's history, a thorough physical examination, and appropriate imaging. Posterior instability is particularly challenging to diagnose and treat because the condition is uncommon and its symptoms are often subtle. Patients with MDI, voluntary instability, or a bony defect require careful assessment to discover the cause of the instability. Most patients respond to a well-designed rehabilitation program; for those who require surgical treatment, predictable results can be achieved using either an open or arthroscopic technique. The use of thermal capsulorrhaphy should be avoided.

## Annotated References

1. Neer CS II, Foster CR: Inferior capsular shift for involuntary inferior and multidirectional instability of the shoulder: A preliminary report. *J Bone Joint Surg Am* 1980;62:897-908.

2. Howell SM, Galinat BJ: The glenoid-labral socket: A constrained articular surface. *Clin Orthop Relat Res* 1989;243:122-125.

3. Harryman DT II, Sidles JA, Harris SL, Matsen FA III: The role of the rotator interval capsule in passive motion and stability of the shoulder. *J Bone Joint Surg Am* 1992;74:53-66.

4. Warner JJ, Deng XH, Warren RF, Torzilli PA: Static capsuloligamentous restraints to superior-inferior translation of the glenohumeral joint. *Am J Sports Med* 1992;20:675-685.

5. Kumar VP, Balasubramaniam P: The role of atmospheric pressure in stabilising the shoulder: An experimental study. *J Bone Joint Surg Br* 1985;67:719-721.

6. Turkel SJ, Panio MW, Marshall JL, Girgis FG: Stabilizing mechanisms preventing anterior dislocation of the glenohumeral joint. *J Bone Joint Surg Am* 1981;63:1208-1217.

7. Rodeo SA, Suzuki K, Yamauchi M, Bhargava M, Warren RF: Analysis of collagen and elastic fibers in shoulder capsule in patients with shoulder instability. *Am J Sports Med* 1998;26:634-643.

8. Self EB Jr: Clinical guidelines for shoulder pain, in Norris TR (ed): *Orthopaedic Knowledge Update: Shoulder and Elbow 2.* Rosemont, IL, American Academy of Orthopaedic Surgeons, 2002, pp 443-467.

   This chapter presents a review of clinical guidelines for the evaluation and management of shoulder pain.

9. Schenk TJ, Brems JJ: Multidirectional instability of the shoulder: Pathophysiology, diagnosis, and management. *J Am Acad Orthop Surg* 1998;6:65-72.

10. Lephart SM, Myers JB, Bradley JP, Fu FH: Shoulder proprioception and function following thermal capsulorrhaphy. *Arthroscopy* 2002;18:770-778.

    Twenty patients with anterior, anteroinferior, or multidirectional glenohumeral instability were treated with thermal capsulorrhaphy. At 6- to 24-month follow-up, no appreciable deleterious effect on proprioception or function was found. Level of evidence: IV.

11. Lephart SM, Borsa PA, Fu FH: Proprioception of the shoulder in healthy, unstable, and surgically repaired shoulders. *J Shoulder Elbow Surg* 1994;3:371-380.

12. Morris AD, Kemp GJ, Frostick SP: Shoulder electromyography in multidirectional instability. *J Shoulder Elbow Surg* 2004;13:24-29.

    Patients with MDI had activity patterns of the anterior, middle, and posterior deltoid that were different from those of individuals with normal shoulders. Activity patterns of the rotator cuff were similar in both groups. Inefficiency of the dynamic stabilizers of the glenohumeral joint may be involved in MDI. Level of evidence: IV.

13. Barden JM, Balyk R, Raso VJ, Moreau M, Bagnall K: Atypical shoulder muscle activation in multidirectional instability. *Clin Neurophysiol* 2005;116:1846-1857.

    MDI is associated with atypical patterns of muscle activity that occur even when highly constrained movements are used to elicit the activity. Glenohumeral hyperlaxity and dysfunctional neuromuscular control of the rotator cuff are contributing factors to the pathoetiology of MDI. Level of evidence: IV.

14. Burkhead WZ Jr, Rockwood CA Jr: Treatment of instability of the shoulder with an exercise program. *J Bone Joint Surg Am* 1992;74:890-896.

15. Gagey OJ, Gagey N: The hyperabduction test. *J Bone Joint Surg Br* 2001;83:69-74.

    In patients with instability, 85% had a range of passive abduction of more than 105°, compared with 90° in the contralateral shoulder. A range of passive abduction of more than 105° is associated with lengthening and laxity of the inferior glenohumeral ligament. Level of evidence: IV.

16. Millett PJ, Clavert P, Hatch GF III, Warner JJ: Recurrent posterior shoulder instability. *J Am Acad Orthop Surg* 2006;14:464-476.

   The current understanding, diagnosis, and treatment of posterior and multidirectional instability of the shoulder are reviewed.

17. Tzannes A, Paxinos A, Callanan M, Murrell GA: An assessment of the interexaminer reliability of tests for shoulder instability. *J Shoulder Elbow Surg* 2004; 13:18-23.

   The load-and-shift, sulcus, and provocative tests (apprehension, augmentation, relocation, and release) are reliable clinical tests for instability in symptomatic patients, if care is taken with respect to arm positioning and if the apprehension test is positive. Level of evidence: III.

18. Tzannes A, Murrell GA: Clinical examination of the unstable shoulder. *Sports Med* 2002;32:447-457.

   A sulcus 2 cm or larger appearing beneath the acromion while the arm is pulled inferiorly is predictive of MDI (likelihood ratio, 9). A positive load-and-shift test is extremely predictive for instability (likelihood ratio, > 80). Level of evidence: V.

19. Misamore GW, Sallay PI, Didelot W: A longitudinal study of patients with multidirectional instability of the shoulder with seven- to ten-year follow-up. *J Shoulder Elbow Surg* 2005;14:466-470.

   In young, athletic patients, the response to nonsurgical treatment of MDI was relatively poor. Only 17 of 57 patients had a satisfactory outcome after 7 to 10 years of nonsurgical treatment. Level of evidence: II.

20. Hamada K, Fukuda H, Nakajima T, Yamada N: The inferior capsular shift operation for instability of the shoulder: Long-term results in 34 shoulders. *J Bone Joint Surg Br* 1999;81:218-225.

21. Yamamoto N, Itoi E, Tuoheti Y, et al: The effect of the inferior capsular shift on shoulder intra-articular pressure: A cadaveric study. *Am J Sports Med* 2006; 34:939-944.

   In seven fresh-frozen cadaver shoulders, the inferior capsular shift procedure decreased joint volume and increased responsiveness of intra-articular pressure to downward loading.

22. Cohen SB, Wiley W, Goradia VK, Pearson S, Miller MD: Anterior capsulorrhaphy: An in vitro comparison of volume reduction. Arthroscopic plication versus open capsular shift. *Arthroscopy* 2005;21:659-664.

   In this in vitro anatomic comparison of procedures, open lateral capsular shift resulted in significantly greater volume reduction than arthroscopic plication. The amount of volume reduction required to eliminate instability caused by capsular laxity remains unknown. Level of evidence: IV.

23. Treacy SH, Savoie FH III, Field LD: Arthroscopic treatment of multidirectional instability. *J Shoulder Elbow Surg* 1999;8:345-350.

24. Gartsman GM, Roddey TS, Hammerman SM: Arthroscopic treatment of multidirectional glenohumeral instability: 2- to 5-year follow-up. *Arthroscopy* 2001;17:236-243.

   Of 47 patients treated arthroscopically for shoulder instability, 94% (44 patients) had a good or excellent outcome at final follow-up; 85% (22 of 26 patients) had returned to their desired level of sports activity. Level of evidence: IV.

25. Hayashi K, Markel MD: Thermal capsulorrhaphy treatment of shoulder instability: Basic science. *Clin Orthop Relat Res* 2001;390:59-72.

   Experimental studies found that joint capsular tissue can be significantly shortened using thermal energy at 70° to 80°. Achievement of shoulder stability relies on initial shrinkage as well as the tissue's healing response. Overtreatment can lead to severe immediate and permanent tissue damage.

26. Wolf RS, Zheng N, Iero J, Weichel D: The effects of thermal capsulorrhaphy and rotator interval closure on multidirectional laxity in the glenohumeral joint: A cadaveric biomechanical study. *Arthroscopy* 2004; 20:1044-1049.

   The effects of thermal capsulorrhaphy and rotator interval closure on glenohumeral laxity were examined in 10 cadaver shoulders. Statistical analysis revealed that rotator interval closure significantly decreased laxity. Thermal capsulorrhaphy did not increase anterior and posterior translation but did decrease inferior translation.

27. Victoroff BN, Deutsch A, Protomastro P, Barber JE, Davy DT: The effect of radiofrequency thermal capsulorrhaphy on glenohumeral translation, rotation, and volume. *J Shoulder Elbow Surg* 2004;13:138-145.

   This cadaver study evaluated changes in resistance to translational forces, rotation, and joint volume in radiofrequency thermal capsulorrhaphy. Significant reduction in glenohumeral translation and volume with only a small loss of rotation was found.

28. Miniaci A, McBirnie J: Thermal capsular shrinkage for treatment of multidirectional instability of the shoulder. *J Bone Joint Surg Am* 2003;85:2283-2287.

   Nineteen patients with MDI were treated with thermal capsular shrinkage. The failure rate was substantial. Recurrence of instability occurred in 47%; stiffness, in 26%; and neurologic symptoms, in 21%. Level of evidence: IV.

29. D'Alessandro DF, Bradley JP, Fleischli JE, Connor PM: Prospective evaluation of thermal capsulorrhaphy for shoulder instability: Indications and results, two- to five-year follow-up. *Am J Sports Med* 2004;32: 21-33.

This nonrandomized prospective study evaluated the indications for and results of thermal capsulorrhaphy in 84 shoulders. At an average 38-month follow-up, the overall results were excellent in 33 (39%), satisfactory in 20 (24%), and unsatisfactory in 31 (37%).

30. Williams RJ III, Strickland S, Cohen M, Altchek DW, Warren RF: Arthroscopic repair for traumatic posterior shoulder instability. *Am J Sports Med* 2003;31: 203-209.

    This is a retrospective review of the arthroscopic repair of 27 patients with a posterior Bankart lesion. All patients had a detached capsulolabral complex. At an average 5.1-year follow-up, 25 patients reported no pain or instability. Level of evidence: IV.

31. Fronek J, Warren RF, Bowen M: Posterior subluxation of the glenohumeral joint. *J Bone Joint Surg Am* 1989;71:205-216.

32. Hurley JA, Anderson TE, Dear W, Andrish JT, Bergfeld JA, Weiker GG: Posterior shoulder instability: Surgical versus conservative results with evaluation of glenoid version. *Am J Sports Med* 1992;20:396-400.

33. Hawkins RJ, Koppert G, Johnston G: Recurrent posterior instability (subluxation) of the shoulder. *J Bone Joint Surg Am* 1984;66:169-174.

34. Pollock RG, Bigliani LU: Recurrent posterior shoulder instability: Diagnosis and treatment. *Clin Orthop Relat Res* 1993;291:85-96.

35. Wolf BR, Strickland S, Williams RJ, Allen AA, Altchek DW, Warren RF: Open posterior stabilization for recurrent posterior glenohumeral instability. *J Shoulder Elbow Surg* 2005;14:157-164.

    This retrospective study evaluated clinical and radiographic outcomes after open posterior stabilization. Open posterior shift was found to be reliable in shoulders with a grade III posterior instability, particularly with a sulcus of grade II or higher. Level of evidence: IV.

36. Costouros JG, Clavert P, Warner, JJ: Trans-cuff portal for arthroscopic posterior capsulorrhaphy. *Arthroscopy* 2006;22:A9-A16.

    Five patients underwent arthroscopic repair of posterior shoulder instability using the trans–rotator cuff portal. The mean ASES score improved from 53 (±15) to 87 (±8). All patients had complete resolution of pain and instability at an average 24-month follow-up.

37. Kim SH, Park JS, Jeong WK, Shin SK: The Kim test: A novel test for posteroinferior labral lesion of the shoulder: A comparison to the jerk test. *Am J Sports Med* 2005;33:1188-1192.

    The Kim test, a novel diagnostic test for detecting a posteroinferior labral lesion of the shoulder, was compared with the jerk test in 172 painful shoulders. The Kim test was more sensitive in detecting a predominantly inferior labral lesion. Level of evidence: I.

38. Kim SH, Ha KI, Yoo JC, Noh KC: Kim's lesion: An incomplete and concealed avulsion of the posteroinferior labrum in posterior or multidirectional posteroinferior instability of the shoulder. *Arthroscopy* 2004; 20:712-720.

    This study clinically described the Kim lesion, which is an incomplete avulsion of the posteroinferior labrum concealed by apparently intact superficial portion. Failure to address this lesion surgically may result in persistent posterior instability. Level of evidence: IV.

39. Kim SH, Kim HK, Sun JI, Park JS, Oh I: Arthroscopic capsulolabroplasty for posteroinferior multidirectional instability of the shoulder. *Am J Sports Med* 2004;32:594-607.

    Thirty-one patients with symptomatic posterior-inferior MDI had labral lesions, including retroversion of the posteroinferior labrum, which were previously unrecognized. Restoration of the labral buttress and capsular tension by arthroscopic capsulolabroplasty successfully stabilized the shoulders.

40. Wolf EM, Eakin CL: Arthroscopic capsular plication for posterior shoulder instability. *Arthroscopy* 1998; 14:153-163.

41. Antoniou J, Duckworth DT, Harryman DT II: Capsulolabral augmentation for the management of posteroinferior instability of the shoulder. *J Bone Joint Surg Am* 2000;82:1220-1230.

42. Kim SH, Ha KI, Park JH, et al: Arthroscopic posterior labral repair and capsular shift for traumatic unidirectional recurrent posterior subluxation of the shoulder. *J Bone Joint Surg Am* 2003;85:1479-1487.

    In all 27 patients who underwent arthroscopic posterior labral repair and capsular shift, shoulder function improved as measured using the University of California Los Angeles, ASES, and Rowe scores at a mean 39-month follow-up. All patients returned to their sports activity with little or no limitation. Level of evidence: IV.

43. Provencher MT, Bell SJ, Menzel KA, Mologne TS: Arthroscopic treatment of posterior shoulder instability: Results in 33 patients. *Am J Sports Med* 2005; 33:1463-1471.

    At a mean 39.1-month follow-up of 33 patients who underwent posterior arthroscopic shoulder stabilization, the mean ASES score was 94.6. Patients with voluntary instability or prior surgery had lower outcome scores. Level of evidence: IV.

44. Bradley JP, Baker CL III, Kline AJ, Armfield DR, Chhabra A: Arthroscopic capsulolabral reconstruction for posterior instability of the shoulder: A prospective study of 100 shoulders. *Am J Sports Med* 2006;34:1061-1071.

    At a 27-month follow-up of 91 athletes with unidirectional posterior shoulder instability after arthroscopic treatment, the mean ASES score improved from 50.36 to

85.66. Stability, pain, and function significantly improved, and 89% of patients were able to return to their sports activity. Level of evidence: II.

45.  Lyons TR, Griffith PL, Savoie FH III, Field LD: Laser-assisted capsulorrhaphy for multidirectional instability of the shoulder. *Arthroscopy* 2001;17: 25-30.

  Laser-assisted capsulorrhaphy was performed on 27 shoulders (26 patients). At a minimum 2-year follow-up, 96% of shoulders remained stable and asymptomatic, and 86% of athletes had returned to their previous level of activity. In 12%, the rating was unsatisfactory.

46.  Wong KL, Williams GR: Complications of thermal capsulorrhaphy of the shoulder. *J Bone Joint Surg Am* 2001;83-A(suppl 2, pt 2):151-155.

  A survey of 378 surgeons on their experience with thermal treatment for shoulder instability revealed recurrent instability rates after laser, monopolar, and bipolar radiofrequency capsulorrhaphy of 8.4%, 8.3%, and 7.1%, respectively. Postsurgical axillary neuropathy affected 1.4% of patients.

# Chapter 10

# Arthroscopic Reconstruction for Anterior Glenohumeral Instability

Brent Ponce, MD

John M. Tokish, MD

## Introduction

Knowledge of shoulder instability has advanced significantly during the past several years. Basic science studies have improved understanding of the pathophysiology of instability, including the role of anatomy, the Bankart lesion, the humeral avulsion of the glenohumeral ligament (HAGL) lesion, and bony deficiency. There has also been dramatic improvement in the arthroscopic diagnosis and treatment of shoulder instability. Many studies have found that the results of arthroscopic procedures now approach or equal those of open procedures. New techniques have been developed to address both the soft-tissue and bony lesions associated with instability.

## Pathoanatomy

Shoulder laxity is defined as asymptomatic, passive translation of the humeral head on the glenoid. Laxity varies widely among individuals. Shoulder instability is the symptomatic pathologic condition associated with pain and discomfort secondary to excessive translation of the glenohumeral joint. Instability can occur acutely as the result of a traumatic subluxation or dislocation or can occur insidiously after years of repetitive stress but without a traumatic event.

Multiple anatomic structures are responsible for stabilizing the shoulder. The soft-tissue static stabilizers include the labrum, glenohumeral ligaments, capsule, and rotator interval. In a normal shoulder, the labrum and rotator cuff provide a stabilizing concavity-compression effect. Stability is also provided by the negative intra-articular pressure of an intact capsule. The osseous static stabilizers include the glenoid and humeral head. The stability they provide is influenced by instrinsic version and conformity as well as the extent of injury. The dynamic shoulder stabilizers include the rotator cuff and scapular stabilizing muscles.

### Labrum and Glenohumeral Ligaments

The labrum is a fibrocartilaginous structure that increases the surface and depth of the glenoid and serves as a chock block or bumper to prevent anterior translation. The Bankart lesion is a tear involving the anteroinferior portion of the labrum; it was formerly considered the essential lesion in shoulder instability. Almost all traumatic anterior dislocations are associated with anteroinferior disruption of the labral attachment to the glenoid. The Bankart lesion is also present in approximately 70% of traumatic subluxations (Figure 1).

The inferior glenohumeral ligament complex (IGHLC) is the primary restraint to anterior translation, most notably when the arm is in abduction and external rotation. Some plastic deformation of the IGHLC occurs during anterior subluxation or dislocation and is an important factor contributing to instability. In cadaver studies, isolated sectioning of the labrum from the glenoid reduces resistance to translation by 20%.[1] Injury to the labrum alone does not lead to recurrent instability; some degree of ligamentous laxity must also be present.

The labrum often detaches medially along the neck of the glenoid instead of in its anatomic position along the edge of the neck of the glenoid and thereby decreases tension on the IGHLC. This condition is called the anterior labroligamentous periosteal sleeve avulsion (ALPSA lesion) (Figure 2). The HAGL lesion is a tear in the capsule on the humeral side; it has been reported to occur in as many as 9.3% of patients with traumatic anterior instability.[2] A reverse HAGL lesion is even more uncommon and is associated with traumatic posterior instability.

Above the equator of the glenoid, the anatomy of the labrum is variable. A sublabral foramen is found in approximately 11% of patients. Repair of a normal sublabral foramen results in excessive tightening of the ligamentous structures. In 2% of patients, the anterosuperior labrum is absent. An absent anterosuperior labrum associated with a thickened, cordlike middle glenohumeral ligament is called the Buford complex. The middle glenohumeral ligament typically arises from the anterosuperior origin of the labrum and crosses the subscapularis obliquely before inserting onto the lesser tuberosity. It limits anterior translation with external

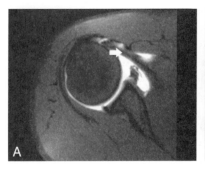

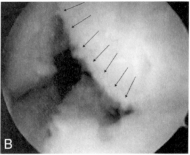

**Figure 1** The Bankart lesion. **A,** Axial MRI showing separation of the anteroinferior glenoid labrum from the glenoid bone. The arrow points to the displaced labrum. **B,** Arthroscopic view from an anterosuperior portal in a right shoulder showing separation of the anteroinferior glenoid labrum from the glenoid. The arrows point to the edge of the glenoid, where the labrum is normally attached.

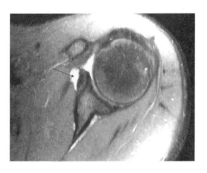

**Figure 2** The ALPSA lesion. MRI showing a labral tear that healed medially to the glenoid neck. At surgery, it was mobilized and advanced to the anterior edge of the glenoid to restore the labral bumper and tension effect. The arrow points to the medially displaced labrum.

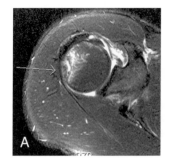

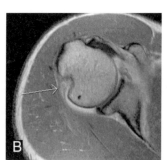

**Figure 3** The Hill-Sachs lesion. **A,** T2-weighted axial MRI showing an acute Hill-Sachs lesion (*arrow*). **B,** Proton density MRI of an engaging Hill-Sachs lesion (*arrow*).

rotation of the arm in midrange abduction. The superior glenohumeral ligament also arises from the anterosuperior edge of the labrum just anterior to the origin of the long head of the biceps. It is an integral part of rotator interval anatomy and primarily resists inferior translation of the adducted shoulder.

The rotator interval lies between the anterior edge of the supraspinatus and the superior edge of the subscapularis. The coracohumeral ligament and superior glenohumeral ligament are the primary structures of the interval. The role of the rotator interval and its component structures remains a subject of debate. Cadaver studies found that the rotator interval contributes to posteroinferior stability.[3] Other cadaver studies found that the rotator interval has a role in anterior stability.[4,5] Excessive tightening of the rotator interval results in a loss of external rotation with the arm in adduction.

### Glenoid and Humeral Head
Shoulder dislocation is associated with bony injury to the glenoid and humeral head. A chondral defect of the glenoid rim is called a glenoid labrum articular disruption lesion. A fracture of the anteroinferior glenoid, called a Bankart fracture, can occur as a traumatic fracture resulting from a single dislocation. Recurrent dislocation can lead to progressive bone loss at the anteroinferior glenoid. Many larger defects require immediate fixation or grafting, if a soft-tissue procedure will not suffice.

An impression fracture of the posterosuperior humeral head is called a Hill-Sachs lesion in a traumatic anterior shoulder dislocation (Figure 3). A traumatic posterior shoulder dislocation may lead to a reverse Hill-Sachs lesion on the anterior aspect of the humeral head. Depending on its size and location, a Hill-Sachs lesion may engage the rim of the glenoid. An engaging Hill-Sachs lesion is treated with bone grafting, humeral head resurfacing, or transfer of the lesser tuberosity into the lesion (the McLaughlin procedure).

## Clinical Evaluation
### History
A thorough history of demographic and injury-related factors, such as the patient's age, the mechanism of injury, the arm positions or activities that cause discomfort, the number of prior dislocations, and the ease of dislocation, can provide insight into the natural history and pathoanatomy of the instability.

Age is one of the most important considerations in the natural history of traumatic shoulder instability. Recurrence is the most common complication in young patients. Randomized studies found an 11% to 16% rate of recurrence after arthroscopic stabilization of traumatic shoulder instability (mean patient age, 22.4 years; range, 16-30 years)[6] and a 47% to 75% rate of recurrence after nonsurgical treatment (mean patient age, 22.4 years; range, 19-26 years).[7] Immediate surgical stabilization should be considered for an active athlete who is younger than 30 years.

In patients who are older than 40 years, rotator cuff tearing is the most common complication of traumatic anterior dislocation. The possibility of a rotator cuff tear should be considered in any patient who is older than 40 years and has significant, persistent weakness within several weeks of a traumatic dislocation.

The mechanism of injury and the position of apprehension are important in determining the direction of instability. A patient with anterior instability has symptoms with the arm in an abducted and externally rotated position. A patient with posterior instability typically has symptoms when the arm is flexed, internally rotated, and adducted. Activities such as carrying a heavy object may elicit symptoms in a patient who has hyperlax shoulders and multidirectional instability. The number of dislocations and the energy associated with dislocation should be considered, as should anatomic factors such as soft-tissue injury and bone loss.

### Physical Examination

Physical examination of the unstable shoulder has been well described, and recent studies have determined the accuracy and utility of special tests for instability. The anterior apprehension, relocation, and anterior drawer tests were found to be specific but not sensitive for instability. The patient's sense of apprehension was found to be a better indicator of instability than the production of pain. The apprehension test was found to have 72% sensitivity and 96% specificity; the likelihood ratio was 20.2.[8] The relocation test was found to have 81% sensitivity and 92% specificity; the likelihood ratio was 10.4. Pain obviated the anterior drawer test in only 13% of patients.

Another study documented the usefulness of the apprehension, relocation, and surprise tests. When all three tests were positive, the mean positive and negative predictive values were 93.6% and 71.9%, respectively. The surprise test was the single most accurate test; its sensitivity was 64%, and its specificity was 99%.[9]

In another study, the interexaminer reliability of tests for shoulder instability was assessed. The load-and-shift, sulcus, and provocative tests (the apprehension, augmentation, relocation, and release tests) are reliable for detecting instability in symptomatic patients if the arm is carefully positioned. Apprehension is the criterion for a positive provocative test. Good or excellent interexaminer agreement was found in most variations of the load-and-shift test; the greatest agreement was found in the 90° abducted position for the anterior direction, with a correlation coefficient of 0.72. With 0° of abduction, the posterior direction correlation coefficient was 0.68 and the inferior direction correlation coefficient was 0.79.[10]

## Outcomes of Arthroscopic Stabilization

The results of early arthroscopic instability surgery were poorer than those of open surgery. Rates of recurrence of instability ranged from 15% to 33%.[11,12] In recent years, however, improved techniques and an increased understanding of the pathophysiology of shoulder instability have corresponded with improved results (Figure 4). Currently, the results of arthroscopy in most primary surgeries are favorable compared with those of open repair. The results are less favorable for some types of revision surgery and for surgery in patients with a soft-tissue insufficiency or a severe bony deficiency on the humeral or glenoid side.[13,14]

Three large case series of 54 to 167 patients examined the results of arthroscopic stabilization and reported unsatisfactory results in 4% to 10%. The outcome scores and rates of return to previous level of sports activities were similar to those reported following open stabilization in historical control groups.[15-17] One of the first studies comparing open and arthroscopic stabilization found a 10% recurrence rate in 89 patients at an average 39-month follow-up. Of the patients who underwent open surgery, 87% had a good or excellent result, compared with 92% of the patients who underwent arthroscopic stabilization.[18]

A prospective, randomized study compared the results of arthroscopic and open stabilization in 60 patients with an isolated Bankart lesion. None of the patients had a recurrence of instability at 2-year follow-up. The only statistically significant difference between the two patient groups was a decrease in the range of motion among patients who underwent open stabilization.[19] In a prospective, randomized study of 64 patients at an average 32-month follow-up, 3 patients had an unsatisfactory result, including 2 who had undergone open stabilization and 1 who had undergone arthroscopic stabilization.[20] Patients who underwent open stabilization had a greater loss of motion. Patients' subjective evaluations were equivalent in the two groups.

## Recent Developments in Arthroscopic Stabilization

### Capsular Plication

Several recent studies evaluated the efficacy of arthroscopic plication techniques in reducing capsular volume and range of motion. In a cadaver model, anteroinferior plication reduced both abduction and external rotation by approximately 20°, anterior translation by 61%, posterior translation by 13%, and inferior translation by 3%.[21] Anterosuperior plication was found to reduce external rotation of the adducted shoulder an average of 30°, and posterosuperior plication was found to reduce internal rotation of the adducted arm an average of 16°.[22] These findings show the manner in which capsulorrhaphy can alter shoulder kinematics and may be relevant in understanding the cause of postsurgical static subluxation and late osteoarthritis (Figure 5).

In a cadaver study, arthroscopic anterior plication resulted in a 22.8% reduction of capsular volume, and

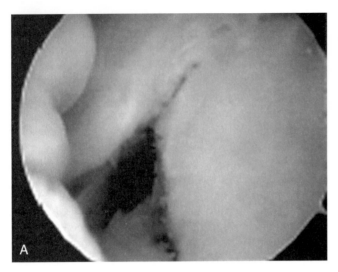
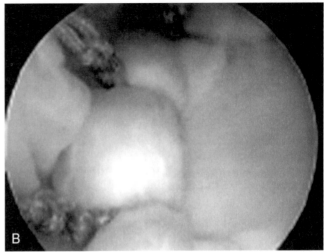

**Figure 4** A Bankart lesion before **(A)** and after **(B)** arthroscopic repair.

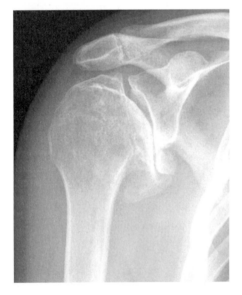

**Figure 5** AP radiograph showing severe degenerative joint disease 23 years after the patient underwent a Putti-Platt procedure.

open capsular shift resulted in a 49.9% volume reduction.[23] A comparison of suture plication and thermal capsulorrhaphy used alone or in combination to reduce capsular volume found that suture plication alone achieved an average volume reduction of 19% and thermal capsulorrhaphy alone achieved an average reduction of 33%. The use of both plication and thermal shrinkage achieved the greatest volume reduction, at an average of 41%.[24] These studies demonstrated that different techniques are effective in reducing the volume of the joint and tightening the ligaments. Intrasurgical decisions continue to be primarily based on the surgeon's judgment.

A cadaver study of three arthroscopic rotator interval closure techniques found a decrease of 6° of flexion, 10° of external rotation, and 3 mm of anterior translation in the adducted arm. No statistically significant differences between the three techniques were noted.[5] In another study, an almost 30% reduction of anterior translation was found immediately following thermal capsulorrhaphy.[25] The early enthusiasm for thermal capsulorrhaphy has waned because of several reported complications and higher-than-expected failure rates. The role of rotator interval closure in instability surgery remains a subject of debate.

### Neurovascular Safety

The proximity of the axillary nerve to capsular plication sutures is of substantial concern. In one cadaver study focusing on the axillary nerve, sutures were placed in five locations (anterior, anteroinferior, inferior, posteroinferior, and posterior), entering the capsule 1 cm away from the glenoid. In 10 shoulder specimens, the anteroinferior and inferior suture locations were closest to the axillary nerve; the average distance was 12.5 mm and 14.4 mm, respectively.[26] A more recent study found that the axillary nerve and the glenoid rim were closest to each other at the 6 o'clock position; the average distance between them at this pont was 12.4 mm.[27] Throughout the course of the axillary nerve, its average distance from the IGHLC was 2.5 mm.

Outside-in portal placement is frequently used in current arthroscopic techniques because it is useful in identifying the ideal placement of the arthroscopic portals. In a cadaver study of five shoulders, six portals (posterior, posterolateral, anterior, 5 o'clock, anterosuperior lateral, and portal of Wilmington) were created using an 18-gauge spinal needle. The distances from the portals to the neurovascular structures were measured, and all of the portals were found to be located more than 20 mm from the axillary nerve, the musculocutaneous nerve, the lateral cord of the brachial plexus, and the axillary artery. The portal-to-cephalic vein distances varied; in one specimen, the vein was pierced. The authors concluded that, although all of the tested portals were safe for the neurovascular structures, using the anterior or 5 o'clock portal could jeopardize the cephalic vein.[28]

### Thermal Capsulorrhaphy

The use of radiofrequency devices in the reduction of capsular volume was initially promising. One early study of thermal capsulorrhaphy found an immediate 40% reduction in anterior translation and a 36% decrease in posterior translation. The clinical results over time were less favorable. A prospective study of 84 unstable shoulders found 39% excellent, 24% satisfactory, and 37% unsatisfactory results at intermediate-term follow-up.[29] The authors recommended against the use of thermal shrinkage because of the high rate of unsatisfactory results. Another study of thermal capsular shrinkage used for anterior instability in 72 patients found that it had no advantage over routine capsular plication and anchor stabilization.[30]

A study of the histology of the capsule after unsuccessful thermal capsulorrhaphy found changes in the collagen, along with denuded synovium, in all shoulders; the capsule was found to be thin in 71%.[31] Even in shoulders that had a successful clinical result, the collagen structure was histologically abnormal for as long as 16 months after thermal capsulorrhaphy.

Because of its location, the axillary nerve is susceptible to injury during capsular shrinkage. One report described injury to the axillary nerve in four patients; heat penetration through the capsule was believed to be the cause.[32] A cadaver study found significant temperature elevation across the axillary nerve and its branches to the teres minor in 11 of 15 specimens after a radiofrequency device was used for thermal capsular shrinkage.[33]

Chondrolysis has been reported following the use of thermal capsulorrhaphy.[34] Because of the devastating complications and a lack of evidence to support its use, thermal capsulorrhaphy has fallen out of favor, and it currently has limited application.

### Suture Knots

Several studies have examined the biomechanical characteristics of knots used in arthroscopic procedures. A study of the failure patterns of six different knots found that their performance was similar; breakage occurred after the suture loops were widened beyond 3 mm. Another study found no significant differences in load to failure among five knot configurations.[35] However, early failure caused by slippage at low tensions occurred when a newer, high-strength suture material was used, in contrast to the Ethibond suture (Ethicon, Somerville, NJ).[36] This finding implies that, although the newer sutures are stronger, they may have relatively low static resistance to slippage and therefore offer less knot security.

In a comparison of square knots with several arthroscopic sliding and sliding-locking knots, all of the tested knots elongated minimally with cyclic load testing. No differences in load at failure were noted in any of the sliding and sliding-locking knots backed with three half hitches, compared with the square knot.[37] This study confirmed that all knots should be backed up with three half hitches, with the posts and direction of the throws alternated. Another study supported the use of three alternating half hitches; the ultimate failure plateau for all knot configurations was reached after three or more alternating half hitches were used. In placing the reinforcing half hitches, switching the post is critical for knot security. Failure to do so makes the knot less reliable.

### Suture Anchors

Metal anchors have excellent strength characteristics, although they are not frequently used in stabilization procedures because of concern about placing metal in close proximity to the articulating surface. Catastrophic chondral injury can result if the anchor loses its fixation and becomes intra-articular. The first anchors were rapidly absorbable and were made of composites of polyglycolic acid. They were associated with significant foreign body reactions that occasionally resulted in cyst formation. Later anchors were made of the homopolymer poly-L-lactic acid. They were designed to degrade at a much slower rate and therefore to decrease the potential for undesired inflammatory reactions. Current anchors are composed of different polymer concentrations so as to vary reabsorption rates while maintaining strength. Additional improvements include the development of stronger sutures, the use of more sutures, and the use of fully threaded designs to increase pullout strength without increasing anchor size. Anchors made of polyetheretherketone, a radiolucent composite plastic whose strength and stiffness combine the characteristics of metal and bioabsorbable materials, are being used more often.[38,39]

In an in vivo study to compare the strength of repairs made using metal and biodegradable anchors, no difference was found in repair strength at any time following implantation.[40] Another study found that, regardless of the anchor used, the weakest point in the repair is the suture rather than the anchor; this was true even if newer, stronger nonabsorbable sutures were used.[41] However, pullout strength was found to be greater when a larger diameter anchor was used.[42] This finding highlights the need for surgeons to critically examine peer-reviewed studies of the implants used during surgery.

Recent reports have been critical of the Suretac device (Acufex Microsurgical, Mansfield, MA), a commonly used early bioabsorbable implant. Early enthusiasm for Suretac's ease of implantation and bioabsorbable characteristics were tempered by reports of foreign body reactions, implant breakage, chondral damage, low rates of return to sports activity, and statistically lower load-to-failure values.[39,43] However, several well-designed clinical outcome studies of the Suretac device found a high rate of success.[7,44,45]

### Recurrence of Instability

Several studies have identified the risk factors for recurrent instability after arthroscopic repair. One recent study identified glenoid bone loss or a large Hill-Sachs lesion, inferior shoulder hyperlaxity (a difference in hyperabduction between the shoulders of more than 20°, using the Gagey test), anteroinferior shoulder laxity, and the use of fewer than three suture anchors as risk factors for recurrence.[13] Other identifiable risk factors for recurrence include the presence of bilateral shoulder instability or poor capsulolabral tissue.[44]

A shoulder with glenoid bone loss is at high risk of recurrence after an arthroscopic stabilization procedure. The cause probably is multifactorial. In a study of 194 arthroscopic stabilizations, 21 patients had a 25% or larger bony defect of the glenoid, and 14 of these patients (67%) had recurrent instability. The bony defects included 11 inverted pear glenoids and three engaging Hill-Sachs lesions. In the 173 patients who did not have a bony defect, the rate of instability was 4% (7 patients), which is comparable to rates after open stabilization.[14] In another study, the combination of glenoid deficiency and inferior hyperlaxity was associated with a 75% recurrence rate.[13]

Most patients with a diagnosis of anterior instability were found to have some anterior bone loss.[46] However, when bone loss of at least 25% occurs, the normal glenoid shape becomes an inverted pear shape. When the length of the glenoid deficiency is equal to the radius of the glenoid, the resistance to dislocation is decreased by 30%. The deficient glenoid is comparable to a golf ball falling off a golf tee that is missing a sizable portion of its concavity. In a patient with a glenoid bone deficiency or an engaging Hill-Sachs lesion, bone grafting to restore the normal articular arc of the glenoid should be strongly considered.[13,46,47]

## Controversies in Arthroscopic Stabilization

Although significant advances have been made in the field of arthroscopic stabilization, several areas of controversy remain.

### Bone Loss

Arthroscopic procedures to treat bony Bankart lesions have had promising early results. In a 2-year follow-up study of 25 patients who were treated with arthroscopic stabilization for an acute bony Bankart lesion, no recurrences of instability were found; 92% (23 patients) returned to their previous level of sports activity.[48]

Of 42 patients with a bony Bankart lesion who were treated with arthroscopic osseous repair, 93% (39 patients) had a good or excellent result; 95% (35 of 37 patients) had returned to their previous level of sports activity at 34-month follow-up.[49] On three-dimensional CT scans, the average glenoid bone loss before surgery was 24.8% and the average bony Bankart fragment was 9.2% of the glenoid. In all patients, the osseous fragment was attached to the labroligamentous complex. Suture anchors were used during repair, and the osseous fragment was retained in restoring the fragment and labroligamentous complex to its anatomic position. After repair, the average passive external rotation was 75° with the arm adducted and 93° with the arm in 90° of abduction. The success reported in this study highlights the potential to address pathology believed to be unresponsive to arthroscopic treatment.

### HAGL Lesions

HAGL lesions are uncommon, and they were previously believed to require open repair. Two recent reports described arthroscopic techniques for the repair of a HAGL lesion.[50,51] Although the arthroscopic repair is technically demanding, the short-term results are promising.

### Accelerated Rehabilitation

In a prospective, randomized study of patients who were not athletes, no difference was found in outcomes after an accelerated or a standard rehabilitation program.[52] Patients who underwent accelerated rehabilitation had less pain in the early postsurgical period and an earlier return to work. Additional research is necessary to validate postsurgical protocols and their application to both athletes and nonathletes.

### Contact Athletes

Open repair has traditionally been recommended for athletes involved in contact sports. Initial results of open and arthroscopic stabilization in these athletes were poor. Failure rates ranged from 23% to 30% after open repair, and they were as high as 70% after arthroscopic repair.[53,54] The results of recent studies are conflicting. Relatively low recurrence rates (between 6.5% and 11%) were reported after arthroscopic stabilization, but high recurrence rates also were reported (between 25% and 29%).[55-57] In comparison, rates between 3% and 13% were reported after open stabilization.[58] Future investigation into these dramatically different rates is required.

## Summary

Advances in arthroscopic glenohumeral ligament reconstruction have led to clinical outcomes equivalent to those of open stabilization. The benefits of arthroscopic stabilization include better intrasurgical visualization, the ability to repair additional pathology, and a decreased rate of subscapularis and other complications associated with open surgery. The identification of risk factors for recurrence, particularly bone loss, is critical to the success of arthroscopic stabilization. Although many questions remain in the treatment of shoulder instability, the currently available information and the success of arthroscopic stabilization have allowed it to become the standard procedure used by many surgeons who treat anterior instability.

## Annotated References

1. Lippitt S, Vanderhooft J, Harris S, Sidles J, Harryman D, Matsen FI: Glenohumeral stability from concavity-compression: A quantitative analysis. *J Shoulder Elbow Surg* 1993;2:27-35.

2. Wolf EM, Cheng JC, Dickson K: Humeral avulsion of glenohumeral ligaments as a cause of anterior shoulder instability. *Arthroscopy* 1995;11:600-607.

3. Harryman DT II, Sidles JA, Harris SL, Matsen FA III: The role of the rotator interval capsule in passive motion and stability of the shoulder. *J Bone Joint Surg Am* 1992;74:53-66.

4. Jost B, Koch PP, Gerber C: Anatomy and functional aspects of the rotator interval. *J Shoulder Elbow Surg* 2000;9:336-341.

5. Plausinis D, Bravman JT, Heywood C, Kummer FJ, Kwon YW, Jazrawi LM: Arthroscopic rotator interval closure: Effect of sutures on glenohumeral motion and anterior-posterior translation. *Am J Sports Med* 2006;34:1656-1661.

   Three interval closures were tested in 12 cadaver shoulders. No differences between the techniques were identified. Average flexion was reduced by 6°; external rotation, 10°; and anterior translation, 3 mm.

6. Kirkley A, Werstine R, Ratjek A, Griffin S: Prospective randomized clinical trial comparing the effectiveness of immediate arthroscopic stabilization versus immobilization and rehabilitation in first traumatic anterior dislocations of the shoulder: Long-term evaluation. *Arthroscopy* 2005;21:55-63.

   At long-term follow-up (mean, 75 months), rates of recurrent instability were 16% after arthroscopic stabilization and 47% after immobilization. Level of evidence: II.

7. Bottoni CR, Wilckens JH, DeBerardino TM, et al: A prospective, randomized evaluation of arthroscopic stabilization versus nonoperative treatment in patients with acute, traumatic, first-time shoulder dislocations. *Am J Sports Med* 2002;30:576-580.

   In a prospective, randomized study, rates of recurrent instability were 11% after arthroscopic stabilization and 75% after immobilization.

8. Farber AJ, Castillo R, Clough M, Bahk M, McFarland EG: Clinical assessment of three common tests for traumatic anterior shoulder instability. *J Bone Joint Surg Am* 2006;88:1467-1474.

   Anterior shoulder instability tests (anterior apprehension, relocation, and anterior drawer) were studied in 363 patients. The tests were found to be specific but not sensitive. Apprehension is a better criterion than pain in a positive apprehension or relocation test. Level of evidence: I.

9. Lo IK, Nonweiler B, Woolfrey M, Litchfield R, Kirkley A: An evaluation of the apprehension, relocation, and surprise tests for anterior shoulder instability. *Am J Sports Med* 2004;32:301-307.

   In three tests, the positive and negative predictive values of a feeling of apprehension were 93.6% and 71.9%, respectively. The surprise test was the single most accurate test (sensitivity = 63.9%, specificity = 98.9%).

10. Tzannes A, Paxinos A, Callanan M, Murrell GA: An assessment of the interexaminer reliability of tests for shoulder instability. *J Shoulder Elbow Surg* 2004; 13:18-23.

    The load-and-shift, sulcus, and provocative tests are reliable clinical tests for instability if the arm is carefully positioned. Apprehension should be used as the criterion, rather than pain, for a positive provocative test.

11. Karlsson J, Magnusson L, Ejerhed L, Hultenheim I, Lundin O, Kartus J: Comparison of open and arthroscopic stabilization for recurrent shoulder dislocation in patients with a Bankart lesion. *Am J Sports Med* 2001;29:538-542.

    In a prospective study of 119 posttraumatic unstable shoulders treated with open (53) or arthroscopic (66) stabilization, the failure rate was 10% for open and 15% for arthroscopic reconstruction at an average 28-month follow-up.

12. Guanche CA, Quick DC, Sodergren KM, Buss DD: Arthroscopic versus open reconstruction of the shoulder in patients with isolated Bankart lesions. *Am J Sports Med* 1996;24:144-148.

13. Boileau P, Villalba M, Héry JY, Balg F, Ahrens P, Neyton L: Risk factors for recurrence of shoulder instability after arthroscopic Bankart repair. *J Bone Joint Surg Am* 2006;88:1755-1763.

    Risk factors were evaluated after 91 consecutive arthroscopic Bankart repairs. At an average 36-month follow-up, the overall failure rate was 15.3%. The risk factors for recurrence included bone loss, inferior hyperlaxity, anteroinferior laxity, and use of three or fewer anchors. Level of evidence: IV.

14. Burkhart SS, De Beer JF: Traumatic glenohumeral bone defects and their relationship to failure of arthroscopic Bankart repairs: Significance of the inverted-pear glenoid and the humeral engaging Hill-Sachs lesion. *Arthroscopy* 2000;16:677-694.

15.  Kim SH, Ha KI, Cho YB, Ryu BD, Oh I: Arthroscopic anterior stabilization of the shoulder: Two to six-year follow-up. *J Bone Joint Surg Am* 2003;85-A:1511-1518.

    An early arthroscopic stabilization study in 167 patients found 95% good or excellent results and 4% failure. Recurrent instability was related to a Bankart lesion greater than 30% of the glenoid circumference. Level of evidence: IV.

16.  Carreira DS, Mazzocca AD, Oryhon J, Brown FM, Hayden JK, Romeo AA: A prospective outcome evaluation of arthroscopic Bankart repairs: Minimum 2-year follow-up. *Am J Sports Med* 2006;34: 771-777.

    In 85 consecutive patients treated with arthroscopic suture anchor repair, the recurrence rate was 10% and the average American Shoulder and Elbow Surgeons Index score was 92. All subscapularis muscle testing was normal. Level of evidence: IV.

17.  Marquardt B, Witt KA, Liem D, Steinbeck J, Pötzl W: Arthroscopic Bankart repair in traumatic anterior shoulder instability using a suture anchor technique. *Arthroscopy* 2006;22:931-936.

    In a prospective study with a minimum 2-year follow-up, 54 consecutive patients were treated with arthroscopic suture anchor stabilization. The overall redislocation rate was 7.5%; 86% returned to previous level of play. Level of evidence: IV.

18.  Kim SH, Ha KI, Kim SH: Bankart repair in traumatic anterior shoulder instability: Open versus arthroscopic technique. *Arthroscopy* 2002;18:755-763.

    At an average 39-month follow-up of 89 shoulders treated with open or arthroscopic stabilization, good or excellent results were found in 87% of the open and 92% of the arthroscopically repaired shoulders. In both groups, the rate of recurrent instability was 10%.

19.  Fabbriciani C, Milano G, Demontis A, Fadda S, Ziranu F, Mulas PD: Arthroscopic versus open treatment of Bankart lesion of the shoulder: A prospective randomized study. *Arthroscopy* 2004;20:456-462.

    At a minimum 2-year follow-up of 60 patients with an isolated Bankart lesion treated with open or arthroscopic stabilization, no recurrence was found. The only significant difference between the groups was a decreased range of motion in the open group. Level of evidence: I.

20.  Bottoni CR, Smith EL, Berkowitz MJ, Towle RB, Moore JH: Arthroscopic versus open shoulder stabilization for recurrent anterior instability: A prospective randomized clinical trial. *Am J Sports Med* 2006; 34:1730-1737.

    At a mean 32-month follow-up of 64 patients after open or arthroscopic stabilization, three failures were found (two open, one arthroscopic). The open stabilization pa-

tients had a greater loss of motion. Subjective evaluations were equal between groups. Level of evidence: I.

21.  Alberta FG, Elattrache NS, Mihata T, McGarry MH, Tibone JE, Lee TQ: Arthroscopic anteroinferior suture plication resulting in decreased glenohumeral translation and external rotation: Study of a cadaver model. *J Bone Joint Surg Am* 2006;88:179-187.

    Testing of a 10-mm suture plication in six cadaver shoulders found a decrease in external rotation and a shift of the center of rotation posteriorly and inferiorly. There was a decrease in anterior (61%), posterior (13%), and inferior (3%) translation.

22.  Gerber C, Werner CM, Macy JC, Jacob HA, Nyffeler RW: Effect of selective capsulorrhaphy on the passive range of motion of the glenohumeral joint. *J Bone Joint Surg Am* 2003;85-A:48-55.

    Anterosuperior capsular plication reduced external rotation by 30° in adduction. Anteroinferior plication reduced abduction by 19° and external rotation by 20°. Posterosuperior plication reduced internal rotation by 16° in adduction. Inferior plication restricted abduction by 28°.

23.  Cohen SB, Wiley W, Goradia VK, Pearson S, Miller MD: Anterior capsulorrhaphy: An in vitro comparison of volume reduction. Arthroscopic plication versus open capsular shift. *Arthroscopy* 2005;21: 659-664.

    Reduction of shoulder volume was evaluated in 15 cadaver shoulders, of which 7 received arthroscopic plication and 8 received open lateral shift. Arthroscopic plication resulted in an average reduction of 22.8% and open lateral shift, an average of 49.9%. Level of evidence: IV.

24.  Karas SG, Creighton RA, DeMorat GJ: Glenohumeral volume reduction in arthroscopic shoulder reconstruction: A cadaveric analysis of suture plication and thermal capsulorrhaphy. *Arthroscopy* 2004;20: 179-184.

    Reduction of shoulder volume was evaluated in 10 cadaver shoulders, of which 5 received arthroscopic suture plication and 5 received thermal capsulorrhaphy. Suture plication resulted in an average reduction of 19.0%; thermal capsulorrhaphy, an average of 33.4%; and combined treatment, an average of 41.0%.

25.  Selecky MT, Tibone JE, Yang BY, McMahon PJ, Lee TQ: Glenohumeral joint translation after arthroscopic thermal capsuloplasty of the rotator interval. *J Shoulder Elbow Surg* 2003;12:139-143.

    Isolated rotator interval thermal capsulorrhaphy decreased anterior translation by almost 30%.

26.  Eakin CL, Dvirnak P, Miller CM, Hawkins RJ: The relationship of the axillary nerve to arthroscopically placed capsulolabral sutures: An anatomic study. *Am J Sports Med* 1998;26:505-509.

27.  Price MR, Tillett ED, Acland RD, Nettleton GS: Determining the relationship of the axillary nerve to the

shoulder joint capsule from an arthroscopic perspective. *J Bone Joint Surg Am* 2004;86-A:2135-2142.

In nine cadaver shoulders, the closest point between the axillary nerve and the glenoid rim was at the 6 o'clock position, with an average distance of 12.4 mm. Throughout its course, the nerve was on average 2.5 mm from the IGHLC.

28. Lo IK, Lind CC, Burkhart SS: Glenohumeral arthroscopy portals established using an outside-in technique: Neurovascular anatomy at risk. *Arthroscopy* 2004;20:596-602.

Examination of the neurovascular structures at risk during placement of glenohumeral arthroscopy portals using an outside-in technique in five cadaver shoulders found that, except for the cephalic vein, all structures were located more than 20 mm from all portals.

29. D'Alessandro DF, Bradley JP, Fleischli JE, Connor PM: Prospective evaluation of thermal capsulorrhaphy for shoulder instability: Indications and results, two- to five-year follow-up. *Am J Sports Med* 2004;32:21-33.

At an average 38-month follow-up, a prospective evaluation of 84 unstable shoulders treated with arthroscopic thermal capsulorrhaphy found excellent results in 33 patients (39%), satisfactory results in 20 (24%), and unsatisfactory results in 31 (37%).

30. Chen S, Haen PS, Walton J, Murrell GA: The effects of thermal capsular shrinkage on the outcomes of arthroscopic stabilization for primary anterior shoulder instability. *Am J Sports Med* 2005;33:705-711.

In an evaluation of the outcomes of 72 patients treated with arthroscopic stabilization using Suretac II tacks, either alone (32) or augmented with thermal capsulorrhaphy (40), the failure rates were found to be similar. Level of evidence: III.

31. McFarland EG, Kim TK, Banchasuek P, McCarthy EF: Histologic evaluation of the shoulder capsule in normal shoulders, unstable shoulders, and after failed thermal capsulorrhaphy. *Am J Sports Med* 2002;30:636-642.

In a histologic evaluation of seven shoulders after unsuccessful thermal capsulorrhaphy, the capsules of 71% were subjectively felt to be thin and attenuated. Denuded synovium (100%), subsynovial edema (43%), and changes in the collagen layer (100%) were found.

32. Greis PE, Burks RT, Schickendantz MS, Sandmeier R: Axillary nerve injury after thermal capsular shrinkage of the shoulder. *J Shoulder Elbow Surg* 2001;10:231-235.

In four patients, axillary nerve injury was observed after radiofrequency capsular shrinkage of the shoulder. Heat penetration through the capsule to the nerve is postulated as the most likely cause of injury.

33. McCarty EC, Warren RF, Deng XH, Craig EV, Potter H: Temperature along the axillary nerve during radiofrequency-induced thermal capsular shrinkage. *Am J Sports Med* 2004;32:909-914.

Arthroscopic thermal capsular shrinkage was found to cause an increase in the temperature of the axillary nerve and its branches in 11 of 15 cadaver shoulders tested in different arm positions.

34. Good CR, Shindle MK, Kelly BT, Wanich T, Warren RF: Glenohumeral chondrolysis after shoulder arthroscopy with thermal capsulorrhaphy. *Arthroscopy* 2007;23:797.

Eight patients developed chondrolysis after thermal energy was used. It is speculated that heating of the joint fluid from any source plays a role in cartilage death.

35. Lieurance RK, Pflaster DS, Abbott D, Nottage WM: Failure characteristics of various arthroscopically tied knots. *Clin Orthop Relat Res* 2003;408:311-318.

Six arthroscopic knots were tested, and performance was found to be similar. The mode of failure in all constructs was widening of the suture loops beyond 3 mm.

36. Abbi G, Espinoza L, Odell T, Mahar A, Pedowitz R: Evaluation of 5 knots and 2 suture materials for arthroscopic rotator cuff repair: Very strong sutures can still slip. *Arthroscopy* 2006;22:38-43.

A comparison of five arthroscopic knots using FiberWire (Arthrex, Naples, FL) and Ethibond found no differences based on knot type. The average load to failure was 276 N with FiberWire and 111 N with Ethibond. However, early failures were seen with FiberWire because of slippage at low tensions.

37. Elkousy HA, Sekiya JK, Stabile KJ, McMahon PJ: A biomechanical comparison of arthroscopic sliding and sliding-locking knots. *Arthroscopy* 2005;21:204-210.

Several arthroscopic sliding and sliding-locking knots were compared with the square knot. All sliding and sliding-locking knots backed with three half-hitches alternating posts and directions of the throws had load at failure comparable to that of the square knot.

38. Barber FA, Herbert MA, Coons DA, Boothby MH: Sutures and suture anchors: Update 2006. *Arthroscopy* 2006; 22:1063.

A comparison of several newer suture anchor designs found higher failure strength for the latest generation suture materials, compared with traditional braided polyester.

39. Burkart A, Imhoff AB, Roscher E: Foreign-body reaction to the bioabsorbable suretac device. *Arthroscopy* 2000;16:91-95.

40. Dejong ES, DeBerardino TM, Brooks DE, Judson K: In vivo comparison of a metal versus a biodegradable suture anchor. *Arthroscopy* 2004;20:511-516.

The strength of absorbable and metal anchor repairs was tested after 0, 6, and 12 weeks of healing, and no differences were found.

41. Barber FA, Herbert MA, Richards DP: Sutures and suture anchors: Update 2003. *Arthroscopy* 2003;19: 985-990.

    Common sutures and suture anchors were tested. Newer, nonabsorbable sutures were found to be significantly stronger than same-sized Ethibond sutures. Screw anchors had higher load values than nonscrew anchors. All anchors were stronger than the suture for which they were designed.

42. Mueller MB, Fredrich HH, Steinhauser E, Schreiber U, Arians A, Imhoff AB: Biomechanical evaluation of different suture anchors for the stabilization of anterior labrum lesions. *Arthroscopy* 2005;21: 611-619.

    Bankart repair strengths using different fixation devices were evaluated in 28 cadaver shoulders. Statistically significant differences were found between 2.4- and 2.8-mm anchors; the smaller diameter anchors had weaker fixation strength values.

43. Sassmannshausen G, Sukay M, Mair SD: Broken or dislodged poly-L-lactic acid bioabsorbable tacks in patients after SLAP lesion surgery. *Arthroscopy* 2006;22:615-619.

    Six patients had postsurgical pain after repair of a superior labrum anterior and posterior lesion repair using a Suretac device. All shoulders had evidence of fixation failure, with no labral healing. Two patients had chondral damage. Level of evidence: IV.

44. DeBerardino TM, Arciero RA, Taylor DC, Uhorchak JM: Prospective evaluation of arthroscopic stabilization of acute, initial anterior shoulder dislocations in young athletes: Two- to five-year follow-up. *Am J Sports Med* 2001;29:586-592.

    At midterm follow-up of 49 dislocations in young athletes treated with arthroscopic repair, the failure rate was 12%. The risk factors were bilateral shoulder instability, a 2+ sulcus sign, and poor capsulolabral tissue.

45. Marquardt B, Witt KA, Götze C, Liem D, Steinbeck J, Pötzl W: Long-term results of arthroscopic Bankart repair with a bioabsorbable tack. *Am J Sports Med* 2006;34:1906-1910.

    At long-term (8.7-year) follow-up of 18 patients with instability who were treated using Suretac, 5.6% required further surgery. The average American Shoulder and Elbow Surgeons Index score was 92. Only 64% had returned to sports. Level of evidence: IV.

46. Lo IK, Parten PM, Burkhart SS: The inverted pear glenoid: An indicator of significant glenoid bone loss. *Arthroscopy* 2004;20:169-174.

    Most of 53 patients with anterior instability were found to have some bone loss anteriorly. The inverted pear glenoid represents bone loss of at least 25% of the width of the inferior glenoid.

47. Burkhart SS, Debeer JF, Tehrany AM, Parten PM: Quantifying glenoid bone loss arthroscopically in shoulder instability. *Arthroscopy* 2002;18:488-491.

    An anatomic investigation in 56 patients and 10 cadaver shoulders identified the bare spot of the glenoid as the center of the inferior glenoid. This finding provides a useful guide for arthroscopic quantification of glenoid bone loss.

48. Porcellini G, Campi F, Paladini P: Arthroscopic approach to acute bony Bankart lesion. *Arthroscopy* 2002;18:764-769.

    At a minimum 2-year follow-up of 25 patients after arthroscopic repair of an acute bony Bankart lesion, the success rate was 92%, with no recurrences, and 23 had returned to their previous sport.

49. Sugaya H, Moriishi J, Kanisawa I, Tsuchiya A: Arthroscopic osseous Bankart repair for chronic recurrent traumatic anterior glenohumeral instability. *J Bone Joint Surg Am* 2005;87:1752-1760.

    At a mean 34-month follow-up, 42 shoulders with an osseous Bankart lesion were evaluated. The average bone loss on CT was 24.8%. Thirty-nine had a good or excellent result, and 35 had returned to their previous level of sports participation. Level of evidence: IV.

50. Spang JT, Karas SG: The HAGL lesion: An arthroscopic technique for repair of humeral avulsion of the glenohumeral ligaments. *Arthroscopy* 2005;21: 498-502.

    A technique for arthroscopic repair of humeral avulsion of the glenohumeral ligaments is described.

51. Richards DP, Burkhart SS: Arthroscopic humeral avulsion of the glenohumeral ligaments (HAGL) repair. *Arthroscopy* 2004;20(suppl 2):134-141.

    A technique for arthroscopic repair of humeral avulsion of the glenohumeral ligaments is described.

52. Kim SH, Ha KI, Jung MW, Lim MS, Kim YM, Park JH: Accelerated rehabilitation after arthroscopic Bankart repair for selected cases: A prospective randomized clinical study. *Arthroscopy* 2003;19: 722-731.

    A prospective, randomized study involving early active range of motion and strengthening found no differences in outcomes. Patients in the accelerated rehabilitation group had less pain and less time to return to work.

53. Uhorchak JM, Arciero RA, Huggard D, Taylor DC: Recurrent shoulder instability after open reconstruction in athletes involved in collision and contact sports. *Am J Sports Med* 2000;28:794-799.

54. Roberts SN, Taylor DE, Brown JN, Hayes MG, Saies A: Open and arthroscopic techniques for the treatment of traumatic anterior shoulder instability in Australian rules football players. *J Shoulder Elbow Surg* 1999;8:403-409.

55. Mazzocca AD, Brown FM Jr, Carreira DS, Hayden J, Romeo AA: Arthroscopic anterior shoulder stabilization of collision and contact athletes. *Am J Sports Med* 2005;33:52-60.

In 18 contact or collision athletes treated with arthroscopic shoulder stabilization, the failure rate was 11%. All patients were able to return to their previous level of sports activity. Level of evidence: IV.

56. Rhee YG, Ha JH, Cho NS: Anterior shoulder stabilization in collision athletes: Arthroscopic versus open Bankart repair. *Am J Sports Med* 2006;34:979-985.

No functional differences were noted between patients who underwent open (32 patients) or arthroscopic (16 patients) stabilization. The failure rate was 25% after arthroscopy and 12.5% after open stabilization. Level of evidence: IV.

57. Cho NS, Hwang JC, Rhee YG: Arthroscopic stabilization in anterior shoulder instability: Collision athletes versus noncollision athletes. *Arthroscopy* 2006; 22:947-953.

At a mean 62-month follow-up after arthroscopic stabilization in 29 athletes, the failure rate was 28.6% in the 14 collision athletes and 6.7% in the noncollision athletes. Level of evidence: IV.

58. Pagnani MJ, Dome DC: Surgical treatment of traumatic anterior shoulder instability in American football players. *J Bone Joint Surg Am* 2002;84-A: 711-715.

At an average 37-month follow-up of 58 American football players after open stabilization of recurrent dislocation (47) or recurrent subluxation (11), the average American Shoulder and Elbow Surgeons Index score was 97, and 52 had returned to play. Treatment was unsuccessful in 2 patients.

# Chapter 11

# Shoulder Injuries in the Throwing Athlete

Jeffrey R. Dugas, MD

*James R. Andrews, MD

## Introduction

Overhead throwing is among the fastest of all human motions. Recorded rotational speeds approach 7,000°/s.[1] The overhead throwing motion in any sport is accomplished by generating potential energy and transforming it into kinetic energy transmitted to the thrown object. In baseball and some other sports, repetitive overhead throwing places enormous stress on the soft-tissue and bony structures of the upper extremity. The common injuries among throwing athletes include a labral tear, rotator cuff strain or tear, biceps tendinitis, and capsular injury.

## Biomechanics

The standard overhead throwing motion can be described in terms of six separate phases (Figure 1). The time required to complete all six phases is approximately 2 seconds, three fourths of which is consumed by the preacceleration phases.[2-4] During the first phase, called the windup, the body readies itself for the throw; there is very little activity and little stress on the upper extremity. In the second phase, early cocking, the throwing arm is abducted by the deltoid and moved by the rotator cuff into an externally rotated position. At the end of the early cocking phase, the arm is at the top of the motion. In the late cocking phase, the arm begins to move toward the target as the lead leg contacts the ground. The arm achieves maximum external rotation, and scapular retraction allows the glenoid to become a stable base for the humerus. As the humeral head approaches maximum external rotation, the anterior structures are taut, leading to an obligate posterior translation of the humeral head. The rotator cuff musculature generates a compression force of 650 N.[1] The acceleration phase begins as the arm initiates internal rotation and ends with release of the ball. The angular velocity of the upper extremity is greatest during the acceleration phase. Despite this tremendous movement, little stress is imposed on the shoulder musculature during acceleration.[5] The deceleration phase begins immediately after the ball is released and ends when humeral internal rotation ceases. Large loads are generated by the rotator cuff muscles as the rapidly rotating arm is slowed and stopped;[1,4] the compressive load on the joint exceeds 1,000 N.[3,5] Any energy not transferred to the ball is dissipated. The follow-through phase concludes the throwing motion. The body returns to a more balanced, stable position. The joint compression forces decrease to less than 400 N.[1,4]

Overhead throwing motions are not identical, and varying arm angles and pitch types probably place different stresses on the shoulder. In a prospective evaluation of 476 young pitchers (age 9 to 14 years), throwing curveballs was found to increase the risk of shoulder pain by 52%.[6] High-speed digitizing was used to study

**Figure 1**  Time-lapsed photograph of the phases of the overhead throwing motion: *(left to right)* windup, early cocking, late cocking, acceleration, deceleration, and follow-through. Most athletes report pain during either the late cocking and early acceleration phases or the deceleration phase.

---

*James R. Andrews, MD is a consultant or employee for Smith & Nephew and Arthrotek.*

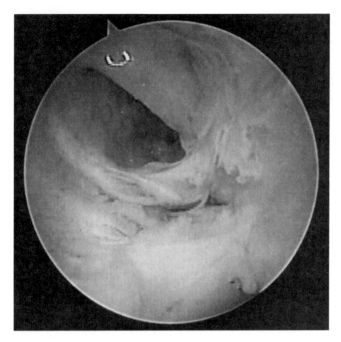

**Figure 2** Arthroscopic view from the posterior portal showing a full-thickness tear of the anteroinferior capsule in a 32-year-old professional pitcher who had reported pain during the late cocking and deceleration phases.

the shoulders of collegiate pitchers; no significant differences were found in the joint loads generated by throwing fastballs and curveballs.[7]

Bony architectural changes in the dominant shoulder of throwing athletes have been a subject of recent attention. For example, humeral and glenoid retroversion were found to be significantly increased in the dominant shoulder of throwing athletes, compared with the nondominant shoulder.[8,9] Retroversion was found to be similar in the dominant and nondominant shoulders of nonthrowing athletes. In throwing athletes, the total arc of motion of the throwing shoulder was not significantly different from the total arc of motion of the nonthrowing shoulder, although the throwing shoulder had significantly increased external rotation and a corresponding decrease in internal rotation. In both throwing and nonthrowing athletes, the total arc of motion in the dominant shoulder was approximately 190°. Another study found that osseous differences between the throwing and nonthrowing shoulders are present when a young athlete reaches maturity. The humeral retroversion of the throwing shoulder is maintained over time, but it decreases with age in the nonthrowing shoulder.[10]

Although increased external rotation is necessary to effectively throw, it provides an opportunity for significant injury. The cause of common undersurface rotator cuff, capsule, and labral pathology is controversial. Fraying and tearing of the superior labrum and the articular undersurface of the rotator cuff has been termed internal impingement; at maximum external rotation, the humeral head and glenoid pinch the posterosuperior labrum and cuff and thereby cause injury.[11] The position of the biceps tendon as the shoulder reaches maximum external rotation is called the peel-back phenomenon. In this position, the biceps tendon is rotated posteriorly, providing tangential pull on its labral attachment to the glenoid.[12] The peel-back phenomenon is a possible cause of type II labral tears in throwers. A biomechanical study provided support for this theory in finding that type II superior labrum anterior and posterior (SLAP) lesions are readily created when stress is placed on the biceps in the externally rotated position; in contrast, tension on the tendon when the arm is in neutral position does not cause this injury.[13] A cadaver study found that decreased internal rotation caused by posterior capsular contracture in the presence of increased external rotation prevents the humeral head from achieving its normal posteroinferior position during the cocking phase of throwing.[14] Instead, the humeral head ends in a posterosuperior position, which may lead to superior labral and posterior rotator cuff pathology. Another hypothesis suggests that the stress on the superior labrum is greatest during the deceleration phase of throwing, and therefore longitudinal tension on the biceps causes typical labral pathology.[15]

The pathomechanics of throwing continue to be studied. Labrum and rotator cuff pathology in the throwing shoulder are probably caused by a combination of mechanisms.

## Pathology

### Capsule and Labrum

The throwing shoulder usually has increased external rotation and concomitantly decreased internal rotation. However, its total arc of motion should equal that of the opposite shoulder. A decrease in total arc of motion is a cause for concern. In many patients, external rotation is preserved and internal rotation is diminished; posterior capsular contracture is a possible etiology of this loss of motion. In the absence of significant trauma, capsular tearing in throwers is uncommon. In a fielder, diving for a batted ball or into a base can lead to a significant shoulder injury, such as a dislocation or combined cuff and capsular injury. In a pitcher, complete capsular disruption can occur, although it is rare. Such an injury can lead to microinstability or macroinstability, capsular synovitis, and altered joint biomechanics because of increased stress on the rotator cuff (Figure 2). No large series of throwers with these types of injuries has been studied.

Tears involving the superior labrum are very common in overhead throwing athletes.[16] Diagnosis and management have improved during the 20 years since the first report of such injuries; MRI has permitted the diagnosis of labral pathology to be confirmed in more than 95% of patients.[17] The most common type of labral

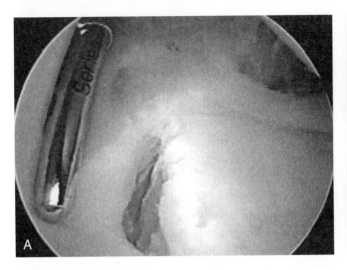
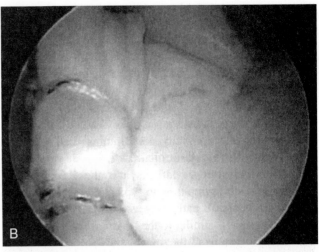

**Figure 3** Arthroscopic views of a typical type II SLAP lesion in a throwing athlete. **A,** Before repair, the glenoid rim is débrided. **B,** The repair is accomplished by reattaching the labrum at the articular margin, rather than further down on the glenoid neck.

pathology in throwers is a type II SLAP tear, in which the superior labrum is detached from the glenoid and the tear involves the biceps anchor[18] (Figure 3). In some patients, the tear extends to the posterior side of the glenoid. In the absence of posterior subluxation or dislocation, true posterior instability is rare in throwers. Labral detachment is more common than dislocation in throwers, and fraying of the labrum without detachment is also common. Fraying typically occurs in the posterosuperior labrum and does not involve the biceps tendon.

Combined injuries of the capsule and labrum are uncommon and difficult to detect. A single traumatic event or continued, prolonged throwing after an initial injury can lead to a combined injury. There have been no peer-reviewed reports on return to play after a combined injury.

### Rotator Cuff

Full-thickness tears of the rotator cuff are rare in throwing athletes, although partial-thickness tears are common. The possibility of a cuff tear combined with instability must be considered if a full-thickness tear is present. Conversely, the presence of a rotator cuff tear should be suspected in a thrower with a dislocation. The most common rotator cuff injury in a throwing athlete is a partial articular surface tear involving the supraspinatus, infraspinatus, or both. A bursal-sided injury to the rotator cuff is unusual, unless the humeral head was forced superiorly, with the cuff striking the undersurface of the acromion.

Rotator cuff weakness is common in the injured thrower. Atrophy of the rotator cuff musculature is most common in the infraspinatus, and its presence should lead the physician to look for neurogenic causes, such as compression on the suprascapular nerve by a ganglion cyst arising from a labral tear. Muscle atrophy may also be caused by impingement or compression on a neurovascular structure within the quadrilateral space or, at a higher level, in the brachial plexus or cervical spine. Weakness of the infraspinatus or supraspinatus often occurs in a thrower who is injured or fatigued, and it should be addressed through active rest and gradual return to throwing.

Glenoid osteochondritis dissecans (OCD), subacromial bursitis and impingement, and biceps tendinitis are among the less common causes of shoulder pain in throwers. Glenoid OCD is rarely reported in throwers and may not be recognized until arthroscopy is performed. The pain is poorly localized within the shoulder, and rest from exercise rarely provides significant improvement. As seen during arthroscopy, the lesion is typically located on the posterior glenoid and is not associated with a labral detachment (Figure 4). The preferred treatment is removal of the loose cartilage fragment, with abrasion of the bony bed to remove the fibrinous tissue and stimulate bleeding.

The symptoms of subacromial and rotator cuff pathology can be difficult to distinguish, although high-quality MRI studies can be helpful. In the absence of intra-articular pathology, a subacromial source should be considered. Relief of symptoms after a diagnostic injection into the subacromial space helps to confirm the diagnosis. Subsequent injection with a corticosteroid may be used, followed by short-term rest, before return to throwing. In a thrower who is older than age 30 years, a continuation of symptoms may require subacromial decompression and bursectomy. A limited acromioplasty is preferable because of the stress placed on the acromion and consequent risk of fracture. Biceps tendinitis is treated using nonsteroidal anti-inflammatory drugs, and, if necessary, corticosteroid injections, in addition to physical therapy and modalities such as iontophoresis, ultrasonography, and electrical stimulation.

## Treatment

### Nonsurgical Treatment

Many throwers with labral or rotator cuff symptoms are initially treated with a 7- to 10-day period of rest from throwing and a course of nonsteroidal anti-inflammatory drugs, followed by rotator cuff strengthening exercises. During this period of active rest, the shoulder is building strength. When the athlete returns to throwing, an accelerated throwing program is initiated, beginning with long tossing and progressing to mound throwing. Inability to progress through this program to normal throwing suggests the presence of a more serious injury. For a thrower whose initial improvement is followed by a recurrence of symptoms, treatment should consist of 3 to 6 weeks of active rest. A lack of improvement after 6 weeks of rest indicates that further investigation is required. MRI, with or without contrast, is the preferred diagnostic imaging method for the thrower's shoulder.[17,19-21]

### Surgical Treatment

Surgical intervention should be considered only after nonsurgical measures have proved unsuccessful. Examination under anesthesia should precede any surgical procedure. Arthroscopic examination of the glenohumeral joint under anesthesia may be useful, using standard shoulder portals. When the joint is insufflated and flow is established, the articular surfaces of the joint, with the labrum, biceps tendon, rotator cuff, and capsule, are examined. Specific attention should be paid to the status of the superior labrum and biceps anchor complex, which is frequently pathologic in the thrower. The joint capsule should be inspected from both the anterior and posterior portals. Any loose bodies can be removed, and labrum and rotator cuff fraying can be gently débrided (Figure 5).

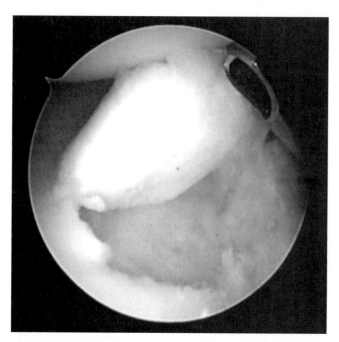

**Figure 4** This typical glenoid OCD is located on the posterior aspect of the glenoid without labral detachment. After excision of the fragment, the bed has been abraded to stimulate the growth of fibrocartilaginous scar tissue.

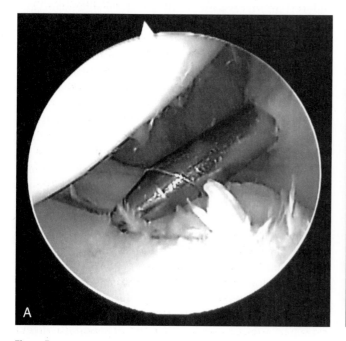 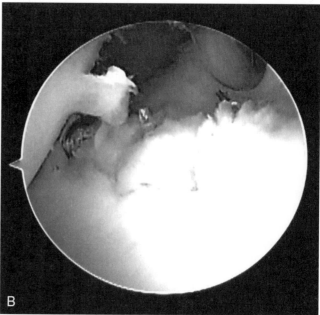

**Figure 5** Arthroscopic views of a frayed posterosuperior labrum in a throwing athlete before **(A)** and after **(B)** débridement. Standard anterior shond posterior portals are used.

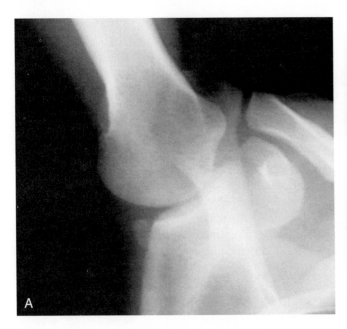
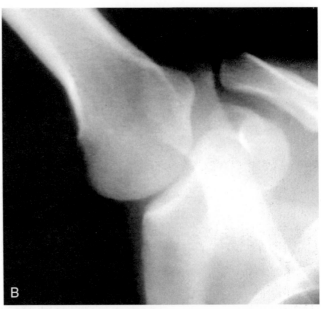

**Figure 6**   West Point plain radiographic views of a shoulder with thrower's exostosis before **(A)** and after **(B)** arthroscopic débridement.

Labral débridement in the arthroscopic treatment of throwers has had mixed results. The rate of good or excellent functional outcomes after labral débridement was 91% in throwers who did not have glenohumeral instability; in those with instability, the rate of fair or poor outcomes was 75%.[22] In another study, 72% of patients had relief during the first year, but only 7% had a good outcome at final follow-up.[23] At 1-year follow-up of 52 consecutive patients, those treated with superior labral débridement had a 78% rate of satisfaction, but only 30% of those treated with anteroinferior labral débridement were satisfied.[24] At 2-year follow up, the numbers decreased to 63% and 25%, respectively. In 46 athletes who underwent labral débridement, 54% had a good or excellent result at an average 31-month follow-up, and 75% of a subset of professional-level throwers achieved a good or excellent result.[25] Outcomes were not correlated with the location of pathology, mechanism of injury, or presence of shoulder laxity or rotator cuff disease. At 48-month follow-up after arthroscopic labral débridement, 62% of baseball pitchers had unimpeded throwing activities.[26] In these studies, the extent of labral pathology was not uniform; some of the studied athletes may have had pathology more severe than fraying or partial-thickness tearing.

Interest in arthroscopic repair of the labrum in athletes has increased during the past 20 years. In a study conducted during the early 1990s, 12 of 13 throwing athletes (92%) returned to preinjury function when a bioabsorbable tack was used because of problems with metallic anchors.[27] In another study using a bioabsorbable tack, only 9 of 17 patients (53%) returned to sports activities.[28] The use of tack fixation in the shoulder has be-

come less common with the advent of arthroscopic suturing techniques and innovations in suture anchor technology. A report of arthroscopic suture anchor fixation of labral tears found that 91% of patients returned to their preinjury level of activity. However, throwing athletes had significantly lower shoulder scores than nonthrowers, and a lower percentage (22%) reported complete recovery of throwing function.[29] Of 31 patients who underwent trans–rotator cuff suture anchor fixation of a superior labral tear, only 16 of 31 returned to preinjury status.[30] At a 41-month follow-up of 40 patients, 75% of the overhead athletes had regained their preinjury functional levels.[31]

Most surgeons now use absorbable suture anchors and nonabsorbable suture material. Many prefer arthroscopic tying of knots, although knotless technology is improving. Studies have found that throwing athletes are at a high risk of superior labral injury and have a low rate of return to preinjury status after surgical repair. The nature of the pathology and the demands on the throwing athlete's shoulder contribute to the unpredictable results of repair. Throwing mechanics, rehabilitation after surgery, and concomitant pathology may be contributing factors.

Thrower's exostosis, or Bennett's lesion of the shoulder, is a bony posteroinferior prominence at the posterior insertion of the inferior glenohumeral ligament. Repetitive throwing may cause traction on this location and lead to formation of an osteophyte. Patients with thrower's exostosis may report posterior shoulder pain during ball release (Figure 6). The joint capsule can be incised arthroscopically with a blunt or sharp instrument on the posterior side of the labrum, directly over the

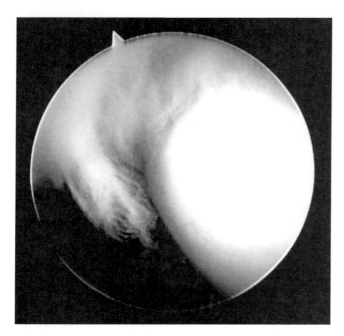

**Figure 7** Undersurface fraying of the supraspinatus in a throwing athlete, representing less than 25% of the cuff thickness. The tear was débrided using a shaver.

exostosis, and the prominence can be burred or shaved down to the level of the native glenoid neck. The defect in the capsule is not repaired to avoid iatrogenically increased tension on the inferior glenohumeral ligament. The prevalence of thrower's exostosis among major league throwers was reported to be more than 20%, based on preseason radiographs; most players do not develop symptoms.[32] In one series of high-level throwers treated for thrower's exostosis, only 55% returned to their preinjury level of competition.[33]

The most common rotator cuff injury is undersurface tearing or fraying involving the supraspinatus, infraspinatus, or both (Figure 7). Such an injury can involve less than 25% or as much as 50% of the thickness of the cuff tissue. The usual treatment is arthroscopic débridement of the tear tissue. In 43 athletes treated with cuff débridement, two groups were distinguished. The first group had acute onset of pain without instability or labral pathology; 86% of these 14 athletes had a satisfactory result, and 64% returned to their preinjury performance level. The second group had a more insidious onset of symptoms, more labral pathology, and worse results; only 45% of the 29 patients returned to their preinjury sports performance level.[34] Nine athletes with subacromial inflammation and no instability had 100% pain relief, although only four returned to their preinjury level. In 75 throwing athletes who underwent arthroscopic débridement for undersurface cuff pathology, only 40% were satisfied with the result, and none of the professional or international-level throwers returned to competition. Satisfaction with the procedure was directly related to the ability to return to competitive

throwing and was inversely related to the preinjury level of play.[35]

The results of rotator cuff repair in athletes have been mixed. In 16 professional players treated with a mini-open repair of a full-thickness rotator cuff tear, only 1 of the 12 pitchers (8%) was able to return to professional-level pitching, although all 12 had a successful return of rotator cuff function with good pain relief.[36] Because of the poor results of open procedures, all-arthroscopic techniques are currently being used. A transtendinous repair is the preferred procedure for a high-grade partial-thickness rotator cuff injury. Five of six overhead throwing athletes (83%) returned to throwing after treatment with transtendinous suturing; two (33%) returned at the same level, and three (50%) returned at a lower level.[37] Eight of nine throwers (89%) who underwent transtendinous repair of a partial-thickness rotator cuff tear had returned to their earlier level of play at a minimum 1-year follow-up.[38]

Because standard surgical approaches have not provided outstanding results, nonsurgical treatment is preferred for a partial-thickness tear in a throwing athlete. Interest in decreasing hyperrotation has led to the development of procedures to limit capsular motion, including thermal capsulorrhaphy and capsular plication. Thermal shrinkage was described as a means of limiting rotational laxity during surgery for standard thrower's pathology.[39] Thermal energy was applied as an adjunct to standard treatment, not as an alternative, and thermal shrinkage improved the rate of return to competitive throwing at the same or a higher level from 61% to 87% at 2-year follow-up.[39] However, complications of thermal capsulorrhaphy have led to some loss of interest in this modality. Capsular plication may prove to be a viable option for treating hyperlaxity in the thrower's shoulder.

Nonsurgical measures should be used extensively for some patients to maximize the potential for healing without surgical intervention. However, some athletes cannot be successfully treated nonsurgically. Surgical treatment should relieve pain without decreasing the thrower's strength and stamina, but a return to play cannot be guaranteed. Much remains to be learned about treating this group of patients.

## Shoulder Injuries in Young Throwing Athletes

Youth baseball injuries appear to be increasing in frequency. Shoulder pathology requiring surgery is occurring more frequently in the shoulders of adolescents. Some years ago, such pathology was limited to the shoulders of elite throwers at upper levels of play. Baseball and other overhead throwing sports are considered developmental sports because the bodily adaptations required for efficient and effective throwing with high velocity tend to occur during the developmental years. An increase in external rotation in the throwing shoulder is necessary to place the young thrower's arm in a position to deliver the ball with sufficient velocity. As the body matures and strengthens with age, the ability to throw harder and for longer periods increases, along with the risk of injury.

It is rare to see a high-level throwing athlete who did not compete at a young age. However, these young athletes are at substantial risk of injury. The nature of the activity, as well as the amount of repetition, can lead to significant pathology. Pitch counts and inning limits are becoming common in youth baseball leagues, and the governing bodies of organized baseball are establishing guidelines. To help reverse the trend toward injury in progressively younger players, physicians must educate young athletic patients, as well as the community, about the risks of year-round baseball schedules, excessively frequent throwing, and dangerous patterns of throwing mechanics.

## Summary

The thrower's shoulder requires a delicate balance of power, flexibility, and stability. The forces acting on the shoulder are tremendous and impart a significant risk of injury. Nonsurgical treatment is usually successful in returning an athlete to competition, although in some patients surgical intervention should be cautiously undertaken. Many youth baseball injuries can be avoided by paying careful attention to pitch counts and proper mechanics and by avoiding year-round baseball.

## Annotated References

1. Fleisig GS, Andrews JR, Dillman CJ, et al: Kinetics of baseball pitching with implications about injury mechanisms. *Am J Sports Med* 1995;23:233-239.

2. Fleisig GS, Dillman CJ, Andrews JR: Proper mechanics for baseball pitching. *Clin Sports Med* 1989;1: 151-170.

3. Pappas AM, Zawacki RM, Sullivan TJ: Biomechanics of baseball pitching: A preliminary report. *Am J Sports Med* 1985;13:216-222.

4. Dillman CJ, Fleisig GS, Andrews JR: Biomechanics of pitching with emphasis upon shoulder kinematics. *J Orthop Sports Phys Ther* 1993;18:402-408.

5. Jobe FW, Moynes DR, Tibone JE, et al: An EMG analysis of the shoulder in pitching: A second report. *Am J Sports Med* 1984;12:218-220.

6. Lyman S, Fleisig GS, Andrews JR, Osinski ED: Effect of pitch type, pitch count, and pitching mechanics on risk of elbow and shoulder pain in youth baseball pitchers. *Am J Sports Med* 2002;30:463-468.

   In 476 pitchers ages 9 to 14 years who were followed for one baseball season, the curveball was associated with a 52% increased risk of shoulder pain, and the slider was associated with an 86% increased risk of elbow pain. A significant relationship was established between the number of pitches thrown per game or per season and the rate of shoulder or elbow pain.

7. Fleisig GS, Kinglsey DS, Loftice JW, et al: Kinetic comparison among the fastball, curveball, change-up and slider in collegiate baseball pitchers. *Am J Sports Med* 2006;34:423-430.

   In 21 healthy collegiate pitchers studied using high-speed videotape, significant kinematic but little kinetic difference was found between the curveball and fastball. The change-up had lower joint kinetics and lower angular velocities than any other pitch. Data were inconclusive for the slider.

8. Crockett HC, Gross LB, Wilk KE, et al: Osseous adaptation and range of motion at the glenohumeral joint in professional baseball pitchers. *Am J Sports Med* 2002;30:20-26.

   Twenty-five professional throwers and 25 nonthrowing athletes underwent upper extremity CT to determine glenoid and humeral head version. In the nonthrowers, average humeral head retroversion between dominant and nondominant arms was not statistically different. In the throwers, the humeral retroversion in the throwing arm was significantly increased compared with the nonthrowing arm, and external rotation in abduction also was increased in the throwing arm.

9. Reagan KM, Meister K, Horodyski MB, Werner DW: Humeral retroversion and its relation to glenohumeral rotation in the shoulder of collegiate baseball players. *Am J Sports Med* 2002;30:354-360.

   In 54 asymptomatic collegiate baseball players, the throwing shoulder had increased external rotation and increased retroversion compared with the nonthrowing shoulder.

10. Yamamoto N, Itoi E, Minagawa H, et al: Why is the humeral retroversion of throwing athletes greater in the dominant shoulders than in non-dominant shoulders? *J Shoulder Elbow Surg* 2006;15:571-575.

    Sixty-six youth baseball players (average age, 12 years) underwent ultrasonography to determine humeral version. The results suggested a decrease in retroversion in the nonthrowing shoulder with increasing age. The conclusion was that humeral retroversion does not increase in the throwing shoulder, but instead it fails to decrease with increasing age, as it does in the nonthrowing shoulder.

11. Walch G, Boileau P, Noel E, et al: Impingement of the deep surface of the supraspinatus tendon on the posterosuperior glenoid rim: An arthroscopic study. *J Shoulder Elbow Surg* 1992;1:238-245.

12. Morgan CD, Burkhart SS, Palmeri M, et al: Type II SLAP lesions: Three subtypes and their relationships to superior instability and rotator cuff tears. *Arthroscopy* 1998;14:553-565.

13. Shepard MD, Dugas JR, Zeng N, Andrews JR: Differences in the ultimate strength of the biceps anchor and the generation of type II superior labrum anterior lesions in a cadaveric model. *Am J Sports Med* 2004;32:1197-1201.

    The biceps tendon was stressed in two directions in matched-paired cadaver shoulders: in line with the fibers of the biceps to mimic longitudinal stress at ball release or in a posterior direction to mimic the peel-back mechanism in hyperexternal rotation. All of the posterior-stressed specimens failed at the bicipital anchor, creating a type II SLAP lesion; none of the in line–stressed specimens failed. The conclusion was that the peel-back mechanism is most likely to be responsible for creation of type II SLAP lesions in throwers.

14. Grossman MG, Tibone JE, McGarry MH, et al: A cadaveric model of the throwing shoulder: A possible etiology of superior labrum anterior-to-posterior lesions. *J Bone Joint Surg Am* 2005;87:824-831.

    Ten cadaver shoulders underwent nondestructive anterior capsular stretching and 10-mm posterior capsular plication, simulating a lax anterior capsule with a posterior capsular contracture, as seen in many throwers. The humeral head rotated posterosuperiorly, potentially causing internal impingement. A posterior contracture does not allow the humerus to externally rotate into its normal posteroinferior position in external rotation.

15. Yeh ML, Lintner D, Luo ZP: Stress distribution in the superior labrum during throwing motion. *Am J Sports Med* 2005;33:395-401.

    In this finite element analysis, the stress at the biceps anchor–glenoid interface was shown to be highest during the deceleration phase of throwing.

16. Andrews JR, Carson WG Jr, McLeod WD: Glenoid labrum tears related to the long head of the biceps. *Am J Sports Med* 1985;13:337-341.

17. Gusmer PB, Potter HG, Schatz JA, et al: Labral injuries: Accuracy of detection with unenhanced MR imaging of the shoulder. *Radiology* 1996;200:519-524.

18. Morgan CD, Burkhart SS, Palmeri M, et al: Type II SLAP lesions: Three subtypes and their relationships to superior instability and rotator cuff tears. *Arthroscopy* 1998;14:553-565.

19. Palmer WE, Brown JH, Rosenthal DI: Labral-ligamentous complex of the shoulder: Evaluation with MR arthrography. *Radiology* 1994;190:645-651.

20. Palmer WE, Brown JH, Rosenthal DI: Rotator cuff: Evaluation with fat-suppressed MR arthrography. *Radiology* 1993;188:683-687.

21. Meister K, Walczak S, Fontenot W, et al: Evaluation of partial undersurface tears of the rotator cuff in the overhand athlete: MRI arthrography versus arthroscopy. *Arthroscopy* 1999;14:451-452.

22. Glasgow SG, Bruce RA, Yacobucci GN, Torg JS: Arthroscopic resection of glenoid labral tears in the athlete: A report of 29 cases. *Arthroscopy* 1992;8:48-54.

23. Altchek DW, Warren RF, Wickiewicz TL, Ortiz G: Arthroscopic labral débridement: A three year follow-up study. *Am J Sports Med* 1992;20:702-706.

24. Cordasco FA, Steinmann S, Flatow EL, Bigliani LU: Arthroscopic treatment of glenoid labral tears. *Am J Sports Med* 1993;21:425-430.

25. Tomlinson RJ Jr, Glousman RE: Arthroscopic debridement of glenoid labral tears in athletes. *Arthroscopy* 1995;11:42-51.

26. Martin DR, Garth WP Jr: Results of arthroscopic debridement of glenoid labral tears. *Am J Sports Med* 1995;23:447-451.

27. Pagnani MJ, Speer KP, Altchek DW, Warren RF, Dines DM: Arthroscopic fixation of superior labral lesions using a biodegradable implant: A preliminary report. *Arthroscopy* 1995;11:194-198.

28. Segmuller HE, Hayes MG, Sales AD: Arthroscopic repair of glenolabral injuries with an absorbable fixation device. *J Shoulder Elbow Surg* 1997;6:383-392.

29. Kim SH, Ha KI, Kim SH, Choi HJ: Results of arthroscopic treatment of superior labral lesions. *J Bone Joint Surg Am* 2002;84-A:981-985.

    In 34 patients (18 throwers) evaluated at an average 33 months after arthroscopic superior labral repair using suture anchors, 94% reported a satisfactory result, and 91% had returned to their preinjury activity level. Throwing athletes had lower rates of satisfaction and return to preinjury function than nonthrowers.

30. O'Brien SJ, Allen AA, Coleman SH, Drakos MC: The trans-rotator cuff approach to SLAP lesions: Technical aspects for repair and clinical follow-up of 31 patients at a minimum of 2 years. *Arthroscopy* 2002;18:372-377.

    In 31 patients evaluated at an average 3.7 years after arthroscopic trans–rotator cuff repair of a type II SLAP lesion, 71% reported good or excellent results, with 52% returning to their preinjury level of sports. No rotator cuff pathology or clinical problems were noted.

31. Ide J, Maeda S, Takagi K: Sports activity after arthroscopic superior labral repair using suture anchors in overhead throwing athletes. *Am J Sports Med* 2005;33:507-514.

    Forty patients, including 22 overuse athletes, were evaluated at an average 41 months after arthroscopic superior labral repair using two absorbable anchors placed at the 1 o'clock and 11 o'clock positions. Good or excellent results were reported in 90%; the throwing athletes had a lower rate of return to full function.

32. Wright RW, Paletta GA Jr: Prevalence of the Bennett lesion of the shoulder in major league pitchers. *Am J Sports Med* 2004;32:121-124.

Of 55 asymptomatic major league pitchers who underwent routine preseason screening radiographs to determine the presence of Bennett's lesion or thrower's exostosis, 12 (22%) were found to have an exostosis. No correlation was found with age, experience, or innings pitched. At follow-up, none required surgical treatment.

33. Meister K, Andrews JR, Batts J, et al: Symptomatic thrower's exostosis: Arthroscopic evaluation and treatment. *Am J Sports Med* 1999;27:133-136.

34. Payne LZ, Altchek DW, Craig EV, Warren RF: Arthroscopic treatment of partial rotator cuff tears in young athletes: A preliminary report. *Am J Sports Med* 1997;25:299-305.

35. Riand N, Boulahia A, Walch G: Posterosuperior impingement of the shoulder in the athlete: Results of arthroscopic débridement in 75 patients. *Rev Chir Orthop Reparatrice Appar Mot* 2002;88:19-27.

   At 2-year follow-up of 75 overhead athletes after arthroscopic débridement of a partial rotator cuff tear, 80% of the supraspinatus lesions had decreased 50% or more in thickness. Only 40% of patients were satisfied with the result, and no professional athletes were satisfied. Concomitant labral pathology was prevalent.

36. Mazoue CG, Andrews JR: Repair of full thickness rotator cuff tears in professional baseball players. *Am J Sports Med* 2006;34:182-189.

   Sixteen professional baseball players were reviewed retrospectively after mini-open repair of a full-thickness rotator cuff tear. Only one player (8%) was able to return to high-level baseball competition. Athletes with this injury should be cautioned as to the poor prognosis for return to competition after mini-open repair.

37. Ide J, Maeda S, Takagi K: Arthroscopic transtendon repair of partial-thickness articular-side tears of the rotator cuff: Anatomical and clinical study. *Am J Sports Med* 2005;33:1672-1679.

   Six overhead athletes underwent transtendinous arthroscopic repair of a high-grade partial tear of the rotator cuff. Only two (33%) had returned to the same or a higher level of play 3 years later.

38. Conway JE: Arthroscopic repair of partial thickness rotator cuff tears and SLAP lesions in professional baseball players. *Orthop Clin North Am* 2001;32: 443-456.

   This is a review of the author's extensive experience in arthroscopic treatment of common pathologies in the thrower's shoulder, with recommendations.

39. Levitz CL, Dugas J, Andrews JR: The use of arthroscopic thermal capsulorrhaphy to treat internal impingement in baseball players. *Arthroscopy* 2001;17: 573-577.

   Patients were treated with traditional arthroscopic débridement or repair of typical thrower's pathology, with or without thermal capsulorrhaphy. Patients who did not receive thermal treatment had an 80% return to competition at 1 year, and 67% were competing 2 years after surgery. Patients who received thermal treatment had a 93% return to competition at 1 year, and 90% were competing at 2 years. No complications were reported.

# Chapter 12

# Complications of Instability Repair

Kevin E. Peltier, MD

George F. Hatch III, MD

John M. Itamura, MD

## Introduction

Instability of the glenohumeral joint is a common clinical condition. For some patients, recurrent glenohumeral instability becomes a debilitating chronic condition that limits daily work-related and recreational activities. Surgical treatment can restore stability and function, allowing most patients to return to work and sports. However, instability repair, like all surgical procedures, carries the risk of complications that can lead to a less than satisfactory outcome. The most common complication is recurrence of instability, which can vary in extent from subtle recurrent subluxation to frank dislocation.

Accurate diagnosis and appropriate initial nonsurgical treatment of glenohumeral instability are essential. An incorrect presurgical diagnosis is a common reason for the recurrence of instability after a glenohumeral stabilization procedure. The inciting factor, direction, and chronicity of the instability must be determined during initial treatment and before surgical treatment is considered.

## Clinical Evaluation

Determination of the nature of the patient's instability begins with a detailed history of instability episodes, including the type of instability (acute traumatic dislocation, subluxation, or microinstability) and its chronicity. The prognosis and treatment options differ for a patient with a single acute dislocation and a patient with a number of dislocation episodes. The direction of the instability (anterior, posterior, inferior, or multidirectional) must be determined through the patient history and physical examination. Records of all treatment should be obtained, including notes related to any earlier surgery on the symptomatic shoulder. Imaging studies showing dislocation should be evaluated for clues to the primary direction of instability, as well as any fracture incurred during the initial injury.

Patient selection is a critical factor in preventing surgical complications. If the patient has concomitant pathology, a stabilization procedure may be more difficult or less likely to succeed. A detailed physical examination and imaging studies can alert the surgeon to the presence of a condition such as a superior labrum anterior and posterior (SLAP) lesion, which can contribute to anterior instability and should be addressed during surgery.[1-3] A humeral-sided avulsion of the glenohumeral ligament (HAGL) lesion or a midsubstance capsular rupture can usually be seen on a magnetic resonance arthrogram.[4] SLAP and HAGL lesions are difficult to treat arthroscopically but must be addressed to avoid a poor surgical outcome.[5] Glenoid or humeral head bone loss is the most common risk factor for recurrence,[6-9] and therefore it must be identified and quantified before surgical treatment. In a patient with a large bony Bankart lesion, a bony reconstruction should be performed with the primary procedure. Patients with psychological difficulties, the ability to voluntarily dislocate the shoulder, or secondary gain issues should be treated cautiously, because surgical failure rates are high in these groups.[5,10]

## Open Versus Arthroscopic Repair

Arthroscopic repair to correct anterior instability has become more popular as techniques and instrumentation have improved. Arthroscopy requires smaller incisions, and it allows the entire glenohumeral joint to be inspected and concomitant pathology to be addressed. It is associated with less postsurgical stiffness and lower morbidity rates. Arthroscopy also permits the surgeon to address instability without tenotomy or splitting of the subscapularis tendon.

When arthroscopic stabilization procedures were first performed, recurrence rates were high and patient satisfaction was poor. Subsequent advances in techniques and instrumentation have permitted capsulolabral pathology to be repaired anatomically and coexistent pathology to be addressed in the entire glenohumeral joint, including the posterior capsule and rotator interval. The implants used in repairing and tensioning the labrum and capsule have evolved from metal staples, soft-tissue tacks, and transglenoid sutures to bioabsorbable suture anchors, which are now the

**Table 1 | Studies of Anterior Instability Recurrence After Arthroscopic Bankart Repair**

| Study | Type of Study | Mean Follow-Up (Months) | Number of Patients | Type of Arthroscopic Fixation | Recurrence Rate | Recurrence Rate After Comparable Open Stabilization |
|---|---|---|---|---|---|---|
| Cole et al[18] (2001) | Retrospective | 54 | 59 | Bioabsorbable tack | 16% | 9% |
| Karlsson et al[16] (2001) | Prospective | 28-36 | 117 | Bioabsorbable tack | 15% | 10% |
| DeBerardino et al[19] (2001) | Prospective | 37 | 58 | Bioabsorbable tack | 12% | – |
| Fabbriciani et al[13] (2004) | Prospective | 24 | 60 | Suture anchor | 0 | 0 |
| Bottoni et al[11] (2006) | Prospective | 32 | 61 | Suture anchor | 3% | 6% |
| Carreira et al[12] (2006) | Prospective | 46 | 85 | Suture anchor | 10% | – |
| Tjoumakaris et al[14] (2006) | Retrospective | 40-56 | 106 | Suture anchor | 1% | 4% |

most common type of implant used in arthroscopic instability surgery.

Both arthroscopic and open anterior stabilization procedures now have low recurrence and failure rates, reported as less than 10% for arthroscopic procedures and less than 11% for traditional open repairs.[11-14] Both types of surgical procedures have a role in treating primary shoulder instability. An open procedure is recommended for a patient who has bone loss, a midsubstance capsular rupture, or a HAGL lesion; or a patient who requires revision surgery.[15] The indications for open and arthroscopic procedures continue to evolve as surgical techniques improve.

The outcomes of open and arthroscopic repair for recurrent anterior shoulder instability have been evaluated in prospective randomized trials. Sixty-four patients underwent an open or arthroscopic stabilization procedure performed by the same surgeon; arthroscopic labral repair was performed using bioabsorbable suture anchors. At a mean 32-month follow-up, no significant difference in clinical failure was found between the two groups. Patients who underwent an open procedure had a longer mean surgical time and a greater postsurgical mean loss of motion than those who underwent an arthroscopic procedure.[11] In another study, patients treated with arthroscopic or open stabilization for traumatic anterior instability had no difference in outcomes or failures.[13]

Studies have found higher recurrence rates after arthroscopic stabilization using bioabsorbable tacks than after open stabilization using suture anchors. In a prospective study of 117 patients with recurrent anterior instability who were treated using bioabsorbable tacks, the recurrence rate was significantly higher in those treated arthroscopically (15%) than in those treated with an open procedure (10%). Patients in the open procedure group lost an average of 10° of abduction and external rotation.[16] A meta-analysis of studies that evaluated open repairs and arthroscopic repairs using bioabsorbable tacks and transglenoid sutures found significantly higher rates of recurrent dislocation after arthroscopic repair (13%) than after open repair (3%).[17] Table 1 compares studies of recurrence in patients treated for anterior instability; those treated using suture anchors had lower recurrence rates than those treated using bioabsorbable tacks.

Recurrence rates of 4% to 8% have been reported after arthroscopic repair for posterior glenohumeral instability.[20,21] In 31 shoulders (19 patients), patients treated with arthroscopic stabilization had statistically better outcomes than patients treated with open repair, as measured using the Rowe and Western Ontario Shoulder Instability Index scores.[22] The contraindications to arthroscopic posterior stabilization are glenoid bony erosion and excessive glenoid retroversion.[10]

The surgeon's knowledge and skill in arthroscopic repair should be a factor in decisions between open and arthroscopic procedures. Arthroscopic posterior stabilization is considered more technically demanding than arthroscopic anterior stabilization because of the difficulty of portal placement and the poor quality of the posterior capsulolabral tissue. The surgeon must determine whether the posterior instability is primarily unidirectional. If it is a component of bidirectional or multidirectional instability (MDI), the anterior, inferior, or posterior capsular laxity also must be addressed in either an arthroscopic or open procedure.[2,5]

## Complications of Arthroscopic Repair

The arthroscopic techniques used to treat glenohumeral instability have improved and increased in number. Failure of arthroscopic treatment can result from poor portal placement, a nonanatomic repair necessitated by difficulty in mobilizing the torn labrum and advancing it to the glenoid rim, or a failure to address other causes of instability, such as a SLAP lesion.[2,3,5] Biomechanical studies have found that SLAP lesions lead to anterior translation of the humeral head.[1,3] In contrast, good clinical results have been reported when a SLAP lesion was addressed during arthroscopic instability repair.[2] Other pathology, such as a HAGL lesion or a capsular rupture, should be identified by diagnostic arthroscopy. Failure to treat these lesions, using either an arthroscopic or open procedure, can lead to clinical failure of the instability repair.[4]

In patients with anterior instability, the height of the labrum on the glenoid is important in restraint against anterior translation. During repair, the labral height must be restored by bringing the labrum up to the edge of the glenoid rim, rather than simply repairing the labrum medially on the glenoid neck. A biomechanical study of arthroscopic anteroinferior capsular plication using suture anchors found that stability can be increased by increasing the height of the capsulolabral bumper.[23] Failure to restore labral height can contribute to failure of arthroscopic instability repair.

## Complications of Suture Anchor and Soft-Tissue Tack Use

Arthroscopic procedures to repair the anterior or posterior capsulolabral structures increasingly rely on the use of suture anchors or soft-tissue tacks to attach the labrum to the glenoid rim. Complications can arise from poor implant placement, suture breakage, inadequate fixation of the anchor, synovitis, or a local reaction to the anchor or suture material.[24,25]

Complications arising from the use of suture anchors have increased with their popularity.[24,26,27] Anchor failure at the suture-to-anchor interface was found to be associated with clinical failures.[27] Osteolysis of the glenoid occurred following the use of suture anchors for anterior instability repair.[28] The number and placement of the anchors is controversial; the use of three or fewer suture anchors in the treatment of anterior shoulder instability was found to be a risk factor for recurrence.[9]

A Bankart lesion, as found at revision surgery, was reported in two studies to be a cause of surgical failure after open or arthroscopic stabilization.[6,9] The glenoid rim must be defined intrasurgically to avoid incorrect anchor placement. Care must be taken to place the anchors deep enough in the glenoid rim to prevent them from pulling out and causing chondral injury to the humeral head. Anchors placed too far onto the articular surface of the glenoid can cause direct chondral injury and lead to diffuse glenohumeral joint chondrolysis.[26]

The use of soft-tissue tacks for anterior shoulder stabilization has led to relatively high rates of recurrence.[16,17,19] The use of bioabsorbable tacks for anterior stabilization led to postsurgical synovitis in as many as 5% of patients.[18]

## Complications of Open Repair

The complications of open surgery are similar to those of arthroscopic surgery. Patients treated with open stabilization had more stiffness in comparison with patients treated with arthroscopic stabilization.[16] Rupture of the subscapularis muscle in association with anterior instability stabilization is a complication unique to open repair, and it should always be considered in the differential diagnosis for a patient who has recurrent instability after an anterior stabilization procedure.[29] Failure to promptly recognize and treat a subscapularis tear can lead to a poor outcome. Careful physical examination is necessary to assess the subscapularis; a patient with a subscapularis deficiency often has increased passive external rotation, as well as positive belly-press and lift-off tests.[30,31] A CT or magnetic resonance arthrogram can be helpful in evaluating the structural integrity of the subscapularis tendon; three-dimensional imaging using the axial and sagittal oblique views allows muscle atrophy to be quantified. Rarely, subscapularis dysfunction is caused by denervation of the muscle after earlier surgery, and for such patients an electromyogram may be helpful. At a mean 36-month follow-up after subscapularis tenotomy used in open shoulder stabilization, 7 of 10 patients had subscapularis insufficiency. No subscapularis ruptures were found, but MRI revealed atrophy and fatty infiltration.[32]

If the subscapularis tendon is deficient or irreparable, a pectoralis major muscle transfer can be used to augment or replace the subscapularis.[30] Pain and stability are usually improved after a transfer of the pectoralis major tendon for anterior shoulder instability.[30,33-35] The patient frequently has limitations on overhead activities after surgery, and the belly-press and lift-off tests usually remain positive.

As in an arthroscopic repair, the anchors used in an open repair must be placed on the glenoid rim rather than the articular surface. An anchor left prominent on the articular surface can lead to chondrolysis. The complication rate is high after open repair using screw placement or staple fixation; hardware failure or migration can cause or contribute to arthropathy.[36]

## Complications in Athletes

Posttraumatic instability is common in athletes involved in contact sports, and many of these patients require surgical treatment to return to their earlier level of athletic competition. Participation in contact sports is itself a risk factor for surgical failure.[7] Open stabilization is usually recommended to decrease the risk of recurrence. However, as arthroscopic techniques have become more popular, they are increasingly used in these athletes. Eighteen athletes involved in high school or collegiate contact or collision sports were arthroscopically treated for anterior instability. All were able to return to their sport; two had recurrent dislocation more than 2 years after return to sport.[37]

For posterior instability in athletes, an open repair has been preferred. However, arthroscopic reconstruction of the posterior capsulolabral structures was shown to be successful in a prospective study of 100 shoulders (91 patients). A subset of contact athletes had no significant differences in outcome, as measured using the American Shoulder and Elbow Surgeons Index score, compared with the entire group; 74% were able to return to their sport at the same level of competition.[38]

## Risk Factors for Recurrence of Instability

The success or failure of surgical techniques used in instability surgery is usually evaluated using the recurrence rate as an outcomes measure. Instability recurrence ranges from subtle subluxation to overt dislocation, and it can be traumatic or atraumatic. A patient with an atraumatic recurrence after surgical stabilization usually has a poorer prognosis than a patient with a traumatic recurrence.

After arthroscopic stabilization using bioabsorbable suture anchors, 14 of 91 consecutive patients with traumatic anterior instability (15%) had recurrent instability at a mean 36-month follow-up.[8] Bone loss (a bony Bankart injury or large Hill-Sachs lesion) was associated with an increased risk of recurrence. The number of suture anchors was found to be critical; in patients with three or fewer anchors, the rate of recurrence was significantly increased. An increased recurrence rate was also found in patients with inferior or anterior glenohumeral hyperlaxity.

Patients with MDI have higher recurrence and failure rates, regardless of surgical method.[5] The recurrence rate is higher after unidirectional repair than after pancapsulorrhaphy.

Several factors can contribute to the failure of a posterior instability repair, including intrasurgical failure to identify and treat a retroverted glenoid, bidirectional or multidirectional instability, or a rotator interval lesion. Recurrence of instability was noted in 19% of 41 patients (44 shoulders) after open posterior stabilization; patients with chondral damage at the time of stabilization and those older than 37 years had the poorest outcomes.[39]

Patients who are able to voluntarily dislocate their shoulder have variable surgical results and are relatively likely to have recurrent instability. Extreme caution

should be using in considering surgery for a patient in this challenging population.

### Bone Loss

Bone loss, especially a defect in the anteroinferior glenoid, is the most common risk factor identified in studies of surgical repair failure. Bone loss in the glenoid has been found in as many as 23% of shoulders with an initial traumatic dislocation and as many as 73% of shoulders with a recurrent dislocation. After arthroscopic or open treatment, an anterior glenoid bony defect was found in 56% of 41 patients who had recurrent instability.[9]

Before surgery, the amount of anterior glenoid bone loss should be evaluated with plain radiography and CT. During surgery, the anteroinferior rim of the glenoid should be inspected. An inverted pear glenoid represents an anteroinferior glenoid bone loss of 25% to 27%.[40] (Figure 1, *A*). In a biomechanical study, the loss of more than half of the maximal anteroposterior diameter of the anteroinferior glenoid led to a 30% or greater loss of dislocation resistance.[41] A glenoid bone loss of this magnitude probably precludes a soft-tissue repair of the glenohumeral joint. Open stabilization is required, using a bone graft to the deficient glenoid.[15,42] The surgeon must address any intrasurgical evidence that a Hill-Sachs lesion is engaging the anteroinferior glenoid, although no studies exist to establish the size at which a Hill-Sachs lesion must be addressed (Figure 1, *B*). A large Hill-Sachs lesion also may be discovered during revision surgery. The use of the glenoid bare spot as a consistent landmark was not supported in a study that found anatomic inconsistency among 20 cadaver shoulders. The use of presurgical CT scans was recommended to quantify glenoid bone loss.[43]

### Thermal Capsulorrhaphy

Although early studies on the use of thermal energy for treatment of glenohumeral instability reported encouraging results,[44-46] most long-term results have been poor. A prospective study evaluated 84 patients treated with thermal capsulorrhaphy for anterior dislocation, anteroinferior instability, or MDI. Thermal capsulorrhaphy was used as an adjunct to surgery if a SLAP or Bankart lesion was repaired and was used alone in patients with MDI. At an average 38-month follow-up, 37% of all patients had an unsatisfactory American Shoulder and Elbow Surgeons Index score, and 45% of the patients treated for MDI had an unsatisfactory score.[44-46] In another group of patients with MDI who were treated with thermal capsulorrhaphy alone, the recurrence rate was high and outcomes were poor.[44] A survey of orthopaedic surgeons found high recurrence rates after thermal capsulorrhaphy was used.[47]

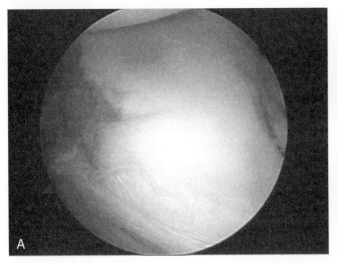
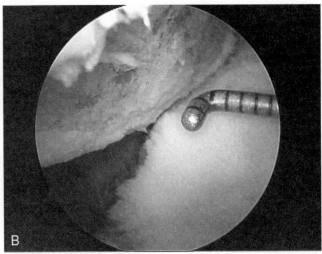

**Figure 1** Arthroscopic evidence of bone loss. **A,** In a shoulder with an anteroinferior fracture of the glenoid, the bare spot can be seen and the amount of bone loss can be estimated. **B,** Evidence of an engaging Hill-Sachs lesion can be seen in this view from a superior portal.

Thermal capsulorrhaphy can result in a loss of capsule integrity ranging from mild attenuation to complete tissue ablation.[44,45] Poor capsular tissue quality can cause significant difficulty during revision surgery. Some surgeons have successfully used a glenoid-based shift if the remaining capsular tissue is thinned but not ablated.[45] Others recommend capsular reconstruction with autograft or allograft tendon.[48,49] Thermal capsulorrhaphy can also result in axillary nerve injury, adhesive capsulitis, or diffuse chondrolysis of the glenohumeral joint.[50] Rapid, destructive chondrolysis has been reported after surgery using either monopolar or bipolar radiofrequency thermal energy. The rate of axillary nerve injury was reported to be approximately 1%; most patients had a sensory injury that was resolved within 3 months, although permanent nerve injury has occurred.[47]

### Capsular Deficiency

Capsular deficiency is a rare condition that has not been well described in relation to instability. It is most often found during revision surgery or after thermal capsulorrhaphy. The soft-tissue deficiency may include the subscapularis, especially after an open repair. Because imaging studies cannot accurately predict the integrity of the capsular tissue, the possibility of a deficiency must be investigated during revision surgery, especially if earlier stabilization surgery included the use of thermal energy.

Soft-tissue autografts or allografts, including hamstring, iliotibial band, anterior tibial, and Achilles tendon grafts, have been used to reconstruct a deficient or irreparable capsule. These techniques had good results in the small reported studies, although return to full sports and other activity was unpredictable.[48,49] After total shoulder arthroplasty, 10 of 236 patients had persistent anterior shoulder instability, which was treated using an Achilles tendon allograft; the results were generally fair to good, with restoration of stability but some loss of motion.[51]

## Other Complications

### Stiffness

Stiffness is uncommon after surgery for open anterior instability, although its incidence may be underreported.[52,53] Some procedures are intended to limit the risk of recurrence by limiting external rotation, and therefore loss of motion has not been considered a complication. Limited external rotation can be expected after capsular reconstruction or revision surgery; the patient should receive this information before surgery. The impact of a loss of external rotation should be considered in selecting the procedure or selectively shifting the capsule. A loss of 10° of external rotation has little functional consequence for most patients, but it can be devastating for a high-level overhead athlete. Overtightening of the shoulder capsule should be avoided because the abnormal kinematics of an overconstrained joint result in altered joint reactive forces, increased shear across the articular cartilage, and premature degenerative arthropathy.[54]

After posterior stabilization, a few patients have stiffness from a loss of internal rotation. In 27 patients treated with arthroscopic posterior stabilization, the mean internal rotation loss was equivalent to one vertebral level.[20] Only 4% of 100 patients treated with arthroscopic capsulolabral reconstruction for posterior instability had limited range of motion at follow-up.[38] Although a slight loss of internal rotation is insignificant for most patients, overhead athletes or swimmers could experience excessive posterior capsular tightness after repair.

## Arthritis

Degenerative disease can occur after any type of instability repair. A patient may develop arthritis during the early postsurgical period or much later. Early degenerative disease is usually related to chondrolysis resulting from thermal capsulorrhaphy or a loose staple, anchor, or other implant. Late development of arthritis is usually the result of overconstraint of the glenohumeral joint, which leads to excessive restriction of motion. Overtightening of the glenohumeral joint can occur during any type of instability repair. Severe overtightening can lead not only to a loss of motion but also to increased contact pressure over a decreased area, leading to chondral injury, or to increased sheer forces along the chondral surfaces, which leads to chondrolysis and early degenerative disease. A loss of external rotation of more than 30%, compared with the contralateral shoulder, increases the risk of capsulorrhaphy arthropathy;[53,55] a capsular release, with or without subscapularis lengthening, can be performed to correct this condition.

Patients who have undergone an open Bankart repair or a Bristow-Latarjet, Putti-Platt, or other procedure for anterior shoulder instability are at increased risk of developing glenohumeral arthritis. A case-control study evaluating patients after total shoulder arthroplasty found that the risk of developing severe arthritis was 10 to 20 times greater in those with a history of shoulder dislocation.[56] Osteoarthritis also occurs in patients after a posterior instability repair; after an open repair for posterior instability, 6 of 26 patients (23%) had degenerative changes.[57]

Most studies of glenohumeral arthritis after instability surgery have focused on the results of open procedures. The incidence of degenerative disease following arthroscopic stabilization has not been established, and a longer follow-up is needed. In a limited number of patients, arthropathy after arthroscopic stabilization was attributed to implant complications or thermal capsulorrhaphy.[24,26,50]

Patients who develop osteoarthritis after instability repair have typically been treated with total shoulder arthroplasty or hemiarthroplasty. Many of these patients are young and active; in one study, the mean patient age was 46 years.[58] Although pain and stiffness improve after arthroplasty, some patients have an unsatisfactory result or require revision surgery because of component failure.[58]

## Infection

Infection must be suspected in any patient who has a difficult course after a surgical procedure. The reported rate of infection after open or arthroscopic shoulder stabilization is approximately 1%.[17] The signs and symptoms of infection may appear soon after surgery (within 6 weeks) or later. Unexplained pain is usually the most important symptom. Fever is not usually present, and white blood cell counts may be normal. Elevated erythrocyte sedimentation rates and C-reactive protein levels may suggest the possibility of infection, although these tests may also be negative. Deep cultures should be obtained, and intravenous antibiotics tailored to the culture results should be administered for 4 to 6 weeks. The patient should be treated with irrigation and débridement, which should be repeated as necessary. Any nonabsorbable suture or anchor material should be removed.

Six patients at one institution had an infection after instability surgery; two had undergone arthroscopic stabilization.[59] Three patients developed an acute infection within 6 weeks, and the other three developed a late infection within 2 years. All of the patients with a late infection had a sinus leading to a retained nonabsorbable suture. None of the patients had a recurrence of instability, although most had stiffness. In two patients, *Propionibacterium acnes* was the pathogen. *P acnes* should be considered as the possible cause of any infection after shoulder instability repair.

## Neurovascular Injury

The axillary nerve, musculocutaneous nerve, and brachial plexus are at risk during open surgery for anterior instability. Injury can result from direct laceration, suture entrapment, or excessive tissue retraction, especially of the coracobrachialis. The shoulder surgeon must be able to locate and isolate the axillary nerve, the musculocutaneous nerve, and parts of the brachial plexus, especially during revision surgery. The greatest reported risk of injury to the axillary and musculocutaneous nerves occurs during the Bristow-Latarjet procedure.[60-62] Revision surgery after an unsuccessful Bristow-Latarjet procedure can be challenging, and exposing the axillary nerve can be difficult. Neurologic complications ranging from postsurgical transient sensory neuropathy to complete motor palsy have been reported from the use of interscalene anesthesia. Although most nerve injuries are transient neurapraxias, which are resolved over time, permanent injuries have been reported.[63,64]

## Results of Revision Surgery

Glenohumeral arthritis, age greater than 30 years, a history of two or more earlier instability surgeries, glenoid bone loss, and a diagnosis of MDI have a negative impact on the outcome of revision anterior shoulder reconstruction.[6] In one study, 81% of the patients had an excellent Rowe score at a mean 49-month follow-up after revision surgery. The authors emphasized that a good outcome can be achieved if pathology discovered during revision surgery is addressed.[9] In a study of open revision surgery, only 78% of patients with multiple earlier stabilization at-

tempts had a good or excellent result, and 22% had an unsatisfactory result.[65] The few studies of revision surgery after unsuccessful posterior instability repair found a higher failure rate than after a primary repair.[10]

Revision surgery can be especially complicated if the initial instability repair was nonanatomic. Some early stabilization procedures, such as the Bristow-Latarjet, Putti-Platt, and Magnuson-Stack repairs, used neighboring anatomic structures or changed the native anatomy to achieve shoulder stability. Revision surgery has a greater risk of complications if the normal anatomic relationships around the shoulder were changed during an earlier procedure.

## Summary

Recurrence of shoulder instability continues to be the most common complication of instability repair. Glenoid bone loss is a common finding at revision surgery for recurrence, and attempts to address it should be made during the initial surgical treatment. Both open and arthroscopic techniques are associated with risks and possible complications. Revision surgery for instability has been found to have relatively poor outcomes and unsatisfactory results. Patients who are treated for glenohumeral instability may develop stiffness, and they are at increased risk of developing glenohumeral arthritis.

## Annotated References

1. Pagnani MJ, Deng XH, Warren RF, Torzilli PA, O'Brien SJ: Role of the long head of the biceps brachii in glenohumeral stability: A biomechanical study in cadavera. *J Shoulder Elbow Surg* 1996;5: 255-262.

2. Gartsman GM, Roddey TS, Hammerman SM: Arthroscopic treatment of bi-directional glenohumeral instability: Two- to five-year follow-up. *J Shoulder Elbow Surg* 2001;10:28-36.

   Fifty-four patients with bidirectional instability (inferior instability with an anterior or posterior component) were treated with an arthroscopic repair of multiple intra-articular lesions, and 91% had a good or excellent result. The surgery was unsuccessful in four patients.

3. McMahon PJ, Burkart A, Mushal V, Debski RE: Glenohumeral translations are increased after a Type II superior labrum anterior-posterior lesion: A cadaveric study of severity of passive stabilizer injury. *J Shoulder Elbow Surg* 2004;13:39-44.

   A 50-N load was applied to cadaver shoulders in the anterior and posterior directions. The loading protocol was repeated after two types of simulated type II SLAP lesions were created, and glenohumeral translation was found to be increased.

4. Bokor DJ, Conboy VB, Olson C: Anterior instability of the glenohumeral joint with humeral avulsion of the glenohumeral ligaments: A review of 41 cases. *J Bone Joint Surg Br* 1999;81:93-96.

5. Millett PJ, Clavert P, Warner JJ: Arthroscopic management of anterior, posterior, and multidirectional shoulder instability: Pearls and pitfalls. *Arthroscopy* 2003;19:86-93.

   Arthroscopic treatment of instability is discussed.

6. Meehan RE, Peterson SA: Results and factors affecting outcome of revision surgery for shoulder instability. *J Shoulder Elbow Surg* 2005;14:31-37.

   Revision surgery for unsuccessful open or arthroscopic anterior glenohumeral stabilization had a satisfactory result in 84% of 24 patients. Factors contributing to poor outcomes included glenohumeral arthritis, age greater than 30 years, two or more earlier instability surgeries, and a bony Bankart lesion.

7. Calvo E, Granizo JJ, Fernandez-Yruegas D: Criteria for arthroscopic treatment of anterior instability of the shoulder. *J Bone Joint Surg Br* 2005;87:677-683.

   In a prospective evaluation of 61 patients after arthroscopic anterior Bankart repair, age less than 28 years, ligamentous laxity, the presence of a fracture of the glenoid rim (> 15% of the articular surface), and postsurgical participation in contact sports were associated with a higher risk of recurrence.

8. Boileau P, Villalba M, Hery JY, Balg F, Ahrens P, Neyton L: Risk factors for recurrence of shoulder instability after arthroscopic Bankart repair. *J Bone Joint Surg Am* 2006;88:1755-1763.

   At a mean 36-month follow-up after arthroscopic Bankart repair, 15% of 91 patients had recurrent instability. The risk factors were bone loss, shoulder hyperlaxity, and three or fewer suture anchors used in the capsulolabral repair.

9. Tauber M, Resch H, Forstner R, Raffl M, Schauer J: Reasons for failure after surgical repair of anterior shoulder instability. *J Shoulder Elbow Surg* 2004;13: 279-285.

   At revision surgery, 56% of 41 patients with recurrent anterior instability had a defect in the anterior bony glenoid rim and 22% had a large capsule. At a mean 49-month follow-up after revision surgery, 81% had an excellent Rowe score.

10. Robinson CM, Aderinto J: Recurrent posterior shoulder instability. *J Bone Joint Surg Am* 2005;87: 883-892.

    Key concepts in the treatment of posterior instability are described.

11. Bottoni CR, Smith EL, Berkowitz MJ, Towle RB, Moore JH: Arthroscopic versus open shoulder stabilization for recurrent anterior instability: A prospective randomized clinical trial. *Am J Sports Med* 2006; 34:1730-1737.

In a prospective randomized trial, 29 patients received open treatment of recurrent anterior instability, and 32 received arthroscopic stabilization. Both groups had improved function after stabilization. Two patients in the open group and one in the arthroscopic-group had an unsatisfactory result. The mean external rotation loss was greater in the open group.

12. Carreira DS, Mazzocca AD, Oryhon J, Brown FM, Hayden JK, Romeo AA: A prosective outcome evaluation of arthroscopic Bankart repairs: Minimum 2-year follow up. *Am J Sports Med* 2006;34:771-777.

At a minimum 2-year (mean 46-month) follow-up, 90% of 85 patients treated with arthroscopic Bankart repair using suture anchors had a good or excellent Rowe score. The recurrence rate was 10% (7 patients); 4 patients had redislocation, and 3 had recurrent subluxation.

13. Fabbriciani C, Milano G, Demontis A, Fadda S, Ziranu F, Mulas PD: Arthroscopic versus open treatment of Bankart lesion of the shoulder: A prospective randomized study. *Arthroscopy* 2004;20:456-462.

In a prospective randomized trial comparing arthroscopic and open treatment of anterior glenohumeral instability, 60 patients were followed for a mean 2 years. Both groups had a low recurrence rate, and no patients treated arthroscopically had recurrent instability.

14. Tjoumakaris FP, Abboud JA, Hasan SA, Ramsey ML, Williams GR: Arthroscopic and open Bankart repairs provide similar outcomes. *Clin Orthop Relat Res* 2006;446:227-232.

A retrospective comparative study of the outcomes of open and arthroscopic treatment for anterior glenohumeral instability found no differences between the groups, using patient-assessed outcomes measures. Both groups had a low rate of recurrent instability. Arthroscopic treatment was found to provide results equal to those of open procedures.

15. Millett PJ, Clavert P, Warner JP: Open operative treatment for anterior shoulder instability: When and why? *J Bone Joint Surg Am* 2005;87:419-432.

Open surgical techniques are reviewed, with their role in the treatment of glenohumeral instability.

16. Karlsson J, Magnusson L, Ejerhed L, Hultenheim I, Ludin O, Kartus J: Comparison of open and arthroscopic stabilization for recurrent shoulder dislocation in patients with a Bankart lesion. *Am J Sports Med* 2001;29:538-542.

In a prospective study, arthroscopic procedures for anterior posttraumatic shoulder instability were performed with tacks, and open procedures used suture anchors. The recurrence rate was 15% in patients treated arthroscopically. Patients treated with an open procedure had a 10% recurrence rate and a 10° loss of external rotation.

17. Freedman KB, Smith AP, Romeo AA, Cole BJ, Bach BR Jr: Open Bankart versus arthroscopic repair with transglenoid sutures or bioabsorbable tacks for recurrent anterior instability of the shoulder: A meta-analysis. *Am J Sports Med* 2004;32:1520-1527.

A meta-analysis of six studies comparing arthroscopic Bankart repair using bioabsorbable tacks or transglenoid sutures with traditional open repair found that redislocation and recurrence were significantly more likely after arthroscopic repair.

18. Cole BJ, Romeo AA, Warner JJ: Arthroscopic Bankart repair with the Suretac device for traumatic anterior shoulder instability in athletes. *Orthop Clin North Am* 2001;32:411-421.

This article reviews the relevant anatomy as well as arthroscopic techniques and possible complications of using the Suretac device for arthroscopic Bankart repair.

19. DeBerardino TM, Arciero RA, Taylor DC, Uhorchak JM: Prospective evaluation of arthroscopic stabilization of acute, initial anterior shoulder dislocations in young athletes: Two to five-year follow up. *Am J Sports Med* 2001;29:586-592.

In a prospective study, 49 shoulders (48 patients) were treated for acute anterior dislocation with arthroscopic stabilization using bioabsorbable tacks. At an average 37-month follow-up, 43 shoulders were stable and the patients had returned to their previous level of activity. Six shoulders (12%) had recurrent instability.

20. Williams RJ III, Strickland S, Cohen M, Altchek DW, Warren RF: Arthroscopic repair for traumatic posterior shoulder instability. *Am J Sports Med* 2003;31: 203-209.

In a retrospective review of 27 shoulders (26 patients) treated arthroscopically, bioabsorbable tack fixation was used to repair posterior labral tears. At a mean 5.1-year follow-up, pain and instability had been relieved in 92% of the patients. Only 2% required an additional procedure.

21. Kim SH, Ha KI, Park JH, et al: Arthroscopic posterior labral repair and capsular shift for traumatic unidirectional recurrent posterior subluxation of the shoulder. *J Bone Joint Surg Am* 2003;85:1479-1487.

Twenty-seven patients with traumatic unidirectional posterior instability were treated with arthroscopic labral repair and posterior capsular shift. At a mean 39-month follow-up, 26 patients had a stable shoulder and were able to return to their previous level of sports activity.

22. Bottoni CR, Franks BR, Moore JH, DeBerardino TM, Taylor DC, Arciero RA: Operative stabilization of posterior shoulder instability. *Am J Sports Med* 2005;33:996-1002.

Nineteen patients were treated arthroscopically for posterior shoulder instability, and 12 were treated with an open procedure. Western Ontario Shoulder Instability Index and Rowe scores were higher in the arthroscopically treated patients. Results were good or excellent in 29 of the 31 shoulders.

23. Alberta FG, ElAttrache NS, Mihata T, McGarry MH, Tibone JE, Lee TQ: Arthroscopic anteroinferior suture plication resulting in decreased glenohumeral translation and external rotation: Study of a cadaver model. *J Bone Joint Surg Am* 2006;88:179-187.

Arthroscopic repair of anterior instability in a cadaver model reestablished labral height and decreased anterior translation. A 1-cm pinch of tissue was taken, and suture anchors were placed on the anteroinferior glenoid.

24. Park HB, Keyurapan E, Gill HS, Selhi HS, McFarland EG: Suture anchors and tacks for shoulder surgery: Part I. The prevention and treatment of complications. *Am J Sports Med* 2006;34:136-144.

Complications arising from the use of suture anchors and tacks in shoulder surgery are discussed.

25. Freehill MQ, Harms DJ, Huber SM, Atlihan D, Buss DD: Poly-L-lactic acid tack synovitis after arthroscopic stabilization of the shoulder. *Am J Sports Med* 2003;31:643-647.

In a retrospective cohort study, 10 of 52 patients treated with arthroscopic shoulder stabilization using poly-L-lactic acid tacks developed pain, and 6 of the 10 developed significant stiffness. All had significant glenohumeral synovitis. Nine of the 10 had gross implant debris at arthroscopic evaluation and débridement.

26. Kaar TK, Schenck RC, Wirth MA, Rockwood CA: Complications of metallic suture anchors in shoulder surgery: A report of 8 cases. *Arthroscopy* 2001;17:31-37.

In a retrospective study of complications of metal suture anchors used during initial surgical treatment, all eight patients had complications, including extraosseous placement and articular damage.

27. Meyer DC, Gerber C: Failure of anterior shoulder instability repair caused by eyelet cutout of absorbable suture anchors. *Arthroscopy* 2004;20:521-523.

This is a case report of a patient with complications from the use of absorbable suture anchors.

28. Athwal GS, Shridharani SM, O'Driscoll SW: Osteolysis and arthropathy of the shoulder after use of bioabsorbable knotless suture anchors: A report of four cases. *J Bone Joint Surg Am* 2006;88:1840-1845.

Four patients developed glenoid osteolysis and arthropathy after bioabsorbable knotless suture anchors were used.

29. Lazarus MD, Harryman DT II: Complications of open anterior stabilization of the shoulder. *J Am Acad Orthop Surg* 2000;8:122-132.

30. Gerber C, Kuechle DK: Isolated rupture of the tendon of the subscapularis muscle: Clinical features of six cases. *J Bone Joint Surg Br* 1991;73:389-391.

31. Gerber C, Hersche O, Farron A: Isolated rupture of the subscapularis tendon. *J Bone Joint Surg Am* 1996;78:1015-1023.

32. Scheibel M, Nikulka C, Dick A, Schroeder RJ, Popp AG, Haas NP: Structural integrity and clinical function of the subscapularis musculotendinous unit after arthroscopic and open shoulder stabilization. *Am J Sports Med* 2007;35:1153-1161.

Ten of 22 patients had an open shoulder stabilization procedure, and 12 had an arthroscopic procedure. Clinical signs of subscapularis insufficiency and MRI findings of atrophy and fatty infiltration were seen after the open procedures.

33. Gerber C, Werner CM, Macy JC, Jacob HA, Nyffeler RW: Effect of selective capsulorrhaphy on the passive range of motion of the glenohumeral joint. *J Bone Joint Surg Am* 2003;85:48-55.

A biomechanical study evaluated the effect of selective capsular plication on passive range of motion in eight human cadaver shoulders. Loss of motion depended on the location of the plication. The study concluded that localized plications of the glenohumeral capsule result in predictable loss of motion.

34. Resch H, Povacz P, Ritter E, Matschi W: Transfer of the pectoralis major muscle for the treatment of irreparable rupture of the subscapularis tendon. *J Bone Joint Surg Am* 2000;82:372-382.

35. Warner JJ: Management of massive irreparable rotator cuff tears: The role of tendon transfer. *Instr Course Lect* 2001;50:63-71.

Techniques are discussed for tendon transfer in irreparable rotator cuff tears and the treatment of subscapularis ruptures.

36. Brophy RH, Marx RG: Osteoarthritis following shoulder instability. *Clin Sports Med* 2005;24:47-56.

The relationship of degenerative arthritis and glenohumeral instability is reviewed.

37. Mazzocca AD, Brown FM Jr, Carreira DS, Hayden J, Romeo AA: Arthroscopic anterior shoulder stabilization of collision and contact athletes. *Am J Sports Med* 2005;33:52-60.

Eighteen athletes involved in contact and collision sports were treated with arthroscopic stabilization for anterior glenohumeral instability. At 24- to 66-month follow-up, all had returned to high school or collegiate sports. Two had experienced recurrent dislocation.

38. Bradley JP, Baker CL III, Kline AJ, Armfield DR, Chhabra A: Arthroscopic capsulolabral reconstruction for posterior instability of the shoulder: A prospective study of 100 shoulders. *Am J Sports Med* 2006;34:1061-1071.

Ninety-one athletes (100 shoulders) with unidirectional posterior shoulder instability were treated with arthroscopic posterior capsulolabral reconstruction. At a mean 27-month follow-up, the mean American Shoulder and Elbow Surgeons Index score had improved significantly. A subgroup of contact athletes had no significant differences

from the entire group. On a magnetic resonance arthrogram, shoulders of patients with posterior instability had significantly greater chondrolabral and osseous retroversion than shoulders of control subjects.

39. Wolf BR, Strickland S, Williams RJ, Allen AA, Altchek DW, Warren RF: Open posterior stabilization for recurrent posterior glenohumeral instability. *J Shoulder Elbow Surg* 2005;14:157-164.

    In a retrospective review of 44 shoulders treated with open posterior stabilization of recurrent posterior glenohumeral instability, patients were reevaluated after 1.8 to 22.5 years. Eight patients (19%) had a recurrence of instability. Patients who had chondral injury at surgery or were older than 37 years at surgery had poorer satisfaction and outcome scores. No progressive radiographic signs of glenohumeral arthritis were seen.

40. Lo IKY, Parten PM, Burkhart SS: The inverted pear glenoid: An indicator of significant glenoid bone loss. *Arthroscopy* 2004;20:169-174.

    A cadaver study of the amount of glenoid bone loss in an inverted pear glenoid found a loss of 27% to 30% of the inferior glenoid. The authors conclude that a bone graft is needed when an inverted pear glenoid is seen during arthroscopy.

41. Gerber C, Nyffeler RW: Classification of glenohumeral joint instability. *Clin Orthop Relat Res* 2002; 400:65-76.

    A classification of glenohumeral instability is described that distinguishes among static, dynamic, and voluntary dislocation.

42. Burkhart SS, De Beer JF: Traumatic glenohumeral bone defects and their relationship to failure of arthroscopic Bankart repairs: Significance of the inverted-pear glenoid and the humeral engaging Hill-Sachs lesion. *Arthroscopy* 2000;16:677-694.

43. Kralinger F, Aigner F, Longato S, Reiger M, Wambacher M: Is the bare spot a consistent landmark for shoulder arthroscopy? A study of 20 embalmed glenoids with 3-dimensional computed tomographic reconstruction. *Arthroscopy* 2006;22: 428-432.

    In an anatomic study of 20 embalmed glenoid specimens, the bare spot was not a consistent landmark. Presurgical CT was recommended to evaluate bony glenoid deficiency.

44. D'Alessandro DF, Bradley JP, Fleischli JE, Connor PM: Prospective evaluation of thermal capsulorrhaphy for shoulder instability: Indications and results. Two- to five-year follow-up. *Am J Sports Med* 2004;32:21-33.

    After thermal capsulorrhaphy, 37% of patients had an unsatisfactory result. The percentage was even higher in patients with MDI. Capsular thinning was found at revision surgery.

45. Park HB, Yokota A, Gill HS, Rassi GE, McFarland EG: Revision surgery for failed thermal capsulorrhaphy. *Am J Sports Med* 2005;33:1321-1326.

    In 14 patients who underwent a revision instability procedure after unsuccessful thermal capsulorrhaphy, recurrent laxity was common, and capsular thinning was also found. However, no patients had capsular ablation, and the quality of the capsular tissue did not affect the revision procedure.

46. Anderson K, Warren RF, Altchek DW, Craig EV, O'Brien SJ: Risk factors for early failure after thermal capsulorrhaphy. *Am J Sports Med* 2002;30: 103-107.

    In a retrospective study, relatively early surgical treatment and multiple recurrent dislocations were determined to be the significant risk factors for early failure after treatment of shoulder instability with thermal capsulorrhaphy.

47. Wong KL, Williams GR: Complications of thermal capsulorrhaphy of the shoulder. *J Bone Joint Surg Am* 2001;83:151-155.

    A survey of 379 orthopaedic surgeons on the use and complications of thermal energy in arthroscopic shoulder procedures found recurrence rates from 7.1% to 8.4%, depending on the type of thermal energy used. Respondents noted potential complications such as capsular insufficiency and axillary nerve injury.

48. Warner JJ, Venegas AA, Lehtinen JT, Macy JJ: Management of capsular deficiency of the shoulder: A report of three cases. *J Bone Joint Surg Am* 2002;84: 1668-1671.

    A surgical technique to reconstruct anterior shoulder capsular deficiency is described.

49. Iannotti JP, Antoniou J, Williams GR, Ramsey ML: Iliotibial band reconstruction for treatment of glenohumeral instability associated with irreparable capsular deficiency. *J Shoulder Elbow Surg* 2002;11: 618-623.

    A surgical technique is described using the iliotibial band for anterior shoulder reconstruction in patients with recurrent instability caused by a loss of capsular tissue and irreparable tearing of the subscapularis.

50. Levine WN, Clark AM Jr, D'Alessandro DF, Yamaguchi K: Chondrolysis following arthroscopic thermal capsulorrhaphy to treat shoulder instability: A report of two cases. *J Bone Joint Surg Am* 2005;87: 616-621.

    Two patients developed severe, rapid chondrolysis after a shoulder instability repair using thermal capsulorrhaphy.

51. Moeckel BH, Altchek DW, Warren RF, Wickiewicz TL, Dines DM: Instability of the shoulder after arthroplasty. *J Bone Joint Surg Am* 1993;75:492-497.

52. Lazarus MD, Sidles JA, Harryman DT, Matsen FA: Effect of a chondral-labral defect on glenoid cavity

and glenohumeral stability: A cadaveric model. *J Bone Joint Surg Am* 1996;78:94-102.

53. Hawkins RJ, Angelo RL: Glenohumeral osteoarthrosis: A late complication of the Putti-Platt repair. *J Bone Joint Surg Am* 1990;72:1193-1197.

54. Harryman DT II, Sidles JA, Clark JM, McQuade KJ, Gibb TD, Matsen FA: Translation of the humeral head on the glenoid with passive glenohumeral motion. *J Bone Joint Surg Am* 1990;72:1334-1343.

55. Walch G, Ascani C, Boulahia A, Nove-Josserand L, Edwards TB: Static posterior subluxation of the humeral head: An unrecognized entity responsible for glenohumeral osteoarthritis in the young adult. *J Shoulder Elbow Surg* 2002;11:309-314.

   Thirteen patients had posterior humeral head subluxation relative to the glenoid and posterior cartilage wear, which could not be corrected surgically. They were believed to represent the first stage of primary glenohumeral arthritis.

56. Marx RG, McCarty EC, Montemurno TD, Altchek DW, Craid EV, Warren RF: Development of arthrosis following dislocation of the shoulder: A case-control study. *J Shoulder Elbow Surg* 2002;11:1-5.

   Ninety-one patients who had undergone total shoulder arthroplasty and 282 control subjects were asked whether they had ever had a shoulder dislocation. A previous dislocation was found to increase the risk of developing shoulder arthritis 10 to 20 times.

57. Fuchs B, Jost B, Gerber C: Posterior-inferior capsular shift for the treatment of recurrent, voluntary posterior subluxation of the shoulder. *J Bone Joint Surg Am* 2000;82:16-25.

58. Sperling JW, Antuna SA, Sanchez-Sotelo J, Schleck C, Cofield RH: Shoulder arthroplasty for arthritis after instability surgery. *J Bone Joint Surg Am* 2002;84:1775-1781.

   Thirty-three patients who developed glenohumeral arthritis after shoulder instability surgery were treated with shoulder arthroplasty. At a minimum 2-year follow-up of 31 patients, significant improvement in pain and external rotation was found. However, 11 of the 31 patients had undergone revision surgery.

59. Sperling JW, Cofield RH, Torchia ME, Hanssen AD: Infection after shoulder instability surgery. *Clin Orthop Relat Res* 2003;414:61-64.

   This is a report of six patients treated for infection after surgical treatment of shoulder instability.

60. Flatow EL, Bigliani LU, April EW: An anatomic study of the musculocutaneous nerve and its relationship to the coracoid process. *Clin Orthop Relat Res* 1989;244:166-171.

61. Bryan WJ, Schauder K, Tullos HS: The axillary nerve and its relationship to common sports medicine shoulder procedures. *Am J Sports Med* 1986;14:113-116.

62. Burkhead WZ Jr, Scheinberg RR, Box G: Surgical anatomy of the axillary nerve. *J Shoulder Elbow Surg* 1992;1:31-36.

63. Bishop JY, Sprague M, Gelber J, et al: Interscalene regional anesthesia for arthroscopic shoulder surgery: A safe and effective technique. *J Shoulder Elbow Surg* 2006;15:567-570.

   In a retrospective chart review, interscalene blocks were found to be effective in 96% of 289 consecutive patients undergoing arthroscopic shoulder surgeries during a 2.5-year period; 4% required general anesthesia because of an inadequate block. Seizures, pneumothoraces, cardiac events, and other major complications did not occur. Minor complications occurred in 1%, and all were transient sensory neuropathies resolved in an average of 5 weeks.

64. Weber SC, Jain R: Scalene regional anesthesia for shoulder surgery in a community setting: An assessment of risk. *J Bone Joint Surg Am* 2002;84:775-779.

   This retrospective study of 218 patients who had scalene block anesthesia during a 3-year period found a number of significant complications. The scalene block was ineffective in 13% of the procedures.

65. Levine WN, Arroyo JS, Pollock RG, Flatow EL, Bigliani LU: Open revision stabilization surgery for recurrent anterior glenohumeral instability. *Am J Sports Med* 2000;28:156-160.

# Section 3

# The Rotator Cuff

Section Editor
Leesa M. Galatz, MD

# Anatomy, Pathogenesis, Natural History, and Nonsurgical Treatment of Rotator Cuff Disorders

Gregory D. Gramstad, MD

Ken Yamaguchi, MD

## Introduction

Rotator cuff disease is one of the most common musculoskeletal disorders. Successful treatment requires a thorough understanding of normal and pathologic anatomy, pathogenesis, and natural history. Basic science research has continued to define rotator cuff and associated anatomy and to elucidate the pathogenesis of rotator cuff disease. Natural history studies have improved the ability to guide treatment using an evidence-based approach.

## Anatomy

The goal of most rotator cuff surgery is anatomic reduction of the ruptured musculotendinous cuff. An understanding of the normal rotator cuff insertion is therefore essential.

The rotator cuff tendon-to-bone insertion has four zones: tendon, fibrocartilage, mineralized fibrocartilage, and bone. The zones do not reconstitute themselves after repair; repaired insertions remain histologically and biomechanically inferior to intact insertions.[1] Thus, it may be important to re-create normal insertional anatomy when attempting repair and to increase the tendon-bone contact area so that the maximum surface area is available for healing. Results from recent studies in which the insertional footprint of the rotator cuff was analyzed have direct implications for characterizing and measuring rotator cuff tears, as well as guiding footprint repair and re-creation.[2-4] Although the different measurement techniques and definitions used in the studies make direct comparisons difficult, the supraspinatus and infraspinatus insertions were found to have similar dimensions: the approximate length is 20 mm, and the approximate medial-lateral width is 15 mm. The supraspinatus and superior subscapularis insertions are approximately 1.5 mm lateral to the articular margin on the anatomic neck.[4] The width of the exposed footprint can be measured to estimate the depth of a partial-thickness tear.

The cuff insertions form a horseshoe pattern that tapers away from the anatomic neck inferiorly; the superior insertion is tendinous, and it becomes more muscular inferiorly. The insertion of the subscapularis is comma shaped and medial to the intertubercular groove; it is tendinous superiorly, tapering away from the anatomic neck and becoming musculocapsular inferiorly[2] (Figure 1). The supraspinatus insertion is tendinous and extends from the posterior intertubercular groove to the anterior tip of the humeral bare area. The infraspinatus frames the humeral bare area, becoming muscular rather than tendinous as it tapers away from the anatomic neck posteriorly. The insertions of the supraspinatus and infraspinatus overlap significantly at the posterior rotator interval. Like the inferior subscapularis, the teres minor has a musculocapsular insertion lateral to the anatomic neck[2] (Figure 2). The insertion is far more inferior and posterior than is generally recognized.

In addition to their role in glenohumeral stability, the rotator interval structures function as primary stabilizers of the long head of the biceps. The coracohumeral and superior glenohumeral ligaments form an intricate sling that resists medial dislocation of the biceps (Figure 3). In addition, superficial fibers from the subscapularis tendon form an annular sling around the proximal biceps, which inserts lateral to the intertubercular groove on the greater tuberosity.[5] Superficial fibers from the anterior supraspinatus blend with these subscapularis fibers to form the roof of the intertubercular groove. A discrete transverse humeral ligament has not been found.[5] Tearing or rupture of the anterior supraspinatus or superior subscapularis can cause injury to the biceps sling and lead to instability of the long head of the biceps. Dislocations of the long head of the biceps are associated with lesions of the biceps sling and rotator cuff.

A posterior rotator interval exists between the supraspinatus and infraspinatus and is defined medially by the scapular spine. Although this interval may have little functional importance, an understanding of its anatomy is important in repair of a large tear. The fibers of the supraspinatus and infraspinatus blend laterally at their insertion on the greater tuberosity, with a 5- to 10-mm overlap. The posterior aspect of the supraspinatus

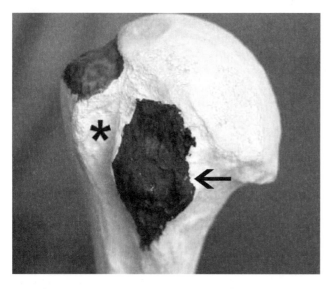

**Figure 1** Subscapularis footprint (*arrow*) on the lesser tuberosity. * = bicipital groove.

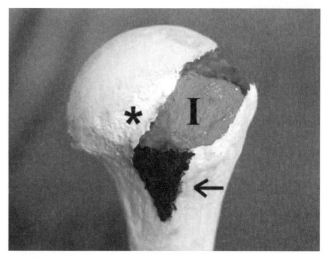

**Figure 2** Posterior cuff footprint on the greater tuberosity. The infraspinatus footprint (I) frames the humeral bare area (*); the musculocapsular teres minor insertion (*arrow*) tapers away from the humeral anatomic neck.

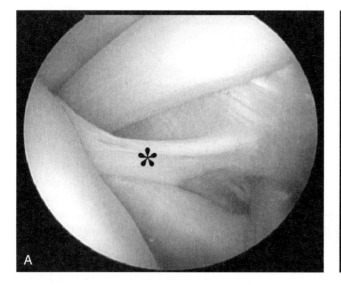

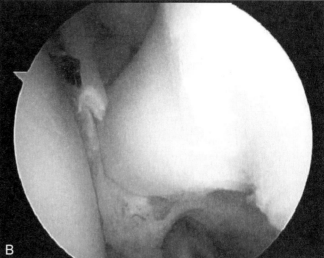

**Figure 3** **A,** Biceps sling (*) seen from a posterior arthroscopic portal. **B,** Medial dislocation of the biceps tendon resulting from a tear of the subscapularis and disruption of the biceps sling.

insertion is generally considered to end at the leading edge of the humeral bare area and deep to the infraspinatus. The infraspinatus inserts more superficially and laterally, wrapping around the supraspinatus fibers at the conjoined portion of the insertion.[2]

Lesions of the suprascapular nerve may be associated with spinoglenoid notch cysts and labral tears, and a relationship with posterior rotator cuff tears has been documented. A cadaver study evaluated the effect of supraspinatus retraction on the takeoff angle of the first motor branch and the resulting tension in the suprascapular nerve.[6] The first motor branch assumed a more acute angle of takeoff with increasing retraction, and in all specimens it was taut with supraspinatus retraction of 2 to 3 cm. The increased tension in the first motor branch from muscular retraction may partially explain the degenerative changes in the supraspinatus muscle. Severe retraction of the infraspinatus causes the nerve to be injured as it is tethered against the spine of the scapula and the spinoglenoid notch and leads to denervation of the infraspinatus.

If nerve injury is suspected as the source of a patient's pain and disability, presurgical electrodiagnostic evaluation may be recommended. Electrodiagnostic evidence of suprascapular nerve denervation was studied in eight patients with massive retracted tears of the posterior rotator cuff; significant reinnervation potentials were found in the two patients who consented to follow-up electromyography after mobilization and partial repair of the rotator cuff.[7] The presence of peripheral or brachial plexopathy can negatively affect the outcome of rotator cuff repair, and presurgical identification of nerve injury is therefore important.

## Etiology and Pathogenesis

The absence of a unified theory of atraumatic rotator cuff disease etiology and pathogenesis suggests that its development is multifactorial. A unified theory would probably include extrinsic elements of primary mechanical impingement and intrinsic elements of primary tendon degeneration from overuse.

Underlying gross instability and macrotrauma are recognized causes of rotator cuff disease. In addition, intrinsic, or overuse, degeneration can cause rotator cuff weakness and dysfunction. The resulting loss of dynamic stability can lead to superior (subacromial) or anterior (subcoracoid) extrinsic functional impingement. Mechanical impingement can cause further microtrauma to the rotator cuff, coracoacromial arch, and subacromial bursa. The accumulation of degeneration and microtrauma leads to ultrastructural changes and then to a vicious cycle of cuff dysfunction, instability, impingement, and injury, leading to further cuff dysfunction and eventually to tearing. Pain is not an essential component of the process; asymptomatic rotator cuff tears exist. However, pain from subacromial bursitis or from the cuff itself can act as a catalyst for the cycle of injury. A congenital anatomic variant such as os acromiale probably can also act as a catalyst. In unstable os acromiale, a primary mechanism of impingement both initiates and accelerates the cycle of injury, leading to ultrastructural damage to the cuff.

### Intrinsic Factors

Patients with symptomatic rotator cuff disease may have weakness and loss of coordinated activation of the rotator cuff and deltoid muscles. An imbalance of muscle fiber diameter and distribution was found in the supraspinatus muscle of patients with symptomatic rotator cuff disease.[8] The fast-twitch fibers, which are responsible for rapid reaction, fine muscle control, and dynamic stability, are more greatly affected, even in the earliest pretear stages. Such changes in rotator cuff form and function can lead to dynamic instability and accentuate both intrinsic and extrinsic impingement.

A study using a novel rat model found that overuse under eccentric muscle-loading conditions caused changes in the supraspinatus similar to those of tendinosis, including an absence of inflammatory cells. Overuse combined with intrinsic injury or external compression affected the histologic and mechanical properties of the supraspinatus more than overuse alone.[9]

The tendons of the rotator cuff appear to undergo degenerative change during normal aging, regardless of external mechanical impingement, and recent studies indicated the way in which these changes can progress to rotator cuff tearing. Some insight into this progression can be gathered from a study of patients with unilateral shoulder pain who underwent bilateral shoulder ultrasonography to evaluate the rotator cuff. An almost-perfect 10-year age distribution was found between patients who had no rotator cuff tear, a unilateral tear, or bilateral tears (at ages 48.7, 58.7, and 67.8 years, respectively). There is a 50% likelihood that a patient with unilateral shoulder pain who is older than 66 years has bilateral rotator cuff tears.[10]

Histologic study of tissue at the site of rotator cuff rupture revealed signs of preexisting degenerative change, primarily in the articular and middle layers of torn cuff tendon stumps.[11] Intratendinous shear forces and differential strain patterns occur during abduction and loading between the articular and bursal surface planes of the supraspinatus.[12,13] These forces are greatest at the articular surface of the tendon insertion, where the tendon is weaker and most partial-thickness tears occur. Granulation tissue at the site of articular-sided partial tears further weakens the cuff insertion and produces factors leading to local osteochondral destruction and cyst formation. Upregulation of apoptosis (programmed cell death) has been found to be directly proportional to the stage of rotator cuff disease, although it is not known whether the upregulation is a cause or effect of tendon injury.

As the cycle of injury continues, macrostructural changes to the supraspinatus tendon and coracoacromial arch accumulate. The subacromial space narrows as a result of swelling of the tendon, thickening and fibrosis of the subacromial bursa, and spurring (enthesophyte formation) on the acromion and coracoacromial ligament insertion. After partial-thickness tearing of the articular segment, strain in the middle and bursal segments increases significantly. The strain on the bursal surface continues to increase with progressive articular-sided tearing and predisposes the remaining tendon to further injury, particularly if intrinsic degeneration is present.[13]

Bursal-sided vascular proliferation is occasionally seen in association with a rotator cuff tear and may be part of a subacromial bursa repair response.[11] In a rat model, chemically induced subacromial bursitis led to dosage-dependent formation of fibrocartilaginous metaplasia in the supraspinatus tendon.[14] Future studies undoubtedly will further address the possible role of subacromial bursitis in tendon degeneration.

### Extrinsic Factors

The bursal surface of the rotator cuff is susceptible to mechanical impingement by the static constraint of the overlying coracoacromial arch. Congenital and developmental variants in anatomy can accentuate the process of impingement. The concept of internal impingement has been expanded to help explain articular-sided lesions of the anterosuperior cuff and biceps.

The presence of a large lateral extension of the acromion was shown to be significantly associated with full-thickness tears of the rotator cuff.[15] The cause may be that the vector of the middle deltoid force is more vertical in shoulders with a higher acromial index (a larger lateral extension), possibly accentuating a tendency for subacromial impingement and mechanical injury to the supraspinatus tendon. Shoulders with glenohumeral osteoarthritis and intact rotator cuffs were associated with a lower acromial index, which would result in a more compressive vector to the middle deltoid force. The association of both coracohumeral stenosis and glenoid inclination and version with rotator cuff tears is controversial.

The coracoacromial ligament, spanning two processes of the same bone, maintains the structure of the coracoacromial arch. The ligament resists widening of the coracoacromial interval (supraspinatus outlet) and has a resting tension that increases during humeral abduction. Basic science research has revealed the osteogenic potential of the coracoacromial ligament insertion and an increased rate of bone turnover at the acromial insertion in the presence of a cuff tear.[16] Dynamic loading of the coracoacromial ligament may stimulate an osteogenic response at the anterior acromial insertion site, leading to enthesophyte formation, stiffening of the coracoacromial arch, and further impingement. There is a strong association between morphologic changes of the acromion and increasing age.[17] The link between acromial shape and a full-thickness cuff tear can also be interpreted as an independent, age-related association between acromial spurring and full-thickness tears. In evaluating acromial morphology and tear etiology, anterolateral acromial spurring should be differentiated from a type III acromion, which is a congenital variant.

Anterosuperior internal impingement has been described as a potential mechanism of anterosuperior articular-sided lesions.[18,19] Combined lesions of the biceps pulley (formed by the superior glenohumeral and coracohumeral ligaments) and the superior articular surface of the subscapularis may result from direct contact with the anterosuperior glenoid rim during forward flexion and internal rotation. This direct contact of the anterosuperior soft tissues with the anterosuperior glenoid rim is similar to the mechanism of posterosuperior internal impingement of the supraspinatus. The point at which the contact becomes pathologic has not been determined.

### Pain

Painless rotator cuff tears are fairly common and are associated with advancing age.[10] Pain can lead to rotator cuff disuse, weakness, compensatory kinematic abnormality, dynamic instability, impingement, and eventually

rotator cuff tearing. The sources of pain and functional disability at the different stages of rotator cuff disease have not been determined, but clearly they extend beyond the presence of a full-thickness tear alone.

Subacromial bursitis may be a significant cause of pain in symptomatic rotator cuff disease, and neurologic and biochemical mechanisms are also recognized. An increased density of sensory nociceptive nerve fibers was identified in the subacromial bursa and coracoacromial ligament in patients with rotator cuff disease.[20,21] Recent investigations of the molecular and biochemical milieu of the subacromial bursa found the presence of messenger RNA expression of inflammatory cytokines, growth factors, and pain-modulating biochemicals (substance P) in surgical patients with symptomatic rotator cuff disease.[21-23]

## Natural History

Spontaneous healing of a rotator cuff tear has occurred in animal models after a surgically created acute injury. There is little evidence, however, that spontaneous healing takes place in humans. It can be assumed that an atraumatic rotator cuff tear will progress over time, although the rate is highly variable. In originally asymptomatic patients with a bilateral tear and unilateral symptoms, the rate of tear progression was found to be 50% at 5 years for those whose shoulders had become symptomatic and 22% for those whose shoulders had remained asymptomatic.[24] The rate of progression in symptomatic tears has not been determined, probably because of a treatment bias. Smaller tears have an intrinsically greater capacity to heal than larger tears.[25] Understanding the progression of symptomatic tear size is critical in determining whether a patient would benefit from early surgical repair. Tears that occur without retraction are not considered irreparable for this purpose. However, irreversible changes on both tendon and bone sides may affect the histology of healing.

Irreversible morphologic and structural changes in the rotator cuff tendons and muscles and the articular cartilage of the glenohumeral joint occur as a function of the size of the tear and the time since tearing. The risks of nonsurgical treatment include the development of permanent alterations in the musculotendinous unit and glenohumeral joint that cannot be reversed or will progress despite treatment. This factor must be considered when determining the best treatment for a patient. Recent studies have improved understanding of the mechanisms and timing of irreversible change.

Torn musculotendinous units are at risk not only of tear size progression but also of retraction, denervation, muscle atrophy, fatty degeneration, and structural or mechanical changes such as stiffness and loss of elasticity. Retraction is weakly associated with tear size. Tear configuration may be more important as the rotator ca-

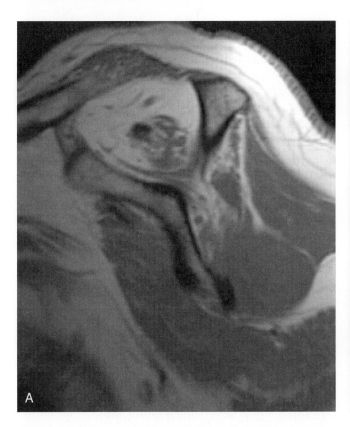
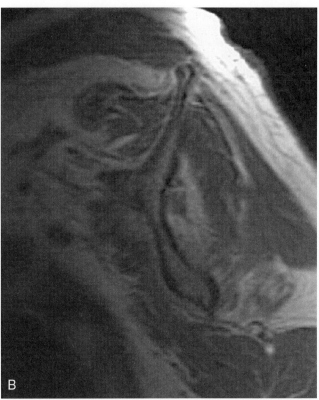

**Figure 4**　Sagittal T1-weighted MRIs of the rotator cuff muscles. **A,** Typical pattern of atrophy in a chronic retracted tear of the supraspinatus. Note the location of the central tendon, with differential atrophy of the superficial portion of the supraspinatus muscle. **B,** Symmetric atrophy and fatty infiltration of the superficial and deep portions of the supraspinatus muscle. This 60-year-old patient had a history of Erb palsy from birth, with a functional recovery.

ble and lateral rotator interval act to prevent retraction of the supraspinatus.[26] Muscle retraction is closely related to fatty infiltration and loss of elasticity.[27] Its effect on strength loss, and therefore on clinical symptoms, is greater than that of detachment alone.[28] Future studies may discover the tear configurations most likely to retract.

Muscle atrophy and interfibrous fatty infiltration are believed to be irreversible, and they may progress despite surgical repair and healing. In a rat model, detachment led to a rapid loss of muscle mass, a time-dependent shift in collagen type, asymmetric alteration in the ratio of fast-twitch to slow-twitch fibers, and increased fibrosis.[29,30] The asymmetry in muscle fiber types suggests that the deep portion of the supraspinatus is associated with postural activity and the superficial portion with high-power activity. Asymmetric atrophy and fatty infiltration were found to affect the superficial (fascial) portion of the muscle more than the deep (scapular) portion.[26] This morphologic feature may be used to differentiate the atrophy of rupture from the symmetric atrophy associated with denervation or disuse (Figure 4). Animal studies of rotator cuff detachment and repair found that measurable irreversible change occurs within 6 to 12 weeks of tendon detachment. Smaller, stiffer muscles were so greatly retracted

and infiltrated with fat that primary repair became impossible as early as 16 weeks after detachment.[27,31,32] The initial changes in morphology, histology, and structural properties are dramatic, and they tend to progress steadily. The time-dependent nature of degenerative alterations in the musculotendinous unit partially explains the observed differences in the reparability and healing of acute and chronic tears.

Although rotator cuff arthropathy rarely develops, a positive correlation was found between rotator cuff tears and the presence of glenohumeral articular cartilage degeneration.[33] Cartilage-degrading enzymes (collagenase and stromelysin) and cartilage catabolic markers (glycosaminoglycans) are elevated in the synovial fluid of patients with a rotator cuff tear.[34] The levels appear to be proportionate to tear size; the increase associated with a massive tear is significant compared with the level associated with an isolated partial-thickness or full-thickness tear of the supraspinatus.

## Nonsurgical Treatment
### Risk Assessment
The literature on nonsurgical treatment is diverse with respect to patient populations, treatments, and outcomes assessment, so that no consensus has been achieved. However, nonsurgical treatment is the appropriate first

**Table 1 | Nonsurgical Treatment Risks in Rotator Cuff Disorders**

| Patient Group | Indication | Risk | Treatment |
|---|---|---|---|
| I | Intact rotator cuff with tendinitis<br>Small partial-thickness tear | Minimal | Nonsurgical |
| II | Symptomatic tear (patient age < 60 years)<br>Small or medium-sized tear (patient age 60 to 65 years)<br>Large, degenerative partial-thickness tear<br>Acute tear (< 3 months' duration) | Significant | Surgical |
| III | Symptomatic tear (patient age > 70 years)<br>Large or massive chronic tear | Already realized | Trial nonsurgical |

treatment of most rotator cuff disease and partial-thickness tearing. The risk of irreversible change must be weighed against the risk of surgical treatment in considering the role of nonsurgical treatment in the care of a full-thickness tear. Rotator cuff tears have been classified based on the relative risk of irreversible change during nonsurgical treatment (Table 1). Group I includes patients at minimal risk of irreversible change to the rotator cuff during prolonged nonsurgical treatment; group II, patients at risk of irreversible change with prolonged nonsurgical treatment; and group III, patients in whom irreversible changes have already occurred. Patients in group I can safely undergo prolonged nonsurgical treatment, and nonsurgical treatment in this group is generally successful. Patients in group II may benefit from early surgical treatment to lessen the risk of irreversible change during nonsurgical treatment. Most patients in group III should receive a trial of nonsurgical treatment.

### Anti-Inflammatory Drugs

The discovery of inflammatory mediators in the subacromial bursa of patients with symptomatic rotator cuff disease suggests that anti-inflammatory drugs may be beneficial in treating painful subacromial bursitis. A recent basic science investigation reported that both dexamethasone and cyclooxygenase-2 (COX-2) inhibitors downregulated an important inflammatory mediator in the subacromial bursa.[35] Another study concluded that the COX-1 pathway is more important than the COX-2 pathway in generating subacromial bursal inflammatory mediators and thereby suggested that the specialized COX-2 inhib-

itors may be less efficacious than nonspecific COX inhibitors.[36]

Subacromial corticosteroid injection has been a mainstay of nonsurgical treatment for many years. However, conflicting clinical results continue to be reported.[37-39] Meta-analyses have provided little conclusive evidence because the treatment groups, steroid types, dosages, and outcomes measures vary widely among even the highest quality studies.[40,41] Subacromial steroid injection is more efficacious in improving symptoms than a placebo and probably oral nonsteroidal anti-inflammatory drugs.[41] Steroids appear to be more efficacious at high dosages (the equivalent of at least 50 mg of prednisone).

Evidence of the deleterious effects of corticosteroid injections is increasing. In a rat model used to investigate the effects of subacromial corticosteroid injections, pathologic and histologic signs of rotator cuff tendon damage have been noted after four or more injections.[42] One injection has been shown to produce a short-term (less than 3 weeks) alteration in the ratio of type III to type I collagen expression, similar to that observed in structural cuff injuries.[43] This finding suggests that short-term activity and therapy modification may be warranted after subacromial corticosteroid injection. Approximately 25% of subacromial injections are misplaced into the muscle of the rotator cuff or deltoid or medial to the medial bursal boundary.[44,45] Inadvertent intramuscular injection is associated with increased postinjection pain. Neither the patient's body mass index nor the clinician's level of confidence significantly affects the accuracy of injection.[44]

### Physical Therapy and Exercise

Exercise was found in a meta-analysis to be beneficial in both short-term recovery and long-term function.[46] Joint mobilization can offer additional benefit. The combination of physical therapy and exercise is effective in treating acute symptoms, although its efficacy in preventing recurrence has not been studied. Ultrasonography, acupuncture, and extracorporeal shock wave therapy have not proved beneficial.[46-48] A self-guided exercise program directed at strengthening dynamic stabilization of the rotator cuff and managing scapular motion abnormalities can be as efficacious as a formal program of physical therapy.[49]

Rehabilitation of the rotator cuff can be difficult if the shoulder is painful. Subacromial pressures have been shown to be affected by arm position and rotator cuff strength.[50] Patients with good external rotation strength at the side have lower subacromial pressures throughout motion than patients with weaker external rotation strength. Subacromial pressures are lowest during external rotation with the arm at the side, compared with internal rotation, abduction, and flexion. External rotation strengthening with the arm at the side may minimize subacromial pressures and pain while enhancing the cuff's ability to act as a humeral head depressor during abduction.

Patients with asymptomatic two-tendon tears of the posterior rotator cuff show increased activity in the subscapularis during elevation and functional tasks. Paradoxically, symptomatic patients show increased activation of the torn cuff muscles and periscapular muscle substitution.[51] This difference could be related to preservation of the anterior-posterior balance in asymptomatic patients, or it could be an adaptive change. Studies designed to determine the most appropriate exercise program for patients with symptomatic irreparable rotator cuff tears are lacking.

## Summary

The successful treatment of rotator cuff disease requires a thorough understanding of rotator cuff anatomy and function and an appreciation of the natural history of rotator cuff disease. The rotator cuff undergoes a natural process of senescence that, combined with mechanical factors, can lead to tearing. The symptoms are poorly correlated with the stage of disease. Pain is the most commonly treated symptom, although its etiology is not well understood. The role of impingement and subacromial bursitis in symptomatic rotator cuff disease continues to be defined. There is evidence that exercise therapy, designed to strengthen the head-depressing function of the cuff, is beneficial in managing symptoms. Anti-inflammatory drugs and injections should be used judiciously in managing subacromial bursitis and painful cuff disease. Natural history studies will continue to be important in defining the indications for surgical intervention.

## Annotated References

1. Galatz LM, Sandell LJ, Rothermich SY, et al: Characteristics of the rat supraspinatus tendon during tendon-to-bone healing after acute injury. *J Orthop Res* 2006;24:541-550.

   In an investigation of the early healing characteristics of rodent supraspinatus tendon repairs, transforming growth factor-β1 was localized to repair tissue and found to coincide with a peak in cell proliferation and density. Repaired tendon insertion sites remained histologically unorganized and biomechanically inferior to uninjured insertion sites after 8 weeks.

2. Curtis AS, Burbank KM, Tierney JJ, Scheller AD, Curran AR: The insertional footprint of the rotator cuff: An anatomic study. *Arthroscopy* 2006;22:609.

   Direct measurement and scanning electron microscopy were used in a cadaver anatomic study of the rotator cuff

insertion and its spatial relationship to identifiable anatomic landmarks.

3. Dugas JR, Campbell DA, Warren RF, Robie BH, Millett PJ: Anatomy and dimensions of rotator cuff insertions. *J Shoulder Elbow Surg* 2002;11:498-503.

   In a cadaver anatomic study of the rotator cuff insertional dimensions, mapping and direct measurement were used to determine the area of insertion and relationship to the articular margin.

4. Ruotolo C, Fow JE, Nottage WM: The supraspinatus footprint: An anatomic study of the supraspinatus insertion. *Arthroscopy* 2004;20:246-249.

   The researchers propose a method for determining the approximate depth of partial-thickness supraspinatus tears.

5. Gleason PD, Beall DP, Sanders TG, et al: The transverse humeral ligament: A separate anatomical structure or a continuation of the osseous attachment of the rotator cuff? *Am J Sports Med* 2006;34:72-77.

   A distinct transverse humeral ligament was not seen in this cadaver anatomic study of the stabilizing structures of the proximal long head of the biceps.

6. Albritton MJ, Graham RD, Richards RS II, Basamania CJ: An anatomic study of the effects on the suprascapular nerve due to retraction of the supraspinatus muscle after a rotator cuff tear. *J Shoulder Elbow Surg* 2003;12:497-500.

   In this cadaver study of the suprascapular nerve and its branching pattern in vivo and after supraspinatus retraction, the researchers theorized that suprascapular neuropathy may occur after significant supraspinatus retraction and may affect muscle atrophy.

7. Mallon WJ, Wilson RJ, Basamania CJ: The association of suprascapular neuropathy with massive rotator cuff tears: A preliminary report. *J Shoulder Elbow Surg* 2006;15:395-398.

   In a prospective consecutive series of eight patients with a massive retracted cuff tear with fatty infiltration, electromyography was used to diagnose denervation of the supraspinatus or infraspinatus. Four patients underwent surgical repair. Two consented to postsurgical electromyography, which found significant reinnervation potentials.

8. Irlenbusch U, Gansen HK: Muscle biopsy investigations on neuromuscular insufficiency of the rotator cuff: A contribution to the functional impingement of the shoulder joint. *J Shoulder Elbow Surg* 2003;12:422-426.

   Histologic analysis of deltoid and suprascapular muscle biopsy revealed that the balance of fast-twitch and slow-twitch fibers shifts in patients with a partial or complete supraspinatus tear.

9. Soslowsky LJ, Thomopoulos S, Esmail A, et al: Rotator cuff tendinosis in an animal model: Role of

extrinsic and overuse factors. *Ann Biomed Eng* 2002; 30:1057-1063.

The authors used a rodent shoulder model to study the effect on the development of rotator cuff tendinosis of extrinsic compression and overuse, as well as overuse in combination with extrinsic compression.

10. Yamaguchi K, Konstantinos D, Middleton WD, Hildebolt CF, Galatz LM, Teefey SA: The demographics and morphological features of rotator cuff disease: A comparison of asymptomatic and symptomatic shoulders. *J Bone Joint Surg Am* 2006;88:1699-1704.

Bilateral ultrasonographic examination was performed in 588 consecutive patients with unilateral shoulder pain. The presence of a partial-thickness or full-thickness rotator cuff tear was found to be highly correlated with increasing age. Symptomatic tears were significantly larger than asymptomatic tears.

11. Hashimoto T, Nobuhara K, Hamada T: Pathologic evidence of degeneration as a primary cause of rotator cuff tear. *Clin Orthop Relat Res* 2003;415:111-120.

The authors describe the histopathologic, histochemical, and morphometric characteristics of medial stumps of torn rotator cuff tendon tissue in an effort to elucidate an etiology of tendon rupture.

12. Huang CY, Wang VM, Pawluk RJ, et al: Inhomogeneous mechanical behavior of the human supraspinatus tendon under uniaxial loading. *J Orthop Res* 2005;23:924-930.

Potential tensile strain gradients between the bursal and articular surfaces of the supraspinatus were evaluated in a cadaver study.

13. Reilly P, Amis AA, Wallace AL, Emery RJ: Supraspinatus tears: Propagation and strain alteration. *J Shoulder Elbow Surg* 2003;12:134-138.

Differential intratendinous strain patterns were studied during static and tensile loading in cadaver shoulders with a full-thickness tear, intratendinous tear, or partial articular-sided tear.

14. Tillander B, Franzen LE, Nilsson E, Norlin R: Carrageenan-induced subacromial bursitis caused changes in the rat's rotator cuff. *J Orthop Res* 2001;19: 441-447.

The authors describe the effect of carrageenan-induced subacromial bursitis on the development of pathologic changes in the rodent supraspinatus tendon.

15. Nyffeler RW, Werner CM, Sukthankar A, Schmid MR, Gerber C: Association of a large lateral extension of the acromion with rotator cuff tears. *J Bone Joint Surg Am* 2006;88:800-805.

In a radiographic investigation of lateral acromial morphology in patients with a proven full-thickness rotator cuff tear and osteoarthritis, as well as normal control sub-

jects, acromiom index was correlated with full-thickness tearing and osteoarthritis.

16. Chambler AF, Pitsillides AA, Emery RJ: Acromial spur formation in patients with rotator cuff tears. *J Shoulder Elbow Surg* 2003;12:314-321.

In patients with a rotator cuff tear, the acromial spur was studied for evidence of secondary bone formation.

17. Speer KP, Osbahr DC, Montella BJ, Apple AS, Mair SD: Acromial morphotype in the young asymptomatic athletic shoulder. *J Shoulder Elbow Surg* 2001;10: 434-437.

Radiographic analysis revealed that the type III acromion is relatively rare in young asymptomatic athletes. It is hypothesized that the higher incidence of type III acromion in older patients may be the result of secondary changes.

18. Gerber C, Sebesta A: Impingement of the deep surface of the subscapularis tendon and the reflection pulley on the anterosuperior glenoid rim: A preliminary report. *J Shoulder Elbow Surg* 2000;9:483-490.

19. Habermeyer P, Magosch P, Pritsch M, Scheibel MT, Lichtenberg S: Anterosuperior impingement of the shoulder as a result of pulley lesions: A prospective arthroscopic study. *J Shoulder Elbow Surg* 2004;13: 5-12.

In 89 patients with a lesion of the proximal long head biceps pulley, the researchers attempted to determine factors influencing the development of anterosuperior impingement.

20. Tamai M, Okajima S, Fushiki S, Hirasawa Y: Quantitative analysis of neural distribution in human coracoacromial ligaments. *Clin Orthop Relat Res* 2000; 373:125-134.

21. Gotoh M, Hamada K, Yamakawa H, Inoue A, Fukuda H: Increased substance P in subacromial bursa and shoulder pain in rotator cuff diseases. *J Orthop Res* 1998;16:618-621.

22. Blaine TA, Kim YS, Voloshin I, et al: The molecular pathophysiology of subacromial bursitis in rotator cuff disease. *J Shoulder Elbow Surg* 2005;14(suppl 1): 84S-89S.

The authors report that the bursal expression of cytokines (tumor necrosis factor and interleukin-1α, -1β, and -6), metalloproteases, and cyclooxygenases (COX-1 and COX-2) was increased in subjects with subacromial bursitis, compared with control subjects. The findings may support the use of anti-inflammatory drugs and surgical bursectomy.

23. Yanagisawa K, Hamada K, Gotoh M, et al: Vascular endothelial growth factor (VEGF) expression in the subacromial bursa is increased in patients with impingement syndrome. *J Orthop Res* 2001;19:448-455.

Vascular endothelial growth factor mRNA expression was detected in the subacromial bursal tissue of patients with rotator cuff disease. It was associated with increased vascularity, synovial proliferation, and shoulder motion pain.

24. Yamaguchi K, Tetro AM, Blam O, Evanoff BA, Teefey SA, Middleton WD: Natural history of asymptomatic rotator cuff tears: A longitudinal analysis of asymptomatic tears detected sonographically. *J Shoulder Elbow Surg* 2001;10:199-203.

    The risk of symptom development and tear progression is reported in a longitudinal natural history study of asymptomatic rotator cuff tears evaluated sonographically.

25. Matthews TJ, Hand GC, Rees JL, Athanasou NA, Carr AJ: Pathology of the torn rotator cuff tendon: Reduction in potential for repair as tear size increases. *J Bone Joint Surg Br* 2006;88:489-495.

    In 40 patients with a chronic full-thickness tear, histologic evidence of reparative and inflammatory changes in the supraspinatus tendon was present in smaller tears and absent in larger tears. The authors conclude that smaller chronic tears have more capacity to heal.

26. Meyer DC, Pirkl C, Pfirrmann CW, Zanetti M, Gerber C: Asymmetric atrophy of the supraspinatus muscle following tendon tear. *J Orthop Res* 2005;23:254-258.

    Supraspinatus tendon tears in painful shoulders were evaluated using MRI for patterns of myotendinous retraction, muscle atrophy, and fatty infiltration. Asymmetrical muscular changes were found to occur after rotator cuff tearing.

27. Gerber C, Meyer DC, Schneeberger AG, Hoppeler H, von Rechenberg B: Effect of tendon release and delayed repair on the structure of the muscles of the rotator cuff: An experimental study in sheep. *J Bone Joint Surg Am* 2004;86:1973-1982.

    Surgical detachment of sheep infraspinatus tendons resulted in profound, progressive changes in muscular attributes. Subsequent attempted repair failed to reverse these changes within 35 weeks.

28. Halder AM, O'Driscoll SW, Heers G, et al: Biomechanical comparison of effects of supraspinatus tendon detachments, tendon defects, and muscle retractions. *J Bone Joint Surg Am* 2002;84:780-785.

    A cadaver biomechanical study evaluated the effects of rotator cuff detachments, defects, and retraction on force transmission through the rotator cuff.

29. Barton ER, Gimbel JA, Williams GR, Soslowsky LJ: Rat supraspinatus muscle atrophy after tendon detachment. *J Orthop Res* 2005;23:259-265.

    Rapid changes in muscle mass and fiber type occur after tendon detachment without repair of the rodent supraspinatus muscle.

30. Yokota A, Gimbel JA, Williams GR, Soslowsky LJ: Supraspinatus tendon composition remains altered long after tendon detachment. *J Shoulder Elbow Surg* 2005;14(suppl 1):72S-78S.

    Qualitative changes occur after detachment without repair of the rodent supraspinatus tendon. Rapid changes in collagen composition occur in the local milieu. The compositional quality of chronic tears is different from that of acute tears.

31. Coleman SH, Fealy S, Ehteshami JR, et al: Chronic rotator cuff injury and repair model in sheep. *J Bone Joint Surg Am* 2003;85:2391-2402.

    A sheep model of infraspinatus detachment was used to determine the effects of immediate and delayed repair on muscle function and tendon elasticity.

32. Safran O, Derwin KA, Powell K, Iannotti JP: Changes in rotator cuff muscle volume, fat content, and passive mechanics after chronic detachment in a canine model. *J Bone Joint Surg Am* 2005;87:2662-2670.

    Surgical detachment of canine infraspinatus tendons led to a time-dependent alteration in muscular attributes. Muscular volume decreased within 6 weeks and then stabilized. At 12 weeks, the tendon had retracted more than 3 cm, had stiffened, and was nonuniformly infiltrated with fat.

33. Feeney MS, O'Dowd J, Kay EW, Colville J: Glenohumeral articular cartilage changes in rotator cuff disease. *J Shoulder Elbow Surg* 2003;12:20-23.

    A cadaver anatomic and histologic study evaluated the correlation between rotator cuff tears and articular cartilage degeneration.

34. Yoshihara Y, Hamada K, Nakajima T, Fujikawa K, Fukuda H: Biochemical markers in the synovial fluid of glenohumeral joints from patients with rotator cuff tear. *J Orthop Res* 2001;19:573-579.

    Synovial fluid from shoulders with a partial-thickness or full-thickness rotator cuff tear was analyzed for the presence of macromolecules involved in cartilage-degrading activity.

35. Kim YS, Bigliani LU, Fujisawa M, et al: Stromal cell-derived factor 1 (SDF-1, CXCL12) is increased in subacromial bursitis and downregulated by steroid and nonsteroidal anti-inflammatory agents. *J Orthop Res* 2006;24:1756-1764.

    The gene expression of inflammatory cytokine stromal cell-derived factor-1 (SDF-1) is increased in the subacromial bursal tissue of patients with bursitis. In cultured bursitis cell lines treated with dexamethasone and a COX-2 inhibitor, the expression of SDF-1 was decreased.

36. Knorth H, Wittenberg RH, Dorfmuller P, et al: [In vitro effects of diclofenac and selective cyclooxygenase-2 inhibitors on prostaglandin release from inflamed bursa subacromialis tissue in patients with subacromial syndrome]. *Orthopade* 2005;34:241-249.

Diclofenac (a nonspecific COX inhibitor) was shown to inhibit prostaglandin $E_2$ release from inflamed subacromial bursal specimens. Selective COX-2 inhibitors were ineffective. The authors conclude that most prostaglandin in subacromial bursal tissue is generated via the COX-1 pathway.

37. Blair B, Rokito AS, Cuomo F, Jarolem K, Zuckerman JD: Efficacy of injections of corticosteroids for subacromial impingement syndrome. *J Bone Joint Surg Am* 1996;78:1685-1689.

38. Alvarez CM, Litchfield R, Jackowski D, Griffin S, Kirkley A: A prospective, double-blind, randomized clinical trial comparing subacromial injection of betamethasone and Xylocaine to Xylocaine alone in chronic rotator cuff tendinosis. *Am J Sports Med* 2005;33:255-262.

    Fifty-eight patients with symptomatic rotator cuff tendinosis or a partial-thickness tear were randomized to injection of Xylocaine alone or with 6 mg of betamethasone. The addition of the steroid did not significantly improve the patient's quality of life or range of motion at any time during the 6-month study.

39. Koester MC, Dunn WR, Kuhn JE, Spindler KP: The efficacy of subacromial corticosteroid injection in the treatment of rotator cuff disease: A systematic review. *J Am Acad Orthop Surg* 2007;15:3-11.

    An evidence-based review of nine randomized controlled trials comparing subacromial steroid injection to placebo in patients with rotator cuff disease is presented. The authors conclude that little reproducible evidence exists to support the efficacy of steroid injection.

40. Buchbinder R, Green S, Youd JM: Corticosteroid injections for shoulder pain. *Cochrane Database Syst Rev* 2003;1:CD004016.

41. Arroll B, Goodyear-Smith F: Corticosteroid injections for painful shoulder: A meta-analysis. *Br J Gen Pract* 2005;55:224-228.

    In an analysis of randomized studies comparing subacromial corticosteroid injection to either an oral nonsteroidal anti-inflammatory drug or placebo for treatment of rotator cuff tendinitis, the authors conclude that steroid injection is effective and may be dose related. One study included patients with adhesive capsulitis.

42. Tillander B, Franzen LE, Karlsson MH, Norlin R: Effect of steroid injections on the rotator cuff: An experimental study in rats. *J Shoulder Elbow Surg* 1999; 8:271-274.

43. Wei AS, Callaci JJ, Juknelis D, et al: The effect of corticosteroid on collagen expression in injured rotator cuff tendon. *J Bone Joint Surg Am* 2006;88:1331-1338.

    The ratio of type III to type I collagen expression, an indicator of injury response, was compared in rats with and without tendon injury after subacromial corticosteroid injection, as well as control and injury-alone groups. The ste-

roid injection elicited an alteration equivalent to that of a structural injury, which returned to baseline within 3 weeks.

44. Henkus HE, Cobben LP, Coerkamp EG, Nelissen RG, van Arkel ER: The accuracy of subacromial injections: A prospective randomized magnetic resonance imaging study. *Arthroscopy* 2006;22:277-282.

    The accuracy of subacromial bursal injections was measured using MRI and found to be no better than 76%. Surgeon confidence was poorly correlated with accuracy, and body mass index had no effect.

45. Mathews PV, Glousman RE: Accuracy of subacromial injection: Anterolateral versus posterior approach. *J Shoulder Elbow Surg* 2005;14:145-148.

    The accuracy of subacromial bursal injection performed through either an anterolateral or posterior approach was assessed using both fluoroscopic and dissection confirmation.

46. Green S, Buchbinder R, Hetrick S: Physiotherapy interventions for shoulder pain. *Cochrane Database Syst Rev* 2003;2:CD004258.

47. Green S, Buchbinder R, Hetrick S: Acupuncture for shoulder pain. *Cochrane Database Syst Rev* 2005;18: CD005319.

    This systematic review of randomized or quasirandomized trials compared acupuncture to other treatment methods or a placebo. Little evidence is available to support or refute the use of acupuncture for shoulder pain.

48. Speed CA, Richards C, Nichols D, et al: Extracorporeal shock-wave therapy for tendonitis of the rotator cuff: A double-blind, randomised, controlled trial. *J Bone Joint Surg Br* 2002;84:509-512.

    In a double-blind, randomized, placebo-controlled trial of extracorporeal shock-wave therapy for treatment of noncalcific rotator cuff tendinitis, no evidence of significant benefit was found.

49. Walther M, Werner A, Stahlschmidt T, Woelfel R, Gohlke F: The subacromial impingement syndrome of the shoulder treated by conventional physiotherapy, self-training, and a shoulder brace: Results of a prospective, randomized study. *J Shoulder Elbow Surg* 2004;13:417-423.

    In a prospective, randomized trial of 60 patients with subacromial impingement treated with exercise-based physiotherapy, a self-guided home program, or a functional brace, all groups showed improvement in pain, mobility, strength, and Constant score. There was no statistically significant difference at any point during the 12 weeks.

50. Werner CM, Blumenthal S, Curt A, Gerber C: Subacromial pressures in vivo and effects of selective experimental suprascapular nerve block. *J Shoulder Elbow Surg* 2006;15:319-323.

The authors directly measured subacromial pressure during active shoulder motion in individuals with normal shoulders. Measurements were repeated after suprascapular nerve paralysis to mimic tears of the supraspinatus and infraspinatus.

51. Kelly BT, Williams RJ, Cordasco FA, et al: Differential patterns of muscle activation in patients with symptomatic and asymptomatic rotator cuff tears. *J Shoulder Elbow Surg* 2005;14:165-171.

Electromyographic activity and kinematic data were recorded during functional tasks in patients with symptomatic and asymptomatic two-tendon rotator cuff tears, as well as individuals with an intact rotator cuff.

# Chapter 14

# Partial-Thickness Rotator Cuff Tears

Jay D. Keener, MD

## Introduction

A partial-thickness rotator cuff tear (PTRCT) is a common cause of shoulder pain and occupational disability. Incomplete tears of the rotator cuff were first characterized by Codman in 1934 as incomplete disruption, intratendinous degeneration, and "rim rent" of the tendinous insertions of the rotator cuff. Neer later introduced mechanical impingement of the superior rotator cuff against the coracoacromial arch as an etiology. Subacromial impingement probably contributes to the development of symptomatic rotator cuff disease; however, debate continues as to the etiology and pathogenesis of PTRCTs. Arthroscopy has allowed PTRCTs to be more accurately characterized, although the treatment roles of repair, débridement, and subacromial decompression have not been clearly delineated. Because of the aging population and the active lifestyle of many older individuals, it is increasingly important for physicians to be able to accurately recognize and treat patients with a PTRCT. Advances in arthroscopic surgical techniques now allow PTRCTs to be effectively treated with minimal morbidity.

## Incidence

Most clinical and cadaver studies have found PTRCTs to be more common than full-thickness rotator cuff tears. The incidence of PTRCTs in cadaver shoulders ranged from 13% to 32%,[1-3] probably reflecting the wide age range of the specimens. The prevalence of rotator cuff disease is strongly associated with age; the peak incidence of PTRCTs is in the fifth and sixth decades of life, whereas for full-thickness tears it is later in life. Clinical studies have found a relatively high incidence of PTRCTs in asymptomatic individuals. An MRI study found that 20% of asymptomatic individuals had a PTRCT; the incidence was highest (26%) in individuals older than 60 years and lowest (4%) in those younger than 40 years.[4] A recent study of bilateral shoulder ultrasonography in a large group of patients with unilateral shoulder pain found a significant incidence of either a partial-thickness or full-thickness tendon tear in the asymptomatic shoulder. The presence of a tear was strongly associated with both the age of the patient (older than 60 years) and the severity of rotator cuff disease in the symptomatic shoulder.[5] In most clinical studies, articular-sided PTRCTs are two to three times more common than bursal-sided tears.[6]

## Anatomy

The tendons of the rotator cuff blend into the articular capsule, coracohumeral ligament, and glenohumeral ligaments before their insertion into the humeral tuberosities. The tendons of the supraspinatus and infraspinatus muscles join to form a single tendon 15 mm proximal to the insertion into the greater tuberosity. Histologic examination of the supraspinatus and infraspinatus tendons reveals five distinct layers,[7] as described in Table 1. The supraspinatus and subscapularis tendons, with the superior glenohumeral and coracohumeral ligaments, contribute to the formation of a sheath that envelopes the biceps tendon as it enters the bicipital groove. A portion of the supraspinatus tendon forms the roof of the sheath, and the subscapularis tendon contributes to

### Table 1 | Layers of the Supraspinatus and Infraspinatus Tendons

| Layer* | Approximate Thickness (mm) | Tissue Type |
| --- | --- | --- |
| 1 | 1 | Coracohumeral ligament fibers interposed with large arterioles |
| 2 | 3-5 | Densely packed parallel tendon fibers |
| 3 | 2-3 | Smaller bundles of collagen with a less uniform orientation than layer 2 |
| 4 | 1 | Loose connective tissue and thick collagen fibrils blending anteriorly with coracohumeral ligament |
| 5 | 1.5-2 | Glenohumeral capsule, consisting of a sheet of interwoven collagen fibers |

*Numbers correspond to relative depth; layer 1 is the most superficial.

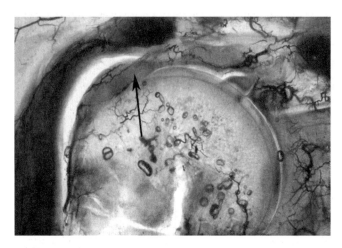

**Figure 1** A coronal plane micrograph of the supraspinatus tendon showing tendon vascularity. The arrow points to the critical zone of vascularity of the articular-sided tendon. *(Reproduced with permission from Stetson WB, Phillips T, Deutsch A: The use of magnetic resonance arthrography to detect partial-thickness rotator cuff tears. J Bone Joint Surg 2006;87:81-88.)*

the floor. The relationship of pathology of the upper subscapularis and anterior supraspinatus tendons to lesions of the biceps tendon is well recognized.

The area and thickness of the footprint insertion onto the humerus differ for each of the rotator cuff tendons. The supraspinatus, infraspinatus, and subscapularis tendons have a mean medial-to-lateral insertion width of 12.7 mm, 13.4 mm, and 17.9 mm, respectively.[8] One recent study found that for the supraspinatus tendon, the medial-to-lateral width of the insertion ranges from 11.6 mm to 12.1 mm at the anterior, middle, and posterior edges of the tendon, and the distance from the articular surface to the medial aspect of footprint insertion ranges from 1.5 mm to 1.9 mm.[9] The average anterior-posterior distance of the supraspinatus and infraspinatus tendons insertions at the point of insertion into the tuberosity is 1.63 cm and 1.64 cm, respectively.[9]

The vascular system of the rotator cuff tendons consists of anastomotic vessels arising from the subscapular and suprascapular arteries, combined with humeral circumflex arteries via the tuberosities.[10] These blood vessels traverse the rotator cuff, and they branch within the second and third layers and along the bursal side of the tendons. The articular side of the rotator cuff is hypovascular compared with the bursal side, and there is a critical zone of hypovascularity in the most lateral portion of the supraspinatus tendon insertion[11] (Figure 1).

## Pathogenesis

The etiology of PTRCTs is controversial. It is likely that both intrinsic and extrinsic factors contribute to the pathogenesis of symptomatic PTRCTs. Most PTRCTs are isolated in the supraspinatus tendon, although involvement of the infraspinatus and upper subscapularis tendons is well recognized. A PTRCT may primarily in-

volve the articular surface, bursal surface, or intratendinous portions of the tendon. The architecture of the supraspinatus tendon dictates that the articular side has an ultimate strength roughly half that of the bursal surface;[12] as a result, most PTRCTs involve this vulnerable aspect of the articular surface of the supraspinatus tendon.

Significant evidence exists to support intrinsic degeneration as an important cause of PTRCTs. The incidence is strongly linked with advancing age. Age-related degenerative changes in the rotator cuff tendons include decreased cellularity, thinning of collagen fascicles, and accumulation of dystrophic tissue. Furthermore, the blood supply to the rotator cuff tendons is compromised with aging, most notably at the articular side of the supraspinatus tendon. Multiple histologic studies support the concept of intrinsic degeneration as the primary etiology of PTRCTs. Cadaver shoulders with no macroscopic evidence of a rotator cuff tear were compared with shoulders with a partial-thickness tear of the supraspinatus tendon; histologic degeneration was observed on both the articular and bursal sides of the normal-appearing tendons, with the articular side showing more advanced degenerative changes. Thinning of the collagen fiber and formation of granulation tissue were more prominent in the tendons with a partial-thickness tear.[1]

The gross appearance and histologic anatomy of the acromion and coracoacromial arch usually are normal in shoulders with an articular-sided PTRCT.[13] A recent clinical study evaluated the pathologic and histologic characteristics of the anterior acromion in 66 patients with a PTRCT. MRI revealed greater pathologic changes in the tendon in shoulders with articular-sided tears, compared with shoulders with bursal-sided tears, although the pathologic changes in the acromion were milder in shoulders with an articular-sided tear.[14]

Mechanical compression and irritation of the rotator cuff may occur as a result of impingement against the coracoacromial arch. However, the role of acromial morphology in the pathogenesis of rotator cuff disease has not been determined. Impingement of the superior rotator cuff tendons against inferior-projecting osteophytes on the anterior third of the acromion and distal clavicle probably contribute to the development of bursal-sided partial-thickness tears. Other extrinsic factors in the pathogenesis of PTRCTs are traumatic injury, glenohumeral instability, and mechanical abutment, such as internal impingement of the articular aspect of the rotator cuff against the posterosuperior labrum and glenoid in throwing athletes. After the supraspinatus has undergone significant attrition, rotator cuff dysfunction may lead to a loss of dynamic stability and secondary impingement or irritation in the subacromial space. This possibility is supported by the clinical observation that many patients with articular-sided tears have signs of

subacromial impingement and respond favorably to subacromial injections. In addition, histologic studies have
found minor inflammatory and attritional changes in the
coracoacromial arch in patients with isolated articular-
surface tears of the supraspinatus.[14]

The presence of a PTRCT alters the strain distribution among the adjacent intact rotator cuff tendons. This
factor may contribute to the progression of a partial-
thickness tear over time. In a cadaver model simulating
a loaded rotator cuff, intratendinous lesions were found
to increase the strain on both the articular and bursal
sides with increasing angles of elevation.[15] Cadaver
studies confirmed that the presence of an articular-sided
partial-thickness tear increases the strain in the middle
and superficial layers of the rotator cuff tendon at angles of elevation greater than 15°.[16] A recent two-
dimensional finite element study found that after creation of articular-sided, bursal-sided, and intratendinous
rotator cuff tears, increased stress distribution occurred
at the site of the tear, with the greatest stress concentrated on the articular surface.[17]

## Natural History

The natural history of an untreated PTRCT is not
known. It is likely that a partial-thickness tear is an intermediate stage in rotator cuff disease and that it eventually becomes a full-thickness tear. Studies have consistently found that patients with a PTRCT are younger
than those with a full-thickness tear.[4,5] However, factors
related to tear propagation and the onset of symptoms
have not been elucidated.

PTRCTs have a limited capacity for spontaneous
healing. Most histologic studies have found fiber thinning and disruption, as well as local granulation tissue,
but little evidence of active repair. PTRCTs retain some
potential for healing at a cellular level, as shown by the
expression of type I procollagen messenger RNA (a
precursor to type I collagen) at the margins of the
tear.[18] However, most clinical evidence suggests that
PTRCTs progress over time. A prospective arthrographic study found that 1 year after initial evaluation,
half of the examined PTRCTs appeared larger, and 25%
had progressed to a full-thickness rotator cuff defect;
less than 10% were considered to be healed.[19] At a minimum 5-year follow-up of shoulders with a PTRCT
treated with arthroscopic débridement and acromioplasty, ultrasonography revealed that 9 of 26 shoulders
(34%) had a full-thickness tear. The authors concluded
that acromioplasty and débridement do not prevent
continued degeneration of the rotator cuff.[20]

## Imaging

Ultrasonography and MRI are the preferred modalities
for evaluating rotator cuff disease, although they are
less accurate in diagnosing PTRCTs than full-thickness

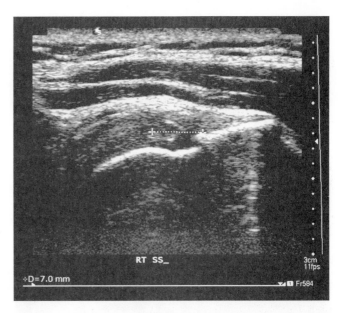

**Figure 2**  A coronal plane ultrasonographic image showing an articular-sided tear of
the supraspinatus tendon involving approximately half of the width of the tendon
insertion.

tears. Ultrasonography is quick and convenient to use,
and it is usually well tolerated by patients. Images of
both shoulders can be easily obtained, and the position
of the extremity can be changed to permit a focused, dynamic examination of the rotator cuff (Figure 2). The
accuracy of ultrasonography depends on the experience
of the ultrasonographer, and consequently it is less
readily available than MRI.

MRI allows the rotator cuff to be defined and concomitant shoulder pathology to be detected. Accuracy is
improved by the addition of intra-articular contrast, especially in detecting articular-sided tears. The development of MRI techniques such as fat suppression, proton
density imaging, and abduction and external rotation
views has improved the visualization of subtle rotator
cuff pathology. The presence of a PTRCT is suggested
by an increased signal in the rotator cuff on T1-
weighted images, without evidence of tendon discontinuity, combined with a signal change on T2-weighted
images indicating a focal defect that is either intratendinous or limited to the articular or bursal surface (Figures 3 and 4). It can be difficult on MRI to differentiate
a high-grade partial-thickness tear from a small full-
thickness tendon tear or to differentiate tendinopathy
from a small partial-thickness tear.

Several recent studies found that the accuracy of
magnetic resonance arthrography (MRA) in PTRCT diagnosis is improved by using more conventional techniques. Fifty patients with chronic shoulder pain were
prospectively evaluated using MRA corroborated by
findings from arthroscopy.[21] The sensitivity and specificity of MRA were 91% and 85%, respectively, with a
positive predictive value of 84% and a false-negative

rate of 9%. Another recent study compared MRA and arthroscopic findings in 275 patients, of whom 139 had a partial-thickness or full-thickness tear at the time of surgery. For full-thickness tears, the sensitivity, specificity, and accuracy of MRA were 96%, 99%, and 98%, respectively; and for partial-thickness tears, they were 80%, 97%, and 95%, respectively. False-negative and false-positive MRA results were predominantly found in small, articular-sided partial-thickness tears.[22] Positioning the shoulder in abduction and external rotation was found to improve accuracy and interobserver reliability in diagnosing PTRCTs using MRA. In this position, tension within the posterior cuff is decreased, and the contrast medium can more easily infiltrate an articular-sided tendon defect.[23]

## Classification

The original classification of rotator cuff disease described three stages: stage I, hemorrhage and cuff edema; stage II, cuff fibrosis; and stage III, cuff tear.[24] PTRCTs were not separately classified; they were considered advanced stage II or early stage III lesions. The currently used classification systems are primarily descriptive and do not address the etiology or natural history of PTRCTs. The Ellman classification system, based on the location, depth, and size of the tendon defect, is most commonly used[25] (Table 2). Tear classification is typically based on the appearance of the tear after débridement in conjunction with arthroscopy. The area of the defect is measured by multiplying the dimensions of the base of the tear and the width of fiber retraction.

## Nonsurgical Treatment

Most patients with a PTRCT have symptoms similar to those of patients with rotator cuff tendinitis or subacromial impingement. The onset of symptoms is usually gradual, and the patient may have a history of overuse without discrete injury. In the absence of severe pain, overt weakness, or images revealing a full-thickness ro-

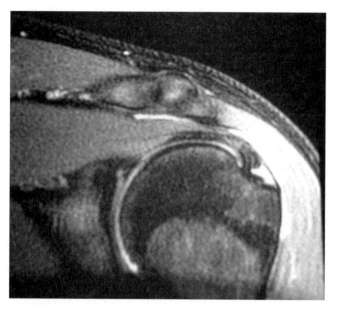

**Figure 3** A coronal plane T2-weighted, noncontrast, fat-suppressed MRI showing a bursal-sided PTRCT of the supraspinatus tendon involving approximately half of the tendon insertion.

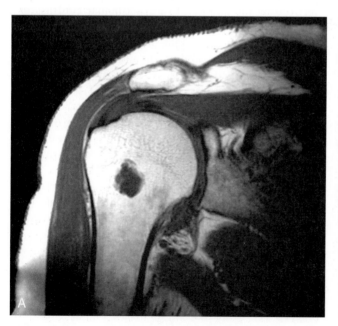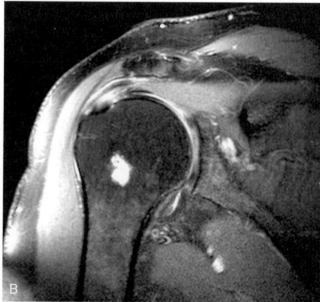

**Figure 4** **A,** An oblique coronal plane, noncontrast MRI study of an intratendinous tear in the supraspinatus tendon, showing a heterogenous signal within the tendon and no obvious tendon disruption. **B,** A fast spin-echo MRI study showing signal intensity within the tendon that suggests high-grade tendinopathy or an intratendinous partial-thickness tear extending to the articular surface.

tator cuff tear, most patients with rotator cuff–derived pain are treated nonsurgically. Activity modification is recommended, with avoidance of overhead or painful activities. Nonsteroidal anti-inflammatory drugs are used to alleviate pain and reduce inflammation, although data are lacking to determine the efficacy of these medications.

Physical therapy is usually recommended, initially to decrease pain and improve shoulder range of motion. Ice, heat, ultrasonography, and electrical stimulation can be used to decrease pain and associated muscle spasms. Many patients with rotator cuff–derived pain have significant tightness of the posterior cuff and capsule, which may affect glenohumeral mechanics during overhead elevation. The therapist addresses posterior capsular mobility using manual mobilization and stretching, and the patient can add self-directed stretching. These exercises are particularly important for overhead athletes. The therapist should identify and address abnormalities in scapulohumeral rhythm and scapular mechanics during overhead motion before initiating strengthening exercises.

As the patient's pain decreases and range of motion improves, attention shifts to improving the strength and endurance of the rotator cuff and scapular stabilizer muscles. Targeted strengthening of the rotator cuff is achieved with a program of progressive resistance exercises using free weights and elastic tubing; the initial strengthening involves arcs of motion outside the zones of mechanical impingement. Strengthening of the scapular stabilizers, particularly the serratus anterior and the lower trapezius, is important for restoring normal scapular mechanics. Proprioceptive training may be necessary to correct scapular dyskinesia and thereby reduce the risk of secondary subacromial impingement. For a higher demand patient or an athlete, eccentric strengthening and plyometric exercises that simulate normal activities should be incorporated into the later stages of rehabilitation.

Subacromial and intra-articular injections are helpful for both diagnosis and therapy. Injections are often used to relieve persistent symptoms, including significant pain while resting or pain that precludes participation in a directed rehabilitation program. Because of the potentially harmful effects of steroids on the articular cartilage and soft tissues of the shoulder, the number of injections is usually restricted to two or three.

## Surgical Treatment

The optimal duration of nonsurgical treatment and the timing of surgery for a PTRCT have not been well defined, although a period of 3 to 6 months of nonsurgical treatment has been recommended before surgical treatment is considered. The necessity and timing of surgery are influenced by patient-specific factors, including physical activity level, tear size, associated pathology, and, for an athlete, the sports-competition schedule.

| Table 2 | Ellman Classification of Partial-Thickness Rotator Cuff Tears | |
|---|---|---|
| **Grade** | **Description** | |
| I | < 3 mm (< 25% of tendon thickness) | |
| II | 3 mm to 6 mm (25% to 50% of tendon thickness) | |
| III | > 6 mm (> 50% of tendon thickness) | |
| **Location** | | |
| A | Articular sided | |
| B | Bursal sided | |
| C | Intratendinous | |

*(Adapted with permission from Ellman H: Diagnosis and treatment of incomplete rotator cuff tears. Clin Orthop Relat Res 1990;254:64-74.)*

A PTRCT can be surgically treated using débridement alone, débridement with acromioplasty, or rotator cuff repair. The choice depends primarily on the depth, size, and location (articular sided or bursal sided) of the tear as well as the quality of the remaining rotator cuff tissue. The treatment must also be considered in the context of the patient's age and activity level.

### Tendon Débridement

Tendon débridement without acromioplasty may be the preferred surgical treatment for a lower demand patient with an articular-sided tear involving less than 50% of the tendon thickness and with healthy-appearing surrounding rotator cuff tissue. Subacromial decompression and acromioplasty may be required, depending on the location of the tear and the presence of signs of mechanical impingement, such as fraying of the coracoacromial ligament or significant inferior projecting acromial osteophytes. The role of acromioplasty has not been clearly delineated; a bursal-sided tear is usually associated with subacromial impingement, and a subacromial decompression with acromioplasty is therefore usually required. For a higher demand patient, such as a manual laborer or athlete, a tear that is larger than 30% of the tendon thickness (> 4 mm) may require repair rather than débridement because of the patient's physical demands and the tendon's limited ability to heal after débridement alone.

A thorough débridement is necessary to fully evaluate the size and depth of the tear and remove degenerative tissue with limited healing capacity. For an articular-sided tear, a shaver is used to remove the frayed capsule and further expose the tendon defect. Degenerative, frayed, and fragmented rotator cuff tissue is removed until healthy-appearing tendon is revealed. Healthy rotator cuff tissue is white and glistening, and the tendon fibers have a longitudinal appearance. A curved shaver and changes in arm position can be used to improve visualization and access to the tear, especially if it is relatively posterior. Inspection of the rotator cuff from the bursal side and débridement, if necessary, are the final steps in the full treatment of an articular-sided tear that is smaller than 50% of the tendon thickness.

A subacromial decompression and acromioplasty are generally indicated if the tear is bursal sided or there are signs of mechanical impingement (fraying of the coracoacromial ligament). The coracoacromial ligament is released from the undersurface of the anterior and lateral acromion using an electrocautery wand. A limited acromioplasty is performed with a high-speed burr to achieve a flat acromial morphology. If hypertrophic inferior osteophytes are present, they are removed from the distal clavicle.

Overhead throwing athletes with rotator cuff disease have unusual requirements. The etiology and pathogenesis of a PTRCT in these patients are unique, although not well defined. The rotator cuff is subjected to rapid, strong eccentric contractions when the arm is decelerated during the follow-through phase of throwing. In addition, mechanical impingement of the articular surface of the rotator cuff against the posterosuperior cuff occurs during the late cocking phase of throwing. The internal impingement can be exacerbated by excessive posterior capsule tightness, subtle anterior instability, or fatigue of the rotator cuff. The rotator cuff is also subjected to high torsional and shear forces as a result of the exaggerated rotation and hyperabduction during the early phases of throwing. A PTRCT in an overhead throwing athlete usually occurs on the articular surface of the supraspinatus and infraspinatus tendons. Tears of the superior and posterosuperior labrum are also often encountered. The PTRCT should be repaired if it is more than 50% of the tendon thickness. Treatment should include débridement or repair of associated labral lesions and débridement of the PTRCT. Acromioplasty is rarely necessary in a throwing athlete. A full return to competitive throwing is difficult after rotator cuff repair.

### Tendon Repair

The size and depth of the tendon defect are the primary factors in determining whether surgical repair is required. However, the recent emphasis on the etiology of the tear may lead to changes in treatment strategy. Because a PTRCT is likely to progress to a full-thickness tear, an age-related degenerative tear may be better treated with repair than débridement. However, clear guidelines are lacking for aggressive surgical treatment. Repair should be considered for a smaller tear (< 30% of the tendon thickness) in a younger or high-demand patient, especially if significant tendinopathy exists in the surrounding tissue. After a small lesion is adequately débrided, the depth of the tear may justify undertaking a repair. An acute PTRCT or a bursal-sided tear involving more than 30% of the tendon thickness warrants a

more aggressive treatment strategy because of the favorable healing environment and the possibility of persistent symptoms after débridement alone.

A PTRCT can be successfully repaired using either an arthroscopic or an open procedure. The choice is primarily dictated by the surgeon's experience and comfort with each technique. The remaining tendon fibers are released either with a shaver or sharply with a knife (Figure 5). Degenerative rotator cuff tissue is removed, and the greater tuberosity is cleared of all soft tissue to expose cortical bone. Tendon-to-bone repair can be performed arthroscopically using suture anchors or through a mini-open incision using suture anchors or bone tunnels. Several suture anchor configurations and suture constructs are available to improve the strength and footprint area of an arthroscopic rotator cuff repair. Side-to-side tendon repair may also be necessary to close intratendinous splits and delaminations.

Another method of repair can be considered for some articular-sided tears. Partial articular-sided supraspinatus tendon avulsions (PASTA lesions) are isolated tears with a healthy-appearing bursal-sided tendon. This type of in situ repair is appropriate for younger patients with a traumatic tear etiology and healthy remaining tissue. At least 25% of the bursal side of the tendon should remain in continuity with the bone for this type of repair to be considered (Figure 6). The tear can be repaired arthroscopically using a suture anchor, leaving the bursal-sided tendon fibers intact. The theoretical advantages of this technique include preservation of the healthy bursal-sided tendon tissue, maintenance of the normal length and tension of the rotator cuff tendon, and restoration of the articular footprint of the tear. The technique requires transtendinous placement of a suture anchor into the greater tuberosity and familiarity with suture shuttling from the joint side to the bursal side of the tendon.

## Surgical Treatment Results

The diagnosis and treatment of PTRCTs have improved as arthroscopy has become more prevalent in treating shoulder disorders. However, few reports have focused on the results of surgical treatment of PTRCTs. In most studies, the outcomes of patients with a PTRCT are grouped with those of patients with less severe or more advanced rotator cuff disease. Most available studies were poorly controlled, with different outcome measures used to assess the response to treatment. Few studies address tendon integrity after tear débridement or repair.

### Tendon Débridement

Débridement with or without acromioplasty usually has a satisfactory outcome if performed for a low-grade PTRCT that involves less than 50% of the tendon thickness. However, no studies support the healing of

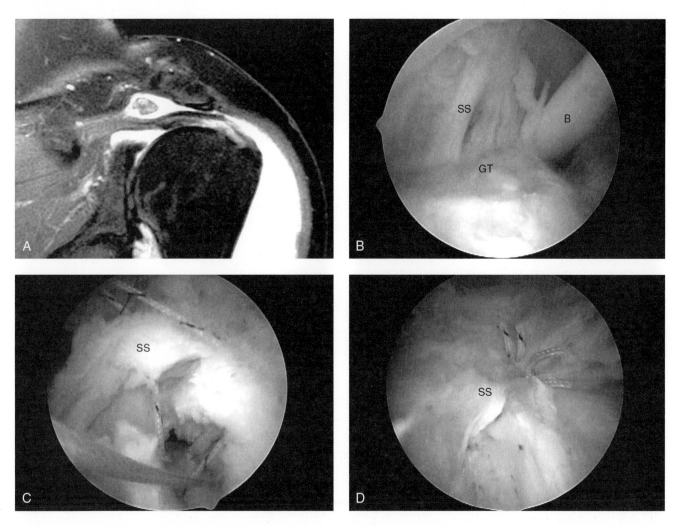

**Figure 5**  **A,** An oblique coronal plane MRA of a high-grade articular-sided PTRCT in the supraspinatus tendon of the left shoulder. **B,** An arthroscopic view of the same shoulder, showing an articular-sided partial-thickness tear of the supraspinatus tendon with adjacent intratendinous delamination. **C,** A bursal-sided view of the same tear from a lateral portal. The high-grade supraspinatus tear has been completed sharply using a knife, a single suture anchor has been placed into the greater tuberosity, and one pair of sutures has been shuttled through the detached tendon. **D,** Two horizontal mattress sutures have been placed arthroscopically to repair the supraspinatus defect. B = biceps tendon, GT = greater tuberosity, SS = supraspinatus tendon.

low-grade PTRCTs after débridement, with or without acromioplasty. Most studies reported satisfactory outcomes in 75% to 88% of PTRCTs at short-term follow-up after arthroscopic débridement, with or without acromioplasty.[26-29] Arthroscopic débridement alone is recommended for articular-sided tears; subacromial decompression and acromioplasty are generally reserved for patients with a small bursal-sided tear or evidence of subacromial impingement at the time of surgery.

The results of arthroscopic débridement alone have been comparable to those of arthroscopic débridement with acromioplasty. Outcomes were assessed in 105 shoulders (105 patients; average age, 51 years) treated with arthroscopic débridement and subacromial decompression and acromioplasty. At the time of surgery, 29 of the shoulders had no rotator cuff tear, and 76 had a PTRCT involving less than 50% of the tendon thick-

ness. At an average 4.5-year follow-up, the L'Insalata Shoulder Rating Questionnaire scores of the patients with a normal rotator cuff and those with a PTRCT were comparable (91 and 89, respectively). Only 8% of patients were noted to have an unsatisfactory result, of whom 38% had a grade II (25% to 50% thickness) bursal-sided tear.[30] A recent study of 62 shoulders (60 patients; average age, 46 years) after complete arthroscopic débridement of a PTRCT without formal subacromial decompression or acromioplasty found that at an average 9.5-year follow-up, only 39% of patients returned for physical examination; 79% had a good or excellent outcome as measured using the University of California Los Angeles (UCLA) Shoulder Scale, in comparison with 86% at 4.5-year follow-up.[31,32] Four patients required additional surgery for repair of a full-thickness rotator cuff tear. The results of surgery were negatively influenced by the depth of the tendinosis. Of

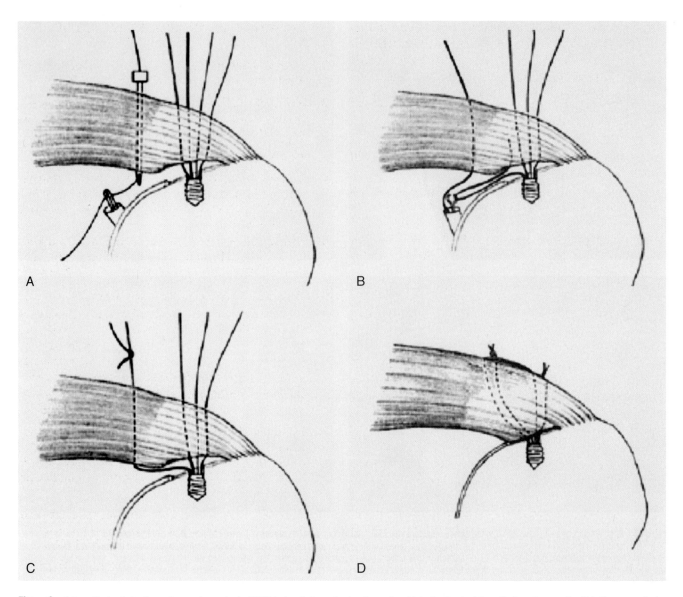

**Figure 6** Schematic drawings of an arthroscopic repair of a PASTA lesion. **A,** An anchor has been placed into the greater tuberosity through a small split in the supraspinatus tendon, and a shuttle suture is passed using a spinal needle through the tendon medial to the tear. **B,** One end of a suture is retrieved through the anterior cannula. **C,** The shuttle relay is used to pass the retrieved suture through the healthy tendon. **D,** The steps are repeated using the remaining three sutures, and knots are tied in the subacromial space to repair the tendon to the greater tuberosity. *(Adapted with permission from Ide J, Maeda S, Takagi K: Arthroscopic transtendon repair of partial-thickness articular-side tears of the rotator cuff: Anatomic and clinical study. Am J Sports Med 2005;33:1672-1679.)*

patients with 50% or more tendon thickness involvement, 54% had a good or excellent result; in comparison, 84% of patients with less than 50% tendon thickness involvement had a good or excellent result. Factors not correlated with the final outcome were the patient's age, gender, or arm dominance or the presence of a bursal-sided tear.

Concern about tear progression and poor tendon healing have limited the use of débridement alone for treating PTRCTs; acromioplasty and débridement have not been shown to prevent progression of rotator cuff disease.[33] These issues have prompted some authors to recommend that smaller PTRCTs be repaired in relatively young or high-demand patients. At a minimum 5-year follow-up of

26 patients (average age, 51.5 years) treated with arthroscopic débridement and acromioplasty for an Ellman grade II PTRCT, physical examination and shoulder ultrasonography revealed nine full-thickness rotator cuff tears, including three bilateral tears.[20] Despite reliable pain relief, the average Constant score remained lower for the postsurgical shoulder than the contralateral shoulder (65 and 84, respectively). The authors concluded that acromioplasty and débridement for PTRCT do not protect the rotator cuff from further degeneration.

### Tendon Repair

The extent of the PTRCT, as measured by the depth of the tear and the quality of the intact tendon fibers, is the primary consideration in the decision to repair the tendon. The available studies of PTRCT repair, whether open or arthroscopic, are limited to higher grade (> 50%) tears. The outcomes of a repair of a high-grade PTRCT are generally comparable to those of débridement of a smaller PTRCT or repair of a small full-thickness tear.[34] Mini-open repair of a PTRCT involving 50% or more of the tendon produced better clinical results and a lower rate of revision than débridement with acromioplasty.[35]

Repair of an isolated articular surface tendon defect without completion of the tear can be considered if the bursal-sided tendon is healthy. This type of repair has been recommended in patients with a PASTA lesion. These patients often are relatively young and have a history of trauma and minimal surrounding tendinopathy. In 22 patients (average age, 42 years), a PASTA lesion was repaired using an arthroscopic transtendon suture anchor repair.[36] The tear depth ranged from 30% to 70% of the tendon thickness, and in 45% of the patients an identifiable trauma had led to the injury. At an average 16-month follow-up, the average UCLA Shoulder Scale score improved from 17.1 to 31.2 points, 86% of patients had a good or excellent result, and 91% were satisfied with the result.

## Summary

PTRCTs are a common cause of shoulder pain. The etiology and pathogenesis of articular-sided tears and bursal-sided tears are probably different, although this point remains controversial. The ability to effectively diagnose and treat these injuries has improved as imaging and arthroscopic techniques have advanced. Appropriate surgical management requires careful inspection of both the articular and bursal sides of the tendon and consideration of factors such as the age and activity level of the patient and any concomitant pathology. For an isolated, low-grade PTRCT that is not extensive, predictably good clinical results can be obtained with débridement, with or without acromioplasty, despite a lack of evidence that tear progression can be prevented. For a high-grade, degenerative PTRCT, more predictable results can be obtained with tendon repair. Because of the likelihood of persistent pain and tear progression, the surgeon should also consider repairing a bursal-sided tear or a low-grade lesion in a high demand patient. An in situ repair is indicated for a tear in a young patient with otherwise healthy tissue, whereas a primary repair may be preferable for a degenerative tear in an older patient.

## Annotated References

1. Sano H, Ishii H, Trudel G, Uhthoff HK: Histologic evidence of degeneration at the insertion of 3 rotator cuff tendons: A comparative study with human cadaveric shoulders. *J Shoulder Elbow Surg* 1999;8:574-579.

2. Lohr JF, Uhthoff HK: The pathogenesis of degenerative rotator cuff tears. *Orthop Trans* 1987;11:237.

3. Yamanaka K, Fukuda H: Pathologic studies of the supraspinatus tendon with reference to incomplete partial thickness tear, in Takagishi N (ed): *The Shoulder.* Tokyo, Japan, Professional Postgraduate Services, 1987, pp 220-224.

4. Sher JS, Uribe JW, Posada A, Murphy BJ, Zlatkin MB: Abnormal findings on magnetic resonance images of asymptomatic shoulders. *J Bone Joint Surg Am* 1995;77:10-15.

5. Yamaguchi K, Ditsios K, Middleton WD, Hildebolt CF, Galatz LM, Teefey SA: The demographic and morphological features of rotator cuff disease: A comparison of asymptomatic and symptomatic shoulders. *J Bone Joint Surg Am* 2006;88:1699-1704.

   Bilateral ultrasonography of 588 patients with unilateral shoulder pain was designed to identify rotator cuff tears and factors related to the development of pain. Age was the primary risk factor for the presence of a rotator cuff tear. The size of the tear was correlated with the presence of pain and severity of rotator cuff disease on the asymptomatic side.

6. Dunteman R, Fukada H, Snyder SJ: Surgical treatment of partial-thickness tears, in Norris TR (ed): *Orthopaedic Knowledge Update: Shoulder and Elbow 2.* Rosemont, IL, American Academy of Orthopaedic Surgeons, 2002, p 163.

7. Clark JM, Harryman DT II: Tendons, ligaments, and capsule of the rotator cuff: Gross and microscopic anatomy. *J Bone Joint Surg Am* 1992;74:713-725.

8. Dugas JR, Campbell DA, Warren RF, Robie BH, Millett PJ: Anatomy and dimensions of rotator cuff insertions. *J Shoulder Elbow Surg* 2002;11:498-503.

   The dimensions of the insertions of the rotator cuff tendons into the humeral tuberosities were studied in 20 cadaver specimens, and the footprint area and dimensions were recorded with a three-dimensional space digitizer. A detailed description of all rotator cuff insertions is included.

9. Ruotolo C, Fow JE, Nottage WM: The supraspinatus footprint: An anatomic study of the supraspinatus insertion. *Arthroscopy* 2004;20:246-249.

   The dimensions of the insertion of the supraspinatus tendon into the greater tuberosity were measured in 17 cadaver specimens.

10. Moseley HF, Goldie I: The arterial pattern of the rotator cuff of the shoulder. *J Bone Joint Surg Br* 1963;45:780-789.

11. Lohr JF, Uhthoff HK: The microvascular pattern of the supraspinatus tendon. *Clin Orthop Relat Res* 1990;254:35-38.

12. Nakijima T, Rokuuma N, Hamada K, Tomatsu T, Fukuda H: Histologic and biomechanical characteristics of the supraspinatus tendon: Reference to rotator cuff tearing. *J Shoulder Elbow Surg* 1994;3:79-87.

13. Ozaki J, Fujimoto S, Nakagawa Y, Masuhara K, Tamai S: Tears of the rotator cuff of the shoulder associated with pathological changes in the acromion: A study in cadavera. *J Bone Joint Surg Am* 1988;70:1224-1230.

14. Ko JY, Huang CC, Chen WJ, Chen CE, Chen SH, Wang CJ: Pathogenesis of partial tear of the rotator cuff: A clinical and pathologic study. *J Shoulder Elbow Surg* 2006;15:271-278.

   MRI was used to grade the severity of pathologic changes in the rotator cuff and the severity of histologic degeneration of the anterior acromion in 66 patients with a PTRCT treated surgically. Articular-sided tears had greater tendinous degeneration than bursal-sided tears but less severe histologic changes of the acromion.

15. Reilly P, Amis AA, Wallace AL, Emery RJ: Supraspinatus tears: Propagation and strain alteration. *J Shoulder Elbow Surg* 2003;12:134-138.

   Strain patterns within cadaver supraspinatus tendons were calculated after the creation of various tendon defects. Increased strain within intact bursal-sided and articular-sided tendon fibers was observed when the tendon was loaded, with greater effects noted at higher angles of elevation.

16. Bey MJ, Song HK, Wehrli FW, Soslowsky LJ: Intratendinous strain fields of the intact supraspinatus tendon: The effect of glenohumeral joint position and tendon region. *J Orthop Res* 2002;20:869-874.

   Tendinous strains adjacent to surgically created articular-sided PTRCTs were determined using MRI in seven cadaver shoulders. Strain increased with higher angles of glenohumeral elevation and, within the adjacent middle and superficial layers of the rotator cuff, with tendon loading.

17. Sano H, Wakabayashi I, Itoi E: Stress distribution in the supraspinatus tendon with partial-thickness tears: An analysis using two-dimensional finite element model. *J Shoulder Elbow Surg* 2006;15:100-105.

   This study examined the effects of different PTRCT patterns on stress distribution within the rotator cuff, using a two-dimensional finite element model. Stress was concentrated at the articular surface in all tear patterns and increased at a higher angle of abduction.

18. Hamada K, Tomonaga A, Gotoh M, Yamakawa H, Fukuda H: Intrinsic healing capacity and tearing process of torn supraspinatus tendons: In situ hybridization study of alpha 1 (I) procollagen mRNA. *J Orthop Res* 1997;15:24-32.

19. Yamanaka K, Matsumoto T: The joint side tear of the rotator cuff: A followup study by arthrography. *Clin Orthop Relat Res* 1994;304:68-73.

20. Kartus J, Kartus C, Rostgard-Christensen L, Sernert N, Read J, Perko M: Long-term clinical and ultrasound evaluation after arthroscopic acromioplasty in patients with partial rotator cuff tears. *Arthroscopy* 2006;22:44-49.

   This retrospective study reported the clinical and ultrasonographic results at a minimum 5-year follow-up of 33 patients with an Ellman grade II PTRCT treated with arthroscopic débridement and acromioplasty. Strength and Constant shoulder scores were lower than in the contralateral shoulder, and 9 of 26 patients had developed a full-thickness rotator cuff tear. Level of evidence: IV.

21. Stetson WB, Phillips T, Deutsch A: The use of magnetic resonance arthrography to detect partial-thickness rotator cuff tears. *J Bone Joint Surg Am* 2005;87(suppl 2):81-88.

   MRA corroborated with arthroscopy was successfully used to evaluate 50 patients with suspected rotator cuff disease.

22. Waldt S, Bruegel M, Mueller D, et al: Rotator cuff tears: Assessment with MR arthrography in 275 patients with arthroscopic correlation. *Eur Radiol* 2007; 17:491-498.

   Conventional MRA was used to evaluate the rotator cuff in 275 patients with shoulder pain, and the findings were compared with surgical findings. Conventional MRA was less accurate in detecting PTRCTs than full-thickness rotator cuff tears but was improved compared with earlier reports.

23. Herold T, Bachthaler M, Hamer OW, et al: Indirect MR arthrography of the shoulder: Use of abduction and external rotation to detect full- and partial-thickness tears of the supraspinatus tendon. *Radiology* 2006;240:152-160.

   Conventional MRA and abduction and external rotation views were used to evaluate 51 patients with rotator cuff disease. Two radiologists reviewed the results and compared them with surgical findings. The abduction and external rotation views improved accuracy and interobserver reliability in the detection of partial-thickness supraspinatus tears.

24. Neer CS II: Anterior acromioplasty for chronic impingement syndrome in the shoulder: A preliminary report. *J Bone Joint Surg Am* 1972;53:41-50.

25. Ellman H: Diagnosis and treatment of incomplete rotator cuff tears. *Clin Orthop Relat Res* 1990;254:64-74.

26. Patel VR, Singh D, Calvert PT, Bayley JI: Arthroscopic subacromial decompression: Results and factors affecting outcome. *J Shoulder Elbow Surg* 1999;8: 231-237.

27. Gartsman GM, Milne JC: Articular surface partial-thickness rotator cuff tears. *J Shoulder Elbow Surg* 1995;4:409-415.

28. Snyder SJ, Pachelli AF, Del Pizzo W, Friedman MJ, Ferkel RD, Pattee G: Partial thickness rotator cuff

tears: Results of arthroscopic treatment. *Arthroscopy* 1991;7:1-7.

29. Payne LZ, Altchek DW, Craig EV, Warren RF: Arthroscopic treatment of partial rotator cuff tears in young athletes: A preliminary report. *Am J Sports Med* 1997;25:299-305.

30. Cordasco FA, Backer M, Craig EV, Klein D, Warren RF: The partial-thickness rotator cuff tear: Is acromioplasty without repair sufficient? *Am J Sports Med* 2002;30:257-260.

    The results of arthroscopic acromioplasty and débridement in 162 patients with rotator cuff tendonitis or a low-grade PTRCT were reported at an average 4.5 years after surgery. The mean L'Insalata score was 90 points. Outcomes were similar, except for lower scores in patients with a high-grade bursal-sided tear. Level of evidence: IV.

31. Budoff JE, Rodin D, Ochiai D, Nirschl RP: Arthroscopic rotator cuff debridement without decompression for the treatment of tendinosis. *Arthroscopy* 2005;21:1081-1089.

    At an average 9.5-year follow-up, 79% of 62 patients with a PTRCT treated with arthroscopic débridement alone had a good or excellent score on the UCLA Shoulder Scale. The outcomes were only slightly less positive than those of the same patients at 4.5-year follow-up. Level of evidence: IV.

32. Budoff JE, Nirschl RP, Guidi EJ: Debridement of partial-thickness tears of the rotator cuff without acromioplasty: Long-term follow-up and review of the literature. *J Bone Joint Surg Am* 1998;80:733-748.

33. Hyvonen P, Lohi S, Jalovaara P: Open acromioplasty does not prevent the progression of an impingement syndrome to a tear: Nine-year follow-up of 96 cases. *J Bone Joint Surg Br* 1998;80:813-816.

34. Wright SA, Cofield RH: Management of partial-thickness rotator cuff tears. *J Shoulder Elbow Surg* 1996;5:458-466.

35. Weber SC: Arthroscopic debridement and acromioplasty versus mini-open repair in the treatment of significant partial-thickness rotator cuff tears. *Arthroscopy* 1999;15:126-131.

36. Waibl B, Buess E: Partial-thickness articular surface supraspinatus tears: A new transtendon suture technique. *Arthroscopy* 2005;21:376-381.

    An arthroscopic repair technique is described for successful treatment of PASTA lesions and preservation of intact bursal-sided tendon fibers. Level of evidence: IV.

# Chapter 15

# Surgical Treatment of Full-Thickness Rotator Cuff Tears

William N. Levine, MD

Gabriel Brown, MD

## Introduction

The widespread use of arthroscopic rotator cuff repair has led to significant advances in arthroscopic surgical techniques and instrumentation. Suture anchor design, insertion technique, and configuration are important biomechanical factors and the subjects of recent study. The clinical use of single-row and double-row arthroscopic repair techniques and their relationship to tendon healing and functional outcomes also are being studied. The integrity of the rotator cuff after arthroscopic repair is being evaluated using MRI, CT arthrography, and ultrasonography. The results of arthroscopic rotator cuff repair are now comparable to those of traditional open or mini-open repair using transosseous suture fixation.

## Biomechanical Research Studies

### Transosseous Tunnel and Suture Anchor Fixation

Several studies have compared rotator cuff fixation using transosseous sutures or suture anchors. In a human cadaver model, transosseous suture fixation was found to allow less motion at the tendon-bone interface than single-row suture anchor fixation after rotator cuff repair.[1] Decreasing motion at the tendon-bone interface is important to allow tendon healing, possibly because motion disrupts formation of the fibrovascular interface tissue that is important for healing. Transosseous tunnel fixation was found to provide more pressure at the tendon-bone interface, thereby increasing the footprint contact area[2] (Figure 1). The mechanical characteristics of transosseous suture fixation may therefore enhance the potential for biologic healing.

### Suture and Tack Fixation

The biomechanical strength of rotator cuff repairs using transosseous sutures was compared with the strength of repairs using a single row of nonsuture-based tacks in human cadaver specimens.[3] A transosseous technique using a modified Mason-Allen suture tied over a bioabsorbable cortical bone augmentation device was found to result in ultimate strength comparable to that of a

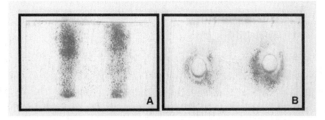

**Figure 1**  Pressure-sensitive film showing rotator cuff tendon-bone interface pressure provided by transosseous suture repair **(A)** and suture anchor mattress repair **(B)**. *(Reproduced with permission from Park MC, Cadet ER, Levine WN, Bigliani LU, Ahmad CS: Tendon-to-bone pressure distributions at a repaired rotator cuff footprint using transosseous suture and suture anchor fixation techniques. Am J Sports Med 2005; 33:1154-1159.)*

single row of two tacks. However, under cyclic loading the bioabsorbable tacks withstood greater initial forces before 50% loss of repair (defined as 5 mm of translation). This finding may be explained by the greater deformability of the sutures compared with the tacks. The tacks failed primarily by cutting through the tendon, and the transosseous sutures failed primarily by rupturing. The strength of either repair was not correlated with age, gender, or bone mineral density. The use of tacks has not become popular, despite their biomechanical advantages, because of their association with mechanical impingement in the subacromial space and early clinical failure.

### Suture Anchor Depth

The effect of anchor depth on the strength of repaired rotator cuff tendons was studied in bovine cadaver shoulders.[4] Clinical failure was defined as more than 3 mm of elongation with cyclic loading. The deep suture anchors failed clinically after fewer loading cycles because of suture cutting into bone. However, load to failure was greater in the deep anchors, possibly because the bone shielded the anchors from early suture abrasion at the anchor eyelet (Figure 2). The proud anchors withstood greater loading cycles before clinical failure, but catastrophic failure occurred earlier than in the deep anchors because of suture breakage resulting from mechanical degradation at the metallic anchor eyelets.

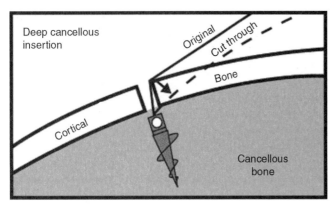

**Figure 2** Standard-depth anchor placement. Cutting of suture into bone shields the suture from early abrasive wear. *(Reproduced with permission from Mahar A, Allred DW, Wedemeyer M, Abbi G, Pedowitz R: A biomechanical and radiographic analysis of standard and intracortical suture anchors for arthroscopic rotator cuff repair. Arthroscopy 2006;22:130-135.)*

Failure of the standard-depth anchors depended on whether the suture was in contact with bone. If the suture was not in contact with bone, the standard-depth anchor failed in a manner similar to that of the proud anchors, and if the suture was in contact with bone, the standard-depth anchor failed in a manner similar to that of the deep anchors. These findings suggest that deep anchor placement may protect the repair against early catastrophic failure but also may hinder healing because of greater gap formation at the bone-tendon junction, as evidenced by early elongation.

A study of suture anchor insertion depth in human cadaver humeri found that displacement of the anchors was greater after deep anchor placement than after standard-depth placement following cyclic loading.[5] However, ultimate failure loads were not influenced by anchor depth. Seven deep anchors and eight standard-depth anchors were tested. Six deep anchors failed at the suture knot, and one pulled out. Four standard-depth anchors failed at the suture knot, three failed at the suture eyelet, and one pulled out. Deep placement of anchors causes greater displacement with cyclic loading, which may impede tendon healing.

### Single-Row and Double-Row Suture Anchor Fixation

Several studies have compared the biomechanical effects of single-row and double-row suture anchor repairs using different suture configurations. In human cadaver supraspinatus tendons repaired with single-row or double-row anchors, smaller gap formation and higher loads to failure were found with the double-row technique.[6] In the single-row technique, two double-loaded anchors were placed in the lateral aspect of the supraspinatus tendon and tied in simple fashion. All failed when the suture pulled out of the tendon. In the double-row technique, anchors were placed in the lateral row as in the single-row technique. In the medial row, two an-

chors were placed, with one horizontal mattress suture configuration in each. Seven of the nine double-row constructs failed when the suture pulled out of the tendon. However, two double-row constructs failed because the greater tuberosity fractured, raising a concern that placing four anchors in the greater tuberosity may cause a stress concentration.

Four different fixation techniques were evaluated in human cadaver supraspinatus tendons.[7] In the two-simple technique, a double-loaded lateral suture anchor was tied in simple fashion. In the arthroscopic Mason-Allen technique, a horizontal mattress knot and a simple knot were tied through a laterally based double-loaded suture anchor. In the massive cuff technique, a horizontal knot was tied entirely within the tendon, and two simple knots were tied through a laterally based double-loaded suture anchor, with both traveling medially over the horizontal stitch. In the double-row technique, the two-simple technique was combined with a horizontal mattress stitch tied through a medially based suture anchor. The ultimate load to failure was higher for the double-row technique than for the other three techniques. In addition, the double-row technique had a lower peak-to-peak elongation (a measure of displacement at higher load cycles) and therefore may result in less gap formation and improved healing. The massive cuff technique was found to be stronger than the arthroscopic Mason-Allen and two-simple techniques. The study recommends using the arthroscopic Mason-Allen or massive cuff technique whenever the double-row technique cannot be used because of arthroscopic placement difficulties.

Four suture anchor configurations were evaluated for the repair of full-thickness supraspinatus tears in a human cadaver model.[8] The single-row repair used three laterally based, double-loaded anchors with sutures tied in a simple fashion. The diamond repair used two laterally based, double-loaded anchors and two medially based anchors placed adjacent to the articular margin; the lateral sutures were tied in simple fashion, and the medial sutures were tied in horizontal mattress fashion. The mattress double-anchor repair used two medially based anchors placed adjacent to the articular margin and two laterally based anchors placed as in the diamond technique; suture material was shuttled from the anteromedial to the anterolateral anchor and tied over the tendon, and the same was done for the two posterior anchors. The modified mattress double-anchor repair differed from the mattress double-anchor repair in that a second suture was tied in each of the medial anchors in a horizontal fashion, in a modified arthroscopic Mason-Allen configuration. The three double-row repair techniques were found to restore the supraspinatus footprint better than the single-row technique. The larger footprint in the double-row repairs improves the potential for tendon-to-bone healing.

There was no difference in load to failure or displacement among the four groups.

### Acute and Delayed Rotator Cuff Repair

Histology, biomechanical performance, and greater tuberosity bone density were studied after supraspinatus repairs that were performed acutely or after a 3-week delay in a rat model.[9] The delayed repair group had more stiffening of the tendon than the acute repair group 10 days after repair, although the acute repair group had more stiffening 56 days after repair. The deterioration in the delayed repairs coincided with decreased greater tuberosity bone density. The authors concluded that both tendon and bone alterations led to poorer healing after a delayed repair.

## Clinical Research Studies

### Open and Arthroscopic Rotator Cuff Repair

Several clinical trials have compared the outcomes of open and arthroscopic rotator cuff repairs. The subjective outcomes of open or mini-open rotator cuff repair were retrospectively compared with those of arthroscopic repair at a mean 33-month follow-up.[10] The study included all of one surgeon's patients who underwent cuff repair with bony reattachment during a 2-year period. At the study period midpoint, an arthroscopic rotator cuff repair technique was used exclusively; patients with all tear sizes were therefore included in both repair groups, with no selection bias. The open procedures used bone tunnels and the Mason-Allen suture technique; the mini-open and arthroscopic procedures used suture anchors. Patients in the arthroscopic group reported better pain relief and greater satisfaction than those in the open and mini-open group. In both groups, patients with small and large presurgical tears had equivalent subjective outcomes. No objective outcomes were reported.

The outcomes of 42 mini-open repairs performed by one surgeon were compared with 42 arthroscopic repairs performed by a second surgeon.[11] The mini-open repairs used suture anchors, except that bone tunnels were used if during surgery it was determined that anchor hold was poor. Anchors were used in the arthroscopic repairs. Patients with massive (> 5 cm) rotator cuff tears were excluded from the study. The patients in the arthroscopic group had fewer medium-sized tears (1 to 3 cm) and more large tears (3 to 5 cm) than patients in the mini-open group. At a minimum 2-year follow-up, there was no difference in outcome between the groups, as measured using the University of California Los Angeles (UCLA) Shoulder Scale and the American Shoulder and Elbow Surgeons (ASES) Shoulder Pain and Disability Index. The authors were not able to comment on the relationship between outcome and tear size because of the small number of patients with large tears and the tear size disparity between the groups.

The authors of a retrospective study reviewed outcomes in 26 patients who underwent a mini-open repair using bone tunnels and 28 patients who underwent an arthroscopic repair using anchors and a simple suture configuration.[12] At a minimum 13-month and an average 33-month follow-up, the groups had equivalent functional improvement. Outcomes could not be evaluated based on tear size because of the limited number of patients with large tears.

MRI was used to evaluate the integrity of the rotator cuff tendon in 32 patients who underwent open or mini-open repair and 40 patients who underwent arthroscopic repair.[13] The open and mini-open repairs used bone tunnels with reinforcement devices and modified Mason-Allen stitches, and the arthroscopic repairs used suture anchors and, if possible, a medial row of tacks. At a minimum 1-year follow-up, there was no statistically significant overall difference between the groups in Constant or ASES scores, visual analog pain scale scores, or retearing rates. In both groups, patients with large tears before surgery had higher rates of retearing, and patients with an intact repair at follow-up had better function. However, patients in the arthroscopic group with a large (> 3 cm) or massive (> 5 cm) rotator cuff tear had a higher rate of retearing, at a statistically significant level; this result might have been confounded by the comparatively large number of massive tears in the arthroscopic group. Cuff integrity was maintained in 62% of the 13 patients with a large or massive tear in the open repair group, compared with 24% of the 21 patients with a large or massive tear in the arthroscopic group. Patients whose repair was intact had better strength in forward elevation and external rotation at the side ($P < 0.01$ and $P < 0.02$, respectively).

Cuff integrity after mini-open or arthroscopic repair was retrospectively compared using ultrasonography.[14] The study involved several surgeons using different techniques. At a minimum 2-year follow-up, no significant differences in outcome scores were found between the 38 patients in the arthroscopic group and the 33 patients in the mini-open group. The two groups had similar retearing rates (24% in the mini-open group and 25% in the arthroscopic group). The retearing rate in both groups was 50% among patients with a tear larger than 3 cm. In both groups, patients with intact cuffs and patients with retearing had equivalent function, as measured using outcomes scales. Patients with intact repairs had better strength in forward flexion ($P = 0.003$) but no difference in external rotation strength ($P = 0.14$), regardless of surgical group.

### Arthroscopic Double-Row Suture Anchor Fixation

Cuff integrity was evaluated at a minimum 24-month follow-up in 52 shoulders of 48 patients treated with arthroscopic double-row suture anchor fixation.[15] The study excluded patients with an irreparable massive tear or a complete subscapularis tendon tear, as well as patients whose surgery did not restore the tendon to an anatomic position on the greater tuberosity. The arthroscopic technique used horizontal mattress knots tied in the medial row, with lateral row repair using either knotless suture anchor devices or standard anchors with sutures tied in simple configuration. The number of anchors in each row ranged from one to three, depending on the size of the tear in the anteroposterior direction. Ultrasonography revealed rotator cuff defects in nine shoulders (17%). Patients with retearing had a relatively large tear before surgery and were found to be weaker in elevation ($P = 0.006$) and external rotation ($P = 0.001$), as measured using dynamometry. The L'Insalata Shoulder Rating Questionnaire scores of patients with a defect did not differ from those of patients with an intact repair.

Cuff integrity after single-row or double-row arthroscopic cuff repair was evaluated in 80 shoulders of 78 patients treated by a single surgeon.[16] Between one and three anchors were used in the single-row repairs, depending on the size of the tear, and the sutures were tied in simple fashion. Near the midpoint of the study, the surgeon made a transition from single-row to double-row fixation. The number of anchors in the double-row repairs ranged from two to five, depending on tear size. The medial row was tied in either a simple or horizontal mattress configuration, depending on whether cuff delamination was present; the lateral row was tied in simple fashion. At a minimum 2-year follow-up, there was no difference between the single-row and double-row groups in functional outcome scores. However, the strength component of the UCLA score approached statistical significance ($P = 0.06$) in favor of the double-row repair group. On MRI, more shoulders were found to have retearing and attenuated cuffs in the single-row group than in the double-row group ($P < 0.01$).

### Tendon Healing After Arthroscopic Repair

Tendon-to-bone healing was studied in 65 patients after arthroscopic repair of an isolated tear of the supraspinatus tendon by a single surgeon.[17] The repair used two or three suture anchors placed in the lateral cortex of the humerus with inverted horizontal mattress suturing in a tension band configuration. The Constant and UCLA scores and the Simple Shoulder Test were used to assess functional outcome at a minimum 6-month follow-up. CT arthrography or MRI (in patients who refused CT arthrography) showed complete healing of the rotator cuff in 46 patients (71%). Tendon healing was significantly associated with strength ($P = 0.001$) and a slight improvement in Constant score ($P = 0.02$). However, tendon healing did not affect pain relief, activity, mobility, or satisfaction. There was an inverse relationship be-

tween tendon healing and patient age ($P < 0.001$); patients with a healed tendon were an average of 10 years younger ($57.8 \pm 9.4$ years) than patients whose tendon did not heal ($68 \pm 7.6$ years).

## Summary

Clinical outcomes of arthroscopic rotator cuff repair are comparable to those of open rotator cuff repair for small and medium-sized tears. Further evaluation of arthroscopic treatment of large and massive rotator cuff tears is needed to determine whether the outcomes of arthroscopic repair in these patients are comparable to those of open repair. Double-row suture anchor fixation is biomechanically superior to single-row fixation, but further clinical studies are needed to determine whether double-row repair results in improved clinical outcome.

## Annotated References

1. Ahmad CS, Stewart AM, Izquierdo R, Bigliani LU: Tendon-bone interface motion in transosseous suture and suture anchor rotator cuff repair techniques. *Am J Sports Med* 2005;33:1667-1671.

   Biomechanical analysis of motion at the tendon-bone interface found superior tendon fixation after transosseous suture repair, compared with suture anchor repair.

2. Park MC, Cadet ER, Levine WN, Bigliani LU, Ahmad CS: Tendon-to-bone pressure distributions at a repaired rotator cuff footprint using transosseous suture and suture anchor fixation techniques. *Am J Sports Med* 2005;33:1154-1159.

   The mean contact area and the mean interface pressure are greater after transosseous suture repair of rotator cuff tendons than after repair using simple suture anchor and suture anchor mattress techniques.

3. Bicknell RT, Harwood C, Ferreira L, et al: Cyclic loading of rotator cuff repairs: An in vitro biomechanical comparison of bioabsorbable tacks with transosseous sutures. *Arthroscopy* 2005;21:875-880.

   The authors compared the strength of human cadaver specimens after rotator cuff repair with bioabsorbable tacks or transosseous sutures. No difference was found in the ultimate strength of repair, although the bioabsorbable tacks withstood greater initial forces to 50% loss of repair.

4. Bynum CK, Lee S, Mahar A, Tasto J, Pedowitz R: Failure mode of suture anchors as a function of insertion depth. *Am J Sports Med* 2005;33:1030-1034.

   Deep anchor placement led to increased early clinical failure (> 3 mm elongation) compared with standard-depth anchor placement in bovine shoulder cadavers. However, deep anchor placement was found to protect the suture from fraying at the anchor eyelet.

5. Mahar AT, Tucker BS, Upasani VV, Oka RS, Pedowitz RA: Increasing the insertion depth of suture an-

chors for rotator cuff repair does not improve biomechanical stability. *J Shoulder Elbow Surg* 2005;14: 626-630.

Following cyclic loading, displacement of suture anchors in human cadaver humeri was found to be greater after deep anchor placement than after standard-depth placement. The ultimate load to failure was similar in the two groups.

6.  Kim DH, Elattrache NS, Tibone JE, et al: Biomechanical comparison of a single-row versus double-row suture anchor technique for rotator cuff repair. *Am J Sports Med* 2006;34:407-414.

    Human cadaver supraspinatus tendons repaired with double-row suture anchor fixation exhibited smaller gap formation and higher load to failure compared with those repaired with single-row suture anchor fixation.

7.  Ma CB, Comerford L, Wilson J, Puttlitz CM: Biomechanical evaluation of arthroscopic rotator cuff repairs: Double-row compared with single-row fixation. *J Bone Joint Surg Am* 2006;88:403-410.

    The repair strength of four different fixation techniques in human cadaver supraspinatus tendons was evaluated. The double-row technique had a higher ultimate load to failure. The massive cuff technique was stronger than the arthroscopic Mason-Allen or two-simple technique.

8.  Mazzocca AD, Millett PJ, Guanche CA, Santangelo SA, Arciero RA: Arthroscopic single-row versus double-row suture anchor rotator cuff repair. *Am J Sports Med* 2005;33:1861-1868.

    Evaluation of four suture anchor configurations for repair of full-thickness supraspinatus tears in a cadaver model found that the three double-row repair techniques restored the supraspinatus footprint better than the single-row technique. There was no difference in load to failure or displacement among the four groups.

9.  Galatz LM, Rothermich SY, Zaegel M, Silva MJ, Havlioglu N, Thomopoulos S: Delayed repair of tendon to bone injuries leads to decreased biomechanical properties and bone loss. *J Orthop Res* 2005;23:1441-1447.

    The effects of immediate repair were compared with those of 3-week delayed repair of supraspinatus tendon tears in a rat model. Inferior tendon-to-bone healing and decreased bone density at the greater tuberosity appeared in the delayed-repair group.

10. Buess E, Steuber KU, Waibl B: Open versus arthroscopic rotator cuff repair: A comparative view of 96 cases. *Arthroscopy* 2005;21:597-604.

    A retrospective evaluation of the subjective outcome of patients with cuff tears of all sizes treated with arthroscopic repair or with open or mini-open repair found that pain relief and patient satisfaction were better in the arthroscopic group at a minimum 15-month follow-up. Level of evidence: IV.

11. Youm T, Murray DH, Kubiak EN, Rokito AS, Zuckerman JD: Arthroscopic versus mini-open rotator cuff repair: A comparison of clinical outcomes and patient satisfaction. *J Shoulder Elbow Surg* 2005;14: 455-459.

    In a study of the outcomes of patients after a mini-open or arthroscopic rotator cuff repair of small to large tears, no differences in UCLA or ASES scores were found at a minimum 2-year follow-up. Level of evidence: III.

12. Sauerbrey AM, Getz CL, Piancastelli M, Iannotti JP, Ramsey ML, Williams GR: Arthroscopic versus mini-open rotator cuff repair: A comparison of clinical outcome. *Arthroscopy* 2005;21:1415-1420.

    A retrospective comparison of the outcomes of mini-open and arthroscopic rotator cuff repair in 54 patients found equivalent functional improvement. Level of evidence: III.

13. Bishop J, Klepps S, Lo IK, Bird J, Gladstone JN, Flatow EL: Cuff integrity after arthroscopic versus open rotator cuff repair: A prospective study. *J Shoulder Elbow Surg* 2006;15:290-299.

    Retearing rates after open and arthroscopic rotator cuff repairs were prospectively determined using MRI at 1-year follow-up. No overall difference in outcome was found, but arthroscopically treated patients with larger tears (> 3 cm) had a higher retearing rate. Level of evidence: II.

14. Verma NN, Dunn W, Adler RS, et al: All-arthroscopic versus mini-open rotator cuff repair: A retrospective review with minimum 2-year follow-up. *Arthroscopy* 2006;22:587-594.

    Cuff integrity was prospectively evaluated using ultrasonography in patients who underwent mini-open or arthroscopic rotator cuff repair. At a minimum 2-year follow-up, no difference was found in overall outcome, regardless of tear size. Level of evidence: III.

15. Anderson K, Boothby M, Aschenbrener D, van Holsbeeck M: Outcome and structural integrity after arthroscopic rotator cuff repair using 2 rows of fixation: Minimum 2-year follow-up. *Am J Sports Med* 2006; 34:1899-1905.

    Patients treated with arthroscopic double-row suture anchor fixation were evaluated for strength and cuff integrity. The functional outcomes of patients with retearing were similar to those of patients with an intact cuff, but these cuffs were weaker in dynamometric measurement. Level of evidence: IV.

16. Sugaya H, Maeda K, Matsuki K, Moriishi J: Functional and structural outcome after arthroscopic full-thickness rotator cuff repair: Single-row versus dual-row fixation. *Arthroscopy* 2005;21:1307-1316.

    The clinical outcomes of single-row and double-row rotator cuff repair were compared. No difference was reported in functional outcome at a minimum 2-year follow-up.

MRI evaluation revealed higher retearing rates in the single-row group. Level of evidence: III.

17.  Boileau P, Brassart N, Watkinson DJ, Carles M, Hatzidakis AM, Krishnan SG: Arthroscopic repair of full-thickness tears of the supraspinatus: Does the tendon really heal? *J Bone Joint Surg Am* 2005;87:1229-1240.

Tendon healing was evaluated using CT arthrography or MRI after arthroscopic repair of the supraspinatus tendon. Tendons that did not heal had less strength. Patients older than 65 years had a decreased likelihood of healing. Level of evidence: IV.

## Chapter 16

# Massive Rotator Cuff Tears

Kenneth C. Lin, MD

*Sumant G. Krishnan, MD

*Wayne Z. Burkhead, MD

## Introduction

The modern understanding of the rotator cuff, rotator cuff tears, and the treatment of tears began during the late 1800s, and a detailed description of the first rotator cuff repair was published in 1911. Knowledge of rotator cuff tears and the ability to treat them continue to expand, and satisfactory results approaching 95% have been reported after repair of rotator cuff tears.[1] A massive rotator cuff tear, typically defined either as a tear larger than 5 cm in combined area or a tear involving two or more tendons,[1] is difficult to repair with satisfactory results. However, the gap in knowledge and techniques is gradually narrowing.

## Anatomy

Knowledge of normal shoulder anatomy and mechanics is necessary to understand massive rotator cuff tears. In the humeroscapular articulation model, the shoulder is seen as two articulations: the glenoid articulates with the humeral head, and the coracohumeral arch articulates with the proximal humerus.[2] In the normal shoulder, these two articulations are concentric, and a secondary function of the substance of the rotator cuff is to act as a spacer between the two. The extrinsic forces acting on the substance of the rotator cuff are small, and, given the concentricity of the two articulations, the functional demands on the rotator cuff as a spacer are minimal. If the rotator cuff is dysfunctional, the dynamic balance of forces (the force couples) maintaining the concentricity of the two articulations can be lost. The loss of force coupling leads to pain and loss of function. The loss of balanced forces required for a patient to become symptomatic explains why some patients with a

confirmed massive rotator cuff tear maintain relatively good active motion and others become pseudoparalytic (Figure 1). The level of function and symptoms depends not on the dimensions of the tear but on the loss of force coupling. The altered forces in a dysfunctional rotator cuff or a cuff tear can allow the humeral head to migrate superiorly as a result of the deltoid vector. The superior migration increases the extrinsic forces on the remaining substance of the rotator cuff, and the demands on its function as a spacer increase. Eventually, the humeral head articulates with the undersurface of the acromion superiorly and possibly with the coracoid anteriorly.

## Clinical Evaluation

The conditions that lead to a massive rotator cuff tear are diverse, and patients' tears are similarly diverse. However, massive rotator cuff tears can be divided into three broad groups: acute, chronic, and acute on chronic. An acute tear results from trauma in an otherwise normal shoulder. Healthy rotator cuff tendon is extremely strong. During normal daily activities the rotator cuff experiences a force of 140 N to 200 N, and its ultimate tensile strength is between 600 N and 800 N into the sixth and seventh decades of life. In patients with no underlying rotator cuff pathology, including many younger patients, a massive rotator cuff tear occurs only after significant trauma. These patients have an acute onset of pain, with significant weakness and even pseudoparalysis. They may have significant ecchymosis that is directly linked to a specific traumatic event.

A chronic tear is at the opposite end of the spectrum. The tearing of the rotator cuff is chronic and degenerative; the patient often reports a minor trauma or no trauma. A minor incident can extend a chronic tear enough to produce symptoms that require medical attention. A patient with a chronic tear usually is older than 60 years; the incidence of rotator cuff pathology increases with age. The tear may not be symptomatic, if the patient has adapted his or her activities to compensate for any deficits. Alternatively, the force couples may

*Sumant G. Krishnan, MD or the department with which he is affiliated has received research or institutional support from Tornier and DePuy Mitek and is a consultant or employee for Tornier and DePuy Mitek. Wayne Z. Burkhead, MD or the department with which he is affiliated has received research or institutional support from Tornier and DePuy Mitek and is a consultant or employee for Tornier.

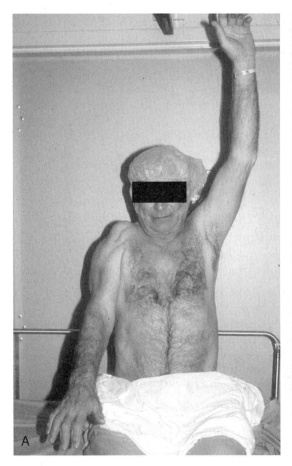
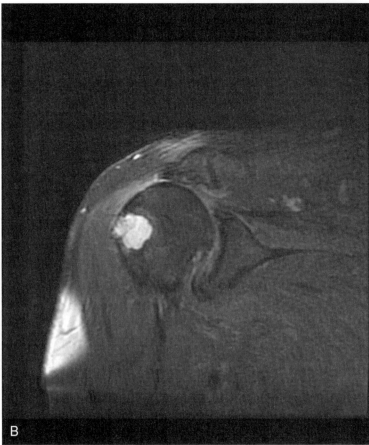

**Figure 1**   A patient with pseudoparalysis. **A,** The loss of active elevation in the right shoulder is the result of a massive rotator cuff tear. **B,** The tear as seen on MRI.

have remained balanced, despite the presence of a tear, allowing for continued good function.

An acute-on-chronic tear has some of the characteristics of an acute tear and a chronic tear. The patient may have some symptoms from a small tear when a new trauma results in a massive, symptomatic tear.

Despite the categorization into three groups, massive rotator cuff tears represent a spectrum of pathology. The patient's physical characteristics, history, anatomy, and tear pathology provide insight into the biology and mechanics of the tear and are important in determining the potential success or failure of each treatment option.

### Physical Examination

The physical examination always begins with an inspection of the contours of the shoulder musculature. Any asymmetry can be the result of atrophy or an altered attitude of the shoulder. Atrophy indicates the presence of either a chronic tear or an associated nerve palsy. Atrophy of the infraspinatus is the most easily observed because of the relatively superficial position of the infraspinatus. A recent study found that suprascapular nerve abnormalities were associated with massive rota-

tor cuff tears or muscle atrophy; electromyography revealed suprascapular neuropathy in association with a massive rotator cuff tear in all patients.[3] Another study found a 30% prevalence of nerve injury associated with rotator cuff tears.[4] The presence of ecchymosis may indicate acute trauma.

Testing of the patient's active range of motion can reveal motion deficits, pseudoparalysis, or pain.[5] Abnormal scapulothoracic motion or dyskinesia may be apparent when the affected shoulder is compared with the contralateral side. A long-standing massive rotator cuff tear can lead to progressive superior or anterosuperior migration of the humeral head. Usually this condition is seen on radiographs, but pronounced anterosuperior migration may appear clinically with attempted overhead elevation. A palpable defect in the deltoid can result from superior migration of the humerus. The Jobe, full can, empty can, belly-press, lift-off, and external rotation strength tests are useful in evaluating the rotator cuff. Lag signs are particularly useful; the external rotation lag sign and hornblower's sign are associated with large and massive tears. Rotator cuff weakness may be present, even in a patient with a chronic tear who has compensated well.

## Imaging Studies

Although the soft tissues of the rotator cuff cannot be directly seen on plain radiographs, radiographic interpretation can yield information about the condition of the cuff.[6] The acromiohumeral distance, which is the space between the inferior surface of the acromion and the most superior part of the proximal humerus, is normally more than 7 mm. It is maintained by the dynamic balance of the forces of the rotator cuff and its space-occupying effect. With loss of balance of the force couples, the humeral head migrates superiorly. A rotator cuff tear is more likely if the acromiohumeral distance is less than 7 mm, and a massive tear is likely if the acromiohumeral distance is less than 5 mm. Superior migration is typically associated with long-standing chronic rotator cuff tearing and fatty infiltration of the torn rotator cuff musculature.[7] As the humeral head shifts superiorly and anteriorly, it can pathologically articulate with the coracoid or the acromion and eccentrically load the superior glenoid. Changes resulting from this abnormal wear, such as rounding off of the greater tuberosity or eccentric wear of the glenoid, may occur in long-standing disease and can be seen on plain radiographs. Arthrography was formerly used for diagnosis in conjunction with plain radiography, but it has been replaced by less invasive modalities.

Ultrasonography is routinely used in some centers for inexpensive evaluation of the rotator cuff. It allows for dynamic evaluation, and high rates of specificity and sensitivity have been reported. However, ultrasonographic examination requires an experienced operator, and interpretation of the results can be operator dependent. As a result, it is not widely used.

CT provides excellent visualization of the bony anatomy of the shoulder, as well as information about the rotator cuff tendon and musculature. CT was used in a study that found a greater likelihood of recurrent cuff tears in tendons whose muscle showed fatty degeneration.[7] In most centers, MRI is used to evaluate the rotator cuff because it offers excellent soft-tissue visualization. The Goutallier system of staging changes in the rotator cuff muscle (grade 0, no fatty deposits; grade 1, some fatty streaking within the muscle; grade 2, more muscle than fat; grade 3, fat equal to muscle; grade 4, more fat than muscle) is based on CT and has been adapted to MRI, although MRI studies tend to overestimate the degree of fatty infiltration[8] (Figure 2).

## Nonsurgical Treatment

The nonsurgical treatment of a massive rotator cuff tear consists of activity modification, the use of nonsteroidal anti-inflammatory drugs, the judicious use of steroid injections, and physical therapy focused on stretching and strengthening. The goals of nonsurgical treatment are pain control and maintenance of as much function as

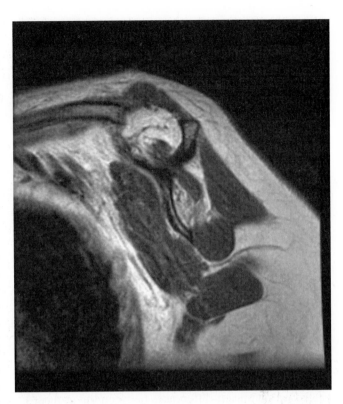

**Figure 2**  A sagittal plane MRI showing near-complete fatty infiltration of the supraspinatus muscle belly.

possible. A report on the nonsurgical management of full-thickness rotator cuff tears found a correlation between the pretreatment duration of symptoms and the extent of pain relief after nonsurgical treatment. Pain improved in 86% of patients with symptoms of 3 months' duration, compared with 56% of patients with symptoms of more than 6 months' duration. However, 94% of the patients had weakness, and 56% had muscle atrophy.[9] These findings are not surprising, given the gradual retraction of the tendon from its insertion site in a rotator cuff tear. Nonsurgical treatment does not produce healing, although the remaining cuff may compensate for the tear, and the symptoms may therefore lessen. A study of asymptomatic rotator cuff tears found that no tears decreased in size during an average of 5 years, and half of the tears eventually became symptomatic. Although the findings did not achieve statistical significance, the study suggested that the onset of pain is correlated with tear progression.[10]

## Surgical Treatment
### Débridement Without Repair

Simple débridement of massive rotator cuff tears has had good results. Of 50 patients treated with an open modified Neer acromioplasty, subacromial decompression, and débridement, 33 had no pain, 10 had occasional pain, and 5 had pain during strenuous activity, at an average 6.5-year follow-up. Most of the patients continued to have weakness, but the average functional score on a modified University of California Los Angeles (UCLA) Shoulder Scale improved from 3.4 before surgery to 7.3 at final review; strength and satisfaction scores improved from 0 to 4.4. Active elevation improved from an average of 105° before surgery to 140° after surgery.[11] Similar results were found in 33 patients treated with subacromial decompression and débridement. The condition of 26 patients improved after surgery, as measured using the American Shoulder and Elbow Surgeons (ASES) Shoulder Index and Constant Shoulder Score. The condition of four patients was worse after surgery, and the condition of three patients was unchanged.[12] Débridement was combined with a tenotomy of the long head of the biceps in patients with an irreparable rotator cuff tear, including older patients who were unwilling to participate in the postsurgical regimen associated with cuff repair.[13] At 57-month follow-up, 87% of the 307 patients were satisfied or very satisfied; the mean Constant score improved from 48.4 before surgery to 67.6 at follow-up. However, a comparison of 41 patients treated with débridement alone or with a débridement–biceps tenotomy combination revealed no significant differences between the groups.[14]

The benefits of subacromial decompression and débridement for the treatment of massive rotator cuff tears appear to lessen over time. Deterioration of results at longer term follow-up was found in rotator cuff tears of all sizes after treatment with arthroscopic subacromial decompression combined with débridement. The deterioration was worst in large and massive tears.[15] In another study, 8% of patients who had undergone débridement had a satisfactory result at a 6- to 9-year follow-up, compared with 87% of those who had undergone repair.[16]

Tuberoplasty has also been used to treat irreparable massive rotator cuff tears. Exostoses are removed from the humerus, and the greater tuberosity is reshaped to create a smooth acromiohumeral articulation. Acromioplasty is specifically avoided, so as to preserve the coracoacromial ligament and prevent iatrogenic anterosuperior escape. Of 20 patients treated with tuberoplasty, 12 had an excellent result and 6 had a good result at a minimum 27-month follow-up. All patients had residual weakness, but 68% were completely pain free.[17] Similarly good results were reported in 23 patients treated with tuberoplasty, at an average 40-month follow-up.[18] However, the long-term results of tuberoplasty have not been studied.

### Primary Repair

Since Codman's first description in 1911, the ability to repair the rotator cuff has improved greatly, along with the understanding of rotator cuff pathology. The results of repairs of massive tears continue to be inferior to those of smaller tears. A histologic study of rotator cuff tears discovered differences based on tear size.[19] In large and massive tears, there was more edema and degeneration, with increased chondroid metaplasia and amyloid deposition. These factors, along with a lack of inflammatory response (seen as an absence of increased fibroblast cellularity and vascular ingrowth), produce a local environment that does not appear to biologically promote tendon healing. In contrast, smaller tears had an increased inflammatory response, with increased fibroblast cellularity and blood vessel proliferation, that creates a local environment favorable for tendon-to-bone healing.

Intrinsic changes in the rotator cuff may predispose a tear to repair failure. CT was used to retrospectively correlate presurgical fatty infiltration of the muscle with repair failure. The degree of presurgical fatty infiltration was correlated with the likelihood of repair failure, and repair was more likely to fail in a massive tear with presurgical fatty infiltration equal to or greater than muscle volume.[7,20]

Extrinsic factors also can contribute to repair failure. In a repair of a massive rotator cuff tear, it may not be possible to adequately mobilize the cuff back to its original insertion. If the cuff can be mobilized, it may be reparable only with excessive tension that predisposes it to failure. As the understanding of the biology of rotator cuff repair has expanded, technical principles such as margin convergence have been developed. In margin convergence, a side-to-side repair of the tendon is used to decrease the necessary mobilization and the strain across the rotator cuff.[21] The clinical consequence of decreasing the strain was reported in 14 patients. Despite the lack of a complete rotator cuff repair, the creation of a smaller tear from the larger one resulted in an average 90° improvement in active elevation, and 13 patients were satisfied with the final result.[21] In a report of the benefits of partial repair in 24 patients, 92% were satisfied with the surgical result, and 83% reported satisfactory pain relief.[22] Even partial repair of a massive tear can result in nerve recovery and functional improvement, although recovery was found to be incomplete and many nerve deficits were permanent.[3]

Good long-term results of massive rotator cuff repair have been reported. The average UCLA Shoulder Scale Score of 30 patients improved from 12.3 before surgery to 31.0 at a mean 65-month follow-up.[23] The average Constant score of 29 patients improved from 49 before surgery to 85 at an average 37-month follow-up. Only 17 of the 29 patients had a structurally successful repair, as determined using MRI. Successful repair was correlated with excellent clinical outcome.[1]

The healing of arthroscopically repaired massive rotator cuff tears has recently been studied. Eighteen patients underwent arthroscopic single-row repair of a chronic large or massive rotator cuff tear. Clinical and ultrasound evaluation at a minimum 12-month follow-up revealed that 17 patients had a recurrent tear. Nonetheless, 16 patients had an improved functional outcome score. Sixteen patients had decreased pain, and 12 reported no pain. Forward elevation improved in all 18 patients, to an average of more than 150°. However, at a minimum 24-month follow-up, the average ASES Shoulder Index score had decreased from 84.6 to 79.9, and the average forward elevation had decreased from 152° to 142°.[24] Another study also found an apparent discrepancy between repair integrity and clinical results. Twenty patients were identified at an average of 3.2 years after rotator cuff repair as having a rerupture or failure to heal. At 7.6 years after surgery, the average Constant score and tear size had not significantly changed; 19 patients continued to be satisfied, and the average Constant score was 88.[25]

### Repair With Augmentation

A cadaver study of the biomechanical effect of a synthetic patch graft found that, if a rotator cuff tear cannot be mobilized back to its original attachment, the interposition of a synthetic patch graft serves to redirect force transmission and improve abduction torque.[26] In a study of the clinical results of allograft used to span irreparable rotator cuff tears, 23 of 28 patients were satisfied with the result at 31-month follow-up, and the mean UCLA Shoulder Scale score had improved from 12.1 to 26.1. However, complete failure of the repair occurred in all patients for whom a magnetic resonance arthrogram was obtained. Because the patients' clinical results were comparable to the results of débridement and subacromial decompression, the authors did not recommend the use of allograft.[27]

Porcine small intestine submucosa was used for augmentation of irreparable massive rotator cuff tears in 11 patients. This bioabsorbable tissue scaffold allows for the ingrowth of repair tissue and has been used in other parts of the body. In seven patients, the xenograft was used as a bridging interpositional graft, and in four patients, the xenograft was used to reinforce a primary repair. Despite the theoretic biologic advantages of this technique, only 1 of 11 was intact at 10-month follow-up, and there was no statistical difference in presurgical and postsurgical shoulder function, as measured using the ASES Shoulder Index.[28] A randomized controlled trial comparing repairs using porcine small intestine submucosa augmentation with repairs using no augmentation found no difference in clinical outcome, using current scoring systems. At 1-year follow-up, 4 of 15 shoulders in the augmentation group were healed, and 9 of 15 shoulders in the no-augmentation group were healed. The authors did not recommend using porcine small intestine submucosa.[29] The use of augmentation devices or patches of any kind remains a subject of controversy.

### Tendon Transfer

A tendon transfer can be considered for a massive rotator cuff tear that is not suitable for a primary repair. A finite element biomechanical model was used to compare tendon transfers, and the calculation determined that transfer of the teres major to the supraspinatus insertion would produce the best functional outcome.[30] Although this finding is of academic interest, the functional and clinical success of a tendon transfer is affected by many variables unaccounted for in a biomechanical model. Therefore, recommendations based on actual clinical results are more difficult to determine.

A number of tendon transfers are used, and the choice partially depends on the location of the tear. The modified L'Episcopo latissimus dorsi transfer is commonly used for posterosuperior tears.[31] The transfer of the latissimus dorsi tendon is attractive because of its great potential for excursion, as well as its relative strength. It affords coverage of the humeral head by acting essentially as a vascularized tendon graft. In addition, retraining of the muscle can improve active external rotation. In 67 patients, pain relief was satisfactory, and flexion improved from an average of 104° to an average of 123°. The functional results were inferior in patients who did not have a functioning subscapularis muscle, and for these patients the latissimus dorsi transfer was found to have no value.[31] This result might be expected because of the inability of the latissimus dorsi to restore a dynamic posterior force couple to the anterior subscapularis-deficient shoulder.

The close proximity of the radial and axillary nerves to the latissimus dorsi insertion is of concern in the latissimus dorsi transfer procedure. A cadaver study of the relative distance from the latissimus dorsi tendon insertion to the radial and axillary nerves with the arm in different positions revealed that external rotation of the arm increases the distance of the axillary and radial nerves from the superior and inferior borders of the latissimus dorsi tendon insertion, respectively.[32] Unfortunately, it is necessary to internally rotate the arm to gain exposure during dissection of the latissimus dorsi tendon from the posterior approach. A careful, adequate exposure is therefore critical.

The latissimus dorsi tendon transfer has been used as a revision procedure after an unsuccessful massive rotator cuff repair. At 51-month follow-up, 14 of 17 patients had significant pain relief and significant improvement in function, as measured using the UCLA Shoulder Scale.[33] Another study found that the results of latissimus dorsi tendon transfer after an unsuccessful rotator cuff repair were significantly inferior to the results of primary tendon transfer.[34] The rate of transfer rupture was substantially higher in the patients treated with salvage transfer than in patients treated with primary transfer.

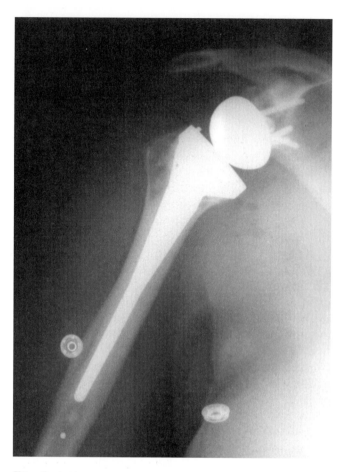

**Figure 3** An AP radiograph showing reverse total shoulder arthroplasty.

A subcoracoid pectoralis major transfer can be used to repair an anterosuperior tear. In a study of the efficacy of a pectoralis major transfer for an isolated subscapularis tear or a combined subscapularis-supraspinatus tear, patients whose transfer was successful had improvements in function and Constant score. Although full active elevation and external rotation were not to be expected, patient satisfaction was high. The authors attributed this result to low presurgical function. Patients with a combined supraspinatus-subscapularis tear did not fare as well as those with an isolated subscapularis tear, although the difference was not statistically significant.[35] Nine of 14 patients with anterosuperior escape caused by massive rotator cuff insufficiency were satisfied at an average 17.5-month follow-up after pectoralis muscle transfer. As in other studies, the patients' function improved, but forward elevation increased only modestly, from 24.4° to 60.8°.[36]

Transfers of other tendons, such as the long head of the triceps, have been successful in limited series,[37] achieving pain improvement and limited improvement in function. However, these transfers have had results inferior to those of repair. Such transfers probably do not have a dynamic function but instead provide a vas-cularized tissue flap that may promote local tendon healing or act as a mechanical spacer between the humeral head and the undersurface of the acromion.

### Arthroplasty

Glenohumeral arthritis develops as a late consequence of the altered, abnormal forces present in a shoulder with a severe rotator cuff deficiency. With loss of the balanced forces of the rotator cuff musculature, the glenohumeral articulation becomes eccentrically loaded, and abnormal wear on the glenoid can lead to painful glenohumeral arthritis. Few successful treatment options are available for glenohumeral arthritis in the severely cuff-deficient shoulder. Although glenohumeral arthritis in an otherwise normal shoulder can be successfully treated with conventional total shoulder arthroplasty, standard arthroplasty is impossible in the cuff-deficient shoulder because of unacceptably high rates of glenoid loosening. Hemiarthroplasty can offer pain relief and some improvement in function, but it has unpredictable long-term results. Of 33 patients treated with hemiarthroplasty for rotator cuff tear arthropathy, approximately 75% had significant improvement of pain, and active elevation improved from an average of 72° before surgery to 91° after surgery.[38]

The introduction of reverse total shoulder arthroplasty has added a treatment option for glenohumeral arthritis in a severely cuff-deficient shoulder (Figure 3). When the concavity-compression effect of the rotator cuff muscles is lost, the superior vector of the deltoid is not balanced by compression of the humeral head into the glenoid. Hence, the patient experiences pseudoparalysis, or inability to elevate the arm above shoulder level, and dynamic anterior-superior subluxation of the humeral head occurs. Conventional unconstrained shoulder arthroplasty cannot restore the altered mechanics of the deficient rotator cuff. As originally described by Grammont, semiconstrained reverse total shoulder arthroplasty medializes the center of rotation of the affected glenohumeral joint and provides a stable fulcrum for active overhead elevation of the arm by the deltoid.[39] A multicenter study reviewed 80 shoulders treated with a reverse total shoulder prosthesis, at a mean 44-month follow-up. The average Constant score improved from 22.6 to 65.6, and 96% of patients had little or no pain. The mean forward elevation improved from 73° to 138°.[39] However, the use of reverse total shoulder arthroplasty for patients with a massive rotator cuff tear and no arthritis is highly controversial. A recent retrospective review of 186 patients who underwent reverse shoulder arthroplasty was completed at a mean 39 months. Although final outcomes varied by etiology, those for patients older than 70 years who had massive, irreparable rotator cuff tearing without arthritis were among the most successful; mean elevation improved from 94° to 143°.[40]

## Summary

The treatment of patients with a massive rotator cuff tear remains challenging, and it must be determined based on a patient's age, symptoms, tear chronicity, and remaining muscle quality. For a younger patient with a symptomatic massive tear, an attempt to restore the force couples of the rotator cuff via primary repair, tendon transfer, or both, must be considered early in the treatment algorithm. For an older patient with a long-standing tear and irreversible fatty changes of the rotator cuff musculature, the morbidity associated with attempted repair or tendon transfer must be weighed against perceived success and quality of life. If nonsurgical or limited surgical treatment is unsuccessful in a patient who is older than 70 years, reverse shoulder arthroplasty may be a viable, although controversial, alternative.

## Annotated References

1. Gerber C, Fuchs B, Hodler J: The results of repair of massive tears of the rotator cuff. *J Bone Joint Surg Am* 2000;82:505-515.

2. Matsen FA, Titelman RM, Lipitt SB, Wirth MA, Rockwood CA Jr: Rotator cuff, in Rockwood CA Jr, Matsen FA (eds): *The Shoulder*, ed 3. Philadelphia, PA, WB Saunders, 2004, pp 795-878.

    The anatomy and biomechanics of the rotator cuff are reviewed.

3. Mallon WJ, Wilson RJ, Basamania CJ: The association of suprascapular neuropathy with massive rotator cuff tears: A preliminary report. *J Shoulder Elbow Surg* 2006;15:395-398.

    Eight patients in a prospective, consecutive series had a massive rotator cuff tear with severe retraction and suprascapular neuropathy. Four patients underwent débridement and partial repair. Active elevation improved from approximately 40° to more than 90°. Two patients recovered suprascapular nerve function.

4. Vad VB, Southern D, Warren RF, Altchek DW, Dines D: Prevalence of peripheral neurologic injuries in rotator cuff tears with atrophy. *J Shoulder Elbow Surg* 2003;12:333-336.

    This retrospective review of 25 patients evaluated the prevalence of neurologic injury in the presence of a rotator cuff tear and muscle atrophy. Electrodiagnostic peripheral neuropathy was found in 28%, most commonly involving the axillary and suprascapular nerves.

5. Hertel R, Ballmer FT, Lombert SM, Gerber C: Lag signs in the diagnosis of rotator cuff rupture. *J Shoulder Elbow Surg* 1996;5:307-313.

6. Saupe N, Pfirrmann CW, Schmid MR, Jost B, Werner CM, Zanetti M: Association between rotator cuff abnormalities and reduced acromiohumeral distance. *AJR Am J Roentgenol* 2006;187:376-382.

    Plain radiographs were used to retrospectively identify three groups of patients based on acromiohumeral distance. The radiographic results were correlated with those of magnetic resonance arthrograms. Reduced acromiohumeral distance was found to be correlated with tear size and fatty degeneration, particularly in the infraspinatus muscle.

7. Goutallier D, Postel JM, Gleyze P, Leguilloux P, Van Driessche S: Influence of cuff muscle fatty degeneration on anatomic and functional outcomes after simple suture of full-thickness tears. *J Shoulder Elbow Surg* 2003;12:550-554.

    Two hundred twenty shoulders that had undergone rotator cuff repair were retrospectively reviewed, and presurgical CT was evaluated for fatty infiltration. Tendons with presurgical fatty infiltration of grade II or higher were more likely to have a recurrent tear.

8. Fuchs B, Weishaupt D, Zanetti M, Hodler J, Gerber C: Fatty degeneration of the muscles of the rotator cuff: Assessment by computed tomography versus magnetic resonance imaging. *J Shoulder Elbow Surg* 1999;8:599-605.

9. Bokor DJ, Hawkins RJ, Huckell GH, Angelo RL, Schickendantz MS: Results of nonoperative management of full-thickness tears of the rotator cuff. *Clin Orthop Relat Res* 1993;294:103-110.

10. Yamaguchi K, Ditsios K, Middleton WD, Hildebolt CF, Galatz LM, Teefey SA: The demographic and morphological features of rotator cuff disease: A comparison of asymptomatic and symptomatic shoulders. *J Bone Joint Surg Am* 2006;88:1699-1704.

    The presence of a symptomatic or asymptomatic rotator cuff tear was confirmed using ultrasonography in 588 patients. Evaluation of demographic and outcome differences found that patient age is most highly correlated with the presence of a tear, and the onset of symptoms, especially pain, is correlated with tear progression.

11. Rockwood CA Jr, Williams GR Jr, Burkhead WZ Jr: Débridement of degenerative, irreparable lesions of the rotator cuff. *J Bone Joint Surg Am* 1995;77:857-866.

12. Gartsman GM: Massive, irreparable tears of the rotator cuff: Results of operative debridement and subacromial decompression. *J Bone Joint Surg Am* 1997;79:715-721.

13. Walch G, Edwards TB, Boulahia A, Nove-Josserand L, Neyton L, Szabo I: Arthroscopic tenotomy of the long head of the biceps in the treatment of rotator cuff tears: Clinical and radiographic results of 307 cases. *J Shoulder Elbow Surg* 2005;14:238-246.

    A review of 307 irreparable rotator cuff tears treated with arthroscopic débridement and tenotomy of the long head of the biceps found a high patient satisfaction rate and improved Constant scores at an average 57-month follow-up. Radiographs revealed continued narrowing of the acromiohumeral distance and worsening glenohumeral arthritis.

14. Klinger HM, Spahn G, Baums MH, Steckel H: Arthroscopic debridement of irreparable massive rotator cuff tears: A comparison of debridement alone and combined procedure with biceps tenotomy. *Acta Chir Belg* 2005;105:297-301.

    A retrospective review of 41 patients treated by a single surgeon with débridement or débridement combined with biceps tenotomy found no difference between the two groups in Constant score or radiographic changes.

15. Zvijac JE, Levy HJ, Lemak LJ: Arthroscopic subacromial decompression in the treatment of full thickness rotator cuff tears: A 3- to 6-year follow-up. *Arthroscopy* 1994;10:518-523.

16. Montgomery TJ, Yerger B, Savoie FH III: A comparison of arthroscopic debridement with open surgical repair for full-thickness tears of the rotator cuff. *J Shoulder Elbow Surg* 1994;3:70-78.

17. Fenlin JM Jr, Chase JM, Rushton SA, Frieman BG: Tuberoplasty: Creation of an acromiohumeral articulation. A treatment option for massive, irreparable rotator cuff tears. *J Shoulder Elbow Surg* 2002;11:136-142.

    Twenty patients underwent a tuberoplasty procedure with reshaping of the greater tuberosity of the humerus, for the treatment of an irreparable rotator cuff tear. At a minimum 27-month follow-up, 95% had a satisfactory result, and 68% were completely pain free. Objective strength deficits persisted.

18. Scheibel M, Lichtenberg S, Habermeyer P: Reversed arthroscopic subacromial decompression for massive rotator cuff tears. *J Shoulder Elbow Surg* 2004;13:272-278.

    Twenty-three patients with an irreparable rotator cuff tear underwent arthroscopic decompression of both the greater tuberosity and acromion, with biceps tenotomy. At a mean 40-month follow-up, 82% were rated excellent or good, but acromiohumeral distance was statistically decreased.

19. Matthews TJ, Hand GC, Rees JL, Athanasou NA, Carr AJ: Pathology of the torn rotator cuff tendon: Reduction in potential for repair as tear size increases. *J Bone Joint Surg Br* 2006;88:489-495.

    Biopsy specimens taken from 40 patients with a chronic rotator cuff tear were examined and compared with biopsy specimens from four uninjured tendons. Cellular and vascular changes indicative of repair and inflammation were most evident in smaller tears and less evident as tear size increased. No correlation appeared with patient age or chronicity of symptoms.

20. Goutallier D, Postel JM, Bernageau J, Lavau L, Voisin MC: Fatty muscle degeneration in cuff ruptures: Pre- and postoperative evaluation by CT scan. *Clin Orthop Relat Res* 1994;304:78-83.

21. Burkhart SS, Athanasiou KA, Wirth MA: Margin convergence: A method of reducing strain in massive rotator cuff tears. *Arthroscopy* 1996;12:335-338.

22. Duralde XA, Bair B: Massive rotator cuff tears: The result of partial rotator cuff repair. *J Shoulder Elbow Surg* 2005;14:121-127.

    A complete repair was attempted in 24 patients with a massive rotator cuff tear, but only a partial repair could be performed. A retrospective review found that 92% were satisfied, 83% had satisfactory pain relief, and average active elevation improved from 114° to 154°.

23. Rokito AS, Cuomo F, Gallagher MA, Zuckerman JD: Long-term functional outcome of repair of large and massive chronic tears of the rotator cuff. *J Bone Joint Surg Am* 1999;81:991-997.

24. Galatz LM, Ball CM, Teefey SA, Middleton WD, Yamaguchi K: The outcome and repair integrity of completely arthroscopically repaired large and massive rotator cuff tears. *J Bone Joint Surg Am* 2004;86-A:219-224.

    Eighteen patients who underwent arthroscopic repair of a rotator cuff tear larger than 2 cm were evaluated at 12 and 24 months. Recurrent tears appeared in 17 patients, and both pain relief and functional outcome deteriorated between 12 and 24 months. The rehabilitation protocol may have contributed to the results.

25. Jost B, Zumstein M, Pfirrmann CW, Gerber C: Long-term outcome after structural failure of rotator cuff repairs. *J Bone Joint Surg Am* 2006;88:472-479.

    Twenty patients identified at 3.2-year follow-up as having a rerupture after arthroscopic rotator cuff repair were reexamined at an average of 7.6 years. Nineteen continued to be satisfied and show improvement, as measured by the Constant score. Constant scores were equivalent at the two follow-ups, and MRI showed no retear progression.

26. Mura N, O'Driscoll SW, Zobitz ME, Heers G, An KN: Biomechanical effect of patch graft for large rotator cuff tears: A cadaver study. *Clin Orthop Relat Res* 2003;415:131-138.

    In a cadaver biomechanical study of 10 specimens repaired with synthetic patch graft, abduction torque was increased when the graft was repaired to the subscapularis.

27. Moore DR, Cain EL, Schwartz ML, Clancy WG Jr: Allograft reconstruction for massive, irreparable rotator cuff tears. *Am J Sports Med* 2006;34:392-396.

    Thirty-two patients underwent reconstruction with patellar tendon, Achilles tendon, or quadriceps tendon allograft. Fifteen patients evaluated with a magnetic resonance arthrogram had structural repair failure. Clinical improvement was comparable to that from débridement and subacromial decompression.

28. Sclamberg SG, Tibone JE, Itamura JM, Kasraeian S: Six-month magnetic resonance imaging follow-up of large and massive rotator cuff repairs reinforced with

porcine small intestinal submucosa. *J Shoulder Elbow Surg* 2004;13:538-541.

Eleven patients with massive rotator cuff tears received a primary repair reinforced with a porcine small intestine submucosa xenograft. MRI showed recurrence in 10 patients. There was no significant difference in presurgical and postsurgical shoulder scores.

29. Iannotti JP, Codsi MJ, Kwon YW, Derwin K, Ciccone J, Brems JJ: Porcine small intestine submucosa augmentation of surgical repair of chronic two-tendon rotator cuff tears: A randomized, controlled trial. *J Bone Joint Surg Am* 2006;88:1238-1244.

Thirty patients with a massive two-tendon rotator cuff tear were randomly assigned to repair without augmentation or repair with porcine small intestine submucosa augmentation. Augmentation did not improve healing rates or clinical outcome, as measured using the Penn Shoulder Score.

30. Magermans DJ, Chadwick EK, Veeger HE, van der Helm FC, Rozing PM: Biomechanical analysis of tendon transfers for massive rotator cuff tears. *Clin Biomech (Bristol, Avon)* 2004;19:350-357.

A biomechanical model was used to simulate latissimus dorsi and teres major tendon transfers. Teres major transfer to the insertion of the supraspinatus was found to provide the best mechanical advantage for humeral elevation and external rotation.

31. Gerber C, Maquieira G, Espinosa N: Latissimus dorsi transfer for the treatment of irreparable rotator cuff tears. *J Bone Joint Surg Am* 2006;88:113-120.

Sixty-seven patients with a massive rotator cuff tear were treated with a latissimus dorsi transfer. At an average 53-month follow-up, Constant and subjective shoulder scores had improved. The benefit was questionable in the absence of a functioning subscapularis.

32. Cleeman E, Hazrati Y, Auerbach JD, Shubin Stein K, Hausman M, Flatow EL: Latissimus dorsi tendon transfer for massive rotator cuff tears: A cadaveric study. *J Shoulder Elbow Surg* 2003;12:539-543.

This anatomic study of 10 cadaver specimens examined the relationships between the latissimus dorsi tendon and the axillary and radial nerves at different arm positions. Internal rotation combined with shoulder abduction was found to decrease the distance from each nerve to the tendon insertion.

33. Miniaci A, MacLeod M: Transfer of the latissimus dorsi muscle after failed repair of a massive tear of the rotator cuff: A two to five-year review. *J Bone Joint Surg Am* 1999;81:1120-1127.

34. Warner JJ, Parsons IM: Latissimus dorsi tendon transfer: A comparative analysis of primary and salvage reconstruction of massive, irreparable rotator cuff tears. *J Shoulder Elbow Surg* 2001;10:514-521.

A retrospective comparison of primary latissimus dorsi transfer to salvage transfer after an unsuccessful rotator cuff repair found statistically worse outcomes after the salvage transfers. In the salvage group patients, 44% of transfers ruptured, compared with 17% of transfers in the primary group patients. The authors conclude that primary transfer leads to more successful results.

35. Jost B, Puskas GJ, Lustenberger A, Gerber C: Outcome of pectoralis major transfer for the treatment of irreparable subscapularis tears. *J Bone Joint Surg Am* 2003;85-A:1944-1951.

Of 28 patients who underwent pectoralis transfer for a chronic subscapularis tear, 23 (82%) were satisfied with the result. The result was less successful if an irreparable supraspinatus tendon tear was also present.

36. Galatz LM, Connor PM, Calfee RP, Hsu JC, Yamaguchi K: Pectoralis major transfer for anterior-superior subluxation in massive rotator cuff insufficiency. *J Shoulder Elbow Surg* 2003;12:1-5.

The outcomes of 14 patients who underwent subcoracoid pectoralis major tendon transfer for a massive anterosuperior rotator cuff tear were reviewed. At a mean 17.5-month follow-up, 77% were satisfied, and 13 had functional improvement in daily activities.

37. Malkani AL, Sundine MJ, Tillett ED, Baker DL, Rogers RA, Morton TA: Transfer of the long head of the triceps tendon for irreparable rotator cuff tears. *Clin Orthop Relat Res* 2004;428:228-236.

Eighteen patients with an irreparable massive rotator cuff tear were reviewed after transfer of the long head of the triceps tendon. At a minimum 2-year follow-up, patients had clinical improvement and a UCLA Shoulder Scale increase from 9.7 to 28.8. The transfer did not result in any loss of elbow extension strength.

38. Sanchez-Sotelo J, Cofield RH, Rowland CM: Shoulder hemiarthroplasty for glenohumeral arthritis associated with severe rotator cuff deficiency. *J Bone Joint Surg Am* 2001;83-A:1814-1822.

This retrospective review evaluated 33 shoulders treated with hemiarthroplasty necessitated by an irreparable rotator cuff tear and associated glenohumeral arthritis. At a mean 5-year follow-up, 27% of the patients continued to have pain, and mean active elevation was only 91°.

39. Sirveaux F, Favard L, Oudet D, Huquet D, Walch G, Mole D: Grammont inverted total shoulder arthroplasty in the treatment of glenohumeral osteoarthritis with massive rupture of the cuff: Results of a multicentre study of 80 shoulders. *J Bone Joint Surg Br* 2004;86:388-395.

In a retrospective, multicenter review of 80 shoulders treated with a Grammont reverse total shoulder prosthesis for rotator cuff tear arthropathy, the Constant score improved from 22.6 to 65.6, and 96% of patients had little or no pain. Forward elevation improved from an average of 73° to 138°.

40. Wall B, Nove-Josserand L, O'Conner DP, Edwards TB, Walch G: Reverse total shoulder arthroplasty: A review of results according to etiology. *J Bone Joint Surg Am* 2007;89:1476-1485.

In a retrospective review of 186 patients who underwent reverse shoulder arthroplasty, the results were correlated with etiology. Although all patient groups had improvement, patients with primary rotator cuff tear arthropathy or a massive irreparable rotator cuff tear had better outcomes.

# Chapter 17

# Factors Affecting the Outcome of Rotator Cuff Surgery

Robert Z. Tashjian, MD

## Introduction

Outcomes assessment has achieved an important position in clinical orthopaedic research during the past several decades. Awareness of the need for well-designed outcomes studies has arisen from concern about differing indications and geographic variations related to some orthopaedic procedures, as well as a generally more challenging health care environment. Physician-designated measures of success, such as fracture healing, lack of deformity, and improvement in motion or strength, are no longer the only criteria for evaluating treatment success. The patient's self-assessment of physical function, general physical and mental health, pain, and ability to perform activities of daily living, work, and sports are now considered at least as important in determining the effects of a treatment.

More than 17 million individuals in the United States are affected by rotator cuff disease, which is the most common shoulder condition treated by orthopaedic surgeons. Thus, factors affecting the outcome of rotator cuff surgery are important to orthopaedic surgeons. In recent years, outcomes instruments have been developed to capture self-assessed patient function, and these and other instruments have been used to identify factors affecting presurgical and postsurgical function in patients with rotator cuff tears. These factors can be used to define surgical indications and establish appropriate patient and surgeon expectations.

## The Evolution of Outcomes Evaluation for Rotator Cuff Surgery

E.A. Codman, a shoulder surgeon and pioneer in radiology and oncology, was also an early researcher of outcomes. He believed that "every hospital should follow every patient it treats, long enough to determine whether or not the treatment has been successful, and then to inquire 'if not, why not?' with a view to preventing similar failures in the future."[1] Several basic outcomes research principles, including the recording of preintervention and postintervention data, originated with Codman.

For outcomes reporting to be possible, a standardized instrument or system must be available to measure results specific to a region of the body, a joint, or a disease (Table 1). Little scientific or statistical analysis was available to guide the development of the initial measurement instruments, including the Neer rating sheet in 1972 and the University of California Los Angeles (UCLA) Shoulder Scale in 1981.[2,3] Both of these instruments measure shoulder pain, motion, strength, and function, as well as patient satisfaction. Their parameters were selected by the authors without direct patient input, and neither scale has been tested for validity or reliability.[4,5] They are routinely used in outcome studies and for patient evaluation after rotator cuff repair.

During the late 1980s and early 1990s, more advanced shoulder outcomes instruments were developed. The Constant-Murley Shoulder Outcome Score includes both physician-derived and patient-reported evaluations of pain, activities of daily living, range of motion, and power.[6] The manner in which the instrument is to be administered is clearly described, and thus its consistency and reliability are improved in comparison with earlier instruments. However, details of the instrument's development are unknown. In addition, its heavy weighting toward physician-derived measurements may effectively misrepresent patient-perceived outcome. The Constant score is the functional score currently recommended by the European Society for Surgery of the Shoulder and the Elbow and the British Elbow and Shoulder Society, despite a relative lack of reliability and validity testing.[7]

The American Shoulder and Elbow Surgeons (ASES) Shoulder Pain and Disability Index was developed in 1993 by an ASES research committee, with contributions from active members of the society. As a patient self-assessment scale, it does not include physician-derived measurements such as strength and motion. To evaluate pain, the ASES questionnaire uses a visual analog scale (VAS). To evaluate function, it uses several Likert-style questions, in which respondents use a numeric scale to indicate the extent to which they agree or disagree with each attitude statement. Although no

**Table 1 | Instruments Used for the Evaluation of Rotator Cuff Disorders**

| Instrument | Date | Scoring Range (Worst to Best) | Domains | Scoring Method (Physician or Patient Assessment) | Testing of Instrument | Shortcomings |
|---|---|---|---|---|---|---|
| Neer Rating Sheet | 1972 | Unsatisfactory, Satisfactory, Excellent | Shoulder pain, active abduction, active external rotation, satisfaction | Physician | None | No patient self-assessment; Unknown development methodology |
| UCLA Shoulder Scale | 1981 | 0-35 | Shoulder pain, function, active forward flexion, strength of forward flexion, satisfaction | Physician | None | No patient self-assessment; Unknown domain-weighting methodology |
| Constant-Murley Shoulder Outcome Score | 1987 | 0-100 | Shoulder pain, function, range of motion, strength | Physician, patient | Limited reliability testing; no validity or responsiveness testing | Unknown development, domain-weighting methodology; Heavy strength and motion weighting (60%) |
| Simple Shoulder Test | 1992 | 0-12 | Shoulder function | Patient | Reliability, validity, responsiveness testing | Unclear item generation, development methodology |
| ASES Shoulder Pain and Disability Index | 1993 | 0-100 | Shoulder pain, function | Patient | Reliability, validity, responsiveness testing | Unknown item selection, weighting methodology |
| Disabilities of the Arm, Shoulder and Hand Questionnaire | 1996 | 0-100 | Upper extremity-related symptoms, functional disability | Patient | Reliability, validity, responsiveness testing | Region specific (less responsive than shoulder-specific instruments) |
| Rotator Cuff Quality-of-Life Measure | 2000 | 0-100 | Rotator cuff symptoms; work, lifestyle, social, emotional issues | Patient | Reliability, validity testing; no responsiveness testing | |
| Western Ontario Rotator Cuff Index | 2003 | 0-100 | Rotator cuff symptoms; work, lifestyle, social, emotional issues; sports ability | Patient | Reliability, validity, responsiveness testing | |

rationale was presented for its item weighting, the ASES Index has been shown to be a valid, reliable, and responsive outcomes measurement tool.[8]

The Simple Shoulder Test (SST) is a patient self-assessment questionnaire published in 1992.[9] Its 12 yes-or-no questions represent important activities of daily living performed by people with normal shoulders, specifically to assess shoulder comfort and function. The ease, reproducibility, sensitivity, reliability, and responsiveness of the SST have been documented in the assessment of several shoulder disorders.[10,11]

In the late 1990s, the American Academy of Orthopaedic Surgeons undertook development of a comprehensive questionnaire for the self-assessment of functional outcomes that could be used to create a national outcomes database. As a component of this program, the Disabilities of the Arm, Shoulder and Hand (DASH) Questionnaire was developed in 1996 to assess symptoms and functional status, with an emphasis on physical function, in patients with an upper extremity musculoskeletal condition. The questions focus on pain, weakness, stiffness, and self-image, as well as the ability to perform occupational functions, family care activities, and daily activities such as dressing, eating, and sleeping.[12] The DASH questionnaire has been validated by other investigators for the assessment of shoulder disorders.[13,14]

Several questionnaires have been developed specifically to evaluate rotator cuff disorders. The Rotator Cuff Quality-of-Life Measure was described in 2000.

It measures work, lifestyle, social, sports, and emotional issues, as well as physical symptoms, and has been found reliable and valid in evaluating rotator cuff disease.[15,16] The Western Ontario Rotator Cuff Index (WORC) was described in 2003.[17] It also measures work, lifestyle, and emotional issues, as well as physical symptoms and sports abilities. Interviews with clinicians and patients were used to generate the questions, in conjunction with a review of other outcomes instruments. The WORC has been shown to be sensitive to functional change and is valid in patients with rotator cuff pathology.[18]

General health status has a significant effect on any shoulder disorder, at a level comparable to that of hypertension, congestive heart failure, acute myocardial infarction, diabetes, or clinical depression,[19] and therefore it should be measured when shoulder outcomes are evaluated. Several general health status instruments have been developed, including the Sickness Impact Profile, the Nottingham Health Profile, and the Medical Outcomes Study Short Form-36 Health Survey (SF-36). The Sickness Impact Profile includes 136 items and often requires a 30-minute interview, and it can be cumbersome to administer in the clinical setting.[20] The Nottingham Health Profile is a 38-item questionnaire that measures sleep impairment, mobility, pain, and energy levels, as well as the effect of health status on work, recreation, and family life.[21] The SF-36 is the health-status measurement instrument most frequently used in the United States. It can be completed in approximately 10 minutes and has been used in many studies evaluating the effectiveness of treatment for orthopaedic disorders, including rotator cuff disorders.[22,23] It is unclear which of these general health status instruments is most useful for evaluating patients with orthopaedic conditions, including rotator cuff disease.[24]

Several factors should be considered when deciding which instruments to use in an outcomes study or critical analysis of published data. The instrument should be validated, reliable, and responsive. Instruments specific to a region, joint, or disease are more sensitive to clinical changes, and, although they do not capture a patient's overall health status, they limit the floor or ceiling effect of a general health status instrument. Therefore, the use of such an instrument is recommended, in addition to a measure of general health status.[10,25] Preintervention and postintervention data should be recorded, as well as objective physician-derived data on strength, motion, and instability.

## Physician-Determined Factors

The outcome of rotator cuff surgery hinges on factors that can generally be categorized as physician determined or patient specific. These factors should be analyzed in evaluating the surgical and nonsurgical options for a patient with rotator cuff disease, to define the risks and benefits of each treatment and decide on the appropriate treatment.

Recent studies on the outcomes of rotator cuff repair evaluated the effect of several physician-determined factors, including the type of surgical procedure (open, mini-open, or complete arthroscopic), the timing of surgery, and the biomechanical construct (single-row or double-row repair). Postsurgical rehabilitation protocols also vary among surgeons, in the absence of an established standard, and can have a significant effect on tendon healing, shoulder motion, and overall shoulder function. In addition, presurgical physician-patient counseling may greatly affect a patient's perception of the outcome.

### Surgical Procedure

A full-thickness rotator cuff tear is surgically treated by débridement or repair. Débridement of full-thickness tears has been only moderately successful, with a satisfactory outcome in 50% to 60% of patients.[26,27] In a patient with a massive, irreparable tear, débridement without repair can decrease pain and improve motion and ability to perform activities of daily living.[27-29] After an isolated biceps tenotomy for an irreparable rotator cuff tear, patients had durable improvement, as measured using the Constant score. Although the arthritic changes associated with a chronic rotator cuff tear progressed, 87% of patients were satisfied at an average 57-month follow-up.[29]

The evidence is relatively strong that repair has better results than débridement without repair. Whether one repair technique is superior to another has not been determined. Patient and tear characteristics, as well as surgeon experience and skill level, are important in the choice of an open, mini-open, or complete arthroscopic repair technique. Arthroscopic and open repairs of a full-thickness tear have been shown to have durable long-term results, with more than 90% of patients reporting good or excellent results.[30,31] Similarly, after a mini-open repair, more than 90% of patients had sustained improvement in WORC and ASES scores at a 5-year follow-up.[32] Several studies have directly compared arthroscopic and open or mini-open repairs.[33-39] No published studies compare open and mini-open repairs.

Rotator cuff repair techniques were evaluated after 96 procedures (12 open, 18 mini-open, 66 complete arthroscopic). The patient group treated with an open or mini-open technique did not differ from the complete arthroscopic group in age, gender, or tear-size characteristics. Both groups had improvement in pain and function at an average 24.6-month follow-up.[34] The complete arthroscopic group had significantly lower VAS pain scores and higher SST scores. The authors concluded that a complete arthroscopic repair improves pain and functional mobility more than an open or mini-open repair. However,

**Table 2 | Clinical Studies of Arthroscopic Double-Row Repairs and Comparisons of Single-Row and Double-Row Repairs**

| Study | Average Follow-up (Months) | Postsurgical Evaluation Method | Average Patient Age (Years) | Patients With Small or Medium-Sized Single-Tendon Tear (n) |
|---|---|---|---|---|
| Charousset et al[52] | 28 | CT arthrography | Double row: 60 Single row: 58 | Double row: 20 Single row: 26 |
| Sugaya et al[53] | 35 | Noncontrast MRI | Double row: 58 Single row: 58 | Double row: 27 Single row: 23 |
| Franceschi et al[54] | 23 | Magnetic resonance arthrography | Double row: 60 Single row: 64 | Double row: 4 Single row: 4 |
| Anderson et al[55] | 30 | Ultrasonography | 58 | 24 (+4 with upper subscapularis and supraspinatus repair) |
| Lafosse et al[56] | 36 | CT arthrography, magnetic resonance arthrography | 52 | 36 |
| Sugaya et al[57] | 14 | Noncontrast MRI | 61 | 56 |
| Huijsmans et al[58] | 22 | Ultrasonography | 59 | 137 |

*Significant difference between overall single-row and double-row retearing rates (*P* < 0.05).

†Significant difference between single-row and double-row retearing rates in small and medium-sized tears.

‡Significant difference between retearing rates in small and medium-sized tears and large and massive tears.

selection bias may have had some part in the differences in the scores of the two groups; the more difficult repairs might have been performed using the open or mini-open approach, and these patients could be expected to have worse scores at follow-up. The lower SST scores of the open and mini-open group were primarily attributable to lower mobility scores. The VAS pain scores of the two groups differed only by 0.7 points, which is statistically significant but unlikely to be clinically relevant.

Several studies directly compared mini-open and complete arthroscopic repairs. In general, both techniques led to overall improvement, as measured using ASES,[35-37,39] SST,[37,38] VAS,[37] and UCLA scores.[33,36,39] The differences between the techniques were not significant. Ultrasonography revealed similar healing rates after repair using a mini-open or complete arthroscopic technique.[37] Only one study reported a significant difference between arthroscopic and mini-open groups; the mini-open repair group had poorer motion 6 weeks and 12 weeks after surgery but not at an average 44.6-month final follow-up.[37] In addition, fibrous ankylosis (< 120° of forward flexion at a 12-week follow-up) developed in 14% of patients in the mini-open group and no patients in the complete arthroscopic group (*P* < 0.05).

Most of the studies comparing techniques were affected by small sample size and lack of prospective randomization. Nonetheless, these studies suggest that, if a tear is reparable, a tendon repair leads to better outcomes than débridement alone, and patient-reported outcomes are similar after mini-open or complete arthroscopic repair. The incidence of early motion loss and frozen shoulder may be higher after mini-open repair than complete arthroscopic repair.

## Surgical Timing

Few studies have addressed the issue of surgical timing. Although most rotator cuff tears occur because of age-related degeneration, in some patients the tear is acute, and early repair after an acute tear has been associated with improved outcome. An acute tear is defined as a full-thickness tear causing a sudden onset of symptoms after a traumatic incident. Patients with an acute tear who underwent repair within 3 weeks had improved active forward elevation compared with those whose tears were repaired between 3 weeks and 3 months after injury.[40] In a study of 29 acute tears (including 20 large or massive tears) repaired within 3 weeks of injury, every tear was found to be completely repairable; active forward elevation improved from an average of 51° before surgery to 167° after surgery, and 92% of patients reported good or excellent final results on the UCLA scale.[41] This study did not include a control group. The authors concluded that early repair is highly successful for a function-limiting tear with a sudden onset of symptoms.

Several animal model studies suggested that irreversible changes can occur after tendon detachment and

**Table 2 Continued | Clinical Studies of Arthroscopic Double-Row Repairs and Comparisons of Single-Row and Double-Row Repairs**

| Patients With Large or Massive Multiple-Tendon Tear (*n*) | Retearing Rate After Double-Row Repair | | | Retearing Rate After Single-Row Repair | | |
|---|---|---|---|---|---|---|
| | Overall | Small or Medium-Sized Tear | Large or Massive Tear | Overall | Small or Medium-Sized Tear | Large or Massive Tear |
| Double row: 11 Single row: 9 | 23% | – | – | 40% | – | – |
| Double row: 14 Single row: 16 | 10%* | 0%† | 29% | 26%* | 13%† | 44% |
| Double row: 26 Single row: 26 | 31% | – | – | 46% | – | – |
| 24 | 17% | – | – | – | – | – |
| 69 | 11% | 0% | 17% | – | – | – |
| 30 | 17% | 5% | 40% | – | – | – |
| 73 | 15% | 7%‡ | 36%‡ | – | – | – |

delayed repair, including rotator cuff muscle atrophy and fatty infiltration.[42] Acute repair has also been shown to lead to more rapid recovery of muscle function and tendon elasticity.[43] A comparison of acute and delayed repair in a rat model found reduced material stress and viscoelastic relaxation in the delayed group, suggesting poorer rotator cuff healing after a delay between injury and repair.[44] In general, the basic science evidence supports clinical findings that early repair is preferable after an acute tear.

## Biomechanical Constructs

Biomechanical constructs with increased strength have been developed for use in complete arthroscopic rotator cuff repair. Single-row suture anchor repairs have led to excellent overall results, although the healing rates are modest. The reported rate of retearing is 29% for a single-tendon posterosuperior tear and 94% for a multiple-tendon posterosuperior tear.[45,46] Suture anchor repair using a single row of lateral anchors was found to restore only 67% of the original footprint of the rotator cuff.[47] The addition of a second row of anchors increases the contact area of the repair by 60%.[48] A double-row suture anchor repair, using medial and lateral rows, was found to improve initial biomechanical strength and restore the normal anatomic rotator cuff insertion.[49-51]

Clinical and structural outcomes have been evaluated after double-row rotator cuff repairs, and several studies have compared healing rates and outcomes after single-row and double-row repairs. The overall retearing rates after double-row repair range from 10% to 31%[52-58] (Table 2). After double-row repair, tendon healing was shown to be correlated with improved pain level,[56] Constant score,[58] UCLA score,[57] Japanese Orthopedic Association score,[57] ASES score,[57] strength,[55,58] and active motion.[8] Tear size was found to be correlated with tendon healing after double-row repair, with larger tears having inferior healing properties compared with smaller tears.[53,55,58] Only one of the studies comparing single-row and double-row repairs reported significantly better healing after a double-row repair compared with a single-row repair; this improvement was seen only in small and medium-sized tears.[53] No significant differences between single-row and double-row repairs were reported with regard to strength, pain, motion, satisfaction, or functional outcome (as measured using the Constant, UCLA, or ASES score).[52-54] Data from double-row repair studies suggest that healing after double-row repair is important because it is associated with improvements in pain, strength, motion, and functional outcome. However, only one study found that double-row repairs offer superior healing (and only in small and medium-sized tears) compared with single-row repairs, with no evidence that the difference leads to an improved outcome.[53]

### Postsurgical Rehabilitation

A successful outcome after rotator cuff surgery depends not only on the surgical repair but also on a properly timed and executed rehabilitation program. No well-designed studies have evaluated the effect of postsurgical rehabilitation on healing or outcome after rotator cuff repair. However, several general principles of rehabilitation are widely accepted. Sling immobilization for a period of 3 to 6 weeks immediately after surgery is recommended to protect the repair. Animal studies have found that repair tension is decreased with immobilization.[59] Postsurgical immobilization resulted in improved tissue quality and viscoelastic properties after cuff repair in a rodent model.[60] Immobilization of the arm in slight abduction may improve rotator cuff vascularity; adduction was shown to decrease the blood supply to the suprapinatus.[61]

### Patient Counseling

Presurgical patient counseling can significantly affect the patient's self-assessed outcome after rotator cuff surgery. Positive expectations of treatment have been found to be correlated with positive outcomes 1 year after rotator cuff repair and specifically with improvement in shoulder pain, shoulder function, quality of life, and general health status.[62] An evaluation of patient expectations found that before surgery for a rotator cuff tear, 48% of patients expected to have complete pain relief after surgery.[63] In general, patients appear to have relatively high expectations before rotator cuff surgery, and these can significantly affect outcome. Surgical counseling may be able to modify expectations to improve outcome.

## Patient-Specific Factors

Patient characteristics, whether controllable or uncontrollable, can have a significant effect on the final outcome after rotator cuff surgery. The patient has control over such factors as smoking habits and the use of nonsteroidal anti-inflammatory drugs (NSAIDs). Factors such as patient age, gender, workers' compensation status, medical comorbidities, and tear-related anatomy (tear size, muscle quality, muscle atrophy, healing) are beyond the patient's control. Significant data suggest that each of these factors can influence outcome after rotator cuff repair.

### Smoking Habits

Basic science evidence suggests that smoking negatively affects healing after repair and therefore influences the final outcome. Nicotine was found to delay tendon-to-bone healing in a rat rotator cuff model; the overall mechanical properties of the repair increased over time in both nicotine-infused and saline control rats, but the nicotine-infused rats had a significant time lag.[64] In general, smoking appears to lead to inferior tendon-healing properties and consequently to poorer outcomes. Nonsmokers had a significantly greater improvement than smokers in UCLA scores after rotator cuff repair.[65]

### NSAID Use

NSAID use was found to have a negative impact on fusion after spine surgery and on bone healing in animal fracture models. Similarly, NSAIDs may alter tendon-to-bone healing. In a rat rotator cuff model, lower failure loads and a disorganized collagen structure were associated with postsurgical NSAID use.[66] Although clinical research is required, limiting the use of NSAIDs after surgery may improve tendon healing and outcomes.

### Age and Gender

Several studies examined the effect of patient age on outcomes after rotator cuff repair. A review of the results of mini-open and complete arthroscopic repair in patients older than 60 years (mean, 70 years) found 87% good or excellent results, as assessed using the UCLA scale at 35-month follow-up.[67] Patients in a similar review had a mean age of 68 years and 81% good or excellent results at 27-month follow-up.[68] In another study, older patients had significantly lower ASES and WORC scores than other patients before rotator cuff repair; the postsurgical scores of all age groups were similar, suggesting greater improvement among older patients.[32] In a study that reported poorer results in older patients, the scoring was significantly skewed toward active motion, and a patient self-report measure was not included.[69] After open repair, older women had the lowest Constant scores, probably because of the scale's strength component.[70] A review of outcomes of rotator cuff repair in patients age 50 years or younger found that 45% had an unsatisfactory result (unrelieved pain, revision surgery, or decreased active motion) at an average 16.2-year follow-up.[71] Another study found that patients younger than 55 years were less willing to undergo further surgery and had poorer satisfaction, pain relief, ability to perform activities of daily living, and ability to resume usual sports or work activities.[72] In general, these study results suggest that older patients score as well or better than younger patients on self-assessment instruments after rotator cuff repair, although they may have less final strength and active motion. Older patients are more likely to tolerate lack of healing than younger patients. Younger patients generally have higher demands and higher expectations of surgery, and therefore they are more likely to be displeased with the results, despite significant gains.

Studies of the effect of patient gender on outcomes after rotator cuff repair differ in their findings. Women were found to have poorer pain relief and postsurgical active motion, as well as lower Neer scores, than men at an average 13.4-year follow-up.[73] However, another study reported that women had significantly higher ASES and Constant scores at an average 13-month follow-up after complete arthroscopic repair.[74] The apparent conflict may be attributable to the use of different surgical techniques, the length of follow-up, or the use of different outcome measures (physician-derived or patient self-assessed). However, it can be concluded that the results of open repairs are slightly worse and the results of arthroscopic repairs are slightly better in women than in men.

### Workers' Compensation Status

Coverage by workers' compensation insurance has been shown to have a significant negative effect on outcomes after an open or mini-open rotator cuff repair; outcomes after complete arthroscopic repair have not been evaluated.[75-77] Patients receiving workers' compensation not only have lower scores on limb-specific and general health status instruments after repair but also are less likely than other patients to return to work after repair.

At a mean 45-month follow-up after an open repair, 54% of patients receiving workers' compensation had a good or excellent UCLA score, compared with 92% of other patients.[75] Only 42% of compensated patients had returned to work, compared with 94% of other patients. Another study found that compensated patients had significantly worse SF-36 scores before and after open rotator cuff repair; this was the only study that used a patient self-assessment questionnaire.[76] High satisfaction rates were reported after open rotator cuff repair; however, compensated patients were significantly less satisfied.[72] At a mean 2-year and 7-year follow-up after mini-open repair, compensated patients had significantly lower UCLA scores (52% and 65%, respectively) than uncompensated patients (84% and 90%).[77] Although none of the studies used a multivariate analysis to exclude confounding factors or examined outcomes after complete arthroscopic repair, it can be concluded that worker's compensation status affects the outcome after repair.

### Medical Comorbidities

Baseline functional outcomes in patients with similar rotator cuff tears are highly variable.[78] Asymptomatic rotator cuff tears are extremely common. The reasons some tears are less symptomatic than others are unknown but related to the presence of medical comorbidities. A study using multivariate analysis to account for confounding variables including age, gender, workers' compensation status, smoking, and rotator cuff tear size found that medical comorbidities have a negative effect on baseline shoulder pain, shoulder function, and quality of life.[79] Comorbidities do not appear to sig-

nificantly affect final postsurgical outcomes. Patients with more severe comorbidities had greater improvement after rotator cuff repair; this finding suggests that comorbidities act as an amplifier of dysfunction.[80] It can be concluded that comorbidities may account for some of the baseline variation in function among patients with rotator cuff tears, but the presence of comorbidities should not be considered a reason to forgo repair or a reason for poor results after repair.

### Tear-Related Anatomy
#### Tear Size

Relatively large tear size has been correlated with poor functional outcome after open or arthroscopic repair. Poor results have been found using measures that are heavily physician weighted (such as strength and Constant and UCLA scores) or patient weighted (such as ASES, SST, and SF-36 scores).

After open rotator cuff repair, 105 patients were evaluated at an average 13.4-year follow-up. Tear size was found to be the most important determinant of outcome with regard to active motion, strength, patient satisfaction, and need for revision surgery.[73] After open repair of a full-thickness tear, an evaluation of 72 patients found that those with a massive tear were significantly less satisfied and had significantly poorer SST, Constant, and UCLA scores than those with a smaller tear.[70] At a 2-year follow-up after open rotator cuff repair, presurgical tear size was highly correlated with Constant score, symptoms of fatigue, and objective measurement of strength.[81] Similar results were found after arthroscopic repair; larger tears were correlated with lower Constant scores and measured strength.[74] A recent comparison of arthroscopic and open repairs found that patients with a small or medium-sized tear had a significantly better UCLA score than those with a large or massive tear, regardless of repair technique.[33] It can be concluded that patients with a relatively large tear have a poorer outcome on physician-weighted measures of function after an open or arthroscopic repair and a poorer outcome on patient-weighted measures of function after an open repair. The effect of tear size on patient self-assessed function after complete arthroscopic repair is unclear.

#### Muscle Atrophy and Fatty Degeneration

The presurgical quality of the rotator cuff muscles significantly affects the final functioning of the repaired tendon. In studies evaluating the relationship of rotator cuff atrophy and fatty degeneration to tendon healing after open or arthroscopic rotator cuff repair, atrophy and fatty degeneration were correlated with poorer healing, and poorer healing was correlated with worse outcomes.[45,82] These studies did not directly correlate atrophy and fatty degeneration with outcome.

One study reported a direct correlation between presurgical rotator cuff fatty degeneration, evaluated using CT, and functional outcomes after open rotator cuff repair.[83] Increases in the global fatty degeneration index (the mean value of muscle fatty degeneration in the supraspinatus, infraspinatus, and subscapularis) were correlated with lower Constant scores at follow-up. In clinical and animal studies, fatty degeneration was not found to be reversible, even after tendon healing.[42,84] Consequently, it can be concluded that presurgical fatty degeneration, and possibly muscle atrophy, are correlated with relatively poor final outcomes, even after the repair has healed.

### Tendon Healing

Tendon healing after open or arthroscopic rotator cuff repair has been extensively studied. Although symptomatic improvement after repair does not depend on healing, healing has been correlated with better results, using both patient self-assessment and physician-derived measures.[45,55-58,82,84-86] Studies that found no correlation between healing and outcome were limited by power.[87,88] Several factors were correlated with improved tendon healing and therefore indirectly with outcome, including relatively young patient age, small tear size, little rotator cuff fatty degeneration, and use of a double-row repair technique rather than a single-row technique.[45,53,86]

SST scores, active flexion, and Constant scores were better in patients having an intact rotator cuff after open repair, as evaluated using ultrasonography.[85,86] Flexion strength and Constant scores were better in patients having an intact cuff after open repair, as evaluated using MRI.[82] Constant scores were also higher in patients with intact tendons after single-row arthroscopic repair of a single tendon tear.[45] Pain levels, strength, active motion, and functional outcomes (as measured using the Constant score, UCLA score, or ASES score) are better in patients with intact tendons after double-row arthroscopic rotator cuff repair.[55-58] The evidence suggests that rotator cuff healing has a significant effect on strength, active motion, and patient self-assessed function and satisfaction after rotator cuff repair.

## Summary

Identifying the factors that influence outcomes after rotator cuff surgery allows surgeons to achieve optimal outcomes and improve patient expectations of surgery. Physician-determined factors influencing outcome after rotator cuff repair include surgical technique, repair construct, and presurgical patient counseling. Open, mini-open, and complete arthroscopic repairs have excellent long-term results; arthroscopic repair techniques offer better early pain control and a lower incidence of postsurgical stiffness compared with open and mini-

open techniques. Double-row repair appears to offer better healing rates than single-row repair, although the effect on final outcome has not been determined. Higher presurgical patient expectations of outcome are predictive of higher self-assessed functional outcome.

Patient-dependent factors influencing outcome after repair include smoking habits, NSAID use, age, gender, medical comorbidities, workers' compensation status, and tear-related anatomy. Smoking has a negative impact on tendon healing and outcome after repair. NSAID use delays tendon healing but has not been shown to affect final outcome. Workers' compensation coverage, relatively large tear size, poor muscle quality, and limited tendon healing all have been shown to negatively affect final outcomes. Self-assessed outcomes of older patients appear to be as good as or better than those of younger patients, although the motion and strength of older patients tend to be worse. Women appear to have slightly better results than men after arthroscopic repair and slightly worse results after open repair. Finally, the presence of comorbidities does not negatively affect improvement after repair.

Further research is required to investigate these relationships. Large, multicenter trials must develop a patient population large enough to adequately prove negative results. Advanced statistical analysis of results would be required to determine potentially confounding variables and truly isolate factors affecting both patient-reported and physician-reported outcomes.

## Annotated References

1. Codman EA: *The Shoulder*. Malaber, FL, Krieger Publishing, 1934, pp 400-410.

2. Neer CS: Anterior acromioplasty for the chronic impingement syndrome in the shoulder: A preliminary report. *J Bone Joint Surg Am* 1972;54:41-50.

3. Amstutz HC, Sew Hoy AL, Clarke IC: UCLA anatomic total shoulder arthroplasty. *Clin Orthop Relat Res* 1981;155:7-20.

4. Kirkley A, Griffin S, Dainty K: Scoring systems for the functional assessment of the shoulder. *Arthroscopy* 2003;19:1109-1120.

   The origin, development, and testing of the ASES Index, the UCLA Shoulder Score, the DASH, the SST, the WORC, the Rotator Cuff Quality-of-Life Measure (RC-QOL), and the Oxford Shoulder Score are discussed.

5. Leggin BG, Iannotti JP: Shoulder outcome measurement, in Iannotti JP, Williams GR (eds): *Disorders of the Shoulder: Diagnosis and Management*. Philadelphia, PA, Lippincott Williams & Wilkins, 1999, pp 1023-1040.

6. Constant CR, Murley AHG: A clinical method of functional assessment of the shoulder. *Clin Orthop Relat Res* 1987;214:160-164.

7. Walton MJ, Walton JC, Honorez L, et al: A comparison of methods for shoulder strength assessment and analysis of Constant score change in patients aged over fifty years in the United Kingdom. *J Shoulder Elbow Surg* 2007;16:285-289.

Normal Constant scores were determined in 108 patients older than age 50 years. The score fell 0.3 points for each successive year. Men scored, on average, 7.5 points higher than women. The authors provide a reference for normal Constant scores and show that scores predictably decline with age.

8. Michener LA, McClure PW, Sennett BJ: American Shoulder and Elbow Surgeons Standardized Shoulder Assessment Form, patient self-report section: Reliability, validity, and responsiveness. *J Shoulder Elbow Surg* 2002;11:587-594.

Sixty-three patients with shoulder dysfunction were evaluated using the ASES Index, the University of Pennsylvania Shoulder Score, and the SF-36. The ASES Index was found to be a reliable, valid, and responsive outcome tool.

9. Lippitt SB, Harryman DT II, Matsen FA III: A practical tool for evaluating function: The simple shoulder test, in Matsen FA, Fu FH, Hawkins RJ (eds): *The Shoulder: A Balance of Mobility and Stability.* Rosemont, IL, American Academy of Orthopaedic Surgeons, 1992, pp 501-518.

10. Beaton D, Richards RR: Assessing the reliability and responsiveness of 5 shoulder questionnaires. *J Shoulder Elbow Surg* 1998;7:565-572.

11. Beaton DE, Richards RR: Measuring function of the shoulder: A cross-sectional comparison of five questionnaires. *J Bone Joint Surg Am* 1996;78:882-890.

12. Hudak PL, Amadio PC, Bombardier C: Development of an upper extremity outcome measure: The DASH (disabilities of the arm, shoulder and hand). The Upper Extremity Collaborative Group. *Am J Ind Med* 1996;29:602-608.

13. Beaton DE, Katz JN, Fossel AH, Wright JG, Tarasuk V, Bombardier C: Measuring the whole or the parts? Validity, reliability, and responsiveness of the Disabilities of the Arm, Shoulder and Hand outcome measure in different regions of the upper extremity. *J Hand Ther* 2001;14:128-146.

In 200 patients evaluated using the DASH and several other outcome measures, the DASH was found to be valid, reliable, and responsive to improvement after treatment of both proximal and distal disorders of the upper extremity.

14. Soohoo NF, McDonald AP, Seiler JG, McGillivary GR: Evaluation of the construct validity of the DASH questionnaire by correlation to the SF-36. *J Hand Surg Am* 2002;27:537-541.

The construct validity of the DASH questionnaire was evaluated at an upper extremity clinic by examining its correlation with the SF-36 in 90 patients. The DASH was found to be a valid measure of health status that is useful in patients with a wide variety of upper-extremity symptoms.

15. Hollinshead RM, Mohtadi NG, Vande Guchte RA, Wadey VM: Two 6-year follow-up studies of large and massive rotator cuff tears: Comparison of outcome measures. *J Shoulder Elbow Surg* 2000;9:373-381.

16. Razmjou H, Bean A, van Osnabrugge V, MacDermid JC, Holtby R: Cross-sectional and longitudinal construct validity of two rotator cuff disease-specific outcome measures. *BMC Musculoskelet Disord* 2006;7: 26.

In 41 participants, the construct validity of the RC-QOL and WORC measures was verified through correlation with each other, the ASES Shoulder Index, and the Upper Extremity Functional Index.

17. Kirkley A, Griffin S, Alvarez C: The development and evaluation of a disease-specific quality of life measurement tool for rotator cuff disease: The Western Ontario Rotator Cuff Index (WORC). *Clin J Sport Med* 2003;13:84-92.

The development of a valid, reliable, disease-specific quality-of-life measurement tool for patients with rotator cuff disease is described. The 21-item WORC was validated using the DASH, the ASES Index, the UCLA Shoulder Scale, the Sickness Impact Profile, and the SF-36. Reliability was found to be very high, and the WORC was found to be more sensitive to change in patients with rotator cuff tears than the other tools.

18. Holtby R, Razmjou H: Measurement properties of the Western Ontario rotator cuff outcome measure: A preliminary report. *J Shoulder Elbow Surg* 2005; 14:506-510.

The construct validity and sensitivity to change of the WORC was tested in rotator cuff patients. The study supports the validity of the WORC for use in patients with rotator cuff disease.

19. Gartsman GM, Brinker MR, Khan M, Karahan M: Self-assessment of general health status in patients with five common shoulder conditions. *J Shoulder Elbow Surg* 1998;7:228-237.

20. Bergner M, Bibbitt RA, Pollard WE, Martin DP, Gilson BS: The sickness impact profile: Validation of a health status measure. *Med Care* 1976;14:57-67.

21. Hunt SM, McKenna SP, McEwen J, Williams J, Papp E: The Nottingham Health Profile: Subjective health status and medical consultations. *Soc Sci Med A* 1981; 15:221-229.

22. Ware J, Snow KK, Kosinski M, Gandek B: *SF-36 Health Survey: Manual and Interpretation Guide.* Boston, MA, The Health Institute, 1993.

23. McKee MD, Yoo DJ: The effect of surgery for rotator cuff disease on general health status: Results of a prospective trial. *J Bone Joint Surg Am* 2000;82:970-979.

24. McQueen DA, Long DL, Schurman JR: Selecting a subjective health status measure for optimum utility in everyday orthopaedic practice. *J Eval Clin Pract* 2005;11:45-51.

   The Nottingham Health Profile was compared with the Western Ontario and McMaster Universities Osteoarthritis Index and the SF-36 and found to produce similar results with higher sensitivity to small outcomes changes.

25. Beaton DE, Richards RR: Measuring function of the shoulder: A cross-sectional comparison of five questionnaires. *J Bone Joint Surg Am* 1996;78:882-890.

26. Gartsman GM: Arthroscopic acromioplasty for lesions of the rotator cuff. *J Bone Joint Surg Am* 1990; 72:169-180.

27. Ellman H, Kay SP, Wirth M: Arthroscopic treatment of full-thickness rotator cuff tears: 2- to 7-year follow-up study. *Arthroscopy* 1993;9:195-200.

28. Gartsman GM: Massive, irreparable tears of the rotator cuff: Results of operative debridement and subacromial decompression. *J Bone Joint Surg Am* 1997; 79:715-721.

29. Walch G, Edwards TB, Boulahia A, Nove-Josserand L, Neyton L, Szabo I: Arthroscopic tenotomy of the long head of the biceps in the treatment of rotator cuff tears: Clinical and radiographic results of 307 cases. *J Shoulder Elbow Surg* 2005;14:238-246.

   After 307 arthroscopic biceps tenotomies performed on irreparable tears or tears in older patients unwilling to participate in rehabilitation, 87% of patients were satisfied at a 57-month follow-up, and Constant scores were improved.

30. Galatz LM, Griggs S, Cameron BD, Iannotti JP: Prospective longitudinal analysis of postoperative shoulder function: A ten-year follow-up study of full-thickness rotator cuff tears. *J Bone Joint Surg Am* 2001;83:1052-1056.

   In 33 patients evaluated 2 years and 10 years after open rotator cuff repair, no changes were seen in raw Constant scores. The authors concluded that the results of open rotator cuff repair do not decline with time.

31. Wolf EM, Pennington WT, Agrawal V: Arthroscopic rotator cuff repair: 4- to 10 year results. *Arthroscopy* 2004;20:5-12.

   At long-term follow-up after arthroscopic rotator cuff repair in 104 patients, 94% had a good or excellent result using the UCLA scale. Level of evidence: IV.

32. Baysal D, Balyk R, Otto D, Luciak-Corea C, Beaupre L: Functional outcome and health-related quality of life after surgical repair of full-thickness rotator cuff tear using a mini-open technique. *Am J Sports Med* 2005;33:1346-1355.

   Eighty-four patients who underwent mini-open rotator cuff repair were found to have significant improvement in shoulder function (ASES score) and health-related qual-

ity of life (WORC) at 1-year follow-up, and the gains were maintained at a minimum 2-year follow-up.

33. Ide J, Maeda S, Takagi K: A comparison of arthroscopic and open rotator cuff repair. *Arthroscopy* 2005;21:1090-1098.

   In 50 patients treated with arthroscopic rotator cuff repair and 50 treated with open repair, there were no differences in UCLA or Japanese Orthopaedic Association scores by technique. Patients with a large or massive tear had a poorer result than those with a small or medium-sized tear, independent of technique. Level of evidence: III.

34. Buess E, Steuber K, Waibl B: Open versus arthroscopic rotator cuff repair: A comparative view of 96 cases. *Arthroscopy* 2005;21:597-604.

   Ninety-six patients in two rotator cuff repair groups (A, mini-open or open; B, complete arthroscopic) were compared at an average 24.6-month follow-up. Group A patients were found to have more pain (VAS) and worse shoulder function (SST) compared with Group B patients.

35. Sauerbrey AM, Getz CL, Piancastelli M, Iannotti JP, Ramsey ML, Williams GR: Arthroscopic versus mini-open rotator cuff repair: A comparison of clinical outcome. *Arthroscopy* 2005;21:1415-1420.

   Fifty-four patients underwent either complete arthroscopic or mini-open rotator cuff repair. At an average 33-month follow-up, there were no significant differences in ASES score improvement.

36. Severud EL, Ruotolo C, Abbott DD, Nottage WM: All-arthroscopic versus mini-open rotator cuff repair: A long-term retrospective outcome comparison. *Arthroscopy* 2003;19:234-238.

   A retrospective review of 35 all-arthroscopic and 29 mini-open rotator cuff repairs found no differences in UCLA or ASES scores. Motion was greater after all-arthroscopic repair at 6- and 12-week follow-up but was not significantly different between groups at an average 44-month follow-up.

37. Verma NN, Dunn W, Adler RS, et al: All-arthroscopic versus mini-open rotator cuff repair: A retrospective review with minimum 2-year follow-up. *Arthroscopy* 2006;22:587-594.

   Seventy-one patients who underwent mini-open or complete arthroscopic rotator cuff repair were evaluated at a minimum of 2 years using the ASES scale, the SST, and shoulder ultrasonography. Recurrent tears were found seven times more often in tears larger than 3 cm, with decreased final strength in shoulders having persistent defects. No difference in outcomes was noted between techniques. Level of evidence: III.

38. Warner JJP, Tetreautl P, Lehtinen J, Zurakowski D: Arthroscopic versus mini-open rotator cuff repair: A cohort comparison study. *Arthroscopy* 2005;21: 328-332.

Nine patients who underwent arthroscopic rotator cuff repair and 12 who underwent mini-open rotator cuff repair were matched for age, gender, dominance, side of injury, history of trauma, and duration of symptoms. At an average 50-month follow-up, there was no significant difference in pain levels, active motion, and SST scores.

39. Youm T, Murray DH, Kubiak EN, Rokito AS, Zuckerman JD: Arthroscopic versus mini-open rotator cuff repair: A comparison of clinical outcomes and patient satisfaction. *J Shoulder Elbow Surg* 2005;14: 455-459.

    Eighty-four patients were evaluated after complete arthroscopic or mini-open rotator cuff repair at a minimum 2-year follow-up. Equivalent UCLA and ASES scores and patient satisfaction were reported; 98.8% were satisfied with the procedure.

40. Bassett RW, Cofield RH: Acute tears of the rotator cuff: The time of surgical repair. *Clin Orthop Relat Res* 1983;175:18-24.

41. Lahteenmaki HE, Virolainen P, Hiltunen A, Heikkila J, Nelimarkka O: Results of early operative treatment of rotator cuff tears with acute symptoms. *J Shoulder Elbow Surg* 2006;15:148-153.

    Of 26 patients treated with open rotator cuff repair within 3 weeks of an acute tear, 85% had no pain at an average 5.9-year follow-up. Active flexion was improved from 51° to 167°, and the satisfaction rate was 96%. Early surgical treatment of tears having a sudden onset of symptoms and poor function is recommended to achieve maximal return of shoulder function.

42. Gerber C, Meyer DC, Schneeberger AG, Hoppeler H, Von Rechenberg B: Effect of tendon release and delayed repair on the structure of the muscles of the rotator cuff: An experimental study in sheep. *J Bone Joint Surg Am* 2004;86:1973-1982.

    The infraspinatus tendons of six sheep were released, encased in a silicone tube for 40 weeks, and reattached. The animals were sacrificed 35 weeks after repair. Fatty infiltration and muscle atrophy of the infraspinatus occurred after release and was not reversed after repair and tendon healing.

43. Coleman SH, Fealy S, Ehteshami JR, et al: Chronic rotator cuff injury and repair model in sheep. *J Bone Joint Surg Am* 2003;85:2391-2402.

    In a chronic rotator cuff tear model using 36 female sheep, early rotator cuff tendon repair resulted in more rapid recovery of force of muscle contraction and tendon elasticity, compared with delayed repair.

44. Galatz LM, Rothermich SY, Zaegel M, Silva MJ, Havlioglu N, Thomopoulos S: Delayed repair of tendon to bone injuries leads to decreased biomechanical properties and bone loss. *J Orthop Res* 2005;23:1441-1447.

    Rat supraspinatus tendon tears received an acute repair or a repair delayed 3 weeks. Material stress was reduced in the delayed group. The viscoelastic properties of the acute-repair group were increased early and decreased late compared with those of the delayed-repair group. This finding indicates inferior rotator cuff healing. The marked decrease in greater tuberosity bone density in the delayed-repair group indicates that bone loss may be a significant factor in poor healing.

45. Boileau P, Brassart N, Watkinson DJ, Carles M, Hatzidakis AM, Krishnan SG: Arthroscopic repair of full-thickness tears of the supraspinatus: Does the tendon really heal? *J Bone Joint Surg Am* 2005;87:1229-1240.

    Sixty-five patients with a chronic, full-thickness supraspinatus tear were followed at least 6 months after arthroscopic repair. The overall retear rate was 29%, and the rate in patients older than 65 years was 57%. Delamination of the infraspinatus or subscapularis and increasing age were negatively associated with tendon healing.

46. Galatz LM, Ball CM, Teefey SA, Middleton WD, Yamaguchi K: The outcome and repair integrity of completely arthroscopically repaired large and massive rotator cuff tears. *J Bone Joint Surg Am* 2004;86: 219-224.

    Eighteen patients with a rotator cuff tear larger than 2 cm in transverse dimension were evaluated at least 12 months after surgery using ultrasonography and ASES scores. Recurrent defects were found in 94%, although scores were significantly improved from baseline. Reevaluation at 2 years revealed worsening ASES scores.

47. Apreleva M, Ozbaydar M, Fitzgibbons PG, Warner JJP: Rotator cuff tears: The effect of the reconstruction method on three-dimensional repair site area. *Arthroscopy* 2002;18:519-526.

    Three-dimensional evaluation of four rotator cuff repair techniques (transosseous simple suture, transosseous mattress suture, single-row suture-anchor simple suture, single-row suture-anchor mattress suture) revealed that the transosseous simple suture technique provided a 20% larger footprint restoration than the other techniques, which covered approximately 67% of the footprint.

48. Tuoheti Y, Itoi E, Yamamoto N, et al: Contact area, contact pressure, and pressure patterns of the tendon-bone interface after rotator cuff repair. *Am J Sports Med* 2005;33:1869-1874.

    In a human cadaver shoulder model, single-row, double-row, and transosseous repairs of full-thickness supraspinatus tears were evaluated for contact area and pressure. Double-row repairs provided significantly more contact area than single-row or transosseous repairs. Single- and double-row repairs had greater contact pressure than transosseous repairs.

49. Kim DH, ElAttrache NS, Tibone JE, et al: Biomechanical comparison of a single-row versus double-row suture anchor technique for rotator cuff repair. *Am J Sports Med* 2006;34:407-414.

Nine matched pairs of human cadaver shoulders had a single-row or double-row repair of a supraspinatus tear, which was then cyclically loaded and tested to failure. Double-row repairs had smaller initial and final-cycle gap formation, lower initial strain over the footprint area, increased repair stiffness, and increased ultimate failure load, compared with single-row repairs.

50. Mazzocca AD, Millett PJ, Guanche CA, Santangelo SA, Arciero RA: Arthroscopic single-row versus double-row suture anchor rotator cuff repair. *Am J Sports Med* 2005;33:1861-1868.

Twenty fresh-frozen human cadaver shoulders were randomly assigned to an arthroscopic rotator cuff repair technique (single-row or one of three different double-row techniques). No differences were found between the single- and double-row repairs in load to failure, although the double-row repairs had a significantly greater supraspinatus footprint width than the single-row repairs.

51. Ma CB, Comerford L, Wilson J, Puttlitz CM: Biomechanical evaluation of arthroscopic rotator cuff repairs: Double-row compared with single-row fixation. *J Bone Joint Surg Am* 2006;88:403-410.

Ten paired human cadaver supraspinatus tendons were split in half. Four different stitch configurations were used for fixation (two-simple, massive cuff, arthroscopic Mason-Allen, and double-row). Double-row fixation had significantly better ultimate tensile strength than any of the single-row fixations.

52. Charousset C, Grimberg J, Duranthon LD, et al: Can a double-row anchorage technique improve tendon healing in arthroscopic rotator cuff repair? A prospective, nonrandomized, comparative study of double-row and single-row anchorage techniques with computed tomographic arthrography tendon healing assessment. *Am J Sports Med* 2007;35:1247-1253.

Healing rates and outcomes were compared in single-row and double-row arthroscopic rotator cuff repairs. No significant differences were found in final Constant scores ($P = 0.4$) or watertight, healed rotator cuffs (60%, single-row and 77%, double-row; $P = 0.13$).

53. Sugaya H, Maeda K, Matsuki K, Moriishi J: Functional and structural outcome after arthroscopic full-thickness rotator cuff repair: Single-row versus dual-row fixation. *Arthroscopy* 2005;21:1307-1316.

After a single-row or double-row arthroscopic rotator cuff repair, 78 patients were evaluated using MRI at an average of 35 months. The retearing rate was significantly lower in the double-row group for smaller tears, and no difference between groups was found for large or massive tears. The UCLA and ASES scores were similar for the two groups. Level of evidence: III.

54. Franceschi F, Ruzzini L, Longo UG, et al: Equivalent clinical results of arthroscopic single-row and double-row suture anchor repair for rotator cuff tears: A randomized controlled trial. *Am J Sports Med* 2007;35:1254-1260.

A prospective, randomized study of 60 patients compared healing rates and outcomes after single-row or double-row arthroscopic rotator cuff repair. At a 2-year follow-up, there was no significant difference in healing rates, UCLA scores, or range of motion ($P > 0.05$).

55. Anderson K, Boothby M, Aschenbrener D, Van Holsbeeck M: Outcome and structural integrity after arthroscopic rotator cuff repair using 2 rows of fixation. *Am J Sports Med* 2006;34:1899-1905.

At an average 30-month follow-up after double-row arthroscopic rotator cuff repair, 17% of 52 shoulders had evidence of retearing on ultrasonography. There was no difference in functional outcome scores between those with an intact repair and those with a defect.

56. Lafosse L, Brozska R, Toussaint B, Gobezie R: The outcome and structural integrity of arthroscopic rotator cuff repair with use of the double-row suture anchor technique. *J Bone Joint Surg Am* 2007;89:1533-1541.

At a minimum 2-year follow-up after arthroscopic double-row rotator cuff repair, 12 of 105 repairs had failed. Patients with retearing had more reported pain than those with an intact repair ($P = 0.014$). Repair integrity did not significantly affect overall Constant score.

57. Sugaya H, Maeda K, Matsuki K, Moriishi J: Repair integrity and functional outcome after arthroscopic double-row rotator cuff repair: A prospective outcome study. *J Bone Joint Surg Am* 2007;89:953-960.

At an average 31-month follow-up of 86 patients after arthroscopic double-row rotator cuff repair, the healing rate was 95% for a small or medium-sized tear, compared with 60% for a large or massive tear, as determined using MRI. Full-thickness retearing was associated with poorer functional outcome and strength ($P < 0.01$).

58. Huijsmans PE, Pritchard MP, Berghs BM, et al: Arthroscopic rotator cuff repair with double-row fixation. *J Bone Joint Surg Am* 2007;89:1248-1257.

At a minimum 12-month follow-up after arthroscopic double-row rotator cuff repair, 83% of 242 patients had an intact repair (of patients with a massive tear, 47%; a large tear, 78%; a medium-sized tear, 93%; a small tear, 88%). Strength and active elevation were better in patients with an intact repair, although repair integrity did not significantly affect pain level.

59. Gerber C, Schneeberger AG, Perren SM, Nyffeler RW: Experimental rotator cuff repair: A preliminary study. *J Bone Joint Surg Am* 1999;81:1281-1290.

60. Thomopoulos S, Williams GR, Soslowsky LJ: Tendon to bone healing: Differences in biomechanical, structural, and compositional properties due to a range of activity levels. *J Biomech Eng* 2003;125:106-113.

A rat rotator cuff model was used to evaluate the effect of active motion on repair healing. Immobilized tendons had superior structural, compositional, and viscoelastic properties, compared with tendons that were exercised.

61. Rathbun JB, Macnab I: The microvascular pattern of the rotator cuff. *J Bone Joint Surg Br* 1970;52:540-553.

62. Henn RF, Tashjian RZ, Kang L, Green A: Patients' expectations predict the outcome of rotator cuff repair. *J Bone Joint Surg Am* 2007;89:1913-1919.

    One hundred twenty-five patients were evaluated before and after rotator cuff repair using the DASH, the SST, and the SF-36. Patients' presurgical expectations of improvement were correlated with higher postsurgical scores. Presurgical expectations were associated with self-reported improvement in function after rotator cuff repair.

63. Mancuso CA, Altchek DW, Craig EV, et al: Patients' expectations of shoulder surgery. *J Shoulder Elbow Surg* 2002;11:541-549.

    Before shoulder surgery, 409 patients with diverse diagnoses were asked about their expectations. The information was used to develop the Hospital for Special Surgery Expectations Survey, which can be used to guide discussion on the goals of shoulder surgery.

64. Galatz LM, Silva MJ, Rothermich SY, Zaegel MA, Havlioglu N, Thomopoulos S: Nicotine delays tendon-to-bone healing in a rat model. *J Bone Joint Surg Am* 2006;88:2027-2034.

    A rat model was used to evaluate the effects of nicotine on rotator cuff tendon healing. In 72 rat repairs evaluated for type I collagen messenger RNA expression and biomechanical properties, the nicotine-infused group had a lag in improvement in biomechanical properties and inferior type I collagen expression compared with the saline control group.

65. Mallon WJ, Misamore G, Snead DS, Denton P: The impact of preoperative smoking habits on the results of rotator cuff repair. *J Shoulder Elbow Surg* 2004;13: 129-132.

    Ninety-five smokers and 125 nonsmokers were evaluated after open rotator cuff repair. Nonsmokers had greater improvement in total UCLA score than smokers and greater improvement in pain scores. More nonsmokers were classified as having a good or excellent result.

66. Cohen DB, Kawamura S, Ehteshami JR, Rodeo SA: Indomethacin and celecoxib impair rotator cuff tendon-to-bone healing. *Am J Sports Med* 2006;34: 362-369.

    The effect of indomethacin and a cyclooxygenase-2–specific NSAID on rotator cuff tendon healing was evaluated in a rat model. Both groups had significantly lower failure loads and decreased collagen organization in the rotator cuff repairs compared with the control group. These results suggest that traditional and selective NSAIDs inhibit tendon-to-bone healing.

67. Grondel RJ, Savoie FH, Field LD: Rotator cuff repairs in patients 62 years of age or older. *J Shoulder Elbow Surg* 2001;10:97-99.

    At a minimum 2-year follow-up after rotator cuff repair, 87% of 93 patients older than age 62 years had a good or excellent result, based on UCLA scores, with a 6% complication rate. Ninety of 92 patients were satisfied. The conclusion is that rotator cuff repair in this age group increases function, decreases pain, and provides a satisfactory result.

68. Rebuzzi E, Coletti N, Schiavetti S, Giusto F: Arthroscopic rotator cuff repair in patients older than 60 years. *Arthroscopy* 2005;21:48-54.

    Of 64 patients older than 60 years who were evaluated at an average 27 months after arthroscopic rotator cuff repair, 81% had a good or excellent result. The authors concluded that arthroscopic rotator cuff repair achieves satisfactory results regardless of age, tear size, or type of repair.

69. Hattrup SJ: Rotator cuff repair: Relevance of patient age. *J Shoulder Elbow Surg* 1995;4:95-100.

70. Romeo AA, Hang D, Bach BR Jr, Schott S: Repair of full thickness rotator cuff tears: Gender, age, and other factors affecting outcome. *Clin Orthop Relat Res* 1999;367:243-255.

71. Sperling JW, Cofield RH, Schleck C: Rotator cuff repair in patients fifty years of age and younger. *J Bone Joint Surg Am* 2004;86:2212-2215.

    Twenty-nine patients who underwent open rotator cuff repair before age 50 years were evaluated at a minimum 13-year follow-up. Repair was associated with long-term pain relief but not with improvement in motion; 45% of patients had an unsatisfactory result. Results of rotator cuff repair in young patients appear to be less favorable than results in a mixed-age patient population.

72. Watson EM, Sonnabend DH: Outcome of rotator cuff repair. *J Shoulder Elbow Surg* 2002;11:201-211.

    Of 667 patients who underwent open rotator cuff repair, 87% were satisfied. The results were less satisfactory in patients covered under workers' compensation, patients who were younger than 55 years, and patients who underwent revision surgery.

73. Cofield RH, Parvizi J, Hoffmeyer PJ, Lanzer WL, Ilstrup DM, Rowland CM: Surgical repair of chronic rotator cuff tears. *J Bone Joint Surg Am* 2001;83: 71-77.

    At an average 13-year follow-up after open rotator cuff repair, 80% of 105 patients were satisfied. Tear size was the most important determinant of active motion, strength, satisfaction, and need for revision (8% required revision).

74. Gartsman GM, Brinker MR, Khan M: Early effectiveness of arthroscopic repair for full-thickness tears of the rotator cuff: An outcome analysis. *J Bone Joint Surg Am* 1998;80:33-41.

75. Misamore GW, Ziegler DW, Rushton JL: Repair of the rotator cuff: A comparison of results in two populations of patients. *J Bone Joint Surg Am* 1995;77: 1335-1339.

76. McKee MD, Yoo DJ: The effect of surgery for rotator cuff disease on general health status. *J Bone Joint Surg Am* 2000;82:970-979.

77. Zandi H, Coghlan JA, Bell SN: Mini-incision rotator cuff repair: A longitudinal assessment with no deterioration of results up to nine years. *J Shoulder Elbow Surg* 2006;15:135-139.

   Seventy-four patients were evaluated at a mean 2 years and again at 7 years after mini-open rotator cuff repair and found to have no deterioration in pain, function, active flexion, or satisfaction, in the absence of reinjury.

78. Duckworth DG, Smith KL, Campbell B, Matsen FA III: Self-assessment questionnaires document substantial variability in the clinical expression of rotator cuff tears. *J Shoulder Elbow Surg* 1999;8:330-333.

79. Tashjian RZ, Henn RF, Kang L, Green A: The effect of co-morbidity on self-assessed function in patients with a chronic rotator cuff tear. *J Bone Joint Surg Am* 2004;86:355-362.

   In 199 patients with a chronic rotator cuff tear evaluated at baseline, a larger number of medical comorbidities was correlated with worse SST, DASH, and SF-36 scores, after several confounding variables were excluded.

80. Tashjian RZ, Henn RF, Kang L, Green A: Effect of medical co-morbidity on self-assessed pain, function, and general health status after rotator cuff repair. *J Bone Joint Surg Am* 2006;88:536-540.

   At 1-year follow-up of 125 patients after rotator cuff repair, patients with more presurgical medical comorbidities had greater improvement from baseline in DASH and VAS shoulder pain and function scores.

81. Iannotti JP, Bernot MP, Kuhlman JR, Kelley JM, Williams GR: Postoperative assessment of shoulder function: A prospective study of full-thickness rotator cuff tears. *J Shoulder Elbow Surg* 1996;5:449-457.

82. Thomazeau H, Boukobza E, Morcet N, Chaperon J, Langlais F: Prediction of rotator cuff repair results by magnetic resonance imaging. *Clin Orthop Relat Res* 1997;344:275-283.

83. Goutallier D, Postel JM, Gleyze P, Leguilloux P, Van Driessche S: Influence of cuff muscle fatty degeneration on anatomic and functional outcomes after simple suture of full-thickness tears. *J Shoulder Elbow Surg* 2003;12:550-554.

   At an average 37-month follow-up after rotator cuff repair, 220 patients were evaluated using MRI or CT arthrography. A recurrent tear was found in 36% of patients, and the percentage was higher in patients with muscle fatty degeneration classified above Goutallier stage I. Constant scores were lower in patients with retearing. Among patients with a watertight repair, the Constant score was lower for those with more muscle fatty degeneration.

84. Gerber C, Fuchs B, Hodler J: The results of repair of massive tears of the rotator cuff. *J Bone Joint Surg Am* 2000;82:505-515.

85. Gazielly DF, Gleyze P, Montagnon C. Functional and anatomical results after rotator cuff repair. *Clin Orthop Relat Res* 1994;304:43-53.

86. Harryman DT II, Mack LA, Wang KY, Jackins SE, Richardson ML, Matsen FA III: Repairs of the rotator cuff: Correlation of functional results with integrity of the cuff. *J Bone Joint Surg Am* 1991;73:982-989.

87. Klepps S, Bishop J, Lin J, et al: Prospective evaluation of the effect of rotator cuff integrity on the outcome of open rotator cuff repairs. *Am J Sports Med* 2004; 32:1716-1722.

   At 1-year follow-up after open rotator cuff repair, clinical evaluation and MRI of 31 patients found a 31% overall tear rate. There was no correlation between postsurgical cuff integrity and functional outcome (ASES and Constant scores).

88. Liu SH, Baker CL: Arthroscopically assisted rotator cuff repair: Correlation of functional results with integrity of the cuff. *Arthroscopy* 1994;10:54-60.

# Chapter 18

# Rotator Cuff Tear Arthropathy

*Christian Gerber, MD

Bernhard Jost, MD

Dominik C. Meyer, MD

## Introduction

Rotator cuff tear arthropathy is a pathologic condition of the glenohumeral joint in which chronic rotator cuff tearing is associated with structural glenohumeral joint destruction. The joint destruction involves humeral head erosion or collapse and, in some patients, glenoid erosion. Rotator cuff tear arthropathy does not encompass rotator cuff disease in which proximal migration of the humeral head is present without advanced structural changes in the joint surfaces. In the Hamada classification of radiographic changes after rotator cuff tearing, only stages IV and V correspond to rotator cuff tear arthropathy[1] (Table 1).

After a massive rotator cuff tear, the shoulder joint is progressively affected by the profoundly altered biomechanical and biologic conditions. The corresponding morphologic changes were recognized as early as the mid 1800s, when tear-associated joint destruction was compared with localized destructive arthritis.[2] The term cuff tear arthropathy was first used by Neer in 1977 to describe shoulder joint destruction secondary to rotator cuff tearing. However, rotator cuff tear arthropathy is still poorly differentiated from similar conditions, and other names, such as senile hemorrhagic shoulder (l'épaule sénile hémorragique) and Milwaukee shoulder, are sometimes used for rotator cuff tear arthropathy or very similar conditions.[1,3]

## Radiographic Classification

In 1990, a system was introduced for classifying radiographic changes in the shoulder after rotator cuff tearing.[1] Five grades were distinguished, based on two parameters: degenerative changes in the glenohumeral joint; and acromiohumeral distance, which is the distance from the top of the humeral head to the undersurface of the acromion, as measured on an anteroposterior radiograph of the shoulder with the arm in neutral rotation. Hamada grades I, II, and III represent chronic rotator cuff tears without arthropathy; rotator cuff tear arthropathy is represented by Hamada grades IV and V.

Seebauer refined the classification of shoulders with massive cuff tears and their development over time, using the parameters of the Hamada classification[4] (Table 2). Hamada grade IV is represented by Seebauer types IA and IIA, and Hamada grade V is represented by Seebauer type IIB. In Seebauer type I, the center of rotation is maintained, and the humeral head is contained within in the coracohumeral arch. In Seebauer type II, the humeral head has lost the center of rotation and no longer is contained within the coracohumeral arch, resulting in anterosuperior escape.

## Etiology and Pathomechanics

The etiology of rotator cuff tear arthropathy, as well as the factors influencing its progression, are not well understood. However, several theories address biomechanical, nutritional, and biochemical factors affecting the evolution of the disease.

*Christian Gerber, MD or the department with which he is affiliated has received research or institutional support from Zimmer Medacta, has received royalties from Zimmer, and is a consultant or employee for Storz.

**Table 1 | Hamada Classification of Rotator Cuff Tear Arthropathy**

| Grade | Acromiohumeral Distance | Characteristics |
|---|---|---|
| I | > 6 mm | |
| II | < 5 mm | |
| III | < 5 mm | Acetabularization of the glenoid and undersurface of the acromion |
| IV | < 5 mm | Grade III changes, with narrowing of the glenohumeral joint space |
| V | < 5 mm | Grade IV changes, with collapse of the humeral head |

**Table 2 | Seebauer Classification of Rotator Cuff Tear Arthropathy**

| Type | Centering | Migration or Translation | Dynamic Stabilization | Stabilization by Coracoacromial Arch |
|------|-----------|--------------------------|-----------------------|--------------------------------------|
| IA | Centered, stable | Minimal superior migration | Present | Present, with acetabularization of coracoacromial arch and femoralization of humeral head |
| IB | Centered, medialized | Minimal superior migration | Compromised | Present, with type IA and medial erosion of the glenoid |
| IIA | Decentered, limited stable | Superior translation | Insufficient | Minimal, with extensive acetabularization with superior medial erosion and femoralization of the humeral head |
| IIB | Decentered, unstable | Anterosuperior escape | Absent | Absent, with deficient anterior structures |

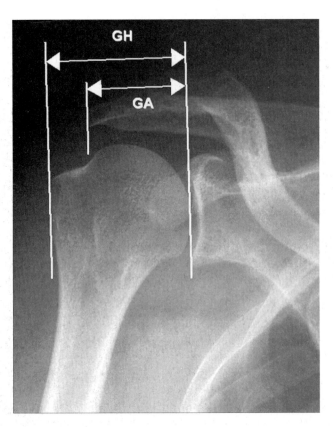

**Figure 1** The lateral extension of the acromion is quantified by calculating the acromion index on a true AP radiograph. The acromion index is calculated by dividing the distance from the glenoid plane to the acromion (GA) by the distance from the glenoid plane to the lateral aspect of the humeral head (GH). The larger the lateral extension of the acromion, the higher the acromion index. *(Reprinted with permission from Nyffeler RW, Werner CM, Sukthankar A, Schmid MR, Gerber C: Association of a large lateral extension of the acromion with rotator cuff tears. J Bone Joint Surg Am 2006;88:800-805.)*

## Biomechanical and Nutritional Factors

Large tears of the rotator cuff tendons may have mechanical and biologic consequences. In cadaver shoulders, the severity of degenerative changes associated with rotator cuff tear arthropathy was positively correlated with the size of the rotator cuff tear.[5] The joint capsule is perforated at the site of the tendon tear, allowing leakage of synovial fluid into the periarticular space and consequent loss of the normal joint milieu and joint pressure. The cartilage, normally nourished by synovial fluid, becomes degraded as a result of the loss of glycosaminoglycans and recurrent hemorrhagic effusions. Loss of negative intra-articular pressure promotes instability and static subluxation of the joint.

As the rotator cuff loses its ability to center the humeral head on the glenoid, the joint loses its fulcrum for abduction with activation of the deltoid muscle. Although the deltoid pulls the humerus proximally, the force is not transformed into abduction. Instead, the sole movement is lifting of the humeral head against the acromion, with eccentric compression against the superior aspect of the glenoid. So-called acetabularization of the glenoid (formation of a socket for the humeral head under the coracoacromial arch) and femoralization of the humerus (erosion of the greater tuberosity) eventually create a neojoint in the subcoracoacromial space.

As the active stabilizing forces of the rotator cuff lose their equilibrium, active range of motion and force transmission decrease. The reduction in active motion jeopardizes cartilage nutrition. Reductions in active loading and movement lead to disuse osteopenia of the humeral head and glenoid, which makes the joint vulnerable to progressive destruction.

The degenerative process is somewhat dependent on temporal and patient-specific factors. It may be influenced by the relationship of the lateral extension of the acromion to the size of the humeral head, which is called the acromion index[6] (Figure 1). If the acromion is narrow, as measured on an AP radiograph, the deltoid functions as the upper aspect of the humeral head, and its contraction may help the rotator cuff contain the head. This anthropometric factor may help limit supe-

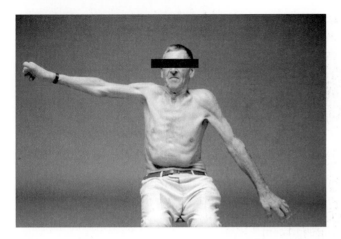

Figure 2 Photograph showing pseudoparesis in the left shoulder of a 65-year-old man.

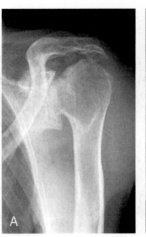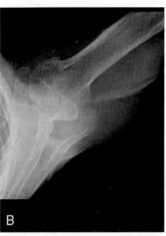

Figure 3 AP **(A)** and axillary **(B)** radiographs showing rotator cuff tear arthropathy in the left shoulder of the patient in Figure 2.

rior subluxation of the joint to Seebauer type IA or IB disease. Conversely, if the acromion extends far laterally and the rotator cuff is torn, there is little to prevent superior subluxation of the humerus. Attrition of the head against the acromion and upper glenoid rim will probably lead to development of Seebauer type IIA or IIB disease.

### Biochemical Factors

The progression of rotator cuff tearing to arthropathy is commonly explained by the formation and deposition of calcium crystals such as octacalcium phosphate and tricalcium phosphate in the synovial tissue and articular cartilage, with release into the synovial fluid. These crystals may undergo phagocytosis by synovial cells, which triggers the release of matrix-degrading proteins (metalloproteinases such as collagenase or stromelysin) and leads to the degradation of the cartilage matrix. The accompanying low-grade inflammatory response initiates cellular and fibroblast proliferation and promotes osteopenia.

## Clinical Evaluation

The clinical symptoms of rotator cuff tear arthropathy are pain and weakness in the shoulder. Pain is often most intense at night but also occurs during work and other daily activities. Weakness results in a loss of active range of motion; passive range of motion is relatively unaffected. The difference between active and passive ranges of motion results in lag signs for elevation and internal and external rotation. If the patient cannot reach approximately 90° of elevation and 0° of external rotation despite full passive range of motion, the shoulder is described as pseudoparalytic or pseudoparetic, for elevation or external rotation, respectively (Figure 2). An attempt to elevate the arm may provoke crepitus and characteristic dynamic superior subluxation of the

shoulder. Static, disabling anterosuperior instability may be present with disruption of the coracoacromial arch. However, in some patients, particularly those with Hamada grade IV/Seebauer type IA or IIA rotator cuff tear arthropathy, active range of motion and abduction strength may be relatively well preserved, despite the presence of a completely ruptured rotator cuff.

Inspection of the shoulder reveals atrophy of the rotator cuff musculature (the supraspinatus and infraspinatus) and, in some patients, atrophy of the deltoid. Frequently, the long head of the biceps is ruptured and the biceps is prominent distally. Profuse leakage of glenohumeral joint fluid into the subacromial space can result in the fluid sign, which is a diffuse swelling of the superficial shoulder, occasionally with subcutaneous ecchymosis. Aspiration of the fluid reveals hemorrhagic effusion; calcium pyrophosphate crystals are usually present, but there are no bacteria.

Plain radiography of a shoulder with rotator cuff tear arthropathy shows Hamada grade IV or V and Seebauer type I or II arthritic changes (Figure 3). CT or MRI reveals severe rotator cuff muscle atrophy and fatty infiltration (usually classified as Goutallier stage III or IV[7]). The joint space is narrowed, the humeral head has collapsed, and the glenoid is often eroded. The joint space is translated medially, leaving a large glenoid cavity seated on a very short, trumpet-shaped scapular neck. Many patients with static superior migration have preferential superior wear of the glenoid. Although more bone remains in the inferior part of the glenoid, the bone is extremely osteopenic because of the lack of contact between the humeral head and glenoid.

## Differentiation of Rotator Cuff Tear Arthropathy From Similar Conditions

More than one condition can lead to the development of a static, superiorly subluxated humeral head with destruction of the rotator cuff, pain, and loss of function. There appears to be no distinction between rotator cuff tear arthropathy and the condition known as senile hemorrhagic shoulder.[8] In Milwaukee shoulder, however, substantial crystal depositions in the remaining soft tissue and cartilage can be seen on plain radiographs.[3,9] In contrast, rotator cuff tear arthropathy is characterized by calcium pyrophosphate crystals that can almost invariably be identified on histologic examination but cannot be discerned on plain radiographs.

Severe osteoarthritis can be identified by the presence of subchondral sclerosis and osteophyte formation on the humeral head and glenoid. Osteoarthritis is characterized by pronounced posterior glenoid erosion, rather than the anterior-superior migration typically found in rotator cuff tear arthropathy. Rheumatoid arthritis and infection are characterized by an intact biceps tendon and marked osteopenia, in addition to other typical symptoms, and therefore they are not easily mistaken for rotator cuff tear arthropathy.

## Nonsurgical Treatment

Joint function is always impaired but sometimes not completely lost in rotator cuff tear arthropathy. In a patient with acetabularization of the glenoid and femoralization of the humerus but minimal joint line destruction, joint function may be surprisingly well preserved, despite an entirely ruptured rotator cuff and biceps tendon. This condition is classified as Seebauer type IA or IB. If joint destruction is not progressing rapidly and the patient can tolerate the symptoms and level of joint function, surgical intervention is not mandatory. Rest, physical therapy, and oral medication can be considered for treating the condition. The goal is to control the patient's pain during activities of daily living.

## Surgical Treatment

If the patient's pain cannot be controlled through nonsurgical treatment or if the disease is progressing rapidly or function is deteriorating, surgical treatment should be considered. Rotator cuff tear arthropathy almost invariably affects patients older than 65 years. The patient's general medical condition and shoulder function should be assessed, and the bone quality of the humerus and glenoid, the integrity of the coracoacromial arch, and the structural and functional integrity of the deltoid muscle should be determined.

A surgical repair of the rotator cuff will fail to heal if static superior subluxation of the humerus has occurred. Tendon transfers, which can successfully treat massive rotator cuff tears, cannot address the arthritic joint destruction that, by definition, is present in rotator cuff tear arthropathy. The goal of treatment is to restore a pain-free shoulder with the best possible function.

### Nonprosthetic Surgery
#### *Arthroscopic Lavage and Débridement*
For a patient with adequate shoulder function, shoulder arthroscopy with lavage and débridement may provide temporary pain relief. Débridement is usually considered inadequate for treating well-established rotator cuff tear arthropathy, and therefore it is performed only for patients whose poor general health precludes other surgical treatment. The surgeon should avoid débridement or weakening of the acromion and the coracoacromial arch (which may be ossified and restrain the humeral head from anterior-superior migration) with an aggressive acromioplasty and release of the coracoacromial ligament.

#### *Glenohumeral Arthrodesis*
Shoulder arthrodesis is rarely considered for treatment of rotator cuff tear arthropathy. Fusion may be difficult to obtain, and the patient may tolerate it poorly. The patient's bone quality and age usually weigh against the procedure; in addition, massive rotator cuff disease is frequently bilateral. The use of shoulder arthrodesis is limited to patients with a history of infection, a severe deltoid deficiency, or axillary nerve palsy, usually after earlier surgery or trauma.

#### *Resection Arthroplasty*
For a patient with a chronic infection as well as a substantial loss of bone stock (usually after several surgical procedures), resection arthroplasty may be the only remaining option. Although the procedure may improve the patient's pain, it results in a completely unstable and uncontrollable flail shoulder.

### Prosthetic Surgery
#### *Reverse Shoulder Prosthetic Surgery*
A reverse (inverse) shoulder prosthesis is used to restore function in shoulders with an intact, functional deltoid and a massive, irreparable rotator cuff tear. It was developed in France during the 1980s[10,11] and has been increasingly used in Europe since the 1990s. The US Food and Drug Administration approved the use of the reverse shoulder prosthesis in 2003, and since then it has been increasingly accepted around the world. The integrity of the coracoacromial arch is irrelevant to use of the reverse shoulder prosthesis. However, sufficient glenoid bone stock and a functioning deltoid are prerequisites for successful implantation.

A reverse prosthesis is used to transform the glenoid into a sphere, called a glenosphere, and to attach a concave socket to the proximal humerus (Figure 4). With shoulder movement, the humerus rotates around the center of the glenosphere, which corresponds to the center of the glenoid; the center of rotation is thereby medialized from the center of the humeral head, and the

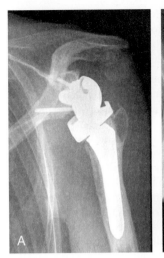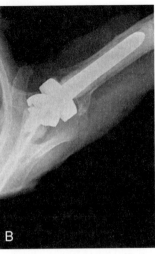

**Figure 4** AP **(A)** and axillary **(B)** radiographs showing implantation of a reverse shoulder prosthesis.

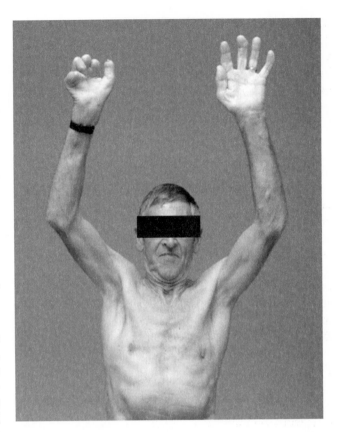

**Figure 5** Photograph taken 1 year after surgery, showing marked improvement in the patient's shoulder function.

lever arm of the deltoid is increased. Mechanically, the deltoid must now generate less force to abduct the arm, and it exerts less tension on the acromion. However, the contraction is potentially slower, and the muscle excursion is longer. Although the reverse shoulder prosthesis restores active rotation,[12] it does not restore external rotation, and the patient has poor control of the arm in space. A transfer of the latissimus dorsi tendon to the anterosuperior humeral head may improve external rotation and arm control.[13,14]

In a multicenter study of 80 reverse shoulder prostheses at 10-year follow-up, the rate of prosthesis replacement was 9%, and the rate of glenoid loosening was 16%.[15] The study found that loosening usually occurred within the first 3 years, and functional deterioration of stable implants began after 6 years. The authors concluded that a reverse shoulder prosthesis should be used to treat only extremely disabling shoulder arthropathy, for which it can adequately restore shoulder function (Figure 5).

### Humeral Head Replacement
If the coracoacromial arch and deltoid function are preserved, the humeral head can be replaced using a hemiprosthesis. The goal of this treatment is articulation of the humerus with the acetabularized upper corner of the subacromial space to form a ball-and-socket joint. Therefore, the preservation of deltoid function and coracoacromial arch integrity is crucial. If possible, the rotator cuff tendons should be repaired to improve anteroposterior balancing and contribute to joint stability.

An extended-head humeral prosthesis has been designed specifically for repair of rotator cuff tear arthropathy. The head of the prosthesis is extended laterally to allow its upper end to articulate with the undersurface of the glenoid. In a recent study of 60 shoulders with Seebauer type IA or IIA rotator cuff arthropathy, patients were treated using this prosthesis.[4] The coracoacromial arch was strictly preserved in all patients, although in some patients the acetabularized glenoid was contoured using a burr. The success rate was 89% at 2-year follow-up, as measured using limited-goal criteria of improvement in pain, motion, and activities of daily living.

Functional recovery after a hemiarthroplasty is inferior to recovery after successful treatment using a reverse prosthesis, and it is much less predictable. Humeral head replacement should be reserved for patients with a contained head that is intact in the coracoacromial arch, as well as preserved overhead elevation. The use of a reverse prosthesis is recommended for pseudoparalytic shoulders.

### Obsolete Prosthetic Surgery
Treatment of rotator cuff tear arthropathy with a conventional total shoulder prosthesis has poor functional results. The head tends to become displaced superiorly, causing eccentric loading to the glenoid rim. In this rocking horse effect, eccentric forces and excessive polyethylene wear lead to early loosening of the glenoid components. Treatment with constrained shoulder prostheses has had similarly catastrophic results because the great load on the glenoid in a constrained joint leads to early loosening.

## Summary

A massive cuff tear may lead to the development of rotator cuff tear arthropathy, which is poorly understood and can be difficult to treat. The two types of rotator cuff tear arthropathy represent two possible patterns of progression. In the first type, the glenoid and coracoacromial arch acetabularize into a socket, and the humerus progressively femoralizes to form a new articulation, which can provide surprisingly good function if the deltoid is intact. Glenohumeral joint destruction may be minimal. Often, patients with this condition are not considered to have rotator cuff tear arthropathy. However, the patient's function progressively deteriorates as the glenohumeral joint degenerates. In the second type, which may evolve from the first, both the humerus and glenoid are rapidly destroyed, and shoulder function is lost. These patients may have poor bone stock and an insufficient coracoacromial arch.

For patients with adequate bone stock and deltoid integrity, the reverse shoulder prosthesis appears to offer recovery of pain-free shoulder function, which is not possible with any other form of treatment. These prostheses must be used judiciously, and it remains to be seen whether the results will be sufficiently durable to justify their widespread use.

## Annotated References

1. Hamada K, Fukuda H, Mikasa M, Kobayashi Y: Roentgenographic findings in massive rotator cuff tears: A long-term observation. *Clin Orthop Relat Res* 1990;254:92-96.

2. Adams R: *A Treatise on Rheumatic Gout, or Chronic Rheumatic Arthritis, of All the Joints.* London, England, J. Churchill, 1857.

3. McCarty DJ, Halverson PB, Carrera GF, Brewer BJ, Kozin F: Milwaukee shoulder: Association of microspheroids containing hydroxyapatite crystals, active collagenase, and neutral protease with rotator cuff defects. I: Clinical aspects. *Arthritis Rheum* 1981;24:464-473.

4. Visotsky JL, Basamania C, Seebauer L, Rockwood CA, Jensen KL: Cuff tear arthropathy: Pathogenesis, classification and algorithm for treatment. *J Bone Joint Surg Am* 2004;86:35-40.

   Sixty shoulders with Seebauer type IA or IIA rotator cuff tear arthropathy underwent hemiarthroplasty using an extended humeral head prosthesis. Limited-goal criteria were used to determine that 89% had a successful result at 2-year follow-up. No progressive glenoid erosion, dislocation, or acromial fracture was found on radiographs.

5. Petersson CJ: Degeneration of the gleno-humeral joint: An anatomical study. *Acta Orthop Scand* 1983;54:277-283.

6. Nyffeler RW, Werner CM, Sukthankar A, Schmid MR, Gerber C: Association of a large lateral extension of the acromion with rotator cuff tears. *J Bone Joint Surg Am* 2006;88:800-805.

   The depressive force of the deltoid on the humeral head during deltoid contraction may prohibit rising of the head and attrition of the cuff against the acromion. To quantify the proportion of the deltoid that pushes on the humeral head, the distance from the glenoid plane to the lateral border of the acromion was divided by the distance from the glenoid plane to the lateral aspect of the humeral head. This acromion index was found to be $0.73 \pm 0.06$ in shoulders with a full-thickness tear, $0.60 \pm 0.08$ in shoulders with osteoarthritis and an intact rotator cuff, and $0.64 \pm 0.06$ in asymptomatic normal shoulders with an intact rotator cuff. The difference between a full-thickness supraspinatus tear and intact rotator cuff was highly significant ($P < 0.0001$). It is unknown whether a large lateral extension of the acromion is a cause or consequence of rotator cuff pathology.

7. Goutallier D, Postel JM, Bernageau J, Lavau L, Voisin MC: Fatty muscle degeneration in cuff ruptures: Pre- and postoperative evaluation by CT scan. *Clin Orthop Relat Res* 1994;304:78-83.

8. De Sèze S, Hubault A, Rampon S: L'épaule sénile hémorragique. L'actualité rhumatologique, in *Expansion Scientifique Française*. Paris, France, 1967, pp 107-115.

9. Garcia GM, McCord GC, Kumar R: Hydroxyapatite crystal deposition disease. *Semin Musculoskelet Radiol* 2003;7:187-193.

   Hydroxyapatite crystal deposition disease is systemic and of unknown etiology. It is caused by para-articular or intra-articular deposition of hydroxyapatite crystals. Any joint can be involved. The shoulder is most commonly affected, and the result is known as Milwaukee shoulder.

10. Grammont P, Trouilloud P, Laffay JP, Deries X: Etude et réalisation d'une nouvelle prothèse d'épaule. *Rhumatologie* 1987;39:407-418.

11. Grammont PM, Baulot E: Delta shoulder prosthesis for rotator cuff rupture. *Orthopedics* 1993;16:65-68.

12. Werner CML, Steinmann PA, Gilbart M, Gerber C: Treatment of painful pseudoparesis due to irreparable rotator cuff dysfunction with the Delta III reverse-ball-and-socket total shoulder prosthesis. *J Bone Joint Surg Am* 2005;87:1476-1486.

    Fifty-eight consecutive patients with painful pseudoparesis (active elevation of $< 90°$) were treated with a reverse shoulder prosthesis. Although the complication rate was 50%, the procedure was found to have substantial potential to improve the condition of patients with severe shoulder dysfunction.

13. Simovitch RW, Helmy N, Zumstein MA, Gerber C: Impact of fatty infiltration of the teres minor muscle on the outcome of reverse total shoulder arthroplasty. *J Bone Joint Surg Am* 2007;89:934-939.

In 42 patients with reverse shoulder prostheses, fatty infiltration of the teres minor was found to be correlated with active external rotation of the shoulder. Stage III or IV fatty infiltration compromises the clinical outcome.

14. Gerber C, Pennington SD, Lingenfelter EJ, Sukthankar A: Reverse Delta-III total shoulder replacement combined with latissimus dorsi transfer: A preliminary report. *J Bone Joint Surg Am* 2007;89: 940-947.

Twelve shoulders with a combined pseudoparesis of anterior elevation and external rotation were treated with a reverse shoulder arthroplasty and a concomitant latissimus dorsi transfer. Both active and external rotation were restored at short term.

15. Guery J, Favard L, Sirveaux F, Oudet D, Mole D, Walch G: Reverse total shoulder arthroplasty: Survivorship analysis of eighty replacements followed for five to ten years. *J Bone Joint Surg Am* 2006;88:1742-1747.

In a multicenter report of 10-year follow-up of 80 shoulders with a reverse shoulder prosthesis, the survival rate was 91% or 84% for prosthesis replacement or glenoid loosening, respectively.

# Chapter 19

# Biologic Augmentation of Rotator Cuff Healing

Jesse McCarron, MD

*Kathleen A. Derwin, PhD

Joseph P. Iannotti, MD, PhD

## Introduction

As many as 30% of patients visit a shoulder surgeon because of rotator cuff pathology, and rotator cuff tears are a common cause of pain and disability. Research findings have increased the ability to determine which rotator cuff tendon tears are likely to heal after open or arthroscopic repair. Although many patients with persistent defects have substantially improved strength, pain, function, and overall satisfaction, the results are even better if the tear partially or completely heals. Between 20% and 70% of larger tears fail to heal after surgery, and the inability to obtain a high healing rate with these tears led clinicians and basic science researchers to investigate methods of augmenting the surgical repair of torn rotator cuffs.[1-3]

During the 1980s, allografts and xenografts using extracellular matrix (ECM) were studied for augmenting the healing of rotator cuff repairs, but their use decreased during the 1990s because of a lack of clinical success. However, improved tissue-processing and cell-based technologies have renewed interest in using ECM grafts for augmenting rotator cuff repairs. The hope is to use the biologic properties of both the host and graft to improve healing.

Several thousand patients receive an ECM graft every year, and many of the procedures involve rotator cuff pathology. The number of patients receiving graft implantation is likely to increase as additional products are developed and surgeons become comfortable with their use. Although only preliminary clinical data are available on the effect of these materials on tendon healing, basic science research has found that significant mechanical and biochemical differences exist among different types of ECM. Good results in animal models have not always led to satisfactory healing or function in

clinical use. Ongoing basic science research using animal models, as well as carefully designed and implemented clinical trials, are needed to fully define the best materials and methods for the biologic enhancement of rotator cuff tears.

## Characteristics of Graft Materials

Cell therapy, growth factors, gene delivery systems, and biologic scaffolds are under investigation for facilitating the healing of rotator cuff repairs. The most commonly used material is a natural ECM. Most ECMs are collagen-rich and of small intestine submucosal (SIS), dermal, or pericardial origin. Although new clinical treatment strategies for biologically enhancing rotator cuff repair are likely to be introduced within the near future, ECM graft use is the only method for which clinically applicable peer-reviewed research has been published.

The optimal mechanical and biochemical qualities of ECM grafts have not been fully determined. However, several basic principles have been established. An ideal ECM graft should have mechanical properties that allow it to share the load of the repaired tendon and enable the tendon-graft construct to resist gap formation and failure. Stiffness and a modulus of elasticity similar to that of intact native tendon are required, as well as the ability to hold a suture under physiologic stress. The ECM material should have biologically active properties that facilitate healing of the tendon to bone. It must be capable of withstanding or even stimulating a cell-based healing response without overly rapid degradation, and it must not create a chronic inflammatory response, allergic reaction, or rejection response from its host.

## Indications for Use

Although graft augmentation has shown promise in animal models, clinical data are inadequate to establish the benefit in healing or function for any patient population. Furthermore, some studies found that some patients had adverse reactions after ECM implantation, including pain, warmth, erythremia, or a sterile inflammatory reaction. Inadequate surgical site healing and

*Kathleen A. Derwin, PhD or the department with which she is affiliated has received research or institutional support from DePuy, Wright Medical, Musculoskeletal Transplant Foundation, and Synthasome, Inc.

**Table 1 | Commercially Available ECM Products**

| Product | Tissue Type | Source | Chemical Cross-Linking | Manufacturer | Commercial Source |
|---|---|---|---|---|---|
| AlloDerm | Dermis | Human | No | LifeCell | LifeCell |
| AlloPatch | Fascia lata | Human | No | Musculoskeletal Transplant Foundation | Musculoskeletal Transplant Foundation |
| Collagen Repair Patch* | Dermis | Porcine | Yes | Tissue Science Laboratories | Zimmer |
| CuffPatch | Small intestine submucosa | Porcine | Yes | Organogenesis | Biomet Sports Medicine |
| GraftJacket | Dermis | Human | No | LifeCell | Wright Medical Technology |
| OrthADAPT | Pericardium | Equine | Yes | Pegasus Biologics | Pegasus Biologics |
| Restore | Small intestine submucosa | Porcine | No | DePuy | DePuy |
| TissueMend | Dermis (fetal) | Bovine | No | TEI Biosciences | Stryker |

*Formerly named Permacol.*

inadequate healing of rotator cuff tears also occurred.[4-6] Based on these early findings, most investigators agree that the use of ECM should be limited to patients at high risk of repair failure after a primary rotator cuff tear repair using an optimal surgical technique.

A rotator cuff tear of medium, large, or massive size or of more than 3 months' duration has a significant likelihood of failing to heal after a primary repair. The risk of repair failure is the most common reason ECM graft augmentation is used. A partial repair of a large tear, leaving a small residual defect, may also benefit from augmentation; the purpose of the graft is to maintain mechanical forces across the defect and create an extrasynovial environment for tendon healing. ECM grafts have also been used as soft-tissue interposition in an irreparable rotator cuff tear. Biologic augmentation has been promoted as a means of hastening healing or improving healing in tissue that would otherwise have less-than-normal strength and biomechanical characteristics.

After a primary repair, a small or medium-sized acute rotator cuff tear heals in most patients. In the absence of clinical data to establish the efficacy of ECM technology or the associated complication rates, its use cannot currently be justified for acute tears of small or medium size.

## Regulatory Aspects

Natural ECM is derived from human or animal tissue that is harvested, processed, sterilized, and marketed for clinical use (Table 1). Like many other allograft products, human-derived ECM is classified as human tissue for transplantation under the Code of Federal Regulations ("Human Tissue Intended for Transplantation," 21 CFR, Pt. 1270). The regulations do not require a new human-derived ECM to undergo premarket review for US Food and Drug Administration (FDA) approval.

Nonhuman ECM graft materials include tissues from porcine, bovine, and equine sources. They are derived from processed and sterilized SIS, dermal, or pericardial tissue. Unlike human-derived ECM, ECM derived from animal tissue requires FDA approval and is regulated as a device rather than as a biologic material or drug. Animal-derived ECM products are FDA Section 510(k) approved "for reinforcement of the soft tissues, which are repaired by suture or suture anchors, during rotator cuff repair surgery" (Tissue Sciences Laboratories, Andover, MA, application for FDA Section 510[k] premarket approval of Permacol cross-linked porcine dermal collagen surgical mesh, 2002). For FDA approval, the safety and effectiveness of the new product's design and manufacture must be equivalent to that of an already-approved device in the same category. A demonstration of clinical efficacy is not required.

## Xenograft Materials
### SIS-Derived Products
#### Basic Science and Animal Research

Animal studies generally support the use of single-layer and multilayer porcine SIS devices to enhance repair of a tendon, meniscus, or ligament (intra-articular or extra-articular).[7-12] SIS appears to promote cell migration into the wound site and is associated with rapid angiogenesis, graft resorption, and constructive remodeling. SIS grafts are resorbed within 3 months of implantation.[8,13,14] Although an acute inflammatory response accompanies SIS implantation,[15] little or no evidence of chronic inflammation or encapsulation has been found.[7,9,12,15] The immune response is consistent with graft resorption and remodeling, rather than rejection.[15] SIS grafts have been found to resist infection, compared with synthetic graft materials.[16]

Subcutaneous implantation of the Restore Orthobiologic Implant (DePuy, Warsaw, IN) into mice and rabbits caused an inflammatory reaction characterized by massive lymphocyte infiltration. Histologic data suggested the presence of nuclear material, as well as mast cell granules, within the Restore material, and molecular methods confirmed the presence of porcine DNA material. Other studies have found that GraftJacket (Wright Medical Technology, Arlington, TN), TissueMend (Stryker, Mahwah, NJ), and Restore, as currently manufactured, are not completely free of nuclear material and cellular debris.[17] Despite the acute inflammatory response and rapid graft resorption seen with SIS materials, peripheral adhesion formation was not found,[8,9] except where the material was used as a full-length intrasynovial tendon graft.[10]

SIS-regenerated tissue is similar to the tissue it was intended to repair.[7,9,11] A study of SIS for interpositional rotator cuff repair in a canine model found no difference in the histologic appearance or failure loads of tendons repaired with or without an SIS graft, after 3 and 6 months.[9] However, the failure strength of both types of repair was significantly less than that of an uninjured tendon. The remodeled tissue was consistent with a tendon phenotype in having an oriented, collagenous matrix. A normal-appearing tendon-to-bone insertion was observed. In a sheep model, an SIS patch was used to augment an infraspinatus tendon repair. At 12 weeks, the stiffness of the augmented repairs was significantly higher than that of unaugmented repairs. However, none of the repairs were intact, and the authors concluded that SIS augmentation was insufficient to prevent anatomic failure of the rotator cuff tendon repair.[18] In a rat model, both acute and chronic supraspinatus tendon tears were repaired using a 10-layer SIS graft. The biomechanical performance of the SIS-grafted tendons was equivalent to that of naturally repaired tendons. The material properties were similar, with a smaller cross-section in the SIS-grafted tendons.[19,20] These findings suggest that, in these animal models, tendon repair with SIS is as satisfactory as natural tendon healing.

In animal models, the biomechanical properties of SIS-regenerated tendon and ligament were usually equal to those of tendons and ligaments repaired without SIS autograft, but they were inferior to those of normal tissue, as late as 6 months after surgery.[7,9,12] Assessments of longer term performance are not available. However, the limited information available from animal models suggest that SIS-derived grafts can be efficacious in clinical use.

### Clinical Application
Two SIS products have been approved by the FDA for human implantation. The Restore and CuffPatch (Biomet Sports Medicine, Warsaw, IN) implants are both of porcine origin. Despite the encouraging results in animal models, the limited available clinical reports suggest that SIS augmentation currently does not improve the likelihood of tendon healing in rotator cuff tears or improve clinical outcome scores. In one series, MRI revealed evidence of failed repair 6 months after surgery in 10 of 11 consecutive patients who underwent open repair of a large or massive rotator cuff tear augmented with the Restore implant.[21] According to results from another prospective, randomized, controlled trial, healing of a large or massive chronic rotator cuff tear repair was 7% less likely to occur if the Restore implant was used ($P = 0.07$).[4] Other studies found that patients had increased pain, local swelling, and sterile fluid accumulation in response to implantation of SIS devices.[5] A prospective clinical trial found that Restore-augmented rotator cuff repairs had a retearing rate equivalent to that of unaugmented repairs at 2-year follow-up, and pain scores and shoulder strength were worse in patients with augmented repairs.[6]

Pathologic and microbiologic testing of tissue and fluid specimens collected from patients who developed an inflammatory reaction revealed that these reactions are consistent with a nonspecific inflammatory response, rather than an allergic or rejection-type reaction. The inflammation may be a reaction to cellular and genetic debris that was not completely removed from the graft material during the manufacturer's processing. Based on these limited early reports, most authors experienced in the use of SIS xenografts do not recommend their use in the augmentation of rotator cuff repairs.[6]

### Dermis-Derived Products
#### Basic Science and Animal Research
In a rat model, subcutaneous implantation of a porcine-derived, cross-linked dermal ECM was well tolerated during a 20-week period. Histologic evaluation revealed a minor chronic inflammatory response, as well as evidence of collagen degradation associated with limited vascular ingrowth.[22]

#### Clinical Application
The FDA has approved two dermis-derived graft materials for human implantation. The chemically cross-linked Collagen Repair Patch (Zimmer, Warsaw, IN) is derived from porcine sources, and the non–cross-linked TissueMend is a fetal bovine derivative.

Collagen Repair Patch has been used clinically to reinforce soft tissue in nonorthopaedic applications, including urogynecologic and plastic reconstructive surgery.[23] The only published report of a clinical orthopaedic application described the use of Permacol, a porcine dermal collagen xenograft for graft interposition in the thumb trapeziometacarpal joint, after a trapeziectomy for treatment of osteoarthritis.[24] The

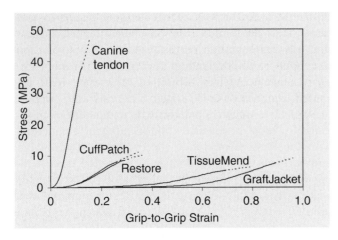

**Figure 1** Stress-strain curves of 4-mm-wide strips of extracellular matrix and normal canine infraspinatus tendon. Dotted lines indicate that the failure point is underrepresented in each curve because every failure occurred at a grip.

xenograft was found to be detrimental to the results of the trapeziectomy, and the study was terminated prematurely because of an apparent adverse reaction to the implant in 6 of the 13 patients. Patients in the xenograft group reported greater pain, were less satisfied with the surgical results, had a longer postsurgical hospital stay, and required more frequent clinical review than patients in the control group. The findings of histologic examination after later removal of three implants were consistent with a foreign body reaction. No peer-reviewed clinical reports have evaluated the role of a cross-linked or non–cross-linked dermis-derived xenograft in tendon or rotator cuff repairs.

### Pericardium-Derived Product
The OrthADAPT Bioimplant (Pegasus Biologics, Irvine, CA) is an equine-derived pericardial xenograft. No peer-reviewed basic science, animal, or clinical reports have been published on the in vivo characteristics of this material.

## Allograft Materials
### Dermis-Derived Products
**Basic Science and Animal Research**
Canine model investigation into the use of human-derived dermis for interpositional rotator cuff repair found that grafted and ungrafted repairs had equivalent failure strength after 3 months. Neither repair was as strong as an intact native tendon. Using histologic criteria, failure at the graft-to-bone interface was found in 2 of the 10 grafted repairs.[25] Three other studies used animal models to evaluate human-derived non–cross-linked dermal ECM as a scaffold for periosteum regeneration. Taken together, these studies provide preliminary evidence that the dermal membrane material allows cellular repopulation, revascularization, and bone defect restoration.[26]

### Clinical Application
GraftJacket is currently the only FDA-approved, commercially available human-derived dermis-based graft product. Its effectiveness in treating diabetic foot ulcers suggests applicability to some types of orthopaedic wounds.[27] Extensive literature is available on the use of acellular dermal grafts such as AlloDerm (LifeCell, Branchburg, NJ) in plastic reconstructive, burn, and dental applications. In a case report, augmentation of a gastrocnemius recession repair of a chronic Achilles tendon rupture led to an early return to activity and a good functional outcome.[28]

### Fascia Lata–Derived Products
**Basic Science and Animal Research**
In the only animal study to evaluate the use of a fascia lata graft for rotator cuff tendon healing, the graft was interposed in a supraspinatus tendon defect in a rabbit model. Histologic analysis 8 weeks after repair revealed reformation of a normal-appearing tendon-to-bone interface, host cell infiltration, and remodeling of the graft material to resemble normal supraspinatus tendon. In 21 rabbits, two graft failures appeared.[29]

### Clinical Application
AlloPatch (Musculoskeletal Transplant Foundation, Edison, NJ) is the only FDA-approved, commercially available fascia lata allograft product. Fascia lata autografts and allografts have been used extensively for soft-tissue reconstruction in orthopaedic, ophthalmologic, and urogynecologic surgery. They have been used to bridge Achilles tendon defects and reconstruct anterior glenohumeral joint capsule deficiencies, with good functional outcomes.[30,31] This material appears to be well tolerated in orthopaedic procedures. The incidence of complications is low, and the biomechanical properties permit significant in vivo tensile forces. However, no published studies are available on the use of this material for the augmentation of rotator cuff repairs.

## Comparative Mechanical Properties
A graft material's derivative tissue type and processing method affect its biomechanical characteristics. Dermis-derived ECM materials are substantially stronger in suture retention load to failure than SIS-derived materials.[32] Conversely, dermis-derived materials have a significantly lower modulus of elasticity than SIS-derived materials.[17] Both dermis-derived and SIS-derived materials require a 10% to 30% stretch before they are capable of bearing any significant load in tension, and they reach the linear portion of the stress-strain curve between 30% and 80% strain. In comparison, fascia lata–derived ECM material and canine infraspinatus tendon require less than 10% stretch before bearing a significant load in tension (Figure 1). Bio-

mechanical studies found that the properties of fascia lata graft materials are on the same order of magnitude as those of canine and human supraspinatus tendon; their load-to-failure ranges are 4 to 16 MPa, 4 to 16 MPa, and 26 to 31 MPa, respectively.[33-35] In both models, failure occurred at the interface between the grip and soft tissue, rather than in the tissue, and therefore the true in vivo strength of these materials is probably greater than reported. Table 2 summarizes the mechanical properties of different graft materials. In comparison, the linear modulus of human infraspinatus tendon in grip-to-grip strain is between 84 and 187 MPa, depending on the tendon region tested.[36]

The data indicate that the biomechanical properties of all commercially available SIS and dermal ECM materials are at least one order of magnitude lower than those of intact native tendon. Whether these materials can be applied in a way that will allow them to bear any significant mechanical load has not been determined. The biomechanical properties of fascia lata–derived ECM materials such as AlloPatch are on the same order of magnitude as human infraspinatus tendon, and therefore these materials are more likely to be able to bear the mechanical loads necessary for improving the overall strength of the repair construct.

## Comparative Biochemical Composition

The commercially available ECM materials are generally similar in biochemical composition to normal tendon tissue (Table 3). The significantly lower hydroxyproline content in GraftJacket than in the other graft materials suggests a lower collagen content. Biochemical analysis of the properties of processed fascia lata graft has found that its collagen content is roughly equivalent to that of normal tendon, with approximately half the chondroitin and dermatan sulfate glycosaminoglycan content of normal tendon.[35] Restore has a sig-

nificantly higher glycosaminoglycan and hyaluronic content than other graft materials. TissueMend, Restore, and GraftJacket all have measurable amounts of residual DNA material, although the amount in TissueMend is significantly higher than that in the other materials. Processed fascia lata and CuffPatch have the smallest amount of residual DNA material.[35]

### Table 2 | Biomechanical Properties of Commercially Available ECM Materials and Native Canine Tendon (Mean ± SD)

| Product | 8% Strain Modulus* (MPa) | Linear Modulus* (MPa) | Suture Failure Load (N) |
|---|---|---|---|
| AlloPatch[†] | 304 ± 52 | 304 ± 52 | – |
| Collagen Repair Patch[‡] | – | – | 128.0 ± 26.3 |
| CuffPatch[‡,§] | 17.0 ± 2.8 | 40.1 ± 15.0 | 32.0 ± 4.1 |
| GraftJacket[‡,§] | 0.3 ± 0.2 | 22.5 ± 5.3 | 229.0 ± 72.0[ǁ] |
| Restore[‡,§] | 14.1 ± 3.6 | 35.5 ± 9.1 | 38.2 ± 2.8 |
| TissueMend[‡,§] | 3.9 ± 2.6 | 15.2 ± 3.5 | 76.0 ± 21.5[¶] |
| Native canine infraspinatus tendon[‡] | 405 ± 86 | 405 ± 86 | – |

*Determined using test strips (4 mm × 30 mm) and grip-to-grip strains.

[†]Data adapted from Derwin KA, Baker AR, Spragg RK, Leigh DR, Farat W, Iannotti JP: Regional variability, processing methods and biophysical properties of human fascia lata extracellular matrix. J Biomed Mater Res A 2008;84:500-507.

[‡]Data from Barber FA, Morley AH, Coon DA: Tendon augmentation grafts: Biomechanical failure loads and failure patterns. Arthroscopy 2006;22:534-538.

[§]Data from Derwin KA, Baker AR, Spragg RK, Leigh DR, Iannotti JP: Commercial extracellular matrix scaffolds for rotator cuff tendon repair: Biomechanical, biochemical and cellular properties. J Bone Joint Surg Am 2006;88:2665-2672.

[ǁ]GraftJacket Extreme was used.

[¶]TissueMend 1.1 was used.

### Table 3 | Biochemical Properties of Commercially Available ECM Materials (Mean ± SD)

| Product | Hydroxyproline (mg/mg dry wt) | Chondroitin Sulfate/ Dermatan Sulfate Glycosaminoglycan (µg/mg dry wt) | Hyaluronan (µg/mg dry wt) | DNA (ng/mg dry wt) |
|---|---|---|---|---|
| AlloPatch[*] | 0.114 ± 0.014 | 0.61 ± 0.30 | 0.31 ± 0.19 | 66 ± 43 |
| Collagen Repair Patch | – | – | – | – |
| CuffPatch[†] | 0.112 ± 0.015 | 0.05 ± 0.01 | 0.05 ± 0.01 | 0.6 ± 0.6 |
| GraftJacket[†] | 0.078 ± 0.013 | 0.27 ± 0.15 | 0.40 ± 0.08 | 134.6 ± 44.0 |
| Restore[†] | 0.102 ± 0.008 | 0.96 ± 0.22 | 0.78 ± 0.22 | 526.8 ± 125.6 |
| TissueMend[†] | 0.122 ± 0.009 | 0.08 ± 0.02 | 0.06 ± 0.02 | 794.6 ± 97.8 |

[*]Data adapted from Derwin KA, Baker AR, Spragg RK, Leigh DR, Farat W, Iannotti JP: Regional variability, processing methods and biophysical properties of human fascia lata extracellular matrix. J Biomed Mater Res A 2008;84:500-507.

[†]Data from Derwin KA, Baker AR, Spragg RK, Leigh DR, Iannotti JP: Commercial extracellular matrix scaffolds for rotator cuff tendon repair: Biomechanical, biochemical and cellular properties. J Bone Joint Surg Am 2006;88:2665-2672.

## Host Response to Chemical Cross-Linking

Chemical cross-linking affects the properties of ECM graft materials. Non–cross-linked materials such as Restore and GraftJacket have the greatest amount of cellular infiltration, especially during the early postsurgical period associated with a more rapid inflammatory response. Chemical cross-linking, as found in CuffPatch, TissueMend, and Permacol, slows cell infiltration into the graft material[37] and is associated with the presence of foreign body giant cells, chronic inflammation, and the accumulation of dense, poorly organized fibrous tissue.[38]

## Surgical Technique

Based on the available data, no specific surgical method or postsurgical rehabilitation protocol can be recommended for using ECM products in rotator cuff repair. The focus of a primary surgical repair should be to optimize the biologic environment for healing and to apply the graft material in a manner that will allow it to provide mechanical support to the repair.

The first step in a primary repair is débridement of all devitalized and mechanically unsound tissue, as identified using qualitative macroscopic criteria. The tendon is then mobilized as much as possible. Using direct advancement, margin convergence, or a rotator interval slide, the full tendon defect is closed, and the tendon is repaired to bone using a double-row technique. The Mason-Allen suture technique should be used wherever possible. The ECM graft should be sutured into place away from the repaired tendon, stretched until taut, then sutured along the opposite side. The material should extend from healthy, intact tendon tissue to the bony insertion site, and it should be closely applied to the native tissue to avoid gaps and allow for host cell infiltration.

After an open repair of a large or massive tear using an ECM patch, the shoulder may be placed in an abduction brace to reduce tension and decrease the risk of gap formation at the repair site.

## Summary

The biologic augmentation of a large, chronic rotator cuff tear repair is an area of extensive ongoing investigation. Success is likely to result from both optimization of surgical technique and development of ECM products that provide early mechanical support to the repair and actively facilitate a biologic environment to stimulate healing. The ECM products currently in clinical use have not yet been found to improve either the biology or mechanics of rotator cuff healing. The human biologic response to these materials has sometimes differed from the response observed in animal models.

Decisions about the clinical application of ECM materials must balance the predicted benefit and the possible complications. Research will lead to improvements in the mechanical and biochemical characteristics of ECM materials, as well as a more detailed understanding of their application. In the future, these materials are likely to improve the healing rates and clinical outcomes of rotator cuff repairs.

## Annotated References

1. Galatz LM, Ball CM, Teefey SA, Middleton WD, Yamaguchi K: The outcome and repair integrity of completely arthroscopically repaired large and massive rotator cuff tears. *J Bone Joint Surg Am* 2004;86: 219-224.

    Eighteen patients were evaluated in a therapeutic study 1 and 2 years after arthroscopic repair of a large rotator cuff tear. There were 17 retears at 1 year, but 16 patients had improved function. The results had deteriorated at 2 years. Level of evidence: IV.

2. Gerber C, Fuchs B, Hodler J: The results of repair of massive tears of the rotator cuff. *J Bone Joint Surg Am* 2000;82:505-515.

3. Rokito AS, Cuomo F, Gallagher MA, Zuckerman JD: Long-term functional outcome of repair of large and massive chronic tears of the rotator cuff. *J Bone Joint Surg Am* 1999;81:991-997.

4. Iannotti JP, Codsi MJ, Kwon Y, Derwin KA, Ciccone J, Brems J: Porcine small intestine submucosa augmentation of surgical repair of chronic two-tendon rotator cuff tears: A randomized, controlled trial. *J Bone Joint Surg Am* 2005;88:1238-1244.

    In a prospective, controlled, randomized clinical trial, 15 of 30 shoulders had a SIS-augmented rotator cuff repair. The repair healed in 4 of 15 shoulders with augmentation compared with 9 of 15 shoulders in the control group ($P = 0.11$). The postsurgical median Penn score was 83 in the augmentation group, compared with 91 in the control group ($P = 0.07$). Level of evidence: II.

5. Malcarney HL, Bonar F, Murrell GAC: Early inflammatory reaction after rotator cuff repair with a porcine small intestine submucosal implant: A report of 4 cases. *Am J Sports Med* 2005;33:907-911.

    Twenty-five patients underwent rotator cuff repair with the Restore Orthobiologic Implant to augment the repaired tendon or fill a defect. Four patients had an inflammatory reaction at a mean 13 days after surgery. Level of evidence: IV.

6. Walton JR, Bowman NK, Khatib Y, Linklater J, Murrell GAC: Restore orthobiologic implant: Not recommended for augmentation of rotator cuff repairs. *J Bone Joint Surg Am* 2007;89:786-791.

    In a case-control study of 15 patients with SIS-augmented and 16 patients with unaugmented rotator cuff repair, 4 patients required revision surgery for a sterile inflammatory reaction at the site of SIS implantation. SIS did not improve functional or structural outcomes. Level of evidence: III.

7. Badylak S, Arnoczky S, Plouhar P, et al: Naturally occurring extracellular matrix as a scaffold for musculoskeletal repair. *Clin Orthop Relat Res* 1999;367: S333-S343.

8. Badylak SF, Tullius R, Kokini K, et al: The use of xenogeneic small intestinal submucosa as a biomaterial for Achilles tendon repair in a dog model. *J Biomed Mater Res* 1995;29:977-985.

9. Dejardin LM, Arnoczky SP, Ewers BJ, Haut RC, Clarke RB: Tissue-engineered rotator cuff tendon using porcine small intestine submucosa: Histologic and mechanical evaluation in dogs. *Am J Sports Med* 2001;29:175-184.

   Porcine SIS was used to replace resected infraspinatus tendon in 21 dogs. The ultimate strength of SIS-regenerated tendons was significantly less than that of native infraspinatus tendons but was similar to that of other primary-repaired tendons at 3 and 6 months.

10. Derwin K, Androjna C, Spencer E, et al: Porcine small intestine submucosa as a flexor tendon graft. *Clin Orthop Relat Res* 2004;423:245-252.

    A canine flexor tendon repair model was used to compare SIS graft reconstruction and intrasynovial flexor tendon autograft reconstruction. After 6 weeks, the SIS reconstruction had host cell infiltration with extensive adhesion formation and impaired tendon function, compared with the flexor tendon autograft repair.

11. Gastel JA, Muirhead WR, Lifrak JT, Fadale PD, Hulstyn MJ, Labrador DP: Meniscal tissue regeneration using a collagenous biomaterial derived from porcine small intestine submucosa. *Arthroscopy* 2001;17:151-159.

    A rabbit model was used to evaluate the gross appearance and histologic healing of meniscal defects reconstructed with SIS scaffold. At 24 weeks after surgery, the SIS reconstructions appeared grossly restored to normal meniscal ultrastructure. Histology showed SIS repopulation with fibrochondrocytes and normal meniscal-like connective tissue.

12. Musahl V, Abramowitch SD, Gilbert TW, et al: The use of porcine small intestinal submucosa to enhance the healing of the medial collateral ligament: A functional tissue engineering study in rabbits. *J Orthop Res* 2004;22:214-220.

    Medial collateral ligament gap injury healing using SIS graft material was evaluated in a rabbit model. SIS-treated ligaments had a 56% increase in stiffness and an approximately 200% increase in failure load compared with untreated ligaments, but they remained mechanically inferior to normal ligaments.

13. Badylak SF, Kropp B, McPherson T, Liang H, Snyder PW: Small intestinal submucosa: A rapidly resorbed bioscaffold for augmentation cystoplasty in a dog model. *Tissue Eng* 1998;4:379-387.

14. Record RD, Hillegonds D, Simmons C, et al: In vivo degradation of 14C-labeled small intestinal submucosa (SIS) when used for urinary bladder repair. *Biomaterials* 2001;22:2653-2659.

    SIS (14C-proline) was used to repair experimental defects in the urinary bladder of 10 dogs. The remodeled tissue resembled normal bladder tissue in structure and function and contained less than 10% of the 14C-proline 3 months after surgery.

15. Allman AJ, McPherson TB, Badylak SF, et al: Xenogeneic extracellular matrix grafts elicit a TH2-restricted immune response. *Transplantation* 2001; 71:1631-1640.

    Histologic examination of SIS-implanted mice revealed an acute inflammatory response that gradually diminished. The graft ultimately became indistinguishable from native tissue. The observations were consistent with graft acceptance.

16. Badylak SF, Wu CC, Bible M, McPherson E: Host protection against deliberate bacterial contamination of an extracellular matrix bioscaffold versus Dacron mesh in a dog model of orthopedic soft tissue repair. *J Biomed Mater Res B Appl Biomater* 2003;67: 648-654.

    Muscular defects were created in a canine model and then repaired using porcine-derived ECM or Dacron mesh and subsequently inoculated with *Staphylococcus aureus* at surgery. Porcine-derived grafts had better resistance to infection than Dacron mesh 28 days after surgery.

17. Derwin KA, Baker AR, Spragg RK, Leigh DR, Iannotti JP: Commercial extracellular matrix scaffolds for rotator cuff tendon repair: Biomechanical, biochemical and cellular properties. *J Bone Joint Surg Am* 2006;88:2665-2672.

    Biomechanical, biochemical, and cellular testing was performed on GraftJacket, CuffPatch, Restore, and TissueMend. All materials required a 10% to 30% stretch before bearing load in tension, with elastic moduli that were one order of magnitude less than that of canine tendon. TissueMend had the highest level of DNA content.

18. Schlegel TF, Hawkins RJ, Lewis CW, Motta T, Turner AS: The effects of augmentation with swine small intestine submucosa on tendon healing under tension: Histologic and mechanical evaluations in sheep. *Am J Sports Med* 2006;34:275-280.

    Infraspinatus tendons were resected and reattached under tension in 26 sheep, with 13 animals receiving SIS augmentation. Biomechanical testing did not reveal a significant difference in load to failure between the augmented and unaugmented groups. Histologic examination showed that none of the patches remained intact during tendon healing.

19. Perry SM, Van Kleunen JP, Gimble JA, Ramsey ML, Soslowsky LJ, Glaser DL: Use of small intestine submucosa in a rat model of acute and chronic rotator cuff tear. *J Shoulder Elbow Surg* 2007;16:179-183.

   A rat model was used for creating and repairing acute and chronic rotator cuff tears with and without SIS augmentation. SIS-augmented and unaugmented repairs were comparable in acute injuries, but SIS-augmented repairs had improved biomechanical characteristics after healing in chronic injuries.

20. Zalavras CG, Gardocki R, Huang E, Stevanovic M, Hedman T, Tibone J: Reconstruction of large rotator cuff tendon defects with porcine small intestinal submucosa in an animal model. *J Shoulder Elbow Surg* 2006;15:224-231.

   Forty supraspinatus tendon defects were created in a rat model, and half were repaired with SIS interposition. At 16 weeks, fibrous ingrowth and neovascularization was seen histologically. Mechanical strength in the SIS group was 78% of normal, compared with 38% of normal in the control group.

21. Sclamberg SG, Tibone JE, Itamura JM, Kasraeian S: Six-month magnetic resonance imaging follow-up of large and massive rotator cuff repairs reinforced with porcine small intestinal submucosa. *J Shoulder Elbow Surg* 2004;13:538-541.

   In a prospective clinical trial of SIS-reinforced or interpositional grafting of massive rotator cuff tears, MRI revealed retearing 6 months after surgery in 10 of 11 patients. No statistically significant difference appeared between presurgical and postsurgical shoulder scores.

22. Macleod TM, Williams G, Sanders R, Green CJ: Histological evaluation of Permacol as a subcutaneous implant over a 20-week period in the rat model. *Br J Plast Surg* 2005;58:518-532.

   Permacol, a porcine-derived, cross-linked collagen matrix, was evaluated for biocompatibility and tissue remodeling in a Sprague-Dawley rat model. At 20 weeks after implantation, Permacol implants had low-grade chronic inflammation and limited vascular ingrowth.

23. Harper C: Permacol: Clinical experience with a new biomaterial. *Hosp Med* 2001;62:90-95.

   This article is a product overview from Tissue Sciences Laboratories, producer of Permacol.

24. Belcher HJ, Zic R: Adverse effect of porcine collagen interposition after trapeziectomy: A comparative study. *J Hand Surg Br* 2001;26:159-164.

   In a controlled, randomized study of SIS graft interposition used in trapeziectomy for treatment of trapeziometacarpal joint osteoarthritis, 6 of 13 patients who received SIS interposition developed a reaction to the implant. They reported more pain and less satisfaction than 13 patients treated without SIS interposition.

25. Adams JE, Zobitz ME, Reach JS Jr, Steinmann SP: Rotator cuff repair using an acellular dermal matrix graft: An in vivo study in a canine model. *Arthroscopy* 2006;22:700-709.

   Human acellular dermal matrix graft was used to repair a full-thickness infraspinatus tendon injury in a canine model. At 12 weeks, the experimental and unaugmented control repairs had equal strength. At 6 months, the experimental and control specimens mimicked normal tendon structure grossly and histologically.

26. Beniker D, McQuillan D, Livesey S, et al: The use of acellular dermal matrix as a scaffold for periosteum replacement. *Orthopedics* 2003;26(suppl 5):S591-S596.

   Rat and porcine animal models were used to evaluate the ability of GraftJacket, a human-derived acellular dermal matrix, to provide a scaffold for bone healing and periosteum replacement. Good cellular infiltration and new bone formation across segmental bone defects were found.

27. Martin BR, Sangalang M, Wu S, Armstrong DG: Outcomes of allogenic acellular matrix treatment of diabetic foot wounds: An initial experience. *Int Wound J* 2005;2:161-165.

   Seventeen patients with diabetic foot ulcers were treated with surgical débridement and application of GraftJacket, a human-derived acellular dermal matrix, with standard wound care techniques. At an average of 8.9 weeks, 89% of ulcers had healed.

28. Lee MS: GraftJacket augmentation of chronic Achilles tendon ruptures. *Orthopedics* 2004;27(suppl 1):S151-S153.

   In this case report, a 64-year-old woman with an Achilles tendon rupture following long-standing tendinitis was treated with a turn-down gastrocnemius flap and GraftJacket augmentation. The patient had good healing and functional outcome at a 6-month follow-up.

29. Sano H, Kumagai J, Sawai T: Experimental fascial autografting for the supraspinatus tendon defect: Remodeling process of the grafted fascia and the insertion into bone. *J Shoulder Elbow Surg* 2002;11:166-173.

   Supraspinatus tendon defects were created in 21 rabbits and repaired with fascia lata grafts. At 8 weeks, histologic examination showed that the tendinous tissue and its insertion were reformed. The distribution of collagen types II and III was similar to that of a normal tendon.

30. Iannotti JP, Antoniou J, Williams GR, Ramsey ML: Iliotibial band reconstruction for treatment of glenohumeral instability associated with irreparable capsular deficiency. *J Shoulder Elbow Surg* 2002;11:618-623.

   At a minimum 2-year follow-up of 7 patients after allograft iliotibial band reconstruction of the anterior glenohumeral joint capsule for recurrent anterior instability, no patients had postsurgical instability, and American Shoulder and Elbow Surgeons scores had improved significantly (*P* < 0.0004). Level of evidence: IV.

31. Haas F, Seibert FJ, Koch H, et al: Reconstruction of combined defects of the Achilles tendon and the overlying soft tissue with a fascia lata graft and a free fasciocutaneous lateral arm flap. *Ann Plast Surg* 2003;51:376-382.

    Five patients were treated with fascia lata autograft reconstruction of a segmental Achilles tendon defect, with fasciocutaneous lateral arm flap coverage. At a minimum 49-month follow-up, all patients had a good functional and cosmetic outcome.

32. Barber FA, Morley AH, Coon DA: Tendon augmentation grafts: Biomechanical failure loads and failure patterns. *Arthroscopy* 2006;22:534-538.

    In an experimental laboratory study, graft materials were mechanically tested for suture retention load to failure. The mean loads to failure were as follows: GraftJacket, 157 N to 229 N (depending on graft thickness); CuffPatch, 32 N; Restore, 38 N; Permacol, 128 N; and TissueMend, 70 N to 76 N (depending on graft thickness).

33. Itoi E, Berglund LJ, Grabowski JJ, et al: Tensile properties of the supraspinatus tendon. *J Orthop Res* 1995;13:578-584.

34. Halder A, Zobitz ME, Schultz KN: Mechanical properties of the posterior rotator cuff. *Clin Biomech (Bristol, Avon)* 2000;15:456-462.

35. Derwin KA, Baker AR, Spragg RK, Leigh DR, Farat W, Iannotti JP: Regional variability, processing methods and biophysical properties of human fascia lata extracellular matrix. *J Biomed Mater Res* A 2008;84:500-507.

    In a structural, biomechanical, and chemical analysis of human-derived fascia lata allograft, little regional variation in structure or biomechanical properties of fascia lata was seen. Standard acellularization and sterilization techniques did not affect the mechanical properties and left little measurable DNA content.

36. Itoi E, Berglund LJ, Grabowski JJ, Schultz FM, Growney ES, Morrey BF, An KN: Tensile properties of the supraspinatus tendon. *J Orthop Res* 1995;13:578-583.

37. Jarman-Smith ML, Bodamyali T, Stevens C, Howell JA, Horrocks M, Chaudhuri JB: Porcine collagen crosslinking, degradation and its capability for fibroblast adhesion and proliferation. *J Mater Sci Mater Med* 2004;15:925-932.

    Permacol, a cross-linked porcine dermis, was compared with un–cross-linked porcine dermis and bovine Achilles tendon for in vitro fibroblast adhesion and matrix degradation. Permacol had slower fibroblast infiltration and decreased matrix degradation than the other tissues.

38. Valentin JE, Badylak JS, McCabe GP, Badylak SF: Extracellular matrix bioscaffolds for orthopaedic applications: A comparative histologic study. *J Bone Joint Surg Am* 2006;88:2673-2686.

    A Sprague-Dawley rat implantation model was used to evaluate the comparative histology of host response to different ECM devices (SIS, GraftJacket, TissueMend, CuffPatch, Permacol). Each device elicited a unique host response with regard to cellularity (*P* < 0.001), vascularity, and presence of multinucleated giant cells (*P* < 0.01).

# Section 4

# Arthroscopy

Section Editors
Jeffrey S. Abrams, MD
Benjamin Shaffer, MD

# Chapter 20

# Arthroscopic Subacromial Decompression

Richard L. Angelo, MD

## Etiology

Subacromial impingement is a common shoulder disorder that can result in significant disability. Damage to the primary external rotator cuff and the long head of the biceps tendon results from mechanical impingement from the anterior one third of the acromion and the coracoacromial ligament. The key pathologic findings include abrasive changes on the bursal surface of the rotator cuff and hypertrophic-inflammatory bursal scarring resulting from a tight subacromial space (outlet stenosis). Degenerative spurs projecting inferiorly from the acromioclavicular joint are believed to contribute to the pathologic process in some patients. Three levels of increasing severity have been described. Stage I is characterized by rotator cuff edema and hemorrhage (considered reversible); stage II, by tendinitis and rotator cuff fibrosis; and stage III, by full-thickness rotator cuff tearing. Anterosuperior shoulder pain, often caused by repetitive overhead activities, is the most consistent symptom. Disability from subacromial impingement primarily affects patients older than 40 years.[1]

Mechanical impingement can play a significant role in rotator cuff pathology. A recent investigation of 50 patients with a diagnosis of impingement syndrome found that bursoscopic findings correlated well with histopathologic changes on the subacromial surface; even patients whose bursoscopic findings were normal had histologic fibrocartilaginous hypertrophy of the excised coracoacromial ligament.[2] In a study of 25 patients who underwent an anterior acromioplasty, the mean subacromial pressures were measured with the arm positioned in 0°, 90°, and 180° of abduction, as well as hyperabduction and cross-body adduction. The presurgical pressures were 11.7, 35.6, 50.1, 51.1, and 57.4 mm Hg, respectively. Following the acromioplasty, the pressures in the same shoulder positions decreased significantly, to 1.6, 7.8, 15.9, 22.8, and 16.5 mm Hg, respectively.[3]

Intrinsic tendinous degeneration is an alternate explanation of progressive rotator cuff dysfunction.[4] As a result of tendinosis, the ability of the rotator cuff, particularly the subscapularis and infraspinatus–teres minor

force couples, to stabilize the humeral head during elevation is significantly compromised. The resulting superior migration of the head may lead to secondary wear and fraying of the involved tendons, particularly the supraspinatus.

The secondary causes of subacromial impingement include scapular dyskinesia from muscular, tendinous, or neurologic dysfunction, which can result in the failure of the scapula to retract and rotate when the arm is raised overhead. Active scapular retraction may be weak or, less commonly, restricted because of pectoralis minor contracture.[5] Dysfunctional scapular patterns leave the acromial roof closed over the superior rotator cuff and contribute to mechanical impingement. A tight posterior capsule is another possible secondary cause. It has been shown to result in a posterosuperior shift of the axis of rotation of the humeral head in the sagittal plane, causing the humeral head to glide superiorly during elevation and external rotation and permitting abrasion of the exterior rotator cuff.[6] A tight posterior capsule has also been associated with a separate entity called internal impingement. In this condition, the posterosuperior shift of the humeral head is believed to allow the greater tuberosity to impact the posterosuperior glenoid and cause partial-thickness articular-sided rotator cuff and posterosuperior labral tears. This proposed mechanism of articular-sided rotator cuff tearing was called into question when it was shown that in normal shoulders, particularly those of throwing athletes, the greater tuberosity makes contact with the posterosuperior glenoid when the shoulder is in a position of full abduction and external rotation.

Occasionally, an unstable os acromiale may contribute to subacromial impingement. It has not been clearly established whether the optimal treatment is resection of the mesoacromial margins followed by internal fixation or arthroscopic removal of the entire anterior free segment. In a retrospective case series, impingement-related pain was completely relieved after subacromial lidocaine injection in all 12 patients (13 shoulders) who had an unstable mesoacromion. Outcome was satisfactory in 11 of the 13 shoulders according to the

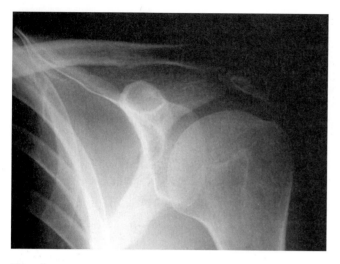

**Figure 1** AP radiograph showing marked lateral acromial downsloping.

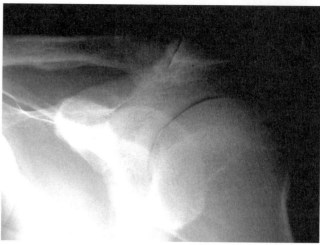

**Figure 2** AP radiograph showing degenerative joint disease with inferior spurring of the acromioclavicular joint.

University of California Los Angeles Shoulder Scale, after modified arthroscopic acromioplasty with removal of the entire mobile anterior acromial fragment. None of the patients had evidence of deltoid detachment, and in all patients the anterior deltoid and rotator cuff muscles had achieved full strength 6 months after surgery, as evaluated by manual muscle testing.[7]

It is important to distinguish patients with primary or secondary mechanical impingement from those with excessive glenohumeral laxity. In younger patients, who are often involved in activities that require overhead arm motion, laxity with excessive anterior-superior translation can cause tendinitis and eventually tendinosis from either rotator cuff stretching or overuse. These patients' anterosuperior shoulder pain is not caused by a tight subacromial space. Therefore, anterior subacromial decompression is not indicated and may worsen the patient's pain. The causes of pathologic glenohumeral instability should be sought and appropriately treated.

## Diagnostic Evaluation

A successful clinical outcome requires obtaining a careful history, a thorough physical examination, and appropriate imaging studies. Pain caused by subacromial impingement typically occurs over the anterior or anterolateral aspect of the shoulder. The discomfort usually worsens with repetitive or forceful overhead activities, and night pain is common. Pain in the region of the trapezius often results from compensatory guarding. If the biceps is significantly involved, the discomfort can extend into the anterior arm. The examination may reveal palpable tenderness over the supraspinatus insertion, greater tuberosity, or anterior acromion, as well as the acromioclavicular region, if that joint is involved. The patient's range of motion may be impaired, especially

flexion, abduction, or internal rotation. The arc of motion from 80° to 120° of elevation in the scapular plane is often painful. Classic impingement signs include pain with either forward hyperflexion, which impinges the supraspinatus against the anterolateral acromion, or maximum internal rotation of the shoulder flexed to 90°, which causes impaction of the greater tuberosity against the deep surface of the acromion. Involvement of the acromioclavicular joint is indicated by tenderness on direct palpation and pain exacerbated by cross-body adduction. Downward pressure on the extended forearm when the shoulder is placed in 90° of flexion, slight adduction, and internal rotation may also cause discomfort. Rotator cuff weakness on examination can be secondary to pain or tendon tearing. Excessive glenohumeral translation is inconsistent with primary subacromial impingement, and it tends to occur in younger patients. The presence of normal scapular mobility, stability, and strength should be confirmed.

The radiographs should include a true AP view to show the degree of lateral slope of the acromion in the coronal plane (Figure 1) and the extent of acromioclavicular degeneration (Figure 2). MRI often shows the relationship of the acromial spurs to underlying rotator cuff pathology (Figure 3). The sagittal acromial profile is determined from the outlet radiographic view. Three types of sagittal acromial profiles are distinguished: type I, relatively flat; type II, having a gentle curve; and type III, having a significant arch or hook on the anterior acromion[8] (Figure 4). Type III has been associated with an increased incidence of rotator cuff pathology. A patient's acromial profile does not appear to change with age. The axillary lateral radiographic view can show acromial spurs projecting anterior to the distal clavicle. Distinct proliferative spurring on the anterior acromion usually represents progressive calcification of the coracoacromial ligament.

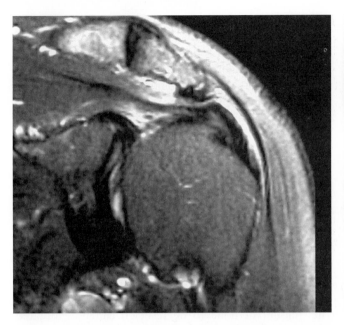

**Figure 3**  Coronal plane MRI showing acromial spur impingement on the rotator cuff.

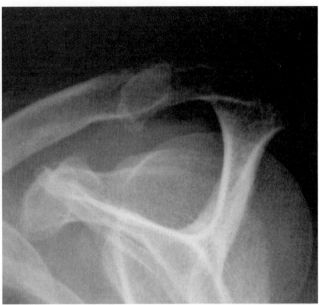

**Figure 4**  Outlet view radiograph showing an acromion with a type III sagittal profile.

It may be necessary to assess the integrity of the rotator cuff. Ultrasonography can be a cost-effective means of studying the rotator cuff tendons, although it is most frequently used in large medical centers, where high study volumes lead to refinements in technique and interpretation and, thus, accuracy. The soft tissues, including the rotator cuff and biceps tendon, can be most comprehensively evaluated using MRI. The extent of rotator cuff tendinosis, as well as partial- and full-thickness tears, can be identified with reasonable accuracy. It is also possible to discern the relationship of impinging bony spurs to the underlying soft tissue and to identify and grade rotator cuff muscle atrophy. Estimating the extent of biceps tendinosis and partial tearing aids in presurgical planning. Imaging of the intra-articular structures can lead to a more comprehensive understanding of the extent of associated pathology.

In a review of 56 patients undergoing an arthroscopic acromioplasty, arthroscopic findings were compared with presurgical radiographic outlet views and T2-weighted parasagittal MRI images for acromial profile shape. Three MRI images were studied: S1, lateral acromial edge; S2, the midacromial region; and S3, lateral aspect of the acromioclavicular joint. The study concluded that outlet view radiographs were superior to any single MRI view for assessing sagittal acromial profile but were inferior to the combination of S1 and S2 MRI views.[9]

Anesthetic injections can be of value in obtaining an accurate diagnosis. Temporary pain relief after injection of 5 cc of 1% lidocaine into the subacromial bursa is a reasonably reliable predictor of a successful outcome following anterior subacromial decompression.[10] Little or no relief of anterolateral shoulder pain suggests that the diagnosis of impingement is incomplete or inaccurate. A posterior approach can be used by passing an 18-gauge spinal needle immediately beneath the posterior acromial margin. Alternatively, because the bursa is a relatively anterolateral structure, accuracy is improved by introducing the needle 1 cm posterior and 2 cm distal to the anterolateral corner of the acromion. At another time, an injection of local anesthetic can be administered into the acromioclavicular joint to help determine the amount of pain caused by acromioclavicular pathology. When acromioclavicular arthritis is present, however, the inferior capsule may be disrupted and permit communication between the acromioclavicular joint and subacromial spaces. As a result, neither an acromioclavicular joint nor a subacromial space injection is completely selective.

## Nonsurgical Treatment

Most patients who have subacromial impingement without significant rotator cuff tendon damage can be successfully treated using nonsurgical measures. However, nonsurgical treatment of subacromial impingement is less effective for a patient with a type III acromial profile than for a patient with a flatter, type I profile.[11] To decrease inflammation, rehabilitation programs recommend the application of ice to the anterolateral shoulder several times daily, the use of nonsteroidal anti-inflammatory drugs, and physical therapy. Stretching to restore glenohumeral and scapulothoracic mobility and strengthening exercises for the rotator cuff, periscapular muscles, and core trunk stabilizers are also essential components. The patient must avoid aggravating physical activities. If these measures fail, a subacromial corticosteroid injection should be considered.

## Arthroscopic Subacromial Decompression
### Indications
The indications for anterolateral acromial resection, as well as the recommended extent of the procedure, have changed during the past several decades because of competing theories regarding the etiology of rotator cuff degeneration. Nonetheless, the value of subacromial decompression in properly selected patients is well established. Evidence of mechanical impingement should be identified before resection of the anterior acromion, regardless of the diagnosis. The findings may include thickened or hemorrhagic bursal tissue, an abraded exterior supraspinatus surface, or a prominent anterolateral bony rim or spur. Occasionally, a thick, excoriated coracoacromial ligament is present, despite a relatively flat acromial profile. It requires débridement and thinning without bone resection.

The symptoms and signs of subacromial impingement should be present for at least 6 months, despite appropriate nonsurgical treatment, before arthroscopic subacromial decompression is considered. In recent years, the need for a routine acromioplasty when the rotator cuff is repaired has been questioned. Some authors believe that a subacromial decompression protects the repair and helps to decrease pain. Others believe that the coracoacromial arch serves a valuable function and should be preserved,[12] or that any bone removal should be limited to smoothing of rough inferior surfaces.[13]

The ability to evaluate extra-articular biceps pathology, as well as subcoracoid impingement, has contributed to a more comprehensive understanding of the causes of anterosuperior shoulder pain. As the understanding of shoulder pathology has grown, the value of thorough arthroscopic evaluation to assess intra-articular and extra-articular pathology has been more fully appreciated. Significant partial-thickness articular-sided rotator cuff, biceps, and labral tears can be readily identified, along with glenohumeral chondral degeneration and loose bodies. It is also important to search for signs of significant adhesive capsulitis, including a thickened, noncompliant, or hemorrhagic capsule, or rotator cuff interval contracture or scarring. Partial anterior acromial resection was originally performed as an open procedure that required detachment and subsequent repair of the deltoid along the anterior acromial margin. Concerns regarding postsurgical failure of the deltoid repair, as well as the evolution and refinement of arthroscopic techniques, have led to the use of arthroscopic techniques for most acromioplasties. With a moderate arthroscopic release of the coracoacromial ligament, the dorsal fascia is left intact and maintains reasonable integrity of the deltoid origin. The coracoacromial ligament scars back to bone. A cadaver study of the effect of an arthroscopic acromioplasty on the acromial attachments of the coracoacromial ligament and anterior fibers of the deltoid found that a bridge of tissue composed of periosteum and collagen fibers of the coracoacromial ligament and deltoid fibers remained attached to the anterosuperior surface of the acromion.[14] However, care must be exercised to avoid excessive bone removal. A simulated arthroscopic acromioplasty was performed in 15 cadaver shoulders, with subsequent histologic evaluation of the anterior acromion, as well as assessment of the deltoid origin and acromial morphology. The researchers found that, with 4 mm of anteroinferior bone resection, 56% (±11%) of the anterior deltoid fibers were detached; with 5.5 mm of bone removed, 77% (±15%) of the fibers were released. The extent of deltoid fibers released was correlated with both acromial thickness and shape.[15]

### Planning
The amount of bone to be resected can be estimated based on radiographic evaluation. Opinion differs on the appropriate extent of bone removal, from simple fine smoothing of the deep acromial surface, to resection limited to the accrued spur, to partial resection of a normal anterior acromion in an attempt to create a flat surface. It is neither possible nor desirable to attempt to create a type I flat profile for every patient. A greatly arched acromial shape cannot be made flat, and the necessarily extensive bone resection risks significantly detaching the deltoid or causing an acromial fracture, especially if the acromion is relatively thin. In patients who have a weak or irreparable rotator cuff tear, the humeral head may gradually escape anterosuperiorly after significant violation of the coracoacromial arch.[16] The options to address this challenging complication are limited.

### Arthroscopic Acromioplasty Technique
Either the beach chair or lateral decubitus position can be used, as determined by the surgeon's familiarity with the orientation or an anticipated need for additional surgical components such as open or arthroscopic rotator cuff repair or biceps tenodesis. The advantages of the beach chair position include an anatomic shoulder orientation; greater freedom of internal and external shoulder rotation; a somewhat easier conversion to an open procedure, if necessary; and simplified airway management. The disadvantages are greater risk in using hypotensive anesthesia, because of the critical minimum systolic pressure necessary to maintain cerebral perfusion; and the need for an assistant or mechanical device to maintain the desired arm position. When the lateral decubitus position is used, the arm is suspended from a boom with a weight of approximately 10 lb. True traction on the arm is seldom necessary; excessive or prolonged traction increases the risk of a neurapraxia.

The surgeon may elect to orient the inferior surface of the acromion vertically, as it truly exists with the patient in the lateral position, or to rotate the camera 90° to place the acromion in a horizontal view, as if the patient were upright.

After the patient is anesthetized and appropriately positioned, padded, and prepped, a skin scribe is used to map the acromion, distal clavicle, and coracoid tip. To minimize bleeding, 25 mL of 0.25% bupivacaine with epinephrine is injected into the subacromial space. The use of hypotensive anesthesia (90 to 100 mm Hg systolic pressure), when medically safe, can assist in maintaining a reasonably clear arthroscopic view. A posterior gleno-humeral portal is marked and established approximately 1.5 cm inferior and 1 cm medial to the posterolateral border of the acromion. The cannula is directed toward the coracoid tip to enter the glenohumeral joint space posteriorly. A thorough diagnostic survey is completed, and any intra-articular pathology is addressed. In particular, the integrity of the long head of the biceps should be assessed, because it is frequently involved in the impingement process. Using a blunt probe, 2 to 3 cm of the extra-articular portion can be drawn into the joint to enhance inspection for damage.

To enter the subacromial bursa, the cannula is withdrawn from the joint and is immediately redirected through the posterior subacromial portal beneath the posteroinferior acromion. The tip of the cannula must be introduced far enough anteriorly to penetrate the posterior wall of the bursa, which is a relatively anterior structure. Once an acceptable view is obtained, a spinal needle is introduced approximately 1 cm posterior and 2.5 cm inferior to the anterolateral corner of the acromion to establish the entry site for the lateral subacromial (LSA) portal. Resection of thickened bursal tissue with a motorized shaver or radiofrequency wand may be necessary to obtain a "room with a view." Soft tissue is removed from the inferior surface of the anterior one third of the acromion. It is not necessary to completely detach the coracoacromial ligament. However, the anterior and anterolateral margins of the acromion, including any osteophytes that have formed because of calcification of the coracoacromial ligament, must be clearly defined. The acromial branch of the thoracoacromial artery is consistently present beneath the coracoacromial ligament at the mid-anterior acromion and usually requires cauterization.

Several methods have been described to accurately resect bone and decompress the subacromial space. In past years, the attempt to create a type I flat acromion in most patients often led to excessive, unnecessary bone removal. In recent years, a more conservative method has been recommended; only the prominent anterior rim of bone and any associated osteophytes are removed. Some authors even promote a very limited smoothing, with preservation of the entire coracoacromial arch.[13] The cutting-block technique has been used

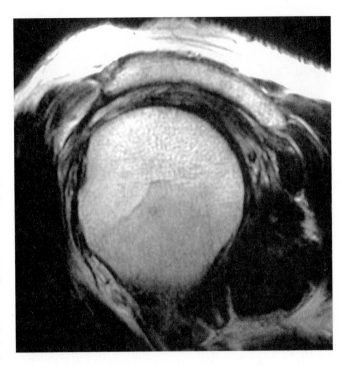

**Figure 5**  Sagittal plane MRI showing a thin type III acromion.

for approximately 15 years, but it carries a significant risk of excessive bone removal. If the shape of the acromion is arched, little or no flat posterior surface may exist in the appropriate plane of resection to use as a true cutting-block guide (Figure 5). Or, if the burr sheath does not rest directly on the posterior rim of bone, the burr approaches the acromial arch at an overly steep angle, and the result is excessive bone removal. Attempts at compensation can result in excessive thinning of the acromion and increased potential for fracture.

A cutting-bar technique is safer than other methods, and it substantially preserves the integrity of the coracoacromial arch. While being viewed from the LSA portal, a barrel-shaped burr is introduced from the posterior subacromial (PSA) portal immediately inferior to the posterior border of the acromion, as in the cutting-block technique. However, the burr tip begins to resect bone from the most inferior extent of the anterior acromion and works progressively superior, instead of beginning near the apex of the acromial arch. It is rarely necessary to resect more than 5 to 7 mm of the bone anteriorly. The plane of this resection does not reach posteriorly to the apex of the acromion if a significant arch is present. When the appropriate level of resection is established in the sagittal plane, the arthroscope is moved to the posterior viewing portal and, with the burr in the LSA portal, enough of the anterolateral aspect of the acromion is removed to make it flush with the initial plane of resection (Figure 6). Slight feathering at the posterior extent of the resection completes the acromioplasty.

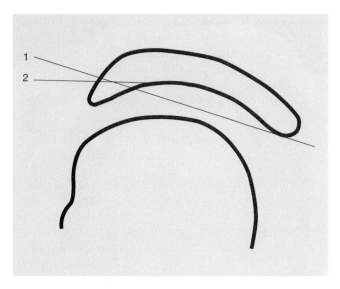

**Figure 6** Diagram of a sagittal acromial profile. Line 1 defines the initial anterior acromial resection using the posterior acromion as a cutting bar. Line 2 defines the final anterior acromial chamfering.

In an alternate method, the burr is first introduced through the LSA portal and is used to establish the depth of anterior resection along the anterior margin of the acromion. The burr is then moved to the posterior portal, where the anterior one fourth of the acromion is carefully planed down to the previously established depth. If presurgical imaging showed significant lateral downsloping of the acromion, the anterolateral rim must be adequately removed, possibly resulting in removal of more bone anterolaterally than anteromedially.

### Distal Clavicle Resection

Controversy exists as to whether coplaning of distal inferior clavicular spurs is preferable to a formal distal clavicular resection or the Mumford procedure. Simple coplaning is readily accomplished by introducing the burr from the lateral acromial portal and removing the inferior clavicular spur along the plane established by the acromioplasty. If a formal partial distal claviculectomy is elected, the arthroscope is placed in the PSA portal. A radiofrequency wand is delivered through the LSA portal and used to remove soft tissue from the inferior distal clavicle. A spinal needle is then introduced just superior and lateral to the tip of the coracoid, which enters anteriorly in the plane of the acromioclavicular joint. Using a motorized burr, resection is begun anteriorly; a 6- to 8-mm depth of resection of the distal clavicle is established using the burr diameter as a reference guide. Bone removal proceeds from anteroinferior to posterosuperior. A 70° arthroscope inserted from either the PSA or the LSA portal may be used to confirm the adequacy of bone removal, especially from the posterosuperior aspect of the clavicle. Final confirmation of appropriate bone removal can be performed from the anterior portal with a 30° arthroscope.

### Rehabilitation

Ice, nonsteroidal anti-inflammatory drugs, and oral analgesics can be used to control postsurgical pain. For the first 3 days after surgery, the patient uses a simple sling and performs 10 minutes of pendulum exercises four times each day. Gentle, progressive passive range of motion exercises are initiated on the fourth day, with the goal of attaining complete passive motion in 3 to 4 weeks. Rotator cuff isometrics are started 1 week after surgery, and progressive resistive rotator cuff and periscapular strengthening exercises are started after 3 weeks. Activity restrictions are lifted by the sixth to eighth week. Formal physical therapy is rarely necessary.

### Complications

Several causes of persistent anterosuperior pain following an acromioplasty have been identified. Inadequate bone resection or decompression of the subacromial space has been considered a common cause of failure, but this belief must be reconciled with the developing opinion that bony resection is rarely necessary and that, at most, a smoothing of the anteroinferior surface of the acromion should considered. Inappropriate acromial resection is detrimental and may lead to the creation of sharp ridges of bone, excessive bone removal, and even acromial fracture. Insufficient posterosuperior bone removal from the distal clavicle may be responsible for persistent postsurgical pain, particularly with shoulder adduction. Hypertrophic subacromial scarring can also lead to a poor result and may contribute to loss of motion. In a comparison study of 36 patients, 18 underwent an open revision decompression for refractory subacromial impingement and 18 underwent a similar arthroscopic procedure. Dense subacromial scarring was present in all patients, and residual prominent bone or an acromial spur was present in 56%. In the arthroscopic group, 94% of patients were satisfied with their revision procedure, compared with 44% in the open group.[17]

Perhaps the most common cause of inadequate pain relief is an inaccurate or incomplete diagnosis. The presurgical finding that most reliably predicts a successful result is a positive subacromial injection test. The test may need to be repeated if it produces only marginal pain relief, to be certain that the lidocaine was accurately introduced into the subacromial bursa. Other shoulder pathologies that may be responsible for persistent pain include glenohumeral instability and an unrecognized or insufficiently treated rotator cuff, biceps, or labral disorder. An excessively tight posterior capsule can lead to secondary impingement of the rotator cuff. A patient with this condition usually responds to an internal rotation stretching program and does not require an arthroscopic posterior capsular release. Infection, bleeding, neurovascular injury, and reflex sympathetic dystrophy are rare following subacromial decompression. Heterotopic ossification is rare after an acromioplasty, but it may occur following distal clavicle resection.

Concern exists that an acromioplasty could possibly destabilize the acromioclavicular joint. A study using 18 cadaver specimens examined the effect of subacromial decompression on the laxity of the acromioclavicular joint. Each shoulder was dissected, and the anterior, posterior, and superior laxity of the intact joint was documented using 100-N loads in each direction. An arthroscopic acromioplasty was then performed, with coplaning of the distal clavicle. When the same loads were again applied, superior compliance was increased by 32% and anterosuperior compliance, by 13%. Although coplaning appeared to increase the mobility of the acromioclavicular joint, the clinical significance of the findings has not been determined.[18]

## Results

A comprehensive review of the literature on open and arthroscopic decompression for subacromial impingement found that the results of the two procedures were not significantly different.[19] The objective success rate in both groups was approximately 80%, and the subjective success rate in both groups was 90%.

In a comparison of arthroscopic and open acromioplasty, 62 patients were evaluated in a prospective, randomized, controlled, and blinded clinical trial. The open and arthroscopic acromioplasty groups were identical with respect to duration of symptoms, shoulder functional demand, age, sex, hand dominance, mechanism of onset, range of motion, strength, joint laxity, and presence of a workers' compensation claim. No significant difference was found between the groups in patient satisfaction, strength, or University of California Los Angeles score. Open acromioplasty appeared to be superior to arthroscopic acromioplasty in pain and functional results. The extent and adequacy of acromial resection may have influenced the results, but a postsurgical radiographic evaluation was not performed.[20]

At an average 32-month follow-up after anterior acromioplasty, 106 consecutive patients of a single surgeon had significant improvements in scores on the American Shoulder and Elbow Surgeons Shoulder Index, the Simple Shoulder Test, and a visual analog pain scale. The scores did not differ by workers' compensation status, although the average time until return to full-duty work differed significantly between the workers' compensation group (13.7 weeks) and the non–workers' compensation group (9.1 weeks). The level of physical work demand directly affected the time to return to full duty, regardless of workers' compensation status.[21]

A retrospective review of 105 patients (107 shoulders) with a normal rotator cuff or a grade I or II partial thickness tear used the L'Insalata outcome questionnaire at an average of 52 months after an anterior acromioplasty. This self-administered questionnaire is a region-specific, validated, 100-point score with domains of global assessment, pain, daily activities, recreational and athletic activities, work satisfaction, and areas for improvement. The average score for the three rotator cuff groups was 90 points. Treatment failure (a score < 70 points) was indicated in three of eight patients (38%) with a bursal-sided tear 3 to 6 mm deep; therefore, an acromioplasty alone was deemed insufficient for this group. There was no evidence after 10 years that the clinical results had deteriorated.[22]

The necessity for an acromioplasty is being debated even for a full-thickness rotator cuff tear. In 96 patients undergoing an open rotator cuff repair performed through a deltoid-splitting approach, an acromioplasty was not performed, and the coracoacromial arch was completely preserved. Sixty-one of the patients completed periodic self-assessments using the Simple Shoulder Test and the Medical Outcomes Study Short Form-36 Health Survey, for a minimum of 2 years and an average of 5 years. The percentage of shoulders that were capable of performing each of the 12 tests on the Simple Shoulder Test significantly improved. Improvement in the number of tests performed was inversely correlated with the number of tendons involved in the repair.[13]

Subcoracoid impingement has received substantially less attention than subacromial impingement, although it is a potential cause of anterior shoulder pain. Reduction of the subcoracoid space can result in impingement of the subscapularis, particularly if the space is less than 7 mm. In a review of 216 patients who had undergone rotator cuff repair and acromioplasty, 11 patients had persistent anterior shoulder pain, localized tenderness at the coracoid process, anterior shoulder pain on horizontal adduction, and a positive subcoracoid block test. Nine patients who had not responded to 6 months of nonsurgical treatment underwent a coracoplasty, and all obtained complete pain relief.[23]

## Summary

Primary subacromial impingement of the rotator cuff caused by outlet stenosis of the coracoacromial arch and a degenerative acromioclavicular joint can result in an abraded rotator cuff, hemorrhagic bursa, anterior acromial spurs, and degeneration of the long head of the biceps tendon. Scapular dyskinesia, a tight posterior capsule, and an os acromiale are significantly less common causes. Patients with excessive glenohumeral laxity may experience rotator cuff tendinitis and eventually tendinosis from overuse, rather than mechanical impingement. Pain when performing forceful or repetitive overhead activities is the most common symptom of subacromial impingement, and positive impingement signs as well as a painful arc from 80° to 120° are the most common examination findings. A positive lidocaine injection test can confirm the diagnosis with reasonable certainty. Radiographs can reveal significant lateral acromial downsloping on the AP view or a type III sagittal profile on the outlet view.

Nonsurgical treatment is successful for approximately 85% of patients with subacromial impingement. Of those who continue to be symptomatic, 80% to 90% have a good or excellent outcome after arthroscopic subacromial decompression. The trend during the past decade has been toward more conservative bone resection and preservation of the coracoacromial arch. If the acromioclavicular joint has significant degeneration and spurring, an arthroscopic partial distal claviculectomy completes the decompression. The most common complication is inaccurate or inappropriate resection of the anterior acromion, and the most serious complication is complete detachment of the coracoacromial ligament in a patient with an irreparable rotator cuff. The loss of integrity of the coracoacromial arch and resulting anterosuperior escapement of the humeral head are extremely difficult to correct. With care and attention to detail, arthroscopic subacromial decompression has a high success rate in appropriately selected patients.

## Annotated References

1.  Neer CS II: Anterior acromioplasty for the chronic impingement syndrome in the shoulder. *J Bone Joint Surg Am* 1972;54A:41-50.

2.  Suenaga N, Minami A, Fukuda K, Kaneda K: The correlation between bursoscopic and histologic findings of the acromion. *Arthroscopy* 2002;18:16-20.

    In 50 patients who underwent an arthroscopic acromioplasty, subacromial bursoscopic findings were well correlated with histopathologic changes on the undersurface and anterior aspect of the acromial arch. Even patients whose bursoscopic findings were normal had fibrocartilaginous hypertrophy at the insertion of the coracoacromial ligament onto the anterior acromion.

3.  Nordt WE III, Garretson RB III, Plotkin E: The measurement of subacromial contact pressure in patients with impingement syndrome. *Arthroscopy* 1999;15: 121-125.

4.  Budoff JE, Nirschl RP, Guidi EJ: Debridement of partial-thickness tears of the rotator cuff without acromioplasty: Long term follow-up and review of the literature. *J Bone Joint Surg Am* 1998;80:733-748.

5.  Ludewig PM, Cook TM: Alterations in shoulder kinematics and associated muscle activity in people with symptoms of shoulder impingement. *Phys Ther* 2000; 80:276-291.

6.  Fitzpatrick MJ, Tibone JE, Grossman M, McGarry MH, Lee TQ: Development of cadaveric models of a thrower's shoulder. *J Shoulder Elbow Surg* 2005; 14(suppl 1):49S-57S.

    In a cadaver model of a thrower's shoulder, the coracohumeral ligament was retained, with the glenoid positioned parallel to the ground and the humerus in 60° elevation in the scapular plane. With posterior capsular plication, the humeral head shifted superiorly with maximal external glenohumeral rotation.

7.  Wright RW, Heller MA, Quick DC, Buss DD: Arthroscopic decompression for impingement syndrome secondary to an unstable os acromiale. *Arthroscopy* 2000;16:595-599.

8.  Nicholson GP, Goodman DA, Flatow EL, Bigliani LU: The acromion: Morphologic condition and age-related changes. A study of 420 scapulas. *J Shoulder Elbow Surg* 1996;5:1-11.

9.  Mayerhoefer ME, Breitenseher MJ, Roposch A, Treitl C, Wurnig C: Comparison of MRI and conventional radiography for assessment of acromial shape. *AJR Am J Roentgenol* 2005;184:671-675.

    Outlet view radiographs and T2-weighted parasagittal MRI images were compared with arthroscopic findings for acromial profile shape. The radiographs were superior for this purpose to any single MRI view but inferior to a combination of S1 and S2 views.

10. Lim JT, Acornley A, Dodenhoff RM: Recovery after arthroscopic subacromial decompression: Prognostic value of the subacromial injection test. *Arthroscopy* 2005;21:680-683.

    After subacromial injection of a local anesthetic and steroid preparation for subacromial impingement syndrome, 101 patients underwent arthroscopic subacromial decompression. A positive presurgical injection test significantly predicted successful arthroscopic subacromial decompression. Level of evidence: III.

11. Wang JC, Horner G, Brown ED, Shapiro MS: The relationship between acromial morphology and conservative treatment of patients with impingement syndrome. *Orthopedics* 2000;23:557-559.

12. Gartsman GM, O'Connor DP: Arthroscopic rotator cuff repair with and without subacromial decompression: A prospective, randomized study of one-year outcomes. *J Shoulder Elbow Surg* 2004;13:424-426.

    To determine whether arthroscopic subacromial decompression changes the outcome of patients with a full-thickness rotator cuff tear and type II acromion, patients received cuff repair with or without acromioplasty. Postsurgical American Shoulder and Elbow Surgeons Shoulder Index scores and functional outcomes did not differ significantly over time.

13. McCallister WV, Parsons IM, Titleman RM, Matsen FA III: Open rotator cuff repair without acromioplasty. *J Bone Joint Surg Am* 2005;87:1278-1283.

    At 2-year follow-up after open rotator cuff repair through a deltoid-splitting approach without formal acromioplasty, the percentage of shoulders that could be used for the Simple Shoulder Test functions increased significantly.

14. Hunt JL, Moore RJ, Krishnan J: The fate of the coracoacromial ligament in arthroscopic acromioplasty: An anatomical study. *J Shoulder Elbow Surg* 2000;9: 491-494.

15. Green A, Griggs S, Labrador D: Anterior acromial anatomy: Relevance to arthroscopic acromioplasty. *Arthroscopy* 2004;20:1050-1054.

    Simulated arthroscopic acromioplasty performed on cadaver shoulders found that the amount of deltoid fiber released was correlated with acromial thickness and shape.

16. Wiley AM: Superior humeral dislocation: A complication following decompression and debridement for rotator cuff tears. *Clin Orthop Relat Res* 1991;263: 135-141.

17. Connor PM, Yamaguchi K, Pollock RG, Flatow EL, Bigliani LU: Comparison of open and arthroscopic revision decompression for failed anterior acromioplasty. *Orthopedics* 2000;23:549-554.

18. Deshmukh AV, Perlmuter GS, Zilberfarb JL, Wilson DR: Effect of subacromial decompression on laxity of the acromioclavicular joint: Biomechanical testing in a cadaveric model. *J Shoulder Elbow Surg* 2004;13: 338-343.

    A cadaver study of the effect of subacromial decompression on the laxity of the acromioclavicular joint found that coplaning appears to increase the compliance of the acromioclavicular joint. The clinical significance of these findings has yet to be determined.

19. Checroun AJ, Dennis MG, Zuckerman JD: Open versus arthroscopic decompression for subacromial impingement: A comprehensive review of the literature from the last 25 years. *Bull Hosp Jt Dis* 1998;57:145-151.

20. Spangehl MJ, Hawkins RH, McCormack RG, Loomer RL: Arthroscopic vs. open acromioplasty: A prospective, randomized, blinded study. *J Shoulder Elbow Surg* 2002;11:101-107.

    Seventy-one patients with impingement syndrome were randomized to arthroscopic or open acromioplasty. Postsurgical improvement, patient satisfaction, University of California Los Angeles score, and strength did not differ significantly between the two groups. Open acromioplasty resulted in superior improvement in pain and function.

21. Nicholson GP: Arthroscopic acromioplasty: A comparison between workers' compensation and non-workers' compensation population. *J Bone Joint Surg Am* 2003;85:682-689.

    At an average 32-month follow-up after arthroscopic subacromial decompression performed by one surgeon, the average American Shoulder and Elbow Surgeons score of 106 patients with impingement syndrome improved from 41.8 to 86.9; the Simple Shoulder Test score, from 5.1 to 10.0, and the visual analog scale pain score, from 6.0 to 1.1. Workers' compensation status was not significantly related to outcome scores but was related to average time to return to full-duty work.

22. Cordasco FA, Backer M, Craig EV, Klein D, Warren RF: The partial-thickness rotator cuff tear: Is acromioplasty without repair sufficient? *Am J Sports Med* 2002;30:257-260.

    A clinical outcome evaluation of arthroscopic acromioplasty was performed in 162 patients with a normal rotator cuff or a grade I or grade II partial-thickness rotator cuff tear. With follow-up extending to 10 years, no evidence appeared that clinically relevant or symptomatic intrinsic rotator cuff pathology progresses in patients with partial-thickness tears treated with arthroscopic anterior acromioplasty.

23. Suenaga N, Minami A, Kaneda K: Postoperative subcoracoid impingement syndrome in patients with rotator cuff tear. *J Shoulder Elbow Surg* 2000;9:275-278.

# Chapter 21

# Arthroscopic Acromioclavicular Resection

Kenneth J. Accousti, MD

Evan L. Flatow, MD

## Introduction

The acromioclavicular (AC) joint is a common source of shoulder pain and disability. It can be the only cause of a patient's pain, or it can contribute to pain from disorders such as subacromial impingement (Table 1). Failure to recognize the contribution of the AC joint to an underlying pathology can lead to unsuccessful treatment and continuing pain.[1]

## Diagnosis

Patients with AC osteoarthritis report pain over the anterosuperior aspect of the shoulder. The pain is exacerbated by movement, especially by cross-body adduction, forward flexion, or internal rotation of the shoulder. During these movements, the acromion is compressed into the distal clavicle, and pain is produced. Patients who have had an AC separation may report instability or snapping with arm movement. Athletes report pain with overhead throwing when the arm is brought forward and across the body during the acceleration and follow-through phases. Weight lifters describe soreness over the distal clavicle that is exacerbated during workouts, especially with bench press, push-up, or dip exercises (Figure 1).

Careful inspection of the AC joint is important. A diagnosis of AC joint pathology is easily made if the patient has a history of trauma or AC separation, but it can be overlooked in a patient with impingement, osteoarthritis, or rotator cuff disease. AC joint degeneration is commonly seen on radiographs of asymptomatic elderly patients. Its presence must be confirmed clinically; the classic tests include direct tenderness to palpation and pain with AP translation.[2] The AC joint is directly anterior to Neviaser's triangle, which is the soft spot between the posterior distal clavicle and scapular spine. Cross-body adduction can elicit discomfort in the posterior aspect of the shoulder, especially in a patient with a tight posterior glenohumeral joint capsule or a superior labrum anterior and posterior (SLAP) tear, and it is important to differentiate this pain from pain occurring directly over the AC joint. Patients with subacromial or subcoracoid impingement also may have pain with cross-body adduction. The O'Brien test (forward flexion with the arm adducted 10° and internally rotated with the thumb down) can be used to elicit pain over a degenerated AC joint. The patient should be asked to specify the location of pain to differentiate between a SLAP tear, which produces posterior or deep pain, and AC arthritis, which produces anterosuperior pain. Adduction, internal rotation, and extension can be used to isolate the posterior AC facet and produce pain, especially after incomplete resection of the distal clavicle.

Although radiographs can be used to confirm the clinical suspicion of AC joint disease, they should not be the sole determinant of whether the AC joint is a source of pain. Standard AP and 30° (scapular plane) AP views of the shoulder, as well as scapular Y and axillary views, are used. In the Zanca view, which is used to isolate the AC joint from the scapula, the x-ray beam is angled 10° to 15° cephalad and is centered over the AC joint; the

### Table 1 | Causes of Primary and Secondary Acromioclavicular Pain

**Primary Pain**

Crystalline arthropathy (gout, pseudogout)

Degenerative arthritis

Distal clavicular osteolysis

Infection

Inflammatory arthropathy (rheumatoid arthritis, systemic lupus erythematosus)

Instability and posttraumatic arthritis (AC separation or fracture)

**Secondary Pain**

Adhesive capsulitis

Calcific tendinitis

Cervical disk disease

Glenohumeral arthritis

Subacromial impingement and rotator cuff disease

Subcoracoid impingement

Visceral afferent stimulation (cardiac, gastrointestinal, pulmonary)

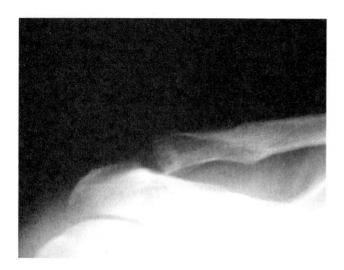

**Figure 1** AP radiograph showing distal clavicular osteolysis in a 24-year-old athlete. The AC joint is widened, and subchondral lytic areas are present in the distal clavicle.

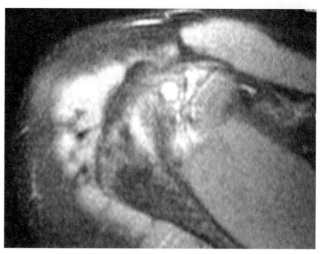

**Figure 2** T2-weighted axial MRI showing AC joint degeneration with subchondral cysts. Bone edema is present in both the distal clavicle and acromion, and the posterior half of the AC joint is tighter.

kilovoltage is decreased to enable better delineation of subtle changes in the distal clavicle, such as osteolysis. Stress-view radiographs, taken with 10- to 15-lb weights in each of the patient's hands, can help in detecting subtle superior-inferior instability, especially when they are compared with radiographs of the opposite shoulder.

MRI and technetium Tc 99m bone scans are more sensitive than radiographs in detecting AC joint pathology, but they are not routinely used because they are costly. AC arthritis is seen on MRI with an increasing frequency related to increasing patient age. However, the condition may be asymptomatic. Bone edema within the distal clavicle or acromion is not seen in asymptomatic individuals, and it is highly predictive of AC pathology[3,4] (Figure 2).

Injection of a local anesthetic and a corticosteroid into the AC joint can relieve the patient's pain and help differentiate between subacromial and AC joint pain; 1 mL of lidocaine and 1 mL of an intermediate- or long-acting corticosteroid such as betamethasone is usually a sufficient dosage. Relief of pain after injection also can be used to predict that the patient would benefit from distal clavicular resection. Insertion of a needle into the AC joint can be difficult, especially if the degenerative changes are advanced and the joint space is narrowed. It is easiest to enter the AC joint anteriorly, where it is widest. The patient must have reproducible symptoms on physical examination at the time of injection.

## Anatomy

The AC joint is a noncongruous, diarthrodial synovial joint. The concave acromial facet and the convex distal clavicle are covered by hyaline cartilage that is separated by a fibrocartilage meniscus. The clavicle acts as a strut to support the shoulder girdle and upper extremity and is the only bony connection between the arm and axial skeleton. The AC joint usually slopes medially in a superior to inferior direction, although individual anatomic differences exist.

The AC joint is supported by the superior and inferior AC capsular ligaments. The superior AC ligament is stronger than the inferior AC ligament, and it is the primary restraint against translation of the distal clavicle in the AP plane. Men have a broader superior AC capsule insertion than women. According to one study, female cadaver shoulders had disruption of the superior AC joint capsule after 5.2 mm of distal clavicular resection, on average.[5] The conoid and trapezoid ligaments are the primary restraints providing superior-inferior stability during large displacement of the clavicle. The lateral margin of the trapezoid ligament insertion on the clavicle is more than 11 mm from the AC joint in both males and females. Most clavicular motion occurs at the sternoclavicular joint, and a relatively small amount of rotation occurs at the AC joint. The acromion can also slide with scapular protraction or retraction and can tilt with arm abduction, relative to the distal clavicle.

## Nonsurgical Treatment

Pain related to the AC joint is initially treated with nonsteroidal anti-inflammatory drugs. Weight lifters who have osteolysis of the distal clavicle should modify their workout and avoid bench press, dip, fly, push-up, and military press exercises. Physical therapy can improve the range of motion and strength of the rotator cuff, deltoid, and parascapular musculature, but it has no specific role in AC joint disease. A lidocaine-corticosteroid injection can be used to reduce pain and inflammation around the AC joint. If infection is suspected, joint aspiration can be performed, but corticosteroids should not be used.

Nonsurgical treatment is usually effective in reducing pain and inflammation in the shoulder. If the symptoms persist for more than 6 months and are interfering with daily activities, distal clavicular resection should be considered.

## Surgical Treatment

Open distal clavicular resection was first described in 1941, and a minimally invasive approach was adopted with the advent of shoulder arthroscopy. Arthroscopic resection permits smaller incisions and preservation of the deltoid and trapezial fascia, which allow for more rapid rehabilitation. Two arthroscopic approaches, the indirect bursal and direct, can be used for distal clavicular resection; long-term follow-up studies have found no difference in outcomes between the two approaches.

The indirect approach allows the surgeon to see the subacromial space and rotator cuff and thus facilitates arthroscopic subacromial decompression and repair of any associated cuff tears. The patient can be positioned in either the beach chair or lateral decubitus position, based on the surgeon's preference. A subacromial viewing portal is used. The arthroscope is placed in a posterior or lateral portal, and an accessory portal is placed into the AC joint from the anterosuperior margin of the AC joint. The superficial landmarks identified at the start of the operation are often difficult to find when swelling caused by saline has begun, and a 1-inch, 19-gauge needle may be helpful in locating the AC joint. A stab incision is made through the skin, and a blunt metal trocar is introduced into the joint to create a smooth path for the radiofrequency probe, shaver, and burr. Precise creation of this portal preserves the superior AC capsule, preventing postsurgical instability.

To improve the ability to see the AC joint, subacromial decompression and bursectomy should be performed first. Resection of the inferior AC joint capsule with radiofrequency cautery and removal of the undersurface of the acromial facet allows excellent visualization of the distal clavicle. The radiofrequency probe and shaver are used to clear any remaining soft tissue and capsule from the inferior portion of the capsule, and the burr is then used to resect 5 to 10 mm of distal clavicle. The acromial facet can be débrided slightly to decrease the amount of distal clavicular resection. The arthroscope should be placed directly into the AC joint to confirm complete resection of the distal clavicle. The posterosuperior portion of the distal clavicle is frequently overlooked; if it is not resected, the patient may have continuing pain.

The direct, superior approach to distal clavicular resection is more technically demanding than the indirect approach. The direct approach is used for patients with isolated AC joint pathology, if the subacromial space does not need to be violated, and for younger patients

with osteolysis, who have wider AC joints and require less bone resection. A viewing portal is created in Neviaser's triangle at the posterior border of the AC joint, and a working portal is placed in the anterior portion of the joint. Standard shoulder arthroscopy instruments are used, but small joint arthroscopes and burrs may be needed to widen the joint so that larger instruments can then be used.

The clinical results of the indirect and direct approaches to distal clavicular resection are similar, although one study found a higher revision rate after use of the direct approach, caused by instability or recurrence of symptoms after inadequate resection.[6] The choice of the indirect or direct approach does not lead to a biomechanical difference in AP translation, if the superior AC ligament was preserved.[7]

The optimal amount of resection is controversial. In the past, as much as 2 cm of distal clavicle was routinely resected. Studies evaluating coracoclavicular and AC ligament insertion onto the distal clavicle and acromion found that 11 mm of resection does not violate the insertion of the trapezoid ligament in either males or females. A smaller resection (5 to 7 mm) should be performed in women to preserve the insertion of the superior AC ligament. Resection of the acromial side of the AC joint decreases the amount of distal clavicular resection needed for adequate decompression and helps preserve the superior AC ligament insertion.

Resection of the distal clavicle in patients with AC joint instability further destabilizes the joint. Biomechanical studies have shown that preexisting instability of the distal clavicle is increased if resection or coplaning is performed without coracoclavicular ligament reconstruction. A combination of subacromial decompression and distal clavicular resection does not lead to instability of the distal clavicle, and the long-term results have been uniformly good to excellent.[8,9] Concern exists about instability following coplaning of the distal clavicle combined with subacromial decompression.[10] However, violation of the inferior AC ligament during coplaning has not led to instability of the distal clavicle or increased AC joint pain after subacromial decompression with clavicular coplaning.[11]

### Rehabilitation

After isolated resection of the distal clavicle, passive range of motion exercises can be started as soon as the patient can tolerate them. Active and active-assisted range of motion exercises are started within 2 weeks of surgery, and resistive exercises are allowed at 3 weeks. Athletes can return to unlimited sports activity at 6 weeks. If rotator cuff repair or coracoclavicular ligament reconstruction was performed, protection with a sling is needed for as long as 6 weeks, depending on the size of the tear repair.

### Complications

The most common complication of arthroscopic distal clavicular resection is continuing pain resulting from inadequate resection. During the procedure, the ability to see the entire AC joint can be hindered by bleeding from the resected edge of the clavicle, as well as soft-tissue edema and medial fat. The result is that the posterosuperior edge of the clavicle is frequently not resected and will continue to cause abutment of the clavicle into the posterior acromial facet. Even after a complete resection, heterotopic ossification can occur, and retained bone fragments attached to the superior capsule can lead to formation of ectopic calcification. Excessive clavicular resection, which violates the coracoclavicular ligaments, leads to instability of the distal clavicle.

## Summary

Failure to recognize and treat AC joint pathology is a common cause of unsatisfactory results after arthroscopic shoulder surgery.[1] All patients should be clinically evaluated for pain and instability in the AC joint. Arthroscopic distal clavicular resection is a proven technique to address AC joint pathology. The risk of complications is minimal if the procedure is performed correctly through either a direct or indirect bursal approach. Concomitant subacromial decompression with coplaning or complete distal clavicular resection has good to excellent results and does not increase AC joint instability. Resection of 7 to 10 mm of distal clavicle may violate the superior AC ligament but not the trapezoid ligament. Partial resection of the acromial facet will decrease the amount needed for an adequate distal clavicular resection and help to preserve the superior AC joint ligament. Common pitfalls include overzealous resection, which leads to instability of the resected distal clavicle, and inadequate resection, especially of the posterosuperior quadrant of the clavicle, which leads to continuing pain. AC joint resection should not be performed in a patient with AC instability unless clavicular stabilization is simultaneously performed to prevent increased instability of the clavicle.

## Annotated References

1. Shaffer BS: Painful conditions of the acromioclavicular joint. *J Am Acad Orthop Surg* 1999;7: 176-188.

2. Walton J, Mahajan S, Paxinos A, et al: Diagnostic values of tests for acromioclavicular joint pain. *J Bone Joint Surg Am* 2004;86:807-812.

   AC tenderness was the most sensitive (96%) but least specific (10%) test for AC joint pathology; the O'Brien test was the most specific (90%) but least sensitive (16%). A positive bone scan and Paxinos test together predicted symptomatic AC joint pathology (99% probability); one negative test reduced the likelihood ratio to 0.03:1. Level of evidence: I.

3. Stein BE, Wiater M, Pfaff HC, Bigliani LU, Levine WN: Detection of acromioclavicular joint pathology in asymptomatic shoulders with magnetic resonance imaging. *J Shoulder Elbow Surg* 2001;10:204-208.

   Of 50 patients with asymptomatic AC joints, 68% of those younger than 30 years had arthritic changes on MRI, and 93% of those age 30 years or older had evidence of arthritic degeneration. The arthritis was more advanced in the older patients but was not correlated with clinical symptoms.

4. Shubin Stein BE, Ahmad CS, Pfaff HC, Bigliani LU, Levine WN: A comparison of magnetic resonance imaging findings of the acromioclavicular joint in symptomatic versus asymptomatic patients. *J Shoulder Elbow Surg* 2006;15:56-59.

   Eighty percent of patients with symptomatic AC disease had reactive bone edema in the distal clavicle or acromion on MRI. No asymptomatic patients had reactive bone edema.

5. Renfree KJ, Riley MK, Wheeler D, Hentz JG, Wright TW: Ligamentous anatomy of the distal clavicle. *J Shoulder Elbow Surg* 2003;12:355-359.

   Dissection revealed no statistical difference between male and female cadaver specimens (41 total specimens) in distance from the distal clavicle to the trapezoid ligament insertion. Resection of less than 11 mm should not violate the lateral insertion of the trapezoid ligament. Resection of more than 5.2 mm of the distal clavicle in women and 7.6 mm in men disrupted the insertion of the superior AC joint capsule, although these data were obtained from only three specimens. Resection from both the acromial and clavicular sides of the AC joint is suggested for preserving the attachment of the superior AC ligament.

6. Levine WN, Soong M, Ahmad CS, Blaine TA, Bigliani LU: Arthroscopic distal clavicle resection: A comparison of bursal and direct approaches. *Arthroscopy* 2006;22:516-520.

   The indirect bursal and direct approaches to arthroscopic distal clavicular excision provided satisfactory results in 66 shoulders (average 6-year follow-up). Four direct-approach patients (10%) required a revision for AP instability or symptom recurrence. The authors believe the direct approach can lead to AP instability if the superior AC capsule is disrupted.

7. Miller CA, Ong BC, Jazrawi LM, et al: Assessment of clavicular translation after arthroscopic Mumford procedure: Direct versus indirect resection. A cadaveric study. *Arthroscopy* 2005;21:64-68.

   Arthroscopic distal clavicular resection was performed on 12 fresh-frozen cadaver shoulders (6 using the direct approach and 6 using the indirect bursal approach). No significant difference was found in anterior or posterior translation.

8.  Martin SD, Baumgarten TE, Andrews JR: Arthroscopic resection of the distal aspect of the clavicle with concomitant subacromial decompression. *J Bone Joint Surg Am* 2001;83:328-335.

    Thirty-one patients (mean age, 36 years; mean follow-up, 58 months) evaluated after distal clavicle resection and subacromial decompression included 25 active in sports and four professional athletes. Patients without a full-thickness rotator cuff tear had no difference in isokinetic strength testing compared with the contralateral shoulder. All patients were satisfied with the outcome.

9.  Kay SP, Dragoo JL, Lee R: Long-term results of arthroscopic resection of the distal clavicle with concomitant subacromial decompression. *Arthroscopy* 2003;19:805-809.

    All 20 patients followed for an average 6 years after combined arthroscopic distal clavicle resection and subacromial decompression had a good or excellent result, as measured using the Constant and University of California

Los Angeles scores; 25% of patients had recurrent calcific density distal to the clavicular resection but were asymptomatic.

10.  Deshmukh AV, Perlmutter GS, Zilberfarb JL, Wilson DR: Effect of subacromial decompression on the laxity of the acromioclavicular joint: Biomechanical testing in a cadaveric model. *J Shoulder Elbow Surg* 2004;13:338-343.

    In 18 fresh-frozen cadaver shoulders, subacromial decompression and coplaning of the distal clavicle increased AP compliance 13% and superior compliance 32%. The clinical significance is unclear, as scarring and re-formation of the AC capsule may help stabilize the AC joint after resection.

11.  Barber FA: Long-term results of acromioclavicular joint coplaning. *Arthroscopy* 2006;22:125-129.

    At 6-year follow-up of 81 patients treated with inferior clavicular osteophyte resection (coplaning), distal clavicular hemiresection of the articular cartilage, or complete distal clavicular resection, coplaning had not compromised the clinical outcome or led to increased AC joint symptoms or further surgery.

# Chapter 22

# Arthroscopic Repair of Full-Thickness Rotator Cuff Tears

*Jeffrey S. Abrams, MD

*Benjamin Shaffer, MD

## Introduction

The understanding and treatment of rotator cuff tears is gradually being transformed as arthroscopic repair techniques evolve. Recent research has emphasized anatomic repair and the use of dual-row attachment, when applicable, to improve repair security.[1-3] Arthroscopy allows for intra-articular assessment and treatment of associated pathology, permits more accurate tear pattern recognition, and facilitates anatomic repair. Because of its minimally invasive nature, arthroscopic cuff repair decreases the risk to the deltoid, the risk of stiffness, and postsurgical pain.[4-7]

Single-tendon tears are ideally suited to arthroscopic repair techniques, but large, massive tears can also benefit.[8-11] Arthroscopic tear pattern assessment allows the surgeon to better appreciate the morphology of the tear and improves the ability to address its components, such as the longitudinal split that accompanies most L-shaped or reverse L-shaped tears.

Patients rated pain relief and satisfaction as good to excellent after cuff repair using an arthroscopic, traditional open, or mini-open approach.[12-21] These results are consistent, despite outcome study findings of postsurgical retearing and compromised tendon integrity after open or arthroscopic repair, as assessed using ultrasonography or MRI.

## Indications and Contraindications for Surgery

Candidates for arthroscopic cuff repair have a full-thickness or significant partial-thickness cuff tear, as well as pain or shoulder dysfunction that has not been relieved by appropriate nonsurgical measures. A young, active patient with an acute tear is an ideal candidate (Table 1). A discrete event or injury may have precipitated the symptoms, although in many patients the onset of symptoms is insidious. No studies have defined the group of patients for whom arthroscopic repair is more appropriate than open repair. However, the perception that surgical morbidity is decreased with arthroscopic repair has probably lowered the threshold for considering arthroscopic repair, particularly in patients older than 70 years who have a large tear that cannot otherwise be repaired.

Surgery is not appropriate for patients whose symptoms are not attributable to the rotator cuff tear, who are being adequately managed by nonsurgical methods, or who will be unable to cooperate with postsurgical rehabilitation. Particularly in older patients, shoulder symptoms may be unrelated to imaging findings.[22-24] Age, tear dimensions, cephalic migration of the humeral head, degree of muscle atrophy, and the presence or degree of fatty infiltration are no longer absolute

## Table 1 | Indications and Contraindications for Arthroscopic Rotator Cuff Repair

**Indications**

Full-thickness cuff tear in a painful shoulder

Acute tear in a young patient

Extension of chronic tear with acute loss of function

Lack of responsiveness to nonsurgical management

Ability to cooperate with postsurgical program and restrictions

**Contraindications**

Symptoms completely or largely attributable to an alternative pathology, such as adhesive capsulitis, glenohumeral arthritis, or cervical radiculopathy

Inability to comply with postsurgical restrictions

Fixed humeral head superior migration, with thinning of the acromion

Rotator cuff arthropathy

Compromised bone stock (relative contraindication)

Chronic, irreparable tear

*Jeffrey S. Abrams, MD or the department with which he is affiliated has received royalties from ConMed Linvatec, holds stock or stock options in Arthrocare Medical, and is a consultant or employee for ConMed Linvatec, Arthrocare Medical, and Wright Medical. Benjamin Shaffer, MD is a consultant for Arthrex.

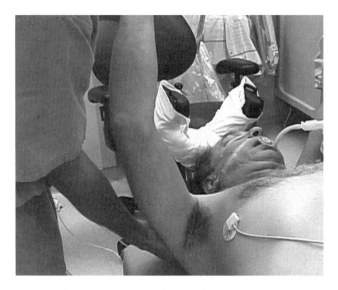

**Figure 1** Examination of the right shoulder under anesthesia, revealing an unexpected restriction in forward elevation.

contraindications to arthroscopic rotator cuff repair. Age has become a relative contraindication, although the established age-related reduction in cuff tendon circulation suggests possible impairment of healing in patients with a chronic tear who are older than 65 years. Satisfactory outcomes in patients with muscle atrophy or fatty infiltration, as detected using CT or MRI, suggest that these rotator cuff tear qualities are not absolute contraindications.[25,26]

Many authors have explored the influence of medical comorbidities on repair outcome. In 125 patients who underwent rotator cuff repair, those with the greatest comorbidity often had the most improvement in shoulder pain, function, and quality-of-life scores. The authors concluded that medical comorbidities should not be a negative factor in determining whether a patient should undergo rotator cuff repair.[27] Cephalic humeral head migration is another relative contraindication to surgical repair, because its presence suggests that the rotator cuff cannot be repaired. Several studies found that superior head translation was reversed following arthroscopic repair, particularly if the subscapularis tendon was also repaired. Recent data revealed that factors including the use of tobacco or nonsteroidal anti-inflammatory drugs can impair rotator cuff healing.[27-29] Compromised bone quality can preclude anchor fixation and may dictate bone grafting of deficient tuberosity to permit rotator cuff repair.[30] Repair is not appropriate for patients with rotator cuff arthropathy.

## Presurgical Planning

Presurgical medical evaluation should focus on physical examination of the shoulder and include assessment of atrophy, range of motion, and the rotator cuff. A thorough orthopaedic examination is necessary to identify any contributing cervical spine, acromioclavicular joint, or glenohumeral joint pathology.

Plain radiographs are required to evaluate the glenohumeral and acromioclavicular joints, as well as subacromial space narrowing and outlet morphology. Cephalic humeral head migration and narrowing of the acromiohumeral distance to less than 6 mm have negative prognostic implications with respect to rotator cuff repair using any technique. MRI and ultrasonography can provide additional information and accurate imaging of a full-thickness rotator cuff tear.[31-33] MRI can help in determining the size and location of the tear, the amount of retraction, and the degree, if any, of muscle atrophy and fatty infiltration. MRI was found to be significantly predictive of arthroscopic findings.[34] MRI with intra-articular contrast enhancement can be useful in a patient who has had earlier shoulder surgery. Ultrasonography is an accurate alternative to MRI, and it has the advantage of permitting dynamic examination of a shoulder component and comparison with the unaffected shoulder. Office-based ultrasonography was found comparable in accuracy to MRI. It led to the correct diagnosis in 37 of 42 shoulders with a full-thickness tear (88%) and 26 of 37 shoulders with a partial-thickness tear (70%), and it was 80% accurate in recognizing normal rotator cuff tendons.[32] However, the implementation of ultrasonography has been limited because it requires a trained ultrasonographer.

Arthroscopic rotator cuff repair requires special instrumentation and implants. Devices for suture passage through tendon, whether in a single-step or two-step approach, are widely available; the diameter of the arthroscopic cannulae must be sufficient to accommodate the suture-passing instruments. Because anchors vary considerably, the surgeon must be familiar with the specific steps required for insertion and deployment. To complete the surgery, a knot pusher and a knot cutter that can cut the newer, reinforced sutures are necessary.

## Surgical Technique
### Examination Under Anesthesia
Examination under regional or general anesthesia is performed to assess any motion restriction (Figure 1). The restriction is usually addressed by gentle manipulation and, if necessary, arthroscopic release.[35] If the restriction is not accompanied by significant hyperemia and synovitis, capsular release and arthroscopic repair can usually be performed together. Alternatively, a second-stage cuff repair can be performed after resolution and clinical recovery from a first-stage manipulation and capsular release.

### Positioning
Arthroscopic rotator cuff repair can be performed with the patient in either the beach chair or the lateral decu-

bitus position. The factors affecting the choice of position are the use of general or scalene block anesthesia; the availability of positioning equipment, such as a head and neck stabilizer and traction and arm-holding devices; the availability of assistants; and the preference of the surgeon. The surgeon must anticipate that conversion to an open repair may be required. Regardless of position, the patient must be carefully padded, and the shoulder girdle must be adequately exposed.

### Portal Placement

The standard posterior glenohumeral arthroscopy portal and a lateral subacromial working portal are used for arthroscopic cuff repair. Several accessory portals distal to the anterior, lateral, and posterior acromial margins are also used (Figure 2). The accessory portals are typically established after the cuff tear is located, using spinal needles for targeting. Formal cannulae are not necessary for every portal; most portals permit percutaneous instrumentation and suture shuttling.

The arthroscope is positioned in the subacromial bursae via the posterior portal, and a lateral portal is created 2 to 3 cm lateral to the anterolateral acromion. This portal provides excellent access to the acromial undersurface, acromioclavicular joint, and supraspinatus and infraspinatus tendons. A puncture or portal for the placement of suture anchors is established adjacent to the lateral border of the acromion to allow a more direct approach to the greater tuberosity for proper insertion and angulation. A superomedial portal, posterior to the acromioclavicular joint, can help in suture shuttling through the supraspinatus. Other periacromial portals are established as necessary for visualization and repair.

### Arthroscopic Evaluation

The surgery begins with arthroscopic evaluation of the glenohumeral joint, rotator cuff, biceps tendon, labrum, articular cartilage, and upper border of the subscapularis. Any concomitant pathology is addressed at this time. Subscapularis tendon tears increasingly are being recognized in patients undergoing rotator cuff repair. The arthroscope is then repositioned in the subacromial space, where a bursectomy is performed to ascertain the location and dimensions of the rotator cuff tear. The surgeon decides on the best method of repairing the tear.

### Subacromial Bursectomy and Decompression

With the arthroscope in the posterior portal, the lateral portal is used to perform the subacromial bursectomy and, if indicated, decompression. The shaver, cautery device, and burr are typically introduced and used through the lateral portal, while being viewed through the posterior portal. A frayed or thickened coracoacromial ligament may be elevated, but complete release or excision

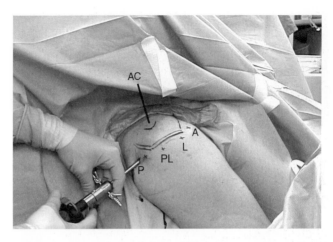

**Figure 2**  The arthroscope placed into a posterior portal in the right shoulder. The acromial margin has been outlined, and potential arthroscopic portals have been marked. A = anterior portal, AC = acromioclavicular joint, L = lateral portal, P = posterior portal, PL = posterolateral portal.

may be contraindicated in large or irreparable tears because compromise of the coracoacromial ligament can destabilize the coracoacromial arch and result in anterosuperior escape.

In either open or arthroscopic surgery, the need for acromioplasty is evaluated on a case-by-case basis.[36-39] A presurgical lateral view radiograph can be used to classify the shape of the acromial profile, an AP view can be used to see the lateral slope of the acromion, and an axillary view can be used to detect any unfused acromial apophysis. Although arthroscopic repairs without acromioplasty have been successful, most arthroscopic surgeons believe that a spur or a Bigliani type III hooked acromion should be smoothed if subacromial stenosis or evidence of subacromial impingement (coracoacromial ligament fraying) is present. Surgeons who routinely perform acromioplasty observe that decompression can improve visualization and allow more space for instrumentation. In addition, it may introduce biologic factors that enhance healing.

Bursectomy is an important aspect of arthroscopic rotator cuff repair. It improves the ability to see the tear, identify the tear pattern, and distinguish the subacromial bursa from true tendon. The bursae may have a role in healing chronic tears in older patients, and therefore the exact amount of resection is controversial.[40,41] A controlled laboratory study of bursa and rotator cuff tissue at the messenger RNA level found an active remodeling process, which suggests that both tissues contribute to rotator cuff healing.[40] Nonetheless, visualization and mobilization of the rotator cuff tear margins are critical to successful repair.

### Tear Pattern Identification

Identifying the tear pattern is an important step in arthroscopic rotator cuff repair. Most tears can be

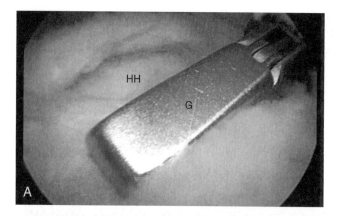

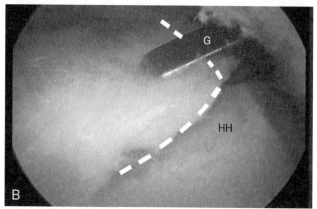

**Figure 3** Arthroscopic views from a posterior portal in the right shoulder. **A,** A grasper inserted from the lateral portal fails to reduce a large, U-shaped rotator cuff tear, despite attempted anterior translation of the posterior rotator cuff component. **B,** Grasping of the anterior rotator cuff tissue shows anatomic reduction of an L-shaped tear (*dashes*) by lateral and posterior translation. G = grasper, HH = humeral head.

classified as crescent, L-shaped, reverse L-shaped, or large U-shaped. A crescent-shaped tear begins as a rotator cuff avulsion and extends anteriorly or posteriorly. A tear with a longitudinal extension may have an L or reverse-L configuration. A large U-shaped tear represents a longitudinal split of an avulsed tendon, with medial retraction.

The tear pattern is best assessed by careful bursectomy, as well as visualization and tissue grasping from different portals. A soft-tissue grasper can attempt tear reduction from multiple directions to discern the pattern (Figure 3). Appreciation of the tear pattern is critical to ensure anatomic repair and minimize tension at the tuberosity attachment. Nonanatomic rotator cuff tendon lateralization, with its excessive tension and high failure rate, has largely fallen into disuse because of the use of arthroscopic techniques and improvement in tear pattern recognition.

### Arthroscopic Releases

Tendon mobilization may be required to approximate retracted chronic tears, particularly if they are relatively large or perceived to be irreparable.[42-44] An anterior ro-

tator interval release, a posterior release between the supraspinatus and infraspinatus tendons, or a superior capsular release between the inferior aspect of the rotator cuff (supraspinatus and infraspinatus) and the superior capsule of the glenohumeral joint can be performed based on the site of tendon immobility. Anterior, lateral, and posterior releases of bursal attachments create adequate mobility for most tears. The placement of a tissue-grasping device or traction sutures helps in identifying the need for additional releases.

An anterior interval release that includes the coracohumeral and superior glenohumeral ligaments is common. This approach is useful in mobilization of the supraspinatus tendon and, in some cases, the subscapularis tendon.[44] In a modification of this technique known as the interval slide, the interval is released, but the most lateral interval tissue is preserved to serve as a reference during the attempt to anatomically repair the rotator cuff.[42-45] When necessary, the subscapularis tendon should be repaired before release. Preservation of normal anatomic landmarks, such as the superior border of the subscapularis, medial biceps pulley, and capsular structures, facilitates anatomic cuff repair. Whether using a traditional release or an interval slide, the surgeon must release soft-tissue attachments between the rotator cuff and the coracoid.

In the posterior interval slide technique, a bipolar device is used to peel the bursa off the posterior margin of the tear, with the arthroscope in the posterior portal, lateral portal, or both. The spine of the scapula is identified, and the interval between the supraspinatus and infraspinatus is identified and released. The posterosuperior capsule can be released. A blunt elevator or grasper mobilizes the supraspinatus and infraspinatus for improved lateral translation. However, care must be taken to avoid injury to the suprascapular nerve, which lies approximately 1.5 cm medial to the glenoid margin. Traction sutures in the cuff margin protect the nerve while the releases are performed. Tendon mobilization is reassessed after each release until sufficient or maximum tendon length has been restored.

### Margin Convergence

An L-shaped tear can grow larger because of tissue detachment from the tuberosities, medial tear extension, muscle and tendon atrophy, or contracture. A large and seemingly irreparable tear can sometimes be easily approximated using tear pattern recognition and margin convergence[46-49] (Figure 4). Repair of the longitudinal tear component must be performed before the tendon-to-bone repair because the longitudinal tear component permits more accurate tear pattern identification and reduces tension on the tendon-to-bone reattachment. Margin convergence also can reduce the angulation of the suprascapular nerve as it passes through the notch.

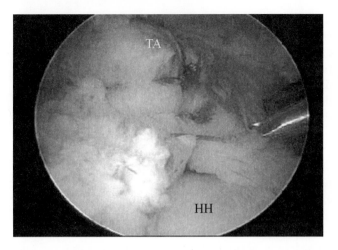

**Figure 4** As seen from a lateral portal in the right shoulder, most of a large, U-shaped tear has been approximated by simple margin convergence. HH = humeral head, TA = tear apex.

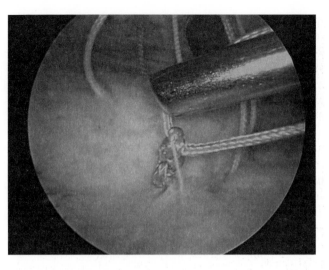

**Figure 5** A single-row suture anchor repair of the right shoulder, seen from the posterior portal.

In performing a margin convergence, the surgeon uses an arthroscopic grasper to assess ideal suture placement for anatomic approximation. Débridement of rotator cuff tear edges using baskets or a shaver can enhance the biologic healing of tendon edges. Care must be taken, however, to abrade rather than remove rotator cuff tissue. Sutures are placed across the longitudinal component, usually from anterior to posterior, beginning at the medial apex of the tear. Several suture passage techniques and materials have been described. As the sutures are tied, the more mobilized area of the rotator cuff (usually posterior) is shifted to bring the tear margins together. After the longitudinal tear component has been addressed, tendon-to-bone repair is considered. The margin convergence may be so effective that it interferes with visualization of the lateral tuberosity. Therefore, the surgeon may prefer to prepare the footprint before tying the most lateral margin convergence sutures.

### Tendon-to-Bone Repair

Even if the humeral head seems to be completely covered using margin convergence, most repairs include a tendon-to-bone reattachment. Following rotator cuff tendon débridement and light decortication to generate a healing response, anchors are placed in the tuberosity at the site of intended reattachment. Controversy exists regarding the optimal biomechanical construct, including the number and placement of anchors and the suture and knot-tying technique.[1,50-60] In a goat rotator cuff model, examination of the biomechanical relationship between the number of suture anchors and strength of the bone-tendon interface found no significant difference in ultimate load-to-failure strength testing after 4 weeks and 8 weeks.[51] In another basic science study, bone quality influenced the strength of anchor place-

ment; in chronic tears, bone in the medial aspect of the tuberosity was stronger than lateral bone.[61]

### Dual-Row Repairs

The first arthroscopic rotator cuff repairs relied on a single-row technique, in which the rotator cuff tendon was reattached to the greater tuberosity using suture anchors (Figure 5). Technical and biomechanical advances included dual-row (two-row) repairs; double-loaded and knotless anchor designs; suture materials with improved strength and handling; and alternative suture-tendon configurations for better tendon security.[55,58-60,62-65] The typical two-row construct contains medial anchors adjacent to the articular surface and secured with mattress sutures, as well as lateral fixation achieved using simple sutures.

Anatomic restoration of the normal rotator cuff footprint using a dual-row attachment technique has been the subject of several basic science investigations[54,55,60,66] (Figure 6). The dual-row construct has been shown to be anatomically and biomechanically superior to single-row repair. A cadaver study found that dual-row anchor fixation ultimately achieves a significantly greater tensile load than three single-row repair models.[55] Another cadaver study found that dual-row repairs lead to higher cyclic and ultimate loads, as well as decreased gap formation, and thus suggested that dual-row repairs, although more technically demanding, are more reliable than single-row repairs.[60] A modification of the dual-anchor technique called transosseous equivalent was the focus of a recent investigation. In securing the tendon both medially and laterally, the technique decreased tendon motion relative to the insertional footprint and thereby enhanced tendon-to-bone stability.[54]

One study of a dual-row technique for arthroscopic repair emphasized reestablishing the normal rotator cuff footprint and increasing the contact area for healing.[66] In vivo examination and measurement of the rotator cuff footprint before and after repair found no uncovered area after a dual-row repair but a 53% uncovered area after a single-row repair.[67] A comparison of the functional and structural outcomes of single-row and dual-row arthroscopic cuff repairs in 78 consecutive patients (80 shoulders) found no difference in functional outcome but an improved structural outcome after use of the dual-row technique.[2] Another comparison study of single-row and three different dual-row constructs found a better contact area in dual-row repairs but no mechanical difference in cyclic and single load-to-failure testing.[3]

### Suture Shuttling and Knot Tying

After medial-row (single-row) anchor placement, sutures are passed through the torn tendon at the site of

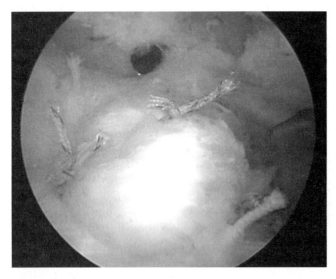

**Figure 6** A dual-row suture anchor repair of the right shoulder, seen from the posterior portal. Mattress sutures have been used medially, and lateral fixation has been achieved using simple sutures.

the intended approximation to bone. Suture passage can be achieved using a variety of techniques (Figure 7). For example, a suture can be passed directly using a single-pass technique, or it can be shuttled in a two-step technique using monofilament suture material as the shuttle device. The surgeon must take care to ensure sufficient distance between suture passage sites, ensure adequate tissue capture, and avoid suture cut-through.

The tendon apposition to bone is secured with knots after suture passage. A variety of suture knot techniques have been described to secure soft tissue to bone. All emphasize secure knots and careful approximation of tissue to ensure optimal healing.[68] The knots can be tied sequentially as each anchor is placed and sutures are passed, or they can be tied after sutures are inserted and passed for all anchors. Knotless suture anchors have also been used, particularly to secure the lateral row in a dual-row repair (Figure 8).

The suture-tendon interface is a weak link in arthroscopic rotator cuff repair.[50,52,56,57,69,70] A bovine model study showed the superiority of a locking-configuration suture to simple or mattress-configuration sutures in resisting gap formation under cyclic loading.[69] However, mattress sutures were found to be more reproducible than complex woven sutures.[50]

Even after accurate tear pattern recognition, generous bursectomy, and adequate releases, some tears are irreparable. Partial repair may provide improvement through the restoration of force couples. Allografts, xenografts, and synthetic augmentation have had mixed results and are now rarely used in arthroscopic cuff repair.[71,72]

## Rehabilitation

Postsurgical protection is required to enhance biologic healing and avoid mechanical failure after an arthroscopic or open rotator cuff repair. Most surgeons prefer postsurgical immobilization using a sling, typically modified to incorporate a small abduction pillow that further

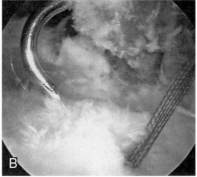
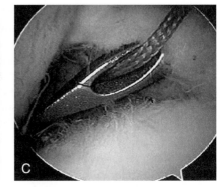

**Figure 7** A left shoulder seen from the posterior portal. **A,** A one-step device facilitates suture passage through the tendon. **B,** In a two-step approach, a hook penetrates the cuff, passes a shuttle suture through the tendon, and shuttles a limb of the suture anchor back through the tendon. **C,** A single-step puncture and suture retrieval can be performed using a penetrating grasper.

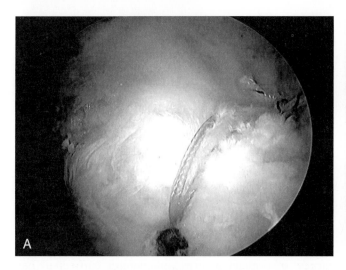
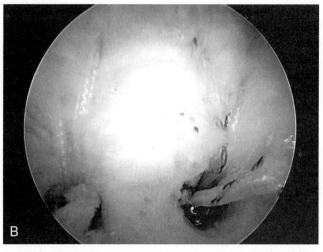

**Figure 8** A left shoulder seen from the anterolateral portal. **A,** A knotless anchor can be used as an alternative to a traditional suture anchor; the mattress sutures from an anteromedial row anchor have been tied, with the sutures left long, and a suture bridge has been created with a laterally placed interference screw. **B,** Inverted mattress sutures are secured laterally to two knotless anchors.

reduces stress on the repair. Scapular strengthening begins early in the postsurgical period. Most protocols discourage active rotator cuff contraction during the first 6 weeks, regardless of the specific tendon repaired. Although active motion usually begins 6 weeks after surgery, repair protection continues for several months because of the slowness of biologic tendon healing. Resistance exercise is usually begun 12 weeks after surgery.

Rehabilitation can be modified based on factors including the location of the tear, confidence in the security of the repair, and the presence of adhesive capsulitis. For example, after repair of a posterosuperior tear, passive external rotation exercises can start on the first day after surgery. Conversely, a subscapularis repair requires restriction of passive external rotation. If motion restriction or inflammatory synovitis was detected during the rotator cuff repair, range-of-motion exercises can be initiated at 3 weeks to minimize the risk of stiffness.

Complete recovery can require a great deal of time. The timing of the patient's return to sports or work is based on the progress of recovery and the demands of the particular sport or activity, but 4 to 6 months is usually required. A manual laborer may require 6 to 9 months before full return to work. A patient receiving workers' compensation benefits may be eligible for a work-hardening program, a functional capacity examination to measure strength deficits, and a limited work schedule before return to full-duty work.

## Outcomes

Outcome studies found a high level of patient satisfaction following arthroscopic rotator cuff repair, comparable to patient satisfaction following open repair.[17,46,73,74]

However, the ability to compare arthroscopic and open repair outcomes is limited because of a relative paucity of well-designed, high-level studies, as well as variability in study design and differences in indications, techniques, surgeon experience, and outcome measures. In a recent study of arthroscopic repair of chronic full-thickness supraspinatus tendon tears using a tension band technique, 62 of 65 consecutive patients were satisfied with the result at an average 29-month follow-up; the improvements in shoulder elevation strength and in Constant and University of California Los Angeles (UCLA) shoulder scores were statistically significant.[73] Evaluation of repair integrity using CT arthrography or MRI 6 months to 3 years after arthroscopic repair showed complete healing in 46 repaired shoulders (71%) and partial healing in 3 shoulders; tendons healed completely in 23 patients (43%) older than 65 years.[14] Of the 16 tears with residual defects, 15 were relatively small. Forward elevation strength was significantly greater in the patients whose rotator cuff tears had healed. Factors that negatively influenced outcome included increasing age and associated delamination of the subscapularis or infraspinatus tendons.

The outcome of arthroscopic repair of 53 isolated supraspinatus tendon tears using a single-row Mason-Allen technique was assessed using Constant score, dynamometry, and open MRI. Constant scores improved for all patients, reaching statistical significance among those with healed cuff tendons. At an average 26-month follow-up, the overall rotator cuff retear rate was 24.5%, and it was higher in patients older than 65 years.[53] However, a retrospective case series examining the influence of patient age on outcome found that 81% of 54 patients with arthroscopically repaired rotator cuff tears of varying sizes had a good or excellent result, regardless of age.[75]

In a retrospective case series of 42 arthroscopically repaired full-thickness rotator cuff tears repaired solely with margin convergence (no tendon-to-bone repair), 41 patients (98%) had a good or excellent result measured using the UCLA Shoulder Scale.[49] In a retrospective study, 71 patients (105 shoulders) evaluated using American Shoulder and Elbow Surgeons (ASES), Constant, and visual analog scales at a minimum 12-month follow-up had improved function, regardless of tear size, with less dramatic gains in strength and motion.[11] A prospective clinical series of 42 patients with large, chronic, retracted tears examined the outcome following an arthroscopic interval and superior capsular release combined with arthroscopic repair. At an average 32-month follow-up, 21 patients had excellent, 6 had good, and 11 had fair outcomes measured using the UCLA scale; 1 had a poor result.[44] At 39-month follow-up of 48 consecutive patients following arthroscopic repair of a medium-to-large tear,[20] 35 had excellent, 11 had good, and 2 had fair results, as assessed using the UCLA and ASES scales; 47 patients (98%) were satisfied with the result.

One recent study examined clinical outcomes after arthroscopic repair of 52 full-thickness tears (average length, 2.47 cm) using a two-row suture anchor technique.[7] At an average 30-month follow-up, all 48 patients had clinical improvement, as assessed using the L'Insalata Shoulder Rating Questionnaire and clinical and strength testing. Nine shoulders (17%) showed evidence of retearing or persistent defect on postsurgical ultrasonography. Patients who had an intact repair had greater strength in elevation and external rotation compared with those who had a lack of repair integrity, although functional scores of the two groups did not differ.

To assess rotator cuff integrity, the functional and anatomic results of single-anchor arthroscopic repair of a large or massive rotator cuff tear were examined in 18 patients.[76] Ultrasonography revealed a 94% tendon defect rate. Nonetheless, patient satisfaction was high, with 16 patients (89%) having improvement in pain and functional ASES score at a minimum 12-month follow-up. However, the results had deteriorated at 2-year follow-up, with only 12 patients (67%) having an ASES score higher than 80 points.

Postsurgical rotator cuff integrity was evaluated in 40 patients following arthroscopic repair and compared with that of a historical control group of 32 patients whose rotator cuff tear had been repaired using an open technique.[77] On MRI, 69% of the open repairs and 53% of the arthroscopic repairs were intact. Smaller tears (< 3 cm) were more likely to be intact (74% open, 84% arthroscopic), and larger tears (> 3 cm) were less likely to be intact (62% open, 24% arthroscopic). The rotator cuff integrity failure rate in larger tears was twice that of smaller tears.

No prospective studies have shown clinical superiority of dual-row arthroscopic repair techniques over single-row techniques. Because tears vary in configuration, a simple comparison may not be useful. The implant costs and additional surgical time required for two-row repair may further undermine its apparent benefits.

The superiority of arthroscopic repair over open repair also has not been established, although arthroscopic repair has theoretic advantages, including anatomic repair, decreased risk of stiffness, and decreased deltoid morbidity. The outcome of cuff repair is more likely to be limited by biologic than technical factors; technical obstacles decline in importance as the surgeon's arthroscopic experience increases. The reported success of primary arthroscopic rotator cuff repair has led to its application in revision repairs. In a heterogenous group of 14 patients (with 2 medium, 1 large, and 11 massive tears; mean tear size, 4.4 cm × 5.5 cm), 13 (93%) were satisfied with arthroscopic revision after unsuccessful earlier surgery. The large or massive tears required extensive dissection, release, and tendon mobilization. At an average 23-month follow-up, there were four excellent, five good, four fair, and one poor result, as measured on the UCLA scale. The importance of proper patient selection and careful attention to rotator cuff mobilization were emphasized in the study report.[78]

## Complications

Retearing is the most common complication of arthroscopic rotator cuff repair. Reported rates of retearing have ranged from 25% after repair of isolated supraspinatus tears[73] to 94% after repair of massive tears.[76] However, many patients achieve pain relief and functional improvement despite residual defects or retearing. Retearing is usually caused by a technical failure of tension-free approximation or a failure of biologic healing, and it probably reflects a lack of repair integrity rather than a reinjury. The incidence of residual or recurrent defects can be especially high after multiple tendon tears. The most recent studies of postsurgical cuff integrity found a decrease in postsurgical cuff defects resulting from surgical technique, instrumentation, implants, or surgeon inexperience.[79]

The presence of postsurgical artifacts can make MRI assessment of repair integrity difficult. Specific sequencing to minimize the difficulty includes inversion recovery and fast spin-echo techniques, rather than fat saturation and conventional spin-echo sequences or gradient-echo sequence techniques.[80] Ultrasonography can provide highly accurate evaluation of postsurgical rotator cuff integrity.[81]

Another common complication is persistent pain because of acromioclavicular joint arthritis or pathology affecting the subscapularis tendon or long head of the biceps tendon.[82] These concomitant conditions are best identified presurgically and addressed intrasurgically.

Stiffness is an uncommon complication of arthroscopic rotator cuff repair. Patients with adhesive capsulitis may have a greater risk of postsurgical stiffness, especially if the repair was combined with manipulation or capsular release. Seventy-two patients with documented stiffness were divided into three groups based on the degree of motion restriction before arthroscopic rotator cuff repair.[35] Group 1 consisted of 42 patients whose total range of motion deficit (TROMD) was 20° or less; in group 2, 24 patients had a TROMD of 25° to 70°; and in group 3, 6 patients had a TROMD greater than 70°. The average TROMD improved in all groups following arthroscopic repair (in group 1, from 10° to 4°; group 2, from 36° to 12°; and group 3, from 89° to 31°). Three patients in group 3 who had adhesive capsulitis showed no or minimal improvement in postsurgical range of motion, and they required a secondary arthroscopic capsular release; their total range of motion averaged 35° at final follow-up. The study concluded that, although arthroscopic rotator cuff repair can be performed in the face of presurgical stiffness, range of motion is not normal after the repair.

Rehabilitation may have value to restore motion before surgical repair, and a two-stage approach, in which restoration of motion is followed by rotator cuff repair, is an alternate strategy for some patients with significant stiffness. If the patient has postsurgical stiffness, surgical and manipulative release should be delayed as long as possible, probably at least 6 months. Recovery of motion can take a relatively long time in the presence of stiffness, and rotator cuff healing takes priority over expanding the range of motion. The risk of stiffness following arthroscopic rotator cuff repair can be minimized by performing an anatomic tension-free repair and minimizing trauma to the deltoid.

Muscle atrophy and dysfunction are an inevitable part of the repair outcome, rather than a complication. Recognizing the condition of the muscles before and after rotator cuff repair is important in determining overall recovery. Except for younger patients with acute tears, patients with a rotator cuff tear usually have muscle atrophy and sometimes fatty infiltration. Some weakness may persist after successful tendon reattachment.

With the exception of repair failure, complications of arthroscopic rotator cuff repair are relatively uncommon.[83] Implant migration, now an uncommon complication, may become more common with the increasing use of different anchor designs.[84] Although neurovascular complications are rare, suprascapular nerve compromise can occur during surgical release and rotator cuff mobilization.[85] To protect the axillary nerve, anteroinferior dissection and avoidance of portal placement more than 5 cm distal to the acromial edge are necessary.

## Summary

Although technically demanding, arthroscopy is increasingly used in repairing full-thickness rotator cuff tears. Arthroscopic rotator cuff repair offers numerous potential advantages, including decreased deltoid morbidity and risk of stiffness, improved tear pattern recognition, and reduced risk of infection. Studies have found outcomes, including pain relief, functional restoration, and patient satisfaction, that are comparable to outcomes following mini-open rotator cuff repair. However, few data currently exist to show the superiority of arthroscopic repair over open repair. Reports of postsurgical cuff integrity have been less positive than subjective and functional results, and MRI and ultrasonography studies have reported varying rates of residual or recurrent defects. Improvements in instrumentation, anchors, and technique, including dual-row repair, may contribute to better outcomes. Despite the technical advances, biologic factors are likely to limit the success of long-term tendon integration and healing into bone and will be the next frontier in arthroscopic rotator cuff repair.

## Annotated References

1.  Anderson K, Boothby M, Aschenbrener D, van Holsbeeck M: Outcome and structural integrity after arthroscopic rotator cuff repair using 2 rows of fixation: Minimum 2-year follow-up. *Am J Sports Med* 2006; 34:1899-1905.

    This study reviewed the clinical and ultrasonographic outcome of 52 shoulders following use of a dual-row suture anchor technique in 48 patients with a reducible full-thickness rotator cuff tear. All patients demonstrated clinical improvement; 17% lacked rotator cuff tear integrity on postsurgical ultrasound imaging. Level of evidence: IV.

2.  Sugaya H, Maeda K, Matsuki K, Moriishi J: Functional and structural outcome after arthroscopic full-thickness rotator cuff repair: Single-row versus dual-row fixation. *Arthroscopy* 2005;21:1307-1316.

    This nonrandomized comparative study examined the functional and structural outcomes of 80 consecutive arthroscopic rotator cuff repairs performed using a single or dual row. The clinical results were comparable, although integrity was better after use of the dual-row technique. Level of evidence: III.

3.  Mazzocca AD, Millett PJ, Guanche CA, Santangelo SA, Arciero RA: Arthroscopic single-row versus double-row suture anchor rotator cuff repair. *Am J Sports Med* 2005;33:1861-1868.

    In a cadaver model, biomechanical testing of single-row repairs and three different dual-row repairs found no difference in cyclic or single load-to-failure testing, although the repair contact area was greater in the dual-row constructs.

4. Yamaguchi K, Levine WN, Marra G, Galatz LM, Klepps S, Flatow E: Transitioning to arthroscopic rotator cuff repair: The pros and cons. *Instr Course Lect* 2003;52:81-92.

The merits and disadvantages of arthroscopic rotator cuff repair are discussed relative to patient expectations, cuff pathoanatomy, and surgical experience.

5. Millstein ES, Snyder SJ: Arthroscopic management of partial, full-thickness, and complex rotator cuff tears: Indications, techniques, and complications. *Arthroscopy* 2003;19(suppl):189-199.

6. Burkhart SS, Lo IKY: Arthroscopic rotator cuff repair. *J Am Acad Orthop Surg* 2006;14:333-346.

This article presents an overview of indications, surgical technique, and outcomes of arthroscopic rotator cuff tear treatment.

7. Abrams JS: Arthroscopic approach to massive rotator cuff tears. *Instr Course Lect* 2006;59-66.

A review of arthroscopic rotator cuff repair indications and surgical technique is presented.

8. Bennett WF: Arthroscopic repair of massive rotator cuff tears: A prospective cohort with 2- to 4-year follow-up. *Arthroscopy* 2003;19:380-390.

Complete arthroscopic repair of a massive rotator cuff tear was found to reduce pain and improve function in 37 patients. The patient satisfaction rate was 95%. Complete coverage was achieved in 78% during initial surgery; the remaining patients had a similar outcome.

9. Jones CK, Savoie FH III: Arthroscopic repair of large and massive rotator cuff tears. *Arthroscopy* 2003;19: 564-571.

At an average 32-month follow-up after arthroscopic repair of a large or massive tear in 50 patients, 88% had a good or excellent outcome, and 98% were satisfied.

10. Bittar ES: Arthroscopic management of massive rotator cuff tears. *Arthroscopy* 2002;18(suppl 9):104-106.

11. Lee E, Bishop JY, Braman JP, Langford J, Gelber J, Flatow EL: Outcomes after arthroscopic rotator cuff repairs. *J Shoulder Elbow Surg* 2006;16:1-5.

A retrospective review of 105 consecutive arthroscopic rotator cuff repairs found significant improvement in outcomes regardless of tear size, as assessed using the ASES, Constant, and visual analog pain scales at a minimum 12-month follow-up. Level of evidence: IV.

12. Wilson F, Hinov V, Adams G: Arthroscopic repair of full-thickness tears of the rotator cuff: 2- to 14-year follow-up. *Arthroscopy* 2002;18:136-144.

Arthroscopic repair of a full-thickness tear in 100 patients had results comparable to those of traditional open repair. Advanced arthroscopic skills and a steep learning curve are required.

13. Verma NN, Dunn W, Adler RS, et al: All-arthroscopic versus mini-open rotator cuff repair: A retrospective review with minimum 2-year follow-up. *Arthroscopy* 2006;22:587-594.

A comparison of 38 rotator cuff tears repaired arthroscopically with a historical control group of 33 shoulders repaired using a mini-open technique found no difference in clinical outcomes or rotator cuff repair integrity at a minimum 2-year follow-up. Level of evidence: III.

14. Sauerbrey AM, Getz CL, Piancastelli M, Iannotti JP, Ramsey ML, Williams GR: Arthroscopic versus mini-open rotator cuff repair: A comparison of clinical outcome. *Arthroscopy* 2005;21:1415-1420.

A retrospective review of 28 arthroscopically repaired rotator cuffs compared with 26 mini-open rotator cuff repairs found no statistically significant difference in clinical outcome at short-term follow-up. Level of evidence: III.

15. Ide J, Maeda S, Takagi K: A comparison of arthroscopic and open rotator cuff repair. *Arthroscopy* 2005;21:1090-1098.

This nonrandomized prospective comparison study evaluated equal groups of 50 patients with rotator cuff tears of varying size that were repaired by arthroscopic or open techniques. All patients had improved clinical outcome scores, but those with small or medium-size tears had better outcomes than those with large or massive tears. Outcomes of arthroscopic and open repair did not significantly differ. Level of evidence: III.

16. Buess E, Steuber KU, Waibi B: Open versus arthroscopic rotator cuff repair: A comparative review of 96 cases. *Arthroscopy* 2005;21:597-604.

Thirty open repairs were compared with 66 arthroscopic repairs in this nonrandomized retrospective case series. Although visual analog scores favored arthroscopic repair, clinical outcomes, as assessed on the Simple Shoulder Test, and overall patient satisfaction were comparable. Level of evidence: III.

17. Tauro JC: Arthroscopic rotator cuff repair: Analysis of technique and results at 2- and 3-year follow-up. *Arthroscopy* 1998;14:45-51.

18. Kim SH, Ha KI, Park JH, Kang JS, Oh SK, Oh I: Arthroscopic versus mini-open salvage repair of the rotator cuff tear: Outcome analysis at 2 to 6 years' follow-up. *Arthroscopy* 2003;19:746-754.

In a comparison of 76 patients treated for a full-thickness tear using an all-arthroscopic technique or a mini-open revision of technically unsuccessful arthroscopic repair, no differences appeared in shoulder scores, pain, and return to activity. Patients with larger tears had lower scores and less predictable recovery.

19. Severud EL, Ruotolo C, Abbott DD, Nottage WM: All-arthroscopic versus mini-open rotator cuff repair: A long-term retrospective outcome comparison. *Arthroscopy* 2003;19:234-238.

At an average 44.6-month follow-up after rotator cuff repair of 64 shoulders, the outcomes and complication rates of all-arthroscopic repair were found to be comparable to those of arthroscopic decompression with mini-open repair. The lower incidence of fibrous ankylosis favors the all-arthroscopic technique, as does a trend toward earlier motion.

20. Murray TF, Lajtai G, Mileski RM, Snyder SJ: Arthroscopic repair of medium to large full-thickness rotator cuff tears: Outcome at 2- to 6-year follow-up. *J Shoulder Elbow Surg* 2002;11:19-24.

This medium-term evaluation of arthroscopic rotator cuff repairs in 48 patients with a medium-sized or large tear, there were 35 excellent, 11 good, and 2 fair results; 1 patient had evidence of a failed repair.

21. Youm T, Murray DH, Kubiak EN, Rokito AS, Zuckerman JD: Arthroscopic versus mini-open rotator cuff repair: A comparison of clinical outcomes and patient satisfaction. *J Shoulder Elbow Surg* 2005;14:455-459.

This retrospective comparison study found that the clinical outcomes of 84 patients who underwent arthroscopic or open rotator cuff repair were similar, with an overall satisfaction rate of 98.8%, regardless of tear size. Level of evidence: III.

22. Yamaguchi K, Ditsios K, Middleton WD, et al: The demographics and morphological features of rotator cuff disease: A comparison of asymptomatic and symptomatic shoulders. *J Bone Joint Surg Am* 2006;88:1699-1704.

This retrospective review of 588 patients who underwent bilateral shoulder ultrasonography found a high correlation between the onset of rotator cuff tearing and increasing age. Level of evidence: III.

23. Milgrom C, Schaffler M, Gilbert S, van Holsbeeck M: Rotator cuff changes in asymptomatic adults: The effect of age, hand dominance, and gender. *J Bone Joint Surg Br* 1995;77:296-298.

24. Sher JS, Uribe JW, Posada A, Murphy BJ, Zlatkin MB: Abnormal findings on magnetic resonance images of asymptomatic shoulders. *J Bone Joint Surg Am* 1995;77:10-15.

25. Goutallier D, Postel JM, Gleyze P, Leguilloux P, Van Driessche S: Influence of cuff muscle fatty degeneration on anatomic and functional outcomes after simple suture of full-thickness tears. *J Shoulder Elbow Surg* 2003;12:550-554.

After repair of a rotator cuff tear using a simple tendon-to-bone suture, 220 shoulders were analyzed for the influence of presurgical fatty degeneration on anatomic and functional outcome. Fatty degeneration was found to be an important prognostic factor.

26. Matsumoto F, Uhthoff HK, Trudel G, Loehr JF: Delayed tendon reattachment does not reverse atrophy and fat accumulation of the supraspinatus: An experimental study in rabbits. *J Orthop Res* 2002;20:357-363.

A rabbit model was used to investigate whether muscle atrophy and fat accumulation after rotator cuff tearing are reversible after successful repair. Fat accumulation was found to be higher after reattachment.

27. Tashjian RZ, Henn RF, Kang L, Green A: The effect of comorbidity on self-assessed function in patients with a chronic rotator cuff tear. *J Bone Joint Surg Am* 2004;86:355-362.

Evaluation of the influence of comorbidities on the clinical outcome of 125 patients 1 year after rotator cuff repair found that the presence of comorbidities does not compromise outcome and should not be a contraindication to repair. Level of evidence: III.

28. Kane SM, Dave A, Haque A, Langston K: The incidence of rotator cuff disease in smoking and nonsmoking patients: A cadaveric study. *Orthopedics* 2006;29:363-366.

This cadaver study examined the relationship between rotator cuff pathology and tobacco use. Increased frequency and severity of rotator cuff pathology was observed in shoulders from individuals who had smoked. The data did not reach statistical significance.

29. Galatz LM, Silva MJ, Rothermich SY, Zaegel MA, Havlioglu N, Thomopoulos S: Nicotine delays tendon-to-bone healing in a rat shoulder model. *J Bone Joint Surg Am* 2006;88:2027-2034.

Nicotine was found to have an adverse effect on rotator cuff healing in a rat model.

30. Burkhart SS, Klein JR: Arthroscopic repair of rotator cuff tears associated with large bone cysts of the proximal humerus: Compaction bone grafting technique. *Arthroscopy* 2005;21:1149.

This article describes a technique by which tuberosity bone defects can be grafted to permit arthroscopic cuff repair. Level of evidence: V.

31. Kluger R, Mayrhofer R, Kröner A, et al: Sonographic versus magnetic resonance arthrographic evaluation of full-thickness rotator cuff tears in millimeters. *J Shoulder Elbow Surg* 2003;12:110-116.

A prospective study compared presurgical magnetic resonance arthrography and ultrasonography with intrasurgical findings to determine tear size in 26 shoulders. No significant difference was found related to tear width or retraction.

32. Iannotti JP, Ciccone J, Buss DD, et al: Accuracy of office-based ultrasonography of the shoulder for the diagnosis of rotator cuff tears. *J Bone Joint Surg Am* 2005;87:1305-1311.

This prospective, multi-institutional study evaluated the accuracy of ultrasonography performed in an orthopaedic surgeon's office on 99 shoulders with a diagnosed rotator cuff condition. The results were compared with those of presurgical MRI as well as the surgical findings. Level of evidence: I.

33. Teefey SA, Rubin DA, Middleton WD, Hildebolt CF, Leibold RA, Yamaguchi K: Detection and quantification of rotator cuff tears: Comparison of ultrasonographic, magnetic resonance imaging, and arthroscopic findings in 71 consecutive cases. *J Bone Joint Surg Am* 2004;86-A:708-716.

    This study examined the accuracy of ultrasonography and MRI for the detection of full-thickness and partial-thickness rotator cuff tears, finding 87% overall accuracy for both imaging tests.

34. Davidson JF, Burkhart SS, Richards DP, Campbell SE: Use of preoperative magnetic resonance imaging to predict rotator cuff tear pattern and method of repair. *Arthroscopy* 2005;21:1428.

    This retrospective study evaluated the predictive value of 55 usable presurgical MRI scans in assessing tear pattern, size, and repairability and found a direct and statistically significant correlation. Level of evidence: III.

35. Tauro JC: Stiffness and rotator cuff tears: Incidence, arthroscopic findings, and treatment results. *Arthroscopy* 2006;22:581-586.

    Seventy-two patients were retrospectively evaluated to determine the influence of presurgical motion restriction on postsurgical stiffness. The range of motion improved, except in three patients with adhesive capsulitis. Level of evidence: IV.

36. Nottage WM: Rotator cuff repair with or without acromioplasty. *Arthroscopy* 2003;19(suppl):229-232.

    A review of the advantages, disadvantages, and support in the literature for performing an acromioplasty during rotator cuff repair is presented.

37. Goldberg BA, Lippitt SB, Matsen FA: Improvement in comfort and function after cuff repair without acromioplasty. *Clin Orthop Relat Res* 2001;390:142-150.

    At a minimum 2 years after 27 full-thickness rotator cuff repairs without deltoid detachment, acromioplasty, or section of the coracoacromial ligament, there was significant improvement in function, comfort, and mental health scores.

38. Lazarus MD, Hosen DM, Kirby CL: Abstract: Rotator cuff repair with and without anterior acromioplasty. A perspective randomized study. *67th Annual Meeting Proceedings*. Rosemont, IL: American Academy of Orthopaedic Surgeons, 2000, p. 596.

39. Gartsman GM, O'Connor DP: Arthroscopic rotator cuff repair with and without arthroscopic subacromial decompression: A prospective, randomized study of one-year outcomes. *J Shoulder Elbow Surg* 2004;13:424-426.

    In this prospective randomized study, 47 patients without and 46 patients with subacromial decompression were compared at a minimum 1-year follow-up and showed no difference in functional outcome. Level of evidence: I.

40. Lo IKY, Boorman R, Marchuk L, Hollinshead R, Hart DA, Frank CB: Matrix molecule mRNA levels in the bursa and rotator cuff of patients with full-thickness rotator cuff tears. *Arthroscopy* 2005;21:645-651.

    In this controlled laboratory study, extracellular matrix molecules from bursal and cuff tissue were examined. Both tissues may contribute to the healing process following repair.

41. Uhthoff HK, Sarkar K: Surgical repair of rotator cuff ruptures: The importance of the subacromial bursa. *J Bone Joint Surg Br* 1991;73:399-401.

42. Lo IKY, Burkhart SS: The interval slide in continuity: A method of mobilizing the anterosuperior rotator cuff without disrupting the tear margins. *Arthroscopy* 2004;20:435-441.

    This study describes the concept and surgical technique of lateral tissue bridge preservation during a rotator interval release in selected patients with massive rotator cuff tears. Level of evidence: V.

43. Lo IKY, Burkhart SS: Arthroscopic repair of massive, contracted immobile rotator cuff tear using single and double interval slides: Technique and preliminary results. *Arthroscopy* 2004;20:22-33.

    The use of a single- or double-interval slide technique led to improvement in active motion, strength, and function in this retrospective cohort of nine patients with massive rotator cuff tears. Level of evidence: IV.

44. Tauro JC: Arthroscopic repair of large rotator cuff tears using the interval slide technique. *Arthroscopy* 2004;20:13-20.

    Forty-two patients with a retracted fixed supraspinatus tear were subjected to an interval slide and release of the rotator cuff interval, contracted coracohumeral ligament, and superior capsule. At an average 32-month follow-up, 27 had an excellent or good result. Level of evidence: IV.

45. Klein JR, Burkhart SS: Identification of essential anatomic landmarks in performing arthroscopic single- and double-interval slides. *Arthroscopy* 2004;20:765-770.

    This article describes the development of single- and double-slide techniques for the release of contracted rotator cuff intervals encountered during arthroscopic repair of massive, immobile rotator cuff tears. Level of evidence: V.

46. Burkhart SS, Danaceau SM, Pearce CE Jr: Arthroscopic rotator cuff repair: Analysis of results by tear size and by repair technique. Margin convergence versus direct tendon-to-bone repair. *Arthroscopy* 2001;17:905-912.

At an average 3-5 year follow-up of 59 patients after arthroscopic rotator cuff repair, 95% had a good or excellent
result, regardless of tear size. U-shaped tears repaired by
margin convergence had results comparable to those of
crescent-shaped tears repaired directly using a tendon-to-
bone technique.

47. Burkhart SS: Arthroscopic repair of massive rotator
cuff tears: Concept of margin convergence. *Tech
Shoulder Elbow Surg* 2000;1:232-239.

48. Burkhart SS, Athanasiou KA, Wirth MA: Margin
convergence: A method of reducing strain in massive
rotator cuff tears. *Arthroscopy* 1996;12:335-338.

49. Wolf EM, Pennington WT, Agrawal V: Arthroscopic
side-to-side rotator cuff repair. *Arthroscopy* 2005;21:
881-887.

This retrospective case series evaluated 42 patients following arthroscopic repair using only a margin convergence technique, with a reported 98% overall good or excellent result at 4-year or 10-year follow-up. Level of
evidence: IV.

50. Schneeberger AG, von Roll A, Kalberer F, Jacob HA,
Gerber C: Mechanical strength of arthroscopic rota-
tor cuff repair techniques: An in-vitro study. *J Bone
Joint Surg Am* 2002;84:2152-2160.

In an in vitro study, arthroscopic rotator cuff repair with
the mattress stitch and bone anchors was found to allow
relatively solid fixation. Holding strength was not improved with the modified Mason-Allen stitch.

51. Fealy S, Rodeo SA, MacGillivray JD, et al: Biomechanical evaluation of the relation between number
of suture anchors and strength of the bone-tendon interface in a goat rotator cuff model. *Arthroscopy*
2006;22:595-602.

A biomechanical comparison of load to failure in a goat
model showed no significant difference in strength between a two-anchor and a four-anchor rotator cuff repair,
as tested at 4 and 8 weeks after repair.

52. Burkhart SS, Diaz Pagan JL, Wirth MA, Athanasiou
KA: Cyclic loading of anchor-based rotator cuff repairs: Confirmation of the tension overload phenomenon and comparison of suture anchor fixation with
transosseous fixation. *Arthroscopy* 1997;13:720-724.

53. Lichtenberg S, Liem D, Magosch P, Habermeyer P:
Influence of tendon healing after arthroscopic rotator cuff repair on clinical outcome using single-row
Mason-Allen suture technique: A prospective, MRI-
controlled study. *Knee Surg Sports Traumatol Arthrosc* 2006;14:1200-1206.

In this study of the influence of rotator cuff integrity on
outcome, the retearing rate was 24.5% after arthroscopic
repair of 53 isolated supraspinatus rotator cuff tears. Compromised integrity negatively influenced postsurgical
strength and Constant score. Patients older than 65 years
had a higher retearing rate. Level of evidence: IV.

54. Ahmad CS, Stewart AM, Izquierdo R, Bigliani LU:
Tendon-bone interface motion in transosseous suture and suture anchor repair rotator cuff repair techniques. *Am J Sports Med* 2005;33:1667-1671.

This controlled cadaver study compared the repair stability of simple suture anchoring and transosseous equivalent. Measurement of motion at the tendon-bone interface revealed significantly less motion with the
transosseous construct, which suggests it is more stable.

55. Ma CB, Comerford L, Wilson J, Puttlitz C: Biomechanical evaluation of arthroscopic rotator cuff repairs: Double-row compared with single-row fixation. *J Bone Joint Surg Am* 2006;88:403-410.

In an in vitro cadaver study, dual-row fixation carried a
significantly higher ultimate tensile load than fixation with
three single-row repair constructs.

56. Ma CB, MacGillivray JD, Clabeaux J, et al: Biomechanical evaluation of arthroscopic rotator cuff
stitches. *J Bone Joint Surg Am* 2004;86:1211-1216.

In an in vitro sheep model, the biomechanical properties
of four suture repair constructs were compared for repair
of a full-thickness rotator cuff tear. The ultimate tensile
load was significantly higher with the described massive
rotator cuff stitch or modified Mason-Allen stitch, in comparison with the simple stitch or horizontal stitch.

57. Cummins CA, Murrell GA: Mode of failure for rotator cuff repair with suture anchors identified at revision surgery. *J Shoulder Elbow Surg* 2003;12:128-133.

Of 342 rotator cuff tears repaired using suture anchors
and a mattress-suturing configuration, 6% required revision surgery, the findings from which suggested that the
weak link in the initial repair was the tendon-suture interface.

58. Burkhart SS, Athanasiou KA: The twist-lock concept
of tissue transport and suture fixation without knots:
Observations along the Hong Kong skyline. *Arthroscopy* 2003;19:613-625.

The twist-lock suture anchor construct, which does not
require the use of knots, was compared with a standard suture anchor construct. Its single-pull loads to failure were
found to be significantly higher than those of the standard
system.

59. Bardana DD, Burks RT, West JR, Greis PE: The effect
of suture anchor design and orientation on suture
abrasion: An in-vitro study. *Arthroscopy* 2003;19:
274-281.

In vitro examination of 17 commonly used suture anchors found that suture anchor eyelet design has an important influence.

60. Smith CD, Alexander S, Hill AM, et al: A biomechanical comparison of single- and double-row fixation in
arthroscopic rotator cuff repair. *J Bone Joint Surg Am*
2006;88:2425-2431.

This cadaver study compared cyclic load and ultimate load to failure in single-row and double-row repairs, finding that gap formation was decreased and strength was increased in double-row constructs.

61. Tingart MJ, Apreleva M, Lehtinen J, Zurakowski D, Warner JJ: Anchor design and bone mineral density affect the pull-out strength of suture anchors in rotator cuff repair: Which anchors are best to use in patients with low bone quality? *Am J Sports Med* 2004; 32:1466-1473.

    This cadaver study evaluated the relationship between suture anchor pull-out strength and bone density, finding that bone quality, anchor type, and anchor placement have a significant impact on anchor failure loads. The authors recommend that suture anchors be placed in the proximal-anterior and middle parts of the greater tuberosity.

62. Millett PJ, Mazzocca A, Guanche CA: Mattress double-anchor footprint repair: A novel, arthroscopic rotator cuff repair technique. *Arthroscopy* 2004;20: 875-879.

    This article describes a surgical technique for arthroscopic rotator cuff repair that enhances tendon-suture security and footprint restoration using a mattress double-anchor technique. Level of evidence: V.

63. Barber FA, Herbert MA, Richards DP: Sutures and suture anchors: Update 2003. *Arthroscopy* 2003;19: 985-990.

    Porcine femurs were used to evaluate several sutures and suture anchors for single-pull load-to-failure strength and failure mode. Screw anchors were found to have higher load-to-failure values than nonscrew anchors; the failure loads of biodegradable anchors were relatively low. All anchors were stronger than the suture for which they were designed.

64. De Carli A, Vadala A, Monaco E, Labianca L, Zanzotto E, Ferretti A: Effect of cyclic loading on new polyblend suture coupled with different anchors. *Am J Sports Med* 2005;33:214-219.

    This biomechanical cadaver study examined the influence of anchor type and suture material on cyclic loading. The FiberWire suture provided stronger fixation but changed the mode of anchor failure; metallic anchors failed via slippage, and absorbable anchors failed via eyelet rupture.

65. Lo IK, Burkhart SS, Athanasiou K: Abrasion resistance of two types of nonabsorbable braided suture. *Arthroscopy* 2004;20:407-413.

    This study of abrasion resistance to cyclic loading compared multiple repair constructs of nonabsorbable suture and anchors. Suture abrasion differed with suture type, anchor type, and testing conditions.

66. Lo IK, Burkhart SS: Double-row arthroscopic rotator cuff repair: Re-establishing the footprint of the rotator cuff. *Arthroscopy* 2003;19:1035-1042.

    A double-row technique for rotator cuff repair is described to reestablish the normal footprint, increase the contact area for healing, and possibly improve clinical results.

67. Brady PC, Arrigoni P, Burkhart SS: Evaluation of residual rotator cuff defects after in-vivo single- versus double-row rotator cuff repairs. *Arthroscopy* 2006; 22:1070-1075.

    In vivo measurement of footprint coverage area in 26 patients found that dual-row repair effectively covered the entire footprint, compared with residual 52.7% lack of coverage in single-row repair.

68. Burkhart SS, Wirth MA, Simonick M, Salem D, Lanctot D, Athanasiou K: Loop security as a determinant of tissue fixation security. *Arthroscopy* 1998;14: 773-776.

69. Koganti AK, Adamson GJ, Gregersen CS, Pink MM, Shankwiler JA: Biomechanical comparison of traditional and locked suture configurations for arthroscopic repairs of the rotator cuff. *Am J Sports Med* 2006;34:1832-1838.

    A controlled laboratory study found that locked configuration sutures were superior to traditional simple and horizontal mattress configurations in resisting gap formation under cyclic loading.

70. Gerber C, Schneeberger AG, Perren SM, Nyffeler RW: Experimental rotator cuff repair: A preliminary study. *J Bone Joint Surg Am* 1999;81:1281-1290.

71. Labbé MR: Arthroscopic technique for patch augmentation of rotator cuff repairs. *Arthroscopy* 2006; 22:1136.

    A single author's experience with arthroscopic application of an augmentation patch is described, with short-term follow-up results in six patients. Level of evidence: V.

72. Mura N, O'Driscoll SW, Zobitz ME, Heers G, An KN: Biomechanical effect of patch graft for large rotator cuff tears: A cadaver study. *Clin Orthop Relat Res* 2003;415:131-138.

    A synthetic patch graft redirected abduction force transmission in a cadaver glenohumeral joint with a rotator cuff defect and was found to be a potential treatment option for otherwise irreparable defects.

73. Boileau P, Brassart N, Watkinson DJ, Carles M, Hatzidakis AM, Krishnan SG: Arthroscopic repair of full-thickness tears of the supraspinatus: Does the tendon really heal? *J Bone Joint Surg Am* 2005;87:1229-1240.

    The functional and structural outcomes of 65 consecutive patients are reported at an average 29-month follow-up after arthroscopic repair of a full-thickness supraspinatus tendon tear. Level of evidence: IV.

74. Gartsman GM, Khan M, Hammerman SM: Arthroscopic repair of full-thickness tears of the rotator cuff. *J Bone Joint Surg Am* 1998;80:832-840.

75. Rebuzzi E, Colett N, Schiavetti S, Giusto F: Arthroscopic rotator cuff repair in patients older than 60 years. *Arthroscopy* 2005;21:48-54.

A retrospective review of 54 patients older than 60 years found that 81% had a good or excellent result following arthroscopic rotator cuff repair that included margin convergence, anchoring, or both. Level of evidence: IV.

76. Galatz LM, Ball CM, Teefey SA, et al: The outcome and repair integrity of completely arthroscopically-repaired large and massive rotator cuff tears. *J Bone Joint Surg Am* 2004;86:219-224.

In a retrospective review of 18 patients with large or massive cuff tears repaired arthroscopically, 17 showed residual or recurrent defect at a minimum 12-month follow-up. Patient satisfaction was high, although clinical deterioration continued between 12-month and 24-month follow-ups. Level of evidence: IV.

77. Bishop J, Klepps S, Lo IK, Bird J, Gladstone JM, Flatow EL: Cuff integrity after arthroscopic versus open rotator cuff repair: A prospective study. *J Shoulder Elbow Surg* 2006;15:290-299.

In a prospective study, clinical examination and imaging were performed on 40 patients following arthroscopic rotator cuff repair and compared with that of a control group of 32 patients following open repair. Clinical outcomes were similar, but rotator cuff repair integrity varied with technique and tear size. Level of evidence: III.

78. Lo IK, Burkhart SS: Arthroscopic revision of failed rotator cuff repairs: Technique and results. *Arthroscopy* 2004;20:250-267.

This case series examined the results of revision arthroscopic rotator cuff repairs in 14 patients who had unsuccessful previous rotator cuff repairs. The technique is technically demanding, and attention to patient selection and surgical detail is important. Level of evidence: IV.

79. Guttmann D, Graham RD, MacLennan MJ, Lubowitz JH: Arthroscopic rotator cuff repair: The learning curve. *Arthroscopy* 2005;21:394-400.

One surgeon found that the surgical time required for 100 consecutive rotator cuff repairs significantly decreased with experience. Level of evidence: IV.

80. Mohana-Borges AV, Chung CB, Resnick D: MR imaging and MR arthrography of the postoperative shoulder: Spectrum of normal and abnormal findings. *Radiographics* 2004;24:69-85.

This article reviews the role of different imaging modalities following rotator cuff repair.

81. Prickett WD, Teefey SA, Galatz LM, Calfee RP, Middleton WD, Yamaguchi K: Accuracy of ultrasound imaging of the rotator cuff in shoulders that are painful postoperatively. *J Bone Joint Surg Am* 2003;85-A: 1084-1089.

In a retrospective review of 44 patients after high-resolution ultrasonographic examination and subsequent shoulder arthroscopy, ultrasonography was found to have led to a correct diagnosis in 40 patients.

82. Boszotta H, Prunner K: Arthroscopically-assisted rotator cuff repair. *Arthroscopy* 2004;20:620-626.

A retrospective 3-year follow-up of 84 patients after arthroscopic repair using a transosseous bone tunnel technique found good clinical results for those with a medium-sized or large rotator cuff tear. Duration of presurgical symptoms, tear size, and long lead biceps tendon pathology were related to outcome. Level of evidence: IV.

83. Weber SC, Abrams JS, Nottage WM: Complications associated with arthroscopic shoulder surgery. *Arthroscopy* 2002;18(suppl 2):88-95.

A review of the literature on complications of arthroscopic shoulder surgery found a rate between 5.8% and 9.5%, although underreporting was considered to be problematic.

84. Mallik K, Barr MS, Anderson MW, Miller MD: Intra-articular migration of a sutureless arthroscopic rotator cuff fixation device. *Arthroscopy* 2003;19:e5-e8.

Intra-articular migration of a sutureless repair device was detected on magnetic resonance arthroscopy 4 months after surgery in this case report.

85. Vad VB, Southern D, Warren RF, Altchek DW, Dines D: Prevalence of peripheral neurologic injuries in rotator cuff tears with atrophy. *J Shoulder Elbow Surg* 2003;12:333-336.

Twenty-five patients with a full-thickness rotator cuff tear and shoulder muscle atrophy underwent electrodiagnostic testing. Seven had an abnormal electromyographic examinations. The prevalence of peripheral neuropathy was 28%; it was significantly associated with increased atrophy.

# Chapter 23

# Arthroscopic Treatment of Partial-Thickness Rotator Cuff Tears

Kelton M. Burbank, MD

*Alan S. Curtis, MD

## Introduction

The importance of partial-thickness rotator cuff tears (PTRCTs) was first recognized by Codman in 1934.[1] Although PTRCTs were included in Neer's classic description of the spectrum of rotator cuff disease, their significance was undervalued.[2,3] Advances in shoulder arthroscopy and imaging techniques, especially MRI, magnetic resonance arthrography, and ultrasonography, have improved the ability to recognize PTRCTs and have led to an apparent increase in their incidence. With improved recognition of PTRCTs, their possible role in the pathophysiology of rotator cuff disease has become a controversial topic. PTRCTs are found in young overhead athletes as well as older, sedentary individuals. Articular-sided tears consistently have been found to be two to three times as prevalent as bursal-sided tears.[4-7] These observations have led researchers to propose intrinsic and extrinsic mechanisms of injury other than outlet impingement. Some have even questioned the need for a subacromial decompression in the treatment of rotator cuff disease.[8,9] The supraspinatus tendon, which is almost always involved in PTRCTs, has a characteristic insertion onto the greater tuberosity.[4-7] This "footprint," particularly its dimensions, has been studied extensively in the hope of improving the diagnosis and treatment of PTRCTs[10-13] (Figure 1). Despite these advances, the best methods of evaluating and treating the different types of PTRCTs remain speculative. The patient's age and activity level as well as the size and location of the tear are important considerations in making treatment decisions. Well-controlled studies are needed.

## Clinical Evaluation

PTRCTs occur in two distinct groups of patients: middle-aged or older individuals who have degenerative rotator cuff pathology; and younger athletes who participate in sports activities requiring repetitive overhead motion, such as baseball, tennis, or swimming. Patients in both groups most commonly complain of pain and stiffness. The pain is typically worse at night. Paradoxically, pain is often worse in a patient with a PTRCT than in a patient with a full-thickness tear, perhaps because of increased levels of substance P or increased strain on the remaining rotator cuff fibers.[14-16] As Codman first noted, patients with a PTRCT have a decreased range of motion, especially with internal rotation. The patient typically has a painful arc of motion between 60° and 120°. Weakness caused by pain, the cuff tear, or both can be assessed manually using the Jobe sign, which is thought to best isolate the supraspinatus.

An overhead athlete may have a history of decreasing performance. The shoulder pain tends to be posterior with the arm abducted and externally rotated. On examination, a glenohumeral internal rotation deficit may be evident. If the tear is progressing, tests for a superior labrum anterior and posterior lesion, such as the Speed's or O'Brien test, may be positive. Subtle signs of instability may also be present. As the rotator cuff becomes weaker, the patient may develop coracoacromial impingement secondary to a lack of rotator cuff stabilization and posterior capsular tightness, with obligate anterior-superior migration of the humeral head.

## Treatment Decision Making

Although the incidence of PTRCTs is not known, MRI and cadaver studies indicate that incidence in asymptomatic individuals increases with age.[17,18] Intratendinous tears are particularly difficult to discover. In addition, the natural history of PTRCTs is not well understood. It appears that PTRCTs are unlikely to heal, and they progress in size. A study that examined 40 PTRCTs

*Alan S. Curtis, MD or the department with which he is affiliated has received miscellaneous nonincome support, commercially-derived honoraria, or other nonresearch-related funding from Arthrex and royalties from DonJoy and Arthrex.

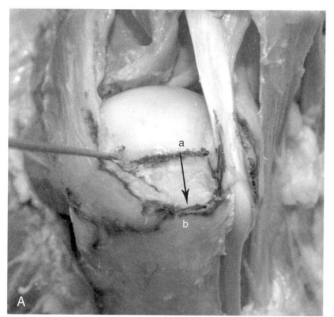
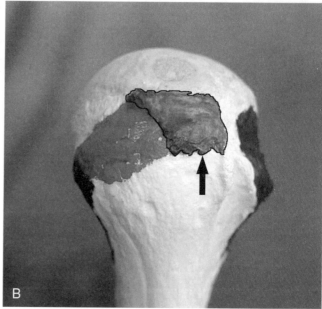

**Figure 1** The supraspinatus footprint. **A,** The tendon has been dissected off to reveal the footprint (a → b = the medial-lateral distance). **B,** Schematic depiction of the supraspinatus footprint (*arrow*).

using arthrography before and after 1 year of nonsurgical treatment found that 80% of the tears increased in size or progressed to a full-thickness tear.[19] Four decreased in size, and four appeared to heal or disappear. No randomized, controlled studies of treatment are available. In light of the epidemiologic difficulties, the lack of consensus on the best treatment of PTRCTs is not surprising.

### Nonsurgical Treatment

The initial treatment of a PTRCT is almost always nonsurgical. Rest, activity modification, nonsteroidal anti-inflammatory drugs, and the application of heat or cold are the treatment mainstays. Physical therapy is a helpful adjuvant, especially if capsular contracture or weakness is present. The goal of physical therapy is to strengthen the rotator cuff muscles and the scapular stabilizers so as to maximize concavity-compression. If physical therapy is not successful, selective cortisone injection may be beneficial. However, a recent review did not support the efficacy of this treatment.[20]

Significant internal rotation contractures require attention in some overhead athletes. An aggressive stretching program is the first step in treatment. Strengthening of the rotator cuff and scapular stabilizers can be initiated after motion returns to normal and pain is under control. Core strengthening to improve the efficiency of the kinetic chain and decrease the strain on the shoulder also can be useful before the athlete begins a gradual return to sports activities.

### Surgical Treatment

Determining the best surgical treatment requires consideration of the depth, location, and area of the tear as well as the patient's age and expectations. For example, the treatment chosen for a PTRCT in a 77-year-old man who wants to play recreational golf should be different from the treatment of a similar tear in a 22-year-old baseball pitcher whose career is at risk. Associated pathology must be assessed; the biceps attachment, labrum, and capsule of the shoulder also may require treatment, especially in a younger patient.

The surgical options generally include débridement, débridement with subacromial decompression, and repair with or without subacromial decompression. A repair can be open, mini-open, or arthroscopic. An articular-sided partial tear can be arthroscopically treated by a transtendon repair or conversion to a full-thickness tear.

## Results of Surgical Treatment
### Arthroscopic Débridement

In reports of tears treated with arthroscopic débridement alone, the percentage of good or excellent results ranged from 50% to 89%.[8,21,22] These retrospective studies did not classify patients by type of tear, and the results must therefore be interpreted with caution.

### Débridement and Subacromial Decompression

Early studies of débridement and decompression included a variety of tear types. In two studies, good or excellent results were reported in 76% or 86% of pa-

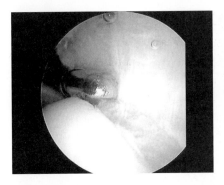

**Figure 2**  A 4.5-mm full-radius shaver is used to débride the edge of the tear and measure the amount of exposed bone.

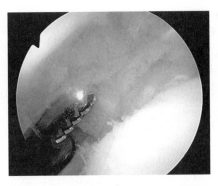

**Figure 3**  Débridement of the footprint using a shaver.

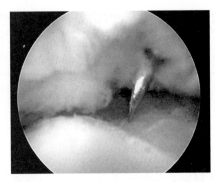

**Figure 4**  Localization of the tear using a spinal needle passed from outside to inside.

tients.[23,24] Another study found similar outcomes with or without subacromial decompression.[25] In a study of athletes younger than age 40 years, patients who had experienced an acute traumatic event had a better result after débridement and acromioplasty than those with an insidious onset of pain.[5] Another study did not find a difference between patients with no tear and patients with an Ellman grade I or II PTRCT treated with subacromial decompression and débridement; the reported rate of success was 92%.[4] (The Ellman classification of PTRCTs is described in chapter 14.) However, poorer results in patients with an Ellman grade IIB tear (38% failure) led to a recommendation that grade IIB and IIIB tears be repaired. A recent retrospective review of débridement and subacromial decompression in 26 type II PTRCTs found that 9 progressed to a full-thickness tear during the 5-year minimum follow-up period, raising questions about the effectiveness of this treatment.[26]

### Repair

A 1999 study compared débridement and subacromial decompression with mini-open repair and subacromial decompression in patients with a grade III tear. Patients who underwent repair with subacromial decompression were found to have better results.[27] In general, patients with a bursal-sided tear had worse results than those with an articular-sided tear. This study concluded that a tear of 50% or more of the tendon thickness (a grade III tear) should be repaired. Another study reported excellent or good results after open repair in 82% of 38 ungraded tears.[7] No difference was noted between patients who underwent acromioplasty and those who underwent coracoacromial ligament resection, or between patients with a bursal-sided, intratendinous, or articular-sided tear. A more recent study reported good or excellent results in 98% of patients with a grade III tear after arthroscopic tear completion and repair.[28] Two other studies reported good or excellent results in 92% or 94% of patients after use of an arthroscopic transtendon approach.[13,29]

Table 1 summarizes the outcome studies on the treatment of PTRCTs. Three recent comprehensive reviews of the literature are available,[36-38] one of which presents a treatment algorithm based on the best current information.[38]

## Surgical Repair of a PASTA Lesion

Although a number of surgical approaches to a partial articular-sided tendon avulsion (PASTA) lesion can successfully be used, an arthroscopic approach is preferable. For an articular-sided lesion, a transtendon technique is used unless the remaining rotator cuff fibers are of poor quality, as they may be in an older patient, or the amount of remaining cuff tissue is insubstantial (generally less than 25% of the insertion). Recent publications have described this technique well.[29,39] For most lesions, a one-anchor repair, is sufficient. If the length of the tear exceeds 1.5 cm, a second anchor can be considered.

Débridement of torn tissue and synovium is done using a shaver whose diameter is known (Figure 2). The extent of detachment from the edge of the articular surface is evaluated. If it is greater than 7 mm, repair should be considered. If the remaining fibers are of poor quality, tear completion and repair using standard arthroscopic technique rather than a transtendon repair, should be performed.

The footprint is prepared through the anterior cannula to a bleeding surface, taking care to preserve the cortical bone for better anchor purchase (Figure 3).

The tear is localized with a spinal needle placed from outside just lateral to the acromion (Figure 4). A portal is created adjacent to the needle, using a number-11 blade through the skin and making a small nick in the supraspinatus in line with its fibers.

A small (6- or 7-mm) cannula is inserted into the lateral portal so that the tip is just visible through the supraspinatus. A 5.5-mm double-loaded or triple-loaded metal anchor is brought through the cannula into the footprint just off the articular surface, taking care to maintain a 45° angle (Figure 5). Although this step can be

## Table 1 | Outcome Studies of Surgical Treatment of PTRCTs

| Study | Number of Patients (Description) | Treatment | Patient Satisfaction Rate (%) | Comments |
|---|---|---|---|---|
| Neer[2] (1972) | 18 | Subacromial decompression only (open) | 94 | |
| Andrews et al[21] (1985) | 34 (young athletes) | Débridement without subacromial decompression | 85 | All patients had a labral tear. |
| Ogilvie-Harris and Wiley[22] (1986) | 57 | Débridement without subacromial decompression | 50 | |
| Esch et al[23] (1988) | 45 | Débridement with subacromial decompression (arthroscopic) | 82 | |
| Ellman[30] (1990) | 20 | Débridement with subacromial decompression (arthroscopic) | 75 | |
| Gartsman[24] (1990) | 40 | Débridement with subacromial decompression (arthroscopic) | 82 | |
| Snyder et al[31] (1991) | 31 (athletes) | Débridement with or without subacromial decompression (arthroscopic) | 84 | Results were similar regardless of whether subacromial decompression was performed. |
| Itoi and Tabata[7] (1992) | 38 | Repair with or without subacromial decompression (open) | 82 | |
| Ryu[32] (1992) | 35 | Subacromial decompression only (arthroscopic) | 86 | |
| Wright and Cofield[33] (1996) | 39 | Repair with subacromial decompression (open) | 85 | |
| Payne et al[5] (1997) | 43 (athletes with traumatic or insidious injury) | Débridement with or without subacromial decompression (arthroscopic) | 72 | Repair also was performed in 2 patients. Patients with a traumatic injury had a better result. |
| Budoff et al[8] (1998) | 79 (athletes) | Débridement with or without subacromial decompression (arthroscopic) | 87 | Acromial osteophyte removal was performed in 42%. |
| Weber[27] (1999) | 65 (Ellman grade III) | Débridement or repair (mini-open) with or without subacromial decompression (arthroscopic) | 94 (mini-open), 45 (arthroscopic) | Repair was more successful than débridement. |
| Conway[34] (2001) | 14 (baseball players) | Repair (arthroscopic) without subacromial decompression | 89 | All tears were intratendinous. |
| Cordasco et al[4] (2002) | 77 (Ellman grades I and II) | Débridement with subacromial decompression (arthroscopic) | 92 | Patients with a bursal-sided tear had a poorer result. |
| Park et al[35] (2004) | 22 (Ellman grade III) | Repair (completion) with subacromial decompression (arthroscopic) | 95 | |
| Duralde and Kimmerly[29] (2005) | 24 | Repair (transtendon) with subacromial decompression | 96 | |
| Ide et al[13] (2005) | 17 | Repair (transtendon) without subacromial decompression | 94 | |
| Deutsch[28] (2007) | 41 | Repair (completion) with subacromial decompression (arthroscopic) | 98 | Subacromial decompression was not performed in 2 patients. |

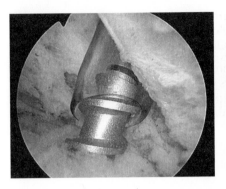

**Figure 5** A metal 5.5-mm anchor is placed through the cannula in the prepared footprint.

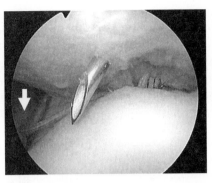

**Figure 6** Spinal needle is used to localize the placement of the first (anterior) suture at the edge of the tear. Absorbable suture or suture shuttle will be passed through the spinal needle and retrieved through the anterior cannula. The suture to be shuttled from the anchor can be seen in the cannula (*arrow*).

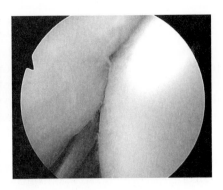

**Figure 7** Reduction of the supraspinatus tear onto the footprint, as seen from inside the joint.

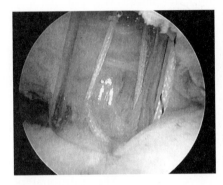

**Figure 8** Sutures being tied in the subacromial space.

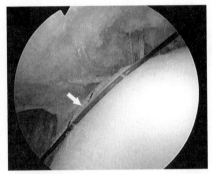

**Figure 9** Absorbable suture is used to shuttle the striped third suture limb (*arrow*) from anterior to posterior. The anterior (white) and posterior (dark) limbs have already been passed.

performed percutaneously, doing so makes subsequent suture retrieval in the subacromial space slightly more difficult.

The first suture to be passed, typically the anterior one, is retrieved through the anterior cannula. A spinal needle is placed percutaneously through the supraspinatus tear. The supraspinatus tendon tear should be penetrated about 1 cm medial and 1 cm anterior to the anchor. A smooth suture or other shuttling device is passed through the needle and retrieved through the anterior portal. The first suture is shuttled through the supraspinatus tendon tear (Figure 6).

This process is repeated for the next suture in the anchor, typically the posterior one. This suture is retrieved through the anterior cannula. The spinal needle is passed through the edge of the supraspinatus tendon tear, this time coming through about 1 cm posterior and 1 cm medial to the anchor. The suture or shuttling device is passed through the spinal needle and retrieved through the anterior portal. The second suture is shuttled back through the supraspinatus. Tension can be placed on the suture ends to check the reduction onto the footprint (Figure 7).

Without changing arm position, the arthroscope is repositioned in the subacromial space, and the sutures are located. If there is significant bursitis, the sutures are retrieved through the anterior portal so they are safe while the bursa is débrided. Alternatively, the bursectomy can be performed before anchor placement. Doing so requires moving the arthroscope back and forth between the joint and the subacromial space, but it does facilitate location and protection of the sutures.

The sutures are tied in the subacromial space through the lateral portal, with the posterior suture tied first. The post should be the limb through the split so the tendon is repaired to the anchor site. The anterior suture is then tied. As the sutures tighten, the supraspinatus becomes dimpled at the edge of the articular surface, re-creating the broad footprint (Figure 8). Subacromial decompression is performed, if indicated.

If a triple-loaded anchor is used, the third suture can be shuttled in the same manner as the other sutures, except that it is placed on either side of the split in the supraspinatus and remains lateral to the other sutures (Figure 9). These suture limbs are then tied across the split in the supraspinatus to repair the small opening.

Alternatively, a free suture (not associated with an anchor) can be passed across the split.

After surgery, the patient is treated using the protocol for a small rotator cuff repair. Protection in a sling is provided for 6 weeks. Passive range of motion of the shoulder and active range of motion of the elbow, wrist, and hand are begun immediately. After 6 weeks, active range of motion of the shoulder is encouraged to restore full motion and prevent stiffness. At 10 weeks, isometric exercises and light resistance are begun, and they progress as tolerated by the patient. At approximately 4 months, most patients can return to their normal activities.

## Summary

PTRCTs are common, and they affect a broad spectrum of patients. The articular side of the supraspinatus tendon is the most commonly affected structure. PTRCTs, particularly intratendinous tears, can be difficult to detect; they have been described as incidental findings in MRI and cadaver studies.[17,18] The treatment recommendations reflect the findings of the available studies, which do not include randomized, controlled trials. The initial treatment should be nonsurgical and should last 3 to 6 months, depending on the patient's age, demands, and response. If surgical treatment is necessary, débridement with or without subacromial decompression is recommended for an Ellman grade IA, IB, or IIA tear. Repair, whether open, mini-open, or arthroscopic, is recommended for a grade IIB, IIIA, or IIIB tear. However, results from a well-designed clinical trial are needed to provide better support for treatment recommendations.

## Annotated References

1. Codman EA: *The Shoulder: Rupture of the Supraspinatus Tendon and Other Lesions in or About the Subacromial Bursa*. Boston, MA, Thomas Todd, 1934.

2. Neer CS II: Anterior acromioplasty for the chronic impingement syndrome in the shoulder: A preliminary report. *J Bone Joint Surg Am* 1972;54:41-50.

3. Neer CS II: Impingement lesions. *Clin Orthop Relat Res* 1983;173:70-77.

4. Cordasco FA, Backer M, Craig EV, Klein D, Warren RF: The partial-thickness rotator cuff tear: Is acromioplasty without repair sufficient? *Am J Sports Med* 2002;30:257-260.

    At a mean 4- to 5-year follow-up of 162 patients after arthroscopic acromioplasty and débridement, patients with a grade IIB partial tear had a significantly higher failure rate. There was no evidence that symptomatic intrinsic rotator cuff pathologic conditions progress in patients with PTRCTs treated with arthroscopic anterior acromioplasty.

5. Payne LZ, Altchek DW, Craig EV, Warren RF:

Arthroscopic treatment of partial rotator cuff tears in young athletes: A preliminary report. *Am J Sports Med* 1997;25:299-305.

6. Ozaki J, Fujimoto S, Nakagawa Y, Masuhara K, Tamai S: Tears of the rotator cuff of the shoulder associated with pathological changes in the acromion: A study in cadavera. *J Bone Joint Surg Am* 1988;70:1224-1230.

7. Itoi E, Tabata S: Incomplete rotator cuff tears: Results of operative treatment. *Clin Orthop Relat Res* 1992;284:128-135.

8. Budoff JE, Nirschl RP, Guidi EJ: Debridement of partial-thickness tears of the rotator cuff without acromioplasty: Long-term follow-up and review of the literature. *J Bone Joint Surg Am* 1998;80:733-748.

9. McCallister WV, Parsons IM, Titelman RM, Matsen FA: Open rotator cuff repair without acromioplasty. *J Bone Joint Surg Am* 2005;87:1278-1283.

    In a prospective study of outcomes at a 2-year minimum and 5-year average follow-up, results were available for 61 of 96 consecutive patients who underwent open rotator cuff repair without acromioplasty or disruption of the coracoacromial ligament. Scores on the Simple Shoulder Test and Short Form-36 Health Survey were significantly improved. Level of evidence: IV.

10. Curtis AS, Burbank KM, Tierney JJ, Scheller AD, Curran AR: The insertional footprint of the rotator cuff: An anatomic study. *Arthroscopy* 2006;22:609.

    This anatomic study delineated the insertional footprints of the four tendons of the rotator cuff. The supraspinatus tendon insertional footprint measured 23 mm × 16 mm. Electron microscopy analysis revealed that the supraspinatus inserts within 1 mm of the edge of the articular surface and fills the sulcus to just beyond the tip of the tuberosity. The authors conclude that a PASTA lesion more than 8 mm from the edge of the articular surface may require repair.

11. Ruotolo C, Fow JE, Nottage WM: The supraspinatus footprint: An anatomic study of the supraspinatus insertion. *Arthroscopy* 2004;20:246-249.

    The supraspinatus insertion in 17 cadavers was found to have an average width of 12.1 mm. The authors conclude that a 50% supraspinatus tear would measure 7 mm from the edge of the articular surface and might require repair.

12. Dugas JR, Campbell DA, Warren RF, Robie BH, Millett PJ: Anatomy and dimensions of rotator cuff insertions. *J Shoulder Elbow Surg* 2002;11:498-503.

    This cadaver study measured the area and dimensions of the rotator cuff tendon insertions and their distance from the articular surface, using two methods.

13. Ide J, Maeda S, Takagi K: Arthroscopic transtendon repair of partial-thickness articular-side tears of the rotator cuff: Anatomical and clinical study. *Am J Sports Med* 2005;33:1672-1679.

In this Japanese study, the average width of the supraspinatus tendon insertion was 9.6 mm in 43 cadaver shoulders, and the mean distance of the tendon insertion from the edge of the articular surface was 0.3 mm. A transtendon repair technique is described. In 17 young patients, there were 14 excellent, 2 good, and 1 fair result. University of California Los Angeles and Japanese Orthopaedic Association shoulder scores significantly improved ($P < 0.01$). Level of evidence:IV.

14. Fukuda H: Partial-thickness rotator cuff tears: A modern view on Codman's classic. *J Shoulder Elbow Surg* 2000;9:163-168.

15. Gotoh M, Hamada K, Yamakawa H, Inoue A, Fukuda H: Increased substance P in subacromial bursa and shoulder pain in rotator cuff diseases. *J Orthop Res* 1998;16:618-621.

16. Bey MJ, Ramsey ML, Soslowsky LJ: Intratendinous strain fields of the supraspinatus tendon: Effect of a surgically created articular-surface rotator cuff tear. *J Shoulder Elbow Surg* 2002;11:562-569.

    MRI was used to quantify intratendinous strains in healthy cadaver shoulder specimens at 15°, 30°, 45°, and 60° of glenohumeral abduction. Comparison with a second set of images taken after an articular-surface PTRCT was created revealed that the tear increased strain in all joint positions except 15°.

17. Sher JS, Uribe JW, Posada A, Murphy BJ, Zlatkin MB: Abnormal findings on magnetic resonance images of asymptomatic shoulders. *J Bone Joint Surg Am* 1995;77:10-15.

18. Lohr JF, Uhthoff HK: The pathogenesis of degenerative rotator cuff tears. *Orthop Trans* 1987;11:237.

19. Yamanaka K, Matsumoto T: The joint side tear of the rotator cuff: A follow-up study by arthrography. *Clin Orthop Relat Res* 1994;304:68-73.

20. Koester MC, Dunn WR, Kuhn JE, Spindler KP: The efficacy of subacromial corticosteroid injection in the treatment of rotator cuff disease: A systemic review. *J Am Acad Orthop Surg* 2007;15:3-11.

    The evidence for using corticosteroid injection to treat rotator cuff disease was investigated. Nine of the 25 articles written between 1966 and 2006 met the inclusion criteria. One study found a clinically important difference in pain relief, and two studies found clinically important improvement in range of motion. The authors concluded that little reproducible evidence exists to support the efficacy of corticosteroid injection in treating rotator cuff disease.

21. Andrews JR, Broussard TS, Carson WG: Arthroscopy of the shoulder in the management of partial tears of the rotator cuff: A preliminary report. *Arthroscopy* 1985;1:117-122.

22. Ogilvie-Harris DJ, Wiley AM: Arthroscopic surgery of the shoulder. *J Bone Joint Surg Br* 1986;68:201-207.

23. Esch JC, Ozerkis LR, Helgager JA, Kane N, Lillott N: Arthroscopic subacromial decompression: Results according to the degree of rotator cuff tear. *Arthroscopy* 1988;4:241-249.

24. Gartsman GM: Arthroscopic acromioplasty for lesions of the rotator cuff. *J Bone Joint Surg Am* 1990; 72:169-180.

25. Snyder SJ: Arthroscopic repair of partial articular supraspinatus tendon avulsions: PASTA lesions of the rotator cuff tendon, in Snyder SJ: *Shoulder Arthroscopy*, ed 2. Philadelphia, PA, Lippincott Williams & Wilkins, 2003, pp 219-229.

26. Kartus J, Kartus C, Rostgård-Christensen L, Sernert N, Read J, Perko M: Long-term clinical and ultrasound evaluation after arthroscopic acromioplasty in patients with partial rotator cuff tears. *Arthroscopy* 2006;22:44-49.

    In a retrospective review, 26 of 33 type II PTRCTs treated with débridement and subacromial decompression were available for evaluation and ultrasonography at a mean 101-month follow-up (minimum, 60 months). Nine had progressed to full-thickness tears, of which two had undergone further surgery.

27. Weber SC: Arthroscopic debridement and acromioplasty versus mini-open repair in the treatment of significant partial-thickness rotator cuff tears. *Arthroscopy* 1999;15:126-131.

28. Deutsch A: Arthroscopic repair of partial-thickness tears of the rotator cuff. *J Shoulder Elbow Surg* 2007; 16:193-201.

    In a prospective analysis of 41 patients with a PTRCT of 50% or more of the tendon thickness, tear completion with arthroscopic repair was performed by one surgeon. All tears involved the supraspinatus tendon, and 80% were articular sided. American Shoulder and Elbow Surgeons Index scores, pain, and satisfaction significantly improved; 40 patients were satisfied with the outcome. Level of evidence: IV.

29. Duralde XA, Kimmerly WS: The technique of arthroscopic repair of partial thickness rotator cuff tears. *Tech Shoulder Elbow Surg* 2005;6:116-123.

    This article offers a step-by-step description of a transtendon repair using a bioabsorbable anchor and a tissue penetrator. At short-term (14-month) follow-up, 20 of the 24 patients had an excellent or good result.

30. Ellman H: Diagnosis and treatment of incomplete rotator cuff tears. *Clin Orthop Relat Res* 1990;254:64-74.

31. Snyder SJ, Pachelli AF, Del Pizzo W, Friedman MJ, Ferkel RD, Pattee G: Partial thickness rotator cuff tears: Results of arthroscopic treatment. *Arthroscopy* 1991;7:1-7.

32. Ryu RK: Arthroscopic subacromial decompression: A clinical review. *Arthroscopy* 1992;8:141-147.

33. Wright SA, Cofield RH: Management of partial-thickness rotator cuff tears. *J Shoulder Elbow Surg* 1996;5:458-466.

34. Conway JE: Arthroscopic repair of partial-thickness rotator cuff tears and SLAP lesions in professional baseball players. *Orthop Clin North Am* 2001;32: 443-456.

The internal impingement process in throwing athletes is described. There is little potential for spontaneous healing of rotator cuff tears and SLAP lesions after débridement.

35. Park JY, Chung KT, Yoo MJ: A serial comparison of arthroscopic repairs for partial- and full-thickness rotator cuff tears. *Arthroscopy* 2004;20:705-711.

36. Fukuda H: The management of partial-thickness tears of the rotator cuff. *J Bone Joint Surg Br* 2003; 85:3-11.

37. Matava MJ, Purcell DB, Rudzki JR: Partial-thickness rotator cuff tears. *Am J Sports Med* 2005;33: 1405-1417.

This comprehensive review of PTRCTs, with 109 references, includes thorough sections on treatment.

38. Wolff AB, Sethi P, Sutton KM, Covey AS, Magit DP, Medvecky M: Partial-thickness rotator cuff tears. *J Am Acad Orthop Surg* 2006;14:715-725.

This review includes techniques for repair of both articular-sided and bursal-sided PTRCTs.

39. Lo IK, Burkhart SS: Transtendon arthroscopic repair of partial-thickness, articular surface tears of the rotator cuff. *Arthroscopy* 2004;20:214-220.

The authors describe their method of transtendon repair using bioabsorbable anchors. For a tear involving less than 1.5 cm of the footprint, one anchor and a tissue penetrator are used. For a tear involving more than 1.5 cm of the footprint, two anchors are used. A unique construct creates a bridge of suture over the rotator cuff, compressing it onto the prepared bone of the footprint.

# Chapter 24

# The Biceps Tendon

Mark W. Rodosky, MD

## Introduction

The long head of the biceps tendon (LHBT) enters the glenohumeral joint through the confines of a complex pulley system composed of soft tissue and bone. The LHBT is a unique structure that has been recognized for many years as a source of shoulder pain. In recent years, knowledge about the pathophysiology, evaluation, and treatment of the LHBT has significantly increased.

## Anatomy

From its origin in the supraglenoid tubercle at the top of the glenoid rim, the biceps tendon travels through the intra-articular space of the glenohumeral joint, turning anteriorly to enter the intertubercular groove at an angle of approximately 35°. The origin and path vary among individuals; the origin can be anterior or posterior to the top of the glenoid rim, or it can arise primarily from the labrum rather than from bone.[1] The tendons may even have isolated slips arising from separate areas of the capsulolabral tissue.[2]

The LHBT is an intracapsular and intra-articular structure, although it is technically extrasynovial. It is encased in a double-tubular investing layer of tendon sheath, which is an extension of the joint capsule's synovial lining. The sheath's two layers form parietal and visceral layers distal to the transverse humeral ligament (THL).[3] In some individuals, the path of the biceps tendon is outside the glenohumeral joint capsule, and the LHBT may not be visible during arthroscopy.

The bony constraint of the LHBT pulley system is provided by the intertubercular groove, which is formed by the junction of the anterior edge of the greater tuberosity and the lateral edge of the lesser tuberosity. The LHBT glides within the groove, constrained by the soft tissue of the pulley system. The width of the groove varies among individuals. The distal part of the groove is stabilized by the THL, which forms its roof. This ligament is a continuation of the interval tissue from the superior aspect, the supraspinatus tendon from the posterolateral aspect, and the subscapularis tendon from the anteromedial aspect.[4] The proximal part of the groove is stabilized by four soft-tissue structures: the superior glenohumeral ligament (SGHL), subscapularis tendon, coracohumeral ligament (CHL), and supraspinatus tendon. Together, these four structures form a funnel-shaped system, called the reflection pulley, which directs and holds the LHBT in the intertubercular groove. The floor of this portion of the pulley system consists of the SGHL, which originates from the anterosuperior labrum adjacent to the supraglenoid tubercle. It crosses laterally to form a U-shaped sling as it inserts beneath the biceps tendon at the floor of the groove and is reinforced by the adjacent subscapularis tendon insertion into the lesser tuberosity[5] (Figure 1). The roof is formed by the CHL, which arises from the coracoid process to form two bands that traverse laterally. The more anterior band inserts into the superior border of the subscapularis tendon, the THL, and the lesser tuberosity. The more posterior band inserts into the greater tuberosity and is reinforced by the tendinous portion of the supraspinatus. The funnel is completed by the union of the anteroinferior SGHL and the posterosuperior CHL.[6]

The LHBT is surrounded by synovial tissue within the biceps groove, often referred to as the biceps hood or sheath. The biceps tendon itself is innervated by a network of sensory sympathetic fibers, which are thought to contribute to the pathogenesis of shoulder pain.[7]

The blood supply of the proximal biceps tendon comes from its attachment at the superior labrum, as well as from a terminal branch of the anterior humeral circumflex artery,[8] which travels through a mesotendon or vincula tendinum to supply the segment of the tendon that occupies the biceps groove. The mesotendon is similar to the vincula tendinum of the digital flexor tendons. It arises from the posterolateral aspect of the biceps groove, where it is continuous with the visceral layer of the LHBT sheath.[9]

## Biomechanics

The precise role of the LHBT remains controversial. One of the first biomechanical studies found that the

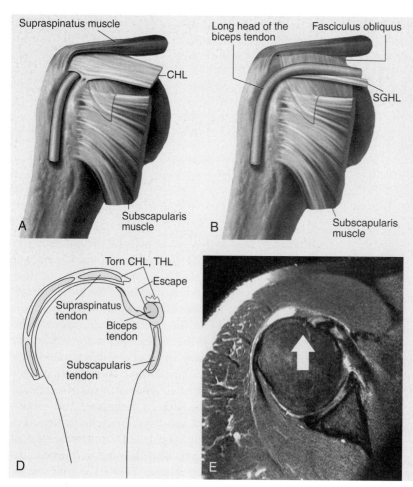

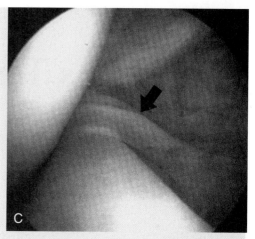

**Figure 1** The biceps groove pulley system. **A,** The roof of the system consists of the CHL reinforced by the supraspinatus tendon and muscle. **B,** The biceps tendon is held within the groove by the pulley system, the floor of which consists of the SGHL reinforced by the subscapularis tendon and muscle. **C,** Arthroscopic view of a normal right shoulder shows the SGHL (*arrow*) below the biceps tendon. **D,** The biceps tendon can escape over the subscapularis tendon, with disruption of the CHL and THL. **E,** Axial MRI of a right shoulder shows subluxation of the biceps tendon (*arrow*) within and under the substance of the subscapularis tendon. (*A and B reproduced with permission from Lichtenberg S, Habermeyer P: Pulley lesion, in Lajtai G, Snyder SJ, Applegate GR, Aitzemuller G, Gerber C (eds): Shoulder Arthroscopy and MRI Techniques. Berlin, Germany, Springer-Verlag, 2003.*)

LHBT can act as a humeral head depressor;[10] this finding supported Neer's contention that the LHBT should be preserved whenever possible.[11] The LHBT was later found to have a role in anterior stability of the shoulder in an overhead throwing position,[12] although electromyographic studies found that the LHBT is not active during simple elevation of the arm, with or without added weight, if the elbow is immobilized.[13,14] Other studies found that the LHBT is active during overhead motion.[15] Based on the premise that the LHBT is active during elevated shoulder motion, other biomechanical studies found that it can stabilize the glenohumeral joint. In these studies, translation of the humeral head on the glenoid was found to be reduced when the LHBT is active.[16-19] Most shoulder surgeons believe that in the presence of pathologic pain, the LHBT is not active and therefore cannot provide biomechanical support.

## Pathophysiology

LHBT pathology can be categorized as inflammatory, traumatic, or instability related. The causes of LHBT pathology are intimately related to the surrounding anatomy of the pulley system and can also be related to major trauma, repetitive microtrauma, or age-related changes. All three subtypes cause debilitating shoulder pain, and they often overlap. For example, an unstable tendon that is sliding in and out of the groove may become inflamed and then partially tear or completely rupture. The subgroups are useful in understanding the pathophysiology and treatment of LHBT conditions.

### Inflammatory Biceps Pathology

The most common pathology is inflammation of the biceps tendon. Inflammation without evidence of associated shoulder pathology is called primary bicipital tenosynovitis (Figure 2). As the biceps tendon travels within the narrow confines of the pulley system, the contact between the tendon and the surrounding structures of the pulley system causes wear and tear on the tendon. This wear and tear can be substantial in someone who participates in an upper extremity sport such as tennis, baseball, or swimming, or whose work requires repeated use of the arm in an overhead position, especially while supporting a heavy load. Nonetheless, primary bicipital tenosynovitis is rare as a result of wear and tear within the groove.

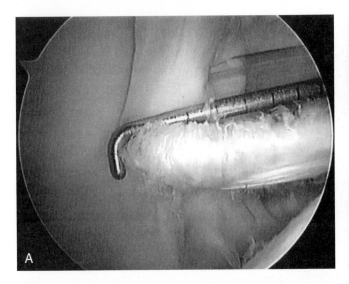 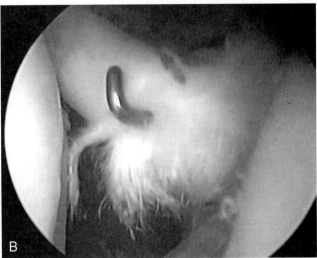

**Figure 2** **A,** In an arthroscopic view of a right shoulder, inflammatory changes are evident when the intertubercular portion of the tendon is displaced into the glenohumeral joint. **B,** In a right shoulder with a substantial partial tear, the probe easily passes through the partially torn biceps tendon.

Certain anatomic conditions can predispose an individual to inflammatory changes of the LHBT within the groove. Anomalies of the biceps groove, including narrowing of its already-slim confines, can add to the repetitive microtrauma that overhead activities inflict on the LHBT.[20] Fractures that result in distortion of the bony confines of the biceps groove also lead to a spectrum of complications, from narrowing of the groove to impingement against bony prominences to partial or complete entrapment from bony fragments.[21] A similar abnormal bony anatomy or increased soft-tissue confinement can be seen with glenohumeral arthritis or after arthroplastic treatment of shoulder fracture or arthritis.[22] As a result, many surgeons recommend biceps tenodesis or tenotomy for all patients undergoing shoulder arthroplasty.[23]

Neer believed that the most common cause of biceps tendinitis is subacromial (extrinsic) impingement.[11] In a recent study, 96% of patients with a partial-thickness or full-thickness LHBT tear had a concurrent supraspinatus tendon tear.[24] Extrinsic factors leading to a rotator cuff tear can also affect the biceps tendon.

Hypertrophic conditions of synovial tissue can result in synovial hypertrophy of the bicipital groove and invasion of the LHBT. This condition can be seen in inflammatory arthritides and pigmented villonodular synovitis.

Inflammation of the LHBT and its surrounding synovial tissue within the groove can lead to significant pain. Most tendinous changes occur in the portion of the tendon that sits in the bony groove when the arm is resting.[25] In the early stages, the tendon appears dull, swollen, and discolored, but it is fully mobile. As the disease progresses, the surrounding soft tissues become thickened and fibrotic, and the blood supply through affected vincula is diminished. Microscopic evaluation of the tendon may reveal round cell infiltration and fiber degeneration.[26] The biceps tendon may become swollen, and the hypertrophic tendon can cause an hourglass deformity, in which the tendon has difficulty sliding and may become entrapped within the groove. This condition is similar to trigger finger syndrome.[27] In some patients, the tendon fixes itself within the groove, causing a loss of external rotation of the glenohumeral joint, particularly when the joint is in a position of lower elevation. With continued inflammation, the LHBT can lose its structural integrity, becoming weak and atrophied.

### Traumatic Biceps Pathology

Any structure in the human body can be overcome by a traumatic force. The most common cause of overpowering force on the biceps tendon is longitudinal traction on the arm. The tendon fails as a result of excessive tension overloading. Another cause of failure is a direct blunt force to the tendon from a fall onto an outstretched arm. A tendon already weakened from inflammation may be more susceptible to trauma.

Repetitive microtrauma from an overhead sports or work activity can also cause biceps tendon pathology. For example, the LHBT can experience a significant repetitive tension load as the arm decelerates during the follow-through phase of throwing. Pain in a throwing athlete often is caused by a diseased tendon and can be completely resolved if the tendon ruptures.

Rupture of the biceps tendon can result in a Popeye deformity. In a patient who is obese or has poorly defined musculature, the deformity may be subtle or nonexistent. Many patients have painful cramping of the biceps muscle belly, which usually disappears within 6 months. Very few patients notice weakness in elbow flexion or forearm supination. In one study, patients with a spontaneous rupture of the LHBT had a 21% loss of supination strength and no loss of elbow flexion strength. After repair, patients had a 10% supination strength loss.[28]

### Instability-Related Biceps Pathology

Instability of the LHBT is caused by an abnormal pulley system, which is most often the result of failure of the soft-tissue restraints. It can also be related to bony disruption of the floor of the pulley system as a direct result of a two-, three-, or four-part fracture of the proximal humerus that has destroyed or distorted the groove and its walls. Instability resulting from damage to the soft-tissue structures is less well understood, but theories based on clinical observation and diagnostic arthroscopy suggest that it is related to both degeneration and trauma. LHBT instability is best discussed in terms of the anatomic structures that form the pulley system.

The most common form of biceps instability is an anteroinferior subluxation of the tendon resulting from a tear in the reflection pulley, most often primarily involving the SGHL insertion at the anteroinferior portion of the mouth of the groove. A tear in the SGHL allows subluxation of the biceps tendon in an anteroinferior direction, toward the upper portion of the subscapularis tendon insertion into the lesser tuberosity. Eventually, tearing of the subscapularis tendon may result, with the biceps tendon sliding into or under the tendon as it tears (Figure 1, *E*). Subluxation is best treated with biceps tenodesis or tenotomy to spare the more important subscapularis tendon from further injury.

Tears of the reflection pulley may be related to a phenomenon called anterosuperior impingement syndrome.[5,29] When the arm is in a position of horizontal adduction and internal rotation, the undersurface of the reflection pulley and the subscapularis tendon impinges against the anterosuperior glenoid rim. In rare instances, superoanterior subluxation of the biceps tendon occurs over the subscapularis tendon (Figure 1, *D*). A tear in the roof of the groove at the CHL is sometimes associated with a supraspinatus tear. In these patients, subluxation or dislocation of the biceps tendon may occur posteriorly at the site of the tear, probably as a result of extrinsic impingement.[11]

Chondromalacia is often seen at the humeral head cartilage adjacent to the mouth of the biceps groove. This biceps tendon footprint is present in 16% of shoulder arthroscopy patients and is frequently associated with glenohumeral instability and rotator cuff tearing.[30]

### Clinical Evaluation

Pain is common in pathologic conditions involving the biceps tendon. In most patients with intrinsic LHBT pathology, the pain is confined to the anterior shoulder, beginning in the area of the biceps groove and radiating

distally toward the muscle belly. However, most such pain is not produced by biceps pathology. Patients with biceps instability may report a painful clicking or snapping in the area of the pulley system with extremes of rotation, especially if the arm is elevated.[31]

Patients whose chronic pain is the result of a partially torn LHBT may experience sudden pain relief as well as cramping after a spontaneous complete rupture.[32] The examiner should look for evidence of a Popeye deformity of the biceps muscle. A slight asymmetry suggests a partial tear or dislocation, and a major deformity suggests a complete rupture. A patient who is overweight may not have visible evidence of deformity. Sometimes complete rupture does not lead to a deformity because the mesotendon or vincula prevents the tendon from retracting past the biceps groove.

The most common pathologic LHBT finding is tenderness over the intertubercular groove.[32] The groove is palpated with the arm in neutral rotation, then in slight external and internal rotation. The examiner should feel the lesser and greater tuberosities rolling beneath the fingertips, with the biceps between the two. Depending on the size and thickness of the patient's deltoid muscle, the biceps may be difficult to palpate.

The Speed's and Yergason tests have long been used to help identify patients with LHBT pathology.[33,34] However, a recent study found that these tests have low, sensitivity and only moderate specificity, and therefore they are unlikely to affect the diagnosis.[35]

Standard radiographs are helpful in diagnosing fractures or deformities involving the biceps pulley system. A biceps groove view parallel to the long axis of the groove can be used to evaluate the architecture of the groove, although it is not usually part of shoulder evaluation. MRI is useful in evaluating the soft-tissue anatomy of the biceps pulley system and the bony architecture of the groove. The sensitivity and specificity of MRI are high for rotator cuff tears involving the pulley system but only low or moderate for most biceps tendon pathologies, although MRI arthrography somewhat improves specificity.[24,36,37] Intra-articular ultrasonography is also only moderately sensitive and specific for most tendon pathology.[38] However, ultrasonography and MRI are more highly sensitive and specific in detecting a complete rupture of the LHBT.[37,38]

### Treatment

A patient with a chronically inflamed or diseased LHBT should be treated with rehabilitation and anti-inflammatory medications for approximately 3 months. Physical therapy is directed at the underlying rotator cuff pathology often associated with biceps tendinitis. If nonsurgical treatment is unsuccessful because of recalcitrant inflammation or significant chronic tendon degeneration, surgery is indicated.

Surgical treatment is directed at the source of the LHBT pathology to alleviate pain and dysfunction. In patients with a bony groove abnormality from an acute fracture, corrective surgery is preferred. In patients with chronic deformity, the LHBT has often been irreversibly damaged, and the groove cannot be surgically corrected.

If the biceps tendon is unstable and inflicting damage on the rotator cuff tendons, surgery is needed to protect the cuff tendons. Procedures to deepen the groove and repair the soft tissue have been described.[39] However, the tendon may become scarred in the groove, or subluxation out of the groove may continue. Biceps tenodesis and tenotomy both prevent further damage to the rotator cuff. No definitive study results are available to clarify the amount of disease that should be present before biceps tenodesis or tenotomy is considered, rather than tenosynovectomy. Tenodesis or tenotomy is probably indicated if the LHBT is unstable, especially if the surrounding rotator cuff tissue is at risk of tearing because of subluxation of the biceps tendon. In addition, tenodesis or tenotomy should be performed if chronic degeneration, tearing, or atrophy is evident in at least 25% of the tendon.[40] A more aggressive approach is acceptable for revision if the patient has symptoms after earlier surgery.[32]

Open biceps tenodesis was traditionally performed using a keyhole technique, in which the LHBT was tied into a knot and placed into a keyhole created at the proximal humerus. Many surgeons abandoned this technique because a small number of postsurgical proximal humeral fractures occurred when the keyhole acted as a stress riser. This technique has been modified into a procedure in which the LHBT is placed into a smaller hole in the intertubercular groove and held with an interference screw. Other procedures fix the tendon at or below the groove using bony fixation with anchors, screw fixation with washers, or soft-tissue fixation to surrounding tissues such as the pectoralis major tendon. Open biceps tenodesis can be performed through a deltoid split, a deltopectoral approach, or a subpectoral approach.[41-43] Arthroscopic biceps tenodesis avoids the morbidity associated with open techniques and is currently the preferred treatment for LHBT pathology.

### The Percutaneous Intra-Articular Transtendon Technique

In the percutaneous intra-articular transtendon technique, the tendon is arthroscopically fixed either to the THL or adjacent rotator cuff or pulley tissue.[44] This simple procedure requires no special hardware and can be performed using two spinal needles, suture material, and standard arthroscopic equipment. Diagnostic arthroscopy is performed with the arm in adduction and forward flexion and the elbow in flexion and supination. This position allows the intertubercular portion of the

biceps tendon, where most pathology exists, to be pulled into the glenohumeral joint with a soft-tissue grabber or probe (Figure 2).

After confirmation of the biceps tendon pathology, the arm is placed in approximately 20° of external rotation, and 1.5 to 2 cm of the proximal biceps tendon is pulled into the joint via the standard anterior cannula, using a soft-tissue grabber, to provide the optimal tension for the prevention of deformity. Starting approximately 2 cm inferior to the anterolateral corner of the acromion, two spinal needles are placed in a percutaneous fashion across the skin, deltoid, THL or lateral rotator cuff interval tissue, and biceps tendon (Figure 3, *A*). The tips of the needles are directly observed traversing the bicipital groove, piercing the biceps tendon, and entering the intra-articular space (Figure 3, *B*). Size 0 polydiaxone monofilament sutures (Ethicon, Cornelia, GA) are passed through the needles and from the shoulder via a standard anterior canula. Each suture is tied to either end of a braided polyester suture and then pulled at the insertion site to shuttle the braided suture through the joint and out through the subacromial space (Figure 3, *C* and *D*). The process is repeated to place a second braided suture. The instruments are moved to the subacromial space via standard portals, and the braided sutures are tied over the THL, using standard arthroscopic knots to secure the biceps tendon in the groove for tenodesis. Suture management and identification in the subacromial space can be simplified by using sutures of two different colors. If a rotator cuff tear is present, the LHBT can be directly sewn to the THL or the adjacent rotator cuff or pulley tissue to perform a soft-tissue tenodesis.

### Suture Techniques

The direct suture technique is similar to the percutaneous intra-articular transtendon technique.[45] The biceps tendon is held in position with a suture or spinal needle, and the intra-articular portion is resected. In the subacromial space, a cannulated suture-passing device is used to sew the LHBT into the groove. The temporary fixation sutures or needles are removed after the biceps tendon is secured in the groove. Another soft-tissue technique involves arthroscopic transfer of the LHBT to the conjoint tendon. The biceps tendon is released from the superior glenoid and brought out of the groove into the subacromial space, where it is attached to the conjoint tendon with arthroscopic sutures.[46]

### Bony Repair Techniques

The success of soft-tissue techniques depends on the presence of intact or adequate THL, rotator cuff, or interval tissue. If these tissues are inadequate, the surgeon must perform a bony repair of the biceps tendon for tenodesis.[47] The quality of the biceps tendon is the most

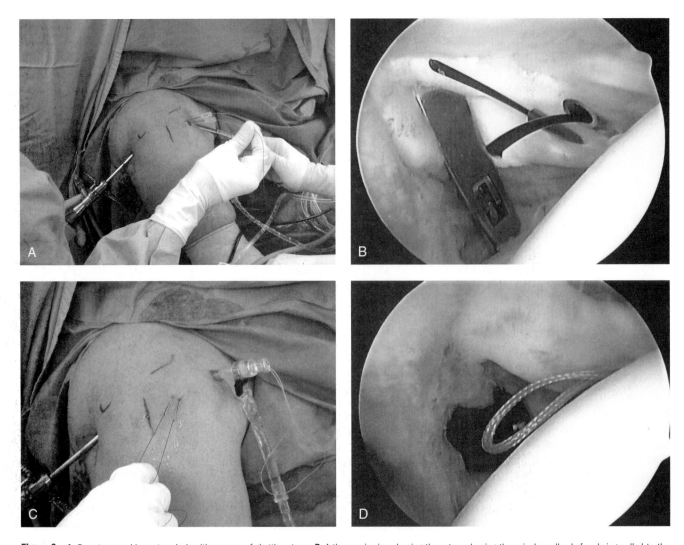

**Figure 3** **A,** Percutaneous biceps tenodesis with passage of shuttle sutures. **B,** Arthroscopic view showing the sutures leaving the spinal needles before being pulled to the outside through the anterior cannula. **C,** Sutures shuttled through in a horizontal mattress fashion. **D,** Arthroscopic view showing mattress loop.

important aspect determining the success or failure of the tenodesis. In arthroscopic biceps tenodesis using suture anchors, a spinal needle is introduced percutaneously to pierce the biceps tendon and is advanced until it becomes lodged into bone at the biceps groove.[48] The needle is located through subacromial arthroscopy, including bursectomy. If the rotator cuff is intact, the THL tissue is resected immediately distal to the needle, until the biceps can be seen within the groove. If the rotator cuff is torn, the biceps is identified directly as it enters the groove. Singly loaded suture anchors are placed either next to or in the groove, and both suture limbs of both anchors are shuttled through the tendon and tied in a mattress fashion. The intra-articular portion of the biceps tendon is excised after secure fixation. If the rotator cuff is intact, the intra-articular resection is easier if the tendon is transected at its insertion into the superior labrum before it exits the glenohumeral joint.

### Interference Screw Fixation

Bioabsorbable interference screw fixation uses a standard cannulated screw system. In the Boileau technique, the 2 cm at the end of the biceps tendon is doubled over, and the two parts are sewn together using a running baseball stitch with a heavy, nonabsorbable suture.[49] A guidewire is passed through the posterior aspect of the humerus away from the axillary nerve and then through the skin, using a Shoulder-Guide (Future Medical Systems, Glen Burnie, MD). The humeral socket is drilled over the guidewire, and a leader pin is placed through the socket. The leader pin is brought out through the posterior shoulder and penetrates the skin at the same place as the guide pin, away from the axillary nerve. A heavy, nonabsorbable suture is placed through the end of the biceps tendon and threaded through the leader pin, which is pulled through the humeral socket and used to pull the tendon back into the subacromial space and into the humeral socket. A guidewire is placed into the socket next to the tendon and used to place the cannulated interference screw. The screw is placed to fix the tendon.

In another interference screw technique, a heavy, nonabsorbable suture is placed through the end of the biceps tendon, and one limb of the suture is drawn through the hole of a leader pin or the cannulated hole of a cannulated interference screw.[40,50] The biceps tendon is placed into the hole with the leader pin or interference screw. The interference screw is advanced to secure the LHBT into the hole. Because it is not necessary to drill a pin that exits the back of the shoulder, the axillary nerve is not at risk of injury from such pins. As a result, most surgeons find this technique safe and easy.

### Arthroscopic Biceps Tenotomy

Arthroscopic biceps tenotomy is a viable surgical option for the treatment of LHBT pathology. The biceps tendon is cut at its origin from the supraglenoid tubercle and left to retract into the arm past the intertubercular groove.[51] However, thin patients can develop a Popeye deformity as a result of this procedure.[52,53] In a recent clinical study, 83% of men and 37% of women had the deformity after arthroscopic tenotomy. This finding indicates that the biceps mesotendon or vincula rarely prevents the tendon from retracting past the intertubercular groove.[52] The deformity can be permanent, and patients should be forewarned. Tenotomy is recommended primarily for older patients.

Most patients achieve pain relief after biceps tenodesis or tenotomy. Many patients are also concerned about cosmesis. Arthroscopic biceps tenodesis is an efficacious means of preventing deformity and preserving elbow strength, as well as relieving pain. Tenotomy is indicated for patients who are older, require a procedure that can be performed quickly, or do not object to the presence of a deformity.

## Summary

The LHBT is an important source of shoulder pain. To effectively diagnose and treat an unstable biceps tendon, it is important to understand the anatomy of the pulley system. Tenodesis or tenotomy are both acceptable treatments for a torn or unstable LHBT. Although a tenotomy is easier to perform, the patient is often left with a deformity or muscle cramping.

## Annotated References

1. Tuoheti Y, Itoi E, Minagawa H, et al: Attachment types of the long head of the biceps tendon to the glenoid labrum and their relationships with the glenohumeral ligaments. *Arthroscopy* 2005;21:1242-1249.

An evaluation of 101 cadaver specimens clarified the types of LHBT attachments to the glenoid labrum and their relationship to the glenohumeral ligaments.

2. Enad JG: Bifurcate origin of the long head of the biceps tendon. *Arthroscopy* 2004;20:1081-1083.

In a case series, 2 of 90 patients undergoing shoulder arthroscopy were found to have a bifurcate origin of the LHBT.

3. Osbahr DC, Diamond AB, Speer KP: The cosmetic appearance of the biceps muscle after long-head tenotomy versus tenodesis. *Arthroscopy* 2002;18:483-487.

In a 5-year retrospective review of 80 patients after tenotomy and 80 after tenodesis, patients were evaluated for the presence of a deformity, pain, or cramping. No difference was found between the two groups or between women and men.

4. Gleason PD, Beall DP, Sanders TG, et al: The transverse humeral ligament: A separate anatomical structure or a continuation of the osseous attachment of the rotator cuff? *Am J Sports Med* 2006;34:72-77.

This anatomic cadaver study found that the THL is a continuation of the surrounding rotator cuff structures.

5. Habermeyer P, Magosch P, Pritsch M, Scheibel MT, Lichtenberg S: Anterosuperior impingement of the shoulder as a result of pulley lesions: A prospective arthroscopic study. *J Shoulder Elbow Surg* 2004;13:5-12.

In 89 patients with an arthroscopically diagnosed pulley lesion, 90% had involvement of the LHBT, and 44% were diagnosed with anterosuperior impingement.

6. Walch G, Nove-Josserand L, Levigne C, Renaud E: Tears of the supraspinatus tendon associated with "hidden" lesions of the rotator interval. *J Shoulder Elbow Surg* 1994;3:353-360.

7. Alpantaki K, McLaughlin D, Karagogeos D, Hadjipavlou A, Kontakis G: Sympathetic and sensory neural elements in the tendon of the long head of the biceps. *J Bone Joint Surg Am* 2005;87:1580-1583.

This study found that the LHBT is innervated by a network of sensory sympathetic fibers, which may play a role in the pathogenesis of shoulder pain.

8. Rathbun JB, McNab I: The microvascular pattern of the rotator cuff. *J Bone Joint Surg Br* 1970;52:540-553.

9. Habermeyer P, Kaiser E, Knappe M, Kreusser T, Wiedmann E: Functional anatomy and biomechanics of the long biceps tendon. *Unfallchirurg* 1987;90:319-329.

10. Kumar VP, Satku K, Balasubramaniam P: The role of the long head of biceps brachii in the stabilization of the head of the humerus. *Clin Orthop Relat Res* 1989;244:172-175.

11. Neer CS II: Anterior acromioplasty for the chronic impingement syndrome in the shoulder. *J Bone Joint Surg* 1972;54:41-50.

12. Rodosky MW, Harner CD, Fu FH: The role of the long head of the biceps muscle and superior glenoid labrum in anterior stability of the shoulder. *Am J Sports Med* 1994;22:121-130.

13. Levy AS, Kelly BT, Lintner SA, Osbahr DC, Speer KP: Function of the long head of the biceps at the shoulder: Electromyographic analysis. *J Shoulder Elbow Surg* 2001;10:250-255.

    Electromyographic activity of the long head of the biceps muscle was evaluated with the elbow extended in a locked brace that prevented flexion and supination. The arm was elevated with a 5-lb weight. No activity was noted in the long head of the biceps muscle.

14. Yamaguchi K, Riew KD, Galatz LM, Syme JA, Neviaser RJ: Biceps activity during shoulder motion: An electromyographic analysis. *Clin Orthop Relat Res* 1997;336:122-129.

15. Jobe FW, Moynes DR, Tibone JE, Perry J: An EMG analysis of the shoulder in pitching. *Am J Sports Med* 1984;12:218-220.

16. Blasier RB, Soslowsky LJ, Malicky DM, Palmer ML: Posterior glenohumeral subluxation: Active and passive stabilization in a biomechanical model. *J Bone Joint Surg Am* 1997;79:433-440.

17. Itoi E, Kuechle DK, Newman SR, Morrey BF, An KN: Stabilising function of the biceps in stable and unstable shoulders. *J Bone Joint Surg Br* 1993;75:546-550.

18. Itoi E, Newman SR, Kuechle DK, Morrey BF, An KN: Dynamic anterior stabilizers of the shoulder with the arm in abduction. *J Bone Joint Surg Br* 1994;76:834-836.

19. Pagnani MJ, Deng XH, Warren RF, Torzilli PA, O'Brien SJ: Role of the long head of the biceps brachii in glenohumeral stability: A biomechanical study in cadavers. *J Shoulder Elbow Surg* 1996;5:255-262.

20. DePalma AF, Callery GE: Bicipital tenosynovitis. *Clin Orthop Relat Res* 1954;3:69-85.

21. Neer CS, Horwitz BS: Fractures of the proximal humeral epiphyseal plate. *Clin Orthop Relat Res* 1965;41:24-31.

22. Tuckman DV, Dines DM: Long head of the biceps pathology as a cause of anterior shoulder pain after shoulder arthroplasty. *J Shoulder Elbow Surg* 2006;15:415-418.

    A retrospective review of eight shoulders in seven patients with biceps pain after shoulder arthroplasty found that tenotomy (four shoulders), tenodesis (three shoulders), and débridement (one shoulder), including subacromial decompression, improved the shoulder arthroplasty outcome.

23. Godeneche A, Boileau P, Favard L, et al: Prosthetic replacement in the treatment of osteoarthritis of the shoulder: Early results of 268 cases. *J Shoulder Elbow Surg* 2002;11:11-18.

    The early results of a study of prosthetic replacement for osteoarthritis are reported, and the common practice of routine biceps tenodesis for patients having arthroplasty surgery is discussed.

24. Beall DP, Williamson EE, Ly JQ, et al: Association of biceps tendon tears of the anterior and superior portions of the rotator cuff. *AJR Am J Roentgenol* 2003;180:633-639.

    In a retrospective evaluation of 111 patients who underwent MRI for shoulder pain followed by arthroscopic or open shoulder surgery, tears of the LHBT were found to have a statistically significant association with tears of the anterosuperior rotator cuff and were highly correlated with tears of the supraspinatus and subscapularis tendons. MRI had a low sensitivity for detecting biceps tendon tears.

25. Neviaser TJ, Neviaser RJ, Neviaser JS: The four-in-one arthroplasty for the painful arc syndrome. *Clin Orthop Relat Res* 1982;163:107-112.

26. Lippmann RK: Bicipital synovitis. *N Y State J Med* 1944;October:2235-2241.

27. Boileau P, Ahrens PM, Hatzidakis AM: Entrapment of the long head of the biceps tendon: The hourglass biceps. A cause of pain and locking of the shoulder. *J Shoulder Elbow Surg* 2004;13:249-257.

    Patients with a hypertrophic lesion of the intra-articular portion of the LHBT, resulting in symptomatic entrapment, were treated with arthroscopic tenotomy (2 patients) or tenodesis (19 patients). The mean Constant score improved from 38 to 76. Level of evidence: IV.

28. Mariani EM, Cofield RH, Askew LJ, Li G, Chao EYS: Rupture of the tendon of the long head of the biceps brachii: Surgical versus nonsurgical treatment. *Clin Orthop Relat Res* 1988;228:233-239.

29. Gerber C, Sebesta A: Impingement of the deep surface of the subscapularis tendon and the reflection pulley on the anterosuperior glenoid rim: A preliminary report. *J Shoulder Elbow Surg* 2000;9:483-490.

30. Sistermann R: The biceps tendon footprint. *Acta Orthop* 2005;76:237-240.

    An observational study of 118 shoulder arthroscopies found chondromalacia beside the bicipital groove in 16% of patients and declared it to be the biceps footprint.

31. Neviaser RJ: Lesions of the biceps and tendonitis of the shoulder. *Orthop Clin North Am* 1980;11:343-348.

32. Sethi N, Wright R, Yamaguchi K: Disorders of the long head of the biceps tendon. *J Shoulder Elbow Surg* 1999;8:644-653.

33. Gilecreest EL, Albi P: Unusual lesions of muscles and tendons of the shoulder girdle and upper arm. *Surg Gynecol Obstet* 1939;68:903-917.

34. Yergason RM: Supination sign. *J Bone Joint Surg Am* 1931;131:160.

35. Holtby R, Razmjou H: Accuracy of the Speed's and Yergason's tests in detecting biceps pathology and slap lesions: Comparison with arthroscopic findings. *Arthroscopy* 2004;20:231-236.

  In consecutive patients with a wide variety of conditions, the Speed's test and Yergason test had moderate specificity. The study found that the tests are not highly consistent and predictive values vary by patient population and setting. Level of evidence: I.

36. Mohtadi NG, Vellet AD, Clark ML, Hollinshead RM, Sasyniuk TM, Fick GH, Burton PJ: A prospective, double-blind comparison of magnetic resonance imaging and arthroscopy in the evaluation of patients presenting with shoulder pain. *J Shoulder Elbow Surg* 2004;13:258-265.

  MRI arthrography was performed within 1 week of shoulder arthroscopy for conditions associated with pain and was compared with intrasurgical arthroscopic findings. Half of the arthroscopically identified partial biceps tendon tears were misidentified on MRI.

37. Zanetti M, Weishaupt D, Gerber C, Hodler J: Tendinopathy and rupture of the tendon of the long head of the biceps brachii muscle: Evaluation with MR arthrography. *AJR Am J Roentgenol* 1998;170:1557-1561.

38. Armstrong A, Teefey SA, Wu T, et al: The efficacy of ultrasound in the diagnosis of long head of the biceps tendon pathology. *J Shoulder Elbow Surg* 2006;15:7-11.

  Ultrasonography was found to reliably diagnose a complete rupture, subluxation, or dislocation of the biceps tendon. However, it is not reliable in detecting an intra-articular partial-thickness tear.

39. Bennett WF: Arthroscopic bicipital sheath repair: Two-year follow-up with pulley lesions. *Arthroscopy* 2004;20:964-973.

  Eighteen patients had lesions of both the subscapularis and supraspinatus involving the pulley system, with less than 50% concomitant biceps disease. All lesions were primarily repaired to stabilize the biceps in the groove. There was one postsurgical biceps disruption, and two patients had inflammation. Level of evidence: IV.

40. Ahmad CS, ElAttrache NS: Arthroscopic biceps tenodesis. *Orthop Clin North Am* 2003;34:499-506.

  A technique for bicep tenodesis using interference screws is described. The tendon is pushed into a hole in the proximal humerus with the screw, which holds the tendon securely in the groove.

41. Edwards TB, Walch G, Sirveaux F, et al: Repair of tears of the subscapularis. *J Bone Joint Surg Am* 2006;88(suppl 1, part 1):1-10.

  Of 84 patients requiring open repair of a subscapularis tear, 54 had an unstable biceps and 10 had a rupture. Forty-eight shoulders underwent tenodesis, 13 underwent tenotomy, and 4 underwent recentering and biceps preservation. The mean Constant score increased from 55 to 79.5 points. Level of evidence: IV.

42. Mazzocca AD, Rios CG, Romeo AA, Arciero RA: Subpectoral biceps tenodesis with interference screw fixation. *Arthroscopy* 2005;21:896.

  The procedure for subpectoral biceps tenodesis with interference screw fixation is described.

43. Wiley WB, Meyers JF, Weber SC, Pearson SE: Arthroscopic assisted mini-open biceps tenodesis: Surgical technique. *Arthroscopy* 2004;20:444-446.

  The procedure for a arthroscopically assisted mini-open biceps tenodesis is described.

44. Sekiya LC, Elkousy HA, Rodosky MW: Arthroscopic biceps tenodesis using the percutaneous intra-articular transtendon technique. *Arthroscopy* 2003;19:1137-1141.

  A technique for percutaneous intra-articular transtendon biceps tenodesis is described. Spinal needles are used to pierce the tendon and pass sutures that are used to secure the biceps tendon in the groove for tenodesis.

45. Castagna A, Conti M, Mouhsine E, Bungaro P, Garofalo R: Arthroscopic biceps tendon tenodesis: The anchorage technical note. *Knee Surg Sports Traumatol Arthrosc* 2006;14:581-585.

  A soft-tissue arthroscopic biceps tenodesis technique is described.

46. Verma NN, Drakos M, O'Brien SJ. Arthroscopic transfer of the long head of the biceps to the conjoint tendon. *Arthroscopy* 2005;21:764.

  Arthroscopic transfer of the LHBT to the conjoint tendon is described as a form of biceps tenodesis.

47. Mazzocca AD, Bicos J, Santangelo S, Romeo AA, Arciero RA: The biomechanical evaluation of four fixation techniques for proximal biceps tenodesis. *Arthroscopy* 2005;21:1296-1306.

  A cadaver study evaluated the cyclic displacement and ultimate failure of four biceps tenodesis techniques (open subpectoral with bone tunnel, arthroscopic suture anchor, open subpectoral interference screw, and arthroscopic interference screw). The failure rate did not differ among the groups.

48. Gartsman GM, Hammerman SM: Arthroscopic biceps tenodesis: Operative technique. *Arthroscopy* 2000;16:550-552.

49. Boileau P, Krishnan SG, Coste JS, Walch G: Arthroscopic biceps tenodesis: A new technique using

bioabsorbable interference screw fixation. *Arthroscopy* 2002;18:1002-1012.

The described technique for arthroscopic tenodesis involves the use of an interference screw. The biceps tendon is drawn into the humerus at the biceps groove and held there with an interference screw. A pin is drilled through the hole and out through the back of the shoulder. A suture is attached to the pin and pulled through the hole to draw the tendon into the hole.

50. Kim S, Yoo J. Arthroscopic biceps tenodesis using interference screw: End-tunnel technique. *Arthroscopy* 2005;21:1405.

An arthroscopic biceps tenodesis technique using an interference screw and an end-tunnel is described. It is similar to a technique used for anterior cruciate ligament reconstruction.

51. Walch G, Edwards TB, Boulahia A, Nove-Josserand L, Neyton L, Szabo I: Arthroscopic tenotomy of the long head of the biceps in the treatment of rotator cuff tears: Clinical and radiographic results of 307 cases. *J Shoulder Elbow Surg* 2005;14:238-246.

In a retrospective review of 307 patients with a rotator cuff tear and LHBT disease who were treated with an arthroscopic biceps tenotomy, 72% were found to have an excellent or good result. Half had an obvious biceps deformity.

52. Kelly AM, Drakos MC, Fealy S, Taylor SA, O'Brien SJ: Arthroscopic release of the long head of the biceps tendon: Functional outcome and clinical results. *Am J Sports Med* 2005;33:208-213.

Fifty-four patients with biceps tendinitis underwent arthroscopic release of the LHBT. Although pain and function improved, 70% developed a Popeye deformity at rest or during active flexion.

53. Wolf RS, Zheng N, Weichel D: Long head of the biceps tenotomy versus tenodesis: A cadaveric biomechanical analysis. *Arthroscopy* 2005;21:182-185.

An anatomic biomechanical cadaver study found a drift past the biceps groove in 40% of specimens after tenotomy with cyclic loading, compared with no specimens after tenodesis.

# Chapter 25

# Subscapularis Tears and Subcoracoid Impingement

Stephen Sohmer, MD, FRCSC

*Ian K.Y. Lo, MD, FRCSC

## Introduction

Tears of the subscapularis are less common than tears of the supraspinatus, and they have received relatively little attention in studies related to the rotator cuff. Subscapularis tears more commonly occur in combination with other rotator cuff tears, rather than in isolation, and partial tears are more common than complete tears. In a study of 314 consecutive shoulder arthroscopies, tears of the subscapularis were found in 19%; 90% of those tears were associated with tears of the supraspinatus.[1] A 27% incidence of subscapularis tears was reported in a study of 165 arthroscopically evaluated shoulders with a disorder of the rotator cuff, labrum, or ligament.[2]

*Ian K.Y. Lo, MD, FRCSC or the department with which he is affiliated has received research or institutional support and royalties from Arthrex and is a consultant or employee for Arthrex.

The main function of the subscapularis is usually described as internal rotation and anterior stabilization of the glenohumeral joint. Recently, the concept of balancing force couples has been emphasized with reference to the subscapularis tendon. A stable fulcrum of glenohumeral motion is possible only when balanced force couples (balanced moments) are present in both the coronal and transverse planes. In a normal shoulder, the tranverse plane force couple consists of a balance of the anterior subscapularis against the posterior infraspinatus and teres minor to effect normal glenohumeral biomechanics (Figure 1). A disruption of the subscapularis leads to an anterior imbalance, a disruption of the transverse plane force couple, an unstable fulcrum of motion, and abnormal biomechanics. Therefore, the restoration of balanced force couples is an important principle of rotator cuff and subscapularis repair. When rotator cuff repair restores the anterior subscapularis and posterior infraspinatus and teres minor forces so that the moments between the two are balanced, function can be

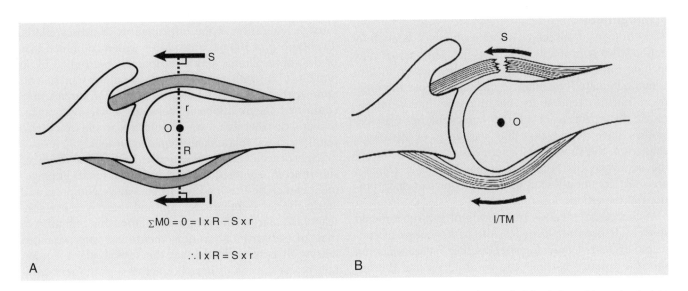

$$\Sigma M0 = 0 = I \times R - S \times r$$

$$\therefore I \times R = S \times r$$

**Figure 1** Axillary views of the transverse plane force couple. **A,** The anterior subscapularis tendon is balanced against the posterior infraspinatus and teres minor tendons. **B,** The transverse plane force couple is disrupted because of a massive tear of the subscapularis tendon. I = infraspinatus, O = center of rotation, R = moment arm of the infraspinatus and teres minor tendons, r = moment arm of the subscapularis tendon, S = subscapularis, TM = teres minor. (*Adapted with permission from Lo IK, Burkhart SS: Current concepts in arthroscopic rotator cuff repair. Am J Sports Med 2003;31:308-324.*)

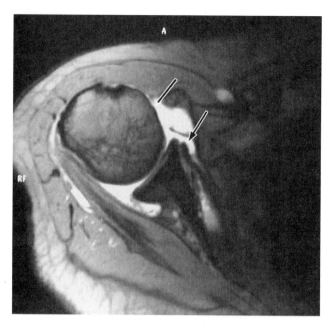

**Figure 2** T2-weighted axial MRI scan showing a decreased coracohumeral distance and a complete tear of the subscapularis tendon. Arrow = edge of the subscapularis tendon, line = coracohumeral distance. *(Reproduced with permission from Lo IK, Parten PM, Burkhart SS: Combined subcoracoid and subacromial impingement in association with anterosuperior rotator cuff tears: An arthroscopic approach. Arthroscopy 2003;19:1068-1078.)*

restored, even in the presence of a persistent supraspinatus defect in the superior rotator cuff.[3,4]

Subcoracoid impingement is direct contact of the coracoid against the subscapularis tendon or lesser tuberosity. It can occur in isolation or in combination with a tear of the subscapularis tendon. This uncommon disorder and its association with subscapularis tendon tears are considered to be similar to subacromial impingement and its relationship to supraspinatus tears.

## Pathogenesis

The etiology of subscapularis tears has not been fully defined but is probably multifactorial. The factors may include intrinsic degeneration, microtrauma or macrotrauma, impaired vascularity, and subcoracoid impingement. Intrinsic tendon degeneration is an important etiologic factor in tears of the subscapularis. Cadaver studies have found that the incidence of histologic changes in the subscapularis tendon is similar to that of the supraspinatus tendon and that histologic changes are most commonly seen in the superior and deep portions of the tendon insertions.[5,6]

Subcoracoid stenosis (narrowing of the subcoracoid space) has been implicated in the pathogenesis of subscapularis tears. Coracohumeral distance, measured as the shortest distance between the coracoid tip and the humerus or lesser tuberosity, as seen on axial CT or MRI, is an indicator of the space available for the subscapularis tendon (Figure 2). In normal shoulders, the coracohumeral distance was found to be 8.7 mm to 11.0 mm, and

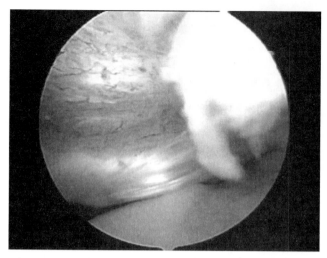

**Figure 3** Posterior arthroscopic view of a tear of the upper 50% of the subscapularis tendon and a corresponding bare subscapularis footprint. The prominent coracoid appears as a bulge anterior to the upper subscapularis tendon, bowstringing the subscapularis fibers. *(Reproduced with permission from Lo IK, Burkhart SS: The etiology and assessment of subscapularis tendon tears: A case for subcoracoid impingement, the roller-wringer effect, and TUFF lesions of the subscapularis. Arthroscopy 2003;19: 1142-1150.)*

it can be as narrow as 6.8 mm with the arm flexed.[7,8] Many authors consider a coracohumeral distance of less than 6 mm as evidence of narrowing.[7-11] A narrower coracohumeral distance is frequently associated with a subscapularis tear. The average coracohumeral distance was measured before surgery using a single axial MRI cut in 35 patients requiring subscapularis repair. The mean distance was 5.0 mm (SD ± 1.7 mm), compared with 10.0 mm (± 1.3 mm) in 35 control subjects having no rotator cuff, subscapularis, or subcoracoid pathology.[12] In 206 consecutive shoulders with rotator cuff tears, 29 had a coracohumeral distance of less than 6 mm measured using CT.[11] A narrowed coracohumeral distance was associated with a combined tear of the supraspinatus and subscapularis and fatty degeneration of the infraspinatus or subscapularis. Twenty-four of 100 patients (24%) with a combined tear of the supraspinatus and subscapularis, but only 3 of 46 patients (7%) with an isolated subscapularis tear, had an abnormal coracohumeral distance. Although studies have confirmed the relationship between a narrow coracohumeral distance and a subscapularis tear, the exact temporal or causal relationship remains unclear.[12,13]

Subcoracoid impingement can occur as a result of subcoracoid stenosis. Although subcoracoid impingement can cause the coracoid to abrasively compress and erode the subscapularis tendon and thereby cause subscapularis tearing, the proposed relationship is similar to that of subacromial impingement and supraspinatus tearing. It is more likely that the subscapularis tendon fails under tension as it arches across a prominent coracoid. During arthroscopy, the surgeon may observe that a patient with subcoracoid stenosis and subcoracoid impingement has bowstringing of the subscapularis tendon across a prominent coracoid (Figure 3). During rotation

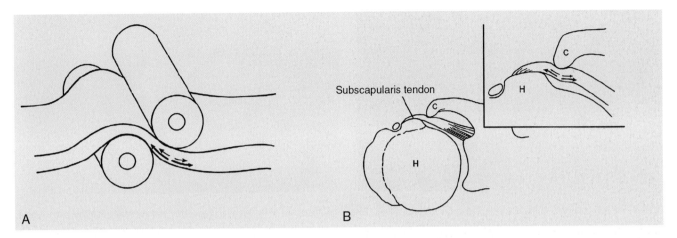

**Figure 4** The roller-wringer effect. **A,** A clothes wringer creates tensile loads on the convex surface of the clothes. **B,** In a patient with subcoracoid impingement, the prominent coracoid indents the superficial surface of the subscapularis tendon, creating tensile forces on the convex articular surface of the subscapularis tendon and possibly leading to tensile undersurface failure of the subscapularis fibers. C = coracoid, H = humerus. *(Reproduced with permission from Lo IK, Burkhart SS: The etiology and assessment of sub-scapularis tendon tears: A case for subcoracoid impingement, the roller-wringer effect, and TUFF lesions of the subscapularis. Arthroscopy 2003;19:1142-1150.)*

of the shoulder, the coracoid can be seen to roll along the subscapularis tendon. A recent theory, the roller-wringer effect, compares subscapularis tearing to the action of an old-fashioned clothes wringer, which squeezes cloth between two rollers to wring out water. In this scenario, the scapularis is squeezed between the coracoid and lesser tuberosity, causing tensile loads on the undersurface of the subscapularis tendon and leading to fiber failure of the articular surface of the subscapularis insertion (Figure 4). This theory is consistent with two observations about subscapularis tears: the most common tear is a partial-thickness articular surface tear, and tendons fail in tension more commonly than in compression.[9]

## Clinical Examination

Pain is usually the primary complaint of a patient with a subscapularis tendon tear. The classic mechanism of injury is a forced external rotation or hyperextension load with the arm in abduction or adduction. However, the patient may not recall a traumatic insult, particularly with a degenerative or multiple-tendon tear. Patients often have a prolonged history of pain with activity, as well as significant disability. They often report pain with activity below shoulder level, which usually does not occur with a posterosuperior cuff tear. The physical findings commonly associated with a subscapularis tendon tear are a painful arc of motion, a decrease in internal rotation strength, and an increase in passive external rotation.

Several clinical signs and tests can be used to evaluate the integrity of the subscapularis tendon. In the lift-off test, the affected arm is internally rotated and extended while the hand is placed on the lumbar region. If the patient is unable to move the arm away from the back by internally rotating the glenohumeral joint, the test result is positive, and the subscapularis tendon is

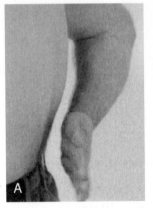
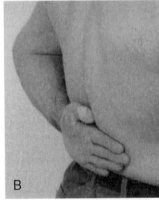

**Figure 5** The lift-off test. **A,** Negative lift-off test of the right shoulder. **B,** Positive lift-off test of the left shoulder. *(Reproduced with permission from Lyons RP, Green A: Subscapularis tendon tears. J Am Acad Orthop Surg 2005;13:353-363.)*

considered to be torn (Figure 5). Although the lift-off test is conclusive in patients with a complete subscapularis tendon tear, it may not yield a positive result if less than 75% of the subscapularis tendon is torn.[14,15] In a modification of the lift-off test, called the subscapularis lag sign, the arm is again positioned on the lumbar region in extension and maximal internal rotation. The patient is asked to hold the arm in this position, and the arm is released by the examiner. The test result is positive if the patient is unable to hold the position and the arm falls back to the lumbar region.[16]

If the patient cannot bring the affected arm into the starting position for the lift-off test because of pain or restricted range of motion, the belly-press test can be used. The patient presses on the abdomen with the palm of the hand and attempts to keep the arm in maximum internal rotation with the elbow anterior to the midcoronal plane of the body (Figure 6). The test is considered positive if

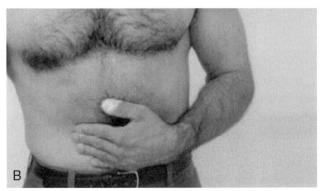

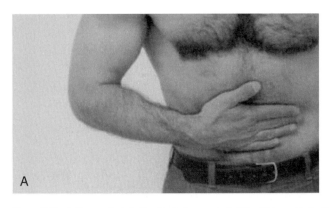

**Figure 6** The belly-press test. **A,** Negative belly-press test of the right arm. **B,** Positive belly-press test of the left arm. *(Reproduced with permission from Lyons RP, Green A: Subscapularis tendon tears.* J Am Acad Orthop Surg *2005;13:353-363.)*

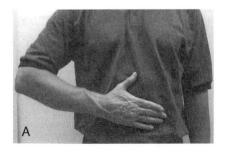

**Figure 7** The Napoleon test. **A,** A negative Napoleon test, indicating normal subscapularis function. The patient can press on the belly with the wrist at 0°. **B,** An intermediate Napoleon test, indicating partial function of the subscapularis. The patient can press on the belly with the wrist flexed 30° to 60°. **C,** A positive Napoleon test, indicating a nonfunctional subscapularis. The patient can press on the belly only by flexing the wrist 90°, using the posterior deltoid rather than subscapularis function. *(Adapted with permission from Burkhart SS, Tehrany AM: Arthroscopic subscapularis tendon repair: Technique and preliminary results.* Arthroscopy *2002;18:454-463.)*

the elbow drops in a posterior direction behind the mid-coronal plane and pressure is exerted on the abdomen by extension of the shoulder.[17,18] The Napoleon test is a variation that accounts for the position of the wrist. In addition to dropping the elbow posteriorly, a patient with a subscapularis tendon tear commonly palmar flexes the wrist against the abdomen (the position seen in portraits of Napoleon). In a study of 25 patients, the amount of wrist flexion was correlated with the size of the subscapularis tendon tear. Patients with a tear of less than 50% of the tendon had a negative Napoleon sign, in which the wrist was fully extended; patients with a partial tear involving more than 50% of the tendon had an intermediate result, in which the wrist was flexed 30° to 60°; and patients with a tear involving the entire subscapularis tendon had a positive Napoleon test, in which the wrist was flexed 90°[14] (Figure 7). The belly-off sign is another modification of the belly-press test. In a positive test, the patient is unable to maintain the palm of the hand on the abdomen when the affected arm is passively brought into flexion and internal rotation (Figure 8). The belly-off sign was found to be more reliable than the lift-off test or belly-press test in detecting partial tears. However, it was less reliable in patients with a significant external rotation insufficiency.[19]

In the recently described bear-hug test, the patient places the hand of the affected side on the opposite shoulder with the fingers extended and the elbow in a forward position (Figure 9). As the patient resists, the examiner attempts to pull the hand away from the shoulder, using an external rotational force perpendicular to the plane of the forearm. If the examiner succeeds, the result is considered positive, indicating a partially or fully torn subscapularis.[15] The lift-off, belly-press, Napoleon, and bear-hug tests were conducted in 68 consecutive patients. During subsequent arthroscopy, subscapularis tendon tears were identified in 29% of the patients; 40% of these tears had not been predicted by any of the presurgical tests.[15] The bear-hug test was found to be the most sensitive (60%), followed by the belly-press test (40%), Napoleon test (25%), and lift-off test (18%). All tests had adequate specificity (92%, 98%, 98%, and 100%, respectively). The presurgical testing was found to be useful in predicting the size of the tear. A positive bear-hug or belly-press test suggested a tear involving at least 30% of the tendon; a positive Napoleon test, a tear of more than 50%; and a positive lift-off test, a tear of more than 75%.

Subcoracoid impingement may accompany subscapularis tendon insufficiency. Although it is rare,

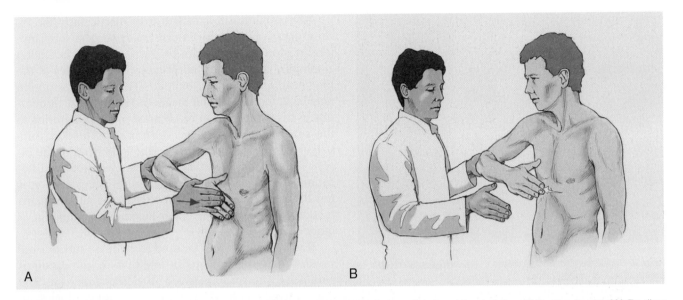

**Figure 8** The belly-off sign. **A,** In the starting position, the affected arm is passively brought into flexion and maximum internal rotation, with the elbow flexed to 90°. The elbow is supported by the examiner's hand while the examiner places the palm on the abdomen. **B,** The patient is asked to keep the wrist straight and actively maintain the position of internal rotation as the examiner releases the wrist while maintaining support at the elbow. If the patient cannot maintain this position, the hand lifts off the abdomen. *(Reproduced with permission from Scheibel M, Magosch P, Pritsch M, Lichtenberg S, Habermeyer P: The belly-off sign: A new clinical diagnostic sign for subscapularis lesions. Arthroscopy 2005;21:1229-1235.)*

subcoracoid impingent is increasingly recognized as a cause of persistent shoulder pain, either in isolation or in combination with a subscapularis tendon tear.[7,8,10,20-25] The pain is probably secondary to impingement between the subscapularis tendon or lesser tuberosity and the coracoid process. Most patients have pain and tenderness in the coracoid and subcoracoid region, as well as a positive coracoid impingement test. The coracoid impingement test is considered positive if pain and clicking are elicited by passive forward flexion, adduction, and internal rotation.[10,21] However, this test has not been evaluated for accuracy, sensitivity, or specificity.

## Diagnostic Imaging

Few studies have evaluated the usefulness of diagnostic imaging in subscapularis tendon assessment. Plain radiography is usually nonspecific, but it can be helpful in ruling out other types of shoulder pathology. In a patient with long-standing subscapularis tendon insufficiency, an axillary radiograph may show static anterior subluxation of the humeral head. Proximal humeral head migration, in association with narrowing of the acromial humeral interval, strongly suggests a massive rotator cuff tear that may include the subscapularis tendon.

Ultrasonography is a relatively inexpensive, noninvasive, and dynamic means of assessing the rotator cuff, although it is highly observer dependent. It was reported to be 100% sensitive and 85% specific in the detection of all rotator cuff lesions, leading to correct identification of six of seven tears of the subscapularis tendon.[26]

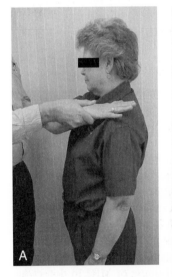
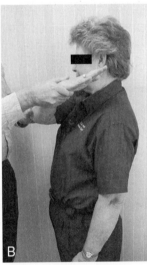

**Figure 9** The bear-hug test. **A,** The patient attempts to hold the starting position by means of resisted internal rotation while the examiner attempts to pull the hand away from the shoulder using external rotation force applied perpendicular to the forearm. **B,** In a positive bear-hug test, the patient cannot hold the hand against the shoulder when the examiner applies an external rotation force. *(Reproduced with permission from Barth JRH, Burkhart SS, de Beer JF: The bear-hug test: A new and sensitive test for diagnosing a subscapularis tear. Arthroscopy 2006;22:1076-1084.)*

In 17 patients with isolated subscapularis tendon tears, ultrasonography revealed 86% of the full-thickness tears. However, ultrasonography is less accurate in detecting partial-thickness tears, particularly small tears of the upper subscapularis tendon.[27,28]

CT arthrography can also be used to confirm the presence of subscapularis tendon tearing. It is more

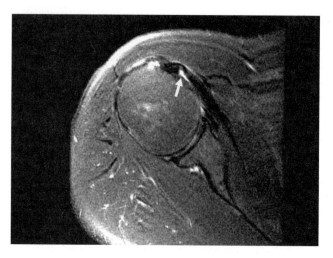

**Figure 10** Axial T2-weighted MRI scan showing a partial thickness subscapularis tendon tear of the right shoulder (*arrow*).

commonly used in Europe than in North America. Extravasation of contrast material from the glenohumeral joint onto the lesser tuberosity is highly suggestive of subscapularis tendon tearing.[29]

MRI is the preferred modality for evaluating rotator cuff pathology. It is used to ascertain the rotator cuff tear pattern and identify concomitant diagnoses. Contrast medium is added to improve the delineation of rotator cuff abnormalities, particularly of upper subscapularis tendon tears. Tears of the subscapularis tendon appear as areas of disorganization or disruption of normal tendon morphology, as well as high signal intensity, on T2-weighted images (Figure 10).

Magnetic resonance arthrography was reported to be 91% sensitive and 86% specific in detecting tears of the subscapularis tendon, although less promising results have also been reported.[30] Full-thickness upper subscapularis tears and partial-thickness tears are commonly missed on MRI. In one study, surgically confirmed subscapularis tendon tears had been presurgically identified on MRI in only 5 of 16 patients (31%).[31] Failure to use T2-weighted axial images and reader inexperience may limit the usefulness of MRI in detecting subscapularis tendon tears.

The chronicity of the tear and the quality of its muscle can be assessed using sagittal oblique MRI or CT images medial to the glenoid. Severe atrophy and fatty degeneration detected on presurgical MRI or CT are usually correlated with poor intrasurgical tendon quality and limited tendon excursion, and they indicate a negative prognosis for subscapularis tendon tear repairability.[32-34] However, some authors believe that the subscapularis tendon usually can be repaired even in the presence of severe atrophy and fatty degeneration. Although the repaired tendon is not functional, it can act as a tenodesis to provide a stable fulcrum of motion.[35]

Abnormalities in adjacent areas, particularly the biceps tendon and rotator interval, may suggest subscapularis tendon tearing. Tears of the subscapularis tendon commonly disrupt the stabilizing reflection pulley of the long head of the biceps tendon (LHBT). The disruption may be detected on axial magnetic resonance arthrography as an extravasation of contrast material anterior to the superior border of the subscapularis tendon. Subscapularis tearing and injury to the long head of the biceps sling usually result in medial subluxation or dislocation of the LHBT. However, if the biceps tendon is not dislocated, detection of a tear of the subscapularis tendon, particularly the upper subscapularis tendon, is more difficult (Figure 11).

Radiography should be used to evaluate subcoracoid stenosis or impingement, in addition to subscapularis pathology. The space between the lesser tuberosity and the coracoid can be decreased by several etiologies, including fracture of the lesser tuberosity, calcific tendinosis, prominence of the coracoid, or surgical factors such as glenoid version alteration or coracoid osteotomy. The surgeon should be aware that proximal humeral migration or static anterior subluxation of the glenohumeral joint can exacerbate narrowing of the subcoracoid space and that narrowing is particularly apparent on an image obtained in the supine position.

The coracoid index is drawn on an axial CT image to measure the lateral projection of the tip of the coracoid to a line tangential to the glenoid face (Figure 12). In 67 patients, the normal projection of the coracoid lateral to this line was 8.2 mm (range, 2.5 mm to 25 mm).[10] Abnormal or excessive projection or angulation of the coracoid beyond this line is believed to indicate a predisposition to subcoracoid stenosis and impingement. The coracohumeral distance (the shortest distance between the coracoid tip and the humerus and lesser tuberosity) is measured on axial CT or MRI and is considered to be an indicator of the space available for the subscapularis tendon.

## Arthroscopic Subscapularis Repair

The arthroscopic repair of a subscapularis tear is a relatively new, evolving procedure. The arthroscopic surgeon should be adept in standard rotator cuff repair before attempting subscapularis repair. Three portals are generally used: a posterior portal for viewing; an anterior portal for anchor placement and suture management; and an anterolateral portal for subscapularis mobilization, preparation of the bone bed, and traction suturing. Familiarity with anterior shoulder anatomy, particularly that of the coracoid area, is essential. Procedures near the coracoid are relatively safe if they are restricted to the lateral aspect of the coracoid and conjoint tendon. In one cadaver study, the axillary and musculocutaneous nerves, the lateral cord of the bra-

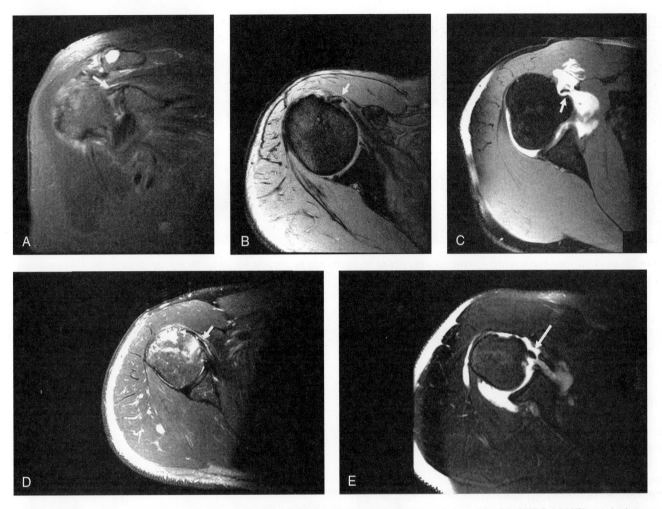

**Figure 11** Biceps pathology associated with subscapularis tendon tears. **A,** Paracoronal MRI scan showing intra-articular rupture of the LHBT. **B,** Axial MRI scan showing a partial subscapularis tendon tear, with the biceps tendon positioned in the bicipital groove. **C,** Axial MRI scan showing a complete subscapularis tendon tear with partial subluxation of the biceps tendon perched on the medial bicipital groove. **D,** Axial MRI scan showing a partial subscapularis tendon tear with subluxation of the biceps tendon into a split of the tendon. **E,** Axial MRI scan showing a complete subscapularis tendon tear, with medial dislocation of the biceps tendon adjacent to the anterior glenoid.

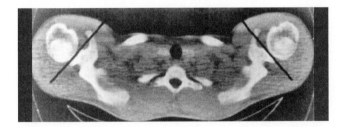

**Figure 12** The coracoid index, a measurement of the projection of the tip of the coracoid lateral to a line drawn tangential to the glenoid face on an axial CT scan. *(Reproduced with permission from Dines DM, Warren RF, Inglis AE, Pavlov H: The coracoid impingement syndrome. J Bone Joint Surg Br 1990;72-B:314-316.)*

chial plexus, and the axillary artery were all located more than 28 mm from the coracoid.[36]

Good visualization is essential during arthroscopic subscapularis repair. The subscapularis tendon and its footprint can easily be identified by using arm positioning, alternative viewing portals, and a 70° arthroscope. The arm can be manipulated into abduction and inter-

nal rotation, drawing the fibers of the subscapularis away from the humeral head and revealing its insertion (Figure 13). To increase the working area in the anterior glenohumeral joint, an assistant can apply posterior translational, abducting force. Evaluation during routine shoulder arthroscopy facilitates recognition and assessment of a pathologic subscapularis tendon.

A subacromial approach can be used as an alternative method of visualizing the subscapularis tendon. The arthroscope is placed in the lateral subacromial portal following bursal débridement. The instruments are introduced through an anterolateral portal, and the coracoacromial ligament is followed inferiorly toward the coracoid and subscapularis tendon. This method provides improved visualization of the bursal surface of the subscapularis tendon, particularly if it is intact, and allows dissection of the axillary nerve.[37] However, axillary nerve dissection is rarely necessary during arthroscopic subscapularis repair. A three-sided (anterior, posterior, and superior) release of the subscapularis tendon,

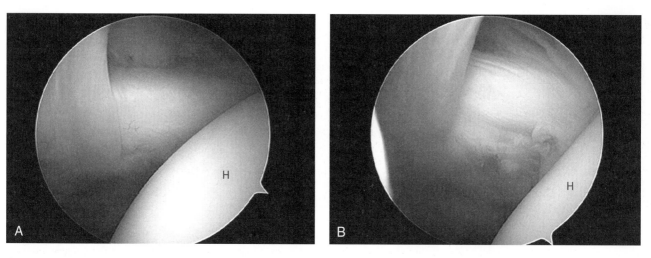

**Figure 13** Arthroscopic views from a posterior glenohumeral portal showing the shoulder with the arm in neutral position **(A)** and internal rotation **(B)**. H = humeral head. *(Reproduced with permission from Lo IK, Burkhart SS: The etiology and assessment of subscapularis tendon tears: A case for subcoracoid impingement, the roller-wringer effect, and TUFF lesions of the subscapularis. Arthroscopy 2003;19:1142-1150.)*

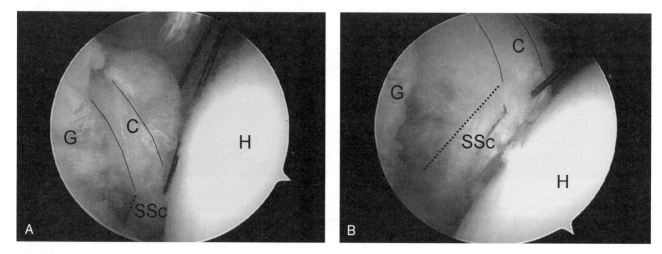

**Figure 14** Posterior-portal arthroscopic views of a right shoulder showing a complete subscapularis tendon tear retracted to the glenoid margin. **A,** A traction stitch has been placed in the superolateral corner of the subscapularis tendon. The soft tissues superior to the superolateral corner of the subscapularis tendon must not be confused with the edge of the subscapularis tendon. This area represents the comma sign. **B,** Traction on the subscapularis tendon reveals the true borders of the subscapularis and shows that the subscapularis tendon has been significantly retracted medially and inferiorly. C = comma sign, G = glenoid, H = humeral head, SSc = subscapularis tendon; dashed line = upper border of the subscapularis tendon, solid line = outline of the comma sign. *(Reproduced with permission from Lo IK, Parten PM, Burkhart SS: Combined subcoracoid and subacromial impingement in association with anterosuperior rotator cuff tears: An arthroscopic approach. Arthroscopy 2003;19:1068-1078.)*

avoiding inferior dissection and the axillary nerve, is usually sufficient for mobilization.[3,4,14,20,35]

Delineating a subscapularis tendon with a partial-thickness or full-thickness, partial-width tear is usually not difficult. However, chronic, complete full-thickness tears of the subscapularis tendon are commonly retracted medially and scarred to the deltoid fascia. Both the lateral and superior borders of the subscapularis stump are obscured, and the tendon can be difficult to locate. The key to locating the subscapularis and differentiating it from the deltoid, conjoint tendon, and coracoacromial ligament is to find the comma sign, which is a comma-shaped arc of tissue at the superolateral border of the subscapularis.[38] The tissue is composed of the

fibers of the medial portion of the coracohumeral ligament, as well as a portion of the superior glenohumeral ligament, which are interdigitated with the superior fibers of the subscapularis tendon at its humeral insertion. The medial portion of the coracohumeral ligament, the superior glenohumeral ligament, and the subscapularis commonly tear as a unit and thus form the comma sign. When the comma sign is identified, the tissue can be followed inferiorly and medially to the superolateral border of the subscapularis tendon. Traction can then be applied to the subscapularis tendon to reveal the entire tendon and muscle unit (Figure 14).

The LHBT also must be addressed during subscapularis tendon repair. Subluxation, dislocation, or rupture

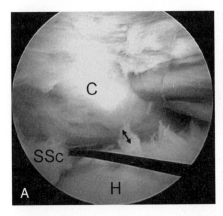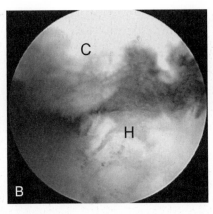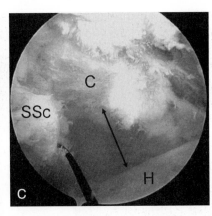

**Figure 15** Posterior arthroscopic views of a right shoulder, using a 70° arthroscope. **A,** A shaver is introduced through an anterosuperolateral portal, the prominent coracoid is palpated, and an initial assessment of the coracohumeral space is made. The minimal space available for the subscapularis tendon (*double-headed arrow*) indicates coraco-humeral stenosis. **B,** Manipulation of the arm in flexion, adduction, and internal rotation reveals coracoid impingement, with contact between the coracoid and the lesser tuberosity of the humerus. **C,** In the completed coracoid resection, the space available for the subscapularis tendon (*double-headed arrow*) has been increased. C = coracoid, H = humeral head, SSc = subscapularis tendon. *(Reproduced with permission from Lo IK, Parten PM, Burkhart SS: Combined subcoracoid and subacromial impingement in association with anterosuperior rotator cuff tears: an arthroscopic approach. Arthroscopy 2003;19:1068-1078.)*

of the LHBT occurs in 31% to 56% of isolated subscap-ularis tendon tears.[18,39] Tears of the subscapularis are usually accompanied by disruption of the adjacent inser-tion of the medial sling, causing medial subluxation of the biceps. If biceps tendon instability is present, the bi-ceps tendon must be treated, because persistent sublux-ation of the biceps can place stress on the subscapularis repair and eventually cause failure. Some authors rec-ommend routine biceps tenodesis or tenotomy, which is associated with improved subjective and objective re-sults, regardless of the presurgical condition of the bi-ceps tendon.[40] For most patients, a biceps tenodesis is preferable to a tenotomy. However, a simple biceps tenotomy is usually sufficient for a patient who is eld-erly and inactive. Arthroscopic bicipital sheath repair with preservation of the biceps tendon has been re-ported in conjunction with subscapularis tearing. The limited results indicate persistent biceps symptoms in 16% of patients.[41-43]

Subcoracoid impingement can also compromise a subscapularis tendon repair. Subcoracoid decompres-sion is usually performed if subcoracoid impingement is confirmed by the following: pain and tenderness in the anterior coracoid region; a positive subcoracoid im-pingement test; imaging and arthroscopic findings of co-racohumeral distance less than 6 mm (Figure 15); and an arthroscopic finding of contact of the coracoid tip against the subscapularis tendon or lesser tuberosity.[20] In one study, subcoracoid decompression was performed in 19% of patients with a combined anterosuperior rota-tor cuff tear (a tear of the subscapularis and supraspina-tus, with or without infraspinatus tearing).[20]

Arthroscopic decompression of the subcoracoid space through a subacromial or intra-articular approach has recently been described. In the subacromial ap-proach, the coracoacromial ligament is used as a land-mark to lead inferiorly and medially to the coracoid.[44] The dissection may require extensive resection of the bursa and fibroadipose tissue to allow visualization of the coracoid, and orientation can be difficult. The intra-articular approach through the rotator interval may be easier to perform, and it allows appropriate orientation of the coracoplasty in the plane of the subscapularis ten-don.[45] The goal of the coracoplasty is to create a 7- to 10-mm space between the coracoid tip and the anterior plane of the subscapularis. Subcoracoid decompression increases the available anterior working space and may protect the repaired subscapularis from abrasion.

Complete tears of the subscapularis are commonly re-tracted medially and require mobilization. A three-sided release that avoids the axillary nerve inferiorly is usually required to gain sufficient mobilization for repair. Ante-rior release of the coracohumeral ligament is usually re-quired, with skeletization of the coracoid, release and de-compression of the subcoracoid space, resection of the rotator interval, and release of the middle glenohumeral ligament and anterior capsule. In performing these re-leases, the continuity of the lateral portion of the rotator interval, called the interval slide in continuity, must be maintained. This tissue helps maintain the integrity of the subscapularis tendon and can greatly facilitate postero-superior rotator cuff repair following subscapularis ten-don repair[4,46] (Figures 16 and 17).

When the subscapularis has been released, the bone bed on the lesser tuberosity is prepared for insertion of the subscapularis tendon. In cadaver studies, the footprint of the subscapularis tendon was found to roughly resem-ble a human ear in shape, with the medial border almost parallel to the longitudinal axis of the humerus and a proximally broad and distally tapered insertion.[47,48] The average superior-to-inferior footprint is 25.8 mm in height (±3.2 mm) and 18.1 mm in width (±1.6 mm)[47] (Figure 18).

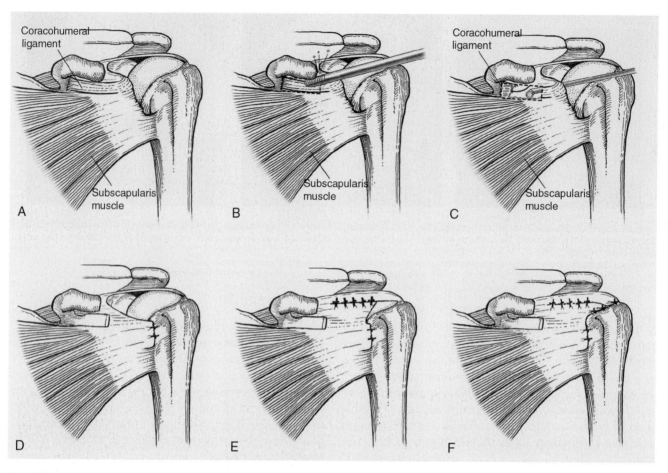

**Figure 16** Anterior view of a left shoulder, showing the interval slide in continuity. **A,** An anterosuperior rotator cuff tear involves 50% of the subscapularis tendon as well as a massive tear of the supraspinatus and infraspinatus tendons. **B,** A coracoplasty is performed to resect the posterolateral aspect of the coracoid tip. Dashed line = the proposed window of the interval slide in continuity. **C,** The posterolateral aspect of the base of the coracoid is exposed, releasing the coracohumeral ligament. The medial rotator interval tissue is excised to create a window through the rotator interval, further releasing and excising the coracohumeral ligament. Care is taken to ensure that the lateral margin of the rotator interval remains intact, maintaining the continuity between the subscapularis tendon and the supraspinatus tendon. **D,** With an interval slide in continuity, the mobility of the subscapularis tendon is improved. The subscapularis tear can now be repaired to bone, leaving a U-shaped posterosuperior rotator cuff tear to be repaired. **E,** The residual U-shaped posterosuperior rotator cuff tear is repaired with side-to-side sutures, using the principle of margin convergence. **F,** The converged margin is repaired to bone in a tension-free manner. *(Reproduced with permission from Lo IK, Burkhart SS: The interval slide in continuity: A method of mobilizing the anterosuperior rotator cuff without disrupting the tear margins. Arthroscopy 2004;20:435-441.)*

By comparing an exposed footprint to data gathered from normal cadavers, the extent of subscapularis tendon tearing can be estimated.

Standard anchor insertion, suture passage, and knot tying are performed following preparation of the bone bed. The currently preferred technique is a double-row repair to reconstruct the broad subscapularis tendon footprint, if the patient has sufficient tendon excursion. In practice, double-row repair may not be easily achievable, and the clinical results of single-row repair generally have been good.[3,4,14,20,42,43] For suture passage, an antegrade technique using a specially designed instrument such as the Scorpion (Arthrex, Inc., Naples, FL) or ExpresSew (Depuy Mitek, Raynham, MA) is less demanding, although shuttling or retrograde passage may be used. Knot tying generally proceeds from inferior to superior, because it can decrease visualization (Figure 19).

After surgery, 6 weeks of sling immobilization is generally recommended, Gentle passive and active-assisted range-of-motion exercises should begin soon after surgery. External rotation should be limited to 0° or as determined during surgery. Progressive active-assisted and active range-of-motion exercises are begun at 6 weeks, and strengthening exercises are begun at 12 weeks after surgery.

## Results

The only available outcomes data on arthroscopic subscapularis tear repairs are from small case series. Arthroscopic repair of 29 shoulders with isolated partial articular-sided tearing of the subscapularis led to an excellent subjective outcome in 18 patients, a good outcome in 10, and a fair outcome in 1.[49] No complications were reported, and the internal rotation strength deficit improved from 32% to 4%. Sixteen of the tears were

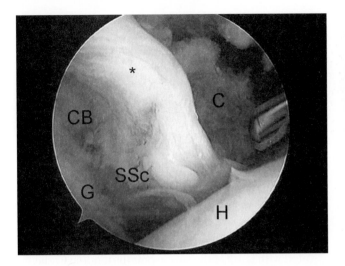

**Figure 17** Posterior arthroscopic view showing a completed interval slide in continuity. The lateral bridge of rotator interval tissue has been maintained; it contains the comma sign and leads to the superolateral aspect of the torn subscapularis tendon. The coracoid tip and coracoid base are visible on either side of the comma sign. C = coracoid tip, CB = coracoid base, G = glenoid, H = humerus, SSc = subscapularis tendon; asterisk = comma sign. *(Reproduced with permission from Lo IK, Burkhart SS: The interval slide in continuity: A method of mobilizing the anterosuperior rotator cuff without disrupting the tear margins. Arthroscopy 2004;20:435-441.)*

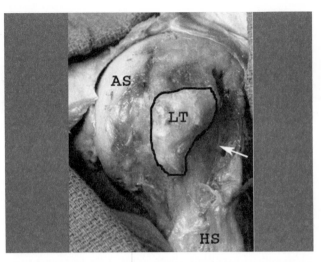

**Figure 18** The lesser tubercle of the proximal humerus is the site of insertion of the subscapularis tendon. The footprint *(outlined)* is defined as the grossly tendinous insertion of the subscapularis tendon. The bicipital groove *(arrow)* abuts the lateral border of the lesser tubercle. AS = articular surface of the humeral head, HS = humeral shaft, LT = lesser tubercle. *(Reproduced with permission from D'Addesi LL, Anbari A, Reish MW, Brahmabhatt S, Kelly JD: The subscapularis footprint: An anatomic study of the subscapularis tendon insertion. Arthroscopy 2006;22:937-940.)*

larger than 1 cm. Tears smaller than 5 mm were débrided. The treatment criteria were not supported by objective data, and the authors noted that further study is needed to determine the indications for débridement or repair.

The first study of arthroscopic repair of full-thickness isolated or combined subscapularis tears reported preliminary results for 25 patients with a mean age of 60.7 years.[14] At a mean 10.7-month follow-up, 92% had an excellent or good result, as determined using the modified University of California Los Angeles Shoulder Scale. One patient had a fair result, and one had a poor result. The University of California Los Angeles score of the eight patients with an isolated subscapularis tear improved, on average, from 10.0 to 32.8. Multitendinous tears involving at least half of the subscapularis, as well as the supraspinatus or infraspinatus, caused profound functional deficits, particularly if proximal humeral head migration was present on radiography. Among the 17 patients with combined tears, 10 had proximal migration of the humeral head, and all had complete presurgical loss of overhead function. Eight of these patients had a durable reversal of proximal humeral migration and restoration of overhead function following surgery. The other two patients had a poor or fair result, with recurrence of proximal migration and little or no change in range of motion.

More recent studies reported similar results 2 to 4 years after arthroscopic repair of isolated or combined tears of the subscapularis tendon. Arthroscopic repair of isolated subscapularis tears in six patients with a complete tear and two patients with a partial tear[42] led to

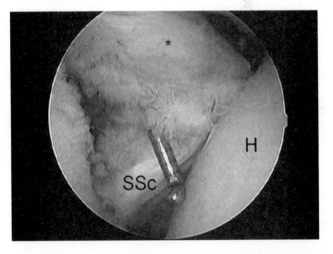

**Figure 19** Arthroscopic intra-articular view from a posterior portal, showing an intact comma sign after subscapularis repair. The hook probe shows the interval slide in continuity. H = humeral head, SSc = subscapularis tendon; asterisk = comma sign. *(Reproduced with permission from Lo IK, Burkhart SS: The interval slide in continuity: A method of mobilizing the anterosuperior rotator cuff without disrupting the tear margins. Arthroscopy 2004;20:435-441.)*

improvement in the mean Constant score from 43 (±9) to 74 (±10); in the visual analog pain scale, from 9 (±1) to 2 (±2); and in the American Shoulder and Elbow Surgeons Index score, from 16 (±13) to 74 (±26). In a report by the same author on arthroscopic repair of 35 combined complete supraspinatus and partial-thickness or full-thickness subscapularis tears, the mean Constant score improved from 53 (±13) to 77 (±10); the visual analog pain scale, from 7 (±3) to 2 (±2); and the American Shoulder and Elbow Surgeons Index score, from 31 (±19) to 80 (±14).[43]

Arthroscopic repair of full-thickness subscapularis tendon tears is an accepted treatment after unsuccessful nonsurgical treatment. However, débridement alone can lead to improvement in carefully selected patients. Large tear size, concomitant disease, and delayed presentation can lead to tendon retraction, muscle atrophy, and fatty infiltration and can complicate treatment and outcome, especially in a patient 65 years or older. Arthroscopic débridement of the subscapularis tear and release of the LHBT was performed in 11 patients whose tears were considered irreparable or who were older and unwilling to participate in the required postsurgical rehabilitation program.[50] The mean patient age was 64 years. At average 33-month follow-up, the mean Constant score improved from 49 to 80. Six patients rated their result as excellent; three, good; one, fair; and one, poor. Releasing a diseased biceps tendon appeared to have a positive effect on outcome; all nine patients who required a biceps release because of subluxation, dislocation, or partial tearing rated the result as excellent or good. The two patients who did not require tendon release had a ruptured biceps tendon or a normal-appearing tendon; they rated the result as fair or poor, respectively.

No consensus exists on treatment algorithms for débridement compared with repair of partial-thickness or full-thickness tears of the subscapularis tendon or treatment of concomitant disease.

## Summary

Knowledge of the pathology and symptoms associated with subscapularis tears and subcoracoid impingement continues to evolve. Arthroscopic repair of the subscapularis tendon is now routine, although basic questions related to treatment have not been answered. In particular, the indications for débridement rather than repair must be defined for all types of lesions, including partial-thickness, partial-width and full-thickness, and complete full-thickness tears. The optimal treatment of concomitant pathology must also be defined.

## Annotated References

1. Kim TK, Rauh PB, McFarland EG: Partial tears of the subscapularis tendon found during arthroscopic procedures on the shoulder: A statistical analysis of sixty cases. *Am J Sports Med* 2003;31:744-750.

   In a study of 314 arthroscopies, partial tears of the subscapularis tendon were not uncommon and were associated with extensive rotator cuff disease. No association with glenohumeral instability was found, although atypical forms of instability were not ruled out.

2. Bennett WF: Subscapularis, medial and lateral head coracohumeral ligament insertion anatomy: Arthroscopic appearance and incidence of "hidden" rotator interval lesions. *Arthroscopy* 2001;17:173-180.

   A study of 165 arthroscopies identified 46 subscapularis tears, 25 hidden rotator interval lesions, and 6 superior glenohumeral-medial head coracohumeral ligament complex plastic deformation lesions.

3. Lo IK, Burkhart SS: Subscapularis tears: Arthroscopic repair of the forgotten rotator cuff tendon. *Techniques Shoulder Elbow Surg* 2002;3:282-291.

4. Burkhart SS, Lo IK: Arthroscopic rotator cuff repair. *J Am Acad Orthop Surg* 2006;14:333-346.

   This article reviews current knowledge of the principles, techniques, instrumentation, and biomechanical rationale for arthroscopic rotator cuff repair.

5. Sakurai G, Ozaki J, Tomita Y, Kondo T, Tamai S: Incomplete tears of the subscapularis tendon associated with tears of the supraspinatus tendon: Cadaver and clinical studies. *J Shoulder Elbow Surg* 1998;7:510-515.

6. Sano H, Ishii H, Trudel G, Uhthoff HK: Histologic evidence of degeneration at the insertion of 3 rotator cuff tendons: A comparative study with human cadaveric shoulder. *J Shoulder Elbow Surg* 1999;8:574-579.

7. Gerber C, Terrier F, Sehnder R, Ganz R: The subcoracoid space: An anatomic study. *Clin Orthop Relat Res* 1987;215:132-138.

8. Friedman RJ, Bonutti PM, Genez B: Cine magnetic resonance imaging of the subcoracoid region. *Orthopedics* 1998;21:545-548.

9. Lo IK, Burkhart SS: The etiology and assessment of subscapularis tendon tears: A case for subcoracoid impingement, the roller-wringer effect, and TUFF lesions of the subscapularis. *Arthroscopy* 2003;19:1142-1150.

   Subcoracoid stenosis and impingement are proposed to cause a roller-wringer effect on the subscapularis tendon, which increases the tensile load on the articular surface of the subscapularis tendon and may lead to tensile undersurface fiber failure of the subscapularis insertion. These factors may collectively contribute to the pathogenesis of subscapularis tears.

10. Dines DM, Warren RF, Inglis AE, Pavlov H: The coracoid impingement syndrome. *J Bone Joint Surg Br* 1990;72:314-316.

11. Nove-Josserand L, Edwards TB, O'Connor DP, Walch G: The acromiohumeral and coracohumeral intervals are abnormal in rotator cuff tears with muscular fatty degeneration. *Clin Orthop Relat Res* 2005;433:90-96.

    The acromiohumeral and coracohumeral intervals were investigated in 206 shoulders with rotator cuff tears. An abnormal coracohumeral interval was associated with a combined tear of the supraspinatus and subscapularis and fatty degeneration of the infraspinatus or subscapularis. Level of evidence: II.

12. Richards DP, Burkhart SS, Campbell Scot E: Relation between narrowed coracohumeral distance and subscapularis tears. *Arthroscopy* 2005;21:1223-1228.

   The coracohumeral distance in 36 shoulders (35 patients) requiring subscapularis repair (5.0 mm, ±1.7 mm) was significantly less than in 35 control subjects (10.0 mm, ±1.3 mm). A significant correlation exists between a narrowed coracohumeral distance and subscapularis repair but not necessarily tear causation. Level of evidence: III.

13. Nove-Josserand L, Boulahia A, Levigne C, Noel E, Walch G: Coracohumeral space and rotator cuff tears. *Rev Chir Orthop Reparatrice Appar Mot* 1999; 85:677-683.

14. Burkhart SS, Tehrany AM: Arthroscopic subscapularis tendon repair: Technique and preliminary results. *Arthroscopy* 2002;18:454-463.

   Arthroscopic subscapularis tendon repair was evaluated in 25 shoulders at an average 10.7-month follow-up. In 92%, the result was good or excellent. The Napolean test was useful in predicting the presence and general size of a subscapularis tear. Combined subscapularis, supraspinatus, and infraspinatus tears are frequently associated with proximal humeral migration and loss of overhead function.

15. Barth JRH, Burkhart SS, de Beer JF: The bear-hug test: A new and sensitive test for diagnosing a subscapularis tear. *Arthroscopy* 2006;22:1076-1084.

   The bear-hug test is described and evaluated in 68 consecutive patients undergoing shoulder arthroscopy. Forty percent of tears were not predicted by any evaluated test. The bear-hug test was the most sensitive (60%). Level of evidence: I.

16. Hertel R, Ballmer FT, Lombert SM, Gerber C: Lag signs in the diagnosis of rotator cuff rupture. *J Shoulder Elbow Surg* 1996;5:307-313.

17. Gerber C, Krushell RJ: Isolated ruptures of the tendon of the subscapularis muscle. *J Bone Joint Surg Br* 1991;73:389-394.

18. Gerber C, Hersche O, Farron A: Isolated rupture of the subscapularis tendon: Results of operative repair. *J Bone Joint Surg Am* 1996;78:1015-1023.

19. Scheibel M, Magosch P, Pritsch M, Lichtenberg S, Habermeyer P: The belly-off sign: A new clinical diagnostic sign for subscapularis lesions. *Arthroscopy* 2005;21:1229-1235.

   The belly-off sign is described and evaluated in 60 patients with injury to the subscapularis musculotendinous unit. It was particularly useful in detecting isolated partial tears and postsurgical insufficiency but less reliable in patients with significant external rotation weakness. Level of evidence: IV.

20. Lo IK, Parten PM, Burkhart SS: Combined subcoracoid and subacromial impingement in association with anterosuperior rotator cuff tears: An arthroscopic approach. *Arthroscopy* 2003;19:1068-1078.

   Eight patients with a combined subscapularis, supraspinatus, and infraspinatus tear of the rotator cuff with subacromial and subcoracoid impingement were treated with arthroscopic subacromial and subcoracoid decompression and rotator cuff repair. At mean 8.8-month follow-up, all patients were satisfied. A high index of suspicion must be maintained for these combined lesions.

21. Ferrick MR: Coracoid impingement: A case report and review of the literature. *Am J Sports Med* 2000; 28:117-119.

22. Gerber C, Terrier F, Ganz R: The role of the coracoid process in the chronic impingement syndrome. *J Bone Joint Surg Br* 1985;67:703-708.

23. Patte D: The subcoracoid impingement. *Clin Orthop Relat Res* 1990;254:55-59.

24. Russo R, Togo F: The subcoracoid impingement syndrome: Clinical, semiologic and therapeutic considerations. *Ital J Orthop Traumatol* 1991;17:351-358.

25. Suenaga N, Nimami A, Kaneda K: Postoperative subcoracoid impingement syndrome in patients with rotator cuff tear. *J Shoulder Elbow Surg* 2000;9: 275-278.

26. Teefey SA, Hasan SA, Middleton WD, Patel M, Wright RW, Yamaguchi K: Ultrasonography of the rotator cuff: A comparison of ultrasonographic and arthroscopic findings in one hundred consecutive cases. *J Bone Joint Surg Am* 2000;82:498-504.

27. Teefey SA, Middleton WD, Payne WT, Yamaguchi K: Detection and measurement of rotator cuff tears with sonography: Analysis of diagnostic errors. *Am J Radio* 2005;184:1768-1773.

   In a prospective evaluation of detection and measurement errors in 71 consecutive patients undergoing presurgical ultrasound and confirmatory arthroscopy, the infrequent detection errors were missed tears or errors resulting from limitations of the test. Measurement errors occurred in patients with large or massive cuff tears.

28. Farin P, Jaroma H: Sonographic detection of tears of the anterior portion of the rotator cuff (subscapularis tendon tears). *J Ultrasound Med* 1996;15:221-225.

29. Walch G, Nove-Josserand L, Levigne C, Renaud E: Tears of the supraspinatus tendon with "hidden" lesions of the rotator interval. *J Shoulder Elbow Surg* 1994;3:353-360.

30. Pfirrmann CW, Zanette M, Weishaupt D, Gerber C, Hodler J: Subscapularis tendon tears: Detection and grading at MR arthrography. *Radiology* 1999;213: 709-714.

31. Tung GA, Yoo DC, Levine SM, Green A: Subscapularis tendon tear: Primary and associated signs on MRI. *J Comput Assist Tomogr* 2001;25:417-424.

   In a study of 16 patients, presurgical diagnosis of subscapularis tear was made in 5. Retrospective review revealed primary signs of a tear in 15; two thirds of these were limited to the cranial third.

32. Goutallier D, Postel JM, Bernageau J, Lavau L, Voison MC: Fatty muscle degeneration in cuff ruptures: Pre- and postoperative evaluation by CT scan. *Clin Orthop Relat Res* 1994;304:78-83.

33. Goutallier D, Postel MN, Bernageau J, Lavau L, Voisin MC: Fatty infiltration of disrupted rotator cuff muscles. *Rev Rheum Engl Ed* 1995;63:415-422.

34. Ticker JB, Warner JJ: Single-tendon tears of the rotator cuff: Evaluation and treatment of subscapularis tears and principles of treatment for supraspinatus tears. *Orthop Clin North Am* 1997;28:99-116.

35. Burkhart SS, Brady PC: Arthroscopic subscapularis repair: Surgical tips and pearls from A to Z. *Arthroscopy* 2006;22:1014-1027.

    Presurgical, intrasurgical, and postsurgical considerations in arthroscopic subscapularis repair are described.

36. Lo IK, Burkhart SS, Parten PM: Surgery about the coracoid: Neurovascular structures at risk. *Arthroscopy* 2004;20:591-595.

    A cadaver dissection study found that the mean distance from the coracoid to the adjacent neurovascular structures (axillary nerve, axillary artery, musculocutaneous nerve, lateral cord) was 28.5 mm (±4.4 mm), which suggested that surgery directly around the coracoid is relatively safe.

37. Paribelli G, Boschi S: Complete subscapularis tendon visualization and axillary nerve identification by arthroscopic technique. *Arthroscopy* 2005;21:1016.

    This article describes visualization of the subscapularis tendon through a lateral subacromial portal using the coracoacromial ligament as a guide toward the coracoid, conjoint tendon, subscapularis tendon, and axillary nerve.

38. Lo IK, Burkhart SS: The comma sign: Arthroscopic guide to the torn subscapularis tendon. *Arthroscopy* 2003;19:334-337.

    The comma sign, an arc formed by a portion of the superior glenohumeral ligament–coracohumeral ligament complex, was found useful in identifying the superolateral corner of the torn subscapularis tendon.

39. Deutsch A, Altchek DW, Veltri DM, Potter HG, Warren RF: Traumatic tears of the subscapularis tendon: Clinical diagnosis, magnetic resonance imaging findings, and operative treatment. *Am J Sports Med* 1997;25:13-22.

40. Edwards TB, Walch G, Sirveaux F, et al: Repair of tears of the subscapularis. *J Bone Joint Surg Am* 2005;87:725-730.

    In a retrospective review of 84 shoulders following open subscapularis repair at mean 45-month follow-up, the mean Constant score improved from 55 to 79.5 points. Tenodesis or tenotomy of the biceps tendon was associated with improved outcome regardless of the presurgical condition of the biceps tendon.

41. Bennett WF: Arthroscopic bicipital sheath repair: Two-year follow-up with pulley lesions. *Arthroscopy* 2004;20:964-973. Level of evidence: IV.

42. Bennett WF: Arthroscopic repair of isolated subscapularis tears: A prospective cohort with 2- to 4-year follow-up. *Arthroscopy* 2003;19:131-143.

    Comparison of patients' presurgical and postsurgical status after arthroscopic repair of an isolated subscapularis tear found a significant difference in all measures except the Constant score at 2- to 4-year follow-up. Magnetic resonance arthrography was found preferable to MRI for visualizing the tear. Level of evidence: IV.

43. Bennett WF: Arthroscopic repair of anterosuperior (supraspinatus/subscapularis) rotator cuff tears: A prospective cohort with 2- to 4-year follow-up. Classification of biceps subluxation/instability. *Arthroscopy* 2003;19:21-33.

    Comparison of patients' presurgical and postsurgical status after arthroscopic repair of an anterosuperior rotator cuff tear found a significant difference in all except the Constant score at 2- to 4-year follow-up. Level of evidence: IV.

44. Karnaugh RD, Sperling JW, Warren RF: Arthroscopic treatment of coracoid impingement. *Arthroscopy* 2001;17:784-787.

    An arthroscopic technique for treating coracoid impingement syndrome is described.

45. Lo IK, Burkhart SS: Arthroscopic coracoplasty through the rotator interval. *Arthroscopy* 2003;19:667-671.

    An intra-articular method of coracoplasty through the rotator interval is described. This technique is easier than a subacromial approach and allows orientation in the plane of the subscapularis tendon.

46. Lo IK, Burkhart SS: The interval slide in continuity: A method of mobilizing the anterosuperior rotator cuff without disrupting the tear margins. *Arthroscopy* 2004;20:435-441.

    This article describes a method of mobilizing tears of the anterosuperior rotator cuff by releasing and resecting a portion of the rotator interval, leaving the lateral margin intact.

47. D'Addesi LL, Anbari A, Reish MW, Brahmabhatt S, Kelly JD: The subscapularis footprint: An anatomic study of the subscapularis tendon insertion. *Arthroscopy* 2006;22:937-940.

    A cadaver study of the subscapularis tendon insertion into the lesser tuberosity found that it resembles a human ear and has a mean height of 25.8 mm (±3.2 mm) and width of 18.1 mm (±1.6 mm).

48. Curtis AS, Burbank KM, Tierney JJ, Scheller AD, Curran AR: The insertional footprint of the rotator cuff: An anatomic study. *Arthroscopy* 2006;22:609.

A cadaver study of rotator cuff tendon insertions into the humerus found that the entire rotator cuff has a horseshoe-shaped insertion that tapers away from the articular surface in a superior-to-inferior direction. The mean maximal insertional length and width of the subscapularis tendon measured 40 mm by 20 mm.

49. Kim SH, Oh I, Park JS, Shin SK, Jeong WK: Intra-articular repair of an isolated partial articular-surface tear of the subscapularis tendon. *Am J Sports Med* 2005;33:1825-1830.

At mean 27-month follow-up of 29 shoulders after arthroscopic repair of isolated partial articular surface tears of the subscapularis tendon, 18 had excellent, 10 had good, and 1 had a fair result. The internal rotation strength deficit improved from 32% to 4%. Level of evidence: IV.

50. Edwards TB, Walch G, Nove-Josserand L, et al: Arthroscopic debridement in the treatment of patients with isolated tears of the subscapularis. *Arthroscopy* 2006;22:941-946.

A retrospective review of 11 carefully selected patients who underwent débridement of a subscapularis tear found that the Constant score improved from 49 to 80 points at mean 34-month follow-up, and 9 patients were satisfied or very satisfied. Level of evidence: IV.

# Chapter 26

# Arthroscopic Treatment of Traumatic Anterior Shoulder Instability

*Robert A. Arciero, MD

*Augustus D. Mazzocca, MD

## Introduction

Shoulder instability results from a complex interaction of epidemiologic, genetic, and injury-related factors. The pathoanatomy is varied, and classifications have been developed to help the orthopaedic surgeon establish a correct diagnosis and formulate a treatment plan. This chapter focuses on recurrent traumatic anterior shoulder instability and the role of arthroscopic stabilization in the surgical treatment of this common disorder.

## Diagnosis

Patients with recurrent traumatic anterior shoulder instability can usually recall a specific episode of trauma that occurred with the arm abducted and externally rotated. They may recall either a spontaneous reduction or a frank dislocation requiring emergency assistance, and they may also report recurrent dislocation or recurrent partial or complete subluxation. Patients who have had a subluxation may recall resolution of symptoms within several days and may even report quickly returning to their sport. The dead arm syndrome is associated with transient subluxation.[1] Reduction with instability lasting 3 to 4 weeks after the trauma indicates a greater degree of capsular or labral disruption.

A patient with recurrent anteroinferior instability may avoid placing the injured shoulder into abduction and external rotation. For these patients, the key physical examination findings are positive apprehension and relocation tests, as well as increased anterior-posterior translation, as determined by a load-and-shift test in the plane of the scapula or with the arm abducted 80° to 90° in neutral rotation in the plane of the scapula. Crepitus elicited by this maneuver often indicates the presence of a labral detachment, which is a key pathologic feature of traumatic anterior shoulder instability.

*Robert A. Arciero, MD or the department with which he is affiliated has received research or institutional support from Arthrex, Smith & Nephew, and Mitek. Augustus D. Mazzocca, MD or the department with which he is affiliated has received research or institutional support from Arthrex.

The natural history of acute traumatic anterior dislocation is open to debate. The rate of recurrence after an initial dislocation is between 65% and 100% in patients who are age 15 to 25 years.

A true AP radiographic view of the shoulder and a modified axillary (West Point) radiographic view can show anterior glenoid erosion, anterior glenoid soft-tissue calcifications, and rim fractures. In a patient with recurrent traumatic anterior instability, these lesions should be carefully evaluated, both to confirm the diagnosis and detect any bony deficiency that may adversely affect nonsurgical, arthroscopic, or open stabilization. CT is valuable for a patient who has had several dislocations, a dislocation that occurred during sleep, or a dislocation that occurred with the arm in relatively little abduction and external rotation; these features may indicate a glenoid or humeral head deficiency. MRI is valuable, although not mandatory, for assessing associated pathology. In a patient with an acute dislocation, the associated hemarthrosis serves as an excellent contrast medium for detecting capsulolabral disruptions, humeral ligament avulsion, and superior and posterior labral tears. In a patient with recurrent shoulder instability, the use of intra-articular gadolinium can improve the ability to assess articular lesions or labral or rotator cuff tears.

## Pathology

The Bankart lesion, which is an avulsion of the inferior capsulolabral complex of the inferior glenohumeral ligament, is a key pathoanatomic finding in patients with recurrent traumatic anterior shoulder instability. Extensive biomechanical research has evaluated the contribution of the glenoid labrum to shoulder stability. In a cadaver model, isolated resection of the labrum increased glenohumeral translation but did not permit complete dislocation, in the absence of ligamentous stretch or injury.[2] A study simulating a capsulolabral disruption found that the circumferential labral attachment to the glenoid is divided into five zones; significant subluxation and dislocation required capsuloligamentous separation from the glenoid of at least three zones.[3]

Arthroscopic investigation found Bankart lesions in 97% of patients with initial traumatic shoulder dislocation requiring reduction.[4] In an MRI study, patients with recurrent shoulder instability had a 19% increase in capsular deformation.[5] The presence of a medially healed Bankart lesion or an anterior labroligamentous periosteal sleeve avulsion (ALPSA) can also be seen on MRI and at arthroscopy. Neviaser was the first to describe this important pathoanatomic variant, which represents an avulsion of the anterior labrum and ligament in which the anterior scapular periosteum remains intact, permitting medial healing of the labrum.[6]

Superior extension of the labral disruption, leading to a concomitant superior labrum anterior and posterior (SLAP) lesion, has been described in acute and recurrent traumatic shoulder instability.[7,8] Posterior extension of the inferior labral disruption or the posteroinferior labrum has also been observed. These more extensive capsulolabral disruptions from the glenoid appear to be associated with high-energy trauma and repeated instability.

Although an uncommon injury, avulsion of the inferior glenohumeral ligament complex from its humeral attachment is seen in patients with acute traumatic initial dislocation or recurrent instability. It can be detected on MRI, particularly if intra-articular contrast has been used. The presence of an extensive lesion is important, because it may indicate the need for an open repair. However, some authors have promoted arthroscopic repair of this lesion.[9]

Patients who have had more than one occurrence of instability, particularly with relatively little abduction or during sleep, should be evaluated for the presence of bony deficiencies. Plain radiographs, particularly the modified axillary view, can show glenoid bone loss, rim fractures, and calcifications. Several other radiographic methods have been used to find a humeral head defect (Hill-Sachs lesion), but they are unreliable. An appropriate history and a markedly positive apprehension test when the arm is in a small amount of abduction and external rotation indicate that CT is required to assess bone loss.

Significant bone defects on the glenoid or humeral head can compromise the outcome of an arthroscopic stabilization procedure. In a cadaver study, a glenoid bone loss of 21% compromised the AP stability of a Bankart repair.[10] A clinical series of 194 arthroscopically examined patients found that the presence of a Hill-Sachs lesion that engaged the glenoid rim when the arm was in abduction and external rotation led to an unacceptably high rate of recurrence of instability after arthroscopic stabilization; an inverted pear appearance of the glenoid indicated substantial anteroinferior glenoid loss.[11]

## Indications

The role of arthroscopic stabilization after an acute primary dislocation of the shoulder is controversial. Several studies have found that primary stabilization is a viable alternative in young, athletic patients, with good predictability and low morbidity. A short-term study of 40 patients between ages 16 and 89 years demonstrated a decrease in recurrence rates after nonsurgical immobilization of the shoulder in external rotation, compared with internal rotation.[12] An imaging study found that, following an anterior shoulder dislocation, reduction and coaption of the capsulolabral complex or Bankart lesion to the scapular neck of the anterior glenoid was best accomplished with the arm in external rotation.[13] Young, active patients are at increased risk of recurrent instability after primary anterior shoulder dislocation. Patients between ages 15 and 25 years old had reported recurrence rates between 65% and 100% after initial dislocation. Several clinical studies found significantly decreased recurrence rates after arthroscopic stabilization in young, high-demand patients with a Bankart lesion and dislocation requiring reduction. Early arthroscopic stabilization of these patients substantially reduced recurrence rates and led to superior outcomes, compared with nonsurgical treatment.[7,14-16] To clarify the role of arthroscopic stabilization in treating primary shoulder dislocation, prospective randomized studies should compare arm immobilization in external rotation with acute primary repair using the newer suture anchoring technique, which permits firm reattachment of the capsulolabral complex using extremely strong suture material and capsular plication. One argument against primary shoulder stabilization in this younger age group is that the surgery is unnecessary in approximately 30% of patients. In one study, the recurrence rate was 65% to 70%.[17] The only prospective randomized study comparing immobilization in internal rotation with arthroscopic repair found lower recurrence rates and improved outcomes after arthroscopic repair.[15]

Most studies found that arthroscopic stabilization using metal staples, transglenoid sutures, and bioabsorbable tacks was associated with a higher rate of recurrent anterior instability than open stabilization.[18-24] However, arthroscopic stabilization for recurrent traumatic anterior shoulder instability using the newer suture anchoring technique is well established. Several clinical studies found that the outcomes of arthroscopic stabilization using the suture anchoring technique rival those of open reconstruction.[25-29] However, patients must be carefully screened to ensure good results.

Expert surgeons have associated bony deficiencies involving the glenoid or humeral head with high recurrence rates after arthroscopic stabilization. A Hill-Sachs defect that engages along the anterior glenoid margin is also associated with high failure rates after arthroscopic stabilization.[11] Bone loss along the anterior glenoid margin can be measured by using a hook or probe during arthroscopic examination under anesthesia, and the arm can be put into a range of motion to determine whether the Hill-Sachs lesion is clinically significant. Anterior glenoid bone loss of more than 20% or an engaging Hill-Sachs lesion is a contraindication to arthroscopic stabilization.[11]

Radiographs are useful in identifying glenoid erosion, rim fractures, and large Hill-Sachs defects. The modified axillary view can be used to estimate anteroinferior glenoid bone loss.[30] The CT sagittal view of the glenoid fossa, particularly in three-dimensional reconstruction, can be used to evaluate the amount of glenoid bone loss. The inferior portion of the glenoid is seen as a circle superimposed on the three-dimensional reconstruction. Bone loss can be estimated by using software or measuring both the diameter of the superimposed circle and the width of the defect.[31]

The presence of an osseous Bankart lesion has been a contraindication to arthroscopic stabilization, but current arthroscopic techniques allow successful mobilization and repair, with resolution of capsular redundancy.[32] Athletes who participate in collision sports were also considered unsuitable for arthroscopic Bankart repair.[33-35] Successful outcomes after arthroscopic stabilization using newer techniques have modified this prohibition, although the topic remains controversial. The outstanding results of open stabilization in American football players serve as a basis of comparison with arthroscopic stabilization results.[36] Suture anchoring techniques have improved outcomes after arthroscopic repair of Bankart lesions in collision-sport athletes.[37,38] Several longer term studies of these athletes found a higher rate of recurrent instability, iatrogenic subscapularis deficiency, and osteoarthritis after open reconstruction.[39-42]

## Arthroscopic Technique

Arthroscopic Bankart repair and capsulorrhaphy requires the surgeon to address the two primary components of recurrent instability: capsulolabral disruption and capsular redundancy. The surgeon must be skilled in shoulder arthroscopy, placement of suture anchors along the anteroinferior quadrant of the glenoid through multiple portals, capsular plication, and arthroscopic knot tying.

General anesthesia, sometimes with an interscalene block, is used for arthroscopic stabilization. An interscalene block is an effective intrasurgical and postsurgical anesthetic that allows administration of postsurgical analgesia. Examination under anesthesia is helpful in determining the degree of translation. The load-and-shift maneuver can be performed with the arm in 80° to 90° of abduction and in the plane of the scapula; the anteroinferior glenohumeral ligament complex and posteroinferior glenohumeral complex can be tested with an-

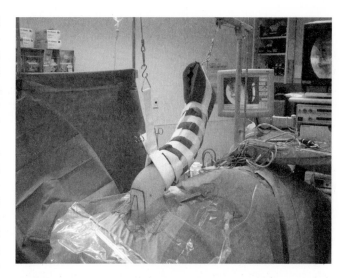

**Figure 1** Patient in the lateral decubitus position. The marking for the posterior portal is shown.

terior and posterior loading, respectively. The presence of crepitus with either maneuver is associated with increased incidence of labral pathology. Inferior translation can be evaluated using the sulcus test, which indicates the competence or laxity of the rotator interval structures (the superior glenohumeral ligament and coracohumeral ligament); if inferior translation does not disappear with external rotation, some authors believe the rotator interval should be closed after completion of the Bankart repair.

The patient can be placed in the beach chair or lateral decubitus position. With sufficient distraction and abduction, the lateral decubitus position allows much better access to the inferior half of the glenohumeral joint (Figure 1). A beanbag can be used to support the patient's torso and maintain 30° of posterior tilt. This position places the face of the glenoid parallel to the floor and facilitates instrumentation and drilling.

Portal placement is fundamental to a successful procedure. Posterior glenohumeral, anterosuperior, and anteroinferior portals are established (Figure 2). The arthroscope can be placed in the anterosuperior portal, and 8 mm or larger cannulae can be placed in both the anteroinferior and posterior portals. From the anterosuperior portal, the surgeon can estimate the extent of glenoid bone deficiency (Figure 3). The posterior portal can provide excellent access to the avulsed capsulolabral complex, as well as the inferior glenohumeral ligament. These three portals are usually sufficient for the procedure. Access to the anteroinferior and posteroinferior glenoid for anchor placement can be gained with percutaneous 3-mm trocars. The trocars can be placed anteriorly through the subscapularis for improved access to the anteroinferior glenoid face or posterolaterally for repair of Bankart lesions that extend posteriorly.

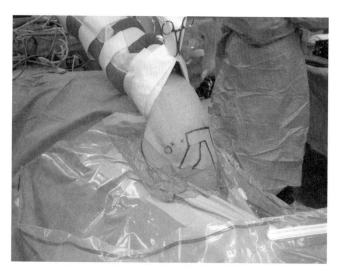

**Figure 2** Patient in the lateral decubitus position. The marking for the anterior portals is shown.

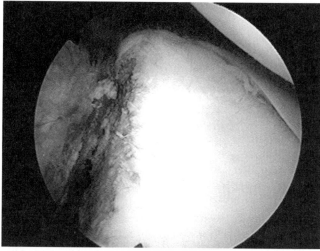

**Figure 3** The right shoulder, as seen from the anterosuperior portal, showing significant anterior glenoid bone loss.

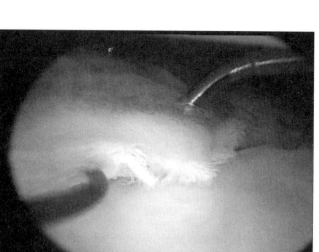

**Figure 4** The right shoulder, as seen from the anterosuperior portal, showing the hook instrument brought in from the posterior portal to allow easy instrumentation and suture placement at the low 6 o'clock position.

All of the intra-articular structures of the shoulder are evaluated arthroscopically, including the biceps anchor and tendon, posterosuperior labrum, glenoid, glenoid fossa, and humeral head. From the anterosuperior portal, the avulsed Bankart lesion can easily be discerned. Often, the lesion is medialized and fibrosed along the anteroinferior scapular neck. The first step is to elevate the capsulolabral disruption from the neck of the scapula until the deep fibers of the subscapularis can be seen through the anterosuperior portal. This step will ensure adequate mobilization of the anteroinferior glenohumeral ligament for retensioning and repositioning. The scapular neck can be abraded with a burr to ensure a bleeding bony bed for healing.

For reattachment and retensioning of the anteroinferior glenohumeral ligament, access to the inferior capsulolabral complex is required. Three methods have been used. In the first, a monofilament traction suture is placed into the anteroinferior glenohumeral ligament while being viewed from the posterior portal; traction is obtained through the anterosuperior portal. By pulling on the mobilized capsulolabral complex in this position, the surgeon can insert shuttling instrumentation through the anteroinferior portal to the most anteroinferior region of the capsulolabral complex.[43] In the second method, a suture punch is placed through a low anterior portal at the 6 o'clock position. The third method involves viewing from the anterosuperior portal and placing the inferiormost suture from the posterior portal (Figure 4). This method guarantees that the capsulolabral complex can be grasped with a monofilament suture or shuttling device at the lowest portion of the glenohumeral ligament.

In the next step, the critical anteroinferior anchor is placed through the anteroinferior portal along the articular edge, approximately 1 cm cephalad from the shuttling suture placement (Figure 5). One limb of the suture housed in the anchor is brought out through the cannula, where another limb of the shuttling suture is housed. A monofilament suture or a commercially available shuttling device permits transfer of the limb in the suture anchor through the inferior capsulolabral complex. Retensioning of the inferior glenohumeral ligament is accomplished when the soft tissue is advanced to the anchor in a more cephalad location and a knot is tied. The normal labral complex is thus reestablished over the articular margin, and the inferior ligament is retensioned (Figure 6). These steps can be repeated with the anchor placed approximately 7 to 8 mm superior along the face of the glenoid, as seen from the anterosuperior portal. At

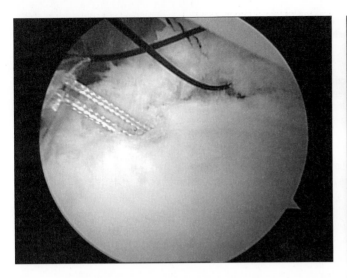

**Figure 5**  The right shoulder, showing the shuttling suture placed inferior to the anchor placement.

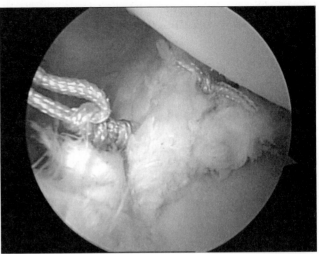

**Figure 6**  The completed capsulolabral attachment with retensioning of the inferior glenohumeral ligament.

least three anchors should be positioned on the inferior quadrant of the glenoid face. If the inferiormost anchor is difficult to place through the anteroinferior portal, it can be placed with a transsubscapular technique using a small trocar. The use of extremely strong suture material allows significant tensioning of the inferior ligament without the risk of suture breakage. This suture material also permits simultaneous capsular plication. A tuck of inferior ligament is taken with a shuttling hook, which is then inserted through the labrum to pass the shuttling suture or device. Knot tying accomplishes a combination of capsular plication and labral repair (Figure 7).

If the injury extends into the superior labrum, the arthroscope is transferred to the posterior portal. A SLAP repair is then performed. If the capsulolabral complex is extended posteriorly, the arthroscope is again placed in the anterosuperior position, and the lesion is addressed through the posterior and anteroinferior portals. Percutaneous posterolateral access, which is created using a small trocar, allows the anchor to be placed posteriorly at the optimum angle from the glenoid. From the posterior portal, the sutures can be shuttled using any number of suture hooks, punches, or shuttling devices. The anteroinferior cannula is also used for shuttling. Capsular plication sutures can be placed separately from the labral repair. The anteroinferior or posteroinferior capsule can be tensioned with a variety of suture hooks or punches by using a tuck technique to grasp a centimeter of tissue, then either performing capsular plication with a monofilament suture or using a shuttling device or monofilament suture to shuttle a nonabsorbable suture.[27,29] The capsular plication is completed with knot tying. In a cadaver model study, the arthroscopic plication technique was effective in reducing translation.[44]

Several authors have promoted routine closure of the rotator interval to improve stabilization, particularly in collision-sport athletes.[27,37] The technique involves using a suture hook to place a size-0 monofilament suture while grasping the upper edge of the medial glenohumeral ligament (Figure 7). The anterosuperior cannula can be backed out just anterior or superficial to the capsule, and a penetrating device can be used to grasp the superior capsular structures and then the suture. The knot is tied through the cannula in the acromial space to effectively retension the contents of the rotator interval. This technique is controversial. Significant loss of external rotation can occur if the rotator interval is vigorously overtensioned. Rotator interval closure should not be performed in overhead throwing athletes, for whom preserving external rotation is important. The routine placement of posteroinferior plication sutures is also controversial. It has been described as an adjunct to arthroscopic Bankart repair in patients who are involved in collision sports or who have significant inferior translation, as demonstrated by the sulcus sign in external rotation.[27,29,37] No validated studies have delineated the indications for or contributions of rotator interval closure to the success of arthroscopic stabilization, with or without posteroinferior plication sutures.

When thermal energy was first introduced to address capsular redundancy, it was widely used because of its ease of application, and several researchers found it to be effective.[45] Surgeons successfully used this technique in elite throwing athletes, particularly professional baseball pitchers with internal impingement. However, high recurrence rates and significant complications appeared over time, including complete capsular necrosis, osteonecrosis of the articular surface, neurologic injury to the axillary nerve, and stiffness.[46,47] Chondrolysis, a devastating complication, has also been associated with this technique.[48] As a

**Table 1 | Studies of Arthroscopic Stabilization Risk Factors and Complications**

| Study | Technique | Patients (*N*) | Follow-up Time (Months) | Recurrence (%) | Risk Factors | Complications |
|---|---|---|---|---|---|---|
| Boileau et al[43] | Suture anchoring | 91 | 36 | 7 (dislocation) 9 (subluxation) | Bone loss in glenoid or humeral head; hyperlaxity; use of fewer than four anchors | |
| Burkhart and DeBeer[11] | Suture anchoring | 194 | 27 | No bone defect: 4 Bone defect: 67 | Inverted pear glenoid; engaging Hill-Sachs lesion | |
| Rhee et al[52] | Metal suture anchoring | 5 | 7-20 | | | Iatrogenic articular damage; protruding anchors |
| Freehill et al[53] | Poly-L-lactic acid tacks | 52 | 8 (average) | | | Pain (19%); stiffness (with intra-articular implant debris); synovitis; articular lesions |
| Athwal et al[54] | Knotless suture anchoring, poly(L-lactide) polymer | 4 | 2-12 | | | Osteolysis, anchor pull-back, glenohumeral arthropathy (with loss of anchor fixation) |
| Wong and Williams[46] | Thermal | 14,277 (survey) | | Laser: 8 Monopolar: 8 Bipolar: 7 | | Capsular attenuation (20%); axillary neuropathy (1%); stiffness |
| Levine et al[48] | Thermal | 2 | | | | Severe chondrolysis |

result, the use of thermal energy has fallen out of favor, and it now has only a limited role as an adjunct in arthroscopic stabilization of recurrent traumatic anterior instability. A recent study found no advantage to the use of thermal energy in addressing capsular redundancy during arthroscopic stabilization.[49] It may have a role in treating overhead throwing athletes with internal impingement, but routine use is not justified.

## Rehabilitation

Studies of animal models found that soft-tissue healing to bone requires 6 to 12 weeks.[50] During this period, the area of soft-tissue repair must be protected. Some believe that inadequate postsurgical immobilization is the cause of the high recurrence rates associated with thermal plication for capsular redundancy. However, one study found that an accelerated rehabilitation program after arthroscopic suture anchor repair did not lead to a higher recurrence rate or negative outcomes. Although the patients were permitted active forward elevation and abduction immediately after surgery, external rotation was restricted for 6 weeks.[26] Requiring immobilization for 4 to 6 weeks after surgery, with early protected range-of-motion exercises, is a reasonable approach.

According to many studies of arthroscopic and open stabilization, an abduction immobilizer is used and Codman exercises are started immediately. Active assisted range-of-motion exercises during the first 6 weeks allow external rotation of 30° and forward elevation of 90°. At 6 weeks after surgery, the full range of motion is permitted, and strengthening exercises are started. The patient is permitted to begin sports activities 5 to 6 months after surgery.

## Pitfalls

Improper patient selection is the most common reason for failure of arthroscopic Bankart repair and capsulorrhaphy. The patient must be evaluated for the presence of significant bony deficiencies, because bone deficiencies of the glenoid or humeral head adversely affect the success of arthroscopic stabilization.[43,51] The procedure can also fail for technical reasons. If the avulsed capsulolabral complex is inadequately mobilized, the retensioning of the inferior glenohumeral ligament may be insufficient. If suture anchors are inappropriately positioned medially on the scapular neck or superiorly, the reattachment of the inferior glenohumeral ligament may be inadequate. The use of fewer than four anchor points has been associated with failure of arthroscopic stabilization.[43] Metal anchors are associated with iatrogenic articular cartilage damage, and biodegradable tacks and bioabsorbable suture anchors are associated with synovitis, chondrolysis, and osteoarthropathy[52-54] (Table 1).

**Table 2 | Studies of Shoulder Repair Techniques**

| Study | Technique | Patients (*N*) | Follow-up Time (Months) | Outcome | Recurrence (%) |
|---|---|---|---|---|---|
| **Transglenoid Sutures, Tacks, Thermal Energy** | | | | | |
| Chen et al[49] | Tacks versus tacks and thermal energy | 72 | Tacks: 58 Tacks and thermal energy: 30 | No difference between groups | Tacks: 21 Tacks and thermal energy: 8 |
| Cole et al[18] | Tacks: Open versus arthroscopic | 59 | 54 | ASES, SF-36: No difference between groups | Open: 18 Arthroscopic: 24 |
| Freedman et al[23] | Tacks and transglenoid sutures: Open versus arthroscopic (meta-analysis) | Open: 156 Arthroscopic: 172 | | Rowe (80 to 100 = good to excellent): Open: 88 Arthroscopic: 71 | Open: 10 Arthroscopic: 20 |
| Marquardt et al[20] | Arthroscopic, bioabsorbable tacks | 18 | 908 (8.7 years) | Rowe: 90 Constant: 91 ASES: 92 | 6 (dislocation or subluxation) |
| Sperber et al[21] | Tacks: Open versus arthroscopic | 56 | 24 | (For stable shoulders only) Rowe: Open: 95 Arthroscopic: 100 Constant: Open: 98 Arthroscopic: 100 | Open: 12 Arthroscopic: 23 |
| Karlsson et al[19] | Tacks: Open versus arthroscopic bioabsorbable | 117 | Open: 36 Arthroscopic: 28 | Rowe: Open: 89 Arthroscopic: 93 Constant: Open: 89 Arthroscopic: 91 | Open: 10 Arthroscopic: 15 |
| Roberts et al[22] | Tacks: Open versus arthroscopic Arthroscopy: Tacks versus transglenoid sutures | 56 | 29 | Rowe: Open: 74 Arthroscopic tacks: 71 Arthroscopic sutures: 56 | Open: 31 Arthroscopic tacks: 38 Arthroscopic sutures: 70 |
| **Arthroscopic Stabilization of Acute Anterior Dislocation** | | | | | |
| Bottoni et al[14] | Tacks versus immobilization | 24 | 36 | SANE: Tacks: 88 Immobilization: 57 | Tacks: 10 Immobilization: 75 |
| Larrain et al[16] | Transglenoid suture anchoring versus nonsurgical treatment | 46 | 67 | Rowe: Anchoring: 96% excellent Nonsurgical: 95% poor | Anchoring: 4 Nonsurgical: 95 |
| Kirkley et al[15] | Transglenoid suturing versus nonsurgical treatment | 31 | 79 | ASES, DASH: No difference between groups WOSI: Higher suturing scores | Lower in suturing group |
| DeBerardino[7] | Tacks | 48 | 37 | SANE: 95 Rowe: 92 Short Form-36: 97 | 12 (failure) |
| **Open Bankart Repair** | | | | | |
| Gill et al[55] | | 56 | 144 (12 years) | 54 excellent or good | 5 (dislocation) |
| Pelet et al[40] | | 30 | 348 (29 years) | Rowe: 80 Constant: 73 Osteoarthritis: 40% | 10 (dislocation) |
| Magnusson et al[39] | | 47 | 69 | Rowe: 90 Constant: 88 | 11 (dislocation) 6 (subluxation) |
| Sachs et al[41] | | 30 | 48 | Constant: 90 WOSI: 83 (Subscapularis function predicted outcome) | 6 (dislocation) 3 (subluxation) |

## Table 2 Continued | Studies of Shoulder Repair Techniques

| Study | Technique | Patients (N) | Follow-up Time (Months) | Outcome | Recurrence (%) |
|---|---|---|---|---|---|
| Pagnani and Dome[36] | | 58 | 37 | ASES: 97<br>Rowe: 94 | 3 (subluxation) |
| Uhorchak et al[42] | | 66 | 47 | ASES: 95<br>Rowe: 80 | 20 (subluxation)<br>12 (rare)<br>8 (multiple)<br>3 (dislocation) |
| **Arthroscopic Bankart Repair Using Suture Anchoring** | | | | | |
| Ide et al[38] | | 55 (contact and noncontact athletes) | 42 | Rowe: 92 | Noncontact: 6<br>Contact: 9.5 |
| Mazzocca et al[37] | Posterior plication, interval closed | 18 (collision- and contact-sport athletes) | 37 | Rowe:<br>Collision: 94<br>Contact: 92<br>SST:<br>Collision: 12<br>Contact: 11<br>ASES:<br>Collision: 89<br>Contact: 88 | 11 (dislocation) |
| Rhee et al[34] | Open versus arthroscopic | 48 (collision-sport athletes) | 72 | VAS, Rowe, Constant: No difference between groups | Open: 12.5<br>Arthroscopic: 25 |
| Cho[35] | Arthroscopic | 29 (collision- and noncollision-sport athletes) | 61 | VAS, Rowe, Constant: No difference between groups | Collision: 17<br>Noncollision: 7 |
| Bottoni et al[25]* | Open versus arthroscopic | 61 | 32 | SANE, SST, WOSI: No difference between groups | Open: 7<br>Arthroscopic: 3 |
| Fabbriciani et al[56]* | Open versus arthroscopic | 60 (strict inclusion criteria) | 24 | Rowe:<br>Open: 86<br>Arthroscopic: 91<br>Constant:<br>Open: 86<br>Arthroscopic: 89 | None |
| Kim et al[26]* | Accelerated rehabilitation versus immobilization | 62 | 31 | UCLA, ASES: No difference between groups | Positive apprehension test:<br>Accelerated rehabilitation: 3<br>Immobilization: 3 |
| Carreira et al[27]† | | 85 | 24 or more | Rowe: 88<br>ASES: 92<br>SST: 11.5 | 5 (dislocation)<br>4 (subluxation) |
| Hayashida et al[57] | Knotless | 47 | 28 | Rowe: 91 | 2 (dislocation)<br>4 (subluxation) |
| Kim et al[28]† | | 167 | 44 | Rowe: 92<br>UCLA: 91<br>ASES: 93 | 4 |
| Mohtadi et al[24]† | Open versus arthroscopic (meta-analysis of 18 articles) | | | | Less instability, better return to sports with open |
| Sugaya et al[32] | Arthroscopic, osseous Bankart | 42 | 34 | Rowe: 94<br>UCLA: 33.6 | 5 (dislocation) |
| Westerheide et al[29]† | Arthroscopic, posterior plication | 67 | 33 | Rowe: 85<br>SST: 11.2<br>WOSI: 85 | 7 (dislocation) |

*Level of evidence I or II*
†*Level of evidence III or IV*

*ASES = American Shoulder and Elbow Surgeons Shoulder Index; DASH = Disabilities of the Arm; Shoulder and Hand Questionnaire; SANE = Single Assessment Numeric Evaluation; SST = Simple Shoulder Test; UCLA = University of California Los Angeles Shoulder Scale; VAS = visual analog scale; WOSI = Western Ontario Shoulder Instability Index.*

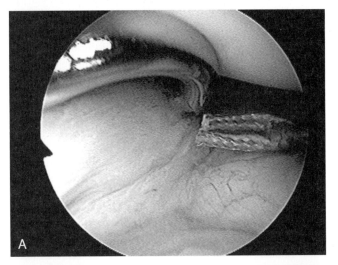

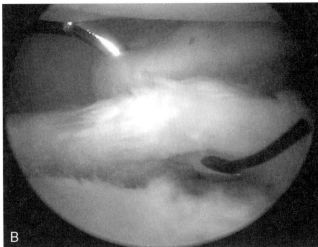

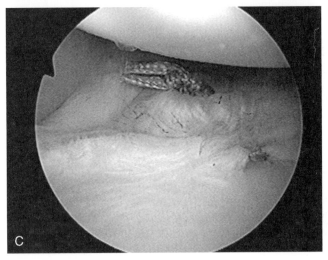

**Figure 7**  **A,** The suture hook is used to grasp a pinch of capsule. **B,** The capsule and labrum are captured with a size-0 monofilament suture. **C,** Nonabsorbable suture within the anchor is shuttled through the capsule and labrum and tied, combining capsular plication and labral repair.

## Summary

Until approximately 10 years ago, only highly skilled surgeons were able to perform shoulder arthroscopy with reliably good results, and the overall recurrence rate after shoulder arthroscopy using tacks and transglenoid sutures was higher than the rate after open reconstruction. However, suture anchoring techniques and nonabsorbable sutures are now commonly used. Table 2 presents the available evidence on the effectiveness of arthroscopic and open shoulder repair techniques. In these studies, the rates of recurrence, including recurrent subluxation, range from 5% to 15% after arthroscopic stabilization. Several long-term studies of the results of open stabilization found higher recurrence rates, particularly of subluxation, than previously reported. Controversy persists as to the use of arthroscopic stabilization in athletes who participate in contact sports; the recurrence rate appears to be lower after open treatment, although the gap is narrowing. In general, outcomes after arthroscopic stabilization have improved with the development of better instrumentation and a greater awareness of the required technical steps, and numerous studies have reported recurrence rates and outcomes similar to those of open procedures.

## Annotated References

1. Rowe CR, Zarins B: Recurrent transient subluxation of the shoulder. *J Bone Joint Surg Am* 1981;63:863-872.

2. Pouliart N, Gagey O: The effect of isolated labrum resection on shoulder stability. *Knee Surg Sports Traumatol Arthrosc* 2006;14:301-308.

   In a cadaver study, a motorized shaver was used to remove the labrum, keeping the capsule intact. The total labrum resection prevented the humeral head from dislocating.

3. Pouliart N, Marmor S, Gagey O: Simulated capsulolabral lesion in cadavers: Dislocation does not result from a Bankart lesion only. *Arthroscopy* 2006;22:748-754.

In a cadaver study, the capsuloligamentous complex was sequentially detached from the glenoid neck, and anterior and inferior stability testing was performed. A dislocation could not be produced by a Bankart lesion alone.

4. Taylor DC, Arciero RA: Pathologic changes associated with shoulder dislocation: Arthroscopic and physical examination findings in first-time, traumatic dislocations. *Am J Sports Med* 1997;25:306-311.

5. Urayama M, Itoi E, Sashi R, Minagawa H, Sato K: Capsular elongation in shoulders with recurrent anterior dislocation: Quantitative assessment with magnetic resonance arthrography. *Am J Sports Med* 2003;31:64-67.

   In a retrospective review of 12 patients with unilateral recurrent anterior shoulder dislocation, the anteroinferior and inferior portions of the shoulder capsule were elongated an average of 19%.

6. Neviaser TJ: The anterior labroligamentous sleeve avulsion lesion: A cause of recurrent instability of the shoulder. *Arthroscopy* 1993;9:17-21.

7. DeBerardino TM, Arciero RA, Taylor DC, Uhorchak JM: Prospective evaluation of arthroscopic stabilization of acute, initial anterior shoulder dislocations in young athletes: Two- to five-year follow-up. *Am J Sports Med* 2001;29:586-592.

   After traumatic anterior shoulder dislocation, 3 patients chose nonsurgical treatment, 6 underwent open repair, and 48 underwent arthroscopic repair. Average patient age was 20 years. At 5-year follow-up, the result of surgical treatments was significantly better than that of nonsurgical treatment.

8. Warner JJ, Kann S, Marks P: Arthroscopic repair of combined Bankart and superior labral detachment anterior and posterior lesions: Technique and preliminary results. *Arthroscopy* 1994;10:383-391.

9. Spang JT, Karas SG: The HAGL lesion: An arthroscopic technique for repair of humeral avulsion of the glenohumeral ligament. *Arthroscopy* 2005;21:498-502.

   A suture anchor technique for arthroscopic repair of a humeral avulsion of the glenohumeral ligament is described to anatomically reapproximate the torn edge of the glenohumeral ligament complex to its humeral head insertion.

10. Itoi E, Lee SB, Berglund LJ, Berge LL, An KN: The effect of a glenoid defect on anteroinferior stability of the shoulder after Bankart repair: A cadaveric study. *J Bone Joint Surg Am* 2000;82:35-46.

11. Burkhart SS, DeBeer JF: Traumatic glenohumeral bone defects and their relationship to failure of arthroscopic Bankart repairs: Significance of the "inverted pear" glenoid and the humeral engaging Hill-Sachs lesion. *Arthroscopy* 2000;16:677-694.

12. Itoi E, Hatakeyama Y, Kido T, et al: A new method of immobilization after traumatic anterior dislocation of the shoulder: A preliminary study. *J Shoulder Elbow Surg* 2003;12:413-415.

   Forty patients with initial shoulder dislocation were assigned to conventional immobilization in internal rotation or a new method of immobilization in external rotation. The recurrence rate was 30% greater in the internal-rotation patients, with an even greater difference in patients younger than 30 years.

13. Itoi E, Sashi R, Minagawa H, Shimizu T, Wakabayashi I, Sato K: Position of immobilization after dislocation of the glenohumeral joint: A study with use of magnetic resonance imaging. *J Bone Joint Surg Am* 2001;83:661-667.

   An MRI study of six patients found that immobilization of the arm in external rotation better approximates the Bankart lesion to the glenoid neck than the conventional internal-rotation position.

14. Bottoni CR, Wilckens JH, DeBerardino TM, et al: A prospective, randomized evaluation of arthroscopic stabilization versus nonoperative treatment in patients with acute, traumatic, first-time shoulder dislocations. *Am J Sports Med* 2002;30:576-580.

   At 36-month follow-up of 12 nonsurgically treated patients and 10 surgically treated patients, arthroscopic stabilization of traumatic first-time anterior shoulder dislocation was found to be effective and safe, significantly reducing the recurrence rate of shoulder dislocation in young athletes compared with conventional nonsurgical treatment.

15. Kirkley A, Werstine R, Ratjek A, Griffin S: Prospective randomized clinical trial comparing the effectiveness of immediate arthroscopic stabilization versus immobilization and rehabilitation in first traumatic anterior dislocations of the shoulder: Long-term evaluation. *Arthroscopy* 2005;21:55-63.

   In a randomized clinical trial, 40 patients younger than 30 years and with a first traumatic anterior shoulder dislocation received immediate anterior stabilization followed by rehabilitation or immobilization. At average 75-month follow-up, there was a small but clinically significant difference between the two groups in the rate of redislocation. Immediate arthroscopic stabilization is recommended for higher level athletes who are younger than 30 years.

16. Larrain MV, Botto GJ, Montenegro HJ, Mauas DM: Arthroscopic repair of acute traumatic anterior shoulder dislocation in young athletes. *Arthroscopy* 2001;17:373-377.

   In a prospective, nonrandomized study of 46 young patients, most of whom were rugby players, 96% of those treated surgically had an excellent result, compared with 5.5% of those treated nonsurgically.

17. Hovelius L, Augustini BG, Fredin H, Johansson O, Norlin R, Thorling J: Primary anterior dislocation of the shoulder in young patients: A 10-year prospective study. *J Bone Joint Surg Am* 1996;78:1677-1684.

18. Cole BJ, L'Insalata J, Irrgang J, Warner JJ: Comparison of arthroscopic and open anterior shoulder stabilization: A two to six-year follow-up study. *J Bone Joint Surg Am* 2000;82:1108-1114.

19. Karlsson J, Magnusson L, Ejerhed L, Hultenheim I, Lundin O, Kartus J: Comparison of open and arthroscopic stabilization for recurrent shoulder dislocation in patients with a Bankart lesion. *Am J Sports Med* 2001;29:538-542.

    A prospective study of 117 patients with symptomatic, recurrent anterior posttraumatic shoulder instability found that both open and arthroscopic reconstruction produced a stable, well-functioning shoulder in the majority of patients. The only significant difference was in external rotation in abduction, which was better in the arthroscopically treated patients.

20. Marquardt B, Witt KA, Gotze C, Liem D, Steinbeck J, Potzl W: Long-term results of arthroscopic Bankart repair with a bioabsorbable tack. *Am J Sports Med* 2006;34:1906-1910.

    At mean 8.7-year follow-up, 18 consecutive patients with traumatic anterior shoulder instability scored an average 91 points on both the Rowe and Constant-Murley scales. The recurrent instability rate was 5.6%. Level of evidence:IV.

21. Sperber A, Hamberg P, Karlsson J, Sward L, Wredmark T: Comparison of an arthroscopic and an open procedure for posttraumatic instability of the shoulder:A prospective, randomized multicenter study. *J Shoulder Elbow Surg* 2001;10:105-108.

    Fifty-six patients were treated for a Bankart lesion with arthroscopic reconstruction using biodegradable tacks or open reconstruction with suture anchors. At 2-year follow-up, a large number of redislocations had occurred in both groups; patients treated arthroscopically had a tendency to more redislocations.

22. Roberts SN, Taylor DE, Brown JN, Hayes MG, Saies A: Open and arthroscopic techniques for the treatment of traumatic anterior shoulder instability in Australian rules football players. *J Shoulder Elbow Surg* 1999;8:403-409.

23. Freedman KB, Smith AP, Romeo AA, Cole BJ, Bach BR Jr: Open Bankart repair versus arthroscopic repair with transglenoid sutures or bioabsorbable tacks for recurrent anterior instability of the shoulder: A meta-analysis. *Am J Sports Med* 2004;32:1520-1527.

    A meta-analysis of open Bankart repair and arthroscopic Bankart repair using bioabsorbable tacks or transglenoid sutures found a 12.6% recurrence rate after arthroscopy and a 3.4% rate after open repair.

24. Mohtadi NG, Bitar IJ, Sasyniuk TM, Hollinshead RM, Harper WP: Arthroscopic versus open repair for traumatic anterior shoulder instability: A meta-analysis. *Arthroscopy* 2005;21:652-658.

    A meta-analysis of 18 articles compared arthroscopic and open repair of traumatic, recurrent anterior shoulder instability. The outcome was more favorable after open repair, with respect to recurrence and return to activity.

25. Bottoni CR, Smith EL, Berkowitz MJ, Towle RB, Moore JH: Arthroscopic versus open shoulder stabilization for recurrent anterior instability: A prospective randomized clinical trial. *Am J Sports Med* 2006;34:1730-1737.

    In a prospective, randomized clinical trial, 61 patients were treated with open or arthroscopic suture anchor stabilization. No differences in outcomes were observed. Failures (recurrent instability and inability to return to work) were observed in 2 of 29 open-technique patients and 1 of 31 arthroscopic-technique patients. Level of evidence: I.

26. Kim SH, Ha KI, Jung MW, Lim MS, Kim YM, Park JH: Accelerated rehabilitation after arthroscopic Bankart repair for selected cases: A prospective randomized clinical study. *Arthroscopy* 2003;19:722-731.

    After arthroscopic Bankart repair using suture anchors, 28 patients received 3 weeks of immobilization with an abduction sling and conventional rehabilitation, and 34 received an accelerated rehabilitation program. The recurrence rate was similar, and none of the patients developed a recurrent dislocation. The accelerated program promoted functional recovery and reduced postsurgical pain.

27. Carreira DS, Mazzocca AD, Oryhon J, Brown FM, Hayden JK, Romeo AA: A prospective outcome evaluation of arthroscopic Bankart repairs: Minimum 2-year follow-up. *Am J Sports Med* 2006;34:771.

    A consecutive series of 85 patients was treated with arthroscopic suture anchor repair featuring a low 5 o'clock portal placed through the subscapularis tendon and posterior plication. The overall recurrence rate was 10%, and 90% had good or excellent results. Level of evidence: IV.

28. Kim SH, Ha KI, Cho YB, Ryu BD, Oh I: Arthroscopic anterior stabilization of the shoulder: Two to six-year follow-up. *J Bone Joint Surg Am* 2003;85-A:1511-1518.

    An evaluation of the results of arthroscopic Bankart repair with use of suture anchors and nonabsorbable sutures in 167 patients found satisfactory recurrence rates, activity, and range of motion.

29. Westerheide KJ, Dopirak RM, Snyder SJ: Arthroscopic anterior stabilization and posterior capsular plication for anterior glenohumeral instability: A report of 71 cases. *Arthroscopy* 2006;22:539-547.

    Arthroscopic anterior reconstruction and posteroinferior pinch tuck capsular plication were performed in 71 shoulders (67 patients) with anterior glenohumeral instability. Five patients (7%) had postsurgical dislocation, 97% returned to normal activity levels, and 90% returned to their previous level of athletics. Level of evidence: IV.

30. Itoi E, Lee SB, Amrami KK, Wenger DE, An KN: Quantitative assessment of classic anteroinferior bony Bankart lesions by radiography and computed tomography. *Am J Sports Med* 2003;31:112.

In cadaver scapulae, the West Point radiographic view and CT were found to be useful in estimating osseous defects of different glenoid lengths.

31. Sugaya H, Moriishi J, Dohi M, Kon Y, Tsuchiya A: Glenoid rim morphology in recurrent anterior glenohumeral instability. *J Bone Joint Surg Am* 2003;85: 878-884.

Three-dimensionally reconstructed CT with elimination of the humeral head was used to evaluate the morphology of the glenoid rim and quantity osseous defects. Fifty percent of shoulders with recurrent anterior glenohumeral instability had an osseous Bankart lesion.

32. Sugaya H, Moriishi J, Kanisawa I, Tsuchiya A: Arthroscopic osseous Bankart repair for chronic recurrent traumatic anterior glenohumeral instability. *J Bone Joint Surg Am* 2005;87:1752-1760.

In an arthroscopic osseous Bankart repair of 42 shoulders (41 patients) with chronic recurrent traumatic glenohumeral instability, a displaced osseous fragment was separated from the glenoid neck before reduction and fixation in the optimal position with suture anchors. The mean Rowe score improved from 33.6 to 94.3 points ($P < 0.01$), and the mean UCLA score, from 20.5 to 33.6 points ($P < 0.01$) at final evaluation.

33. Gill TJ, Zarins B: Open repairs for the treatment of anterior shoulder instability. *Am J Sports Med* 2003; 31:142-153.

Open surgical techniques for treatment of anterior shoulder instability are reviewed.

34. Rhee YG, Ha JH, Cho NS: Anterior shoulder stabilization in collision athletes: Arthroscopic versus open Bankart repair. *Am J Sports Med* 2006;34:979-985.

In a comparison of collision athletes with recurrent instability after open Bankart repair or arthroscopic Bankart repair using suture anchors and tacks, the outcome measures were similar. Postsurgical recurrent instability was observed in 25% of arthroscopic-repair patients and 12.5% of open-repair patients. Level of evidence: IV.

35. Cho NS, Hwang JC, Rhee YG: Arthroscopic stabilization in anterior shoulder instability: Collision athletes versus noncollision athletes. *Arthroscopy* 2006;22:947-953.

Athletes who participate in collision sports and other athletes underwent arthroscopic Bankart repair using suture anchors and tacks. The outcomes measures were similar, but higher recurrent instability occurred in the collision-sport group (28%) than in the other group (6.7%). Level of evidence: IV.

36. Pagnani MJ, Dome DC: Surgical treatment of traumatic anterior shoulder instability in American football players. *J Bone Joint Surg Am* 2002;84:711-715.

After open anterior shoulder stabilization, 55 of 58 American football players had a good or excellent result, and 52 returned to playing football for at least 1 year. One patient stopped playing because of recurrent instability. Postsurgical stability appeared to be superior to that reported after arthroscopic stabilization in this population.

37. Mazzocca AD, Brown FM Jr, Carreira DS, Hayden J, Romeo AA: Arthroscopic anterior shoulder stabilization of collision and contact athletes. *Am J Sports Med* 2005;33:52-60.

Eighteen collision- and contact-sport athletes were treated with arthroscopic suture anchor repair for recurrent instability. Rotator interval closure was performed in selected patients. Recurrent dislocations occurred in two collision-sport athletes (11%) and no contact-sport athletes. All returned to their sport. Level of evidence: IV.

38. Ide J, Maeda S, Takagi K: Arthroscopic Bankart repair using suture anchors in athletes: Patient selection and postoperative sports activity. *Am J Sports Med* 2004;32:1899-1905.

A prospective cohort group of athletes was treated with arthroscopic stabilization using a suture anchor technique. Rowe scores improved from 30 to 92 points, and the overall recurrence rate was 7%. No difference in recurrence was observed between contact and noncontact athletes.

39. Magnusson L, Kartus J, Ejerhed L, Hultenheim I, Sernert N, Karlsson J: Revisiting the open Bankart experience: A four- to nine-year follow-up. *Am J Sports Med* 2002;30:778-782.

Retrospective review of 54 shoulders found that, in the long term, the open Bankart procedure resulted in an unexpectedly high rate of recurrent instability.

40. Pelet S, Jolles BM, Farron A: Bankart repair for recurrent anterior glenohumeral instability: Results at twenty-nine years' follow-up. *J Shoulder Elbow Surg* 2006;15:203-207.

At 29-year follow-up of 30 patients, 10% had recurrent dislocation. The global rate of osteoarthritis was 40%, with five patients needing total shoulder arthroplasty. The average Rowe and Constant scores were lower than scores for normal shoulders, at 20 points and 13 points, respectively.

41. Sachs RA, Williams B, Stone ML, Paxton L, Kuney M: Open Bankart repair: Correlation of results with postoperative subscapularis function. *Am J Sports Med* 2005;33:1458-1462.

The integrity and strength of the subscapularis muscle was the only factor correlated after open Bankart repair with overall patient satisfaction and outcomes scores on the Western Ontario Shoulder Instability Index. Level of evidence: II.

42. Uhorchak JM, Arciero RA, Huggard D, Taylor DC: Recurrent shoulder instability after open reconstruction in athletes involved in collision and contact sports. *Am J Sports Med* 2000;28:794-799.

43. Boileau P, Villalba M, Hery JY, Balg F, Ahrens P, Neyton L: Risk factors for recurrence of shoulder instability after arthroscopic Bankart repair. *J Bone Joint Surg Am* 2006;88:1755-1763.

At mean 36 months following arthroscopic stabilization of recurrent anterior traumatic shoulder instability, 14 (15.3%) of 91 consecutive patients had recurrent instability. The risk of recurrence was significantly related to the presence of a glenoid or humeral bone defect (glenoid compression fracture, $P = 0.01$; large Hill-Sachs lesion, $P = 0.05$). Recurrence was significantly higher in patients with inferior ($P = 0.03$) or anterior ($P = 0.01$) shoulder hyperlaxity or fewer than four anchors ($P = 0.03$).

44. Alberta FG, Elattrache NS, Mihata T, McGarry MH, Tibone JE, Lee TQ: Arthroscopic anteroinferior suture plication resulting in decreased glenohumeral translation and external rotation: Study of a cadaver model. *J Bone Joint Surg Am* 2006;88:179-187.

Six intact cadaver shoulders were tested after capsular stretching and arthroscopic capsular plication. Plication reduced anterior translation and external rotation, and it resulted in a shift of the glenohumeral center of rotation posteriorly.

45. Miniaci A, Codsi MJ: Thermal capsulorrhaphy for the treatment of shoulder instability. *Am J Sports Med* 2006;34:1356-1363.

This update on the use of thermal energy to treat shoulder instability discusses basic science concepts, clinical studies, postsurgical care rationale, and complications.

46. Wong KL, Williams GR: Complications of thermal capsulorrhaphy of the shoulder. *J Bone Joint Surg Am* 2001;83(suppl 2, pt 2):151-155.

A survey of 379 surgeons found promising short-term results of use of thermal energy for treatment of shoulder instability, with low rates of recurrent instability. However, capsular insufficiency was found with recurrent instability.

47. D'Alessandro DF, Bradley JP, Fleischli JE, Connor PM: Prospective evaluation of thermal capsulorrhaphy for shoulder instability: Indications and results, two- to five-year follow-up. *Am J Sports Med* 2004;32:21-33.

At average 38-month follow-up, 37% of 84 shoulders treated with arthroscopic thermal capsulorrhaphy had an unsatisfactory result on several outcome measures. The use of this technique should be tempered until studies document its efficacy.

48. Levine WN, Clark AM Jr, D'Alessandro DF, Yamaguchi K: Chondrolysis following arthroscopic thermal capsulorrhaphy to treat shoulder instability: A report of two cases. *J Bone Joint Surg Am* 2005;87:616-621.

Two young athletes who developed severe chondrolysis following thermal capsulorrhaphy were treated with humeral head resurfacing and lateral meniscal allograft.

49. Chen S, Haen PS, Walton J, Murrell GA: The effects of thermal capsular shrinkage on the outcomes of arthroscopic stabilization for primary anterior shoulder instability. *Am J Sports Med* 2005;33:705-711.

A comparison of arthroscopic Bankart repair using bioabsorbable tacks with or without thermal capsulorrhaphy found no difference in outcomes or recurrence rates. The addition of thermal shrinkage resulted in neither benefit nor harm. Level of evidence: III.

50. Rodeo SA, Arnoczsky SP, Torzilli PA, Hidaka C, Warren RF: Tendon-healing in a bone tunnel: A biomechanical and histological study in the dog. *J Bone Joint Surg* 1993;75-A:1795-1803.

51. Tauber M, Resch H, Forstner R, Raffl M, Schauer J: Reasons for failure after surgical repair of anterior shoulder instability. *J Shoulder Elbow Surg* 2004;13:279-285.

Of 41 patients with recurrent anterior shoulder instability after failed arthroscopic Bankart repair (25 patients) or open stabilization (16 patients), 23 (56%) had a defect of the anterior bony glenoid rim at revision surgery, 9 (22%) had a large capsule, 2 (5%) had a laterally torn capsule, and 7 (17%) had a typical Bankart lesion with good capsule quality.

52. Rhee YG, Lee DH, Chun IH, Bae SC: Glenohumeral arthropathy after arthroscopic anterior shoulder stabilization. *Arthroscopy* 2004;20:402-406.

In a report of five patients with iatrogenic arthropathy after arthroscopic Bankart repair using a metallic suture anchors, the authors caution that proper surgical technique is required and recommend aggressive early evaluation and radiography if unusual mechanical symptoms appear.

53. Freehill MQ, Harms DJ, Huber SM, Atlihan D, Buss DD: Poly-L-lactic acid tack synovitis after arthroscopic stabilization of the shoulder. *Am J Sports Med* 2003;31:643-647.

Retrospective review of 52 patients after arthroscopic stabilization using an average of 2.2 poly-L-lactic acid tacks found that pain developed in 10 patients at an average of 8 months, and progressive stiffness developed in 6 of the 10. Nine of these patients had gross implant debris, and evidence of glenohumeral synovitis was seen in all 10.

54. Athwal GS, Shridharani SM, O'Driscoll SW: Osteolysis and arthropathy of the shoulder after use of bioabsorbable knotless suture anchors: A report of four cases. *J Bone Joint Surg Am* 2006;88:1840-1845.

In four patients with severe osteolysis of the glenoid and destructive, progressive glenohumeral arthropathy after the use of bioabsorbable knotless anchors, loss of anchor fixation may have resulted in anchor loosening, pistoning, and osteolysis. Eventual backing out of the anchor led to articular damage.

55. Gill TJ, Micheli LJ, Gebhard F, Binder C: Bankart repair for anterior instability of the shoulder: Long-term outcome. *J Bone Joint Surg Am* 1997;79:850-857.

56. Fabbriciani C, Milano G, Demontis A, Fadda S, Ziranu F, Mulas PD: Arthroscopic versus open treatment of Bankart lesion of the shoulder: A prospective randomized study. *Arthroscopy* 2004;20:456-462.

Sixty patients with traumatic anterior shoulder instability underwent surgical repair of an isolated Bankart lesion (30 arthroscopic suture anchor repairs and 30 open procedures). No recurrence was reported. Constant and Rowe scores were not significantly different in the two groups. Arthroscopic repair with suture anchors was found to be an effective surgical technique for this purpose.

57. Hayashida K, Yoneda M, Mizuno N, Fukushima S, Nakagawa S: Arthroscopic Bankart repair with knotless suture anchor for traumatic anterior shoulder instability: Results of short-term follow-up. *Arthroscopy* 2006;22:620-626.

Forty-seven patients with traumatic recurrent anterior shoulder instability but no severe glenoid bone defect underwent arthroscopic Bankart repair with knotless suture anchors. At 2-year follow-up, 87% had a good or excellent result. The recurrence rate was 6.4%. Three patients had a directly related complication (backing out of the anchor or breakage of the anchor suture loop).

# Chapter 27

# Multidirectional Instability

*Richard K.N. Ryu, MD

## Introduction

Multidirectional instability (MDI) of the shoulder lacks a precise definition, and that fact can cause difficulty in evaluating the published results of nonsurgical and surgical treatment. A typical patient with MDI has generalized ligamentous laxity and develops symptomatic laxity in the absence of trauma or as a result of repetitive microtrauma, such as that experienced by an overhead throwing athlete. All patients with MDI have "uncontrollable and involuntary inferior dislocation or subluxation secondary to redundancy of the ligaments and inferior capsule."[1] The direction of instability can be anterior, posterior, or both, and it always includes an inferior component. The question of whether MDI is better treated with rehabilitation or surgery remains unanswered.

## Pathoanatomy

A complex balance of static and dynamic stabilizers produces a functional, stable shoulder. Instability is not synonymous with laxity. However, laxity can become symptomatic, and symptomatic laxity is probably the basis of MDI development. Unlike patients with traumatic instability, those with MDI usually do not have a Bankart lesion; instead, capsular patholaxity is present. Some patients with long-standing shoulder instability have secondary labral damage, even if the instability is atraumatic.[2]

The role of the rotator interval in MDI is well established. The rotator interval influences the amount of translation, especially inferiorly and posteriorly; conversely, imbrication of the rotator interval leads to restored inferior and posterior stability when the shoulder is flexed forward.[3] The superior glenohumeral ligament (SGHL) is important in providing stability to inferior-superior translation with the shoulder adducted. The coracohumeral ligament may be less important in providing stability than previously thought.[4]

An assessment of the possible contribution of collagen and elastin to MDI found that collagen from patients with unidirectional instability or MDI differed from that of individuals with a normal capsule, suggesting a possible systemic basis for the generalized ligamentous laxity commonly found in patients with MDI.[5] However, the biopsy samples used in this study were taken from the anterosuperior capsule and did not represent the inferior quadrant.

Loss of negative intra-articular pressure is another possible contributor to the ubiquitous inferior component of MDI. Some authors believe that the greater shoulder volume associated with a symptomatically lax shoulder reduces the negative pressure phenomenon, as in the venting of an intact joint. If negative intra-articular pressure is difficult to maintain, the ability to respond to an inferior load may be compromised. Cadaver studies found that, even after capsular imbrication and despite capsular reduction, simple venting of the capsule can lead to recurrent inferior laxity.[6]

Diminutive labral anatomy may also hinder the compression-concavity phenomenon. In symptomatic patients with a primary posteroinferior instability pattern, MRI studies revealed not only more glenoid retroversion but also a decrease in labral height, which led to diminished glenoid depth.[7]

The role of neuromuscular dysfunction continues to be questioned. Several researchers have linked shoulder instability patterns to neuromuscular dyskinesia involving the scapulothoracic articulation. A study comparing patients with normal shoulders, MDI, or multidirectional laxity discovered differences in muscle-firing patterns in the deltoid and, to a lesser extent, the rotator cuff. The delayed muscle activity and muscle imbalance were believed to contribute to asynchronous, less effective activity of the dynamic shoulder stabilizers.[8] A similar study of isolated anterior instability found activation suppression of the supraspinatus, subscapularis, biceps, and pectoralis major. The authors postulated that compromised dynamic muscular function could contribute to symptoms of persistent instability.[9] Whether these neuromuscular aberrations are the cause or the result of

*Richard K.N. Ryu, MD or the department with which he is affiliated holds stock or stock options in KFx.

shoulder instability has yet to be established. However, treatment of associated scapular dyskinesia is an integral part of MDI rehabilitation.

The natural history of MDI is also not well established. A study that followed patients with atraumatic shoulder instability for more than 3 years found age at onset to be significant in predicting whether the instability would progress. Younger patients had a greater risk of progressive instability. Spontaneous resolution of symptoms occurred in approximately 10%, and it occurred nine times more frequently among patients who abstained from overhead throwing activities than those who did not.[10] These findings indicate that recovery with activity modification is clearly possible and that the younger a patient is at onset, the greater the risk of progressive symptoms.

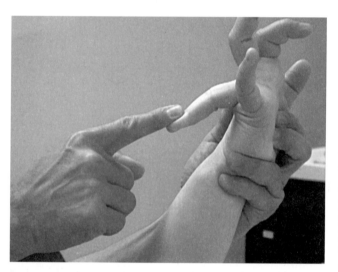

**Figure 1**  Metacarpal hyperlaxity.

## Clinical Evaluation

Patients typically develop symptoms of MDI before reaching 30 years of age. In some patients, atraumatic MDI progressively worsens until it affects basic activities, such as typing or reaching overhead. These patients sometimes have periscapular discomfort, numbness, or tingling in the hand. More frequently, patients have generalized ligamentous laxity with symptoms that worsen after participation in a forceful repetitive overhead activity, such as swimming, gymnastics, or volleyball. Infrequently, a single traumatic episode leads to development of symptomatic MDI. Evidence of significant trauma is usually not found during surgery. In contrast, a patulous capsule and interval are routinely found. A Bankart-type lesion is less common.

As an ailment of capsular redundancy and ligament insufficiency, MDI often has an insidious onset. Frank subluxation is found after the instability worsens. The patient's pain is frequently consistent with rotator cuff disease brought about by capsular dysfunction, and a thorough examination is required to ascertain the correct diagnosis. Age at onset, associated elbow recurvatum, metacarpal hyperlaxity (Figure 1), and a history of a repetitive overhead activity are significant factors in determining that capsular insufficiency, rather than rotator cuff disease, is the source of the patient's shoulder pain. The most important finding is generalized laxity with shoulder instability in more than one direction and, invariably, an inferior component. Patients with MDI of an atraumatic origin have global laxity in the anterior, posterior, and inferior directions. Those with a repetitive microtraumatic etiology superimposed on ligamentous laxity may have anteroinferior or posteroinferior instability. The sulcus sign (Figure 2), which is a cleft below the acromial border, is generated by axial distraction of the adducted shoulder and is consistent with inferior

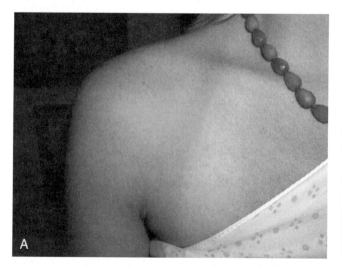

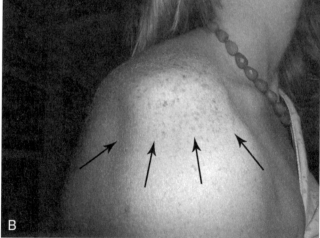

**Figure 2**  The sulcus sign. **A,** Shoulder without traction. **B,** Cleft (*arrows*) appears with axial loading.

translation of the joint. The sulcus sign should not appear when the shoulder is externally rotated, increasing tension within the SGHL. A persistent sulcus cleft in external rotation confirms the patulous nature of the rotator interval, including the SGHL. Some patients with this condition can voluntarily subluxate or dislocate their shoulders in multiple directions, although they may do so unwillingly. These patients should be distinguished from those whose voluntary instability is associated with behavioral or psychiatric issues; in this subgroup of patients, surgery should be avoided.

## Treatment Outcomes

MDI is initially treated through a rehabilitation program emphasizing correct scapulothoracic mechanics in conjunction with strengthening. Although the reported efficacy of nonsurgical treatment varies, it can be an effective alternative to surgery. In one study, 80% of all patients with atraumatic instability and 88% of the subgroup with MDI were successfully treated using only rehabilitation.[11] A long-term evaluation of nonsurgical treatment for MDI found that 33% of the patients required surgery; of the remaining patients, almost half had a satisfactory outcome based on shoulder instability scores.[12]

The goal of surgery for recalcitrant MDI, whether the surgery is open or arthroscopic, is to reduce capsular volume without significantly compromising the patient's range of motion or function. Neer's seminal work on a laterally based capsular shift[1] was a turning point in the ability to offer effective surgical treatment of MDI, although concerns have been raised as to the correctness of the presurgical diagnoses in this study. (More than half of the patients reported their symptoms after significant trauma.) A study of 43 shoulders more than 2 years after an inferior capsular shift procedure found that 9% had recurrent subluxation, and an additional 24% had continued apprehension correlated with residual inferior and posterior translation.[13] This study is compelling because more than two thirds of the patients had generalized ligamentous laxity without a history of significant trauma and only seven shoulders had a Bankart lesion; these findings are consistent with a diagnosis of MDI. In another study, 96% of the patients had an excellent or good result at an average 5-year follow-up of 52 shoulders treated for MDI with an inferior capsular shift procedure. Almost 90% had returned to sports activity, although not at their preinjury level.[14] Other studies confirmed the efficacy of surgical management of MDI using an open inferior capsular shift procedure; the reported success rates routinely approached 90%. However, the study populations were not uniform, and the diagnosis of MDI tended to be overly inclusive.

Several cadaver studies found that an arthroscopic approach can be successful in achieving adequate volume reduction. In one study, anteroinferior capsular suture plication using 10-mm plication sutures effectively reduced anterior translation and external rotation in cadaver specimens; in addition, anterior capsular labral height was improved almost 3.5 mm.[15] Another cadaver study used progressively larger plication distances to calculate the volume reduction achieved with an arthroscopic plication technique. The authors concluded that arthroscopic plication methods reliably reduced volume and that a definite relationship existed between the amount of tissue captured and the extent of volume reduction.[16] Researchers compared open, laterally based inferior shifting to arthroscopic capsular plication to determine capsular volume reduction, finding a 50% reduction with an open approach. In contrast, an arthroscopic approach using three plication sutures, based anteriorly, inferiorly, and posteriorly, reduced volume approximately 23%. The authors concluded that an open approach was preferable for patients requiring significant tissue shifting, although additional plication sutures might improve the volume reduction.[17]

The clinical results of arthroscopic treatment of MDI have been encouraging. At a minimum 2-year follow-up of 19 consecutive shoulders treated for MDI with arthroscopic capsular plication, 13 excellent and 5 good outcomes were recorded, with no complications. However, the primary pathology at surgery was excessive capsular laxity in 9 patients and Bankart pathology in 7 patients.[18] A study evaluating 47 patients with MDI treated with an arthroscopic capsular shift found a 93% success rate at 3-year follow-up. Twenty-six patients had not reported a traumatic episode, and only 10 Bankart lesions were noted at surgery.[19]

Several studies investigated the effectiveness of volume reduction after arthroscopic thermal capsulorrhaphy. One study compared an open capsular shift and thermal capsulorrhaphy; capsular volume was reduced 50% after an open capsular shift and 30% after thermal shrinkage.[20] Although thermal treatment of MDI was once popular because of its simplicity and ease of application, diminished longer term results and the significant risk of complications, including capsular necrosis, chondrolysis, and neurovascular injury, have caused it to fall out of favor. A 2-year follow-up of 19 patients found a 47% failure rate and a 21% rate of iatrogenic transient axillary nerve dysesthesia.[21] A similar study of 53 patients with MDI found that 41% had an unsatisfactory outcome and 14% had transient axillary nerve injury.[22]

## Nonsurgical and Surgical Treatment
### Rehabilitation
The initial treatment of a patient with MDI should focus on rehabilitation and strengthening. Scapulothoracic articulation and core strengthening should be the foundations of treatment, although the rotator cuff musculature also deserves attention. Gentle, slowly progressive

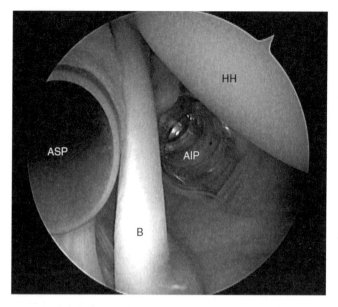

**Figure 3** Intrasurgical photograph showing the anterosuperior portal (ASP) for viewing and the anteroinferior portal (AIP) for instrumentation. B = biceps, HH = humeral head.

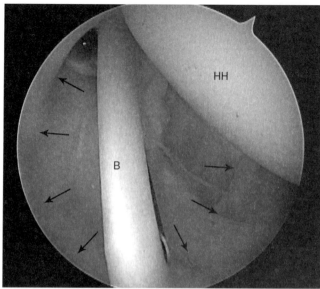

**Figure 4** Intrasurgical photograph showing the patulous rotator interval (*arrows*). B = biceps, HH = humeral head.

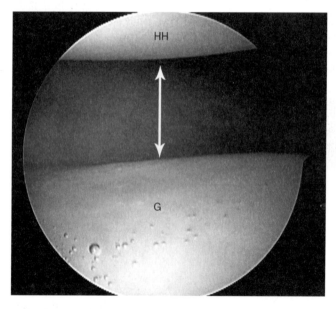

**Figure 5** Intrasurgical photograph showing a positive drive-through sign (*arrow*). G = glenoid, HH = humeral head.

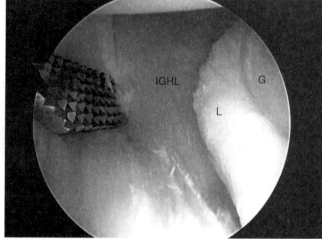

**Figure 6** Intrasurgical photograph taken from the anterosuperior portal, showing ligaments carefully rasped to generate a healing response. G = glenoid, IGHL = inferior glenohumeral ligament, L = labrum.

exercises, in conjunction with significant activity modification, must be performed for at least 3 months before the efficacy of the regimen is determined.

### Arthroscopic Surgery

Surgery can be performed with the patient in either the supine or the lateral decubitus position. A thorough examination is performed under anesthesia, and the findings are compared with the contralateral extremity. Confirming the primary direction of instability as anterior or posterior is of paramount importance for surgical planning. (The inferior component is always present.)

When the degree and direction of instability have been determined, a posterior portal is established. A slightly inferior and lateral placement, compared with the usual location, facilitates posterior instrumentation for both capsular and labral surgery. Dual anterior portals are established at the superior and inferior extent of the rotator interval (Figure 3). The glenohumeral space is carefully inspected, as are the rotator interval, which is usually patulous (Figure 4), and the labrum and its attachment, which may be roughened but rarely detached. Occasionally, Bankart-type labral separations are found and must be addressed. The biceps anchor is usually intact. An articular-sided partial rotator cuff tear is sometimes found. Axial and lateral traction on the humeral

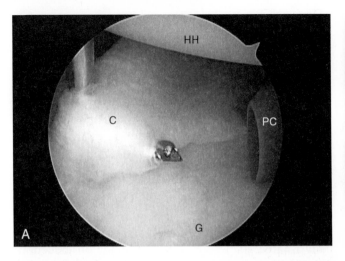
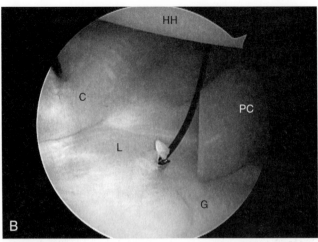

**Figure 7** Intrasurgical photographs showing capsular tissue captured with first pass and shifted superiorly before the labrum is engaged **(A)** and suture hook passing through the labrum as the second step, with passage of absorbable suture **(B)**. C = capsular tissue, G = glenoid, HH = humeral head, L = labrum, PC = posterior cannula.

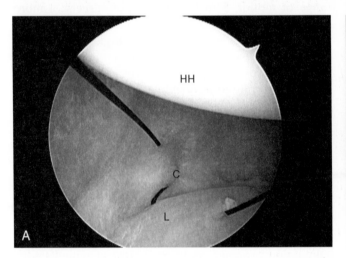
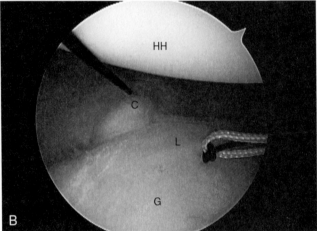

**Figure 8** Intrasurgical photographs taken from the anterosuperior portal, showing pinch-tuck suture in place **(A)** and retrograde shuttling of permanent suture through the capsular tissue **(B)**. C = capsular tissue, G = glenoid, HH = humeral head, L = labrum.

head leads to a positive drive-through sign, in which the humeral head separates from the glenoid (Figure 5). The arthroscope can be easily driven across the joint from posterior to anteroinferior; this maneuver is usually not possible in a stable shoulder. Although a drive-through sign is not pathognomonic for MDI, its presence, in conjunction with a consistent history and a finding of instability on the examination under anesthesia, serves to confirm the diagnosis.

The primary direction of pathologic translation, which usually is anteroinferior, is addressed first. The ligaments are carefully roughened with a rasp to avoid thinning the already-compromised capsular tissue (Figure 6). A suture hook is then passed in a pinch-tuck fashion, in which capsular tissue is captured lateral to the glenoid and reapproximated to the labrum. To help prevent overtightening of the joint, the capsular tissue is penetrated inferiorly, 1 to 2 cm from the labral rim

and at or below the level of the glenoid (Figure 7). Placing the arm in 40° to 50° of abduction can also prevent overtightening. The axillary nerve is at risk, although careful attention to positioning in abduction and slight forward flexion can minimize the likelihood of complications. After the capsular layer is captured, the hook is passed through the labrum, which is usually intact. An absorbable suture is passed and retrieved, then used as a shuttling device to carry nonabsorbable suture through the capsule (Figure 8). This sequence is repeated to achieve a horizontal mattress configuration. Tying the knot on the labral side of the sutures pushes the capsular tissue and labrum onto the glenoid face, re-creating labral height and increasing the depth of the glenoid (Figure 9). This procedure can be repeated as necessary to ablate the inferior capsular pouch, effectively shifting tissue from inferior to superior.

After the primary direction of instability has been treated, the opposite side is shifted to balance the capsule and avoid creating iatrogenic instability in the opposite direction (Figure 10). Finally, the rotator interval is closed to diminish the inferior pouch. Several techniques can be used. Passing sutures through the SGHL and retrieving them through the middle glenohumeral ligament allows a simple, satisfactory closure (Figure 11). Careful arm positioning in 25% of external rotation helps prevent motion loss.

There is no consensus as to whether absorbable or nonabsorbable suture material is preferable. The optimal number of sutures and the exact amount of volume reduction required for successful arthroscopic stabilization of MDI also have not been determined. Undercorrection can fail to relieve the symptoms of instability, but overconstraint of the joint can lead to early arthrosis and disabling functional limitations.

### Postsurgical Immobilization

Postsurgical treatment is facilitated by using an external rotation brace with the arm in 10° to 15° of abduction and external rotation. In patients treated for primary posteroinferior instability, the brace should be externally rotated 20° to 30°, with 10° to 15° of abduction. This position is maintained for 6 weeks before motion exercises are initiated. The goal is to achieve a full range of motion 5 to 6 months after surgery; a more rapid return to full motion can compromise the desired stability. Despite the prolonged postsurgical immobilization, arthroscopic plication for MDI rarely leads to permanent stiffness because the patient usually has an underlying generalized ligamentous laxity.

### Summary

Patients with MDI typically do not have a history of trauma. They have generalized ligamentous laxity that has become pathologic, frequently as a result of repetitive overhead activities. In addition, asynchronous dynamic shoulder function can contribute to instability symptoms. Bankart lesions are found infrequently.

The initial treatment consists of a well-supervised rehabilitation program. More than 50% of patients with

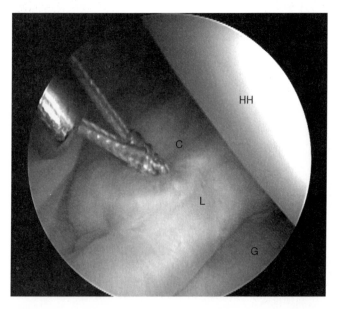

**Figure 9** Intrasurgical photograph showing reconstitution and widening of labral dimensions. C = capsular tissue, G = glenoid, HH = humeral head, L = labrum.

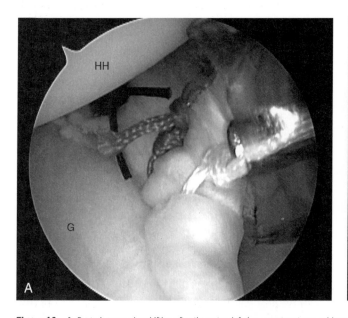

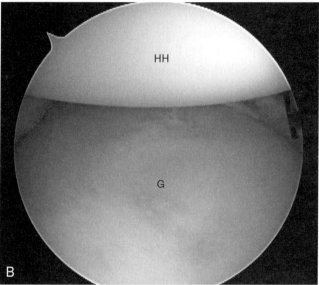

**Figure 10** **A,** Posterior capsular shifting after the anteroinferior component was addressed. **B,** As seen from the anterosuperior portal, the humeral head is balanced and well centered on the glenoid face after panscapular plication. G = glenoid, HH = humeral head.

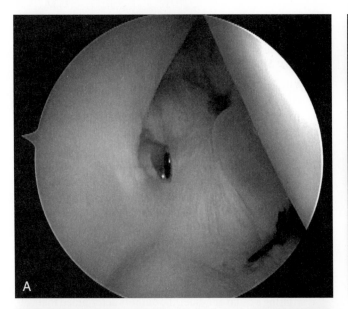

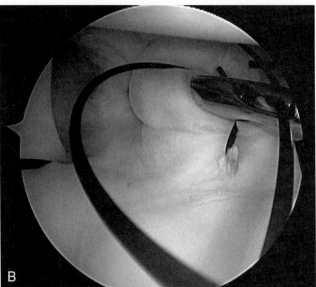

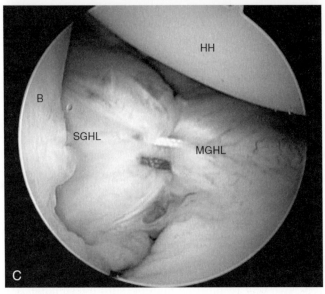

**Figure 11** Intrasurgical photographs showing rotator interval closure technique. **A,** Passing the suture through the SGHL. **B,** Retrieving the suture with a grasper through the middle glenohumeral ligament. **C,** Closing the interval with an approximation of the SGHL and the middle glenohumeral ligament. B = biceps, G = glenoid, HH = humeral head, L = labrum, MGHL = middle glenohumeral ligament, SGHL = superior glenohumeral ligament.

MDI have improvement if activity modification is pursued concomitantly. For those with persistent instability and pain, surgical stabilization is warranted. Both the open and arthroscopic techniques must reduce capsular volume to be successful. Numerous studies have concluded that either approach is effective, although neither the precise amount of tissue shifting nor a standardized surgical technique has yet been elucidated.

## Annotated References

1. Neer CS, Foster CR: Inferior capsular shift for involuntary inferior and multidirectional instability of the shoulder: A preliminary report. *J Bone Joint Surg Am* 1980;62:897-908.

2. Werner AW, Lichtenberg S, Schmitz H, Nikolic A, Habermeyer P: Arthroscopic findings in atraumatic shoulder instability. *Arthroscopy* 2004;20:268-272.

In this prospective case series, the authors detail arthroscopic findings in atraumatic shoulder instability. Classic Bankart lesions were noted in 30%, non-Bankart pathology in 44%, articular-sided partial cuff tears in 7%, and superior labral anterior and posterior pathology in 12%. Level of evidence: IV.

3. Harryman DT, Sidles JA, Harris SL, Matsen FA: The role of the rotator interval in passive motion and stability of the shoulder. *J Bone Joint Surg Am* 1992;74:53-66.

4. Warner JJ, Deng X, Warren RF, Torzilli PA: Static capsuloligamentous restraints to superior-inferior translation of the glenohumeral joint. *Am J Sports Med* 1992;20:675-685.

5. Rodeo SA, Suzuki K, Yamauchi M, Bhargava M, Warren RF: Analysis of collagen and elastic fibers in shoulder capsule in patients with shoulder instability. *Am J Sports Med* 1998;26:634-643.

6. Yamamoto N, Itoi E, Tuoheti Y, et al: The effect of the inferior capsular shift on shoulder intra-articular pressure. *Am J Sports Med* 2006;34:939-944.

In this cadaver study, intra-articular pressure was measured after imbricating and venting the capsule to assess the role of negative intra-articular pressure on stability. Imbrication facilitated favorable intra-articular pressure, but venting led to recurrent instability, despite the prior imbrication.

7. Kim SK: Arthroscopic treatment of posterior and multidirectional instability. *Oper Tech Sports Med* 2004;12:111-121.

This review article details pathology, pertinent physical examination findings, surgical findings, and surgical technique available to treat posterior instability and MDI of the shoulder.

8. Morris AD, Kemp GJ, Frostick SP: Shoulder electromyography in multidirectional instability. *J Shoulder Elbow Surg* 2004;13:24-29.

Electromyography studies revealed altered muscle activity and imbalance affecting shoulder girdle coordination in patients with MDI. The effect was more noteworthy on the deltoid than on the rotator cuff musculature.

9. Myers JB, Ju Y, Hwang J, McMahon PJ, Rodosky MW, Lephart SM: Reflexive muscle activation alterations in shoulders with anterior glenohumeral instability. *Am J Sports Med* 2004;32:1013-1021.

This study of reflexive muscle activation in shoulders with anterior instability found suppression and slowed activation of major muscle groups.

10. Kuroda S, Sumiyoshi T, Moriishi J, Maruta K, Ishige N: The natural course of atraumatic shoulder instability. *J Shoulder Elbow Surg* 2001;10:100-104.

The natural course of shoulder instability was followed in 341 patients (573 shoulders) for an average 4.5 years. Spontaneous recovery occurred in 50 patients and was related to age and discontinuation of overhead sports.

11. Burkhead WZ, Rockwood CA: Treatment of instability of the shoulder with an exercise program. *J Bone Joint Surg Am* 1992;74:890-896.

12. Misamore GW, Sallay PI, Didelot W: A longitudinal study of patients with multidirectional instability of the shoulder with seven- to ten-year follow up. *J Shoulder Elbow Surg* 2005;14:466-470.

This long-term study evaluated the results of treatment of MDI with rehabilitation exercises. At an average 8-year follow-up, 21 of the 57 patients had undergone surgical treatment. Of the nonsurgical patients, 17 were rated as having excellent or good results, and the remaining 19 were rated as having poor results. Level of evidence: III.

13. Cooper RA, Brems JJ: The inferior capsular-shift procedure for multidirectional instability of the shoulder. *J Bone Joint Surg Am* 1992;74:1516-1521.

14. Pollock RG, Owens JM, Flatow EL, Bigliani LU: Operative results of inferior capsular shift procedure for multidirectional instability of the shoulder. *J Bone Joint Surg Am* 2000;82:919-928.

15. Alberta FG, ElAttrache NS, Mihata T, McGarry MH, Tibone JE, Lee TQ: Arthroscopic anteroinferior suture plication resulting in decreased glenohumeral translation and external rotation. *J Bone Joint Surg Am* 2006;88:179-187.

In a cadaver study, the authors determined that arthroscopic anteroinferior capsular plication effectively reduced anterior translation and external rotation. The glenohumeral center of rotation moved posteriorly and inferiorly following the plication.

16. Flanigan DC, Forsythe T, Orwin J, Kaplan L: Volume analysis of arthroscopic capsular shift. *Arthroscopy* 2006;22:528-533.

Using a cadaver model, the authors determined that volume reduction in a shoulder can be reliably achieved and is a direct function of the amount of tissue captured with the plication technique.

17. Cohen SB, Wiley W, Goradia VK, Pearson S, Miller MD: Anterior capsulorrhaphy: An in vitro comparison of volume reduction. Arthroscopic plication versus open capsular shift. *Arthroscopy* 2005;21:659-664.

In this cadaver study, joint volume reduction was measured using open and arthroscopic plication techniques. Although the open shift led to a 50% reduction, compared with 23% achieved arthroscopically, the authors concluded that additional arthroscopic suture placement might have permitted a greater reduction in capsular volume. Level of evidence: IV.

18. McIntyre LF, Caspari RB, Savoie FH: Arthroscopic treatment of multidirectional shoulder instability: Two year results of a multiple suture technique. *Arthroscopy* 1997;13:418-425.

19. Gartsman GM, Roddey TS, Hammerman SM: Arthroscopic treatment of multidirectional glenohumeral instability: 2- to 5-year follow-up. *Arthroscopy* 2001;17:236-243.

The results of arthroscopic technique in repair of multidirectional glenohumeral instability were studied in 47 patients, of whom 44 had a successful result. The surgical treatment must be individualized to address the multiple lesions in the shoulder.

20. Luke TA, Rovner AD, Karas SG, Hawkins RJ, Plancher KD: Volumetric change in the shoulder capsule after open inferior capsular shift versus arthroscopic thermal capsular shrinkage: A cadaveric model. *J Shoulder Elbow Surg* 2004;13:146-149.

The authors compared capsular volume reduction using open treatment and thermal treatment in a cadaver model. The open shift resulted in a capsular volume reduction of

50%, compared with 30% achieved using the thermal technique.

21. Miniaci A, Codsi MJ: Thermal capsulorrhaphy for the treatment of shoulder instability. *Am J Sports Med* 2006;34:1356-1363.

    The current status of thermal capsulorrhaphy is reviewed, including indications, failures, and complications. Level of evidence: IV.

22. D'Alessandro DF, Bradley JP, Fleischli JE, Connor PM: Prospective evaluation of thermal capsulorrhaphy for shoulder instability: Indications and results, two to five year follow-up. *Am J Sports Med* 2004;32: 21-33.

    In an evaluation of the outcome of thermal treatment for instability patients, including a subgroup of patients with MDI, longer term follow-up revealed a subgroup failure rate exceeding 40%. Level of evidence: II.

# Chapter 28

# Posterior Shoulder Instability

Fotios P. Tjoumakaris, MD

James P. Bradley, MD

## Introduction

Posterior instability of the glenohumeral joint accounts for approximately 5% of all shoulder instability, and trauma is believed to be the cause in half of these patients.[1,2] Posterior shoulder instability has been considered a diagnostic and therapeutic challenge. However, surgeons are increasingly aware of the condition and the need to identify patients at risk. With the development of advanced imaging modalities and arthroscopic repair techniques, the ability to diagnose and successfully treat posterior shoulder instability has improved.

## Pathoanatomy

Several architectural abnormalities, including soft-tissue and bone abnormalities of the glenohumeral joint, are associated with posterior instability of the shoulder. Deficiencies in the rotator interval, a structure that is vital in providing static stability to the shoulder and particularly in limiting inferior and posterior joint translations when the arm is adducted,[3,4] can significantly contribute to pathologic laxity in patients who have increased inferior and posterior translations of the glenohumeral joint. This capsular defect of the interval may have implications for surgical intervention, particularly in patients with a traumatic posterior instability. A recent study using magnetic resonance arthrography (MRA) investigated chondrolabral changes in shoulders with atraumatic posterior shoulder instability. In 33 affected shoulders, the glenoid was shallower compared with age-matched normal shoulders, and there was more osseous and chondrolabral retroversion in the middle and inferior glenoid. The study did not determine whether these differences were etiologic or pathologic.[5] In some patients an incomplete, concealed avulsion of the posteroinferior labrum, called the Kim lesion, is a contributing factor to recurrent instability.[6] The Kim lesion appears arthroscopically as a crack at the junction of the posteroinferior glenoid articular cartilage and labrum, and a complete detachment of the deeper labrum from the glenoid rim can be identified. Two other factors have also been identified as contributing to the development of posterior instability: a reverse humeral avulsion of the glenohumeral ligaments and a posterior labrocapsular periosteal sleeve avulsion (POLPSA).[7,8]

Several dynamic restraints provide shoulder stability. The muscular forces surrounding the shoulder contribute greatly to the concavity compression effect on the humeral head within the glenoid.[9] Of the rotator cuff muscles, the subscapularis provides the most resistance to posterior translation of the shoulder. Proper coordination and mechanical functioning of the scapulothoracic muscles is also necessary to achieve adequate glenohumeral stability. Scapular winging acts as a compensatory mechanism to prevent posterior subluxation of the humeral head in some patients, although in other patients scapular winging is the primary etiology of the subluxation.[1] According to a study of a group of eight elite golfers with posterior shoulder instability, fatigue developed in the serratus anterior muscle during competitive play; the authors postulated that this fatigue contributed to scapulothoracic asynchrony and may have resulted in posterior shoulder instability and subsequent subacromial impingement.[10] Identifying the patient's scapulothoracic dyskinesia on physical examination is therefore essential for coordinating an effective rehabilitation program.

## Diagnosis

The surgeon should maintain a high level of suspicion whenever the diagnosis of posterior shoulder instability is a possibility. Recurrent posterior subluxation is more common than frank posterior instability, but its ambiguous signs and symptoms, including pain and shoulder fatigue with activity, make clinical diagnosis difficult. Traumatic instability with dislocation is characteristically found in victims of trauma or electrocution, seizure patients, or athletes in contact sports; recurrent posterior subluxation is more likely to occur in overhead throwing athletes. In a recent study of collegiate football players, 50% of the 336 athletes reported a history of shoulder injuries, and 4% of these injuries were classified as posterior instability.[11] Offensive and defensive linemen

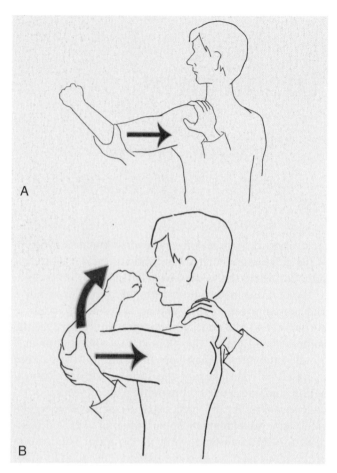

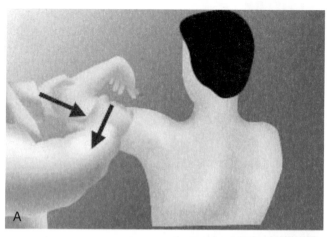

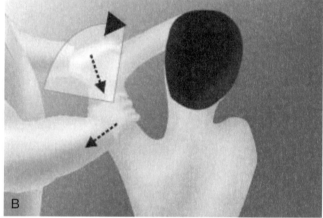

**Figure 1** The jerk test. **A,** Axial force is applied on the arm in 90° of abduction and internal rotation. **B,** The arm is horizontally adducted while the axial load is maintained. *(Reproduced with permission from Kim SH, Park JC, Park JS, et al: Painful jerk test: A predictor of success in nonoperative treatment of posteroinferior instability of the shoulder. Am J Sports Med 2004;32:1849-1855.)*

**Figure 2** The Kim test. **A,** With the patient seated and the arm in 90° of abduction, the examiner holds the elbow and lateral aspect of the proximal arm and applies a strong axial loading force. **B,** With the arm elevated diagonally to 45°, the examiner applies downward and backward force to the proximal arm. *(Reproduced with permission from Kim SH, Park JS, Jeong WK, et al: The Kim test: A novel test for posteroinferior labral lesion of the shoulder. A comparison to the jerk test. Am J Sports Med 2005;33:1188-1192.)*

were more likely than other players to report symptomatic posterior instability.

A thorough shoulder examination is warranted in all patients who have minor shoulder complaints and are in an at-risk athletic group. Early identification of patients with signs of instability, based on clinical suspicion, may increase the likelihood of an effective program to prevent instability.

## Physical Examination

Recent studies have attempted to correlate physical examination findings with treatment outcomes in patients with posterior shoulder instability. Eighty-nine shoulders (81 patients) with posterior instability and a positive clunk during the jerk test (Figure 1) underwent nonsurgical treatment. In a follow-up jerk test, pain was correlated with failure of nonsurgical treatment.[12] This finding can be useful in identifying patients likely to benefit from early surgical stabilization. The Kim test, a

recently described physical examination maneuver, can help in the diagnosis of posteroinferior shoulder instability.[13] With the patient's arm in 90° of abduction and diagonally elevated to 45°, an axial load is applied to the elbow, and a downward and posterior force is applied to the upper arm (Figure 2). A sudden onset of posterior shoulder pain constitutes a positive test result, regardless of an accompanying posterior clunk of the humeral head. It is important to apply a firm axial compression force to the glenoid surface near the humeral head; to provide countersupport, the patient should sit against the back of a chair rather than on a stool. A combination of the Kim test and the jerk test was found to be 97% sensitive in detecting a posteroinferior labral lesion. A posterior skin dimple over the posteromedial deltoid of both shoulders, as identified on physical examination, was found to be 62% sensitive and 92% specific in detecting posterior instability.[14]

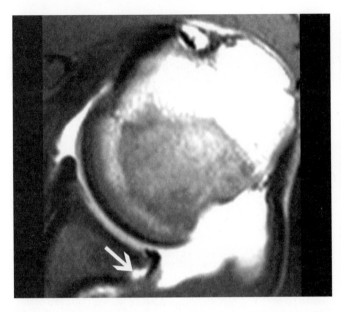

**Figure 3** MRA showing a small reverse Hill-Sachs lesion in conjunction with a POLPSA (*arrow*).

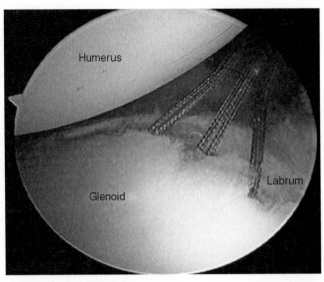

**Figure 4** Arthroscopic view from the anterosuperior portal, which is the main portal used for visualization. The posterior portal is used for anchor placement and instrumentation of the posterior labrum and capsular structures.

## Imaging

In most patients with posterior shoulder instability, plain radiographic findings are normal, although in some patients bone defects appear in the anterior humeral head (a reverse Hill-Sachs lesion) or the posterior glenoid. MRA is the most useful modality for identifying lesions in the posterior capsule and labral complex.[15] The MRA findings that suggest posterior shoulder instability are posterior translation of the humeral head relative to the glenoid, posterior labrocapsular avulsion, posterolabral injury, humeral avulsion of the posterior band of the inferior glenohumeral ligament, and POLPSA (Figure 3). MRA-identified pathoanatomy was used to differentiate four types of posterior labral lesions: type I, an incomplete detachment; type II (Kim lesion), an incomplete and concealed detachment; type III, chondrolabral erosion; and type IV, a flap tear of the posteroinferior labrum.[16] Dynamic ultrasonography has been shown to effectively quantify glenohumeral laxity, although studies comparing the efficacy of this imaging technique with that of MRI and data comparing ultrasonographic findings with surgical evaluation are not available.[17]

## Treatment

Treatment recommendations for posterior instability have evolved along with the understanding of its pathoanatomy. Physical therapy is the mainstay of treatment, although nonsurgical treatment is often not successful and surgical stabilization is required. Several open surgical techniques are used, the most common of which is a deltoid-preserving posterior capsular shift. Arthroscopic posterior shoulder stabilization has been performed with increasing frequency during the past several years. Arthroscopic intervention allows the surgeon to diagnose and selectively address the pathology responsible for the instability, whether it is labral, capsular, or a combination.

Osseous and capsular defects identified before surgery, such as an engaging reverse Hill-Sachs lesion, a posterior glenoid deficiency or retroversion, or capsular rents or insufficiency arising from revision surgery, usually require an open approach. A humeral head osteoarticular allograft, bone grafting of the posterior glenoid, glenoid wedge osteotomy to correct retroversion, or open posterior capsular shift is used to correct the defect.

## Technique

The arthroscopic technique most commonly used to address posterior shoulder instability is suture anchor fixation of the posterior labrum. Whether capsular plication is also required depends on the severity and chronicity of the instability. The lateral decubitus position is usually preferred, because it offers the surgeon good visualization and access to the posterior glenohumeral joint. The anterosuperior portal is used for viewing, and the posterior portal is used for working (Figure 4); additional portals may be necessary for accurate anchor placement. Suture anchors are placed along the posterior glenoid rim in an inferior-to-superior direction. The labrum, with or without accompanying capsule, is secured to the articular margin to restore the length-tension relationship of the posterior band of the inferior glenohumeral ligament (Figure 5). The repair is complete when the avulsed labrum and capsule are securely restored to the glenoid articular margin (Figure 6).

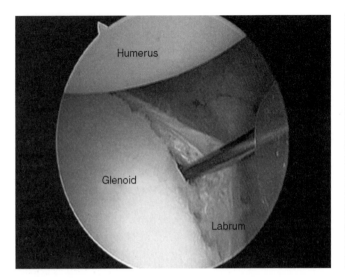

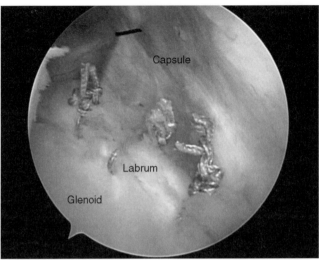

**Figure 5** Arthroscopic view from the anterior portal showing three suture anchors placed along the posterior glenoid after preparation of the labrum and capsule for repair.

**Figure 6** The posterior labrum and capsule have been restored to the articular margin of the posterior glenoid, and the posterior portal has been closed after removal of the working cannula.

**Table 1 | Studies of Arthroscopic Posterior Shoulder Stabilization**

| Study | Shoulders (Number) | Follow-up (Months) | Recurrence (%) | Pathology |
|---|---|---|---|---|
| Bottoni et al[24] | 19 | 40 | 5.2 | Traumatic, unidirectional |
| Bradley et al[21] | 100 | 27 | 11.0 | Athletic, unidirectional |
| Goubier et al[22] | 13 | 34 | 0 | Traumatic/atraumatic, unidirectional/ multidirectional |
| Kim et al[16] | 27 | 39 | 3.7 | Traumatic, unidirectional |
| Provencher et al[25] | 33 | 39 | 12.1 | Traumatic/atraumatic, unidirectional |
| Williams et al[23] | 27 | 61 | 8.0 | Traumatic, unidirectional |

## Outcomes

A review of 33 shoulders found good results after an open capsular shift, with only 13% of patients reporting a recurrence 2 years later.[18] A review of 44 shoulders treated with a similar technique found a 19% recurrence rate at a longer term follow-up; this finding echoes those of earlier studies.[19] All 10 patients who underwent an unusual surgery called posterior addition acromioplasty reported good results, with no recurrent dislocation or subluxation after 9.5 years.[20]

Recent studies of arthroscopic techniques have found excellent results at short-term and intermediate-term follow-up, with recurrence rates of 12% or lower[16,21-25] (Table 1). In the largest series, 100 shoulders underwent arthroscopic posterior capsulolabral reconstruction for unidirectional posterior instability; after 2 years, 89% of the patients were able to return to their athletic activities with little or no limitation. The success of this technique in a demanding athletic population has led to its application in other patients with unidirectional posterior instability. The durability of this technique is indicated by a similar series in which 27 patients with traumatic posterior instability underwent arthroscopic repair; after 5 years, 92% reported an absence of instability or pain.[23]

Although arthroscopic capsular plication and capsulolabral reconstruction are currently the preferred techniques, thermal capsulorrhaphy was also studied for treatment of isolated posterior shoulder instability.[26] Eleven of the 14 patients had a good outcome after 2 years. However, the documented failure of this technique for patients with mulitidirectional or anterior instability has decreased enthusiasm for its use in treating posterior shoulder instability. In another study of 84 patients who received thermal capsulorrhaphy to treat anterior, anteroinferior, or multidirectional instability, 37% had instability or pain at an average 38-month follow-up.[27] This finding indicates that thermal capsulorrhaphy may not provide a satisfactory long-term result.

## Summary

Posterior shoulder instability is both a diagnostic and therapeutic challenge for the orthopaedic surgeon. Advances in physical examination techniques and the addition of MRA enable surgeons to better identify the precise pathology responsible for the condition. The transition from open surgical techniques to arthroscopic techniques is permitting the repair to be tailored to the pathology, and this development may in part explain recent outcome improvements. Further study is needed to determine the durability of results achieved by current arthroscopic approaches to the treatment of posterior glenohumeral instability.

## Annotated References

1. Robinson CM, Aderinto J: Recurrent posterior shoulder instability. *J Bone Joint Surg Am* 2005;87: 883-892.

   The authors of this review of posterior shoulder instability diagnosis and treatment conclude that, as lesion-specific surgery becomes more prevalent, arthroscopic outcomes will continue to improve.

2. Arciero RA, Mazzocca AD: Traumatic posterior shoulder subluxation with labral injury: Suture anchor technique. *Tech Shoulder Elbow Surg* 2004;5:13-24.

   This outline of the etiology, pathomechanics, presentation, and evaluation of patients with posterior shoulder subluxation includes an arthroscopic technique for treatment of the condition.

3. Harryman DT II, Sidles JA, Harris SL, Matsen FA III: The role of the rotator interval capsule in passive motion and stability of the shoulder. *J Bone Joint Surg Am* 1992;74:53-66.

4. Cole BJ, Rodeo SA, O'Brien SJ, et al: The anatomy and histology of the rotator interval capsule of the shoulder. *Clin Orthop Relat Res* 2001;390:129-137.

   A rotator interval defect was found in the majority of 47 fetal and 10 adult cadaver rotator interval regions. The complete absence of tissue in 28 of 37 fetal specimens with a defect suggests that the defect is congenital.

5. Kim SH, Noh KC, Park JS, et al: Loss of chondrolabral containment of the glenohumeral joint in atraumatic posteroinferior multidirectional instability. *J Bone Joint Surg Am* 2005;87:92-98.

   In a study of 33 shoulders with posteroinferior instability, as evaluated by MRI and compared with age-matched normal shoulders, greater retroversion of both the osseous and chondrolabral portions of the middle and inferior glenoid was found in the unstable shoulders, as well as a more common shallow glenoid. Level of evidence: IV.

6. Kim SH, Ha KI, Yoo JC, et al: Kim's lesion: An incomplete and concealed avulsion of the posteroinferior labrum in posterior or multidirectional posteroinferior instability of the shoulder. *Arthroscopy* 2004; 20:712-720.

   In reporting a new clinical entity, termed Kim lesion, the authors recommend completing the labral tear and reattaching the labrum and posterior band of the inferior glenohumeral ligament to the posterior glenoid rim to prevent recurrent posterior shoulder instability.

7. Safran O, Defranco MJ, Hatem S, et al: Posterior humeral avulsion of the glenohumeral ligament as a cause of posterior shoulder instability: A case report. *J Bone Joint Surg Am* 2004;86-A:2732-2736.

   This case report describes a patient with an MRI-proven posterohumeral avulsion of the glenohumeral ligament from the humerus, resulting in posterior shoulder instability. Level of evidence: V.

8. Yu JS, Ashman CJ, Jones G: The POLPSA lesion: MR imaging findings with arthroscopic correlation in patients with posterior instability. *Skeletal Radiol* 2002; 31:396-399.

   The features of the POLPSA lesion were evaluated using MRI in six male athletes with posterior shoulder instability.

9. Lee SB, An KN: Dynamic glenohumeral stability provided by three heads of the deltoid muscle. *Clin Orthop Relat Res* 2002;400:40-47.

   The dynamic glenohumeral stability provided by three heads of the deltoid was quantified using a new biomechanical parameter, the dynamic stability index.

10. Hovis WD, Dean MT, Mallon WJ, et al: Posterior instability of the shoulder with secondary impingement in elite golfers. *Am J Sports Med* 2002;30:886-890.

    Posterior glenohumeral instability associated with subacromial impingement is reported in a retrospective review of eight elite golfers.

11. Kaplan LD, Flanigan DC, Norwig J, et al: Prevalence and variance of shoulder injuries in elite collegiate football players. *Am J Sports Med* 2005;33:1142-1146.

    Among players with shoulder injuries identified by the National Football League Scouting Combine, 50% reported a history of shoulder injury, of which posterior shoulder instability was 4%. Offensive and defensive linemen were most commonly affected.

12. Kim SH, Park JC, Park JS, et al: Painful jerk test: A predictor of success in nonoperative treatment of posteroinferior instability of the shoulder. *Am J Sports Med* 2004;32:1849-1855.

    In a case study of 89 shoulders with posterior instability and a positive clunk on the jerk test, patients who experienced pain during a follow-up test were more likely to require surgical intervention for a posterior labral lesion than patients who reported no pain. Level of evidence: IV.

13. Kim SH, Park JS, Jeong WK, et al: The Kim test: A novel test for posteroinferior labral lesion of the shoulder. A comparison to the jerk test. *Am J Sports Med* 2005;33:1188-1192.

The Kim test can be combined with the jerk test to diagnose posterior instability with 97% sensitivity. The test is positive if an axial force applied to the humeral head in a diagonally upward and posterior direction produces pain in the shoulder. Level of evidence: I.

14. Von Raebrox A, Campbell B, Ramesh R, et al: The association of subacromial dimples with recurrent posterior dislocation of the shoulder. *J Shoulder Elbow Surg* 2006;15:591-593.

    Fourteen patients with posterior instability were compared with age-matched control subjects. A posterior dimple sign was found to be associated with posterior instability, with a sensitivity of 62% and a specificity of 92%. Level of evidence: III.

15. Tung GA, Hou DD: MR arthrography of the posterior labrocapsular complex: Relationship with glenohumeral joint alignment and clinical posterior instability. *AJR Am J Roentgenol* 2003;180:369-375.

    MRA was used to investigate the relationship between tears of the posterior labrocapsular complex and glenohumeral alignment, as well as the presence and extent of posterior labrocapsular tears in patients with posterior instability.

16. Kim SH, Ha KI, Park JH, et al: Arthroscopic posterior labral repair and capsular shift for traumatic unidirectional recurrent posterior subluxation of the shoulder. *J Bone Joint Surg Am* 2003;85-A:1479-1487. Level of evidence: IV.

    Arthroscopic posterior labral repair and caspular shift was found to be a reliable procedure for treating unidirectional recurrent posterior subluxation of traumatic origin, providing stability, pain relief, and functional restoration.

17. Borsa PA, Jacobson JA, Scibek JS, et al: Comparison of dynamic sonography to stress radiography for assessing glenohumeral laxity in asymptomatic shoulders. *Am J Sports Med* 2005;33:734-741.

    This study of dynamic ultrasonography to evaluate 33 asymptomatic shoulders found it to be a valid and repeatable method of determining glenohumeral laxity.

18. Rhee YG, Lee DH, Lim CT: Posterior capsulolabral reconstruction in posterior shoulder instability: Deltoid saving. *J Shoulder Elbow Surg* 2005;14:355-360.

    Thirty-three shoulders underwent open deltoid-saving, posterior capsulolabral reconstruction for recurrent posterior shoulder instability. At 25-month follow-up, four patients (13.3%) had recurrent instability. After exclusion of those with voluntary dislocation, the success rate was 92.6%. Level of evidence: IV.

19. Wolf BR, Strickland S, Williams RJ, et al: Open posterior stabilization for recurrent posterior glenohumeral instability. *J Shoulder Elbow Surg* 2005;14:157-164.

    A retrospective review of 44 shoulders after an open posterior capsular shift for posterior shoulder instability

found a 19% recurrence rate. Patients older than 37 years at the time of surgery and those found to have chondral damage had poor results. Level of evidence: IV.

20. Scapinelli R: Posterior addition acromioplasty in the treatment of recurrent posterior instability of the shoulder. *J Shoulder Elbow Surg* 2006;15:424-431.

    Ten patients with recurrent posterior shoulder instability underwent an inverted scapular spine bone graft to the posterior border of the acromion. At long-term follow-up (9.5 years), all reported a satisfactory outcome, with no recurrent instability. Level of evidence: IV.

21. Bradley JP, Baker CL III, Kline AJ, et al: Arthroscopic capsulolabral reconstruction for posterior instability of the shoulder: A prospective study of 100 shoulders. *Am J Sports Med* 2006;34:1061-1071.

    One hundred shoulders of athletes were evaluated after arthroscopic posterior capsulolabral reconstruction for unidirectional posterior instability. At a mean 27-month follow-up, 89% of patients were able to return to their sport, and 67% reported returning to their pre-injury level of competition and function. Level of evidence: II.

22. Goubier JN, Iserin A, Duranthon LD, et al: A 4 portal arthroscopic stabilization in posterior shoulder instability. *J Shoulder Elbow Surg* 2003;12:337-341.

    An arthroscopic stabilization technique to treat posterior instability, using four portals, is presented as used in 11 patients (13 shoulders). According to the authors, the technique facilitates access to the posteroinferior glenoid and reduces the rate of postsurgical instability.

23. Williams RJ III, Strickland S, Cohen M, et al: Arthroscopic repair for traumatic posterior shoulder instability. *Am J Sports Med* 2003;31:203-209.

    The results of arthroscopic repair of a posterior Bankart lesion of traumatic origin were evaluated in 27 shoulders (26 patients) at a mean 5.1-year follow-up. The procedure was found to be an effective means of eliminating pain and instability.

24. Bottoni CR, Franks BR, Moore JH, et al: Operative stabilization of posterior shoulder instability. *Am J Sports Med* 2005;33:996-1002.

    Nineteen shoulders underwent arthroscopic surgical stabilization for posterior shoulder instability, and 12 underwent open surgical stabilization. There was one recurrence in each group. The Rowe and Western Ontario Shoulder Instability Index scores were better in the arthroscopic group. Level of evidence: IV.

25. Provencher MT, Bell SJ, Menzel KA, et al: Arthroscopic treatment of posterior shoulder instability: Results in 33 patients. *Am J Sports Med* 2005;33:1463-1471.

    Thirty-three patients underwent arthroscopic posterior stabilization with suture anchors or capsular plication. At latest follow-up, four patients had recurrent instability and three had pain; these seven patients had earlier surgery or voluntary subluxation. Level of evidence: IV.

26. Bisson LJ: Thermal capsulorrhaphy for isolated posterior instability of the glenohumeral joint without labral detachment. *Am J Sports Med* 2005;33:1898-1904.

Fourteen shoulders (11 patients) with isolated posterior instability, without labral detachment, underwent thermal capsulorrhaphy. Ten of 11 patients who were immobilized for 6 weeks had good or excellent results, compared with one of three patients who were not immobilized. At a minimum 26-month follow-up, thermal capsulorrhaphy com-

bined with postsurgical immobilization was found effective in treating posterior instability. Level of evidence: IV.

27. D'Alessandro DF, Bradley JP, Fleischli JE, et al: Prospective evaluation of thermal capsulorrhaphy for shoulder instability: Indications and results, two to five year follow up. *Am J Sports Med* 2004;32:21-33.

Eighty-four shoulders with anterior, multidirectional, or anteroinferior instability were treated with thermal capsulorrhaphy after unsuccessful nonsurgical treatment. At average 38-month follow-up, 37% of patients reported an unsatisfactory result. Level of evidence: II.

# Chapter 29

# Arthroscopic Treatment of the Arthritic Shoulder

Stephen C. Weber, MD

Jeffrey I. Kauffman, MD

Carol A. Parise, PhD

## Introduction

Techniques for the arthroscopic treatment of shoulder arthritis have advanced significantly during recent years. The pioneering research primarily concerned diagnosis, especially in the early stages, when shoulder arthritis is often not detectable on radiographs.[1,2] Treatment of serendipitously identified lesions was limited to lavage and débridement, and little information on functional outcomes was available.

The outcomes of arthroplasty, especially in patients younger than 60 years, have been better defined in recent years. Although results have improved, in one study half of the patients who underwent arthroplasty for shoulder arthritis before the age of 50 years had an unsatisfactory outcome, regardless of whether the glenoid was resurfaced.[3] Poor outcomes and limited durability associated with shoulder arthroplasty have led to renewed interest in nonarthroplastic treatment, and especially in techniques that can be performed arthroscopically. Reasonably satisfactory results at midterm (approximately 48 months) have been reported after arthroscopic débridement for shoulder arthritis, and substantial outcomes data are now available. For other new techniques, only encouraging preliminary results are available.

## Classification

Arthritis of the shoulder can be classified as inflammatory or noninflammatory (Table 1). The unifying factor among the inflammatory arthropathies is the presence of significant synovitis, for which arthroscopic synovectomy is usually recommended. Recent studies found that synovectomy and arthroscopic treatment offer significant benefits for patients with rheumatoid arthritis, although in some patients the disease continued to progress. The most significant benefits occurred in patients who had relatively limited arthritis, as seen on presurgical radiographs.[4]

Gout is uncommon in the shoulder and rarely requires arthroscopic treatment. However, patients with ankylosing spondylitis or psoriatic arthritis commonly have concomitant acromioclavicular arthritis, which re-

quires surgical resection. Calcium pyrophosphate deposition is common in degenerative arthritis, but the best method of surgical treatment is unclear.

Because significant synovitis is not normally present in noninflammatory arthritis, synovectomy is not usually required. The arthroscopic treatment varies depending on associated findings and surgeon preference. Noninflammatory arthritic change in the shoulder is most often classified using the Outerbridge system, which was first developed for the knee[5] (Table 2). Recent data showed that both the Outerbridge and radiographic classifications are useful in predicting the outcome of arthroscopic treatment. Among the many available radiographic systems, the Samilson classification is most widely used to predict and assess the outcome of arthroscopic treatment of the shoulder[6] (Table 3). Chondrolysis, a condition that is challenging to treat, is usually degenerative and has become more common with the use of thermal capsulorrhaphy.[7]

## Nonsurgical Treatment

Nonsurgical treatment is the mainstay of shoulder arthritis management. Anti-inflammatory drugs offer symptomatic relief of pain, and gentle physical therapy may bring about significant improvement in range of motion. Steroid injections can be beneficial for both inflammatory and noninflammatory conditions. The US Food and Drug Administration has not approved viscosupplementation for shoulder conditions, but its use has

| Table 1 | Classification of Glenohumeral Arthritis | |
|---|---|
| **Inflammatory** | **Noninflammatory** |
| Ankylosing spondylitis | Capsulorrhaphy arthropathy |
| Calcium pyrophosphate deposition | Charcot arthritis |
| Gout | Postinstability arthritis |
| Psoriatic arthritis | Posttraumatic osteoarthritis |
| Rheumatoid arthritis | Primary osteoarthritis |
| Systemic lupus erythematosus | Septic arthritis |

been beneficial in the knee and it may offer similar short-term benefits in the shoulder.

## Surgical Treatment

Surgical treatment should be considered only if nonsurgical treatment has been unsuccessful in reducing pain and improving function.

The patient should be counseled about restrictions on using an arthritic shoulder. Any surgical treatment requires permanent activity modification beginning during the postsurgical period; heavy lifting, high-impact activities, and manual labor can be expected to degrade the surgical outcome. Therefore, it is usually advisable to initiate activity modification before surgery is considered.

### Débridement and Lavage

Outcomes data on arthroscopic débridement and lavage for glenohumeral arthritis reveal short-term improvement with minimal complications (Table 4). The longer term results are somewhat less encouraging, although still positive. Radiographic scores based on the Samilson classification were highly correlated with function at the final follow-up (mean, 60 months); the finding that only 20% of the patients required arthroplasty at final follow-up indicates that débridement delays the need for arthroplasty in many patients[13] (Figure 1). This result is significant, given the risk of implant loosening after arthroplasty in younger patients. In almost all studies, higher grade articular lesions and more severe radiographic changes were associated with longer term inferior results in the shoulder, as in the knee.[15]

Débridement techniques vary, but most involve lavage, mechanical smoothing of the articular surfaces, and removal of any loose bodies (Figure 2). Anterior capsular release to remove the standard internal rotation contracture has had good results.[16,17] Removal of the usual osteophyte on the anteroinferior humerus has had

| Table 2 | Outerbridge Classification of Noninflammatory Shoulder Arthritis | |
|---|---|
| **Grade** | **Cartilage Description** |
| I | Softening or blistering |
| II | Fissuring or fibrillation |
| III | Deep ulceration |
| IV | Exposed bone |

| Table 3 | Samilson Radiographic Classification of the Arthritic Shoulder | |
|---|---|
| **Grade** | **Description** |
| I | No changes |
| II | Mild arthrosis with osteophyte < 3 mm |
| III | Moderate arthrosis with osteophyte 3 to 7 mm and some joint space irregularity |
| IV | Severe arthrosis with osteophytes > 7 mm, joint space narrowing, and sclerosis |

| Table 4 | Reported Outcomes After Arthroscopic Débridement for Shoulder Arthritis | | | | |
|---|---|---|---|---|---|
| **Study** | **Number of Shoulders** | **Procedure** | **Mean Follow-up, Months (Range)** | **Mean Patient Age, Years (Range)** | **Results** |
| Bishop et al[8] | 26 (radiographic stage III or IV) | Abrasion arthroplasty and capsular débridement | 56 | NA | 18 excellent/good |
| Cameron et al[9] | 61 | Shaver débridement and capsular release | 34 (12-79) | 49 (21-73) | 88% significant pain relief |
| Ellman et al[1] | 18 | Shaver débridement and acromioplasty | N/A | 51 (21-67) | 100% good/excellent at short-term follow-up |
| Ellowitz et al[10] | 18 (grade IV chondral lesions) | Shaver débridement and acromioplasty | (12-73) | (38-79) | 14 excellent/good, 4 fair |
| Guyette et al[11] | 36 | Shaver débridement and acromioplasty | 60 (26-152) | 61 (34-87) | Correlation between outcome and presurgical radiographic finding |
| Safran and Baillargeon[12] | 18 (grade IV chondral lesions) | Shaver débridement and bursectomy | 24 (12-50) | 64 (42-85) | 78% good/excellent, 22% fair/poor |
| Weber and Kauffman[13] | 40 | Shaver débridement | 60 (24-168) | 57.8 | 28% excellent/good, 72% fair/poor; 20% conversion to arthroplasty at follow-up |
| Weinstein et al[14] | 27 | Shaver débridement | 34 (12-63) | 47 (27-72) | 80% good/excellent |

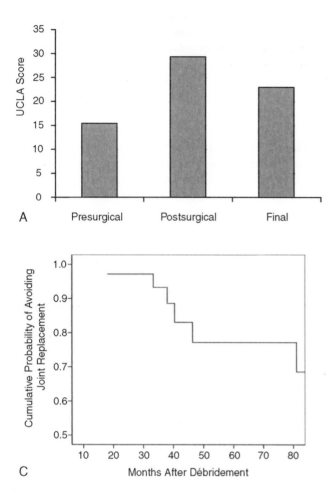

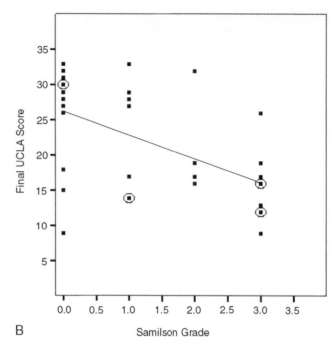

**Figure 1** Graphs of short-term and longer term outcomes after arthroscopic shoulder débridement. **A,** Presurgical, early postsurgical, and final (mean, 60-month) University of California Los Angeles (UCLA) activity scores, showing a significant decline over time. **B,** Pearson correlation coefficient (0.430, $P < 0.02$) of UCLA scores at final measurement, compared with Samilson radiographic scores. (Circles represent two patients with identical scores; final UCLA score unavailable for one patient.) **C,** Shoulders requiring arthroplasty over time.

mixed success,[18] and concern has been expressed about the proximity of the axillary nerve. Glenoplasty to restore the glenoid to a concave configuration in a patient with posterior subluxation and a biconcave glenoid is controversial.[19] Necessary concomitant procedures, such as acromioplasty or acromioclavicular resection, should be performed despite the presence of articular cartilage. Several studies found that these procedures provide good outcome despite the presence of arthritis.[11,19] The longer term results and low complication rates are arguments in favor of the use of débridement and acromioplasty as the initial treatment of mild to moderate glenohumeral arthritis. However, a patient older than 60 years who has Samilson grade III or IV changes may be better treated with arthroplasty because the results of arthroplasty in older patients tend to be superior to those in younger patients.

## Marrow Stimulation Techniques

Marrow stimulation techniques such as microfracture have been used successfully to treat arthritis of the knee. Most reports of shoulder treatment are anecdotal,

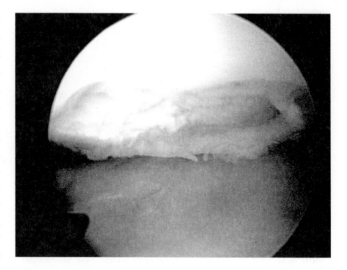

**Figure 2** Outerbridge grade IV articular cartilage lesion of the humerus after débridement and lavage.

although limited data are available.[20] Microfracture of focal lesions of the humerus or glenoid, using a procedure developed for the knee, appears promising, although supporting data are lacking (Figure 3).

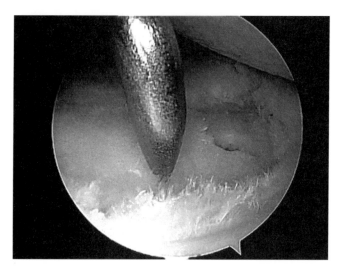

**Figure 3**   Microfracture of Outerbridge grade IV articular cartilage lesion of the glenoid.

## Osteochondral Autograft Transfer

The results of osteochondral autograft transfer in the knee have been excellent. The first results from a similar procedure in the shoulder were promising, although donor site morbidity from the knee was a significant complication.[21] An open procedure was described. However, the procedure could be performed arthroscopically, as it is in the knee. Osteochondral autograft transfer probably should be used only for patients with focal lesions for whom established techniques, such as débridement, have been unsuccessful.

## Autogenous Chondrocyte Transfer

Autogenous chondrocyte transfer has been widely used in the knee to manage Outerbridge grade IV lesions. (Implantation is not a truly arthroscopic procedure.) Results for the shoulder should be as good or better because weight bearing is not a concern. Autogenous chondrocyte transfer was used successfully to treat the shoulder of a patient with large lesions created by chondrolysis secondary to thermal capsulorrhaphy.[22]

## Arthroscopic Interposition Arthroplasty

The short-term results of interposition arthroplasty in association with prosthetic humeral resurfacing have been encouraging[23] and have led to an attempt to perform arthroscopic interposition arthroplasty without prosthetic replacement. Preliminary work with interposition arthroplasty using lateral meniscus[24] or an acellular orthobiologic xenograft[25] has had encouraging results. Six of 11 patients had 90% improvement, with complete resolution of pain at 8-month to 20-month follow-up. Five had no improvement, and one subsequently underwent a hemiarthroplasty. Avoiding prosthetic replacement in younger patients has significant advantages, but long-term outcome data are lacking. The procedures are technically challenging. However, complications have been minimal and do not appear to have significantly affected any subsequent arthroplasties.

## Results

Outerbridge grade III and IV lesions are often found incidentally while a patient is being evaluated arthroscopically for a procedure such as acromioplasty. The patient should be treated with débridement and lavage of the articular cartilage injuries. Long-term follow-up revealed few complications in patients whose presurgical radiographs showed no changes.[13] For patients whose radiographs show changes associated with glenohumeral arthritis, the treatment is more problematic. If the patient is older and has a sedentary lifestyle, treatment can be deferred until the patient is ready for arthroplasty. The results of arthroplasty are generally good, and the risk that the patient will require revision surgery is low. For a younger, active patient whose radiographs show Samilson grade III or IV arthritis, choosing treatment is more difficult. Arthroplasty frequently is unsuccessful in these patients, and revision surgery will almost certainly be required at a later time. Débridement and lavage, which have good short-term results, probably are the best initial treatment after unsuccessful nonsurgical treatment. Capsular release can also be beneficial in restoring glenohumeral centering and improving external rotation. Microfracture can be considered for patients with focal lesions because it does not significantly increase the morbidity of the procedure and may be beneficial.

Few long-term data are available on the treatment of patients who do not want to consider arthroplasty. Encouraging preliminary results have been reported on autogenous chondrocyte transfer and interposition arthroplasty, which have the advantage of not compromising the ability to perform a subsequent arthroplasty, if necessary.[20]

## Complications

The expected complications are the same for most arthroscopic interventions, and more complicated procedures are expected to result in more complications. Few complications have been reported after débridement and lavage. Interposition arthroplasty has the antigenicity and infection complications associated with the implanted material, whether it is a xenograft or allograft.

## Summary

The arthroscopic treatment of glenohumeral arthritis has progressed significantly. The satisfactory results of lavage and débridement are now well established in the midterm. Aside from arthroplasty, the preliminary results of arthroscopic treatments for arthritis are encouraging in younger patients, but longer term results are needed before these procedures can be generally recommended.

## Annotated References

1. Ellman H, Harris E, Kay S: Early degenerative joint disease simulating impingement syndrome: Arthroscopic findings. *Arthroscopy* 1992;8:482-487.

2. Cofield RH: Arthroscopy of the shoulder. *Mayo Clin Proc* 1983;58:501-508.

3. Sperling JW, Cofield RH, Rowland CM: Minimum 15 year follow-up of Neer hemiarthroplasty and total shoulder arthroplasty in patients 50 years and younger. *J Bone Joint Surg Am* 1998;80:464-473.

4. Smith AM, Sperling JW, O'Droscoll SW, Cofield RH: Arthroscopic shoulder synovectomy in patient with rheumatoid arthritis. *Arthroscopy* 2006;22:50-56.

   In 16 shoulders (13 patients) with rheumatoid arthritis but no associated cuff tears, pain relief and modest motion improvement were found 5.5 years after arthroscopic shoulder synovectomy. The procedure had limited benefit for patients with more advanced disease.

5. Outerbridge R: The etiology of chondromalacia patellae. *J Bone Joint Surg Br* 1961;43:752-758.

6. Samilson RL, Prieto V: Dislocation arthropathy of the shoulder. *J Bone Joint Surg Am* 1983;65:456-460.

7. Petty DH, Jazrawi LM, Estrada LS, Andrews JR: Glenohumeral chondrolysis after shoulder arthroscopy: Case reports and review of the literature. *Am J Sports Med* 2004;32:509-515.

   Glenohumeral chondrolysis, a devastating complication of shoulder arthroscopic surgery, most often occurred with the use of thermal techniques. The results of treatment were poor. According to the authors, "The diffuse nature of the cartilage degeneration makes cartilage regeneration processes unlikely to succeed."

8. Bishop JY, Flatow EL: Management of glenohumeral arthritis: A role for arthroscopy? *Orthop Clin North Am* 2003;34:559-566.

   Arthroscopy was assessed for the treatment of glenohumeral arthritis and found to be useful in selected patients.

9. Cameron BD, Galatz LM, Ramsey ML, Williams GR, Iannotti JP: Non-prosthetic management of grade IV osteochondral lesions of the glenohumeral joint. *J Shoulder Elbow Surg* 2002;11:25-32.

   Of 61 patients with a grade IV osteochondral lesion of the glenohumeral joint who were treated with arthroscopic debridement, 88% had significant improvement in pain and function.

10. Ellowitz AS, Rosas R, Quick DC, Rodosky MW, Buss DD: The benefit of arthroscopic subacromial decompression for impingement in patients found to have unsuspected glenohumeral osteoarthritis. *Orthop Trans* 1997;21:1135-1136.

11. Guyette TM, Bae H, Warren RF, Craig E, Wickiewicz TL: Results of arthroscopic subacromial decompression in patients with subacromial impingement and glenohumeral degenerative joint disease. *J Shoulder Elbow Surg* 2002;11:299-304.

    Patients who had mild or moderate glenohumeral degenerative joint disease experienced durable improvement in shoulder function after arthroscopic subacromial decompression. Results were less predictable in patients with severe degenerative joint disease.

12. Safran MR, Baillargeon D: The role of arthroscopy in the treatment of glenohumeral arthritis. *Sports Med Arthros Rev* 2004;12(2):139-145.

    A prospective evaluation of 18 patients with grade IV lesions who were treated solely with bursectomy found that 78% had significant pain relief at an average 24-month follow-up.

13. Weber SC, Kauffman JI: Abstract: Arthroscopic debridement for glenohumeral osteoarthritis: Long-term follow-up. *72nd Annual Meeting Proceedings*. Rosemont, IL: American Academy of Orthopaedic Surgeons, 2005, p 512.

    Forty patients had 86% good or excellent results 6 months after arthroscopic débridement, but only 33% had good or excellent results at final follow-up (3 to 14 years; mean, 5 years). Nonetheless, only 20% required arthroplasty by final follow-up. The final outcome was highly correlated with the amount of arthritis seen on presurgical radiographs.

14. Weinstein DM, Bucchieri JS, Pollock RG, Flatow EL, Bigliani LU: Arthroscopic debridement of the shoulder. *Arthroscopy* 2000;16:471-476.

15. Aaron RK, Skolnick AH, Reinert SE: Arthroscopic debridement for osteoarthritis of the knee. *J Bone Joint Surg Am* 2006;88:936-943.

    The severity of presurgical radiographic changes in the knee is highly predictive of outcomes after arthritic débridement. Failure to stratify results based on radiographs may inappropriately bias studies against arthroscopic débridement of degenerative joints.

16. Holloway GB, Schenk T, Williams GR, Ramsey ML, Iannotti JP: Arthroscopic capsular release for the treatment of refractory postoperative or postfracture shoulder stiffness. *J Bone Joint Surg Am* 2001;83:1682-1687.

    Fifty patients with stiffness were treated with arthroscopic release. At a 20-month follow-up, all patients had improved motion. Patients with idiopathic adhesive capsulitis had the most improvement in pain.

17. O'Driscoll SW: Abstract: Arthroscopic glenoidplasty and osteocapsular arthroplasty for advanced glenohumeral osteoarthritis. *67th Annual Meeting Proceedings*. Rosemont, IL: American Academy of Orthopaedic Surgeons, 2000, pp 193-194.

18. Andrews JR: Abstract: Arthroscopic debridement for glenohumeral arthritis. *67th Annual Meeting*

*Proceedings.* Rosemont, IL: American Academy of Orthopaedic Surgeons, 2000, pp 190-192.

19. Simpson NS, Kelley JG: Extra-glenohumeral joint shoulder surgery in rheumatoid arthritis: The role of bursectomy, acromioplasty, and distal clavicle excision. *J Shoulder Elbow Surg* 1994;3:66-69.

20. McCarty LP III, Cole BJ: Nonarthroplasty treatment of glenohumeral cartilage lesions. *Arthroscopy* 2005; 21:1131-1142.

    A review of open and arthroscopic treatment of glenohumeral arthritis assesses newer techniques and presents preliminary experience with microfracture, chondrocyte transfer, and osteochondral autograft transfer.

21. Scheibel M, Bartl C, Magosch P, Lichtenberg S, Habermeyer P: Osteochondral autologous transplantation for the treatment of full-thickness articular cartilage defects of the shoulder. *J Bone Joint Surg Br* 2004;86-B:991-997.

    Of eight patients treated with osteochondral autologous transplantation in the humerus, six were pain free and two were improved at a mean 32-month follow-up. Donor site morbidity at the knee was the most important complication. Although an open procedure was described, an arthroscopic procedure could be performed, as described for the knee. Despite treatment, most patients had disease progression.

22. Romeo AA, Cole BJ, Mazocca AD, Fox JA, Freeman KB, Joy E: Autologous chondrocyte repair of an articular defect in the humeral head. *Arthroscopy* 2002;18: 925-929.

    Autologous chondrocyte repair was used to treat a young patient with chondrolysis secondary to thermal treatment, with an excellent result. This staged arthroscopic-open procedure is used in patients with a large defect after failure of a simple procedure.

23. Burkhead WZ, Hulton KS: Biologic resurfacing of the glenoid with hemiarthroplasty of the shoulder. *J Shoulder Elbow Surg* 1995;4:263-270.

24. Pennington WT, Bartz BA: Arthroscopic glenoid resurfacing with meniscal allograft: A minimally invasive alternative for treating glenohumeral arthritis. *Arthroscopy* 2005;21:1517-1520.

    This is the only peer-reviewed report of an arthroscopic glenoid resurfacing technique. Ten patients reported subjective short-term improvement.

25. Brislin KJ, Savoie FH, Field LD, Ramsey JR: Surgical treatment for glenohumeral arthritis in the young patient. *Tech Shoulder Elbow Surg* 2004;5:165-169.

    The authors' technique for arthroscopic interposition arthroplasty using a porcine orthobiologic patch yielded good results in the first 20 patients, with no reported complications. A spherical humeral head was a requirement for the procedure.

# Chapter 30

# Superior Labrum Anterior and Posterior Injury

F. Alan Barber, MD

## Introduction

The system of classifying superior labrum anterior and posterior (SLAP) injuries has been expanded and made more precise since the condition was first described.[1,2] The current challenges are to differentiate labral pathology from normal labral variation or the effects of aging and to identify clinically significant lesions.

## Classification

Several mechanisms of SLAP injury have been proposed. A SLAP injury can result from biceps traction overload (which can occur when the long head of the biceps acts as a decelerator of the arm during the follow-through phase of throwing); acceleration of the arm during the late cocking phase of throwing; a tight posterior capsule; shearing forces on the superior biceps labral complex created by a fall onto an outstretched arm;[3] a sudden forced abduction and external rotation of the shoulder (which can happen, for example, when a baseball runner slides headfirst into base); or the forces applied during a motor vehicle crash by a shoulder belt (which restrains the ipsilateral chest wall and causes the shoulder to roll around the belt). Acceptance of one mechanism as valid for a particular patient need not exclude others.

The value of any classification system is in providing an organized method for evaluating an injury, which can positively affect the treatment algorithm. Table 1 summarizes the current 10-type classification of SLAP lesions. A type I lesion consists of fraying on the inner margin of the superior labrum (Figure 1, *A*). It is considered by some to represent a normal degenerative change resulting from the retreat of blood supply from the superior labrum that comes with increasing age. A meniscus-like superior labrum (a meniscoid labrum), in which a similar degenerative fraying of the inner rim occurs, can be considered a normal type I variant. Although type I is the most common, type II is the most common clinically significant type of SLAP lesion. A type II injury occurs when the superior labrum pulls away from the superior glenoid tubercle at the attach-

ment of the biceps tendon (Figure 1, *B*). Type II can be further classified by anatomic location relative to the biceps tendon; the three subtypes are anterior, posterior, and combined anterior and posterior[4] (Figure 2). The anterior subtype, a labral avulsion from the anterosuperior quadrant of the glenoid, is the most common. The posterior subtype, a labral avulsion in the posterosuperior quadrant of the glenoid, is the most common in throwing athletes. The combined subtype, an avulsion of both the anterosuperior and posterosuperior quadrants of the glenoid, is the least common. When traction is applied to the biceps tendon of a patient with a posterior or combined type II injury, the force on the tendon shifts from anterior-horizontal to posterior-vertical. This force is transmitted to the labrum at the biceps tendon base, and the detached labrum slides medially or peels away from the posterosuperior glenoid.[4]

**Table 1 | Classification of SLAP Lesions**

| Type* | Description |
| --- | --- |
| I | Degenerative fraying on inner rim |
| II | Superior labral detachment at biceps insertion |
| III | Bucket-handle tear of superior labrum with no elevation of biceps-labral attachment |
| IV | Bucket handle tear extending into biceps with tendon damage |
| V | Bankart lesion extending superiorly to include the biceps attachment |
| VI | Anterior or posterior labral flap with a type II biceps elevation |
| VII | Biceps attachment separation extending into the middle glenohumeral ligament |
| VIII | Type II with posterior labral extension |
| IX | Type II with circumferential labral tearing |
| X | Type II with posterior inferior labral separation |

*Types I through IV were originally described by Snyder;[1] types V through VII, by Maffet, Gartsman, and Moseley;[5] types VIII through X, by Powell, Nord, and Ryu.[6]

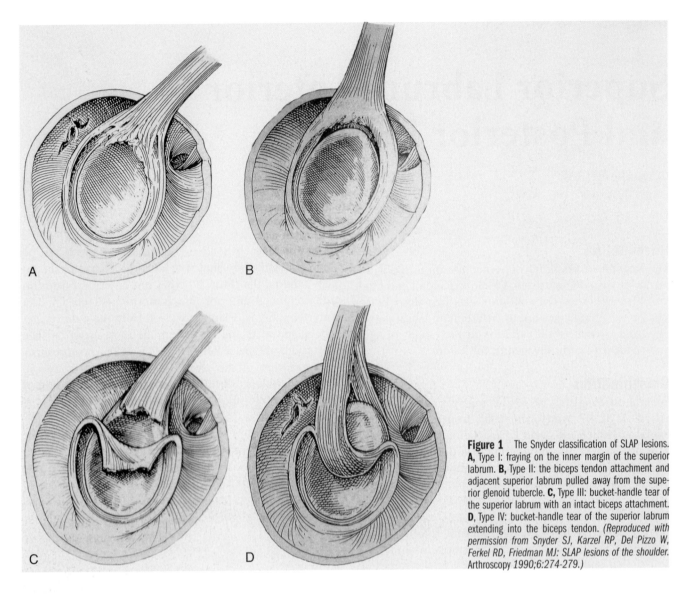

**Figure 1** The Snyder classification of SLAP lesions. **A,** Type I: fraying on the inner margin of the superior labrum. **B,** Type II: the biceps tendon attachment and adjacent superior labrum pulled away from the superior glenoid tubercle. **C,** Type III: bucket-handle tear of the superior labrum with an intact biceps attachment. **D,** Type IV: bucket-handle tear of the superior labrum extending into the biceps tendon. *(Reproduced with permission from Snyder SJ, Karzel RP, Del Pizzo W, Ferkel RD, Friedman MJ: SLAP lesions of the shoulder. Arthroscopy 1990;6:274-279.)*

A type III SLAP lesion is a bucket-handle tear of the superior labrum, usually extending from anterior to posterior at the biceps insertion (Figure 1, *C*). In contrast to type II, there is no elevation of the biceps-labral attachment from the glenoid. A type IV lesion is a bucket-handle labral tear that extends into the biceps tendon, resulting in a split in the tendon attachment (Figure 1, *D*).

The classification system has been expanded to include SLAP lesions associated with shoulder instability[5] (Figure 3). Type V is a Bankart lesion extending superiorly to the biceps attachment. Type VI is an anterior or posterior labral flap with a type II biceps elevation. Type VII is a biceps attachment separation that extends into the middle glenohumeral ligament. Type VIII is a type II SLAP lesion with posterior labral extension; type IX, a type II lesion with circumferential labral tearing; and type X, a type II lesion with posterior inferior labral separation[6] (Figure 4). As awareness of labral pa-

thology increases, more variations probably will be added to the classification system; one probable addition is a type II lesion with articular cartilage avulsions and loose bodies[7] (Figure 5).

The overall incidence of SLAP tears is low. In the original study, they were found in only 28 (4%) of 700 patients undergoing arthroscopy, and half of the 28 were type II.[1] In a study of 2,375 patients after shoulder procedures, 140 (5.9%) had a SLAP injury, of which 77 (55%) were type II.[8] Of 530 shoulders that underwent glenohumeral arthroscopy, 32 (6%) had a SLAP lesion, of which 17 (53%) were type II.[9] Of 544 shoulders undergoing arthroscopy for varied diagnoses, 139 (26%) had SLAP injuries, of which 29 (5.3%) were type II and 103 (74%) were degenerative type I.[10] In 712 patients undergoing shoulder arthroscopy, the incidence of SLAP injury was 6.2% using the original classification system and 11.8% using the expanded system.[5] Patients younger than 40 years were more likely to have a clini-

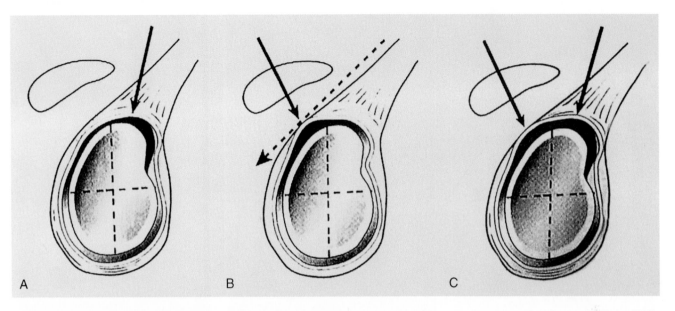

**Figure 2** The three SLAP type II subtypes. **A,** Anterior. **B,** Posterior. **C,** Combined anterior and posterior. *(Reproduced with permission from Burkhart SS, Morgan CD: The peel-back mechanism: Its role in producing and extending posterior type II SLAP lesions and its effect on SLAP repair rehabilitation. Arthroscopy 1998;14:637-640.)*

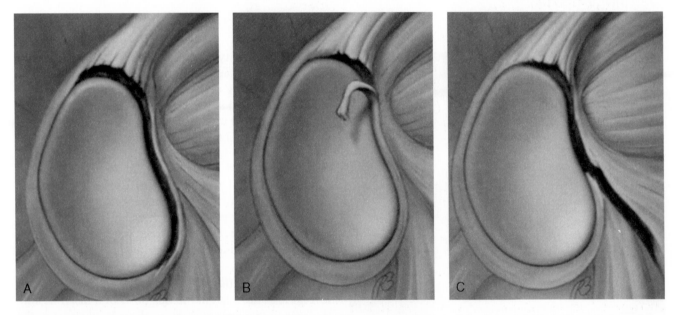

**Figure 3** The Maffet and Gartsman classification of SLAP lesions associated with instability. **A,** Type V: Bankart lesion that extends superiorly to the biceps attachment. **B,** Type VI: anterior or posterior labral flap with a type II biceps elevation. **C,** Type VII: biceps attachment separation that extends into the middle glenohumeral ligament. *(Reproduced with permission from Powell SE, Nord KD, Ryu RK: The diagnosis, classification and treatment of SLAP lesions. Oper Tech Sports Med 2004;12:99-110.)*

cally significant type II lesion, and their most common symptom was shoulder instability. In contrast, those age 40 years or older who were diagnosed with a type II lesion were frequently found to have either rotator cuff pathology or glenohumeral arthritis.

## Clinical Evaluation

Clinically significant SLAP lesions are most often found in three groups: men younger than 40 years whose dominant arm is affected after many years of high-performance overhead activities; military personnel; and people with a specific history of shoulder trauma or instability. A history of a fall onto an outstretched hand or a motor vehicle crash during which the patient was wearing a shoulder belt suggests the presence of a SLAP injury.[1,4,5,11] The primary diagnostic challenge is to differentiate a clinically significant superior labral injury (a true SLAP injury) from its normal variants and from degenerative changes. A patient's history and associated diagnoses are the most important considerations;

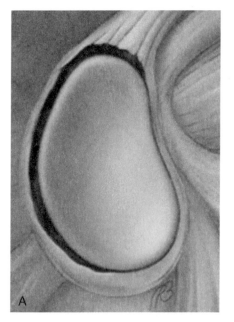
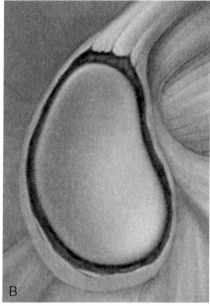
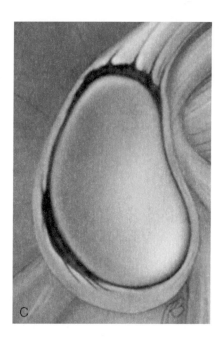

**Figure 4** Classification of additional types of SLAP lesions. **A,** Type VIII: type II with posterior labral extension. **B,** Type IX: type II with circumferential labral tearing. **C,** Type X, type II with a posteroinferior labral separation. *(Reproduced with permission from Powell SE, Nord KD, Ryu RK: The diagnosis, classification and treatment of SLAP lesions.* Oper Tech Sports Med *2004;12:99-110.)*

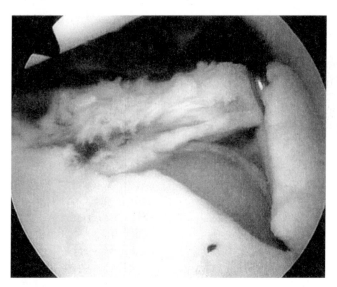

**Figure 5** A new SLAP variant, consisting of a type II SLAP lesion with articular cartilage avulsion and loose bodies. *(Reproduced with permission from Choi NH, Kim SJ: Avulsion of the superior labrum.* Arthroscopy *2004;20:872-874.)*

the secondary considerations include the patient's report of a mechanism of injury consistent with a SLAP injury, as well as the results of the clinical examination and imaging studies, and, finally, the outcome of surgical treatment.

The symptoms, which may appear suddenly or over time, include clicking and popping in the shoulder, often accompanied by anterior shoulder pain and reduced function. The ability to throw, serve, or swim, as well as the speed of such movements, may be decreased. In an overhead throwing athlete, pain during attempted overhead activities and inability to throw at the preinjury velocity are referred to as dead arm syndrome.[12,13]

The presence of a SLAP lesion should be anticipated and not discovered incidentally during surgery. A true type II SLAP lesion is not associated with significant glenohumeral arthritis or a rotator cuff tear. If one of these conditions is present, the superior labral variation is most likely part of the degenerative process, and a surgical procedure to attach the labrum to the superior glenoid is unlikely to affect the clinical outcome.

### Physical Examination

Several tests are used in the diagnosis of a SLAP lesion. Their common element is the application of stress to the biceps anchor by torsional or tensile loading during shoulder manipulation. The O'Brien test positions the arm in 10° adduction and 90° of forward flexion[14] (Figure 6). With the patient's forearm in full pronation (thumb pointing downward), the examiner resists forward flexion by pushing down on the wrist. Next, with the patient's hand in full supination (palm facing upward), the examiner again resists forward flexion. The experience of pain when the forearm is in pronation but not supination is considered a positive test result. Tenderness at the acromioclavicular joint combined with local tenderness to palpation indicates acromioclavicular joint pathology; here, too, less pain with the palm up than with the thumb down constitutes a positive test.

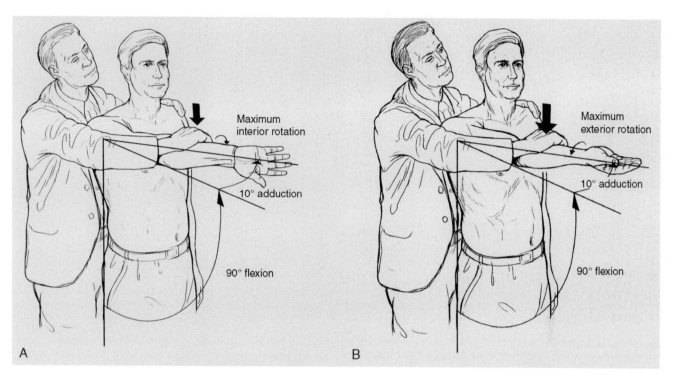

**Figure 6** The O'Brien active compression test. **A,** The patient's arm is forward flexed to 90°, adducted 10° to 15°, and maximally internally rotated. The patient is instructed to resist as the examiner applies a uniform downward force. **B,** The patient maximally supinates the arm, and the maneuver is repeated. *(Adapted with permission from O'Brien SJ, Pagnani MJ, Fealy S, McGlynn SR, Wilson JB: The active compression test: A new and effective test for diagnosing labral tears and acromioclavicular joint abnormality. Am J Sports Med 1998;26:610-613.)*

In a positive Speed's test, pain is produced at the anterior bicipital groove by resisted forward flexion with the shoulder flexed at 90° and the forearm fully supinated.[24] A lack of internal rotation in comparison with the opposite shoulder suggests that the posterior capsule is tight. A positive Speed's test can also be caused by bicipital tendinitis. In the most accurate method of measuring internal rotation, the patient is supine, and the examiner stabilizes the scapula by pressing on the anterior shoulder. In a throwing athlete, the dominant arm may have more external rotation than is considered normal and correspondingly less internal rotation, although the total arc of motion should remain 180°.

Unfortunately, the results of these and other tests are often inconsistent. In the literature, the initial report of some tests, including the modified O'Brien test,[14] the crank test,[15] and the anterior slide test,[16] was not independently validated by other studies.[17,18] The relocation test of Jobe[18] was found accurate by some authors[20] but not by others.[21] The biceps load test[22] and the pain provocative test[23] have not been validated by other authors. The Speed's test[24] and a loss of internal rotation not resolved by a short course of physical therapy[4] are also commonly used to assess SLAP injuries. Despite concerns about their reliability,[25] all of these tests have a role in the physical examination of the shoulder.

### Imaging Studies

Diagnostic imaging studies cannot consistently identify SLAP tears, although plain radiographs should be obtained to rule out obvious bony problems. The addition of gadolinium to MRI improves the ability to define the superior labrum. Community-read MRI scans were reported to have only 51% accuracy, but they were significantly more sensitive if arthrography was performed with MRI ($P = 0.0002$); two fellowship-trained musculoskeletal radiologists read the same MRI studies with 62% and 69% accuracy, 60% and 67.5% sensitivity, and 71% and 76.5% specificity.[26]

Some anatomic variations of the superior labrum can confound the diagnostic accuracy of MRI. A normal sublabral separation from the glenoid surface is common, varying from a slight crease to a sulcus measuring 1 to 2 mm or more. These anatomic variations are not pathologic but may appear on magnetic resonance arthrography (MRA). In contrast, the presence of a ganglion or sublabral cyst, often associated with suprascapular nerve compression, suggests the presence of a SLAP lesion.[27]

### Arthroscopic Evaluation

A type III, IV, or VI SLAP lesion is easily diagnosed using arthroscopy, because of the bucket-handle component

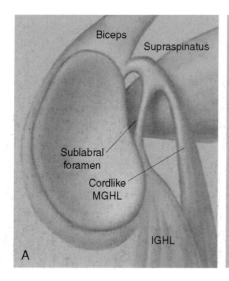
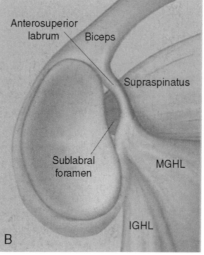
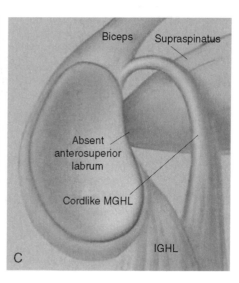

**Figure 7** Normal anatomic variants of the anterior labrum. **A,** A cordlike middle glenohumeral ligament (MGHL). **B,** A large sublabral foramen. **C,** The Buford complex, consisting of an absent anterosuperior labrum and a cordlike MGHL inserted directly at the base of the biceps tendon. IGHL = inferior glenohumeral ligament. *(Courtesy of Scott E. Powell, MD, Burbank, CA.)*

in types III and IV and the labral flap in type VI. The diagnosis of a type II lesion is more difficult and, therefore, presurgical assessment is important. The arthroscopic diagnosis is usually defined by three elements, called the type II SLAP triad: sublabral chondromalacia of the superior glenoid, fraying of the undersurface of the labrum, and a sulcus or gap larger than 5 mm between the labrum and articular cartilage. Occasionally, a sublabral hemorrhage is observed in the acute setting.

A superior sublabral cyst is often found with a type II SLAP lesion,[28] and communication with the glenohumeral joint is often associated with development of this structure. Elevation of the superior labrum exposes the communication, and a labral repair corrects the deformity. In a study of 546 patients who underwent arthroscopic shoulder surgery, 73 (13%) had a normal anatomic variation in the anterior labrum resulting in anterior sublabral holes[29] (Figure 7). A cordlike middle glenohumeral ligament was found in 47 patients (8.6%), and a large sublabral foramen was found in 18 (3.3%). The Buford complex, found in 8 patients (1.5%), is the absence of the anterosuperior labrum, with direct insertion of a cordlike middle glenohumeral ligament at the base of the biceps tendon.[29-31]

The most common of the type II subtypes, the anterior type, primarily involves the attachment of the labrum anterior to the biceps tendon[32] (Figure 2). If anterosuperior instability also exists, as evidenced by damage to the superior glenohumeral ligament, this type of injury can become a superior labrum anterior rotator cuff lesion with fraying of the anterior supraspinatus tendon.[33] In an anterior labral injury of the anterior or combined anterior and posterior subtype, a biceps root disruption exists and a firm biceps attachment to the superior glenoid is lacking. As a result, the labrum can be readily displaced by a

probe. In a posterior labral injury of the posterior or combined subtype, a positive peel-back sign is present; the entire superior biceps–labrum complex can be displaced medially from the posterosuperior glenoid using a probe or a maneuver in which the arm is taken out of traction, abducted 90°, and externally rotated.

A type II SLAP lesion results in microinstability of the glenohumeral joint, and the increased laxity between the glenoid and the humeral head allows an arthroscope inserted through the posterior portal to be moved from the anterosuperior area of the joint along the anterior glenoid edge to the anteroinferior aspect of the joint. This maneuver, called the drive-through sign, can be used in all type II SLAP lesions.

## Nonsurgical Treatment

A SLAP injury initially should be treated with rest, anti-inflammatory drugs, stretching, and strengthening of specific muscles. Throwing athletes and other overhead athletes may have decreased internal rotation, and an arc of shoulder motion of less than 180° indicates a tight posterior capsule. Weakness of the scapular stabilizers and scapular dyskinesis may result in scapular winging and asymmetric motion of the arm. A stretching program to attain full motion, especially with internal rotation, should be undertaken before any surgical intervention. If symptoms persist after 3 months of nonsurgical treatment, surgery is indicated.

## Surgical Treatment

SLAP lesions are surgically treated using arthroscopy. For a type I lesion, the treatment is débridement of the labral fraying. For a type II lesion, reattachment of the superior labrum to achieve a stable biceps–superior labral anchor is performed. A type III or IV lesion requires débridement

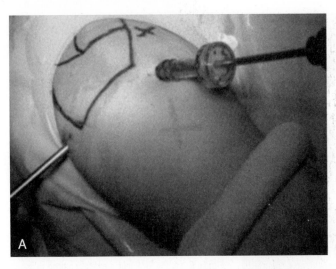
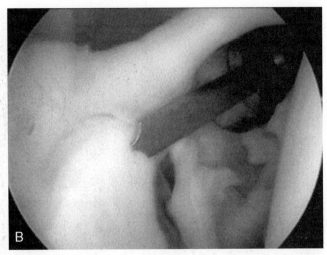

**Figure 8** **A,** Using a standard posterior portal for viewing, the surgeon places the working cannula in the lateral anterosuperior portal, located near the anterior edge of the acromion. **B,** The drill can reach the superior glenoid at a 30° angle. *(Reproduced with permission from Buess E, Schneider C: Simplified single-portal V-shaped SLAP repair. Arthroscopy 2006;22:680.)*

of the bucket-handle tear. In addition, a type IV lesion may require a suture repair of the associated biceps tear or a biceps tenodesis, depending on the extent of the biceps tendon damage. For types V, VI, and VII, any glenohumeral shoulder instability should be corrected with reattachment of the superior labrum, and a type VI flap should be débrided. To repair a type VIII, IX, or X lesion, the labrum should be reattached and any flaps débrided. Elimination of the drive-through and peel-back signs indicates that the repair is adequate.

After a thorough examination is performed under anesthesia, appropriate arthroscopic portals should be established, including a standard posterior viewing portal and an anteroinferior instrumentation portal. The anteroinferior portal should be located midway between the anterior acromial margin and the coracoid to allow access to the labral attachment for managing sutures and passing instruments in front of and behind the biceps anchor. A third, more superior portal should be placed for anchor insertion and suture management. The placement of this anchor varies with the location of the labral detachment. For an anterior type II detachment, the usual anterosuperior portal is sufficient. For a posterior or combined type II detachment, a second anchor should be placed posterior to the biceps tendon origin. This area cannot be reached through an anterosuperior portal, and a more posterior transcuff portal placed 1 cm lateral and 2 cm anterior to the posterolateral acromial corner allows accurate anchor placement.

A lateral anterosuperior portal in the rotator cuff interval, approximately 3 cm more lateral than the normal anterosuperior portal, allows access to the labrum both anterior and posterior to the biceps anchor[34] (Figure 8). Portal placement that avoids piercing the rotator cuff is believed to decrease the incidence of night pain and promote improved performance in athletes.[35]

The goal of surgical repair is to securely reattach the biceps-labral complex to the glenoid to eliminate the peel-back and drive-through signs. Because of problems associated with the use of translabral tacks, suture anchors are now the preferred method of biceps-labral fixation. An anterior type II repair requires one suture anchor, placed either beneath or slightly anterior to the biceps tendon origin; in this location, a mattress suture or two simple sutures can fix both sides of the biceps origin. A posterior or combined type II repair requires a suture anchor placed posterior to the biceps origin to fully stabilize the posterosuperior labrum.

The usual steps in a SLAP repair include careful probing to assess the nature of the biceps and superior labral injury and débridement of any degenerated tissue (Figures 9 and 10). The superior labrum is elevated away from the glenoid to expose the glenoid neck. This step is followed by débridement and abrasion of the area to prepare it for the biceps-labral reattachment. Caution is required during abrasion of the superior glenoid to avoid removing cortical bone; simple roughening of the bone surface to create a bleeding bed is sufficient. Next, the appropriate suture anchor or anchors are inserted into the superior glenoid articular cartilage margin at an angle (usually 45°) that will carry the anchor into the bone without cutting medially or laterally into the articular cartilage; the thickness of the superior glenoid varies with the location. After the anchor is in place, the sutures are passed through the labral tissue and a simple or mattress stitch is created.

### Postsurgical Treatment

A type II SLAP repair significantly decreases the patient's presurgical internal and external rotation and translation.[36] The primary challenge during the postsurgical period is to prevent stiffness. Immobilization should be avoided. Instead, the patient can use a sling

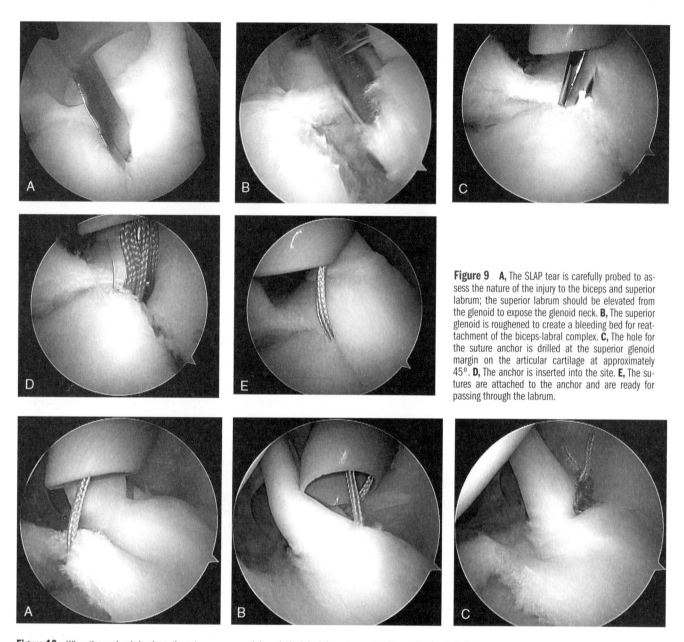

**Figure 9** **A,** The SLAP tear is carefully probed to assess the nature of the injury to the biceps and superior labrum; the superior labrum should be elevated from the glenoid to expose the glenoid neck. **B,** The superior glenoid is roughened to create a bleeding bed for reattachment of the biceps-labral complex. **C,** The hole for the suture anchor is drilled at the superior glenoid margin on the articular cartilage at approximately 45°. **D,** The anchor is inserted into the site. **E,** The sutures are attached to the anchor and are ready for passing through the labrum.

**Figure 10** When the anchor is in place, the sutures are passed through the labral tissue to create either a simple stitch **(A)** or a mattress stitch **(B)**, and the knot is tied **(C)**.

for comfort, with encouragement to periodically remove the arm from the sling and perform external rotation movements to stretch the posterior capsule. After 3 weeks, the use of the sling is discontinued, and pendulum exercises with elbow flexion and extension are permitted. No flexion above shoulder level is allowed, even for activities such as face washing or hair combing, and elbow flexion exercises requiring the lifting of more than 1 lb are avoided for the first 6 weeks. At 6 weeks, strengthening of the rotator cuff, scapular stabilizers, biceps, and deltoid muscles is initiated.

For throwing athletes, an interval throwing program can begin on a level surface at 4 months. Strengthening, especially of the posterior capsule, and stretching are continued. Throwing from the mound can begin at 6 months, and the patient is usually ready for a full release to activity at 7 months. Athletes involved in contact sports usually can return to activity without restriction at 3 months, if they are not involved in throwing or another overhead activity.[37] Nonthrowing athletes or nonathletes may have a better outcome than overhead throwing athletes after a SLAP repair,[38-40] and throwing athletes may have a better outcome than gymnasts.[41]

## Complications

The most common complication after a SLAP repair is stiffness with loss of motion, which can be prevented by appropriate postsurgical treatment. Failure to make the correct diagnosis can also result in complications. The superior labrum undergoes degeneration with increasing age, and the presence of a mobile biceps-labral attachment does not indicate a pathologic SLAP lesion requiring surgery. In a patient who is older than 40 years or has glenohumeral arthritis or a rotator cuff tear, surgery to repair the superior labrum may lead to a poor outcome because the primary source of the symptoms was not addressed.

Bioabsorbable poly-L-lactic acid polymer tacks can cause continuing pain and postsurgical disability. Failure of bioabsorbable tacks and chondral injury were factors associated with inadequate SLAP lesion healing in second-look arthroscopies.[42] Synovitis and foreign-body granuloma formation were reported to cause pain and stiffness after tack repair,[43,44] as well as device breakage and early loosening, also leading to loose bodies, massive synovitis, stiffness, and pain.[45] Metal suture anchors also have been reported to cause severe chondral damage.[46] The technique for obtaining access to the superior labrum can affect the duration of night pain as well as functional and patient satisfaction scores. In one study, the results were better when the rotator interval piercing technique was used rather than a rotator cuff piercing technique,[40] although the authors earlier reported problem-free use of trans–rotator cuff portals.[47] Failure to correct associated subacromial impingement can also lead to a poor oucome.[39,40]

## Summary

The SLAP lesion is uncommon except in young, active populations, such as military personnel,[48] in which trauma occurs with relative frequency. The typical SLAP injury is found in the dominant arm of a male overhead or throwing athlete who is younger than age 40 years; or a person who has experienced a shoulder dislocation, a fall onto an outstretched arm, or a motor vehicle crash while wearing a shoulder belt.

True SLAP lesions are found in fewer than 10% of all shoulder arthroscopies. They may be confused with normal anterior labral variants, which are found in 13% of shoulder arthroscopies. Clinical examination and diagnostic imaging are unreliable, and the diagnosis can be confirmed only by arthroscopy. However, a high level of suspicion should be required before arthroscopy is undertaken. Although a SLAP lesion may be observed in conjunction with glenohumeral instability, a labral abnormality found incidentally or associated with glenohumeral arthritis or a rotator cuff tear is probably not a clinically significant SLAP lesion and does not warrant repair.

## Annotated References

1. Snyder SJ, Karzel RP, Del Pizzo W, Ferkel RD, Friedman MJ: SLAP lesions of the shoulder. *Arthroscopy* 1990;6:274-279.

2. Andrews JR, Carson WG Jr, McLeod WD: Glenoid labrum tears related to the long head of the biceps. *Am J Sports Med* 1985;13:337-341.

3. Clavert P, Bonnomet F, Kempf JF, Boutemy P, Braun M, Kahn JL: Contribution to the study of the pathogenesis of type II superior labrum anterior-posterior lesions: A cadaveric model of a fall on the outstretched hand. *J Shoulder Elbow Surg* 2004;13: 45-50.

   Cadaver shoulder specimens were used to evaluate a fall onto an outstretched hand. A forward fall consistently produced a type II SLAP lesion, but a backward fall did not. Shear forces were a major factor in producing these lesions.

4. Burkhart SS, Morgan CD: The peel-back mechanism: Its role in producing and extending posterior type II SLAP lesions and its effect on SLAP repair rehabilitation. *Arthroscopy* 1998;14:637-640.

5. Maffet MW, Gartsman GM, Moseley B: Superior labrum-biceps tendon complex lesions of the shoulder. *Am J Sports Med* 1995;23:93-98.

6. Powell SE, Nord KD, Ryu RK: The diagnosis, classification and treatment of SLAP lesions. *Oper Tech Sports Med* 2004;12:99-110.

   The SLAP classification system is expanded by descriptions of types VII, IX, and X.

7. Choi NH, Kim SJ: Avulsion of the superior labrum. *Arthroscopy* 2004;20:872-874.

   Superior labral detachment with cartilage loss and exposed glenoid is described.

8. Snyder SJ, Banas MP, Karzel RP: An analysis of 140 injuries to the superior glenoid labrum. *J Shoulder Elbow Surg* 1995;4:243-248.

9. Handelberg F, Willems S, Shahabpour M, Huskin JP, Kuta J: SLAP lesions: A retrospective multicenter study. *Arthroscopy* 1998;14:856-862.

10. Kim TK, Queale WS, Cosgarea AJ, McFarland EG: Clinical features of the different types of SLAP lesions: An analysis of one hundred and thirty-nine cases. Superior labrum anterior posterior. *J Bone Joint Surg Am* 2003;85:66-71.

    Of 544 patients undergoing shoulder arthroscopy, 139 (26%) were found to have a SLAP lesion (types I to IV). The type varied by patient population. Level of evidence: IV.

11. Ruotolo C, Nottage WM, Flatow EL, Gross RM, Fanton GS: Controversial topics in shoulder arthroscopy. *Arthroscopy* 2002;18(2, suppl 1):65-75.

Of 544 patients undergoing shoulder arthroscopy, 25% were found to have a SLAP lesion (types I to IV). Patient age younger than 40 years was associated only with instability, and patient age 40 years or older was associated with a supraspinatus tear and humeral ostearthritis.

12. Burkhart SS, Morgan CD, Kibler WB: Shoulder injuries in overhead athletes: The "dead arm" revisited. *Clin Sports Med* 2000;19:125-158.

13. Burkhart SS, Morgan CD, Kibler WB: The disabled throwing shoulder: Spectrum of pathology. Part II: Evaluation and treatment of SLAP lesions in throwers. *Arthroscopy* 2003;19:531-539.

14. O'Brien SJ, Pagnani MJ, Fealy S, McGlynn SR, Wilson JB: The active compression test: A new and effective test for diagnosing labral tears and acromioclavicular joint abnormality. *Am J Sports Med* 1998;26:610-613.

15. Liu SH, Henry MH, Nuccion SL: A prospective evaluation of a new physical examination in predicting glenoid labral tears. *Am J Sports Med* 1996;24:721-725.

16. Kibler WB: Specificity and sensitivity of the anterior slide test in throwing athletes with superior glenoid labral tears. *Arthroscopy* 1995;11:296-300.

17. Stetson WB, Templin K: The crank test, the O'Brien test, and routine magnetic resonance imaging scans in the diagnosis of labral tears. *Am J Sports Med* 2002;30:806-809.

In 65 patients, arthroscopy revealed that presurgical O'Brien and Crank tests were not sensitive in detecting glenoid labral tears and were often falsely positive.

18. McFarland EG, Kim TK, Savino RM: Clinical assessment of three common tests for superior labral anterior-posterior lesions. *Am J Sports Med* 2002;30:810-815.

In 426 patients, arthroscopy revealed 39 SLAP tears. A comparison of normal shoulders with shoulders having a SLAP tear failed to find diagnostic accuracy in the active compression, anterior slide, and compression rotation tests.

19. Jobe CM: Superior glenoid impingement: Current concepts. *Clin Orthop Relat Res* 1996;330:98-107.

20. Guanche CA, Jones DC: Clinical testing for tears of the glenoid labrum. *Arthroscopy* 2003;19:517-523.

The findings of the Speed's, anterior apprehension, Yergason, O'Brien, Jobe relocation, and Crank tests were compared with surgical findings. Only the O'Brien test (63% sensitive, 73% specific) and Jobe relocation test (44% sensitive, 87% specific) were correlated with the presence of a labral tear.

21. Mileski RA, Snyder SJ: Superior labral lesions in the shoulder: Pathoanatomy and surgical management. *J Am Acad Orthop Surg* 1998;6:121-131.

22. Kim SH, Ha KI, Ahn JH, Kim SH, Choi HJ: Biceps load test II: A clinical test for SLAP lesions of the shoulder. *Arthroscopy* 2001;17:160-164.

The biceps load test II was performed in 127 patients and found to be an effective tool for diagnosing SLAP lesions.

23. Mimori K, Muneta T, Nakagawa T, Shinomiya K: A new pain provocation test for superior labral tears of the shoulder. *Am J Sports Med* 1999;27:137-142.

24. Gilecreest EL, Albi P: Unusual lesions of muscles and tendons of the shoulder girdle and upper arm. *Surg Gynecol Obstet* 1939;68:903-917.

25. Holtby R, Razmjou H: Accuracy of the Speed's and Yergason's tests in detecting biceps pathology and SLAP lesions: Comparison with arthroscopic findings. *Arthroscopy* 2004;20:231-236.

In 152 patients with shoulder pain, the Speed's and Yergason tests were evaluated against surgical findings. They were found to be only moderately specific (Speed's, 75%; Yergason, 79%), with insufficiently consistent results and variable predictive value. Level of evidence: I.

26. Reuss BL, Schwartzberg R, Zlatkin MB, Cooperman A, Dixon JR: Magnetic resonance imaging accuracy for the diagnosis of superior labrum anterior-posterior lesions in the community setting: Eighty-three arthroscopically confirmed cases. *J Shoulder Elbow Surg* 2006;15:580-585.

According to this study, MRI was inaccurate in diagnosis of SLAP lesions. MRI and magnetic resonance arthroscopy of 83 surgically confirmed type II SLAP lesions were evaluated by community and musculoskeletal-trained radiologists. Community radiologists identified 51% of the SLAP lesions and were more accurate using magnetic resonance arthroscopy than MRI (*P* = 0.0002). Musculoskeletal radiologists were more accurate than community radiologists.

27. Westerheide KJ, Karzel RP: Ganglion cysts of the shoulder: Technique of arthroscopic decompression and fixation of associated type II superior labral anterior to posterior lesions. *Orthop Clin North Am* 2003;34:521-528.

Arthroscopic techniques allow decompression of ganglion cysts and repair of the associated labral lesions, thereby decreasing cyst recurrence and allowing earlier rehabilitation and a more rapid return to normal activities.

28. Westerheide KJ, Dopirak RM, Karzel RP, Snyder SJ: Suprascapular nerve palsy secondary to spinoglenoid cysts: Results of arthroscopic treatment. *Arthroscopy* 2006;22:721-727.

Shoulder ganglion cysts with suprascapular nerve compression are often associated with labral lesions, including SLAP tears. Arthroscopic techniques allow decompression of the ganglion cysts and repair of the labral lesions.

29. Rao AG, Kim TK, Chronopoulos E, McFarland EG: Anatomical variants in the anterosuperior aspect of

the glenoid labrum: A statistical analysis of seventy-three cases. *J Bone Joint Surg Am* 2003;85:653-659.

Three anterosuperior labrum variations were found in 13% of 546 patients: a sublabral foramen (3.3%); a sublabral foramen with a cordlike middle glenohumeral ligament (8.6%); and an absent anterosuperior labrum with a cordlike middle glenohumeral ligament, which is known as the Buford complex (1.5%).

30. Bents RT, Skeete KD: The correlation of the Buford complex and SLAP lesions. *J Shoulder Elbow Surg* 2005;14:565-569.

Six (2.5%) of 235 patients in a military population had a Buford complex (cordlike middle glenohumeral ligament and absent anterosuperior labrum). Five (83.3%) of the six and 40 (17.5%) of the remaining 229 patients had a SLAP lesion.

31. Ilahi OA, Labbe MR, Cosculluela P: Variants of the anterosuperior glenoid labrum and associated pathology. *Arthroscopy* 2002;18:882-886.

A sublabral foramen was found in 20 shoulders during 108 consecutive arthroscopies (18.5%), and a Buford complex was found in 7 (6.5%). More SLAP lesions were found in these 27 shoulders (56%) than in the rest of the study population (12%).

32. Morgan CD, Burkhart SS, Palmeri M, Gillespie M: Type II SLAP lesions: Three subtypes and their relationships to superior instability and rotator cuff tears. *Arthroscopy* 1998;14:553-565.

33. Savoie FH III, Field LD, Atchinson S: Anterior superior instability with rotator cuff tearing: SLAC lesion. *Orthop Clin North Am* 2001;32:457-461.

The superior labrum anterior rotator cuff lesion is described as a definable clinical entity with satisfactory surgical results.

34. Buess E, Schneider C: Simplified single-portal V-shaped SLAP repair. *Arthroscopy* 2006;22:680.

This report describes the lateral anterosuperior portal in the rotator interval, which is located about 3 cm more laterally than the standard anterosuperior portal and does not violate the rotator cuff tendon or muscle.

35. Cohen DB, Coleman S, Drakos MC, et al: Outcomes of isolated type II SLAP lesions treated with arthroscopic fixation using a bioabsorbable tack. *Arthroscopy* 2006;22:136-142.

A study of 41 isolated type II SLAP repairs treated with arthroscopic bioabsorbable tack fixation found that outcomes were significantly poorer if the rotator cuff was pierced. The symptoms included night pain.

36. Panossian VR, Mihata T, Tibone JE, Fitzpatrick MJ, McGarry MH, Lee TQ: Biomechanical analysis of isolated type II SLAP lesions and repair. *J Shoulder Elbow Surg* 2005;14:529-534.

Type II SLAP lesions were studied in six cadaver shoulders before and after arthroscopic repair. Slap lesions caused a significant increase in all motion ranges, which was significantly decreased after repair.

37. Funk L, Snow M: SLAP tears of the glenoid labrum in contact athletes. *Clin J Sport Med* 2007;17:1-4.

A retrospective cohort study found that SLAP tears were common in rugby players and could be diagnosed using magnetic resonance arthrography (76% sensitivity). Arthroscopic repair offers excellent results and a return to sport at an average of 2.6 months after surgery.

38. Kim SH, Ha KI, Kim SH, Choi HJ: Results of arthroscopic treatment of superior labral lesions. *J Bone Joint Surg Am* 2002;84-A:981-985.

Thirty-two of 34 patients had a satisfactory outcome at a mean 33 months after arthroscopic repair of an isolated superior labral lesion. The results were less satisfactory for patients who participated in overhead sports.

39. Coleman SH, Cohen DB, Drakos MC, et al: Arthroscopic repair of type II superior labral anterior posterior lesions with and without acromioplasty: A clinical analysis of 50 patients. *Am J Sports Med* 2007;35:749-753.

A combined type II SLAP repair and acromioplasty had no negative effect and prevented residual clinical impingement. At 3.4-year follow-up, L'Insalata and American Shoulder and Elbow Surgeons scores were similar in the two groups; 21% of SLAP-repair patients and no combined-procedure patients had postsurgical clinical impingement.

40. Cohen DB, Coleman S, Drakos MC, et al: Outcomes of isolated type 2 SLAP lesions treated with arthroscopic fixation using a bioabsorbable tack. *Arthroscopy* 2006;22:136-142.

Evaluation at 3.7-year follow-up of 41 bioabsorbable tack repairs of a type II SLAP lesion found only 71% overall patient satisfaction. Patients with a rotator cuff piercing technique had significantly lower American Shoulder and Elbow Surgeons Index scores and night pain; athletes had poorer outcomes than nonathletes. Level of evidence: III.

41. Rhee YG, Lee DH, Lim CT: Unstable isolated SLAP lesion: Clinical presentation and outcome of arthroscopic fixation. *Arthroscopy* 2005;21:1099.

A retrospective review of SLAP repairs found that the most common presurgical symptoms were pain (100%) and clicking (57%). A positive compression rotation test was the most common sign. Seventy-six percent of athletes returned to their sport after repair, and throwing athletes did better than other athletes ($P = 0.011$). Level of evidence: IV.

42. Sassmannshausen G, Sukay M, Mair SD: Broken or dislodged PLLA bioabsorbable tacks in patients after SLAP lesion surgery. *Arthroscopy* 2006;22:615-619.

Bioabsorbable poly-ʟ-lactic acid tacks used for SLAP repair can break or dislodge, resulting in pain, mechanical symptoms, and chondral injury. Arthroscopy may be needed to remove tack fragments identified on MRI and restabilize the labral lesion. Level of evidence: IV.

43. Segmuller HE, Hayes MG, Saies AD: Arthroscopic repair of glenolabral injuries with an absorbable fixation device. *J Should Elbow Surg* 1997;6:383-392.

44. Edwards DJ, Hoy G, Saies AD, Hayes MG: Adverse reactions to an absorbable shoulder fixation device. *J Shoulder Elbow Surg* 1994;3:230-233.

45. Burkhart A, Imhoff AB, Roscher E: Foreign-body reaction to the bioabsorbable Suretac device. *Arthroscopy* 2000;16:91-95.

46. Kaar TK, Schenck RC, Wirth MA, Rockwood CA: Complications of metallic suture anchors in shoulder surgery: A report of 8 cases. *Arthroscopy* 2001;17:31-37.

The use of metallic suture anchors is common and effective, but there can be significant complications. Proper anchor placement is important.

47. O'Brien SJ, Allen AA, Coleman SH, Drakos MC: The trans–rotator cuff approach to SLAP lesions: Technical aspects for repair and a clinical follow-up of 31 patients at a minimum of 2 years. *Arthroscopy* 2002;18: 372-377.

The trans–rotator cuff approach was found to allow improved placement of a biodegradable fixation device or suture anchors into the superior labrum and not to compromise the function of the rotator cuff.

48. Kampa RJ, Clasper J: Incidence of SLAP lesions in a military population. *J R Army Med Corps* 2005;151: 171-175.

In shoulder arthroscopies performed on 70 military and 108 civilian patients, the incidence of SLAP lesions in the military patients was found to be 38.6%, compared with 11.1% in the civilian patients.

# Chapter 31

# Paralabral Cysts of the Shoulder

Charles L. Getz, MD

*Matthew L. Ramsey, MD

Gerald R. Williams, MD

## Introduction

Paralabral cysts were regarded as a curiosity until the mid 1980s, and only sporadic case reports appeared in the orthopaedic literature. The widespread availability of MRI during the past 20 years has led to improved evaluation of the soft-tissue structures of the shoulder. As a result, paralabral cysts are now recognized as an uncommon, although not rare, cause of shoulder pain and dysfunction.

## Pathology

Paralabral cysts develop as a result of pathology of the labrum, labroglenoid interface, or capsule. An injury can create a one-way valve mechanism that allows egress of synovial fluid from the joint but prevents its return. The fluid collects as it leaves the joint and becomes a discreet, walled-off structure. A review of MRI studies obtained during a 2-year period found that 20 of 593 patients (3%) had a paralabral cyst. In each of these patients, an adjacent labral tear was present.[1] A similar review found that 50 of 2,211 patients (2%) had a paralabral cyst on MRI; 57% were posterior, 21% were anterior, 14% were superior, and 8% were inferior. A labral tear was present in only 26 (52%) of the affected patients.[2] Therefore, it appears that detachment of the labrum is probably not the only mechanism by which fluid escapes from the joint.

Paralabral cysts in the spinoglenoid notch are frequently associated with posterosuperior labral pathology. Paralabral cysts in other locations have different clinical implications. Superior labral tears have been reported to cause cysts in the suprascapular fossa, with subsequent compression of the suprascapular nerve to both the supraspinatus and infraspinatus.[3] Inferior paralabral cysts, which are associated with inferior labral tears, have been reported to cause compression of the axillary nerve similar to that seen in quadrilateral space

syndrome.[4,5] The reported association of anterior paralabral cysts with anteroinferior labral tears and anterior instability is thought to be incidental.[6]

## Anatomy of the Spinoglenoid Notch

Formation of a paralabral cyst in the spinoglenoid notch can result in suprascapular nerve impairment. The anatomy of the suprascapular nerve, as it passes from the suprascapular fossa along the posterior glenoid neck and lateral to the scapular spine, is shown in Figure 1. In a cadaver study, the motor branch of the suprascapular nerve innervated the supraspinatus within 1 cm of the

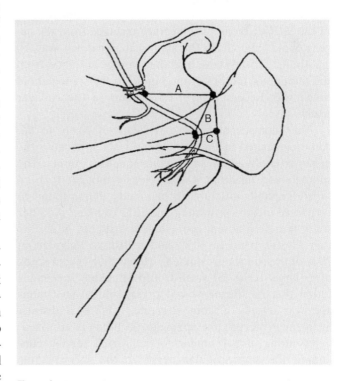

**Figure 1** Diagram of the posterior scapula illustrating the passage of the suprascapular nerve inferior to the transverse scapular ligament, as well as innervation of the spinati. A = supraglenoid tubercle to suprascapular notch (3 cm; range, 2.5-3.9 cm), B = supraglenoid tubercle to base of scapular spine (2.5 cm; range, 1.9-3.2 cm), C = midline posterior glenoid rim to base of scapular spine (1.8 cm; range, 1.4-2.5 cm). *(Reproduced with permission from Bigliani LU, Dalsey RM, McCann PD: An anatomical study of the suprascapular nerve. Arthroscopy 1990;6:301-305.)*

---

*Matthew L. Ramsey, MD is a consultant or employee for Zimmer.*

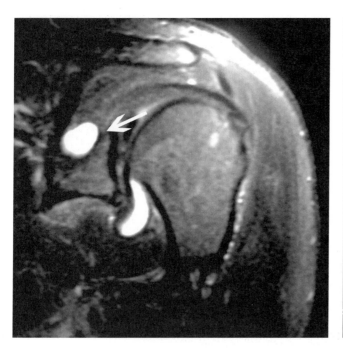

**Figure 2** A coronal T2-weighted MRI study showing a round, smooth cyst (*arrow*) at the base of the spine of the scapula and posterior glenoid rim.

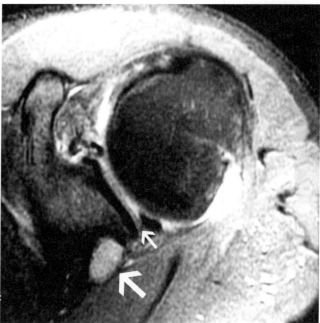

**Figure 3** An axial short-tau inversion recovery image showing a round, homogenous cyst (*large arrow*) in the spinoglenoid notch, associated with a posterolabral detachment. The tear between the labrum and glenoid is shown (*small arrow*).

suprascapular notch in all 90 specimens, and the inferior branch of the suprascapular nerve innervated the infraspinatus within 1 cm of the spinoglenoid notch in 80 of the 90 specimens.[7] The average distance from the supraglenoid tubercle to the suprascapular notch was 3.0 cm (range, 2.5-3.9 cm), and the average distance from the midline of the posterior glenoid to the spinoglenoid notch was 1.8 cm (range, 1.4-2.5 cm) in the cadaver study.

The suprascapular nerve is relatively likely to become entrapped in the spinoglenoid notch because the nerve is confined to an osseoligamentous tunnel. The spinoglenoid ligament was previously thought to be a highly variable structure. In one study, it was found to be absent in 50% of women and 13% of men.[8] Another study found an absent spinoglenoid ligament in 20%, a thin fibrous band in 60%, and a distinct ligament in 20% of the specimens studied.[9] However, a recent study of a large series of fresh-frozen shoulder specimens found that the ligament was present in all specimens and was usually a stout structure.[10] When a distinct ligament is present, the spinoglenoid notch is an osseoligamentous tunnel similar to the carpal tunnel, containing the suprascapular nerve to the infraspinatus and its venous plexus. Cysts and other space-occupying lesions probably create more pressure on the neurovascular bundle when they occur in a tunnel than in a less restricted location. Therefore, the suprascapular nerve is more vulnerable to entrapment by cysts in the spinoglenoid notch.

## Evaluation

No single physical examination finding is diagnostic for a spinoglenoid cyst. Patients with spinoglenoid cysts most commonly complain of posterior shoulder pain,[2,11] and pain with accompanying weakness is also common. There have been isolated reports of shoulder weakness without pain. Most patients are young, active, and male, and their dominant side is more likely to be affected. Posterior shoulder muscle atrophy and shoulder external rotation weakness are present, as they are with rotator cuff tears and other neurologic conditions. Examination findings consistent with a superior labrum anterior and posterior (SLAP) or posterolabral tear may be present in patients with labral pathology.

## Diagnostic Studies

A paralabral cyst has a characteristic appearance on MRI.[2,12,13] The lesion is round and homogenous, but it may contain thin septations (Figures 2 through 4). It appears bright on a T2-weighted image and dark on a T1-weighted image. A heterogenous or irregular appearance may indicate that the lesion is a tumor rather than a cyst. Myxoid tumors, synovial cell sarcomas, and peripheral nerve sheath tumors appear hyperintense on a T2-weighted image and hypointense on a T1-weighted image.[12] Intravenous gadolinium enhances the entire solid tumor, but only the rim of a cyst.

Intravenous gadolinium should also be used if a spinoglenoid lesion has a tubular rather than a spherical appearance. The underlying pathology may be associated with dilated venous structures. Of six patients found to have vascular dilatation on MRI, the three who underwent spinoglenoid ligament release were found to have dilated venous structures corresponding to the preoperative imaging. Their condition improved following surgery.[13]

Although contrast is not needed to see a paralabral cyst on MRI, intra-articular gadolinium is useful in seeing the labrum and detecting a labral injury. Occasionally, contrast flow can be seen through a labral tear into a paralabral cyst.[2]

Electromyography (EMG) is a well-established means of evaluating nerve dysfunction. It is useful in detecting suprascapular nerve entrapment,[14,15] as well as any functional alterations, and determining appropriate treatment. Even if examination findings are consistent with infraspinatus weakness, confirmation of the site of nerve entrapment can be helpful in surgical planning. EMG can also document the return of nerve function after surgery.

## Treatment and Results

In several case reports, inferior paralabral cysts causing axillary nerve dysfunction responded to open decompression, and the patients recovered nerve function.[4,5] Anterior cysts do not cause nerve dysfunction, but they are associated with anteroinferior labral detachment.[6,16] The resulting shoulder instability is caused by the Bankart lesion rather than the cyst. The indication for surgical treatment of an anterior paralabral cyst is recurrent instability. Decompression of an anterior cyst is incidental to the labral repair and does not by itself correct shoulder instability. Anterior cysts not associated with instability are thought to be incidental and are simply observed.

Nonsurgical treatment is recommended for spinoglenoid cysts and cysts of the suprascapular fossa that are found incidentally and are normal on EMG. In general, other possible causes of shoulder pain should dictate the treatment plan. However, surgical management is indicated after other causes have been eliminated, particularly if the cyst is accompanied by a labral tear.

Observation is indicated for a cyst that is causing pain but no nerve dysfunction, because spontaneous resolution is believed to occur in 10% to 17% of patients.[3,11] After several months of observation, treatment of the cyst is recommended if the pain persists or if weakness develops. Surgery should be considered for a patient with a cyst that is causing suprascapular nerve dysfunction. Table 1 outlines studies that have examined the surgical treatment alternatives. An open posterior approach to the shoulder has been used, with or without osteotomy of the acromion.[17,18,27,28] However, the open approach does not allow treatment of concurrent intra-articular pathology and therefore may not resolve pain or prevent cyst recurrence.[1,16,25] Drainage guided by CT,

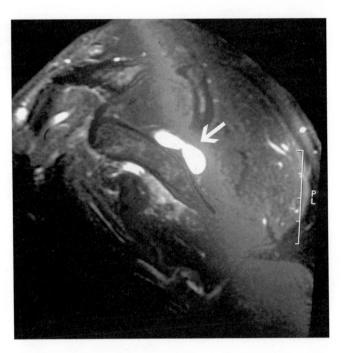

**Figure 4**  A T2-weighted sagittal MRI study showing a cyst (*arrow*) extending superiorly into the suprascapular fossa and inferiorly into the infraspinatus fossa; only the nerve to the infraspinatus is affected.

ultrasonography, or MRI is effective in decompressing spinoglenoid cysts.[19,29-31] This treatment appears to be reliable in draining the cyst and carries little risk to the patient; it does not require anesthesia and allows quick recovery. However, image-guided drainage does not address the intra-articular pathology, and the rate of persistent or recurrent symptoms is high. Cyst recurrence has been reported,[1,11,14,22] and in one study three of four patients who underwent ultrasonography-guided drainage had a recurrence at 4 months.[2]

Several arthroscopic methods are increasingly being used to address intra-articular pathologies.[1,3,11,14,15,19,22,25,26] Direct decompression of the cyst is performed through an intra-articular capsulotomy or beneath the labral detachment and is followed by labral repair, if necessary. Alternatively, repair of a labral injury is followed by image-guided drainage of the cyst. In a third method, the labral injury is repaired or, if no injury exists, a capsulotomy is performed; external pressure is then applied to the spinoglenoid notch in an attempt to break open the cyst. Cyst decompression is performed when there is a flow of characteristic yellow fluid.

The results of arthroscopic paralabral cyst treatment are encouraging. After arthroscopic cyst decompression, with or without labral repair, eight patients had average improvement in their Constant score from 70 to 93 and in their Simple Shoulder Test score from 7.75 to 11. One patient developed a frozen shoulder, and one developed a smaller recurrent cyst.[24] In a study of 16 patients 40 months after direct arthroscopic cyst decompression, the

**Table 1 | Studies of Paralabral Cyst Treatment**

| Study | Technique, Number of Patients | Outcome, Number of Patients |
|---|---|---|
| Skirving et al[17] (1994) | Open, 3 | Improvement, 2; improvement with recurrence of symptoms and cyst, 1 |
| Takagishi et al[18] (1994) | Open, 3 | EMG and clinical improvement, 3 |
| Tirman et al[1] (1994) | Open, 2; arthroscopic with aspiration or open excision, 8 | Recurrence with unaddressed SLAP, 1 |
| Fehrman et al[19] (1995) | Arthroscopic evaluation and open excision (SLAP bed curetted when present), 6 | Excellent arthroscopic evaluation, 5; fair, 1 |
| Iannotti and Ramsey[20] (1996) | Arthroscopic SLAP repair and cyst decompression, 3 | MRI resolution and clinical improvement, 3 |
| Chochole et al[21] (1997) | Extensive débridement of SLAP with no repair or decompression, 1 | MRI and clinical improvement, 1 |
| Moore et al[3] (1997) | Nonsurgical, 6<br>Arthroscopic, 5<br>Arthroscopic and open, with later repair, 5<br>Open, 6 | Cyst resolution, 1; no improvement, 4<br>Improvement, 4; failure and later SLAP repair, 1<br>Pain improvement, 5<br>Clinical improvement and partial cyst resolution on MRI, 3 |
| Leitschuh et al[22] (1999) | Ultrasonography-guided drainage, 1 | Symptom return and SLAP repair, 1 |
| Piatt et al[11] (2002) | Nonsurgical, 19<br>Arthroscopic, 10<br>Non-image-guided needle aspiration, 11<br>Arthroscopic SLAP débridement or repair, 6 | Patient satisfaction, 10; cyst resolution, 2<br>Patient satisfaction, 10<br>Recurrent or residual cyst, 5<br>Patient satisfaction, 4 |
| Chen et al[14] (2003) | Arthroscopic SLAP repair and cyst decompression, 3 | Patient satisfaction with normal EMG and no recurrence on MRI, 3 |
| Westerhide and Karzel[23] (2003) | Arthroscopic cyst decompression and SLAP repair or débridement, 14 | Patient satisfaction, 10; improved SST score, 10 (overall improvement from 4.3 to 11.5) |
| Lichtenberg et al[24] (2004) | Arthroscopic SLAP repair or capsulotomy with cyst decompression, 8 | Complete cyst resolution, 7; small cyst recurrence, 1; frozen shoulder, 1; overall improvement in Constant score from 70 to 93, and SST score from 7.75 to 11 |
| Abboud et al[15] (2006) | Arthroscopic direct cyst decompression with SLAP repair, 8; with SLAP débridement, 8 | Patient satisfaction, 16; improved ASES score, 16; no difference in outcome between groups |
| Baums et al[25] (2006) | Arthroscopic indirect cyst decompression through SLAP with SLAP repair, 1 | Normal EMG with no recurrence on MRI and 94 Constant score, 1 |
| Youm et al[26] (2006) | Arthroscopic indirect cyst decompression through SLAP, with SLAP repair, 10 | Patient satisfaction, 10; recurrence, 0 |

*ASES = American Shoulder and Elbow Surgeons Shoulder Index, SST = Simple Shoulder Test.*

need for labral repair in 8 of the patients did not significantly affect the outcome. The average American Shoulder and Elbow Surgeons score improved from 68 to 92.[15]

A study of 10 patients after indirect cyst decompression and SLAP repair found that all were satisfied at an average 10.7-month follow-up, and repeat scanning revealed no recurrences.[26] In a study of a similar technique, the blush of cyst rupture was not seen in several of the 14 patients, and no attempt at cyst decompression was made. The average Simple Shoulder Test score had improved from 4.3 to 11.5 at 51-month follow-up.[23]

Several small series reported that abnormalities seen on EMG were resolved 6 to 9 months after decompression.[15,25] Atrophy of the infraspinatus may remain, despite clinical improvement.[20]

## Summary

Although paralabral cysts are increasingly recognized as a source of shoulder pain and dysfunction, the optimal treatment is still being defined. Recurrence appears to be linked to residual labral pathology in patients who undergo open cyst excision, image-guided drainage, or arthroscopic treatment. Cysts appear to recur less frequently after arthroscopic treatment than after open cyst excision or image-guided drainage, which do not permit intra-articular pathology to be evaluated or addressed. Both open and arthroscopic surgical interventions have produced better results than observation or image-guided drainage. However, the risks associated with surgery, as well as the rehabilitation required after a SLAP repair, increase the desirability of observation or image-guided drainage for some patients.

## Annotated References

1. Tirman PF, Feller J, Janzen DL, et al: Association of glenoid labral cysts with labral tears and glenohumeral instability: Radiologic findings and clinical significance. *Radiology* 1994;190:653-658.

2. Tung GA, Entzian D, Stern JB: MR imaging and MR arthrography of paraglenoid labral cysts. *AJR Am J Roentgenol* 2000;174:1707-1715.

3. Moore TP, Fritts HM, Quick DC: Suprascapular nerve entrapment caused by supraglenoid cyst compression. *J Shoulder Elbow Surg* 1997;6:455-462.

4. Sanders TG, Tirman PF: Paralabral cyst: An unusual cause of quadrilateral space syndrome. *Arthroscopy* 1999;15:632-637.

5. Robinson P, White LM, Lax M, et al: Quadrilateral space syndrome caused by glenoid labral cyst. *AJR Am J Roentgenol* 2000;175:1103-1105.

6. Yukata K, Imada K, Yoshizumi Y, et al: Intra-articular ganglion cyst (paralabral cyst) of the shoulder associated with recurrent anterior dislocation: A case report. *J Shoulder Elbow Surg* 2002;11:95-97.

7. Bigliani LU, Dalsey RM, McCann PD: An anatomical study of the suprascapular nerve. *Arthroscopy* 1990;6:301-305.

8. Kaspi A, Yanai J, Pick CG: Entrapment of the distal suprascapular nerve: An anatomical study. *Int Orthop* 1988;12:273-275.

9. Cummins CA, Anderson K, Bowen M, et al: Anatomy and histological characteristics of the spinoglenoid ligament. *J Bone Joint Surg Am* 1998;80:1622-1625.

10. Plancher KD, Peterson RK, Johnston JC: The spinoglenoid ligament: Anatomy, morphology, and histological findings. *J Bone Joint Surg Am* 2005;87:361-365.

    Fifty-eight fresh-frozen cadaver shoulders were dissected to evaluate the presence and morphology of the spinoglenoid ligament.

11. Piatt BE, Hawkins RJ, Fritz RC, et al: Clinical evaluation and treatment of spinoglenoid notch ganglion cysts. *J Shoulder Elbow Surg* 2002;11:600-604.

    Of 73 patients with spinoglenoid notch cysts, 65 had a posterosuperior labral tear. All patients reported pain at a mean 20.5-month follow-up. Patients underwent nonsurgical treatment (19), attempted needle aspiration (11), arthroscopic treatment of the labral defect with no cyst excision (6), or surgical cyst excision with the tear fixed in an arthroscopic or open procedure (27). The satisfaction rates were 53%, 64%, 67%, and 97%, respectively.

12. Sherman PM, Sanders TG, De Lone DR: A benign soft tissue mass simulating a glenoid labral cyst on unenhanced magnetic resonance imaging. *Mil Med* 2004;169:376-378.

    In this case report, a peripheral nerve sheath tumor in the spinoglenoid notch was enhanced by the addition of intravenous gadolinium to aid in differentiating the mass from a cyst.

13. Carroll KW, Helms CA, Otte MT, et al: Enlarged spinoglenoid notch veins causing suprascapular nerve compression. *Skeletal Radiol* 2003;32:72-77.

    Distended veins in the spinoglenoid notch may be readily apparent on MRI and should be distinguished from paralabral ganglion cysts compressing the suprascapular nerve in the absence of labral tears, especially if percutaneous aspiration of a ganglion cyst is considered.

14. Chen AL, Ong BC, Rose D: Arthroscopic management of spinoglenoid cysts associated with SLAP lesions and suprascapular neuropathy. *Arthroscopy* 2003;19:E15-E21.

    In three patients, presurgical and postsurgical electromyography and MRI revealed cyst resolution and return of suprascapular nerve function after arthroscopic spinoglenoid cyst excision and labral repair.

15. Abboud JA, Silverberg D, Glaser DL, et al: Arthroscopy effectively treats ganglion cysts of the shoulder. *Clin Orthop Relat Res* 2006;444:129-133.

    The outcomes of eight patients with labral pathology and eight without labral pathology who underwent arthroscopic treatment are compared. Level of evidence: III.

16. Ferrick MR, Marzo J: Ganglion cyst of the shoulder associated with a glenoid labral tear and symptomatic glenohumeral instability: A case report. *Am J Sports Med* 1997;25:717-719.

17. Skirving AP, Kozak TK, Davis S: Infraspinatus paralysis due to spinoglenoid notch ganglion. *J Bone Joint Surg Br* 1994;76:588-591.

18. Takagishi K, Saitoh A, Tonegawa M, et al: Isolated paralysis of the infraspinatus muscle. *J Bone Joint Surg Br* 1994;76:584-587.

19. Fehrman DA, Orwin JF, Jennings R: Suprascapular nerve entrapment by ganglion cysts: A report of six cases with arthroscopic findings and review of the literature. *Arthroscopy* 1995;11:727-734.

20. Iannotti JP, Ramsey M: Arthroscopic decompression of a ganglion cyst causing suprascapular nerve compression. *Arthroscopy* 1996;12:739-745.

21. Chochole MH, Senker W, Meznik C: Glenoid-labral cyst entrapping the suprascapular nerve: Dissolution after arthroscopic debridement of an extended SLAP lesion. *Arthroscopy* 1997;13:753-755.

22. Leitschuh PH, Bone CM, Bouska W: Magnetic resonance imaging diagnosis, sonographically directed percutaneous aspiration, and arthroscopic treatment of a painful shoulder ganglion cyst associated with a SLAP lesion. *Arthroscopy* 1999;15:85-87.

23. Westerheide KJ, Karzel R: Ganglion cysts of the shoulder: Technique of arthroscopic decompression and fixation of associated type II superior labral anterior to posterior lesions. *Orthop Clin North Am* 2003;34:521-528.

   The diagnosis and treatment of ganglion cysts of the shoulder is discussed, with associated labral lesions.

24. Lichtenberg S, Magosch P, Habermeyer P: Compression of the suprascapular nerve by a ganglion cyst of the spinoglenoid notch: The arthroscopic solution. *Knee Surg Sports Traumatol Arthrosc* 2004;12:72-79.

   In six patients who underwent arthroscopic treatment of a spinoglenoid cyst, the cysts were decompressed by external pressure and labral tears were repaired. If no tear was present, capsulotomy was performed. Level of evidence: IV.

25. Baums MH, Seil R, Kettler M, et al: Treatment option in a SLAP-related ganglion cyst resulting in suprascapular nerve entrapment. *Arch Orthop Trauma Surg* 2006;126:621-623.

   In a case report of recurrent spinoglenoid cyst following open excision, the patient was successfully treated with arthroscopic SLAP repair and indirect cyst decompression.

26. Youm T, Matthews PV, El Attrache NS: Treatment of patients with spinoglenoid cysts associated with superior labral tears without cyst aspiration, debridement, or excision. *Arthroscopy* 2006;22:548-552.

   Successful outcomes were reported in 10 consecutive patients with SLAP tear and cyst. The cysts were decompressed by external pressure, and labral tears were repaired arthroscopically. Two patients had labral repair only, without cyst decompression. Level of evidence: IV.

27. Hirayama T, Takemitsu Y: Compression of the suprascapular nerve by a ganglion at the suprascapular notch. *Clin Orthop Relat Res* 1981;155:95-96.

28. Neviaser TJ, Ain BR, Neviaser R: Suprascapular nerve denervation secondary to attenuation by a ganglionic cyst. *J Bone Joint Surg Am* 1986;68:627-629.

29. Fritz RC, Helms C, Steinbach L: Suprascapular nerve entrapment: Evaluation with MR imaging. *Radiology* 1992;182:437-444.

30. Chiou HJ, Chou YH, Wu JJ, et al: Alternative and effective treatment of shoulder ganglion cyst: Ultrasonographically guided aspiration. *J Ultrasound Med* 1999;18:531-535.

31. Winalski CS, Robbins MI, Silverman SG, Davies JA: Interactive magnetic resonance image-guided aspiration therapy of a glenoid labral cyst: A case report. *J Bone Joint Surg Am* 2001;83-A:1237-1242.

# Chapter 32

# Complications of Arthroscopic Shoulder Surgery

Felix H. Savoie III, MD

J. Randall Ramsey, MD

*Larry D. Field, MD

## Introduction

The increased popularity of shoulder arthroscopy has been accompanied by an increase in reported complications. The most comprehensive analysis found a 0.76% incidence of complications in more than 14,000 arthroscopic subacromial decompression procedures.[1] A 4.8% rate and a 10.6% rate were reported among patients having arthroscopic shoulder surgery.[2,3] The incidence of complications can be reduced if the necessary precautions are integrated into the patient's care before, during, and after surgery.

## Presurgical Considerations

The nonsurgical treatment options should be exhausted before surgical intervention is scheduled. A thorough patient history should include the original injury and all earlier treatments, with an evaluation of the success or failure of each treatment. The physical examination should include careful assessment of the patient's passive and active range of motion. Unrecognized adhesive capsulitis, degenerative joint disease, or noninflammatory capsular contractures can lead to poor surgical results and a need for revision surgery; these conditions are easily recognized by testing range of motion while observing the scapula and spine for excessive contribution to the observed motion. The inferior capsule can be evaluated by inferior glide testing.

A complete neurologic examination is also required, because unrecognized neurologic injury can lead to poor results and persistent symptoms. Muscular atrophy, poor scapular control, or decreased sensation may indicate a neurologic injury.

The history and physical examination findings must be corroborated by diagnostic imaging. MRI is the preferred method, although the error rate is believed to be 15% or higher. The rate may be higher in community settings than in university teaching programs.[4] Artifact and signal changes associated with earlier surgery may be factors in MRI for patients being considered for revision surgery. A saline or gadolinium injection can improve the accuracy of MRI in these patients. Dynamic ultrasonography may be more useful than MRI in evaluating postsurgical soft-tissue defects, and CT arthrography with three-dimensional reconstruction can be used if bone defects are suspected. If nerve injury is suspected, the patient may benefit from electromyography or a nerve conduction study performed by a neurologist with a particular interest in shoulder disorders.

After the diagnostic evaluation is completed, the patient and surgeon should meet to formulate appropriate treatment. If necessary, the patient should be referred to the primary care physician for medical clearance; timely presurgical medical consultation can decrease the risk of postsurgical complications including deep vein thrombosis, pulmonary embolism, and death. Additional laboratory testing or other medical testing may be recommended for a patient at high risk of complications.

Pulmonary complications, including spontaneous pneumothorax unrelated to the surgery or interscalene block use, have been reported in patients with asthma who smoke cigarettes.[5] Published reports of thromboembolic events after arthroscopic surgery may stimulate the more routine use of compressive or pulsatile pressure stockings, heparin, enoxaparin or related compounds, and acetylsalicylic acid.[3] The use of these and other measures should be based on the recommendation of the patient's primary care physician.

Many pathologic conditions can be managed arthroscopically. However, most advanced surgical procedures require specialized equipment and skilled assistance. Following the surgery, regular therapy and family support are required. These considerations should be addressed before surgery to minimize the risk of complications during the surgery and the recovery period.[4,6-8]

---

*Larry D. Field, MD is a consultant or employee for Smith & Nephew.

# Intrasurgical Complications

## Anesthesia

The risks related to the use of anesthesia are the same in arthroscopic surgery as in other surgical procedures. However, arthroscopic surgery has additional risks related to specific positioning requirements, the length of the surgery, use of laryngeal mask airway management, and hypotensive anesthesia. Fluid overload has been reported during lengthy arthroscopic procedures, as well as airway compromise resulting from excessive fluid dissection.[2] Cerebral ischemia, hyponatremia, and hypertension caused by epinephrine in the infusion fluids also have been reported.[9]

Interscalene blocks, either alone or in conjunction with general anesthesia, are increasingly being used during shoulder arthroscopy. The associated complications include pneumothorax, phrenic nerve injury, seizures, and, in a few patients, permanent nerve injury. Transient paralysis of the recurrent laryngeal nerve or elevation of the hemidiaphragm because of phrenic nerve blockage may occur but is usually harmless.[2,5,9-14]

Skin slough has occurred in a few patients after skin infiltration by a local anesthetic containing epinephrine.[4,6-8]

## Positioning

Shoulder arthroscopy can be performed in the lateral decubitus position or the beach chair position, using single-traction or dual-traction devices. Either position is safe for most patients. However, as in any surgical procedure, excessive pressure from traction or prolonged surgical time can injure the neurovascular structures. Most neurologic injuries from traction and positioning are transient, although at least four permanent brachial plexus stretch injuries have been reported.[2,15] For shoulder arthroscopy in either position, limiting longitudinal traction to 12 lb and lateral traction to 7 lb has been recommended, with a surgical time limit of 2 hours.[2,15]

In the beach chair position, the patient's head and neck must be supported to prevent traction injuries or compressive cervical spine or brachial plexus injuries. Both transient and permanent neurologic injuries have been reported after surgery in the beach chair position.[13] The most common complication is transient brachial plexopathy, which has an incidence as high as 7%.[13] The greatest strain on the brachial plexus was found to occur with the unsupported arm in 10° of abduction and 0° of flexion.[13] The use of an arm support is encouraged to maintain a 45° or greater abduction and thereby prevent neurologic injury.[4] Unusual nerve complications associated with the head-positioning device include transient dysfunction of the hypoglossal and auricular nerves.[2,5,9,10,14]

The lateral decubitus position can also lead to neurologic injury from excessive traction. Judicious use of weight (determined based on arm size, with a maximum constant weight of 12 lb to maintain the arm in the proper position) usually minimizes the likelihood of permanent injury. Periodic release of the lateral joint distraction traction (at a maximum force of 7 lb) can also minimize neurologic injury when dual traction is used, in either the beach chair or lateral decubitus position. Incorrect placement of arm traction sleeves and compressive wraps can cause pressure injury to the antebrachial cutaneous nerves. In the lateral position, the arm on the nonsurgical side can be injured because of brachial plexus compression caused by failure to pad the axilla. Similarly, in the hip on the nonsurgical side, prolonged compression without proper cushioning can cause contusion of the lateral femoral cutaneous nerve. Unusual transient injuries have been reported in the radial nerve of the surgical arm and the peroneal nerve of the leg on the nonsurgical side.[2,11,12,15]

## Portals

Proper portal placement is essential in any arthroscopic procedure. The standard posterior portal is made in the joint line through the raphe in the infraspinatus muscle. A too-lateral placement can damage the infraspinatus tendon, and the articular cartilage can be damaged when the surgeon attempts to view the glenohumeral joint. A superior or inferior placement can damage the infraspinatus muscle, and an excessively medial placement can damage the articular cartilage of the humeral head. If the portal placement is too medial and inferior, the axillary nerve is at risk in the quadrangular space.

The placement of additional portals depends on the procedure. An anterior rotator interval portal lateral to the coracoid is standard in diagnostic arthroscopy. A low anteroinferior portal is used in routine anterior capsulolabral reconstruction performed for traumatic anterior instability with an inferior capsular shift. Before this portal is created, spinal needle testing is used to determine the inferior and lateral placement needed for reaching the inferior structures and inserting the anchor at an appropriate angle on the glenoid. In the beach chair position, a transsubscapularis portal may be necessary to allow inferior access during surgery performed to correct instability. However, the portal can damage the subscapularis tendon, which is thick in this area and may bind the cannula or instruments. In the lateral decubitus position, a transsubscapularis portal is not used because the area is too close to the musculocutaneous nerve. Alternative anterior portals inferior to the subscapularis are close to the axillary nerve and should be used carefully, if at all.[4,6-8] In general, modern instrumentation and techniques have eliminated the need for transsubscapularis and alternative anterior portals.

The anterosuperior portal is often used for suture management, visualization during anterior and posterior reconstruction, and anchor placement during a superior labrum anterior and posterior (SLAP) repair. The portal is established from a point near the anterolateral corner of the acromion, and it traverses the deltoid muscle and bursa before entering the glenohumeral joint at the most superior aspect of the rotator interval. Placement too close to the acromion can damage the deltoid tendon. Posterior placement can damage the tendon of the supraspinatus and the rotator cuff.

The posterosuperior portal (the portal of Wilmington) has been used for access to a posterosuperior SLAP tear. The portal is established under direct visualization using an outside-in technique. It is usually located near the posterolateral acromion and traverses the muscular part of the infraspinatus.

The Neviaser portal, used for suture placement and retrieval, is established in the V formed by the posterolateral clavicle and the medial aspect of the acromion. The suprascapular nerve lies directly below this area and can be injured by a too-vertical placement. The instruments used through this portal traverse the muscular part of the supraspinatus; anterior-to-posterior movement should be minimized to prevent disruption of the muscle-tendon junction.

Additional portals can be established around the coracoid for arthroscopic acromioclavicular reconstruction. All should be in line with or lateral to the coracoid. A portal placed medial to the coracoid traverses the brachial plexus area and increases the risk of injury to these structures.[4] For bursal surgery, a posterior, lateral, or anterior portal can be created with less risk of injury to associated structures, if it is above or even with the level of the supraspinatus and is directed into the bursa and not downward toward the neurovascular structures.

### Technique

Most technical errors are related to anchor and suture management (Table 1). Proper placement of anchors in the glenoid requires cornering on the junction of the glenoid face and neck; the purpose is to obtain bone adequate for avoiding pullout and subsequent articular cartilage injury. Anchors inserted onto the articular surface of the glenoid or humerus must be placed deep into the subchondral bone to prevent exposure when the articular cartilage later thins because of age or arthritis. Anchors inserted into the greater tuberosity during a rotator cuff repair can pull out or migrate because of poor bone quality or degenerative cysts. After insertion and before suture passage, every anchor placed into the shoulder should be tested to determine the adequacy of fixation.

Proper suture management is required to prevent tangling and rupture. Accessory portals can be used for

**Table 1 | Intrasurgical Technical Considerations and Related Complications**

| Risk Factor | Representative Complications |
|---|---|
| Imprecise portal placement | Muscle, tendon, nerve damage |
| Improper anchor placement | Pullout, migration |
| Improper suture retrieval | Tangling, rupture |
| Choice of suture material | Breakage, crepitus, tissue damage |
| Thermal capsulorrhaphy | Capsular damage, chondrolysis, nerve injury |
| Edema | Deviation of trachea, respiratory compromise |
| Knot placement | Mechanical impingement |

suture storage until retrieval is necessary. The anchor should be watched as the suture is pulled; the suture should move through the soft tissue without moving through the anchor.

Anchors of any material can migrate within the bone over time. Plastic and bioabsorbable anchors, especially tack-type implants, have also been associated with fragmentation, breakage, and loose body formation. Polyglycolic acid tacks have been associated with the formation of cysts and giant cell tumors in the early postsurgical period.[2,15-19]

Some complications, including crepitus and damage to surrounding soft tissue, are directly related to the suture material. In a study of 116 patients, no association was found between chondrolysis and suture material.[20] The strength of the currently used FiberWire sutures (Arthrex, Naples, FL) significantly decreases the risk of suture breakage. The FiberWire suture is a permanent material, and the position of the suture must be carefully evaluated during the repair; an incorrectly placed knot can cause mechanical impingement of the surrounding articular cartilage, rotator cuff, or bursal tissue. Synovitis has been associated with fraying of FiberWire and other permanent sutures, but this complication appears to be rare and related to mechanical debris generated during the cutting of the suture. The use of sharp cutting instruments may prevent excessive fraying and creation of mechanical debris.

The frequency of instrument breakage appears to be declining. However, a magnetic retriever should always be available during surgery for use if breakage occurs.

The reported complications of thermal capsulorrhaphy include capsular damage, chondrolysis, nerve injury, and more difficult revision surgery. The relationship of chondrolysis to specific technical factors has yet to be elucidated, although thermal devices used intra-articularly, pain pump catheters, local anesthesia, and suture materials have been implicated.[18] The thermal destruction of capsular tissues can be minimized by intermittent use of the probe, capsule striping rather than covering, and postsurgical shoulder immobilization for at least 4 weeks.

Fluid-related complications are usually associated with the use of a pump. Edema can be severe immediately after surgery, but it usually diminishes rapidly after the inflow is stopped.[12] The use of normal saline or lactated Ringer's solution seems to minimize the risk. However, excessive insufflation of the soft tissues can result in deviation of the trachea and respiratory compromise, necessitating intensive ventilation support. It is important to maintain low pressure and monitor the soft tissue to prevent fluid-related complications. An arbitrary 2-hour time limit is useful in preventing excessive fluid buildup. Air in the pump line can cause an air embolism when the patient is in the beach chair position.[5]

### Judgment

In reconstructive surgery, the surgeon must determine proper anchor and suture placement, evaluate the effect of the repair, and look for additional pathologies, such as a humeral avulsion of the glenohumeral ligament. In a repair of an unstable shoulder, the surgeon must check that the completed repair is anatomically correct and that the instability is no longer present. In a rotator cuff repair, the shoulder must be checked for adequacy of the repair when the arm is placed in adduction and when it is moved to internal and external rotation.

Knot placement on the anchor side rather than on the soft-tissue side can lead to mechanical impingement on the articular cartilage of the humeral head (after a Bankart repair) or on the rotator cuff (after a SLAP repair). Impingement can also occur if knotless anchors are used or if the suture crosses the articular cartilage as it is passed from the anchor to the repaired tissue. Impingement of the knot on the rotator cuff appears to be a significant complication during a posterior SLAP repair to correct internal impingement in a throwing athlete, when the knot impinges on the infraspinatus in abduction and external rotation. The surgeon should check for impingement by placing the arm in abduction and external rotation when the repair is completed. More than two suture knots placed on the top of the rotator cuff can cause impingement on the coracoacromial arch when the arm is in some positions. The surgeon should evaluate for the presence of impingement before the procedure is completed.

## Postsurgical Complications
### Infection

The reported incidence of infection after shoulder arthroscopy is less than 2%. *Staphylococcus aureus* is the most commonly isolated organism, although unusual organisms such as *Propionibacterium* are also found.[1] The use of perisurgical antibiotics has been recommended, although no conclusive statistical evidence is available to support this practice.[1] Minimizing surgical time and maintaining sterility can also decrease the risk of infection. Patient medical and nutritional status is the factor most highly correlated with the incidence of infection.

### Immobilization

Both mechanical and biologic factors should be considered in determining the patient's immobilization position. The repair must be protected while the patient is allowed to function as normally as possible. The patient must be positioned to induce the maximum blood flow into the repaired area; opposite-limb exercises can be used to improve circulation. Cold therapy may be useful in decreasing swelling and increasing circulation to the surgical site. The healing environment can be improved by providing a nutritious diet with vitamin and mineral supplementation.

An abduction sling can be used after a rotator cuff repair; the best position for increasing blood flow into the critical area is 30° to 45° of abduction.[21] Immobilization in a sling with the arm at the side has been recommended after open surgery to prevent abduction contractures, but this position reduces the blood supply to the repaired rotator cuff and puts the repair under tension.[21]

The surgeon must consider the rate at which the tissues heal to bone in determining when and how often the shoulder should be moved. At least 6 weeks is usually required before the repaired structures have healed sufficiently to tolerate stress. Motion that does not produce stress on the repair can be allowed before 6 weeks have elapsed.

The use of cyclooxygenase-2 inhibitors and most other nonsteroidal anti-inflammatory drugs should be avoided during the first week after surgery (the inflammatory phase of healing). Research is being conducted into factors that may increase the speed of healing.

### Rehabilitation

Complications can result from any level of exercise. The use and timing of postsurgical exercise are controversial, and the basic science of healing should be considered in decision making. Early attention to scapular position is essential in the rehabilitation of an injured shoulder. Most physicians advise patients to begin an individualized home exercise program early in the postsurgical period. The program should allow movement within the rehabilitation safe zone, as determined during surgery. Damage to the repaired shoulder during early physical therapy frequently results from poor communication between the therapist and the surgeon, who is responsible for determining the goals of early therapy, the rehabilitation safe zone, and the limits of motion.

Postsurgical capsulitis was formerly thought to be rare after arthroscopic rotator cuff surgery. However, a recent study found a 10% incidence at 3-month follow-up, with a 1% incidence of stiffness requiring surgical release.[3] Judicious use of steroids 3 months after surgery can help the patient regain motion. Arthroscopic release and removal of subbursal adhesions is the preferred treatment if steroid use is not successful and manipulation is not possible because of the risk of fracture or retearing a repaired rotator cuff.

### Return to Work or Play

Reinjury or discomfort when the patient returns to work or play is relatively common after shoulder surgery. The restoration of the injured shoulder achieved with physical therapy may be sufficient for most routine activities but not for the stress inherent in physical labor or a sport. Many therapists now offer work conditioning or work hardening for patients who have a physically demanding occupation. A gradual return to work activities may allow the patient to regain normal use and endurance without undue stress on the shoulder. Total body conditioning, including integrated rehabilitation and core strengthening exercise, is essential to the process.

Early scapular, core, and integrated rehabilitation are essential before a return to sports activity, as are open-chain plyometric exercises. Sport-specific conditioning should be completed and documented. If high-speed performance is part of the activity, it must be part of the rehabilitation.

## Summary

Arthroscopy is among the safest methods of surgically treating the shoulder, but the standard surgical risks of infection, failure to heal, and medical complications are present. The technical demands of arthroscopic surgery have correspondingly increased the risk of complications. Proper attention to the patient's anatomy, technical factors, and the postsurgical course should minimize the possibility of complications.

## Annotated References

1. Small NC: Complications in arthroscopy: The knee and other joints. Committee on Complications of the Arthroscopy Association of North America. *Arthroscopy* 1986;2:253-258.

2. Curtis AS, Snyder SJ, Delpizzo W, Ferkel RD, Karzel RP: Complications of shoulder arthroscopy. *Arthroscopy* 1992;8:395.

3. Brislin KJ, Field LD, Savoie FH: Complications after arthroscopic rotator cuff repair. *Arthroscopy* 2007; 23:124-134.

A retrospective review of 263 patients 3 months after arthroscopic rotator cuff repair found a 10.6% rate of complications, including stiffness (23 patients, 22 of whom had an uneventful resolution), failure to heal, infection, reflex sympathetic dystrophy, deep vein thrombosis, and death from an unrelated cause (1 patient each). These data establish a baseline complication rate for arthroscopic rotator cuff repair. Level of evidence: IV.

4. Severud EL, Ruotolo C, Abbott DD, Nottage WM: All-arthroscopic versus mini-open rotator cuff repair: A long-term retrospective outcome comparison. *Arthroscopy* 2003;19:234-238.

In a retrospective study of 64 shoulders, outcomes and complication rates after all-arthroscopic cuff repair were comparable to those of arthroscopic decompression with mini-open repair. There was a lower incidence of fibrous ankylosis and a trend to better early motion in the group treated with all-arthroscopic repair.

5. Oldman M, Peng Pi P: Pneumothorax after shoulder arthroscopy: Don't blame it on regional anesthesia. *Reg Anesth Pain Med* 2004;29:382-383.

A spontaneous pneumothorax developed after routine shoulder arthroscopy in a healthy 41-year-old man. No interscalene block had been used, and there were no associated risk factors. A postsurgical pneumothorax is not always the result of inadvertent puncture during surgery or regional anesthesia.

6. Gartsman GM: Arthroscopic Rotator Cuff Repair. *Clin Orthop Relat Res* 2001;390:95-106.

The advantages of arthroscopic surgery for repair of full-thickness rotator cuff tears must be balanced against the technical difficulty of the method, which limits its application to surgeons skilled in open and arthroscopic shoulder surgery.

7. Grondel RJ, Savoie FH, Field LD: Rotator cuff repairs in patients 62 years of age or older. *J Shoulder Elbow Surg* 2001;10:97-99.

Evaluation of repair of a rotator cuff tear in 97 shoulders (92 patients, age 62 years or older) found that 87% had a good or excellent result in terms of function, pain, and satisfaction.

8. Murray TF, Lajtai G, Mileski RM, Snyder SJ: Arthroscopic repair of medium to large full-thickness rotator cuff tears: Outcome at 2- to 6-year follow-up. *J Shoulder Elbow Surg* 2002;11:19-24.

At medium-term follow-up after 48 arthroscopic repairs of medium-sized or large rotator cuff tears, 44 of 45 patients were satisfied with the result. There were no complications requiring surgery, and 46 shoulders had a good or excellent result. One patient had evidence of repair failure.

9. Pohl A, Cullen DJ: Cerebral ischemia during shoulder surgery in the upright position: A case series. *J Clin Anesth* 2005;17:463-469.

Four patients with minimal risk factors sustained permanent neurologic injury during surgery in the beach chair position. Cranial blood flow may be decreased in this position, and blood pressure should be maintained at 80% of the presurgical resting value.

10. Haile DT, Frie ED, Hall BA, Spring J: Transient postoperative aphonia following instillation of bupivacaine into the shoulder joint. *Can J Anaesth* 2006;53: 212-213.

    A pain pump catheter was used for analgesia after a left shoulder arthroscopy, and the patient developed aphonia (complete loss of ability to speak) lasting 7 hours.

11. Esmail AN, Getz CL, Schwartz DM, et al: Axillary nerve monitoring during arthroscopic shoulder stabilization. *Arthroscopy* 2005;21:665-671.

    In 20 consecutive patients, activity within the axillary nerve was monitored during arthroscopic thermal and labral reconstructive procedures. Four of the 11 patients undergoing thermal capsulorrhaphy had a temporary increase in motor latency; no patients undergoing labral repair had changes. Level of evidence: II.

12. Lo IK, Burkhart SS: Immediate postoperative fluid retention and weight gain after shoulder arthroscopy. *Arthroscopy* 2005;21:605-610.

    Fluid retention during arthroscopic surgery was analyzed in 53 patients. Surgical time was strongly correlated with weight gain, and no complications were reported.

13. Bishop JY, Sprague M, Gelber J, et al: Interscalene regional anesthesia for shoulder surgery. *J Bone Joint Surg Am* 2005;87:974-979.

    Of 547 patients who had interscalene anesthesia performed by anesthesiologist trained in regional anesthesia, only 12 (2.3%) had minor complications.

14. Polzhofer GK, Peterson W, Hassenpflug J: Thromboembolic complication after arthroscopic shoulder surgery. *Arthroscopy* 2003;19:E129-E132.

    A patient had venous pulmonary thromboembolism after shoulder arthroscopy, which was partly caused by irritation of the subclavian vein from compression of the motor-driven shaver.

15. Weber SC, Abrams JS, Nottage WM: Complications associated with arthroscopic shoulder surgery. *Arthroscopy* 2002;18(suppl):88-95.

    A review of complications of arthroscopic shoulder surgery and their treatment found that the incidence was low.

For newer procedures, it is estimated at 5.8% to 9.5%. Underreporting makes assessing the incidence rates difficult.

16. Sassmannshausen G, Sukay M, Mair SD: Broken or dislodged poly-L-lactic acid bioabsorbable tacks in patients after SLAP lesion surgery. *Arthroscopy* 2006;22:615-619.

    After unsuccessful SLAP surgery, six patients had repair with bioabsorbable poly-L-lactic acid tacks. All tacks broke, and the lesions did not heal. MRI and repeat arthroscopy are recommended for symptoms of more than 6 months' duration after surgery. Level of evidence: IV.

17. Degreef I, Debeer P: Heterotopic ossification of the supraspinatus tendon after rotator cuff repair: A case report. *Clin Rheumatol* 2006;25:251-253.

    In a patient who had a rotator cuff repair in the presence of axillary nerve paralysis, postsurgical severe heterotopic ossification developed within the supraspinatus.

18. Levine WN, Clark AM Jr, D'Alessandro DR, et al: Chondrolysis following arthroscopic thermal capsulorrhaphy to treat shoulder instability: A report of two cases. *J Bone Joint Surg Am* 2005;87:616-621.

    The authors postulate that chondrolysis following thermal capsulorrhaphy is a cartilage basement membrane disorder not related to the use of heat probes, bupivacaine, cold fluids, preservatives, or suture and anchor materials. Nonetheless, the association with temperature probes should preclude capsule shrinkage for most patients.

19. Freehill MQ, Harms DJ, Humber SM, et al: Poly-L-lactic acid tack synovitis after arthroscopic stabilization of the shoulder. *Am J Sports Med* 2003;31: 643-647.

    Of 52 patients who underwent arthroscopic stabilization with an average of 2.2 poly-L-lactic acid tacks, 10 developed pain and 6 developed stiffness. All 10 had evidence of glenohumeral synovitis, and 3 had significant chondral damage on the humeral head.

20. Clavert P, Warner JJ: Panacryl synovitis: Fact or fiction? *Arthroscopy* 2005;21:200-203.

    Synovitis related to degradation of the Panacryl suture material was found in 1 of 116 patients. Level of evidence: IV.

21. Lohr JF, Uthoff HK: The microvascular pattern of the supraspinatus tendon. *Clin Orthop Relat Res* 1990;254:35-38.

# Section 5

# Arthritis and Arthroplasty

Section Editor
Michael Pearl, MD

# Chapter 33

# Nonarthroplastic Treatment of Glenohumeral Arthritis

*Theodore A. Blaine, MD

Sara Edwards, MD

## Introduction

Many arthritic conditions can affect the glenohumeral joint, including osteoarthritis, rheumatoid arthritis, osteonecrosis, posttraumatic arthritis, rotator cuff tear arthropathy, and postcapsulorrhaphy arthropathy. The most common is osteoarthritis, a slowly progressing disease that leads to cartilage thinning and ultimately to complete cartilage loss. A patient with osteoarthritis of the glenohumeral joint typically has pain and limited motion, leading to significantly decreased function and impairment of general health. Fortunately, several nonsurgical treatment options exist, including pharmacotherapy and physical therapy. Although shoulder arthroplasty is a reliable surgical solution for glenohumeral osteoarthritis, several nonarthroplastic treatments are available and may be preferable for some patients.

## Pathophysiology

Regardless of its primary cause, glenohumeral arthritis involves degradation and loss of articular cartilage. Other mechanical factors contribute to disease progression. As the subchondral plate stiffens, increased shear force in the cartilage layer alters the ultrastructure of the cartilage, increasing its water content and precipitating a cascade of events in the cartilage substance that results in inability to tolerate applied forces. As the cartilage becomes degraded, increasing friction within the affected joint induces mechanical destruction of the remaining cartilage. The adjacent bone is subjected to increased stress, which leads to subchondral sclerosis and microfissuring of the bone surface. Synovial fluid is compressed through the small fissures and forms cysts. Incongruence of the joint leads to painful loss of motion. Loose bodies may be present, as well as a large volume of clear yellow synovial fluid that is high in catabolic markers of cartilage degradation.

Osteoarthritis is primarily an osseous disease. However, it also affects the soft tissues of the shoulder. The contracted anterior capsule and subscapularis tendon limit external rotation and force the humeral head posteriorly. Posterior glenoid wear and erosion result from posterior subluxation of the humeral head; the reported incidence is as high as 45%.

Chronic posterior subluxation can lead to a redundant and attenuated posterior capsule. The synovium may become thickened, inflamed, and friable. The rotator cuff is usually intact, and full-thickness rotator cuff tears are not commonly found during arthroplasty. In a series of 110 shoulders undergoing replacement for osteoarthritis, only 4 (3.6%) had a full-thickness rotator cuff tear.[1]

The hallmark of inflammatory arthritis is chronic inflammation. Cartilage autoantigen (types II, IX, and XI collagen, aggrecan, and link protein), in conjunction with a major histocompatibility class II receptor by the antigen-presenting cell, is believed to initiate the inflammatory cascade. A complex interplay of inflammatory cells leads to synovial hypertrophy and destruction of articular cartilage. The most important cytokines in the etiology of inflammatory arthritis have been identified as tumor necrosis factor-$\alpha$ and interleukin-1. Inhibition of these cytokines eliminated the process of erosive arthritis in animal models.[2]

The pathology of noninflammatory arthritis is distinct from and less well understood than that of inflammatory arthritis. A cascade of cellular and biochemical events leads to the breakdown of articular cartilage, followed by insufficient cartilage repair. The biochemical events associated with osteoarthritis include a loss of collagen matrix, resulting in an increase in water content, alterations in proteoglycan composition, and an increase in proteolytic enzymes and cytokines. The acceleration of cartilage degradation and repair processes increases the production of cartilage breakdown products and the synthesis of cartilage proteoglycans.

*Theodore A. Blaine, MD is a consultant or employee for Sanofi-Aventis.

## Clinical Evaluation

### History

A typical patient reports the insidious onset of an unremitting dull ache in the shoulder. Stiffness and loss of function are common. A patient with severe osteoarthritis has difficulty performing activities of daily living. A patient whose osteoarthritis is less severe has muscle fatigue and difficulty with functions at the extreme of motion, such as reaching upward. The patient may have positional night pain that differs from the pain characteristic of rotator cuff disease. Cervical spondylosis is frequently present in patients with osteoarthritis and must be ruled out because symptoms of cervical disease can mimic those of a primary glenohumeral disorder.

### Physical Examination

The patient's shoulder contours, bony prominences, muscle atrophy, and deformity should be examined with both shoulders fully exposed. The cervical spine is thoroughly examined by assessing range of motion and performing the Spurling test. Neurologic sensory and motor function is assessed, and active and passive range of motion in elevation, external rotation, and internal rotation is measured and recorded. If the arthritis is advanced, capsular tightness and joint incongruity become severe, and the shoulder may be restricted to scapulothoracic motion. Because scapular movement does not contribute significantly to glenohumeral rotation, limitation of external rotation is a sensitive physical finding for shoulder arthritis.

### Imaging Studies

Cartilage pathology cannot be seen radiographically, and therefore the incidence of early shoulder arthritis may be underappreciated. The difficulty is compounded because the shoulder is not a weight-bearing joint. AP views in neutral, internal, and external rotation in the plane of the scapula are recommended, as well as axillary and supraspinatus outlet views. The classic radiographic findings include a narrowed joint space, subchondral sclerosis and cyst formation, flattened humeral and glenoid surfaces, and a ring of osteophytes around the humeral anatomic neck. The axillary view is most useful in evaluating posterior subluxation, glenoid wear, and joint space narrowing.

CT and MRI are rarely necessary. If the patient has severe posterior glenohumeral subluxation and glenoid wear, CT can be used during planning for glenoid resurfacing to assess the glenoid bone stock and version. MRI can be used to detect the presence of a rotator cuff tear.

## Nonsurgical Treatment

A patient with glenohumeral osteoarthritis initially should be treated for relief of symptoms using activity modification, anti-inflammatory drugs, acetaminophen, moist heat, and gentle physical therapy.[3,4] Corticosteroid injections into the glenohumeral joint can be helpful for a patient who wishes to postpone surgical intervention.

### Physical Therapy

Physical therapy is recommended to maintain motion and strength, but it should not be so aggressive as to aggravate the patient's condition. Unlike a patient with adhesive capsulitis, a patient with glenohumeral osteoarthritis should not be encouraged to push through the pain because structural changes associated with arthritis often mechanically block motion. Presurgical physical therapy for a patient with glenohumeral osteoarthritis should be focused on increasing the range of motion within mechanical limits and improving rotator cuff and scapulothoracic muscle strength.

A rheumatoid shoulder is likely to become stiff, so early treatment of any loss of motion is beneficial. To avoid exacerbating the inflammation, it is important for the patient to avoid excessive stretching or strengthening of an acutely inflamed shoulder. Active-assisted exercises can be performed after the inflammation subsides to improve strength and function.

### Pharmacotherapy

The use of oral nonsteroidal anti-inflammatory drugs (NSAIDs) is considered first-line systemic pharmacotherapy for patients with shoulder pain. In a small number of controlled clinical trials, both conventional NSAIDs and cyclooxygenase-2 (COX-2) selective inhibitors were found to be effective in patients with shoulder pain.[5] Unfortunately, a high risk of adverse gastrointestinal effects is associated with conventional NSAIDs, and an increased cardiovascular risk is associated with both conventional NSAIDs and COX-2 inhibitors.[6,7] The renal, hematologic, dermatologic, and adverse neurologic effects associated with NSAIDs also limit their use; elderly patients may be at particular risk. NSAIDs can also blunt the effects of diuretics, β-blockers, angiotensin-converting enzyme inhibitors, and angiotensin type-2 receptor antagonists in patients with hypertension and thereby lead to a loss of blood pressure control. NSAIDs can interfere with digoxin levels, potentiate anticoagulants, and interact with platelet inhibitors, thus leading to an increased risk of bleeding. A short course of NSAID therapy is generally recommended for patients with shoulder pain because the cardiovascular effects of NSAIDs and COX-2 inhibitors have been found only after long-term therapy (> 2 to 3 months). A proton pump inhibitor, which was found in clinical trials to heal ulcers and decrease the risk of ulcer recurrence, can be coadministered to decrease adverse gastrointestinal effects.

Acetaminophen is a reasonable alternative to NSAIDs for pain relief, although it too can increase the risk of cardiovascular disease. Two prospective cohort studies, of women 34 to 53 years of age and 51 to 77 years of age, found that women who took more than 500 mg per day of acetaminophen had a significantly higher risk than control subjects of developing hypertension, regardless of the age group.[8] The benefit of acetaminophen compared with NSAIDs is the decreased risk of adverse gastrointestinal effects.

Opioid analgesics can be used in a fixed-dose combination with a NSAID or acetaminophen. This treatment is usually for patients with moderate or severe pain. Opioids are not usually recommended for patients with significant respiratory depression, although the safety concerns vary with the product. The potential for abuse of opioids is significant.

A rheumatologist should coordinate the medication therapy of a patient with inflammatory arthritis of the shoulder. A number of available medications, including salicylates, analgesics, NSAIDs, gold, corticosteroids, chloroquine, sulfasalazine, D-penicillamine, methotrexate, and tumor necrosis factor blockers, can decrease symptoms and the rate of disease progression. The patient should be monitored for adverse effects.

Topical and intramuscular NSAID therapy was found to be effective for the short-term treatment of shoulder pain,[9] but it has not been investigated in randomized controlled trials compared with other therapies. Gallium nitrate, a topical ointment that inhibits interleukin-1β and tissue plasminogen activator, was shown to provide pain relief in a small case series of patients with arthritis.[10]

Corticosteroid injections are commonly used to treat shoulder pain. Current guidelines recommend subacromial injection of a mixture of a local anesthetic and a short-acting corticosteroid for patients with a rotator cuff disorder that has not responded to physical therapy or NSAIDs.[11] The considerable variability in response to corticosteroid injections may reflect the degree of inflammation involved in a patient's acute pathology. Steroid injections may be most beneficial in patients with inflammatory disease and less effective in those with long-term pain, such as from osteoarthritis. Other variables affecting the outcome may be needle placement, anatomic site of inflammation, the frequency and dose of injection, and the type of corticosteroid.

Current guidelines do not specifically recommend corticosteroid injections for patients with glenohumeral osteoarthritis.[11] Nevertheless, corticosteroid injections are widely used in clinical practice for patients with shoulder pain of any etiology, and occasionally they are used in conjunction with physical therapy as an initial treatment for shoulder pain. Response to the injection is usually rapid, and pain relief may enhance the benefits achieved with physical therapy.

An increasing body of evidence supports the use of intra-articular injection of a sodium hyaluronate preparation for patients with shoulder pain.[12-15] The hyaluronans are large polysaccharide molecules found naturally in the synovial fluid. They help create a viscous environment that cushions joints and preserves normal function. Several biologic and biomechanical effects may play a role in pain inhibition, such as the enhancement of endogenous hyaluronan and cartilage synthesis and inhibition of cartilage degradation, inflammation, and secondary pain mediators. Hyaluronans are used extensively in the management of osteoarthritis of the knee, and clinical trial results have documented their effectiveness.[16-18] Small-scale studies of patients with rotator cuff tears, extra-articular arthritis of the shoulder, adhesive capsulitis, or shoulder osteoarthritis found that hyaluronic acid injections have significant benefit in relieving pain, improving range of motion, and decreasing the use of oral analgesics.

## Nonarthroplastic Surgical Treatment

The primary indications for surgical treatment of glenohumeral osteoarthritis are pain and loss of function that persists after nonsurgical management. Shoulder arthroplasty is rarely performed to improve function or range of motion, unless the patient has pain. The patient's general health, activity level, and motivation should be considered. Progressive bone loss, especially on the glenoid side, is one of many factors that may influence decision making. The timing of shoulder arthroplasty is not straightforward; patients are usually advised to delay reconstructive surgery as long as possible. Active infection and complete functional loss of both the rotator cuff and deltoid muscles are absolute contraindications to arthroplasty.

Prosthetic arthroplasty has become the standard treatment of severe shoulder osteoarthritis. However, other surgical options should also be part of the surgeon's armamentarium.

### Open Débridement and Soft-Tissue Balancing

One study found uniformly poor results after open release, débridement, removal of osteophytes, and soft-tissue balancing for osteoarthritis.[19] However, 10 patients with osteoarthritic changes were successfully treated with open release of the subscapularis and anterior capsule, after previous anterior instability surgery. All patients had decreased pain and increased external rotation at an average 3.5-year follow-up.[20] The goal is to normalize shoulder joint biomechanics through soft-tissue balancing, so that the joint forces are more evenly distributed and articulation involves the less affected cartilage surfaces.

### Arthroscopic Débridement

Patients with early glenohumeral osteoarthritis who are not candidates for prosthetic replacement may benefit from arthroscopic irrigation and débridement. Synovial

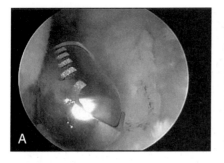
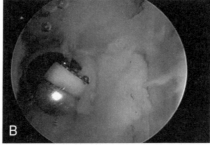
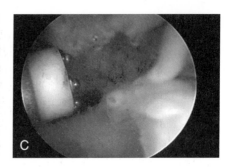

**Figure 1** Arthroscopic view of a left glenohumeral joint from the posterior portal. **A,** Débridement of loose, unstable cartilage flaps is performed using an arthroscopic shaver. Note the severe cartilage wear on the posterior glenoid. **B,** Synovial débridement is performed using electrocautery. **C,** Capsular release of the posterior capsule is performed between the posterior labrum and the overlying rotator cuff.

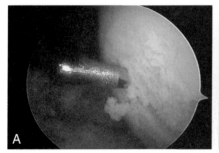
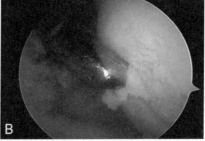
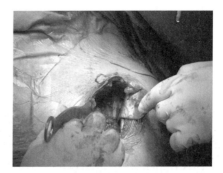

**Figure 2** Arthroscopic view of a left glenohumeral joint from the posterior portal, showing severe wear of the humeral head. **A,** A chondral pick is positioned over the focal defect. **B,** The chondral pick is seated in the focal defect to stimulate an ingrowth of bone marrow cells from the subchondral bone.

**Figure 3** The glenoid exposed in preparation for meniscal allograft implantation. A Fukuda retractor is used to retract the humeral head, and a spiked Darrach retractor is placed on the anterior scapular neck.

débridement is followed by débridement of any loose, unstable cartilage flaps; capsular release is an important component of the procedure (Figure 1). If focal cartilage defects are present, chondral picking or drilling may be performed to stimulate pluripotent cells from the subchondral bone marrow to populate the defect (Figure 2). This technique is not recommended if the patient has severe degeneration or global cartilage defects.

Coexistent conditions contributing to the symptoms, such as subacromial impingement, can be addressed during surgery. In a review of 36 patients who had arthroscopic subacromial decompression in addition to glenohumeral débridement, the results were satisfactory (L'Insalata score, 90) in patients with Outerbridge grade I, II, or III changes. The results were less satisfactory (L'Insalata score, 50) in patients with an Outerbridge grade IV change.[21] Intermediate-term results indicated that the procedure produces significant pain relief and, therefore, may delay the need for arthroplasty. Results after arthroscopic treatment of 49 patients with early glenohumeral osteoarthritis were 93% good or excellent at an average 4.3-year follow-up.[22] However, the condition of 75% of the patients worsened following arthroscopic débridement. Arthroscopy is contraindicated in patients with severe arthritis, complete loss of joint space, large osteophytes, or posterior glenohumeral subluxation.

## Biologic Resurfacing

Biologic resurfacing is an option for treating patients with glenohumeral arthritis. Typically, a lateral meniscus allograft has the best configuration to match the native glenoid[23] (Figures 3 and 4). It is usually performed, with or without humeral resurfacing, on young patients who are not candidates for shoulder arthroplasty, and the results have been variable.[24] Both open and arthroscopic techniques have been described.[25,26] The allograft can be implanted with a rim of suture anchors around the glenoid; suture anchors are then passed through the edge of the allograft and advanced to the glenoid using a parachute technique (Figure 5). Arthroscopic resurfacing of the joint with meniscal allograft and porcine soft tissue graft has been described,[25] but no long-term results are available.

## Resection Arthroplasty

The success of prosthetic arthroplasty has significantly limited the need for humeral head resection. This procedure is used only in the presence of resistant infection or after an unsuccessful arthroplasty with extensive bone loss, if reimplantation is contraindicated.[27] Although the procedure may relieve pain, it results in poor function and range of motion because the fulcrum of the shoulder is

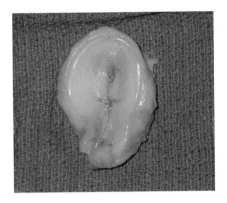

**Figure 4** A lateral meniscus allograft as sutured and fashioned to match the elliptical shape of the native glenoid, in preparation for implantation.

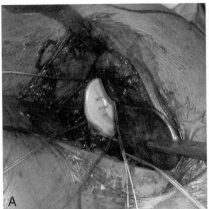

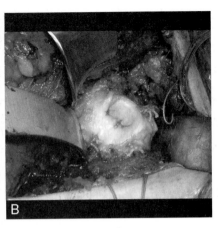

**Figure 5** Suture anchors implanted around the glenoid rim. **A,** The sutures are passed through the rim of the meniscal allograft using a parachute technique. The allograft is then advanced to the glenoid over the sutures. **B,** The sutures are tied to secure the meniscus to the glenoid.

lost. Active forward elevation is typically limited to between 40° and 90°, with little or no active internal or external rotation.[28] Resection arthroplasty currently has no role in the treatment of primary osteoarthritis with preserved bone stock and functional musculature.

### Glenohumeral Arthrodesis

Since the introduction of shoulder arthroplasty, the need for glenohumeral arthrodesis has markedly diminished. Shoulder fusion is indicated for a patient with combined deltoid and rotator cuff paralysis, which can occur because of an upper brachial plexus injury; an active, chronic low-grade infection; or severe bone loss following radical shoulder-girdle tumor resection. It can also be indicated after an unsuccessful reconstructive procedure.[29,30] It is rarely required for the treatment of primary osteoarthritis. The technique includes reconstruction with or without intercalary allograft bone at the glenohumeral articulation. Salvage to shoulder arthroplasty has not been successful, and, therefore, shoulder arthrodesis should be regarded as a last resort.[31]

## Summary

Several nonarthroplastic options exist for the treatment of osteoarthritis of the shoulder. All patients with glenohumeral arthritis should undergo a trial of nonsurgical therapy before any surgical intervention. The surgeon must especially be familiar with nonarthroplastic options for the management of arthritis in younger patients and patients unable to receive a prosthesis.

## Annotated References

1. Pollock RG, Higgs GB, Codd TP, et al: Total shoulder replacement for the treatment of primary glenohumeral osteoarthritis. *J Shoulder Elbow Surg* 1995;4:S12.

2. Ratcliffe A, Flatow EL, Roth N, et al: Biochemical markers in synovial fluid identify early osteoarthritis of the glenohumeral joint. *Clin Orthop Relat Res* 1996;330:45-53.

3. Meislin RJ, Sperling JW, Stitik TP: Persistent shoulder pain: Epidemiology, pathophysiology, and diagnosis. *Am J Orthop* 2005;34(suppl 12):5-9.

   Persistent shoulder pain is common and often has a multifactorial etiology (bursitis, tendinitis, rotator cuff tear, adhesive capsulitis, impingement syndrome, osteonecrosis, glenohumeral osteoarthritis, or traumatic injury). This review focuses on persistent shoulder pain associated with rotator cuff disorders, adhesive capsulitis, and glenohumeral osteoarthritis. Level of evidence: V.

4. Moskowitz RW, Blaine TA: An overview of treatment options for persistent shoulder pain. *Am J Orthop* 2005;34(suppl 12):10-15.

   The treatment options for persistent shoulder pain include physical therapy, rest, heat, and administration of oral analgesics. The use and benefit of intra-articular corticosteroid injections and sodium hyaluronate are described. Level of evidence: V.

5. Raffa RB, Clark-Vetri R, Tallarida RJ, Wertheimer AI: Combination strategies for pain management. *Expert Opin Pharmacother* 2003;4:1697-1708.

   Combination strategies for the use of oral analgesics can decrease the incidence of adverse effects and lead to synergy between the medications. Basic science, clinical, and pharmacoeconomic issues related to analgesic combinations are discussed.

6. Graham DJ: COX-2 inhibitors, other NSAIDs, and cardiovascular risk: The seduction of common sense. *JAMA* 2006;296:1653-1656.

Cardiovascular risk factors related to the use of COX-2 inhibitors and traditional anti-inflammatory drugs are summarized.

7. Graham DJ, Campen D, Hui R, et al: Risk of acute myocardial infarction and sudden cardiac death in patients treated with cyclo-oxygenase 2 selective and non-selective non-steroidal anti-inflammatory drugs: Nested case-control study. *Lancet* 2005;365: 475-481.

Data from patients ages 18 to 84 years who were treated with a NSAID showed an increased risk of serious coronary heart disease with the use of rofecoxib compared with celecoxib. Naproxen did not protect against serious coronary heart disease. Level of evidence: III.

8. Forman JP, Stampfer MJ, Curhan GC: Non-narcotic analgesic dose and risk of incident hypertension in US women. *Hypertension* 2005;46:500-507.

Hypertension is a common problem that can be exacerbated by the use of anti-inflammatory drugs, particularly acetaminophen and NSAIDs. Aspirin was not found to increase hypertension in women.

9. Spacca G, Cacchio A, Forgacs A, Monteforte P, Rovetta G: Analgesic efficacy of a lecithin-vehiculated diclofenac epolamine gel in shoulder periarthritis and lateral epicondylitis: A placebo-controlled, multicenter, randomized, double-blind clinical trial. *Drugs Exp Clin Res* 2005;31:147-154.

In a randomized, controlled trial, 158 patients received diclofenac gel or a placebo. Significant improvement, measured using the visual analog pain score, was achieved by using the topical gel for the treatment of shoulder arthritis.

10. Eby G: Elimination of arthritis pain and inflammation for over 2 years with a single 90 mm, topical 14% gallium nitrate treatment: Case reports and review of actions of gallium III. *Med Hypotheses* 2005;65:1136-1141.

Gallium III, an inhibitor of bone resorption, was reported to be effective in the treatment of arthritis in animal models. This case series describes the efficacy of gallium III treatment for osteoarthritis and adhesive capsulitis in several human patients.

11. American Academy of Orthopaedic Surgeons: *AAOS Clinical Guideline on Shoulder Pain Support Document.* Rosemont, IL, American Academy of Orthopaedic Surgeons, 2001.

This document provides clinical guidelines for the diagnosis, nonsurgical treatment, and surgical treatment of different shoulder pain etiologies.

12. Shibata Y, Midorikawa K, Emoto G, et al: Clinical evaluation of sodium hyaluronate for the treatment of patients with rotator cuff tear. *J Shoulder Elbow Surg* 2001;10:209-216.

A randomized, controlled comparison of the efficacy of subacromial injection of cortisone or sodium hyaluronate

in patients with a rotator cuff tear found no significant difference in outcome or pain relief.

13. Ramonda R, Franceschini M, Leardini G: Treatment of shoulder periarthritis with hyaluronic acid. *Riv It Biol Med* 1998;18(suppl 2):51.

14. Itokazu M, Matsunaga T: Clinical evaluation of high-molecular-weight sodium hyaluronate for the treatment of patients with periarthritis of the shoulder. *Clin Ther* 1995;17:946-955.

15. Leardini G, Perbellini A, Franceschini M, et al: Intra-articular injections of hyaluronic acid in the treatment of painful shoulder. *Clin Ther* 1988:10:521-526.

16. Altman RD, Moskowitz R: Intraarticular sodium hyaluronate (Hyalgan) in the treatment of patients with osteoarthritis of the knee: A randomized clinical trial. Hyalgan Study Group. *J Rheumatol* 1998;25:2203-2212.

17. Lo GH, LaValley M, McAlindon T, Felson DT: Intra-articular hyaluronic acid in treatment of knee osteoarthritis: A meta-analysis. *JAMA* 2003;290:3115-3121.

18. Wang CT, Lin J, Chang CJ, Lin YT, Hou SM: Therapeutic effects of hyaluronic acid on osteoarthritis of the knee: A meta-analysis of randomized controlled trials. *J Bone Joint Surg Am* 2004;86-A:538-545.

A meta-analysis of 20 blinded, randomized controlled trials compared intra-articular injections of hyaluronic acid and a placebo to treat osteoarthritis of the knee. Hyaluronic acid injection was found to decrease symptoms. Patients who were older than 65 years or had advanced osteoarthritis were less likely to benefit. Level of evidence: II.

19. Neer CS II: Replacement arthroplasty for glenohumeral arthritis. *J Bone Joint Surg* 1974;56A:1-13.

20. MacDonald PB, Hawkins RJ, Fowler PJ, et al: Release of the subscapularis for internal rotation contracture and pain after anterior repair for recurrent anterior dislocation of the shoulder. *J Bone Joint Surg* 1992; 74A:734-737.

21. Guyette TM, Bae H, Warren RF, Craig E, Wickiewicz TL: Results of arthroscopic subacromial decompression in patients with subacromial impingement and glenohumeral degenerative joint disease. *J Shoulder Elbow Surg* 2002;11:299-304.

A retrospective review of 36 patients with arthroscopic subacromial decompression and concurrent glenohumeral degenerative joint disease found improved shoulder function and pain relief in patients with mild to moderate arthritis. Those with more advanced arthritis had less consistent results.

22. Weinstein DM, Bucchieri JS, Pollock RG, Flatow EL, Bigliani LU: Arthroscopic debridement of the shoulder for osteoarthritis. *Arthroscopy* 2000;16:471-476.

23. Creighton RA, Cole BJ, Nicolson GP, Romeo AA, Lorenz EP: Effect of lateral meniscus allograft on shoulder articular contact areas and pressures. *J Shoulder Elbow Surg* 2007;16:367-372.

   A cadaver study found that biologic resurfacing with a lateral meniscus allograft of the glenohumeral joint is supported by decreased forces (a statistically significant decrease in total force and a decrease in contact area) on the glenoid surface. Level of evidence: I.

24. Sperling JW, Steinmann SP, Cordasco FA, Henshaw DR, Coons DA, Burkhead WZ: Shoulder arthritis in the young adult: Arthroscopy to arthroplasty. *Instr Course Lect* 2006;55:67-74.

   This review article describes nonarthroplastic treatment alternatives for young adult patients with shoulder arthritis. Arthroscopic treatment or interposition arthroplasty can provide symptomatic relief without radically compromising future procedures. Level of evidence: V.

25. Pennington WT, Bartz BA: Arthroscopic glenoid resurfacing with meniscal allograft: A minimally invasive alternative for treating glenohumeral arthritis. *Arthroscopy* 2005;21:1517-1520.

   An arthroscopic method of glenoid resurfacing with a meniscal allograft is described for patients with an arthritic condition of the glenohumeral joint. Level of evidence: IV.

26. Themistocleous GS, Zalavras CG, Zachos VC, Itamura JM: Biologic resurfacing of the glenoid using a meniscal allograft. *Tech Hand Up Extrem Surg* 2006;10:145-149.

   In a technique developed to allow secure fixation of a meniscal allograft to the glenoid in combination with hemiarthroplastic replacement of the humeral head, the meniscal horns are sutured together to fashion an ovoid allograft that closely matches the circumference of the glenoid. The wedge shape of the meniscus may enhance stability and improve pain relief. Level of evidence: V.

27. Braman JP, Sprague M, Bishop J, Lo IK, Lee EW, Flatow EL: The outcome of resection shoulder arthroplasty for recalcitrant shoulder infections. *J Shoulder Elbow Surg* 2006;15:549-553.

   In a retrospective case series, none of seven patients who underwent resection arthroplasty following infection after shoulder arthroplasty had a satisfactory outcome using Neer's criteria, although all were able to reach their opposite axilla, back pocket, perineum, and mouth. Level of evidence: IV.

28. Cofield RH: Shoulder arthrodesis and resection arthroplasty. *Instr Course Lect* 1985;34:268-277.

29. Wilde AH, Brems JJ, Boumphrey FR: Arthrodesis of the shoulder: Current indications and operative technique. *Orthop Clin North Am* 1987;18:463-472.

30. Gonzalez-Diaz R, Rodriguez-Merchan EC, Gilbert MS: The role of shoulder fusion in the era of arthroplasty. *Int Orthop* 1997;21:204-209.

31. Sperling JW, Cofield RH: Total shoulder arthroplasty after attempted shoulder arthrodesis: Report of three cases. *J Shoulder Elbow Surg* 2003;12:302-305.

   This three-patient study suggests that patients may have improved pain after conversion of attempted arthrodesis to arthroplasty, although functional improvements are minimal. The status of the rotator cuff tendons and muscles appears to affect functional outcome.

# Chapter 34

# Humeral Anatomy and Reconstruction

Samer S. Hasan, MD, PhD

## Introduction

Prosthetic shoulder arthroplasty is effective in restoring comfort and function in patients whose normal shoulder anatomy has been altered by a condition such as primary osteoarthritis, secondary arthritis resulting from earlier instability, capsulorrhaphy, fracture or other trauma, osteonecrosis, or inflammatory arthritides, including rheumatoid arthritis. As a result, prosthetic shoulder arthroplasty is becoming more common; in 2004, approximately 29,000 procedures were performed in the United States.[1] There are two types of prosthetic shoulder arthroplasty procedures: total shoulder arthroplasty, which includes resurfacing of both the humeral head and glenoid; and resurfacing of the humeral head, which is accomplished by either hemiarthroplasty or surface replacement.

Modern shoulder arthroplasty began with the development of the Neer prosthesis in the early 1950s.[2] A decade later, prosthesis use had expanded from the treatment of certain proximal humerus fractures to the treatment of fracture sequelae and arthritis. As the concept of total joint arthroplasty gained acceptance during the 1970s, glenoid resurfacing became more common. During the 1980s, second-generation modular implants, which offered different head and stem sizes, replaced the original Neer monobloc design. The goal of third-generation prosthetic designs is to replicate normal shoulder anatomy more accurately than the second-generation implants. These implants have ushered in an era of prosthetic adaptability, although controversy remains as to the extent to which adaptability is necessary to achieve optimal shoulder function. Other factors, such as surgical indications, surgical technique (including soft-tissue release and implant positioning), perisurgical care, and rehabilitation are also important determinants of a patient's outcome, and their impact may exceed that of a novel prosthetic design.

## Anatomy

Rigorous study of the shoulder anatomy relevant to prosthetic geometry began during the 1990s. The initial studies found wide variability in normal humeral anatomy.[3,4] Subsequent studies applied this variability to shoulder arthroplasty and prosthetic design, determining that normal humeral geometry differs substantially from that of typical humeral implants.[3,5-9]

Humeral anatomy can by defined by several important metrics (Figure 1). The orthopaedic axis of the humerus is defined using the center of the humeral intramedullary canal or, equivalently, the center of the best-fitting reamer within that canal.[3,10] Anatomic studies found that the center of the humeral head typically is not along this axis but instead is offset in both the coronal and transverse planes (Figure 2). This offset varies but is typically medial and posterior.[3,5,8,11]

The humeral head is retroverted with respect to the humeral shaft, although the degree of retroversion is highly variable. Retroversion can be defined with respect to proximal and distal references. The three proximal references are the plane of the articular surface, a line connecting the center of rotation to the central point on the articular surface, and a line connecting the greater tuberosity to the central point on the articular surface.[12] The distal reference is the transepicondylar axis or the long axis of the forearm. The bicipital groove has been proposed as a reference if the distal humeral anatomy is distorted.[3,13] Its usefulness as a reference may be limited, however, because it rotates internally from proximal to distal[14] and its relationship to the articular surface is highly variable.[14,15] Retroversion was found to vary from -5° to 55°, depending on the methodology used, with an average of 20° to 30°.[5,7,11]

The proximal humerus, unlike the proximal femur, has no neck, and therefore the inclination angle is actually a head-shaft angle.[12] Several studies found that the mean inclination angle is 40°, although it varies substantially, from 30° to more than 50°.[5,8,11] These measurements are somewhat imprecise because the base of the articular surface is irregular and can only be approximated by a plane; in addition, the conical shape of the proximal humeral canal precludes precise determination of the orthopaedic axis.[8,16] A cadaver study of paired

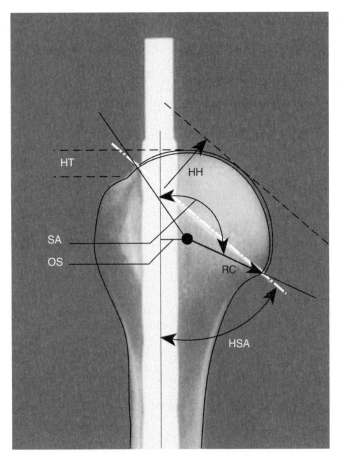

**Figure 1** Radiograph marked to show the center of rotation (*black dot*), base of the articular surface (*dashed white line*), orthopaedic axis (*vertical black line*), head height (HH), head-shaft angle (HSA), head-to-tuberosity height (HT), medial offset (OS), radius of curvature (RC), and surface arc (SA). (*Reproduced with permission from Pearl ML, Volk AG: Coronal plane geometry of the proximal humerus relevant to prosthetic arthroplasty. J Shoulder Elbow Surg 1996;5:320-326.*)

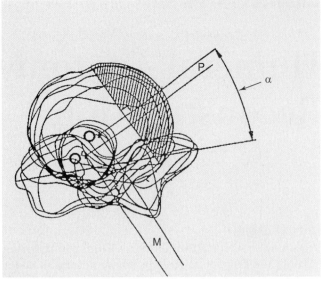

**Figure 2** Schematic drawing of the offset in the transverse plane; the offset is variable but typically is medial and posterior. α = retroversion angle, M = medial offset, P = posterior offset. (*Adapted with permission from Boileau P, Walch G: The three-dimensional geometry of the proximal humerus: Implications for surgical technique and prosthetic designs. J Bone Joint Surg Br 1997;79:859.*)

humeri found significant differences in head inclination between the right and left shoulders.[11]

The articular surface of the proximal humerus varies in size and orientation. It is essentially spherical, particularly in its central portion.[16] The size of the articular surface is defined by two metrics: the radius of curvature and the head height or thickness of the articular surface. The radius of curvature ranges from 20 mm to 30 mm, and it is typically smaller in women than in men.[4,5,8,11,12] One study found that the radius of curvature was greater in the coronal plane than in the transverse plane.[4] The head height ranges from 15 mm to 21 mm.[4,5,8,11] Although the dimensions of these two metrics vary greatly, they are highly correlated with each other: the head height measurement is typically three quarters of the radius of curvature, regardless of head size.[4,8] The trigonometric relationship of the surface arc to the head height and radius of curvature is as follows: surface arc = 180 – 360 arcsin[1 – (head height)/(radius of curvature)]/π. Consequently, the surface arc is approximately 150°.[8]

The position of the humeral head can be defined by the relationship of the top of the humeral head to the top of the greater tuberosity. This head-to-tuberosity height ranges from 2 mm to 10 mm.[4,8] It is not correlated with the radius of curvature or the head height.[8] Regardless of humeral head size, the articular surface is inclined relative to the shaft; although the angle of the incline varies, the articular surface does not rise more than 10 mm above the tuberosities.[8]

## Humeral Head Implants

The design of modular humeral head implants that can replicate normal anatomy is based on the interrelationships of the metrics. Using elegant computer simulations, researchers found second-generation press-fit implants to be generally inadequate for re-creating normal humeral anatomy.[9] An optimization algorithm was developed that allows a surgeon to select the second-generation head-and-stem combination that will least displace the patient's articular surface and center of rotation. The prosthetic systems selected using this algorithm displace the center of rotation superiorly and laterally. To compensate for this shift, a smaller head may be chosen, resulting in a decrease of 11° to 41° in the articular surface arc[9] (Figure 3). Cemented second-generation implants may re-create normal anatomy better than cementless implants because the humeral implant can be positioned within the cement mantle to compensate for constraints imposed by implant design.[4] The newer, third-generation implants are more adaptable, and they can be implanted without the use of cement.[4,6]

The surgeon's ability to replicate normal anatomy is increased if a range of humeral head sizes is available. However, the complexity of intrasurgical decision making and potential for errors are also increased. The cost of maintaining a large inventory of humeral head implants in different sizes is also a consideration.

The use of modular humeral head-and-stem implants is intended to permit a more anatomic replacement. However, modular implants have a prosthetic collar-and-taper lock mechanism that suspends the head from the osteotomy, often by several millimeters, and this gap between the collar and humeral head diminishes the surface arc available for glenohumeral motion[17] (Figure 3). The head must be larger than the collar, so that the collar cannot abrade the glenoid at the limits of the arc of motion.[16] Some humeral head designs have a peripheral chamfer, which reduces the articular surface arc,[10] and newer humeral head designs have a recessed base that fits over the collar to eliminate the gap between the humeral head and the collar.[5]

The extent to which the normal humeral head must be replicated anatomically is unclear. Joint destruction often precludes a truly anatomic replacement.[16] Nonetheless, it is usually undesirable to use an implant with a radius of curvature markedly different from that of the resected humeral head. The normal shoulder is a highly conforming joint; a small amount of translation is possible because both the labrum and articular cartilage are reversibly deforming.[18] Prosthetic components are not deformable, so the radius of curvature of the native glenoid and labrum must exceed that of the humeral head to allow for physiologic translation.[16,19]

Anatomic studies suggest that a mismatch of 2 mm to 6 mm re-creates normal glenohumeral translation during active arm movement.[4,6,18] If the radius of curvature of the humeral head matches that of the glenoid, then the joint is conforming and no translation is possible without loading the rim.[19] If the radius of curvature of the humeral head replacement is too small, then abnormal glenohumeral kinematics may result. The humeral head may translate excessively on the glenoid, and the tuberosity may impinge on the acromion and internally on the glenoid rim.[20] A smaller-than-average humeral head may produce point loading on the glenoid and accelerate chondral wear.[10]

Glenohumeral kinematics also are influenced by the thickness of the humeral head replacement. Decreasing the thickness by only 5 mm reduces the surface arc available for differential motion and diminishes glenohumeral rotation by 24° in the coronal plane.[21] Increasing the thickness of the humeral head replacement leads to a similar motion loss; a 5-mm increase reduces glenohumeral rotation by 20° to 26° and results in earlier obligate translation of the humeral head on the glenoid.[19]

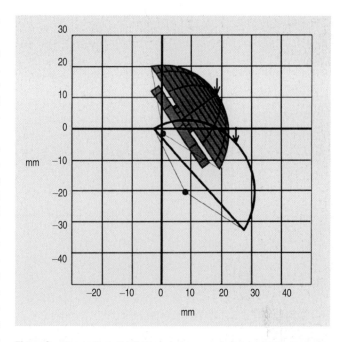

**Figure 3** Diagram illustrating the typical discrepancy between native humeral anatomy and a best-fit prosthesis selected using computer simulation. The prosthesis has a greater head-to-tuberosity height and a smaller articular surface arc. The gap between the prosthesis head and the collar contributes to the decrease in surface arc. *(Reproduced with permission from Pearl ML, Kurutz S: Geometric analysis of commonly used prosthetic systems for proximal humeral replacement. J Bone Joint Surg Am 1999;81: 666.)*

A thicker implant also increases the potential for rotator cuff strain and injury.[10] As a result, overstuffing the glenohumeral joint is not recommended. Smaller prosthetic heads within the anatomic range perform better than larger heads.[19]

## Humeral Osteotomy

The humeral osteotomy is a critical step in prosthetic shoulder arthroplasty, regardless of the type of implant used. However, the strategy for humeral osteotomy is determined by the type of implant. A third-generation system, which has a variable prosthetic inclination, typically allows humeral head resection at the base of the articular surface. Circumferential removal of peripheral osteophytes before the osteotomy facilitates the definition of this plane. The osteotomy must not violate the superior and posterior rotator cuff insertions, which are easily palpable and serve as useful intrasurgical reference points.[7,10]

The extent to which a third-generation stem can accommodate the osteotomy depends on the available prosthetic inclinations. Implants with an inclination angle of 38° or 44° accommodated 95% of shoulders when a 3° mismatch from the native angle was allowed.[11] Most third-generation implants currently in use have several inclination angles.

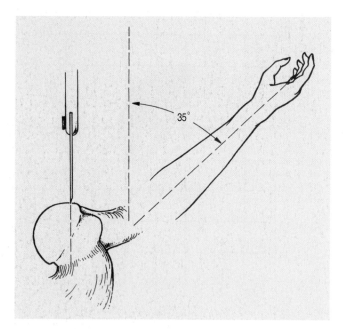

**Figure 4** Drawing showing that the use of the forearm axis to guide the osteotomy in a predetermined but excessive amount of retroversion will injure the posterior rotator cuff insertion if the native shoulder has considerably less retroversion. *(Reproduced with permission from Pearl ML, Volk AG: Retroversion of the proximal humerus in relationship to prosthetic replacement arthroplasty. J Shoulder Elbow Surg 1995;4: 286-289.)*

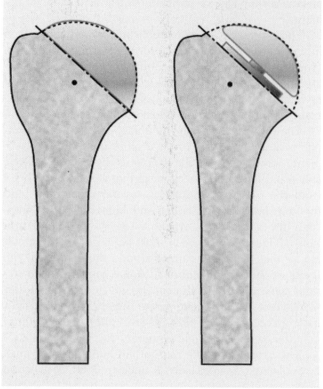

**Figure 5** Drawing showing the decrease in articular surface arc after an optimally placed osteotomy and humeral head replacement using a second-generation implant. *(Adapted from Pearl ML, Romeo AA, Wirth MA, Yamaguchi K, Nicholson GP, Creighton RA: Decision making in contemporary shoulder arthroplasty. Instr Course Lect 2005;54:74.)*

In contrast to third-generation implants, second-generation implants have a fixed angle of inclination. The osteotomy should be performed at this angle, using a cutting guide, so that the humeral head replacement will fit the proximal humerus well. Either an intramedullary or extramedullary cutting guide can be used, although an intramedullary guide may be less likely to tilt into excess varus or valgus. After subscapularis and capsular release, the humeral head is rotated externally, and the guide is positioned in the desired retroversion. Most guides have a rod that projects at a fixed angle, such as 30°, and is aligned with the forearm. Because of the wide variability in humeral head retroversion, the osteotomy should be performed so that it is in line with the anatomic neck,[16] thus lessening the possibility that the rotator cuff insertion will be violated by an errant oscillating saw or osteotome (Figure 4). The relationship of the cutting guide to the forearm or epicondylar axis and the posterior cuff insertion should be inspected as the osteotomy is being performed.

After the retroversion has been determined, the cutting guide must be positioned at the appropriate height. The cut will violate the supraspinatus insertion if it is too low and will leave a portion of the humeral head surface uncovered by the implant if it is too high. After the osteotomy has been performed and the proximal humerus has been prepared to accept the prosthetic stem, the trial component can serve as a midsurgical cutting guide, allowing for revision of the initial osteotomy.[16] Because the fixed inclination angle of a second-generation implant may not match the humeral inclination angle, portions of the articular surface may be left uncovered, even after an optimally placed osteotomy (Figure 5).

The prosthetic humeral head rests on a stem, and the position of the stem within the humeral canal is critical to restoring normal glenohumeral kinematics. The final position of the prosthetic stem is influenced by implant morphology (including metaphyseal flare and fin placement) and implant texture (rough, smooth, or fluted).[12] Some types of implant stems are available in 1-mm diameter increments, and others are available in 2-mm increments.[12] Some stems are available in one length, and others in two or more lengths.

Factors specific to the humeral anatomy, such as humeral retroversion, are also important in positioning the prosthetic stem. The morphology of the proximal humeral metaphysis is often overlooked. The volume, proximal-to-distal taper, bone density, and cortical thickness of this region vary widely.[12,22] In a narrow, tapered metaphysis, a thick stem may not be properly seated, and as a result the position of the prosthetic humeral head will be proud.

The center of rotation of the humeral head usually does not coincide with the orthopaedic axis, in either the transverse or coronal plane. Instead, the center of rotation is offset, typically medial and posterior to the orthopaedic axis. When a second-generation implant is used, the proximal humerus can be prepared to help restore this offset, and a smaller implant can be inserted with cement and selectively positioned within the cement mantle.[5] In contrast, a third-generation implant incorporates an eccentric locking of the Morse taper between the modular head and stem; the prosthetic humeral head is rotated until it matches the osteotomy surface[5,6] (Figure 6). This design feature offers greater flexibility in restoring the offset and, coupled with variable inclination, limits the need for considering implant design before or during the osteotomy.

## Cemented and Press-Fit Fixation

The original technique for insertion of the humeral component (in patients with a condition other than fracture) relies on macrolocking into the proximal humeral bone; methylmethacrylate cement is not used.[23] Midterm and long-term follow-up after use of this Neer press-fit implant found that no revision surgery was needed because of humeral component loosening.[24] When glenoid resurfacing became popular, debate arose over the optimal technique for humeral fixation. If the glenoid was to be resurfaced, cementing the humeral component was recommended to protect the humeral prosthetic interface from polyethylene wear debris and decrease the likelihood of loosening.[25] Clinically relevant loosening is rare after either cemented or cementless fixation, although radiographs revealed a higher rate of loosening in cementless humeral stems than in cemented stems.[26] Recent advances in glenoid implant design and preparation have resulted in a substantial reduction in the production of wear particles, and therefore humeral component loosening secondary to osteolysis now is quite unlikely.[25]

Cylindrical stems may be more prone to humeral loosening than tapered press-fit stems;[27] higher rates of loosening were reported with cylindrical stems.[28] A prospective, multicenter radiographic study of 127 shoulder arthroplasties performed using a tapered press-fit metaphyseal stem found no humeral component subsidence or shift in position at a minimum 2-year follow-up.[29] Seventy-five of the shoulders had radiolucency around the distal tip, generally less than 1 mm wide; only two shoulders had radiolucency around the proximal stem.

The use of cement in the medullary canal can be problematic. Intramedullary cement pressurization can lead to harmful systemic emboli, and cement extravasation from bone can injure the radial nerve or other structures. Revision shoulder arthroplasty is becoming more common and has led to a heightened appreciation

**Figure 6** Photograph of the prosthetic head offset mechanism in two representative implant systems (DuPuy, Warsaw, IN, *top*; Tornier, Stafford, TX, *bottom*). Rotating the head around an offset-locking mechanism correspondingly alters the offset in the transverse and coronal planes.

of complications during extraction of a well-fixed humeral component, especially after a fracture of the humeral shaft.[27] Removal of a cementless humeral stem during revision surgery is easier than removal of a cemented stem, unless bony ingrowth is present (as sometimes occurs with a proximally or fully coated humeral stem). Cementless humeral implants are relatively easy to implant because they do not require additional preparation of the humeral canal, such as brushing and lavage, or the use of a cement restrictor. Because cement curing is not required, operating room time and overall costs are reduced. These factors have contributed to the resurgent popularity of cementless components in shoulder arthroplasty.

The use of cemented humeral stems also has certain advantages. Cementing an implant allows the position of the stem to be adjusted within the intramedullary canal to correct for a mismatch in anteroposterior or mediolateral offset. A cemented implant can be positioned proud or in slight varus or valgus during cement curing to correct for any imperfections in the preparation of the proximal humerus. Biomechanical studies found that a cemented stem

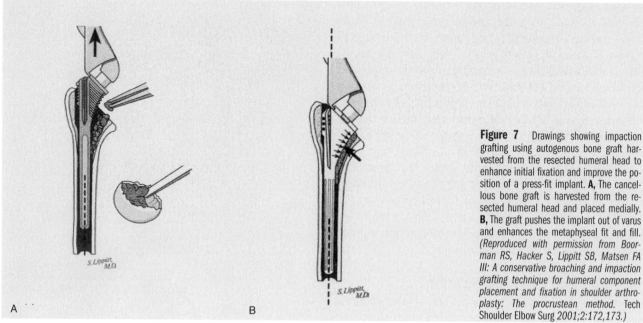

**Figure 7** Drawings showing impaction grafting using autogenous bone graft harvested from the resected humeral head to enhance initial fixation and improve the position of a press-fit implant. **A,** The cancellous bone graft is harvested from the resected humeral head and placed medially. **B,** The graft pushes the implant out of varus and enhances the metaphyseal fit and fill. *(Reproduced with permission from Boorman RS, Hacker S, Lippitt SB, Matsen FA III: A conservative broaching and impaction grafting technique for humeral component placement and fixation in shoulder arthroplasty: The procrustean method. Tech Shoulder Elbow Surg 2001;2:172,173.)*

has greater torsional stability than a cementless stem.[30] This is an important consideration in the treatment of a four-part proximal humerus fracture, in which the prosthesis is implanted directly into the intramedullary canal. A cemented stem may also be preferable for implantation into osteoporotic bone (such as that found in patients with rheumatoid arthritis) or a humeral implant revision. In these situations, the surgeon must be prepared to use cement to insert the implant.

When the metaphyseal bone is carefully prepared and a modern implant is used, humeral loosening does not appear to be a clinically relevant complication. A cementless implant is usually an attractive choice in primary shoulder arthroplasty performed for degenerative joint disease. The stability of the press fit can be enhanced by placing morcellized bone graft, harvested from the resected humeral head, around the prosthesis during final seating[27] (Figure 7). This grafting technique enhances the bone stock and reduces the void between the prosthesis and the humerus. It permits relatively easy component extraction, if revision is needed. Because cancellous bone is compressible, a stable press fit is achieved in a safer manner than is allowed by a diaphyseal fit in broached cortical bone. Most importantly, the bone graft can be packed medially to push the humeral component out of varus or anteriorly to decrease implant angulation and improve head positioning, without the use of cement.[27]

## Humeral Implant Malpositioning

Optimal function after shoulder arthroplasty depends on proper implant positioning, after proper humeral bone preparation and humeral head sizing. An implant malpo-

sitioning of 8 mm superiorly, inferiorly, anteriorly, or posteriorly was found to result in a statistically significant decrease in passive glenohumeral motion, similar to that caused by using an excessively thick humeral head.[31] However, an articular malpositioning of no more than 4 mm may produce only a small, clinically irrelevant alteration in humeral translation and range of motion.[31]

If the humeral head implant placement is too inferior, the greater tuberosity may abut against the acromion during abduction and elevation, or the undersurface of the rotator cuff may contact the glenoid and cause rotator cuff abrasion.[16,31] A superior placement of the humeral head implant tensions the overlying supraspinatus tendon excessively and tightens the inferior capsule at lower abduction angles, thereby limiting abduction.[12] Placement of a humeral head implant 5 mm or 10 mm too high was found to result in a mean reduction of 10° or 16°, respectively, in the maximum abduction angle.[32] Superior placement also displaces the center of rotation upward in relation to the line of the action of the rotator cuff and thereby decreases the abduction moment arms of the infraspinatus and subscapularis by as much as 100%.

An anterior humeral head implant placement may place excessive tension on the subscapularis tendon.[12] This tendon is typically incised during the shoulder arthroplasty approach and is later repaired; an anterior placement may increase the risk of subscapularis failure. Posterior implant placement may stretch the posterior capsule and rotator cuff. Decreased range of motion caused by component malpositioning can lead to capsular contracture and obligate glenohumeral translation.[19,31]

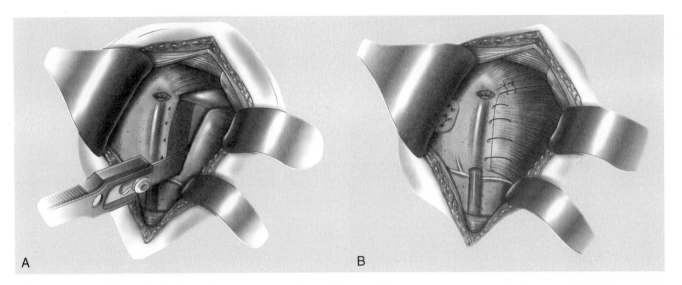

**Figure 8** Drawings showing osteotomy of the lesser tuberosity **(A)** and final repair **(B)**. This technique has been proposed to decrease the incidence of subscapularis failure following shoulder arthroplasty. *(Reproduced with permission from Gerber C, Pennington SD, Yian EH, Pfirrmann CA, Werner CM, Zumstein MA: Lesser tuberosity osteotomy for total shoulder arthroplasty: Surgical technique.* J Bone Joint Surg Am 2006;88(suppl 1):170-177.)

## Surgical Technique

Because every implant is designed to fit in a certain manner, the choice of implant affects aspects of the surgical technique, such as the osteotomy and preparation of the humeral canal. Prosthetic hemiarthroplasty is performed with the patient in a semisitting position in which the arm can be draped and positioned freely in space. An oblique anterior incision overlying the deltopectoral interval is made so that it courses over or is just medial to the coracoid process and ends at or just proximal to the level of the deltoid tubercle. The cephalic vein is retracted laterally with its deltoid feeders, and the clavipectoral fascia is incised lateral to the conjoint tendon. The subscapularis is managed either by simple tenotomy, leaving a cuff of tissue medially for later repair, or by a sharp release off the lesser tuberosity. A sharp release often includes the underlying capsule as a single layer, so that the tendon and capsule can be repaired medially along the osteotomy site as a single thick layer of tissue.[10] Subscapularis release and subsequent repair at the osteotomy site are used to gain external rotation postsurgically, if the presurgical external rotation at the side was less than 20°. Every centimeter of tendon advancement results in an approximately 20° gain in external rotation.[33]

The subscapularis release technique has recently become a topic of controversy. If the anterior capsule is released and a third-generation implant is used, external rotation improves after shoulder arthroplasty without subscapularis advancement.[6] Recent studies suggested that the incidence of clinically relevant subscapularis disruption after tendon-to-tendon or tendon-to-bone repair may be higher than previously reported.[34,35] Subscapularis healing after repair may be enhanced by a lesser tuberosity osteotomy,[36] which is equivalent to release of the subscapularis with an underlying wafer of lesser tuberosity and allows bone-to-bone healing to occur (Figure 8). This technique produced consistent bone-to-bone healing at short-term follow-up[37] but may not produce gains in external rotation equivalent to those from subscapularis release and medialized repair.

If the patient has a severe internal rotation contracture that allows passive external rotation of less than 0° at the side, as is common in capsulorrhaphy arthropathy, a subscapularis coronal Z lengthening can be performed to gain external rotation.[38] However, the advantage gained by using this technique must be weighed carefully against the risk of tendon compromise.

Regardless of the manner in which the subscapularis tendon is incised, it should be released circumferentially to mobilize the tendon and facilitate repair. The anterior capsule, which is pathologically stiff in an arthritic shoulder, should be released; any adhesions between the subscapularis and overlying structures such as the coracoid, axillary nerve, and conjoint tendon should also be released.[10] In a total shoulder arthroplasty, additional releases can be performed during glenoid exposure. If the joint is concentric, without posterior glenoid erosion or posterior subluxation, the posterior capsule should be released to prevent obligate anterior translation of the humeral head away from the tight posterior capsule.[19]

The biceps tendon in an arthritic shoulder is often diseased or partly torn and can be a source of pain after shoulder arthroplasty.[38] No consensus exists on biceps tendon management during shoulder arthroplasty; either tenotomy or tenodesis is performed, or the tendon is not manipulated.[39] Consensus is also lacking as to management of the coracoacromial ligament. It can be

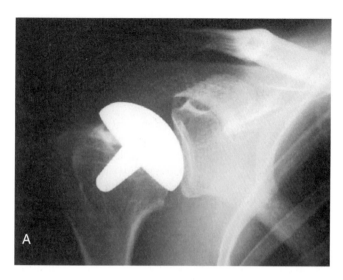
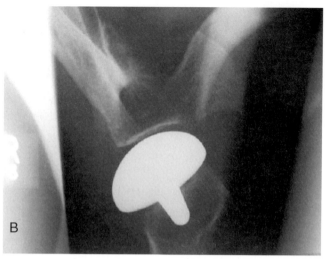

**Figure 9** AP **(A)** and axillary lateral **(B)** radiographs showing proper positioning of a resurfacing implant. *(Reproduced with permission from Copeland SA, Levy O, Brownlow HC: Resurfacing arthroplasty of the shoulder. Tech Shoulder Elbow Surg 2003;4:208.)*

partially or completely released to achieve exposure, which facilitates placement of retractors underneath the acromion to expose the supraspinatus insertion. Alternatively, the ligament can be preserved as an important static stabilizer.[10] The coracoacromial ligament should never be released during arthroplasty if an irreparable or marginally reparable rotator cuff tear is present because of the possibility of anterosuperior escape.[40]

## Resurfacing Arthroplasty

A traditional hemiarthroplasty requires humeral head resection and uses an intramedullary stem. However, implants designed to resurface the articular surface with a cap are available. Modern resurfacing arthroplasty offers several advantages (Figure 9). Only the remaining cartilage and underlying subchondral bone are removed before resurfacing; the humeral bone stock is preserved. Resurfacing arthroplasty is therefore attractive for young patients who may require later surgery. Because these implants do not have a stem, they can be used if the intramedullary canal is already filled with cement, the stem of an elbow replacement, or a humeral internal fixation device.[41] The absence of a stem also eliminates the risk of a shaft stress fracture, a fat embolus, or hypotension associated with intramedullary canal reaming and cementation. Resurfacing arthroplasty is an attractive option for a patient with posttraumatic arthritis caused by a proximal humeral malunion or arthritis arising from a congenital humeral anomaly.[41]

In theory, a resurfacing arthroplasty should enable the normal anatomy to be replicated without the constraints imposed by metaphyseal or canal geometry. In practice, replicating normal anatomy is often difficult with this technique because a humeral head deformity can prevent accommodation of the resurfacing implant after limited subchondral reaming.

Current resurfacing arthroplasty techniques use a porous-coated or hydroxyapatite-coated implant intended for press-fit use. The initial fixation depends on meticulous machining of the humeral head. After ingrowth is achieved, these implants may be difficult to remove. Some porous-coated designs appear to have rates of clinically relevant loosening higher than those of stemmed press-fit implants.[42] The long-term effectiveness of resurfacing arthroscopy is not yet known; only a few studies have been published.[42,43] Concomitant glenoid implantation has been described as more technically challenging during resurfacing arthroplasty than during conventional total shoulder arthroplasty because the remaining humeral head may impede glenoid visualization and preparation.[41,42]

Resurfacing arthroplasty should not be considered a less invasive alternative to conventional shoulder arthroplasty. Resurfacing should not be performed through a mini-open deltoid-splitting incision in patients with an intact or reparable rotator cuff. Such an exposure is inadequate for the capsular release and removal of peripheral osteophytes that are essential for optimal recovery of shoulder motion. Instead, the surgical approach used for resurfacing should be identical to that used for traditional hemiarthroplasty.

## Total Shoulder Arthroplasty Versus Hemiarthroplasty

During the past 50 years, the indications for shoulder hemiarthroplasty have expanded from fracture to posttraumatic arthritis and several degenerative conditions. The status of the glenoid, humerus, and rotator cuff, as well as the activity demands of the patient, must be carefully assessed in deciding whether total shoulder arthroplasty or hemiarthroplasty is preferable.[44]

A hemiarthroplasty is sufficient if the glenoid is not diseased. Proximal humerus fracture malunion or posttraumatic arthritis sometimes does not greatly affect the glenoid, and in these patients hemiarthroplasty is the preferred procedure. Hemiarthroplasty is often considered for stage IV osteonecrosis, which is characterized by humeral collapse and arthritis but not by substantial glenoid involvement.[45,46] Some acute three-part and four-part proximal humerus fractures are best treated with hemiarthroplasty and repair of the tuberosities, but without glenoid resurfacing.

Hemiarthroplasty alone is preferable if the glenoid is dysplastic or medialized from a severe erosive disease, such as rheumatoid arthritis, and cannot accommodate an implant. If posterior glenoid erosion or an abnormal glenoid version is profound, augmentation of the glenoid with a structural bone graft is needed, and a hemiarthroplasty can be performed to articulate with the reconstructed glenoid. In addition, a hemiarthroplasty should be performed if the durability of an implanted glenoid component is an important consideration. Some patients with cuff tear arthropathy may benefit from hemiarthroplasty; a conventional glenoid component should not be implanted because of accelerated glenoid loosening resulting from eccentric loading. Glenoid implantation in young, very active patients is controversial because of the possibility of glenoid loosening. These concerns have prompted the development of nonprosthetic strategies for treating glenoid arthrosis.

The outcome of hemiarthroplasty depends on the presurgical condition of the glenohumeral joint, as well as the underlying diagnosis. In a review of consecutive hemiarthroplasties performed for conditions other than fracture, an absence of glenoid erosion was associated with significantly greater improvement in shoulder function and comfort.[47] Shoulders that had undergone prior surgery had less improvement in function, and shoulders with an intact rotator cuff had significantly greater improvement in strength. Shoulders with rheumatoid arthritis, capsulorrhaphy arthropathy, or cuff tear arthropathy had the least functional improvement, and those with osteonecrosis or primary or secondary degenerative joint disease had the greatest improvement.

In a study of patients with a concentric glenoid, 86% had a satisfactory result after hemiarthroplasty, compared with 63% of patients with a nonconcentric glenoid.[48] The patients with a nonconcentric glenoid were more likely to have a loss of forward elevation and external rotation; pain relief was similar in the two groups. The authors concluded that hemiarthroplasty should be performed only if the patient has a concentric glenoid because it affords a better fulcrum for glenohumeral motion. Another study evaluated the progression of glenoid erosion after hemiarthroplasty in eight young, active patients by accurately measuring glenohumeral joint space on serial axillary radiographs.[49] Progressive

glenoid wear was found in all patients, with a 68% decrease in glenohumeral joint space at a mean 43-month follow-up. Patients with a residual joint space narrower than 1 mm had a lower outcome score than patients with a wider joint space.

Other recent studies reported outcomes of hemiarthroplasty for the treatment of shoulder arthritis. Sixty-four shoulders carefully selected for hemiarthroplasty had a concentric glenoid with eburnated bone, a nonconcentric glenoid that could be converted to a smooth concentric surface, or a humeral head centered within the glenoid after soft-tissue balancing.[50] At a minimum 5-year follow-up, most of the stems had either no radiolucency or distal radiolucency. At a minimum 2-year follow-up after hemiarthroplasty of 36 shoulders with inflammatory arthritis,[51] significant clinical improvement was found to be unrelated to disease severity. Patients in whom the prosthesis was adapted to restore native glenohumeral alignment had more improvement in quality of life, use of the arm, and range of motion than patients whose glenohumeral alignment was not restored.

Several well-designed randomized clinical studies compared outcomes of hemiarthroplasty with those of total shoulder arthroplasty for the treatment of osteoarthritis. Compared with total shoulder arthroplasty, hemiarthroplasty was found to cause less morbidity and to be less costly.[52] However, at 3-year follow-up, 3 of the 25 patients who underwent hemiarthroplasty had required conversion to total shoulder arthroplasty because of residual pain related to glenoid erosion. The patients who underwent hemiarthroplasty had less forward elevation than those who underwent total shoulder arthroplasty. Another study found no significant differences in quality of life between patients treated with total shoulder arthroplasty and those treated with hemiarthroplasty;[53] 2 of 21 patients who underwent hemiarthroplasty required conversion to total shoulder arthroplasty.

Some study findings suggest that the results after hemiarthroplasty are somewhat inferior to the results after total shoulder arthroplasty. A meta-analysis of hemiarthroplasty and total shoulder arthroplasty found that, at a minimum 2-year follow-up, pain scores were significantly lower and improvement in forward elevation was significantly greater in patients who underwent total shoulder arthroplasty.[54] A large, multicenter study in which a third-generation humeral implant was used found that, at a minimum 2-year follow-up, patients who underwent total shoulder arthroplasty had better functional outcome and subjective assessment than patients who underwent hemiarthroplasty, regardless of patient age or rotator cuff status.[55,56]

The long-term outcomes after hemiarthroplasty for osteoarthritis have been especially disappointing in younger patients, who have relatively high expectations and demands. Sixty percent of patients age 50 years or younger were dissatisfied with their result at a minimum 15-year follow-up after hemiarthroplasty.[57] The survival rates for hemiarthroplasty after 10 and 15 years were substantially lower than those for total shoulder arthroplasty, primarily because rates of revision for glenoid erosion after hemiarthroplasty far exceed rates for glenoid implant loosening after total shoulder arthroplasty.[57,58]

## Future Directions

Hemiarthroplasty, whether performed alone or in conjunction with glenoid replacement, produces reliable and durable improvement in comfort and function for most patients with end-stage arthritis. The possible complications include postsurgical stiffness, subscapularis tearing, shoulder instability, and implant loosening. The existing techniques for soft-tissue release and subscapularis management must be refined to allow maximum mobility and function and minimize the risk of complications. Studies are needed to compare cemented and cementless hemiarthroplasty, so that specific indications and contraindications can be established for each technique. The development of evidence-based guidelines for total shoulder arthroplasty, hemiarthroplasty, humeral resurfacing, and biologic glenoid resurfacing would be helpful in treating young, active patients with advanced osteoarthritis.

The extent of the modularity or implant variability needed for optimal shoulder function is poorly understood. No statistically significant differences were found in a study of outcomes after total shoulder arthroplasty using a modular humeral prosthesis with a variable head diameter, a nonmodular prosthesis with a variable head diameter, or a nonmodular prosthesis with a fixed head diameter; hemiarthroplasty was not specifically studied.[59] The study did not find that humeral component modularity is important in determining outcomes but suggested that surgeons can adjust techniques such as osteotomy and soft-tissue release to compensate for any limitations of the humeral implant. The costs associated with the choice of specific implant designs, large inventories, prolonged surgical learning curves, and increased complication rates should be included in any analysis of new techniques.

Proper surgical technique is important because even a subtle implant malpositioning can adversely affect shoulder mobility and stability. Malpositioning can result from an improper osteotomy or improper selection or implantation of the prosthesis. In addition, meticulous soft-tissue releases and repair of the subscapularis tendon are essential for optimal shoulder function.

Shoulder arthroplasty is an infrequently performed procedure; most orthopaedic surgeons perform only one or two per year.[60] Studies have found inferior outcomes and higher complication rates after shoulder arthroplasty performed by low-volume surgeons at low-volume hospitals.[61,62] There may be a substantial discrepancy between the average outcome of hemiarthroplasty, which is skewed by results from many low-volume surgeons, and published reports, which are from the highest volume surgeons. High-volume surgeons are more likely to perform total shoulder arthroplasty to treat osteoarthritis.[63] It is questionable whether shoulder arthroplasty should be performed by a surgeon who has relatively little experience in the techniques.

## Summary

Hemiarthroplasty, or humeral head replacement, is an effective treatment for end-stage refractory glenohumeral arthritis, whether it is performed alone or coupled with glenoid replacement in a total shoulder arthroplasty. Third-generation humeral head replacement designs have improved the ability to address severe joint deformity and replicate the variable humeral anatomy. Resurfacing arthroplasty is a bone-conserving alternative that may be an attractive option for younger patients with arthritis. Meticulous attention to surgical technique, including carefully placed humeral head osteotomy, thorough débridement of osteophytes, and capsular releases, as well as management of the subscapularis tendon, is more important for the success of surgery than the choice of implant. Hemiarthroplasty should be considered if the glenoid is uninvolved, if the quality or quantity of glenoid bone is deficient, or if the glenoid surface will be loaded excessively or eccentrically after surgery. The precise indications for choosing hemiarthroplasty rather than total shoulder arthroplasty are continuing to evolve.

## Annotated References

1. Joint replacements from head to toe. American Academy of Orthopaedic Surgeons. http://www.aaos.org/Research/stats/Joint%20Replacements%20from%20Head%20to%20toe.pdf. Accessed July 30, 2007.

2. Neer CS II: Articular replacement for the humeral head. *J Bone Joint Surg Am* 1955;37:215-228.

3. Ballmer FT, Sidles JA, Lippitt SB, Matsen FA III: Humeral head prosthetic arthroplasty: Surgically relevant geometric considerations. *J Shoulder Elbow Surg* 1993;2:296-304.

4. Iannotti JP, Gabriel JP, Schneck SL, Evans BG, Misra S: The normal glenohumeral relationships: An anatomical study of one hundred and forty shoulders. *J Bone Joint Surg Am* 1992;74:491-500.

5. Boileau P, Walch G: The three-dimensional geometry of the proximal humerus: Implications for surgical technique and prosthetic designs. *J Bone Joint Surg Br* 1997;79:857-865.

6.  Walch G, Boileau P: Prosthetic adaptability: A new concept for shoulder arthroplasty. *J Shoulder Elbow Surg* 1999;8:443-451.

7.  Pearl ML, Volk AG: Retroversion of the proximal humerus in relationship to prosthetic replacement arthroplasty. *J Shoulder Elbow Surg* 1995;4:286-289.

8.  Pearl ML, Volk AG: Coronal plane geometry of the proximal humerus relevant to prosthetic arthroplasty. *J Shoulder Elbow Surg* 1996;5:320-326.

9.  Pearl ML, Kurutz S: Geometric analysis of commonly used prosthetic systems for proximal humeral replacement. *J Bone Joint Surg Am* 1999;81:660-671.

10. Matsen FA III, Lippitt SB, Sidles JA, Harryman DT II: *Practical Evaluation and Management of the Shoulder*. Philadelphia, PA, WB Saunders, 1994, pp 151-219.

11. Robertson DD, Yuan J, Bigliani LU, Flatow EL, Yamaguchi K: Three-dimensional analysis of the proximal part of the humerus: Relevance to arthroplasty. *J Bone Joint Surg Am* 2000;82:1594-1602.

12. Pearl ML: Proximal humeral anatomy in shoulder arthroplasty: Implications for prosthetic design and surgical technique. *J Shoulder Elbow Surg* 2005; 14(suppl):99S-104S.

    The author summarizes a decade of research into the variability of proximal humeral anatomy and its relevance to shoulder arthroplasty and prosthetic design.

13. Tillet E, Smith M, Fulcher M, Shankin J: Anatomic determination of humeral head retroversion: The relationship of the central axis of the humeral head to the bicipital groove. *J Shoulder Elbow Surg* 1993;2: 255-263.

14. Itamura J, Dietrick T, Roidis N, Shean C, Chen F, Tibone J: Analysis of the bicipital groove as a landmark for humeral head replacement. *J Shoulder Elbow Surg* 2002;11:322-326.

    In 21 cadaver humeri, CT studies revealed that the course of the bicipital groove from proximal to distal undergoes substantial internal rotation.

15. Kummer FJ, Perkins R, Zuckerman JD: The use of the bicipital groove for alignment of the humeral stem in shoulder arthroplasty. *J Shoulder Elbow Surg* 1998;7: 144-146.

16. Pearl ML, Romeo AA, Wirth MA, Yamaguchi K, Nicholson GP, Creighton RA: Decision making in contemporary shoulder arthroplasty. *Instr Course Lect* 2005;54:69-85.

    The authors present a thorough review of anatomic, implant, and disease-specific factors that influence decision making during shoulder arthroplasty.

17. Pearl ML, Kurutz, Robertson DD, Yamaguchi K: Geometric analysis of selected press fit prosthetic systems for proximal humeral replacement. *J Orthop Res* 2002;20:192-197.

    The geometry of four second-generation press-fit prosthetic systems was compared with the anatomy of 60 hu-
    meral specimens. The gap created by the prosthetic collar and Morse taper hindered the ability of a prosthetic system to replicate normal humeral anatomy. The system with the greatest range of geometric options produced the lowest mean displacement of the center of rotation and a superior anatomic fit.

18. Karduna AR, Williams GR, Williams JL, Iannotti JP: Glenohumeral joint translations before and after total shoulder arthroplasty: A study in cadavera. *J Bone Joint Surg Am* 1997;79:1166-1174.

19. Harryman DT, Sidles JA, Harris SL, Lippitt SB, Matsen FA III: The effect of articular conformity and the size of the humeral head component on laxity and motion after glenohumeral arthroplasty: A study in cadavera. *J Bone Joint Surg Am* 1995;77:555-563.

20. Ballmer FT, Lippitt SB, Romeo AA, Matsen FA III: Total shoulder arthroplasty: Some considerations related to glenoid surface contact. *J Shoulder Elbow Surg* 1994;3:299-306.

21. Jobe CM, Iannotti JP: Limits imposed on glenohumeral motion by joint geometry. *J Shoulder Elbow Surg* 1995;4:281-285.

22. Hacker SA, Boorman RS, Lippitt SB, Matsen FA III: Impaction grafting improves the fit of uncemented humeral arthroplasty. *J Shoulder Elbow Surg* 2003; 12:431-435.

    In 10 randomly assigned paired cadaver humeri, preparation and insertion of a press-fit humeral prosthesis was performed with or without cancellous impaction autografting. CT studies revealed that impaction grafting reduced the void and improved the quality of fit between the humerus and the proximal two thirds of the prosthesis.

23. Neer CS II: Follow-up notes on articles previously published in the journal: Articular replacement for the humeral head. *J Bone Joint Surg Am* 1964;46: 1607-1610.

24. Neer CS II: Replacement arthroplasty for glenohumeral osteoarthritis. *J Bone Joint Surg Am* 1974;56: 1-13.

25. Klimkiewicz JJ, Iannotti JP, Rubash HE, Shanbhag AS: Aseptic loosening of the humeral component in total shoulder arthroplasty. *J Shoulder Elbow Surg* 1998;7:422-426.

26. Chin PY, Sperling JW, Cofield RH, Schleck C: Complications of total shoulder arthroplasty: Are they fewer or different? *J Shoulder Elbow Surg* 2006;15: 19-22.

    Early and late complications during a single surgeon's extensive decade-long experience with shoulder arthroplasty are compared with those tabulated earlier to look for changes in the type and frequency of complications.

27. Boorman RS, Hacker S, Lippitt SB, Matsen FA III: A conservative broaching and impaction grafting technique for humeral component placement and

fixation in shoulder arthroplasty: The procrustean method. *Tech Shoulder Elbow Surg* 2001;2:166-175.

The described impaction grafting technique uses cancellous bone harvested from the resected humeral head to improve humeral component positioning and enhance the quality of fit between the humerus and the prosthesis.

28. Torchia ME, Cofield RH, Settergren CR: Total shoulder arthroplasty with the Neer prosthesis: Long-term results. *J Shoulder Elbow Surg* 1997;6:495-505.

29. Matsen FA III, Iannotti JP, Rockwood CA Jr: Humeral fixation by press-fitting of a tapered metaphyseal stem: A prospective radiographic study. *J Bone Joint Surg Am* 2003;85:304-308.

In 127 patients with osteoarthritis, subsidence or shift in position did not occur after implantation of a press-fit humeral prosthesis with a tapered metaphyseal stem, although 59% had radiolucency at the distal tip. Level of evidence: IV.

30. Harris TE, Jobe CM, Dai QG: Fixation of proximal humeral prostheses and rotational micromotion. *J Shoulder Elbow Surg* 2000;9:205-210.

31. Williams GR Jr, Wong KL, Pepe MD, et al: The effect of articular malposition after total shoulder arthroplasty on glenohumeral translations, range of motion, and subacromial impingement. *J Shoulder Elbow Surg* 2001;10:399-409.

In a cadaver model, anterior-posterior and superior-inferior articular offsets as small as 4 mm were found to be sufficient to cause statistically significant increases in subacromial contact and decreases in glenohumeral range of motion.

32. Nyffeler RW, Sheikh R, Jacob HA, Gerber C: Influence of humeral prosthesis height on biomechanics of glenohumeral abduction: An in vitro study. *J Bone Joint Surg Am* 2004;86:575-580.

Superior malpositioning of the prosthetic humeral head leads to stiffness and loss of abduction strength and displaces the center of rotation upward in relation to the rotator cuff muscles, possibly leading to long-term supraspinatus tendon failure.

33. MacDonald PB, Hawkins RJ, Fowler PJ, Miniaci A: Release of the subscapularis for internal rotation contracture and pain after anterior repair for recurrent anterior dislocation of the shoulder. *J Bone Joint Surg Am* 1992;74:734-737.

34. Miller SL, Hazrati Y, Klepps S, Chiang A, Flatow EL: Loss of subscapularis function after total shoulder replacement: A seldom recognized problem. *J Shoulder Elbow Surg* 2003;12:29-34.

Widespread dysfunction of the repaired subscapularis tendon was found after total shoulder arthroplasty. Two thirds of all studied patients had abnormal lift-off and belly-press tests, and 92% of these patients were unable to tuck in a shirt. Level of evidence: IV.

35. Miller BS, Joseph TA, Noonan TJ, Horan MP, Hawkins RJ: Rupture of the subscapularis tendon after shoulder arthroplasty: Diagnosis, treatment, and outcome. *J Shoulder Elbow Surg* 2005;14:492-496.

The symptoms of subscapularis rupture after shoulder arthroplasty include pain, decreased internal rotation strength, increased external rotation mobility, and instability. Despite subscapularis repair and, if needed, augmentation with pectoralis transfer, decreased functional outcomes were observed. Level of evidence: IV.

36. Gerber C, Yian EH, Pfirrmann CA, Zumstein MA, Werner CM: Subscapularis muscle function and structure after total shoulder replacement with lesser tuberosity osteotomy and repair. *J Bone Joint Surg Am* 2005;87:1739-1745.

The authors describe the technique of lesser tuberosity osteotomy and repair. Follow-up imaging revealed excellent bone-to-bone healing of the lesser tuberosity, without subscapularis rupture, but also increased fatty infiltration of the subscapularis. Level of evidence: IV.

37. Green A, Norris TR: Shoulder arthroplasty for advanced glenohumeral arthritis after anterior instability repair. *J Shoulder Elbow Surg* 2001;10:539-545.

Shoulder arthroplasty for end-stage glenohumeral arthritis arising after anterior instability repair reliably improved function, comfort, and range of motion. Most patients had undergone a nonanatomic repair. Two thirds of the patients required subscapularis lengthening and anterior capsular release for severe internal rotation contractures. Level of evidence: IV.

38. Tuckman DV, Dines DM: Long head of the biceps pathology as a cause of anterior shoulder pain after shoulder arthroplasty. *J Shoulder Elbow Surg* 2006; 15:415-418.

In eight shoulders treated for anterior shoulder pain involving the biceps muscle after shoulder arthroplasty, arthroscopic or open tenodesis and débridement resulted in improved shoulder comfort, mobility, and function. Level of evidence: IV.

39. Fama G, Edwards TB, Boulahia A, et al: The role of concomitant biceps tenodesis in shoulder arthroplasty for primary osteoarthritis: Results of a multicentric study. *Orthopedics* 2004;27:401-405.

Comparison of outcomes following shoulder arthroplasty with or without biceps tenodesis revealed that patients who underwent tenodesis fared better than those who did not. The authors conclude that biceps tenodesis is a useful adjunct to shoulder arthroplasty for osteoarthritis.

40. Hockman DE, Lucas GL, Roth CA: Role of the coracoacromial ligament as restraint after shoulder hemiarthroplasty. *Clin Orthop Relat Res* 2004;419:80-82.

In a cadaver model, coracoacromial ligament section produced increased anterosuperior translation following hemiarthroplasty. The authors caution that the coracoacromial ligament should be preserved to enhance glenohumeral joint stability.

41. Copeland SA, Levy O, Brownlow HC: Resurfacing arthroplasty of the shoulder. *Tech Shoulder Elbow Surg* 2003;4:199-210.

   The indications for surface replacement arthroplasty of the shoulder and the technique are described in detail by the developer of the first contemporary surface replacement system and his associates.

42. Levy O, Copeland SA: Cementless surface replacement arthroplasty of the shoulder: 5- to 10-year results with the Copeland mark-2 prosthesis. *J Bone Joint Surg Br* 2001;83:213-221.

   The results of surface replacement arthroplasty performed for different types of shoulder arthritis were reviewed at a minimum 5-year follow-up. Patients with primary osteoarthritis had the best results, and patients with a cuff tear or posttraumatic arthropathy had the worst results. The overall rate of revision surgery was 8%. Level of evidence: IV.

43. Levy O, Copeland SA: Cementless surface replacement arthroplasty (Copeland CSRA) for osteoarthritis of the shoulder. *J Shoulder Elbow Surg* 2004; 13:266-271.

   In a study of the intermediate-term outcome of 79 surface replacements for osteoarthritis, significant improvements were noted, regardless of whether a glenoid implant was used. Complications were infrequent, although four revisions were performed following total shoulder arthroplasty. Level of evidence: IV.

44. Krishnan SG, Harkins DC, Burkhead WZ: Total shoulder versus hemiarthroplasty: Elements in decision making. *Tech Shoulder Elbow Surg* 2004;5:208-213.

   The authors present a thorough review of the indications for total shoulder arthroplasty and hemiarthroplasty.

45. Hasan SS, Romeo AA: Nontraumatic osteonecrosis of the humeral head. *J Shoulder Elbow Surg* 2002;11: 281-298.

   The pathogenesis, etiology, natural history, diagnosis, and treatment of nontraumatic osteonecrosis of the shoulder are reviewed. The indications for shoulder arthroplasty are included.

46. Mansat P, Huser L, Mansat M, Bellumore Y, Rongieres M, Bonnevialle P: Shoulder arthroplasty for atraumatic avascular necrosis of the humeral head: Nineteen shoulders followed up for a mean of seven years. *J Shoulder Elbow Surg* 2005;14:114-120.

   The authors report on the results of shoulder arthroplasty for nontraumatic osteonecrosis. At a mean 7-year follow-up, 16 of 19 shoulders had an excellent or satisfactory result, but motion deficits were common. Patients with postradiation necrosis fared the worst. Level of evidence: IV.

47. Hettrich CM, Weldon E III, Boorman RS, Parsons IM IV, Matsen FA III: Preoperative factors associated with improvements in shoulder function after humeral hemiarthroplasty. *J Bone Joint Surg Am* 2004;86: 1446-1451.

   In a study of the influence of presurgical factors on shoulder function after hemiarthroplasty, shoulders with rheumatoid arthritis and rotator cuff tear arthropathy had the least functional improvement, and shoulders with osteonecrosis and osteoarthritis had the greatest improvement. Glenoid erosion adversely affected outcome. Level of evidence: II.

48. Levine WN, Djurasovic M, Glasson JM, Pollock RG, Flatow EL, Bigliani LU: Hemiarthroplasty for glenohumeral osteoarthritis: Results correlated to degree of glenoid wear. *J Shoulder Elbow Surg* 1997;6: 449-454.

49. Parsons IM IV, Millett PJ, Warner JJ: Glenoid wear after shoulder hemiarthroplasty: Quantitative radiographic analysis. *Clin Orthop Relat Res* 2004;421: 120-125.

   The progression of glenoid erosion following hemiarthroplasty was evaluated using serial axillary radiographs in eight young, active patients. Progressive glenoid wear was found in all patients, and patients with the narrowest residual joint spaces fared the worst. Level of evidence: IV.

50. Wirth MA, Tapscott RS, Southworth C, Rockwood CA Jr: Treatment of glenohumeral arthritis with a hemiarthroplasty: A minimum five-year follow-up outcome study. *J Bone Joint Surg Am* 2006;88: 964-973.

   Outcomes significantly improved after hemiarthroplasty in 64 shoulders with a concentric glenoid, a nonconcentric glenoid that could be converted to a smooth concentric surface, or a humeral head centered within the glenoid after soft-tissue balancing. Level of evidence: IV.

51. Collins DN, Harryman DT II, Wirth MA: Shoulder arthroplasty for the treatment of inflammatory arthritis. *J Bone Joint Surg Am* 2004;86:2489-2496.

   In 36 shoulders with inflammatory arthritis studied after treatment with hemiarthroplasty, significant improvement was independent of disease severity. Improvement was greatest if prosthetic adaptability enabled a restoration of glenohumeral alignment. Level of evidence: II.

52. Gartsman GM, Roddey TS, Hammerman SM: Shoulder arthroplasty with or without resurfacing of the glenoid in patients who have osteoarthritis. *J Bone Joint Surg Am* 2000;82:26-34.

53. Lo IK, Litchfield RB, Griffin S, Faber K, Patterson SD, Kirkley A: Quality-of-life outcome following hemiarthroplasty or total shoulder arthroplasty in patients with osteoarthritis: A prospective, randomized trial. *J Bone Joint Surg Am* 2005;87:2178-2185.

   A randomized study of 42 patients after hemiarthroplasty or total shoulder arthroplasty for osteoarthritis found no difference between the two treatment groups in disease-specific and general quality-of-life measures. Level of evidence: I.

54. Bryant D, Litchfield R, Sandow M, Gartsman GM, Guyatt G, Kirkley A: A comparison of pain, strength, range of motion, and functional outcomes after hemiarthroplasty and total shoulder arthroplasty in patients with osteoarthritis of the shoulder: A systematic review and meta-analysis. *J Bone Joint Surg Am* 2005;87:1947-1956.

Meta-analysis of four randomized clinical trials comparing hemiarthroplasty and total shoulder arthroplasty for the treatment of osteoarthritis found that total shoulder arthroplasty led to a better functional outcome than hemiarthroplasty at a minimum 2-year follow-up. Level of evidence: I.

55. Edwards TB, Kadakia NR, Boulahia A, et al: A comparison of hemiarthroplasty and total shoulder arthroplasty in the treatment of primary glenohumeral osteoarthritis: Results of a multicenter study. *J Shoulder Elbow Surg* 2003;12:207-213.

A retrospective review of almost 700 shoulder arthroplasties found that 94% of patients who underwent total shoulder arthroplasty and 86% of patients who underwent hemiarthroplasty had a good or excellent result. Patients in the total shoulder arthroplasty group had better pain, mobility, and activity scores.

56. Pfahler M, Jena F, Neyton L, Sirveaux F, Molé D: Hemiarthroplasty versus total shoulder prosthesis: Results of cemented glenoid components. *J Shoulder Elbow Surg* 2006;15:154-163.

This retrospective review of 705 total shoulder arthroplasties and 469 hemiarthroplasties using the same type of shoulder prosthesis found that total shoulder arthroplasty led to better functional outcomes and subjective results than hemiarthroplasty. The superiority of total shoulder arthroplasty appeared to be independent of patient age or rotator cuff status.

57. Sperling JW, Cofield RH, Rowland CM: Minimum fifteen-year follow-up of Neer hemiarthroplasty and total shoulder arthroplasty in patients aged fifty years or younger. *J Shoulder Elbow Surg* 2004;13:604-613.

At a minimum 15-year follow-up, unsatisfactory results were found after 60% of Neer hemiarthroplasties and 48% of total shoulder arthroplasties in patients age 50 years or younger. Almost 75% of radiographs showed either glenoid erosion or lucencies. The estimated 20-year survival rate for hemiarthroplasty and total shoulder arthroplasty was 75% and 84%, respectively.

58. Sperling JW, Cofield RH, Rowland CM: Neer hemiarthroplasty and Neer total shoulder arthroplasty in patients fifty years old or less: Long-term results. *J Bone Joint Surg Am* 1998;80:464-473.

59. Churchill RS, Kopjar B, Fehringer EV, Boorman RS, Matsen FA III: Humeral component modularity may not be an important factor in the outcome of shoulder arthroplasty for glenohumeral osteoarthritis. *Am J Orthop* 2005;34:173-176.

The authors found no statistical difference in outcomes after total shoulder arthroplasty using a modular humeral prosthesis with a variable head diameter, a nonmodular prosthesis with a variable head diameter, or a nonmodular prosthesis with a fixed head diameter.

60. Hasan SS, Leith JM, Smith KL, Matsen FA III: The distribution of shoulder replacement among surgeons and hospitals is significantly different than that of hip or knee replacement. *J Shoulder Elbow Surg* 2003;12:164-169.

This study of the 1998 database of the Center for Medical Consumers in the state of New York revealed that more than 40% of surgeons who performed hip or knee replacements performed 10 or more such procedures. In contrast, only 3% (10 surgeons) who performed shoulder replacements performed 10 or more such procedures; 75% performed only 1 or 2 procedures.

61. Hammond JW, Queale WS, Kim TK, McFarland EG: Surgeon experience and clinical and economic outcomes for shoulder arthroplasty. *J Bone Joint Surg Am* 2003;85:2318-2324.

An analysis of Maryland discharge data from 1994 to 2000 revealed that patients of surgeons who performed a relatively high number of shoulder arthroplasties had lower complication rates and hospital lengths of stay than patients of lower volume surgeons. Level of evidence: II.

62. Jain N, Pietrobon R, Hocker S, Guller U, Shankar A, Higgins LD: The relationship between surgeon and hospital volume and outcomes for shoulder arthroplasty. *J Bone Joint Surg Am* 2004;86:496-505.

This study of a national outcomes database used sophisticated statistical tools to determine that patients who undergo total shoulder arthroplasty or hemiarthroplasty performed by a high-volume surgeon or in a high-volume hospital are more likely to have a good outcome. Level of evidence: III.

63. Jain NB, Hocker S, Pietrobon R, Guller U, Bathia N, Higgins LD: Total arthroplasty versus hemiarthroplasty for glenohumeral osteoarthritis: Role of provider volume. *J Shoulder Elbow Surg* 2005;14:361-367.

The authors studied a national outcomes database to estimate the risk-adjusted association between provider volume and the selection of total shoulder arthroplasty. High-volume surgeons were more likely than low-volume surgeons to perform a total shoulder arthroplasty.

# Chapter 35

# Glenoid Resurfacing

*John W. Sperling, MD

## Introduction

Patients with glenohumeral arthritis must be carefully evaluated to determine whether shoulder arthroplasty with glenoid resurfacing is appropriate. The indications for glenoid resurfacing, as well as the relative advantages of different component designs, are the subject of significant debate.

## Clinical Evaluation and Patient Counseling

The surgeon should begin the evaluation of a patient with glenohumeral arthritis by gaining a thorough understanding of the patient's symptoms, motivation, and ability to comply with postsurgical restrictions and rehabilitation. A careful physical examination and appropriate imaging studies can facilitate surgical planning and help the surgeon anticipate the surgical components that will be required.

### History

The patient's primary symptoms and their severity must be determined, as well as the duration of symptoms and any alleviating or aggravating factors. Other important factors include the patient's occupation, recreational pursuits, history of trauma, and specific treatment goals (including pain relief, increased strength, and increased range of motion).

A focused review of systems is required. If joints other than the shoulder are involved, the treatment plan must address the order in which the joints will be treated. The possibility of preexisting neurologic disease should be considered. Pain in glenohumeral arthritis is typically centered in the central or anterolateral aspect of the shoulder; pain in a radicular pattern extending the length of the arm may have a neurologic component, and the possibility of cervical spine pathology or peripheral nerve compression should be investigated. Weight loss, a cough, or shortness of breath may indi-

cate systemic or lung disease. Rarely, shoulder pain is found to be a symptom of lung cancer.

Records from any earlier evaluation and treatment can help the surgeon determine whether the appropriate nonsurgical measures have been exhausted. A history of metabolic or rheumatologic disease may suggest earlier decision making related to shoulder arthroplasty. A compilation of the patient's concomitant medical conditions and a complete list of medications are necessary to understanding the patient's overall health.

### Physical Examination

The examination should begin with an inspection for muscular atrophy, cervical range of motion, and tenderness. A bilateral examination of the upper extremities includes the wrists, elbows, and shoulders. The neurovascular examination includes an assessment of strength, sensation, and reflexes. The Spurling test is performed to discover cervical radiculopathy.

The strength of the deltoid and periscapular muscles is tested. Active and passive shoulder abduction, as well as external and internal rotation, are evaluated and recorded. Range of motion is measured and described to detect anterosuperior humeral head escape or altered scapular motion. A scale of 1 to 5 is usually used to grade internal rotation, external rotation, flexion, extension, and abduction.

### Imaging Studies

The routine radiographic series includes an axillary view and a 40° posterior oblique view with internal and external rotation. An AP view is helpful in evaluating the superior-inferior and medial-lateral acromiohumeral distance. A patient with significant glenoid erosion may have a decrease in the amount of humeral head offset from the lateral border of the acromion; specifically, the lateral border of the humeral head may be medial to the lateral edge of the acromion (Figure 1). Superior subluxation of the humeral head and a decrease in the acromiohumeral distance, as seen in an AP view, is associated with rotator cuff deficiency. The AP view is also

---

*John W. Sperling, MD is a consultant or employee for Biomet.

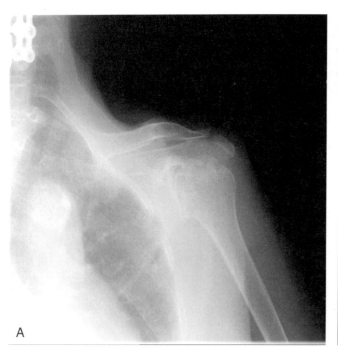
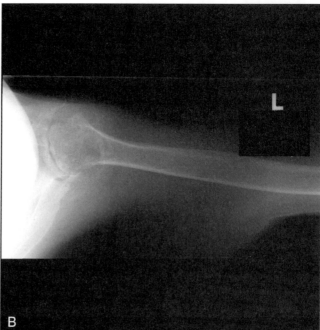

**Figure 1** Severe glenoid erosion seen on AP **(A)** and axillary **(B)** radiographs.

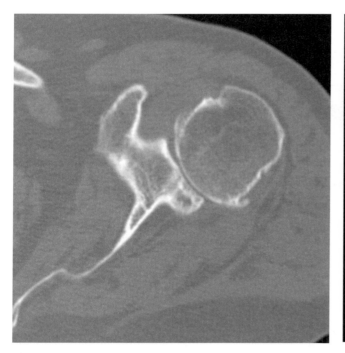

**Figure 2** CT scan showing a biconcave glenoid.

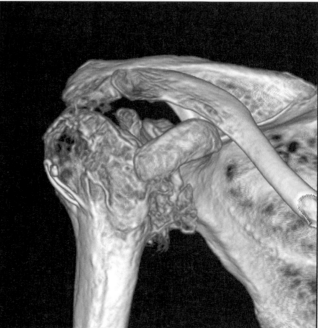

**Figure 3** Three-dimensional CT scan showing a humeral malunion.

helpful in determining cortical thickness, bone density, and humeral canal size. The axillary view allows assessment of glenoid version, glenoid erosion, and glenohumeral subluxation.

CT provides important information as to glenoid version and the degree of glenoid bone loss (Figure 2). In patients with posttraumatic arthritis, three-dimensional CT allows evaluation of the humerus and glenoid (Figure 3).

### Patient Counseling

A specific diagnosis can be determined by integrating the findings of the history, physical examination, and imaging studies. The treatment options are then discussed

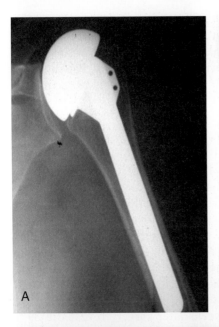
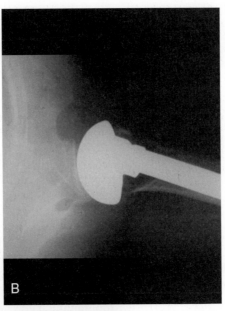
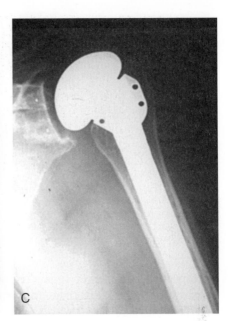
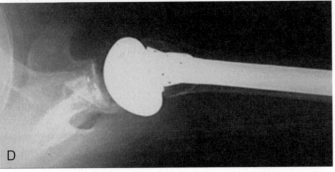

**Figure 4** AP **(A)** and axillary **(B)** radiographs of a patient who had continuing pain after a hemiarthroplasty for osteoarthritis. AP **(C)** and axillary **(D)** radiographs of the patient after revision TSA.

with the patient. The decision must be made as to whether glenoid resurfacing should be pursued and, if so, the type of glenoid resurfacing to be used. It is critical to understand the patient's goals and expectations of surgery. Clearly, the primary indication for shoulder arthroplasty is pain relief.

Total shoulder arthroplasty (TSA) is usually performed in a patient with glenoid wear who has an intact or repairable rotator cuff tear. The patient is counseled that the likelihood of achieving good or excellent pain relief after TSA is 90%. In contrast, the likelihood of good pain relief after hemiarthroplasty is 80% to 85%. Painful glenoid arthritis after a hemiarthroplasty is probably the most common reason revision surgery is required (Figure 4). TSA should not be performed unless the patient is willing to accept the associated restrictions. A standard glenoid component should not be used in a patient with severe glenoid bone deficiency or an irreparable rotator cuff tear.

## Biologic Resurfacing

Concern about the longevity of glenoid resurfacing has led to interest in using biologic materials for joint interposition. Before the evolution of modern arthroplasty,

shoulder fusion was considered for relatively young, active patients, and the results were satisfactory in approximately 80% of patients.[1] However, some patients had continued scapulothoracic pain and restricted motion. Interposition arthroplasty using a variety of biologic surfaces has been considered for younger patients because it allows preservation of glenoid bone stock for future procedures. In the first-described biologic resurfacing of the glenoid with hemiarthroplasty placement, 26 shoulders (24 patients) underwent interposition arthroplasty using anterior shoulder capsule, autogenous fascia lata, or Achilles tendon allograft[2] (Figure 5). A long-term study of 36 shoulders after hemiarthroplasty with biologic resurfacing found that the mean American Shoulder and Elbow Surgeons Index score improved from 39 to 91 points. Neer's criteria were used in determining that 18 shoulders had an excellent result; 13, a satisfactory result; and 5, an unsatisfactory result.[3]

## Total Shoulder Arthroplasty Versus Hemiarthroplasty

Whether TSA or hemiarthroplasty is preferable for treating osteoarthritis remains a subject of controversy. A

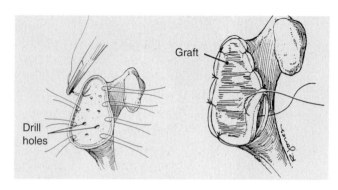

**Figure 5** A soft-tissue graft for interposition arthroplasty. **A,** Preparation. **B,** Placement. *(Reproduced with permission from Burkhead WZ, Hutton KS: Biologic resurfacing of the glenoid with hemiarthroplasty of the shoulder. J Shoulder Elbow Surg 1995; 4:263-270.)*

retrospective multicenter review of 601 TSAs and 89 hemiarthroplasties performed for osteoarthritis found that TSA was associated with significantly better functional outcome scores and pain relief at a minimum 2-year follow-up.[4] A review of 92 TSAs and 62 hemiarthroplasties in patients who were age 50 years or younger found that both procedures provided significant long-term improvement in pain, motion, and final outcome. Each of the patients was followed at least 15 years, or until revision surgery was required. No significant difference was found between TSA and hemiarthroplasty in pain, range of motion, or Neer rating. The 10-year survival rate of TSA was superior to that of hemiarthroplasty; early revision for painful glenoid arthritis was required in 12 patients who had undergone hemiarthroplasty. There was no significant difference in overall survival.[5]

Fifty-one shoulders with osteoarthritis, a concentric glenoid, and an intact rotator cuff were randomly assigned to receive a TSA or hemiarthroplasty. TSA was found to provide significantly greater pain relief. No revisions were required in the TSA group; three revisions were required for painful glenoid arthritis in the hemiarthroplasty group.[6] In another prospective study, 42 patients with osteoarthritis were randomly assigned to receive a TSA or hemiarthroplasty. The quality-of-life scores of the two groups did not significantly differ at a minimum 2-year follow-up. Two patients in the hemiarthroplasty group had required revision to a TSA because of painful glenoid arthritis.[7]

Thirty-seven TSAs and 28 hemiarthroplasties were performed in patients with an intact rotator cuff. At a mean 4.3-year follow-up, the mean American Shoulder and Elbow Surgeons Index score had improved from 37 to 91 in the TSA group and from 42 to 84 in the hemiarthroplasty group. The authors concluded that TSA was modestly superior in the medium term.[8]

Patients with rheumatoid arthritis were evaluated at a mean 11.6-year follow-up after TSA in 187 shoulders and hemiarthroplasty in 95 shoulders. Patients in both groups had marked pain relief and improved motion. Among patients with an intact rotator cuff, TSA resulted in superior pain relief and improvement in abduction, compared with hemiarthroplasty. Patients with an intact rotator cuff also were less likely to require revision surgery after TSA.[9]

## Glenoid Components
### Design
Glenoid component design may affect the risk of component loosening. Sixty-six TSAs were performed in patients with osteoarthritis, using either a keeled flat-back or keeled convex-back glenoid component. Radiographs taken immediately after surgery and 2 years later showed better results with the keeled convex-back component than with the keeled flat-back component.[10] In another study, 23 shoulders received a keeled glenoid component and 20 received a pegged component. Radiographs taken 6 weeks after surgery revealed a 39% rate of periprosthetic lucency in the shoulders with the keeled component and a 5% rate in the shoulders with the pegged component.[11]

### Preparation
Glenoid preparation may also affect the potential for glenoid component loosening. Thirty-seven shoulders received a cemented all-polyethylene flat-back glenoid component after standard curettage preparation, and 35 received the same component after bone compaction to prepare the keel slot. On the immediate postsurgical radiograph, more shoulders in the curettage group had lucent lines (38%) than in the bone compaction group (11%). The progression of lucent lines on later radiographs was also higher in the curettage group. The authors concluded that preparation of the keel slot with bone compaction appears to provide better fixation.[12]

A number of other methods are available to prepare the glenoid bone before implanting the component, although they have not been formally studied. In a typical current preparation, the bone surface is cleaned with pulsatile lavage and carefully dried with sponges. The technology is evolving to include the possible use of high-pressure air for cleaning and thrombin-soaked sponges for drying. Research is needed to clarify the use and relative benefits of new methods and techniques.

### Fixation
Interest in the use of cementless metal-backed glenoid components is increasing. In a prospective randomized study, 40 shoulders received either a cemented all-polyethylene glenoid component or a cementless metal-backed component. At a minimum 3-year follow-up, the survival of the cementless metal-backed components was significantly less than that of the cemented all-polyethylene components. The incidence of radiolucency

was greater in the all-polyethylene components and is a matter of concern.[13]

In a review of 147 shoulders with a cementless metal-backed glenoid component, the overall survival rate was 95% after 5 years and 85% after 10 years. The failure rate appeared to be higher in shoulders with a cementless metal-backed component than in shoulders with a cemented all-polyethylene component. Excessive polyethylene wear and screw breakage, leading to a higher failure rate, were cited as common complications associated with the uncemented metal-backed design.[14]

The effect of cementing technique on glenoid component fixation has recently been studied. In an investigation of cement placement using a syringe or finger pressure, as well as cement placement on the back of the glenoid component, the syringe was found to provide better fixation of a pegged glenoid component than finger pressure. Placing cement on the back of the glenoid component increased fixation by filling out irregularities after reaming.[15]

### Treatment of a Failed Component

Glenoid component loosening is an important concern related to TSA. The ability to evaluate patients for component loosening has improved, and there have been several recent reports on the treatment outcome of this complication.

Glenoid component loosening was assessed in 47 TSAs using fluoroscopically guided radiography and CT. CT was found to be more sensitive in detecting component loosening.[16] Of 24 patients who underwent component removal and glenoid bone grafting to treat component loosening, 22 had satisfactory pain relief at a mean 33-month follow-up. At a mean 11-month follow-up, 4 of the patients had received a second revision to a TSA, which resulted in satisfactory pain relief. Radiographs revealed graft subsidence in 10 of the remaining 20 patients. The authors concluded that bone grafting during revision may allow later placement of a glenoid component, if the pain persists.[17]

Forty-eight shoulders underwent glenoid component revision; 18 had component removal and bone grafting, and 30 had placement of a new glenoid component. At a mean 4.9-year follow-up, the patients who received a new glenoid component were significantly more satisfied than those who underwent removal and bone grafting.[18]

### Summary

Biologic resurfacing of the glenoid may be a reasonable option for a relatively young patient with glenohumeral osteoarthritis. However, TSA remains the preferred treatment for advanced glenohumeral osteoarthritis. Future improvements in surgical technique and implant design should lead to increased longevity of glenoid resurfacing.

## Annotated References

1. Cofield RH: Shoulder arthrodesis and resection arthroplasty of the shoulder. *Instr Course Lect* 1985;34: 268-277.

2. Burkhead WZ, Hutton KS: Biologic resurfacing of the glenoid with hemiarthroplasty of the shoulder. *J Shoulder Elbow Surg* 1995;4:263-270.

3. Krishnan SG, Nowinski RJ, Harrison D, Burkhead WZ: Humeral hemiarthroplasty with biologic resurfacing of the glenoid for glenohumeral arthritis: Two to fifteen-year outcomes. *J Bone Joint Surg Am* 2007; 89:727-734.

   A retrospective study of 36 shoulders after hemiarthroplasty and biologic resurfacing of the glenoid found 18 excellent, 13 satisfactory, and 5 unsatisfactory results, using Neer's criteria.

4. Edwards TB, Kadakia NR, Boulahia A, et al: A comparison of hemiarthroplasty and total shoulder arthroplasty in the treatment of primary glenohumeral osteoarthritis: Results of a multicenter study. *J Shoulder Elbow Surg* 2003;12:207-213.

   Follow-up at a minimum 2 years after TSA or hemiarthroplasty used physical examination, Constant score, and radiographic evaluation to conclude that TSA provides results superior to those of hemiarthroplasty in patients with primary osteoarthritis.

5. Sperling JW, Cofield RH, Rowland CM: Minimum fifteen-year follow-up of Neer hemiarthroplasty and total shoulder arthroplasty in patients aged fifty years or younger. *J Shoulder Elbow Surg* 2004;13: 604-613.

   At a minimum 15-year follow-up of 62 hemiarthroplasties and 92 TSAs in patients age 50 years or younger, both procedures provided significant improvement in pain and motion. There was no significant difference in pain, motion, and final outcome.

6. Gartsman GM, Roddey TS, Hammerman SM: Shoulder arthroplasty with or without resurfacing of the glenoid in patients who have osteoarthritis. *J Bone Joint Surg Am* 2000;82:26-34.

7. Lo IK, Litchfield RB, Griffen S, Faber K, Patterson SD, Kirkley A: Quality of life outcome following hemiarthroplasty or total shoulder arthroplasty in patients with osteoarthritis: A prospective, randomized trial. *J Bone Joint Surg Am* 2005;87:2178-2185.

   In a prospective study of 42 patients randomly assigned to receive a hemiarthroplasty or a TSA, no significant differences were found between the two groups in quality-of-life scores at a minimum 2-year follow-up.

8. Orfaly RM, Rockwood CA, Esenyel CZ, Wirth MA: A prospective functional outcome study of shoulder arthroplasty for osteoarthritis with an intact rotator cuff. *J Shoulder Elbow Surg* 2003;12:214-221.

This prospective study found a modest superiority of TSAs compared with hemiarthroplasty.

9. Sperling JW, Cofield RH, Schleck C, Harmsen WS: Total shoulder arthroplasty versus hemiarthroplasty for rheumatoid arthritis of the shoulder: Results of 303 consecutive cases. *J Shoulder Elbow Surg* 2007; 16:683-690.

Patients with rheumatoid arthritis had improvement in pain, active abduction, and external rotation after either TSA or hemiarthroplasty. Among patients with an intact rotator cuff, TSA appears to be preferred for pain relief, improved abduction, and lower risk of revision surgery.

10. Szabo I, Buscayret F, Edwards TB, Nemoz C, Boileau P, Walch G: Radiographic comparison of flat back and convex back glenoid components in total shoulder arthroplasty. *J Shoulder Elbow Surg* 2005; 14:636-642.

The radiographic results of convex-back keeled glenoid components were found to be better than those of keeled flat-back components.

11. Gartsman GM, Elkousy HA, Warnock KM, Edwards TB, O'Connor DP: Radiographic comparison of pegged and keeled glenoid components. *J Shoulder Elbow Surg* 2005;14:252-257.

The rate of radiographic lucency was significantly less in pegged glenoid components than in keeled glenoid components.

12. Szabo I, Buscayret F, Edwards TB, et al: Radiographic comparison of two glenoid preparation techniques in total shoulder arthroplasty. *Clin Orthop Relat Res* 2005;431:104-110.

In a comparison of the radiographic outcomes of 66 TSAs using two types of glenoid components, the keeled convex-back glenoid component was found to have a better outcome than the keeled flat-back glenoid component.

13. Boileau P, Avidor C, Krishnan SG, Walch G, Kempf JF, Mole D: Cemented polyethylene versus uncemented metal-backed glenoid components in total shoulder arthroplasty: A prospective, double-blind, randomized study. *J Shoulder Elbow Surg* 2002;11:351-359.

At a minimum 3-year follow-up, the survival rate of cementless metal-backed glenoid components was signifi-cantly less than that of cemented all-polyethylene glenoid components.

14. Martin SD, Zurakowski D, Thornhill TS: Uncemented glenoid component in total shoulder arthroplasty: Survivorship and outcome. *J Bone Joint Surg Am* 2005;87:1284-1292.

A review of 147 shoulders with a cementless glenoid component found a higher failure rate compared with all-polyethylene glenoid components, at a similar follow-up. Excessive polyethylene wear as well as screw breakage were common in the metal-backed glenoid components.

15. Nyffeler RW, Meyer D, Sheikh BJ, Gerber C: The effect of cementing technique on structural fixation of pegged glenoid components in total shoulder arthroplasty. *J Shoulder Elbow Surg* 2006;15:106-111.

Placement of cement with a syringe resulted in better fixation than finger pressure in preparing a pegged glenoid component. Placing cement on the back of the glenoid component improved fixation.

16. Yian EH, Werner CM, Nyffeler RW, et al: Radiographic and computed tomography analysis of cemented pegged polyethylene glenoid components in total shoulder arthroplasty. *J Bone Joint Surg Am* 2005;87:1928-1936.

CT scans were found to be a more sensitive method of evaluating glenoid component loosening than fluoroscopically guided radiography.

17. Phipatanakul WP, Norris TR: Treatment of glenoid loosening and bone loss due to osteolysis with glenoid bone grafting. *J Shoulder Elbow Surg* 2006;15: 84-87.

Of 24 patients treated for glenoid component loosening, 18 had satisfactory pain relief, including 4 who had received a second revision to TSA with a satisfactory outcome.

18. Antuna SA, Sperling JW, Cofield RH, Rowland CM: Glenoid revision surgery after total shoulder arthroplasty. *J Shoulder Elbow Surg* 2001;10:217-224.

In a retrospective review of 48 shoulders after glenoid component revision, patients who underwent placement of a new glenoid component were significantly more satisfied than those who underwent removal and bone grafting.

# Chapter 36

# Arthroplasty for Acute and Chronic Fractures

François Sirveaux, MD, PhD

*Daniel Molé, MD

## Introduction

Neer reported initial encouraging results after arthroplasty for proximal humerus fractures.[1,2] Many surgeons have tried to replicate Neer's results, but the data often have revealed less than satisfactory outcomes. Most have reported good pain relief but disappointing functional results. Analyses of clinical failures have led to many changes in prosthetic design and surgical technique. Some of the factors affecting the outcome after surgery are patient related or fracture related and cannot be modified; health status and fracture severity are two of these factors. Arthroplasty is appropriate for elderly patients with a comminuted four-part fracture or occasionally a three-part fracture. The reverse prosthesis has been suggested as an alternative for fracture treatment in elderly patients because good results have been reported after the reverse prosthesis was used for other indications in this patient population. This chapter reviews the latest published information regarding arthroplasty for fractures and briefly discusses future considerations in this rapidly changing area of shoulder surgery.

## Presurgical Assessment

The goal of surgical treatment for a proximal humerus fracture is to obtain an anatomic reconstruction while preserving the vascularity of the humeral head. Prosthetic replacement of the humeral head is indicated if stability cannot otherwise be restored or if humeral head necrosis is likely. Primary hemiarthroplasty is performed for displaced four-part fractures, with or without humeral head dislocation; head-split fractures; impaction fractures with involvement of more than 40% of the articular surface; and some three-part fractures with marked displacement and diminished bone stock. Although the indications for shoulder hemiarthroplasty have changed little during the past several years, some selection criteria have been modified in response to

complications, failures, and improvements in internal fixation techniques.

### Patient-Related Factors

Patient assessment is essential before hemiarthroplasty. It includes evaluation of both the impaired shoulder and the patient's general health status. Proximal humerus fractures are the third most common type of fracture in elderly patients, after hip and distal radius fractures, and their incidence has increased dramatically. Between 1970 and 2002, a 243% age-adjusted increase in incidence was found in women and a 153% increase was found in men.[3] This trend, in conjunction with the increasing size of the elderly population, led to an estimate that the number of proximal humerus fractures in elderly patients could triple by 2030. Shoulder replacement surgery is likely to be required to treat many of these fractures. Several studies found that patient age significantly affects the results of surgery. A review of 66 patients treated with shoulder hemiarthroplasty for fracture identified the factors associated with poor outcome.[4] Tuberosity migration was more common in women older than 75 years. A delayed rehabilitation protocol was therefore recommended for these patients. A retrospective multicenter study of 167 patients found that poor outcomes and poor subjective results in elderly patients correlates with lack of tuberosity healing. This study also established that elderly patients are no more likely than younger patients to accept pain and loss of motion.[5] Another study found that patients age 65 years or younger have a better range of motion after hemiarthroplasty than patients who are older.[6] These results were attributed to poor bone quality, poor general health status, and the presence of medical comorbidities in patients older than 65 years.

Neurologic deficits, tobacco usage, and alcohol consumption can jeopardize the results of surgical treatment for a proximal humerus fracture.[7] These factors were included in two statistical models using multiple regression analysis to predict a patient's Constant score 1 year after surgery (Tables 1 and 2). The presurgical as-

---

*Daniel Mole, MD or the department with which he is affiliated has received royalties from Tornier.*

**Table 1 | Early Multiple Regression Model Used Before Surgery to Predict Constant Score at 1 Year**

**Predicted Constant Score =**
127.3 - (0.8 × age) - (12.5 × neurologic deficit) - (2.1 × weekly alcohol consumption) - (1.9 × daily tobacco consumption).

| Age | Neurologic Deficit | Presurgical Factors | |
|---|---|---|---|
| | | **Alcohol Consumption (Units per Week)** | **Tobacco Consumption (Cigarettes per Day)** |
| Number of years | 0 = No deficit<br>1 = Neurologic deficit | 0 = None<br>1 = 1-10<br>2 = 11-20<br>3 = 21-30<br>4 = > 30 | 0 = None<br>1 = 1-10<br>2 = 11-20<br>3 = 21-30<br>4 = > 30 |

*(Adapted with permission from Robinson CM, Page RS, Hill RM, Sanders DL, Court-Brown CM, Wakefield AE: Primary hemiarthroplasty for treatment of proximal humeral fractures. J Bone Joint Surg Am 2003;85:1215-1223.)*

**Table 2 | Multiple Regression Model Used 6 Weeks After Surgery to Predict Constant Score at 1 Year**

**Predicted Constant Score =**
118.0 - (0.7 × age) - (11.9 × neurologic deficit) - (10.9 × revision) - (7.6 × prosthesis position) - (5.9 × tuberosity position).

| Age | Neurologic Deficit | Postsurgical Factors | | |
|---|---|---|---|---|
| | | **Revision** | **Prosthesis Position*** | **Tuberosity Position** |
| Number of years | 0 = No deficit<br>1 = Neurologic deficit before surgery | 0 = No revision<br>1 = Revision within first 6 weeks | 0 = Anatomically positioned or displaced < 5 mm<br>1 = Displaced superiorly or inferiorly by 5-10 mm<br>2 = Displaced superiorly or inferiorly by > 10 mm | 0 = Anatomically positioned or displaced < 10 mm<br>1 = Displaced 10-20 mm<br>2 = Displaced > 20 mm |

*Position of the center of the prosthetic head relative to the central axis of the glenoid.

*(Adapted with permission from Robinson CM, Page RS, Hill RM, Sanders DL, Court-Brown CM, Wakefield AE: Primary hemiarthroplasty for treatment of proximal humeral fractures. J Bone Joint Surg Am 2003;85:1215-1223.)*

sessment must also include the patient's immune status, because immunosuppressive therapy, as well as diabetes mellitus, malignant lesions, and rheumatoid arthritis, increases the risk of infection.[8] It is important to evaluate the patient's ability to comply with postsurgical activity restrictions and rehabilitation.

### Fracture-Related Factors

The primary indication for hemiarthroplasty is the presence of a four-part fracture. Osteosynthesis of a four-part fracture should be considered in view of the disappointing reported functional results of hemiarthroplasty. The reported rate of humeral head necrosis ranges from 26% to 75% in a four-part fracture. It is possible to use a minimally invasive technique for osteosynthesis even in elderly patients.[9] Hemiarthroplasty is recommended only for an elderly, sedentary patient with poor bone quality and a displaced articular fracture.[10] Most valgus-impacted fractures are amenable to fixation, even in elderly patients. Minimal displacement of the medial aspect of the humeral metaphysis and integrity of the me-

dial periosteum were considered to be determinants of humeral head blood supply.[11] In another study, the length of the dorsomedial metaphyseal extension and the integrity of the medial hinge were found to be the most relevant predictors of ischemia.[12]

Presurgical radiographs are essential to evaluate the anatomy of the proximal humerus. Full-length scaled radiographs of the injured and contralateral humeri may be taken. At least two radiographic orthogonal views are necessary to analyze the fracture pattern. CT is useful in analyzing a complex fracture[13,14] and provides information about the status of the cuff by revealing fatty infiltration of the muscle. However, a deficient cuff is not usually present with a three-part or four-part fracture.[15] A cadaver study found that CT measurements of humeral head retroversion are reproducible and that the angles vary little from side to side.[16] The retroversion on the unimpaired side was used as a reference during surgery in six patients treated with hemiarthroplasty for fracture, and the study findings suggest that a presurgical CT of the contralateral side may be useful in implant positioning.[16]

Several studies focused on the optimal timing of surgery. Patients who were surgically treated within the first 2 weeks after injury were found to have better scores on the American Shoulder and Elbow Surgeons Shoulder Index than those treated later.[15] Two other studies concluded that the optimal time for surgery is between 6 and 10 days after injury.[17,18] The delay allows for treatment of medical comorbidities, resolution of some of the hematoma and tissue swelling around the shoulder joint, complete radiographic and CT studies to identify a possible occult fracture, and patient education as to the expected results and potential complications. After 20 days, the ability to mobilize and fix the tuberosities may be compromised by early healing or bone resorption.[17] Another study found that shoulders surgically treated within 14 days of injury achieve a greater range of motion in abduction than those treated later.[19]

## Surgeon-Related Factors

Hemiarthroplasty for a proximal humerus fracture is a demanding procedure, and a relationship has been found between outcomes and the number of procedures a surgeon performs. A multicenter study of 167 patients found that patients treated by surgeons who performed fewer than 15 hemiarthroplasty procedures for fracture per year had inferior clinical results and a lower rate of tuberosity healing.[5] A study of the relationship between surgeon and hospital volume and the outcomes of shoulder arthroplasty in the United States found a higher rate of complications and a longer average hospital stay after hemiarthroplasty performed by surgeons who performed only one shoulder arthroplasty per year, compared with surgeons who performed more than five shoulder arthroplasties per year.[20] More than 75% of shoulder surgeons in the state of New York performed only one or two shoulder replacements a year.[21] It can be extrapolated from this information that most hemiarthroplasties for fracture are performed by a surgeon who is inexperienced in the procedure. Little evidence-based literature is available to guide surgeons' decision making.[22]

## Hemiarthroplasty

### Technique

The deltopectoral approach is traditionally used for humeral head replacement (HHR), although the anterosuperior approach has become popular for the treatment of a proximal humerus fracture and placement of a reverse prosthesis.[23,24] The axillary nerve must be identified if a distal exposure is required. No clinical reports are available to support the theoretic advantages of the anterosuperior approach.

After the humeral head and the tuberosities are identified, strong nonabsorbable sutures are placed around the tuberosities at the tendon insertion. Gentle manipulation of the tuberosities is recommended to preserve the periosteal attachment between the tuberosities and the humeral shaft. The bicipital groove and the superior border of the pectoralis major can be used as landmarks for prosthesis positioning.[25,26] The role of the long head of the biceps is controversial. Some surgeons believe that, because the long head of the biceps may be entrapped in the fragment, a systematic tenotomy and tenodesis should be performed.[17,25,27] Others preserve the biceps as a landmark for tensioning.[13] No studies have found biceps tenotomy to have a statistically significant effect.

The results of hemiarthroplasty are strongly influenced by the restoration of the proximal humeral anatomy. A correlation was found between poor functional results and malpositioning of the prosthesis in height or retroversion.[4] Lengthening of the humerus of more than 10 mm and shortening of more than 15 mm after hemiarthroplasty had a significant detrimental effect on the final Constant Shoulder Score. Excessive prosthetic retroversion (> 40°) significantly affected the Constant score, as did range of motion in active anterior elevation and external rotation. After 16 hemiarthroplasties for fracture, the position of the prosthesis was analyzed using CT and the results were compared with the anatomy of the contralateral upper humerus.[28] A difference in retroversion of less than 10° and a difference in length of less than 14 mm were correlated with a higher Constant score.

The position of the tuberosity relative to the prosthesis is crucial and is correlated with outcome.[4,15,28] In the frontal plane, the position of the greater tuberosity in relation to the top of the head defines the head-to-tuberosity distance (HTD). In cadaver specimens, the HTD ranged from 3 to 20 mm (average, 8 ± 3 mm).[29] A correlation was found between the HDT and the functional result after hemiarthroplasty for fracture; the ideal HTD value was found to be between 5 and 10 mm.[15,18] Another study found that a slightly distal position (10 to 16 mm) is preferable because the prosthetic design used in the study produces less lateral offset than other designs.[30] In the more distal position, the tuberosity overlaps the shaft and thereby increases the bony contact between the greater tuberosity and the diaphysis.

Lateralization of the greater tuberosity is important for restoring the lever arm of the rotator cuff. The humeral offset refers to the distance between the center of the glenoid and the lateral cortex of the greater tuberosity. Loss of humeral offset was found to be correlated with poor clinical outcome.[18] Lateral offset can be restored by adding a lateral graft between the prosthesis and the greater tuberosity or by using a prosthesis with a larger body proximally to compensate for bone loss (Figure 1).

Techniques have been developed to improve prosthesis positioning. The first step is to restore humeral

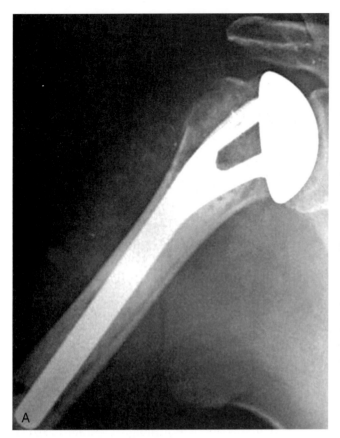
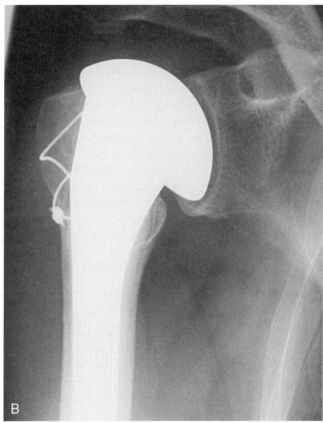

**Figure 1** Restoration of the humeral offset using a low-profile prosthesis with lateral graft (Aequalis Fracture, Tornier St. Imier, France) **(A)** or a bulky prosthesis (Epoca, Argomedical Cham, Switzerland) **(B)**. *(Courtesy of Professor R. Hertel, Bern, Switzerland.)*

length. The bone loss at the proximal shaft can be determined using radiographs and a template. Comparison radiographs of the opposite, uninjured side are often useful in assessing the extent of fracture at the medial calcar. During surgery, the trial component is introduced into the medullary canal. Proper prosthesis height can be approximated using soft-tissue tension, which should allow anteroposterior translation of the humeral head of approximately 50% and inferior translation of approximately 50% of the glenoid height.[13] Specialized intramedullary or transosseous devices have been developed to stabilize the trial prosthesis within the canal. An external jig can be used both to stabilize the trial prosthesis and reproduce the length of the humerus. The jig helps to maintain the proper height and correctly position the tuberosities.[27] The restoration of the so-called gothic arch creates a reproducible landmark during surgery, especially when visualized with fluoroscopy[17] (Figure 2). This technique led to an 81% rate of tuberosity healing. The superior border of the pectoralis major was found to be an accurate landmark for restoration of the humeral length. The distance between the superior border of the pectoralis major and the top of the humeral head is normally 5.5 cm (±0.5 cm).[31]

Version is the second important factor in positioning. Most studies recommend an average 20° to 30° of retroversion, which can be achieved by flexing the patient's elbow to 90° and placing the arm in 20° to 30° of external rotation while fixing the prosthesis in neutral position.[4,13] The head of the prosthesis should face the glenoid when the arm is in neutral position. In a cadaver study, the mean distance from the equatorial plane of the humeral head to the center of the distal part of the bicipital groove was found to be 8.5 mm.[26] This landmark can be used to determine retroversion. Excessive retroversion can lead to loss of fixation because of posterior migration of the greater tuberosity when the arm is internally rotated[4] (Figure 3).

The tuberosities are fixed using a combination of vertical and horizontal sutures. There is currently no indication for using an uncemented stem. Before cementing the prosthesis, two holes are drilled for the vertical sutures. A distal intramedullary plug is used to achieve cement pressurization in the humeral canal. In a patient with severe osteoporosis, the intramedullary plug should not be used because excessive pressurization can damage the humerus.[8] Excess cement is removed from the proximal part of the prosthesis to avoid compromising the healing of the tuberosities.

Fixation of the tuberosities is the most important part of the procedure. Strong, nonabsorbable suture or wire is used to achieve secure horizontal and vertical

fixation. The sutures are placed at the tendon-bone junction rather than through the bone of the tuberosities. The vertical sutures create a tension band effect between the tuberosities and the shaft (Figure 4). If severe tuberosity comminution is present, a Krakow weave suture can be used in the tendon to improve the fixation.[32] A cadaver study found that a circumferential medial cerclage suture improved fixation and interfragmentary stability.[33] The circumferential suture or wire can be passed through a medial hole or around the neck of the prosthesis.[4,33] Feathering of the lateral cortex of the proximal humerus was recommended to provide a bleeding surface for the tuberosity that overlaps the shaft.[13] It is especially important to fit the lateral bone graft under the greater tuberosity before tying the sutures. To ensure an arc of tension-free rotation, the greater tuberosity can be fixed with the arm in internal rotation, and the lesser tuberosity can be fixed with the arm in external rotation; the horizontal suture should be tied first to prevent overreducing the greater tuberosity. The cancellous graft taken from the head must be applied between the tuberosities and at the tuberosity-shaft junction to enhance healing. An AP radiograph can be taken during surgery to assess the position of the tuberosities before final fixation.[34]

## Prosthesis Design

Tuberosity malpositioning and migration are the main causes of failure after a hemiarthroplasty for fracture. A multicenter study found that prosthetic design affects tuberosity healing,[5] and specialized designs have been developed specifically for use in fractures. Most fracture stems can be adapted to fit the intramedullary canal appropriately and are designed to be used with cement. A long stem must be available for use in a fracture with diaphyseal extension. A modular head is preferable for recreating the normal anatomy. A new modular prosthesis with an enlarged rim on the head and 10 to 14 holes around the circumference allows the bone-tendon junc-

tion of the cuff to be fixed to the periphery via the holes.[35] The soft-tissue repair created using this prosthesis is designed to prevent migration of the tuberosities and permit early rehabilitation.

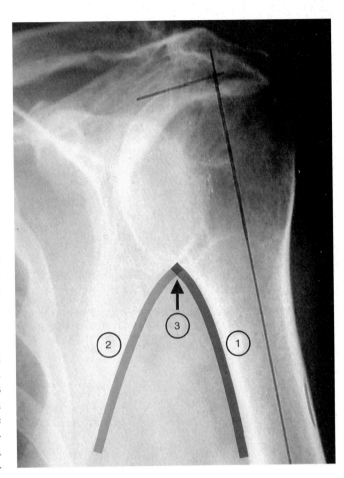

**Figure 2** The gothic arch of a normal shoulder. 1 = medial border of the proximal humerus, 2 = lateral border of the scapula to the base of the glenoid surface, 3 = joining of the lines to create the gothic arch shape. *(Reproduced with permission from Krishnan SG, Pennington SD, Burkhead WL: Shoulder arthroplasty for fracture: Restoration of the "gothic arch." Tech Shoulder Elbow Surg 2005;6:57-66.)*

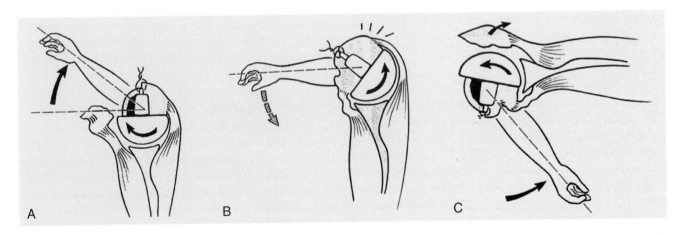

**Figure 3 A,** Excessive retroversion of the prosthesis forces the surgeon to fix the tuberosity with the arm in external rotation. **B,** The retroversion leads to suture pullout with the arm in neutral position. **C,** The retroversion leads to further disruption of the construct in internal rotation. *(Courtesy of Professor P. Boileau, Nice, France.)*

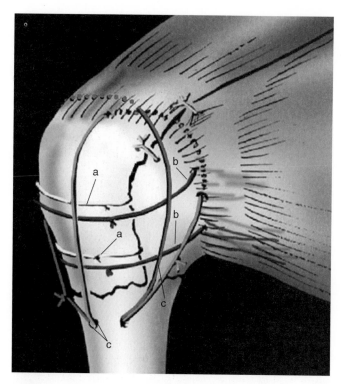

**Figure 4** The six-suture configuration consists of two horizontal sutures for the greater tuberosity (a), two horizontal sutures around the lesser and greater tuberosities (b), and two vertical tension band sutures (c). *(Reproduced with permission from Krishnan SG, Pennington SD, Burkhead WL: Shoulder arthroplasty for fracture: Restoration of the "gothic arch." Tech Shoulder Elbow Surg 2005;6:57-66.)*

Fracture-specific prosthesis design has advanced during the past several years. A low-profile fracture prosthesis was reported to cause only half as much tuberosity migration or malunion as a standard design stem, although the difference in clinical results was not significant in this retrospective comparison.[27] The use of a fracture-design prosthesis led to complete healing of the tuberosities in 50% of patients, compared with 29% of patients when a standard prosthesis was used.[36] However, the study included too few patients to reveal a significant difference in clinical outcomes. Another study also reported a high rate of tuberosity healing (81%) using a fracture prosthesis.[17]

### Rehabilitation

The patient's safe arc of motion at the end of the procedure can help define the range of passive motion during the first phase of rehabilitation.[25] Three-dimensional analysis of shoulder girdle mobility 1 to 6 years after hemiarthroplasty for fracture revealed that glenohumeral motion was reduced in relation to scapulothoracic motion.[19] The healing of the tuberosities should be evaluated radiographically 6 weeks after surgery, at which time active-assisted mobilization can start. Strengthening exercises should be initiated 12 weeks after surgery.

Minor variations in the rehabilitation program have been reported, but their influence on outcome has not been determined; for example, no immobilization combined with early passive motion was described in one study.[37] Ideally, the patient is able to return to daily activities 6 months after surgery. Although one study found no statistical improvement in Constant score from 6 months to 1 year after surgery,[7] some surgeons recommend that stretching and strengthening exercises be continued for 1 year after surgery.[13,38]

## Reverse Shoulder Arthroplasty

The use of a reverse prosthesis for proximal humerus fractures is not new; Grammont used a reverse prosthesis in 22 patients with an acute fracture or a fracture sequela between 1989 and 1993, but his results were not published. When used for massive rotator cuff tears or tumor resection, the reverse design restored active mobility in elevation, despite the loss of cuff function.[39-42] Poor results after hemiarthroplasty for fracture are clearly related to tuberosity migration or nonunion, which leads to inferior rotator cuff function. The reverse prosthesis improves shoulder function after revision for a failed hemiarthroplasty.[40,43] The reverse prosthesis is a promising alternative for the treatment of proximal humerus fractures in selected elderly patients (Figure 5). Little peer-reviewed research has been published on reverse prosthesis use for fracture. One study of early results reported a rather alarming rate of complications, including reflex sympathetic dystrophy, other neurologic complications, dislocation, calcification, and scapular notching.[44]

The advantages and risks of using a reverse prosthesis must be weighed in deciding whether it is appropriate for the patient. The reverse prosthesis is constrained, and concerns have been raised regarding its longevity.[45] It has a better survival rate when used in patients with cuff tear arthropathy than in patients with other etiologies, such as rheumatoid arthritis or trauma, or when used for revision surgery.[45] Although the indications are evolving, it appears that as techniques and prosthetic designs improve, reverse arthroplasty will play a prominent role in the future treatment of proximal humerus fractures.

## Fracture Sequelae
### Classification and Prognosis

Patients who require a shoulder arthroplasty for fracture sequelae are usually younger than patients treated with shoulder arthroplasty for other indications. Multiple studies reported unpredictable results and a high rate of complications after treatment of fracture sequelae. Fracture sequelae can be classified as nonunion or malunion of the proximal humerus, articular incongruence without distortion of the proximal humerus, or

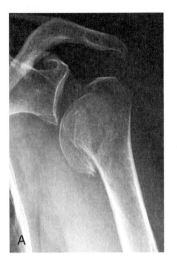
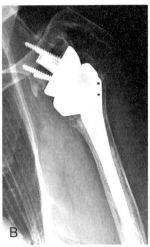
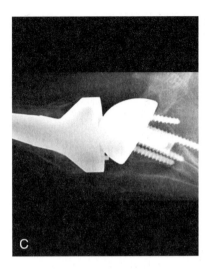

**Figure 5**  **A,** AP radiograph showing a four-part displaced fracture of the left shoulder in an 82-year-old woman. **B,** Postsurgical AP radiograph showing a reverse prosthesis with tuberosity fixation. **C,** Axillary radiograph showing healing of the tuberosities around the prosthesis at 1-year follow-up. **D,** The patient had recovered active anterior elevation and active external rotation at 1-year follow-up.

secondary osteonecrosis.[46-48] Three types of malunions are distinguished based on radiologic characteristics. Type I is a malposition of the greater or lesser tuberosity; type II, an articular incongruity; and type III, a malalignment of the articular surface (45° or more of rotational deformity of the articular surface with respect to the diaphysis, in any of three planes).[47]

Alternatively, fracture sequelae can be categorized on the basis of anatomic distortion, head and tuberosity position, and the need for an osteotomy of the greater tuberosity. Types I and II are secondary to an intracapsular, impacted compression fracture that leaves the greater tuberosity in continuity with the diaphysis; types III and IV are secondary to a major extracapsular, displaced fracture with rotational deformity of the greater tuberosity.[48] This classification system was validated in 203 patients treated with an unconstrained shoulder prosthesis and was found to be strongly correlated with the results of unconstrained prosthesis use. It is further discussed in chapter 39.

### Hemiarthroplasty

HHR is indicated for patients with joint incongruity or secondary degenerative changes.[47,49] The results are strongly influenced by the etiology and extent of initial deformity.[46-48,50,51] Hemiarthroplasty for surgical neck nonunion is controversial and is best reserved for nonunion associated with osteoporosis, severe cavitation of the head, or glenohumeral arthritis. At a minimum 5-year follow-up of 25 patients after treatment of surgical neck nonunion with hemiarthroplasty, pain was significantly improved but functional results were poor, with an average of 88° of active anterior elevation.[51] In 13 of 25 patients (62%), the results were unsatisfactory; 12 of 25 patients (48%) had failure related to nonunion,

malunion, or resorption of the greater tuberosity. The authors highlighted the risk of postsurgical instability and the importance of secure tuberosity fixation, recommending the addition of a bone graft. In another study, similar results were achieved in 28 patients, with an average adjusted Constant score of 45.[46] Disappointing results were also reported in 22 patients who had a mean Constant score of 36, 63° of active anterior elevation, a 32% complication rate, and a 13% revision rate.[48] The authors concluded that severe tuberosity malunion is a relative contraindication for hemiarthroplasty and, if possible, stabilization using a graft or HHR using a low-profile prosthesis should be performed to improve the healing of the tuberosity.

Shoulder replacement can provide pain relief and functional improvement for a patient with a posterior locked dislocation. Six patients were treated with total shoulder arthroscopy (TSA) and six were treated with HHR; after a minimum of 5 years, two patients had an early recurrence of dislocation, and three required revision.[52] Three patients treated with TSA and two treated with HHR had an unsatisfactory result. In a multicenter study, 25 patients had a locked dislocation or fracture-dislocation (type II sequela).[48] The average pain score on a 15-point scale significantly improved, from 5.5 before surgery to 12.5 at a minimum 2-year follow-up (range, 24 to 96 months). The average Constant score improved from 28 to 61. The patients gained an average of 44° in active anterior elevation and 36° in external rotation. The average Constant score of the patients treated with TSA was higher than that of patients treated with HHR. Complications appeared in 32%, and 24% required revision surgery. The authors concluded that, because of glenoid erosion, TSA is preferable to HHR if the dislocation has been present for many years.

The technical recommendations for shoulder arthroplasty include adapting the posterior offset of the head, grafting the glenoid in patients with bone deficiency, and immobilizing the arm in neutral or external rotation during the first 4 to 6 weeks.

Osteotomy of the tuberosity for proximal humeral malunion has a detrimental effect.[46,48,50] Types I and II fracture sequelae do not require osteotomy and are therefore differentiated from types III and IV fracture sequelae, which do require osteotomy.[48] Patients with a type I or II fracture sequela had a significantly higher Constant score than patients with a type III or IV sequela (62 and 42, respectively), and patients with a type I sequela had a substantially lower rate of complications than those with a type IV sequela (16% and 32%, respectively). Every complication impaired the results of surgery. Another study found similar results; in patients with a tuberosity osteotomy, the mean elevation was 86°, compared with 119° in patients without an osteotomy.[50] The osteotomy often led to nonunion, malunion, or resorption of the tuberosity, which jeopardized the surgical results.[48,50] It is preferable to avoid osteotomy of the greater tuberosity by adapting the prosthesis to the deformity, using a small stem or a stem with lateral offset. In 12 patients, the humeral components were malpositioned to accommodate the deformity; none of these patients required revision surgery for humeral component loosening.[50] Difficulty related to positioning of the stem because of the deformity in proximal humeral malunion has led some surgeons to promote a resurfacing replacement,[53] but no data have been published on the results.

Several negative prognostic factors have been identified. Pain relief was decreased in patients who had undergone surgical treatment of the initial fracture, developed humeral head osteonecrosis, or had arthroplasty within 2 years of the fracture.[50] Considering the predictably poor results of surgery, a type IV sequela was considered a relative contraindication to unconstrained shoulder replacement.[48]

## Future Considerations

Considering the potential increase in the number of patients who will need shoulder arthroplasty for fracture in the future, it is necessary to improve the reproducibility of the procedure so that the results do not depend on the experience of the surgeon. Every parameter in surgical decision making must be thoroughly considered. Patient selection is of great importance, even though patient compliance is difficult to anticipate before surgery. Presurgical CT and imaging of the contralateral side may aid in restoring the anatomy. As has been clearly demonstrated, the quality of surgical technique is a factor determining the results. Computer-assisted surgery may be helpful in reproducing the anatomy, especially retroversion. The addition of biologic substrates may enhance healing of the tuberosities. In the long term, it must be considered that the results of hemiarthroplasty deteriorate with time because of glenoid erosion, especially when used for an acute or chronic fracture in a young patient.[54,55] Alternatives to shoulder replacement and additional biologic resurfacing for young patients will increasingly be of interest.[56]

Exploration of the use of the reverse prosthesis for fracture is only beginning. Implant design and surgical technique can be improved, as they were for hemiarthroplasty. Studies are needed to clarify the role of tuberosity fixation, although clinical follow-up is difficult because advanced patient age at the time of surgery means that a high percentage of patients are expected to die during the study period.

## Summary

Although arthroplasty for fracture of the proximal humerus is an established procedure, many are challenging its effectiveness and reconsidering its role. Few studies have reported excellent outcomes after hemiarthroplasty for acute fracture, as originally reported by Neer. However, severe fractures that are not amenable to osteosynthesis do require treatment, either as acute injuries or late mechanical problems of the glenohumeral joint. As patient populations continue to age, these fractures will become not only more common but also more difficult to treat effectively. The reverse shoulder prosthesis may offer opportunities to restore function lost after severe fracture in elderly patients.

## Annotated References

1. Neer CS II: Displaced proximal humeral fractures: Classification and evaluation. *J Bone Joint Surg Am* 1970;52:1077-1089.

2. Neer CS II: Displaced proximal humeral fractures: II. Treatment of three-part and four-part displacement. *J Bone Joint Surg Am* 1970;52:1090-1103.

3. Palvanen M, Kannus P, Niemi S, Parkkari J: Update in the epidemiology of proximal humeral fractures. *Clin Orthop Relat Res* 2006;442:87-92.

   Epidemiologic data on proximal humerus fractures were collected from the Finnish National Register from 1970 to 2002. Overall and age-adjusted incidence increased during the three decades, especially among elderly women. If the trend continues, the number of proximal humerus fractures will triple during the next three decades.

4. Boileau P, Krishnan SG, Tinsi L, Walch G, Coste JS, Molé D: Tuberosity malposition and migration: Reasons for poor outcomes after hemiarthroplasty for displaced fractures of the proximal humerus. *J Shoulder Elbow Surg* 2002;11:401-412.

In 65 patients at a mean 27-month follow-up after hemiarthroplasty for a displaced proximal humerus fracture, the factors associated with failure of tuberosity osteosynthesis were poor initial position of the prosthesis (excessive height or retroversion), poor position of the greater tuberosity, and the combination of age older than 75 years and female gender.

5. Kralinger F, Schwaiger R, Wambacher M, et al: Outcome after primary hemiarthroplasty for fracture of the head of the humerus: A retrospective multicentre study of 167 patients. *J Bone Joint Surg Br* 2004;86: 217-219.

A multicenter retrospective study of 167 hemiarthroplasties for fracture from 12 Austrian hospitals compared different types of prostheses. At a mean 29-month follow-up, 79% of the patients had mild or no pain, and the mean overall Constant score was 55. Tuberosity healing was influenced by patient age, prosthesis design, and the number of hemiarthroplasties performed at the institution. Level of evidence: III.

6. Prakash U, McGurty DW, Dent JA: Hemiarthroplasty for severe fractures of the proximal humerus. *J Shoulder Elbow Surg* 2002;11:428-430.

The outcomes of 22 patients followed for a mean 33 months after hemiarthroplasty for proximal humerus fracture are described. Pain relief was the most predictable outcome. Most patients were satisfied, and the results were better in younger patients.

7. Robinson CM, Page RS, Hill RM, Sanders DL, Court-Brown CM, Wakefield AE: Primary hemiarthroplasty for treatment of proximal humeral fractures. *J Bone Joint Surg Am* 2003;85:1215-1223.

In a 13-year study of 138 patients after hemiarthroplasty for proximal humerus fracture, the overall rate of prosthesis survival was 97% at 1 year and 94% at 10 years. The overall modified Constant score was 64. Factors predictive of 1-year Constant score are defined.

8. Plausinis D, Kwon YW, Zuckerman JD: Complications of humeral head replacement for proximal humeral fractures. *Instr Course Lect* 2005;54:371-380.

The incidence and complications of HHR were analyzed by reviewing published studies. Infection, nerve injury, intrasurgical fracture, instability, complications related to the tuberosities and cuff, component-related complications, heterotopic ossifications, glenoid complications, and stiffness are emphasized. Level of evidence: V.

9. Aschauer E, Resch H: Four-part proximal humeral fractures: ORIF, in Warner JJ, Iannotti JP, Flatow E (eds): *Complex and Revision Problems in Shoulder Surgery*, ed 2. Philadelphia, PA, Lippincott Williams & Wilkins, 2005, pp 289-309.

The principles and the techniques of osteosynthesis for four-part fractures are discussed, with a detailed description of the percutaneous technique developed by Resch. Level of evidence: V.

10. DeFranco MJ, Brems JJ, Williams GR Jr, Iannotti JP: Evaluation and management of valgus impacted four-part proximal humerus fractures. *Clin Orthop Relat Res* 2006;442:109-114.

Pathoanatomy and prognostic factors related to valgus impacted fractures are described, as well as the less invasive techniques for osteosynthesis. Level of evidence: V.

11. Iannotti JP, Ramsey ML, Williams GR Jr, Warner JJ: Nonprosthetic management of proximal humeral fractures. *Instr Course Lect* 2004;53:403-416.

Presurgical assessment and classification of proximal humerus fracture are described, with the factors to be considered in choosing among immobilization, osteosynthesis (including different techniques), and humeral head replacement. Level of evidence: V.

12. Hertel R, Hempfing A, Stiehler M, Leunig M: The risk of necrosis following proximal humeral fracture, in Boileau P (ed): *Shoulder Arthroscopy and Arthroplasty: Current Concepts 2006*. Montpellier, France, Sauramps Medical, 2006, p 194.

The predictive factors for necrosis are discussed. Radiologic and intrasurgical findings were identified in a prospective study of 100 patients with intracapsular fracture. Dorsomedial metaphyseal extension and the medial hinge of the fracture were found to be the most relevant factors in ischemia. Level of evidence: II.

13. Dines DM, Tuckman D, Dines J: Hemiarthroplasty for complex four-part fracture of the proximal humerus: Technical considerations and surgical technique. *Univ Pennsyl Orthop J* 2002;15:29-36.

The indications, surgical technique, and results of hemiarthroplasty for complex four-part fractures of the proximal humerus are described.

14. Mora Guix JM, Gonzalez AS, Brugalla JV, Carril EC, Banos FG: Proposed protocol for reading images of humeral head fractures. *Clin Orthop Relat Res* 2006; 448:225-233.

The authors' protocol, using 17 parameters on radiographs and 11 parameters on CT to assess proximal humerus fractures, was evaluated in 30 patients. Combined radiographs and CT have the best interobserver and intraobserver reliability in fracture assessment. Level of evidence: III.

15. Mighell MA, Kolm GP, Collinge CA, Frankle MA: Outcomes of hemiarthroplasty for fractures of the proximal humerus. *J Shoulder Elbow Surg* 2003;12: 569-577.

A review of 71 patients treated with hemiarthroplasty found that 93% were pain free and satisfied with the result. The mean American Shoulder and Elbow Surgeons Index score was 76. Healing of the greater tuberosity more than

2 cm below the humeral head was correlated with a poor functional result.

16. Hernigou P, Duparc F, Hernigou A: Determining humeral retroversion with computed tomography. *J Bone Joint Surg Am* 2002;84-A:1753-1762.

   A study of 120 cadaver humeri found that retroversion of the proximal part of the humerus can be reliably measured using CT.

17. Krishnan SG, Pennington S, Burkhead W: Shoulder arthroplasty for fracture: Restoration of the "gothic arch." *Tech Shoulder Elbow Surg* 2005;6:57-66.

   The medial calcar of the humerus was used as a surgical landmark to adapt the height of the prosthesis during hemiarthroplasty for fracture. Thirty-two patients had short-term functional improvement compared with an earlier series. Level of evidence: IV.

18. Demirhan M, Kilicoglu O, Altinel L, Eralp L, Akalin Y: Prognostic factors in prosthetic replacement for acute proximal humerus fractures. *J Orthop Trauma* 2003;17:181-188.

   In 32 patients evaluated at a mean 35-month follow-up, presurgical delay, difficulty with tuberosity fixation, and tuberosity position were the factors influencing clinical outcome. Lateralization of the tuberosities was related to a better outcome, and distal transfer was related to a poorer outcome.

19. Becker R, Pap G, Machner A, Neumann WH: Strength and motion after hemiarthroplasty in displaced four-fragment fracture of the proximal humerus: 27 patients followed for 1-6 years. *Acta Orthop Scand* 2002;73:44-49.

   Isometric strength measurement and three-dimensional motion analysis were performed on the surgically treated and contralateral shoulders of 27 patients. Impaired function appeared to be caused by reduced glenohumeral mobility rather than muscle strength, and the outcome was better after early rather than late hemiarthroplasty.

20. Jain N, Pietrobon R, Hocker S, Guller U, Shankar A, Higgins LD: The relationship between surgeon and hospital volume and outcomes for shoulder arthroplasty. *J Bone Joint Surg Am* 2004;86-A:496-505.

   Surgeon and hospital volume were found to influence the rate of postsurgical complications and the length of hospital stay after TSA or hemiarthroplasty. Level of evidence: III.

21. Hasan SS, Leith JM, Smith KL, Matsen FA III: The distribution of shoulder replacement among surgeons and hospitals is significantly different than that of hip or knee replacement. *J Shoulder Elbow Surg* 2003;12:164-169.

   More than 40% of hip or knee replacement surgeons in New York State were found to have performed 10 or more replacements in 1998. In contrast, only 3% of shoulder replacement surgeons performed 10 or more replacements.

22. Misra A, Kapur R, Maffulli N: Complex proximal humeral fractures in adults: A systematic review of management. *Injury* 2001;32:363-372.

   In 24 published reports on the clinical outcomes of treatment of three- and four-part proximal humerus fractures, nonsurgically treated patients had more pain and poorer range of motion. Fixation produced better restoration of anatomy. The data are inadequate for evidence-based decision making.

23. Seebauer L, Walter W, Keyl W: Reverse total shoulder arthroplasty for the treatment of defect arthropathy. *Oper Orthop Traumatol* 2005;17:1-24.

   The indications and contraindications for use of the reverse prosthesis are analyzed in detail and the surgical technique is described. The authors developed a four-type functional and biomechanical classification for arthropathies associated with cuff deficiency. Level of evidence: V.

24. Webb M, Funk L: An anterosuperior approach for proximal humeral fractures. *Tech Shoulder Elbow Surg* 2006;7:77-81.

   The anterosuperior approach was modified for internal fixation and hemiarthroplasty. The authors describe the method for extending the approach inferiorly and exposing, mobilizing, and protecting the axillary nerve. Level of evidence: V.

25. Gerber A, Warner JJ: Hemiarthroplasty for management of complex proximal humerus fractures: Preoperative planning and surgical solution, in Warner JJ, Iannotti JP, Flatow E (eds): *Complex and Revision Problems in Shoulder Surgery,* ed 2. Philadelphia, PA, Lippincott Williams & Wilkins, 2005, pp 311-329.

   The technique of hemiarthroplasty for proximal humerus fractures is discussed, with a detailed description of prosthesis positioning. Level of evidence: V.

26. Hempfing A, Leunig M, Ballmer FT, Hertel R: Surgical landmarks to determine humeral head retrotorsion for hemiarthroplasty in fractures. *J Shoulder Elbow Surg* 2001;10:460-463.

   A study to determine criteria for adjusting retrotorsion when the proximal bicipital groove is destroyed found that adjusting the retrotorsion of the prosthetic component to the distal bicipital groove is adequate.

27. Boileau P, Coste JS, Ahrens P, Staccini P: Prosthetic shoulder replacement for fracture: Results of the multicentre study, in Walch G, Boileau P, Molé D (eds): *2000 Shoulder Protheses: Two to Ten Years Follow-up*. Montpellier, France, Sauramps Medical, 2001, pp 561-573.

   In a retrospective multicenter study of shoulder replacement for fractures, 431 patients were reviewed clinically and radiologically. Epidemiologic data and clinical results are reported by type of prosthesis. The prognostic factors were found to be malposition or migration of the tuberosities, restoration of height and retroversion, use of the fracture jig, immobilization, and rehabilitation. Level of evidence: III.

28. Christoforakis JJ, Kontakis GM, Katonis PG, et al: Relevance of the restoration of humeral length and retroversion in hemiarthroplasty for humeral head fractures. *Acta Orthop Belg* 2003;69:226-232.

At 46-month follow-up after hemiarthroplasty for proximal humerus fracture, patients who had a difference in retroversion of less than 10° and a difference in length between fractured and sound humeri of less than 14 mm had a very good clinical outcome.

29. Iannotti JP, Gabriel JP, Schneck SL, Evans BG, Misra S: The normal glenohumeral relationships: An anatomical study of one hundred and forty shoulders. *J Bone Joint Surg Am* 1992;74:491-500.

30. Loebenberg MI, Jones DA, Zuckerman JD: The effect of greater tuberosity placement on active range of motion after hemiarthroplasty for acute fractures of the proximal humerus. *Bull Hosp Jt Dis* 2005;62: 90-93.

The influence of greater tuberosity position on clinical results is analyzed in a retrospective study of 23 patients after hemiarthroplasty for fracture, and the position is compared with that of 50 normal proximal humeri. The authors conclude that the greater tuberosity must be placed 10 to 16 mm below the humeral head. Level of evidence: III.

31. Murachovsky J, Ikemoto RY, Nascimento LG, Fujiki EN, Milani C, Warner JJ: Pectoralis major tendon reference (PMT): A new method for accurate restoration of humeral length with hemiarthroplasty for fracture. *J Shoulder Elbow Surg* 2006;15:675-678.

In a cadaver study of 20 paired humeri, the pectoralis major tendon was found to be a useful landmark in restoring humeral length in complex proximal humerus fractures.

32. Frankle MA, Mighell MA: Techniques and principles of tuberosity fixation for proximal humeral fractures treated with hemiarthroplasty. *J Shoulder Elbow Surg* 2004;13:239-247.

Recent developments in prosthesis design and tuberosity fixation are described, and biomechanics are discussed to support the fixation technique promoted by the authors. Level of evidence: V.

33. Frankle MA, Ondrovic LE, Markee BA, Harris ML, Lee WE III: Stability of tuberosity reattachment in proximal humeral hemiarthroplasty. *J Shoulder Elbow Surg* 2002;11:413-420.

A cadaver study found that hemiarthroplasty for four-part proximal humerus fractures should incorporate a circumferential medial cerclage to decrease interfragmentary motion and strain, maximize fracture stability, and facilitate rehabilitation.

34. Boileau P, Sinnerton RJ, Chuinard C, Walch G: Arthroplasty of the shoulder. *J Bone Joint Surg Br* 2006; 88:562-575.

This overview of recent advances in prosthesis design for TSA and hemiarthroplasty for acute fracture and sequelae includes the reverse prosthesis. Level of evidence: V.

35. De Wilde LF, Berghs BM, Beutler T, Ferguson SJ, Verdonk RC: A new prosthetic design for proximal humeral fractures: Reconstructing the glenohumeral unit. *J Shoulder Elbow Surg* 2004;13:373-380.

The authors developed a new model of hemiarthroplasty for fracture and performed biomechanical testing with two types of tuberosity fixation. The prosthesis is designed to improve tuberosity fixation by adding sutures fixed through the cuff and around the head of the prosthesis. Level of evidence: III.

36. Loew M, Heitkemper S, Parsch D, Schneider S, Rickert M: Influence of the design of the prosthesis on the outcome after hemiarthroplasty of the shoulder in displaced fractures of the head of the humerus. *J Bone Joint Surg Br* 2006;88:345-350.

A standard anatomic implant or an implant designed for fracture was used in 39 patients. The implant designed for fracture allowed for increased tuberosity healing, although no significant difference was found in functional results. Level of evidence: III.

37. Brems JJ: Shoulder arthroplasty in the face of acute fracture: Puzzle pieces. *J Arthroplasty* 2002;17 (suppl 1):32-35.

The surgical principles and techniques that allow anatomic reconstruction of the proximal humerus are reviewed and discussed, emphasizing tuberosity placement and fixation.

38. Abrutyn D, Dines D: Secure tuberosity fixation in shoulder arthroplasty for fractures. *Tech Shoulder Elbow Surg* 2004;5:177-183.

Tuberosity reconstruction in hemiarthroplasty for fracture is described, with an emphasis on achieving secure and anatomic tuberosity fixation. Level of evidence: V.

39. Sirveaux F, Favard L, Oudet D, Huquet D, Walch G, Molé D: Grammont inverted total shoulder arthroplasty in the treatment of glenohumeral osteoarthritis with massive rupture of the cuff: Results of a multicentre study of 80 shoulders. *J Bone Joint Surg Br* 2004;86:388-395.

In a retrospective multicenter study of 80 patients, the authors propose a new classification of glenoid erosion in cuff-deficient shoulders, emphasizing the problem of the glenoid notch. The status of the teres minor influences recovery of external rotation.

40. De Wilde L, Mombert M, Van Petegem P, Verdonk R: Revision of shoulder replacement with a reversed shoulder prosthesis (Delta III): Report of five cases. *Acta Orthop Belg* 2001;67:348-353.

This short retrospective study is the first of patients with a reverse prosthesis for revision of shoulder replacement.

The mean Constant score improved from 14 to 62. Level of evidence: IV.

41. Seebauer L: Reverse prosthesis through a superior approach for cuff tear arthropathy. *Tech Shoulder Elbow Surg* 2006;7:13-26.

   A new classification of cuff tear arthropathy, based on pathomechanical and morphologic findings, is described, with a technique using a superior approach. In 56 patients reviewed retrospectively at a mean 39-month follow-up, the rate of inferior glenoid bone erosion was 19%. Level of evidence: IV.

42. Hatzidakis AM, Norris TR, Boileau P: Reverse shoulder arthroplasty indications, technique, and results. *Tech Shoulder Elbow Surg* 2005;6:135-149.

   In an overview of the history, biomechanics, and results of reverse prosthesis use, the surgical approach is described in detail.

43. Paladini P, Collu A, Campi E, Porcellini G: The inverse prosthesis as a revision prosthesis in failures of shoulder hemiarthroplasty. *Chir Organi Mov* 2005; 90:11-21.

   In seven patients treated with hemiarthroplasty revision using a reverse prosthesis, the Constant score improved from 23 to 49. The authors suggest that the reverse prosthesis is an effective alternative solution for revision.

44. Bufquin T, Hersan A, Hubert L, Massin P: Reverse shoulder arthroplasty for the treatment of three- and four-part fractures of the proximal humerus in the elderly. *J Bone Joint Surg Br* 2007;89-B:516-520.

   The clinical outcome was satisfactory at a mean 22-month follow-up of 41 patients (mean age, 78 years) after reverse shoulder arthroplasty, although complications were common.

45. Guery J, Favard L, Sirveaux F, Oudet D, Molé D, Walch G: Reverse total shoulder arthroplasty: Survivorship analysis of eighty replacements followed for five to ten years. *J Bone Joint Surg Am* 2006;88:1742-1747.

   This analysis of the reverse prosthesis at medium-term follow-up (mean, 69 months) includes the influence of etiology on results. The cumulative survival curve was calculated by etiology, and arthropathies with a massive cuff defect were found to have a better outcome than other etiologies. Level of evidence: IV.

46. Mansat P, Guity MR, Bellumore Y, Mansat M: Shoulder arthroplasty for late sequelae of proximal humeral fractures. *J Shoulder Elbow Surg* 2004;13:305-312.

   In a retrospective study of 28 patients after shoulder replacement for fracture sequelae (8 TSA and 20 hemiarthroplasties), the results were satisfactory in 64%. The outcome is influenced by the status of the rotator cuff and the need for greater tuberosity osteotomy.

47. Ritzman T, Iannotti JP: Malunions of the proximal humerus, in Warner JJ, Iannotti JP, Flatow E (eds):

*Complex and Revision Problems in Shoulder Surgery*. Philadelphia, PA, Lippincott Williams & Wilkins, 2006, pp 347-464.

   Clinical and radiologic assessment of proximal humeral malunion is described in detail by type of malunion (two-part anatomic neck, two-part greater tuberosity, two-part lesser tuberosity, surgical neck, three- or four-part malunion). Level of evidence: V.

48. Boileau P, Chuinard C, Le Huec JC, Walch G, Trojani C: Proximal humerus fracture sequelae: Impact of a new radiographic classification on arthroplasty. *Clin Orthop Relat Res* 2006;442:121-130.

   This is a retrospective evaluation of 203 patients who received a nonconstrained prosthesis for fracture sequelae. The authors define four types of sequelae and show that the surgical results were influenced by sequela type.

49. Beredjiklian PK, Iannotti JP, Norris TR, Williams GR: Operative treatment of malunion of a fracture of the proximal aspect of the humerus. *J Bone Joint Surg Am* 1998;80:1484-1497.

50. Antuna SA, Sperling JW, Sanchez-Sotelo J, Cofield RH: Shoulder arthroplasty for proximal humeral malunions: Long-term results. *J Shoulder Elbow Surg* 2002;11:122-129.

   Of 50 shoulders with proximal humeral malunion treated with hemiarthroplasty or TSA and followed for a mean 9 years, 12 had an excellent Neer result rating, 13 a satisfactory result, and 25 an unsatisfactory result (including all shoulders with tuberosity malunion or resorption).

51. Antuna SA, Sperling JW, Sanchez-Sotelo J, Cofield RH: Shoulder arthroplasty for proximal humeral nonunions. *J Shoulder Elbow Surg* 2002;11: 114-121.

   At a mean 6-year follow-up of 25 patients who underwent hemiarthroplasty or TSA because of pain or functional impairment from a proximal humeral nonunion, 1 had an excellent Neer result rating, 11 a satisfactory result, and 13 an unsatisfactory result.

52. Sperling JW, Pring M, Antuna SA, Cofield RH: Shoulder arthroplasty for locked posterior dislocation of the shoulder. *J Shoulder Elbow Surg* 2004;13: 522-527.

   Twelve patients were reviewed at a mean 9-year follow-up after shoulder arthroplasty for locked posterior dislocation. The data suggest that shoulder arthroplasty for locked posterior dislocation provides pain relief and improved motion. Recurrent posterior instability usually appears during the early postsurgical period.

53. Copeland S, Funk L, Levy O: Surface-replacement arthroplasty of the shoulder. *Curr Orthop* 2002;16: 21-31.

54. Sperling JW, Cofield RH, Rowland CM: Minimum fifteen-year follow-up of Neer hemiarthroplasty and total shoulder arthroplasty in patients aged fifty

years or younger. *J Shoulder Elbow Surg* 2004;13: 604-613.

In 114 patients younger than 50 years who were treated with shoulder arthroplasty (78 HHR and 36 TSA), there was marked long-term pain relief and improvement in motion at a minimum 15-year follow-up. A moderate rate of hemiarthroplasty revision was required for painful glenoid arthritis. In patients treated with HHR, 60% had an unsatisfactory result, compared with 48% in patients treated with TSA.

55.   Parsons IM, Millett PJ, Warner JJ: Glenoid wear after shoulder hemiarthroplasty: Quantitative radiographic analysis. *Clin Orthop Relat Res* 2004;421: 120-125.

Erosion on the glenoid is analyzed in eight patients after hemiarthroplasty, using a digitizing device at a mean 43-month follow-up. Glenoid cartilage erosion can be expected after HHR in young, active individuals; the wear may adversely affect function or necessitate conversion to TSA.

56.   Cameron B, Iannotti JP: Alternatives to total shoulder arthroplasty in young patients. *Tech Shoulder Elbow Surg* 2004;5:135-145.

The surgical alternatives to TSA include arthroscopic débridement, glenoidplasty, capsular release, synovectomy, corrective osteotomy, core decompression, and soft-tissue interposition arthroplasty. Level of evidence: V.

# Chapter 37

# Arthroplasty in the Cuff-Deficient Shoulder

*Gregory P. Nicholson, MD

## Introduction

A chronic, massive rotator cuff tear with degenerative joint disease is termed cuff tear arthropathy (CTA).[1] It is clinically characterized by pain and poor active motion, with almost-normal passive motion. However, the level of shoulder function varies among patients, even in the presence of significant CTA. Many patients are unaware of the condition until the onset of shoulder pain. Surgical intervention for a shoulder with CTA is challenging because of the degenerative changes. If no other satisfactory option exists, a reverse shoulder arthroplasty can be used in a patient whose shoulder has a cuff deficiency, joint damage, poor active motion, and pain. The reverse shoulder arthroplasty has been available in the United States for the past 3 years but has been used in Europe for more than 10 years.

## Etiology

CTA is an age-related degenerative disease. Most patients are older than 60 years, and their rotator cuff tear has developed over a long period of time. The shoulder adapts as the humeral head is elevated through the defect in the rotator cuff and contacts the acromion. The coracoacromial arch becomes the new fulcrum of the humeral head, and other osseous adaptive changes occur on the humeral head. The greater tuberosity is rounded off, the acromion becomes concave, and a new acromiohumeral articulation forms. The patient may have surprisingly little pain and good function and may be unaware of the presence of the condition. However, repeated nonphysiologic contact of the humeral head with the acromion and superior glenoid can cause cartilage and osseous wear with fluid production. Pain, crepitus, and loss of function can result. With further bony

erosion and progressive cuff damage, shoulder function may deteriorate, and a relatively minor trauma may precipitate the appearance of shoulder symptoms. The patient's adaptive shoulder balance may be disrupted by an extension of the preexisting chronic rotator cuff tear, leading to significant pain and loss of function. Although the degenerative condition was already present, the trauma exposed the shoulder's vulnerability.

A diagnosis of end-stage CTA is based on the patient's history, physical examination, and radiographic studies. The etiology of rotator cuff deficiency leading to arthritis and shoulder dysfunction must be considered. Rheumatoid arthritis, neuropathic arthropathy, septic arthritis, and failed rotator cuff repair with loss of coracoacromial arch containment are other possible diagnoses.

A cuff deficiency with joint destruction can result from an unsuccessful rotator cuff repair. The cuff tissue may now be irreparable. Even if a repair is possible, atrophy and fatty infiltration of the rotator cuff muscle bellies would compromise postsurgical function. Poor active motion and pain are common. The patient almost always has coracoacromial arch violation, causing anterosuperior instability with attempted active elevation; the instability is sometimes disabling.[2,3] A rotator cuff repair failure with anterosuperior instability can readily be identified from the patient's surgical history, physical examination findings, and MRI. Such a patient does not have the degenerative and adaptive changes characteristic of CTA and is usually 5 to 10 years younger than patients with CTA. Reverse arthroplasty may be the only option available to achieve reliable pain relief, stability, and function.

A proximal humerus fracture can lead to cuff deficiency and symptomatic shoulder dysfunction because of tuberosity malunion or nonunion with rotator cuff dysfunction. Widely displaced tuberosities indicate that the rotator cuff has been split, and the humeral head will become herniated through the gap. The process can occur after nonsurgical or surgical treatment. Arthroplasty can be used to treat this form of shoulder joint destruction and cuff deficiency.[4]

---

*Gregory P. Nicholson, MD or the department with which he is affiliated has received research or institutional support from EBI, royalties from Innomed and Zimmer, holds stock or stock options in Zimmer, and is a consultant or employee for Zimmer.*

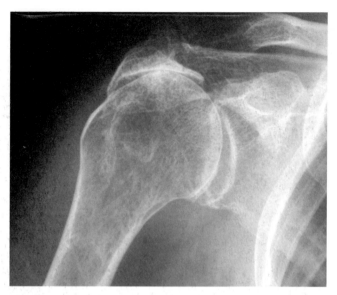

**Figure 1** An AP radiograph of a right shoulder, showing the humeral head elevation and new acromiohumeral articulation typical of CTA. This shoulder does not have significant glenohumeral joint erosion.

A shoulder that has undergone an unsuccessful total shoulder arthroplasty or hemiarthroplasty for CTA or fracture may require a revision arthroplasty.[5]

## Patient Evaluation

### History

The surgeon must be aware of any earlier surgery around the patient's shoulder, especially attempts at rotator cuff repair in the presence of coracoacromial arch violation. Trauma such as a fall, dislocation, or fracture also must be documented, as well as any history of inflammatory arthritis, infection, or gout (with the number of prescribed steroid injections). The surgeon must review the patient's medications, with particular attention to antimetabolites or corticosteroids.

### Physical Examination

Patients typically have a progressive loss of motion and strength, with increasing pain; night pain is common. The ability to use the hand away from the body can be compromised. An internal rotation drop sign may appear as the forearm falls into internal rotation when the patient attempts to reach out or hold the hand as if to shake hands. The presence of this sign usually signifies extensive involvement of the infraspinatus. The patient may have had a minor trauma that exposed the vulnerability of the affected shoulder, resulting in significant pain and shoulder dysfunction.

Physical examination usually reveals poor active motion and almost-normal passive motion. From behind, atrophy of the supraspinatus and infraspinatus can be seen. Excessive fluid production under the deltoid may lead to an inflated appearance under the deltoid. Strength testing can elicit weakness during external ro-

tation. Crepitus may be noted during both active and passive motion, but there may be surprisingly little pain. The term pseudoparalysis is used to describe the functionally disabling condition of a patient who has poor active elevation (less than 45°) and little or no pain.[6] Another important finding is anterosuperior instability with the humeral head riding out from underneath the coracoacromial arch when elevation is attempted.

### Imaging Studies

Plain radiographs are essential, including a true AP view of the glenohumeral joint, an axillary view, and a Y scapular view. If the patient does not have advanced osseous changes, CT or MRI can disclose the size and location of the rotator cuff tear and, more importantly, the status of the rotator cuff muscle bellies. These studies can help the surgeon assess the repairability of the rotator cuff tear. However, in most patients with advanced CTA, the adaptive and degenerative changes can be seen on plain radiographs, and advanced imaging studies are not required.

A pattern of superior wear with significant adaptive changes and concavity of the acromion can be seen on radiographs (Figure 1). Another pattern of relatively centralized wear between the humeral head and the glenoid with significant loss of glenoid bone stock can occur. There may be destructive arthropathy in the humeral head, glenoid, and acromion. It is unknown whether these three patterns represent different points in the process of degeneration or different responses to the chronic cuff deficiency. Proposed radiographic classifications of glenoid-side and acromial-side degenerative changes seen in patients with CTA are qualitative and have not been directly correlated with presurgical function and pain or with treatment outcomes.[7,8] It must be remembered that a shoulder with an irreparable rotator cuff tear does not always progress to painful, symptomatic CTA.

## Nonsurgical Treatment

A corticosteroid injection can be used to decrease inflammation and fluid production, control pain, and allow physical therapy. Therapeutic exercises can be completed at home and should not cause pain. These exercises should focus on the remaining structures, which usually include part of the teres minor and subscapularis, as well as the anterior deltoid. The patient should be informed of the amount of improvement to be expected in active motion, strength, and function. Isometric and closed chain exercises are easiest for an elderly patient to perform and can help the patient gain 5° to 15° of motion and stability. Closed chain exercises for the anterior deltoid can improve the ability to use the hand away from the body. The patient may be satisfied with these gains, if pain relief can be maintained.

## Surgical Treatment

The primary indication for surgical intervention is pain relief. The active forward elevation and shoulder function of patients during this disease process can be somewhat variable. Some patients have almost no pain but extremely poor function with the inability to actively elevate the arm above the horizontal or even use the hand away from the body at waist height. Treating these patients is particularly challenging because they have a painless pseudoparalysis of the shoulder. Hemiarthroplasty will not restore active elevation ability in a patient who has pseudoparalysis. Any surgery on CTA is a limited-goals procedure for pain relief and improved function of the shoulder for activities of daily living.

### Hemiarthroplasty

For a patient with CTA who has an active elevation of at least 60°, as well as pain that is unresponsive to nonsurgical treatment and no history of coracoacromial arch surgery, the preferred treatment is hemiarthroplasty. Total shoulder arthroplasty with resurfacing of the glenoid using an unconstrained shoulder design has no advantages over hemiarthroplasty. Extended-head designs are available, but their use has not been shown to offer an advantage over hemiarthoplasty in improving pain or motion. Arthrodesis is poorly tolerated in elderly patients and is not recommended.

Hemiarthroplasty can predictably relieve unremitting pain in patients with CTA.[9-11] The results are most consistent for patients who have not had an earlier rotator cuff repair or acromioplasty with coracoacromial arch violation. Improvement in functional ability, particularly active elevation, has not been predictable after hemiarthroplasty. Patients and surgeons should expect an average active elevation of approximately 90°. Progressive bone changes in the acromion and glenoid have occurred after hemiarthroplasty (Figure 2), and erosion has been correlated with increasing pain and decreasing function with follow-up over 2 years.[10]

No prognostic factor has been identified that correlates with why some patients achieve better active elevation and shoulder function than others after hemiarthroplasty. However, relatively poor results are quite clearly associated with earlier rotator cuff surgery and coracoacromial arch violation. Hemiarthroplasty is not indicated if the patient has coracoacromial arch violation because anterosuperior instability will result.

### Reverse Shoulder Arthroplasty

Reverse shoulder arthroplasty was approved for use in the United States in 2004, after being used in Europe since 1991.[12,13] When no other satisfactory option is available, reverse shoulder arthroplasty is indicated for the treatment of irreparable rotator cuff deficiency, poor active motion, pain, and joint damage from arthritis, a fracture, or an unsuccessful earlier implantation.

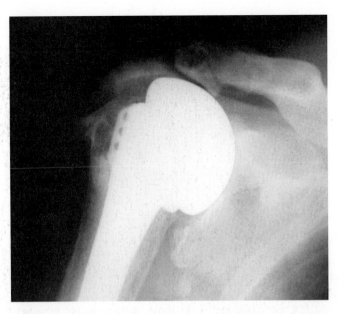

**Figure 2** An AP radiograph of a right shoulder 2 years after hemiarthroplasty for CTA. Superior glenoid bone erosion and erosion into the acromion and distal clavicle are apparent. The patient was relatively pain free for 2 years before developing pain and recurrent fluid production.

The earliest reverse arthroplastic implant designs had a lateral center of rotation, and glenoid implant failure was common due to force placed on the implant-bone interface. The newer designs shift the center of rotation to a more medial and inferior position, placing the center of rotation at the glenoid baseplate–scapular bone interface. The forces are decreased at the implant-bone interface, and the mechanical advantage of the deltoid is enhanced. The potential for forward elevation is improved, although the semiconstrained design may limit external and internal rotation.[14] The Grammont implant is the reverse prosthesis with the longest record of use. It is a semiconstrained inverse shoulder implant that moves the center of rotation medially and inferiorly and relies on the deltoid for stability and function.[12,14]

An in vivo study of the dynamics of normal, rotator cuff–deficient, post–total shoulder arthroplasty, and post–reverse arthroplasty shoulders found that shoulders with a reverse shoulder implant had kinematic and kinetic patterns similar to those of normal shoulders. The semiconstrained design of the reverse implant kept the intersection of the differing motion axes relatively constant.[15]

### *Indications*

Reverse shoulder arthroplasty can be performed for a patient with CTA, pseudoparalysis of the shoulder (with or without significant pain), an unsuccessful rotator cuff repair with anterosuperior instability and coracoacromial arch violation, or unsuccessful fracture care with tuberosity and rotator cuff problems. The patient should be older than 65 years and have pain, poor active

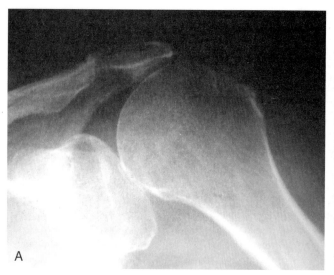
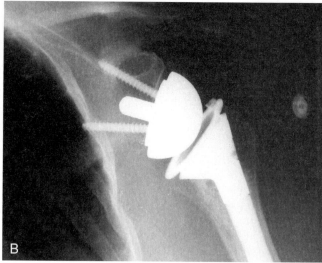

**Figure 3** **A,** An AP radiograph of a left shoulder, showing humeral head elevation and adaptive changes on the acromion and humerus. The patient had pain and poor active motion. **B,** An AP radiograph of the same shoulder 6 months after reverse arthroplasty. Note the desirable inferior position of the glenoid component on the glenoid and the slight inferior tilt position.

elevation (usually < 60°), and irreparable cuff tissue. No other satisfactory option should exist. Age is an important factor because of concerns about the longevity of implants.[4-8,12,13] Also among the prerequisites for a reverse arthroplasty are a functioning deltoid muscle and adequate glenoid bone stock for secure implantation of the glenoid component.

The contraindications to reverse arthroplasty include neurologic or structural deltoid dysfunction, glenoid wear or destruction that would preclude secure implantation of the glenoid component, and active infection. The relative contraindications include age younger than 65 years and the presence of rheumatoid arthritis, as well the surgeon's lack of experience with shoulder arthroplasty.[5,8] Rotator cuff dysfunction and deficiency, as well as joint destruction, are almost always present in patients with rheumatoid arthritis, and therefore the condition would seem to be well suited for treatment with reverse arthroplasty. However, bone stock on the glenoid side is often poor in patients with rheumatoid arthritis, and this factor can lead to early implant failure. Reverse arthroplasty for rheumatoid arthritis has had poor results, with an early failure rate.[5,16]

Reverse arthroplasty is preferable to hemiarthroplasty if the patient has extremely poor active elevation, previous coracoacromial arch violation, or anterosuperior instability of the humeral head. Reverse arthroplasty is also used after an unsuccessful hemiarthroplasty for CTA or a fracture.

### Technical Considerations

Reverse shoulder arthroplasty is a total shoulder replacement that requires exposing the inferior glenoid rim. It is not a rotator cuff repair. Either the deltopec-

toral or superior approach can be used.[8] The deltopectoral approach may allow improved exposure to the inferior glenoid in either a primary or revision procedure, as well as a better inferior placement and an inferior tilt for the glenoid component[6,8,17,18] (Figure 3). In revision surgery for a patient with an existing implant, the deltopectoral approach is more extensile and is recommended. The superior approach can be used for a primary procedure. There are anecdotal reports that the superior approach results in a lower incidence of instability because it does not require subscapularis tenotomy.

Placing the glenosphere distally on the glenoid provided the best balance of the adduction and abduction arc of motion, while avoiding inferior impingement that could lead to scapular notching.[17] An inferior tilt of 10° produced better biomechanical forces across the glenoid component than a neutral position. A superiorly tilted or superiorly placed position was found to be poor with regard to both scapular impingement of the humeral component and forces across the implant.[18]

### Results

Interest in reverse shoulder arthroplasty is rapidly increasing in the United States, and a number of peer-reviewed reports have been published. The pace and scope of research is more advanced in Europe, where the implant has been used during a longer period of time and correspondingly longer follow-up times are available.

The results of reverse arthroplasty must be interpreted in the context of other procedures in the same patient population. Compared with hemiarthroplasty, reverse arthroplasty is better able to provide active for-

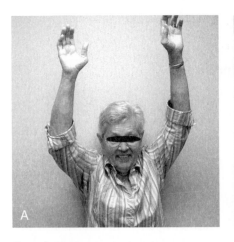
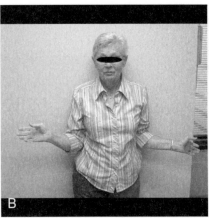
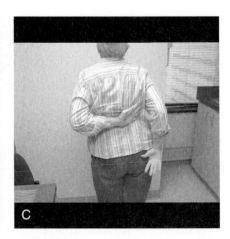

**Figure 4**    Photographs taken 1 year after a reverse arthroplasty for CTA. The patient is pain free and satisfied with her level of function. **A,** Active elevation is greater than 140°. **B,** Active external rotation on the affected side is 20° and not equal to that of the opposite side. **C,** Active internal rotation is limited to the buttock level.

ward elevation in patients with CTA. However, external rotation is not significantly improved[4-8,13] (Figure 4). In a multicenter study of age- and diagnosis-matched groups, reverse arthroplasty was shown to have a 20-point advantage over hemiarthroplasty in Constant scores and a 40° advantage in active forward elevation.[7] Reverse arthroplasty significantly relieved pain in patients with CTA (96% reported little or no pain), and the average active forward elevation was 138° (a 40° gain of elevation). The outcome scores were not affected by age, gender, surgical approach, or radiologic extent of arthritis.[7]

In a report on reverse arthroplasty for painful pseudoparalysis and massive cuff deficiency, function and pain were significantly improved at an average 38-month follow-up. Average active forward elevation improved 58°, and the postsurgical Constant score averaged 64%.[6] However, this study revealed the disadvantages of reverse arthroplasty, pointing out the need for careful patient selection and patient education about potential complications. The complication rate was 50%, and 33% of the patients required an additional surgical procedure. A hematoma formed in 12 patients, requiring surgical drainage in 7. Five patients had a dislocation, and four of them required revision surgery. The authors concluded that while complications were frequent, they rarely affected the outcome, and the patients' condition was significantly improved by the procedure.[6]

In the same study, scapular notching appeared in 96% of the patients available for radiographic follow-up. However, the presence of notching was not correlated with clinical outcome.[6] In other studies, scapular notching was identified in 64% of patients at an average 44-month follow-up[7] and in 24.5% of patients at 6- to 12-month follow-up.[8] The notch did not appear to progress over time and did not affect clinical results at mid-term follow-up. The patients gained predictable pain relief, as well as an average active forward elevation of 145°.[8]

An implant design featuring a lateralized glenosphere was developed to avoid humeral component impingement on the inferior scapula. No inferior scapular notching has appeared at an average 33-month follow-up of 60 reverse arthroplasties using this design. Patients' average active elevation and outcome scores were significantly improved, and pain relief was consistently achieved. This implant appears to provide the potential for better external rotation than Grammont-type devices. However, 10 patients (17%) had a total of 13 complications, and 8 revision procedures were required in 7 patients (12%) who had device failure on the glenoid side.[19]

In general, reverse arthroplasty provides significant pain relief and the potential for substantial improvement in active elevation in patients with cuff deficiency, pain, and poor elevation and function. Active external rotation was not improved when a Grammont-type implant was used. However, rates of complications and revision surgery are high.[4-6] The scapular notching seen on radiographs is of concern, although its impact on clinical results has been difficult to define.[4-6,8] Presurgical function was poor in patients who underwent reverse arthroplasty, and the procedure produced consistent results and high patient satisfaction.[4-8,13,19]

### Complications

The most common complications of reverse shoulder arthroplasty are hematoma formation, infection, instability, implant failure, scapular notching, and glenoid component loosening. Reported rates of revision surgery are as high as 33%.[4-8,19]

Because of concerns about the longevity of the reverse implant, it is recommended for use only in patients who are older than 65 years and have relatively low activity demands. An analysis of implant survival over time revealed a significant decline at two critical points after reverse arthroplasty. The first occurred approximately 3 years after the arthroplasty and was believed to reflect early implant loosening, probably resulting from surgical technique, poor patient bone stock (as in rheumatoid arthritis), or the difficulty of revision surgeries. The second point was approximately 6 years after the arthroplasty and reflected progressive functional deterioration and increased pain. The authors concluded that reverse arthroplasty should be used only for older, less functionally demanding patients. It is best suited to patients with CTA and should be limited in patients with rheumatoid arthritis.[5]

The complication rate after reverse arthroplasty is essentially doubled when the procedure is used in revision surgery.[4-6] Reverse arthroplasty is a useful salvage option for revision surgery after failure of an implant or a fracture repair. However, improvement in active elevation greatly depends on the status of the teres minor muscle in patients undergoing revision surgery; if the teres minor is compromised, the patient will have poorer elevation and function.[4] Infection rates are higher after a revision, and this factor must be considered before a reverse arthroplasty is performed.[4-6]

Although most authors recommend restriction of reverse arthroplasty to patients older than 65 years, the average age in the reported series was between 68 and 73 years.[4-8,12,13,19] Every patient does not require a reverse shoulder replacement for cuff-deficient arthritis, and every surgeon should not attempt the operation. The surgeon should be experienced in shoulder arthroplasty, as this is an arthroplasty, not a rotator cuff operation. The procedure has the ability to significantly improve the patient's shoulder function and quality of life. However, poor patient selection and poor surgical technique can lead to an untenable result.

## Summary

Reverse shoulder arthroplasty has been available in the United States for more than 3 years and is being performed in increasing volume worldwide in patients with cuff deficiency and arthritic shoulder conditions. Clinical and basic science research is increasing the information available to surgeons and patients. The reverse shoulder arthroplasty provides the potential for improved active elevation compared with hemiarthroplasty. It is indicated for patients older than 65 years with irreparable cuff deficiency, joint damage with pain, and active elevation of less than 60°, if no other satisfactory option exists. Glenoid component longevity, implant instability, and scapular notching are matters of concern. Although reported complication rates are high, patient satisfaction has also been high, and outcomes have been consistent. Not every patient requires a reverse arthroplasty, but the procedure has shown great promise for carefully selected patients. Longer term follow-up studies and continued basic science research are needed as different de-

signs become available and more patients undergo reverse shoulder arthroplasty.

## Annotated References

1.  Neer CS II, Craig EV, Fukuda H: Cuff-tear arthropathy. *J Bone Joint Surg Am* 1983;65:1232-1244.

2.  Nicholson GP: Treatment of anterior superior shoulder instability with a reverse ball and socket prosthesis. *Operative Techniques Orthop* 2003;13:235-241.

    The indications and surgical technique for reverse shoulder arthroplasty are reviewed.

3.  Nicholson GP: Current concepts in reverse shoulder replacement. *Curr Opin Orthop* 2006;17:306-309.

    The indications, results, and complications of reverse arthroplasty for a cuff-deficient shoulder are reviewed.

4.  Boileau P, Watkinson D, Hatzidakis AM, Hovorka I: The Grammont reverse shoulder prosthesis: Results in cuff tear arthritis, fracture sequelae, and revision arthroplasty. *J Shoulder Elbow Surg* 2006; 15:527-540.

    Primary reverse arthroplasty has better results for CTA than for other conditions. The complication rate is higher after revision surgery than after primary surgery.

5.  Guery J, Favard L, Sirveaux F, Oudet D, Molé D, Walch G: Reverse total shoulder arthroplasty. *J Bone Joint Surg Am* 2006;88:1742-1747.

    The survival of Grammont-type reverse arthroplastic implants is analyzed. Two breaks in the survival curve were seen, corresponding to mechanical issues after 3 years and deterioration of function after 6 years.

6.  Werner CM, Steinmann PA, Gilbart M, Gerber C: Treatment of painful pseudoparesis due to irreparable rotator cuff dysfunction with the Delta III reverse-ball-and-socket total shoulder prosthesis. *J Bone Joint Surg Am* 2005;87:1476-1486.

    This large series reports significant improvement in pain relief and function obtained by reverse replacement. It also highlights potential problems and reports a high incidence of scapular notching and complications.

7.  Sirveaux F, Favard L, Oudet D, Huquet D, Walch G, Molé D: Grammont inverted total shoulder arthroplasty in the treatment of glenohumeral osteoarthritis with massive rupture of the cuff. *J Bone Joint Surg Br* 2004;86:388-395.

    In a multicenter study comparing hemiarthoplasty and reverse arthroplasty for CTA, better Constant scores and active elevation were achieved with reverse arthroplasty. A radiographic classification is outlined.

8.  Seebauer L, Walter W, Keyl W: Reverse total shoulder arthroplasty for the treatment of defect arthropathy. *Oper Orthop Traumatol* 2005;17(1):1-24.

This is an excellent description of the superior surgical approach and surgical technique for reverse shoulder arthroplasty, with a report of the results of a large clinical series.

9. Pollock RG, Deliz ED, McIlveen SJ, et al: Prosthetic replacement in rotator cuff-deficient shoulders. *J Shoulder Elbow Surg* 1992;1:173-186.

10. Sanchez-Sotelo J, Cofield RH, Rowland CM: Shoulder hemiarthroplasty for glenohumeral arthritis associated with severe rotator cuff deficiency. *J Bone Joint Surg Am* 2001;83:1814-1822.

    This longer term follow-up series found that after 2 to 3 years, hemiarthroplasty begins to show radiographic changes and increasing pain. Level of evidence: IV.

11. Zuckerman JD, Scott AJ, Gallagher MA: Hemiarthroplasty for cuff tear arthropathy. *J Shoulder Elbow Surg* 2000;9:169-172.

12. Grammont PM, Baulot E: Delta shoulder prosthesis for rotator cuff rupture. *Orthopedics* 1993;16:65-68.

13. Boulahia A, Edwards TB, Walch G, Baratta RV: Early results of a reverse design prosthesis in the treatment of arthritis of the shoulder in elderly patients with a large rotator cuff tear. *Orthopedics* 2002;25:129-133.

    Promising results are reported for reverse arthroplasty in this early series.

14. Boileau P, Watkinson D, Hatzidakis AM, Balg F: Grammont reverse prosthesis: Design, rationale, and biomechanics. *J Shoulder Elbow Surg* 2005;14 (suppl):147S-161S.

    This is an excellent review of the biomechanical principles of reverse shoulder arthroplasty.

15. Mahfouz M, Nicholson GP, Komistek R, Hovis D, Kubo M: In vivo determination of the dynamics of normal, rotator cuff-deficient, total and reverse replacement shoulder. *J Bone Joint Surg Am* 2005; 87(suppl 2):107-113.

    A sophisticated method allowed in vivo evaluation of the dynamics of different shoulder conditions and implants.

16. Rittmeister M, Kerschbaumer F: Grammont reverse total shoulder arthroplasty in patients with rheumatoid arthritis and nonreconstructible rotator cuff lesions. *J Shoulder Elbow Surg* 2001;10:17-22.

    A high rate of reverse implant failure was seen in this small series of patients with rheumatoid arthritis.

17. Nyffeler RW, Werner CML, Gerber C: Biomechanical relevance of glenoid component positioning in the reverse Delta III total shoulder prosthesis. *J Shoulder Elbow Surg* 2005;14:524-528.

    In a cadaver study, the inferior glenoid component position was found to be optimal for motion and to avoid inferior impingement.

18. Harman M, Frankle M, Vasey M, Banks SL: Initial glenoid component fixation in "reverse" total shoulder arthroplasty: A biomechanical evaluation. *J Shoulder Elbow Surg* 2005; 14(suppl):162S-167S.

    The inferior tilt of the glenoid component provided compressive forces across the baseplate during range of motion.

19. Frankle M, Siegal S, Pupello D, Saleem A, Mighell M, Vasey M: The reverse shoulder prosthesis for glenohumeral arthritis associated with severe rotator cuff deficiency: A minimum two-year follow-up study of sixty patients. *J Bone Joint Surg Am* 2005;87:1697-1705.

    In a report of the results of a reverse prosthesis design, patient satisfaction was high, although complications were reported. Scapular notching was not seen.

# Section 6

# Trauma and Fractures

Section Editor
Herbert Resch, MD

# Chapter 38

# Treatment of Proximal Humerus Fractures

Andreas Hartmann, MD

Herbert Resch, MD

## Introduction

Proximal humerus fractures account for approximately 5% of all fractures. They are third in frequency among all types of fractures. Osteoporosis is a risk factor for proximal humerus fractures, and the incidence therefore increases with patient age.[1] Recent studies have confirmed that the incidence is increasing with aging of the population.[2] Many innovative fixation devices and techniques have recently been developed that are contributing to the treatment of proximal humerus fractures.

## Anatomy

Several anatomic characteristics of the proximal humerus must be considered in decision making before fracture treatment. The main blood supply to the proximal humerus flows through the branches of the axillary artery. The ascending branch of the anterior humeral circumflex artery with its intraosseous continuation, the arcuate artery, is the most important contributor to the blood supply of the proximal humerus and is almost always compromised in a four-part fracture.[3,4] In some fractures, intraosseous anastomoses to the posterior humeral circumflex artery and its smaller ascending branches along the inferior capsule can maintain some blood supply to the articular fragment.[3] Severe comminution of the medial metaphysis of the proximal humerus or the presence of a short medial metaphyseal segment (< 1 cm) is a predictor of humeral head ischemia.[5,6]

The proximal humerus fractures into several predictable segments: the shaft, the head, the greater tuberosity, and the lesser tuberosity. Proximal humerus fractures are classified as having two, three, or four parts, based on displacement and angulation.[7] The fracture line between the tuberosities normally is located a few millimeters lateral to the bicipital groove. This consistent fracture characteristic is important to understand, as it is useful during fracture reduction maneuvers.

The rotator cuff covers the humeral head like a helmet. The four muscles that make up the rotator cuff are the subscapularis, the supraspinatus, the infraspinatus, and the teres minor. Their attachment to individual fracture fragments influences the displacement of the fragments. The force vectors of the four rotator cuff muscles displace the fragments in their respective directions. Greater displacement of the fracture segments is associated with a higher risk of disruption of the blood supply to the humeral head and consequent osteonecrosis. A higher energy injury results in more severe fracture displacement as well as more severe soft-tissue injury.

## Epidemiology and Etiology

Many fractures of the proximal humerus are fractures of senescence. They frequently occur in patients with osteoporosis, and women are affected twice as often as men. In a 32-year study of all patients who were admitted to a Finnish hospital with a proximal humerus fracture, overall incidence and mean patient age increased during the study period.[8] The data from this study were used to predict that the incidence of proximal humerus fractures will triple during the next three decades. A 60-year-old woman is estimated to have an 8% risk of a proximal humerus fracture during her remaining lifetime.[9] In people older than 60 years, 97% of proximal humerus fractures result from a simple fall involving a direct blow to the shoulder.[10,11] In contrast, proximal humerus fractures in younger people are often caused by high-energy trauma.

The presence of osteoporosis complicates the surgical treatment of any proximal humerus fracture. Fixation of an osteoporotic fracture is more likely to fail, and the final radiologic and functional outcomes are more likely to be compromised.[12] A study of 239 patients hospitalized for fracture treatment found that only 13% had normal bone density.[13] To prevent fractures in the elderly population, it is urgent that bone density measurement and osteoporosis treatment become health care priorities.

## Associated Injuries

A proximal humerus fracture in an elderly patient usually results from a low-energy fall. A fracture-dislocation or a fracture resulting from high-energy trauma is much more likely to be associated with neurovascular injuries. The axillary nerve can be injured during a shoulder fracture-dislocation; in most patients, the injury results in axonotmesis, and a full recovery can be expected. An injury to the brachial vessels can occur during high-energy trauma, and most such vascular injures involve arterial intimal lesions that disrupt the blood supply. Vascular injuries are easily missed because of extensive collateral circulation in the upper extremity. Therefore, a high level of suspicion should be maintained during the initial evaluation. Routine angiograms are not recommended. However, a diminished pulse, unusual pallor, expanding hematoma, or changing neurologic examination is an indication that the patient should be further evaluated for vascular injury.

Observation usually is sufficient after an isolated axillary nerve injury, although an injury of the entire brachial plexus may require surgical treatment. Vitamin B supplementation can facilitate recovery from nerve injury. A vascular injury is usually treated with reconstructive surgery.

## Classification

Proximal humerus fractures are generally described according to fracture anatomy and mechanism of injury. In Neer's system, proximal humerus fractures are classified based on the involvement of the articular surface, the greater tuberosity, the lesser tuberosity, and the shaft.[7] Neer defined significant displacement as more than 1 cm of translation or more than 45° of angulation in any major fracture fragment. Neer's simple classification remains the most widely used system for proximal humerus fractures. More recent systems, such as the Mittlmeier five-part theory,[14] are descriptive but not useful in clinical decision making.

The AO-ASIF classification system contains three main groups and nine subgroups (a total of 27 groups). The system's complexity makes it unsuitable for routine clinical use. The Neer system was found to have better interobserver and intraobserver reliability than the AO-ASIF system. However, the reliability of the Neer classification system is still in question. In one study, only 30% of fractures received equivalent scores from five observers at different levels of training.[15] When CT three-dimensional imaging was used, interobserver reliability doubled.[16]

A true valgus impacted fracture has unique features. The mechanism of injury in an impacted fracture is compression of the articular surface onto the glenoid through the abducted arm. There is never great displacement of the shaft or the articular segment. The humeral head is fractured into a valgus position onto the shaft. Valgus impacted three- and four-part fractures have a much better outcome after fixation than more displaced fractures. The blood supply to the humeral head is maintained by the blood vessels of the medial

hinge and the intact periosteal tissue on the lateral cortex. The intact soft-tissue sleeve allows a controlled, accurate reduction to be performed using ligamentotaxis.[17,18]

## Clinical Examination

A thorough neurovascular examination must be performed. If the fracture is associated with dislocation, the risk of concomitant blood vessel injury increases as much as 30%.[19] Doppler ultrasonography or angiography can be used if the diagnosis is in doubt.

Tenderness over the greater tuberosity suggests the presence of a fracture. A nondisplaced or minimally displaced fracture of the greater tuberosity is overlooked in as many as 53% of initial evaluations.[20]

The radiologic examination includes a trauma series with a true AP view of the shoulder, an axillary view, and a tangential or Y scapular view. The radiographs may reveal that the greater tuberosity is displaced posteriorly because of the pull of the supraspinatus and infraspinatus muscles. The lesser tuberosity and the shaft may be displaced medially by the subscapularis and pectoralis major muscles.[21] The humeral head may be pushed into valgus because of depression forces or displaced medially in a surgical neck fracture. In an anterior glenohumeral fracture-dislocation, the head can be displaced far inferiorly and medially into the subcoracoid region. Posterior fracture-dislocations are easily missed; therefore, it is particularly important to obtain an axillary view.

CT is recommended if any doubt exists as to the degree or position of the displaced fracture parts. If fracture lines extend into the head segment or if a head-split fracture is present, CT is essential in decision making regarding reconstruction.

An intact rotator cuff is important in regaining full postsurgical function after fixation or humeral head replacement. The rotator cuff is usually intact in an elderly patient with a proximal humerus fracture. However, if the rotator cuff is compromised and poor postsurgical cuff function is anticipated, the surgeon should consider performing a reverse shoulder arthroplasty.

## Treatment Decision Making

Humeral head vascularity, fracture pattern, bone quality, and overall geometry are important considerations in determining the appropriate treatment. Osteoporosis influences the degree of comminution, the magnitude of cancellous defects secondary to impaction, and the likelihood of fixation failure or loss of reduction. An osteoporotic fracture is often more appropriately treated with arthroplasty than with reduction and internal fixation. A hemiarthroplasty may be the most suitable option for a highly comminuted fracture or a fracture-dislocation with poor bone quality. Successful joint arthroplasty requires anatomic reduction and healing of the tuberosities to restore exact humeral head geometry. Height and version are also important considerations.

Although the pattern and associated characteristics of the fracture are the most important considerations, surgeon experience and patient comorbidities also influence the choice of treatment and the outcome. Vascularity of the humeral head determines the risk of osteonecrosis. Vascularity is often preserved through an intact medial hinge, and it is compromised by extensive horizontal translation of the head relative to the shaft. The high risk of future osteonecrosis must also be considered in a head-split fracture or a fracture associated with a dislocation.

The optimal treatment of a four-part fracture remains controversial. A review of evidence-based studies to evaluate the results of nonsurgical treatment, internal fixation, and arthroplasty concluded that insufficient evidence is available to determine the optimal intervention for a displaced four-part fracture.[22] A meta-analysis including 24 studies of three- and four-part fractures was conducted from 1969 to 1999 to compare nonsurgical treatment, open reduction and internal fixation, and arthroplasty.[23] Nonsurgically treated patients had more pain and a poorer range of motion than those treated using either fixation or arthroplasty. The patients treated with fixation had better restoration of anatomy. There was no significant difference in functional range of motion between those treated with arthroplasty and those treated with fixation.

An overview of 33 studies of the treatment of displaced fractures found limitations including differing patient selection criteria, surgical procedures, and outcome measurements, as well as small study populations.[24] Only three randomized studies were published. The overall conclusion was that good results can be achieved using minimally invasive reduction and fixation to treat displaced two-, three-, and four-part fractures in older patients. Plating and nonsurgical treatment can be successful in defined subgroups. The studies did not support the general use of primary arthroplasty for four-part fractures.

A prospective, randomized study compared nonsurgical treatment with tension band wiring in three- and four-part fractures.[25] Forty patients with a mean age of 74 years were either nonsurgically treated or surgically treated using tension band wiring. The 100-point Constant Shoulder Score, which assigns a maximum of 15 points for pain, 20 for activity, 40 for motion, and 25 for strength, was used to measure outcome. At a 36-month follow-up of 29 patients, the average Constant score was 65 points for the nonsurgically treated patients and 60 points for the surgically treated patients.

Until larger comparative studies are available to determine the validity of the trends found in the existing small studies, treatment decisions are likely to continue to be based on the surgeon's experience and preference.

## Nonsurgical Treatment

Nonsurgical treatment is best used for nondisplaced or minimally displaced two-part and three-part fractures. In these fractures, the rotator cuff and periosteum are often uninterrupted. Along with the joint capsule, these soft-tissue structures work like a sleeve to stabilize the fractured proximal humerus against further displacement. Although nonsurgical treatment after closed reduction has been recommended for a stable fracture,[26] it is preferable to stabilize the reduced fracture with internal fixation because of the risk of loss of fixation. Studies suggest that nonsurgical treatment of comminuted four-part fractures has poor results.[27] The average Constant score was 65.5 points after nonsurgical treatment of valgus impacted fractures.[28] However, the average Constant score was only 47 points at 10-year follow-up after nonsurgical treatment of comminuted four-part fractures, although patients reported a high level of satisfaction.[29]

During nonsurgical treatment, the injured arm is immobilized in a sling for 3 to 4 weeks. In stable fracture patterns, early physical therapy has a positive influence on the outcome.[30] During the first week, the patient begins to use pendulums. After some types of fractures, the patient can progress to passive exercises in 2 to 3 weeks. Shoulder rotation increases the risk of tuberosity displacement; therefore, rotational motion should begin 5 to 6 weeks after injury. Active and active-assisted motion also begins approximately 5 weeks after injury.

## Surgical Treatment

General anesthesia with a scalene block is recommended for most surgical procedures. The purposes of the scalene block are to allow a lighter anesthesia to be used and to reduce postsurgical pain. In a high-risk patient, the use of a scalene block alone can be considered.

The patient is placed in the beach chair position, with the arm draped free. The image intensifier is best placed parallel to the patient to allow radiographs to be taken in the axillary and AP planes without torquing the patient's arm.

A superior deltoid-splitting or deltopectoral approach is chosen based on the type of fracture, the treatment method, and the preference of the surgeon. The deltoid-splitting approach is less invasive and is preferred for treatment of an isolated fracture of the greater tuberosity or for antegrade intramedullary nailing. Because of the risk of damage to the axillary nerve, the split in the deltoid muscle must be restricted to 5 cm. A deltoid-splitting approach was recommended for use with plating; at 3-month follow-up, study participants had a mean Constant score of 74 points.[31]

The deltopectoral approach is preferred for a multiple-part fracture being fixed with plating. However, fixation of a dorsally displaced major tuberosity can be challenging if this approach is used. The deltopectoral approach allows excellent exposure and visualization, which are necessary when the fracture extends distally. The soft tissues must be protected during the procedure to avoid additional damage to the blood supply of the proximal humerus. Tuberosity reduction is achieved by placing sutures through the bone-tendon junction of all three rotator cuff muscles. The sutures act as reins to pull the tuberosities into anatomic position. If the deltopectoral approach has been used, the procedure can easily be converted into an arthroplasty, if necessary. The conversion is more difficult if a deltoid-splitting approach is used.

Bony stability, which is critical for successful fixation, is influenced not only by osteoporosis but also by differential bone densities within the proximal humerus. The posterior and medial regions of the humeral head have the greatest bone density. Screws or other fixation devices should therefore be directed toward these regions to ensure the greatest possible fixation strength.[32,33]

The selection of an implant should be based on the patient's age, bone quality, fracture pattern, and associated injuries as well as the ability to achieve closed reduction and the displacement of fracture fragments.

A comparison of percutaneous and open treatment found a significantly lower risk of osteonecrosis (12.7% versus 50%) in patients treated with closed reduction and percutaneous pinning.[34] Although the patients in this study were equally distributed by age and fracture type, only 14.5% received open treatment. To minimize the risk of osteonecrosis after open treatment, the use of a limited exposure, a limited dissection of the soft tissues, and a minimal amount of hardware has been recommended.[35]

Internal fixation of complex fractures of the proximal humerus can produce reliably good results if anatomic reduction is obtained, regardless of the surgical procedure used.[36] At a mean 63-month follow-up, 32 patients with a mean age of 44.9 years had an average Constant score of 78 points. In 35% of these patients, partial or total osteonecrosis of the humeral head lowered the average Constant score to 66 points. Two patients required revision to arthroplasty.

Few randomized studies have been published to compare the treatment options. The available studies use different outcomes measures, and the patient groups differ with respect to patient age and fracture patterns. The surgical procedures vary within studies; for example, open fixation is sometimes added to a closed reduction method. Most of the studies are small and relatively underpowered. No general treatment recommendations can be derived from them.[24]

### Closed Reduction and External Fixation
External fixation is rarely used to treat a fracture of the upper arm. In one recent study, 62 consecutive patients, most of whom had a two-part proximal humerus fracture, were treated with an external fixator.[37] At a mean 18-month follow-up, their mean Constant score was 86 points. One infection but no osteonecrosis occurred; 2 patients required revision to a hemiprosthesis because of pain. These data suggest that that external fixation can be considered for a two-part fracture.

### Closed Reduction and Percutaneous Fixation
Kirschner wires were commonly used for fixation in the past. Wire loosening, loss of fixation, and pin infection were recurring complications. Although the use of threaded wires somewhat improves fixation, loosening continues to occur in elderly patients, who are the majority of those requiring surgical treatment of a proximal humerus fracture. Many devices and methods have been developed in an attempt to achieve stability without loosening. Some surgeons use cannulated screws, and others prefer using multiple pins in different planes.[38,39] One method uses intramedullary pins inserted from far distal through a special device called the Humerusblock (Synthes, Bettlach, Switzerland).

The findings of recent studies on closed reduction and percutaneous fixation[38,40-49] are outlined in Table 1. Comparing the patient ages and fracture distribution reported in these studies with functional results can be useful in surgical decision making. The most common complications reported in the studies were osteonecrosis and infection. In one of the earliest studies, the Constant scores were 85.4 points for 9 patients with a three-part fracture and 82.5 points for 18 patients with a four-part fracture; 13 of the four-part fractures were valgus impacted, and 8 did not have significant lateral displacement.[38] The mean patient age was 54 years, which is relatively young.

Fixation using the Humerusblock is shown in Figure 1. The subcapital fracture is reduced under intensifier imaging with the arm in adduction and internal rotation and with simultaneous traction applied to the arm. If closed reduction is not possible using positioning and traction, an elevator is introduced percutaneously into the fracture gap posterior to the biceps groove. The patient's arm is held adducted in the neutral position by the surgical assistant, and a 5-cm skin incision is performed on the lateral side of the upper arm, approximately 4 cm below the lateral aspect of the subcapital fracture. After blunt soft-tissue dissection to the bone, a guiding device that includes the Humerusblock is positioned exactly on the lateral side of the cortex of the humerus and is fixed, first with a thin wire and then with a self-cutting cannulated screw. The screw is not tightened. The Humerusblock guide device can be tilted in the sagittal and frontal planes as much as 20°. This adjustment ensures that the 2.2- or 2.5-mm Kirschner wires brought in through the guiding tubes of the setting

**Table 1 | Recent Studies of Percutaneous Pinning**

| Study | Mean Follow-Up Period (Months) | Mean Patient Age (Years) | Patients (N) | Two-Part Fractures (n) | Three-Part Fractures (n) | Four-Part Fractures (n) | Outcomes Measure (Mean Score) |
|---|---|---|---|---|---|---|---|
| Jaberg et al[40] (1992) | 36 | 63 | 48 | 32 | 8 | 5* | Saillant: 70% good or excellent |
| Resch et al[38] (1997) | 24 | 54 | 27 | 0 | 9 | 18 | Constant: 85.4 points, three-part fracture; 82.5 points, four-part fracture |
| Herscovici et al[41] (2000) | 40 | 54 | 41 | 21 | 16 | 4 | Modified ASES: 78, two-part fracture; 70, three-part fracture; 37, four-part fracture |
| Wachtl et al[42] (2000) | 17 | 52 | 53 | 23 | 12 | 15 | Constant: 63 points |
| Khodadadyan-Klosterman et al[43] (2002) | 16.5 | 56 | 18 | 0 | 19 | 5 | Constant: > 90 points, 7 patients; > 80 points, 8 patients; > 70 points, 2 patients; < 70 points, 1 patient |
| Takeuchi et al[44] (2002) | 29 | 65 | 41 | 41 | 0 | 0 | Neer: excellent, 25 patients; satisfactory, 12 patients; unsatisfactory, 3 patients; failure, 1 patient |
| Werner et al[45] (2002) | 36 | 56 | 14 | 3 | 4 | 7 | Constant: 70 points |
| Gorschewsky et al[46] (2005) | 12 | 70 | 95 | 32 | 43 | 22 | Constant: 76 points |
| Tamai et al[47] (2005) | 13 | 75 | 31 | 20 | 7 | 4 | Japanese Shoulder: 78 |
| Fenichel et al[48] (2006) | 30 | 50 | 50 | 24 | 26 | 0 | Constant: 81 points |
| Keener[49] (2007) | 35 | 61 | 36 | 11 | 9 | 16 valgus | ASES: 83.4; Constant: 73.9 points |

ASES = American Shoulder and Elbow Surgeons Index.
*Excluding patients with severe disability.

device can be correctly positioned in the humeral head. The pins must be located in the center of the head, as seen on an AP radiograph, to provide the best possible resistance to valgus and varus stress. The pins should also be centered, as seen on an axillary radiograph. The pins should not perforate the articular surface; inadvertent perforation increases the risk of postsurgical pin migration.

After fixation of the articular segment to the shaft, the tuberosities are reduced by using a pointed hook to pull them into anatomic position. The tuberosities are fixed percutaneously using cannulated titanium screws. The wires are usually left in place for 3 to 4 weeks. In approximately 20% of patients, the Kirschner wires perforate the head segment before removal. If perforation occurs, the wires must be withdrawn before the patient can begin exercising.

Good results were obtained when Kirschner wires were inserted through the lateral cortex of the proximal humerus using a similar technique, with some variation in the manner of securing the pins.[44,45,47] The favorable results from this technique were thus substantiated.

This method of closed reduction relies on ligamentotaxis. The intact periosteal connection between the tuberosities and the shaft facilitates the reduction by distal tension on the periosteum inferiorly and superior tension on the rotator cuff. In a severely displaced fracture, the soft-tissue sleeve is disrupted, and the effect of ligamentotaxis is lost. Fractures with more displacement are at greater risk of loss of fixation, osteonecrosis, malunion, or nonunion. Although the amount of displacement is an important prognostic factor, many published studies do not take into account the severity of individual fractures, and comparisons of the studies are therefore difficult.

Schanz screws (Mikromed, Katowicka, Poland), dynamic hip screws, or 2-mm Kirschner wires were used in two-, three-, and four-part fractures.[41] Pinning failed in all four of the four-part fractures, and the authors advised against the use of percutaneous pinning in four-part

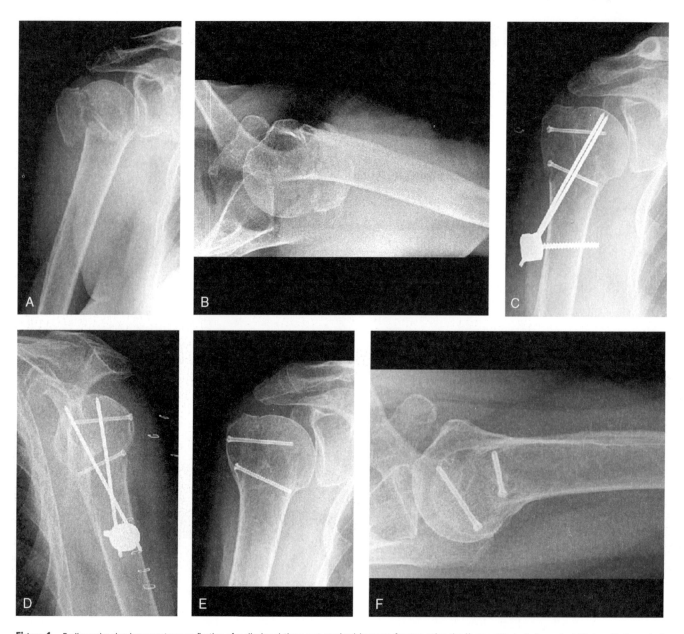

**Figure 1** Radiographs showing percutaneous fixation of a displaced three-part proximal humerus fracture using the Humerusblock. **A,** Presurgical AP view. **B,** Presurgical axillary view. **C,** Postsurgical AP view. **D,** Postsurgical outlet view. **E,** Postsurgical AP view at 12-month follow-up. **F,** Postsurgical axillary view at 12-month follow-up.

fractures. In 15% of 41 patients, loosening of the pins occurred. The Schanz and dynamic hip screws were found to resist loosening much better than the Kirschner wires.

In a multicenter study of 35 patients who underwent percutaneous pinning, the average American Shoulder and Elbow Surgeons (ASES) Index score was 83.4, and the average Constant score was 73.9 points. Although four patients had a malunion and four developed arthritis, neither of these factors affected final outcome.[49] A study of the use of threaded pins in 50 patients with a two- or three-part fracture found good results. The average Constant score was 81 points. No loosening was reported, although superficial infection occurred in 10% and loss of fixation in 14%.[48]

*Intramedullary Nailing*

A laboratory study found that intramedullary fixation provided better biomechanical fixation than percutaneous pinning.[50] Biomechanical testing of intramedullary fixation with an interlocking nail in osteoporotic bone led to excellent fixation.[51] Two types of nails are available, one of which is bent a few degrees to simplify its introduction. The insertion site for the bent nail is near the tendon-bone junction of the rotator cuff, which is a weak point when a fracture of the greater tuberosity is present. The other type of nail is straight and is introduced through the center of the humeral head, risking a fracture of the articular segment. The nail is locked using a spiral blade or interlocking screws inserted at dif-

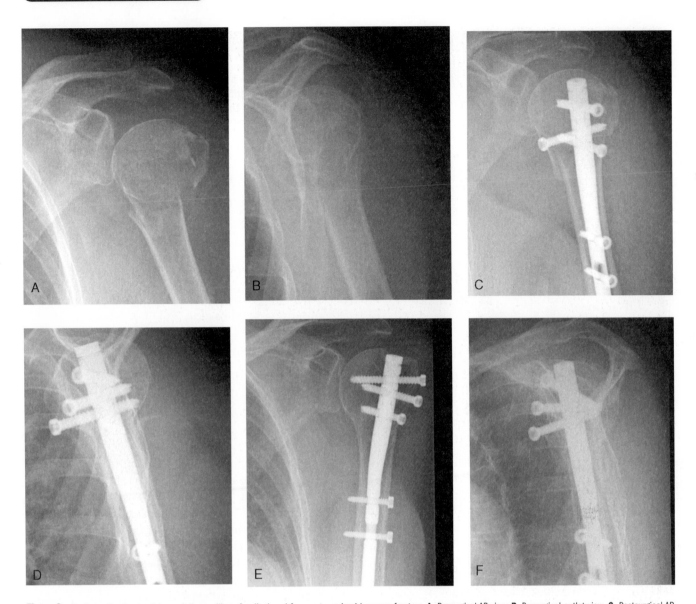

**Figure 2** Radiographs showing intramedullary nailing of a displaced four-part proximal humerus fracture. **A,** Presurgical AP view. **B,** Presurgical outlet view. **C,** Postsurgical AP view. **D,** Postsurgical outlet view. **E,** Postsurgical AP view at 15-month follow-up. **F,** Postsurgical outlet view at 15-month follow-up. *(Courtesy of Oliver Trapp, MD, Murnau, Germany.)*

ferent angles with an appropriate jig. The screws provide rigid fixation of the tuberosities. If necessary, additional fixation of the tuberosities is provided by heavy sutures passed through the rotator cuff tendon and tied around the ends of the screws (Figure 2). Care must be taken to avoid damaging the axillary nerve or the long head of the biceps tendon.

The primary disadvantage of intramedullary nailing is that nail insertion requires an incision into the rotator cuff, which can result in persistent pain and disability. In a biomechanical study, intramedullary fixation was found to be more rigid than either plating or pinning and produced a very stable construct.[52] Some surgeons believe that the construct can be too rigid and prevent

healing. The interlocking nails are relatively new devices, and no long-term studies are available to confirm their biomechanical advantage in clinical practice.

Retrograde intramedullary fixation offers an alternative to the anterograde approach. Ideally, the retrograde approach avoids complications associated with the rotator cuff. In one study of intramedullary pinning from the distal humerus, patients had an average Constant score of 63 points; 42% of 53 patients had a pin perforation at the articular segment.[42] The results were excellent in a similar small study.[43]

In the largest available study of retrograde intramedullary fixation, fractures were stabilized with very good results using a titanium helix wire turned

**Table 2 | Recent Studies of Intramedullary Nailing**

| Study | Mean Follow-up Period (Months) | Mean Patient Age (Years) | Patients (N) | Patients at Follow-up (n) | Two-Part Fractures (n) | Three-Part Fractures (n) | Four-Part Fractures (n) | Outcomes Measure (Mean Score) |
|---|---|---|---|---|---|---|---|---|
| Adedapo and Ikpeme[55] (2001) | 12 | 69 | 34 | 23* | | 10 | 6 | Neer: 89, three-part fracture; 60, four-part fracture |
| Rajasekhar et al[56] (2001) | 18 | 64 | 30 | 25 | 23 | 4 | 0 | Constant: > 75 points, 13 patients; 50-75 points, 7 patients; < 50 points, 5 patients |
| Mittlmeier et al[14] (2003) | ≥ 12 | 69 | 221 | 64 | 19 | 34 | 11 | Constant: 75 points |
| Stedtfeld et al[57] (2003) | ≥ 12 | 69 | 95 | 45 | | | | Constant: 86 points |
| Mathews and Lobenhoffer[54] (2004) | 13 | 81 | 41 | 36 | 16 | 22 | 3 | Constant: 57 points |
| Park et al[53] (2006) | 39 | 62 | 26 | 26 | 7 | 18 | 1 | Neer: 90 |

*Includes 7 patients with three- or four-part fracture and associated shaft fracture.*

through the medullary canal from distal. Complications appeared in 12% of 95 patients.[46]

Twenty-six patients with a mean age of 62 years were treated using open intramedullary nailing with tension bands and locking sutures.[53] At 39-month follow-up, the average ASES score was 85 points, and the average Neer score was 90 points. More than one type of nail was used in the study. Three patients required additional surgery for arthrolysis or conversion to a prosthesis.

In patients with a mean age of 81 years, fractures were treated using the Targon nail (Aesculap, Tuttlingen, Germany).[54] The mean raw Constant score was 57 points, and the age-adjusted Constant score was 86%. No loss of fixation occurred, although one patient experienced fracture displacement after a second fall. One fracture of the shaft occurred but healed without surgery.

In another large study, 64 patients with a mean age of 69 years were treated using the Targon nail.[14] The average Constant score was 75 points at a minimum 12-month follow-up. Complications occurred in 51% of the patients. The complications included stiffness, infection, osteonecrosis, nonunion, and backing out of the screws (in 23%).

The findings of recent studies on intramedullary fixation are outlined in Table 2. The Polarus nail (Acumed, Hillsboro, OR) was used to treat three-part, four-part, and other combined shaft fractures.[55] At a mean 12-month follow-up, patients with a three-part fracture had a Neer score of 89 points, and those with a four-part fracture had

a score of 60 points. Interlocking intramedullary nails were found to be quite stable. Fixation of the tuberosities is difficult because the angle of the screws is predetermined by the configuration of the nail. The rate of screw complications was high in association with intramedullary nailing in the proximal humerus. This device is best used in fractures that extend into the shaft and in metaphyseal comminuted fractures. Whether insertion through the rotator cuff is a disadvantage is debatable.

The Bilboquet device (Stryker Implant, Cestas, France) is a two-part titanium implant that consists of a circular staple impacted into the humeral head and a stem fitting into the humeral shaft. Of 26 patients treated using this device, results were excellent in 9, good in 9, fair in 6, and poor in 2 at mean 26-month follow-up.[58]

## Open Reduction and Internal Fixation

Open reduction and internal fixation is indicated for higher energy injuries in younger patients, especially after an unsuccessful closed reduction. It can be performed using sutures, tension band wire, or plates.

Twenty-eight shoulders (27 patients) with a two- or three-part fracture were treated with suture-only fixation.[59] Of the 22 two-part fractures, 13 were fractures of the greater tuberosity only. The mean patient age was 64 years, and the mean follow-up period was 59 months. Radiographs showed that all shoulders healed without

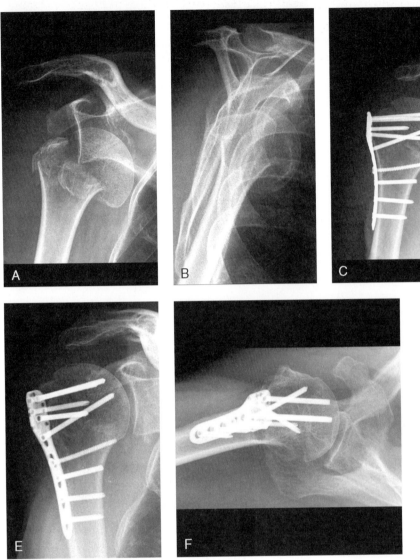

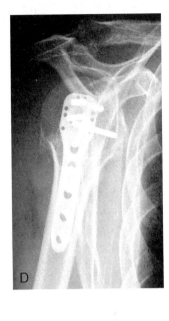

**Figure 3** Radiographs showing the use of a locking plate for a displaced four-part proximal humerus fracture. **A,** Presurgical AP view. **B,** Presurgical outlet view. **C,** Postsurgical AP view. **D,** Postsurgical outlet view. **E,** Postsurgical AP view at 6-month follow-up. **F,** Postsurgical axillary view at 6-month follow-up. *(Courtesy of Michael Plecko, MD, Graz, Austria.)*

evidence of osteonecrosis of the humeral head. The average ASES score was 87.1 points. For slightly displaced greater tuberosity fractures, suture-only fixation treatment is a viable option. In contrast, suture fixation has inadequate stability in surgical neck fractures.

A 10-year follow-up of 60 patients with a three- or four part fracture treated with a T plate found that results were excellent in 30%, good in 57%, and poor in 13%, as measured using the Constant score.[60] The rate of osteonecrosis was 37%. In another study, more than 50% of the patients had a four-part fracture; the average Constant score was 63 points, and the complication rate was 7%.[61] In 93 patients with rheumatoid arthritis who were treated for proximal humerus fracture, the overall complication rate was 58%; 22 shoulders required additional surgery.[62] This study reaffirmed that complications after surgical treatment of proximal humerus fractures are common in patients with rheuma-

toid arthritis and highlighted the difficulty of treating these patients.

The introduction of fixed-angle locking screws increased the popularity of plating for proximal humerus fractures. Biomechanical studies found that locking plates had significantly greater stability than the buttress plate, blade plate, or T plate[63,64] (Figure 3). The locking plate is superior in stiffness, torsional resistance, ultimate load, and displacement. Furthermore, the multidirectional screw insertion into the center of the humeral head increases the pull-out strength of the locking plate.[65-67]

Biomechanical studies found that optimal screw fixation can be obtained by using the longest screws possible and directing the screws in diverging or converging directions. The best bone is in the medial and posterior part of the humeral head, and it is advantageous to direct some screws into this dense bone.[33] Proper

**Table 3 | Recent Studies of Fixed-Angle Plating**

| Study | Mean Follow-up Period (Months) | Mean Patient Age (Years) | Patients (*N*) | Patients at Follow-up (*n*) |
|---|---|---|---|---|
| Hintermann et al[71] (2000) | 39 | 72 | 42 | 38 |
| Mückter et al[72] (2001) | 10 | 70 | 47 | 31 |
| Wijgman et al[60] (2002) | 120 | 48 | 109 | 60 |
| Lungershausen et al[68] (2003) | 14 | 64 | 51 | 24 |
| Robinson[73] (2003) | 12 | 67 | 29 | 25 |
| Wanner et al[69] (2003) | 17 | 67 | 71 | 60 |
| Björkenheim et al[74] (2004) | 12 | 67 | 72 | 72 |
| Lill et al[31] (2004) | 3 | 63 | 35 | 29 |
| Burton et al[75] (2005) | 17 | 62 | 19 | 13 |
| Frankhauser et al[61] (2005) | 12 | 64 | 29 | 29 |
| Plecko and Kraus[76] (2005) | 31 | 58 | 64 | 36 |
| Koukakis et al[77] (2006) | 16 | 62 | 20 | 20 |

positioning of the screws is difficult, and most plates are designed to guide the positioning. The Humeral Suture Plate (Arthrex, Naples, FL) has a polyaxial, fixed-angle mechanism; the screw angle can be varied as much as 30°.

Loss of fixation after the use of fixed-angle plates was found to be 4%, compared with 22% after the use of conventional plates.[68] However, the study did not find that the use of the fixed-angle plate produced significantly better functional results. The average adjusted Constant score was 73% for the shoulders treated with the fixed-angle plate and 69% for those treated with a conventional plate.

To increase stability, an alternative technique used two one-third tubular plates placed at a 90° angle.[69] This plate application provided great torsional stiffness and primary stability. At a mean 17-month follow-up, 61 of the 71 patients treated using this technique had an average Constant score of 61 points.

Longer plates are necessary for fractures extending to the shaft with metaphyseal comminution. The use of a longer plate on the lateral humerus is somewhat limited because of the proximity of the deltoid insertion. Helical plating, in which the plate curves distally from the lateral to the anterior side to avoid the deltoid insertion, has been proposed.[70] The greatest danger in performing plate fixation percutaneously arises from the musculocutaneous nerve, which can be found a mean 13.5 cm distal to the greater tuberosity.

Although the stability of fixed-angle plates is well established, long-term functional results have yet to be determined. The most recent studies, as listed in Table 3, are too small to allow a definitive statement about the usefulness of fixed-angle plating in various patient groups.[31,60,61,68,69,71-77] However, the results appear to be better in less comminuted fractures. For patients with any type of fracture who were treated using a conventional plate, the average Constant score ranged from 61 to 80 points; for patients treated with a fixed-angle device, the range was 63 to 83 points. The range of complications was 2% to 38%.

Open reduction and internal fixation leads to a good functional outcome. Although biomechanical studies found better results after the use of a fixed-angle plate, the functional results are equal to those reported for other types of plates.

The complication rates reported in some studies of locked plating are unacceptably high. However, many of

## Table 3 Continued | Recent Studies of Fixed-Angle Plating

| Two-Part Fracture (*n*) | Three-Part Fracture (*n*) | Four-Part Fracture (*n*) | Outcomes Measure (Mean Score) | Plate Design |
|---|---|---|---|---|
| 0 | 34 | 8 | Constant: 73 points | Blade |
| 23 | 20 | 0 | Constant: 83 points | PlanTan[†] |
| 0 | 40 | 20 | Constant: excellent, 30%*; good, 57%*; poor, 13%* | T or cerclage wires |
| 8 | 8 | 3 | Neer: 72 | Königsee[‡] |
| | 5 | 20 | Constant: 80 points | Buttress or screws |
| 10 | 33 | 17 | Constant: 61 points | Double |
| 38 | 22 | 12 | Constant: 77 points | Philos[§] |
| 8 | 16 | 5 | Constant: 74%* | Locking Proximal Humeral Plate[‖] |
| 6 | 7 | 0 | Constant: 74%* | PlanTan[†] |
| 5 | 15 | 9 | Constant: 75 points | Locking Proximal Humeral Plate[‖] |
| 8 | 9 | 19 | Constant: 63 points | Locking Proximal Humeral Plate[‖] |
| 5 | 11 | 4 | Constant: 76%* | Philos[§] |

*Age- and gender-adjusted score.
[†] PlanTan Medizintechnik, Lambrechtshagen, Germany
[‡] Königsee Implantate, Königsee-Aschau, Germany
[§] Synthes, Stratec Medical, Mezzovico, Switzerland
[‖] Mathys, Bettlach, Switzerland

these complications may be associated with a lack of surgical experience with the newer implants. The risk of complications can be minimized by ensuring that the humeral head screws are the correct height and length. To prevent screw protrusion into the joint, the screws should be 5 mm shorter than the measured distance. For additional stability, the tuberosities should be fixed to the plate and to each other using heavy sutures. Soft tissues and intact periosteal sleeves should be protected to preserve the blood supply to the fracture fragments.

### Primary Arthroplasty

A high risk of osteonecrosis or loss of fixation is the accepted indication for primary arthroplasty of a proximal humerus fracture. Osteonecrosis or loss or fixation is particularly likely after a head-split fracture, a fracture with 50% fragmentation of the articular surface, or a fracture-dislocation or nonreconstructable fracture in an older patient. The use of primary or secondary arthroplasty for some other types of fractures is a subject of debate. Some surgeons prefer immediate fracture reconstruction and secondary arthroplasty for fractures with nonunion, malunion, or osteonecrosis.

Healing of the tuberosities and their attached rotator cuff tendons is crucial in functional outcome after arthroplasty.[78,79] The surgeon must ensure that the fracture prosthesis is inserted at the correct height; the top of the implant head should be 5 mm higher than the top of the greater tuberosity, and retroversion should be 20° to 25°. Proper healing of the tuberosities depends on a secure fixation in anatomic position. In the largest available study, the average Constant score of patients with nonunited or malpositioned tuberosities was 49 points; if the tuberosities were healed in an incorrect position, the score was 53 points; if the tuberosities were healed anatomically, the score was 64 points.[79] Tenodesis of the long head of the biceps tendon should be performed, and soft tissues should be protected to preserve blood supply to the tuberosities. Postsurgical rehabilitation should be gentle because aggressive early mobilization appears to have a detrimental influence on healing of the tuberosities.

Studies have not yet defined the indications for using a reverse shoulder prosthesis, and recommendations therefore cannot be made. In an older patient with a large rotator cuff deficiency, the reverse prosthesis can be considered as an option.

## Table 4 | Recent Studies of Proximal Humerus Arthroplasty

| Study | Mean Follow-up Period (Months) | Mean Patient Age (Years) | Patients (N) | Patients at Follow-up (n) | Outcomes Measure (Mean Score) | Tuberosity Disintegration | Prosthesis |
|---|---|---|---|---|---|---|---|
| Bosch et al[80] (1998) | 42 | 65 | 39 | 25 | Constant: 54 points | | Neer II* |
| Zyto et al[81] (1998) | 39 | 71 | 27 | 27 | Constant: 46 points | 11% | Neer II* Biomodular[†] |
| Becker et al[82] (2002) | 45 | 67 | 27 | 27 | Constant: 45 points | | Global[‡] |
| Mighell et al[83] (2003) | 36 | 66 | 71 | 71 | ASES: 77 | 22% | Global[‡] |
| Schittko et al[84] (2003) | ≥ 6 | | 58 | 43 | Constant: 55 points | | Ortra[§] |
| Schmal et al[85] (2004) | 14 | 70 | 20 | 17 | Constant: 52 points | 82% | Epoca[ǁ] |
| Kralinger et al[79] (2004) | 29 | 70 | 167 | 167 | Constant: 55 points | 46% | Various |
| Grassi and Tajana[86] (2005) | 62 | 71 | 51 | 48 | Constant: 58 points | 45% | |
| Gierer et al[87] (2006) | 12 | 73 | 24 | 18 | Constant: 56 points | 69% | Epoca[ǁ] |

*ASES = American Shoulder and Elbow Surgeons Index.*
*Smith & Nephew, Memphis, TN*
[†] *Biomet, Warsaw, IN*
[‡] *Depuy, Warsaw, IN*
[§] *Zimmer, Freiburg, Germany*
[ǁ] *Argomedical, Gifhorn, Germany*

Recent studies of the results of arthroplasty in treating proximal humerus fractures[79-87] are outlined in Table 4. Some studies did not distinguish between primary and secondary implantation. The range of Constant scores was 45 points to 58 points, which is very low compared with other types of reconstructive surgery. The rate of tuberosity malposition or nonunion remains high (between 11% and 82%). Some surgeons believe a prosthesis design is needed that is narrow in the metaphyseal area to leave space for bone grafting.[88]

Presurgical planning and the use of a fracture jig should facilitate the correct positioning of the fragments. A combination of vertical sutures through a bone tunnel in the diaphysis and horizontal cerclage sutures around the tuberosities and the implant appears to provide the strongest, tightest fixation of the tuberosities.[89] Several surgeons recommend that exercising be avoided for 4 weeks after surgery to promote tuberosity healing.[88]

A systematic review of the literature identified 24 reports of patients with three- and four-part fractures who were treated nonsurgically, with internal fixation, or with arthroplasty. The studies were small and used varying outcome measures. In general, the patients treated nonsurgically had the worst outcomes in terms of pain and range of motion. Restoration of anatomy was best achieved with fixation. There was no overall difference in range of motion between the patients treated with internal fixation and those treated with arthroplasty.[23] It is clear that currently available literature is inadequate for evidence-based decision making.

## Summary

The vascularity and bone quality of different regions of the proximal humerus must be considered in the treatment of proximal humerus fractures. Osteoporosis and the anatomy of the vessels are factors that require an understanding of the different fracture patterns, as well as osteonecrosis. The results of minimally invasive and open treatment have been similar, and the options for fracture fixation are still under discussion. Reconstruction is preferable to humeral head replacement whenever possible. The functional outcome of arthroplasty is poor, but patient satisfaction is acceptable. Prospective studies are needed to compare the different treatment methods.

## Annotated References

1. Green A, Norris T: Proximal humerus fractures and fracture dislocations, in Jupiter J, ed: *Skeletal Trauma*, ed 3. Philadelphia, PA, Saunders, 2003, pp 1532-1624.

2. Kannus P, Palvanen M, Niemi S, Parkkari J, Vuori I: Osteoporotic fractures of the proximal humerus in elderly Finnish persons: Sharp increase in 1970-1998 and alarming projections for the new millennium. *Acta Orthop Scand* 2000;71:465-470.

3. Brooks CH, Revell WJ, Heatley FW: Vascularity of the humeral head after proximal humeral fractures. An anatomical cadaver study. *J Bone Joint Surg Br* 1993;75:132-136.

4. Gerber C, Schneeberger AG, Vinh TS: The arterial vascularization of the humeral head: An anatomical study. *J Bone Joint Surg Am* 1990;72:1486-1494.

5. Resch H, Beck E, Bayley I: Reconstruction of the valgus-impacted humeral head fracture. *J Shoulder Elbow Surg* 1995;4:73-80.

6. Hertel R, Hempfing A, Stiehler M, Leunig M: Predictors of humeral head ischemia after intracapsular fracture of the proximal humerus. *J Shoulder Elbow Surg* 2004;13:427-433.

   A prospective surgical evaluation protocol was used in 100 intracapsular proximal humerus fractures to measure circulation and determine predictors for ischemia, subject to fracture type.

7. Neer CS: Displaced proximal humeral fractures: Part 1. Classification and evaluation. *J Bone Joint Surg Am* 1970;52:1077-1089.

8. Palvanen M, Kannus P, Niemi S, Parkkari J: Update in the epidemiology of proximal humeral fractures. *Clin Orthop Relat Res* 2006;442:87-92.

   A small patient population is represented in this retrospective data evaluation of patients admitted to a hospital with proximal humerus fractures during a period of more than 30 years. Level of evidence: IV.

9. Lauritzen JB, Schwarz P, Lund B, McNair P, Transbol I: Changing incidence and residual lifetime risk of common osteoporosis-related fractures. *Osteoporos Int* 1993;3:127-132.

10. Court-Brown CM, Garg A, McQueen MM: The epidemiology of proximal humeral fractures. *Acta Orthop Scand* 2001;72:365-371.

    Data were acquired prospectively in this epidemiologic study of all consecutive patients with proximal humerus fractures in a Scottish hospital that serves all trauma patients in an area with a 700,000-person population.

11. Palvanen M, Kannus P, Parkkari J: Injury mechanisms of osteoporotic upper limb fractures. *J Bone Miner Res* 2000;15:S539.

12. Sadowski C, Riand N, Stern R, Hoffmeyer P: Fixation of fractures of the proximal humerus with the PlantTan humerus fixator plate: Early experience with a new implant. *J Shoulder Elbow Surg* 2003; 12:148-151.

    Of seven patients treated with a new plate for humeral fixation, the four patients who were older than 75 years had a 100% failure rate.

13. Astrand J, Thorngren KG, Tägil M: One fracture is enough! Experience with a prospective and consecutive osteoporosis screening program with 239 fracture patients. *Acta Orthop* 2006;77:3-8.

    A prospective, consecutive osteoporosis screening program was conducted in 239 patients with fracture in an orthopaedic center in Sweden. Only 13% patients had bone mineral density values in the normal range.

14. Mittlmeier TWF, Stedtfeld HW, Ewert A, Beck M, Frosch B, Gradl G: Stabilization of proximal humeral fractures with an angular and sliding stable antegrade locking nail (Targon PH). *J Bone Joint Surg Am* 2003;85:136-146.

    In this case series, the Targon intramedullary nail was found to have good results, although the complication rate was more than 50%. Approximately half of the complications were caused by backing out of the locking screws.

15. Sidor ML, Zuckerman JD, Lyon T, Koval K, Cuomo F, Schoenberg N: The Neer classification system for proximal humeral fractures: An assessment of interobserver reliability and intraobserver reproducibility. *J Bone Joint Surg Am* 1993;75:1745-1750.

16. Edelson G, Kelly I, Vigder F, Reis ND: A three-dimensional classification for fractures of the proximal humerus. *J Bone Joint Surg Br* 2004;86:413-425.

    Proximal humerus fractures were classified using cadaver specimens and radiographs. Three-dimensional CT was found to be invaluable in assessing proximal humerus fractures. An interobserver reliability study found a strong kappa coefficient of 0.69.

17. Resch H, Aschauer E, Povacz P, Ritter E: Closed reduction and fixation of articular fractures of the humeral head. *Tech Shoulder Elbow Surg* 2000;1: 154-162.

18. Iannotti JP, Ramsey ML, Williams GR, Warner JJP: Nonprosthetic management of proximal humeral fractures. *J Bone Joint Surg Am* 2003;85:1578-1593.

    Methods of fixation for different types of proximal humerus fractures are presented.

19. Zuckerman JD: Fractures of the proximal humerus: Diagnosis and management, in Iannotti JP (ed): *Disorders of the Shoulder: Diagnosis and Management*. Philadelphia, PA, Lippincott Williams & Wilkins, 1999, pp 639-685.

20. Ogawa K, Yoshida A, Ikegami H: Isolated fractures of the greater tuberosity of the humerus: Solutions to recognizing a frequently overlooked fracture. *J Trauma* 2003;54:713-717.

A retrospective evaluation of 99 radiographs found that 59% of fractures of the greater tuberosity were overlooked. This condition can be effectively diagnosed by detecting tenderness on the lateral wall of the greater tuberosity.

21. Neer CS: Four-segment classification of proximal humeral fractures: Purpose and reliable use. *J Shoulder Elbow Surg* 2002;11:389-400.

    The 1970 Neer classification system and its 1975 revision are reviewed and explained.

22. Bhandari M, Matthys G, McKee MD: Four part fractures of the proximal humerus. *J Orthop Trauma* 2004;18:126-127.

    A literature review found only five randomized, controlled trials, with insufficient evidence to determine the optimal intervention for a displaced four-part fracture.

23. Misra A, Kapur R, Maffulli N: Complex proximal humeral fractures in adults: A systematic review of management. *Injury* 2001;32:363-372.

    In this systematic literature review of treatment for three- and four-part fractures, 24 reports met the inclusion criteria. The data did not reveal evidence-based decision making in the treatment of complex proximal humerus fractures.

24. Tingart M, Bathis H, Bouillon B, Tiling T: The displaced proximal humeral fracture: Is there evidence for therapeutic concepts? *Chirurg* 2001;72:1284-1291.

    A literature review of proximal humerus fractures found 3 randomized, 4 prospective, and 26 retrospective studies. Only limited scientific evidence on the treatment of displaced proximal humerus fractures was found.

25. Zyto K, Ahrengart L, Sperber A, Tornkvist H: Treatment of displaced proximal humeral fractures in elderly patients. *J Bone Joint Surg Br* 1997;79:412-417.

26. Hepp P: Voigt C, Josten C: The conservative treatment of proximal humeral fractures, in Lill H (ed): *Die proximale Humerusfraktur.* Stuttgart, Germany, Thieme, 2006, pp 40-45.

    Nondisplaced proximal humerus fractures can be treated nonsurgically, and acceptable results can be expected in two- and three-part fractures. Nonsurgical treatment is optional in patients with risk factors.

27. Lill H, Bewer A, Korner J, et al: Conservative treatment of displaced proximal humeral fractures. *Zentralbl Chir* 2001;126:205-210.

    Of 52 nonsurgically treated patients, 37 were evaluated at a mean 20-month follow-up. Treatment of two- and three-part fractures had good results, despite malunions. Poor results after nonsurgical treatment of four-part fractures indicate that these should be treated surgically.

28. Court-Brown CM, Cattermole H, McQueen MM: Impacted valgus fractures (B1.1) of the proximal humerus: The results of non-surgical treatment. *J Bone Joint Surg Br* 2002;84:504-508.

    A retrospective analysis of 125 patients after nonsurgical treatment of a valgus-impacted proximal humerus fracture found an 80% mean adjusted Constant score. These fractures should be treated nonsurgically.

29. Zyto K: Non-operative treatment of comminuted fractures of the proximal humerus in elderly patients. *Injury* 1998;29:349-352.

30. Koval KJ, Gallagher MA, Marsicano JG, Cuomo F, McShinawy A, Zuckerman JD: Functional outcome after minimally displaced fractures of the proximal part of the humerus. *J Bone Joint Surg Am* 1997;79:203-207.

31. Lill H, Hepp P, Rose T, Konig K, Josten C: The angle stable Locking-Proximal-Humerus-Plate (LPHP®) for proximal humeral fractures using a small anterior-lateral-deltoid-splitting-approach: Technique and first results. *Zentralbl Chir* 2004;129:43-48.

    The technique for using a new implant is presented. In a prospective study of 29 patients, 11 had complications at 3-month follow-up.

32. Tingart MJ, Bouxsein ML, Zurakowski D, Warner JP, Apreleva M: Three-dimensional distribution of bone density in the proximal humerus. *Calcif Tissue Int* 2003;73:531-536.

    Bone density was quantified in different areas of the humeral head, and bone sites that may provide stronger fixation for implants are identified.

33. Lill H, Hepp P, Gowin W, et al: Age- and gender-related distribution of bone mineral density and mechanical properties of the proximal humerus. *Rofo* 2002;174:1544-1550.

    In a study of 70 cadavers, a high correlation between age and bone mineral density was found in female specimens.

34. Kralinger F, Irenberger A, Lechner C, Wambacher M, Golser K, Sperner G: Comparison of open versus percutaneous treatment for humeral head fracture. *Unfallchirurg* 2006;109:406-410.

    In a retrospective analysis of 83 patients after open or closed reduction for proximal humerus fracture, the patients treated with open reduction had a significantly higher incidence of osteonecrosis.

35. Hertel R: Fractures of the proximal humerus in osteoporotic bone. *Osteoporos Int* 2005;16(suppl 2):S65-S72.

    Current treatment options for proximal humerus fractures in patients with osteoporosis are reviewed, and the author's preferences are presented.

36. Gerber C, Werner CML, Vienne P: Internal fixation of complex fractures of the proximal humerus. *J Bone Joint Surg Br* 2004;86:848-855.

In a retrospective study of 34 consecutive articular fractures of the proximal humerus after open reduction and internal fixation in patients with good bone quality, complete or partial osteonecrosis occurred in 12 patients (35%). All other patients had reliable shoulder function.

37. Martin C, Guillen M, Lopez G: Treatment of 2- and 3-part fractures of the proximal humerus using external fixation: A retrospective evaluation of 62 patients. *Acta Orthop* 2006;77:275-278.

    A retrospective evaluation of 62 consecutive proximal humerus fractures after external fixation found satisfactory results. The mean Constant score was 84 points.

38. Resch H, Povacz P, Frohlich R, Wambacher M: Percutaneous fixation of three- and four-part fractures of the proximal humerus. *J Bone Joint Surg Br* 1997;79: 295-300.

39. Hartmann A, Resch H: Closed reduction, percutaneous screw fixation and fixed angle wire stabilization, in Lill H (ed): *Die proximale Humerusfraktur*. Stuttgart, Germany, Thieme, 2006, pp 79-84.

    The principles of closed reduction for proximal humerus fracture are presented, as well as the technique for fixation using the Humerusblock.

40. Jaberg H, Warner JJP, Jakob RP: Percutaneous stabilization of unstable fractures of the humerus. *J Bone Joint Surg Am* 1992;74:508-515.

41. Herscovici D, Saunders DT, Johnson MP, Sanders R, DiPasquale T: Percutaneous fixation of proximal humeral fractures. *Clin Orthop Relat Res* 2000;375: 97-104.

42. Wachtl SW, Marti CB, Hoogewoud HM, Jakob RP, Gautier E: Treatment of proximal humerus fracture using multiple intramedullary flexible nails. *Arch Orthop Trauma Surg* 2000;120:171-175.

43. Khodadadyan-Klostermann C, Raschke M, Fontes R, et al: Treatment of complex proximal humeral fractures with minimally invasive fixation of the humeral head combined with flexible intramedullary wire fixation: Introduction of a new treatment concept. *Langenbecks Arch Surg* 2002;387:153-160.

    In a prospective study, 24 patients with a three- or four-part fracture received closed reduction and retrograde pinning with elastic nails. At 1-year follow-up, 45% had a satisfactory result, as measured using the Neer and Constant scores.

44. Takeuchi R, Koshino T, Nakazawa A, Numazaki S, Sato R, Saito T: Minimally invasive fixation for unstable two-part proximal humeral fractures: Surgical techniques and clinical results using J-nails. *J Orthop Trauma* 2002;16:403-408.

    A retrospective case study of 41 unstable two-part fractures fixed with retrograde pinning found an excellent result in 61% and a satisfactory result in 90%, as measured using the Neer score.

45. Werner A, Bohm D, Ilg A, Gohlke F: Intramedullary wire fixation of proximal humeral fractures: Modified Kapandji technique. *Unfallchirurg* 2002;105: 332-337.

    In a retrospective study, 14 of 29 patients were evaluated at a minimum 24-month follow-up. In this group, there were 3 two-part, 4 three-part, and 7 four-part fractures. The mean Constant score was 70 points.

46. Gorschewsky O, Puetz A, Klakow A, Pitzl M, Neumann W: The treatment of proximal humeral fractures with intramedullary titanium helix wire by 97 patients. *Arch Orthop Trauma Surg* 2005;125: 670-675.

    Ninety-seven patients with a proximal humerus fracture were treated using an intramedullary titanium helix wire. At 1-year follow-up, 41 patients had a very good result; 24, a good result; 16, a satisfactory result; and 14, a poor result. The average Constant score was 76 points, and the average University of California Los Angeles score was 30.7 points.

47. Tamai K, Ohno W, Takemura M, Mashitori H, Hamada J, Saotome K: Treatment of proximal humeral fractures with a new intramedullary nail. *J Orthop Sci* 2005;10:180-186.

    A new device for intramedullary nailing is presented. In 31 patients, the mean Japanese Orthopaedic Association Shoulder Score was 78 at a mean 13-month follow-up.

48. Fenichel I, Oran A, Burstein G, Perry M: Percutaneous pinning using threaded pins as a treatment option for unstable two- and three-part fractures of the proximal humerus: A retrospective study. *Int Orthop* 2006;30:153-157.

    A retrospective study of 50 patients with a two- or three-part fracture found an average Constant score of 81 points at a mean 2.5-year follow-up after treatment with percutaneous pinning.

49. Keener JD, Parsons BO, Flatow EL, Rogers K, Williams GR, Galatz LM: Outcomes after percutaneous reduction and fixation of proximal humeral fractures. *J Shoulder Elbow Surg* 2007;16:330-338.

    In 27 of 35 patients treated with percutaneous pinning, the mean ASES and Constant scores at a mean 35-month follow-up were 83.4 and 73.9 points, respectively.

50. Wheeler DL, Colville MR: Biomechanical comparison of intramedullary and percutaneous pin fixation for proximal humeral fracture fixation. *J Orthop Trauma* 1997;11:363-367.

51. Ito K, Hungerbuhler R, Wahl D, Grass F: Improved intramedullary nail interlocking in osteoporotic bone. *J Orthop Trauma* 2001;15:192-196.

    In a biomechanical study, intramedullary nailing with a bladelike device was found to be 41% stiffer and 20% stronger than nailing with conventional locking bolts.

52. Lill H, Hepp P, Korner J, et al: Proximal humeral fractures: How stiff should an implant be? A comparative

mechanical study with new implants in human specimens. *Arch Orthop Trauma Surg* 2003;123:74-81.

A comparative mechanical study of new implants in cadaver specimens found that implants with low stiffness and greater elasticity appear to minimize the peak stresses at the bone-implant interface and are therefore particularly suitable for fracture fixation in osteoporotic bone.

53. Park JY, An JW, Oh JH: Open intramedullary nailing with tension band and locking sutures for proximal humeral fracture: Hot air balloon technique. *J Shoulder Elbow Surg* 2006;15:594-601.

At a mean 39-month follow-up, 26 consecutive patients treated with nailing and locking sutures were evaluated. The average Neer and ASES scores were 90 and 85, respectively.

54. Mathews J, Lobenhoffer P: Results of intramedullary nailing of unstable proximal humeral fractures in geriatric patients with a new antegrade nail system. *Unfallchirurg* 2004;107:372-380.

In a retrospective study of 41 geriatric patients treated with the Targon nail, 32 patients had a mean Constant score of 57 points at a mean 13-month follow-up.

55. Adedapo AO, Ikpeme JO: The results of internal fixation of three- and four-part proximal humeral fractures with the Polarus nail. *Injury* 2001;32:115-121.

Twenty-three patients with a displaced three- or four-part fracture of the proximal humerus were treated using the Polarus intramedullary interlocking nail. At 1-year follow-up, the median Neer scores for patients with three- and four-part fractures were 89 and 60, respectively.

56. Rajasekhar C, Ray PS, Bhamra MS: Fixation of proximal humeral fractures with the Polarus nail. *J Shoulder Elbow Surg* 2001;10:7-10.

Thirty patients with a fracture of the proximal humerus received internal fixation using an intramedullary locked nail. At a mean 18-month follow-up, 20 of 25 patients (80%) had a satisfactory or excellent functional outcome, as measured using the Constant score.

57. Stedtfeld HW, Attmanspacher W, Thaler K, Frosch B: Fixation of humeral head fractures with antegrade intramedullary nailing. *Zentralbl Chir* 2003;128:6-11.

In a prospective study, 45 patients treated using the Targon nail had a mean Constant score of 85.7 points at 1-year follow-up.

58. Doursounian L, Grimberg J, Cazeau C, Jos E, Touzard RC: A new internal fixation technique for fractures of the proximal humerus: The Bilboquet device. A report on 26 cases. *J Shoulder Elbow Surg* 2000;9:279-288.

59. Park MC, Murthi AM, Roth NS, Blaine TA, Levine WN, Bigliani LU: Two-part and three-part fractures of the proximal humerus treated with suture fixation. *J Orthop Trauma* 2003;17:319-325.

Of 28 patients with a proximal humerus fracture treated with nonabsorbable rotator cuff–incorporating sutures, 78% had an excellent result at an average 4.4-year follow-up. The mean ASES score was 87.1.

60. Wijgman AJ, Roolker W, Patt TW, Raaymakers ELFB, Marti RK: Open reduction and internal fixation of three and four-part fractures of the proximal part of the humerus. *J Bone Joint Surg Am* 2002; 84:1919-1925.

In a retrospective long-term study of 109 patients with a three- or four-part fracture treated using a T plate or cerclage wires, 52 of 60 patients (87%) had a good or excellent result at 10-year follow-up, as measured using the Constant score.

61. Frankhauser F, Boldin C, Schippinger G, Haunschmid C, Szyszkowitz R: A new locking plate for unstable fractures of the proximal humerus. *Clin Orthop Relat Res* 2005;430:176-181.

In a prospective cohort study, 26 patients with fractures treated with a locking proximal humerus plate had a mean Constant score of 75 points at 12-month follow-up. Level of evidence: II.

62. Smith AM, Sperling JW, Cofield RH: Complications of operative fixation of proximal humeral fractures in patients with rheumatoid arthritis. *J Shoulder Elbow Surg* 2005;14:559-564.

Nine proximal humerus fractures were evaluated in patients with rheumatoid arthritis. Physicians and patients should be aware of the high rates of complications and unsatisfactory results after surgery in patients with rheumatoid arthritis.

63. Weinstein DM, Bratton DR, Ciccone WJ, Elias JJ: Locking plates improve torsional resistance in the stabilization of three-part proximal humeral fractures. *J Shoulder Elbow Surg* 2006;15:239-243.

Biomechanical tests compared the use of an angled blade plate and a locking plate in a reconstructed three-part proximal humerus fracture. The locking plate was found to provide better torsional fatigue resistance and stiffness than the blade plate.

64. Hessmann MH, Hansen WSM, Krummenauer F, Pol TF, Rommens M: Locked plate fixation and intramedullary nailing for proximal humerus fractures: A biomechanical evaluation. *J Trauma* 2005;58:1194-1201.

Four implants were tested in a biomechanical study. The proximal humerus nail and the rigid internal fixator were found to be stronger than the semielastic locked plate or the Synthes T plate in fixation of unstable subcapital proximal humerus fractures.

65. Wagner M: General principles for the clinical use of the LCP. *Injury* 2003;34:B31-B42.

This review article outlines the principles and practice of correctly using locking plates. It is a significant contribution to the understanding of locking plates as an important innovation.

66. Liew ASL, Johnson JA, Patterson SD, King GJW, Chess DG: Effect of screw placement on fixation in the humeral head. *J Shoulder Elbow Surg* 2000;9: 423-426.

67. Lill H, Korner J, Glasmacher S, et al: The crossed screw osteosynthesis of proximal humeral fractures. *Unfallchirurg* 2001;104:852-859.

   A retrospective study of 21 patients treated using two crossed screws and, when necessary, a tension band, found that 71% had a good or excellent result at a mean 18-month follow-up. The complication rate was 29%.

68. Lungershausen W, Bach O, Lorenz CO: Locking plate osteosynthesis for fractures of the proximal humerus. *Zentralbl Chir* 2003;128:28-33.

   A retrospective study compared results for 51 patients treated using a locking plate and 32 patients treated using percutaneous wires. At a mean 1-year follow-up, there was no significant difference, as measured using the Neer score; patients treated using a locking plate had a mean score of 72, and those treated using percutaneous wires had a mean score of 68.

69. Wanner GA, Wanner-Schmid E, Romero J, et al: Internal fixation of displaced proximal humeral fractures with two one-third tubular plates. *J Trauma* 2003;54:536-544.

   Sixty consecutive patients were treated using two one-third tubular plates. Retrospective evaluation at a mean 17-month follow-up found that 63% had a good or excellent result, as measured using the Constant score.

70. Gardner MJ, Griffith MH, Lorich DG: Helical plating of the proximal humerus. *Injury* 2005;36:1197-1200.

   This cadaver study evaluated possible injury to the musculocutaneous nerve during plating. Avoiding the identified nerve-location danger zone can make percutaneous screw placement a safer procedure.

71. Hintermann B, Trouillier HH, Schafer D: Rigid internal fixation of fractures of the proximal humerus in older patients. *J Bone Joint Surg Br* 2000;82:1107-1112.

72. Mückter H, Herzog L, Becker M, Vogel W, Meeder PJ, Buchholz J: Angle- and rotation-stable internal fixation of proximal humerus fractures with the Humerus Fixator Plate: Early clinical experience with a newly developed implant. *Chirurg* 2001;72:1327-1335.

   Thirty-one patients treated with the Humerus Fixator Plate were studied at a mean 10-month follow-up. The mean Constant score was 83 points. In 13% of patients, screw protrusion led to implant removal.

73. Robinson CM: Severely impacted valgus proximal humeral fractures: Results of operative treatment. *J Bone Joint Surg Am* 2003;85:1647-1655.

   Twenty-five patients with a valgus-impacted fracture were treated with open reduction and internal fixation with cement augmentation. At 1-year follow-up, the median Constant score was 80 points, and the Disabilities of the Arm, Shoulder and Hand Questionnaire score was 22 points. Level of evidence: IV.

74. Björkenheim JM, Pajarinen J, Savolainen V: Internal fixation of proximal humeral fractures with a locking compression plate: A retrospective evaluation of 72 patients followed for a minimum of 1 year. *Acta Orthop Scand* 2004;75:741-745.

   Seventy-two patients treated using the Philos plate were evaluated at a minimum 12-month follow-up. The mean Constant score was 77 points.

75. Burton DJC, Wells G, Watters A, Schilders E, Venkateswaran B: Early experience with the PlantTan fixator plate for 2 and 3 part fractures of the proximal humerus. *Injury* 2005;36:1190-1196.

   The humerus fixator plate was used in 15 patients with a proximal humerus fracture. At a mean 17-month follow-up, the mean Constant score of the affected shoulder was 74% of that of the unaffected shoulder. The procedure was not recommended for elderly patients.

76. Plecko M, Kraus A: Internal fixation of proximal humerus fractures using the locking proximal humerus plate. *Oper Orthop Traumatol* 2005;17:25-50.

   Approximately 36 patients treated using a locking plate were evaluated at 1-year follow-up. The mean Constant score was 63 points, and the mean Disabilities of the Arm, Shoulder and Hand Questionnaire score was 18 points.

77. Koukakis A, Apostolou CD, Taneja T, Korres DS, Amini A: Fixation of proximal humerus fractures using the PHILOS plate. *Clin Orthop Relat Res* 2006; 442:115-120.

   At 1-year follow-up of 18 patients treated using a locking plate, the mean Constant score was 76 points. Level of evidence: IV.

78. Boileau P, Krishnan SG, Tinsi L, Walch G, Coste JS, Molé D: Tuberosity malposition and migration: Reasons for poor outcomes after hemiarthroplasty for displaced fractures of the proximal humerus. *J Shoulder Elbow Surg* 2002;11:401-412.

   The results of hemiarthroplasty for displaced proximal humerus fracture were evaluated in 66 consecutive patients. At a mean 27-month follow-up, the mean Constant score was 56 points.

79. Kralinger F, Schwaiger R, Wambacher M, et al: Outcome after primary hemiarthroplasty for fracture of the head of the humerus: A retrospective multicentre study of 167 patients. *J Bone Joint Surg Br* 2004;86: 217-219.

   In a multicenter retrospective study, 167 patients were evaluated 1 year after fracture arthroplasty. The mean Constant score was 55 points. However, only 42% of the patients were able to raise the arm above 90°.

80. Bosch U, Skutek M, Fremerey RW, Tscherne H: Outcome after primary and secondary hemiarthroplasty in elderly patients with fractures of the proximal humerus. *J Shoulder Elbow Surg* 1998;7:479-484.

81. Zyto K, Wallace WA, Frostick SP, Preston BJ: Outcome after hemiarthroplasty for three- and four-part fractures of the proximal humerus. *J Shoulder Elbow Surg* 1998;7:85-89.

82. Becker R, Pap G, Machner A, Neumann WH: Strength and motion after hemiarthroplasty in displaced four-fragment fracture of the proximal humerus: 27 patients followed for 1-6 years. *Acta Orthop Scand* 2002;73:44-49.

  At a mean 4-year follow-up of 27 patients after hemiarthroplasty for a displaced four-part fracture, the mean Constant score was 45 points.

83. Mighell MA, Kolm GP, Collinge CA, Frankle MA: Outcomes of hemiarthroplasty for fractures of the proximal humerus. *J Shoulder Elbow Surg* 2003;12: 569-577.

  At a minimum 2-year follow-up of 71 patients after hemiarthroplasty for a proximal humerus fracture, the mean ASES score was 77 points.

84. Schittko A, Braun W, Ruter A: Experiences with the OrTra® prosthesis in primary prosthetic replacement of fractures of the humeral head: Indication, technique and results. *Zentralbl Chir* 2003;128:12-16.

  At a minimum 6-month follow-up of 43 patients after fracture arthroplasty, the mean Constant score was 55 points, and pain relief was good. Shoulder function was unsatisfactory.

85. Schmal H, Klemt C, Sudkamp NP: Evaluation of shoulder arthroplasty in treatment of four-fragment fractures of the proximal humerus. *Unfallchirurg* 2004;107:575-579.

  At a mean 14-month follow-up of 17 patients after hemiarthroplasty for a displaced four-part fracture, the mean Constant score was 52 points.

86. Grassi FA, Tajana MS: Partial prosthetic replacement of the shoulder in fractures and fracture-dislocations of the proximal humerus. *Chir Organi Mov* 2005;90: 179-190.

  At a mean 5.2-year follow-up of 48 patients after partial shoulder replacement for fracture and fracture-dislocation of the proximal humerus, the mean Constant score was 57.8 points.

87. Gierer P, Simon C, Gradl G, et al: Complex proximal humerus fractures: Management with a humeral head prosthesis? Clinical and radiological results of a prospective study. *Orthopade* 2006;35:834-839.

  At 1-year follow-up of 24 patients with a complex proximal humerus fracture treated with arthroplasty, the mean Constant score was 56 points, and the University of California Los Angeles score was 27.

88. Sanchez-Sotelo J: Proximal humerus fractures. *Clin Anat* 2006;19:588-598.

  This review article presents humeral head vascularity, fracture patterns, bone quality, and overall geometry and draws conclusions about nonsurgical treatment, internal fixation, and hemiarthroplasty.

89. Frankle MA, Mighell MA: Techniques and principles of tuberosity fixation for proximal humeral fractures treated with hemiarthroplasty. *J Shoulder Elbow Surg* 2004;13:239-247.

  This review article presents fracture arthroplasty geometry and fracture patterns, with a description of correct tuberosity fixation and an overview of literature from 1995 to 2000.

# Chapter 39

# Sequelae of Proximal Humerus Fractures

*Pascal Boileau, MD

Lionel Neyton, MD

## Introduction

The sequelae of proximal humerus fractures (malunion and nonunion) require challenging surgical reconstruction.[1-3] A reliable functional result frequently is difficult to achieve because of the extent of bone loss, the resulting deformity, and the complexity of the surgical technique.[3-8] It is crucial that the patient understands the prognosis before a surgical treatment decision is reached. Patients treated for sequelae of proximal humerus fractures usually are younger and more active than patients treated for osteoarthritis.[3,6,8,9]

Until recently, decision making as to the surgical treatment of proximal humerus fracture sequelae was hampered by the lack of an accurate classification system. The patient populations in the published studies were small, and the lesions were heterogeneous.[3,5,6,8-16] A new surgical classification system, based on two multicenter studies of the results of shoulder arthroplasty for proximal humerus fracture sequelae, has improved the ability to predict surgical results.[17,18] The studied arthroplasties used either an unconstrained anatomic prosthesis or a constrained reverse prosthesis.[19,20]

## Physiopathology and Surgical Classification

Isolated tuberosity nonunions and malunions are relatively simple to treat. Tuberosity malunions are fixed with arthroscopic or open reduction and internal fixation using sutures or screws. Isolated fractures of the lesser tuberosity are rare and usually are associated with posterior dislocation. Greater tuberosity fractures are more common and frequently are associated with nonunion or malunion. The most common deformity is residual posterior displacement as a result of rotator cuff forces.

Malunions and nonunions involving the humeral head articular surface as well as the tuberosities are classified into two groups that differ in natural history,

prognosis, and functional outcome[17,18] (Figure 1). The relationship between the mechanism of the initial fracture and its sequela is summarized in Table 1.

In the first group (sequelae types I and II), sequelae are secondary to an impacted intracapsular fracture. A type I sequela results from a fracture with minimal displacement, such as a valgus-impacted fracture or a fracture with mild varus displacement of the proximal fragment. A type II sequela results from an anterior or posterior dislocation or fracture-dislocation. Type I and type II sequelae have tuberosity-diaphysis continuity and mild to moderate deformity of the proximal humerus.

In the second group (sequelae types III and IV), the sequelae are secondary to a disimpacted, displaced extracapsular fracture. A type III malunion or nonunion results from a displaced surgical neck fracture, with no displacement of the greater tuberosity in relation to the humeral head. In a type IV sequela, a severe malunion of the tuberosity leads to a severe deformity of the proximal humerus.

Clinical classification of complex proximal humerus fracture sequelae is straightforward.[17-19] True AP and axillary radiographs or CT studies are used to decide whether each of the following is present: mild, acceptable deformity of the proximal humerus anatomy; anterior or posterior dislocation of the head fragment; isolated nonunion or malunion of the surgical neck; or severe, unacceptable deformity of the proximal humerus anatomy.

The key factors in determining the treatment of complex proximal humerus fracture sequelae can be summarized as distortion of the proximal humeral anatomy, tuberosity-diaphysis continuity, and the need for a greater tuberosity osteotomy (Figure 2). If the anatomic distortion is moderate and tuberosity-diaphysis continuity is present, as in a type I or II sequela, an unconstrained arthroplasty can be performed without a greater tuberosity osteotomy, and a good functional result can be expected. The mildly distorted anatomy of the proximal humerus should be accepted, and the prosthesis and technique should be modified to accommodate the distorted anatomy.

---

*Pascal Boileau, MD or the department with which he is affiliated has received royalties from Tornier, Inc.

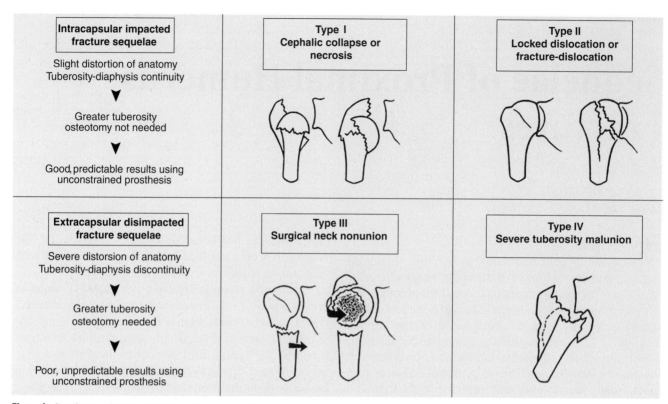

**Figure 1** Classification of proximal humerus fracture sequelae. *(Adapted with permission from Boileau P, Chuinard C, Le Huec JC, Walch G, Trojani C: Proximal humerus fracture sequelae: Impact of a new radiographic classification on arthroplasty. Clin Orthop Relat Res 2006;442:121-130.)*

**Table 1 | Relationship of Initial Fracture, Mechanism of Injury, and Sequelae**

| Initial Fracture | Mechanism of Injury | Fracture Characteristics | | Fracture Sequelae | |
|---|---|---|---|---|---|
| | | **Humeral Head** | **Greater Tuberosity** | | |
| Intracapsular Impacted | Medial-lateral compression | Valgus or varus impaction | Connected to the diaphysis | Mild, acceptable deformation of proximal humerus anatomy Diaphysis and epiphysis continuity | Type I: Cephalic collapse or necrosis |
| | Anterior-posterior compression | Impaction, posterior or anterior dislocation | | | Type II: Locked anterior or posterior dislocation or fracture-dislocation |
| Extracapsular Disimpacted | Rotation, translation | Disimpaction, rotation | Disconnected from the diaphysis | Major, unacceptable deformation of proximal humerus anatomy Diaphysis and epiphysis discontinuity | Type III: Surgical neck nonunion or malunion |
| | Compression, rotation, shearing | Disimpaction, dislocation (anterior-posterior or medial-lateral) | | | Type IV: Severe tuberosity malunion or nonunion |

A greater tuberosity osteotomy is consistently associated with a poor result during proximal humerus reconstruction. Therefore, with a malunion where a greater tuberosity osteotomy would be required to implant an unconstrained prosthesis (as in type III) or a tuberosity-diaphysis discontinuity with severe tuberosity malunion (as in type IV), alternatives should be considered. Type III should be treated with open reduction and internal fixation. Reverse arthroplasty should be considered for type IV.

This classification system does not take into account the possible presence of osteoporosis, a rotator cuff tear, or capsular retraction. Nonetheless, it is a coherent pathophysiologic categorization of the sequelae of proximal humerus fractures, allowing the surgical indications, technical issues, and prognosis to be clearly defined during presurgical planning and patient counseling.

The classification system also does not include isolated nonunion or malunion of the greater or lesser tuberosity, for which arthroplasty is not usually indicated. Osteosynthesis is the preferred treatment.

## Shoulder Arthroplasty for Proximal Humerus Fracture Sequelae

The findings of two large multicenter studies of unconstrained and reverse arthroplasty for proximal humerus fracture sequelae are summarized in Table 2.[19-21]

### Unconstrained Anatomic Arthroplasty

Between 1991 and 1998, an unconstrained prosthesis was used to treat 221 shoulders with proximal humerus nonunion or malunion.[19] The prosthesis was modular and adaptable to allow variable head size, head offset, and neck inclination angle. The mean patient age at the time of surgery was 61 years (range, 19 to 87 years).

Sixty patients (27%) had an earlier surgical attempt to reduce and fix the acute fracture.

Standard presurgical and postsurgical radiographs were available for 203 patients (92%). The presurgical radiographs were used to identify 137 sequelae of an impacted fracture with humeral head collapse or necrosis (type I), 25 locked dislocations or fracture-dislocations (type II), 22 sequelae of a displaced fracture with nonunion of the surgical neck (type III), and 19 sequelae of a displaced fracture with severe

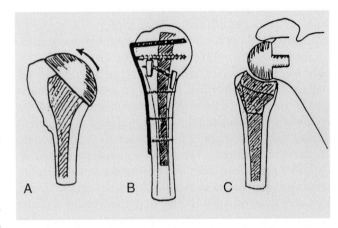

**Figure 2**  Surgical treatment of fracture sequelae, by type. **A,** Unconstrained prosthesis, used for type I and II sequelae. **B,** Open reduction and internal fixation with peg bone graft, used for type III sequelae. **C,** Reverse prosthesis, used for type IV sequelae. *(Adapted with permission from Boileau P, Chuinard C, Le Huec JC, Walch G, Trojani C: Proximal humerus fracture sequelae: Impact of a new radiographic classification on arthroplasty. Clin Orthop Relat Res 2006;442:121-130.)*

| Table 2 \| Functional Results of Reverse and Unconstrained Shoulder Arthroplasty for Proximal Humerus Fracture Sequelae (N = 243)[19,20] | | | | | |
|---|---|---|---|---|---|
| **Arthroscopic Procedure, by Sequela Type** | **Patients (n)** | **Constant Score (%)** | **Adjusted Constant Score (%)** | **Active Elevation** | **External Rotation*** |
| **Type I** | | | | | |
| Reverse | 8 | 60 | 88 | 117° | 18° |
| Unconstrained | 137 | 61 | 81 | 125° | 32° |
| **Type II** | | | | | |
| Reverse | 5 | 57 | 84 | 118° | 16° |
| Unconstrained | 25 | 61 | 78 | 117° | 28° |
| **Type III** | | | | | |
| Reverse | 7 | 41 | 58 | 86° | 1° |
| Unconstrained | 22 | 36 | NA | 63° | 28° |
| **Type IV** | | | | | |
| Reverse | 20 | 55 | 75.5 | 127° | -1° |
| Unconstrained | 19 | 42 | 55 | 81° | 12° |
| **Total** | | | | | |
| Reverse | 40 | 53 | 75 | 114° | 4° |
| Unconstrained | 203 | 57 | NA | 112° | 30° |

*\* Internal rotation after reverse arthroplasty was at the sacrum level in all sequela types. Internal rotation data for unconstrained arthroplasty are not available.*

tuberosity malunion or nonunion (type IV). Of the 221 procedures, 97 were total shoulder arthroplasties (44%), and the remaining 124 were hemiarthroplasties. Osteotomy with complete detachment of the greater tuberosity was performed in all patients with nonunion of the surgical neck (type III) because the prosthesis implantation required the tuberosities to be separated. Osteotomy of the greater tuberosity was performed in all patients with severe tuberosity malunion (type IV) because of the unacceptable anatomic distortion.

The results were evaluated at a mean 42-month follow-up (range, 24 to 96 months). Fifty-nine complications (27%) occurred, and revision surgery was required in 27 shoulders (12%). This study confirmed that unconstrained shoulder arthroplasty has predictably good results for treatment of type I and type II fracture sequelae, if it is performed without an osteotomy of the greater tuberosity. The slightly distorted anatomy of the proximal humerus should be accepted, and the prosthesis and technique should be modified to accommodate the distorted anatomy. The use of an adaptable prosthesis with adjustable offsets and inclination can be helpful. Treatment of type III or type IV fracture sequelae using a greater tuberosity osteotomy had poor results, and the conclusion was that a different treatment must be used for these patients.

### Constrained Reverse Arthroplasty

A constrained reverse arthroplasty was used between 1992 and 2002 to treat 40 patients.[20] The average patient age at the time of surgery was 72.9 years (range, 57 to 86 years). Twenty-four patients (60%) had earlier surgical treatment of the initial fracture. Eight patients had cephalic collapse and necrosis (type I), 5 had a chronic locked dislocation (type II), 7 had a surgical neck nonunion (type III), and 20 had a severe malunion (type IV). Of the 40 patients, 10 (25%) had complications, and 9 (22%) required revision surgery. The complications included infection in four patients (requiring resection arthroplasty in two), instability in two patients, glenoid fracture in one patient (requiring conversion to hemiarthroplasty), stiffness in one patient (requiring arthroscopic arthrolysis), axillary nerve palsy in one patient, and a fracture below the stem in one patient (requiring open reduction and internal fixation). At a mean 38-month follow-up (range, 24 to 95 months), reverse arthroplasty was found to have good results in patients with type I, II, or IV sequelae. The results were poor in patients with a surgical neck nonunion (type III); five of the seven patients had complications. Among all patients with type IV sequelae, those treated with a reverse prosthesis had a much better result than those treated with an unconstrained prosthesis. Patients with type I or type II sequelae had good pain relief and elevation after treatment with a reverse prosthesis, but those treated with an unconstrained prosthesis had better external rotation.

## Indications for Unconstrained or Reverse Arthroplasty

The findings of these studies of unconstrained and reverse shoulder arthroplasty in patients with proximal humerus fracture sequelae should be interpreted with caution. The patients treated with reverse arthroplasty were older, and fewer patients were treated with reverse than with unconstrained arthroplasty. The surgeon's choice should be guided by the fracture sequelae type, as well as the patient's age. Reverse arthroplasty should be used cautiously in patients younger than 70 years. In a younger patient with a type IV sequela, all other options should be considered, and reverse arthroplasty should be delayed until the patient reaches age 65 to 70 years.

The results of unconstrained and reverse arthroplasty are generally equivalent when used for type I fracture sequelae (cephalic collapse or necrosis with slight distortion of the anatomy), except that external rotation is better after unconstrained arthroplasty. In addition, unconstrained arthroplasty is associated with a much lower complication rate. It is preferred for patients with a type I fracture sequela to restore both active elevation and external rotation. Patients with a compromised or torn rotator cuff may benefit from reverse arthroplasty.

Either unconstrained or reverse arthroplasty can be used in a patient with a type II sequela (locked dislocation or fracture-dislocation). Unconstrained arthroplasty may be preferable for a chronic posterior dislocation. A chronic anterior dislocation, which is subject to persistent anterior instability, may be more stable with reverse arthroplasty.

Unconstrained and reverse arthroplasty both have poor functional results after treatment of type III sequelae (surgical neck nonunion).[4,15,17,18,22-24] Nonarthroplastic intramedullary bone peg graft and internal fixation are recommended, especially if the humeral head is intact. Humeral head replacement or tuberosity fixation with bone graft should be considered if the surgical neck nonunion is associated with tuberosity nonunion, severe humeral head cavitation, or osteoarthritis.

Reverse arthroplasty is the only satisfactory treatment of type IV fracture sequelae (severe distortion of proximal humeral anatomy with tuberosity malunion). Unconstrained arthroplasty requires a greater tuberosity osteotomy, and the poor healing of the greater tuberosity negatively affects the outcome.[4,9,25] Reverse arthroplasty leads to acceptable results, including active anterior elevation of 127° and a mean Constant score of 55 points, despite nonunion or malunion of the greater tuberosity.[20] Patients and surgeons should be aware that

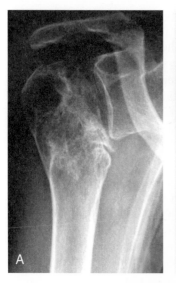

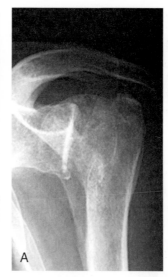

**Figure 3** Cephalic collapse with necrosis following a four-part impacted fracture (type I sequela). **A,** AP radiograph showing tuberosity-diaphysis continuity and slight distortion of the anatomy. **B,** AP radiograph showing reconstruction with an unconstrained prosthesis. Almost no bone has been cut, and the prosthesis stem has been inserted through the impacted necrotic head fragment. Active elevation and external and internal active rotation have been restored.

**Figure 4** A locked posterior fracture-dislocation (type II sequela) that was misdiagnosed for 7 months. **A,** AP radiograph showing tuberosity-diaphysis continuity and slight distortion of the anatomy. The humeral head is impacted on the posterior glenoid rim, and signs of necrosis appear. **B,** AP radiograph showing good results after reconstruction with an unconstrained prosthesis.

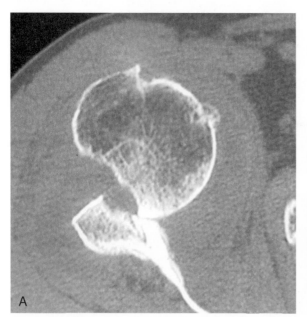

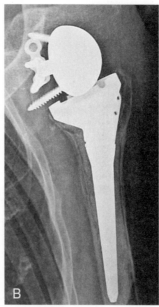

**Figure 5** A locked anterior fracture-dislocation (type II sequela). **A,** CT scan showing a chronic unreduced anterior dislocation with severe anterior glenoid bone loss. **B,** AP radiograph showing reverse arthroplasty with concomitant glenoid bone grafting.

the results of reverse arthroplasty for fracture sequelae are inferior to the results of reverse arthroplasty for rotator cuff tear arthropathy, and the rates of complications and revision surgery are higher.

## Technical Recommendations

In type I sequelae, a modular, adaptable unconstrained prosthesis is of particular benefit because it allows the prosthetic head to be placed in anatomic position relative to the greater tuberosity.[4-6] If sequelae have been present for more than 6 months, chondrolysis or severe

glenoid erosion probably has developed, and total shoulder arthroplasty is therefore preferable to hemiarthroplasty. Hemiarthroplasty may provide incomplete pain relief, which can limit or prevent motion and lead to a persistently stiff shoulder. The goal of the procedure is to position the uppermost point of the prosthetic head at the anatomic level, 5 mm above the greater tuberosity (Figure 3). It is possible to restore the anatomy with only slight distortion and without a tuberosity osteotomy; only a slight head cut is usually needed. A greater tuberosity osteotomy must be avoided at all

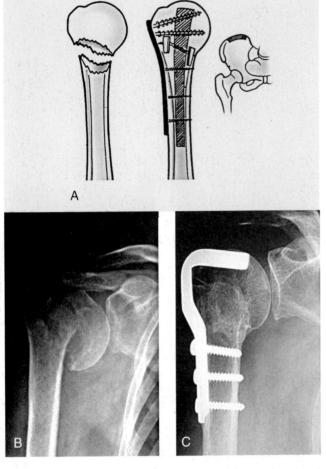

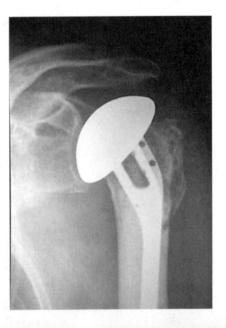

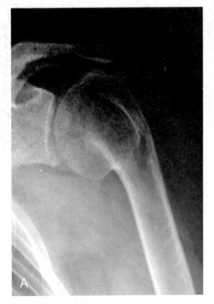

costs. In a patient with severe head collapse, no cut is needed, and the reamer is passed directly through the impacted head fragment. The prosthetic head should be anatomically sized, and the surgeon should not hesitate to use a small cemented stem in a valgus position. In a patient with severe distortion at the diaphysis level, a shortened stem or a resurfacing head can be used. To enter the joint, it is preferable to detach the lesser tuberosity with an osteotome rather than to cut the subscapularis tendon.

Surgical decision making for type II sequelae is influenced by the direction of the dislocation. For a posterior fracture-dislocation, unconstrained arthroplasty can

**Figure 6** A surgical neck nonunion (type III sequela). **A,** Diagram of the peg bone graft technique, in which a 7-cm intramedullary peg bone graft is taken from the iliac crest. **B,** AP radiograph showing the head fragment, which is small but alive. **C,** AP radiograph at 5-year follow-up, showing osteosynthesis with a blade plate and intramedullary peg bone graft. The functional result was excellent.

**Figure 7** A surgical neck nonunion (type III sequela). AP radiograph showing a low-profile prosthesis, which allows ample bone graft placement between the tuberosities and shaft.

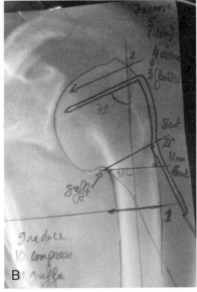

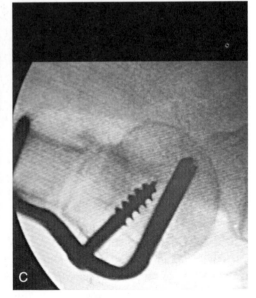

**Figure 8** An isolated surgical neck malunion (type III sequela). **A,** AP radiograph showing varus deformity. **B,** Presurgical template of the osteotomy at the level of the malunion. **C,** Perisurgical fluoroscopic study showing internal fixation with a 90° blade plate.

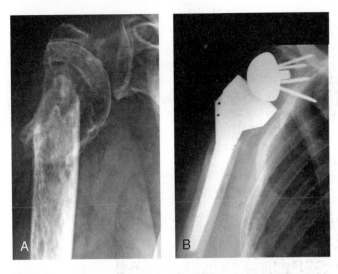

**Figure 9** Disimpacted fracture with severe tuberosity malunion (type IV sequela). **A,** AP radiograph showing severe anatomic distortion and severe tuberosity malunion and nonunion. **B,** AP radiograph showing proud positioning of the reverse prosthesis and proximal bone loss; neck extension was used to restore humeral length and avoid instability. The patient had an acceptable functional outcome.

lead to a good result (Figure 4). The prosthesis is usually oriented with minimal retroversion and sometimes is placed in neutral retroversion.[26,27] A posterior offset of the prosthetic head may be necessary to cover a posteriorly displaced greater tuberosity. After surgery, the patient must use a neutral or external rotation brace for a period of 4 to 6 weeks to prevent recurrent posterior instability.[22] For a locked anterior fracture-dislocation, reverse arthroplasty is the preferred treatment (Figure 5).

Type III sequelae should not be treated with arthroplasty because prosthesis implantation often prevents union of the tuberosities to the humeral shaft. Open reduction and internal fixation is usually preferred.[1,5,6,9,23,26] The head fragment is usually alive, although it may be small, and two surgical options can therefore be considered. If there is minimal humeral head cavitation or osteoarthritis, an intramedullary bone peg graft and internal fixation can be successful[28] (Figure 6). If severe humeral head cavitation or osteoarthritis is present, implantation of a low-profile prosthesis improves the likelihood of

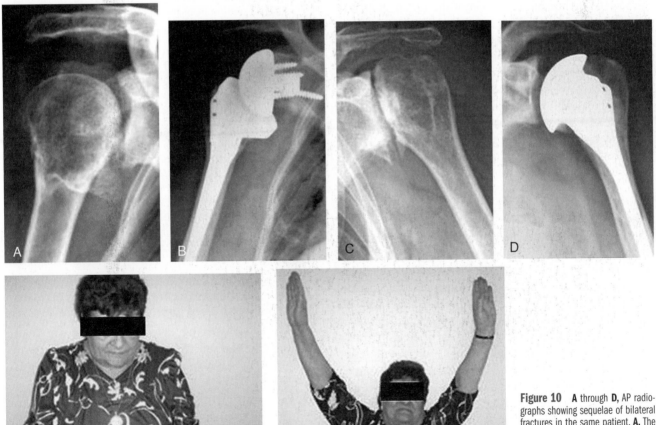

**Figure 10** **A** through **D,** AP radiographs showing sequelae of bilateral fractures in the same patient. **A,** The right shoulder, with a type IV sequela. **B,** The right shoulder after reverse arthroplasty. **C,** The left shoulder, with a type I sequela. **D,** The left shoulder after unconstrained arthroplasty. **E** and **F,** Although active elevation was restored in both shoulders, the patient had better active external rotation in the left shoulder.

healing by allowing copious bone graft to be placed between the epiphysis and diaphysis (Figure 7). Union of the tuberosities to the shaft should be the primary goal. If the surgical neck malunion is isolated, deformity correction with an osteotomy restores the anatomy and is recommended (Figure 8).

In type IV sequelae, reverse arthroplasty is preferable for pain relief and functional improvement (Figures 9 and 10). However, prosthetic instability, humeral fracture, or infection may occur. Infection is always a risk if the shoulder has had earlier surgical treatment. The presence of infection should be ruled out using presurgical laboratory test results and aspiration under fluoroscopy. In a patient with a possible low-grade infection, a two-stage procedure can be used. Bone loss in the proximal epiphysis may dictate a distal placement of the prosthesis; prosthetic instability can result. Scaled radiographs of both humeri can be used to determine the correct placement of the prosthesis and avoid humeral shortening and instability. An intrasurgical fracture is often related to poor exposure of the diaphysis because of the medial retraction of the tuberosities. The surgeon should not hesitate to excise the greater tuberosity to improve the exposure; the tuberosities should be reattached around the prosthesis, if possible. The use of a hybrid reverse prosthesis with a cemented stem and cementless epiphysis can maximize the likelihood of tuberosity healing to the shaft. Rupture or weakness of the external rotation muscles can result from longstanding distortion of the proximal anatomy; a latissimus dorsi and teres major transfer, in combination with reverse arthroplasty, can improve external rotation.

## Summary

Three key factors must be considered before treatment of proximal humerus fracture sequelae: the distortion of the proximal humeral anatomy, the tuberosity-diaphysis continuity, and the need for a greater tuberosity osteotomy. If distortion of the anatomy is moderate and tuberosity-diaphysis continuity is present, as in type I and type II sequelae, an unconstrained shoulder prosthesis can be implanted, and a good functional result can be expected. Shoulders with tuberosity-diaphysis discontinuity or severe anatomic distortion (type III and type IV sequelae) require a greater tuberosity osteotomy, which almost always has a poor functional outcome. For a surgical neck nonunion (type III), the recommended treatment is an intramedullary peg bone graft with osteosynthesis. If head cavitation is severe or osteoarthritis is present, a low-profile prosthesis can be used. For a severe tuberosity malunion or nonunion (type IV), reverse arthroplasty is the recommended treatment.

## Annotated References

1. Neer CS II, Watson KC, Stanton FJ: Recent experience in total shoulder replacement. *J Bone Joint Surg Am* 1982;64:319-337.

2. Neer CS: Nonunion of the surgical neck of the humerus. *Orthop Trans* 1983;3:389.

3. Neer CS: *Shoulder Reconstruction*. Philadelphia, PA, WB Saunders, 1990.

4. Norris TR, Turner JA, Bovill D: Nonunion of the upper humerus: An analysis of the etiology and treatment in 28 cases, in Post M, Morrey BF, Hawkins RJ (eds): *Surgery of the Shoulder*. St. Louis, MO, Mosby-Year Book, 1990, p 63.

5. Antuna SA, Sperling JW, Sanchez-Sotelo J, Cofield RH: Shoulder arthroplasty for proximal humeral malunions: Long term results. *J Shoulder Elbow Surg* 2002;11:122-129.
   After hemiarthroplasty or total shoulder arthroplasty in 50 shoulders with proximal humerus malunion, significant pain relief and improvement in range of motion were found at a mean 9-year follow-up. The result was poorer if surgical treatment of the initial fracture or greater tuberosity osteotomy was required during arthroplasty.

6. Beredjiklian PK, Ianotti JP, Norris TR, Williams GR: Operative treatment of malunion of a fracture of the proximal aspect of the humerus. *J Bone Joint Surg Am* 1998;80:1484-1497.

7. Dines DM, Klarren RF, Altcheck DW, Moeckel B: Posttraumatic changes of the proximal humerus: Malunion, nonunion, and osteonecrosis: Treatment with modular hemiarthroplasty or total shoulder arthroplasty. *J Shoulder Elbow Surg* 1993;2:11-21.

8. Watson KC: Indications and considerations of shoulder replacement in post-traumatic conditions, in Köbel R, Helbig B, Blauth W (eds): *Shoulder Replacement*. Berlin, Germany, Springer-Verlag, 1987, pp 129-133.

9. Keene JS, Huizenga RE, Engber WD, Rogers SC: Proximal humeral fractures: A correlation of residual deformity with long term function. *Orthopedics* 1983;6:173.

10. Lee CK, Hansen HR: Post-traumatic avascular necrosis of the humeral head in displaced proximal humeral fractures. *J Trauma* 1981;21:788-791.

11. Norris TR, Turner JA: Late prosthetic shoulder arthroplasty for displaced proximal humerus fractures. *J Shoulder Elbow Surg* 1995;4:271-280.

12. Pritchett JW: Prosthetic replacement for chronic unreduced dislocations of the shoulder. *Clin Orthop Relat Res* 1987;216:89-93.

13. Razemon JP, Baux S: Les séquelles des fractures de l'extrémité supérieure de l'humérus. *Rev Chir Orthop Reparatrice Appar Mot* 1969;55:387-496.

14. Lee CK, Hansen HR: Post-traumatic avascular necrosis of the humeral head in displaced proximal humeral fractures. *J Trauma* 1981;21:788-791.

15. Rowe CR, Zarins B: Chronic unreduced dislocations of the shoulder. *J Bone Joint Surg Am* 1982;64: 494-505.

16. Mansat P, Guity MR, Bellumore Y, Mansat M: Shoulder arthroplasty for late sequelae of proximal humeral fractures. *J Shoulder Elbow Surg* 2004;13:305-312.

    Malunion of the greater tuberosity can be tolerated if it does not compromise acceptable positioning of the humeral component. However, an osteotomy must be performed for malunion of the greater tuberosity with major displacement, and the results are unpredictable.

17. Boileau P, Walch G, Trojani C, Sinnerton R, Romeo AA, Veneau B: Sequelae of fractures of the proximal humerus: Surgical classification and limits of shoulder arthroplasty, in Walch G, Boileau P (eds): *Shoulder Arthroplasty*. New York, NY, Springer-Verlag, 1999, pp 349-358.

18. Boileau P, Trojani C, Walch G, Krishnan SG, Romeo A, Sinnerton R: Shoulder arthroplasty for the treatment of the sequelae of fractures of the proximal humerus. *J Shoulder Elbow Surg* 2001;10:299-308.

    Fracture sequelae are classified based on an anatomic scheme. Predictably good results were obtained without greater tuberosity osteotomy in shoulders with slight malunion (types I and II). Less favorable, unpredictable results were obtained after severe malunion (types III and IV) requiring greater tuberosity osteotomy for prosthesis implantation.

19. Boileau P, Chuinard C, Le Huec JC, Walch G, Trojani C: Proximal humerus fracture sequelae: Impact of a new radiographic classification on arthroplasty. *Clin Orthop Relat Res* 2006;442:121-130.

    At a mean 42-month follow-up, the results of the largest reported study of arthroplasty for fracture sequelae (203 shoulders) validated the classification of fracture sequelae. Treatment of fracture sequelae according to the classification is recommended. Level of evidence: IV.

20. Neyton L, Garaud P, Boileau P: Results of reverse shoulder arthroplasty in proximal humerus fracture sequelae, in Walch G, Boileau P, Molé D, Favard L, Lévigne C, Sirveaux F (eds): *Reverse Shoulder Arthroplasty*. Montpellier, France, Sauramps Medical, 2006.

21. Constant CR, Murley AH: Clinical method of functional assessment of the shoulder. *Clin Orthop Relat Res* 1987;214:160-164.

22. Antuna SA, Sperling JW, Sanchez-Sotelo J, Cofield RH: Shoulder arthroplasty for proximal humeral nonunions. *J Shoulder Elbow Surg* 2002;11: 114-121.

    Patients who have functional impairment resulting from nonunion of the humeral surgical neck after unsuccessful internal fixation, severe osteoporosis, cavitation of the humeral head, or secondary osteoarthritis may benefit from arthroplasty. Although function is not completely restored, pain relief and subjective satisfaction can be achieved.

23. Duralde XA, Flatow EL, Pollock RG, Nicholson GP, Self EB, Bigliani LU: Operative treatment of nonunions of the surgical neck of the humerus. *J Shoulder Elbow Surg* 1996;5:169-180.

24. Healy WL, Jupiter JB, Kristiansen TK, White RR: Nonunion of the proximal humerus, in Post M, Morrey BF, Hawkins RJ (eds): *Surgery of the Shoulder*. St. Louis, MO, Mosby-Year Book, 1990, p 59.

25. Jakob RP, Miniani A, Anson PS: Four part valgus impacted fractures of the proximal humerus. *J Bone Joint Surg Br* 1991;73:295-298.

26. Boileau P, Walch G: The three-dimensional geometry of the proximal humerus: Implications for surgical technique and prosthetic design. *J Bone Joint Surg Br* 1997;79:857-865.

27. Flatow EL, Neer CS II: Chronic anterior dislocation of the shoulder. *J Shoulder Elbow Surg* 1993;2:2-10.

28. Scheck M: Surgical treatment of nonunions of the surgical neck of the humerus. *Clin Orthop Relat Res* 1982;167:255-259.

# Chapter 40

# Clavicular Fractures

Jan Nowak, MD, PhD

## Introduction

Fractures of the clavicle account for approximately 3% of all fractures and 44% of fractures of the shoulder girdle.[1] The treatment of clavicular fractures varies widely and traditionally has been based on experience and local practice, rather than science. The indications for surgery have been unclear, and the scientific evidence has been insufficient for formulating evidence-based treatment protocols. There were no large, long-term studies on which to determine the fracture types or other risk factors associated with sequelae or nonunion. Recent studies have provided data that help to answer many clinical questions. Surgical indications and techniques have been studied, and the indications for acute-phase and delayed procedures to treat malunion or nonunion have been clarified. Optimal radiographic techniques have been determined. Recent studies with a high level of evidence have yielded results that can be applied in clinical practice.

## Anatomy and Kinematics

### Ligament Attachments

The clavicle is not present in animals that use their forelimbs for standing. In humans, the clavicle provides bony protection for the subclavicular vessels and the brachial plexus. The clavicle is S shaped, rotating upward and translating posteriorly during elevation of the arm to provide clearance and prevent compression of the underlying neurovascular structures.

The clavicle provides a bony framework for muscle origins and insertions. Many of the muscles that originate and insert on the clavicle are critical for the biomechanical functioning of the scapula and active movement of the arm. The clavicle transmits the supporting forces of the trapezius muscle to the scapula through the coracoclavicular ligaments.

On the lateral end of the clavicle, the coracoclavicular ligaments suspend the upper extremity and the scapula from the clavicle. The coracoclavicular ligaments function as a single ligament but consist of two parts. The cone-shaped conoid ligament runs in a posterome-

dial direction from the medial base of the coracoid process to the conoid tubercle of the clavicle. The trapezoid-shaped trapezoid ligament runs in an anterolateral direction from the base of the coracoid process to the trapezoid line on the undersurface of the acromial part of the clavicle. These ligaments vary widely among individuals. The conoid ligament is located approximately 24 mm from the distal clavicle, and the trapezoid ligament is located approximately 11 mm from the distal clavicle. Resection of more than 7 mm of the distal clavicle in men and 5 mm in women may violate the superior acromioclavicular ligament.[2]

On the medial end of the clavicle, the costoclavicular ligament is attached to the first costal cartilage and runs to the impression on the undersurface of the sternal part of the clavicle. A safe resection length from the inferior articular surface of the medial end of the clavicle to the most medial insertion of the costoclavicular ligament is 10 mm.[3]

### Bony Anatomy

The clavicle is shaped like an S that is concave on the anterolateral aspect and convex on the anteromedial aspect. When a fracture occurs, the clavicle is shortened, and the lateral fragment becomes angulated inferiorly and rotated medially. Measurement of cortical thickness in 196 cadaver specimens revealed that the medial ventral cortex and the dorsal acromial cortex are the thinnest regions of the clavicle. The diameter of the medullary canal is approximately 7 mm at its narrowest part, and therefore reaming is not necessary before a 3.5-mm titanium nail is inserted. The primary difficulties in nail placement result from the S curvature of the clavicle.[4]

## Imaging

Two radiographic projections, a 0° AP view and a 35° to 45° cephalic tilt view, are adequate for a thorough evaluation of almost any type of clavicular fracture, including a transverse fracture and a fracture with complete displacement and shortening.[5-7] A fracture of the medial part of the clavicle is the only type for which CT is

| Table 1 | Risk Factors for Sequelae or Nonunion After Clavicular Fracture | |
|---|---|---|
| **Factor** | **Increased Risk** | |
| | **Sequelae** | **Nonunion of Middle Part of Clavicle** |
| Fracture displacement with no bony contact | X | X |
| Fracture comminution | X | X |
| Fracture comminution with transversally placed fragments | X | |
| Shortening at fracture site | X | |
| Advanced age | X | X |
| Female gender | | X |

required for full analysis. Three-dimensional CT reconstruction can be helpful in evaluating a medial clavicular fracture or dislocation.

## Treatment Decision Making

Nonsurgical treatment of clavicular fractures has been preferred, regardless of fracture type or patient characteristics. However, recent studies found that the long-term results of nonsurgical treatment are not as favorable as previously believed.[8] Prospective, matched, randomized controlled comparisons of primary surgical treatment and nonsurgical treatment have identified patients at risk for sequelae including cosmetic defects, pain, weakness, malunion, and nonunion. This information helps guide surgical decision making. Table 1 outlines the risk factors for sequelae and nonunion of the clavicle midshaft. Shortened, displaced fractures are most likely to have adverse sequelae at short-term and long-term follow up.[5-7] The factors affecting the likelihood of malunion or nonunion include fracture type, location, comminution, displacement, gender, and age. The ability to identify the factors associated with unsatisfactory outcomes allows the surgeon to determine the optimal treatment for the patient.

### Risk Factors for Sequelae

More than 200 patients were prospectively evaluated 6 months and 10 years after fracture. At 10-year follow-up, some type of sequela was found in 46%: 29% had pain during activity, 27% had a cosmetic defect, and 9% had pain at rest. In addition, 7% had a nonunion.[6,7,9] A transverse, midshaft displaced fracture without any bony contact was at the greatest radiographic risk for sequelae; the sequelae included pain at rest, pain during activity, and cosmetic defects. In most patients at 10-year follow-up, the estimated odds ratios for each of these sequelae was between 3 and 4, indicating a relatively high risk.

Cosmetic defect was the only outcome significantly associated with fracture location; the risk of a poor cosmetic result was increased if the fracture was located in the middle third of the shaft. Fractures of the lateral third were not associated with an increased risk of sequelae. A comminuted fracture was significantly associated with a poor cosmetic result, regardless of gender. Gender was found to affect the risk only for nonunion.[7,9]

Bayonet apposition, defined as overlapping or shortening at the fracture site, significantly predicted cosmetic defects at 10-year follow-up. The estimated odds ratio was almost 4.

The difference in length between the injured and uninjured clavicles cannot be used to predict the likelihood of sequelae because intraindividual differences between the clavicles exist regardless of whether a clavicular injury is present.

### Risk Factors for Nonunion

The rate of nonunion of clavicular fractures after 6 months is only 5% to 7%.[9,10] In a prospective study of 868 patients with a radiographically confirmed fracture of the clavicle, a 6% incidence of nonunion was found.[10] Univariate analysis found significant association between the risk of nonunion after a diaphyseal fracture and incrementally advancing age, female gender, complete displacement of the fracture with no bony contact, and fracture comminution. Multivariate analysis found that each of these factors was independently predictive of nonunion. Fracture angulation, translation, or shortening was not significantly predictive of nonunion.

Surgical treatment is not necessary for every clavicular nonunion. The functional demands of the patient must be considered. Although older patients are at a higher risk of nonunion, they often have relatively low functional demands.[10] The risks related to anesthesia must also be evaluated.

## Surgical Treatment

### Lateral Clavicular Fracture

Clavicular hook-plate fixation provides stable fixation of an acute lateral fracture and allows early rehabilitation. A prospective study of 31 patients found solid healing and good functional results after clavicular hook-plate fixation.[11] The plates must be removed after union to prevent the hook from causing acromial osteolysis. A comparison of clavicular hook-plate and Kirschner wire fixation found an unacceptable rate of complications after Kirschner wires were used.[12] In a prospective study of 32 patients, placement of a transacromial Knowles pin for fixation of unstable Neer type II fractures also led to solid healing.[13]

## Middle Clavicular Fracture

A number of different methods are available for intramedullary fixation of an acute middle clavicular fracture. Twelve athletes were treated using a flexible titanium nail inserted from the sternal end of the clavicle. Closed reduction was used in half of the 12 fractures; one nonunion resulted, and no patients developed a postsurgical infection. The nail was removed after 1 year. The 12 patients could be mobilized early, although they could not quickly return to high physical demand activities.[14] Another prospective study of the same intermedullary fixation technique for a displaced midshaft clavicle fracture found similarly good results, with minor complications at an average 1-year follow-up.[15]

Elastic stable intramedullary nailing was compared with figure-of-8 bandaging in a prospective study of approximately 60 patients with matched fracture types. The surgically treated patients had significantly better results in all tested variables.[16]

Plate fixation of midshaft clavicle fractures is widely used. The plate is usually placed superiorly. However, infraclavicular placement was considered safe as used in a study of 89 patients.[17] A rigid plate was used to treat 39 high-demand semiprofessional athletes with a displaced fracture. Radiographic union was found in 90% (35 patients) after 3 months. However, 18% (7 patients) developed a postsurgical wound infection. Refracture and nonunion each occurred in 5% (2 patients). The high rate of complications was attributed to an early return to high-demand activities.[18] Acute fractures appear to heal with fewer complications when elastic titanium nails are used, compared with plate fixation.

Plate fixation and nonsurgical treatment were compared in a multicenter prospective, randomized study.[8] At 1-year follow-up of 132 patients, seven nonunions and nine malunions had occurred among the 67 surgically treated patients; there were two nonunions and no malunions in the 65 nonsurgically treated patients. The surgically treated patients had significantly improved scores on the Disabilities of the Arm, Shoulder and Hand Questionnaire and the Constant Shoulder Score. In the nonsurgically treated patients, there was a direct relationship between greater displacement at the fracture site and lower scores on the Disabilities of the Arm, Shoulder and Hand Questionnaire. If the fracture has any of the characteristics listed in Table 1, it should be treated surgically.

## Malunion

Paresthesia and pain triggered by using the arm above shoulder level have been described in patients with a hypertrophic malunion. The symptoms are explained by a mechanical conflict between the clavicle and the underlying first rib, if the fracture has healed with excessive callus formation. Similar symptoms appear after a displaced fracture with shortening or a transverse fracture, with excessive callus formation. The symptoms may develop months after the accident, and neurophysiologic findings may be negative. These factors are important from legal and insurance, as well as medical, standpoints.

Shortening with anterior rotation of the distal fragment, inferior translation of the distal fragment, and protraction of the shoulder with pseudowinging of the scapula can occur after malunion of a clavicular fracture, resulting in a characteristic deformity with pain and impaired function, regardless of excessive callus formation. In a prospective study, eight patients were initially treated nonsurgically. The symptoms disappeared after the callus was removed; internal fixation was not performed, and shortening was not addressed.[19] In another study, 15 patients with malunion of a displaced fracture had chronic pain, neurologic symptoms, and cosmetic and functional dissatisfaction.[20] The symptoms were reported a mean 3 years after injury (range, 1 to 15 years). The patients were treated with corrective osteotomy and plate fixation; no intercalary bone graft was used. Patient satisfaction was good, and half of the neurologic symptoms were eliminated. One patient experienced nonunion. It can be concluded that initial surgical stabilization would have been preferable for the patients in these two studies, whose fractures were associated with the risk factors listed in Table 1. Although the results of late surgery were acceptable, these patients endured symptoms that could have been prevented by initial surgical treatment.

## Nonunion

Surgeons should attempt to identify all acute fractures that may lead to nonunion and should treat these fractures surgically. A hypertrophic nonunion usually heals as soon as it is stabilized. Good results have been reported regardless of whether an intramedullary nail, cannulated screw, or plate was used.

Surgical treatment of an atrophic nonunion is challenging, and very few recent, prospective studies are available to guide surgeons in determining the best treatment method. Some studies have retrospectively reviewed both atrophic and hypertrophic nonunions, fixed with or without bone grafting. With the development of the locking compression plate, postsurgical stability and healing of atrophic nonunions have improved significantly.

External and plate fixation of atrophic nonunions were compared in a prospective study of 24 fractures. Patients in both groups received autogenous bone graft. Those who were treated with plate fixation had more rapid, reliable healing. Patients found the external frame to be cumbersome.[21]

## Author Recommendations

Two guidelines derived from experience are useful in considering acute treatment of a transverse clavicular fracture that is displaced without bony contact.

The 7-day, 70-year rule refers to the initial period of approximately 5 to 7 days during which a fracture stabilizes; fracture shortening and displacement are less severe after 1 week than immediately after the fracture. The patient's upper body posture at that time can be said to predict his or her appearance at approximately age 70 years. Immediately after the fracture, a 20° inferior- or superior-view radiograph frequently is taken. A 0° AP and a 45° inferior radiograph can be taken 1 week after the fracture, and the patient's first appointment with the surgeon can take place at that time.

Multidirectional instability of the shoulder is often associated with joint laxity in the glenohumeral joint, with chaos of the proprioceptive elements. Chaos of the proprioceptive elements also occurs in patients with multidirectional instability after a clavicular fracture, especially those who have the risk factors outlined in Table 1. Patients with multidirectional instability develop pain, and later lengthening of the clavicle does not achieve pain reduction. Stabilization of a fracture should always be considered if risk factors and joint laxity are present after 5 to 7 days.

## Summary

The treatment of clavicular fractures has been a subject of recent study, and a stronger evidence base is now available for many current treatment recommendations. Several risk factors for a less than satisfactory outcome have been identified, including complete displacement, comminution, shortening, relatively advanced age, and female gender. Surgery should be considered for a patient who has one or more of these factors.

## Annotated References

1. Postacchini F, Gumina S, De Santis P, Albo F: Epidemiology of clavicle fractures. *J Shoulder Elbow Surg* 2002;11:452-456.

   This is a report of an epidemiologic study of 535 isolated clavicle fractures treated in a large metropolitan hospital over an 11-year period.

2. Renfree KJ, Riley MK, Wheeler D, Hentz JG, Wright TW: Ligamentous anatomy of the distal clavicle. *J Shoulder Elbow Surg* 2003;12:355-359.

   Insertional variations in supporting ligaments of the acromioclavicular joint were studied in 41 cadaver specimens, especially with respect to gender.

3. Bisson LJ, Dauphin N, Marzo JM: A safe zone for resection of the medial end of the clavicle. *J Shoulder Elbow Surg* 2003;12:592-594.

   Dissection of 86 cadaver sternoclavicular joints determined the distance (safe resection length) from the inferior articular surface of the medial end of the clavicle to the most medial insertion of the costoclavicular ligament (1.2 ± 0.3 cm in men, 1.0 ± 0.2 cm in women).

4. Andermahr J, Jubel A, Elsner A, et al: Anatomy of the clavicle and the intramedullary nailing of midclavicular fractures. *Clin Anat* 2006;20:48-56.

   Anatomic variations in the clavicle of relevance to intramedullary fixation were analyzed in 196 cadaver specimens. The clavicle was found to have gender- and side-specific features.

5. Basamania C, Craig E, Rockwood C Jr: Fractures of the clavicle, in Rockwood C Jr, Matsen FA III, Wirth M, Lippitt S (eds): *The Shoulder*, ed 3. Philadelphia, PA, Saunders, 2004, pp 455-520.

   Clavicular fractures are thoroughly described.

6. Nowak J, Holgersson M, Larsson S: Sequelae from clavicular fractures are common: A prospective study of 222 patients. *Acta Orthop* 2005;76:496-502.

   In 222 patients with a clavicular fracture followed for 6 months, the risk of persistent symptoms after nonsurgical treatment was far higher than expected.

7. Nowak J, Holgersson M, Larsson S: Can we predict long-term sequelae after fractures of the clavicle based on initial findings? A prospective study with nine to ten years of follow-up. *J Shoulder Elbow Surg* 2004;13:479-486.

   Based on two radiographic projections (0° and 45°), the risk of sequelae was predicted for 208 patients 5 to 7 days after the initial fracture.

8. Canadian Orthopaedic Trauma Society: Nonoperative treatment compared with plate fixation of displaced midshaft clavicular fractures: A multicenter, randomized clinical trial. *J Bone Joint Surg Am* 2007; 89:1-10.

   This elegant study removes all doubt as to whether displaced fractures of the middle part of the clavicle should be treated surgically, especially if the fracture has transversely placed fragments. Level of evidence: I.

9. Nowak J, Mallmin H, Larsson S: The aetiology and epidemiology of clavicular fractures: A prospective study during a two-year period in Uppsala, Sweden. *Injury* 2000;31:353-358.

10. Robinson CM, Court-Brown CM, McQueen MM, Wakefield AE: Estimating the risk of nonunion following nonoperative treatment of a clavicular fracture. *J Bone Joint Surg Am* 2004;86-A:1359-1365.

    Based on initial radiographs, the risk factors for nonunion of the middle part of the clavicle were predicted for 581 patients.

11. Meda PV, Machani B, Sinopidis C, Braithwaite I, Brownson P, Frostick SP: Clavicular hook plate for

lateral end fractures: A prospective study. *Injury* 2006;37:277-283.

All 31 patients treated with a clavicular hook plate for lateral end fracture achieved clinical and radiographic union at a mean 12 weeks, with good function.

12. Flinkkila T, Ristiniemi J, Hyvonen P, Hamalainen M: Surgical treatment of unstable fractures of the distal clavicle: A comparative study of Kirschner wire and clavicular hook fixation. *Acta Orthop Scand* 2002;73: 50-53.

In a study of 22 patients treated using Kirschner wires and 17 treated using a clavicular hook-plate, shoulder symptoms were reduced and function adequately restored by both methods. Complications were unacceptably frequent with the Kirschner wires.

13. Fann CY, Chiu FY, Chuang TY, Chen CM, Chen TH: Transacromial Knowles pin in the treatment of Neer type 2 distal clavicle fractures: A prospective evaluation of 32 cases. *J Trauma* 2004;56:1102-1105.

Thirty-two patients with an unstable distal clavicle fracture were treated using a single transacromial Knowles pin without repair of the torn ligament. At a mean 80-month follow-up, all patients had excellent results with solid union.

14. Jubel A, Andemahr J, Bergmann H, Prokop A, Rehm KE: Elastic stable intramedullary nailing of midclavicular fractures in athletes. *Br J Sports Med* 2003;37:480-483.

In 12 high-performance athletes, intramedullary fixation of displaced midclavicular fracture was successful in terms of clinical outcome and rapid resumption of sports activities.

15. Kettler M, Schieker M, Braunstein V, Konig M, Mutschler W: Flexible intramedullary nailing for stabilization of displaced midshaft clavicle fractures: Technique and results in 87 patients. *Acta Orthop* 2007;78: 424-429.

A study of 87 patients at a 13-month follow-up found that flexible intramedullary nailing, a minimally invasive technique for stabilization of displaced midshaft clavicle fractures, has minor risks and complications.

16. Jubel A, Andermahr J, Prokop A, Lee JI, Schiffer G, Rehm KE: Die Behandlung der diaphysären Klavikelfraktur. Vergleich der Frühergebnisse nach Rucksackverband und elastisch stabiler intramedullärer Nagelung. [Treatment of midclavicular fractures in adults: Early results after rucksack bandage or elastic stable intramedullary nailing]. *Unfallchirurg* 2005;108:707-714.

At 6-month follow-up of 27 patients treated nonsurgically using a figure-of-8 bandage and 27 treated using minimally invasive intramedullary fixation with a titanium pin, the surgically treated patients had better functional, satisfaction, pain, and cosmetic results.

17. Coupe BD, Wimhurst JA, Indar R, Calder DA, Patel AD: A new approach for plate fixation of midshaft clavicular fractures. *Injury* 2005;36:1166-1171.

An intraclavicular surgical approach was used in 89 patients during a 9-year period and was found to be a safe approach to an otherwise hazardous procedure.

18. Verborgt O, Pittoors K, Van Glabbeek F, Declercq G, Nuyts R, Somville J: Plate fixation of middle-third fractures of the clavicle in the semi-professional athlete. *Acta Orthop Belg* 2005;71:17-21.

Rigid plate fixation of a middle-third clavicular fracture was found to provide good results in 29 semiprofessional athletes and may permit early return to sports activity, at the expense of a significant risk of complications.

19. Nowak J, Stalberg E, Larsson S: Good reduction of paresthesia and pain after excision of excessive callus formation in patients with malunited clavicular fractures. *Scand J Surg* 2002;91:369-373.

In eight patients with hypertrophic callus after a malunited clavicular fracture, excess callus and scar tissue were removed without stabilizing osteosynthesis. Paresthesia, numbness, pain, and headache were significantly reduced after surgery and had not recurred at an average 20-month follow-up.

20. McKee MD, Wild LM, Schemitsch EH: Midshaft malunions of the clavicle. *J Bone Joint Surg Am* 2003; 85:790-797.

In 15 patients with malunion after nonsurgical treatment of a displaced midshaft clavicular fracture, with orthopaedic, neurologic, and cosmetic complications, corrective ostotomy resulted in satisfaction and improved upper-extremity scores in most patients.

21. Nowak J, Rahme H, Holgersson M, Lindsjo U, Larsson S: A prospective comparison between external fixation and plates for treatment of midshaft nonunions of the clavicle. *Ann Chir Gynaecol* 2001;90: 280-285.

Eleven patients were treated with external fixation and 13 with internal fixation using a 3.5-mm reconstruction plate. All had autologous cancellous bone graft. At long-term follow-up, the reconstruction plate was found to be preferable because of faster and more reliable healing.

# Chapter 41

# Humeral Shaft Fractures

P.M. Rommens, MD, PhD

## Introduction

Humeral shaft fractures account for approximately 7% of all fractures in adults. They can result from direct trauma, such as from a motor vehicle crash, or indirect rotational trauma, which occurs in some types of sports injuries or falls. Humeral shaft fractures are most frequently found in younger men and older women. In patients younger than 40 years, especially men, humeral shaft fractures typically result from high-energy trauma. These patients are more likely to have a comminuted fracture, multiple associated injuries, or concomitant soft-tissue injury. In patients older than 60 years, isolated humeral shaft fractures typically occur as a result of low-energy trauma, such as a fall from a standing or sitting position. These simple fractures have little or no associated soft-tissue damage.

Traditionally, most humeral shaft fractures were treated nonsurgically. In recent years, the principles of treatment and indications for surgery have been strongly influenced by patients' increasing functional demands and improvements in implant design and techniques.

## Clinical Evaluation

A patient with a humeral shaft fracture has acute, severe pain in the upper extremity. Axial deviation and rotational deformity are present, and the upper arm may be shortened. Swelling and hematoma are visible at the fracture site and may extend to the entire upper arm. Fewer than 10% of patients have an open fracture or severe soft-tissue injury. An open fracture rarely results from low-energy trauma, and the soft-tissue injury generally is minimal or moderate.

Because neurovascular damage is a common complication of a humeral shaft fracture, a thorough neurovascular examination should be performed. Radial nerve palsy occurs in more than 10% of patients, especially if the fracture affects the middle or lower third of the humeral shaft. Isolated median or ulnar nerve palsy is uncommon and is usually associated with a brachial plexus lesion. Injury of the brachial artery is rare and always occurs as a result of high-energy or penetrating trauma.

Absence of radial or ulnar pulses or distal ischemia strongly suggests a brachial artery injury, which requires immediate repair in conjunction with stabilization of the fracture.

Conventional radiographs in two planes perpendicular to each other are used to diagnose humeral shaft fractures. The x-ray beam, not the arm, should be rotated because rotation of the arm will occur at the fracture site rather than at the shoulder. Radiographs of the shoulder and elbow joints also should be taken. The radiographs must be examined carefully to identify or exclude the presence of secondary fractures or fissures extending into the adjacent joints. The use of other imaging techniques is unnecessary. CT and MRI are not useful immediately after injury, although they can be helpful in a patient who has delayed healing, pseudarthrosis, or deep infection.

Before treatment is begun, the radiographs should be studied in conjunction with a thorough examination of the soft tissues and neurovascular structures surrounding the fracture.

## Classification

Three categories of humeral shaft fractures are distinguished in the AO-ASIF comprehensive system.[1] In type A, the fracture has a simple configuration; after reduction, there is complete contact between the main fracture fragments. Type A1 is a spiral fracture, type A2 is an oblique fracture with obliquity of less than 45°, and type A3 is a transverse fracture. A third fracture fragment is always present in a type B lesion; after reduction, the contact between the main fracture fragments is incomplete. Type B1 is a spiral fracture with a third spiral fragment, type B2 is an oblique or transverse fracture with an additional wedge fragment, and type B3 is an oblique or transverse fracture with several additional wedge fragments. A type C fracture is the most complex; after reduction, there is no contact between the main fracture fragments. Type C1 is a double spiral fracture, type C2 is a segmental fracture, and type C3 is a multifragmented or comminuted fracture.

A closed soft-tissue injury is classified using the Tscherne system, and an open soft-tissue injury is classified using the Gustilo system.[2,3]

## Treatment Decision Making

Fractures of the humeral shaft are painful and unstable, and they hinder upper extremity function. Many fractures require acute stabilization, usually by placing the upper extremity in an adduction bandage attached to the thorax. Other treatment modalities may be considered depending on the fracture configuration, the patient's functional demands, and the patient's willingness to tolerate the treatment. Nonsurgical treatment, closed reduction and external fixation, closed reduction and internal fixation, or open reduction and internal fixation may be appropriate. Each treatment has advantages and disadvantages.

## Nonsurgical Treatment

The humerus is circumferentially covered by muscles and has an excellent blood supply. It therefore has an excellent ability to heal. Because the arm is not a weight-bearing extremity, perfect alignment of the fracture fragments is not essential. Axial and rotational deviations, as well as shortening of as much as 2 cm, are cosmetically acceptable and can be functionally compensated for by the shoulder and elbow joints. The distinguished surgeon Lorenz Böhler believed that humeral shaft fractures should be treated nonsurgically,[4] despite the advantages of surgical treatment.

The upper arm can be adequately stabilized using one of several different methods. During the acute phase, it is sufficient to use either a circumferential bandage around the fractured arm and the thorax or a Gilchrist bandage with the upper arm in adduction and internal rotation. The upper arm also can be aligned using a plaster of Paris splint, which is attached dorsally from the axilla to the wrist. If the fracture is located between the rotator cuff and the pectoralis muscle, the humeral head is abducted and internally rotated. If the fracture is between the pectoralis and deltoid muscles, the proximal fragment is adducted and the distal fragment is laterally displaced. If the fracture line is distal from the deltoid muscle, the proximal fragment is abducted. A fracture proximal to the brachioradialis and the extensors has a distal fragment that is rotated laterally. After alignment and splinting, the entire arm is brought into adduction and internal rotation and then is immobilized using a collar and cuff. The hanging arm cast, in which a weight is attached to the lower arm, is not recommended because it distracts the fracture site and hinders healing. A hanging arm cast should be considered only as a temporary measure to achieve an acceptable alignment of fracture fragments.

Within 1 to 2 weeks after the injury, the swelling and pain subside, and the splint or adduction bandage is replaced by a functional brace that is used until the fracture heals.[5] To prevent stiffness, passive and active-assisted movement of the shoulder and elbow joints is followed by active range-of-motion exercises. Rotation of the upper arm is not allowed until bridging callus is visible at the fracture site.

Nonsurgical treatment usually leads to successful healing. The rate of nonunion is less than 5%,[3] and the average time required for healing is less than 3 months. However, few data are available to describe shoulder and elbow function or muscle force at the conclusion of treatment.[6]

Nonsurgical treatment is valid for an acute humerus fracture, provided that uneventful healing can be expected. It is contraindicated if the fracture is at high risk of nonunion or other complications. In addition, the patient must be well informed and understand that successful nonsurgical treatment requires a long immobilization period and that axis deviation, shortening, temporary muscle atrophy, and stiffness of the adjacent joints may occur.

## Surgical Treatment

The absolute indications for surgery include an associated vascular injury, a severe open fracture, the presence of multiple traumatic injuries, and unacceptable alignment of the fracture fragments after closed reduction.[7] The relative indications for surgery include the presence of a transverse, short oblique, or spiral fracture; bilateral fractures; a fracture in a patient with an unstable thorax; extension of the fracture into the shoulder or elbow joint; a combined humerus-forearm fracture (a floating elbow); a fracture with primary radial nerve palsy, and a fracture in a patient who is obese or is uncooperative with nonsurgical treatment.

Each of these indications has an obvious rationale. Damage to the artery requires urgent surgical repair, and the fracture can be stabilized during surgery. An open fracture requires débridement, as well as soft-tissue débridement to avoid wound infection; stabilization of the fracture is necessary to provide a stable environment for wound healing. A patient with multiple injuries benefits from early stabilization of fractures of the long bones, which can improve the ability to move freely as soon as the patient's general condition allows. Fractures at the proximal or distal end of the humeral diaphysis may cause unacceptable shortening or axial deviation. Axial deviation that recurs after closed reduction should be corrected surgically. In a transverse or short oblique fracture, the area of bone contact may be too small and the fracture instability too great for uneventful healing. In a spiral fracture, direct bone contact may be prevented by intercalating muscle bellies. In bilateral fractures, nonsurgical treatment precludes the use of either upper extremity in the activities of daily living. In a patient with an unstable thorax, an adduction bandage further hinders breathing. If the humeral shaft fracture is accompanied by a fracture of the humeral head or an intra-articular fracture of the distal humerus that requires surgical treatment, both fractures can be stabilized during one surgical procedure. If the patient has a floating elbow, both the humeral shaft fracture and the forearm must be stabilized. In an obese patient, nonsurgical stabilization using a cast or splint may be compromised by the presence of a very thick soft-tissue mantle. An uncooperative patient might dismantle the bandage. These and other difficulties can be avoided by early surgical fixation of the fracture.

The humeral shaft fracture may be associated with primary radial nerve palsy. No definitive treatment of this combination of injuries exists. Discussion continues as to whether surgical exploration and release of the nerve should be performed with stabilization of the fracture.

Each of the techniques for surgical fixation of humeral shaft fractures has advantages, disadvantages, and possible complications.[8]

### Plate Osteosynthesis

Open reduction and internal fixation using plates and screws has for decades been the preferred method for surgical stabilization of humeral shaft fractures.[9-11] This technique allows anatomic reduction of fracture fragments and rigid fixation, enabling early active postsurgical motion. Because the humeral shaft is round and small in cross-section, parallel drilling of a row of screws may cause a fissure or secondary fracture line to form through the plate drill holes. Loosening of the screws and plate, especially during rotational movement of the upper arm, may create additional fractures. A broad dynamic compression plate with screw holes in two rows should be used. Alternatively, the screw holes should be drilled in different directions. The screws should engage a minimum of six to eight cortices at each side of the fracture. The plate can be used as a buttress. Alternatively, fracture compression can be obtained by eccentric positioning of some screws in the plate. In a spiral or long oblique fracture or a fracture with a large wedge fragment, lag screws are used outside or inside the plate holes. The use of an internal plate fixator with angle-stable (locking) screws is recommended in a patient with osteoporosis.

The location of the fracture determines the surgical approach to the humeral shaft. The course of nerves and vessels adjacent to the humeral shaft must be precisely determined to avoid iatrogenic damage.

### Fractures of the Proximal Third

The deltopectoral approach is used for surgical fixation of a fracture of the proximal third of the humeral shaft.

The patient is positioned in the beach chair position or supine. The affected arm is positioned on a radiolucent side table so that the entire fracture area will be visible under x-ray image intensification. The incision begins below the coracoid process and runs in the deltopectoral groove distally and laterally. The deltoid muscle is retracted laterally, and the pectoralis, long head of the biceps, and coracobrachial muscles are retracted medially. Damage to the cephalic vein is prevented by protecting it laterally with the deltoid muscle. Other neurovascular structures are at less risk because of their distance from the surgical approach area. The distal attachment of the deltoid muscle can be elevated for better exposure of the fracture. The plate is carefully contoured and attached to the anterolateral surface of the humerus. After plate fixation and irrigation, a drain is placed deep into the wound. The position of the muscles is reapproximated using single stitches, and the subcutaneous tissue and the skin are closed separately. The drain is removed the second day after surgery. Active motion is allowed as soon as possible, usually after 1 or 2 days (Figure 1).

### Fractures of the Middle Third

For fixation of a fracture of the middle third of the humeral shaft, the patient is placed supine. The arm is positioned on a radiolucent side table so that the entire area of the fracture will be visible under image intensification. The deltopectoral approach used for fractures of the proximal third is extended distally along the lateral aspect of the biceps. Proximally, the humeral shaft is exposed along the deltopectoral interval. Distally, the anterolateral cortex of the humeral shaft is exposed by longitudinal splitting of the brachial muscle. Special attention must be paid to the course of the musculocutaneous and radial nerves. The musculocutaneous nerve runs ventral to the brachialis muscle. As the radial nerve leaves the posterior compartment of the arm, it perforates the lateral intermuscular septum and then enters the anterior compartment. Regardless of the approach used, the radial nerve is at particular risk during plate fixation of the humerus. After plate fixation and irrigation, a drain is placed, the position of the muscle is reapproximated using single stitches, and the subcutaneous tissue and the skin are closed separately. The drain is removed the second day after surgery. Active motion is allowed as soon as possible, usually after 1 or 2 days.

### Fractures of the Distal Third

For fixation of a fracture of the distal third of the humeral shaft, the patient is placed in a prone or lateral position. The affected arm is positioned in 90° of shoulder abduction on a radiolucent side table; the elbow is flexed at 90°, and the hand is directed toward the floor. The entire fracture area must be visible under image intensification. A strict dorsal skin incision, in line with

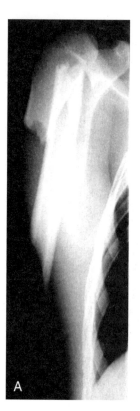
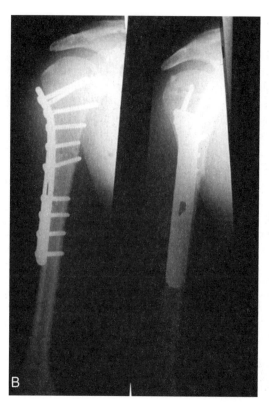
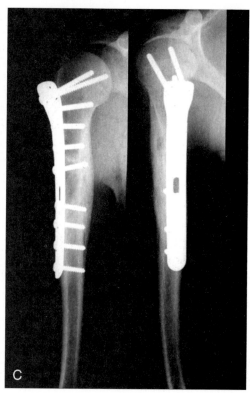

**Figure 1** **A,** AP radiograph showing a proximal transverse shaft fracture with significant shortening in a 15-year-old boy who was involved in a bicycle collision. **B,** Postsurgical AP and lateral radiographs showing anterolateral plating of the fracture. **C,** AP and lateral radiographs taken at 6-month follow-up. The patient had full shoulder and elbow function.

the humeral diaphysis, begins distally at the tip of the olecranon and extends as far proximal as needed. The deep approach is chosen based on the precise location of the fracture. If the fracture is located far proximal to the olecranon fossa, the dorsal cortex of the humerus is exposed through longitudinal splitting of the triceps muscle. In a more distal fracture, medial or lateral mobilization of the triceps muscle is recommended. In a fracture with a very distal extension, olecranon osteotomy can be considered.

The exposure and mobilization of the radial nerve is challenging. The nerve crosses the dorsal cortex of the humeral shaft at the transition between the middle and proximal thirds. It becomes more lateral as it travels distally along the humerus. Placement of a plate between the radial nerve and the bone surface is frequently required, and damage to the nerve from traction must be avoided during the fracture exposure, reduction maneuvers, and plate placement.

After plate insertion and irrigation, the triceps muscle is closed using single stitches. A drain is placed deep to the triceps muscle, and another drain is placed in the subcutaneous tissue. The subcutaneous tissue and skin are closed separately. The drains are removed on the second day after surgery. Active motion is allowed as soon as possible (Figure 2).

## Complications of Humeral Plating

Between 5% and 10% of patients have delayed healing and pseudarthrosis after a humeral plating procedure, primarily because surgical manipulation and periosteal stripping deprived fracture fragments of their blood supply. Distraction of fracture fragments or a bone defect in a comminuted fracture can lead to nonunion. Osteonecrosis after severe trauma is relatively infrequent. Screw loosening or plate breakage can lead to instability at the fracture site, with loss of fixation and pseudarthrosis. Severe osteoporosis or a weak bone-implant construct, which can occur if a short plate and a small number of screws were used, can place the fracture fixation at risk of failure. Revision plating is always required, usually in combination with cancellous bone grafting.[12] Infection can result from severe primary soft-tissue contamination after an open fracture or surgical contamination. Deep infection is rare because of the humeral shaft's excellent soft-tissue coverage.

Secondary radial nerve palsy is a specific complication of plate osteosynthesis when posterior plating of the shaft is used. If the plate extends proximally to the radial groove, the nerve must be exposed and mobilized to bring the plate onto the dorsal cortex. For anterolateral plating of the humerus, the nerve must be mobilized distally to avoid injury. Patients with neurapraxia have a good prognosis, although recovery of function

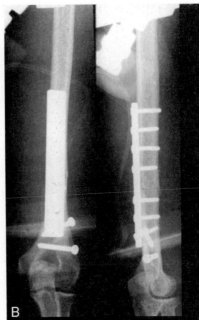
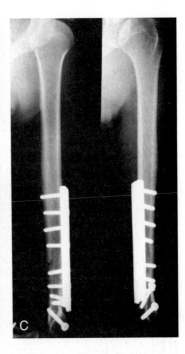

**Figure 2** **A,** Presurgical lateral radiograph of a left-arm floating elbow (distal humerus fracture and complete proximal lower arm fracture) in a 21-year-old man who was involved in an automobile crash. **B,** Postsurgical AP and lateral radiographs showing dorsal plate osteosynthesis using a broad dynamic compression plate (Synthes, West Chester, PA). Lag screws were added for stabilization of the intra-articular extension of the fracture. **C,** Oblique radiographs taken at 16-week follow-up. The patient had full shoulder and elbow function.

may take several months.[13] Damage to the ulnar or median nerve or the brachial artery is rare. After surgery, the neurovascular structures of the extremity must be examined to detect any surgical damage.

### Intramedullary Nailing

The use of intramedullary rods has become the standard treatment for femoral and tibial shaft fractures. Healing is usually uneventful, with a rapid functional recovery and a low rate of complications. Although intramedullary nailing of humeral shaft fractures has been used for more than 50 years, it has been widely accepted only during the past decade. The older intramedullary implants bear the name of their inventors (Rush pins and Ender, Hackethal, and Prévot nails). They are flexible, small in diameter, and noninterlocked. They are introduced into the canal in an antegrade or retrograde fashion through small entry portals in the metaphyseal region. If the entire medullary canal is occupied by hardware, the construct has adequate stability. The rods are not fixed to the bone. The resulting complications include proximal or distal migration, with perforation of the shoulder or elbow joint; instability caused by loosening; and shortening caused by telescoping of the fracture fragments.

Flexible nails are widely used for stabilization of humeral shaft fractures in children and adolescents. Modern intramedullary rods intended for use in adult humeral shaft fractures are more rigid and can be interlocked statically or dynamically. They can sometimes be used to obtain interfragmentary compression. Solid, cannulated, and hollow nails are available. The thicker nails are inserted after reaming, and the thinner nails can be introduced without reaming. The nails can be introduced in antegrade or retrograde fashion; each approach has slightly different indications as well as drawbacks.[14,15]

### Antegrade Nailing

Antegrade nailing is best used for a midshaft or distal fracture.[16,17] Precise reduction is more difficult and the likelihood of achieving stability is lower if antegrade nailing is used for a proximal fracture. The patient is placed in the beach chair position, with the upper extremity positioned on an arm support so that the broken humeral shaft and the shoulder joint will be visible on image intensification. The skin incision runs anteriorly from the lateral edge of the acromion and is only 2 cm long. The muscle fibers of the deltoid muscles are split, the subacromial bursa is opened, and the supraspinatus tendon is identified. The tendon is carefully split in line with its fibers and separated to expose the cartilage of the humeral head. The entry portal for the nail is situated medial to the attachment of the supraspinatus tendon in the lateral cartilage area of the humeral head. The nail is inserted with careful rotational movements until its distal end reaches the fracture line. The fracture is reduced under image intensification, and the distal fragment is engaged with the tip of the nail. The nail is further introduced until it reaches its final position. In a cannulated nail, the correct length can be read on the

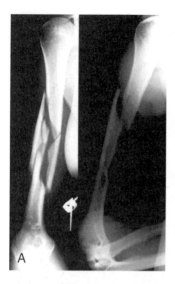
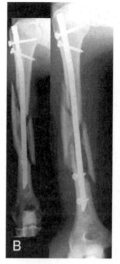
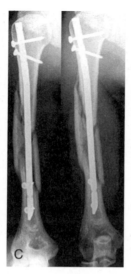
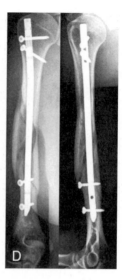
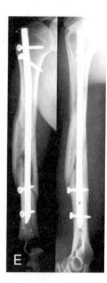

**Figure 3** **A,** Presurgical AP and lateral radiographs of a closed multifragmental fracture of the right humerus in a 27-year-old man who was involved in a motorcycle crash. **B,** Postsurgical AP and oblique radiographs showing antegrade nailing with double interlocking proximally and distally. **C,** AP and oblique radiographs taken at 4-week follow-up. **D,** AP and lateral radiographs taken at 16-week follow-up. **E,** AP and lateral radiographs taken at 1-year follow-up, before hardware removal. The patient had full shoulder and elbow function.

inserted guidewire. The length of a solid nail must be measured before surgery, using the contralateral arm or the reduced injured arm. At the insertion point, the nail must not protrude proximal to the articular surface of the humeral head. Double interlocking at each side of the fracture is recommended. Distraction at the fracture site must be avoided. With some types of nails, closure of the fracture gap or interfragmentary compression is achieved by using a compression device. The positioning of the nail and screws is controlled in two planes under image intensification. The supraspinatus tendon is closed with separate stitches. A drain is placed between the supraspinatus tendon and the deltoid muscle; the deltoid muscle, subcutaneous tissue, and skin are closed consecutively. The arm is placed in a collar-and-cuff bandage, and the drain is removed on the second day. Active motion of the shoulder and elbow is allowed as soon as possible. Because the nail-bone construct has the least stiffness in the rotational plane, rotational movements of the arm are forbidden until bridging callus can be seen on radiographs (Figure 3).

### Retrograde Nailing

Retrograde nailing is more demanding than antegrade nailing, but it has the advantage of being totally extra-articular.[14,18-21] Retrograde nailing is best used in a midshaft or proximal fracture. The patient is placed in the prone position, with the broken arm placed on a radiolucent side table and the lower arm hanging downward. The entire humeral shaft and the elbow and shoulder joints must be visible in two planes on image intensification. The dorsal midline skin incision begins at the tip of the olecranon and runs 10 cm proximally. The triceps tendon is split longitudinally, and the dorsal cortex above

the olecranon fossa is exposed. An entry portal measuring 20 mm by 10 mm is made in the center of the triangle between the medial and lateral supracondylar ridge and the roof of the olecranon fossa. The distal humerus is prepared for nail insertion using hand reamers of increasing diameter, and the nail is inserted with careful rotational movements. The proximal fragment is picked up with the tip of the nail under image intensification. Hand force and rotational movements are used to further insert the nail until the tip reaches the proximal metaphyseal area. At least two interlocking bolts are placed at each side of the fracture. The wound is irrigated, and the layers are closed. One Redon drain is placed at the entry portal; it is removed after 24 to 48 hours. As with antegrade nailing, the patient must avoid rotational movements until bridging callus is seen on radiographs. This technique, if strictly followed, does not disturb the elbow or shoulder joint, and excellent shoulder and elbow function can ultimately be expected (Figure 4).

### Complications of Intramedullary Nailing

The typical complications of antegrade nailing are subacromial impingement and damage to the rotator cuff, which result in chronic shoulder pain and loss of shoulder function.[22,23] These complications can be prevented by careful preparation of the entry portal and countersinking of the nail base below the level of the articular cartilage. Proximal interlocking can cause damage to the axillary nerve, which can be avoided by meticulous dissection of the path between the skin and bone before drilling and insertion of the bolt. Damage to the radial nerve may result from stretching of the nerve during manipulation of fracture fragments or improper placement of the nail. If the damage is detected after surgery,

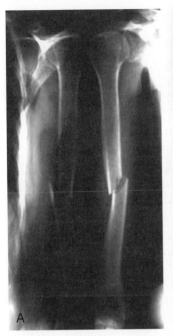
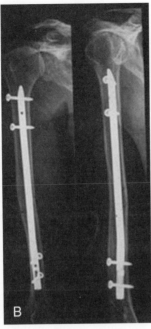
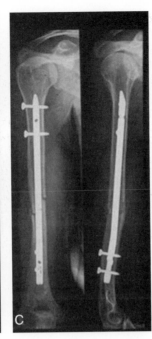
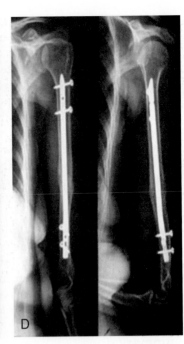

**Figure 4** **A,** Presurgical AP and lateral radiographs of a closed oblique midshaft fracture of the left humerus in a 67-year-old woman after a low-energy fall. **B,** Postsurgical AP and lateral radiographs showing retrograde nailing with double interlocking proximally and distally. No interfragmentary compression was used. **C,** AP and lateral radiographs taken at 4-week follow-up. **D,** AP and lateral radiographs taken at 16-week follow-up. The patient had full shoulder and elbow function.

the radial nerve should be explored as soon as possible to ensure that its continuity is preserved and that it is not intercalated between fracture fragments. In retrograde nailing, a supracondylar fracture at the level of the entry portal is an important iatrogenic complication that necessitates plate fixation.

Delayed union and nonunion result from suboptimal fracture alignment or inadequate stability. If hypertrophic nonunion occurs, stability must be enhanced; exchange nailing with a thicker nail and interfragmentary compression can be used. For atrophic nonunion, stability is best achieved with compression plating.[12,24] Cancellous bone grafting is also performed to augment healing of an atrophic nonunion. Deep infection and vascular complications are rare after nailing.

### External Fixation

External fixation is currently used only for a severe open, contaminated fracture or a fracture that has become infected after previous treatment.[25] In a patient with multiple fractures, external fixation of a grossly unstable humeral fracture can be used as a temporary primary treatment.[26] To avoid complications, the surgeon must determine the safe zones for pin placement. The pins of the external fixator are placed in the proximal third and distal third of the humeral shaft. To avoid damage to the radial nerve, pins are never inserted into the middle third. In the proximal third, pins are placed from lateral to medial through the deltoid muscle; the deltoid is spread bilaterally, and a drill guide is used to

protect the axillary nerve. In the distal third, pins are placed from posterior to anterior through the triceps muscle. Three pins are placed on each side of the fracture and connected with one or two bridging bars. Alignment is achieved by closed means.

Wound treatment includes regular débridement, irrigation, and secondary wound closure or split skin grafting, with the external fixator in place. The fixator can be left in place until wound healing, or it can be removed and stability achieved using plate osteosynthesis or nailing, if no acute signs of infection are present. Because of the perforation of the deltoid and triceps muscles by the fixator pins, the patient has limited postsurgical range of motion in the shoulder and elbow joints, and mobilization may be painful.

Several complications are associated with external fixation. External fixator pins perforate skin and muscle bellies and therefore can be responsible for wound and pin track infections. If pin loosening occurs, the stability of the entire construct diminishes. Malalignment, delayed union, or nonunion may result. Fixator pins may perforate the brachial artery or the ulnar, median, or axillary nerve. Very proximal or distal pin placement may lead to pin perforation of the shoulder or elbow joint, with the danger of intra-articular infection.

## Humeral Shaft Fracture With Radial Nerve Palsy

Humeral shaft fracture with radial nerve palsy is a specific entity that has been discussed for many years.

Primary radial nerve palsy previously was not considered to require surgical treatment. In more than 90% of patients, it results from neurapraxia; the patient recovers with nonsurgical treatment after a period of weeks or months. Some surgeons prefer early surgical exploration, in which the nerve is exposed at the level of the fracture and, if axonotmesis is present, the nerve is directly repaired with suture. The fracture is stabilized during the same procedure. The success rate after surgical treatment is not significantly different from that of nonsurgical treatment. If clinical and electromyographic recovery of radial nerve function is not seen after 3 months, surgical nerve release with restoration of continuity is recommended.

Secondary radial nerve palsy can occur after closed fracture manipulation, plate osteosynthesis, nailing, or external fixation. The treatment is not controversial. Early exploration of the nerve is uniformly recommended to ascertain nerve continuity and free trajectory.

## Summary

Humeral fractures can be treated nonsurgically or surgically. Surgical treatment has absolute and relative indications, and it is being used more frequently because of considerations related to patient comfort, pain relief, and early functional recovery. Plate osteosynthesis remains a valid treatment for most types of fractures. Intramedullary nailing using an antegrade or retrograde technique is gaining popularity as a safe, less invasive procedure. External fixation is rarely indicated. With correct surgical technique and careful soft-tissue treatment, complications such as radial or axillary nerve palsy, subacromial impingement, and iatrogenic supracondylar fracture can be avoided. Uneventful healing can be expected in more than 90% of patients, if good fracture alignment and adequate stability are achieved through surgical or nonsurgical treatment.

## Annotated References

1. Müller ME, Nazarian S, Koch P: *Classification AO des fractures.* Berlin, Germany, Springer-Verlag, 1987.

2. Oestern HJ, Tscherne H, Sturm J, Nerlich M: Classification of severity of injury. *Unfallchirurg* 1985;88: 465-472.

3. Gustilo RB, Mendoza RM, Williams DN: Problems in the management of type III (severe) open fractures: A new classification of type III open fractures. *J Trauma* 1984;24:742-746.

4. Böhler L: Gegen die operative Behandlung von Oberarmschaftbrüchen. *Langenbecks Arch Chir* 1964;308:465-470.

5. Sarmiento A, Kinman PB, Galvin EG, et al: Functional bracing of fractures of the shaft of the humerus. *J Bone Joint Surg Am* 1977;59:596-601.

6. Wallny T, Westermann K, Sagebiel C, et al: Functional treatment of humeral shaft fractures: Indications and results. *J Orthop Trauma* 1997;11:283-287.

7. Bell MJ, Beauchamp CG, Kellam JK, et al: The results of plating humeral shaft fractures in patients with multiple injuries: The Sunnybrook experience. *J Bone Joint Surg Br* 1985;67:293-296.

8. Blum J, Rommens PM: Surgical approaches to the humeral shaft. *Acta Chir Belg* 1997;97:237-296.

9. Heim D, Herkert F, Hess P, et al: Surgical treatment of humeral shaft fractures: The Basel experience. *J Trauma* 1993;35:226-232.

10. McCormack RG, Brien D, Buckley RE, et al: Fixation of fractures of the shaft of the humerus by dynamic compression plate or intramedullary nail: A prospective, randomised trial. *J Bone Joint Surg Br* 2000;82: 336-339.

11. Chapman JR, Henley MB, Agel J, et al: Randomised prospective study of humeral shaft fracture fixation: Nails versus plates. *J Orthop Trauma* 2000;14: 162-166.

12. Marti RK, Verheyen CC, Besselaar PP: Humeral shaft non-union: Evaluation of uniform surgical repair in fifty-one patients. *J Orthop Trauma* 2002;16: 108-115.

    Fifty-one patients were treated for aseptic nonunion with surgical exploration of the radial nerve through an anterolateral approach, as well as neurolysis, decortication, compression plating, and cancellous bone grafting. Consolidation was achieved in all patients; 96% of the patients considered the result excellent or good.

13. Rommens PM, Vansteenkiste F, Stappaerts KH, Broos PL: [Indications, dangers and results of surgical treatment of humerus fractures]. *Unfallchirurg* 1989;92:565-570.

14. Blum J, Janzing H, Gahr R, Langendorff HS, Rommens PM: Clinical performance of a new medullary humeral nail: Antegrade versus retrograde insertion. *J Orthop Trauma* 2001;15:342-349.

    In 57 retrograde and 27 antegrade nailing procedures, the rate of perisurgical complications was equivalent. There was no difference in functional outcome after healing. Five fractures, all with retrograde nailing, required secondary surgery. Retrograde nailing is technically more demanding.

15. Scheerlinck T, Handelberg F: Functional outcome after intramedullary nailing of humeral shaft fractures: Comparison between retrograde Marchetti-Vincenzi and antegrade unreamed AO nail. *J Trauma* 2002;52:60-71.

    A retrograde approach to the humeral medullary cavity using a Marchetti-Vincenzi nail resulted in better shoulder function and similar elbow function, in comparison with an antegrade approach using an AO unreamed humeral nail.

16. Demirel M, Turhan E, Dereboy F, Ozturk A: Interlocking nailing of humeral shaft fractures: A retrospective study of 114 patients. *Indian J Med Sci* 2005; 59:436-442.

After antegrade locked nailing in 114 patients, primary union was observed in 109 and transient postsurgical radial nerve palsy in 4; 105 had excellent or satisfactory recovery of shoulder and elbow function. Antegrade locked nailing is reliable and efficient.

17. Lin J, Hou SM: Antegrade locked nailing for humeral shaft fractures. *Clin Orthop Relat Res* 1999;365: 201-210.

18. Blum J, Machemer H, Baumgart F, Schlegel U, Wahl D, Rommens PM: Biomechanical comparison of bending and torsional properties in retrograde intramedullary nailing of humeral shaft fractures. *J Orthop Trauma* 1999;13:344-350.

19. Rommens PM, Blum J: Retrograde nailing of humeral shaft fractures with the unreamed humeral nail (UHN). *Tech Orthop* 1998;13:51-60.

20. Rommens PM, Blum J, Runkel M: Retrograde nailing of humeral shaft fractures. *Clin Orthop Relat Res* 1998;350:26-39.

21. Rommens PM, Blum J: Retrograde locked nailing of humeral shaft fractures using the unreamed humeral nail (UHN). *Orthop Traumatol* 1999;7:251-259.

22. Bhandari M, Devereaux PJ, McKee MD, Schemitz EH: Compression plating versus intramedullary nailing of humeral shaft fractures: A meta-analysis. *Acta Orthop* 2006;72:279-284.

Three studies involving a total of 155 patients found that plate fixation of humeral shaft fractures may reduce the risk of reoperation and shoulder impingement. The cumulative evidence is inconclusive, and a larger study is needed to confirm the findings.

23. Dimakopoulos P, Papadopoulos AX, Papas M, Panagopoulos A, Lambiris E: Modified extra rotator-cuff entry point in antegrade humeral nailing. *Arch Orthop Trauma Surg* 2005;125:27-32.

Thirty-two patients underwent successful antegrade nailing through a modified insertion point located 1 cm below the crest of the greater tuberosity. Excellent active shoulder function was established in 98%. This extra–rotator cuff entry point is beneficial for the shoulder's postsurgical function.

24. Lin J, Hou SM, Hang JS: Treatment of humeral shaft delayed unions and nonunions with humeral locked nails. *J Trauma* 2000;48:695-703.

25. Zinman C, Norman D, Hamoud K, et al: External fixation for severe open fractures of the humerus caused by missiles. *J Orthop Trauma* 1997;11:536-539.

26. Dougherty PJ, Silverton C, Yeni Y, Tashman S, Weir R: Conversion from temporary external fixation to definitive fixation: Shaft fractures. *J Am Acad Orthop Surg* 2006;14:S124-S127.

Temporary external fixation is the most common method of initially stabilizing a diaphyseal fracture in an at-risk patient. The best time to perform definitive fixation without increasing the risk of infection and nonunion is unknown, and future research is needed.

# Section 7

Elbow Trauma, Fracture, and Reconstruction

Section Editor
Matthew L. Ramsey, MD

# Chapter 42

# Elbow Injuries and the Throwing Athlete

*Christopher S. Ahmad, MD

## Introduction

Throwing places unique demands on the elbow and leads to predictable patterns of injury. In particular, young throwing athletes compete in an increasingly demanding athletic environment and face a correspondingly increased risk of injury to the elbow. Biomechanical research, new physical examination maneuvers, and better imaging techniques are improving knowledge of elbow injury patterns. Nonsurgical and surgical methods of treatment are also advancing. Surgical techniques have become less invasive, and they are supported with clinical results and biomechanical studies.

## Throwing-Related Elbow Anatomy and Biomechanics

The anterior oblique ligament, posterior oblique ligament, and transverse ligament make up the medial ulnar collateral ligament (UCL) complex. The anterior oblique ligament is the strongest of the three and the primary stabilizer to valgus stress. The anterior oblique ligament is functionally composed of anterior and posterior bands that provide reciprocal function in resisting valgus stress throughout the range of flexion-extension. The anterior band is tight in extension, and the posterior band is tight in flexion. The goal of surgical reconstruction is to reproduce the functional anatomy of the anterior oblique ligament.

During the acceleration phase of throwing, the elbow reaches an angular velocity of 3,000° per second as it extends from 110° to 20° of flexion. This speed corresponds to a 64 N/m valgus torque. The combination of valgus torque and rapid extension generates a tensile stress along the medial side (the UCL, flexor-pronator mass, and medial epicondyle), a shear stress in the posterior compartment (the posteromedial tip of the olecranon and olecranon fossa), and a compression force of

*Christopher S. Ahmad, MD or the department with which he is affiliated has received research or institutional support from Arthrex, Inc.

as much as 500 N on the lateral side of the radiocapitellar joint. On the medial side, the force exceeds the known ultimate tensile strength of UCL cadaver specimens, which is 33 N/m, and creates an obvious risk of injury.[1]

Muscle dynamic stabilization may help protect the UCL. In a cadaver model, the flexor carpi ulnaris was found to be a primary dynamic contributor to valgus stability, and the flexor digitorum superficialis was found to be a secondary stabilizer.[2] These muscular dynamic forces must be taken into account in medial UCL injury prevention, nonsurgical treatment, and surgical exposure.

In the posterior compartment, the olecranon is repeatedly and forcefully driven into the olecranon fossa during throwing. Shear forces on the medial aspect of the olecranon tip and olecranon fossa can cause injury and osteophyte formation. This constellation of injuries is called valgus extension overload syndrome.[3] The relationship between the posterior compartment of the elbow and the UCL is becoming clear. In a study of professional baseball players who underwent olecranon débridement, 25% developed valgus instability and eventually required UCL reconstruction.[4] This finding suggests that both the olecranon and the UCL contribute to valgus stability. A cadaver biomechanical study found that sequential partial resection of the posteromedial aspect of the olecranon caused increases in elbow valgus angulation.[5] Another cadaver study confirmed that strain in the UCL increases as posteromedial olecranon resection increases beyond 3 mm.[6] These studies conclude that aggressive olecranon resection to treat posteromedial impingement places the UCL at risk of injury.

An alternate proposal is that subtle valgus instability may lead to symptomatic posteromedial impingement. A cadaver study finding that UCL injury results in contact pressure alterations in the posterior compartment explains the formation of osteophytes on the posteromedial olecranon.[7] This study concludes that patients with posteromedial impingement pain should be critically evaluated for concomitant UCL injuries.

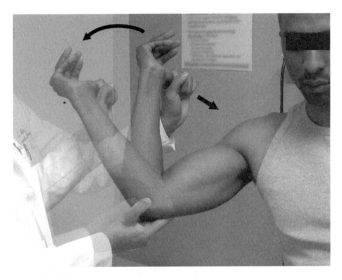

**Figure 1** The moving valgus stress test. The arrows indicate the valgus stress applied while the elbow is moved from flexion to extension.

Different baseball pitches produce different amounts of torque. The fastball and slider pitches generate the greatest force on the shoulder and elbow, and the curveball pitch generates the highest elbow valgus stress. The change-up pitch produces less torque on the elbow and is therefore safer for the pitcher than either the curveball or the fastball. A study of young baseball pitchers found that the better players are more likely to pitch fastballs and curveballs, pitch more often, and play on more teams.[8] These factors contribute to overloading the elbow and making it more vulnerable to injury. At present, the most effective means of mitigating the likelihood of injury is to limit the number of pitches.

## Clinical Evaluation

### Physical Examination

The physical examination of the medial elbow focuses on the UCL, medial epicondyle, and flexor-pronator mass. UCL injury is indicated by point tenderness directly over the UCL or near its origin and insertion. Valgus instability is tested by flexing the patient's elbow between 20° and 30° to unlock the olecranon from its fossa, while applying valgus stress. In the milking maneuver, the patient or the examiner pulls on the patient's thumb to create valgus stress, with the patient's forearm supinated and the elbow flexed beyond 90°. In the moving valgus stress test, which is a modification of the milking maneuver, valgus torque is applied to the elbow until the shoulder reaches its limit of external rotation. The elbow is then flexed and extended with the torque held constant. The test is considered positive if the medial elbow pain is reproduced at the UCL and is at its most intense when the elbow is flexed between 70° and 120° (Figure 1). The moving valgus stress test was found to be highly sensitive (100%) and specific (75%)

compared with UCL arthroscopic assessment or open exploration.[9]

Medial epicondylitis may be confused with a UCL injury, and the two conditions may coexist. The patient has tenderness at the common flexor origin just distal to the medial epicondyle, as well as pain with resisted pronation or flexion of the wrist. Flexor-pronator avulsion can coexist with a UCL tear; the patient has more obvious weakness and a palpable defect just distal to the epicondyle. The ulnar nerve should be assessed for subluxation and the Tinel sign.

The posterior compartment examination focuses on the olecranon. Pain is elicited in the posterior compartment. Pronation, valgus, and extension forces indicate valgus extension overload. Tenderness and crepitus over the posteromedial olecranon are evaluated. The lateral elbow examination assesses the radial head and capitellum and can determine the presence of a synovial plica. Crepitus in the radiocapitellar joint can signify chondromalacia or capitellar osteochondritis dissecans (OCD). In a positive flexion-pronation test, pain localized in the lateral aspect of the elbow is reproduced during flexion-extension of the pronated forearm. This finding suggests the presence of a synovial plica in the radiocapitellar joint.

### Imaging Studies

Imaging of the elbow begins with standard radiography, including the AP, lateral, and axial views. The elbow is assessed for joint space narrowing, osteophytes, and loose bodies. Valgus stress radiographs can be used to measure the medial joint line opening; an opening larger than 3 mm is often considered diagnostic of valgus instability.[10] However, it should be remembered that the uninjured, asymptomatic dominant elbow of a professional baseball pitcher has a mild increase in valgus elbow laxity compared with the nondominant elbow.[11]

Conventional MRI is useful in identifying chronic thickening of the UCL, an obvious full-thickness UCL tear, or a traumatic tear of flexor-pronator origin (Figure 2). Magnetic resonance arthrography enhanced with intraarticular gadolinium improves the ability to diagnose a partial undersurface tear. Dynamic ultrasonography has recently been studied as a means of evaluating the UCL and detecting increased laxity with valgus instability. Ultrasonography is noninvasive, inexpensive, and dynamic, but operator experience is required for its use.

In a radiographic study of throwers ages 9.5 to 12 years, hypertrophy of the medial humeral epicondyle appeared in all pitchers and catchers and in 90% of fielders.[12] Separation of the medial epicondyle was found in 63% of the pitchers, 70% of the catchers, and 50% of the fielders; fragmentation was found in 19% of the pitchers, 40% of the catchers, and 15% of the fielders. Elbow soreness was reported by 49% of those with separation and 56% of those with fragmentation. The higher incidence of medial epicondylar separation and fragmentation among catchers may be related to the increased stress on the elbow during throwing from the squatting position.

## Conditions Causing Medial Elbow Pain

### Medial Epicondylitis

Medial epicondylitis is rare compared with lateral epicondylitis and is caused by activities that require repetitive wrist flexion or forearm pronation. It most commonly occurs as a result of high-energy valgus forces among baseball pitchers, golfers, and participants in racquet sports. Medial epicondylitis is characterized by pain along the medial elbow that is increased by resisted forearm pronation or wrist flexion. Nonsurgical treatment involves rest and the use of ice, nonsteroidal anti-inflammatory drugs (NSAIDs), and sometimes corticosteroid injection, followed by guided rehabilitation and return to sports participation. Modification of the throwing or swing motion, as well as modification of the racquet or other equipment, should be considered. Surgical treatment is necessary if nonsurgical treatment is unsuccessful. It involves excision of the pathologic portion of the tendon, repair of the resulting defect, and reattachment of the origin of the flexor pronator muscle group to the medial epicondyle. Surgical treatment produces substantial subjective relief, although objective strength deficits may persist.

### Medial Epicondylar Apophysitis

In a skeletally mature thrower, the UCL accepts the valgus stress and is more likely to be injured than the medial apophysis. A skeletally immature athlete is more likely to injure the medial apophysis. Patients report a gradually increasing onset of medial elbow pain and stiffness during throwing. Medial epicondylar apophysitis is suggested by the presence of tenderness and swelling over the epicondyle and occasionally a flexion contracture. Early in the disease process, plain radiographs are negative, but later radiographs reveal irregular ossification of the medial epicondylar apophysis. If left untreated, the apophysis may widen or separate, and fragmentation may result. The initial nonsurgical treatment is rest and avoidance of pitching for at least 4 to 6 weeks. If the medial epicondyle physis widens more than 3 to 5 mm, open reduction and internal fixation is indicated and appears to yield good results.[13]

### UCL Injury

Nonsurgical treatment of a UCL injury includes a 6- to 12-week period of rest from throwing, with flexor-pronator strengthening. If the patient has relief of symptoms and the physical examination findings are normal, a return to throwing can begin, using optimal throwing

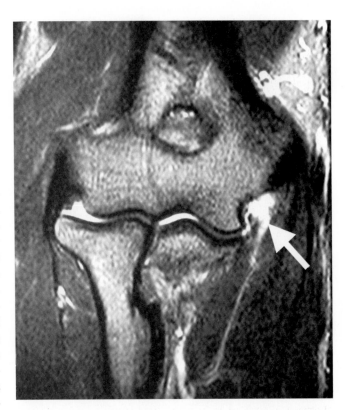

**Figure 2** MRI showing a tear of the UCL (*arrow*). *(Reproduced with permission from Ahmad CS, ElAttrache NS: MUCL Reconstruction in the Overhead Athlete. Techniques in Orthopedics: Surgical Management of Complex Elbow Problems: Update 2006;21: 290-298.)*

mechanics. In a study of 31 throwing athletes with a UCL injury who were treated with as much as 3 months of rest and rehabilitation, 42% had returned to their earlier level of competition at an average 24.5 weeks after diagnosis.[14] No history or physical examination features were found to predict which athletes responded to nonsurgical treatment.

### Jobe Technique

The original Jobe technique for UCL reconstruction used a tendinous transection and reflection of the flexor-pronator mass, submuscular transposition of the ulnar nerve, and creation of humeral tunnels to penetrate the posterior humeral cortex. This technique provided excellent exposure at the cost of morbidity to the flexor-pronator mass and ulnar nerve. Several modifications have lessened the technical demands of the procedure and decreased the soft-tissue morbidity. A muscle-splitting approach avoids the necessity of detaching the flexor-pronator mass and can be used with or without subcutaneous transposition of the ulnar nerve. The technique for bone tunnel creation has been modified to direct the tunnels anteriorly on the humeral epicondyle, so as to avoid ulnar nerve injury as the graft is passed in a figure-of-8 fashion (Figure 3). This modified Jobe technique is the standard surgical procedure for UCL

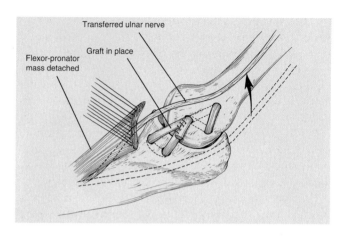

**Figure 3** A classic Jobe UCL reconstruction. *(Reproduced from Ahmad CS, ElAttrache NS: Elbow valgus instability in the throwing athlete.* J Am Acad Orthop Surg *2006;14:693-700.)*

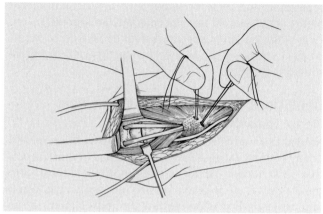

**Figure 4** Docking reconstruction with graft limbs tensioned into the humeral docking tunnel. *(Reproduced from Ahmad CS, ElAttrache NS: Elbow valgus instability in the throwing athlete.* J Am Acad Orthop Surg *2006;14:693-700.)*

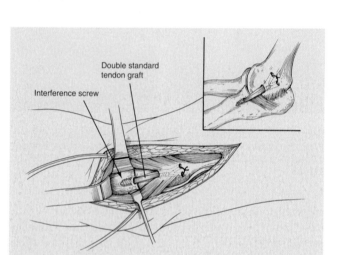

**Figure 5** Hybrid reconstruction with interference screw fixation on the ulna and docking fixation on the humerus. *(Reproduced from Ahmad CS, ElAttrache NS: Elbow valgus instability in the throwing athlete.* J Am Acad Orthop Surg *2006;14:693-700.)*

reconstruction, and it enables as many as 93% of throwing athletes to return to competition.[15]

### Docking Technique

The docking technique is a further modification of the Jobe technique that simplifies graft passage, tensioning, and fixation. Both the Jobe and docking techniques use a muscle-splitting approach with humeral tunnel creation on the ulna. With the docking technique, the inferior docking tunnel is drilled to a depth of 15 mm using a 4-mm burr or drill. Two small exit tunnels, separated by a distance of 5 mm to 1 cm, are created to allow suture passage from the primary humeral docking tunnel. The graft is passed through the ulnar tunnel from anterior to posterior, and the posterior limb of the graft is passed into the humeral docking tunnel. The length of the anterior limb of the graft is adjusted to allow the

graft to be tensioned within the humeral docking tunnel. Pulling on the sutures tensions the graft into the humeral docking tunnel. The sutures are tied over the bony bridge (Figure 4).

One hundred consecutive overhead throwing athletes underwent UCL reconstruction with the docking technique. At a mean 36-month follow-up, 90% had been able to play at their earlier level or a higher level of competition for more than 12 months.[16] A modification of the docking technique using a four-strand palmaris longus graft for reconstruction was performed in 25 elite professional and collegiate baseball players. At a minimum 2-year follow-up, 92% were able to return to their preinjury level of competition.[17]

### Hybrid Interference Screw Fixation Technique

New techniques for UCL reconstruction are being evaluated in the laboratory, with the goal of reconstructing the central isometric fibers of the native ligament and fixing the graft with interference screws.[1] A hybrid technique has been developed to achieve ulnar fixation with an interference screw and humeral fixation using the docking technique (Figure 5). It offers several advantages over the docking technique. Fewer drill holes are required. Only one central tunnel is created, rather than two tunnels with an intervening bony bridge on the ulna, and therefore less dissection is required in the muscle-splitting approach. Creation of the posterior ulnar tunnel, which is in close proximity to the ulnar nerve, is not required. Finally, graft passage is less difficult; an interference screw is used in the single tunnel. In a biomechanical evaluation of interference screw fixation in cadavers, the strength of the graft fixation was found to be 95% that of an intact UCL under valgus load.[1] Clinical follow-up data are not currently available, however, for the interference screw and hybrid techniques.

## Ulnar Neuritis

A throwing athlete may develop ulnar neuritis secondary to nerve traction from valgus stress, nerve compression from adhesions, osteophyte formation, flexor muscle hypertrophy, or nerve irritation from subluxation. A patient has paresthesia in the fourth and fifth digits during or after throwing, and a positive Tinel sign can be elicited at the cubital tunnel. The nonsurgical treatment involves rest and the use of ice, NSAIDs, and physical therapy, followed by a gradual return to throwing. The condition can be treated surgically with ulnar neurolysis and submuscular or subcutaneous anterior ulnar nerve transposition (Figure 6). Excellent results have been reported in throwing athletes after anterior subcutaneous transposition of the ulnar nerve; an average 12 weeks is required until return to play.[18]

## Conditions Causing Posterior Elbow Pain
### Posteromedial Impingement or Valgus Extension Overload

In isolated valgus extension overload, elbow pain occurs during the deceleration phase of throwing as the elbow reaches terminal extension. The pain is localized in the posteromedial aspect of the olecranon. The patient may report limited extension (caused by impinging posterior osteophytes) or locking and catching (caused by loose bodies). Pain in the posterior compartment can be elicited by snapping the elbow into extension and accentuated by applying valgus stress.

AP, lateral, oblique, and axial views of the elbow may reveal posteromedial olecranon osteophytes or loose bodies within the articulation. CT and MRI may be used to further define loose bodies and osteophytes.

Nonsurgical treatment includes activity modification, intra-articular cortisone injection, and NSAIDs. A period of rest from throwing is required, followed by a progres-

sive throwing program. The patient should receive instruction in pitching to detect and correct any flaws that might have contributed to the injury. Surgical treatment is indicated for a patient who has symptoms of posteromedial impingement after nonsurgical treatment. Arthroscopic débridement or a limited-incision arthrotomy is performed to decompress the posterior compartment (Figure 7). Resection is limited to osteophytes and maximum of 3 mm of olecranon to avoid increased strain on the medial collateral ligament. Arthroscopy limits morbidity and allows a complete diagnostic assessment of the elbow.

The presence of UCL insufficiency is a relative contraindication to isolated olecranon débridement. Basic science studies found that olecranon resection increases both valgus angulation of the elbow and the strain on the UCL during valgus stress.[5,6] In addition, UCL insufficiency causes contact alterations in the posteromedial compartment that can lead to symptomatic chondrosis and osteophyte formation manifested as valgus

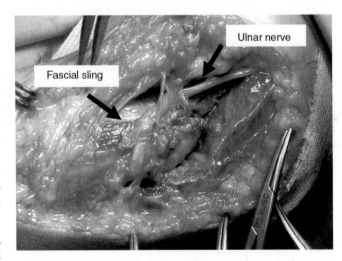

**Figure 6** Ulnar nerve transposition with creation of a stabilizing fascial sling.

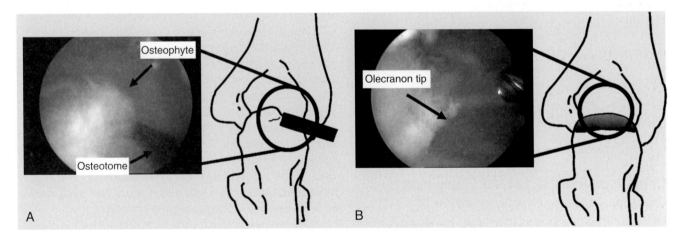

**Figure 7** Surgical treatment of posteromedial impingement. **A,** An osteotome is used to remove the osteophyte. **B,** The olecranon tip is contoured with a motorized burr. *(Adapted from Ahmad CS, ElAttrache NS: Arthroscopic posteromedial decompression for valgus extension overload syndrome, in Yamaguchi K, King GJW, McKee M, O'Driscoll SW [eds]: Advanced Reconstruction: Elbow. Rosemont, IL, American Academy of Orthopaedic Surgeons, 2007, p 56.)*

## Table 1 | Classification of Elbow OCD

| Grade | Description | Treatment |
|-------|-------------|-----------|
| I | Smooth but soft cartilage | Drilling, if symptomatic |
| II | Fibrillation or fissuring of cartilage | Removal of cartilage to stable rim and drilling |
| III | Exposed bone with fixed osteochondral fragment | Removal of osteochondral fragment and drilling |
| IV | Loose but nondisplaced fragment | Removal of fragment and drilling |
| V | Displaced fragment with loose body | Drilling or mosaicplasty |

*(Data from Baumgarten TE, Andrews JR, Satterwhite YE: The arthroscopic classification and treatment of osteochondritis dissecans of the capitellum. Am J Sports Med 1998;26: 520-523.)*

extension overload syndrome.[7] The UCL insufficiency may become symptomatic following posteromedial decompression. Therefore, a careful history, physical examination, and advanced imaging studies are important to avoid overlooking UCL injury or valgus instability.

### Olecranon Stress Fracture

The triceps contracts forcefully on the olecranon during the acceleration phase of throwing. In a child with open physes, the strong triceps contractions to the olecranon apophysis cause a shear and distracting force. Repeated triceps contractions can result in olecranon apophysitis and ultimately in stress fracture of the olecranon apophysis. A patient has posterior elbow pain, weakness, and a decreased range of motion. The symptoms are worst during the acceleration and follow-through phases of throwing. Physical examination findings include tenderness over the olecranon and pain during resisted extension. Plain radiographs usually show widening or fragmentation of the olecranon physis and sclerosis, as compared with the contralateral side. A bone scan or MRI can be used to confirm the presence of a stress fracture.

The initial treatment of olecranon apophysitis includes activity modification, physical therapy, and the use of NSAIDs and ice. Surgical treatment is indicated after 3 to 6 months of nonsurgical treatment for a patient with refractory symptoms and a documented lack of olecranon apophyseal closure. A single cannulated 6.5- or 7.3-mm cancellous screw is placed down the intramedullary canal to cross the fracture site or unfused apophysis.

## Conditions Causing Lateral Elbow Pain

### Capitellar Osteochondritis Dissecans

OCD is more common in skeletally immature athletes than in adults. It arises from repetitive and excessive compressive forces generated by large valgus stresses on the elbow during throwing. Other factors contributing to the development of OCD include a genetic predisposition and a tenuous end-artery vascular supply to the capitellum. Blood is supplied to the capitellum by two end arteries (the radial recurrent and interosseous recurrent arteries), and blood flow can be disrupted during repetitive microtrauma.

A patient with OCD reports elbow pain and stiffness that are relieved by rest. If not addressed, the symptoms progress to locking or catching caused by the formation of intra-articular loose bodies. Physical examination reveals lateral elbow tenderness and loss of extension.

Capitellar OCD lesions are classified based on the status and stability of the overlying cartilage, as outlined in Table 1.[19] The initial treatment of a lesion of any grade involves activity modification, avoidance of throwing and related sports activities, and NSAID use. For acute symptoms, an elbow brace may be used for a short period. If the lesion is not detached or frank loose bodies are not present, throwing and related sports activities are restricted for 4 weeks, and physical therapy is begun. When strength and motion are recovered, a progressive throwing program is undertaken. The program begins with short-distance tossing and progresses to long-distance tossing and to throwing from the mound at reduced effort and finally at full effort. The patient should be instructed in proper pitching mechanics. Return to the preinjury level of performance is achieved in approximately 3 to 4 months.

Surgical treatment is indicated if nonsurgical treatment is unsuccessful. Diagnostic arthroscopy to confirm the stability of the overlying cartilage is followed by drilling of the lesion with a 2-mm smooth pin.

Immediate surgical treatment is indicated if the patient has a grade III, IV, or V lesion, particularly if mechanical symptoms are present. The surgery begins with diagnostic arthroscopy and assessment of the overlying cartilage. Loose bodies are removed, and the cartilage is contoured to a stable rim using shavers and curets. If the lesion does not require mosaicplasty, it is treated with antegrade drilling, with perforations separated by 2 to 3 mm to introduce marrow elements and create a fibrocartilage healing response (Figure 8).

Mosaicplasty, a technique for transferring multiple osteochondral autografts, is an option for treatment of a large capitellar OCD lesion (Figure 9). The advantages of mosaicplasty include the ready availability of donor cartilage-bone plugs, the ability to cover defects of different sizes, and the use of native hyaline cartilage containing active, mature chondrocytes. In theory, the function of native articular cartilage used for grafting is better than that of fibrocartilage, which has been shown to have inferior biomechanical properties.[20]

A 13-year-old male baseball catcher with a large capitellar lesion that engaged the radial head was treated with mosaicplasty combined with a distal humeral osteotomy through an open approach. Plain radiographs taken

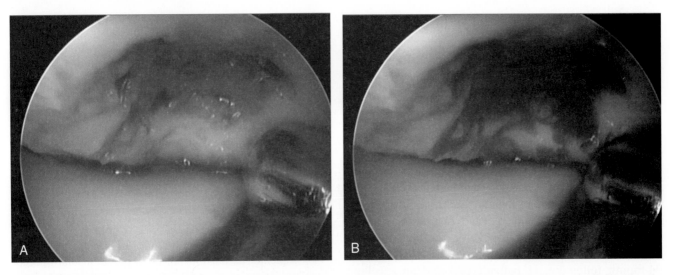

**Figure 8** Surgical treatment of a capitellar OCD lesion. **A,** After antegrade drilling, perforations in the lesion are visualized from the posterolateral portal. **B,** Blood from the bone marrow occupies the defect.

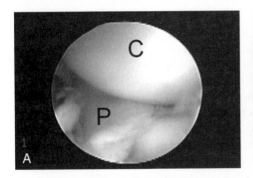
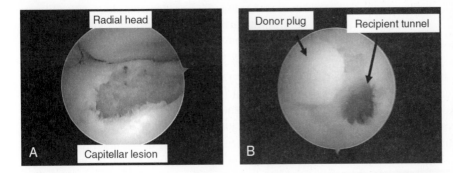

**Figure 9** Surgical treatment of a capitellar OCD lesion with mosaicplasty. **A,** The capitellar lesion. **B,** The first osteochondral autograft in place and flush with surrounding articular surface. **C,** The completed mosaicplasty with osteochondral graft plugs. *(Adapted from ElAttrache NS, Ahmad CS: Mosaicplasty for capitellar osteochondritis dissecans, in Yamaguchi K, King GJW, McKee M, O'Driscoll SW [eds]: Advanced Reconstruction: Elbow. Rosemont, IL, American Academy of Orthopaedic Surgeons, 2007, pp 180, 182.)*

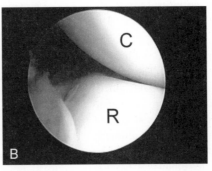

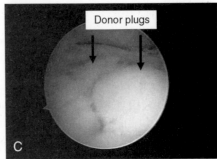

**Figure 10** Arthroscopic views of a radiocapitellar plica before excision **(A)** and after excision **(B)**. C = capitellum, P = plica, R = radial head.

10 months after surgery showed osteotomy union and disappearance of the capitellar lesion. During a second open surgical procedure to improve elbow motion, the osteochondral plugs grafted to the capitellum were found to have a smooth articular surface indistinguishable from that of the surrounding articular cartilage. The patient was active in sports including baseball, judo, and sumo wrestling at 35-month follow-up.[21]

Panner's disease is a capitellar OCD that occurs in children younger than 10 years. It is commonly associated with baseball, softball, gymnastics, or wrestling and not strictly with repetitive throwing, as other forms of OCD are. Usually it is self-limiting with no long-term sequelae. The initial radiographs reveal fissuring and irregularity of the capitellum. Subsequent radiographs show reossification, and the patient has a corresponding resolution of symptoms. Panner's disease is treated with rest from the sports activity that caused the condition, as well as the use of NSAIDs and ice.

## Radiocapitellar Plica

Lateral synovial plica of the elbow was recently identified as a cause of lateral elbow pain. Twelve patients who were throwing athletes or golfers were arthroscopically treated for posterolateral elbow impingement resulting from a synovial plica.[22] All of the patients had posterolateral elbow pain, and seven reported clicking or catching; no patients had lateral epicondylitis. A thickened, hypertrophic lateral synovial plica was removed in all patients. Eight (67%) had associated synovitis and inflammation of the adjacent capsular tissue requiring additional débridement, and seven (58%) had chondromalacia with visible changes in the articular cartilage, involving the capitellum and posterolateral distal humerus in five and the radial head in two. At a mean 34-month follow-up, 11 patients reported an excellent outcome. Figure 10 shows a radiocapitellar plica before and after arthroscopic resection.

## Summary

The complex forces acting on the elbow during throwing place the elbow at risk of injury. The development of more precise physical examination maneuvers and newer imaging techniques has led to greater accuracy in the diagnosis of these elbow injuries. Advanced surgical treatment options emphasize the reproduction of normal anatomy and biomechanics while surgical morbidity of the muscles is minimized.

## Annotated References

1. Ahmad CS, Lee TQ, ElAttrache NS: Biomechanical evaluation of a new elbow ulnar collateral ligament reconstruction using interference screw fixation. *Am J Sports Med* 2003;31:332-337.

   Cadaver elbows underwent kinematic testing with an intact, released, and reconstructed ligament. The medial UCL reconstruction technique created single bone tunnels at the isometric anatomic insertion sites on the medial epicondyle and sublime tubercles; graft fixation was achieved with soft-tissue interference screws. The ultimate moment for intact elbows (34.0 N·m) was not significantly different from that of the reconstructed elbows (30.6 N·m). Release of the medial UCL caused a significant increase in valgus instability. Reconstruction restored valgus stability to near that of the intact elbow.

2. Park MC, Ahmad CS: Dynamic contributions of the flexor-pronator mass to elbow valgus stability. *J Bone Joint Surg Am* 2004;86:2268-2274.

   Six cadaver elbows were tested at 30° and 90° of flexion with no other constraints to motion, and a full UCL tear was simulated. Muscle forces were simulated on the basis of the centroids and physiologic cross-sectional areas of individual muscles. The flexor carpi ulnaris is the primary sta-

bilizer, and the flexor digitorum superficialis is a secondary stabilizer. The pronator teres provides the least dynamic stability.

3. Wilson FD, Andrews JR, Blackburn TA, McCluskey G: Valgus extension overload in the pitching elbow. *Am J Sports Med* 1983;11:83-88.

4. Andrews JR, Timmerman LA: Outcome of elbow surgery in professional baseball players. *Am J Sports Med* 1995;23:407-413.

5. Kamineni S, Hirahara H, Pomianowski S, et al: Partial posteromedial olecranon resection: A kinematic study. *J Bone Joint Surg Am* 2003;85:1005-1011.

   In a study of the kinematic effects of increasing valgus and varus torque and posteromedial olecranon resection, sequential partial resection of the posteromedial aspect of the olecranon resulted in stepwise increases in valgus angulation with valgus torque. Although no single critical amount of olecranon resection was identified, valgus angulation of the elbow increased in association with all resections, with a marked increase associated with a 9-mm resection. Bone removal from the olecranon should therefore be limited to osteophytes.

6. Kamineni S, ElAttrache NS, O'Driscoll LW, et al: Medial collateral ligament strain with partial posteromedial olecranon resection: A biomechanical study. *J Bone Joint Surg Am* 2004;86:2424-2430.

   Using an electronic tracking device in seven cadaver elbows, the strain in the anterior bundle of the UCL was found to increase with increasing flexion angle, valgus torque, and olecranon resection beyond 3 mm. The nonuniform change in strain suggests that resections of the posteromedial aspect of the olecranon of more than 3 mm may jeopardize the anterior bundle.

7. Ahmad CS, Park MC, ElAttrache NS: Elbow medial ulnar collateral ligament insufficiency alters posteromedial olecranon contact. *Am J Sports Med* 2004;32:1607-1612.

   Seven elbow cadaver specimens were tested with partial and full tears of the medial UCL, using pressure-sensitive film placed in the posteromedial compartment. The UCL altered contact area and pressure between the posteromedial trochlea and olecranon. This finding helps explain the development of posteromedial osteophytes.

8. Fleisig GS, Kingsley DS, Loftice JW, et al: Kinetic comparison among the fastball, curveball, change-up, and slider in collegiate baseball pitchers. *Am J Sports Med* 2006;34:423-430.

   In a study of 21 healthy collegiate pitchers using a high-speed automated digitizing system, elbow force was found to be less in the change-up than in other pitches, and elbow varus torque was greater in the fastball and curveball pitches than in the change-up. Elbow flexion torque was greater in the curveball than in the change-up. The curveball and change-up were found to have different kinematics from the fastball, as in earlier studies. The resultant joint loads were similar in the fastball and curveball. The low kinetics in the change-up implies that it is the safest.

9. O'Driscoll SW, Lawton RL, Smith AM: The "moving valgus stress test" for medial collateral ligament tears of the elbow. *Am J Sports Med* 2005;33:231-239.

Twenty-one patients underwent surgical intervention for medial elbow pain caused by medial collateral ligament insufficiency or another abnormality of chronic valgus overload. The presurgical moving valgus stress test was highly sensitive (100%, 17 of 17 patients) and specific (75%, 3 of 4 patients) compared with assessment of the medial collateral ligament by surgical exploration or arthroscopic valgus stress testing.

10. Conway JE, Jobe FW, Glousman RE, Pink M: Medial instability of the elbow in throwing athletes: Treatment by repair or reconstruction of the ulnar collateral ligament. *J Bone Joint Surg Am* 1992;74:67-83.

11. Ellenbecker TS, Mattalino AJ, Elam EA, Caplinger RA: Medial elbow joint laxity in professional baseball pitchers: A bilateral comparison using stress radiography. *Am J Sports Med* 1998;26:420-424.

12. Hang DW, Chao CM, Hang YS: A clinical and roentgenographic study of Little League elbow. *Am J Sports Med* 2004;32:79-84.

Of 343 Little League players, 58% of pitchers, 63% of catchers, and 47% of fielders had soreness. Radiographic examination revealed hypertrophy of the medial humeral epicondyle. Changes in the medial epicondyle may be an adaptive physiologic reaction to the excessive valgus stress of throwing.

13. Farsetti P, Potenza V, Caterini R, Ippolito E: Long-term results of treatment of fractures of the medial humeral epicondyle in children. *J Bone Joint Surg Am* 2001;83:1299-1305.

Forty-two patients with an isolated fracture of the medial humeral epicondyle with displacement of > 5 mm at average age 12 years were evaluated at average age 45 years. The long-term results of nonsurgical treatment were similar to the results of open reduction and internal fixation. Nonunion of the epicondylar fragment, which was present in most patients treated only with a cast, did not adversely affect the functional results. Surgical excision of the medial epicondylar fragment should be avoided because the long-term results are poor.

14. Rettig AC, Sherrill C, Snead DS, Mendler JC, Mieling P: Nonoperative treatment of ulnar collateral ligament injuries in throwing athletes. *Am J Sports Med* 2001;29:15-17.

Thirty-one throwing athletes with UCL injuries underwent nonsurgical treatment that included a minimum of 3 months' rest with rehabilitation exercises. Forty-two percent returned to their previous level of competition at an average 24.5 weeks after diagnosis. Patient history and physical examination were not useful in predicting the success of nonsurgical treatment.

15. Thompson WH, Jobe FW, Yocum LA, Pink MM: Ulnar collateral ligament reconstruction in athletes: Muscle-splitting approach without transposition of the ulnar nerve. *J Shoulder Elbow Surg* 2001;10: 152-157.

Eighty-three highly competitive athletes with medial elbow instability underwent reconstruction of the anterior band of the UCL without transposition of the ulnar nerve, using a muscle-splitting approach. After surgery, 5% had transient ulnar nerve symptoms that were resolved with nonsurgical treatment. At 2- to 4-year follow-up, 93% of those who had not had an earlier surgical procedure had an excellent result. All were able to return to their sport. The modified procedure yielded a decreased complication rate and improved outcomes.

16. Dodson CC, Thomas A, Dines JS, Nho SJ, Williams RJ, Altchek DW: Medial ulnar collateral ligament reconstruction of the elbow in throwing athletes. *Am J Sports Med* 2006;34:1926-1932.

One hundred consecutive overhead throwing athletes were treated with surgical reconstruction using the docking technique. All patients underwent routine arthroscopic assessment, and the ulnar nerve was transposed in 22. At a mean 36-month follow-up, 90% were able to compete at the same or a higher level of sports. Level of evidence: IV.

17. Paletta GA Jr, Wright RW: The modified docking procedure for elbow ulnar collateral ligament reconstruction: 2-year follow-up in elite throwers. *Am J Sports Med* 2006;34:1594-1598.

Twenty-five elite professional or collegiate baseball players were assessed at a minimum 2 years after elbow UCL reconstruction using the modified docking procedure with a four-strand palmaris longus graft. Twenty-three (92%) were able to return to their preinjury level of competition. One had a transient postsurgical ulnar nerve neurapraxia, and one had a stress fracture of the ulnar bone bridge after a full return to pitching. Level of evidence: IV.

18. Rettig AC, Ebben JR: Anterior subcutaneous transfer of the ulnar nerve in the athlete. *Am J Sports Med* 1993;21:836-839.

19. Baumgarten TE, Andrews JR, Satterwhite YE: The arthroscopic classification and treatment of osteochondritis dissecans of the capitellum. *Am J Sports Med* 1998;26:520-523.

20. Furukawa T, Eyre DR, Koide S, et al: Biochemical studies on repair cartilage resurfacing experimental defects in the rabbit knee. *J Bone Joint Surg Am* 1980; 62:79-89.

21. Nakagawa Y, Matsusue Y, Ikeda N, Asada Y, Nakamura T: Osteochondral grafting and arthroplasty for

end-stage osteochondritis dissecans of the capitellum: A case report and review of the literature. *Am J Sports Med* 2001;29:650-655.

Mosaicplasty combined with a distal humeral osteotomy using an open approach is described in a 13-year-old male baseball catcher with a large capitellar lesion that allowed engagement of the radial head. Ten months after surgery, plain radiographs showed osteotomy union and disappearance of the capitellar lesion.

22. Kim DH, Gambardella RA, ElAttrache NS, Yocum LA, Jobe FW: Arthroscopic treatment of posterolateral elbow impingement from lateral synovial plicae in throwing athletes and golfers. *Am J Sports Med* 2006;34:438-444.

Nine male and three female patients, mean age 21.6 years, included seven baseball pitchers, two softball players, and three golfers. All patients had posterolateral elbow pain, 58% had clicking or catching, and 25% had swelling or effusion. Mean time from symptom onset to treatment was 9.25 months, and average follow-up time was 33.8 months. A thickened synovial lateral plica was débrided in all patients. Ninety-two percent reported an excellent outcome with a mean elbow score of 92.5. The average time from surgery to return to competitive play was 4.8 months. One patient had medial elbow instability that later required reconstructive surgery.

# Chapter 43

# Acute, Recurrent, and Chronic Elbow Instability

April D. Armstrong, MD, BSc(PT), MSc, FRCSC

## Introduction

During the past several years, more comprehensive knowledge of elbow anatomy and biomechanical principles has led to the ability to obtain a stable concentric reduction of the elbow and to restore a functional range of motion. It is now better understood that the bony and soft-tissue constraints of the elbow are equally important in providing stability to the elbow. Recent studies have delineated surgical approaches that are consistent with biomechanical principles, and new physical examination tests have advanced the diagnosis of recurrent instability.

## Elbow Constraints

The elbow joint is highly congruous and therefore inherently stable. Its stability is provided by both static and dynamic constraints. The three primary static constraints are the ulnohumeral bony articulation, the anterior bundle of the medial collateral ligament (MCL), and the lateral collateral ligament (LCL) complex. The elbow is considered stable if these three constraints are intact. The secondary static constraints include the capsule, the radiocapitellar articulation, and the common flexor and extensor origins (Figure 1). The capsule has most of its stabilizing effect when the elbow is extended.[1] All muscles that cross the elbow joint apply a compressive force that contributes to dynamic stability, although the primary dynamic constraints are the anconeus, triceps, and brachialis muscles.

## Acute Elbow Dislocation

An acute elbow dislocation can be simple or complex. A simple elbow dislocation does not involve osseous injury. However, a dislocation with a small osseous fracture fragment at the epicondyles or coronoid that does not affect stability is still considered a simple elbow dislocation. A complex elbow dislocation involves an osseous injury of the distal humerus, proximal ulna, or proximal radius that affects joint stability. Complex elbow dislocations are not as common as simple elbow dislocations, but they are much more difficult to treat.

Complex dislocations have a higher rate of complications related to recurrent instability, stiffness, and post-traumatic arthritis.

### Simple Elbow Dislocation

Simple elbow dislocations are categorized by the direction of the dislocation and the resulting location of the proximal radius and ulna in relation to the distal humerus. A simple dislocation can occur in an anterior, posterior, medial, lateral, or divergent pattern. Posterior dislocations are the most common; they are subdivided into posterior, posterolateral, and posteromedial dislocations. Valgus force on the elbow, combined with axial load, supination, or external rotation of the forearm, may be responsible for a posterolateral dislocation.[2,3] The elbow contacts the ground in an extended position, producing an axial load; as the elbow progressively flexes, an eccentric contraction of the medial head of the triceps produces an external rotation moment at the

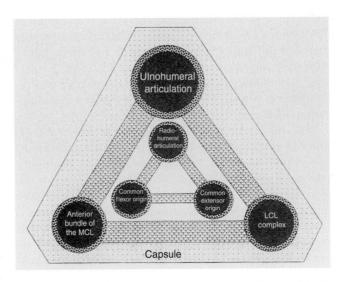

**Figure 1** The static constraints of the elbow can be thought of in terms of the defenses of a fortress. The ulnohumeral articulation, the anterior bundle of the MCL, and the LCL complex are primary constraints. The capsule, the radiocapitellar articulation, and the common flexor and extensor origins are secondary restraints. (*Reproduced with permission from the Mayo Foundation.*)

**Table 1 | Stages of Soft-Tissue Disruption**

| Stage | Description |
|-------|-------------|
| 1 | Disruption of the lateral ulnar collateral ligament (LUCL) |
| 2 | Disruption of the other lateral ligamentous structures and the anterior and posterior capsule |
| 3 | Disruption of the medial portion of the lateral ulnar collateral ligament (MUCL): |
| | 3A Partial MUCL disruption |
| | 3B Complete MUCL disruption |
| | 3C Distal humerus stripped of soft tissue; severe instability resulting in dislocation or subluxation |

*(Adapted with permission from O'Driscoll SW: Acute, recurrent, and chronic elbow instabilities, in Norris TR (ed): Orthopaedic Knowledge Update: Shoulder and Elbow, ed. 2. Rosemont, IL, American Academy of Orthopaedic Surgeons, 2002, pp 313-324.)*

ulnohumeral joint (supination), while an internal rotation moment on the humerus is created by the shoulder internal rotators and adductors. The mechanical axis of the elbow joint is displaced medially, creating a valgus moment on the elbow joint. A recent biomechanical study suggested that a combination of axial load, external rotation of the forearm, and varus leads to posterior dislocation.[4] This finding implies that more than one mechanism can cause posterior dislocation.

The nature of the soft-tissue injury that occurs in elbow dislocation is a subject of controversy. Biomechanical studies found that a progressive circular disruption of soft tissues occurs during a posterolateral elbow dislocation, starting laterally and progressing medially; the anterior bundle of the MCL is either disrupted or left intact.[2] The three-stage spectrum of instability outlined in Table 1 conflicts with clinical and biomechanical studies findings, which indicate that the MCL is disrupted in all posterior elbow dislocations.[1,3,5] This conclusion suggests the possibility of more than one soft-tissue injury pattern in an elbow dislocation. Regardless of the pattern, formulating an appropriate treatment plan and rehabilitation protocol requires understanding the implications of the patient's soft-tissue injury.

The treatment algorithm for a simple elbow dislocation has shifted from prolonged immobilization toward early range-of-motion exercises to minimize postinjury contracture (Figure 2). The muscle-loading forces of the elbow tend to stabilize the joint to protect the soft-tissue injury; the bony architecture itself is highly congruous.

After reduction of an elbow dislocation, the treatment plan is dictated by the stability of the joint, as assessed through the full range of motion. Flexion and extension should be performed in pronation, supination, and neutral rotation. After a posterior elbow dislocation, the elbow usually becomes more unstable as it approaches extension. Postreduction radiographs in two planes, taken with the elbow at 90° and with the appro-

priate forearm rotation, can be used to confirm a concentric reduction. Widening of the ulnohumeral joint may indicate a persistent subluxation of the joint. Static widening of the ulnohumeral joint seen on a lateral radiograph is called the drop sign.[6]

Because of the compressive forces of muscle loading, a dislocated ulnohumeral joint often anatomically reduces itself when the joint is actively mobilized. If necessary, a congruous joint can be restored by changing the forearm position, splinting, or surgical treatment. A prolonged incongruous alignment predisposes the joint to recurrent instability and arthrosis. If the LCL complex has been disrupted but the MCL is intact, the elbow may be more stable with the forearm in pronation.[7-9] If the LCL is intact and the MCL is ruptured, the elbow may be more stable with the forearm in supination.[9,10] If both ligaments are disrupted, the elbow may be placed in neutral rotation to protect both the medial and lateral ligamentous structures. Widening of the ulnohumeral joint may indicate the presence of an entrapped osteochondral fragment or entrapped soft tissue, both of which require surgical intervention. A posterior impaction fracture of the capitellum is sometimes detected, but it does not affect the stability of the joint. It is analogous to the Hill-Sachs lesion in the shoulder.[11] If the elbow is found to be stable on examination and if AP and lateral plain radiographs show a concentric reduction, the patient's elbow may be placed in a sling and early active rehabilitation initiated. If the elbow is unstable with extension beyond 90°, it should be splinted at 90°, with appropriate forearm rotation, for 5 to 7 days. Surgical treatment should be considered if stability cannot be achieved with 60° or more of elbow flexion because using an extension block is difficult with greater flexion and carries a high risk of flexion contracture.

At the first follow-up appointment, the splint should be removed and active range-of-motion exercises initiated. Active motion has been shown to provide compressive stability to the joint. In contrast, passive motion can accentuate the instability and increase the risk of heterotopic ossification. A hinged brace with an appropriate extension block and forearm rotation is used to allow motion throughout the stable arc. The extension block is typically used for a period of 3 to 4 weeks, and radiographs are taken weekly to confirm that the reduction is stable and anatomic. The extension blocking is progressively decreased, so that after 6 weeks the patient has full extension. As soon as mobilization of the elbow begins, forearm pronation and supination with the elbow at 90° can be safely performed to prevent a rotational contracture.

## Complex Elbow Dislocation

Ligament repair is important in the treatment of a complex elbow fracture-dislocation. Critical soft tissues or

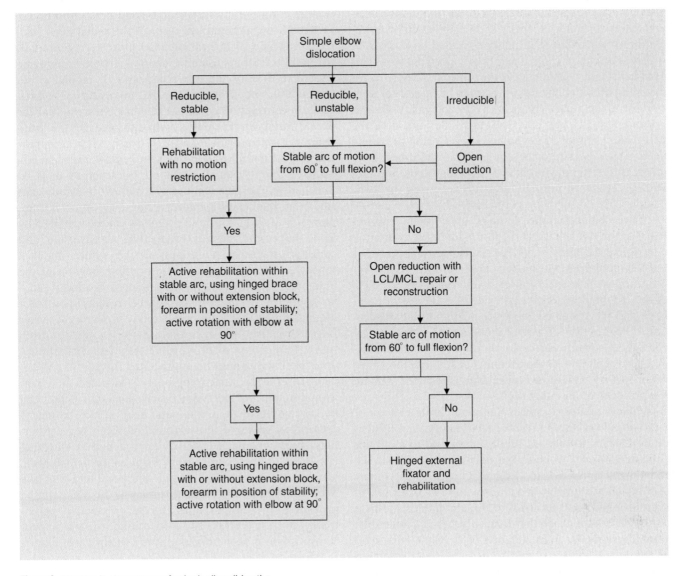

**Figure 2** Algorithm for the treatment of a simple elbow dislocation.

cartilage may be injured, including the LCL, MCL, and common extensor and flexor pronator origins. Osteochondral injury to the capitellum and trochlea may have occurred. Recent research has focused on the terrible triad and varus posteromedial rotatory types of complex elbow instability. Both bony and soft-tissue injury associated with these dislocations must be addressed to limit the risk of recurrent instability, stiffness, and late arthrosis.

### Terrible Triad Dislocation
The terrible triad injury is an elbow dislocation with a radial head and coronoid fracture. Recent biomechanical studies assessed the interplay between bony and soft-tissue damage in the terrible triad complex and confirmed the importance of the radial head as an important secondary valgus stabilizer.[12] Resection of a radial head with an intact MCL does not create pure val-

gus instability.[1,13] However, gross valgus instability results if the radial head is removed and the MCL is deficient, which is often the case in a terrible triad injury. Replacing the radial head can improve valgus stability but does not restore the stability found with a native radial head and MCL insufficiency.[13-16] Internal fixation of a radial head fracture improves joint stability, but only if the joint can be fixed with a construct that is as stable and as strong as the native radial head.[16] Otherwise, a radial head replacement should be performed, taking care to restore the normal length of the radius to maximize its stabilizing benefits and avoiding overstuffing or understuffing the radiocapitellar joint.[17] Repair or reconstruction of the anterior bundle of the MCL can restore a valgus stability almost equivalent to that of an uninjured elbow.[13]

The radial head may act as a varus and external rotatory stabilizer of the elbow, and isolated radial head resection may lead to subluxation of the joint under varus and external rotatory loads.[4,14,18] In cadaver elbows, simulation of a terrible triad injury by radial head excision with a deficient LCL significantly worsened the varus and external rotatory instability of the joint. Replacing the radial head provided increased varus and external rotatory stability to the joint, although considerable laxity was still present. Stability was not restored to the joint until the LCL was repaired.[18] This finding suggests that the radial head is an important constraint to varus and external rotatory forces, although it is less important than the LCL. Specific attention must be given to repairing the LCL complex after a radial head fracture.[4,14,18-20]

Biomechanical studies revealed the combined importance of the radial head and coronoid fracture present in a terrible triad injury.[21,22] If the radial head was removed but the medial and lateral ligaments were left intact, significant posterolateral rotatory laxity was created. If 30% of the coronoid was then removed, the joint was destabilized and the result was complete ulnohumeral dislocation. Implantation of a rigid metal radial head without coronoid reconstruction restored stability to the joint. Radial head replacement alone could not stabilize the elbow when 50% to 70% of the coronoid was resected, despite the presence of an intact MCL and LCL.[22]

Clinical outcome studies analyzed the use of treatment algorithms in the terrible triad injury, with a focus on developing a standard surgical approach to minimize complications.[23,24] It is increasingly recognized that the radial head, coronoid, and LCL play a key role in elbow stability after a terrible triad injury. The risk of recurrent joint instability and arthrosis of the ulnohumeral joint is high.[24-26] Resection of the radial head is not advisable; the radiocapitellar joint supports 60% of the axial load of the elbow joint,[27-29] and with radial head resection this load is transferred to the ulnohumeral joint. The development of ulnohumeral arthrosis is thus accelerated, although the extent to which the arthrosis is associated with the initial traumatic event is not known.

The use of a standard surgical approach for a terrible triad injury results in improved stability and decreased arthrosis[23,30-32] (Figure 3). The standard approach is to repair the damaged tissues in sequential order from deep to superficial; that is, from coronoid–anterior capsule to radial head, LCL, common extensor origin, MCL, flexor-pronator origin, and hinged external fixator. A posterior midline incision or combined lateral and medial incision can be used; the posterior midline incision is considered more versatile because it allows access to both medial and lateral structures and may carry less risk to the cutaneous nerves.[33] Thick fasciocutaneous flaps are elevated to expose the Kocher interval. The common extensor origin and LCL complex are often avulsed from the lateral condyle, and working through injured tissues may help to preserve vital soft-tissue restraints.

The coronoid fracture is addressed first. Often it can be fixed using an approach through the radial head fracture, especially if the radial head must be replaced. A coronoid fracture is usually classified as type I, involving less than 10% of the coronoid; type II, involving between 10% and 50%; or type III, involving more than 50%. In an isolated coronoid fracture, the potential for elbow instability increases with the size of the fragment.[21,34] Even a small coronoid fracture has an important impact on elbow stability if the elbow has been dislocated.[23,24,35] A small coronoid tip fracture may be attached to the anterior capsule, and the anterior capsule is an important stabilizer if the dislocation is complex.[36,37] A small coronoid fragment can be repaired by using lasso-type sutures to encircle the capsule and coronoid fragment, then passing the suture material through drill holes in the corresponding portion of the ulna and tying it over the subcutaneous border. A similar approach can be used for a larger comminuted coronoid fragment that cannot be fixed with screws. A larger fragment is fixed anatomically using screw fixation from the posterior ulna to capture the fragment. If the coronoid fragment cannot be approached through the radial head, a separate medial approach is required. A flexor-pronator splitting technique can be used. Dissection can be carried through a traumatic rent in the tissues, if present, to preserve the surrounding soft tissues. Alternatively, the medial side can be approached by elevating the flexor carpi ulnaris from distal to proximal while protecting the insertion of the anterior bundle of the MCL on the sublime tubercle. Injury to the MCL can be prevented by discontinuing further dissection proximally after the fracture site is identified. An ulnar nerve transposition is recommended if the flexor carpi ulnaris is elevated.

Elevation of the flexor carpi ulnaris is often necessary to fix a coronoid fracture of the anteromedial facet, which has recently been identified as critical to the stability of the elbow.[35] The fracture involves the sublime tubercle in addition to the coronoid. Because the anterior bundle of the MCL is attached to the sublime tubercle, the instability pattern is significantly worse than with a coronoid fracture alone. The congruence of the ulnohumeral joint is more significantly disrupted because the fracture involves the entire anteromedial facet, and the MCL is insufficient as a result of the involvement of the sublime tubercle. A coronoid fracture involving the anteromedial facet is best identified on an AP radiograph of the elbow. Anteromedial plate fixation is often required to provide rigid fixation of a large fracture fragment and restore stability.

The radial head is addressed after fixation of the coronoid. A strong, stable anatomic fixation of the radial head is preferred. Small fragments (< 25% of the circumference of the radial head) can be excised if they do not affect the stability of the joint, leaving the residual radial head

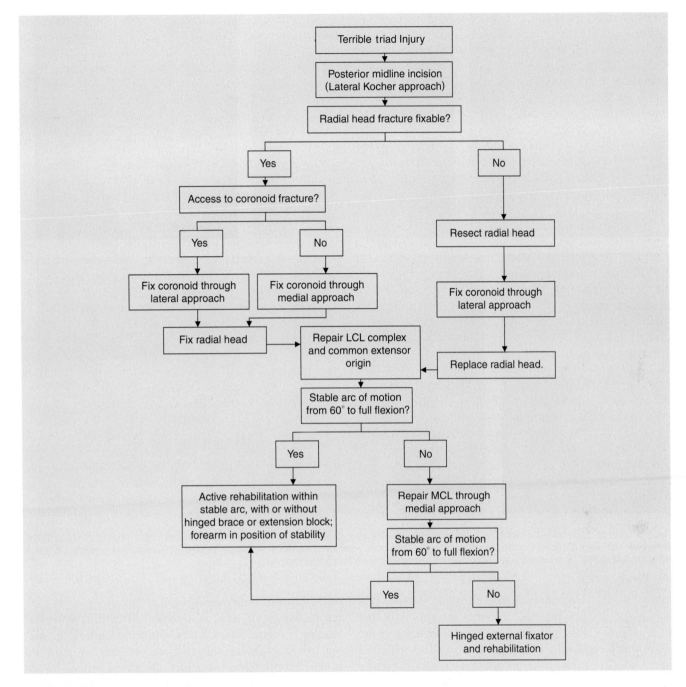

**Figure 3**  Algorithm for the treatment of a terrible triad injury.

intact.[19] If fixation is not possible, the radial head should be replaced using a metal implant. The lateral reconstruction is completed by repairing the LCL at the isometric point on the humerus and repairing the common extensor origin to the lateral condyle.[38] These repairs usually result in stability of the elbow, although the MCL and flexor-pronator origin should be repaired if necessary to achieve stability. Often a rent in the flexor-pronator muscle group extends downward to the MCL complex. Tissue for repair may not be available, unless the MCL is avulsed from its origin or insertion. If adequate stability cannot be restored

after these repairs, the use of a hinged external fixator is recommended.

After surgery, the elbow is placed at 90° in a well-padded splint, with the forearm positioned for maximal stability. Early range-of-motion exercises are initiated, using a protocol similar to that used for a simple elbow dislocation.

### Varus Posteromedial Rotatory Instability
Varus posteromedial rotatory instability was first described only recently.[35,39] It is characterized as either a

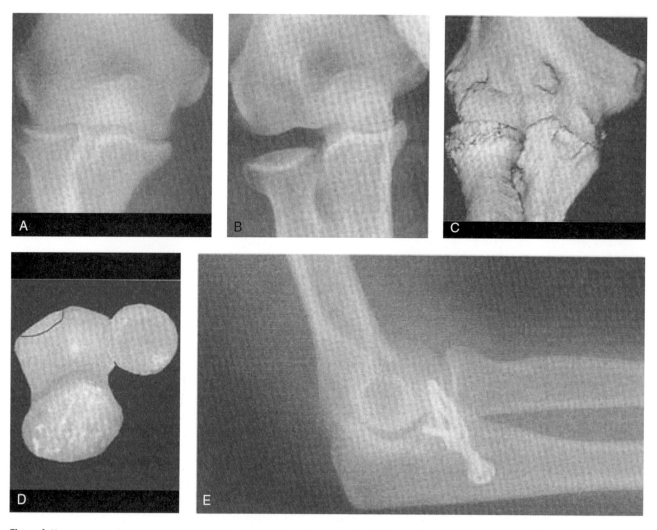

**Figure 4** Varus posteromedial rotatory instability. **A,** Stress radiograph showing varus opening. **B,** Stress radiograph showing apparent medial narrowing caused by rotatory ulnohumeral subluxation. **C,** CT with three-dimensional reconstruction showing the anteromedial location of the fracture. **D,** Schematic illustration of the fracture. **E,** Lateral radiograph showing anatomic reduction and rigid fixation. (*Reproduced with permission from the Mayo Foundation.*)

minimally displaced anteromedial coronoid fracture or a comminuted coronoid fracture with disruption of the LCL complex. This injury results in incongruence of the joint, which can lead to early posttraumatic arthritis. Patients who appear to have an isolated coronoid fracture must be evaluated for potential joint instability or lack of congruence. Because only subtle radiographic findings may be present, such as asymmetric loss of the medial joint space on an AP view, a high level of investigational vigilance is required[39] (Figure 4).

A new classification system for fractures of the coronoid incorporates the clinically important anteromedial fragment (Figure 5). A fracture of the coronoid tip does not extend into the sublime tubercle or coronoid body; an anteromedial fracture extends into the anterior half of the sublime tubercle; and a basal fracture involves the coronoid body and extends through more than 50% of its height. The anteromedial subtype is the fracture pattern of interest in varus posteromedial rotatory instability. The

mechanism of injury is believed to involve a varus posteromedial rotation (pronation of the forearm) with axial loading.[35] As the elbow flexes with axial loading, the medial trochlea rides up onto the anteromedial coronoid and is sheared off. After the injury, the elbow articulates incongruously under axial and varus stress, with point loading at the fracture site on the anteromedial ulna. This pattern of articulation leads to early arthrosis.

An AP radiograph may reveal asymmetric loss of the medial joint space and malalignment of the elbow in a varus position. The radiohumeral joint line may be widened if significant LCL disruption is present. A lateral radiograph may reveal a double crescent sign, in which the depressed anteromedial fragment appears as a double subchondral density. CT can be used to confirm the diagnosis.

Varus posteromedial rotatory instability should be treated by anatomically reducing the anteromedial fragment using a medial approach. An anteromedial

| Fracture Type | Subtype | Description |
|---|---|---|
| Tip | 1 | ≤ 2 mm of coronoid height |
| | 2 | > 2 mm of coronoid height |
| | | |
| Anteromedial | 1 | Anteromedial rim |
| | 2 | Anteromedial rim and tip |
| | 3 | Anteromedial rim and sublime tubercle (± tip) |
| | | |
| Basal | 1 | Coronoid body and base |
| | 2 | Transolecranon basal coronoid fracture |

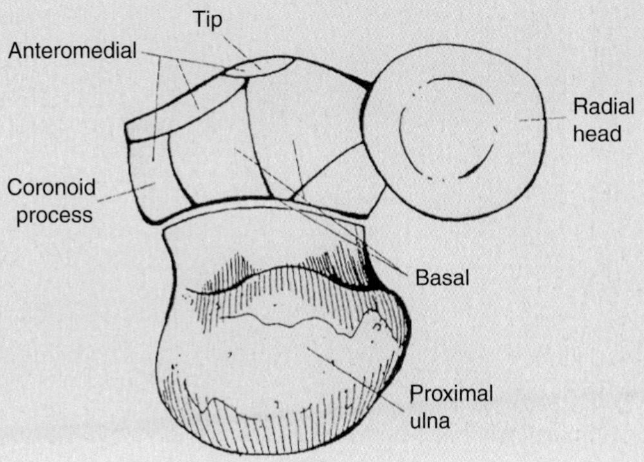

**Figure 5** The O'Driscoll coronoid fracture classification system. *(Reproduced from O'Driscoll SW, Jupiter JB, Cohen MS, Ring D, McKee MD: Difficult elbow fractures: Pearls and pitfalls. Instr Course Lect 2003;52:113-134).*

buttress plate is usually required for fixation. An LCL repair is critical to decrease the varus load to the elbow, and ulnar nerve transposition should be considered. If stability is not achieved, the use of a hinged external fixator should be considered.

## Recurrent Elbow Instability
### Posterolateral Rotatory Instability
The term posterolateral rotatory instability refers to recurrent subluxation of the elbow caused by injury to the LCL complex. The LCL complex is made up of the lateral ulnar collateral ligament (LUCL), the radial collateral ligament, the annular ligament, and the accessory collateral ligament. The exact role of each component of the LCL complex is a subject of controversy, although the traditional belief is that the LUCL plays an important role in posterolateral rotatory instability.[40-46] Recently, it has been suggested that the LCL complex functions as one structure, and neither the LUCL nor

the radial collateral ligament has a separate stabilizing function.[41,43] Because the LCL is under continual stress during everyday activities, an insufficiency of this ligament can be disabling. In contrast, patients often are unaware of an MCL insufficiency, unless a sports or occupational activity subjects the elbow to a repetitive valgus load.

Injury to the LCL complex usually results from trauma, such as a fall onto an outstretched arm; an iatrogenic injury, most likely from an aggressive lateral epicondylitis release; or a long-standing cubitus varus deformity, such as a malunion after a childhood supracondylar fracture.[47,48] The injury causes laxity of the LCL and the lateral capsule, which allows posterior subluxation of the radial head when the forearm is supinated, the elbow is slightly flexed, and valgus stress is applied. In this position, the ulnohumeral joint rotates and the radiocapitellar joint is compressed to allow posterior subluxation of the radial head. Supination

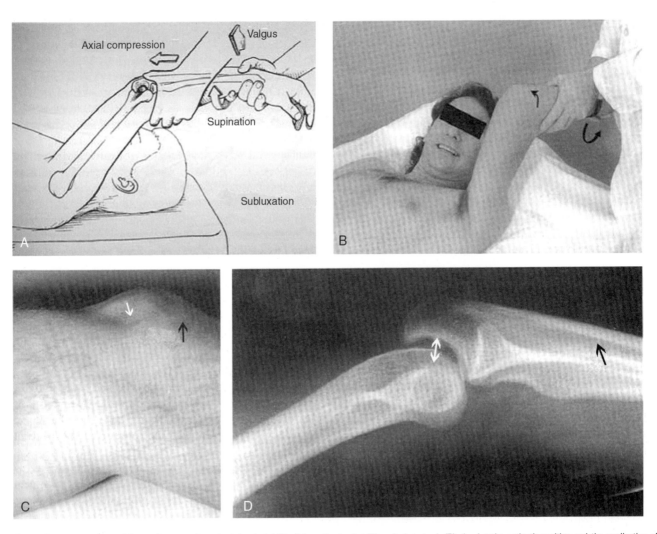

**Figure 6** The lateral pivot-shift test for posterolateral rotatory instability. Schematic drawing **(A)** and photograph **(B)** showing the patient's position and the application of valgus supinated force, causing subluxation. **C,** Photograph showing the rotation of the radius and ulna off of the humerus (*dark arrow*) and the skin dimpled behind the radial head (*light arrow*). **D,** Lateral stress radiograph showing the radius and ulna supinated away from the humerus (*dark arrow*) and leaving a gap in the ulnohumeral articulation and the radial head posterior to the capitellum (*light arrow*). (A and D, reproduced from O'Driscoll SW, Jupiter JB, Cohen MS, Ring D, McKee MD: Difficult elbow fractures: Pearls and pitfalls. Instr Course Lect 2003;52:113-134; B and C, reproduced from Frymoyer JW [ed]: Orthopaedic Knowledge Update 4. Rosemont, IL, American Academy of Orthopaedic Surgeons, 1993, pp 335-352.)

stresses the LCL complex, and slight flexion unlocks the olecranon from the olecranon fossa and allows the ulnohumeral joint to rotate.

Patients with posterolateral rotatory instability describe a painful locking, catching, or clicking of the elbow, particularly during extension or weight bearing. They also may describe a sensation of instability. The pivot-shift test of the elbow is traditionally used to detect posterolateral rotatory instability (Figure 6). The patient is supine, the arm is raised overhead, the forearm is supinated with the elbow extended, and a valgus supinated force is applied to the elbow. In this position, the radial head is subluxated. The elbow is slowly flexed while the valgus supinated force is maintained. As the elbow is flexed, the radiocapitellar joint is eventually reduced; dimpling of the skin may appear before the joint is reduced. A clunk or subluxation usually does not oc-

cur if the patient is awake. This test is uncomfortable for an awake patient, who may show apprehension, and is more reliable if the patient is under anesthesia. The key radiographic findings are posterolateral subluxation or dislocation of the radial head, with widening of the ulnohumeral joint as the radius and ulna rotate as a unit away from the distal humerus; the semilunar notch of the ulna is rotated away from the trochlea. The proximal radioulnar joint has a normal appearance. The subluxation occurs immediately before continued elbow flexion causes joint reduction.

Three other tests for posterolateral rotatory instability are available and may be more clinically useful. The posterolateral drawer test is similar to the Lachman test for the knee. With the elbow flexed at 90°, the proximal forearm is forced from an anterior to a posterolateral translational direction in an attempt to subluxate the

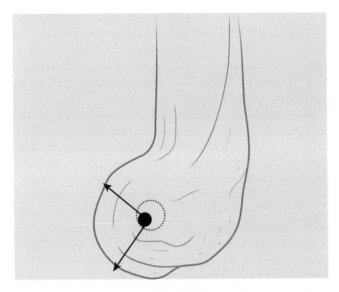

**Figure 7** The burr hole should be drilled slightly posterior and proximal to the isometric center of rotation to keep the graft tensioned in extension.

joint. The test is positive if subluxation is observed or the patient reports a sensation of instability. For the floor push-up sign, the patient is asked to push upward from a prone position with the forearms maximally supinated and pronated. The test is positive if instability occurs or if the patient is reluctant to fully extend the elbows with the forearm supinated but not with the forearm pronated. The chair push-up test requires the patient to sit with the elbows flexed at 90°, the forearms supinated, and shoulders abducted beyond shoulder width. The patient uses the hands to push up from the chair armrest and, in a positive test, shows apprehension or instability as the elbow is extended. The chair push-up test was reported to have greater sensitivity than the traditional posterolateral rotatory instability test in a comparison of patients who were not under anesthesia.[49,50] In the relocation test, which is a modification of the chair push-up test, the examiner's thumb is placed over the radial head to prevent posterolateral subluxation while the chair push-up test is performed. The patient reports decreased pain and instability as the examiner pushes over the radial head.[49]

Reconstruction is the preferred treatment to correct a chronic symptomatic LCL insufficiency. In the original procedure, a tendon graft was passed through two drill holes bridging the crista supinatoris on the ulna and three drill holes in the humerus, the most important of which was at the isometric point. The graft was passed in a figure-of-8 fashion and sutured to itself.[46] In the docking technique, similar drill holes in the ulna are used, but both tendon ends are docked at the humeral isometric point of insertion for the LCL, and sutures are passed through smaller drill holes to tie over a bone bridge at the lateral supracondylar ridge.[51] The single strand technique uses only one drill hole at the crista su-

pinatoris and another drill hole at the humeral isometric point; fixation is accomplished using either interference screws or sutures tied over bone tunnels.[52,53] The triceps tendon technique either leaves the ulna insertion intact and weaves the tendon through the capsule to the humeral isometric point or uses the middle fascia of the triceps as a tendon graft for single strand reconstruction.[54-56]

Only limited studies of LCL reconstruction have been published, reporting on different techniques. Long-term outcome data are required to determine the feasibility of these techniques. A retrospective review of different LCL reconstruction techniques at a mean 6-year follow-up found better results in patients whose primary symptom was instability rather than pain. The results were more predictable if the posterolateral rotatory instability had a traumatic cause rather than an iatrogenic or unknown cause.[57]

Regardless of the technique, the isometric placement of the humeral attachment is critical in LCL reconstruction. The isometric point is at the center of the capitellum, which is distal to the lateral epicondyle. At the point of isometry, the distance to all articular margins of the capitellum is equal. To keep the graft tensioned with elbow extension, the burr hole at the isometric point should be drilled so that the isometric center of rotation is at the anterodistal edge of the hole. This is the position most likely to provoke posterolateral rotatory instability (Figure 7).

All of the reconstruction techniques are premised on the inadequacy of a primary repair to achieve posterolateral rotatory stability. Often the quality of the LCL tissue is inadequate, and an augmented reconstruction provides better results than a primary repair alone. Ligament augmentation has been described using a hamstring (semitendinosus, gracilis), Achilles, triceps fascia, plantaris, palmaris, or long toe extensor tendon graft or a ligament augmentation device.[51-56]

### Valgus Elbow Instability

Valgus elbow instability is much less common than posterolateral rotatory instability. It most often occurs in throwing athletes, especially baseball pitchers, as a result of repetitive overuse. Some athletes describe hearing a popping sound when the ligament completely ruptured. Valgus elbow instability can also develop as a result of trauma, such as simple elbow dislocation. Traditionally, it has been considered clinically insignificant. Posttraumatic valgus elbow instability may be more common than has been believed, and it may have a more significant association with elbow arthrosis. Long-term follow-up studies after a simple elbow dislocation found that 15% to 35% of patients had chronic valgus elbow instability; 50% of these patients had elbow arthrosis.[58-60]

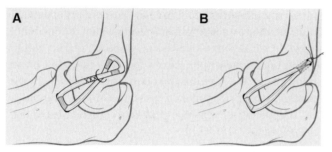

**Figure 8** Traditional techniques for MCL reconstruction. **A,** Figure-of-8 technique. **B,** Docking technique.

MCL insufficiency is difficult to diagnose, and the diagnosis relies heavily on the patient's history and physical examination results. A throwing athlete has medial elbow pain, particularly during the late acceleration phase of throwing, as well as diminished throwing accuracy and velocity. The specific physical examination tests for valgus instability include the valgus stress test, the milking maneuver, and the moving valgus stress test,[61] which is described in Chapter 42. Stress radiography, MRI, and arthroscopy may also be useful in establishing the diagnosis, and interest in the use of ultrasonography as a diagnostic tool has increased.[62-66]

The MCL is composed of the anterior bundle, the posterior bundle, and the transverse ligament. The anterior bundle of the MCL is the primary valgus stabilizer of the elbow. MCL insufficiency may be linked to posteromedial elbow pain; this condition is known as valgus extension overload. Biomechanical cadaver studies found an association between MCL insufficiency and increased contact forces at the posteromedial compartment of the elbow.[67,68] Osteophytes, loose bodies, soft-tissue inflammation, and swelling may develop. The patient may describe a joint effusion, locking, crepitus, and decreased range of motion at the end of the extension range. Radiography, CT, or MRI can reveal loose bodies or osteophytes on the borders of the posterior fossa. Loose bodies and osteophytes have been found in asymptomatic throwers, and therefore the natural history of this pathology is unclear.[69] If nonsurgical treatment is unsuccessful in a symptomatic patient, a conservative arthroscopic resection of the posteromedial osteophytes can be used. To prevent increased strain on the MCL, the bone resection should be limited to osteophytes and leave all native olecranon bone intact.[68,70,71] Although the anterior bundle of the MCL is not truly isometric, its fibers are almost isometric. The isometric point is located close to the anatomic axis of rotation at the center of the trochlea.[72,73] It is important to identify this point during anatomic reconstruction of the ligament.

Every patient should initially be treated nonsurgically. The flexor-pronator mass, particularly the flexor carpi ulnaris, acts as an important dynamic stabiliz-er,[74,75] and strengthening of this musculature is an important component of rehabilitation. No history or physical examination findings have been determined to predict the success of nonsurgical treatment. In a study of 31 throwing athletes, 42% had returned to their sport at an average of 25 weeks after diagnosis.[76]

If nonsurgical treatment is unsuccessful, MCL reconstruction is preferred to primary surgical repair. The original MCL reconstruction technique used detachment of the flexor-pronator mass, ulnar nerve transposition, and a figure-of-8 reconstruction (Figure 8). All currently used techniques, including the docking and interference screw techniques, recognize the importance of the flexor-pronator mass as a dynamic stabilizer, and use a flexor-pronator splitting approach.[77] Ulnar nerve transposition is not routinely advised because of the high incidence of ulnar nerve complications associated with earlier reconstruction techniques.[78] After figure-of-8 reconstruction with a modified muscle-splitting approach and without ulnar nerve transposition, 82% of patients returned to their sport; 93% of those with no earlier surgery returned to their sport.[79]

In the docking technique, a triangular graft configuration is used. Two drill holes bridge the sublime tubercle, and one drill hole is placed at the humeral anatomic point of isometry. Both limbs of the tendon graft are docked into the humeral drill hole, and sutures are brought through separate puncture holes and tied over a bone bridge. The reported rates of return to sport were 90% to 97% at 1-year follow-up.[80-83] The interference screw reconstruction technique, reported only in biomechanical cadaver studies, relies on single drill holes in the ulna and the humerus. Conflicting results have caused concern that early failure can occur at the point of interference screw fixation.[84,85] A biomechanical study compared four reconstruction techniques: figure-of-8, docking, interference screw, and single strand using an Endobutton (Smith & Nephew, Andover, MA) for ulnar fixation.[85] Under a repetitive valgus load, the peak load to failure of all reconstructed ligaments was inferior to that of the native ligament. No difference in strength was identified between the docking and Endobutton constructs, which were found to be stronger than the figure-of-8 and interference screw constructs. Clinical and biomechanical studies support the docking procedure as an effective means of treating MCL insufficiency.

## Chronic Elbow Instability

Chronic elbow instability is uncommon, and it is better prevented than treated. Surgical reconstruction is challenging, and damage to the articular surface often precludes achievement of a full range of motion or pain relief. The patient must understand that the best result is a functional range of motion and moderate pain relief.

Achieving these goals is more likely if the chronic elbow dislocation is simple rather than complex.

The traditional method of repairing a chronic elbow dislocation is open reduction with extensile release of the contracted soft tissues, including the capsule and collateral ligaments, reconstruction of the collateral ligaments and bone injuries, and application of a hinged elbow external fixator. The results have been satisfactory.[86] The hinged external fixator maintains ulnohumeral joint reduction with or without distraction, allows early range of motion, and protects the ligament repair or reconstruction during postsurgical healing. Only small case series have been reported, and it appears that anatomic reduction of the joint with an external fixator unloads the soft-tissue sleeve to allow it to heal in an optimal position.[87]

For a chronic complex elbow dislocation, reconstruction of osseous injuries and repair or reconstruction of the ligaments is important.[88,89] Interposition arthroplasty must be considered if the articular destruction is greater than 50% or if the patient is physiologically too young for a joint arthroplasty. An autologous fascia lata is usually used for the graft; it is sutured to the distal end of the humerus with anchors or drill holes. The results have been inconsistent, and only limited motion gains and pain control can be expected.

## Summary

An elbow dislocation must be taken seriously. The surgeon must analyze the available treatments carefully to achieve a good outcome using a well-organized, stepwise approach. Research will continue to improve knowledge of the intricate relationships between bone and soft tissues and will improve the ability to diagnose and treat elbow instability.

## Annotated References

1.  Deutch SR, Jensen SL, Tyrdal S, Olsen BS, Sneppen O: Elbow joint stability following experimental osteoligamentous injury and reconstruction. *J Shoulder Elbow Surg* 2003;12:466-471.

    In a cadaver model, LCL repair was found to be important in restoring stability to the elbow after a fracture dislocation, even in the absence of radial head resection.

2.  O'Driscoll SW, Morrey BF, Korinek S, An KN: Elbow subluxation and dislocation: A spectrum of instability. *Clin Orthop Relat Res* 1992;280:186-197.

3.  Sojbjerg JO, Helmig P, Kjaersgaard-Andersen P: Dislocation of the elbow: An experimental study of the ligamentous injuries. *Orthopedics* 1989;12:461-463.

4.  Deutch SR, Jensen SL, Olsen BS, Sneppen O: Elbow joint stability in relation to forced external rotation: An experimental study of the osseous constraint. *J Shoulder Elbow Surg* 2003;12:287-292.

    In a cadaver model, elbow flexion, varus stress, and forearm external rotation were found to produce posterior elbow dislocation.

5.  Josefsson PO, Gentz CF, Johnell O, Wendeberg B: Surgical versus non-surgical treatment of ligamentous injuries following dislocation of the elbow joint: A prospective randomized study. *J Bone Joint Surg Am* 1987;69:605-608.

6.  Coonrad RW, Roush TF, Major NM, Basamania CJ: The drop sign, a radiographic warning sign of elbow instability. *J Shoulder Elbow Surg* 2005;14:312-317.

    The authors define the radiographic drop sign, which is a measure of persistent instability of the elbow.

7.  Dunning CE, Zarzour ZD, Patterson SD, Johnson JA, King GJ: Muscle forces and pronation stabilize the lateral ligament deficient elbow. *Clin Orthop Relat Res* 2001;388:118-124.

    In a cadaver model, passive pronation of the forearm or muscle activity was found to stabilize the LCL-deficient elbow.

8.  Jensen SL, Olsen BS, Seki A, Ole Sojbjerg J, Sneppen O: Radiohumeral stability to forced translation: An experimental analysis of the bony constraint. *J Shoulder Elbow Surg* 2002;11:158-165.

    In a cadaver biomechanical model, as much as 60% of the force transmitted through the elbow joint was found to occur at the radiohumeral articulation.

9.  Pomianowski S, O'Driscoll SW, Neale PG, Park MJ, Morrey BF, An KN: The effect of forearm rotation on laxity and stability of the elbow. *Clin Biomech (Bristol, Avon)* 2001;16:401-407.

    A cadaver study found that pronation increases the varus-valgus laxity of the elbow in an MCL-deficient elbow. Forearm rotation should be considered during clinical examination of elbow instability.

10. Armstrong AD, Dunning CE, Faber KJ, Duck TR, Johnson JA, King GJ: Rehabilitation of the medial collateral ligament-deficient elbow: An in vitro biomechanical study. *J Hand Surg Am* 2000;25:1051-1057.

11. Faber KJ, King GJ: Posterior capitellum impression fracture: A case report associated with posterolateral rotatory instability of the elbow. *J Shoulder Elbow Surg* 1998;7:157-159.

12. Morrey BF, Tanaka S, An KN: Valgus stability of the elbow: A definition of primary and secondary constraints. *Clin Orthop Relat Res* 1991;265:187-195.

13. Jensen SL, Deutch SR, Olsen BS, Sojbjerg JO, Sneppen O: Laxity of the elbow after experimental excision of the radial head and division of the medial collateral ligament: Efficacy of ligament repair and radial head prosthetic replacement. A cadaver study. *J Bone Joint Surg Br* 2003;85:1006-1010.

In a cadaver model, repair of the MCL in the elbow was found to be superior to isolated radial head prosthetic replacement in restoring valgus and internal rotatory instability.

14. Beingessner DM, Dunning CE, Gordon KD, Johnson JA, King GJ: The effect of radial head excision and arthroplasty on elbow kinematics and stability. *J Bone Joint Surg Am* 2004;86-A:1730-1739.

    A biomechanical study of the effect on elbow kinematics and stability of radial head excision, with or without radial head replacement, determined that radial head replacement alone is insufficient for the treatment of complex fractures. Collateral ligament injury also must be addressed.

15. King GJ, Zarzour ZD, Rath DA, Dunning CE, Patterson SD, Johnson JA: Metallic radial head arthroplasty improves valgus stability of the elbow. *Clin Orthop Relat Res* 1999;368:114-125.

16. Pomianowski S, Morrey BF, Neale PG, Park MJ, O'Driscoll SW, An KN: Contribution of monoblock and bipolar radial head prostheses to valgus stability of the elbow. *J Bone Joint Surg Am* 2001;83-A:1829-1834.

    In a cadaver model, a bipolar radial head replacement was found to restore valgus stability in an MCL-deficient elbow but to function less well than a native radial head.

17. Van Glabbeek F, Van Riet RP, Baumfeld JA, et al: Detrimental effects of overstuffing or understuffing with a radial head replacement in the medial collateral-ligament deficient elbow. *J Bone Joint Surg Am* 2004;86-A:2629-2635.

    A biomechanical study of the effect on elbow laxity and radiocapitellar joint pressure of lengthening or shortening radial neck length found that restoring normal radial length is important during a radial head replacement.

18. Jensen SL, Olsen BS, Tyrdal S, Sojbjerg JO, Sneppen O: Elbow joint laxity after experimental radial head excision and lateral collateral ligament rupture: Efficacy of prosthetic replacement and ligament repair. *J Shoulder Elbow Surg* 2005;14:78-84.

    An experimental study of the effect on elbow joint laxity of radial head excision and LCL division, as well as radial head replacement and ligament repair, found that radial head replacement and LCL repair restore stability. LCL repair is more critical.

19. Beingessner DM, Dunning CE, Gordon KD, Johnson JA, King GJ: The effect of radial head fracture size on elbow kinematics and stability. *J Orthop Res* 2005;23:210-217.

    A biomechanical study of the effect of radial head fracture size and ligament injury on elbow kinematics found that fixing fractures of one third or less of the articular surface may have biomechanical advantages.

20. Hall JA, McKee MD: Posterolateral rotatory instability of the elbow following radial head resection. *J Bone Joint Surg Am* 2005;87:1571-1579.

    A retrospective review of 42 patients after radial head resection found clinical and radiographic evidence of posterolateral rotatory instability in 17%. This diagnosis should be considered in patients with elbow pain who have a history of radial head resection. Level of evidence: III.

21. Closkey RF, Goode JR, Kirschenbaum D, Cody RP: The role of the coronoid process in elbow stability: A biomechanical analysis of axial loading. *J Bone Joint Surg Am* 2000;82-A:1749-1753.

22. Schneeberger AG, Sadowski MM, Jacob HA: Coronoid process and radial head as posterolateral rotatory stabilizers of the elbow. *J Bone Joint Surg Am* 2004;86-A:975-982.

    In a biomechanical study of the role of the radial head and coronoid process as posterolateral rotatory stabilizers, both were found to contribute significantly to stability.

23. Pugh DM, Wild LM, Schemitsch EH, King GJ, McKee MD: Standard surgical protocol to treat elbow dislocations with radial head and coronoid fractures. *J Bone Joint Surg Am* 2004;86-A:1122-1130.

    A standard surgical approach to treatment of complex elbow dislocations was found to have good clinical results. Level of evidence: III.

24. Ring D, Jupiter JB, Zilberfarb J: Posterior dislocation of the elbow with fractures of the radial head and coronoid. *J Bone Joint Surg Am* 2002;84-A:547-551.

    In a study of 11 patients with a terrible triad injury, the importance of addressing the radial head, coronoid fracture, and LCL is highlighted.

25. Josefsson PO, Gentz CF, Johnell O, Wendeberg B: Dislocations of the elbow and intraarticular fractures. *Clin Orthop Relat Res* 1989;246:126-130.

26. Sanchez-Sotelo J, Romanillos O, Garay EG: Results of acute excision of the radial head in elbow radial head fracture-dislocations. *J Orthop Trauma* 2000;14:354-358.

27. Amis AA, Dowson D, Wright V: Muscle strengths and musculo-skeletal geometry of the upper limb. *Eng Med* 1979;8:41-48.

28. Halls AA, Travill A: Transmission of pressures across the elbow joint. *Anat Rec* 1964;150:243-247.

29. Morrey BF, An KN, Stormont TJ: Force transmission through the radial head. *J Bone Joint Surg Am* 1988;70:250-256.

30. Chapman CB, Su BW, Sinicropi SM, Bruno R, Strauch RJ, Rosenwasser MP: Vitallium radial head prosthesis for acute and chronic elbow fractures and fracture-dislocations involving the radial head. *J Shoulder Elbow Surg* 2006;15:463-473.

Sixteen patients with an unreconstructable acute fracture of the radial head or residual instability from a previously treated fracture received a metal radial head prosthesis. A retrospective review found that radial head replacement yielded satisfactory results. Level of evidence: III.

31. McKee MD, Pugh DM, Wild LM, Schemitsch EH, King GJ: Standard surgical protocol to treat elbow dislocations with radial head and coronoid fractures: Surgical technique. *J Bone Joint Surg Am* 2005; 87(suppl 1, pt 1):22-32.

    A step-by-step standard surgical approach is described for complex elbow fracture-dislocations with a radial head and coronoid fracture.

32. Popovic N, Gillet P, Rodriguez A, Lemaire R: Fracture of the radial head with associated elbow dislocation: Results of treatment using a floating radial head prosthesis. *J Orthop Trauma* 2000;14:171-177.

33. Dowdy PA, Bain GI, King GJ, Patterson SD: The midline posterior elbow incision: An anatomical appraisal. *J Bone Joint Surg Br* 1995;77:696-699.

34. Hull JR, Owen JR, Fern SE, Wayne JS, Boardman ND: Role of the coronoid process in varus osteoarticular stability of the elbow. *J Shoulder Elbow Surg* 2005;14:441-446.

    In a biomechanical study investigating the role of the coronoid process in varus osteoarticular stability of the elbow, the coronoid is identified as a key varus stabilizer.

35. O'Driscoll SW, Jupiter JB, Cohen MS, Ring D, McKee MD: Difficult elbow fractures: Pearls and pitfalls. *Instr Course Lect* 2003;52:113-134.

    This review addresses important concepts of complex elbow fractures.

36. Ablove RH, Moy OJ, Howard C, Peimer CA, S'Doia S: Ulnar coronoid process anatomy: Possible implications for elbow instability. *Clin Orthop Relat Res* 2006;449:259-261.

    An anatomic study to quantify the capsular and brachialis attachments of the coronoid process revealed that coronoid tip fractures include disruption of the anterior capsule. This finding explains the development of instability with these fractures.

37. Doornberg JN, van Duijn J, Ring D: Coronoid fracture height in terrible-triad injuries. *J Hand Surg Am* 2006;31:794-797.

    A CT analysis of coronoid fractures in terrible triad injuries found that fragment height is variable. A classification system based on fracture morphology and injury pattern may be preferable.

38. McKee MD, Schemitsch EH, Sala MJ, O'Driscoll SW: The pathoanatomy of lateral ligamentous disruption in complex elbow instability. *J Shoulder Elbow Surg* 2003;12:391-396.

Disruption of the LCL was found in all 62 patents with elbow dislocation. Addressing this ligament is an integral part of surgical intervention.

39. Sanchez-Sotelo J, O'Driscoll SW, Morrey BF: Medial oblique compression fracture of the coronoid process of the ulna. *J Shoulder Elbow Surg* 2005;14: 60-64.

    In a case report of the oblique medial compression fracture of the coronoid, the radiographic and clinical implications are highlighted.

40. Cohen MS, Hastings H II: Rotatory instability of the elbow: The anatomy and role of the lateral stabilizers. *J Bone Joint Surg Am* 1997;79:225-233.

41. Dunning CE, Zarzour ZD, Patterson SD, Johnson JA, King GJ: Ligamentous stabilizers against posterolateral rotatory instability of the elbow. *J Bone Joint Surg Am* 2001;83-A:1823-1828.

    In a cadaver model, elbow instability was detected only if the entire ligament was cut, not if the radial collateral ligament or LCL was left intact.

42. Imatani J, Ogura T, Morito Y, Hashizume H, Inoue H: Anatomic and histologic studies of lateral collateral ligament complex of the elbow joint. *J Shoulder Elbow Surg* 1999;8:625-627.

43. McAdams TR, Masters GW, Srivastava S: The effect of arthroscopic sectioning of the lateral ligament complex of the elbow on posterolateral rotatory stability. *J Shoulder Elbow Surg* 2005;14:298-301.

    Sequential sectioning of the LCL complex and lateral musculature found that injury to both the radial collateral ligament and LUCL was required to produce instability. The overlying musculature was also important for stability.

44. Olsen BS, Sojbjerg JO, Nielsen KK, Vaesel MT, Dalstra M, Sneppen O: Posterolateral elbow joint instability: The basic kinematics. *J Shoulder Elbow Surg* 1998;7:19-29.

45. Seki A, Olsen BS, Jensen SL, Eygendaal D, Sojbjerg JO: Functional anatomy of the lateral collateral ligament complex of the elbow: Configuration of Y and its role. *J Shoulder Elbow Surg* 2002;11:53-59.

    In a cadaver model, the LCL was found to function as a Y structure, not as an isolated linear ligament.

46. O'Driscoll SW, Bell DF, Morrey BF: Posterolateral rotatory instability of the elbow. *J Bone Joint Surg* 1991;73-A:440-446.

47. Beuerlein MJ, Reid JT, Schemitsch EH, McKee MD: Effect of distal humeral varus deformity on strain in the lateral ulnar collateral ligament and ulnohumeral joint stability. *J Bone Joint Surg Am* 2004;86-A:2235-2242.

    A biomechanical study of the relationship between cubitus varus, strain in the LCL complex, and posterolateral rotatory instability found that cubitus varus deformity increased the strain on the LCL and increased posterolateral rotatory instability.

48. O'Driscoll SW, Spinner RJ, McKee MD: Tardy posterolateral rotatory instability of the elbow due to cubitus varus. *J Bone Joint Surg Am* 2001;83-A: 1358-1369.

    The authors report stretching of the LCL complex and posterolateral rotatory instability secondary to chronic cubitus varus deformity.

49. Arvind CH, Hargreaves DG: Table top relocation test: New clinical test for posterolateral rotatory instability of the elbow. *J Shoulder Elbow Surg* 2006; 15:500-501.

    The tabletop relocation test was performed in eight patients before and after LCL reconstruction and was found to be reliable.

50. Regan W, Lapner PC: Prospective evaluation of two diagnostic apprehension signs for posterolateral instability of the elbow. *J Shoulder Elbow Surg* 2006; 15:344-346.

    The posterolateral rotatory instability test, chair push-up test, and floor push-up test are described, as tested in eight patients. The chair push-up test was effective in diagnosing posterolateral rotatory instability and more sensitive than the posterolateral rotatory instability test in patients who were awake. Level of evidence: II.

51. Mehta JA, Bain GI: Posterolateral rotatory instability of the elbow. *J Am Acad Orthop Surg* 2004;12: 405-415.

    This article reviews posterolateral rotatory instability of the elbow.

52. King GJ, Dunning CE, Zarzour ZD, Patterson SD, Johnson JA: Single-strand reconstruction of the lateral ulnar collateral ligament restores varus and posterolateral rotatory stability of the elbow. *J Shoulder Elbow Surg* 2002;11:60-64.

    In a cadaver model, both single-strand and double-strand ligament reconstructions were found to restore varus and posterolateral elbow stability.

53. Lehman RC: Lateral elbow reconstruction using a new fixation technique. *Arthroscopy* 2005;21: 503-505.

    This article describes a single-strand LCL reconstruction.

54. DeLaMora SN, Hausman M: Lateral ulnar collateral ligament reconstruction using the lateral triceps fascia. *Orthopedics* 2002;25:909-912.

    A technique is described for reconstructing the LCL of the elbow using the lateral triceps fascia.

55. Eygendaal D: Ligamentous reconstruction around the elbow using triceps tendon. *Acta Orthop Scand* 2004;75:516-523.

A LCL reconstruction using the triceps tendon is described. The procedure was successful in 13 of 14 patients.

56. Olsen BS, Sojbjerg JO: The treatment of recurrent posterolateral instability of the elbow. *J Bone Joint Surg Br* 2003;85:342-346.

    In 18 patients, the LCL of the elbow was reconstructed using a triceps tendon graft.

57. Sanchez-Sotelo J, Morrey BF, O'Driscoll SW: Ligamentous repair and reconstruction for posterolateral rotatory instability of the elbow. *J Bone Joint Surg Br* 2005;87:54-61.

    In a retrospective review of 12 direct LCL repairs and 33 LCL reconstructions using a variety of techniques, reconstruction was found to have better results than direct repair, regardless of technique. Patients had better subjective results if instability was the primary symptom, rather than pain. Level of evidence: III.

58. Eygendaal D, Verdegaal SH, Obermann WR, van Vugt AB, Poll RG, Rozing PM: Posterolateral dislocation of the elbow joint: Relationship to medial instability. *J Bone Joint Surg Am* 2000;82:555-560.

59. Josefsson PO, Johnell O, Gentz CF: Long-term sequelae of simple dislocation of the elbow. *J Bone Joint Surg Am* 1984;66:927-930.

60. Mehlhoff TL, Noble PC, Bennett JB, Tullos HS: Simple dislocation of the elbow in the adult: Results after closed treatment. *J Bone Joint Surg Am* 1988;70: 244-249.

61. O'Driscoll SW, Lawton RL, Smith AM: The "moving valgus stress test" for medial collateral ligament tears of the elbow. *Am J Sports Med* 2005;33:231-239.

    The moving valgus stress test for assessing valgus instability was highly sensitive (100%) and specific (75%) compared with assessment during surgical exploration or arthroscopic valgus stress testing. Level of evidence: II.

62. Jacobson JA, Propeck T, Jamadar DA, Jebson PJ, Hayes CW: US of the anterior bundle of the ulnar collateral ligament: Findings in five cadaver elbows with MR arthrographic and anatomic comparison. Initial observations. *Radiology* 2003;227:561-566.

    The anterior bundle of the MCL was identified using ultrasonography in five cadaver elbows.

63. Miller TT, Adler RS, Friedman L: Sonography of injury of the ulnar collateral ligament of the elbow: Initial experience. *Skeletal Radiol* 2004;33:386-391.

    A study of the sonographic appearance of MCL injuries found that tears of the MCL appeared as nonvisualization of the ligament or alteration of the normal morphology.

64. Nazarian LN, McShane JM, Ciccotti MG, O'Kane PL, Harwood MI: Dynamic US of the anterior band of the ulnar collateral ligament of the elbow in asymptomatic major league baseball pitchers. *Radiology* 2003;227:149-154.

A dynamic ultrasonographic technique was used in evaluating the anterior band of the MCL in professional baseball pitchers.

65. Sasaki J, Takahara M, Ogino T, Kashiwa H, Ishigaki D, Kanauchi Y: Ultrasonographic assessment of the ulnar collateral ligament and medial elbow laxity in college baseball players. *J Bone Joint Surg Am* 2002; 84-A:525-531.

    Ultrasonography is described for evaluation of the MCL of the elbow.

66. Ward SI, Teefey SA, Paletta GA, et al: Sonography of the medial collateral ligament of the elbow: A study of cadavers and healthy adult male volunteers. *AJR Am J Roentgenol* 2003;180:389-394.

    Sonography was used to identify and measure the size of the anterior bundle of the normal MCL of the elbow in 30 healthy men and five cadaver specimens.

67. Ahmad CS, Park MC, Elattrache NS: Elbow medial ulnar collateral ligament insufficiency alters posteromedial olecranon contact. *Am J Sports Med* 2004;32: 1607-1612.

    In a biomechanical study of the effect of MCL injury on the posteromedial compartment of the elbow, MCL insufficiency was found to alter the contact area and pressure between the posteromedial trochlea and olecranon.

68. Kamineni S, ElAttrache NS, O'Driscoll LW, et al: Medial collateral ligament strain with partial posteromedial olecranon resection: A biomechanical study. *J Bone Joint Surg Am* 2004;86-A:2424-2430.

    A biomechanical study of the effect of sequential resection of the posteromedial olecranon on the strain of the MCL found that resection of the olecranon of 3 mm or greater jeopardized the function of the anterior bundle of the MCL.

69. Kooima CL, Anderson K, Craig JV, Teeter DM, van Holsbeeck M: Evidence of subclinical medial collateral ligament injury and posteromedial impingement in professional baseball players. *Am J Sports Med* 2004;32:1602-1606.

    In a descriptive review of elbow MRI in 16 asymptomatic professional baseball players, MCL abnormalities were present in 86%, and findings consistent with posteromedial impingement were present in 81%.

70. Andrews JR, Timmerman LA: Outcome of elbow surgery in professional baseball players. *Am J Sports Med* 1995;23:407-413.

71. Kamineni S, Hirahara H, Pomianowski S, et al: Partial posteromedial olecranon resection: A kinematic study. *J Bone Joint Surg Am* 2003;85-A:1005-1011.

    The kinematic effects of posteromedial olecranon resection on valgus elbow stability were investigated in a cadaver model. The authors recommend resection only of osteophytes, not of normal bone.

72. Armstrong AD, Ferreira LM, Dunning CE, Johnson JA, King GJ: The medial collateral ligament of the elbow is not isometric: An in vitro biomechanical study. *Am J Sports Med* 2004;32:85-90.

    In a biomechanical study, true isometry of the anterior bundle of the MCL was not identified, although an almost isometric area was located on the lateral aspect of the attachment site of the anterior bundle of the MCL on the medial epicondyle close to the anatomic axis of rotation.

73. Ochi N, Ogura T, Hashizume H, Shigeyama Y, Senda M, Inoue H: Anatomic relation between the medial collateral ligament of the elbow and the humero-ulnar joint axis. *J Shoulder Elbow Surg* 1999;8:6-10.

74. Hamilton CD, Glousman RE, Jobe FW, Brault J, Pink M, Perry J: Dynamic stability of the elbow: Electromyographic analysis of the flexor pronator group and the extensor group in pitchers with valgus instability. *J Shoulder Elbow Surg* 1996;5:347-354.

75. Park MC, Ahmad CS: Dynamic contributions of the flexor-pronator mass to elbow valgus stability. *J Bone Joint Surg Am* 2004;86-A:2268-2274.

    In a biomechanical study of the dynamic contribution of the muscles around the elbow with MCL insufficiency, the flexor carpi ulnaris was identified as the primary stabilizer and the flexor digitorum as a secondary stabilizer.

76. Rettig AC, Sherrill C, Snead DS, Mendler JC, Mieling P: Nonoperative treatment of ulnar collateral ligament injuries in throwing athletes. *Am J Sports Med* 2001;29:15-17.

    Of 31 throwing athletes treated nonsurgically for an MCL injury, 42% returned to their earlier level of competition.

77. Smith GR, Altchek DW, Pagnani MJ, Keeley JR: A muscle-splitting approach to the ulnar collateral ligament of the elbow: Neuroanatomy and operative technique. *Am J Sports Med* 1996;24:575-580.

78. Jobe FW, Stark H, Lombardo SJ: Reconstruction of the ulnar collateral ligament in athletes. *J Bone Joint Surg Am* 1986;68:1158-1163.

79. Thompson WH, Jobe FW, Yocum LA, Pink MM: Ulnar collateral ligament reconstruction in athletes: Muscle-splitting approach without transposition of the ulnar nerve. *J Shoulder Elbow Surg* 2001;10: 152-157.

    In 83 athletes, a muscle-splitting approach without ulnar nerve transposition was used for reconstruction of the anterior band of the MCL.

80. Dodson, CC, Thomas A, Dines JS, Nho SJ, Williams RJ, Altcheck DW: Medial ulnar collateral ligament reconstruction of the elbow in throwing athletes. *Am J Sports Med* 2006;34:1926-1932.

    Clinical experience with the docking procedure for MCL instability is reported. At a mean 36-month follow-up,

90% of patients were able to compete at the same or a higher level than before MCL injury. Level of evidence: III.

81. Hyman J, Breazeale NM, Altchek DW: Valgus instability of the elbow in athletes. *Clin Sports Med* 2001; 20:25-45.

    This is a review of valgus instability of the elbow and the preferred method of treatment.

82. Paletta GA Jr, Wright RW: The modified docking procedure for elbow ulnar collateral ligament reconstruction: 2-year follow-up in elite throwers. *Am J Sports Med* 2006;34:1594-1598.

    A modified docking MCL reconstruction technique for MCL insufficiency in elite athletes is described. At a mean 11.5 months, 92% of patients had returned to their preinjury level of competition. Level of evidence: III.

83. Rohrbough JT, Altchek DW, Hyman J, Williams RJ, Botts JD: Medial collateral ligament reconstruction of the elbow using the docking technique. *Am J Sports Med* 2002;30:541-548.

    One year after a docking technique was used to repair MCL insufficiency, 92% of patients had returned to sports activity.

84. Ahmad CS, Lee TQ, ElAttrache NS: Biomechanical evaluation of a new ulnar collateral ligament reconstruction technique with interference screw fixation. *Am J Sports Med* 2003;31:332-337.

    In a cadaver model, MCL reconstruction using interference screws was able to restore elbow kinematics.

85. Armstrong AD, Dunning CE, Ferreira LM, Faber KJ, Johnson JA, King GJ: A biomechanical comparison of four reconstruction techniques for the medial collateral ligament-deficient elbow. *J Shoulder Elbow Surg* 2005;14:207-215.

    In a biomechanical comparison, the peak load to failure of MCLs repaired using four reconstruction techniques was less than that of a native MCL. The strength of the docking and Endobutton techniques was equivalent, and both had greater strength than the figure-of-8 or interference screw technique.

86. McKee MD, Bowden SH, King GJ, et al: Management of recurrent, complex instability of the elbow with a hinged external fixator. *J Bone Joint Surg Br* 1998; 80:1031-1036.

87. Jupiter JB, Ring D: Treatment of unreduced elbow dislocations with hinged external fixation. *J Bone Joint Surg Am* 2002;84-A:1630-1635.

    Five patients achieved a stable, mobile joint after open reduction and hinged external fixation of a chronic unreduced elbow dislocation.

88. Ring D, Hannouche D, Jupiter JB: Surgical treatment of persistent dislocation or subluxation of the ulnohumeral joint after fracture-dislocation of the elbow. *J Hand Surg Am* 2004;29:470-480.

    The results of surgical reconstruction of persistent posttraumatic elbow instability with an external hinged fixator are reviewed. A stable joint was achieved in six patients, with an average arc of motion of 99°. Five of the patients had radiographic signs of arthrosis. Level of evidence: III.

89. Ruch DS, Triepel CR: Hinged elbow fixation for recurrent instability following fracture dislocation. *Injury* 2001;32(suppl 4):SD70-SD78.

    Application of an articulated external fixator was an alternative to complete osseous and ligamentous reconstruction in achieving elbow stability in five patients with chronic unreduced elbow fracture dislocation.

# Chapter 44

# Elbow Stiffness

Mark S. Cohen, MD

## Introduction

The elbow is the joint that most commonly develops posttraumatic stiffness. This propensity has been attributed to several factors, including the congruous nature of the elbow, the presence of three articulations (the ulnohumeral, radiocapitellar, and proximal radioulnar) within a synovial cavity, and the close relationship of the joint capsule to the intracapsular ligaments and surrounding muscles.[1] The elbow capsule itself plays a role in arthrofibrosis. After even relatively minor trauma, the capsule can undergo structural and biochemical alterations that lead to thickening, decreased compliance, and loss of motion.[2] Prolonged immobilization of the elbow after trauma is an additional risk factor for the development of stiffness. After open or arthroscopic surgery for restricted elbow motion, most well-selected patients achieve improved function and pain relief.

## Surgical Treatment

### Patient Selection

Contracture release can be considered for a patient with restricted elbow motion and flexion of less than approximately 110° to 115° or a flexion contracture of at least 25° to 30°. Usually the patient has undergone an unsuccessful course of supervised physical therapy, including proper splinting. A congruous joint with an adequate ulnohumeral joint space, at least centrally, is also required. Joint congruity usually can be documented using plain radiographs, although CT is occasionally required, especially after trauma. Adequate soft-tissue coverage of the surgical site is preferred, as well as an interval from injury to surgery of at least 3 to 4 months to allow resolution of posttraumatic inflammation.

Achievement of optimal surgical results depends on the patient's participation in a structured rehabilitation program. Therefore, surgical release of a contracted elbow is contraindicated if a patient is unable or unwilling to comply with extensive postsurgical therapy; adolescents in particular may not be sufficiently dedicated to improving their elbow motion. If the ulnohumeral joint is incongruous, a simple release may not lead to improved motion and may actually worsen the pain. Patients who are candidates for elbow release surgery typically have no pain within their allowable arc of motion, although pain at the extremes of motion is common. Patient selection for surgery is not affected by the severity of the contracture, the number of earlier surgical procedures, or the presence of a limited amount of heterotopic bone.

If severe posttraumatic arthritis is present in the ulnohumeral articulation, any surgical procedure must be of a salvage type, such as interposition arthroplasty using a soft-tissue resurfacing of the joint, with or without distraction using an articulated hinged fixator. For some patients, hemiarthroplasty or total joint arthroplasty may be indicated.

### Open Technique

Improvement of elbow flexion requires posterior release of any soft-tissue structures that may be tethering the joint, including the posterior joint capsule and the triceps muscle and tendon, which can adhere to the humerus. In addition, anterior removal of any bony or soft-tissue impingement is required, including osteophytes from the coronoid process and bony or soft-tissue overgrowth of the coronoid and radial fossae (Figure 1). For full flexion, there must be a concavity above the humeral trochlea and capitellum to accept the coronoid centrally and the radial head laterally. In an elbow with long-standing lack of flexion, the posteromedial joint capsule, which is also referred to as the posterior bundle of the medial collateral ligament, can be a substantial limitation. This structure, which forms the floor of the cubital tunnel, is taut in flexion and often must be released. The ulnar nerve is also an important consideration.

Improvement of elbow extension requires removal of posterior impingements between the olecranon tip and the olecranon fossa. Any tethering soft tissues must be released anteriorly; these may include the anterior joint capsule and adhesions between the brachialis and the humerus (Figure 1).

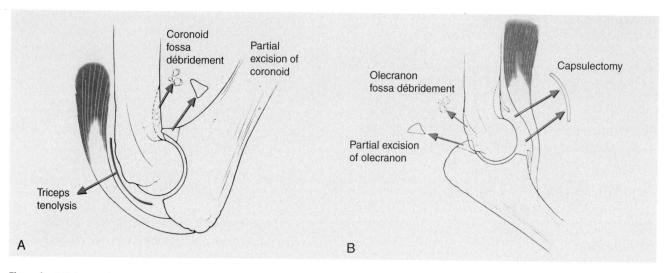

**Figure 1** **A,** To improve flexion, posterior soft-tissue tethers including the joint capsule and triceps are released, and anterior impingement is removed, typically between the coronoid and coronoid fossa of the humerus. If necessary, a concavity is created laterally above the capitellum to accept the radial head (radial fossa). **B,** To improve extension, posterior impingement is removed at the olecranon tip, and the anterior capsule and brachialis are released. *(Courtesy of Hill Hastings II, MD, Indianapolis, IN.)*

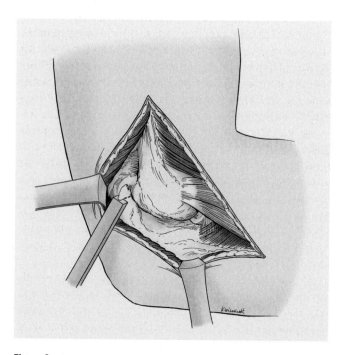

**Figure 2** Exposure of the posterolateral ulnohumeral joint. The anconeus and triceps are reflected posteriorly to expose the posterior capsule, olecranon tip, and olecranon fossa and to allow visualization and débridement of the posterior joint, with removal of any bony impingement. *(Copyright Mark S. Cohen, MD, Chicago, IL.)*

Elbow release surgery is typically performed under regional anesthesia, using a long-acting block that also provides postsurgical muscular relaxation and pain control. An indwelling axillary catheter also can be used to provide effective anesthesia. The location of the skin in-

cision is less important than the selection of the deep interval for joint release. A lateral, medial, or combined deep approach can be used to release the elbow both anteriorly and posteriorly. The joint can be approached through limited medial and lateral skin incisions or through a long posterior skin incision that provides both medial and lateral access to the joint. The presence of earlier skin incisions must be considered in presurgical planning.

The lateral deep approach typically uses a Kocher-type skin incision that begins along the supracondylar humeral ridge and passes distally in the interval between the anconeus and the extensor carpi ulnaris.[3-5] Dissection is carried proximally beneath the humeral epicondyle and along the supracondylar ridge of the humerus, thereby reflecting both the anconeus and triceps posteriorly. The ulnohumeral joint is exposed, and any lateral joint spurs are resected. A triceps tenolysis is performed using an elevator to release any adhesions between the muscle and the posterior humerus. Posteriorly, the olecranon fossa is cleared of any fibrous or bony tissue that could inhibit terminal extension, and the tip of the olecranon is resected if evidence of overgrowth or impingement is present (Figure 2).

The posterior aspect of the radiocapitellar joint (the lateral gutter) can be inspected by excising the elbow capsule through the lateral soft spot, which is just proximal to the conjoined lateral collateral and annular ligament complex. Loose bodies and proliferative synovitis are often found in this sulcus. Any osteophytes or bony overgrowths behind the capitellum are removed because these can limit the recovery of elbow extension.

Dissection is carried anteriorly by sliding along the anterior humeral supracondylar ridge and distally by muscle splitting between the extensor carpi radialis longus and brevis. With continued dissection, the extensor carpi radialis longus and brachialis are elevated to expose the entire anterior joint capsule. The capsule is elevated and resected. The radial and coronoid fossae are cleared of any bony or fibrous tissue, and the tip of the coronoid is removed if impingement is present in flexion (Figure 3).

After complete anterior and posterior capsular release and débridement, the elbow is extended under direct visualization by applying firm pressure to the forearm. Usually the joint is brought to almost full extension. Flexion is also achieved by gentle manipulation. In a patient with a long-standing elbow contracture, the brachialis or triceps muscle, or both, may be tight and inhibit full terminal elbow extension or flexion. Such a myostatic contracture can be stretched for several minutes during the procedure, although postsurgical therapy is needed to overcome the contracture. Motion is optimally limited only by muscular contracture with soft end points. Severe contracture of the posteromedial capsule can limit recovery of elbow flexion. In some patients, a separate limited medial approach may be necessary to decompress the ulnar nerve and release this capsule.

A similar deep medial approach is an alternative to the lateral approach.[6] It involves a medial or posterior incision with exposure of all flexor-pronator muscular origins. A medial incision requires careful identification and protection of the medial antebrachial cutaneous nerve branches, which are commonly found distal to the epicondyle. The ulnar nerve is released well proximal and distal to the joint and is retracted anteriorly for protection. The triceps is then elevated posteriorly from the intermuscular septum and the humerus, exposing the medial and posterior ulnohumeral joints. The posterior joint is released and débrided. The posteromedial joint capsule (posterior bundle of the medial collateral ligament) can be sharply released through this approach.

Dissection continues along the humeral supracondylar ridge and distally down through the posterior third of the flexor-pronator muscle origin. This procedure protects the important anterior bundle of the medial collateral ligament, which lies beneath the humeral origin of the flexor carpi ulnaris. The flexor-pronator and brachialis muscles are reflected anteriorly, exposing the anterior joint capsule. The capsule is then released and excised to allow visualization and débridement of the anterior joint, including the coronoid and radial fossae. The ulnar nerve is usually transposed anteriorly into a subcutaneous position. Care must be taken to ensure that the nerve is not compressed or tethered proximally or distally. The muscular intervals are closed over a drain.

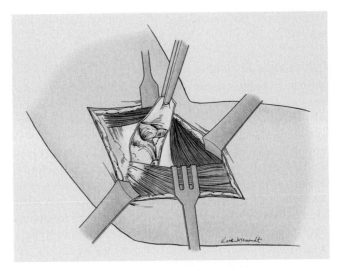

**Figure 3** Isolation and excision of the anterior joint capsule, which is usually thickened and adhering to the anterior humerus and the joint. The capsule is formally excised, removing a thick strip from lateral to medial to expose the joint proper, and débridement is performed as required. *(Copyright Mark S. Cohen, MD, Chicago, IL.)*

The advantages of the lateral deep approach include simplicity, use of a muscular plane that avoids superficial sensory nerves, access to all three joint articulations, and, possibly, less muscular morbidity with respect to the extensor and flexor-pronator muscular origins. However, the lateral exposure does not allow the ulnar nerve to be addressed, if necessary. The advantages of the medial deep approach include the ability to expose and decompress the ulnar nerve, as well as improved cosmesis (a less visible scar). The medial exposure also facilitates direct release of the posteromedial ulnohumeral joint capsule, which can limit flexion in patients with severe contracture. The primary disadvantage of the medial deep approach is that it does not allow lateral joint pathology to be addressed. These approaches are not mutually exclusive, and both can be used through a long posterior incision.

Understanding of the ulnar nerve and its role in elbow stiffness has evolved considerably. The nerve lies along the medial joint capsule in the cubital tunnel, and it may adhere to the surrounding soft tissues after trauma. Ulnar neuritis, manifested as tingling and numbness in the ulnar digits or medial joint pain in flexion, occasionally is a cause of posttraumatic elbow stiffness. The normal tension and compression of the ulnar nerve during elbow flexion is magnified in a posttraumatic stiff elbow. It is recommended that the ulnar nerve be released or transposed whenever nerve symptoms are present or when tension signs exist (a positive Tinel sign or positive elbow flexion test). Transposition is also recommended if a significant elbow extension contracture exists because significant improvement in joint flexion can acutely precipitate ulnar nerve symptoms. It is generally recommended that ulnar nerve release or transposition be considered if elbow flexion is less than 90°.

### Arthroscopic Technique

Interest in arthroscopic release of the stiff elbow is increasing, and the indications are evolving.[7-9] The surgical principles are the same as for open elbow release. Knowledge of the pathophysiology of elbow stiffness is required, as well as advanced skills in elbow arthroscopy, especially for treatment of complex contractures. In general, contractures associated with osteoarthritis of the elbow are easier to treat than those associated with posttraumatic conditions of the elbow. Surgery involving a posttraumatic contracture with thickening and adherence to the joint capsule, scarring, and myostasis can be especially difficult. Posttraumatic joint contracture severely limits joint distention. Multiple portals are required and fluid management is essential. The use of arthroscopic joint retractors is helpful in visualization.

The goals of arthroscopic treatment of elbow stiffness parallel those of open treatment. All elements of stiffness need to be understood and completely addressed. However, the methods used to achieve the goals are quite different. The joint must be entered, and a working space must be established. In a contracted joint, stripping of the capsule from the supracondylar region may be required. After the working space is established, the capsule must be defined as a distinct structure before it can be resected. Retractors placed through accessory portals may be required to maintain the working space after the capsule is stripped from the humerus.

The bony work typically precedes capsular excision. Osteophytes are resected from the processes and fossae to reestablish the normal anatomic relationships. The capsule is resected only if it is identifiable as a distinct structure. If the capsule cannot be defined or if the pericapsular structures cannot be separated from the capsule, arthroscopic release should be abandoned in favor of an open release.

In very experienced hands, the arthroscopic procedure appears to have results equivalent to those of an open procedure. However, long-term results are not yet available. The arthroscopic procedure clearly has a learning curve for the surgeon. The complications include nerve injury, excessive fluid extravasation, and iatrogenic chondral injury.[10]

## Postsurgical Treatment

A number of effective postsurgical treatment programs can be used after elbow release surgery. In some programs, continuous passive motion is used to help maintain the motion gained during surgery, beginning when the patient is in the recovery room and extending until the following morning.[3,11] Formal therapy commonly begins on the first day after surgery. The dressing is removed, and edema is controlled using an elastic compression bandage or sleeve. Active and active-assisted elbow motion is combined with intermittent continuous passive motion. Static progressive elbow bracing is begun; flexion and extension are alternated, as determined based on the presurgical deficit and early progress of the elbow. A several-week course of indomethacin, a nonsteroidal anti-inflammatory drug (NSAID), is commonly prescribed to prevent heterotopic ossification and limit inflammation of the joint and soft tissues during rehabilitation.

The patient must be motivated to follow the postsurgical treatment program and must understand the commitment required. If a severe loss of motion was present, the home program can extend 3 to 6 months after surgery. An appropriately selected patient can expect recovery of a functional arc of elbow motion as well as pain relief.[3,5,7,8]

The use of a dynamic splint that applies constant tension to the soft tissues for as long as 23 hours per day was formerly popular. However, a patient-adjusted static brace is much more effective for the elbow than a dynamic splint. This brace uses the principle of passive progressive stretching to allow stress-relaxation of the soft tissues. It is used for much shorter periods of time and is better tolerated by patients.

## Complications

The most common complication of elbow release surgery involves the ulnar nerve and is related to improvement in elbow flexion. Ulnar nerve tension increases during elbow flexion, and improvement in motion can precipitate symptoms if the nerve was even slightly compromised by the trauma and subsequent contracture. Although no proven motion guidelines are available, release or transposition of the ulnar nerve is recommended during surgery for a patient who had ulnar nerve symptoms or a significant extension contracture before surgery. If in doubt, the surgeon should decide in favor of ulnar nerve release or transposition to decrease the risk of complication.

## Heterotopic Ossification

Heterotopic ossification is defined as inappropriate formation of mature lamellar bone in a nonosseous location.[12,13] The elbow is uniquely predisposed to heterotopic ossification, for reasons that remain unclear, and heterotopic bone can be an independent factor leading to joint stiffness. Heterotopic ossification should be distinguished from periarticular calcification, which is the formation of amorphous calcium deposits, most often in the capsule or collateral ligaments after injury. Periarticular calcification is common and has minimal clinical significance.

Heterotopic ossification of the elbow most often occurs after direct joint trauma and appears to be at least partly related to the severity of the injury. It is reported to occur in approximately 3% of simple elbow dislocations and as many as 20% of fracture-dislocations. It is also found below the level of the spinal cord injury after neural axis trauma and after isolated closed head trauma (in 5% to 10% of patients), most commonly on the hemiplegic side. Between 75% and 90% of patients with both head and elbow injury develop heterotopic ossification.[8] These are the patients at highest risk for this complication. Heterotopic bone is also found in the elbow of 1% to 3% of patients with burns and is related to burn severity rather than location.[14]

Heterotopic ossification was formerly believed to be caused by vigorous passive motion of the elbow during therapy. The relationship has not been proven and is not considered clinically relevant. Nevertheless, forceful and repeated manipulation of a stiff elbow probably should be avoided because it leads to the development of heterotopic bone in experimental models. Formerly, a delay of 2 or 3 days before surgical intervention after elbow trauma was considered an independent risk factor for heterotopic ossification. This association has not been supported in the literature. However, multiple surgical insults during the first 7 to 14 days after trauma appear to increase the patient's risk of developing ectopic bone.[8]

The pathophysiology of heterotopic ossification is not completely understood. The condition involves inappropriate differentiation of pluripotent mesenchymal stem cells into osteoblastic cell lines. Osteogenic precursor cells, an inductive agent (most likely a growth factor), and an environment conducive to osteogenesis are required.[12,13] An increase in circulating osteoblastic growth factors was identified after closed head injury.[15] The inappropriately developing bone is histologically identical to native bone, except that it is more metabolically active and lacks a true periosteal layer. Heterotopic ossification is seen with certain HLA foci, and this association suggests a genetic predisposition to the condition.[8]

There is no effective treatment for heterotopic ossification. The use of diphosphonates only delays bone mineralization.[8,12] Prophylaxis for high-risk patients is therefore especially important. NSAID use is effective if begun within 3 to 5 days of the trauma. Indomethacin, ibuprofen, naproxen, and aspirin all have been shown to be beneficial. These agents disrupt the prostaglandin pathway and in experimental models inhibit the migration and differentiation of stem cells.[3,12] The optimal duration of NSAID therapy is unclear; effectiveness has been reported within a range of 5 days to 6 weeks.[8]

Low-dose external beam radiation is the preferred means of prophylaxis for heterotopic ossification. It is thought to inhibit the differentiation of stem cells, which

are particularly radiosensitive.[16] A single dose of 600 to 700 cGy is administered 2 to 4 days after trauma, using a limited-field technique to decrease soft-tissue exposure. Radiation-induced sarcoma has not been reported after exposure to less than 3,000 cGy.[8]

Early active mobilization of the elbow after trauma appears to lessen the likelihood the patient will develop heterotopic ossification and to hasten functional recovery. Clinical data are available to support the benefits, although the mechanism is not well understood.[8] It is not known whether passive joint mobilization offers the same benefits.

Although the process of heterotopic ossification begins with the initial insult, the condition becomes evident 2 to 12 weeks later. A patient with heterotopic ossification often has local soft-tissue swelling, tenderness, warmth, and progressive loss of elbow motion. This inflammation-mediated condition sometimes is mistaken for an infection, especially during the perisurgical period. Pain usually is not the primary symptom, although it is present at the extremes of motion. Laboratory studies reveal a transient decrease in serum calcium and an increase in inorganic phosphate. The serum alkaline phosphatase level begins to rise within 2 to 4 weeks, and at approximately 3 months it reaches three to four times the normal level. As heterotopic ossification develops, technetium bone scans reveal an increase in metabolic activity; the level can remain abnormal for considerably longer than 1 year. Serial bone scans were formerly used to assess biologic activity and the maturity of the process. However, to diminish the potential for recurrence, intervention was not recommended until bone scan results had returned to normal and the process was metabolically quiescent, often after 12 to 18 months. The prognostic value of laboratory and bone scan findings has not been proved, and these tests are no longer used in the evaluation or treatment of heterotopic ossification of the elbow.

Plain radiography is the most effective method of evaluating heterotopic ossification and following its progression. Within several weeks of the trauma, an ill-defined, fluffy periarticular density can be identified (Figure 4). Over time, the margins become more distinct and trabeculation appears. Radiographic maturity, which is defined as the appearance of sharp cortical margins, commonly requires 3 to 5 months. In most patients, surgical intervention can safely be undertaken at radiographic maturity. It may be prudent to wait longer in skeletally immature patients because nonbridging heterotopic bone may be resorbed over time in these patients.

Heterotopic bone can form in a localized or diffuse pattern that may not follow anatomic tissue planes. Its development does not necessarily result in a loss of motion or function, and surgical resection is indicated only if the patient has functional impairment. Anterior

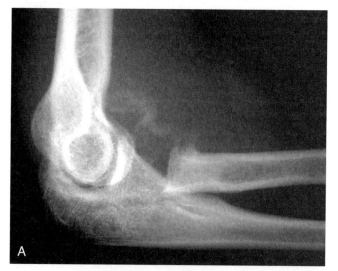

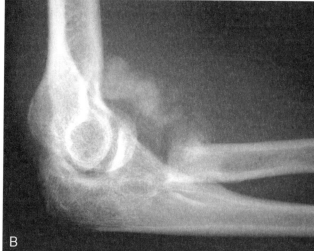

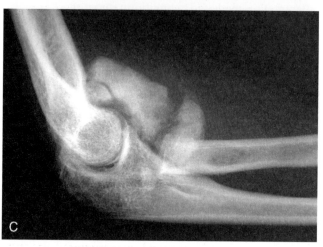

**Figure 4** The process of heterotopic ossification seen in lateral radiographs taken over time. **A,** Four weeks after trauma, an ill-defined fluffy density appears. **B,** At 8 weeks, the ectopic bone has consolidated; the borders are poorly defined. **C,** At 16 weeks, sharp cortical margins are apparent, and the ossification appears to be mature. Resection can proceed when radiographic maturity occurs.

heterotopic bone most commonly forms beneath the brachialis muscle and is separated from the anterior articular surface by an area of radiolucency. Posterior heterotopic bone often forms in continuity with the joint beneath the triceps; this is the most common pattern leading to complete ankylosis.

Although in most patients plain radiographs are adequate for assessing heterotopic bone formation and planning surgical resection, CT may be useful to define the status of the ulnohumeral joint and the geometry of the ectopic bone if the bone formation is complex. CT with three-dimensional reconstruction can be particularly helpful. For most patients, early surgical intervention at radiographic maturity is preferable to limit capsular and ligamentous contracture, muscle atrophy, and cartilage degeneration and allow a more rapid return to function. Early surgical intervention also may be technically easier.

The choice of surgical approach for heterotopic ossification excision about the elbow depends in part on the location and extent of the ectopic bone. Burrs, curets, osteotomes, and rongeurs are used to excise the bone. The radial, medial, and ulnar nerves are identified and pro-

tected as needed. For posterior heterotopic ossification, partial or complete elevation of the triceps from the olecranon is required. The ulnar nerve may be found to be totally encased in a shell of bone, even if the patient had no neurologic symptoms. Because there often is no apparent difference in the quality or appearance of the heterotopic bone and the host cortex, resection is facilitated by the use of intrasurgical fluoroscopy. For anterior heterotopic ossification, the usual approach is medial or lateral, and both approaches may be required if ossification is extensive. The choice does not depend on the skin incision, and either approach normally can be used without violation of the collateral ligaments. The lateral deep approach allows the radiocapitellar and proximal radioulnar joints to be addressed, and the medial deep approach allows decompression of the ulnar nerve and the ulnohumeral exposure.

After surgery, patients usually undergo a formal rehabilitation program. Although some evidence suggests that prophylaxis to decrease the risk of recurrence is not always necessary,[8] most patients are treated with a NSAID or low-dose radiation.

The results of heterotopic bone resection about the elbow depend in part on the severity of the condition and the patient's presurgical functional limitations. A functional arc of joint motion can be achieved even in patients with long-standing ulnohumeral joint ankylosis.[17] Residual spasticity and incomplete neurologic recovery of the upper extremity are correlated with an increased recurrence rate. Partial regrowth of heterotopic bone can occur but is clinically significant only if it limits elbow motion. A recurrence that causes functional limitation is rare.

## Summary

Loss of motion is not uncommon after trauma to the elbow. If nonsurgical measures fail to improve the patient's range of motion and function, surgical intervention may be indicated. Recovery of mobility typically requires the release of the elbow capsule and soft tissue as well as any bony impingement. Because the outcome of surgery partly depends on the patient's participation in postsurgical treatment, patient selection is essential. Fortunately, an appropriately selected, highly motivated patient usually achieves a functional arc of elbow motion after surgery is performed.

## Annotated References

1. Modabber MR, Jupiter JB: Current concepts review: Reconstruction for post-traumatic conditions of the elbow joint. *J Bone Joint Surg Am* 1995;77:1431-1446.

2. Cohen MS, Schimel DR, Masuda K, Hastings H, Muehleman C: Structural and biochemical evaluation of the elbow capsule following trauma. *J Shoulder Elbow Surg* 2007;16:484-490.

   The elbow capsule clearly plays a role in posttraumatic contracture. Microscopic and immunohistochemical evaluation of structural and biochemical alterations in the elbow capsule after trauma found significant thickening of the capsule and extensive disorganization of the collagen fiber bundle arrangement, as well as increased levels of specific cytokines involved in connective tissue turnover.

3. Cohen MS, Hastings H: Post-traumatic contracture of the elbow: Operative release using a lateral collateral sparing approach. *J Bone Joint Surg Br* 1998;80: 805-812.

4. Cohen MS, Hastings H: Capsular release for contracture of the elbow: Operative technique and functional results. *Orthop Clin North Am* 1999;30: 133-139.

5. Mansat P, Morrey BF: The column procedure: A limited lateral approach for extrinsic contracture of the elbow. *J Bone Joint Surg Am* 1998;80:1603-1615.

6. Kasparyan NG, Hotchkiss RN: Dynamic skeletal fixation in the upper extremity. *Hand Clin* 1997;13: 643-663.

7. Ball CM, Meunier M, Galatz LM, Calfee R, Yamaguchi K: Arthroscopic treatment of post-traumatic elbow contracture. *J Shoulder Elbow Surg* 2002;11: 624-629.

   At a minimum 1-year follow-up after arthroscopic release in 14 patients with posttraumatic contracture of the elbow, flexion had improved from a mean 118° to 133°, and extension had improved from 35° to 9°. All patients had functional improvement, and no arthroscopy-related complications were reported.

8. Jupiter JB, O'Driscoll SW, Cohen MS: The assessment and management of the stiff elbow. *Instr Course Lect* 2003;52:93-112.

   The classification, diagnosis, nonsurgical treatment, and open and arthroscopic surgical treatment of elbow stiffness are reviewed, as well as the assessment and management of heterotopic ossification. The difficult combination of stiffness associated with nonunion of the distal humerus is discussed.

9. Savoie FH, Nunley PD, Field LD, Savoie FH: Arthroscopic management of the arthritic elbow: Indications, technique, and results. *J Shoulder Elbow Surg* 1999;8:214-219.

10. Haapaniemi T, Berggren M, Adolfsson L: Complete transection of the median and radial nerves during arthroscopic release of post-traumatic elbow contracture. *Arthroscopy* 1999;15:784-787.

11. Gates HS, Sullivan FL, Urbaniak JR: Anterior capsulotomy and continuous passive motion in the treatment post-traumatic flexion contracture of the elbow. *J Bone Joint Surg Am* 1992;74:1229-1234.

12. Ellerin BE, Helfet D, Parikh, et al: Current therapy in the management of heterotopic ossification of the elbow: A review with case studies. *Am J Phys Med Rehabil* 1999;78:259-271.

13. Summerfield SL, DiGiovanni C, Weiss AP: Heterotopic ossification of the elbow. *J Shoulder Elbow Surg* 1997;6:321-332.

14. Gaur A, Sinclair M, Caruso E, Peretti G, Zaleske D: Heterotopic ossification around the elbow following burns in children: Results after excision. *J Bone Joint Surg Am* 2003;85-A:1538-1543.

   Eight patients (10 elbows) were treated surgically for motion-limiting heterotopic ossification of the elbow after burns at an average 17 months after injury. At follow-up, all 9 available elbows had an improved arc of motion (average, 57°), and no recurrences had occurred. Patient selection, surgical resection, and rehabilitation are discussed.

15. Bidner SM, Rubins IM, Desjardins JV, et al: Evidence for a humeral mechanism for enhanced osteogenesis after head injury. *J Bone Joint Surg Am* 1990;72:1144-1149.

16. Heyd R, Strassmann G, Schopohl B, Zamboglou N: Radiation therapy for the prevention of heterotopic

ossification at the elbow. *J Bone Joint Surg Br* 2001; 83:332-334.

Nine patients underwent surgical resection of clinically significant heterotopic bone about the elbow. All received perisurgical radiation (600 to 1,000 cGy). At a mean 8-month follow-up, no recurrent heterotopic bone was observed, and eight patients had improved clinically. The efficacy of radiation therapy is discussed as an adjunct to surgical resection of heterotopic bone about the elbow.

17. Ring D, Jupiter JB: Operative release of complete ankylosis of the elbow due to heterotopic bone in patients without severe injury of the central nervous system. *J Bone Joint Surg Am* 2003;85-A:849-857.

After surgical release of complete ankylosis of the elbow in seven patients (11 elbows) after burns and eight patients (9 elbows) after trauma, four patients in the burn group and three in the trauma group failed to regain at least 80° of motion. Six patients underwent a repeat release. At an average 40-month follow-up, the average arc of elbow motion was 81° in the patients with burns and 94° in the patients with trauma. Surgery to regain elbow motion in patients with complete ankylosis is worthwhile and safe, despite the frequent need for repeat surgery.

# Chapter 45

# Elbow Arthritis

Raymond A. Klug, MD

Bradford O. Parsons, MD

## Introduction

Arthritis is less common in the elbow than in other large joints such as the hip, knee, or shoulder. The common symptomatic forms are rheumatoid arthritis (RA), posttraumatic arthritis (PTA), and primary osteoarthritis (OA). Recent treatment advances have led to a decline in the number of rheumatoid arthritis patients undergoing orthopaedic surgery. However, the incidence of posttraumatic elbow arthritis is increasing as the population ages.

Elbow arthritis encompasses varying degrees of articular cartilage loss, bony deformity, intrinsic or extrinsic contracture, laxity, and neurologic symptoms. The relative contribution of each symptom and, therefore, the treatment, differs with the disease process. The goals of treatment are to restore articular congruity, maintain joint stability, restore function, and alleviate pain. Advances in surgical technique and implant design are creating new treatment options.

## Rheumatoid Arthritis

RA is the most common form of elbow arthritis. Between 20% and 50% of patients with RA have elbow involvement. In contrast, approximately 90% of patients have hand or wrist involvement, and 80% have shoulder involvement. Isolated elbow RA occurs in fewer than 5% of patients.

### Patient Evaluation

RA is a systemic disease, and pain originating in the elbow can limit the functioning of other parts of the involved upper extremity. Most patients have elbow pain both at rest and with activity. Pain with activity occurs at the extremes and midarc of motion and is secondary to progressive synovitis. Synovitis resolves itself spontaneously in a few patients, but in most patients it persists and progresses unless treated. Progressive synovitis can lead to articular and periarticular destruction of the normal ligamentous and osseous architecture, resulting in painful instability and functional loss. The need for pain relief often leads to obligate elbow flexion and superimposed extrinsic contracture, with end-range motion loss and pain. In this unique situation, laxity and stiffness can coexist. Synovial proliferation can lead to compression of the ulnar nerve or, less commonly, the radial nerve. The neurologic symptoms vary, but the result is a painful, weak, unstable, and stiff joint. The degree of ligamentous laxity, osseous deformity, and joint contracture, as well as neurologic involvement and skin integrity, is determined through physical examination.

Radiographic evaluation requires AP and lateral views. The Mayo Clinic classification (Figure 1, Table 1) stages disease severity using radiographic and clinical findings and can be used to guide treatment. CT can be used to further delineate osseous changes. MRI is usually not necessary, but it may be helpful if the diagnosis is unclear or oncologic lesions are suspected. Electrophysiologic studies are performed in patients who have neurologic symptoms.

### Nonsurgical Treatment

The first-line drugs for the treatment of patients with RA include nonsteroidal anti-inflammatory drugs (NSAIDs) and oral corticosteroids; the second-line drugs include methotrexate, sulfasalazine, and hydroxychloroquine. Disease-modifying antirheumatic drugs, such as D-penicillamine, methotrexate, and sulfasalazine, are also used. Recently, tumor necrosis factor-α antagonists, including etanercept, infliximab, and adalimumab, have been shown to be efficacious.[1] The success of these medications has led to a decline in the number of patients who require surgical treatment. Some patients with symptomatic elbow RA benefit from occupational therapy, splinting for contractures, bracing for joint instability, or occasional intra-articular corticosteroid injections for painful synovitis.

If nonsurgical treatment is unsuccessful, surgical intervention may be required. For less severe disease, the mainstay of surgical treatment is open or arthroscopic synovectomy. For patients with advanced disease, total elbow arthroplasty (TEA) may be required.

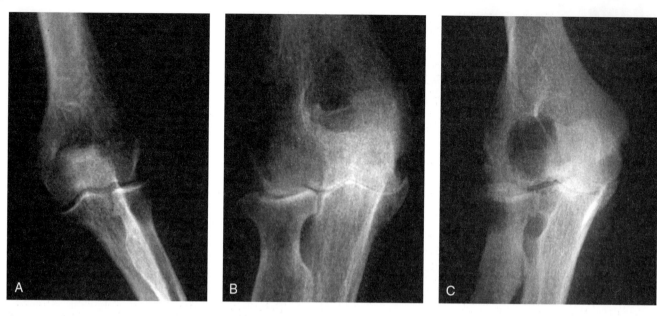

**Figure 1** AP radiographs showing the progression of changes in an elbow with RA. **A,** In Mayo grade I, the radiographic appearance is relatively normal, although osteopenia is present. **B,** In Mayo grade II, periarticular cysts appear, with loss of articular cartilage joint space. **C,** In Mayo grade III, more extensive cyst formation occurs, with loss of subchondral osseous architecture, although the joint remains relatively congruent.

| Table 1 | Mayo Clinic Classification of the Rheumatoid Elbow | |
| --- | --- |
| **Grade** | **Description** |
| I | No radiographic abnormalities, except periarticular osteopenia with accompanying soft-tissue swelling <br> Mild to moderate synovitis |
| II | Mild to moderate joint space reduction with little or no architectural distortion <br> Recalcitrant synovitis that cannot be managed with NSAIDs alone |
| III | Variable reduction in joint space, with or without cyst formation <br> Architectural alteration, such as thinning of the olecranon or resorption of the trochlea or capitellum <br> Variable synovitis, which may be quiescent |
| IV | Extensive articular damage, with subchondral bone loss and joint subluxation or ankylosis <br> Minimal synovitis |

*Data from Morrey BF, Adams RA: Semiconstrained arthroplasty for the treatment of rheumatoid arthritis of the elbow. J Bone Joint Surg Am 1992;74:479-490.*

## Synovectomy

Open synovectomy, with or without radial head excision, provides excellent early pain relief in patients with Mayo grade I or grade II disease,[2,3] although symptoms often recur. Synovectomy may also be helpful for a patient with more advanced disease, but the results are less reliable if the patient has significant joint destruction.

Radial head excision originally was a standard part of open synovectomy, but it is controversial and is now often avoided. Recent biomechanical data revealed that the radial head is an important secondary stabilizer of the normal elbow.[4,5] In the patient with RA, the disease process may attenuate the ligamentous constraints about the elbow, and radial head resection can accelerate the progression of instability and arthrosis. In arthroscopic synovectomy, which is becoming a more common procedure, the entire joint can routinely be visualized, and therefore the increased anterior exposure achieved by radial head excision is unnecessary. Recent studies found that radial head débridement during synovectomy can yield results equivalent to those of radial head excision.[6]

Compared with traditional open procedures, arthroscopic elbow surgery offers the advantages of less soft-tissue damage, less postsurgical pain, and a quicker recovery. For the surgeon, it offers better visualization of the entire joint, which can eliminate the need for radial head excision. The types of elbow pathologies that can be managed arthroscopically have increased because of improvements in technique, instrumentation, and understanding of three-dimensional arthroscopic anatomy and neurovascular relationships.

Elbow arthroscopy is a technically difficult procedure. Synovectomy of the rheumatoid elbow is perhaps the most difficult and complex arthroscopic elbow procedure because of the presence of anatomic distortions and pathologic tissues. The risk of neurovascular injury during elbow arthroscopy is greatest if the patient has loss of normal osseous architecture and a stiff, unstable elbow.[7] Thus, while elbow arthroscopy is an attractive option for treating symptomatic patients with RA, the surgeon must have expertise in performing the proce-

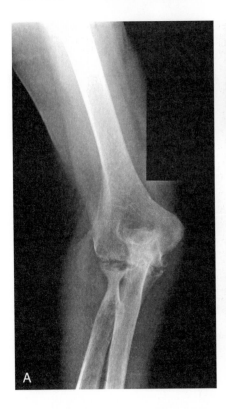

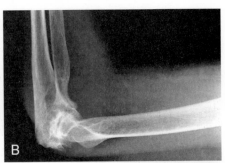

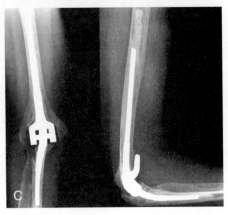

**Figure 2** Radiographs of an elbow with Mayo grade III rheumatoid involvement. **A,** AP view. **B,** Lateral view. **C,** AP and lateral radiographs showing a satisfactory result 6 years after TEA using a Coonrad-Morrey semiconstrained prosthesis. *(Reproduced from Morrey BF, O'Driscoll SW: Elbow arthritis, in Norris TR (ed): Orthopaedic Knowledge Update: Shoulder and Elbow. Rosemont, IL, American Academy of Orthopaedic Surgeons, 1997, pp 379-386.)*

dure as well as a thorough understanding of technique and neurovascular anatomy.

Good or excellent results after arthroscopic synovectomy were reported in 93% of patients, although only 57% of the 14 elbows maintained those results at an average 42-month follow-up.[8] Two elbows had transient neurapraxia of the radial or ulnar nerves, which was resolved within 3 months. Arthroscopic synovectomy was recommended only for patients who are younger than 50 years; have more than 90° of flexion; and have Mayo grade I, II, or III changes. Recent studies found good or excellent pain relief and function at an average 8-year follow-up.[9,10] One study compared the results of arthroscopic and open synovectomy in 58 elbows of patients with RA. Both groups had good results at an average 13-year follow-up. However, patients with substantial loss of motion (an arc less than 90°) had better functional outcomes after arthroscopic synovectomy.[11]

### Total Elbow Arthroplasty

TEA historically has been the most commonly performed procedure for RA, with good results.[12-15] The alternatives to TEA in patients with advanced disease include distraction interposition arthroplasty, distal humeral hemiarthroplasty, and surface replacement. Outside the United States, unlinked (resurfacing) implant designs are most commonly used for elbow replacement in patients with RA. In the United States, linked (semiconstrained) implants are more commonly used. An unlinked implant requires the presence of almost normal osseous and ligamentous architecture to maintain its stability, whereas in

a linked implant stability is conferred by the prosthesis. Reports of early loosening and failure of linked, highly constrained implants led to increased use of unlinked implants. However, some unlinked implants become dislocated as ligamentous stability is lost in patients with progressive RA. The newer linked implants are less constrained and better able to mimic the kinematic sloppy-hinge nature of the elbow. These factors remove the risk of implant dislocation. The use of these implants has improved implant loosening and survival rates, which are now similar to those of unlinked implants.

Recent studies found excellent pain relief, functional improvement, and implant survival after TEA using both linked and unlinked designs. A review of 58 Souter-Strathclyde unlinked prostheses (Stryker UK, Newbury, England) that were used in patients with RA found improvement in the Mayo Elbow Performance Score from 30 to 83 at an average 9-year follow-up. Survival was 70% and 53% at 10 and 16 years, respectively.[12] Similar longevity was observed after TEA using the Kudo type-3 unlinked prosthesis (Biomet, Warsaw, IN).[13]

A recent study of 18 rheumatoid elbows treated with the Gschwend-Scheier-Bahler III (GSB III) semiconstrained elbow prosthesis (Zimmer, Warsaw, IN) found substantial improvements in motion (to an average 33° flexion-extension), Mayo score, and patient satisfaction at an average 7.6-year follow-up.[14] A long-term study of 41 elbows treated using the Coonrad/Coonrad-Morrey semiconstrained prosthesis (Zimmer) found implant survival with good functional results of 50% at 14 years and 25% at 20 years[15] (Figure 2). One study compared

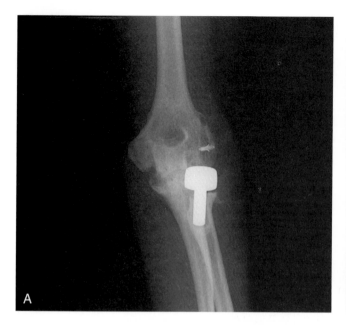

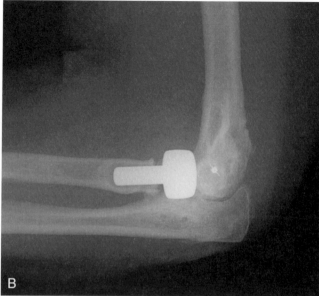

**Figure 3** Radiographs showing a radial head replacement and ulnohumeral degenerative changes after surgical repair of a terrible triad fracture-dislocation with early arthrosis and persistent instability. **A,** AP view. **B,** Lateral view.

survival of the Souter-Strathclyde, Kudo, and Coonrad-Morrey implants at 61, 67, and 68 months, respectively. Although pain relief was excellent and flexion was improved in all three groups, the Coonrad-Morrey implant had the highest survival rate. The authors concluded that the newer linked implants prevent dislocation without increasing the risk of loosening.[16]

The most recent innovation is the linkable design, which is an unconstrained implant that later can be converted to a constrained implant, if instability becomes a problem.[17] These devices may offer the best of both worlds; an implant can be placed in an unconstrained manner to minimize wear and loosening, but it can be converted to a constrained implant if necessary. Long-term studies are not yet available on linkable elbow prostheses.

## Posttraumatic Arthritis

The incidence of PTA has increased substantially during the past 20 years. PTA can occur after an intra-articular fracture or dislocation. Patients with PTA often are younger and more physiologically demanding than patients with other etiologies of the elbow. Frequently, they have alteration of the osseous anatomy because of malunion or nonunion and associated ligamentous instability. Many have had earlier surgery as a result of trauma.[18] They may have symptomatic hardware, indolent infection, neurologic deficits, or ulnar nerve transposition. The treatment of PTA can be complex. Because the pathologies are different in each patient, algorithmic approaches often cannot be used.

### Patient Evaluation

Patients with PTA frequently report pain at the extremes or midarc of motion as well as stiffness. The possible sources of pain include damage to the articular surface, stiffness, neurologic deficits, prominent hardware, and infection. Stiffness frequently has both intrinsic and extrinsic causes. Scarring around nerves, especially the ulnar nerve, can also inhibit motion and cause pain. Mechanical symptoms can result from osteophyte or loose body formation, retained hardware, or the articular incongruity itself. Because of articular malunion or prominent hardware, patients with PTA often have more severe articular deformation than patients with OA.

The patient's motion, stability, soft-tissue integrity, neurologic status, and infection status should be assessed. AP and lateral radiographs are critical in assessing changes in osseous architecture around the joint, as well as any hardware (Figure 3). CT is helpful in further delineating osseous changes. Laboratory studies, including C-reactive protein level, erythrocyte sedimentation rate, and complete blood cell count with differential, are performed to rule out indolent infection. Patients with neurologic symptoms are evaluated using electrophysiologic studies.

### Treatment

A patient with PTA is initially treated with NSAIDs, activity modification, and occupational or physical therapy. Bracing or splinting can be helpful for a patient with instability or contracture. If conservative measures are not successful, surgical treatment is indicated. Open or arthroscopic débridement and capsular release to treat mild degenerative conditions, including osteophytes, loose bodies, and soft-tissue contractures, can relieve pain and restore function in a properly selected patient. However, the feasibility of an arthroscopic procedure should be carefully considered because earlier surgery may have distorted the neurovascular anatomy.

Unlike patients with OA, many patients with PTA have advanced articular destruction and associated instability. In such patients, joint débridement is associated with high rates of failure, symptomatic recurrence, and disease progression. TEA can be considered in patients with lower physical demands who are older than 65 years, but it is not suitable for most patients with PTA because of their relative youth and high activity level. Although the short-term results of TEA in such patients have been excellent, revision surgery is often required because of aseptic loosening or bushing wear.[19] The results of TEA in patients with PTA are less favorable than the results in patients with RA, probably for two reasons: patients with PTA tend to have a higher activity level, and the osseous malunion and soft tissue contractures commonly seen in PTA alter the forces placed on the implant.[20,21]

When TEA is performed in a patient with PTA, the altered anatomy and forces on the elbow usually dictate the use of a linked implant rather than an unlinked implant. Two years after TEA with a linked implant, 83% of relatively active patients had a good or excellent outcome. However, 27% had complications, including loosening, implant fracture, and early bushing wear.[22] At an average 51-month follow-up after TEA with a linked implant, 15 patients had a 73% satisfaction rate and a 20% loosening rate.[23] Newer designs that can be used as either an unlinked or linked implant may prove useful in patients with PTA. Additionally, the use of hemiarthroplasty is being explored for patients with PTA or acute elbow trauma.

Interposition arthroplasty, which is often the better procedure for a patient with PTA, involves the release of all contractures, ulnohumeral joint recontouring, collateral ligament reconstruction, and application of a distracting hinged external fixator. The joint is débrided, and the distal humerus is resurfaced with soft tissue, such as dermis, allograft material, or fascia, which is attached using suture anchors or drill holes. A hinged external fixator is used to distract the joint and maintain stability. Interposition arthroplasty is the preferred procedure for patients who have midarc and terminal range-of-motion pain, stiffness, and articular derangement too severe for débridement alone to be successful. The contraindications include gross instability that cannot be reconstructed, as from significant bone loss or nonunion; active infection; or inability or unwillingness to tolerate the external fixator. One study found that 69% of patients with PTA had satisfactory pain relief at an average of 63 months,[24] and more recent reports corroborated this finding.[25] Interposition arthroplasty is often used as a bridging option to treat patients who are too young for TEA. One study reported reasonably satisfactory results after conversion to TEA of elbows previously treated with interposition arthroplasty.[26]

## Osteoarthritis

Only 1% to 2% of patients with arthritis of the elbow have primary OA, which is characterized by osteophyte formation, capsular contracture, and variable loose body formation. Unlike OA in more commonly affected joints, OA in the elbow is characterized by relative sparing of joint space early in the disease process. It usually affects the dominant arm of a male patient who is younger than 50 years and performs repetitive heavy labor or, less commonly, a repetitive sports activity. OA of the elbow is rare in women or in the nondominant arm.[27]

### Patient Evaluation

A patient with OA typically reports stiffness, end-range pain with forced flexion or extension, and mechanical symptoms such as locking or clicking of the joint. Pain is uncommon in the midarc of motion or at rest. Most patients have loss of elbow extension, often resulting from posterior osteophytic impingement and associated soft-tissue contracture. As the disease progresses, loss of flexion and forearm rotation can occur. A superimposed extrinsic capsular contracture can exacerbate stiffness. The mechanical symptoms commonly result from the presence of loose bodies or osteophytes about the elbow. Osteophytes and contractures can also impinge on the ulnar nerve and cause dysfunction and pain.

AP and lateral views are used in radiographic evaluation of the elbow. The dominant finding in OA is the presence of osteophytes, which often have encroached on the olecranon and coronoid fossae of the distal humerus and the corresponding edges of the olecranon and coronoid. Radiocapitellar osteophytes and loose bodies may also be present.[28] Usually, the joint space appears relatively normal, unless the disease is severe (Figure 4). CT, especially with three-dimensional reconstruction, can delineate the osteophytes. MRI is not usually helpful in evaluating patients with primary OA.

### Treatment

The initial treatment of symptomatic elbow OA involves a combination of rest, activity modification, anti-inflammatory drugs, and, occasionally, corticosteroid injections. NSAIDs are often used to relieve pain and reduce inflammation. Cortisone injections may provide temporary relief, but they are rarely a long-term solution. Occupational therapy may be helpful in relieving inflammation and alleviating soft-tissue contracture. Splinting can be used to improve the range of motion in a patient with a superimposed soft-tissue contracture.

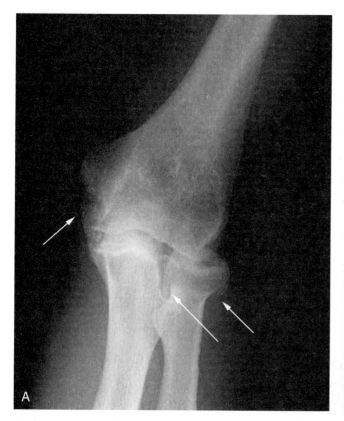 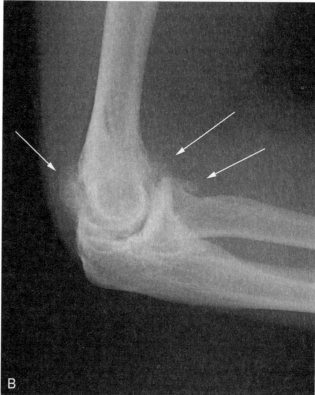

**Figure 4**   Radiographs showing typical primary OA of the elbow. Osteophytes (*arrows*) have encroached on the olecranon and coronoid fossa, and the disease has progressed to involve the radiocapitellar joint. **A,** AP view. **B,** Lateral view.

However, the end range of motion frequently is limited because of osteophyte impingement, which is unlikely to improve with splinting; splinting may instead exacerbate the inflammation and pain.

Surgical treatment is indicated if nonsurgical treatment is unsuccessful. The traditional surgical treatment of OA of the elbow involves open débridement of the joint, removal of osteophytes, and capsular release with or without fenestration of the olecranon fossa.[28-34] TEA and interposition arthroplasty are infrequently performed for OA of the elbow.

The Outerbridge-Kashiwagi arthroplasty uses a posterior approach to the elbow.[31] Impingement is relieved, and osteophytes are removed posteriorly along the olecranon and its fossa through a window in the olecranon fossa. Osteophytes are removed anteriorly along the coronoid via a window in the distal humerus. Wide capsular release or exposure cannot be performed using this procedure.[28]

A patient with significant disease or an extrinsic contracture contributing to stiffness is often treated using ulnohumeral arthroplasty, which is a more extensive débridement with osteophyte excision and a column release to improve motion. An extensive exposure, not possible with the posterior triceps-splitting approach used in Outerbridge-Kashiwagi arthroplasty, is required for wide débridement. It is achieved using a lateral or

medial column approach or a posterior approach with large medial and lateral skin flaps to expose the joint.[35] Patients who have ulnar nerve symptoms are treated either with release of the entrapped nerve or formal transposition. Similarly, patients with a loss of flexion greater than 110° that has persisted for more than 3 months should undergo ulnar nerve release and possibly transposition. The flexion limitation may be caused by an entrapped ulnar nerve, and forced flexion under anesthesia without nerve release can lead to permanent nerve injury.[29]

In most studies, the short-term results of open ulnohumeral arthroplasty have been good to excellent. The predictors of a favorable outcome include symptoms originating less than 2 years before surgery, significant pain before surgery, and ulnar nerve symptoms. A lack of mechanical symptoms is associated with a less favorable response to débridement.[30] After open débridement, 26 athletes and 24 manual laborers had pain relief and improved range of motion at an average of 60 months. All patients were able to return to sports or work, although 5 or more years later 40% of the patients had radiographic changes and recurrent symptoms, often including flexion contractures.[31] In another study, pain relief was satisfactory in 34 of 46 elbows, and the motion arc had increased an average of 23° at an average 80-month follow-up.[29] At an average 10-year follow-up of 33 elbows, the mean arc

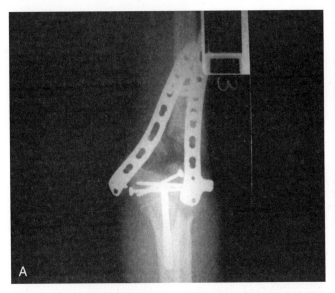
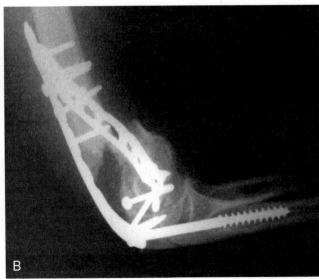

**Figure 5** Radiographs of the elbow of an elderly patient who developed a periarticular nonunion of a distal humerus fracture, requiring conversion to TEA to improve elbow function. **A,** AP view. **B,** Lateral view.

of motion had increased 24° (7° extension, 17° flexion), and the results were considered satisfactory in 85% of patients; 76% were able to return to strenuous labor.[36] Loss of extension occurred over time in most of the 19 patients who were followed more than 10 years, but the flexion gains persisted. All of these patients had radiographic evidence of osteophyte recurrence at the coronoid and olecranon tips and their respective fossae, but the radiographic findings were not correlated with symptom recurrence. A study of 17 patients found similar objective results at an 85-month follow-up. Patient-derived subjective outcomes were better than objective results, and this finding may indicate that patient satisfaction following ulnohumeral arthroplasty is higher than previously believed.[37]

Arthroscopic osteocapsular arthroplasty is the arthroscopic equivalent of ulnohumeral arthroplasty. It involves débridement of osteophytes and loose bodies and capsular release with or without olecranon fossa fenestration. An initial report of arthroscopic débridement in 24 patients who had both ulnohumeral and radiocapitellar degeneration found decreased pain in all patients and an average motion increase of 81° after 32 months. Eighteen of the patients had a radial head excision.[38] Nonetheless, most surgeons do not perform radial head resection with arthroscopic débridement for primary OA because this procedure can lead to abnormal biomechanics, laxity of the arthritic elbow, and the inferior long-term results associated with progressive arthrosis of the ulnohumeral joint. Recent studies have shown that arthroscopic débridement without radial head resection can be successful. The results were good or excellent in 21 of 25 patients, with a 21° average increase in arc of motion at 67-month follow-up. These results

suggest that radial head excision is unnecessary and should be avoided in patients with moderate or severe radiocapitellar arthritis.[6] At 26 months after arthroscopic osteocapsular arthroplasty, 11 patients had a mean 73° increase in flexion-extension and statistically significant improvement in pain control and patient satisfaction.[39]

Although open or arthroscopic débridement is the standard surgical treatment of elbow OA, interposition arthroplasty or TEA may be considered for a patient with advanced disease. However, the indications for these procedures should be scrutinized because a younger, active patient with OA often has early implant failure or requires soft-tissue arthroplasty. For a patient who is not a candidate for débridement or who has had unsuccessful results after débridement, interposition arthroplasty is preferable to TEA. However, results after interposition arthroplasty have been less consistent in patients with primary OA than in patients with PTA.[40] For active patients with primary OA, TEA is rarely the preferred procedure because of the risk of polyethylene wear and loosening. In 14 elbows, early failure, including component fracture and osteolysis with aseptic loosening, occurred in 21%.[41,42]

## Flail Elbow

A flail elbow is caused by chronic dislocation, periarticular nonunion, or a grossly unstable elbow secondary to advanced rheumatic disease. Although a flail elbow may not be truly arthritic in nature, the surgical treatment often requires reconstruction with TEA; therefore, flail elbow can be considered within the spectrum of disease seen in patients with elbow arthritis. The condition is rarely seen in the United States, and there are few options for treating it. Some patients have little pain, and others gain stability and function by using an orthosis. Five patients with chronic elbow dislocation were treated with some success using a distracting hinged external fixator.[43]

For most patients, functional limitations and constant pain require consideration of surgical treatment, usually replacement arthroplasty. After a linked-implant TEA, 16 of 19 patients with a flail elbow had a satisfactory outcome and a functional arc of motion.[44] Another study of six patients corroborated these findings.[45] TEA was also used with success in elderly patients with a distal humeral nonunion[46,47] (Figure 5). Recent studies have reported excellent outcomes, with pain improvement and restoration of function in selected patients.[46,47]

## Complications and Revision Arthroplasty

Improved implant designs, as well as advances in understanding pathologic anatomy, normal elbow biomechanics, and kinematics, have led to improved surgical outcomes with infrequent complications. To avoid complications, especially nerve injury, after procedures such as arthroscopic osteocapsular arthroplasty, synovectomy, or capsular release, the surgeon must have expertise and a thorough understanding of the three-dimensional anatomy of the elbow.

Some complications, including infection, nerve injury, and stiffness, are associated with the surgical treatment of all arthritic joints. Aseptic loosening, instability (predominantly associated with unlinked implants), and triceps insufficiency also occur. After a TEA, 2% to 5% of patients become infected, most frequently with *Staphylococcus epidermidis* or *Staphylococcus aureus*.[48] These patients often require a staged revision using antibiotics, although a patient with an early *S. aureus* infection can sometimes be successfully treated with aggressive irrigation and débridement.

When revision arthroplasty is necessary, osseous reconstruction often requires impaction grafting or allograft reconstruction in conjunction with implant replacement. In the future, the longevity of TEA may be improved by intervention earlier in the disease process, the development of linkable prosthetic designs, a greater understanding of polyethylene wear patterns, and improvements in polyethylene surface design.[49-53]

## Summary

Treatment of the arthritic elbow, like treatment of other arthritic joints, requires a thorough understanding of pathophysiology and etiology, as well as current treatment options. Many patients are successfully treated using nonsurgical methods, and others can be successfully treated surgically. Improvements in arthroscopic techniques and implant design, as well as increased under-

standing of pathologic anatomy and conditions associated with elbow arthritides, have led to improved surgical outcomes. Pain relief and functional improvement can be achieved in patients who are appropriately selected and treated.

## Annotated References

1. Lipsky PE, van der Heijde DM, St Clair EW, et al: Infliximab and methotrexate in the treatment of rheumatoid arthritis. *N Engl J Med* 2000;343:1594-1602.

2. Alexiades MM, Scott TS, Figgie MP, Inglis AE: Minimum ten year follow-up study for elbow synovectomy for rheumatoid arthritis. *Trans Orthop* 1990;14:255.

3. Kauffman JI, Chen AL, Stuchin S, Di Cesare PE: Surgical management of the rheumatoid elbow. *J Am Acad Orthop Surg* 2003;11:100-108.

   Advancements in prostheses and surgical techniques have led to reliably successful elbow arthroplasty in patients with severe RA of the elbow.

4. Beingessner DM, Dunning CE, Gordon KD, Johnson JA, King GJ: The effect of radial head excision and arthroplasty on elbow kinematics and stability. *J Bone Joint Surg Am* 2004;86-A:1730-1739.

   Eight cadaver elbows were studied in an in vitro simulator, and valgus angulation and rotational kinematics were determined. In specimens with intact ligaments, varus-valgus laxity increased after radial head excision but was corrected after radial head arthroplasty.

5. Schneeberger AG, Sadowski MM, Jacob HA: Coronoid process and radial head as posterolateral rotatory stabilizers of the elbow. *J Bone Joint Surg Am* 2004;86-A:975-982.

   Posterolateral rotatory displacement of the ulna was measured in seven intact elbows under varus and supinating forces. Excision of the radial head with intact collateral ligaments caused a mean posterolateral rotatory laxity of 18.6° (*P* < 0.0001).

6. Kelly EW, Bryce R, Coghlan J, Bell S: Arthroscopic debridement without radial head excision of the osteoarthritic elbow. *Arthroscopy* 2007;23:151-156.

   Of 25 elbows treated for radiocapitellar arthritis by débridement and capsular release without radial head excision, 24 were "better" or "much better" at an average follow-up of 67 months; The average motion arc improved by 21°. Level of evidence: IV.

7. Kelly EW, Morrey BF, O'Driscoll SW: Complications of elbow arthroscopy. *J Bone Joint Surg Am* 2001; 83-A:25-34.

   After 473 elbow arthroscopies, a serious complication occurred in 4 and a minor complication in 50, including 12 transient nerve palsies. The most significant risk factors for

development of a temporary nerve palsy were a diagnosis of RA and contracture.

8. Lee BP, Morrey BF: Arthroscopic synovectomy of the elbow for rheumatoid arthritis: A prospective study. *J Bone Joint Surg Br* 1997;79:770-772.

9. Fuerst M, Fink B, Ruther W: Survival analysis and longterm results of elbow synovectomy in rheumatoid arthritis. *J Rheumatol* 2006;33:892-896.

   Synovectomy was performed on 85 elbows with RA, and 61 were examined clinically at a mean of 8.7 years. Morrey scores significantly improved, especially because of effective pain relief. Level of evidence: IV.

10. Horiuchi K, Momohara S, Tomatsu T, Inoue K, Toyama Y: Arthroscopic synovectomy of the elbow in rheumatoid arthritis. *J Bone Joint Surg Am* 2002; 84-A:342-347.

    Arthroscopic synovectomy was evaluated in 21 elbows at a minimum of 42 months (mean, 97 months), using the Mayo Elbow Performance Score and radiographic findings. One of the most favorable indications was a grade I or II presurgical radiographic rating.

11. Tanaka N, Sakahashi H, Hirose K, Ishima T, Ishii S: Arthroscopic and open synovectomy of the elbow in rheumatoid arthritis. *J Bone Joint Surg Am* 2006;88: 521-525.

    Arthroscopic or open synovectomy was performed in 58 elbows with RA. At an average 13-year follow-up, 48% of patients had mild or no pain after arthroscopic synovectomy and 70% had mild or no pain after open synovectomy. Level of evidence: III.

12. Landor I, Vavrik P, Jahoda D, Guttler K, Sosna A: Total elbow replacement with the Souter-Strathclyde prosthesis in rheumatoid arthritis: Long-term follow-up. *J Bone Joint Surg Br* 2006;88:1460-1463.

    At a mean 9.5-year follow-up, 58 Souter-Strathclyde total elbow replacements were reviewed. The mean Mayo Elbow Performance Score improved from 30 to 82. Thirteen elbows (22.4%) had been revised. The Kaplan-Meier survival rates at 10- and 16-year follow-up were 70% and 53%, respectively. Level of evidence: IV.

13. Thillemann TM, Olsen BS, Johannsen HV, Sojbjerg JO: Long-term results with the Kudo type 3 total elbow arthroplasty. *J Shoulder Elbow Surg* 2006;15: 495-499.

    At a mean 9.5-year follow-up after TEA using an unlinked Kudo type-3 implant, the prostheses had survived in 67.9% of eight elbows available for examination; the mean survival of all implants was 8.7 years. Level of evidence: IV.

14. Kelly EW, Coghlan J, Bell S: Five- to thirteen-year follow-up of the GSB III total elbow arthroplasty. *J Shoulder Elbow Surg* 2004;13:434-440.

    Eighteen elbows with the GSB III elbow prosthesis were evaluated at an average of 7.6 years after TEA. All patients were satisfied, with a mean Mayo Elbow Performance Score of 91. Mean flexion-extension and supination-pronation arcs improved 33° and 67°, respectively. Level of evidence: IV.

15. Aldridge JM III, Lightdale NR, Mallon WJ, Coonrad RW: Total elbow arthroplasty with the Coonrad/Coonrad-Morrey prosthesis: A 10- to 31-year survival analysis. *J Bone Joint Surg Br* 2006;88:509-514.

    Twenty-one of 41 elbows were functional 10 to 14 years after Coonrad/Coonrad-Morrey elbow arthroplasty, 10 were functional 15 to 19 years later, and 10 were functional 20 to 31 years later. There were 14 complications and 13 revisions. Level of evidence: IV.

16. Little CP, Graham AJ, Karatzas G, Woods DA, Carr AJ: Outcomes of total elbow arthroplasty for rheumatoid arthritis: Comparative study of three implants. *J Bone Joint Surg Am* 2005;87:2439-2448.

    Patients treated for RA with TEA were stratified into three 33-patient groups by type of implant (Souter-Strathclyde, Kudo, or Coonrad-Morrey). At a minimum 61-month follow-up, the Coonrad-Morrey implant had better 5-year survivorship than the other implants. Focal osteolysis adjacent to the ulnar components was seen in 16% of Coonrad-Morrey TEAs, with 8% progressing to frank loosening. Level of evidence: III.

17. Gramstad GD, King GJ, O'Driscoll SW, Yamaguchi K: Elbow arthroplasty using a convertible implant. *Tech Hand Up Extrem Surg* 2005;9:153-163.

    Use of an anatomic convertible implant allows great versatility in choosing hemiarthroplasty or unlinked or linked TEA. Conversion from an unlinked to a linked constraint (or vice versa) can be performed at any time in a minimally invasive fashion.

18. Morrey BF: Post-traumatic contracture of the elbow: Operative treatment, including distraction arthroplasty. *J Bone Joint Surg Am* 1990;72:601-618.

19. Moro JK, King GJ: Total elbow arthroplasty in the treatment of posttraumatic conditions of the elbow. *Clin Orthop Relat Res* 2000;370:102-114.

20. Lee BP, Adams RA, Morrey BF: Polyethylene wear after total elbow arthroplasty. *J Bone Joint Surg Am* 2005;87:1080-1087.

    Of 12 patients who underwent an isolated bushing exchange for polyethylene wear, 7 had PTA and 5 had RA; 9 had extensive deformity. The revision was performed an average 7.9 years after implantation. At final follow-up, all patients had functioning elbows. Level of evidence: IV.

21. Wright TW, Hastings H: Total elbow arthroplasty failure due to overuse, C-ring failure, and/or bushing wear. *J Shoulder Elbow Surg* 2005;14:65-72.

    Ten patients had C-ring or bushing wear after a Coonrad-Morrey TEA. The average time to revision was 60 months. The common associated factors were PTA (3

patients), supracondylar nonunion (5 patients), male sex, young age, and high activity level. Level of evidence: II.

22. Schneeberger AG, Adams R, Morrey BF: Semicon-strained total elbow replacement for the treatment of post-traumatic osteoarthrosis. *J Bone Joint Surg Am* 1997;79:1211-1222.

23. Schneeberger AG, Meyer DC, Yian EH: Conrad-Morrey total elbow replacement for primary and re-vision surgery: A 2- to 7.5-year follow-up study. *J Shoulder Elbow Surg* 2007;16(suppl 3):S47-S54.

   After a Coonrad-Morrey TEA for PTA, 73% of 15 pa-tients had a satisfactory outcome at 51-month follow-up, using the Mayo Elbow Performance Score. Ten (66%) had mild or no pain, and 5 had moderate or severe pain. The loosening rate was 20%. Level of evidence: IV.

24. Cheng SL, Morrey BF: Treatment of the mobile, pain-ful arthritic elbow by distraction interposition ar-throplasty. *J Bone Joint Surg Br* 2000;82:233-238.

25. Hausman MR, Birnbaum PS: Interposition elbow ar-throplasty. *Tech Hand Up Extrem Surg* 2004;8: 181-188.

   Interposition arthroplasty, combined with hinged exter-nal fixation, is an alternative to TEA and may be prefera-ble in younger, more active patients who anticipate heavier use.

26. Blaine TA, Adams R, Morrey BF: Total elbow arthro-plasty after interposition arthroplasty for elbow ar-thritis. *J Bone Joint Surg Am* 2005;87:286-292.

   TEA using a linked semiconstrained implant was evaluated at average 10-year follow-up in 12 patients who had an earlier interposition arthroplasty. The aver-age Mayo Elbow Performance Score improved from 32.1 before surgery to 80.4 at follow-up ($P < 0.001$). Level of evidence: IV.

27. Doherty M, Preston B: Primary osteoarthritis of the elbow. *Ann Rheum Dis* 1989;48:743-747.

28. Tsuge K, Mizuseki T: Debridement arthroplasty for advanced primary osteoarthritis of the elbow: Re-sults of a new technique used for 29 elbows. *J Bone Joint Surg Br* 1994;76:641-646.

29. Antuna SA, Morrey BF, Adams RA, O'Driscoll SW: Ulnohumeral arthroplasty for primary degenerative arthritis of the elbow: Long-term outcome and com-plications. *J Bone Joint Surg Am* 2002;84-A:2168-2173.

   Ulnohumeral arthroplasty in 46 elbows with primary OA were reviewed at an average 80-month follow-up. Mayo Elbow Performance Scores were excellent for 26, good for 8, fair for 4, and poor for 8. Thirteen reported ul-nar nerve symptoms, for which surgery was required in six.

30. Forster MC, Clark DI, Lunn PG: Elbow osteo-arthritis: Prognostic indicators in ulnohumeral de-bridement. The Outerbridge-Kashiwagi procedure.

*J Shoulder Elbow Surg* 2001;10:557-560.

   At a mean 39-month follow-up of 35 patients (36 el-bows) after ulnohumeral débridement for elbow OA, 81% were satisfied. Mean flexion-extension arc, pain score, and locking were significantly improved, although some patients had pain at rest.

31. Kashiwagi D: Osteoarthritis of the elbow joint, in Kashiwagi D (ed): *Elbow Joint Proceedings of the In-ternational Congress in Japan.* Amsterdam, Nether-lands: Elsevier, 1986, pp 177-188.

32. Morrey BF: Primary degenerative arthritis of the el-bow: Treatment by ulnohumeral arthroplasty. *J Bone Joint Surg Br* 1992;74:409-413.

33. Oka Y: Debridement for osteoarthritis of the elbow in athletes. *Int Orthop* 1999;23:91-94.

34. Oka Y: Debridement arthroplasty for osteoarthrosis of the elbow: 50 patients followed mean 5 years. *Acta Orthop Scand* 2000;71:185-190.

35. Mansat P, Morrey BF: The column procedure: A lim-ited lateral approach for extrinsic contracture of the elbow. *J Bone Joint Surg Am* 1998;80:1603-1615.

36. Wada T, Isogai S, Ishii S, Yamashita T: Débridement arthroplasty for primary osteoarthritis of the elbow. *J Bone Joint Surg Am* 2004;86-A:233-241.

   Thirty-three elbows with primary OA were available for follow-up at a mean 121 months after treatment with dé-bridement arthroplasty; 19 elbows were followed more than 10 years. The mean arc of movement improved 24°, and 76% of patients returned to strenuous labor. Level of evidence: IV.

37. Tashjian RZ, Wolf JM, Ritter M, Weiss AP, Green A: Functional outcomes and general health status after ulnohumeral arthroplasty for primary degenerative arthritis of the elbow. *J Shoulder Elbow Surg* 2006;15: 357-366.

   Eighteen elbows with primary OA were evaluated at a mean 85 months after ulnohumeral arthroplasty. The mean elbow flexion arc improved 16°, and the mean forearm rotation arc improved 35°. Self-assessed patient outcomes were better than as determined by categorical scoring sys-tems. Level of evidence: III.

38. Savoie FH III, Nunley PD, Field LD: Arthroscopic management of the arthritic elbow: Indications, tech-nique, and results. *J Shoulder Elbow Surg* 1999;8: 214-219.

39. Krishnan SG, Harkins DC, Pennington SD, Harrison DK, Burkhead WZ: Arthroscopic ulnohumeral ar-throplasty for degenerative arthritis of the elbow in patients aged under fifty years. *J Shoulder Elbow Surg* 2007:16;443-448.

   At 26 months after ulnohumeral arthroplasty for degen-erative arthritis, 11 patients with a mean age of 36 years had a 73° improvement in mean arc of motion ($P < 0.01$). Sub-

jective report of pain improved from 9.2 to 1.7, and subjective satisfaction improved from 1.8 to 9.0. Level of evidence: IV.

40. Fox RJ, Varitimidis SE, Plakseychuk A, Vardakas DG, Tomaino MM, Sotereanos DG: The Compass Elbow Hinge: Indications and initial results. *J Hand Surg Br* 2000;25:568-572.

41. Espag MP, Back DL, Clark DI, Lunn PG: Early results of the Souter-Strathclyde unlinked total elbow arthroplasty in patients with osteoarthritis. *J Bone Joint Surg Br* 2003;85:351-353.

   A retrospective review of 11 Souter-Strathclyde primary TEAs in 10 patients with OA found that, although no patients had symptoms, there was radiographic evidence of loosening in three humeral and two ulnar components, one of which ultimately required revision.

42. Kozak TK, Adams RA, Morrey BF: Total elbow arthroplasty in primary osteoarthritis of the elbow. *J Arthroplasty* 1998;13:837-842.

43. Jupiter JB, Ring D: Treatment of unreduced elbow dislocations with hinged external fixation. *J Bone Joint Surg Am* 2002;84-A:1630-1635.

   Treatment of an unreduced dislocation of the elbow using open reduction and hinged external fixation as late as 30 weeks after injury was found to restore a stable, mobile joint without the need for tendon lengthening or transfer, ligament reconstruction, or deepening of the trochlear notch of the ulna.

44. Ramsey ML, Adams RA, Morrey BF: Instability of the elbow treated with semiconstrained total elbow arthroplasty. *J Bone Joint Surg Am* 1999;81:38-47.

45. Mighell MA, Dunham RC, Rommel EA, Frankle MA: Primary semi-constrained arthroplasty for chronic fracture-dislocations of the elbow. *J Bone Joint Surg Br* 2005;87:191-195.

   Six patients with chronic elbow dislocation were treated with primary semiconstrained TEA. The most dramatic improvement was in function. The mean American Shoulder and Elbow Surgeons Index score improved 5.2 times ($P < 0.001$), and the mean total range of movement increased from 33° to 121° ($P < 0.001$). Level of evidence: IV.

46. McKee MD, Jupiter JB: Semiconstrained elbow replacement for distal humeral nonunion. *J Bone Joint Surg Br* 1995;77:665-666.

47. Morrey BF, Adams RA: Semiconstrained elbow replacement for distal humeral nonunion. *J Bone Joint Surg Br* 1995;77:67-72.

48. Yamaguchi K, Adams RA, Morrey BF: Infection after total elbow arthroplasty. *J Bone Joint Surg Am* 1998;80:481-491.

49. Ferlic DC, Clayton ML: Salvage of failed total elbow arthroplasty. *J Shoulder Elbow Surg* 1995;4:290-297.

50. Kamineni S, Morrey BF: Proximal ulnar reconstruction with strut allograft in revision total elbow arthroplasty. *J Bone Joint Surg Am* 2004;86-A:1223-1229.

   Twenty-two elbows were followed for an average of 4 years after treatment of a proximal ulnar bone deficiency with allograft bone struts after aseptic failure of TEA. The mean Mayo Elbow Performance Score improved from 34 before surgery to 79. Level of evidence: IV.

51. King GJ, Adams RA, Morrey BF: Total elbow arthroplasty: Revision with use of a non-custom semiconstrained prosthesis. *J Bone Joint Surg Am* 1997;79: 394-400.

52. Loebenberg MI, Adams R, O'Driscoll SW, Morrey BF: Impaction grafting in revision total elbow arthroplasty. *J Bone Joint Surg Am* 2005;87:99-106.

   Impaction grafting was performed in 12 patients undergoing revision TEA. At an average 72-month follow-up, 8 had radiographic incorporation. The remaining four elbows were revised because of loosening (two elbows), implant fracture (one), or infection (one). Level of evidence: IV.

53. Renfree KJ, Dell PC, Kozin SH, Wright TW: Total elbow arthroplasty with massive composite allografts. *J Shoulder Elbow Surg* 2004;13:313-321.

   Ten patients who underwent massive allograft prosthetic composite TEA were evaluated after 6.5 years. Pain and stability had improved modestly, but functional outcomes were disappointing. Three patients were unable to use the elbow. Level of evidence: IV.

# Chapter 46

# Radial Head Fractures

*David Ring, MD, PhD

## Introduction

The understanding of fractures of the radial head has improved in recent years, but optimal treatment is still controversial. It is important to distinguish between a stable fracture of the radial head, which is an isolated injury without an associated complete ligament injury or unstable fracture of the ulna, and an unstable fracture, which is associated with a more complex and unstable injury of the elbow or forearm. An apparently isolated fracture with more than 2 mm of displacement, which is relatively uncommon, should raise the suspicion of concomitant injury. Restriction of forearm rotation by a stable, isolated fracture of the radial head is uncommon; the primary risk is elbow stiffness. An unstable, displaced fracture usually is part of a complex injury of the elbow or forearm in which the radial head is an important contributor to forearm and elbow stability. In an unstable fracture, the radial head should either be repaired through open reduction and internal fixation (ORIF) or replaced with a prosthesis. There is some evidence that ORIF of a complex articular fracture having more than three articular fragments may lead to early failure, nonunion, and restriction of forearm rotation.[1] In an unstable, displaced fracture, excision without prosthetic replacement should be performed with great caution.

## Anatomy and Biomechanics
### The Displaced Fracture

An unstable, displaced fracture of the radial head, whether it is a partial or complete articular fracture

*David Ring, MD, PhD or the department with which he is affiliated has received research or institutional support from AO Foundation, Small Bone Innovations, Wright Medical, Smith & Nephew, Accumed, and Tornier; miscellaneous non-income support, commercially-derived honoraria, or other nonresearch-related funding from Wright Medical, Smith & Nephew, and Small Bone Innovations; royalties from Hand Innovations; holds stock or stock options in Mimedex, Inc and Illuminos, Inc; and is a consultant or employee for Wright Medical, Smith & Nephew, Accumed, and Tornier.

(Mason type II or III), is usually associated with additional fracture or ligament injury.[2,3] A retrospective study of 333 radial head fractures in adult patients at a tertiary care medical center found that 110 of the fractures were displaced; 46 of these involved part of the radial head, and 64 involved the entire radial head. Because the original Mason classification was used in this study, the definition of displacement is somewhat unclear. An associated fracture or soft-tissue injury was found in 118 of the 333 patients (39%), 53 (16%) had a coronoid fracture, and 45 (14%) had an elbow dislocation. Fifty percent of the displaced partial articular fractures were associated with another fracture or ligament injury of the elbow or forearm.[2] In another study, 24 patients with an acute displaced fracture of the radial head but no documented elbow dislocation or forearm tenderness were evaluated using MRI. There was evidence of injury to the medial collateral ligament (MCL) in 13 patients; injury to the lateral collateral ligament, in 18; and injury to both ligaments, in 12. Capitellar osteochondral defects were present in 7 patients; capitellar bone bruises, in 23; and loose bodies, in 22.[3] Apparently isolated fractures of the radial head with more than 2 mm of displacement are uncommon, and in many of these fractures some ligament or osteochondral injury is present. It is possible that these injuries represent a transition between stable, isolated injuries and obvious elbow or forearm fracture-dislocations.

A biomechanical study found that all aspects of the radial head have similar subchondral bone properties. The implication is that subluxation or dislocation, rather than an inherent weakness in this area, creates most anterolateral radial head fractures.[4] The anterolateral quadrant is fractured as the radial head subluxates or dislocates posteriorly.

### The Ligament-Deficient Elbow

Repair or reconstruction of the radial head is most important for a displaced fracture with an associated fracture or ligament injury. Several biomechanical studies addressed the role of the radial head in the ligament-

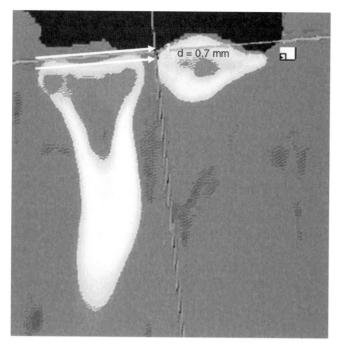

**Figure 1** Quantitative analysis of CT studies of the elbow suggests that the most distal part of the radial head articular surface (*top arrow*) is, on average, 1 mm more proximal than the lateral edge of the coronoid process at the lesser sigmoid notch (bottom arrow). Some surgeons prefer to use the center of the dish of the radial head, which should be roughly even with the coronoid at the lesser sigmoid notch. A more proximal radial head prosthesis may be too large. d = distance on a line parallel to the radius between the two measurements; for this patient, the distance is 7 mm.

deficient elbow. A study of passive and active elbow motion and pivot-shift testing using an in vitro elbow simulator found that, with the ligaments intact, a fracture as small as one third of the anterolateral radial head affects valgus angulation and external rotation of the ulna relative to the humerus.[5] Small fractures also contributed to gross instability when the ligaments were disrupted.

A biomechanical study of cadaver elbows with a fractured radial head and cut MCL found comparable restoration of varus and valgus laxity after either fixation with a plate and screws or replacement with a metal prosthesis.[6] In another study, replacement of the radial head with one of three metal prostheses (two bipolar and one monoblock) decreased valgus laxity in an MCL-deficient elbow. One bipolar implant had greater laxity with the forearm in neutral rotation; this finding suggests that prosthesis mobility may compromise stability.[7]

In another biomechanical study, elbow instability was found to be much worse with concomitant fracture of the coronoid. Posterolateral rotatory laxity of the elbow averaged 5.4° in an intact elbow, 9° after surgical exposure of the radial head, and 18.6° after radial head excision. The elbow became dislocated with excision of the radial head and 30% of the coronoid process, even if the collateral ligaments were intact. Radial head re-

placement prevented dislocation unless the coronoid loss was more than 50%, when reconstruction of the coronoid was also necessary to prevent dislocation.[8]

### The Interosseous Ligament–Deficient Forearm

Several biomechanical studies defined the importance of radiocapitellar contact in the interosseous ligament–deficient elbow (the Essex-Lopresti lesion) and its variants. If the radial head is fractured or excised and the interosseous ligament remains intact, distal ulnar loads are limited to less than half of the applied wrist force. If the interosseous membrane is damaged, almost the entire applied wrist force is shifted to the ulna.[9] Insertion of a metal radial head prosthesis maintains the distal ulnar forces at normal levels, when the radius is restored to its original anatomic length, regardless of forearm rotation position. In an interosseous ligament–deficient forearm, the use of a larger radial head prosthesis lowers distal ulnar loads correspondingly.[10] A combination of radial head replacement and interosseous ligament reconstruction improves the longitudinal stability of the forearm and the load transfer at the wrist and elbow more than either procedure alone.[11]

### The Radial Head Prosthesis

Biomechanical and radiologic-anatomic studies established the importance of radial head prosthesis sizing and provided guidelines for determining appropriate size. Radial neck lengthening or shortening of 2.5 mm or more significantly changes varus-valgus laxity and ulnar rotation in a MCL-deficient elbow.[12] Quantitative CT analysis of intact forearms found that the distal articular surface of the radial head, as assessed intrasurgically, should be roughly even with the distal limit of the lesser sigmoid notch of the coronoid process[13] (Figure 1). After arthroplasty using a metallic radial head, radiocapitellar contact area was decreased approximately two thirds relative to the native joint. Use of a smaller implant created a slightly larger contact area, and contact area decreased as joint flexion angle increased.[14]

## Patterns of Injury

Fractures of the radial head were first classified by Mason, in an era when fractures were excised or treated nonsurgically.[15] A nondisplaced fracture that could be treated nonsurgically was designated as type I; a displaced fracture involving part of the radial head, as type II; and a comminuted fracture of the entire head of the radius, which was best treated by excision, as type III. Type II fractures presented a treatment dilemma because some had a poor result, even though most of the head was intact.

The Morrey modification of the Mason classification included fractures of the radial neck and a quantitative definition of displacement as involving more more than

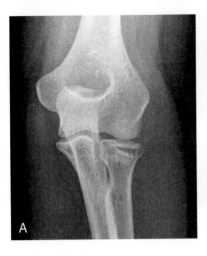
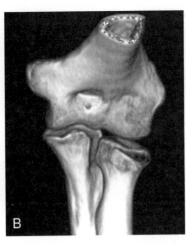

**Figure 2** **A,** AP radiograph showing a fragment that appears to be displaced at least 2 mm. **B,** Three-dimensional CT reconstruction showing the fragment impacted into a stable position.

2 mm, with a fragment of 30% or more of the displaced articular surface.[16] A fracture-dislocation of the elbow was classified as Mason type IV, following Johnston's suggestion.[17] However, inclusion of the radial neck fracture was not useful because these fractures are treated differently and should be considered separately. The inclusion of fracture-dislocation also was not useful because fractures of the radial head are associated with a variety of complex injury patterns and must be characterized regardless of injury pattern. Finally, few data support the quantitative definition of displacement offered in this system.

The Hotchkiss modification of the Mason classification reflects current treatment options.[18] Type I is a minimally displaced fracture that can be successfully treated nonsurgically; type II is a displaced partial head fracture that blocks forearm rotation and can be repaired with ORIF; and type III is an irreparable fracture that requires excision, with or without prosthetic replacement. Although this classification is conceptually useful, the method of distinguishing displaced from nondisplaced fractures and repairable from irreparable fractures is incompletely defined.

In the AO-ASIF Comprehensive Classification of Fractures of Long Bones, fractures of the proximal radius and ulna are combined in a way that is not useful for patient management.[19] However, this system usefully distinguishes fractures with more than three fragments from those with two or three major fragments. The presence of more than three fragments is associated with a much higher risk of early failure, nonunion, and loss of forearm rotation after ORIF.[1] Other factors that may be important in treatment but are not well accounted for in current classification systems include lost fragments, which are common in displaced fractures; fragments that are too small to be repaired and must be discarded; fragments with little or no subchondral bone; fragments with osteoporotic bone; impaction and deformation of fracture fragments; and metaphyseal bone loss. Partial resection of the radial head has long been

associated with inferior results, as well as difficulty in ORIF.[1,20] Therefore, when lost fragments, fragments too small to fix, or fragments with inadequate bone quality are found, the surgeon should consider performing a resection of the radial head, with prosthetic replacement if associated injuries are present. Deformation of the radial head can hinder forearm rotation after surgical fixation of an impacted fracture, and therefore it may be preferable to avoid surgical fixation of such a fracture. Metaphyseal bone loss and impaction occur even in a displaced partial radial head fracture, and using a plate may be superior to using screws alone to fix such a fracture.

## Nonsurgical Treatment

Most partial articular fractures of the radial head are impacted fractures that are not associated with dislocation or fracture-dislocation of the elbow (Figure 2). Recent data emphasize that elbow stiffness is the main risk after a stable, isolated radial head fracture and that nonsurgical treatment is associated with very good long-term results.[21,22]

A prospective, randomized comparison of elbow mobilization begun immediately or 5 days after a minimally displaced fracture of the radial head found that patients with immediate mobilization had greater comfort, flexion, strength in supination, and elbow function 7 days after injury, although the difference had disappeared 4 weeks after surgery.[23] The study authors used these findings to support early mobilization, but they can also be used to argue that a short period of immobilization is not detrimental if elbow exercises are initiated within approximately 1 week.

Nonunion of a stable, minimally displaced fracture of the radial head and neck can occur, but it is usually asymptomatic and may not be diagnosed. The true incidence is therefore unknown. A small study confirmed that nonunion of the radial neck after nonsurgical treatment is usually asymptomatic and does not require

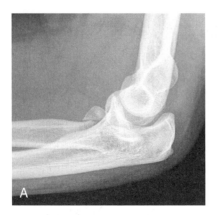
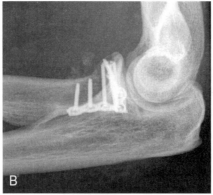
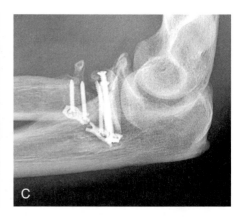

**Figure 3** **A,** Lateral radiograph of a displaced fracture of the entire radial head, associated with dislocation of the elbow. **B,** Lateral radiograph taken 1 month after ORIF using a plate and screws. **C,** Lateral radiograph taken 8 months later, showing nonunion and implant failure.

treatment, and fractures not united after 1 year may eventually heal.[24]

Long-term follow-up studies found good results after displaced partial articular fracture of the radial head and neck. One hundred patients with a so-called uncomplicated or isolated fracture of the radial head (a displaced fracture of the radial head without an apparent associated fracture or ligament injury) were evaluated an average 19 years after injury.[21] Displacement was defined using the Broberg and Morrey modification of the Mason classification. It is possible that many of the patients had an undiagnosed, MRI-detectable associated ligament injury. Among the 88 patients who were treated nonsurgically, only 9 (10%) had a secondary resection of the radial head; 84% had a good outcome, according to the very strict Steinberg classification. Unfortunately, patients with fractures of the radial neck or radial head and patients who were treated nonsurgically or surgically were all studied together.

A second study focused on a subgroup of the same patients with partial articular fractures displaced more than 2 mm.[22] Of the 49 patients, 6 (12%) had undergone a delayed radial head resection within 6 months of injury, for undocumented reasons. Forty patients (82%) had no complaints at an average 19 years after fracture. The 34 who returned for clinical evaluation had slight differences in flexion, extension, and supination compared with their opposite side. There was more arthrosis in the injured elbow than in the uninjured elbow, although neither the motion loss nor the arthrosis was clinically important.

Despite the unanswered questions in these studies (Why was a delayed radial head resection performed in some patients? Was it necessary or useful? How many of the fractures had unrecognized elbow dislocation?), they established that long-term results can be excellent after nonsurgical treatment of apparently isolated fractures of the radial head displaced more than 2 mm. These results may be difficult to improve upon with sur-

gical treatment. The value of surgical intervention would need to be established through collection of comparable data in a prospective, randomized trial.

## Surgical Treatment
### Open Reduction and Internal Fixation
A retrospective review of ORIF in 56 patients (30 with a partial articular fracture of the radial head and 26 with a fracture of the entire head) found good results in patients with an isolated, single-fragment partial head fracture or a fracture of the entire head with three or fewer fragments. The results were less positive in patients with a partial head fracture that was comminuted or widely displaced, indicating an association with a more complex injury pattern. The results were poor in patients with a fracture of the entire head if the fracture had more than three fragments; among 14 patients with this type of fracture, 6 had a nonunion, 3 had early failure, and 4 had poor forearm rotation[25] (Figure 3). This study confirmed that ORIF is best used for apparently isolated and minimally displaced fractures, for which ORIF is least needed. This finding must be kept in mind in considering new treatments such as arthroscopy-assisted pin or screw fixation of an isolated fracture.[26] In other words, the results of nonsurgical treatment are so good that the role of surgical treatment should not be overstated. The most complex fractures, which have more than three fragments and involve the entire head, are almost always associated with elbow or forearm instability. They should be treated with prosthetic arthroplasty rather than ORIF to avoid the risk of early failure and recurrent instability. The best treatment of a displaced partial head fracture or a whole head fracture with limited fragmentation is less well established and may depend on the overall injury pattern.

### Radial Head Excision
Excision of the radial head is a viable option, although the procedure must be used with caution for a fracture-dislocation of the elbow or forearm. At an average

18-year follow-up, 61 patients treated with radial head excision had good results.[27] No difference was found between patients treated with primary or delayed radial head excision. The four most symptomatic elbows had associated elbow dislocation. The motion of the injured arm was similar to that of the uninjured arm; mild arthrosis was present in many of the injured elbows.

In a retrospective study of consecutive patients with a displaced fracture of the entire head of the radius (Mason type III), patients treated with ORIF had less elbow arthrosis, more strength, and better functional scores than patients treated with excision; however, the longer follow-up of the patients with excision may be a factor in the findings.[28] Another retrospective series reported similar results.[29] Surprisingly, there were no early failures or nonunions among the patients treated with ORIF.[30]

Patients treated with radial head excision may be at risk for posterolateral rotatory instability,[31] possibly because of a combination of absent radiocapitellar contact and insufficiency of the lateral collateral ligament.

### Prosthetic Replacement

Several retrospective studies found that arthroplasty using a metal radial head prosthesis is safe and effective in patients treated for an acute fracture-dislocation or its sequelae.[32-38] The prosthesis helps restore elbow stability and has few drawbacks, although some studies found that impingement, capitellar erosion, or limitation of flexion can develop, probably as a result of overstuffing with an excessively long or large prosthesis.[38-40] The most complete long-term data are for the loose polished stem implant,[33,35,37,41] although data on the fixed-stem monoblock and fixed-stem bipolar radial head prostheses are also becoming available.[32,42] Polyethylene wear–induced osteolysis is becoming a concern with bipolar prostheses, although no data have yet been published. No comparative studies have established the superiority of any one type of implant concept. In a cadaver study, the use of an allograft radial head instead of a prosthesis was not beneficial.[43]

Most complications after placement of a metal radial head prosthesis have been related to the use of an overly large prosthesis. Loss of flexion, capitellar erosion, and synovitis have been associated with an oversized prosthesis, particularly one that is too long[39,40] (Figure 4).

Two retrospective studies confirmed the ability of a metal radial head prosthesis to contribute substantially to reconstruction in a patient with posttraumatic elbow instability.[44,45] Radiocapitellar contact is a critical component of elbow stability, and repair of the radial head is usually not possible in salvage surgery.

### Treatment of Fracture-Dislocation

Several recent retrospective series found potential complications after treatment of fracture-dislocations of the

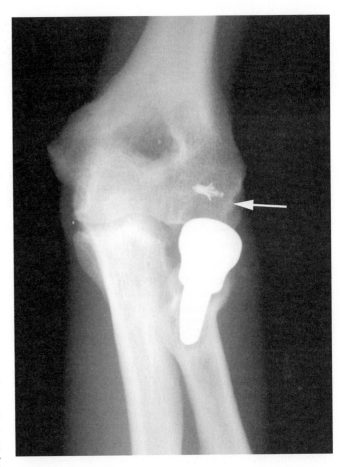

**Figure 4** AP radiograph showing subluxation of the joint, radiocapitellar wear, and synovitis after use of a prosthesis that was too long. The arrow points to a large cyst in the capitellum.

elbow, particularly if radiocapitellar contact is not restored.[46-48] Surgical protocols that include restoration of radiocapitellar contact with either radial head ORIF or prosthetic replacement were associated with better results.[49]

## Current Treatment Principles

Several principles of treatment for fractures of the radial head can be derived from study findings and experience. These principles are outlined in Table 1.

### Minimally Displaced, Isolated Fractures

A patient with a minimally displaced, isolated fracture of the radial head usually can be successfully treated with a temporary sling for comfort and early active and active-assisted exercises to restore elbow mobility. The indications for surgical treatment are uncertain. A radiographic finding that a patient has a fragment larger than one third of the radial head diameter and displacement of more than 2 mm is not helpful in determining whether surgery is needed because such patients have had good long-term results after nonsurgical treatment.[21] Surgery

**Table 1 | Principles of Treating Fractures of the Radial Head**

Displacement of a fracture of the radial head implies an associated ligament injury or fracture. It is important not to miss an injury such as dislocation with a fracture of the radial head and coronoid (the so-called terrible triad of the elbow) or a fracture-dislocation of the forearm (the Essex-Lopresti lesion).

An apparently isolated displaced fracture of the radial head, without a complete ligament injury of the elbow or forearm or an unstable fracture of the ulna, is relatively uncommon.

MRI often reveals that an apparently isolated displaced fracture of the radial head is associated with a subclinical ligament tear and osteochondral injury. The implication is that some subluxation is required to create displacement.

An apparently isolated partial articular fracture of the radial head can be successfully treated nonsurgically, even if it is displaced. The role of surgical treatment is unclear.

The most important function of the radiocapitellar articulation is to stabilize a traumatically destabilized elbow or forearm. The radiocapitellar articulation may also act to slow or limit the development of ulnohumeral arthrosis.

Treatment of a complex fracture of the radial head with ORIF is unreliable. However, ORIF of a straightforward fracture of the radial head that is part of a complex fracture can help restore stability of the forearm and elbow.

Metal prosthetic replacement of a fractured radial head helps restore stability, although overstuffing the prosthesis must be avoided. The long-term function of a metal-on-cartilage articulation has not been completely evaluated.

is probably necessary if a true bony hindrance of forearm rotation is present. This condition is uncommon, and intra-articular reexamination and aspiration conducted several days after the injury may reveal that the patient's motion restriction is caused by pain.

For a minimally displaced, isolated partial fracture of the radial head, ORIF is straightforward and can restore radial head anatomy. Salvage surgery requires excision, with or without a prosthetic replacement, and cannot fully reproduce the native anatomy. Biomechanical data suggest that even small displaced fragments can affect elbow kinematics,[5] and this factor may be important in patients with high physical demands. Good scientific data from prospective, randomized trials are needed to better establish the role of ORIF in these relatively simple injuries.

### Displaced Fractures

Displaced fractures almost invariably are part of a more complex injury of the elbow or forearm. Articulation between the radial head and capitellum is a critical component of elbow and forearm stability. Excision should be used sparingly and with great caution. If lost fragments, metaphyseal bone loss, fraction impaction or de-

formation, irreparable fragments, or more than three articular fragments are present, prosthetic replacement may be preferable to ORIF, which can be used for a straightforward fracture. In using a metal prosthesis, the surgeon must take care not to overstuff the joint. Attention must be paid to the safe zone to avoid impingement at the proximal radioulnar joint.

### Complications

A patient with a minimally displaced, isolated fracture of the radial head is at risk of elbow stiffness and nonunion. Nonunion is usually asymptomatic, and therefore its true incidence is unknown. Nonunion is not clinically important. Stiffness is best avoided by active elbow motion within a few days of injury.

A patient with an apparently isolated partial articular fracture of the radial head with more than 2 mm of displacement may have a more complex injury, such as an unrecognized Essex-Lopresti lesion. Elbow stiffness and restriction of forearm rotation may result. Restriction of forearm rotation is uncommon; it can be successfully treated by excision of the radial head, although this treatment is controversial if the elbow and forearm ligaments are healed and intact.

A displaced fracture of the radial head associated with another fracture or ligament injury can contribute to elbow instability. The optimal treatment of this type of radial head fracture is ORIF or prosthetic head replacement. Early fixation failure, nonunion, and restriction of forearm motion by an implant are common complications of ORIF, and therefore ORIF is best used for very simple fractures with good bone quality. Prosthetic replacement is a useful method of restoring elbow stability in the short term, and it appears to cause few complications in the medium term (average, 10 years) if the prosthesis is not too large. Prostheses that are too large are associated with capitellar erosion, loss of flexion, pain, and synovitis.

### Summary

The treatment of minimally displaced fractures of the radial head is consistent with good long-term results. Elbow stiffness is the most common complication, and the role of surgical treatment is uncertain. Displaced fractures of the radial head are usually associated with other fractures or ligament injuries. The radial head is an important stabilizer of the elbow and forearm. Preservation of radiocapitellar contact is an important element in the treatment of a displaced radial head fracture that is part of a complex injury pattern. Relatively simple fractures (three or fewer reparable articular fragments) can be treated with ORIF, but more complex fractures are treated with prosthetic replacement.

## Annotated References

1. Ring D, Quintero J, Jupiter JB: Open reduction and internal fixation of fractures of the radial head. *J Bone Joint Surg Am* 2002;84:1811-1815.

   In 56 patients treated with ORIF, 13 of the 14 patients who had more than three articular fragments had an unsatisfactory result, including 6 with nonunion, 3 with early failure, and 4 with restricted forearm rotation.

2. van Riet RP, Morrey BF, O'Driscoll SW, Van Glabbeek F: Associated injuries complicating radial head fractures: A demographic study. *Clin Orthop Relat Res* 2005;441:351-355.

   Of 333 radial head fractures (Mason type I, 67%; type II, 14%; type III, 19%), 39% were associated with other fractures or soft-tissue injuries, including coronoid fracture (16%) and elbow dislocation (14%).

3. Itamura J, Roidis N, Mirzayan R, Vaishnav S, Learch T, Shean C: Radial head fractures: MRI evaluation of associated injuries. *J Shoulder Elbow Surg* 2005;14:421-424.

   In 24 patients with an acute radial head fracture (Mason type II or III) without documented dislocation or tenderness at the distal radioulnar joint, MRI revealed injury to the MCL in 13, to the lateral collateral ligament (LCL) in 18, and to both the MCL and the LCL in 12. Capitellar osteochondral defects were revealed in 7, capitellar bone bruises in 23, and loose bodies in 22.

4. Gordon KD, Duck TR, King GJ, Johnson JA: Mechanical properties of subchondral cancellous bone of the radial head. *J Orthop Trauma* 2003;17:285-289.

   In a study of 13 cadaver elbows, there were no differences in mean indentation modulus across the four quadrants. The anterior quadrants had higher local yield strength than the posterior quadrants.

5. Beingessner DM, Dunning CE, Gordon KD, Johnson JA, King GJ: The effect of radial head fracture size on elbow kinematics and stability. *J Orthop Res* 2005;23:210-217.

   In a study of six cadaver elbows, shear load decreased incrementally with wedge excisions between 20° and 120° and was always less than 0.8 N at wedge sizes above 120°.

6. Charalambous CP, Stanley JK, Siddique I, Powell E, Ramamurthy C, Gagey O: Radial head fracture in the medial collateral ligament deficient elbow: Biomechanical comparison of fixation, replacement and excision in human cadavers. *Injury* 2006;37:849-853.

   In five cadaver elbows with a two-part radial head fracture and MCL injury, radial head fixation had superior varus laxity compared with radial head replacement, as well as superior varus and valgus laxity compared with radial head excision.

7. Pomianowski S, Morrey BF, Neale PG, Park MJ, O'Driscoll SW, An KN: Contribution of monoblock and bipolar radial head prostheses to valgus stability of the elbow. *J Bone Joint Surg Am* 2001;83-A:1829-1834.

   In a sequential cutting study of cadaver elbows, the greatest laxity was observed after release of the MCL with resection of the radial head. Laxity was always greater in pronation than in neutral rotation or supination, regardless of the angle of flexion. The Judet bipolar implant was associated with increased laxity in neutral rotation, compared with monoblock prostheses.

8. Schneeberger AG, Sadowski MM, Jacob HA: Coronoid process and radial head as posterolateral rotatory stabilizers of the elbow. *J Bone Joint Surg Am* 2004;86:975-982.

   Posterolateral rotatory laxity averaged 5.4° in intact elbows and 18.6° after excision of the radial head. Complete dislocation occurred after removal of an additional 30% of the height of the coronoid, despite intact ligaments. Implantation of a rigid radial head prosthesis stabilized the elbows; a bipolar prosthesis had greater residual laxity. Elbows with a defect of 50% to 70% of the coronoid could not be stabilized by radial head replacement alone; additional coronoid reconstruction restored stability.

9. Shepard MF, Markolf KL, Dunbar AM: Effects of radial head excision and distal radial shortening on load-sharing in cadaver forearms. *J Bone Joint Surg Am* 2001;83-A:92-100.

   In an intact cadaver elbow, varus alignment increased the force on the distal part of the ulna (27.9% versus 7.1% of the applied wrist force) and the interosseous membrane (51.2% versus 4.0%), compared with valgus alignment. After excision of the radial head, the values (42% versus 58.8%) did not change with varus or valgus alignment.

10. Markolf KL, Tejwani SG, O'Neil G, Benhaim P: Load-sharing at the wrist following radial head replacement with a metal implant: A cadaveric study. *J Bone Joint Surg Am* 2004;86-A:1023-1030.

    Force in the distal part of the ulna and proximal displacement of the radius were measured as the wrist was axially loaded in neutral, varus, and valgus elbow alignment. Metal radial head prostheses restored the distal ulnar forces and proximal placement of the radius to that of the intact forearm. Using an oversized prosthesis (+4 mm) further decreased these values.

11. Pfaeffle HJ, Stabile KJ, Li ZM, Tomaino MM: Reconstruction of the interosseous ligament unloads metallic radial head arthroplasty and the distal ulna in cadavers. *J Hand Surg Am* 2006;31:269-278.

    Proximal radial migration and forearm force vectors were measured under a direct axial compressive load in five conditions: the interosseous ligament intact, the interosseous ligament reconstructed with a double-bundle flexor carpi radialis construct, the radial head excised, metallic radial head arthroplasty completed, and the interosseous ligament reconstruction cut. Double-bundle flexor carpi radialis reconstruction effectively restored the forces of the intact forearm, but ligament reconstruction and radial head arthroplasty, alone or combined, could not restore forces after radial head resection and interosseous ligament sectioning.

12. Van Glabbeek F, Van Riet RP, Baumfeld JA, et al: Detrimental effects of overstuffing or understuffing with a radial head replacement in the medial collateral-ligament deficient elbow. *J Bone Joint Surg Am* 2004;86:2629-2635.

    In six cadaver elbows after MCL release, radial neck lengthening of 2.5 mm decreased varus-valgus laxity and ulnar rotation with the ulna tracking in varus and external rotation, and it increased pressure on the radiocapitellar articulation. Shortening of 2.5 mm increased varus-valgus laxity and ulnar rotation with the ulna tracking in valgus and internal rotation.

13. Doornberg JN, Linzel DS, Zurakowski D, Ring D: Reference points for radial head prosthesis size. *J Hand Surg Am* 2006;31:53-57.

    In 17 CT studies of normal proximal ulnae and radii, the average distance between the planes defined by the radial head articular surface and the coronoid central ridge was –0.8 mm.

14. Liew VS, Cooper IC, Ferreira LM, Johnson JA, King GJ: The effect of metallic radial head arthroplasty on radiocapitellar joint contact area. *Clin Biomech (Bristol, Avon)* 2003;18:115-118.

    A cadaver study applied 100-N loads at three different flexion angles. The contact area of the prosthetic radial head decreased by approximately two thirds relative to the native radiocapitellar joint. It increased with the use of a smaller implant or a lower flexion angle.

15. Mason ML: Some observations on fractures of the head of the radius with a review of one hundred cases. *Br J Surg* 1959;42:123-132.

16. Morrey BF: Radial head fractures, in Morrey BF (ed): *The Elbow and Its Disorders.* Philadelphia, PA, WB Saunders, 1985, p. 355.

17. Johnston GW: A follow-up of one hundred cases of fracture of the head of the radius. *Ulster Med J* 1952; 31:51-56.

18. Hotchkiss RN: Displaced fractures of the radial head: Internal fixation or excision. *J Am Acad Orthop Surg* 1997;5:1-10.

19. Müller ME, Nazarian S, Koch P, Schatzker J: *The Comprehensive Classification of Fractures of Long Bones.* Berlin, Germany, Springer-Verlag, 1990.

20. Carstam N: Operative treatment of fractures of the upper end of the radius. *Acta Orthop Scand* 1950;19: 502-526.

21. Herbertsson P, Josefsson PO, Hasserius R, Karlsson C, Besjakov J, Karlsson M: Uncomplicated Ma-son type-II and III fractures of the radial head and neck in adults: A long-term follow-up study. *J Bone Joint Surg Am* 2004;86:569-574.

    At an average 19 years after injury, reexamination of 100 patients with an apparently isolated displaced fracture of the radial head (28 of whom had an acute or delayed radial head excision) found that 84 had a good outcome according to the very strict Steinberg classification and 77 had no symptoms in the injured elbow. The average flexion was 2° less and the average extension was 4° less than that of the uninjured elbow. Level of evidence: IV.

22. Akesson T, Herbertsson P, Josefsson PO, Hasserius R, Besjakov J, Karlsson MK: Primary nonoperative treatment of moderately displaced two-part fractures of the radial head. *J Bone Joint Surg Am* 2006; 88:1909-1914.

    Of 49 patients with a large partial fracture of the radial head displaced 2 to 5 mm, 6 had a delayed radial head resection. At final evaluation, 40 had no subjective complaints. Average flexion and supination was 2° less and extension was 4° less than that of the uninjured elbow.

23. Liow RY, Cregan A, Nanda R, Montgomery RJ: Early mobilisation for minimally displaced radial head fractures is desirable: A prospective randomised study of two protocols. *Injury* 2002;33:801-806.

    In 60 patients, a minimally displaced fracture of the radial head was mobilized either immediately or 5 days after injury. The patients with immediate mobilization had less pain, greater flexion, greater strength in supination, and better elbow function 7 days after injury, although there were no differences at 1 month.

24. Ring D, Psychoyios VN, Chin K, Jupiter JB: Nonunion of nonoperatively treated fractures of the radial head. *Clin Orthop Relat Res* 2002;398:235-238.

    Five patients had documented nonunion of a nonsurgically treated radial head fracture.

25. Ring D: Open reduction and internal fixation of fractures of the radial head. *Hand Clin* 2004;20:415-427.

    This review article suggests that minimally displaced, isolated fractures are well treated both nonsurgically and with screw fixation. Unstable, displaced fractures may require prosthetic replacement to restore forearm and elbow stability because internal fixation may be difficult or unreliable.

26. Rolla PR, Surace MF, Bini A, Pilato G: Arthroscopic treatment of fractures of the radial head. *Arthroscopy* 2006;22:233-236.

    The results of arthroscopically assisted reduction and percutaneous cannulated screw fixation of minimally displaced, isolated fractures of the radial head are described.

27. Herbertsson P, Josefsson PO, Hasserius R, Besjakov J, Nyqvist F, Karlsson MK: Fractures of the radial head and neck treated with radial head excision. *J Bone Joint Surg Am* 2004;86:1925-1930.

Evaluation of long-term outcomes of primary or delayed radial head excision for treatment of radial head and neck fractures found that the result was often good or fair. The outcome was associated with fracture type (Mason type IV fractures had the worst results), rather than the timing of excision.

28. Ikeda M, Sugiyama K, Kang C, Takagaki T, Oka Y: Comminuted fractures of the radial head: Comparison of resection and internal fixation. *J Bone Joint Surg Am* 2005;87:76-84.

    At an average 10-year follow-up of 15 patients treated with radial head resection and an average 3-year follow-up of 13 patients treated with ORIF, elbow motion was comparable. The patients treated with excision were weaker and had more arthrosis.

29. Pilato G, De Pietri M, Vernieri W, Bini A: The surgical treatment of fractures of the radial head: A comparison between osteosynthesis and capitellectomy. *Chir Organi Mov* 2004;89:213-222.

    At an average 44.6-month follow-up after surgery, 20 patients with a displaced Mason type II or III fracture were evaluated with radiography. Signs of arthrosis were present in 90% of those treated with excision and 20% of those treated with osteosynthesis.

30. Ikeda M, Yamashina Y, Kamimoto M, Oka Y: Open reduction and internal fixation of comminuted fractures of the radial head using low-profile mini-plates. *J Bone Joint Surg Br* 2003;85:1040-1044.

    Ten patients with a severely comminuted fracture of the entire radial head had a repair using low-profile mini-plates. After implant removal, nine patients had a satisfactory result.

31. Hall JA, McKee MD: Posterolateral rotatory instability of the elbow following radial head resection. *J Bone Joint Surg Am* 2005;87:1571-1579.

    Seven (17%) of 42 patients evaluated for elbow or forearm complaints after radial head resection were diagnosed with posterolateral rotatory elbow instability on the basis of characteristic clinical and radiographic findings.

32. Ashwood N, Bain GI, Unni R: Management of Mason type-III radial head fractures with a titanium prosthesis, ligament repair, and early mobilization. *J Bone Joint Surg Am* 2004;86-A:274-280.

    Sixteen patients with a Mason type III radial head fracture and collateral ligament injury were treated with a titanium radial head prosthesis. Thirteen had a satisfactory result, and there were no major complications.

33. Chapman CB, Su BW, Sinicropi SM, Bruno R, Strauch RJ, Rosenwasser MP: Vitallium radial head prosthesis for acute and chronic elbow fractures and fracture-dislocations involving the radial head. *J Shoulder Elbow Surg* 2006;15:463-473.

    Of 16 patients treated using a metal radial head replacement for an acute or chronic fracture, 15 had a satisfactory result. There was a trend toward greater disability and poorer motion in the delayed treatment group.

34. Dotzis A, Cochu G, Mabit C, Charissoux JL, Arnaud JP: Comminuted fractures of the radial head treated by the Judet floating radial head prosthesis. *J Bone Joint Surg Br* 2006;88:760-764.

    Of 14 patients who received a cemented bipolar radial head replacement, 12 had a satisfactory result. The mean score on the Disabilities of the Arm, Shoulder and Hand questionnaire was 24.

35. Harrington IJ, Sekyi-Otu A, Barrington TW, Evans DC, Tuli V: The functional outcome with metallic radial head implants in the treatment of unstable elbow fractures: A long-term review. *J Trauma* 2001;50:46-52.

    Among 20 patients reviewed an average of 12.1 years after a metal prosthetic (loose spacer) radial head was used to restore elbow stability, there were 12 excellent, 4 good, 2 fair, and 2 poor results.

36. Loreto CA, Rollo G, Comitini V, Rotini R: The metal prosthesis in radial head fracture: Indications and preliminary results. *Chir Organi Mov* 2005;90:253-270.

    Ten patients who received radial head replacement after elbow or forearm fracture-dislocation were followed for an average of 2 years and found to have good elbow and wrist function, despite a 40% periprosthetic lucency rate.

37. Moro JK, Werier J, MacDermid JC, Patterson SD, King GJ: Arthroplasty with a metal radial head for unreconstructible fractures of the radial head. *J Bone Joint Surg Am* 2001;83-A:1201-1211.

    Among 25 patients with a metal radial head replacement for an unreconstructible fracture, 17 had a satisfactory result. All unsatisfactory results were related to comorbid conditions, including secondary gain. Seventeen had asymptomatic radiolucency around the stem of the prosthesis.

38. Wretenberg P, Ericson A, Stark A: Radial head prosthesis after fracture of radial head with associated elbow instability. *Arch Orthop Trauma Surg* 2006;126:145-149.

    Eighteen patients treated with radial head replacement for acute traumatic instability were evaluated an average 4 years after treatment. Five prostheses had been extracted because of poor range of motion, and 7 of the 13 retained prostheses had radiolucent lines.

39. Birkedal JP, Deal DN, Ruch DS: Loss of flexion after radial head replacement. *J Shoulder Elbow Surg* 2004;13:208-213.

    Six patients had decreased elbow flexion caused by impingement of a metal prosthesis on the capitellum.

40. Van Riet RP, Van Glabbeek F, Verborgt O, Gielen J: Capitellar erosion caused by a metal radial head

prosthesis: A case report. *J Bone Joint Surg Am* 2004; 86-A:1061-1064.

In this case study, a radial head prosthesis that was too long caused difficulty with the capitellum.

41. Grewal R, MacDermid JC, Faber KJ, Drosdowech DS, King GJW: Comminuted radial head fractures treated with a modular metallic radial head arthroplasty: Study of outcomes. *J Bone Joint Surg Am* 2006;88:2192-2200.

Twenty-six patients with an unreconstructible comminuted radial head fracture and associated elbow injuries were treated with a modular metallic radial head arthroplasty. Prospective evaluation found slight to moderate deficits in range of motion and strength compared with the opposite side. All elbow joints remained stable, no implant required revision, and there was no evidence of overstuffing of the joint.

42. Smets S, Govaers K, Jansen N, Van Riet R, Schaap M, Van Glabbeek F: The floating radial head prosthesis for comminuted radial head fractures: A multicentric study. *Acta Orthop Belg* 2000;66:353-358.

43. Karlstad R, Morrey BF, Cooney WP: Failure of fresh-frozen radial head allografts in the treatment of Essex-Lopresti injury: A report of four cases. *J Bone Joint Surg Am* 2005;87:1828-1833.

This study confirms that allograft radial heads are not successful for the treatment of chronic Essex-Lopresti lesions.

44. Brinkman JM, Rahusen FT, de Vos MJ, Eygendaal D: Treatment of sequelae of radial head fractures with a bipolar radial head prosthesis: Good outcome after 1-4 years follow-up in 11 patients. *Acta Orthop* 2005; 76:867-872.

In 11 patients who received a cemented bipolar radial head prosthesis for elbow instability after elbow fracture-dislocation, all elbows were stabilized, and no signs of loosening, fracture, or heterotopic ossification appeared. Two patients required revision for subluxation of a prosthesis that was too large, and one patient had erosion of the capitellum.

45. Ring D, Hannouche D, Jupiter JB: Surgical treatment of persistent dislocation or subluxation of the ulnohumeral joint after fracture-dislocation of the elbow. *J Hand Surg Am* 2004;29:470-480.

Thirteen consecutive patients had ulnohumeral instability after a fracture-dislocation of the elbow, with adequate articular surfaces and adequate, stable alignment of the olecranon. After treatment with temporary hinged external fixation, preservation, or reconstruction of both the coronoid process and radiocapitellar contact, as well as repair or reconstruction of the LCL complex, 10 achieved satisfactory elbow function.

46. Celli A, Nicoli E: Fractures of the radial head associated with dislocation of the elbow. *Chir Organi Mov* 2004;89:7-19.

Nineteen of 31 patients with a fracture of the radial head associated with dislocation of the elbow had an unsatisfactory result, primarily because of secondary stiffness and instability.

47. Lill H, Korner J, Rose T, Hepp P, Verheyden P, Josten C: Fracture-dislocations of the elbow joint: Strategy for treatment and results. *Arch Orthop Trauma Surg* 2001;121:31-37.

In a study of 28 patients with a fracture-dislocation of the elbow joint, 12 were treated with a two-step procedure (initial closed reduction and immobilization, with secondary open surgery) and 9 were treated nonsurgically. Nineteen patients (68%) had an unsatisfactory result, and 10 patients (36%) underwent secondary surgery.

48. Ring D, Jupiter JB, Zilberfarb J: Posterior dislocation of the elbow with fractures of the radial head and coronoid. *J Bone Joint Surg Am* 2002;84-A:547-551.

Of 11 elbows with a terrible triad elbow injury, 7 became redislocated in a splint after manipulative reduction and 5 (including all 4 treated with resection of the radial head) became redislocated after surgical treatment. Seven elbows had an unsatisfactory result.

49. Pugh DM, Wild LM, Schemitsch EH, King GJ, McKee MD: Standard surgical protocol to treat elbow dislocations with radial head and coronoid fractures. *J Bone Joint Surg Am* 2004;86-A:1122-1130.

Thirty-six consecutive patients with a terrible triad injury were treated with fixation or replacement of the radial head; fixation of the coronoid fracture, if possible; repair of associated capsular and lateral ligamentous injuries; and, in selected patients, repair of the MCL or adjuvant hinged external fixation. Twenty-eight patients (78%) had a satisfactory result, and only one had recurrent instability.

# Chapter 47

# Fractures of the Distal Humerus

Joaquin Sanchez-Sotelo, MD, PhD

## Introduction

The distal humerus fracture is one of the most difficult elbow injuries to treat. In a substantial number of patients, nonunion, stiffness, and posttraumatic arthritis may complicate the course of the injury and lead to an unsatisfactory outcome. Advances in imaging studies and fixation techniques have provided more reproducible methods of evaluating and treating distal humerus fractures. CT has a valuable role in the evaluation of distal humerus fractures, and arthroplasty has emerged as a reliable option for treating severe injuries in elderly, low-demand patients.

## Evaluation

Distal humerus fractures occur most commonly among individuals in two age groups. Patients younger than 50 years typically have a distal humerus fracture as the result of high-energy trauma. Patients older than 60 years may have a highly comminuted fracture from a low-energy injury secondary to osteopenia. The goals of the initial evaluation are to understand the nature of the fracture and determine the presence of preexisting symptomatic elbow pathology; the extent of soft-tissue injuries, especially if the fracture is open; and the presence of associated musculoskeletal or neurovascular injuries.

Lateral and AP radiographs of the elbow should be examined to identify the location of the fracture lines and the severity of comminution. Care should be taken not to overlook small, low articular shearing fractures. The complex morphology of the distal humerus and the possible presence of fracture displacement with overlapping fragments make it difficult to appreciate the full extent of the injury. CT with three-dimensional reconstruction is essential for evaluating relatively complex injuries and is especially useful in revealing the extent of articular involvement. Traction radiographs, taken while the patient is under anesthesia, are also useful in determining the extent of injury.

## Classification

The two most important categories of distal humerus fractures are those affecting the articular surface with-out extension above the level of the olecranon fossa and those extending into the humeral shaft.

Although none of the classification systems for distal humerus fractures is perfect, the AO-ASIF Comprehensive Classification of Fractures of the Long Bones is most commonly used in the peer-reviewed literature to identify periarticular fractures, including distal humerus fractures.[1] Twenty-seven different injury patterns are identified. A fracture is initially classified as extra-articular (type A), partial articular (type B), or complete articular (type C). Each type is further classified based on the fracture pattern. Extra-articular fractures include those with ligamentous avulsion (A1), no comminution (A2), and comminution (A3). Partial intra-articular fractures are identified as lateral column (B1), medial column (B2), or coronal shear fractures (B3). Complete articular fractures include those with no comminution (C1), comminution at the supracondylar level (C2), and comminution at the articular level (C3). Each of these groups is divided into three subgroups (1, 2, and 3) based on the degree of fragmentation.

### Articular Fractures

The spectrum of articular fractures has been recognized only recently.[2] A fracture of the capitellum is the classic articular fracture of the distal humerus. Fractures of the capitellum can be osteochondral (a Hahn-Steinthal fracture) or involve most of the capitellum (a Kocher-Lorenz fracture), often extending over the capitellotrochlear ridge to include part of the trochlea. More extensive articular fractures can shear most of the articular surface and extend into the lateral or medial epicondyle (Figure 1). Such injuries are associated with a relatively poor prognosis, and successful treatment usually requires an olecranon osteotomy or triceps reflection.

### Columnar Fractures

Columnar fractures extend into the medial and lateral columns above the olecranon fossa. They may be supracondylar, intercondylar, or supraintercondylar with some supracondylar or articular comminution (Figure 2).[1]

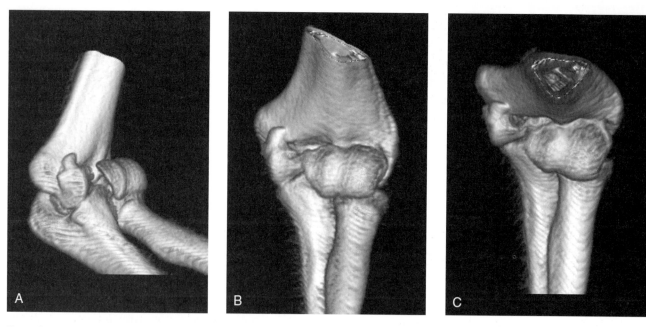

**Figure 1** Articular fractures of the distal humerus without extension into the columns have a wide range of complexity and are best characterized using CT with three-dimensional reconstruction. **A** through **C,** Three-dimensional CT reconstruction images showing the same articular fracture involving the capitellum and trochlea.

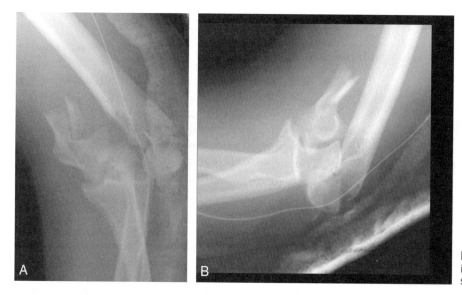

**Figure 2** AP **(A)** and lateral **(B)** radiographs showing a supraintercondylar distal humerus fracture with substantial comminution.

## Internal Fixation

Internal fixation is the treatment of choice for most fractures of the distal humerus. Although treatment is often challenging, improved fixation techniques and appropriate postsurgical management allow fracture healing and good functional results in many patients.

### Surgical Approach

The surgical approach used in treating a fracture of the distal humerus is chosen based on the fracture pattern and treatment strategy.[3] An articular fracture affecting the capitellum is best addressed through a lateral approach. A more complex articular fracture or a colum-nar fracture is best approached through an olecranon osteotomy[4] or mobilization of the extensor mechanism.[5,6] A simple columnar fracture can be fixed by working on both sides of the triceps; this bicolumnar approach is also commonly used for elbow arthroplasty.[7] The ulnar nerve is routinely transposed to an anterior subcutaneous position, except when a lateral approach to an articular fracture is used.

An articular fracture affecting the lateral side of the joint surface can be safely addressed through a lateral approach. The classic Kocher approach provides good exposure, although it can compromise the integrity of the lateral collateral ligament complex.[3] The Kaplan ap-

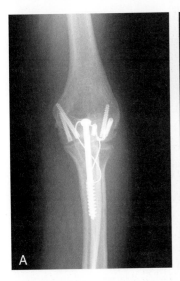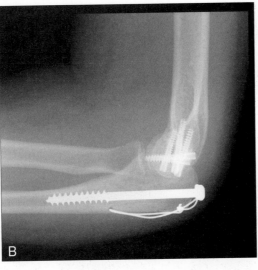

**Figure 3** AP **(A)** and lateral **(B)** radiographs after internal fixation of the complex articular fracture shown in Figure 1, using multiple headless compression screws.

proach, which involves detachment of the anterior half of the extensor-supinator group from the lateral column anterior to the lateral epicondyle, provides a more ample exposure, especially for fractures that extend medially into the trochlea.[8]

An olecranon osteotomy provides excellent exposure for a relatively complex articular fracture or a supraintercondylar fracture.[4] Several osteotomy configuration and fixation techniques are available. A chevron-shaped osteotomy is more stable than a transverse osteotomy; it can be initiated with an oscillating saw and completed with an osteotome to minimize cartilage damage and create an irregular surface at the articular side to promote stability and healing. Plate or tension band fixation with a single screw or two Kirschner wires is commonly used for fixation of the osteotomy. Plates are associated with a greater risk of wound complications, if skin viability was compromised by the injury.

Some surgeons prefer to use a triceps-reflection or split approach to avoid the possibility of nonunion of the olecranon osteotomy, preserve the anconeus muscle, and preserve an intact ulna for use either as a template in reconstructing the distal humerus or after an intrasurgical decision to proceed with arthroplasty. The nature of the fracture sometimes must be assessed during surgery before deciding to proceed with internal fixation or arthroplasty. In this circumstance, preservation of the ulna is extremely helpful, because healing of an olecranon osteotomy in conjunction with elbow replacement may be compromised by the more limited options for fixation of the osteotomy, the need to remove additional bone for implantation of the component, and the possible detrimental effects of polymethylmethacrylate on fracture healing. Triceps reflection from medial to lateral, called the Bryan-Morrey approach, provides a relatively limited exposure but maintains the continuity of the extensor mechanism distally.[5] The triceps-reflecting anconeus pedicle approach provides better

exposure for fracture fixation, but it completely detaches the extensor mechanism from the ulna.[6] Both approaches may be associated with residual weakness in terminal extension.

### Surgical Techniques
#### Articular Fractures
Most articular fractures can reliably be fixed using a combination of headless compression screws, such as Herbert or Acutrac screws, and threaded pins (Figure 3). In some articular fractures, substantial comminution along the lateral or medial epicondyle requires the use of a plate.[2] A fracture with extensive articular comminution and cartilage damage may benefit from neutralization and distraction, achieved by adding dynamic external fixation for a period of 3 to 6 weeks.

#### Columnar Fractures
New surgical principles and the development of precontoured periarticular plates have improved the likelihood of a successful outcome, even in a fracture with extensive comminution.[9] In such an injury, a stable construct is best achieved by applying two parallel plates so that the maximum fixation is obtained in the distal fragments and interfragmentary compression takes place at the supracondylar level. The goal is to allow early unprotected rehabilitation that will restore a functional range of motion.[10,11]

A series of surgical steps has been developed to facilitate the application of the principles of maximum distal fixation and true supracondylar compression.[11] In contrast to earlier recommendations, the current practice is to avoid initial screw fixation of the articular fragments. All screws used distally pass through the plates to provide not only articular fixation but also plate anchorage (Figure 4). The reduced fracture is initially fixed with Steinmann pins. The principles of plate fixation

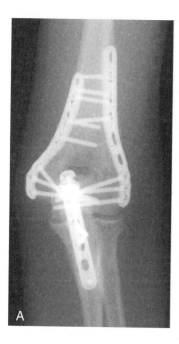

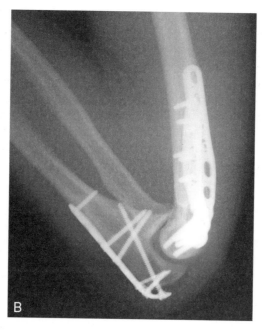

**Figure 4** AP **(A)** and lateral **(B)** radiographs after stable fixation of a distal humerus fracture, achieved by maximum distal fixation of the parallel plates using multiple screws and compression at the supracondylar level.

hold that as many screws as possible are placed across the articular fragments to provide multiple points of fixation. In addition, interlocking screws from the lateral and medial sides increase the stability of the construct. Small articular fragments may be fixed to the main fragments using threaded or absorbable pins.

Compression at the supracondylar level is achieved by using reduction clamps, inserting screws in the compression mode, and slightly undercontouring the plates. If satisfactory bone apposition and compression at the supracondylar level preclude an anatomic reduction, the fracture may be shortened 5 mm to 2 cm. The distal fragment must be offset anteriorly to clear space for the coronoid process and radial head in flexion, and bone must be removed posteriorly to create a new olecranon fossa and allow elbow extension.[12] This amount of humeral shortening is associated with a very small decrease in extension strength.[13]

The role of locking plate technology in the fixation of distal humerus fractures is still undefined. Locking plates have the potential to provide similar fracture stability with less hardware. The angle of screw insertion is predetermined in most systems, and the ability of the surgeon to choose an orientation to accommodate the fracture's complex regional morphology and configuration is therefore compromised.

## Postsurgical Treatment

The goals of postsurgical treatment are to minimize swelling, achieve a functional range of motion, and avoid complications. If stable fixation has been achieved, the condition of the soft tissues is the only factor to be considered in determining the safety of early motion. Immediately after surgery, the elbow is elevated and immobilized in ex-

tension using a bulky compression dressing. Elbow motion can be initiated on the first or second day after surgery, in the maximum range of motion tolerated by the patient. Some surgeons prefer to use a continuous passive motion machine. Depending on the condition of the soft tissues, the patient's tolerance, and the surgeon's preference, continuous passive motion can be used for a few days or as long as 3 to 4 weeks. A dynamic or static progressive splint can be used when continuous passive motion is discontinued or if improvements in motion are slow to occur.

More than one surgical procedure may be required for sequential débridement of an open fracture or definitive fixation after a suboptimal attempt. Consideration should be given to decreasing the risk of heterotopic ossification by using indomethacin or single-dose radiation therapy to the soft tissues of the anterior and posterior aspects of the elbow, shielding the fracture site so that healing is not compromised.

## Results and Complications
### Articular Fractures
Satisfactory results have been reported after the fixation of most fractures involving the capitellum. The results of internal fixation of the spectrum of articular distal humerus fractures have been reported only recently. In 21 patients with different patterns of articular fracture stabilized with implants buried beneath the articular surface, only one early loss of fixation occurred.[2] Six patients (30%) required additional surgery for stiffness. The final outcome was satisfactory in 16 patients (75%).

### Columnar Fractures
Studies of internal fixation of columnar fractures of the distal humerus using current techniques are summarized

in Table 1. The results of the available studies are difficult to compare because of variations in the severity of injuries and the accuracy of range-of-motion measurements. Improvements in fixation techniques have led to lower rates of hardware failure and nonunion. However, range of motion is not reliably restored in all patients. The most commonly reported complications are infection, nonunion, stiffness with or without heterotopic ossification, need for removal of the hardware used for fixation of the olecranon osteotomy, and posttraumatic osteoarthritis or osteonecrosis requiring interposition arthroplasty or elbow replacement.

## Arthroplasty
### Rationale and Indications
Joint arthroplasty is a well-accepted treatment for some types of fractures, including those of the proximal humerus or femoral neck. The successful use of elbow implants in patients with rheumatoid arthritis and some other conditions prompted the use of elbow arthroplasty in patients with distal humerus fracture. Elbow arthroplasty is indicated only in carefully selected patients who are older than approximately 70 years and have preexisting symptomatic pathology (such as a fractured rheumatoid elbow) or a low comminuted fracture with substantial osteopenia and severe damage to the articular surface.[22] Elbow arthroplasty is contraindicated if the patient has high physical demands, the fracture is amenable to stable internal fixation, or the fracture is open.

Total elbow arthroplasty offers several advantages in the treatment of distal humerus fractures. The extensor mechanism can be left undisturbed, no postsurgical protection is required, functional range of motion is relatively easy to achieve, and pain and limited motion secondary to nonunion, malunion, or posttraumatic osteoarthritis are avoided. The most important disadvantages are the risk of implant-related complications and the need to limit use of the upper extremity so as to minimize polyethylene wear.

Some studies have reported good results after distal humerus hemiarthroplasty with column fixation, as an alternative to resection of the fragments followed by a total elbow arthroplasty.[23] Distal humerus hemiarthroplasty eliminates the risk of complications associated with the presence of polyethylene or an ulnar component.[24] However, the surgical approach requires violation of the extensor mechanism. In addition, the need for healing of the columns is not eliminated, and instability or symptomatic changes may occur in the articular surfaces of the unresurfaced ulna and radial head. Further study is needed to determine the role of distal humerus hemiarthroplasty in distal humerus fractures.

### Surgical Technique
Semiconstrained total elbow arthroplasty is the recommended technique for elbow replacement in an acute fracture.[25] The ulnar nerve is subcutaneously transposed, and the joint is approached by working on both sides of the triceps. Subperiosteal resection of the fractured articular fragments provides a working space for broaching and implantation. Bone graft from the resected fragments is placed behind the humeral flange. Antibiotic-loaded polymethylmethacrylate is routinely used for implant fixation. The implants are linked after the components are fully seated. The common origins of the flexor-pronator and extensor-supinator muscles are then sutured to the triceps to seal the joint (Figure 5).

After surgery, the elbow is immobilized with an anterior splint in full extension and is elevated for 24 to 48 hours. Active range-of-motion exercises are initiated. Recovery of functional, painless motion can be expected in 2 to 3 months. A permanent restriction on lifting is required; the patient is advised to avoid using the affected side for one-time lifting of more than 5 lb or repeated lifting of more than 1 lb.

### Results and Complications
Use of a semiconstrained total elbow replacement was first reported in 21 elderly patients with a distal humerus fracture.[22] The overall results were excellent in 15 patients and good in 5 patients, with a range of motion of 25° to 130°. Similar results were reported in other studies[26-28] (Table 2). In 43 patients followed for an average of 7 years, the mean Mayo Elbow Performance Score was 93 points, and the range of motion was 24° to 132°. Five patients required revision surgery.[29] The only comparative study of elbow replacement and internal fixation evaluated 24 fractures in women older than 65 years. Elbow replacement was found to provide better motion and better overall results than internal fixation.[30]

Resection of the humeral condyles is routinely performed as part of this surgical technique and does not appear to adversely affect function. A comparison of 16 elbow replacements with preservation of the humeral condyles and 16 elbow replacements with resection of the condyles revealed no differences in motion or strength.[31]

## Summary and Future Directions
A fracture of the distal humerus often represents a severe threat to upper extremity function. Recent advances in understanding and treating these injuries have led to better outcomes. CT with three-dimensional reconstruction is useful in appreciating the variety and complexity of articular and columnar fractures, selecting the optimal surgical technique for a particular

**Table 1 | Studies of Internal Fixation of Distal Humerus Fractures Affecting the Humeral Columns**

| Study | Patients, Number | Patient Age, Years Mean (Range) | Follow-up, Months Mean (Range) | AO Fracture Type, Number | Open Fractures, Number (%) |
|---|---|---|---|---|---|
| Jupiter et al[14] (1985) | 34 | 57 (17-79) | 70 (25-139) | C1, 13 C2, 2 C3, 19 | 14 (41) |
| Henley et al[15] (1987) | 33 | 32 (15-61) | 18.3 | C1, 23 C2, 8 C3, 2 | 14 (42) |
| Sanders and Sackett[16] (1990) | 17 | 51 (12-85) | > 24 | C1, 4 C2, 3 C3, 10 | 7 (41) |
| McKee et al[17] (2000) | 25 | 47 (19-85) | 37 (18-75) | C, 25 | 0* |
| McKee et al[18] (2000) | 26 | 44 (17-78) | 51 (10-141) | C1, 5 C2, 13 C3, 8 | 26 (100) |
| Pajarinen and Bjorkenheim[19] (2002) | 21 | 44 (16-81) | 24 (10-41) | C1, 6 C2, 12 C3, 3 | 5 (24) |
| Gofton et al[20] (2003) | 23 | 53 (16-80) | 45 (14-89) | C1, 3 C2, 11 C3, 9 | 7 (30) |
| Soon et al[21] (2004) | 15 | 43 (21-80) | 12 (2-27) | B, 3 C1, 4 C2, 4 C3, 4 | |
| Sanchez-Sotelo et al[9] (2007) | 32 | 58 (16-99) | 24 (12-60) | A3, 3 C2, 4 C3, 25 | 13 (44) |

**Table 1 Continued | Studies of Internal Fixation of Distal Humerus Fractures Affecting the Humeral Columns**

| Range of Motion | Results (Measure) | Complications, Number | Revision Surgery, Number |
|---|---|---|---|
| 30°-120° (76% of patients) | Satisfactory, 79% (Jupiter Rating System) | Nonunion, 2<br>Refracture, 1<br>Olecranon osteotomy nonunion, 2<br>HO, 1<br>Ulnar neuropathy, 4<br>Median neuropathy, 1 | Hardware removal, 24<br>Capsulectomy, 3<br>HO removal, 1<br>Nerve decompression, 4 |
| Mean: 19° extension, 126° flexion | Satisfactory, 92% (25 patients; Jupiter Rating System) | Hardware failure, 5<br>Infection, 2<br>Olecranon osteotomy nonunion, 2<br>HO, 2 | Repeat internal fixation, 2<br>Tension band wiring removal, 6<br>Olecranon osteotomy, repeat internal fixation, 2 |
| 55°-140° (mean, 108°) | Satisfactory, 76% (Jupiter Rating System) | Delayed union, 2<br>Infection, 2<br>Pulmonary embolism, 1<br>Ulnar neuropathy, 1 | Hardware removal, 3<br>Ulnar nerve decompression, 1 |
| 55°-140° (mean, 108°) | Mean, 20; range, 0-55 (DASH) | Ulnar neuritis, 3<br>Transient radial nerve palsy, 1<br>Nonunion, 1<br>Malunion, 1 | Tension band wiring removal, 3<br>Repeat internal fixation, 1<br>Elbow release, 2 |
| 55°-140° (mean, 97°) | Mean, 23.7; range, 0-57.5 (DASH)<br>Satisfactory, 60% (MEPS) | Septic nonunion, 1<br>Delayed union, 4<br>Transient radial nerve palsy, 1 | Repeat internal fixation, 3 |
| 98°-116° (mean, 107°) | Satisfactory, 56% (OTA) | Deep infection, 1<br>Nonunion, 2<br>Traumatic nerve injury, 3<br>Olecranon osteotomy nonunion, 1 | Repeat internal fixation, 2 |
| Mean, 122° (extension loss, 19° ± 12°; flexion loss, 142° ± 6°) | Mean, 12; range, 0-38 (DASH)<br>Subjective satisfaction, 93%<br>Satisfactory, 87% (MEPS) | Deep infection, 1<br>Olecranon osteotomy nonunion, 2<br>HO, 3<br>Osteonecrosis, 1<br>Reflex sympathetic dystrophy, 1<br>Capitellar nonunion, 1 | Olecranon osteotomy, repeat internal fixation, 2<br>Elbow release, 3<br>Capitellar internal fixation, 1 |
| 45°-145° (mean, 109°) | Satisfactory, 86% (MEPS) | Transient ulnar neuritis, 2<br>Hardware failure, 3<br>Nonunion, 1 | Total elbow arthroplasty, 1<br>Repeat internal fixation, 3<br>Elbow manipulation or release, 4 |
| Extension, 0°-55° (mean, 26°); flexion, 80°-150° (mean, 124°) | Satisfactory, 83% (MEPS) | Delayed union, 1<br>Ulnar neuropathy, 6<br>HO, 5<br>Infection, 1 | Wound débridement or coverage, 4<br>Bone grafting, 1<br>HO removal, 4<br>HO removal and distraction arthroplasty, 1<br>Triceps reconstruction, 1 |

*Closed fractures only.

DASH = Disabilities of the Arm, Shoulder and Hand Questionnaire, HO = type II heterotopic ossification (restricting motion), MEPS = Mayo Elbow Performance Score, OTA = Orthopaedic Trauma Association rating.

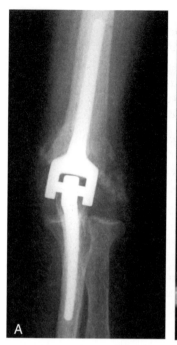
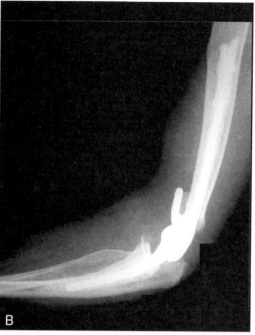

**Figure 5** AP **(A)** and lateral **(B)** radiographs showing total elbow arthroplasty in an elderly patient with substantial comminution and osteopenia.

**Table 2 | Studies of Total Elbow Arthroplasty in Selected Patients With Distal Humerus Fracture**

| Study | Patients, Number | Patient Age, Mean Years | Follow-up, Mean | Range of Motion | Mayo Elbow Performance Score | Complications |
|---|---|---|---|---|---|---|
| Cobb and Morrey[22] (1997) | 21 | 72 | 3.3 years | 25°-130° | Excellent, 15 Good, 5 | Ulnar component fracture, 1 |
| Ray et al[28] (2000) | 7 | 82 | 3 years | 20°-103° | Excellent, 5 Good, 2 | Superficial infection, 1 |
| Gambirasio et al[26] (2001) | 10 | 84 | 17.8 months | 23.5°-125° | Mean, 94 Range, 80-100 | None |
| Garcia et al[27] (2002) | 16 | 73 | 3 years | 24°-125° | Mean, 93 Range, 80-100 | None |
| Frankle et al[30] (2003) | 12 | 72 | 3.75 years | 15°-120° | Excellent, 11 Good, 1 | Disengagement, 1 Superficial infection, 2 |
| Kamineni and Morrey[29] (2004) | 43 | 67 | 7 years | 24°-132° | Mean, 93 | Revision surgery required, 5 |

fracture, and planning the surgery. Simple lateral-sided articular fractures are usually fixed through a lateral approach, but more complex fractures extending to the medial side of the joint are better fixed by mobilizing the extensor mechanism. Innovative internal fixation strategies that maximize plate anchorage in the distal fragments and interfragmentary compression represent a major advancement in the treatment of columnar fractures. Simultaneously, total elbow arthroplasty has been shown to provide excellent results in selected elderly patients with preexisting elbow pathology and substantial osteopenia and comminution.

Future research should focus on the development of less invasive techniques, including arthroscopically assisted fracture reduction and fixation of some injuries. Newer implants with locking-screw technology may allow the use of less hardware without decreasing the stability of the construct. Pharmacologic strategies designed to prevent the development of stiffness or heterotopic ossification, such as the use of indomethacin and botulinum toxin (Botox), may lead to a more predictable recovery of motion. Improvements in implant design, fixation, and wear may lessen the risk of complications after elbow arthroplasty. The role of hemiarthroplasty has yet to be defined.

## Annotated References

1. Muller ME, Nazarian S, Koch P, Schatzker J (eds): *The Comprehensive Classification of Fractures of the Long Bones.* Berlin, Germany, Springer-Verlag, 1990.

2. Ring D, Jupiter JB, Gulotta L: Articular fractures of the distal part of the humerus. *J Bone Joint Surg Am* 2003;85:232-238.

   Satisfactory results were reported for 20 of 21 articular fractures treated with internal fixation. The average arc of motion was 96°. Ten patients required additional surgery; six of the procedures were for stiffness.

3. Morrey BF: Anatomy and surgical approaches, in Morrey BF (ed): *Joint Replacement Arthroplasty.* Philadelphia, PA, Churchill-Livingstone, 2003, pp 269-285.

   The indications and surgical approaches used for the fixation of distal humerus fractures are described.

4. Ring D, Gulotta L, Chin K, Jupiter JB: Olecranon osteotomy for exposure of fractures and nonunions of the distal humerus. *J Orthop Trauma* 2004;18:446-449.

   Forty-five consecutive chevron-shaped olecranon osteotomies were fixed with two Kirschner wires and two figure-of-8 tension wires. There was fixation failure, and 12 patients required hardware removal. Properly performed olecranon osteotomy was associated with a low complication rate.

5. Bryan RS, Morrey BF: Extensive posterior exposure of the elbow: A triceps-sparing approach. *Clin Orthop Relat Res* 1982;166:188-192.

6. O'Driscoll SW: The triceps-reflecting anconeus pedicle (TRAP) approach for distal humeral fractures and nonunions. *Orthop Clin North Am* 2000;31:91-101.

7. Alonso-Llames M: Bilaterotricipital approach to the elbow: Its application in the osteosynthesis of supracondylar fractures of the humerus in children. *Acta Orthop Scand* 1972;43:479-490.

8. Kaplan EB: Surgical approach to the proximal end of the radius and its use in fractures of the head and neck of the radius. *J Bone Joint Surg Am* 1941;23:86-92.

9. Sanchez-Sotelo J, Torchia ME, O'Driscoll SW: Complex distal humeral fractures: Internal fixation with a principle-based parallel-plate technique. *J Bone Joint Surg Am* 2007;89:961-969.

   Thirty-two complex distal humerus fractures were treated with internal fixation using parallel plates with multiple distal long screws. Union was obtained in all except one, and the mean flexion-extension arc was 99°. Five patients required additional surgery to treat elbow stiffness.

10. Schemitsch EH, Tencer AF, Henley MB: Biomechanical evaluation of methods of internal fixation of the distal humerus. *J Orthop Trauma* 1994;8:468-475.

11. Sanchez-Sotelo J, Torchia ME, O'Driscoll SW: Principle-based internal fixation of distal humerus fractures. *Tech Hand Up Extrem Surg* 2001;5:179-187.

    This is the first detailed description of an internal fixation technique using two parallel plates with multiple long distal screws to obtain maximum distal fixation and compression at the supracondylar level.

12. O'Driscoll SW, Sanchez-Sotelo J, Torchia ME: Management of the smashed distal humerus. *Orthop Clin North Am* 2002;33:19-33.

    In this description of the principles of treating the most severe injuries, with extensive articular comminution and severe soft-tissue disruption, metaphyseal shortening is reported to facilitate fixation.

13. Hughes RE, Schneeberger AG, An KN, Morrey BF, O'Driscoll SW: Reduction of triceps muscle force after shortening of the distal humerus: A computational model. *J Shoulder Elbow Surg* 1997;6:444-448.

14. Jupiter JB, Neff U, Holzach P, Allgower M: Intercondylar fractures of the humerus: An operative approach. *J Bone Joint Surg Am* 1985;67:226-239.

15. Henley MB, Bone LB, Parker B: Operative management of intra-articular fractures of the distal humerus. *J Orthop Trauma* 1987;1:24-35.

16. Sanders RA, Sackett JR: Open reduction and internal fixation of delayed union and nonunion of the distal humerus. *J Orthop Trauma* 1990;4:254-259.

17. McKee MD, Wilson TL, Winston L, Schemitsch EH, Richards RR: Functional outcome following surgical treatment of intra-articular distal humeral fractures through a posterior approach. *J Bone Joint Surg Am* 2000;82:1701-1707.

18. McKee MD, Kim J, Kebaish K, Stephen DJ, Kreder HJ, Schemitsch EH: Functional outcome after open supracondylar fractures of the humerus: The effect of the surgical approach. *J Bone Joint Surg Br* 2000;82:646-651.

19. Pajarinen J, Bjorkenheim JM: Operative treatment of type C intercondylar fractures of the distal humerus: Results after a mean follow-up of 2 years in a series of 18 patients. *J Shoulder Elbow Surg* 2002;11:48-52.

    Only 56% of 18 patients with an AO type C distal humerus fracture had a satisfactory result. Patients older than 40 years and those immobilized longer than 3 weeks after surgery had relatively poor results.

20. Gofton WT, Macdermid JC, Patterson SD, Faber KJ, King GJ: Functional outcome of AO type C distal humeral fractures. *J Hand Surg Am* 2003;28:294-308.

    In a review of the outcomes of internal fixation using two plates (60%) or three plates (40%) in 23 type C fractures, the complication rate was 48%. However, most complications were minor, and the mean subjective satisfaction rate was 93%.

21. Soon JL, Chan BK, Low CO: Surgical fixation of intra-articular fractures of the distal humerus in adults. *Injury* 2004;35:44-54.

    Fifteen patients with intra-articular distal humerus fractures were followed for 1 year after internal fixation with one or two plates. Four patients required additional intervention for joint stiffness, and three required revision to a total elbow arthroplasty. The remaining patients had a good or excellent result.

22. Cobb TK, Morrey BF: Total elbow arthroplasty as primary treatment for distal humeral fractures in elderly patients. *J Bone Joint Surg Am* 1997;79:826-832.

23. Parsons M, O'Brien RJ, Hughes JS: Elbow hemiarthroplasty for acute and salvage reconstruction of intra-articular distal humerus fractures. *Tech Shoulder Elbow Surg* 2005;6:87-97.

24. Shifrin PG, Johnson DP: Elbow hemiarthroplasty with 20-year follow-up study: A case report and literature review. *Clin Orthop Relat Res* 1990;254: 128-133.

25. Kamineni S, Morrey BF: Distal humeral fractures treated with noncustom total elbow replacement: Surgical technique. *J Bone Joint Surg Am* 2005; 87(suppl 1):41-50.

    A surgical technique for semiconstrained noncustom cemented total elbow arthroplasty in acute distal humerus fractures is described. The benefits of the bicolumnar approach are outlined.

26. Gambirasio R, Riand N, Stern R, Hoffmeyer P: Total elbow replacement for complex fractures of the distal humerus: An option for the elderly patient. *J Bone Joint Surg Br* 2001;83:974-978.

    Semiconstrained elbow arthroplasty for treatment of an acute distal humerus fracture provided satisfactory results in 10 patients. Mean arc of motion was 23° of extension to 125° of flexion, and there were no complications.

27. Garcia JA, Mykula R, Stanley D: Complex fractures of the distal humerus in the elderly: The role of total elbow replacement as primary treatment. *J Bone Joint Surg Br* 2002;84:812-816.

Fifteen of 16 patients had a satisfactory result after elbow arthroplasty for a distal humerus fracture. The mean arc of motion was 24° of extension to 125° of flexion, and there were no complications.

28. Ray PS, Kakarlapudi K, Rajsekhar C, Bhamra MS: Total elbow arthroplasty as primary treatment for distal humeral fractures in elderly patients. *Injury* 2000;31:687-692.

29. Kamineni S, Morrey BF: Distal humeral fractures treated with noncustom total elbow replacement. *J Bone Joint Surg Am* 2004;86:940-947.

    Forty-nine total elbow arthroplasties for the treatment of a distal humerus fracture were followed for an average of 7 years. The mean arc of motion was 24° to 131°, and the mean Mayo Elbow Performance Score was 93 points. However, complications were reported in 14 elbows (29%), and there were 10 revisions, 5 of which included implant revision.

30. Frankle MA, Herscovici D Jr, DiPasquale TG, Vasey MB, Sanders RW: A comparison of open reduction and internal fixation and primary total elbow arthroplasty in the treatment of intraarticular distal humerus fractures in women older than age 65. *J Orthop Trauma* 2003;17:473-480.

    Better outcomes and a lower complication rate were reported after elbow arthroplasty compared with internal fixation in a group of 24 women older than 65 years. Three patients treated with internal fixation required additional surgery to replace the elbow.

31. McKee MD, Pugh DM, Richards RR, Pedersen E, Jones C, Schemitsch EH: Effect of humeral condylar resection on strength and functional outcome after semiconstrained total elbow arthroplasty. *J Bone Joint Surg Am* 2003;85:802-807.

    No differences were found in elbow range of motion, grip strength, or strength in flexion, extension, pronation, or supination in patients with either preservation or resection of the humeral condyles at the time of elbow arthroplasty.

# Chapter 48

# Proximal Ulnar Fractures and Fracture-Dislocations

Robert G. Turner, MB, BCh, FRCS

Graham J.W. King, MD, MSc, FRCSC

## Introduction

Approximately 10% of all upper limb fractures are fractures of the proximal ulna. These injuries vary in severity from a simple, nondisplaced fracture to a complex fracture with associated ulnohumeral joint dislocation, ligamentous injury, or radial head fracture. An understanding of the relevant anatomy, injury patterns, and treatment options is essential for treating fractures of the proximal ulna.

## Anatomy

The ulna can easily be palpated along most of its length, from the triceps insertion to the tip of the styloid. The proximal tip of the olecranon is covered by the triceps tendon and is therefore difficult to palpate. The subcutaneous position of the ulna causes it to be especially vulnerable to direct trauma.

The elbow is a complex hinge joint, and the ulna is an important part of its distal articulation. The olecranon and coronoid process form the greater sigmoid notch, which has an ellipsoidal contour and an arc of approximately 190°. The greater sigmoid notch articulates with the trochlea of the humerus. The density of the bone in the coronoid and olecranon is greater than that of the bone in the middle of the sigmoid notch, and the central area is therefore relatively vulnerable to fracture. The coronoid process lies anterior to the olecranon process and acts as a barrier to posterior translation. Fracture of the coronoid frequently accompanies posterior dislocation of the elbow. The olecranon process prevents anterior translation of the ulna relative to the humerus. The olecranon process and the coronoid contribute to varus-valgus stability of the elbow. Ulnohumeral joint stability is further enhanced by a central longitudinal ridge on the olecranon that articulates with a central groove on the trochlea.

Although the articular surface between the olecranon and coronoid is covered with hyaline cartilage, there is a transverse bare area approximately midway between them (Figure 1). The surgeon must be aware of this

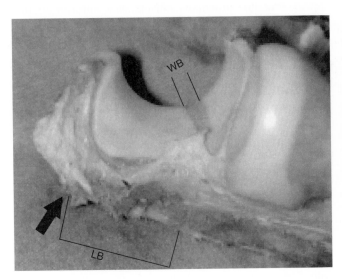
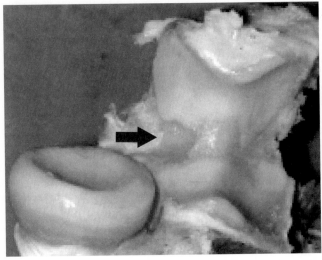

**Figure 1** The olecranon bare area between the proximal and distal portions of the greater sigmoid notch is devoid of articular cartilage. **A,** Lateral view of a disarticulated right proximal radius and ulna. LB = distance from the palpable tip of the olecranon (*arrow*) to the bare area (mean, 2.1 cm; range, 1.4 to 2.5 cm), WB = width of the bare area (mean, 0.53 cm; range, 0.13 to 0.97 cm). **B,** Anterior view of a proximal ulnar articular surface, showing a wide bare spot (*arrow*). (*Adapted with permission from Wang AA, Mara M, Hutchinson DT: The proximal ulna: An anatomic study with relevance to olecranon osteotomy and fracture fixation. J Shoulder Elbow Surg 2003;12:293-296.*)

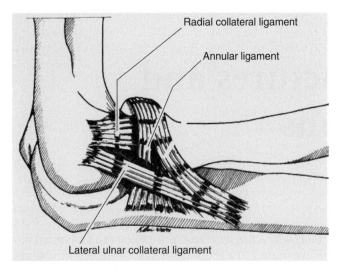

**Figure 2**　The lateral elbow ligaments. *(Reproduced with permission from Safran MR, Baillargeon D: Soft-tissue stabilizers of the elbow. J Shoulder Elbow Surg 2005; 14[suppl 1]:S179-S185.)*

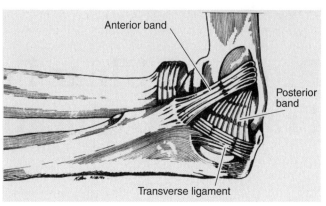

**Figure 3**　The medial elbow ligaments. *(Adapted with permission from Safran MR, Baillargeon D: Soft-tissue stabilizers of the elbow. J Shoulder Elbow Surg 2005; 14[suppl 1]:S179-S185.)*

anatomic feature; an attempt to oppose articulating cartilage in this region would result in overcompression of the fracture,[1] which would narrow the olecranon fossa and produce an incongruent ulnohumeral joint. The bare area should be chosen for an olecranon osteotomy to minimize damage to the surrounding hyaline cartilage. The coronoid broadens medially to form the sublime tubercle, which provides the site for insertion of the anterior band of the medial collateral ligament (MCL) and is an important contributor to varus stability.

The lateral collateral ligament (LCL) is the major stabilizer against varus stress.[2] The LCL consists of the radial collateral ligament, the annular ligament, and the lateral ulnar collateral ligament (Figure 2). The annular ligament originates on and inserts into the anteroposterior margins of the lesser sigmoid notch of the ulna. The radial collateral ligament arises from the lateral epicondyle and inserts into the annular ligament. The lateral ulnar collateral ligament originates on the lateral epicondyle, passes over the annular ligament, and curves to insert into the tubercle of the supinator crest of the ulna.

On the medial side, the MCL is divided into the anterior band, the posterior band, and the transverse ligament (Figure 3). The MCL is the primary stabilizer of the elbow to valgus force, and the radial head is an important secondary stabilizer.[3] The origin of the MCL is from the central 65% of the anteroinferior surface of the medial epicondyle. The anterior band inserts along the medial aspect of the coronoid process, near the sublime tubercle. The posterior band, a fan-shaped thickening of the capsule, forms the floor of the cubital tunnel. It inserts along the midportion of the medial margin of the semilunar notch. The transverse ligament consists of

horizontal capsular fibers between the tip of the olecranon and the coronoid.

The triceps has a thick, broad insertion onto the posterior olecranon and extends to become confluent with the periosteum of the ulna. The triceps does not insert into the tip of the olecranon process; such an insertion would create impingement in the olecranon fossa. The tip can therefore be clearly visualized during elbow arthroscopy. The triceps tendon can be split to accommodate a posterior plate, although some surgeons favor positioning the plate on top of the tendon.

Anteriorly, the brachialis has a broad insertion into the midportion of the coronoid and extends distally onto the ulnar metaphysis. The brachialis does not insert into the tip of the coronoid process, which, like the olecranon process, is easily visualized arthroscopically. Small coronoid tip fractures typically have attached anterior capsule but not brachialis muscle. Just anterior to this muscle lies the anterior interosseous nerve, which is at risk of penetration by a Kirschner wire or drill bit. The ulnar nerve lies just behind the medial humeral epicondyle; it travels between the humeral and ulnar heads of the flexor carpi ulnaris, ultimately lying under the flexor carpi ulnaris on the anteromedial side of the ulna.

## Mechanism of Injury and Clinical Assessment

Olecranon fractures occur as a result of direct or indirect trauma, or both. Direct trauma, such as a fall onto the tip of the olecranon, can cause a simple fracture. A more severe direct force can produce a comminuted fracture resulting from the force of the olecranon against the distal humerus, which is frequently responsible for the presence of impacted joint surface fragments found at surgery. In an indirect trauma, such as a fall onto an outstretched hand, the forced contraction of the triceps on the olecranon produces an avulsion-type fracture or a simple transverse fracture.

Most olecranon fractures in patients older than 60 years occur as a result of a simple fall. In patients younger than 60 years, an olecranon fracture may be associated with a high-energy injury occurring during a motor vehicle crash, fall, or assault. Although olecranon fractures typically occur in isolation, a full history and examination should be performed to exclude the presence of other injuries. In particular, the clavicle, shoulder, arm, forearm, wrist, and hand should be carefully assessed.

The neurovascular status of the limb should be assessed and documented. Subsequent surgery may result in injury to nerves around the elbow, including the median, anterior interosseous, and ulnar nerves, and initial documentation is important in determining whether the injury resulted from the initial trauma or the surgery.

The subcutaneous position of the olecranon enables fracture fragments and the intervening hematoma to be easily palpated. The skin overlying the fracture should be inspected for abrasions or punctures, the presence of which influences the timing of surgery. As many as 31% of olecranon fractures are open fractures.[4]

It is important to assess the patient's ability to extend the arm against gravity, although extending the arm may be difficult because of pain. Inability to extend the arm implies disruption of the extensor mechanism. Tenderness or bruising anteriorly may suggest the presence of a coronoid or radial head fracture. Tenderness or bruising laterally may suggest a radial head fracture or lateral ligamentous injury.

## Imaging

A true lateral radiograph allows assessment of the degree of comminution, the amount of disruption to the articular surface, the presence of an associated elbow subluxation, and the integrity of the coronoid process. Obtaining this essential radiograph can be difficult, and the surgeon may be required to help position the patient properly. An associated injury such as dislocation of the radiohumeral joint, fracture of the coronoid process, or fracture of the radial head significantly affects elbow stability, and the possible presence of such an injury should be carefully considered in assessing radiographs.

The congruence of the ulnohumeral joint can be difficult to evaluate. The alignment of the coronoid with the trochlea should be examined. However, mild subluxation is often missed. If the center of the radial head is not aligned with the center of the capitellum, the presence of ulnohumeral subluxation or dislocation is suggested. Radiocapitellar alignment is particularly important in evaluating a child, who may have a plastic deformity of the ulna associated with a radial head dislocation; this is the Monteggia-type injury most frequently overlooked in emergency departments.

An AP radiograph allows the olecranon fracture pattern to be identified as oblique, transverse, or comminuted and reveals the presence of an associated injury of the radial head or capitellum. A radiocapitellar radiograph is required for evaluation of the radiocapitellar joint and should be obtained if injury to radiocapitellar structures is suspected.

CT studies and radiographs of the contralateral elbow are useful in planning the reconstruction of a comminuted fracture. CT also is useful in assessing fractures of the coronoid or radial head.

The coronoid should be carefully assessed on radiographs. Recently, there has been increased interest in anteromedial coronoid fractures, which are thought to be caused by varus and posteromedial rotatory forces and are frequently associated with disruption of the LCL. The shadow of the anteromedial fragment may be subtle on the AP view, and the ulnohumeral joint may appear asymmetric with loss of the medial joint space. If the displacement is severe, the elbow may be misaligned in varus. The radiohumeral joint line may be variably widened if a disruption of the lateral ulnar collateral ligament is present. On the lateral view, a double crescent sign may be seen.[5] (The intact lateral coronoid produces a radiographic density crescent parallel to the humeral joint surface, and the displaced anteromedial coronoid produces a second radiographic density crescent that is not parallel to the humeral joint surface.)

## Classification

Several classification systems exist for proximal ulnar fractures, although none of them is universally accepted. The Mayo classification of olecranon fractures is simple, relevant, and useful in planning treatment[6] (Table 1). Displacement, comminution, and ulnohumeral instability are considered in the Mayo system. A type I fracture is nondisplaced or minimally displaced. In type II, the proximal fragment is displaced without elbow instability. In type III, the proximal fragment is displaced, with instability of the ulnohumeral joint. Fractures of each type are further classified as noncomminuted (subtype A) or comminuted (subtype B).

The Orthopaedic Trauma Association uses the AO-ASIF classification system of olecranon fractures. Fractures of the proximal radius and ulna are divided into three broad categories. Type A is an extra-articular fracture involving the metaphysis of the radius or ulna; type B is an intra-articular fracture of the radius or ulna; type B1 is an intra-articular fracture of the olecranon alone. Type C is an intra-articular fracture of both the radial head and olecranon. This classification system encompasses a broad range of injury patterns and is not useful in fracture treatment.

The Schatzker classification is based on olecranon fracture configuration. It is more complex than the Mayo system but less useful in practice.

**Table 1 | Mayo Classification of Olecranon Fractures**

| Type | Description | Subtype | |
|------|-------------|---------|---|
| | | **A (Noncomminuted)** | **B (Comminuted)** |
| I | Minimal or no displacement | | |
| II | Displacement of the proximal fragment with no ulnohumeral joint instability | | |
| III | Displacement of the proximal fragment with ulnohumeral joint instability | | |

**Table 2 | Bado Classification of Monteggia Fractures**

| Type | Description | Illustration |
|------|-------------|--------------|
| I | Fracture of the middle or proximal third of the ulna with anterior dislocation of the radial head | |
| II | Fracture of the middle or proximal third of the ulna with posterior dislocation of the radial head | |
| III | Fracture of the ulna distal to the coronoid process with lateral dislocation of the radial head | |
| IV | Fracture of the middle or proximal third of the ulna with anterior dislocation of the radial head and fracture of the proximal third of the radius | |

Fracture of the proximal one third of the ulna with dislocation of the radial head (Monteggia fracture) was first described in 1814, before the development of radiography. The direction of dislocation of the radial head is classified using the popular Bado system (Table 2). Bado type I is anterior; type II, posterior; type III, lateral; and type IV, any direction with a diaphyseal fracture of the radius. Anterior and lateral Monteggia fractures may be associated with injury to the posterior interosseous nerve. A lateral dislocation (Bado type III) occurs most commonly in children. An anterior dislocation (type I) is most common in children and young adults, and a posterior dislocation (type II) occurs primarily in people who are older than 40 years. Type I injuries are the most common, accounting for 65% of injuries. Type IV is the least common, accounting for only 1% of injuries.[7]

A coronoid fracture can occur in association with a fracture of the olecranon or radial head or a dislocation or subluxation of the elbow, or it can occur in isolation. A separate system is available for classifying coronoid fractures.[8]

## Treatment Decision Making

Patient age, bone quality, associated injuries, and activity level, as well as fracture size, displacement, comminution, and dislocation, should be considered in treatment decision making.

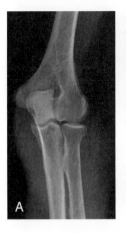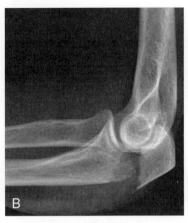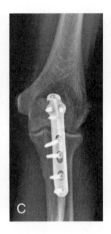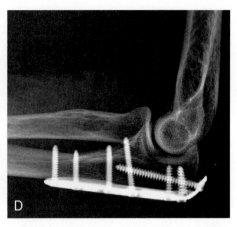

**Figure 4** AP **(A)** and lateral **(B)** radiographs of a displaced Mayo type IIA fracture of the olecranon in an 83-year-old woman. AP **(C)** and lateral **(D)** radiographs showing anatomic reduction of the fracture with a precontoured plate. Longitudinal screws were inserted through the plate at the olecranon tip.

## Olecranon Fractures

### Mayo Types IA and IB

A stable, minimally displaced or nondisplaced fracture of the olecranon is uncommon. If the extensor mechanism is intact, as indicated by the elbow's ability to extend against gravity, the fracture can be treated with a brief period of immobilization. Radiographs should be obtained after 1, 2, 4, and 6 weeks and carefully assessed for signs of displacement.

### Mayo Type IIA

Mayo type IIA comprises simple transverse or oblique fractures. A transverse fracture can be treated using tension band wire or plate fixation (Figure 4). Tension band wires should not be used to treat an oblique fracture because the resulting forces can produce translation of the fracture and an articular step-off.

### Mayo Type IIB

Dorsal comminution can cause widening of the sigmoid notch, and articular-side comminution can cause narrowing of the sigmoid notch. The tension band technique should not be used. Instead, a neutralization technique such as plate fixation is recommended.

Excision of the proximal fragment and advancement of the triceps insertion may be appropriate in a patient with low functional demands. This treatment is infrequently used, and the surgeon must confirm the stability of the elbow before it is considered. The collateral ligaments, radial head, and coronoid process must be intact. Biomechanical testing of elbow stability after excision of varying amounts of olecranon revealed that as much as 50% of the proximal ulna can be excised without affecting elbow function.[3] Subsequent studies of the effect of excising the posteromedial olecranon found an alteration in MCL strain, which suggests that olecranon excision should be avoided in younger patients with relatively high physical demands.[4]

### Mayo Types IIIA and IIIB

A transolecranon fracture-dislocation is classified as a type III injury. Stable anatomic reduction and restoration of the contour and dimensions of the trochlear notch are essential. If the olecranon is extensively comminuted, the trochlea can be used as a template for fracture reduction. Realignment of the ulna usually restores the radioulnar relationship because the intact interosseous ligament maintains stability, even if the annular ligament is torn. After fixation of the proximal ulna, the alignment of the radial head and capitellum should be inspected. Malalignment is assumed to be caused by malreduction of the ulna, unless another cause is established.

Plate fixation is generally recommended for a type III fracture. Like a type IIA fracture, a type IIIA fracture can be treated using tension band wires only if the fracture is transverse (Figure 5).

## Complex Proximal Ulnar Fractures and Fracture-Dislocations

Elbow dislocations can be classified as simple or complex. A fracture is not present in a simple dislocation but is present in a complex dislocation. In contrast to an anterior transolecranon fracture-dislocation, a posterior fracture-dislocation usually is associated with a fracture of the coronoid and radial head. Injury to the LCL also is common, and therefore the LCL should be inspected during surgery.

A concomitant radial head fracture that requires surgical attention can be approached by working through the proximal ulnar fracture or using a Boyd, Kocher, Kaplan, or extensor digitorum communis–splitting approach.

An olecranon fracture that extends into the proximal ulna usually can be approached by extending the posterior incision distally. A fracture of the medial aspect of the proximal ulnar shaft often involves the

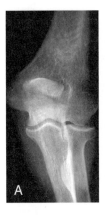
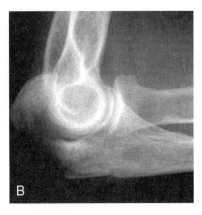
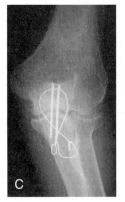
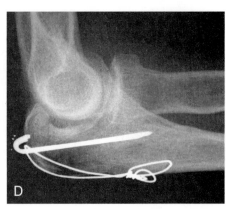

**Figure 5** AP **(A)** and lateral **(B)** radiographs of a Mayo type IIIA olecranon fracture in a 59-year-old man. AP **(C)** and lateral **(D)** radiographs showing the results of incorrect treatment using tension band wire. Note the articular step and narrowing of the greater sigmoid notch. The tension band wire has been improperly applied, with the Kirschner wires failing to penetrate the anterior cortex.

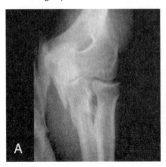
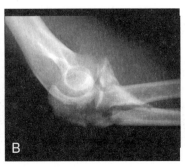
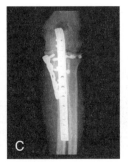
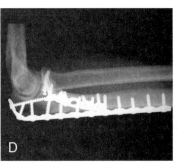

**Figure 6** AP **(A)** and lateral **(B)** radiographs of a Monteggia fracture (Bado type II) in a 50-year-old man. Radial head fracture and coronoid fracture are present, as is common in posterior fracture-dislocations. AP **(C)** and lateral **(D)** radiographs showing anatomic reduction of the fracture using a contoured plate. The ulna bows distally towards the ulnar side, and the distal end of the plate can therefore be seen on the radial aspect of the ulna. An additional plate was used for the coronoid fracture, and screws were used for the radial head fracture.

coronoid or sublime tubercle, which requires particular attention for anatomic reduction and stable fixation.

Elevating the flexor carpi ulnaris from the proximal aspect of the ulna usually allows adequate coronoid exposure. Alternatively, the coronoid can be approached through the olecranon fracture or, when addressing a radial head injury, through the lateral exposure. The coronoid can be secured using a screw placed through the olecranon plate, an antiglide plate, or transosseous sutures.

Ulnohumeral stability should be evaluated during surgery. If the joint is unstable, the LCL should be inspected and repaired. If necessary, the origin of the LCL should be reattached to the lateral epicondyle using a bone anchor or drill holes through the bone.

## Monteggia Fractures

A Monteggia fracture in a child is often associated with plastic deformation of the ulna. This injury is often missed. Inspection of the radiocapitellar joint is essential to diagnose and confirm the reduction of this fracture. A child with plastic deformation or a greenstick fracture can be treated with closed reduction and cast immobilization for 3 to 6 weeks. The risk of subsequent displacement can be decreased by immobilization in

110° of flexion and full supination to tighten the interosseous membrane.[9] A complete fracture in a child should be treated with open reduction and internal fixation with a plate. Transverse fractures have been successfully treated using an intramedullary nail.[10]

Delayed treatment of a childhood Monteggia injury is difficult. An ulnar osteotomy usually is required. Débridement of interposing soft tissue in the radiohumeral joint, shortening of the radius, and reconstruction of the annular ligament using triceps fascia also may be advisable.[11]

A Monteggia fracture-dislocation in an adult requires plate fixation. Reconstructing a comminuted fracture is often difficult and may require a distraction device on the ulna to aid in radiohumeral joint reduction and maintain ulnar length while the plate is applied.

A Bado type II injury (posterior fracture-dislocation) is usually a high-energy injury. It may result in fracture of the coronoid process or radial head, which should undergo fixation (Figure 6). Ligamentous injury also can occur, leading to ulnohumeral instability. The LCL complex should be repaired if posterolateral instability is present, even though placing the arm in pronation with supplementary support from a hinged brace often is successful.

## Nonsurgical Treatment

Immobilization in full extension may improve the reduction of a Mayo type I fracture. However, this type of immobilization is poorly tolerated by the patient and often results in diminished flexion. Immobilization between 45° and 90° of flexion is preferable. Although active flexion is permitted after 3 weeks, it is limited to 90° until radiographic evidence of fracture healing is available. Radiographs should be obtained after 1, 2, 4, and 6 weeks and carefully assessed for signs of displacement.[12]

## Surgical Treatment

### Patient Positioning

The lateral decubitus position can be used, with the patient's arm placed over a well-padded support. Alternatively, the patient can be positioned supine, with the arm placed across the chest. However, the arm is not as well supported in this position. To prevent the arm from falling away from the body and keep it in position, a sandbag or saline bag is placed under the ipsilateral scapula and the arm is placed on a rolled-up surgical drape. The use of a tourniquet is recommended. The surgery can be performed using general anesthesia or a regional block.

### Incision and Approach

The ulna can be approached through a posterior midline incision just lateral or medial to the tip of the olecranon. Some surgeons prefer a curvilinear incision, which curves around the tip of the olecranon before becoming linear in line with the ulna. Neither of these incisions causes scarring over the tip of the olecranon. Exposure of the coronoid process by elevation of the flexor pronator mass may be required, depending on the fracture type. Isolating or transposing the ulnar nerve is necessary only if the fracture is severely comminuted or the patient has a preexisting ulnar neuropathy.

The fracture is exposed, the hematoma is removed, and the periosteum is elevated approximately 2 mm on either side of the fracture to assess the reduction. To ensure an anatomic reduction, a complex fracture of the olecranon requires exposure of the articular surface of the olecranon. A simple fracture is reduced through a more limited exposure, and the articular reduction is evaluated fluoroscopically.

### Tension Band Wiring

Tension band wiring is used only for noncomminuted transverse fractures of Mayo type IIA or IIIA. Tension band compression of an oblique fracture can displace the fracture as the bones translate along the line of obliquity, and tension band compression of a comminuted fracture results in collapse and maltracking or impingement at the elbow joint.

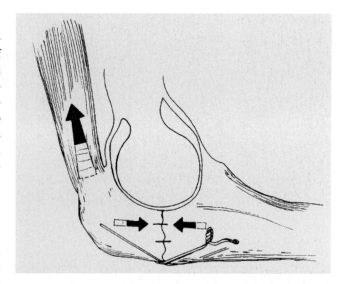

**Figure 7** Forces resulting from tension band wiring. The extensor force of the triceps *(large arrow)* is converted during motion into dynamic compression just below the articular surface *(small arrows). (Adapted with permission from Müller ME, Allgöwer M, Schneider R, Willenegger H [eds]: Manual of Internal Fixation: Techniques Recommended by the AO-ASIF Group, ed 3. Berlin, Germany, Springer-Verlag, 1991, p 19.)*

It is believed that properly performed tension band wiring converts the extensor force of the triceps into a dynamic compressive force along the articular surface (Figure 7). Two Kirschner wires and a figure-of-8 wire loop should be used. Because Kirschner wires tend to back out, some authors recommend using 6.5- or 7.3-mm longitudinal cancellous screws as an alternative. The shaft of the ulna curves and widens distally, and therefore a screw may be difficult to position or fail to achieve adequate purchase within the canal.

Two parallel 1.6- or 2.0-mm Kirschner wires are used, with a figure-of-8 loop constructed of 18-gauge wire. Kirschner wires are inserted at the proximal end of the olecranon. They can be passed longitudinally within the canal, although penetration of the anterior cortex is recommended to decrease the possibility of wire migration.[13] If the wires pass too far through the anterior cortex, there is a risk of injury to the anterior interosseous nerve. The surgeon usually feels a change in resistance as the wire reaches the second cortex and at that point stops advancing the wire. The anterior metaphysis is triangular, and radiographic assessment of the extent of anterior penetration is often misleading. The distal tips of the wires can impinge on the radial tuberosity or soft tissues and produce a mechanical block to rotation. This complication can avoided by inserting the Kirschner wires at 30° of ulnar angulation to the posteromedial crest of olecranon and at 30° to the sagittal plane.[14] The position of the radius should be noted during wire insertion. Forearm pronation should be avoided because it places the radius and ulna in close proximity. Pronation and supination should be checked after wire insertion to confirm there is no impingement (Figure 8). Care

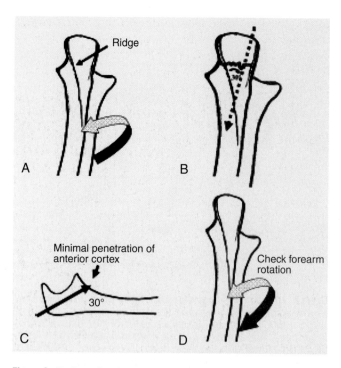

**Figure 8** Kirschner wire placement in tension band wiring. **A,** After reduction, the forearm is supinated and the posteromedial ridge of the olecranon is identified. **B,** A Kirschner wire is inserted by aiming toward the anterior cortex in the coronal plane at 30° of ulnar angulation in relation to the posteromedial ridge of the olecranon. **C,** Anterior cortical penetration is limited to the absolute minimum required. The optimal angle in the sagittal plane is 30°. **D,** When fixation is complete, forearm rotation is evaluated. *(Reproduced with permission from Candal-Couto JJ, Williams JR, Sanderson PL: Impaired forearm rotation after tension-band-wiring fixation of olecranon fractures: Evaluation of the transcortical K-wire technique. J Orthop Trauma 2005;19: 480-482.)*

should be taken not to place the Kirschner wires too far ulnarly to avoid risk of injury to the ulnar nerve.

To place the wire loop, a 16-gauge intravenous cannula is passed under the triceps tendon so that it lies directly against the bone and just above the Kirschner wires (Figure 9, *A*). The central metal trocar needle is removed from the cannula and replaced by the 18-gauge wire. The cannula is removed, leaving the wire deep to the triceps tendon. A transverse hole in good cortical bone is drilled into the ulna distal to the fracture. The wire is made into a figure-of-8, and one end is passed through the hole. Two twisted knots are constructed in the wire, and these are tightened sequentially to produce compression at the fracture site. The ends of the knots are cut and bent against the cortex, taking care that the wires are not prominent on the subcutaneous border of the ulna.

A scalpel is used to make a vertical nick in the triceps tendon at the site of each Kirschner wire (Figure 9, *B*). The Kirschner wires are backed out 5 mm, and their ends are twisted over and impacted into the tip of the olecranon with a mallet and punch to ensure the tips are deep to the triceps.

The elbow should be checked for stability and flexion, extension, pronation, and supination before the wound is closed. Despite careful attention, prominent hardware frequently causes irritation; as many as 81% of patients require removal of symptomatic hardware.[15]

Tension band wire fixation uses the AO principle of converting posterior tensile forces to articular compressive forces. A recent biomechanical study tested the technique in 10 cadaver specimens with a simulated

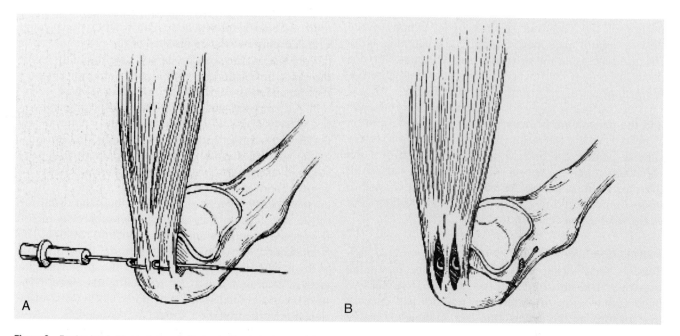

**Figure 9** Tension band wiring technique. **A,** The tension band wire is passed deep to the triceps tendon, above the Kirschner wires, using a 16-gauge or larger intravenous cannula. **B,** Fibers of the triceps tendon are split to allow the bent end of the Kirschner wire to be impacted firmly against the bone. *(Reproduced from Hak DJ, Golladay GJ: Olecranon fractures: Treatment options. J Am Acad Orthop Surg 2000;8:266-275.)*

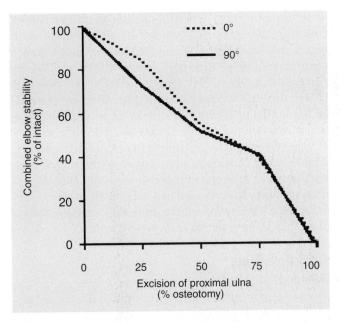

**Figure 10** The effects of olecranon excision on elbow stability. With the elbow flexed and extended, the stability of the elbow is altered as a function of the proportion of olecranon resected; approximately 50% of the stabilizing force of the ulna to resist axial displacement and rotation is lost if the proximal 50% of the articulation is removed. *(Reproduced with permission from Morrey BF, An KN: Stability of the elbow: Osseous constraints. J Shoulder Elbow Surg 2005;14[suppl 1]:174S-178S.)*

transverse olecranon fracture. Simulated elbow motion did not produce compression across the osteotomy gap in any of the specimens.[16]

## Plate Fixation

Plate fixation can be used for a Mayo type II or type III olecranon fracture, a Monteggia injury, or a fracture involving the coronoid and proximal ulna. The use of one-third tubular plates is not recommended because they can fail in a greatly comminuted fracture. Pelvic reconstruction plates are typically used. However, if the fracture extends distal to the coronoid, a dynamic compression plate is preferred because it is stronger. Precontoured plates are readily available and can be used.

The dorsum is the tension side of the ulna and is easy to expose surgically. The plate can be contoured as necessary. A longitudinal screw should be inserted into the most proximal hole to improve stability.[17] The proximal portion of the plate can be placed on top of the distal triceps insertion. This placement is particularly useful in a very proximal fracture or a comminuted proximal fracture; alternatively, the triceps can be split to allow the plate to lie directly on the bone.

In a displaced olecranon fracture (Mayo type III), the coronoid can be inspected through the opening between the olecranon and ulna. If a coronoid fracture is present, it can be reduced and temporarily held with a Kirschner wire until the olecranon is reduced. The coronoid often can be secured by passing a screw through or

adjacent to the dorsal plate. Sutures passed through the coronoid fragment and the ulnar shaft can be used to secure a relatively small coronoid fracture. A coronoid fracture also can be exposed by a medial approach through the flexor pronator muscles.

The surgeon should take care to reconstruct the articular surface in a comminuted fracture of the olecranon, avoiding the bare area on the articular surface. The dorsal surface can be used as a guide for alignment of the fragments. In a comminuted fracture, the curve of the trochlea can be used as a template for restoration of the articular surface of the olecranon. Areas of bone loss may require supplementation with a bone graft. Cancellous bone graft is used for a smaller defect, and corticocancellous bone graft is used for a larger defect. After provisional fracture fixation with Kirschner wires, a dorsal plate is applied and fixed using cancellous screws into the olecranon and cortical screws into the ulnar shaft distally. Care should be taken to direct the screws ulnarly to avoid impingement on the radial head in the proximal radioulnar joint and allow placement of an axial screw more radially. The elbow should be checked for stability and flexion, extension, pronation, and supination before wound closure.

In treating a Monteggia fracture or a Mayo type III olecranon fracture, the radial head should be inspected on radiographs to ensure it is in line with the center of the capitellum after the proximal ulna is reduced. If the radial head is not in line, malreduction of the ulna is assumed to be responsible unless another cause is established.

## Olecranon Excision With Triceps Advancement

Internal fixation of olecranon fractures usually is recommended to produce good healing with bone-to-bone contact and permit early motion. Olecranon excision should be reserved for treating a comminuted fracture in a patient with poor bone quality and low physical demands or a severely comminuted open fracture in a patient with higher physical demands. It can also be used as a salvage procedure after unsuccessful internal fixation. Elbow stability should be confirmed before this procedure is considered. Olecranon excision is contraindicated for a Mayo type III fracture.

Biomechanical testing found that as much as 50% of the olecranon can be excised without compromising stability[3] (Figure 10). However, one study found that 11 of 12 patients had a good or excellent result after excision of as much as 70% of the olecranon.[18]

After the olecranon tip fragment is excised, the triceps tendon is reattached using nonabsorbable Krakow locking sutures passed through drill holes in the proximal ulna. It has been recommended that the tendon be attached adjacent to the articular surface to create a sling for the trochlea.[6] Recent biomechanical studies recommended attachment toward the nonarticular surface to increase the triceps moment arm and reduce extension weakness.[19]

### Postsurgical Treatment

After surgery, the elbow should be splinted in extension. Active elbow flexion and gravity-assisted extension usually can be initiated on the first or second day after surgery. A weak fixation or poor tissue quality may dictate a delay in mobilization. Patients can use a static progressive extension splint while sleeping for as long as 12 weeks after surgery. A collar and cuff can be used for no more than 6 weeks to rest the arm during the day. The routine use of nonsteroidal anti-inflammatory drugs is not recommended as prophylaxis for heterotopic ossification in simple fractures, but its use is recommended in fracture-dislocations. Strengthening exercises are initiated after fracture union is confirmed radiographically.

## Results and Outcomes

### Olecranon Excision With Triceps Advancement

After olecranon excision with triceps advancement or open reduction and internal fixation using different methods, 107 patients had similar results for pain, function, elbow stability, and degenerative joint disease.[20] However, the 3.6-year mean (2-year minimum) follow-up period may have been insufficient to assess the patients for arthrosis. In cadaver elbows with olecranon fractures that were surgically treated using tension band wire or olecranon excision with triceps advancement, fixation re-created the normal joint stresses. However, the triceps advancement models had abnormally elevated stresses in the remaining articular segment.[21] Olecranon excision with triceps advancement therefore should be reserved for patients who are older or have low functional demands.

### Tension Band Wiring

In a prospective randomized study of elbows with a displaced fracture after treatment with either tension band wiring or one-third tubular plates, loss of reduction and development of a significant articular step (2 mm or more) were 10 times more common in the elbows treated with tension band wiring.[22] Functional and radiographic outcomes were better in the elbows treated with plate fixation. Other recent studies of the outcomes of treatment for olecranon fractures found that patients with a comminuted fracture or a Mayo type III fracture had poorer outcomes after tension band wiring.[23,24]

### Open Reduction and Internal Fixation

Hardware removal is more frequently required in patients who had tension band wiring than in patients who had plate fixation. After plate fixation of Mayo type II and type III olecranon fractures, Disabilities of the Arm, Shoulder and Hand Questionnaire scores were consistent with almost-normal elbow function, and Medical Outcomes Study Short Form-36 Health Survey scores were consistent with normal elbow function.[25] Twenty percent of patients had symptoms requiring plate removal; this rate is lower than that reported for removal of tension band wiring. No difference in outcomes was found between Mayo type II and type III fractures.

The recommended treatment of olecranon fractures is plate fixation. Tension band wiring should be reserved for the treatment of simple transverse fractures. The surgeon must be aware that surgical exploration often reveals unexpected comminution in a fracture that appeared on radiographs to be a simple transverse fracture.

## Complications

### Infection

The use of prophylactic antibiotic drugs at the time of surgery reduces the likelihood that the patient will develop a postsurgical infection. If the skin overlying the ulna is greatly damaged, surgery may be delayed for a few days until the condition of the skin improves. A low-grade postsurgical infection can be treated with débridement of the wound and fracture site, and antibiotic drugs should be used until the fracture has united. The hardware can then be removed. A high-grade infection requires antibiotic treatment, hardware removal, and débridement, with or without an antibiotic-impregnated cement spacer. The subsequent reconstruction is often difficult.

### Neurologic Injury

The ulnar nerve, median nerve, or anterior interosseous nerve may be injured during tension band wiring.[26-28] Plate fixation also places nerves at risk, although the anterior interosseous nerve is at greater risk of injury from tension band wires.

### Irritation From Hardware

The hardware used for fracture repair lies almost directly under the skin and is often bothersome, especially when the patient leans on the elbow to stabilize the arm during daily activities. The rate of removal of tension band wires is as high as 81%.[15] Tension band loops can be a source of patient distress, especially at the knots. The axial Kirschner wire often backs out, even if it was placed deep to the triceps and engaged in the anterior ulnar cortex. Although plate removal is less frequently required, problematic symptoms can develop regardless of the type of plate used.

### Failure of Fixation

Tension band wire fixation can fail if it is used for any fracture configuration other than a simple transverse olecranon fracture. Plate or tension band wire fixation of any type of fracture can fail if overly vigorous physical therapy is begun too soon after surgery. Caution is especially important if thin plates are used to treat fractures that extend distal to the coronoid because these plates are subject to significant forces and can bend or break.

### Ulnohumeral Instability

Ulnohumeral instability most often results from inadequate reduction of the ulnar fracture and can be corrected by a revision fixation. To protect the fixation during healing of an extremely comminuted olecranon or coronoid fracture, hinged external fixation can be used for 4 to 6 weeks.

### Arthrosis

Damage to the articular surface at the time of injury increases the patient's risk of developing arthrosis.[24] A comminuted fracture can be difficult to reconstruct, and residual incongruity is a risk factor for posttraumatic arthrosis.

### Posttraumatic Contractures and Heterotopic Ossification

Contractures sometimes occur after elbow trauma. Normal elbow function is achieved if the arc of elbow motion includes a range of 30° to 130°. If the patient has significant loss of motion that does not respond to therapy and splinting, surgery can be performed to excise the contracted capsule and heterotopic bone. Prophylactic radiation and nonsteroidal anti-inflammatory drugs can reduce the likelihood that the patient will develop heterotopic ossification.

## Summary

Fractures of the olecranon are common, and they present technical challenges. Careful patient evaluation and radiographic assessment are necessary before embarking on treatment. Surgery usually is required. Although tension band wire fixation has been popular, plate fixation generally leads to a better functional outcome. Patients more frequently request later removal of tension band wires than plates.

## Annotated References

1. Wang AA, Mara M, Hutchinson DT: The proximal ulna: An anatomic study with relevance to olecranon osteotomy and fracture fixation. *J Shoulder Elbow Surg* 2003;12:293-296.

   An anatomic analysis of ulnar length and diameter, the site of the varus curve, and the site and size of the bare area are presented.

2. Safran MR, Baillargeon D: Soft-tissue stabilizers of the elbow. *J Shoulder Elbow Surg* 2005;14(suppl 1): 179S-185S.

3. Morrey BF, An KN: Stability of the elbow: Osseous constraints. *J Shoulder Elbow Surg* 2005;14(suppl 1): 174S-178S.

   This article presents a discussion of the biomechanical aspects of the bony elements of the elbow, with all soft-tissue constraints excised. As much as 50% of the olecranon can be excised without compromising elbow function. The coronoid was found to be the most important stabilizer.

4. Kamineni S, ElAttrache NS, O'Driscoll SW, et al: Medial collateral ligament strain with partial posteromedial olecranon resection: A biomechanical study. *J Bone Joint Surg Am* 2004;86:2424-2430.

   Posteromedial olecranon excision is performed for extension impingement osteophytosis. This cadaver biomechanical study found that the strain in the anterior bundle of the MCL increases with increasing flexion angle, valgus torque, and olecranon resection of more than 3 mm.

5. Sanchez-Sotelo J, O'Driscoll S, Morrey B: Medial oblique compression fracture of the coronoid process of the ulna. *J Shoulder Elbow Surg* 2005;14:60-64.

   An oblique, medial compression fracture of the coronoid is subtle and sometimes missed on routine assessment. It may be associated with joint subluxation or dislocation. The currently accepted classification system may not fully characterize fractures of the coronoid.

6. Cabenela ME, Morrey BF: Fractures of the proximal ulna and olecranon, in Morrey BF (ed): *The Elbow and Its Disorders*, ed 2. Philadelphia, PA, WB Saunders, 1993, pp 405-428.

7. Wolfgang G, Burke F, Bush D, et al: Surgical treatment of displaced olecranon fractures by tension band wiring technique. *Clin Orthop Relat Res* 1987; 224:192-204.

8. O'Driscoll SW, Jupiter JB, Cohen MS, Ring D, McKee MD: Difficult elbow fractures: Pearls and pitfalls. *Instr Course Lect* 2003;52:113-134.

   Fractures of the distal humerus, coronoid, trochlea, radial head, and radial neck are discussed, as well as trans-olecranon fracture-dislocations. A new classification of coronoid fractures relevant to fracture treatment is introduced.

9. Speed JS, Boyd HB: Treatment of fractures of the ulna with dislocation of the head of the radius. *JAMA* 1940;115:1699-1704.

10. Ring D, Waters PM: Operative fixation of Monteggia fractures in children. *J Bone Joint Surg Br* 1996;78: 734-739.

The soft-tissue stabilizers of the elbow are described. The static soft-tissue stabilizers consist of the anterior and posterior joint capsule and the MCL and LCL complexes. Additional stability is conferred by the dynamic muscles crossing the elbow joint.

11. Ring D, Jupiter JB, Waters PM: Monteggia fractures in children and adults. *J Am Acad Orthop Surg* 1998; 6:215-224.

12. Mezzera M, Hotchkiss R: Fractures and dislocations of the elbow, in Rockwood CA, Heckman JD, Bucholz RW (eds): *Rockwood and Green's Fractures in Adults*, ed 5. Philadelphia, PA, Lippincott Williams and Wilkins, 2001, pp 921-951.

    Diagnosis and treatment of elbow fractures and dislocations are described.

13. Heim U, Pfeiffer KM: *Internal Fixation of Small Fractures: Technique Recommended by the AO-ASIF Group*, ed 3. New York, NY, Springer, 1988, p 112.

14. Candal-Couto JJ, Williams JR, Sanderson PL: Impaired forearm rotation after tension-band-wiring fixation of olecranon fractures: Evaluation of the transcortical K-wire technique. *J Orthop Trauma* 2005;19:480-482.

    Biomechanical testing was performed to assess the risk of mechanical block to rotation. Clinical case studies describe impaired rotation because of wire protruding into the radius or surrounding soft tissue. Level of evidence: IV.

15. Karlsson MK, Hasserius R, Besjakov J, Karlsson C, Josefsson PO: Comparison of tension-band and figure-of-eight wiring techniques for treatment of olecranon fractures. *J Shoulder Elbow Surg* 2002;11: 377-382.

    In a nonrandomized, retrospective review (mean, 18 years) of patients who underwent one of two tension band wiring procedures, 81% required hardware removal. More than 50% of the fractured elbows had degenerative changes including joint space narrowing, subchondral cysts, subchondral sclerosis, and osteophytes, and 6% had osteoarthritis. Level of evidence: IV.

16. Hutchinson DT, Horwitz DS, Ha G, Thomas CW, Bachus KN: Cyclic loading of olecranon fracture fixation constructs. *J Bone Joint Surg Am* 2003;85: 831-837.

    In a biomechanical study of 10 cadaver elbows fixed with tension band wire or 7.3-mm screws with or without tension band wires, cyclic loading simulated active range of motion and the action of pushing up from a chair. The performance of screw fixation was better than that of tension band wire fixation. The AO principle of converting posterior tensile forces to articular compressive forces was not supported.

17. Gordon MJ, Budoff JE, Yeh ML, Luo ZP, Noble PC: Comminuted olecranon fractures: A comparison of plating methods. *J Shoulder Elbow Surg* 2006;15: 94-99.

    In a comparison of fixation using a posterior plate, a posterior plate with longitudinal screws, and a dual medial-lateral plate, the posterior plate with longitudinal screws was found to be 48% stronger than the dual plate.

18. Inhofe PD, Howard TC: The treatment of olecranon fractures by excision of fragments and repair of the extensor mechanism: Historical review and report of 12 fractures. *Orthopedics* 1993;16:1313-1317.

19. Didonna ML, Fernandez JJ, Lim TH, Hastings H II, Cohen MS: Partial olecranon excision: The relationship between triceps insertion site and extension strength of the elbow. *J Hand Surg Am* 2003;28: 117-122.

    Ten cadaver elbows were placed in different degrees of flexion. Loads were applied to the triceps, and the generated forces were recorded. A 50% olecranon excision was performed, and the anterior and posterior triceps attachments were tested. The posterior attachment has a mechanical advantage; the greatest differences are at increasing positions of elbow extension, where triceps strength is functionally more important.

20. Gartsman GM, Sculco TP, Otis JC: Operative treatment of olecranon fractures. Excision or open reduction with internal fixation. *J Bone Joint Surg Am* 1981;63:718-721.

21. Moed BR, Ede DE, Brown TD: Fractures of the olecranon: An in vitro study of elbow joint stresses after tension-band wire fixation versus proximal fracture fragment excision. *J Trauma* 2002;53:1088-1093.

    In eight pairs of cadaver elbows, open reduction and internal fixation was performed using tension band wiring or triceps advancement. Pressure at the joint was recorded. Internal fixation restores the normal biomechanics of the elbow joint. Proximal fragment excision results in abnormally elevated joint stresses and an increased risk of arthrosis.

22. Hume MC, Wiss DA: Olecranon fractures. A clinical and radiographic comparison of tension band wiring and plate fixation. *Clin Orthop Relat Res* 1992;285: 229-235.

23. Rommens PM, Kuchle R, Schneider RU, Reuter M: Olecranon fractures in adults: Factors influencing outcome. *Injury* 2004;35:1149-1157.

    In a retrospective review of 95 consecutive olecranon fractures, 95% of which were treated with tension band wiring, migration was found in 9.5%, reintervention was necessary in 14.7%, and suboptimal fixation (wires not parallel to or breaching anterior cortex) was found in 26%. The incidence of arthrosis was 3.4 times greater in patients with suboptimal fixation. Hardware had been removed in two thirds of the patients. Patients with a comminuted or Mayo type III fracture had a more restricted range of motion and more arthrosis. Level of evidence: IV.

24. Villanueva P, Osorio F, Commessatti M, Sanchez-Sotelo J: Tension-band wiring for olecranon fractures: Analysis of risk factors for failure. *J Shoulder Elbow Surg* 2006;15:351-356.

    In 37 consecutive elbow fractures treated with tension band wiring, the incidence of arthrosis was higher in Mayo type III fractures. Olecranon fractures with associated elbow instability, radial head fracture, or coronoid fracture did less well than isolated olecranon fractures. Level of evidence: IV.

25. Bailey CS, MacDermid J, Patterson SD, King GJ: Outcome of plate fixation of olecranon fractures. *J Orthop Trauma* 2001;15:542-548.

Twenty-five patients underwent plate fixation of an olecranon fracture; 14 were Mayo type II, and 11 were Mayo type III. The mean Disabilities of the Arm, Shoulder and Hand Questionnaire scores were consistent with almost-normal elbow function and the Short Form-36 Health Survey scores, with normal elbow function. Twenty percent had plate removal. No difference in outcomes was found between type II and III fractures. Level of evidence: III.

26. Thumroj E, Jianmongkol S, Thammaroj J: Median nerve palsy after operative treatment of olecranon fracture. *J Med Assoc Thai* 2005;88:1434-1437.

This is a case report of median nerve injury in olecranon fracture treatment. Level of evidence: V.

27. Parker JR, Conroy J, Campbell DA: Anterior interosseus nerve injury following tension band wiring of the olecranon. *Injury* 2005;36:1252-1253.

In this case report, several passes of the Kirschner wire were required to achieve an AO-type fixation of the olecranon, resulting in anterior interosseus nerve injury. The palsy was resolved within 6 months. Level of evidence: V.

28. Ishigaki N, Uchiyama S, Nakagawa H, Kamimura M, Miyasaka T: Ulnar nerve palsy at the elbow after surgical treatment for fractures of the olecranon. *J Shoulder Elbow Surg* 2004;13:60-65.

In this case report of four patients, three had ulnar nerve palsy caused by ulnar nerve irritation from fracture fragments in a comminuted fracture, and one had palsy caused by an osteophyte in association with inflammation from wire migration. Level of evidence: V.

# Section 8

# Miscellaneous Shoulder Topics

Section Editor
John W. Sperling, MD

# Chapter 49

# Adult Traumatic Brachial Plexus Injuries

Alexander Y. Shin, MD

*Robert J. Spinner, MD

Allen T. Bishop, MD

## Introduction

Most injuries to the brachial plexus result from a motor vehicle crash (typically involving a motorcycle), a vehicle striking a pedestrian, a vehicle rollover, or a vehicle striking a fixed object. The brachial plexus can be injured by penetrating trauma as well as blunt trauma. In addition, an iatrogenic injury to the brachial plexus can occur, especially during shoulder surgery. Most brachial plexus injuries are part of a closed injury and result from traction, compression, or both.

Although the incidence of brachial plexus injuries is difficult to ascertain, it is rising in many institutions throughout the world.[1-6] Contributing factors include the increasing popularity of dangerous or extreme sporting activities and powerful motor sports, as well as the increasing likelihood of surviving a high-speed motor vehicle crash because of safety features such as airbags. Most patients with a brachial plexus injury are males age 15 to 25 years.[5,7,8] Patients suffer significant physical disability, psychological distress, and socioeconomic hardship.

The recommended treatment of complete root avulsion has varied widely during the past 50 years, and the reported results of treatment have been fair to dismal. The standard approach in the years following World War II was surgical reconstruction by shoulder fusion, elbow bone block, and finger tenodesis.[9] During the 1960s, the favored treatment was above-elbow transhumeral amputation combined with shoulder fusion in slight abduction and flexion.[10] Regardless of the treatment, many patients during this period exclusively used the hand on the unaffected side within 2 years of injury, and therefore few outcomes were considered successful.[11] The primitive surgical reconstruction did not produce good results, although amputation and shoulder fusion performed within 24 months of injury usually had an adequate result. The loss of glenohumeral motion caused by a brachial plexus injury limited the effective-ness of body-powered devices. A manual laborer usually was better able to accept a hook prosthesis than an office worker with a similar injury.[11]

Recent advances in brachial plexus reconstruction have led to improved results. Increased understanding of the pathophysiology of nerve injury and repair as well as advances in microsurgical techniques have permitted reliable restoration of elbow flexion and shoulder abduction and, in some patients, useful prehension of the hand.

## Anatomy and Mechanisms of Injury

### Anatomy of the Brachial Plexus

The brachial plexus typically is formed from five cervical nerve roots, C5 through T1 (Figure 1). C4 contributes to some extent in 28% to 62% of patients, and T2 contributes in 16% to 73% of patients.[12] A brachial plexus with a C4 contribution is called prefixed, and a plexus with a T2 contribution is called postfixed.

The true form of the brachial plexus, as described by Kerr based on the dissection of 175 cadaver specimens, has five separate sections: roots, trunks, divisions, cords, and terminal branches. The roots are formed by the coalescence of the ventral and dorsal nerve rootlets as they pass through the spinal foramen[12] (Figure 2). The dorsal root ganglion holds the cell bodies of the sensory nerves and lies within the confines of the spinal canal and foramina. An avulsion of the spinal roots from the spinal cord is known as a preganglionic injury. In a central preganglionic injury, the nerve is avulsed directly from the spinal cord; in a peripheral preganglionic injury, rootlets are ruptured proximal to the dorsal root ganglion. An injury distal to the dorsal root ganglion is referred to as postganglionic. The distinction between preganglionic and postganglionic injury is important in determining the necessary type of surgical reconstruction.

The C5 and C6 roots merge to form the upper trunk, C7 becomes the middle trunk, and the C8 and T1 roots merge to form the lower trunk. At Erb's point, C5 and C6 merge, and the suprascapular nerve emerges. Each trunk forms anterior and posterior divisions, which pass

*Robert J. Spinner, MD or the department with which he is affiliated has received royalties from Mayo Medical Ventures.

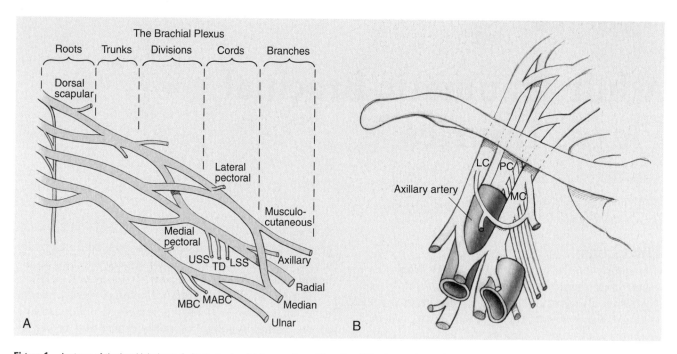

**Figure 1** Anatomy of the brachial plexus. **A,** Roots, trunks, divisions, cords, and branches. LSS = lower subscapular, MABC = medial antebrachial cutaneous, MBC = medial brachial cutaneous, TD = thoracodorsal, USS = upper subscapular. **B,** The lateral (LC), posterior (PC), and medial (PC) cords. *(Reproduced with permission from the Mayo Foundation.)*

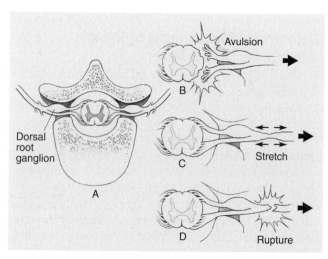

**Figure 2** Anatomy of the brachial plexus roots and the three types of injury. **A,** The roots are formed by the coalescence of the ventral (motor) and dorsal (sensory) rootlets as they pass through the spinal foramen. **B,** An avulsion injury pulls the rootlets out of the spinal cord. **C,** A stretch injury attenuates the nerve. **D,** A rupture results in a complete discontinuity of the nerve. *(Reproduced with permission from the Mayo Foundation.)*

beneath the clavicle. The posterior divisions merge to become the posterior cord, and the anterior divisions of the upper and middle trunk merge to form the lateral cord. The anterior division of the lower trunk forms the medial cord. The lateral cord splits into two terminal branches: the musculocutaneous nerve and the lateral cord contribution to the median nerve. The posterior cord forms the axillary and radial nerves. The medial cord becomes the ulnar nerve and the medial cord contribution to the median nerve.

A few terminal branches begin in the roots, trunks, or cords. The branches from the C5 root go to the phrenic nerve, the dorsal scapular nerve (the rhomboid muscles), and the long thoracic nerve (the serratus anterior muscle). The branches from C6 and C7 also contribute to the long thoracic nerve. The branches from the upper trunk include the suprascapular nerve (supraspinatus and infraspinatus muscles) and the nerve to the subclavius muscle. The lateral cord branches go to the lateral pectoral nerve. The posterior and medial cords each have three branches: the posterior cord branches proximal to distal to the upper subscapular nerve, the thoracodorsal nerve, and the lower subscapular nerve. The medial cord branches go to the medial pectoral nerve, the medial antebrachial cutaneous nerve, and the medial brachial cutaneous nerve.

The sympathetic ganglion for T1 lies in close proximity to the T1 root and provides sympathetic outflow to the head and neck. Avulsion of the T1 root interrupts the T1 sympathetic ganglion and results in Horner syndrome (Figure 3), which consists of miosis (contraction of the pupil), enophthalmos (sinking of the eyeball into the orbit), ptosis (drooping of the eyelid), and facial anhidrosis (absence of sweating).

### Mechanisms of Injury

Brachial plexus lesions more frequently affect the supraclavicular region than the retroclavicular or infraclavicular level. The nerve roots and trunks are more commonly affected than the divisions, cords, or terminal

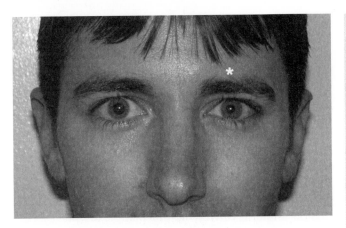

**Figure 3** A patient with Horner syndrome. After a left-side lower trunk avulsion injury interrupting the T1 sympathetic ganglion, this patient has the characteristic miosis and ptosis (*asterisk*). *(Reproduced with permission from the Mayo Foundation.)*

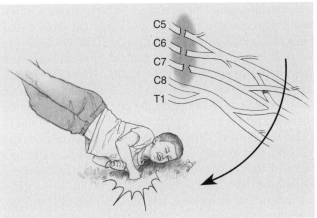

**Figure 4** Upper brachial plexus injuries occur when the head and neck are violently moved away from the ipsilateral shoulder, resulting in a stretch, avulsion, or rupture of the upper roots (C5 through C7) with preservation of the lower roots (C8-T1). *(Reproduced with permission from the Mayo Foundation.)*

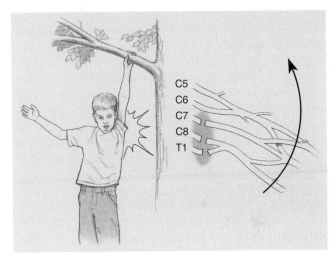

**Figure 5** The lower elements of the plexus (C8-T1) can be injured with abduction and traction, such as occurs if the arm is pulled above the head. This pattern can lead to preganglionic or postganglionic injury to the lower neural elements of the brachial plexus. *(Reproduced with permission from the Mayo Foundation.)*

branches. Double-level injuries recently have been more widely recognized, especially in the nerves that are relatively fixed to surrounding structures, such as the axillary nerve. In the supraclavicular region, a traction injury can occur if the head and neck are violently moved away from the ipsilateral shoulder; the injury is often to the C5-C6 roots or the upper trunk (Figure 4). A traction injury to the brachial plexus can also result from violent abduction of the arm, as can occur if the arm is violently pulled into a machine. If the arm is abducted over the head with significant force, traction occurs in the lower elements of the brachial plexus (the C8-T1 roots) or lower trunk (Figure 5). A compression injury to the brachial plexus is most likely to occur between the clavicle and the first rib. A direct blow can cause injury to the neural structures of the brachial plexus around the coracoid process. Iatrogenic injury to the brachial plexus can occur during a shoulder procedure, often as the result of inadvertent suture placement around the nerves.

The types and mechanisms of brachial plexus injury can be effectively summarized by Narakas' law of seven 70s, an estimate based on examination of 1,000 patients during an 18-year period.[13] Of all traumatic brachial plexus injuries, 70% resulted from road traffic accidents. Of the crashes, 70% involved a motorcycle or bicycle. Of the cyclists, 70% had multiple injuries. Of all patients, 70% had a supraclavicular lesion. Of those with a supraclavicular lesion, 70% had at least one avulsed root. Of patients with a root avulsion, at least 70% had an avulsion of a lower root (C7, C8, or T1). Of patients with lower root avulsion, almost 70% had persistent pain.

## Clinical Evaluation

### Physical Examination

A patient with a brachial plexus injury often has other traumatic injuries requiring immediate stabilization. A high level of suspicion for a brachial plexus injury should be maintained during emergency department examination of a patient with a significant shoulder girdle injury. Often the patient is initially obtunded or sedated, and careful observation is required as the patient becomes more coherent. If the patient is awake and cooperative, an experienced, systematic examiner can perform a detailed examination of the brachial plexus and its terminal branches in a few minutes.

The median, ulnar, and radial nerves can be quickly checked by examining the patient's finger and wrist motion. Elbow flexion and extension can be examined to determine musculocutaneous and high radial nerve function. Examination of shoulder abduction can determine the functioning of the axillary nerve, a branch of the posterior cord. Examination of wrist extension, elbow extension, and shoulder abduction can help determine the condition of the posterior cord. An injury to the posterior cord can affect both deltoid function and the muscles innervated by the radial nerve. The latissimus dorsi, which is innervated by the thoracodorsal nerve (a branch of the posterior cord), can be palpated in the posterior axillary fold and can be felt to contract when the patient coughs or holds a hand against the buttocks. The pectoralis major is innervated by the medial and lateral pectoral nerves, which are branches of the medial and lateral cords, respectively. The lateral pectoral nerve innervates the clavicular head, and the medial pectoral nerve innervates the sternal head of the pectoralis major. The entire pectoralis major can be palpated from superior to inferior as the patient adducts the arm against resistance.

The suprascapular nerve is a terminal branch at the trunk level, proximal to the cord level. Its condition can be assessed by examining external rotation as well as abduction of the shoulder. If the patient's brachial plexus condition is chronic, the posterior aspect of the shoulder is often significantly atrophied near the infraspinatus muscle. Supraspinatus muscle atrophy is difficult to detect clinically because the trapezius muscle covers most of the supraspinatus. Axillary nerve function and rotator cuff integrity should also be evaluated because loss of shoulder flexion, rotation, and abduction can be caused by a significant injury to the rotator cuff or deltoid.

Some clinical examination findings suggest a preganglionic injury. For example, the presence of Horner syndrome suggests a root avulsion at the C8-T1 level. The presence of injury to the long thoracic nerve or dorsal scapular nerve suggests a proximal preganglionic injury because these nerves originate at the root level. If the C5 root is avulsed (a preganglionic injury), careful examination will reveal atrophy of the rhomboid and parascapular muscles. The long thoracic nerve is formed from the roots of C5 through C7 and innervates the serratus anterior. It is more than 20 cm long and vulnerable to injury as it descends along the chest wall. Injury to the long thoracic nerve results in significant scapular winging when the patient attempts to forward elevate the arm. The dorsal scapular nerve is derived from C4-C5, often at a foraminal level, and innervates the rhomboid muscles. The patient must be observed from the posterior to fully evaluate the status of the serratus anterior and rhomboid muscles.

Neighboring cranial nerves must be considered during motor testing. For example, the spinal accessory nerve that innervates the trapezius muscle is occasionally injured during neck or shoulder trauma affecting the brachial plexus. The integrity of the spinal accessory nerve is important because of its potential for use in a nerve transfer.

Nerve distributions should be checked, especially in the autonomous zones, during a careful sensory or autonomic examination. Root-level dermatome sensation can be unreliable in determining levels of injury because of overlap from other nerves or anatomic variation.

The patient's active and passive range of motion should be recorded, and reflexes should be assessed. To discover evidence of concomitant spinal cord injury, the patient should be examined for lower limb strength, sensory levels, and increased or pathologic reflexes. Nerve percussion is especially helpful. Acute pain over a nerve suggests the presence of a rupture, and absence of percussion tenderness over the brachial plexus suggests an avulsion. An advancing Tinel sign may suggest a recovering lesion.

A vascular examination should also be performed, in which the examiner feels for distal pulses or thrills and listens for bruits. Vascular injury sometimes is found with an infraclavicular lesion or a severe injury such as scapulothoracic dissociation. It is possible to rupture the axillary artery in a significant brachial plexus injury. The likelihood of such an injury should be evaluated, and a vascular surgical consultation should be obtained before any brachial plexus intervention.

## Imaging

Radiography can provide clues to neurologic injury associated with a traumatic injury to the neck or shoulder girdle. The standard radiographs include cervical spine, shoulder, and chest views. Cervical spine radiographs should be examined for the presence of a cervical fracture, which could put the spinal cord at risk. A transverse process fracture of the cervical vertebrae may indicate a root avulsion. A fracture of the clavicle may indicate trauma to the brachial plexus. A chest radiograph can reveal a fracture of the first or second rib and suggest damage to the overlying brachial plexus. Careful review of chest radiographs can provide information about any earlier rib fractures, which can become important if intercostal nerves are considered for use in nerve transfer. In addition, an injury to the phrenic nerve is associated with paralysis of the hemidiaphragm.

Arteriography may be indicated if vascular injury is suspected, and magnetic resonance angiography is useful to confirm the patency of any earlier vascular repair or reconstruction. CT combined with myelography can be instrumental in defining the level of a possible nerve root injury.[14,15] Ninety brachial plexus lesions were examined using myelography and were classified; the results were compared with the level of lesions found during intrasurgical electrophysiologic investigation. This study found that myelography can be reliable and useful in presurgical assessment of the level of the lesion in each injured root.[15] After an avulsion of a cervical root, the dural sheath heals with development of a pseudomeningocele. Immediately after injury, a blood clot in the area of the nerve root avulsion often displaces dye from the myelogram. To allow time for any blood clots to dissipate and a pseudomeningocele to fully form, CT with myelography should be performed 3 to 4 weeks after the injury. A pseudomeningocele seen on CT with myelography strongly suggests the presence of a root avulsion.

MRI has improved during the past several years, and it can now be helpful in evaluating a patient with a suspected nerve root avulsion.[16-18] MRI is noninvasive and can show much of the brachial plexus. (In contrast, CT with myelography shows only possible nerve root injury.) MRI can reveal large neuromas and associated inflammation, edema, and atrophy after trauma. It is helpful in detecting mass lesions in spontaneous neuropathy affecting the brachial plexus or its terminal branches. After acute trauma, CT with myelography is the best means of detecting nerve root avulsion. However, as MRI evaluation of the brachial plexus continues to improve, it may eventually eliminate the need for the more invasive myelography.

### Electrodiagnostic Studies

Appropriately used and correctly interpreted electrodiagnostic studies are integral to presurgical and intrasurgical decision making. They can help in confirming the diagnosis, locating lesions, defining the severity of axon loss and the completeness of a lesion, eliminating other conditions from the differential diagnosis, and revealing subclinical recovery or unrecognized subclinical disorders. Electrodiagnostic studies therefore are important as an adjunct, but not a substitute, for a thorough patient history, physical examination, and imaging studies. When all results are considered, a decision can be made about proceeding with surgical intervention.

For closed injuries, baseline electromyography (EMG) and nerve conduction velocity studies are best performed 3 to 4 weeks after the injury, after wallerian degeneration has occurred. Serial electrodiagnostic studies can be performed every few months in conjunction with a physical examination to document and quantify ongoing reinnervation or denervation.

EMG tests the muscles at rest and during activity. Signs of denervation, such as fibrillation potentials, can be seen in proximal muscles as early as 10 to 14 days after injury and, in more distal muscles, within 3 to 6 weeks. Reduced recruitment of motor unit potentials can be seen as soon as weakness from a lower motor neuron injury occurs. The presence of active motor units with voluntary effort and few fibrillations at rest is associated with a good prognosis, compared with the absence of motor units and many fibrillations. EMG can be helpful in needle examination to distinguish preganglionic and postganglionic lesions in muscles that are proximally innervated by root-level motor branches, such as the cervical paraspinal, rhomboid, and serratus anterior muscles.

Nerve conduction velocity studies should accompany EMG. In posttraumatic brachial plexus lesions, the amplitudes of compound muscle action potentials are generally low or absent. Sensory nerve action potentials are important in determining whether a lesion is preganglionic or postganglionic. Sensory nerve action potentials are preserved in lesions proximal to the dorsal root ganglia. Because the sensory nerve cell body is intact and inside the dorsal root ganglion, nerve conduction velocity studies often show that the sensory nerve action potential is normal and motor conduction is absent, although the patient is insensate in the associated dermatome. Sensory nerve action potentials are absent in postganglionic or combined preganglionic and postganglionic lesions. Because sensory innervation is overlapping, especially in the index finger, caution is required in determining that a specific nerve has a preganglionic injury based on the sensory nerve action potentials alone.

Electrodiagnostic studies have limitations. The skill and experience of the physician performing the study and interpreting the result are key to the validity of EMG and nerve velocity conduction studies. EMG can reveal evidence of early recovery in muscles, such as the emergence of nascent potentials, a decreased number of fibrillation potentials, or the appearance of an increased number of motor unit potentials. These findings may precede clinically apparent recovery by weeks or months. However, recovery shown on EMG is not always correlated with clinically relevant recovery, in terms of the extent or quality of regeneration. It merely indicates that an unknown number of fibers have reached muscles and established motor end plate connections. Conversely, evidence of reinnervation may not be detected on EMG in complete lesions, despite ongoing regeneration, if the end organs are distal.

Electrodiagnostic studies must be used to guide decision making during brachial plexus surgery. It is well known that the external appearance of a nerve is not correlated with its histologic appearance and does not provide reliable information about the ability of the nerve to recover spontaneously. A combination of intrasurgical electrodiagnostic techniques can be used to gather information before a surgical decision is made. Nerve action potentials and somatosensory-evoked potentials can be used routinely, occasionally with compound muscle action potentials. The use of nerve action potentials allows the surgeon to test a nerve directly across a lesion, detect reinnervation months before it can be seen using conventional EMG techniques, and distinguish between neurapraxia or mild axonotmesis (when a nerve action potential is present) and severe axonotmesis or neurotmesis (when a nerve action potential is absent). The presence of a nerve action potential across a lesion indicates axon preservation or significant regeneration. Studies using primates suggested that the presence of a nerve action potential indicates the viability of thousands of axons, rather than the hundreds of axons revealed by other techniques.[19] The presence of a nerve action potential predicts good recovery after neurolysis without further treatment such as neuroma resection or grafting. More than 90% of patients with a preserved nerve action potential progress to clinically significant recovery.

The presence of nerve action potentials can indirectly help distinguish between preganglionic and postganglionic injury. In a patient with severe neurologic loss, a higher conduction velocity with large amplitude and short latency indicates a preganglionic injury. In contrast, a flat tracing suggests that adequate regeneration is not occurring and is consistent with a repairable postganglionic lesion or an irreparable combined preganglionic-postganglionic lesion. In an irreparable lesion, sectioning the nerve back to the intraforaminal level would not reveal good fascicular structure.

The presence of an intrasurgical somatosensory-evoked potential suggests continuity between the peripheral nervous system and the central nervous system via a dorsal root. A positive response is determined by the integrity of a few hundred intact fibers. The actual state of the ventral root is not tested directly by this technique but is inferred from the state of the sensory nerve rootlets, although the correlation between dorsal and ventral root avulsions is not always perfect. Somatosensory-evoked potentials are absent in postganglionic or combined preganglionic-postganglionic lesions. Motor-evoked potentials can be used to assess the integrity of the motor pathway via the ventral root. This technique, using transcranial electrical stimulation, has now been approved for use in the United States.[20] Compound muscle action potentials are not useful in complete distal lesions because of the time necessary for regeneration into distal muscles, but they are useful in partial lesions, where the size of the compound muscle action potential is proportional to the number of functioning axons. Although these techniques have limitations and present technical challenges, they can help guide treatment when performed by an experienced neurologist or electrophysiologist.

## Surgical Decision Making

The three most important factors in the surgical treatment of brachial plexus injuries are patient selection, exact timing of surgery, and prioritization of the restoration of upper arm function. Surgery should be performed if there has been no clinical or electrical evidence of recovery or there is no hope of spontaneous recovery. Deciding whether a patient can benefit from

surgery and timing the surgery are among the most difficult decisions in peripheral nerve surgery, despite improvements in imaging and electrodiagnostic studies. During the observation period, the patient should receive physical therapy to prevent contractures and strengthen functioning muscles.

The timing of surgery depends on the mechanism and type of injury. Immediately after a sharp, open injury, exploration and primary repair of the injured portion of the brachial plexus are indicated to facilitate end-to-end repair of the injured nerves. After an open injury with avulsion of the nerve caused by a blunt object, the ends of the lacerated nerve should be tagged and maintained at length, and the repair should be performed 3 to 4 weeks later. By this time, the injured nerve ends are demarcated and access to the zone of nerve injury is better. Most neural lesions from gunshot wounds should be observed for several months because they frequently recover spontaneously and rarely are in discontinuity.

The timing of surgery for a stretch injury is more controversial. The mechanism and type of the injury, the physical examination and imaging findings, and the preference of the surgeon are important factors. Performing surgery soon after the injury may allow insufficient time for spontaneous reinnervation, but waiting too long can lead to unnecessary failure of the motor end plate and thus to failure of reinnervation. If complete root avulsion is strongly suspected, exploration and reconstruction can best be performed 3 to 6 weeks after the injury. Routine exploration is performed 3 to 6 months after the injury, if reinnervation has been inadequate. Delayed surgery (performed after 6 months) and late surgery (performed after 12 months) have relatively poor results because the time for the nerve to regenerate to the target muscles is greater than the survival time of the motor end plate after denervation.

Injuries to the brachial plexus that result from a surgical procedure involving the shoulder or neck should be given particularly close attention. If a nerve injury is suspected, documentation of presurgical motor and sensory function, as well as careful postsurgical examination, can help in identifying the affected nerves. Serial examinations and electrodiagnostic testing should be conducted during the next 3 months. If recovery does not occur during that time, surgical exploration and repair or reconstruction of injured nerves should be performed.

Most surgeons consider restoration of elbow flexion to be the highest surgical priority for a flail upper extremity. Other priorities, in descending order of importance, are shoulder abduction and stability, hand sensibility, wrist extension and finger flexion, wrist flexion and finger extension, and intrinsic function of the hand.

## Surgical Treatment

Primary brachial plexus surgery may include direct nerve repair, neurolysis, nerve grafting, and nerve transfers as well as soft-tissue procedures such as free-functioning muscle transfer. Secondary surgery may be necessary to restore some function or augment a partial recovery of function. The secondary surgery can include soft-tissue reconstruction procedures such as tendon and muscle transfer or free muscle transfer or bony procedures such as arthrodesis or osteotomy, but it typically does not include nerve procedures. Often a combination of techniques is used, and the surgeon thus requires a broad surgical armamentarium.

### Direct Nerve Repair

Primary repair of nerve ends is performed after a sharp injury, such as a laceration, or after incarceration of a nerve by suture in a focal area, such as can happen to the axillary nerve in a shoulder stabilization procedure. This technique cannot be applied to a stretch injury.

### Neurolysis

External neurolysis is a prerequisite to intrasurgical electrical studies. Neurolysis can be performed alone if the nerve is in continuity and a nerve action potential is obtained across the lesion.[21]

### Intraplexal Nerve Grafting

Nerve grafting can be performed if the surgeon encounters a rupture or a postganglionic neuroma that does not conduct a nerve action potential across the lesion. In such a patient, the nerve has maintained viable motor axons at a postganglionic level because of its connection to the spinal cord; these axons can be grafted to specific targets. Interpositional grafts, typically using cable grafts of sural or other cutaneous nerves, are coapted between nerve stumps without excess tension. Ideally, C5 should be targeted for shoulder abduction (the suprascapular and axillary nerves); C6, for elbow flexion (the musculocutaneous nerve); and C7, for elbow extension (the radial nerve).

### Nerve Transfer

Nerve transfer, also termed neurotization, can be performed if the injury is preganglionic. This procedure increasingly is being used to accelerate recovery by decreasing the distance between the site of nerve repair and the end organ. A functioning but less important nerve (or part of a nerve) is transferred distally to the more important nonfunctioning nerve. Nerve transfers ideally should be performed within 6 months of the injury. After the first 6 months, they may be preferable to grafting.

A variety of nerves can be used as a source for neurotization. Some of the more common are the spinal accessory nerve (cranial nerve XI), the motor and sensory intercostal nerves, and the medial pectoral nerve. Recently, the use of a fascicle of a functioning ulnar nerve (the Oberlin transfer) or the median nerve in patients with intact C8 and T1 nerves has allowed a rapid and powerful return of elbow flexion. The phrenic nerve and contralateral C7 or hemicontralateral C7 nerve have been used during the past two decades to expand the pool of extraplexal donor nerves and improve outcomes.[22,23] The use of the deep cervical plexus nerve or hypoglossal nerve (cranial nerve XII) has also been reported, although the results have been poor.[24]

The average number of myelinated axons varies among the donor nerves. The spinal accessory nerve typically has approximately 1,700 axons, the phrenic nerve has 800 axons, a single intercostal motor nerve has 1,300 axons, and the contralateral C7 nerve has approximately 23,800 axons.[25] It is desirable to maximize the number of myelinated axons per target function while minimizing donor site morbidity. Several series have reported acceptable morbidity using the contralateral C7 and phrenic nerves, but long-term studies are not available.[23-26]

Neurotization for shoulder abduction can be easily obtained by nerve transfer of the spinal accessory nerve or phrenic nerve to the suprascapular nerve. The benefits of using one of these two nerves are that no additional interposition nerve grafts are needed, and a direct coaptation of the nerves is possible (Figure 6). If additional nerve sources are available, neurotization of the axillary nerve or nerve grafting from C5 to the axillary nerve is recommended to provide additional shoulder stability and abduction.

Neurotization for elbow flexion can be performed by using intercostal nerves directly (Figure 7) or using the spinal accessory nerve with an interpositional graft. The biceps motor branch can be targeted rather than the entire musculocutaneous nerve. By separating the biceps motor branch from the lateral antebrachial cutaneous nerve in a retrograde manner, it is possible to transfer the maximum number of motor axons directly to the biceps muscle and gain length in the recipient nerve, eliminating the need for interpositional grafts (if intercostal nerves are used) and shortening the length of an accessory nerve graft. The phrenic nerve can be used with an interpositional graft to the musculocutaneous nerve.

Two popular options exist for reconstructing elbow flexion after an upper trunk avulsion injury. The medial pectoral nerve can be transferred to the musculocutaneous nerve or the biceps branch. Alternatively, the Oberlin transfer, in which a fascicle from the ulnar nerve is transferred to the motor branch of the biceps, can be used with excellent results[24] (Figure 8). A double neurotization may be preferred, in which an ulnar fascicle is transferred to the biceps branch and a median nerve

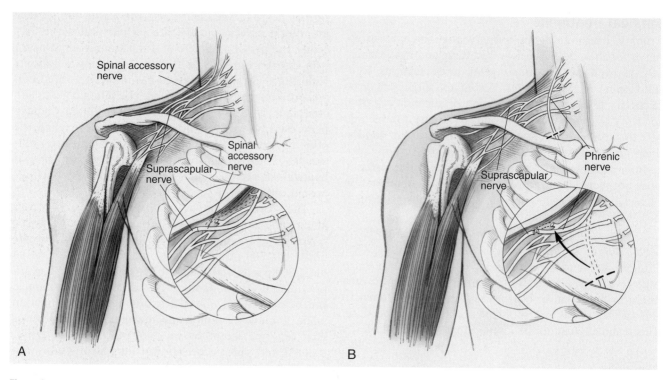

**Figure 6** Neurotization for shoulder abduction performed in the supraclavicular exposure, using the spinal accessory nerve **(A)** or the phrenic nerve **(B)**. *(Reproduced with permission from the Mayo Foundation.)*

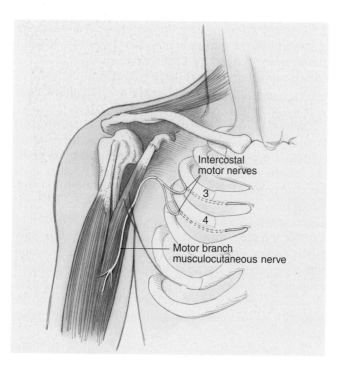

**Figure 7** Neurotization for elbow flexion using the intercostal nerves. *(Reproduced with permission from the Mayo Foundation.)*

fascicle is transferred to the brachialis branch.[27,28] Shoulder function can be restored by performing a double nerve transfer: a spinal accessory nerve transfer to the suprascapular nerve and a triceps branch transfer to the posterior axillary nerve. In a posterior approach to the axillary nerve, an intact triceps branch can be transferred to the axillary nerve[29-31] (Figure 9). Excellent results have been reported from using these combinations of nerve transfers.[32]

In a patient with a complete plexus avulsion injury, the contralateral or hemicontralateral C7 can be used with a vascularized ulnar nerve graft or sural nerve grafts to bring a large number of motor axons to the injured side.[23,26,32] It can also be used with a vascularized ulnar nerve graft to innervate the median nerve, in the hope of obtaining useful finger flexion and protective sensation in the median nerve distribution (Figures 10 and 11); or with nerve grafts to the axillary and suprascapular nerves to achieve shoulder stablity.

## Outcomes of Nerve Transfer

Neurotization for elbow flexion and shoulder stability has been found effective in restoring muscle function. A critical meta-analysis evaluated 1,028 nerve transfers, as reported in 27 studies.[33] Twenty-six studies reported 965 nerve transfers for elbow flexion restoration. On the British Medical Council scale (M0 = paralysis, M1 = trace contraction, M2 = active movement with gravity eliminated, M3 = movement against gravity, M4 = movement against gravity and some resistance, M5 = normal), 71% of the transfers to the musculocutaneous nerve achieved at least M3 flexion, and 37% achieved M4 flexion. The two most commonly used donor nerves

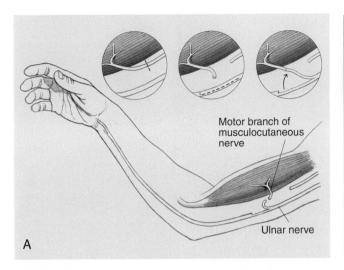

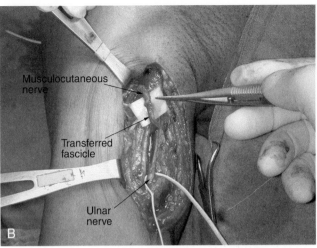

**Figure 8** **A,** Fascicle transfer to the motor branch of the biceps to obtain elbow flexion. **B,** Photograph showing the fascicles from the ulnar nerve transferred to the motor branch of the biceps. *(Reproduced with permission from the Mayo Foundation.)*

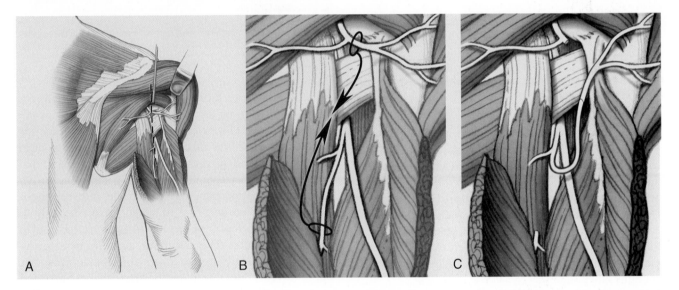

**Figure 9** Posterior transfer of a triceps branch to the axillary nerve to restore deltoid function. **A,** Posterior approach to the quadrilateral space and triangular interval. **B,** Identification of the axillary nerve and triceps branch. **C,** Division and coaption of the axillary nerve and triceps branch. *(Reproduced with permission from the Mayo Foundation.)*

were the intercostal (54%) and the spinal accessory (39%). An intercostal nerve graft achieved M3 flexion in 72% of patients; only 47% of patients achieved M3 flexion after an interpositional nerve graft. If the spinal accessory nerve was transferred to the musculocutaneous nerve, 77% of patients gained M3 elbow flexion, and 29% of those patients gained M4 flexion. After an Oberlin transfer of two fascicles of the ulnar nerve to the musculocutaneous nerve, 97% of patients achieved M3 flexion, and 94% achieved M4 flexion.

For restoration of shoulder abduction, eight studies and 123 transfers were evaluated in the meta-analysis.[33] Seventy-three percent of patients achieved M3 shoulder abduction, and 26% of those patients achieved M4 abduction. The spinal accessory nerve was used in 41%,

and the intercostal nerves were used in 26%. Achievement of M3 abduction was significantly better with the spinal accessory nerve (98%) than the intercostal nerves (56%). However, patients with a good result had only 45° of shoulder abduction.

Outcome analysis research on brachial plexus injuries is needed. Unfortunately, it is still unknown which method of treatment produces the best outcomes for a patient with a C5 and C6 rupture or severe neuroma. The surgical alternatives are a graft from C5 and C6 or nerve transfers closer to the end organ.

### Free Muscle Transfer

Advances in microsurgical techniques have led to innovations in surgical reconstruction of the upper extremity

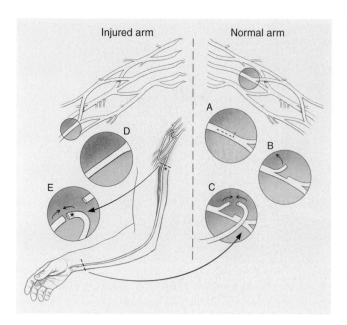

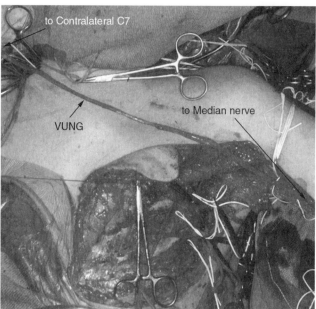

**Figure 10** A hemicontralateral C7 transfer used with a vascularized ulnar nerve graft to reinnervate the median nerve for finger flexion and sensation. **A,** C7 is identified in the normal arm. **B,** A distal hemicontralateral cut into C7 creates a C7 stump. **C,** The hemicontralateral C7 stump is coapted to the distal portion of the vascularized ulnar nerve. **D,** The median nerve in the injured arm is divided. **E,** The proximal end of the vascularized ulnar nerve is coapted to the median nerve. *(Reproduced with permission from the Mayo Foundation.)*

**Figure 11** The vascularized ulnar nerve reaching across the chest to the contralateral C7. VUNG = vascularized ulnar nerve graft. *(Reproduced with permission from the Mayo Foundation.)*

after brachial plexus injury. In a free-functioning muscle transfer, a muscle and its neurovascular pedicle are transplanted to a new location to assume a new function. The muscle is powered by neurotizing the motor nerve to the flap, and the circulation of the transferred muscle is restored with microsurgical anastomosis of the donor and recipient vessels. Within several months, the transferred muscle begins to be innervated by the donor nerve. Eventually it begins to contract and gain independent function.

Free-functioning muscle transfers were first used in patients with an injury more than 12 months old, because restoration of function to a long-denervated muscle was not successful using neural reconstruction. This technique has also been used as a salvage procedure after unsuccessful nerve reconstruction.[34-37] Free muscle transfer has now been incorporated into a strategy for early reconstruction in patients to obtain grasping function or augment elbow flexion power.

Free muscle transfers are most commonly used to provide reliable elbow flexion.[5,38-42] A variety of free-functioning muscles can be transferred, including the latissimus dorsi (with the thoracodorsal nerve), the rectus femoris (femoral nerve), and the gracilis (anterior division of the obturator nerve). The gracilis is commonly used in brachial plexus reconstruction because of its proximally based neurovascular pedicle, which allows earlier reinnervation, and its long tendon, which reaches into the forearm for hand reanimation. The gracilis can

be used to restore biceps function,[43,44] wrist extension, or finger flexion or as a double-muscle transfer in the novel two-stage Doi procedure.[5,6,45] When the gracilis is transferred for elbow flexion, its major vascular pedicle should be placed in proximity to the thoracoacromial trunk in the infraclavicular fossa by passing the proximal gracilis tendon beneath the clavicle and securing it to its superior border. It is tunneled subcutaneously to the antecubital fossa, where it will later be secured to the biceps tendon. The obturator nerve branch to the gracilis is typically repaired to the spinal accessory nerve or two intercostal motor nerves; the harvested length of either should be as long as possible to allow direct nerve repair distal to the clavicle. The gracilis tendon is woven into the biceps tendon distally (Figure 12).

The Doi double free-functioning gracilis muscle transfer may achieve prehension in patients with a complete brachial plexus lesion.[5] The goals of this two-stage procedure are to restore elbow flexion and extension as well as wrist extension and finger flexion. In the first stage, the brachial plexus is explored, and a free-functioning gracilis is harvested and neurotized by the spinal accessory nerve (Figure 13). The gracilis is proximally attached to the clavicle and distally routed under the brachioradialis to the radial wrist digit extensors. The vascular anastomoses are to the thoracoacromial artery and venae comitantes or another available venous outflow. In the second stage, performed 2 to 3 months later, the second gracilis is harvested, and the motor and sensory intercostal nerves from the third through sixth intercostal spaces are harvested (Figure 14). The gracilis is

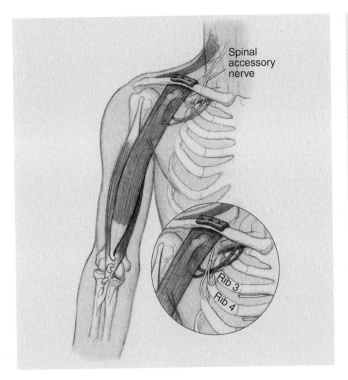

**Figure 12** A free muscle transfer of the gracilis used for elbow flexion, showing the proximal end of the gracilis secured to the clavicle, vascular inflow and outflow via the thoracoacromial trunk, and the muscle powered by the spinal accessory nerve or intercostal motor nerves (*shown in inset*). (*Reproduced with permission from the Mayo Foundation.*)

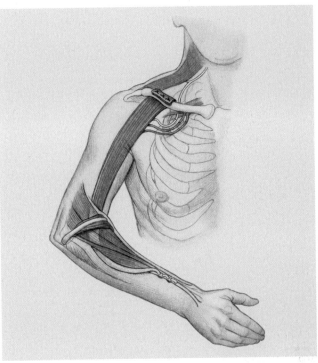

**Figure 13** First stage of a Doi free muscle transfer of the gracilis, showing the gracilis neurotized by the spinal accessory nerve and anastomosed to the thoracoacromial trunk. (*Reproduced with permission from the Mayo Foundation.*)

attached proximally to the second rib, then routed subcutaneously along the medial side of the arm and attached to the finger flexor tendons. It is neurotized with two of the motor intercostal nerves, and the sensory intercostal nerves are neurotized to the median nerve to provide palmar sensation. The new vascular supply of this second transferred gracilis is provided by the thoracodorsal vessels. The two remaining motor intercostal nerves are neurotized to triceps branches.

In a slight modification of the first stage of the original Doi double free muscle transfer, the gracilis muscle can be secured to wrist extensors, rather than finger extensors, to promote finger flexion through a tenodesis effect.[5,6,39,40,42,44-47] To create a more effective pulley with diminished bowstringing of the tendon, the gracilis tendon is routed underneath the lacertus fibrosus. A more effective pulley should improve muscle excursion and strengthen wrist extension.

A Doi double free muscle transfer restored good or excellent elbow flexion in 96% of patients.[5] One-year follow-up of eight patients after the second-stage transfer found that transfer for combined elbow flexion and wrist extension resulted in lower overall elbow flexion strength compared with transfer for elbow flexion alone. Seventy-nine percent of the free-functioning innervated muscle transfers for elbow flexion alone (a single transfer) and 63% of similar transfers for combined motion

(a first-stage Doi procedure) achieved at least M4 elbow flexion strength ($P > 0.05$). This result is not surprising, in that the muscles must use some of their strength and excursion to extend the wrist or digits and invariably lose some power and degree of flexion because of bowstringing at the elbow.[48]

After the double free muscle procedure, grasping function relies on the recovery of some triceps function to stabilize the elbow during contraction of the gracilis muscle, as well as recovery of adequate muscle strength and absence of significant adhesions. Sixty-five percent of patients achieved more than 30° of total active motion of the fingers after the second muscle transfer,[46] which is sufficient only for rudimentary grasping in many patients. However, grasping function is difficult to achieve using other methods. Earlier efforts to restore prehension after a brachial plexus injury were unsuccessful because of the distance between the nerve repair site and motor end plates and the resulting prolonged reinnervation time. Therefore, these reported results must be regarded as a significant advance in treating otherwise irreparable avulsion injuries. In an alternative procedure offering the possibility of hand function after root avulsion injury, the contralateral C7 nerve is combined with a vascularized ulnar nerve conduit.[24,25,35] A recent study described the potential for achieving hand function using an extended phrenic nerve that is harvested thoracoscopically, lengthened with a nerve graft,

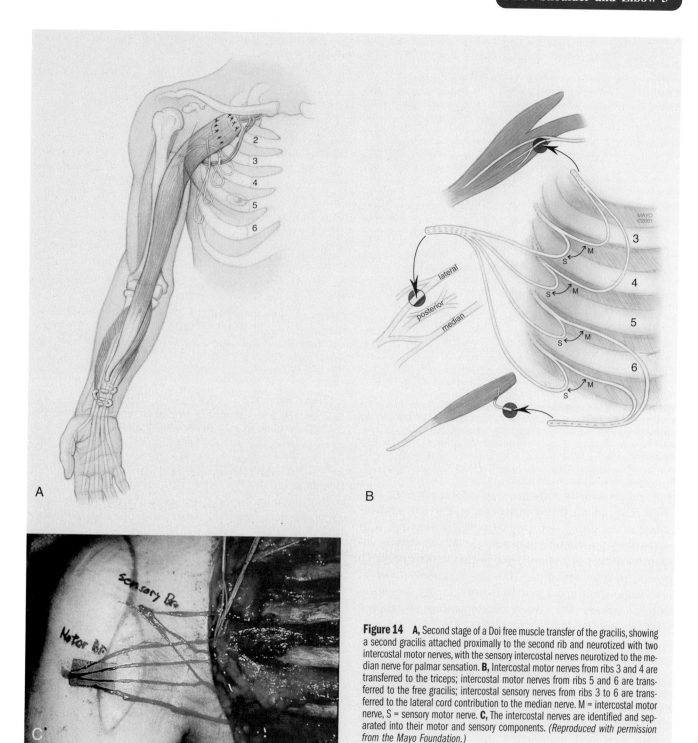

**Figure 14** **A,** Second stage of a Doi free muscle transfer of the gracilis, showing a second gracilis attached proximally to the second rib and neurotized with two intercostal motor nerves, with the sensory intercostal nerves neurotized to the median nerve for palmar sensation. **B,** Intercostal motor nerves from ribs 3 and 4 are transferred to the triceps; intercostal motor nerves from ribs 5 and 6 are transferred to the free gracilis; intercostal sensory nerves from ribs 3 to 6 are transferred to the lateral cord contribution to the median nerve. M = intercostal motor nerve, S = sensory motor nerve. **C,** The intercostal nerves are identified and separated into their motor and sensory components. *(Reproduced with permission from the Mayo Foundation.)*

and directed to the posterior portion of the median nerve.[49]

## Postsurgical Treatment

The patient must understand the limitations of surgical reconstruction before it is undertaken. Recovery of nerve function is a slow, arduous, and sometimes disheartening process. The growth rate of a newly grafted or transferred nerve is 1 mm per day, or 1 inch per month. After a long transfer, such as a hemicontralateral C7 nerve graft, 2 to 3 years may elapse before even early clinical results can be seen. The shorter the distance to the target muscle, the more rapidly reinnervation occurs.

While waiting for reinnervation, the patient must undertake physical therapy to keep the joints of the upper extremity supple and prevent joint contractures. A resting plastic splint can be used in conjunction with daily range-of-motion exercises for the shoulder, elbow, wrist, and digits. For patients with evidence of regeneration after nerve transfers, it can be helpful to learn how to use the new nerve to move the previously denervated muscle. The efficacy of electrical stimulation in preserving muscle and motor end plates is controversial. However, electrical stimulation can be psychologically beneficial because it allows the patient to see the muscles contract during the long recovery period. Assessment of recovery is recommended at 3- to 4-month intervals after surgery for a minimum of 2 years, and preferably for 5 years.

### Secondary Reconstruction

Secondary reconstruction should be considered for patients who have not recovered motor function or for whom function can be improved or refined by a relatively minor surgical intervention. The options for secondary reconstruction include tendon transfer, free-functioning muscle transfer, shoulder arthrodesis, and wrist and hand arthrodesis. A tendon transfer can lead to a gratifying result for a patient who has made a partial recovery and would benefit from additional function. The procedure is usually delayed until the maximum motor recovery has occurred after the original procedure.

A free-functioning muscle transfer can be performed for secondary reconstruction to improve the strength of a weakly reinnervated biceps or triceps muscle or to improve the strength of finger flexors, provided that the finger joints are supple. Arthrodesis can be useful in secondary reconstructive surgery for the shoulder, wrist, or hand. Shoulder fusion can be performed as a salvage procedure for a persistently painful subluxating shoulder. Shoulder fusion is not desirable as a primary reconstructive technique because most patients prefer voluntary shoulder abduction if it can be achieved through nerve reconstruction.[36] Bony procedures such as humeral rotational osteotomy, thumb axis arthrodesis, bone-block opponensplasty, and finger joint arthrodesis also can improve function.

## The Future of Brachial Plexus Surgery

Brachial plexus surgery is evolving. In the past, benign neglect and amputation were acceptable treatment options. Newer techniques and surgical experience have led to improved outcomes and permitted surgeons to achieve prehension in some patients. Despite these advances, the results are in general still disappointing. The return of function is often limited, and neuropathic pain, especially deafferentiated pain, may persist. Frequently patients are unable to return to work or must adapt their activities to their limited abilities.

The future promises exciting developments in neurobiologic strategies, imaging techniques, and surgical approaches. Basic research should focus on the motor neuron, to slow cell death and facilitate growth across the interface of the central and peripheral nervous systems; nerve repair, to improve the nerve-to-nerve interface; the area distal to the nerve repair site, to enhance nerve regeneration; and the motor end plate, to delay its dissolution. Understanding the mechanisms of neuropathic pain will be as important as improving function. New imaging modalities and techniques will allow differentiation among nerve lesions to determine the extent of degeneration and the potential for regeneration, which can guide the timing and type of surgery. The current innovative surgical strategies are a suggestion of future developments, which may include more aggressive nerve transfers, creative free muscle techniques, and invasive direct reimplantation of spinal nerves into the spinal cord.[50-53] The addition of neurotrophic factors or anti-scarring agents may improve both the rate and efficacy of nerve regeneration.

## Summary

Injuries to the brachial plexus in an adult patient can be intimidating to the orthopaedic surgeon, who may also be treating concomitant injuries. For the patient and family, the injury and its results can be devastating and difficult to comprehend. A thorough understanding of the complex anatomy of the brachial plexus, as well as clinical evaluation, imaging, electrodiagnostic studies, and treatment options and their timing, can enable the surgeon to offer optimal care to the patient with a brachial plexus injury.

## Annotated References

1. Allieu Y, Cenac P: Is surgical intervention justifiable for total paralysis secondary to multiple avulsion injuries of the brachial plexus? *Hand Clin* 1988;4: 609-618.

2. Azze RJ, Mattar Júnior J, Ferreira MC, Starck R, Canedo AC: Extraplexual neurotization of brachial plexus. *Microsurgery* 1994;15:28-32.

3. Brandt KE, Mackinnon SE: A technique for maximizing biceps recovery in brachial plexus reconstruction. *J Hand Surg Am* 1993;18:726-733.

4. Brunelli G, Monini L: Direct muscular neurotization. *J Hand Surg Am* 1985;10:993-997.

5. Doi K, Muramatsu K, Hattori Y, et al: Restoration of prehension with the double free muscle technique following complete avulsion of the brachial plexus: Indications and long-term results. *J Bone Joint Surg Am* 2000;82:652-666.

6. Doi K, Kuwata N, Muramatsu K, Hottori Y, Kawai S: Double muscle transfer for upper extremity

reconstruction following complete avulsion of the brachial plexus. *Hand Clin* 1999;15:757-767.

7. Malone JM, Leal J: Underwood J, et al: Brachial plexus injury management through upper extremity amputation with immediate postoperative prostheses. *Arch Phys Med Rehabil* 1982;63:89-91.

8. Allieu Y: Evolution of our indications for neurotization: Our concept of functional restoration of the upper limb after brachial plexus injuries. *Chir Main* 1999;18:165-166.

9. Hendry HAM: The treatment of residual paralysis after brachial plexus lesions. *J Bone Joint Surg Br* 1949; 31:42.

10. Fletcher I: Traction lesions of the brachial plexus. *Hand* 1969;1:129-136.

11. Yeoman PM, Seddon HJ: Brachial plexus injuries: Treatment of the flail arm. *J Bone Joint Surg Br* 1961; 43:493-500.

12. Kerr A: Brachial plexus of nerves in man: The variations in its formation and branches. *Am J Anat* 1918; 23:285-395.

13. Narakas AO: The treatment of brachial plexus injuries. *Int Orthop* 1985;9:29-36.

14. Carvalho GA, Nikkhah G, Matthies C, Penkert G, Samii M: Diagnosis of root avulsions in traumatic brachial plexus injuries: Value of computerized tomography myelography and magnetic resonance imaging. *J Neurosurg* 1997;86:69-76.

15. Nagano A, Ochiai N, Sugioka H, Hara T, Tsuyama N: Usefulness of myelography in brachial plexus injuries. *J Hand Surg Br* 1989;14:59-64.

16. Walker AT, Chaloupka JC, de Lotbiniere AC, Wolfe SW, Goldman R, Kier EL: Detection of nerve rootlet avulsion on CT myelography in patients with birth palsy and brachial plexus injury after trauma. *AJR Am J Roentgenol* 1996;167:1283-1287.

17. Doi K, Otsuka K, Okamoto Y, Fujii H, Hattori Y, Baliarsing AS: Cervical nerve root avulsion in brachial plexus injuries: Magnetic resonance imaging classification and comparison with myelography and computerized tomography myelography. *J Neurosurg* 2002;96(suppl 3):277-284.

The authors establish their MRI technique as reliable and reproducible in assessing cervical nerve roots in brachial plexus injury.

18. Gupta RK, Mehta VS, Banerji AK, Jain RK: MR evaluation of brachial plexus injuries. *Neuroradiology* 1989;31:377-381.

19. Nakamura T, Yabe Y, Horiuchi Y, Takayama S: Magnetic resonance myelography in brachial plexus injury. *J Bone Joint Surg Br* 1997;79:764-769.

20. Tiel RL, Happel LT Jr, Kline DG: Nerve action potential recording method and equipment. *Neurosurgery* 1996;39:103-108.

21. Burkholder LM, Houlden DA, Midha R, Weiss E, Vennettilli M: Neurogenic motor evoked potentials: Role in brachial plexus surgery. Case report. *J Neurosurg* 2003;98:607-610.

The coupling of motor-evoked potentials, sensory-evoked potentials, and nerve action potentials can augment intrasurgical electrophysiologic testing.

22. Kim DH, Cho YJ, Tiel RL, Kline DG: Outcomes of surgery in 1019 brachial plexus lesions treated at Louisiana State University Health Sciences Center. *J Neurosurg* 2003;98:1005-1016.

The technique of nerve action potentials was validated in a large study of brachial plexus lesions.

23. Gu YD, Ma MK: Use of the phrenic nerve for brachial plexus reconstruction. *Clin Orthop Relat Res* 1996; 323:119-121.

24. Chuang DC: Neurotization procedures for brachial plexus injuries. *Hand Clin* 1995;11:633-645.

25. Gu YD, Chen DS, Zhang GM, et al: Long-term functional results of contralateral C7 transfer. *J Reconstr Microsurg* 1998;14:57-59.

26. Songcharoen P, Wongtrakul S, Mahaisavariya B, Spinner RJ: Hemi-contralateral C7 transfer to median nerve in the treatment of root avulsion brachial plexus injury. *J Hand Surg Am* 2001;26: 1058-1064.

In a large study, hemilateral-contralateral C7 transfer provided M3 finger flexion in 30% of patients and S3 recovery in the median nerve area in 50%. Donor morbidity was 3%.

27. Liverneaux PA, Diaz LC, Beaulieu JY, Durand S, Oberlin C: Preliminary results of double nerve transfer to restore elbow flexion in upper type brachial plexus palsies. *Plast Reconstr Surg* 2006;117:915-919.

Safe, rapid recovery was achieved in 15 patients treated with a combined double fascicular nerve transfer for elbow flexion.

28. Mackinnon SE, Novak CB, Myckatyn TM, Tung TH: Results of reinnervation of the biceps and brachialis muscles with a double fascicular transfer for elbow flexion. *J Hand Surg Am* 2005;30:978-985.

Double nerve transfer for elbow flexion targeting the biceps and brachialis muscles can produce excellent recovery.

29. Alnot JY, Rostoucher P, Oberlin C, Touam C: C5-C6 and C5-C6-C7 traumatic paralysis of the brachial plexus of the adult caused by supraclavicular lesions [in French]. *Rev Chir Orthop Reparatrice Appar Mot* 1998;84:113-123.

30. Leechavengvongs S, Witoonchart K Uerpairojkit C, Thuvasethakul P: Nerve transfer to deltoid muscle using the nerve to the long head of the triceps: Part II. A report of 7 cases. *J Hand Surg Am* 2003;28:633-638.

The introduction of a novel nerve transfer led to improved shoulder abduction. Average abduction was 124° with dual innervation of the shoulder.

31. Witoonchart K, Leechavengvongs S, Uerpairojkit C, Thuvasethakul P, Wongnopsuwan V: Nerve transfer to deltoid muscle using the nerve to the long head of the triceps: Part I. An anatomic feasibility study. *J Hand Surg Am* 2003;28:628-632.

A direct triceps branch transfer to the axillary nerve was found to be feasible in an anatomic study.

32. Leechavengvongs S, Witoonchart K, Uerpairojkit C, Thuvasethakul P, Malungpaishrope K: Combined nerve transfers for C5 and C6 brachial plexus avulsion injury. *J Hand Surg Am* 2006;31:183-189.

Double innervation of the shoulder via nerve transfers (from spinal accessory to suprascapular nerve and from triceps branch to axillary nerve) was found to provide rapid, excellent recovery.

33. Merrell GA, Barrie KA, Katz DL, Wolfe SW: Results of nerve transfer techniques for restoration of shoulder and elbow function in the context of a meta-analysis of the English literature. *J Hand Surg Am* 2001;26:303-314.

This meta-analysis of nerve transfers for shoulder abduction and elbow flexion well summarizes the results achieved in 27 studies. Fascicular transfers were just gaining popularity when this report was written.

34. Ruch DS, Friedman AH, Nunley JA: The restoration of elbow flexion with intercostal nerve transfers. *Clin Orthop Relat Res* 1995;314:95-103.

35. Songcharoen P, Mahaisavariya B, Chotigavanich C: Spinal accessory neurotization for restoration of elbow flexion in avulsion injuries of the brachial plexus. *J Hand Surg Am* 1996;21:387-390.

36. Mikami Y, Nagano A, Ochiai N, Yamamoto S: Results of nerve grafting for injuries of the axillary and suprascapular nerves. *J Bone Joint Surg Br* 1997;79: 527-531.

37. Chuang DC, Yeh MC, Wei FC: Intercostal nerve transfer of the musculocutaneous nerve in avulsed brachial plexus injuries: Evaluation of 66 patients. *J Hand Surg Am* 1992;17:822-828.

38. Akasaka Y, Hara T, Takahashi M: Free muscle transplantation combined with intercostal nerve crossing for reconstruction of elbow flexion and wrist extension in brachial plexus injuries. *Microsurgery* 1991;12: 346-351.

39. Doi K, Sakai K, Fuchigami Y, Kawai S: Reconstruction of irreparable brachial plexus injuries with reinnervated free-muscle transfer: Case report. *J Neurosurg* 1996;85:174-177.

40. Doi K, Shigetomi M, Kaneko K, et al: Significance of elbow extension in reconstruction of prehension with reinnervated free-muscle transfer following complete brachial plexus avulsion. *Plast Reconstr Surg* 1997;100:364-372.

41. Manktelow RT, Zuker RM, McKee NH: Functioning free muscle transplantation. *J Hand Surg Am* 1984; 9A:32-39.

42. Doi K, Sakai K, Kuwata N, Ihara K, Kawai S: Double free-muscle transfer to restore prehension following complete brachial plexus avulsion. *J Hand Surg Am* 1995;20:408-414.

43. Chung DC, Carver N, Wei FC: Results of functioning free muscle transplantation for elbow flexion. *J Hand Surg Am* 1996;21:1071-1077.

44. Doi K, Sakai K, Ihara K, Abe Y, Kawai S, Kurafuji Y: Reinnervated free muscle transplantation for extremity reconstruction. *Plast Reconstr Surg* 1993;91: 872-883.

45. Doi K: New reconstructive procedure for brachial plexus injury. *Clin Plast Surg* 1997;24:75-85.

46. Doi K, Sakai K, Kuwata N, Ihara K, Kawai S: Reconstruction of finger and elbow function after complete avulsion of the brachial plexus. *J Hand Surg Am* 1991; 16:796-803.

47. Doi K, Hattori Y, Kuwata N, et al: Free muscle transfer can restore hand function after injuries of the lower brachial plexus. *J Bone Joint Surg Br* 1998;80: 117-120.

48. Barrie KA, Steinmann SP, Shin AY, Spinner RJ, Bishop AT: Gracilis free muscle transfer for restoration of function after complete brachial plexus avulsion. *Neurosurg Focus* 2004;16:E8.

Functioning free muscle transfer using the gracilis muscle can reliably produce good elbow flexion, neurotized by spinal accessory or intercostal nerves, as part of a brachial plexus reconstructive paradigm.

49. Zhao X, Lao J, Hung LK, Zhang GM, Zhang LY, Gu YD: Selective neurotization of the median nerve in the arm to treat brachial plexus palsy: An anatomic study and case report. *J Bone Joint Surg Am* 2004; 86A:736-742.

A novel neurotization strategy for regaining hand function uses an extended phrenic nerve lengthened with a nerve graft and directed to the posterior position of the median nerve.

50. Fournier HD, Menei P, Khalifa R, Mercier P: Ideal intraspinal implantation site for the repair of ventral root avulsion after brachial plexus injury in humans: A preliminary anatomical study. *Surg Radiol Anat* 2001;23:191-195.

The authors propose that reimplantation should be directed through the ventral root exit zone to a depth of 2 mm in the ventromedial region of the ventral grey horn, rather than into the white matter of the lateral aspect of the spinal cord.

51. Fournier HD, Mercier P, Menei P: Lateral interscalenic multilevel oblique corpectomies to repair ventral root avulsions after brachial plexus injury in humans: Anatomical study and first clinical experience. *J Neurosurg* 2001;95(suppl 2):202-207.

An anterior approach to the ventral rootlets is promoted for use in reimplantation. It avoids the laminectomy-facetectomy that is necessary from a posterior approach and affords more direct access to the ventral site of reimplantation.

52. Carlstedt T, Anand P, Hallin R, Misra PV, Noren G, Seferlis T: Spinal nerve root repair and reimplantation of avulsed ventral roots into the spinal cord after brachial plexus injury. *J Neurosurg* 2000;93(suppl 2): 237-247.

53. Bertelli JA, Ghizoni MF: Brachial plexus avulsion injury repairs with nerve transfers and nerve grafts directly implanted into the spinal cord yield partial recovery of shoulder and elbow movements. *Neurosurgery* 2003;52:1385-1390.

Nerve root reimplantation into the spinal cord resulted in limited recovery.

# Chapter 50

# Evaluation and Treatment of Pediatric Brachial Plexus Palsy

Michael Pearl, MD

## Natural History

The reported incidence of brachial plexus palsy ranges from 1 to 4.6 per 1,000 births by vaginal delivery.[1,2] Despite advances in obstetric care, the incidence of the condition appears to be increasing, possibly because of increased birth weights. The reported rates of brachial plexus birth-related palsy (BPBP) vary regionally and are influenced by the method of data capture; in addition, the reported rates of recovery are influenced by the definition used for recovery. The commonly held belief that 80% to 90% of children with BPBP recover must be reconsidered if orthopaedic sequelae are included. In one study, a persistent restriction in passive range of shoulder motion was observed in 56% of children who did not have complete neurologic recovery by 3 weeks of age, although many of these children were reported to later achieve a "good functional recovery."[3] The percentage of children who require later surgical treatment for contractures also varies but in one study was reported as 27% of 74 children.[4] In addition, more than half of the children with BPBP have abnormal glenohumeral anatomy on MRI.[5]

Although neurologic injury at birth may include the entire brachial plexus, it most often involves the upper trunk. The injury varies in severity and may be transient. The child may have nearly complete neurologic recovery of antigravity biceps and deltoid function, usually observed by 2 months of age. A child with transient injury does not require microsurgical intervention. At the other extreme of severity, the child may develop a permanent flail arm. This condition usually occurs in association with a complete plexus lesion and avulsion of the cervical spinal nerve roots, and the child will fare poorly without microsurgical intervention. When the nerve roots are avulsed, microsurgery is limited to nerve transfers from uninvolved areas such as the intercostal and spinal accessory nerves. For a child with a brachial plexus injury of intermediate severity, the indications for microsurgery remain a subject of controversy.

The timing of brachial plexus exploration and grafting in the absence of biceps recovery varies by institution, but the range is 3 to 9 months of age. The surgeon must choose a treatment protocol based on incomplete knowledge of the natural history of these injuries because the available studies include neurosurgical intervention at different times during patients' first year. Further complicating the understanding of the effectiveness of neurosurgical intervention are the secondary musculoskeletal procedures that usually are part of the treatment regimen. In addition, recent studies have reported that glenohumeral deformities affect many patients, and it is evident that earlier analyses attributing functional results to nerve surgery, releases, or transfers are suspect unless they differentiated between children with and without marked skeletal deformities.

Regardless of whether microsurgery is performed, it is clear that an internal rotation contracture of the shoulder is the most common condition requiring treatment in children who do not fully recover[3-10] (Figure 1). The contracture results from an imbalance between the strength of the internal rotators (primarily the subscapularis) and the external rotators (primarily the infraspinatus). If left untreated, the contracture leads to a progressive glenohumeral deformity characterized by posterior displacement of the humeral head on an increasingly dysplastic and deformed glenoid (Figure 2). A false articulation then forms on the posterior aspect of the glenoid, becomes progressively retroverted, and may lead to an array of deformities that have been described as flat, biconcave, and convex (pseudoglenoid) (Figure 3). A number of classification systems have been proposed.[3,7,11-13] All of them recognize that with increasing deformity the glenohumeral joint has increasing posterior displacement from its normally centered and concentric position, and the normal concave shape of the glenoid becomes increasingly convex (Figure 4). In an advanced deformity, the humeral head articulates with the posterior aspect of the convex glenoid, and it becomes increasingly misshapen and retroverted.[14]

Institutional protocols for the treatment of contractures and deformities vary widely, and therefore it is difficult to compare study results. Efforts to standardize

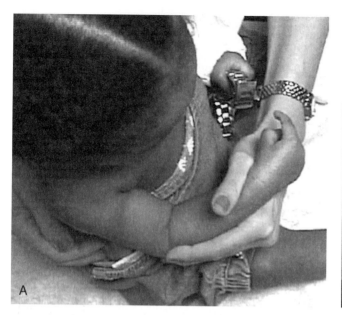
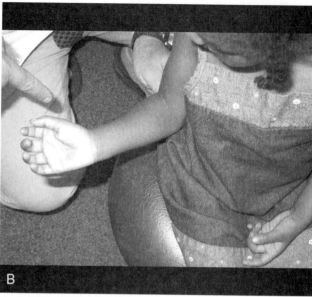

**Figure 1** **A,** Maximum passive external rotation range (~20°) in an 11-month-old girl with BPBP. Scapular motion is controlled, and the elbow is held at the side. **B,** Two years after arthroscopic release, the child has active external rotation equal to the passive range as she tries to reach for the examiner's finger. The examiner is holding the child's elbow against her side. *(Reproduced with permission from Pearl ML, Edgerton BW, Kazimiroff PA, Burchette RJ, Wong K: Arthroscopic release and latissimus dorsi transfer for shoulder internal rotation contractures and glenohumeral deformity secondary to brachial plexus birth palsy. J Bone Joint Surg Am 2006;88:564-574.)*

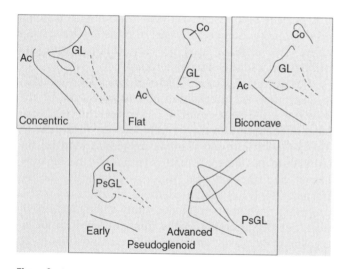

**Figure 2** Schematic drawings showing the spectrum of glenoid morphology, from a normal concentric glenoid to a pseudoglenoid. Ac = acromion, GL = glenoid, Co = coracoid process, PsGL = pseudoglenoid. *(Reproduced with permission from Pearl ML, Edgerton BW: Glenoid deformity secondary to brachial plexus birth palsy. J Bone Joint Surg Am 1998;80:659-667.)*

methods of evaluation are ongoing, and some consistent observations are emerging.

## Clinical Evaluation

Musculoskeletal and neurologic examination of an infant or young child is difficult because of the patient's fear of the examination, inability to comprehend directions, and lack of coordination as a result of undeveloped motor function. The patient, especially an infant, may eagerly reach for an attractive overhead object,

such as a lollipop or shiny key, and thereby provide a strong indication of active elevation. However, the effectiveness of similar inducements to move in other directions is less predictable. Because of the child's age and other factors, a complete motor examination can be only approximated. An alternative to the muscle-grading systems commonly used for adults, such as that of the British Medical Council, must be used.

The Hospital for Sick Children in Toronto's Active Movement Scale is a response to the limitations of the British Medical Council system, primarily in recognizing that the strength of a weak muscle should not be graded against gravity if it is uncertain whether the muscle can function when gravity is eliminated.[15] As a result, the first four grades of strength in the Active Movement Scale are devoted to achieving a full, active range of motion with gravity eliminated (Table 1). This system is particularly useful in evaluating infants for neurologic surgery. These patients are especially weak, and their inability to comply with commands means that grading must be based on observation. The Active Movement Scale does not allow strength to be measured effectively in the context of significant limitations in passive range of motion. In addition, it is unlikely that the ability to achieve a full range of motion with gravity eliminated is required for generating appreciable force in specific positions of a joint. Therefore, a muscle with a low score, indicating an incomplete range of motion with gravity eliminated, may be stronger in some midrange positions than a muscle with a higher score assigned on the basis of the muscle's ability to achieve a full passive range of motion.

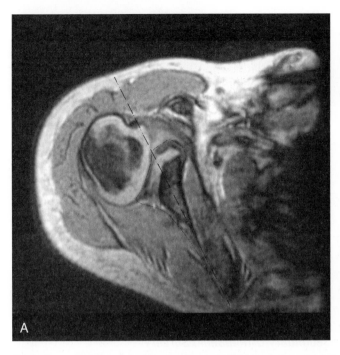
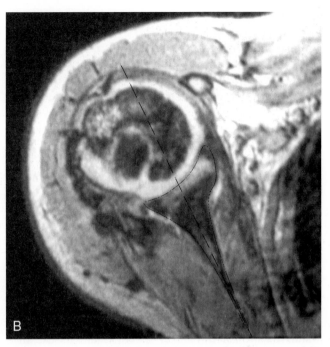

**Figure 3**  T2-weighted three-dimensional gradient echo MRI images of a patient before and after arthroscopic release and latissimus dorsi transfer. **A,** A pseudoglenoid in a child age 4 years, 7 months. **B,** Two years after surgery, the pseudoglenoid has remodeled to a concentric joint with a round humeral head well centered on the glenohumeral joint. *(Reproduced with permission from Pearl ML, Edgerton BW, Kazimiroff PA, Burchette RJ, Wong K: Arthroscopic release and latissimus dorsi transfer for shoulder internal rotation contractures and glenohumeral deformity secondary to brachial plexus birth palsy. J Bone Joint Surg Am 2006;88:564-574.)*

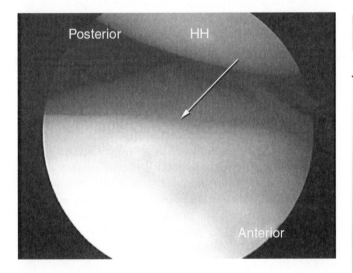

**Figure 4**  Arthroscopic view of the left shoulder of a 2-year-old child with a pseudoglenoid, showing a convex glenoid with a central ridge *(arrow)* separating the anterior and posterior aspects. HH = humeral head. *(Reproduced with permission from Pearl ML: Arthroscopic release of shoulder contracture secondary to birth palsy: An early report on findings and surgical technique. Arthroscopy 2003;19:577-582.)*

| Table 1 | The Active Movement Scale of the Hospital for Sick Children in Toronto | |
|---|---|
| **Observation*** | **Muscle Grade** |
| **With Gravity Eliminated** | 0 |
| No contraction | 1 |
| Contraction, no motion | 2 |
| Motion ≤ ½ range | 3 |
| Motion ≥ ½ range | 4 |
| **Against Gravity** | |
| Motion ≤ ½ range | 5 |
| Motion ≥ ½ range | 6 |
| Full motion | 7 |

*Grading of a complete range of motion with gravity eliminated is necessary before grading against gravity.*

A reliability study of the Toronto Active Movement Scale and the Mallet score, which is also commonly used, was conducted in an ongoing effort to standardize evaluations between medical centers.[16] The participating examiners were able to use the scales reliably, but it is unclear whether the study findings can be extrapolated to evaluations conducted at other, disparate institutions over long periods of time. More importantly, the effectiveness of these and other scales and the extent to which they comprehensively reflect recovery of muscle and limb function are not addressed by measures of reliability. The widely used Mallet score, for example, focuses on improvements in external rotation and is almost useless in children younger than 2 years.

## Imaging

Studies assessing the development of the glenohumeral deformity that occurs in most children with incomplete recovery from BPBP have only recently become available. Fortunately, understanding of this deformity has evolved considerably during the past decade. It is now clear that the deformity results from persistent internal rotation contractures, which are best measured by passive range of external rotation with the arm at the side. Future studies should compare patients based on the presence of such a contracture and, in patients with a contracture, the status of their glenohumeral development.

Ultrasonography, arthrography, and MRI have been used to study the morphology of the pediatric glenohumeral joint in children with BPBP.[5-7,11,14,17-21] The exact role and relative advantages of each modality are undecided, although most institutions now favor MRI. Ultrasonography is noninvasive, and the results are immediately available, but the level of image detail is poor. Arthrography offers more detailed images than ultrasonography, but it is invasive and is most often used while the patient is under anesthesia for surgical intervention. MRI offers the greatest detail and potential for standardization. However, it is costly, and its use in a young child often requires general anesthesia.

## Surgical Treatment
### Neurologic Microsurgery
Microscopic neurosurgical intervention should be used only for the most severe brachial plexus injuries and only during the first year of life, after which it is believed to be ineffective. This surgery never achieves complete neurologic improvement and always leaves a residual impairment. Regardless of whether a child with an incomplete early neurologic recovery receives microsurgical intervention, orthopaedic procedures must be considered in the future.

The prognosis for natural recovery in a child with an avulsion injury is quite poor. Microsurgical intervention is recommended before the child reaches age 3 months, although the treatment is limited to nerve transfer; grafting is not possible in the absence of a healthy proximal nerve root.[22,23]

For a child with an intraplexus rupture, the return of antigravity biceps strength is the primary criterion in determining the need for brachial plexus exploration and nerve reconstruction. Controversy persists as to the need for and timing of microsurgical intervention for children with an intraplexus rupture. The recommended timing ranges from 3 to 9 months of age.[24,25] However, there is no doubt that increasing delay in the return of biceps function leads to decreasing spontaneous recovery. Children who did not develop biceps function before age 5 months were found to do less well in spontaneous recovery than similarly affected children who received microsurgical intervention.[26] The surgical indications continue to be refined, and some institutions recommend a comprehensive evaluation of muscles

other than the biceps to predict the likelihood of recovery.[27]

It is particularly difficult to discern which neurologic lesions would do as well with late secondary orthopaedic intervention (without early microsurgery) as with early microsurgery and later secondary procedures. No studies have conclusively found that microsurgery in combination with secondary orthopaedic procedures resulted in better outcomes than secondary orthopaedic procedures alone. Nonetheless, contemporary practice is predicated on the belief that microsurgery improves outcomes. A long-term study of 22 children whose biceps recovery was delayed until age 3 to 6 months and who did not have brachial plexus microsurgery found that the function of these children was comparable to the reported function of children who had brachial plexus microsurgery.[24] The confusion has been increased by reports of clinical success after a wide array of secondary procedures.

### Secondary Orthopaedic Surgery
Internal rotation contracture and the resulting glenohumeral deformity have been reported in children as young as 5 months.[5] The contracture will not resolve spontaneously and therefore can be treated at any time, although the child's parents may accept the need for surgery more readily if it is preceded by a period of formal physical therapy. In addition, surgery is somewhat more easily performed in children older than age 1 year than on younger children. During the past 20 years, the three prevailing surgical treatments have involved contracture release with or without a muscle transfer to augment external rotation power. These procedures include an anterior capsular release with Z-plasty lengthening of the subscapularis, with or without transfer of muscles for external rotation;[28] a partial pectoralis major release, with transfer of the latissimus dorsi and teres major;[9] and subscapularis slide, with or without a latissimus dorsi transfer.[8] For children with extensive glenohumeral deformity, the prevailing treatment recommendation has been to avoid a soft-tissue procedure in favor of a rotational osteotomy of the humerus, to rotate the arm into a more functional position of external rotation.[29] Good results have recently been described after two additional treatments: arthroscopic release of the internal rotation contracture, with or without latissimus transfer;[10,30] and open anterior release, with derotational osteotomy of the humerus to rotate the humerus into internal rotation after soft-tissue releases, if excessive retroversion compels an external rotation contracture of the arm.[31,32]

To reconcile these seemingly disparate approaches, it must be recognized that the internal rotation contracture is caused by loss of the normal balance between external rotation and internal rotation, principally because of infraspinatus weakness. Therefore, even a procedure that tips this balance by reducing internal rotation strength, augmenting external rotation strength, or both may be somewhat effective. It must also be recognized that the commonly used clinical scoring systems, especially the Mallet score, are probably too crude to distinguish between the results of the various approaches.

### Formal Anterior Approach
The first surgical releases, as described by Fairbanks during the early 20th century and modified by Sever, used a traditional anterior deltopectoral approach. To decrease the likelihood of recurrent internal rotation contracture, a version of the L'Episcopo transfer of the latissimus dorsi and teres major was added. Modifications of this procedure are still performed at many centers, and some recent studies are available. Ten patients were followed for an average of 30 years after release of the upper half of the pectoralis major, the entire subscapularis, and the anterior capsule, with transfer of the latissimus dorsi and teres major to the pectoralis major stump.[28] The patients' gains in external rotation deteriorated over time, and five patients had significant degenerative changes at the glenohumeral joint.

Concerns about the results of the anterior approach include a poor cosmetic result, possible anterior dislocation, and functionally significant external rotation contractures. Some modifications have addressed these concerns; one such modification achieves better cosmesis by using an incision in the skin lines from the coracoid to the axilla.[33,34] The latissimus transfer is performed by step cutting the tendon insertion, rerouting the released tendon posteriorly, and securing it to the remaining latissimus tendon anteriorly. The subscapularis is released, sometimes with the pectoralis and teres major. Release of the anterior capsule is avoided.

Recent descriptions of the anterior approach that warn against releasing the anterior capsule nonetheless acknowledge that it is not possible to restore external rotation and reduce the glenohumeral joint unless the capsule is released.[31,32] These studies postulate that, in addition to anterior soft-tissue contracture, excessive retroversion of the humerus compels an external rotation contracture in many patients after the glenohumeral joint is reduced. For these patients, an internal rotational osteotomy has been recommended as part of the surgery.[31]

### Hoffer Modification of the L'Episcopo Transfer
In a frequently used surgical approach originally devised by Hoffer, a cosmetic incision in the axillary crease is used to release the inferior fibers of the pectoralis major and transfer the combined tendons of the latissimus dorsi and teres major muscles to the posterior rotator cuff. This procedure has resulted in functional improvement in many children. The advocates of this procedure warn against releasing the anterior capsule or subscapularis to avoid anterior dislocation or creation of an external rotation contracture. Recent studies found that, despite improvements in shoulder function, this procedure did not improve the glenohumeral deformity in many patients.[9,35] This surgical approach is probably most effectively used for external rotation weakness in the absence of a severe, firmly entrenched internal rotation contracture and glenohumeral deformity.

### Release of the Subscapularis Origin
In an approach originated by Carlioz and Brahimi, the subscapularis is released from its origin along the ventral, medial border of the scapula and then reflected distally.[36] For children who are older than 4 years or have had an unsuccessful earlier release, transfer of the latissimus dorsi tendon to the posterolateral rotator cuff is also recommended. This procedure avoids the anterior capsule and in theory preserves some subscapularis function. It clearly tips the balance between internal and external rotation strength in favor of the weak external rotators. In one study, however, this procedure failed to adequately release the capsular contracture in 5 of 25 children, and an anterior approach was also required during the procedure.[6] A long-term follow-up study of 203 children found deterioration in many of the functional gains observed during the early postsurgical period, resulting in significant functional limitations in adulthood. This finding appears to be consistent with the few very long-term studies available.[8]

### Arthroscopic Subscapularis Tenotomy and Capsular Release
The first study of arthroscopic release reported promising early results[30] (Figure 5), and a 2-year minimum follow-up study not only confirmed the efficacy of the procedure but also found that elimination of the internal rotation contracture led to remarkable remodeling of the glenohumeral deformity.[10] The surgical protocol used the following recommendations: children younger than 3 years received only an arthroscopic release, and older children simultaneously received a latissimus dorsi transfer.[8] Fifteen of the 19 younger children who underwent isolated arthroscopic release had sufficient external rotation strength with the contracture eliminated to maintain a functional range of both active and passive external rotation (Figure 1, *B*). Four of the 19 children received a subsequent successful latissimus dorsi transfer for recurrence of the contracture or insufficient external rotation strength. All 14 older children treated with simultaneous release and latissimus dorsi transfer maintained their gains in external rotation. Most of the children with glenohumeral deformity had normalization of the glenohumeral joint with increased sphericity of the humeral head and centralization of the head on the glenoid (Figure 3, *B*).

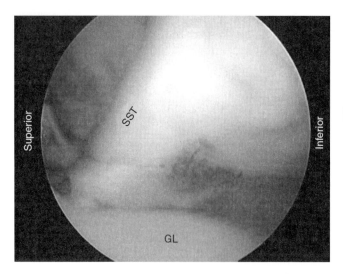 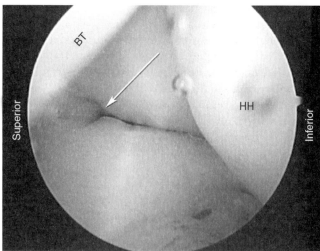

**Figure 5** **A,** The subscapularis tendon as seen from the posterior portal. **B,** Subscapularis tenotomy with an electrocautery device (*arrow*). BT = biceps tendon, GL = glenoid, HH = humeral head, SST = subscapularis tendon. *(Reproduced with permission from Pearl ML: Arthroscopic release of shoulder contracture secondary to birth palsy: An early report on findings and surgical technique.* Arthroscopy 2003;19:577-582.)

Procedures that tip the balance of the shoulder rotators toward external rotation, either by sacrificing internal rotator strength or augmenting external rotator power, inevitably weaken internal rotation or diminish the range of internal rotation. This loss of internal rotation was observed and documented using the arthroscopic approach as well as other techniques. Earlier studies of other techniques did not sufficiently analyze the loss of internal rotation to allow for meaningful comparison. Recent studies suggest that procedures that carry less risk of limiting internal rotation are less effective in restoring external rotation and improving glenohumeral deformity than those that treat the contracture effectively. Accordingly, long-standing concerns about releasing the subscapularis and the anterior capsule must be tempered by evidence that not doing so fails to release all contractures and leaves many posteriorly displaced, deformed glenohumeral joints without the possibility of remodeling. Arthroscopic release allows for specific attention to the subscapularis and anterior capsule. It therefore appears to avoid the risks of earlier open procedures that required the release of multiple superficial structures, such as the pectoralis major.

### Other Considerations

In a child who has active elevation of less than 90°, weakness in elevation is functionally limiting. Usually, the child's passive range of motion is much greater than active range of motion. Procedures including upper trapezius detachment from the acromion and insertion on the humerus and latissimus transfer to the supraspinatus have been described to restore active elevation, but there are no recent reports of success. Paralysis of active elevation remains a largely unresolved difficulty, and ag-

gressive surgical intervention is likely to be disappointing. However, if a significant internal rotation contracture is present in addition to limited active elevation, improving the range of external rotation can markedly improve the child's ability to reach by allowing the hand to be placed in a higher position.

External rotation contractures do not result in posterior displacement of the glenohumeral joint or significant deformity but can be functionally disabling when they result from release of internal rotation contractures. Internal rotational osteotomies of the humerus may be required in some children who have marked difficulty reaching their midline or performing personal care activities.

Consideration of any procedure to improve shoulder function should include a realistic assessment of the child's ability to use the hand and any limitations at the elbow. A nonfunctioning hand will be no more useful if it can be placed in more positions. An elbow that cannot be extended because of an extreme flexion contracture or an absent triceps may impede reaching to a far greater extent than the limitations at the shoulder.

### Summary and Future Directions

Brachial plexus palsy continues to occur secondary to injury during the birth process, and it can result in permanent impairment in upper extremity function. Although most injuries are transient, those that do not recover spontaneously can be severe and require neurosurgical intervention. Controversy persists regarding the timing of neurosurgery, but most surgeons agree that failure to achieve antigravity biceps function by 6 months of age warrants plexus exploration and grafting if possible. Many children whose injuries are not severe enough to require neurosurgery within the first year of life will later manifest external rotation weakness and internal rotation contractures at the shoulder.

A child with incomplete recovery from BPBP faces many difficulties. Efforts continue to prevent BPBP through improvements in obstetric care. Refinement of microsurgical techniques will continue to improve neurologic outcomes, and secondary orthopaedic procedures may eventually become unnecessary. For the foreseeable future, however, these secondary procedures are the mainstay for improving function in children with BPBP. No existing surgical technique can restore normal elevation in a shoulder that is unable to achieve a horizontal position. Fortunately, multiple options exist for treating the most common consequence of BPBP, which is external rotation weakness and the resultant internal rotation contracture. The options best suited to a specific child are determined based on the degree of contracture, the age of the child, and the status of glenohumeral development. Recent studies have found that earlier techniques and published clinical data did not adequately account for glenohumeral deformity. Treatment protocols must aim to reestablish a centered glenohumeral joint in the young child to allow for optimal skeletal development.

## Annotated References

1. Chauhan SP, Rose CH, Gherman RB, Magann EF, Holland MW, Morrison JC: Brachial plexus injury: A 23-year experience from a tertiary center. *Am J Obstet Gynecol* 2005;192:1795-1800.

   This 23-year study from a tertiary medical center found that the incidence of BPBP was 1 in every 1,000 births by vaginal delivery, with permanent sequelae occurring in 1 in every 10,000.

2. Hoeksma AF, Wolf H, Oei SL: Obstetrical brachial plexus injuries: Incidence, natural course and shoulder contracture. *Clin Rehabil* 2000;14:523-526.

3. Hoeksma AF, Ter Steeg AM, Dijkstra P, Nelissen RG, Beelan A, de Jong BA: Shoulder contracture and osseous deformity in obstetrical brachial plexus injuries. *J Bone Joint Surg Am* 2003;85-A:316-322.

   Fifty-two children with BPBP were followed from within 6 weeks of delivery to a mean age of 3.7 years. In children whose neurologic recovery was delayed by more than 3 weeks, 54% had shoulder contracture and 26% had osseous deformity.

4. Bisinella GL, Birch R: Obstetric brachial plexus lesions: A study of 74 children registered with the British Paediatric Surveillance Unit (March 1998-March 1999). *J Hand Surg Br* 2003;28:40-45.

   Seventy-four children with BPBP identified from a British registry were followed from birth for a minimum of 2 years. Thirty-nine (52.7%) spontaneously recovered, and

29 (39.3%) regained good function. However, 20 (27%) required surgical correction for secondary deformity of the glenohumeral joint.

5. van der Sluijs JA, van Ouwerkerk WJ, de Gast A, Wuisman PI, Nollet F, Manoliu RA: Deformities of the shoulder in infants younger than 12 months with an obstetric lesion of the brachial plexus. *J Bone Joint Surg Br* 2001;83:551-555.

   MRI of 16 children younger than 1 year of age (mean, 5.2 months) who had incomplete recovery from BPBP found a convex glenoid in 7 children and a biconcave glenoid in 3.

6. Pearl ML, Edgerton BW: Glenoid deformity secondary to brachial plexus birth palsy. *J Bone Joint Surg Am* 1998;80:659-667.

7. Kozin SH: Correlation between external rotation of the glenohumeral joint and deformity after brachial plexus birth palsy. *J Pediatr Orthop* 2004;24:189-193.

   A correlation between the degree of internal rotation contracture with retroversion of the glenoid and posterior displacement of the glenohumeral joint was found using MRI studies in 33 children.

8. Pagnotta A, Haerle M, Gilbert A: Long-term results on abduction and external rotation of the shoulder after latissimus dorsi transfer for sequelae of obstetric palsy. *Clin Orthop Relat Res* 2004;426:199-205.

   A long-term follow-up study of 203 children who received a latissimus dorsi transfer found progressive loss of abduction beginning 6 years after surgery.

9. Waters PM, Bae DS: Effect of tendon transfers and extra-articular soft-tissue balancing on glenohumeral development in brachial plexus birth palsy. *J Bone Joint Surg Am* 2005;87:320-325.

   Clinical and radiographic follow-up studies of 25 children treated with tendon transfer found clinical improvement but no improvement in glenohumeral deformity on MRI. Level of evidence: IV.

10. Pearl ML, Edgerton BW, Kazimiroff PA, Burchette RJ, Wong K: Arthroscopic release and latissimus dorsi transfer in the treatment of shoulder internal rotation contractures and glenohumeral deformity secondary to brachial plexus birth palsy. *J Bone Joint Surg Am* 2006;88:564-574.

   After arthroscopic release of internal rotation contractures supplemented by latissimus dorsi transfer, this study of 33 children found excellent improvement in external rotation with striking remodeling of glenohumeral deformity. Level of evidence: IV.

11. Moukoko D, Ezaki M, Wilkes D, Carter P: Posterior shoulder dislocation in infants with neonatal brachial plexus palsy. *J Bone Joint Surg Am* 2004;86:787-793.

A prospective ultrasonographic study of 134 consecutive children with BPBP found posterior displacement of the glenohumeral joint in 8% as early as age 6 months.

12. Hui JH, Torode IP: Changing glenoid version after open reduction of shoulders in children with obstetric brachial plexus palsy. *J Pediatr Orthop* 2003;23: 109-113.

   In 23 children who had open reduction and tendon lengthening surgery for posterior shoulder dislocation secondary to BPBP, CT studies revealed a 31% decrease in glenoid retroversion after surgery.

13. Kon DS, Darakjian AB, Pearl ML, Kosco AE: Glenohumeral deformity in children with internal rotation contractures secondary to brachial plexus birth palsy: Intraoperative arthrographic classification. *Radiology* 2004;231:791-795.

   A correlative study of arthrographic and arthroscopic findings for 64 children found characteristic deformity of the glenohumeral joint from internal rotation contractures.

14. van der Sluijs JA, van Ouwerkerk WJ, de Gast A, Wuisman P, Nollet F, Manoliu RA: Retroversion of the humeral head in children with an obstetric brachial plexus lesion. *J Bone Joint Surg Br* 2002;84: 583-587.

   Humeral retroversion in 33 consecutive infants with BPBP (mean age, 1 year 10 months) was measured using MRI. Children older than 12 months had increased retroversion on the affected side compared with the contralateral side (29.9° and 19.6°, respectively).

15. Curtis C, Stephens D, Clarke HM, Andrews D: The active movement scale: An evaluative tool for infants with obstetrical brachial plexus palsy. *J Hand Surg Am* 2002;27:470-478.

   In a two-part reliability study of the Active Movement Scale, the findings of two physical therapists examining 63 infants were compared at different intervals (Part A), and the findings of 10 therapists examining 10 infants were compared (Part B). Favorable kappa statistics (Part A) and analysis of variance (Part B) were observed.

16. Bae DS, Waters PM, Zurakowski D: Reliability of three classification systems measuring active motion in brachial plexus birth palsy. *J Bone Joint Surg Am* 2003;85-A:1733-1738.

   In a test-retest intraobserver and interobserver reliability study of 80 children, the findings of two examiners using the modified Mallet Classification, the Toronto Test Score, and the Hospital for Sick Children in Toronto Active Movement Scale were compared. Positive correlations were noted for individual and aggregate scores.

17. Saifuddin A, Heffernan G, Birch R: Ultrasound diagnosis of shoulder congruity in chronic obstetric brachial plexus palsy. *J Bone Joint Surg Br* 2002;84: 100-103.

   In an study of 22 children with shoulder deformity secondary to BPBP (average age, 4.75 years), 17 shoulders found incongruent on ultrasonography also were found incongruent at surgery; 3 found incongruent on ultrasonography were not found incongruent at surgery. The diagnostic accuracy of ultrasonography was 82%.

18. Poyhia TH, Nietosvaara YA, Remes VM, Kirjavainen MO, Peltonen JI, Lamminen AE: MRI of rotator cuff muscle atrophy in relation to glenohumeral joint incongruence in brachial plexus birth injury. *Pediatr Radiol* 2005;35:402-409.

   In 39 children with internal rotation contractures, MRI studies revealed diffuse atrophy of rotator cuff muscles and increased glenoid retroversion with posterior displacement of the glenohumeral joint.

19. Pearl ML, Edgerton BW, Kon DS, et al: Comparison of arthroscopic findings with magnetic resonance imaging and arthrography in children with glenohumeral deformities secondary to brachial plexus birth palsy. *J Bone Joint Surg Am* 2003;85:890-898.

   In a comparison of MRI, arthrographic, and arthroscopic findings, 61% of children undergoing surgical intervention for internal rotation contractures secondary to BPBP had glenohumeral deformity. The severity of contracture was correlated with the existence of deformity ($P = 0.001$).

20. van der Sluijs JA, van Ouwerkerk WJ, Manoliu RA, Wuisman PI: Secondary deformities of the shoulder in infants with an obstetrical brachial plexus lesions considered for neurosurgical treatment. *Neurosurg Focus* 2004;16:E9.

   MRI studies of 26 children showed characteristic deformity of the glenohumeral joint.

21. van der Sluijs JA, van der Meij M, Verbeke J, Manoliu RA, Wuisman PI: Measuring secondary deformities of the shoulder in children with obstetric brachial plexus lesion: Reliability of three methods. *J Pediatr Orthop B* 2003;12:211-214.

   An MRI reliability study of 30 shoulders in 29 children found good reliability between three systems in measuring glenoid version and humeral subluxation.

22. Chuang DC, Mardini S, Ma HS: Surgical strategy for infant obstetrical brachial plexus palsy: Experiences at Chang Gung Memorial Hospital. *Plast Reconstr Surg* 2005;116:132-142.

   A single surgeon's experience with microsurgical plexus reconstruction in 78 children found that the surgery had better results when performed early.

23. Noaman HH, Shiha AE, Bahm J: Oberlin's ulnar nerve transfer to the biceps motor nerve in obstetric brachial plexus palsy: Indications, and good and bad results. *Microsurgery* 2004;24:182-187.

   A successful Oberlin transfer was performed in seven children. This procedure was recommended after breech delivery with avulsion of C5 and C6 nerve roots, late presentation with good recovery of shoulder function, or neuroma-in-continuity of the upper trunk with good nerve intrasurgical conduction for the shoulder muscles but no biceps activity.

24. Smith NC, Rowan P, Benson LJ, Ezaki M, Carter PR: Neonatal brachial plexus palsy: Outcome of absent biceps function at three months of age. *J Bone Joint Surg Am* 2004;86-A:2163-2170.

    A prospective study of 170 patients found good shoulder function (Mallet grade IV) in the absence of biceps function at age 3 months.

25. DiTaranto P, Campagna L, Price AE, Grossman JA: Outcome following nonoperative treatment of brachial plexus birth injuries. *J Child Neurol* 2004;19: 87-90.

    Ninety-one children treated nonsurgically had good to excellent function at follow-up, if critical marker muscles recovered British Medical Council level M4 function by age 6 months.

26. Waters PM: Comparison of the natural history, the outcome of microsurgical repair, and the outcome of operative reconstruction in brachial plexus birth palsy. *J Bone Joint Surg Am* 1999;81:649-659.

27. Nehme A, Kany J, Sales-De-Gauzy J, Charlet JP, Dautel G, Cahuzac JP: Obstetrical brachial plexus palsy: Prediction of outcome in upper root injuries. *J Hand Surg Br* 2002;27:9-12.

    A retrospective review of upper root BPBP injuries found that high birth weight, timing of return of elbow flexion, and early C7 involvement were the best early predictors of outcome, when used in combination but not alone.

28. Kirkos JM, Kyrkos MJ, Kapetanos GA, Haritidis JH: Brachial plexus palsy secondary to birth injuries. *J Bone Joint Surg Br* 2005;87:231-235.

    A 30-year average follow-up study of 10 shoulders (10 patients) after latissimus dorsi transfer found that gains in external rotation persisted for 10 years and then deteriorated.

29. Waters PM, Bae DS: The effect of derotational humeral osteotomy on global shoulder function in brachial plexus birth palsy. *J Bone Joint Surg Am* 2006;88: 1035-1042.

    Forty-three patients underwent derotational osteotomy of the humerus for internal rotation contractures and glenoid dysplasia at an average age of 7.6 years. Most Mallet score functions noticeably improved.

30. Pearl ML: Arthroscopic release of shoulder contracture secondary to birth palsy: An early report on findings and surgical technique. *Arthroscopy* 2003;19: 577-582.

    Forty-one children with internal rotation contractures from BPBP underwent arthroscopic release at a mean age of 3.5 years; older children received a latissimus dorsi transfer. In this early report, arthroscopic release achieved 45° or more external rotation in all patients except a 12-year-old child with marked deformity.

31. Kambhampati SB, Birch R, Cobiella C, Chen L: Posterior subluxation and dislocation of the shoulder in obstetric brachial plexus palsy. *J Bone Joint Surg Br* 2006;88:213-219.

    In a prospective study, 183 consecutive patients (101 with subluxation and 82 with dislocation) were treated with anterior release. In 70 patients, the procedure was supplemented by internal rotation osteotomy for excessive retroversion, obligating an external rotation contracture.

32. van der Sluijs JA, van Ouwerkerk WJ, de Gast A, Nollet F, Winters H, Wuisman PI: Treatment of internal rotation contracture of the shoulder in obstetric brachial plexus lesions by subscapular tendon lengthening and open reduction: Early results and complications. *J Pediatr Orthop B* 2004;13:218-224.

    Of 19 children who underwent anterior shoulder release, 8 developed functionally disturbing external rotation contractures of the shoulder.

33. Zancolli EA, Zancolli ER Jr: Palliative surgical procedures in sequelae of obstetric palsy. *Hand Clin* 1988;4:643-669.

34. Zancolli EA, Zancolli ER III: Reconstructive surgery in brachial plexus sequelae, in Gupta A, Kay S, Scheker L (eds): *The Growing Hand*. London, England, Mosby, 2000, pp 805-823.

35. Kozin SH, Chafetz RS, Barus D, Filipone L: Magnetic resonance imaging and clinical findings before and after tendon transfers about the shoulder in children with residual brachial plexus birth palsy. *J Shoulder Elbow Surg* 2006;15:554-561.

    Twenty-three children underwent transfer of the latissimus dorsi and teres major at an average age of 5.3 years. One year after surgery, MRI revealed no change. Transfers improved overall shoulder motion but did not reduce humeral head subluxation or enhance glenohumeral joint realignment.

36. Carlioz H, Brahimi L: [Place of internal disinsertion of the subscapularis muscle in the treatment of obstetric paralysis of the upper limb in children]. *Ann Chir Infant* 1971;12:159-167.

# Chapter 51

# Postsurgical Shoulder Rehabilitation

Kevin E. Wilk, PT, DPT

Michael M. Reinold, PT, DPT, ATC, CSCS

## Introduction

Rehabilitation plays a vital role in the ultimate functional outcome of shoulder surgery. The most significant clinical challenge is to allow early tissue healing while restoring motion, strength, and function. Achieving this delicate balance between stability and mobility is often difficult for the orthopaedic team.

Rehabilitation is a gradual process that requires patience and willingness to make adjustments. The emphasis is on allowing the repaired tissues to heal, gradually restoring motion, initiating protected muscle-strengthening exercises, and increasing function. The ultimate goal is to return patients to their desired level of activity without pain or restrictions.

Each of the numerous surgical procedures performed at the glenohumeral joint requires a significantly different rehabilitation program. Rehabilitation should proceed in a sequential, progressive fashion that is organized into several phases. Each phase builds on the preceding phase and has specific goals, exercises, and precautions. The process should proceed as safely and expeditiously as possible, with attention to avoiding the development of postsurgical complications, including stiffness. The program for a specific patient is based on several factors, including the type of injury, tissue classification, the type of surgical procedure, the desired activity level, and specific patient characteristics (Table 1).

## Rehabilitation Principles and Phases

Before designing a postsurgical rehabilitation program, the clinician should consider six basic rehabilitation principles (Table 2). A multiple-phase, criteria-based approach is recommended, with each phase consisting of specific exercises and goals (Tables 3 and 4).

The primary goal of phase I, the immediate postsurgical phase, is to prevent excessive scarring while avoiding too-aggressive motion that would compromise the surgical repair. This maximal-protection phase is designed to protect the healing soft tissues, prevent the negative effects of immobilization, reestablish dynamic joint stability, and diminish postsurgical pain and inflammation. The type of surgical procedure, the method of fixation, and the current tissue status dictate the allowed range of motion (ROM). Motion is used in a restricted, protected arc that is intended to nourish the articular cartilage, assist in collagen tissue synthesis and collagen organization, and promote healing. Early motion helps decrease the patient's pain through neuromuscular modulation.[1-4]

Dynamic joint stabilization exercises are performed with the patient maintaining a static joint position as the therapist facilitates a muscle cocontraction (Figure 1). The static joint position should be carefully chosen to prevent excessive stress on tissue affected by the surgical procedure. Submaximal isometrics are performed to initiate voluntary muscle contractions of the rotator cuff muscles, which help prevent muscle atrophy and loss of motor control. Most human shoulder musculature

### Table 1 | Patient-Specific Factors Affecting Rehabilitation Program Design

Type of instability
Type of surgical procedure, exposure, graft tissue, fixation method
Response to surgery
Status of tissue (hyperelastic, normal, hypoelastic)
Status of dynamic stabilization (muscle-bone, muscle strength and balance, proprioceptive ability)
Healing ability (rapid or slow)
Activity levels (past, present, future expectations)
Physician beliefs concerning rehabilitation

### Table 2 | Principles of Rehabilitation

Healing tissue must not be overstressed.
The effects of immobilization must be minimized.
The patient must fulfill specific criteria to progress.
The rehabilitation program must be based on current scientific and clinical research.
The rehabilitation program must be tailored to the individual patient.
The rehabilitation program must use a team approach that includes the physician, the therapist, and the patient.

## Table 3 | Rehabilitation Phases and Goals

### I. Immediate Postsurgical Phase
Protect the healing tissue and maintain static stability.
Minimize the negative effects of immobilization.
Reestablish dynamic joint stability.
Diminish postsurgical pain and inflammation.

### II. Intermediate Phase
Reestablish full range of motion.
Normalize arthrokinematics.
Enhance neuromuscular control.
Improve muscle strength.

### III. Advanced Strengthening Phase
Enhance strength, power, and endurance.
Improve muscle balance.
Monitor functional motion.

### IV. Return-to-Activity Phase
Return gradually to functional sports, work, and other activities.
Maintain muscle strength and flexibility.

## Table 4 | Criteria for Progress Between Phases

### Phase I to Phase II
Satisfactory static stability
Diminishing pain and inflammation
Adequate muscle control
Baseline dynamic stability

### Phase II to Phase III
Full, nonpainful functional ROM
Good muscle strength (a score of 4 on the 5-point Manual Muscle Test Scale)
Satisfactory static stability on clinical examination
Satisfactory dynamic stability

### Phase III to Phase IV
Full functional ROM
Adequate static stability
Satisfactory dynamic stability
Good muscle strength and endurance
Satisfactory clinical examination

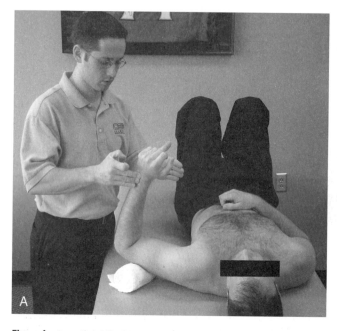 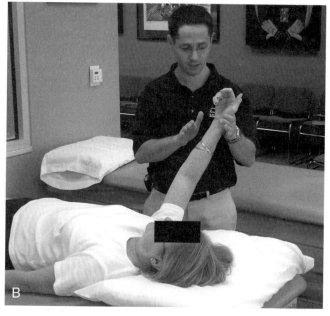

**Figure 1** Dynamic stabilization drills. The clinician provides a gentle isometric contraction, alternating the plane of resistance. **A,** External and internal rotation cocontractions with rhythmic stabilization. **B,** Rhythmic stabilization at 100° of shoulder flexion and 10° of horizontal abduction.

consists of a roughly equal combination of slow-twitch and fast-twitch muscle fibers,[5] and immobilization has a greater effect on slow-twitch fibers. Pain and inflammation can inhibit voluntary muscle activation and impede the rehabilitation process. The therapist should attempt to control pain and inflammation by judiciously using modalities such as ice and electrical stimulation, in addition to guarded motion and isometric exercises.

Several criteria must be met before the patient enters phase II, the intermediate phase: satisfactory static stability, diminishing pain and inflammation, adequate

muscle control, and baseline dynamic stability. In phase II, the advancement of shoulder mobility is emphasized. The patient's ROM is gradually increased through active-assisted and passive ROM exercises, stretching, and joint mobilization techniques, as needed. The guidelines for motion progression are based on the type of surgical procedure, the method of fixation, and the patient's tissue status, as well as the clinician's assessment of the quantity and end feel of motion. For example, a patient with less-than-desirable motion who has a firm or hard end feel receives more aggressive stretching than a patient who has a capsular or soft end feel. Joint mobilization techniques are used to restore normal motion and correct asymmetric capsular tightness. The flexibility of the anterior capsule and posterior capsule should be comparable, and correcting asymmetric capsular tightness should be a critical goal. Tightness of one side compared with the opposite side will lead to excessive humeral head displacement in the opposite direction from the tightness and ultimately to abnormal joint arthrokinematics.[6-8] Other phase II goals include improvement in muscle strength and enhancement of neuromuscular control. The techniques include proprioceptive neuromuscular facilitation with rhythmic stabilization,[9,10] neuromuscular control drills,[11,12] and isolated muscle-strengthening isotonic exercises for the rotator cuff and scapular muscles.

Toward the end of phase II, an overhead athlete can begin aggressive stretching to gradually increase motion past 90° of external rotation. External rotation of 115° (±5°) is necessary to allow an athlete to begin throwing. Strengthening exercises focus on reestablishing muscle balance, particularly the external rotation–internal rotation unilateral muscle ratio. The thrower's 10 exercise program can be initiated. These exercises are based on electromyographic studies documenting the efficacy of each movement.[13,14]

The patient should meet several criteria before entering phase III, the advanced strengthening phase: full, nonpainful functional motion, good muscle strength (a score of at least 4 on the 5-point Manual Muscle Test Scale), satisfactory static stability on clinical examination, and dynamic joint stability. Phase III is directed toward improving the patient's strength, power, and endurance while maintaining the shoulder joint's functional ROM. Progressive resistance exercises are used to reestablish muscle balance and significant strength for the patient's desired functional activities. Thus, a suitable ratio should be achieved between the posterior and anterior muscles, rotator cuff and deltoid muscles, and retractor and protractor scapular muscles. The desirable ratios are 62% to 70% for external rotation–internal rotation, 66% to 72% for posterior rotator cuff–deltoid muscles, and approximately 100% for retractor–protractor scapular muscles.[15-18] Muscle balance and dynamic joint stability should be achieved before initiating aggressive strengthening exercises such as plyometrics or functional activities such as throwing and swimming.

During phase III, muscle endurance training is emphasized, in addition to eccentric muscle training and advanced proprioceptive training.[19] When the rotator cuff muscles have reached a significant level of fatigue, the humeral head becomes displaced superiorly with simple arm movements such as shoulder abduction.[20] Muscular endurance training is designed to enhance dynamic functional joint stability and prevent fatigue-induced sublux-

ation. Plyometric training drills are designed to train the shoulder and upper body to produce and dissipate forces. These exercises generally increase an athlete's shoulder motion and gradually increase the functional stress on the shoulder joint.

The criteria that must be met before the patient enters phase IV, the return-to-activity phase, are full functional ROM, adequate static and dynamic stability, satisfactory muscle strength and endurance, and a satisfactory clinical examination. When these criteria are met, the patient is ready to initiate a controlled, gradual return to full, unrestricted sports or daily activities. An athlete receives an interval program designed for return to a specific sport.[21] Any constraints necessitated by the patient's tissue status or healing process should be considered before a functional program is initiated. Other goals are to maintain muscle strength, dynamic stability, and functional shoulder motion established in the preceding phase. A program of maintenance stretching and strengthening exercises should be initiated.

## Procedure-Specific Rehabilitation Guidelines
### Instability Procedure

Several factors can directly affect a rehabilitation program after surgery to correct shoulder instability. The type of surgery (open or arthroscopic), the type of procedure (such as Bankart lesion repair, capsular shift, plication, or shrinkage), and the method of capsule fixation should be carefully considered. The rehabilitation program should be adjusted if the subscapularis muscle was compromised to gain exposure to the capsule in an open procedure. The direction of instability (anterior, posterior, or multidirectional) must also be considered. The expected rate of progress for a patient with a first-time unidirectional traumatic dislocation is different from that of a patient with recurrent multidirectional instability. Many patients have an appreciable degree of congenital laxity that can be determined by examining the contralateral shoulder. The greater the congenital laxity, the slower the rate of ROM progression will be. Patients who exhibit a positive sulcus on the uninvolved shoulder rarely have difficulty regaining motion in the postsurgical shoulder. The patient's tissue status is a third critical factor on which to base the expected rate of rehabilitation progress. A patient with significant tissue laxity or hyperlaxity will progress more slowly than a patient with more normal collagen tissue. Patients with congenital atraumatic laxity have some collagen formation after surgery; these patients should be moved through rehabilitation much more slowly than young overhead athletes who have traumatic or acquired laxity, normal collagen tissue, and an excellent postsurgical healing response. In a patient who forms collagen rapidly after surgery (a so-called rapid healer), the rehabilitation program should be monitored and accelerated as necessary to prevent loss of motion and formation of contractures.

The status of the patient's dynamic stabilizers must be considered. Someone who has good or excellent muscle development and strength, dynamic stability, and proprioceptive abilities should progress more rapidly than someone who has a slender, underdeveloped body and nonathletic shoulder girdle musculature.

### Bankart Lesion Procedure

The rehabilitation program after arthroscopic stabilization of a Bankart-type lesion is significantly different from the program after open stabilization. The initial postsurgical rehabilitation is much slower in the arthroscopically stabilized shoulder because the strength of arthroscopic tissue fixation is somewhat tenuous during the first 4 to 6 weeks, and care must be taken to avoid disturbing the soft-tissue repair.[22,23]

Several programs for rehabilitation after arthroscopic stabilization have been published.[5,24-28] Some promote immobilization for 3 to 6 weeks after surgery, followed by guarded motion with gradual restoration of motion. Most agree that shoulder abduction and external rotation should be restricted or limited for 4 to 6 weeks, that a strengthening program should be initiated after 4 to 8 weeks, and that contact sports and other strenuous sports should be restricted for 6 months.[5,23,28]

It is recommended that the patient be placed in an immobilizing brace immediately after surgery. The brace is used continuously for 2 to 3 weeks. The affected arm is kept in a sling during daily activities for 3 to 4 weeks and is worn during sleep through week 4. For the first 2 weeks after surgery, the patient is allowed to perform active-assisted and passive ROM exercises. Active-assisted motion is initially restricted to 60° of forward flexion, 45° of internal rotation, and 5° to 10° of external rotation, with the arm placed in 20° of abduction. Passive ROM exercises are performed for shoulder flexion and abduction to a maximum of 90° and are performed for external and internal rotation to the patient's tolerance, with the arm in 20° of abduction. These ranges are strictly enforced to avoid potentially deleterious forces on the anteroinferior aspect of the glenohumeral capsule, where the surgical procedure was performed.

The use of the sling is usually discontinued during week 3 or 4, based on clinical assessment of the patient's response to surgery, stability, and pain level. Occasionally, the patient is encouraged to continue using a shoulder immobilizer while sleeping to restrict uncontrolled shoulder motions and positions. Active-assisted and passive ROM exercises are continued to gradually improve abduction, external rotation, flexion, and internal rotation. After 4 weeks, active-assisted and passive motion are increased; they are still restricted to 90° of shoulder

elevation, 15° to 20° of external rotation, and 60° of internal rotation. To restore dynamic joint stability, the patient performs light strengthening exercises, such as rhythmic stabilization for the external rotation–internal rotation muscles and submaximal isometrics for the entire shoulder musculature.

During the first 6 weeks, the therapist must be careful to avoid overstressing the healing tissue and soft-tissue fixation. A gradual restoration of motion helps avoid the negative effects of immobilization and assists in collagen formation and organization.

Full ROM can be expected by weeks 9 and 10. External rotation should be approximately 85° to 90°. During week 12, a throwing athlete's shoulder is aggressively stretched past 90° of external rotation; the goal is external rotation of 115° (±5°). All strengthening exercises gradually intensify, with the goal of improving rotator cuff and scapular strength, restoring muscle balance, and enhancing the dynamic stabilization of the glenohumeral joint complex.

After approximately 13 to 15 weeks, activities such as light swimming, plyometrics, and golf club swings are permitted. An interval throwing program or another interval sport program can be initiated during week 16 if the patient has met the criteria for phase IV.[21] A return to contact and other strenuous sports is usually permitted 7 to 9 months after surgery, with a return to competitive throwing after 9 to 12 months.

Rehabilitation after an open Bankart procedure progresses in a similar fashion, although more rapid ROM restoration is allowed. The patient typically wears a sling for protection during the first 2 weeks. Progressive ROM exercises are initiated approximately 2 weeks earlier than after an arthroscopic procedure. Progress is cautious during the first 2 to 4 weeks, and full passive ROM is expected by week 7 or 8. This progression protects against excessive scar tissue formation and loss of motion.

### Capsular Plication Procedure

Motion is allowed immediately after a capsular plication procedure, but aggressive stretching is avoided. Aggressive external rotation, elevation, or shoulder extension is not allowed. Gentle active-assisted and passive ROM exercises are allowed during the first 2 weeks to stimulate the proliferation of collagen tissue. During week 3, external and internal rotation can be performed at 45° of abduction. External rotation is allowed to approximately 30°, and internal rotation is allowed until the patient can touch his or her side. Active-assisted flexion is allowed to 90°, with gradual progression past 90° during week 4. During week 5, external and internal rotation can be performed at 90° of abduction. By week 6, the goal is to attain 75° of external rotation, and by week 8, to have 90° of external rotation at 90° of abduction. By weeks 6 to 8, flexion is usually at 170° to 180°. For an overhead athlete, particularly a baseball pitcher, external rotation of approximately 115° is desirable. This goal is achieved gradually and no earlier than week 12.

Isometric muscle-training drills and exercises begin immediately after surgery. Nonpainful, submaximal isometric exercises are used during the first 7 to 10 days. Approximately 10 to 14 days after surgery, a light isotonic program is begun, emphasizing external rotation and scapular muscle strengthening. At week 5, an athlete is allowed to progress to the thrower's 10 exercise program. Approximately 8 weeks after surgery, plyometric drills are allowed using both hands and with restricted external rotation. Ten to 14 days later, one-hand drills are incorporated. An aggressive strengthening program begins at week 12 and continues to week 16. The patient's response to the surgery and the strengthening program dictates adjustments to the program. A gradual return to throwing begins at week 16.[21] A return to contact sports activity is usually allowed after 6 to 8 months, and a return to overhead sports activity, after 9 to 12 months.

### Anterior Capsular Shift Procedure

After an open capsular shift procedure, a somewhat aggressive program is recommended for overhead athletes. Most other patients progress cautiously to avoid overstressing their healing tissue. During weeks 1 to 3, active-assisted ROM exercises for external and internal rotation are performed to the patient's tolerance, with the arm in 30° of abduction. During weeks 2 to 4, ROM and stretching exercises gradually progress. Active-assisted ROM exercises for external and internal rotation are performed with the arm in 45° of abduction, with the goal of achieving 45° of external and internal rotation by week 4. Tubing exercises may be initiated for strengthening of the external and internal shoulder rotators. Rhythmic stabilization drills and cocontraction also are performed.

External and internal rotation stretching is performed at 90° of abduction beginning during week 4 for overhead athletes and week 6 for other patients. An overhead athlete should have 90° of external rotation and 45° to 55° of horizontal abduction by week 8 and should gradually progress to full throwing motion during weeks 8 to 12. For other patients, 80% to 90% of motion is often restored by week 10; the remaining motion is regained over time with a return to functional activities. An athlete usually can return to unrestricted sports activity within 6 to 9 months, depending on the sport, position, skill level, and progress of rehabilitation.

### SLAP Lesion Procedure

The rehabilitation program after surgical intervention involving a superior labrum anterior and posterior (SLAP) lesion depends on the severity and type of lesion, the type of procedure (débridement or repair), and concomitant procedures necessitated by underlying glenohumeral joint instability. The rehabilitation program should emphasize restoring and enhancing the dynamic stability of the glenohumeral joint while ensuring that adverse stresses are not applied to healing tissue.

The patient's mechanism of injury must be fully understood before rehabilitation guidelines are determined. For a patient whose SLAP injury was the result of a compressive injury, such as a fall onto an outstretched hand, weight-bearing exercises should be avoided to minimize compression and shear on the superior labrum. A patient with a traction injury should avoid resisted or eccentric biceps contractions. A patient with a peel-back lesion should avoid excessive external shoulder rotation during surgical healing.

Although the efficacy of rehabilitation after a SLAP lesion procedure has not been established, rehabilitation guidelines have been developed based on clinical experience and basic science studies on the mechanics of the glenoid labrum and the pathomechanics of SLAP lesions.[29-38]

### Type I or III SLAP Lesion Débridement

A type I or type III SLAP lesion normally is treated by simple arthroscopic débridement of the frayed labrum without an anatomic repair.[38] The rehabilitation program can be somewhat aggressive in restoring motion and function because the biceps-labrum anchor to the glenoid rim is stable and intact. The rate of progression is determined based on the presence and extent of concomitant lesions and the patient's tolerance. The patient usually wears a sling for comfort during the first 3 to 4 days after surgery. Active-assisted and passive ROM exercises are initiated immediately after surgery. Full passive ROM can be expected within 10 to 14 days after surgery. Flexion ROM exercises are performed to the patient's tolerance. External and internal rotation exercises in the scapular plane are initiated at 45° of glenohumeral abduction and usually are advanced to 90° of abduction 4 or 5 days after surgery.

Shoulder musculature training can begin with the patient performing submaximal isometric exercises during the first week. Light isotonic strengthening of the shoulder and scapular musculature, with the exception of the biceps, is initiated during week 2. External and internal rotation, tubing, side-lying external rotation, prone rowing, prone horizontal abduction, and prone external rotation exercises are included. Active elevation exercises, such as scapular plane elevation and lateral raises, are also begun. Light biceps resistance usually is not initiated until 2 weeks after surgery to prevent irritation of the débridement site. Early, aggressive elbow flexion and forearm supination exercises, particularly eccentric exercises, should be used only with caution.

The patient is advanced to controlled weight-training activities during postsurgical weeks 4 to 6. In an athlete, plyometric exercises can be initiated between weeks 4 and 5 to train the upper extremity to absorb and develop external forces. The athlete is allowed to begin a gradual return to sport-specific activities between postsurgical weeks 7 and 10, typically using an interval sport program. The rate of return to overhead sports activity often depends on the extent of concomitant injuries. For example, an athlete who has undergone débridement involving 20% to 30% penetration of the rotator cuff usually begins an interval sport program between postsurgical weeks 7 and 10, but an athlete with more extensive pathology may need to delay initiation of the interval sport program as long as 4 months.[21]

### Type II SLAP Lesion Repair
In a type II SLAP lesion, the labrum-biceps complex is detached from the glenoid rim. Frequently, a peel-back lesion is also present.[30] This injury can result from a fall, traction force, a motor vehicle crash, or sports activity,[38] and it is common among overhead throwing athletes. The initial goal of rehabilitation is to ensure that the forces and loads on the repaired labrum are appropriately controlled. It is important to determine the extent of the lesion, its exact location, and the number of suture anchors before constructing the rehabilitation program. For example, the progress of rehabilitation would be slower for a patient whose SLAP repair used three anchors than for a patient whose repair required only one anchor because of the extent of pathology and tissue involvement. The anatomic repair is more extensive in a SLAP type II lesion than in a type I or II lesion because of the reattachment of the biceps tendon anchor,[38] and postsurgical rehabilitation must be delayed to allow healing.

To protect the healing structures from excessive motion, the patient is instructed to sleep in a shoulder immobilizer and to wear a sling during the day for the first 4 weeks after surgery. Gradual, protected ROM exercises are performed below 90° of elevation. During the first 2 weeks, external and internal rotation ROM exercises are performed passively in the scapular plane to approximately 10° to 15° of external rotation and 45° of internal rotation. The initial external rotation ROM exercises are performed cautiously to minimize strain on the labrum through the peel-back mechanism. Four weeks after surgery, the patient is instructed to begin external and internal rotation ROM exercises at 90° of shoulder abduction and to begin flexion motion above 90° of elevation. Motion is gradually increased, with the goal of restoring full ROM (90° to 100° of external rotation at 90° of abduction) by 8 weeks after surgery and progressing to thrower's motion (external rotation of

approximately 115° [±5°]) by week 12. Restoration of motion is usually accomplished with minimal difficulty.

The submaximal isometric exercises performed immediately after surgery are designed to prevent shoulder atrophy. No biceps contractions are permitted for 8 weeks. The use of external and internal rotation exercise tubing is initiated during weeks 3 and 4, and the program progresses to include lateral raises, scapular plane elevation, prone rowing, and prone horizontal abduction by week 6. A full isotonic exercise program, such as the thrower's 10 program, is initiated by week 7 or 8. Strengthening exercises for the external rotators and scapular stabilizers are emphasized.

Resisted biceps activity (elbow flexion or forearm supination) is not allowed during the first 8 weeks to protect healing of the biceps anchor. Aggressive strengthening of the biceps is avoided for the first 12 weeks. Weight-bearing exercises usually are not performed for at least 8 weeks to avoid creating compression and shearing forces on the healing labrum. Two-hand plyometric exercises and more advanced strengthening activities are allowed at weeks 10 to 12, progressing to an interval sport program at postsurgical week 16.[21] The criteria for phase IV are used to determine whether an interval sport program can be initiated. The patient is usually ready for a return to sports activity 9 to 12 months after surgical repair of a type II SLAP lesion.

### Type IV SLAP Lesion Repair
Surgical repair of a type IV SLAP lesion includes a biceps repair, resection of the biceps frayed area, or tenodesis. The postsurgical progress of ROM and other exercises is similar to progress after a type II SLAP lesion repair.[38] Individual rehabilitation programs differ significantly based on the extent of biceps involvement. If the biceps was resected, biceps muscle contractions can begin 6 to 8 weeks after surgery. If the patient underwent a biceps tear repair or biceps tenodesis, resisted or active biceps exercises should be avoided during the first 3 months to allow the soft tissue to heal. Light isotonic strengthening for elbow flexion is initiated between weeks 12 and 16 and gradually progresses as determined by the patient's tolerance. Full resisted biceps activity is incorporated during weeks 16 to 20. Progression to sport-specific activities, such as plyometric exercises and an interval sport program, is allowed on the same schedule as after a type II SLAP repair.

### Rotator Cuff Repair Procedure
Rehabilitation after rotator cuff repair surgery has evolved during the past decade as patients' functional demands have increased. A slightly more aggressive progression has become possible because of improved surgical techniques using stronger fixation methods and requiring minimal deltoid involvement. Earlier

rehabilitation programs after a traditional open procedure used a slower progression of active ROM and strengthening exercises to allow soft-tissue healing. Prolonged rehabilitation, loss of motion, residual postsurgical pain, and a delayed return to functional activities were potential complications. A mini-open or arthroscopic procedure allows a more aggressive rehabilitation approach that minimizes the risk of these complications and ensures that patients can return to functional activities as quickly and safely as possible.

A patient's postsurgical rehabilitation program is determined based on the size of the rotator cuff tear, the type of surgical procedure, and the quality of the tissue. A type I tear is smaller than 1 cm with good tissue, a type II tear is medium sized to large (1 cm to 5 cm) with adequate tissue, and a type III tear is massive (larger than 5 cm) with poor tissue. A separate, slightly more cautious protocol is used after arthroscopic repair of a small or medium-sized tear, based on observed fixation strength.[39]

Rehabilitation is usually initiated within the first few days after surgery. The initial goals are to maintain the integrity of the repair, gradually increase passive ROM, diminish postsurgical pain and inflammation, and retard muscle atrophy. The patient is instructed to avoid lifting objects away from the body if they are heavier than 20 lb. A 30° to 45° abduction brace is used during the first 2 to 4 weeks after an arthroscopic or mini-open repair. A sling is used for support during the first 10 to 14 days following mini-open repair of a type I or II tear.

Reestablishing passive motion expeditiously while maintaining the integrity of the repair is of paramount importance during the early phases of rehabilitation. Active-assisted and passive ROM exercises are performed by a physical therapist and include flexion in the scapular plane and external and internal rotation at 45° of abduction in the scapular plane. As the patient's ROM increases, external and internal rotation exercises can be performed at greater degrees of abduction, progressing to 75° and finally to 90° by 2 to 3 weeks after surgery. Full passive ROM (180° of flexion, 90° to 100° of external rotation, and 55° to 65° of internal rotation) should be achieved within 4 weeks after a mini-open repair and 5 weeks after an arthroscopic repair. The more extensive the tear, the slower the progression must be to allow adequate tissue healing.

Rotator cuff inhibition is prevented immediately following surgery through the use of submaximal isometric exercises. The patient's voluntary contraction during submaximal isometric shoulder exercises can be enhanced by neuromuscular electrical stimulation of the posterior rotator cuff (Figure 2). The patient performs rhythmic stabilization exercises in the supine position during the first 11 to 14 days after surgery. These exercises are performed gently and are designed not to improve muscle strength but to restore dynamic stabili-

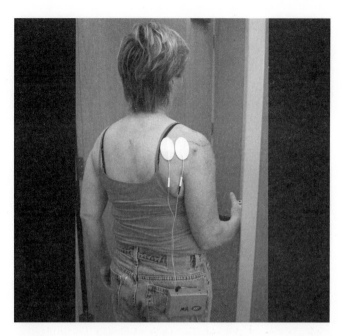

**Figure 2** After a rotator cuff repair, isometric external rotation of the shoulder can be enhanced by neuromuscular electrical stimulation of the posterior rotator cuff using the 300PV™ neuromuscular stimulation device (Empi, St. Paul, MN). The patient performs the exercise while applying the electrical stimulation.

zation of the glenohumeral joint by facilitating cocontraction of the surrounding musculature.

Active ROM exercises can be initiated when adequate dynamic stabilization of the glenohumeral joint is achieved. Four weeks after surgery, external and internal rotation exercises are performed at 0° of arm abduction using mild resistance. External rotation using manual resistance is performed in the supine position. As strength returns, side-lying external rotation may be initiated. External rotation strengthening is emphasized to avoid prolonged weakness of the posterior rotator cuff, which has been observed among patients who have undergone rotator cuff repair.[40] Prone exercises, such as rowing and horizontal abduction, are included to emphasize the strength of the posterior shoulder and scapular muscles.

By week 5 or 6 after a mini-open repair or by week 6 or 7 after repair of a type III tear or an arthroscopic repair, sufficient balance between the external and internal rotators usually exists, and active ROM exercises are permitted, including standing abduction and elevation in the scapular plane with external rotation. The patient must be able to actively elevate the arm without shoulder or scapular hiking before weight is added to the exercises. If the patient exhibits a shoulder shrug sign, the manual resistance, rhythmic stabilization, and tubing exercises are continued until proper shoulder elevation is achieved. The patient can also begin active elevation exercises in the side-lying position to minimize the effect of gravity until the shrug sign is diminished (Figure 3). Active ROM exercises are initially per-

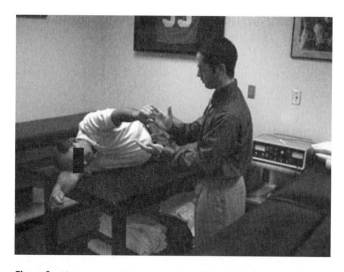

**Figure 3** After a rotator cuff repair, a gravity-minimized side-lying position is useful for flexion in the scapular plane with manual resistance. The clinician can apply manual resistance and rhythmic stabilization in this position.

formed using the weight of the arm; approximately 1 lb is added every 10 to 14 days. A full progressive-resistance isotonic strengthening program for the rotator cuff, scapulothoracic, and shoulder musculature is initiated by week 8.

A return to light functional activities is allowed at the discretion of the physician and when the patient's tolerance allows, at approximately week 8 to 12. Patients are permitted to begin a strengthening program at approximately week 12, depending on the size of the repair and the tissue quality. Weight is gradually added from week 16 to 20. An interval golf program may begin at week 12, and an interval tennis program at week 20 to 22. The progression through an interval program to return to functional and sports activities ensures that the amount of force applied to the shoulder gradually increases without compromising the integrity of the repair.[21] Most patients return to full, unrestricted functional activities 6 to 7 months after surgery.

## Summary

Postsurgical rehabilitation is vital to the overall outcome of shoulder surgery. Rehabilitation after each surgical procedure has specific goals and precautions. Appropriately designed rehabilitation programs avoid overstressing the healing tissue while gradually restoring motion, strength, and function. A successful program should include early controlled motion and emphasize rotator cuff and scapular strength, dynamic stability, and neuromuscular control, allowing the patient to return to sports and functional activities as quickly and safely as possible.

## Annotated References

1. Dehne E, Tory R: Treatment of joint injuries by immediate mobilization based upon the spinal adaptation concept. *Clin Orthop Relat Res* 1971;77: 218-232.

2. Salter RB, Hamilton HW, Wedge JH: Clinical application of basic science research on continuous passive motion for disorders of injuries and synovial joints. *J Orthop Res* 1984;1:325-333.

3. Tipton CM, Matthes RD, Maynard JA, Carey RA: The influence of physical activity on ligaments and tendons. *Med Sci Sports* 1975;7:165-175.

4. Haggmark T, Eriksson E, Jansson E: Muscle fiber type changes in human muscles after injuries and immobilization. *Orthopaedics* 1986;9:181-189.

5. Wickiewicz TL, Pagnani MJ, Kennedy K: Rehabilitation of the unstable shoulder. *Sports Med Arthrosc* 1993;1:227-235.

6. Harryman DT, Sidles JA, Clark JM, et al: Translation of the humeral head on the glenoid with passive glenohumeral motion. *J Bone Joint Surg Am* 1990;72: 1334-1338.

7. Wilk KE, Andrews JR: Rehabilitation following arthroscopic subacromial decompression. *Orthopedics* 1993;16:349-358.

8. Hawkins RJ, Angelo RL: Glenohumeral osteoarthrosis: A late complication of the Putti-Platt procedure. *J Bone Joint Surg Am* 1990;72:1193-1197.

9. Knott M, Voss DE: *Proprioceptive Neuromuscular Facilitation*, ed 2. New York, NY, Harper & Row, 1968.

10. Wilk KE, Arrigo CA: Current concepts in the rehabilitation of the athlete's shoulder. *J Orthop Sports Phys Ther* 1993;18:365-375.

11. Davies GJ, Dickoff-Hoffman S: Neuromuscular testing and rehabilitation of the shoulder complex. *J Orthop Sports Phys Ther* 1993;18:449-456.

12. Wilk KE, Arrigo CA: An integrated approach to upper extremity exercises. *Orthop Phys Ther Clin N Am* 1992;9:337-349.

13. Reinold MM, Wilk KE, Fleisig GS, et al: Electromyographic analysis of the rotator cuff and deltoid musculature during common shoulder external rotation exercises. *J Orthop Sports Phys Ther* 2004;34: 385-394.

   Intramuscular electrodes were used to analyze muscle activity of the rotator cuff and deltoid during seven shoulder exercises. Side-lying external rotation was found to have the highest infraspinatus and teres minor activity. Prone horizontal abduction yielded the highest activity in the middle and posterior deltoid and supraspinatus.

14. Reinold MM, Ellerbush MT, Barrentine SW, et al: Electromyographic analysis of the supraspinatus and

deltoid muscles during rehabilitation exercises. *J Orthop Sports Phys Ther* 2002;32:A43.

> Electromyographic electrodes were placed into the supraspinatus, middle deltoid, and posterior deltoid to analyze three exercises commonly used to strengthen and test the supraspinatus. No significant differences in supraspinatus activity were found.

15. Wilk KE, Arrigo CA, Andrews JR: The strength characteristics of the internal and external rotator muscles in professional baseball pitchers. *Am J Sports Med* 1993;21:61-69.

16. Davies GJ: Macrotraumatic shoulder injuries, in Davies GJ (ed): *A Compendium of Isokinetics in Clinical Usage*, ed 4. Onalaska, WI, S&S Publishers, 1992, pp 433-480.

17. Paine RM, Voight M: The role of the scapula. *J Orthop Sports Phys Ther* 1993;18:386-391.

18. Wilk KE, Andrews JR, Arrigo CA: The abductor and adductor strength characteristics of professional baseball pitchers. *Am J Sports Med* 1995;23:307-311.

19. Lephart SM, Warner JP, Borsa PA, Fu FH: Proprioception of the shoulder joint in healthy, unstable surgically repaired shoulders. *J Shoulder Elbow Surg* 1994;3:371-380.

20. Wickiewicz TH, Chen SK, Otis JC, Warren RF: Glenohumeral kinematics in a muscle fatigue model: A radiographic study. *Orthop Trans* 1995;18:126.

21. Reinold MM, Wilk KE, Reed J, et al: Interval sport programs: Guidelines for baseball, tennis, and golf. *J Orthop Sports Phys Ther* 2002;32:293-298.

> An interval sport program is commonly used in conjunction with a specific rehabilitation program to better prepare the athlete for a return to competition. Comprehensive programs for baseball, tennis, and golf are discussed.

22. Shall LM, Crowley PW: Soft tissue reconstruction in the shoulder: Comparison of suture anchors, absorbable staples and absorbable tacks. *Am J Sports Med* 1994;22:715-718.

23. Warner JJP, Miller M, Marks P: Arthroscopic Bankart repair with Suretac device: Clinical and experimental observations. *Arthroscopy* 1995;11:2-20.

24. Morgan CD: Arthroscopic transglenoid suture repair. *Oper Tech Orthop Surg* 1991;1:171-179.

25. Grana WA, Buckley P, Yates C: Arthroscopic Bankart suture repair. *Am J Sports Med* 1993;21:348-353.

26. Arciero RA, Wheeler JH, Ryan JB, McBride JT: Arthroscopic Bankart repair vs. non-operative treatment for acute, initial anterior shoulder dislocations. *Am J Sports Med* 1994;22:589-594.

27. Wolf E, Wilk R, Richmond J: Arthroscopic Bankart repair using suture anchors. *Oper Tech Orthop Surg* 1991;1:184-191.

28. Altchek DW: Arthroscopic shoulder stabilization using a bioabsorbable fixation device. *Sports Med Arthrosc* 1992;1:266-271.

29. Andrews JR, Carson WR: The arthroscopic treatment of glenoid labrum tears in the throwing athlete. *Orthop Trans* 1984;8:44-49.

30. Burkhart SS, Morgan CD: The peel-back mechanism: Its role in producing and extending posterior type II SLAP lesions and its effect on SLAP repair rehabilitation. *Arthroscopy* 1998;14:637-640.

31. Cooper DE, Arnoczky SP, O'Brien SJ, Warren RF, DiCarlo E, Allen AA: Anatomy, histology, and vascularity of the glenoid labrum: An anatomical study. *J Bone Joint Surg Am* 1992;74:46-52.

32. Myers TH, Zemanovic JR, Andrews JR: The resisted supination external rotation test: A new test for the diagnosis of SLAP lesions. *Am J Sports Med* 2005;33: 1315-1320.

> By re-creating the peel-back mechanism, the resisted supination external rotation test was found to be more accurate in diagnosing SLAP tears in 40 overhead throwing athletes than two other commonly used tests.

33. Nam EK, Snyder SJ: The diagnosis and treatment of superior labrum, anterior and posterior (SLAP) lesions. *Am J Sports Med* 2003;31:798-810.

> Shoulder arthroscopy has greatly improved the diagnosis and treatment of injury to the labrum and biceps tendon; the treatment is directly correlated with the type of labral injury. Anatomy, biomechanics, classification, diagnosis, and treatment are discussed.

34. Pagnani MJ, Deng XH, Warren RF, Torzilli PA, Altchek DW: Effect of lesions of the superior portion of the glenoid labrum on glenohumeral translation. *J Bone Joint Surg Am* 1995;77:1003-1010.

35. Rodosky MW, Harner CD, Fu FH: The role of the long head of the biceps muscle and superior glenoid labrum in anterior stability of the shoulder. *Am J Sports Med* 1994;22:121-130.

36. Shepard MF, Dugas JR, Zeng N, Andrews JR: Differences in the ultimate strength of the biceps anchor and the generation of type II superior labral anterior posterior lesions in a cadaveric model. *Am J Sports Med* 2004;32:1197-1201.

> The loading patterns of the biceps in the late cocking and deceleration phases of the throwing motion were simulated in 16 cadaver shoulders. The late cocking phase was found to produce significantly more stress to the biceps and superior labrum.

37. Vangsness CT Jr, Jurgenson SS, Watson T, et al: The origin of the long head of the biceps from the scapula and glenoid labrum: An anatomical study of 100 shoulders. *J Bone Joint Surg Br* 1994;76:951-954.

38. Wilk KE, Reinold MM, Dugas JR, et al: Current concepts in the recognition of superior labral (SLAP) lesions. *J Orthop Sports Phys Ther* 2005;35:273-291.

Accurate diagnosis of the extent and type of labral injury is critical for both the surgeon and the therapist. General anatomy and biomechanics are discussed, with specific clinical testing, current concepts in surgical treatment, and postsurgical treatment.

39. Waltrip RL, Zheng N, Dugas JR, Andrews JR: Rotator cuff repair: A biomechanical comparison of three techniques. *Am J Sports Med* 2003;31:493-497.

Double- or single-layer rotator cuff repair was performed on 12 matched pairs of cadaver shoulders. The double-layer repair had a significantly higher number of cycles to failure than either of the two single-layer repair techniques.

40. Rokito AS, Zuckerman JD, Gallagher MA, et al: Strength after surgical repair of the rotator cuff. *J Shoulder Elbow Surg* 1996;5:12-16.

# Chapter 52

# Calcific Tendinitis

Seth L. Sherman, MD

Robert G. Marx, MD

## Introduction

Calcific tendinitis is a common disorder of the shoulder in which multifocal, cell-mediated calcification in or around a living tendon is usually followed by spontaneous phagocytic resorption.[1] The tendon reconstitutes itself after resorption or surgical removal of the calcium deposit.[2] Although the etiology of calcific tendinitis remains controversial, circumscribed tissue hypoxia and localized tissue pressure may be triggers for the disease process.[2,3] In some patients with calcific tendinitis, acute or chronic pain is caused by inflammation around the calcium deposits.[2] Mild or moderate chronic pain may be present during the formative, calcium deposition phase, although this phase is latent and asymptomatic in most patients. The acute, resorptive phase may be characterized by an abrupt onset of severe pain that limits function. The pain may be caused by inflammation or secondary to rotator cuff impingement from bursal irritation, thickening, or deposit prominence. Chronic glenohumeral stiffness can also result from calcific tendinitis.

## Epidemiology

Most patients with calcific tendinitis are 30 to 50 years old, and women are affected approximately 1.5 times as often as men.[2,4] As many as 10% of patients have bilateral deposits. The reported incidence ranges from 2.7% to 63% of the general population; it varies with the clinical and radiographic criteria used in the study.[5] More than 30% of patients with insulin-dependent diabetes mellitus develop tendon calcification;[2] patients with diabetes are more likely than other patients to have asymptomatic deposits. Approximately 25% of patients with calcific tendinitis have a rotator cuff tear, although these patients are likely to have a relatively small amount of calcification.[2] In approximately 80% of patients, the disease occurs in the supraspinatus tendon, 1.5 to 2 cm from the tendinous insertion at the greater tuberosity.[2,4] There may a genetic susceptibility to calcific tendinitis; patients were found to have an increased frequency of the HLA-A1 antigen.[1]

## Pathogenesis

The mechanism of calcific tendinitis was first believed to involve degenerative calcification. This theory held that tendon fiber degeneration precedes calcification in the critical zone at the hypovascular bone-tendon junction.[6] Age-related wear leads to tendon fiber degeneration, followed by focal hyalinization, fibrillation, and eventual detachment from the surrounding normal tendon fibers.[1,2] The necrotic debris becomes calcified in a process that corresponds histologically with necrosis of tenocytes and intracellular accumulation of calcium in the form of microspheroliths or psammomas.

More recent studies have rejected the degenerative calcification model and proposed reactive calcification as the mechanism.[1,2] These studies point out that the degenerative calcification model has several limitations. It fails to consider that incidence does not increase with patient age (the typical patient is in the fifth decade of life); that the disease is self-limiting; and that the histologic, morphologic, and ultrastructural features of

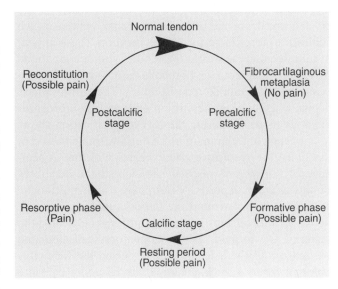

**Figure 1** Schematic representation of the progressive phases of calcific tendinitis. *(Adapted from Uhthoff HK, Loehr JW: Calcific tendinopathy of the rotator cuff: Pathogenesis, diagnosis, and management. J Am Acad Orthop Surg 1997;5:183-191.)*

**American Academy of Orthopaedic Surgeons**

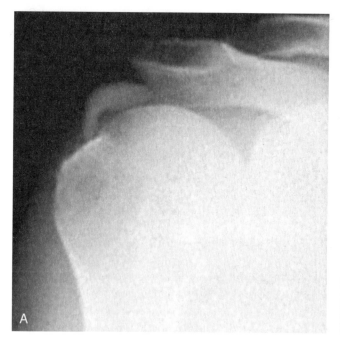
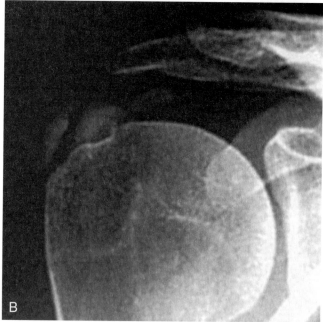

**Figure 2** AP radiographs showing calcifications. **A,** Dense, rounded, and sharply delineated calcification (DePalma type II, Gärtner type III). **B,** Multilobar, radiodense, and sharply delineated calcification (Gärtner type II). *(Reproduced with permission from Porcellini G, Paladini P, Campi F, Paganelli M: Arthroscopic treatment of calcifying tendinitis of the shoulder: Clinical and ultrasonographic follow-up findings at two to five years. J Shoulder Elbow Surg 2004;13:503-508.)*

degenerative calcification are different from those observed in patients with calcific tendinitis. In addition, the model does not differentiate between insertional tendon calcification and intrasubstance calcification.[1]

The active mediation of calcification by cells in a viable environment is called reactive calcification.[1,2] The process has three stages (Figure 1). During the first, precalcific stage, the predisposed site undergoes fibrocartilaginous metaplasia of tenocytes into chondrocytes. The second, calcific stage has three phases: formative, resting, and resorptive. During the formative phase, calcium crystals are deposited primarily in matrix vesicles, which coalesce to form large foci of calcification. These appear in multifocal areas within the tendon and are separated by fibrocartilaginous or fibrocollagenous tissue. The deposits have a chalklike consistency.[1,2] The resting phase begins when calcium deposition ends and the fibrocartilaginous tissue bordering the foci of calcification shows no evidence of inflammation.[2] After a variable period of inactivity, the resorptive phase begins with the appearance of thin-walled vascular channels at the periphery of the calcium deposits. Macrophages and multinucleated giant cells surround the deposits and phagocytose debris as the calcium is resorbed. Morphologically, the material is formed by inflammatory cell-mediated breakdown of the calcium deposit during the formative phase; it forms a thick, creamy material under pressure during the resorptive phase. During the final, postcalcific stage, granulation tissue with young fibroblasts and new vascular channels remodels the space occupied by

the resorbing calcium deposits. With scar maturation, type III collagen is replaced with type I collagen. The tendon heals with subsequent fiber realignment.[1,2]

The reactive calcification theory describes the pathogenesis of the disease based on morphologic studies. However, the factors causing the initial fibrocartilaginous transformation within the tendon and the factors leading to the onset of the resorptive period remain elusive.

## Classification

The DePalma and Kruper classification describes two radiographic types, which are clinically correlated with the resorptive and formative phases. Type I, usually seen during the resorptive phase in patients with acute pain, has a fluffy, fleecy appearance with a poorly defined periphery; an overlying crescentic streak indicates rupture of the calcium deposit into the subacromial bursa. Type II corresponds to subacute or chronic disease in the formative phase and is characterized by discrete, homogenous deposits with uniform density and a well-defined periphery. Radiographic change can be seen from type II to type I but never from type I to type II[1,7,8] (Figure 2).

The commonly used Gärtner classification system is also based on the radiographic appearance of the calcification. Type I is homogenous in structure and has well-defined borders; type II is heterogeneous with a sharp outline or homogenous without a defined border; and type III is cloudy and translucent[8] (Figure 3).

## Clinical Evaluation

Calcific tendinitis is usually diagnosed by a thorough patient evaluation that includes a detailed history, a focused physical examination, and basic radiographic studies.[6] The initial radiographs should include AP, internal and external rotation, scapular Y, and axillary views to determine the location of the deposits and reveal possible impingement.[2] Supraspinatus tendon deposits can be seen on a neutral rotation view; infraspinatus or teres minor deposits, an internal rotation view; and subscapularis tendon deposits, an external rotation view.[1] The scapular Y view can help in determining whether the calcification is causing impingement. CT can be useful if the calcium deposits are not clearly visible on plain radiographs. On T1-weighted MRI images, calcium deposits appear as areas of decreased signal intensity. T2-weighted images frequently reveal a perifocal band of increased signal intensity consistent with edema.[1] MRI can also be helpful in determining the presence of an associated rotator cuff tear.

It is important to distinguish calcific tendinitis from a rotator cuff tear because the treatment of the two conditions is inherently different.[6] The clinical presentation of calcific tendinitis depends on the stage and extent of disease. The formative phase is rarely symptomatic.[3] Acute symptomatic episodes usually occur during the resorptive phase because of edema and the sudden increase in intratendinous pressure.[3] For approximately 50% of patients diagnosed during the resorptive phase, the primary complaints are shoulder pain, especially at night, and decreased range of motion.[5] On radiographs, these patients have cloudy, translucent tendon calcification without clear circumscription (DePalma type I, Gärtner type III). The patients with the worst pain and symptoms usually have the best prognosis, for reasons that are not entirely clear. It is possible that robust acute inflammation more readily clears the deposits and leads into the postcalcific healing phase.

There is a strong tendency to self-healing by spontaneous resorption of the deposits. Within approximately 2 to 3 weeks of the onset of symptoms, the patient usually regains a normally functioning joint, with or without treatment. However, the condition does not always follow this pattern, and the natural cycle can be blocked at any point.[9] In these patients, the symptoms are related to the presence of dense, sharply delineated calcifications (DePalma type II, Gärtner types I and II) that can become chronic and debilitating.[5] The calcification sometimes leads to a rotator cuff tear.[9] Although the symptoms disappear as the calcification disappears, the time required for spontaneous resolution of calcification and the related symptoms often represents an unacceptably long interference with the patient's quality of life. In one study, calcifications disappeared in 9.3% of patients within 3 years of the initial diagnosis.[10] In another

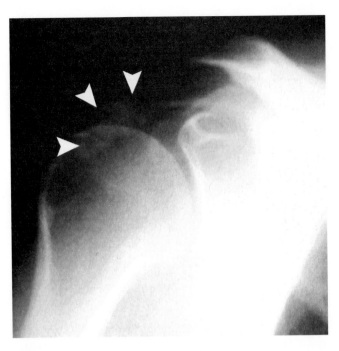

**Figure 3** AP radiograph showing fluffy, indistinct calcification (*arrowheads*) corresponding to Gärtner type III. (*Reproduced with permission from Hurt G, Baker CL Jr: Calcific tendinitis of the shoulder.* Orthop Clin North Am 2003;34:567-575.)

study, calcifications disappeared in 27.1% of patients within 10 years.[11] A third study reported that calcifications with sharp margins and a homogeneous or heterogeneous structure disappeared spontaneously in 33% of patients within 3 years.[12]

## Treatment

Proper treatment of calcific tendinitis of the rotator cuff requires distinguishing between the resorptive and formative phases. The goals of treatment are pain reduction and the disappearance of calcium deposits. Physical therapy, oral nonsteroidal anti-inflammatory drugs (NSAIDs), subacromial corticosteroid injections, needle lavage, and extracorporeal shock-wave therapy (ESWT) are the mainstays of nonsurgical treatment of acute and chronic disease. Open or arthroscopic surgery is reserved for patients who had unsuccessful nonsurgical treatment.

### The Resorptive Phase (Acute Calcific Tendinitis)

In a patient who has clinical and radiographic signs of the resorptive phase (severe, acute-onset shoulder pain; decreased range of motion; Gärtner type III radiographic findings), spontaneous resolution of the disease can be anticipated.[1] The treatment of these patients should be focused on controlling pain, decreasing inflammation, relieving intratendinous pressure, and maintaining range of motion. Steroid injections are effective in decreasing pain and inflammation for patients with acute symptoms, although there is no evidence that

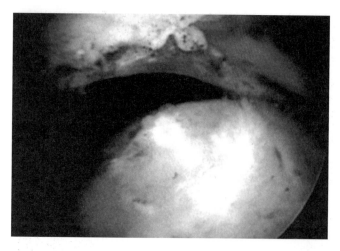

**Figure 4** Arthroscopic view of the bursal side showing evidence of a calcific deposit in the rotator cuff tendon. *(Reproduced with permission from Hurt G, Baker CL Jr: Calcific tendinitis of the shoulder. Orthop Clin North Am 2003;34:567-575.)*

steroid injections facilitate calcium resorption[13] and frequent injections may be harmful to the tendon structure.[6] A short course of NSAIDs is often useful in pain control, although there is no evidence that they alter the natural progression of the disease.[1,13]

During the resorptive phase of calcific tendinitis, the use of treatments such as ESWT, radiotherapy, and arthroscopic and open surgical procedures is not indicated. Supportive measures and gentle physical therapy to maintain range of motion usually lead to a favorable outcome.

Needle lavage is often extremely useful during the resorptive stage to decrease intratendinous pressure.[2] Lavage is performed in the operating room or radiology suite. The preferred technique uses an inflow-outflow setup with two large-bore needles and injection of 2% lidocaine.[1] The clinical response to needle lavage has been favorable; in one study, more than 70% of patients had improvement in pain.[2] Needle aspiration and lavage using ultrasonography or image intensification was reported to eliminate between 28% and 76% of calcium deposits.[4] Most calcifications are likely to be resorbed spontaneously, without intervention, in patients with acute symptoms. Therefore, completely eliminating deposits with needle lavage is less important than decreasing intratendinous pressure and pain.

### The Formative Phase (Chronic Calcific Tendinitis)

Chronic, debilitating calcific tendinitis has been the focus of much recent research. Patients with chronic, debilitating calcific tendinitis are in the formative phase of the disease, with Gärtner type I or type II radiographic findings. Although the natural history of calcification is unclear in these patients, spontaneous resolution does not usually occur. Standard nonsurgical treatments have been unsuccessful. Treatments ranging from ESWT to

open and arthroscopic surgery have been used to address patients' functional concerns.

ESWT is gaining popularity as a treatment for chronic calcific tendinitis of the rotator cuff. Sound waves are used to create substantial differences in pressure at the interface of anatomic structures having different acoustic impedances.[14] Although the mechanism of action is not fully understood, ESWT has been used to target calcium deposits for resorption. A recent review of 16 studies, including 5 randomized controlled trials, found moderate evidence that high-energy ESWT is effective for chronic calcific tendinitis when the shock waves are focused on the calcium deposit.[15] High-energy ESWT was found to be superior to low-energy ESWT or placebo treatment, and ESWT was found more effective than transcutaneous electrical nerve stimulation.[15,16] The clinical and radiographic outcomes of ESWT appear to be significantly better when three-dimensional computer-assisted navigation is used to locate the calcium deposit.[14] Another recent randomized, controlled study found that, in comparison with ESWT alone, ultrasonography-guided needle lavage in combination with high-energy ESWT significantly improved calcium deposit elimination, led to better clinical results, and decreased the need for surgery.[4] All of these studies suggest a relationship between residual calcium deposits and eventual clinical outcome, but this relationship has yet to be fully explored.

Surgical treatment of calcific tendinitis is most helpful for patients who are in a chronic formative phase, especially if impingement symptoms are present. Approximately 10% of all patients have shoulder pain that is unresponsive to nonsurgical treatment and requires surgical treatment.[2] Open or arthroscopic excision of calcium deposits reliably leads to pain relief.[3] The indications for surgery include symptom progression, constant pain that interferes with activities of daily living, and lack of improvement after nonsurgical treatment.[2] Open surgical procedures have had very good results. Studies have consistently found that 82% to 88% of patients rate the subjective outcome as excellent; the improvement in the Constant score is as much as 100%.[3] The outcomes of recent arthroscopic surgical procedures appear to be equivalent to those of open procedures. Arthroscopic surgery offers better cosmesis, a shorter length of stay, and a shorter rehabilitation time without compromising patient outcome, and it has become the preferred method of surgical treatment for calcific tendinitis[1] (Figures 4 and 5). Studies of arthroscopic removal of rotator cuff calcifications found that 79% to 94% of patients had excellent shoulder function and subjective satisfaction; the average age- and gender-corrected Constant scores were 85 points or higher.[3]

The arthroscopic treatment of calcific tendinitis is technically demanding. It can be difficult to locate the calcium deposits within the tendon and determine the amount of resection needed, while avoiding compromise of the surrounding healthy tendon. Postsurgical recovery requires 3 to 6 months because the tendon and subacromial bursa heal slowly. Pain relief is gradual and progressive, and it may extend over the entire first year. Nonetheless, most patients are able to return to work within 6 weeks.[3] Complications of the arthroscopic technique, although uncommon, have been reported to include frozen shoulder, hematoma, and residual impingement because of inadequate resection (requiring repeat surgery and possible subacromial decompression).[3,17] The amount of calcium deposit for which resection is necessary, the use of subacromial decompression acromioplasty, and the routine exploration of the glenohumeral joint are controversial topics in arthroscopic treatment.

The reported rates of complete calcium deposit removal range from 40% to 88%.[3] A large study with a 2-year follow-up found that a successful outcome depended only on the absence of calcium deposits, and a high Constant score was inversely related to the number and size of residual calcium deposits.[9] The complete removal of all calcifications was therefore recommended.

Another large study found that more than 90% of patients had excellent shoulder function and satisfaction at 2-year follow-up, although only 44% had immediate and complete removal of calcification.[3] The study concluded that complete removal of calcification is not absolutely necessary, and partial resection, with preservation of surrounding healthy tendon, is sufficient for an excellent functional outcome. Prospective, randomized studies are needed to settle the ongoing debate.

Studies of routine subacromial decompression found that good results were obtained regardless of whether subacromial decompression was used.[3,9,18] Some surgeons argue that decompression is not routinely indicated because it does not improve outcomes and leads to a moderate decrease in postsurgical strength.[9] In general, it has been suggested that subacromial decompression should be performed if intrasurgical signs of mechanical irritation appear on the undersurface of the acromion or the calcium deposits cannot be completely removed without causing significant tendon damage.[3] For patients with obvious inflammatory changes around a calcium deposit or with large deposits that bulge into the subacromial space and cause obvious mechanical impingement, acromioplasty is not routinely indicated because it does not address the underlying condition.

Routine exploration of the glenohumeral joint is often part of the arthroscopic treatment of calcific tendinitis, although the deposits are removed through a bursal approach. Few studies have addressed the desirability of entering the joint. At 3-month follow-up, duration of pain and time to return to work were found to be significantly greater in patients who underwent routine glenohumeral exploration; however, Constant scores and re-

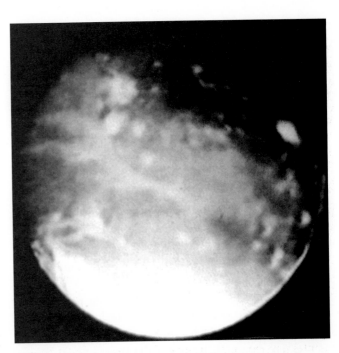

**Figure 5**  Arthroscopic view showing the snowstorm effect, which is often seen with arthroscopic needle lavage or débridement of calcific tendinitis. *(Reproduced with permission from Hurt G, Baker CL Jr: Calcific tendinitis of the shoulder. Orthop Clin North Am 2003;34:567-575.)*

sidual deposit size were not affected at 6-month follow-up.[18] Although a larger prospective evaluation is needed, routine glenohumeral exploration appears to be detrimental to short-term outcome and not essential in the arthroscopic treatment of calcific tendinitis.

## Summary

Calcific tendinitis is a common shoulder disorder of unknown etiology that involves calcium deposition and resorption within a rotator cuff tendon. Most affected patients are 30 to 50 years old. Most calcifications occur 1.5 to 2 cm from the insertion of the supraspinatus tendon. Calcific tendinitis is a process of reactive formation involving three stages: precalcific, calcific (formative, resting, and resorptive), and postcalcific. The diagnosis is made through patient history, physical examination, and imaging studies. Patients in the resorptive phase may have acute-onset shoulder pain, decreased range of motion, and Gärtner type III calcium deposits. These patients are best treated using NSAIDs, subacromial injections, gentle physical therapy, and, for some patients, needle lavage. Spontaneous resolution with subsequent tendon healing usually occurs within 2 to 3 weeks. Patients in the formative phase may have chronic, progressive shoulder pain and Gärtner type I or type II deposits. High-energy ESWT, with or without ultrasonography-guided needle lavage, has been successful in these patients. For 10% of patients, surgery is indicated after unsuccessful nonsurgical treatment.

Open and arthroscopic procedures have had equivalent outcomes (patient satisfaction 79% to 94%, Constant score > 85). Arthroscopic treatment offers improved cosmesis, a shorter hospital stay, and a shorter rehabilitation period. Controversies in arthroscopic treatment include the amount of calcium deposit resection necessary for functional improvement, the use of routine subacromial decompression, and the benefit of glenohumeral joint exploration.

## Annotated References

1. Uhthoff HK, Loehr JW: Calcific tendinopathy of the rotator cuff: Pathogenesis, diagnosis, and management. *J Am Acad Orthop Surg* 1997;5:183-191.

2. Hurt G, Baker CL Jr: Calcific tendinitis of the shoulder. *Orthop Clin North Am* 2003;34:567-575.

   This comprehensive review discusses the pathogenesis, radiographic evaluation, and nonsurgical and surgical treatment of calcific tendinitis.

3. Seil R, Litzenburger H, Kohn D, Rupp S: Arthroscopic treatment of chronically painful calcifying tendinitis of the supraspinatus tendon. *Arthroscopy* 2006;22: 521-527.

   Fifty-four patients, mean age 45.4 years, underwent arthroscopic removal of calcific tendinitis of the supraspinatus. At 24-month follow-up, the mean Constant score improved from 32.8 to 90.9. Thirty-one percent were pain free or had achieved maximum pain relief at 3 months; 28% had achieved maximum pain relief at 12 months. Seventy-eight percent returned to work within 6 weeks, and 92% were satisfied with the outcome. Complete removal of the deposits did not appear to be essential,

4. Krasny C, Enenkel M, Aigner N, Wlk M, Landsiedl F: Ultrasound-guided needling combined with shock-wave therapy for the treatment of calcifying tendinitis of the shoulder. *J Bone Joint Surg Br* 2005;87: 501-507.

   A prospective, randomized controlled trial compared ESWT with ultrasonography-guided needling followed by high-energy ESWT for the treatment of chronic calcific tendinitis of the shoulder. Forty patients received each treatment, and the mean follow-up time was 4.1 months. The combined treatment led to a disappearance of deposits in 60% of patients and avoidance of surgery in 80%, compared with 32.5% and 55%, respectively, in patients who received only ESWT. The patients who received the combined treatment also had significantly better clinical results.

5. Cacchio A, Paoloni M, Barile A, et al: Effectiveness of radial shock-wave therapy for calcific tendinitis of the shoulder: Single-blind, randomized clinical study. *Phys Ther* 2006;86:672-682.

   Calcifications disappeared completely in 86% of 90 patients who received radial shock-wave therapy and partial-ly disappeared in 13.4%. Only 8.8% of the control-group patients had partial disappearance of calcifications, and none had total disappearance. Radial shock-wave therapy led to a significant reduction in pain and improved shoulder function after 4 weeks.

6. Moretti B, Garofalo R, Genco S, Patella V, Mouhsine E: Medium-energy shock wave therapy in the treatment of rotator cuff calcifying tendinitis. *Knee Surg Sports Traumatol Arthrosc* 2005;13:405-410.

   Fifty-four patients with calcific tendinitis underwent medium-energy ESWT. At 1-month and 6-month follow-ups, 70% had a satisfactory functional result. The deposits disappeared in 54% and were less than half the original size in 35%. No complications were reported.

7. DePalma AF, Kruper JS: Long-term study of shoulder joints afflicted with and treated for calcific tendinitis. *Clin Orthop Relat Res* 1961;20:61-72.

8. Gärtner J, Heyer A: [Calcific tendinitis of the shoulder.] *Orthopade* 1995;24:284-302.

9. Porcellini G, Paladini P, Campi F, Paganelli M: Arthroscopic treatment of calcifying tendinitis of the shoulder: Clinical and ultrasonographic follow-up findings at two to five years. *J Shoulder Elbow Surg* 2004;13:503-508.

   Ninety-five shoulders (63 patients) underwent clinical and ultrasonographic evaluation at a mean 36-month follow-up after arthroscopic treatment of calcific tendinitis. Ultrasonography revealed no cuff tears. At 24-month follow-up, the Constant score was inversely related to the number and size of residual calcifications in all patients. Outcome was strongly related only to the presence of residual calcification, and complete removal of deposits was therefore recommended.

10. Bosworth BM: Calcium deposits in the shoulder and subacromial bursitis: A survey of 12,122 shoulders. *JAMA* 1941;116:2477-2482.

11. Wagenhauser JF: Die periarthropatie-syndrome. *Therapiewoche* 1972;37:3187-3192.

12. Gärtner J: [Tendinosis calcarea: Results of treatment with needling.] *Z Orthop Ihre Grenzgeb* 1993;131: 461-469.

13. Vad VB, Solomon J, Adin DR: The role of subacromial shoulder irrigation in the treatment of calcific rotator cuff tendinosis: A case series. *Arch Phys Med Rehabil* 2005;86:1270-1272.

    Twenty-eight patients underwent fluoroscopy-guided subacromial shoulder irrigation followed by corticosteroid injection for the treatment of chronic calcific tendinitis after unsuccessful nonsurgical treatment. At 1-year follow-up, 85.7% had significantly improved satisfaction, as measured using the L'Insalata Shoulder Rating Questionnaire and visible numeric pain score.

14. Sabeti-Aschraf M, Dorotka R, Goll A, Trieb K: Extracorporeal shock wave therapy in the treatment of calcific tendinitis of the rotator cuff. *Am J Sports Med* 2005;33:1365-1368.

A prospective, randomized single-blind study of 50 patients compared the use of low-energy ESWT and three-dimensional computer-assisted navigation with the use of ESWT and patient-to-therapist feedback. Patients in both groups had significantly improved Constant-Murley and visual analog scores at 12-week follow-up, although the results were significantly better in the patients who had received ESWT and computer-assisted navigation.

15. Harniman E, Carette S, Kennedy C, et al: Extracorporeal shock wave therapy for calcific and noncalcific tendonitis of the rotator cuff: A systematic review. *J Hand Ther* 2004;17:132-151.

This review of 16 studies, including 5 randomized controlled studies, found moderate evidence that high-energy ESWT is effective for chronic calcific tendinitis of the shoulder if the shock waves are focused at the calcific deposit.

16. Gerdesmeyer L, Wagenpfeil S, Haake M, et al: Extracorporeal shock wave therapy for the treatment of chronic calcifying tendonitis of the rotator cuff: A randomized controlled trial. *JAMA* 2003;290:2573-2580.

A randomized, controlled double-blind study compared the use of high-energy ESWT, low-energy ESWT, and placebo treatment for chronic calcific tendinitis. Both high-energy and low-energy ESWT had a beneficial effect on shoulder function and patient-rated pain score. Both resulted in decreased calcification size at 3-, 6- and 12-month follow-up, compared with placebo treatment. High-energy ESWT appeared to provide better results than low-energy ESWT.

17. Jacobs R, Debeer P: Calcifying tendinitis of the rotator cuff: Functional outcome after arthroscopic treatment. *Acta Orthop Belg* 2006;72:276-281.

Sixty-one shoulders were treated with arthroscopic excision, subacromial bursa débridement, and shaving. At a mean 15-month follow-up, modified Constant and Disabilities of the Arm, Shoulder and Hand scores significantly improved (from 33.4 to 66.8 and from 49.7 to 17.3, respectively). Acromioplasty or residual calcification did not affect final outcome. Frozen shoulder occurred in 18%. Level of evidence: IV.

18. Sirveaux F, Gosselin O, Roche O, Turell P, Molé D: Postoperative results after arthroscopic treatment of rotator cuff calcifying tendonitis, with or without associated glenohumeral exploration. *Rev Chir Orthop Reparatrice Appar Mot* 2005;91:295-299.

In a retrospective study of 64 patients treated arthroscopically for chronic calcific tendinitis of the rotator cuff using a bursal approach either in isolation or with glenohumeral exploration, no difference in Constant score or deposit disappearance was found at 6-month follow-up. The average duration of pain and time to return to work (11 weeks and 12 weeks, respectively) were significantly higher in patients who underwent glenohumeral exploration, compared with the remaining patients (6 weeks and 5 weeks, respectively).

# Chapter 53

# Frozen Shoulder

Adam M. Smith, MD

## Introduction

Few musculoskeletal conditions are more puzzling than frozen shoulder. It is one of the more commonly encountered shoulder conditions, affecting an estimated 2% to 5% of the general population. Patients with frozen shoulder often have intense pain and severe loss of motion, and they have no other intrinsic or extrinsic shoulder condition that would limit motion or function.

The difficulty of defining frozen shoulder has contributed to uncertainty about its pathogenesis and incidence. Frozen shoulder was recognized as early as 1872. Codman first used the term in 1934 to describe a syndrome of shoulder pain with restriction of elevation and external rotation, although he did not identify the etiology of the condition.[1] It is now clear that frozen shoulder can be a primary or a secondary disorder.

Idiopathic, or primary, frozen shoulder is defined as a significant limitation of active and passive motion in all planes, with an unknown etiology.[2] The term adhesive capsulitis is sometimes used to identify frozen shoulder. However, this term implies the presence of an inflammation of the shoulder capsule with joint adhesions, which has not been found in patients with frozen shoulder. The term idiopathic or primary frozen shoulder is therefore preferred.

## Etiology

The etiology of frozen shoulder is not well understood. An examination of contracted capsular biopsy specimens led Neviaser in 1945 to describe frozen shoulder as an inflammatory condition,[3] although other researchers have questioned his conclusion. The dense fibroblast and myofibroblast cells interposed with collagen material found in capsular specimens are more consistent with a capsular fibrosis similar to Dupuytren disease.[4-6]

Contracture of the coracohumeral ligament and rotator interval tissue is increasingly recognized in association with frozen shoulder. The rotator cuff interval is the triangular space bordered medially by the coracoid, inferiorly by the upper edge of the subscapularis, and superiorly by the anterior edge of the supraspinatus.

Capsular tissue and coracohumeral and superior glenohumeral ligament tissue lie in the interval.[7] Contracture of the coracohumeral ligament limits external rotation of the shoulder when the arm is at the side. The presence of contracted tissue in the rotator cuff interval is believed to lead to severe loss of motion, especially external rotation. Contracture and thickening of the coracohumeral ligament of the rotator cuff interval are pathognomonic for frozen shoulder.

Fibrosis of the rotator cuff interval tissue in patients with frozen shoulder is consistent with severe limitation of motion. However, other pathology remains unexplained. The intra-articular synovitis found during the acute pain phase does not clearly match any of the associated fibrotic diseases, which are usually painless in their early stages. It is possible that the etiology and histology of frozen shoulder vary between groups of patients.

## Associated Disease Processes

Several medical conditions have been associated with idiopathic frozen shoulder, including systemic diseases such as diabetes, cardiac disease, and hypothyroidism, as well as other medical conditions such as ipsilateral arm trauma.[8] The reported incidence of frozen shoulder in patients with diabetes is 10% to 36%. The nature of the strong association between frozen shoulder and diabetes is not understood. Patients with insulin-dependent diabetes tend to have more severe limitation of motion and are more resistant to nonsurgical treatment than patients with non–insulin-dependent diabetes.[9]

## Diagnosis

Idiopathic frozen shoulder appears to progress through three phases, which are identified as acute pain or inflammation, severe stiffness or fibrosis, and residual impairment. Although some patients recall a relatively trivial event in which the shoulder was strained or injured, the onset of pain is usually insidious. During the acute pain phase, patients often have disabling night pain that interferes with sleep, and the pain can be difficult to control. Physical examination reveals a global limitation of active and passive motion, with significant loss of external rotation. The end points of motion are firm, and capsular stretching causes severe pain. The shoulder may be diffusely tender to palpation, and gentle motion may be difficult to tolerate, even with the arm at the side. The patient's strength may be limited because of pain. The pain often radiates into the strap muscles of the neck, the upper and lower trapezius, the anterior shoulder muscles, and the upper arm. Scapular motion is dyskinetic, and nonneurologic winging is frequently observed.

As the acute pain phase diminishes, patients are left with a stiff shoulder and pain at the end points of motion. Shoulder motion improves gradually, often over several weeks or months. Even though the outcome of nonsurgical treatment is usually considered to be satisfactory, on objective examination most patients continue to have some limitation in motion after several months. Follow-up of more than 2 years found that 50% of patients diagnosed with frozen shoulder had residual mild pain, stiffness, or both.[10]

Other causes of shoulder stiffness must be ruled out during the process of making the diagnosis. Frozen shoulder can be confused with numerous other conditions; the symptoms occur in patients who have rotator cuff tearing, fracture, glenohumeral arthritis, or postsurgical arthrofibrosis. However, the loss of motion in idiopathic frozen shoulder by definition occurs in the absence of any other joint pathology and is associated with relatively normal radiographic studies.

Standard radiographs should be obtained to rule out other pathology that would limit motion, such as glenohumeral arthritis or an underlying articular deformity. If physical examination findings are consistent with frozen shoulder and radiographic findings are negative, advanced imaging studies are not necessary for diagnosis. Arthrography of the affected shoulder may reveal obliteration of the inferior pouch and subscapular recess, as well as diminished capsular volume. MRI may reveal diminished capsular volume with thickening of the coracohumeral ligament and abnormalities similar to synovitis at the superior border of the subscapularis tendon.[11] In addition, MRI can be used to assess for an intra-articular deformity.

## Nonsurgical Treatment
### Medications
Although nonsteroidal anti-inflammatory drugs are often prescribed during the acute pain phase, their effect is usually limited. Oral narcotic drugs can be used in the short term for pain control, especially at night. Oral corticosteroids also have been used in an attempt to control pain. Patients treated with oral corticosteroids and physical therapy were compared with patients treated with physical therapy only. Night pain improved more

rapidly in the patients treated with oral corticosteroids; there were no differences between the two patient groups in pain at rest or with motion.[12]

Corticosteroid injections into the intra-articular glenohumeral or subacromial space have been routinely used. Well-designed randomized controlled studies have found that intra-articular injections decreased pain in the short term compared with physical therapy alone.[13] There was no difference after 16 weeks between patients who had received a corticosteroid injection and those who had received a placebo injection.

The use of corticosteroids in patients with diabetes is of concern. Elevated blood glucose levels have been observed with relatively high dosages of oral corticosteroids. The effect of intra-articular injections on blood glucose has not been well defined. In one small study, frequent examination of 18 patients over a 2-week period found no significant effect of intra-artcular corticosteriod injection on blood glucose levels.[14]

Although patients respond favorably to corticosteroid injections, the accuracy of non–image-enhanced injections into the intra-articular or subacromial space has been called into question. Studies have found that only 70% of injections into the subacromial space without radiographic guidance were correctly placed,[15] and only 27% of intra-articular glenohumeral injections were correctly placed.[16] This lack of accuracy has stimulated interest in using fluoroscopy or ultrasonography for guiding injection placement.[17,18] A randomized study compared the short-term outcomes of injections administered into the subacromial space, with or without ultrasonographic guidance. Patients whose injection was placed with ultrasonographic guidance had significantly less pain and better function.[18]

### Brisement
Brisement is a procedure designed to distend the shoulder capsule in patients with frozen shoulder. It has been described for use in the physician's office.[19,20] Intra-articular injection of a local anesthetic is followed by distention of the shoulder capsule using a saline and corticosteroid injection. The results of this procedure are promising, but they have been examined only in poorly controlled studies with a limited number of patients.

### Physical Therapy
For decades, the principal treatment for frozen shoulder has been physical therapy using gentle stretching. Excellent clinical results have been reported.[21] However, a satisfactory return of motion often requires several months and sometimes as much as 1 year of treatment. In a study of 62 patients at a minimum of 2 years after treatment, the average range of motion was 157° of forward elevation, 65° of external rotation, and internal

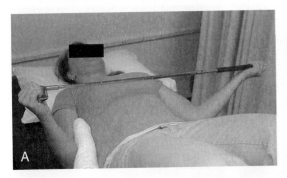

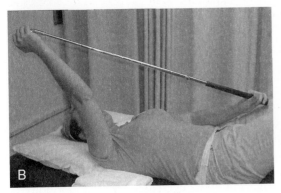

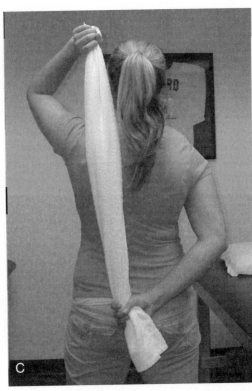

**Figure 1** Simple home-based exercises allow progress at the patient's own pace, are easy to teach, and are effective in the treatment of frozen shoulder. Objects such as a golf club or towel can be used to facilitate external rotation (A), elevation (B), and internal rotation (C).

rotation to the fifth thoracic vertebra. However, 30% of patients had residual limitation of motion compared with the contralateral shoulder; the limitation was in external rotation in half of these patients.[22] Other studies found similar limitations and deficiencies using validated outcomes measures such as the Disabilities of the Arm, Shoulder and Hand Questionnaire, although 90% of patients reported a satisfactory outcome.[23]

Controlled studies of the effect of physical therapy on long-term outcome are difficult to assess because the results of physical therapy are usually combined with those of other treatments. Some studies have concluded that improvement is more rapid with supervised therapy,[17] and others have recommended the use of home-based therapy only (Figure 1). In a prospective study of 77 patients with idiopathic frozen shoulder followed for 24 months, patients were treated with intense physical therapy, which included manual stretching and passive motion, or with supervised neglect, which included a gentle home exercise program with stretching only to pain tolerance.[23] Surprisingly, the patients treated with supervised neglect had a better outcome, based on the Constant score; 89% had a satisfactory outcome, compared with 63% of the patients treated with intense therapy.

## Surgical Treatment

Surgical treatment is indicated for a motivated patient who has recalcitrant shoulder stiffness after 6 to 12 months of nonsurgical treatment. Frozen shoulder should not be surgically treated during the acute pain (inflammation) phase.

### Manipulation Under Anesthesia

Gentle manipulation of the shoulder under anesthesia has for many years been a mainstay of surgical treatment. Of 19 patients examined at a mean 15 years after the initial procedure, 16 had no pain, and only 1 required subsequent shoulder surgery.[24] Although most of the numerous studies of shoulder manipulation reported favorable outcomes, a study of shoulder manipulation combined with corticosteroid injection found that approximately 40% of patients had moderate or severe disability 3 months after manipulation.[25] Many studies report the results of manipulation in association with the results of other treatments, leading to difficulty in assessing the efficacy of manipulation alone. However, a study of the outcomes of 24 patients after manipulation of the shoulder with or without a corticosteroid injection found no significant difference in pain or range of motion.[26]

Most researchers agree that manipulation should be gentle and should include stabilization of the scapula using a short lever arm on the humerus. Abduction, external rotation, and internal rotation are slowly and gradually increased. The surgeon typically feels tearing of the capsular structures, and motion is restored during the procedure. In a smaller number of patients, the capsule is stretched with no palpable tearing. There is no known difference in the outcome of tearing or stretching of the capsule, if motion is restored.

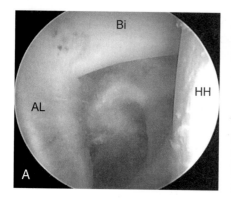
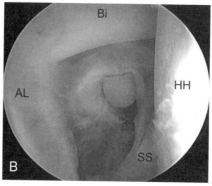
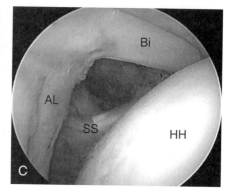

**Figure 2** The intra-articular anterior view of the shoulder from the posterior viewing portal. **A,** Obliteration of the rotator cuff interval and dense tissue formation can be seen. The subscapularis is obscured by fibrosis of the rotator cuff interval and the anterior labrum (AL); the superior glenohumeral ligament is adhesed and confluent with the rotator cuff interval. Bi = biceps tendon, HH = humeral head. **B,** An ablation device has been inserted into the anterior midglenoid portal. The subscapularis (SS) has been defined, and resection of the rotator cuff interval has begun. **C,** The entire rotator cuff interval has been excised, and the subscapularis and anterior labrum are well defined. The patient had complete freedom of external rotation after excision.

Shoulders undergoing manipulation under anesthesia were arthroscopically examined after motion was restored to assess the structural damage to the shoulder resulting from the procedure.[27] Twelve of the 30 patients had new damage to the shoulder, including a superior labrum anterior and posterior (SLAP) lesion in 4, anterior labral detachment in 4 (1 of whom had an osteochondral defect), partial subscapularis tearing in 3, and middle glenohumeral ligament tearing in 2. None of the patients had a fracture or nerve injury. Manipulation of the shoulder probably leads to tearing only of the inferior capsular pouch and does not selectively release the contracted rotator cuff interval. The effect of damage to the shoulder during manipulation is not well understood.

## Open Surgery

Open surgical treatment for frozen shoulder has been used successfully after failed manipulation.[6] A deltopectoral incision is preferred for maximum visualization. The subacromial space is defined, and any subdeltoid adhesions are released with care to protect the axillary nerve laterally. The biceps is identified as it tracks laterally through the bicipital groove, and the coracoid can be palpated medially. Both are useful landmarks in identifying the rotator cuff interval. The rotator cuff interval and coracohumeral ligament are excised to restore external rotation. If the subscapularis continues to be immobile, a Z-plasty of the subscapularis is performed, and the anterior capsule of the shoulder is separated. Inferior and posterior capsulotomy may be necessary to restore abduction and internal rotation, respectively. If dissection of the inferior capsule or complete release of the subscapularis is necessary, care should be taken to dissect the axillary nerve, which may be adhering to the densely contracted capsular tissue.

## Arthroscopic Surgery

Arthroscopic capsular release has become an important surgical treatment for frozen shoulder, although it was once considered an ancillary procedure with little diagnostic or therapeutic benefit.[28] The procedure is minimally invasive and offers decreased surgical morbidity, a shorter hospital stay, and decreased postsurgical pain, with significant gains in motion and pain relief. However, arthroscopic capsular release can be difficult and should be performed only by a surgeon with expertise in shoulder arthroscopy.

The arthroscopic release technique has been well described.[29-31] Presurgical communication with the anesthesiologist regarding hypotensive anesthesia can help minimize intrasurgical bleeding. Patient positioning is dependent on surgeon preference. Gaining access to the joint can be difficult, requiring care to avoid iatrogenic injury to the chondral surfaces. Insufflation of the joint with saline helps to distract the joint space before the working cannulas are inserted. A smaller blunt metal trocar and cannula can be used through the typical posterior portal and followed by dilation of the portal to allow the larger cannulas to be introduced.

Visualization can be difficult because of the constrained capsular volume; the biceps tendon serves as the key surgical landmark to delineate the superior aspect of the rotator cuff interval (Figure 2). An anterior portal is established in the rotator cuff interval, and a shaver is used to excise the inflamed synovium that is usually adhering to the anterosuperior aspect of the joint.

A needle-tip cautery device is used to release the coracohumeral ligament and the rotator cuff interval. The subscapularis is usually engulfed in thickly adhering interval tissue and can be difficult to define. A 70° arthroscope is useful when incision of the interval is carried down to the level of the superior aspect of the subscapularis. Incision of the rotator cuff interval is usually sufficient to release the subscapularis and allow external rotation to be restored. If deficits remain, the anterior capsular structures, including the middle glenohumeral ligament, should also be released (to the 5-o'clock position in a right shoulder).

Internal rotation contractures are addressed by release of the posterior capsule. The arthroscope is placed into the anterior portal, and needle-tip cautery is used to divide the posterior capsule from the level of the biceps to the posteroinferior glenohumeral ligament. Care should be taken to avoid damage to the superficially located infraspinatus muscle.

Gentle manipulation usually provides a palpable tearing of the remaining inferior capsule, restoring full range of motion. Arthroscopic dissection of the inferior capsule risks injury to the axillary nerve, which in cadaver specimens was located an average of only 12.4 mm to the glenoid rim at the 6-o'clock position and only 2.5 mm deep to the inferior capsular structures.[32] This anatomy is distorted in patients with frozen shoulder, who often have thickening of the capsular and ligamentous tissues.

## Summary

Most patients with idiopathic frozen shoulder can be treated nonsurgically, using a combination of intra-articular corticosteroid injections and gentle passive physical therapy. Although the result is usually satisfactory, the time required for maximal outcome can be as much as 1 year. The residual functional deficits can be substantial, despite diminished pain. Manipulation under anesthesia is effective for pain relief and provides durable gains in motion. If manipulation is unsuccessful, systematic arthroscopic capsular release has proved to be safe and effective.

## Annotated References

1. Codman EA: Tendinitis of the short rotators, in *The Shoulder: Rupture of the Supraspinatus Tendon and Other Lesions in or About the Subacromial Bursa.* Boston, MA, Thomas Todd and Co, 1934, pp 216-234.

2. Zuckerman JD, Cuomo F: Frozen shoulder, in Matsen FA III, Fu FH, Hawkins RJ (eds): *The Shoulder: A Balance of Mobility and Stability.* Rosemont, IL, American Academy of Orthopaedic Surgeons, 1993, pp 253-267.

3. Neviaser JS: Adhesive capsulitis of the shoulder. *J Bone Joint Surg Am* 1945;27:211-222.

4. Bunker TD, Anthony PP: The pathology of frozen shoulder: A Dupuytren-like disease. *J Bone Joint Surg Br* 1995;77:677-683.

5. Omari A, Bunker TD: Open surgical release for frozen shoulder: Surgical findings and results of the release. *J Shoulder Elbow Surg* 2001;10:353-357.

   Twenty-five patients had open surgical treatment of primary frozen shoulder. Pathologic specimens revealed obliteration of the rotator cuff interval and thickening of the coracohumeral ligament with a dense matrix of type III collagen, fibroblasts, and myofibroblasts. Good or excellent results were noted in 20 patients.

6. Ozaki J, Nakagawa Y, Sakurai G, Tamai S: Recalcitrant chronic adhesive capsulitis of the shoulder: Role of contracture of the coracohumeral ligament and rotator interval in pathogenesis and treatment. *J Bone Joint Surg Am* 1989;71:1511-1515.

7. Jost B, Koch PP, Gerber C: Anatomy and functional aspects of the rotator interval. *J Shoulder Elbow Surg* 2000;9:336-341.

8. Reeves B: The natural history of the frozen shoulder syndrome. *Scand J Rheumatol* 1975;4:193-196.

9. Massoud SN, Pearse EO, Levy O, Copeland SA: Operative management of the frozen shoulder in patients with diabetes. *J Shoulder Elbow Surg* 2002;11: 609-613.

   The treatment of 43 diabetic patients with recalcitrant primary frozen shoulder was reviewed at a mean 35 months. Patients with type I diabetes were more likely to require arthroscopic release than patients with type II diabetes.

10. Shaffer B, Tibone JE, Kerlan RK: Frozen shoulder: A long-term follow-up. *J Bone Joint Surg Am* 1992;74: 738-746.

11. Mengiardi B, Pfirrmann CW, Gerber C, Hodler J, Zanetti M: Frozen shoulder: MR arthrographic findings. *Radiology* 2004;233:486-492.

    Magnetic resonance arthrograms of 22 patients with frozen shoulder were compared with those of matched control subjects. Thickening of the coracohumeral ligament and rotator cuff interval, as well as obliteration of the fat triangle between the coracohumeral ligament and the coracoid process, were findings characteristic of frozen shoulder.

12. Binder A, Hazleman BL, Parr G, Roberts S: A controlled study of oral prednisolone in frozen shoulder. *Br J Rheumatol* 1986;25:288-292.

13. Ryans I, Montgomery A, Galway R, Kernohan WG, McKane R: A randomized controlled trial of intra-articular triamcinolone and/or physiotherapy in shoulder capsulitis. *Rheumatology (Oxford)* 2005;44: 529-535.

    Eighty patients with frozen shoulder were examined in a randomized, placebo-controlled trial to compare outcomes after treatment with triamcinolone injection and physical therapy. At 6 weeks, pain and function were improved in patients receiving injection and therapy. At 16 weeks, both groups had improved similarly.

14. Amoretti N, Grimaud A, Brocq O, et al: Shoulder distension arthrography in adhesive capsulitis. *Clin Imaging* 2006;30:254-256.

    The results of 27 patients were examined after capsular distention for frozen shoulder.

15. Yamakado K: The targeting accuracy of subacromial injection to the shoulder: An arthrographic evaluation. *Arthroscopy* 2002;18:887-891.

    "Blind" subacromial injection was accurate in only 70% of shoulders. Accurate subacromial and intradeltoid injections offered comparable pain relief.

16. Sethi PM, Kingston S, ElAttrache N: Accuracy of anterior intra-articular injection of the glenohumeral joint. *Arthroscopy* 2005;21:77-80.

    This study assessed the accuracy of anterior intra-articular shoulder injections without radiologic assistance in 41 awake patients. Only 26.8% of attempted anteriorly placed injections were actually intra-articular.

17. Carette S, Moffet H, Tardif J, et al: Intra-articular corticosteroids, supervised physiotherapy, or a combination of the two in the treatment of adhesive capsulitis of the shoulder: A placebo-controlled trial. *Arthritis Rheum* 2003;48:829-838.

    A combination of intra-articular injection and home-based physical therapy was found effective for improvement of shoulder pain and disability in patients with frozen shoulder. Supervised physical therapy and injection provided faster improvement in shoulder range of motion.

18. Naredo E, Cabero F, Beneyto P, et al: A randomized comparative study of short term response to blind injection versus sonographic-guided injection of local corticosteroids in patients with painful shoulder. *J Rheumatol* 2004;31:308-314.

    Forty-one patients were examined in a prospective, blinded, randomized comparison of intra-articular injection and sonography-guided cortisone injection. Six weeks after injection, pain and function were significantly improved in patients who underwent guided injection.

19. Callinan N, McPherson S, Cleaveland S, Voss DG, Rainville D, Tokar N: Effectiveness of hydroplasty and therapeutic exercise for treatment of frozen shoulder. *J Hand Ther* 2003;16:219-224.

    Sixty patients with frozen shoulder who underwent hydroplasty with physical therapy were reviewed retrospectively. Distention of the glenohumeral joint was achieved with a 10-mL injection of a combination of bupivacaine, lidocaine, and corticosteroid followed by an injection of 30 mL of chilled sterile normal saline. Gains in all planes of motion were noted, with only 3% of patients having continued night pain.

20. Fareed DO, Gallivan WR Jr: Office management of frozen shoulder syndrome: Treatment with hydraulic distension under local anesthesia. *Clin Orthop Relat Res* 1989;242:177-183.

21. Miller MD, Wirth MA, Rockwood CA Jr: Thawing the frozen shoulder: The "patient" patient. *Orthopedics* 1996;19:849-853.

22. Griggs SM, Ahn A, Green A: Idiopathic adhesive capsulitis: A prospective functional outcome study of nonoperative treatment. *J Bone Joint Surg Am* 2000;82-A:1398-1407.

23. Diercks RL, Stevens M: Gentle thawing of the frozen shoulder: A prospective study of supervised neglect versus intensive physical therapy in seventy-seven patients with frozen shoulder syndrome followed up for two years. *J Shoulder Elbow Surg* 2004;13:499-502.

    Seventy-seven patients with idiopathic frozen shoulder were examined prospectively to compare intensive physical therapy with exercise within the limit of pain (supervised neglect). Supervised neglect yielded better pain relief and motion than intensive physical therapy.

24. Farrell CM, Sperling JW, Cofield RH: Manipulation for frozen shoulder: Long-term results. *J Shoulder Elbow Surg* 2005;14:480-484.

    Nineteen frozen shoulders were evaluated at an average 15 years after manipulation under anesthesia. Patients had significant improvement in elevation and external rotation; 16 had little or no pain, and 18 required no further surgery. The average American Shoulder and Elbow Surgeons Index score was 80.

25. Dodenhoff RM, Levy O, Wilson A, Copeland SA: Manipulation under anesthesia for primary frozen shoulder: Effect on early recovery and return to activity. *J Shoulder Elbow Surg* 2000;9:23-26.

26. Kivimaki J, Pohjolainen T: Manipulation under anesthesia for frozen shoulder with and without steroid injection. *Arch Phys Med Rehabil* 2001;82:1188-1190.

    Twenty-four patients underwent manipulation of a frozen shoulder. Twelve also had a corticosteroid injection. Injection with lidocaine and betamethasone did not enhance the effect of manipulation.

27. Loew M, Heichel TO, Lehner B: Intraarticular lesions in primary frozen shoulder after manipulation under general anesthesia. *J Shoulder Elbow Surg* 2005;14:16-21.

    Thirty shoulders with primary frozen shoulder underwent manipulation under anesthesia followed by arthroscopic assessment. Hemarthrosis occurred in all shoulders with capsular tearing. Four had a new SLAP lesion, four had anterior labral detachment (one with osteochondral damage), three had a partial subscapularis tear, and two had a middle glenohumeral ligament tear.

28. Neviaser RJ, Neviaser TJ: The frozen shoulder: Diagnosis and management. *Clin Orthop Relat Res* 1987;223:59-64.

29. Jerosch J: 360 degrees arthroscopic capsular release in patients with adhesive capsulitis of the glenohu-

meral joint: Indication, surgical technique, results. *Knee Surg Sports Traumatol Arthrosc* 2001;9: 178-186.

Twenty-eight patients with primary frozen shoulder had arthroscopic capsular release. Functional outcomes and range of motion in all planes improved significantly.

30. Pollock RG, Duralde XA, Flatow EL, Bigliani LU: The use of arthroscopy in the treatment of resistant frozen shoulder. *Clin Orthop Relat Res* 1994;304: 30-36.

31. Warner JJ, Allen A, Marks PH, Wong P: Arthroscopic release for chronic, refractory adhesive capsulitis of

the shoulder. *J Bone Joint Surg Am* 1996;78:1808-1816.

32. Price MR, Tillett ED, Acland RD, Nettleton GS: Determining the relationship of the axillary nerve to the shoulder joint capsule from an arthroscopic perspective. *J Bone Joint Surg Am* 2004;86:2135-2142.

An anatomic study of nine cadaver shoulders found that the average distance between the axillary nerve and the midportion of the glenoid rim was 12.4 mm. The average distance between the axillary nerve and the inferior glenohumeral ligament (capsule) was only 2.5 mm.

# Chapter 54

# Anesthesia and Analgesia for Shoulder and Elbow Surgery

Terese T. Horlocker, MD

## Introduction

Regional techniques for anesthesia are well suited to shoulder and elbow surgical procedures. To provide postsurgical analgesia and allow early limb mobilization, continuous catheter techniques can be used. Although the benefits of regional anesthesia are well established for patients undergoing shoulder or elbow surgery, the surgical site may be adjacent to neural structures, as in total shoulder arthroplasty or fixation of a proximal humerus fracture. Thus, the management of anesthesia and analgesia is in part based on the patient's evolving neurologic status and must take into account the need for perisurgical serial neurologic examinations, which are not possible in the presence of a regional block. The patient's anticipated rehabilitation goals and any history of adverse effects or interaction with systemic analgesia must also be considered. Meticulous regional anesthesia technique, careful patient positioning, and serial neurologic examinations are necessary to reduce the incidence of neurologic dysfunction and optimize the surgical outcome.

## Intrasurgical Anesthesia Management
### Shoulder and Upper Arm Surgery

Surgery involving the shoulder and humerus can be performed under regional or general anesthesia.[1] Reconstructive shoulder surgery, including total shoulder arthroplasty and rotator cuff repair, presents the anesthesiologist with unique management and positioning considerations. Interscalene or supraclavicular brachial plexus blockade alone can provide excellent surgical anesthesia with careful positioning and appropriate sedation (Figures 1 and 2). However, general anesthesia, or a combination of general and regional anesthesia, is often chosen because access to the patient's airway is limited during surgical procedures involving the shoulder and upper arm. An interscalene block can be administered before the surgical incision is performed or after postsurgical determination of upper extremity neurologic function. A presurgical interscalene block reduces the intrasurgical requirement for volatile anesthetic and

opioids and, in theory, provides preemptive analgesia; however, postsurgical evaluation of neurologic function cannot be performed until resolution of the block. Interscalene block produces ipsilateral diaphragmatic paresis and a 25% loss of pulmonary function for the duration of the block, and its use is therefore contraindicated in patients with severe pulmonary disease.[2-4]

Advances in needle, catheter, and nerve stimulator technology have improved the ability to localize neural structures and have led to higher success rates. The selection of a regional technique depends on the surgical site. The interscalene approach is preferred for use in shoulder surgery because it is the most proximal technique (Figure 1). In contrast, the more distal supraclavicular (Figure 2), infraclavicular, or axillary (Figure 3) approach is preferred for elbow surgery to provide adequate blockade of the lower trunk, which is not blocked with the interscalene technique. Single-injection brachial plexus techniques have been used. However, the

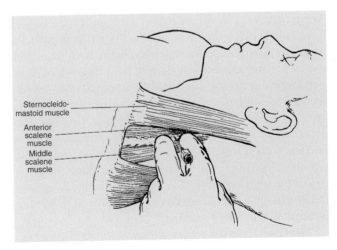

**Figure 1** Administration of an interscalene block. The fingers palpate the interscalene groove, and a 22- to 25-gauge, 4-cm needle is inserted perpendicular to the skin at a 45° caudad and slightly posterior angle until a paresthesia (usually C5 and C6 dermatomes) or nerve stimulator response is elicited. This response usually occurs at a superficial level. Thirty mL of local anesthetic is injected. *(Reproduced with permission from Wedel DJ, Horlocker TT: Nerve blocks, in Miller RD [ed]: Miller's Anesthesia, ed 6. New York, NY, Churchill Livingstone, 2005, pp 1685-1717.)*

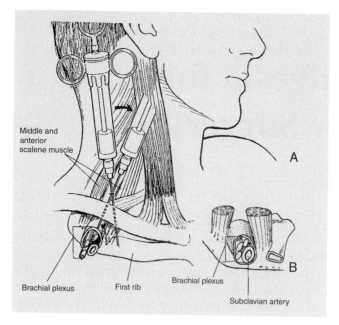

**Figure 2** **A,** Administration of a supraclavicular block. The interscalene groove is identified at the clavicular level, typically 1.5 to 2.0 cm posterior to the midpoint of the clavicle; the subclavian artery is palpated to confirm the landmark. A 22-gauge, 4-cm needle is directed in a caudad, slightly medial, and posterior direction until a paresthesia or motor response is elicited or the first rib is encountered. If the first rib is encountered without elicitation of a paresthesia, the needle can be systematically walked anteriorly and posteriorly along the rib until the plexus or the subclavian artery is located. Location of the artery provides a useful landmark; the needle can be withdrawn and reinserted in a more posterolateral direction, usually resulting in a paresthesia or motor response. Upon localization of the brachial plexus, 20 to 30 mL of solution is injected. **B,** The upper, middle, and lower trunks are compactly arranged at the level of the first rib. *(Reproduced with permission from Wedel DJ, Horlocker TT: Nerve blocks, in Miller RD [ed]: Miller's Anesthesia, ed 6. New York, NY, Churchill Livingstone, 2005, pp 1685-1717.)*

duration of effect may not be sufficient to substantially improve analgesia or outcome.[5-7]

### Nerve Injury

Interscalene block should be used with caution in patients who have preexisting brachial plexopathy because of the risk of perisurgical exacerbation of neurologic deficits. A postsurgical neurologic deficit is documented in 4% of patients who undergo total shoulder arthroplasty, and the brachial plexus is injured in 3% of these patients. The nerve injury is at the level of the nerve trunks, which is also the level at which an interscalene block is performed. It is therefore impossible to determine whether the etiology of the injury is surgical or anesthesia related. Such an injury usually is a neurapraxia and is resolved in 90% of patients within 3 to 4 months.[8]

Nerve injury often occurs in association with upper extremity trauma. Radial nerve palsy is identified in as many as 20% of patients with a humeral shaft fracture. Injury to the axillary nerve and brachial plexus is associated with a proximal humerus fracture. The significant incidence of neurologic deficits is an important reason for clinical examination before administration of regional anesthesia.

### Patient Positioning

Shoulder and upper arm surgical procedures are typically performed using the beach chair position, in which the patient is placed in a 10° to 20° reverse Trendelenburg position to promote venous return, with flexion at the hips and knees. The patient is shifted laterally to the edge of the operating table to allow unrestricted surgical access to the upper extremity. The patient's hips must be secured to prevent unnecessary lateral movement, and the head and neck must be firmly supported by the operating table and secured in a neutral position; excessive rotation or flexion of the head away from the surgical side results in a stretch injury to the brachial plexus. Care also must be taken to avoid pressure on the eyes and ears. Access to the patient's face and airway is limited after surgical draping, and therefore all airway connections should be tightened and possibly reinforced with tape. Hypotension and bradycardia, which occur in as many as 20% of patients, can be minimized by gradually moving the patient into the beach chair position, providing adequate hydration, and administering atropine or β-blockade.

A tourniquet cannot be used during a proximal upper extremity surgical procedure, and significant blood loss may occur. Arterial cannulation may be helpful for direct blood pressure measurement and hemoglobin concentration monitoring during total shoulder arthroplasty or reduction of a humerus fracture. In theory, a venous air embolism can occur during a shoulder procedure because the surgical site is higher than the heart; however, this complication has not been reported in the literature. To allow prompt diagnosis and treatment of a venous air embolism, patients with a documented right-to-left shunt may be monitored with precordial Doppler ultrasonography or transesophageal echocardiography.

### Elbow Surgery

Surgical procedures involving the distal humerus, elbow, or forearm are commonly performed under regional anesthesia. The supraclavicular, infraclavicular, and axillary approaches to the brachial plexus are reliable and provide consistent anesthesia to the four major nerves (median, ulnar, radial, and musculocutaneous; Figure 3). However, a small but definite risk of pneumothorax is associated with a supraclavicular block, and it is therefore unsuitable for use in an outpatient procedure. Pneumothorax typically occurs 6 to 12 hours after hospital discharge, so a postsurgical chest radiograph is not helpful. To eliminate the need for hospital readmission, the lung may be reexpanded using a small Teflon catheter under fluoroscopic guidance. Chest tube placement is advised for a pneumothorax larger than 20% of lung volume. An infraclavicular or axillary approach to the brachial plexus eliminates the risk of a pneumothorax and provides reliably adequate anesthesia for surgery near the elbow.[8]

## Postsurgical Analgesia

Patients undergoing major upper extremity surgery experience substantial postsurgical pain. Lack of adequate postsurgical analgesia impedes early physical therapy and rapid rehabilitation, which are important for maintaining joint range of motion and facilitating hospital discharge. Analgesia after major upper extremity surgery has typically been provided through an intravenous patient-controlled analgesia (PCA) device. However, opioids administered through a PCA device do not consistently provide adequate pain relief, and they often cause sedation, constipation, pruritus, and nausea and vomiting. Recent clinical studies have consistently reported that, compared with systemic opioids, a continuous brachial plexus block provides a superior quality of analgesia and a better surgical outcome, with fewer adverse effects.[5,9,10] These reports suggest that continuous peripheral techniques may be the optimal analgesic method after major shoulder or elbow surgery. Appreciation of the indications, benefits, and adverse effects of both conventional and novel analgesic approaches is paramount for maximizing rehabilitation and patient satisfaction.

### Multimodal Analgesia

Not surprisingly, the efficacy and adverse effects of analgesic therapy are major determinants of patient satisfaction. In a prospective survey of 10,811 patients, moderate or severe postsurgical pain and severe nausea and vomiting were associated with patient dissatisfaction, after adjusting for patient and surgical factors.[11] Multimodal analgesia is a multidisciplinary approach to pain management. The goal is to maximize the positive aspects of the treatment while limiting adverse effects. Because many of the adverse effects of analgesic therapy are both opioid related and dose dependent, limiting perisurgical opioid use is an important principle of mul-

timodal analgesia. The use of single-injection and continuous brachial plexus techniques, with a combination of opioid and nonopioid analgesic agents for breakthrough pain, offers superior pain control, attenuation of the stress response, and a decreased need for opioids.

### Conventional Opioid Analgesia
#### Parenteral Opioids

Despite their common, well-defined adverse effects, opioid analgesics are widely used for postsurgical pain relief. Systemic opioids can be administered orally, intravenously, or intramuscularly. Current analgesia regimens typically use intravenous PCA during the first 24 to

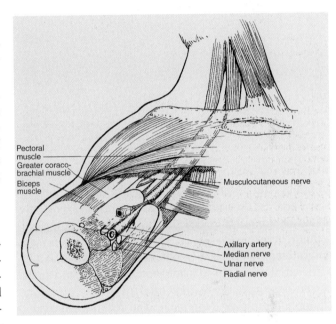

**Figure 3** Administration of an axillary block. The arm is abducted at a right angle to the body, and the axillary artery is identified. Proximal needle placement and maintenance of distal digital pressure facilitate the proximal spread of the local anesthetic. Several methods of identifying the brachial plexus, including transarterial injection and elicitation of paresthesia or motor response, are reported to have good results. In general, the use of multiple injections (identifying more than one peripheral nerve) can shorten the onset of anesthesia and increase blockade reliability. *(Reproduced with permission from Wedel DJ, Horlocker TT: Nerve blocks, in Miller RD [ed]: Miller's Anesthesia, ed 6. New York, NY, Churchill Livingstone, 2005, pp 1685-1717.)*

**Table 1 | Intravenous Opioids Used in Patient-Controlled Analgesia**

| Analgesic | Bolus Dose | Lockout Interval | 4-Hour Maximum Dosage | Infusion Rate* |
|---|---|---|---|---|
| Fentanyl | 10-20 µg | 5-10 min | 300 µg | 20-100 µg/h |
| Hydromorphone | 0.1-0.2 mg | 5-10 min | 3 mg | 0.1-0.2 mg/h |
| Meperidine | 5-25 mg | 5-10 min | 200 mg[†] | 5-15 mg/h |
| Morphine sulfate | 0.5-2.5 mg | 5-10 min | 30 mg | 1-10 mg/h |

*A background infusion is not recommended for opioid-naïve patients.
[†]In a healthy patient, meperidine dosage should be limited to 800 mg during the first 24 h and 600 mg every 24 h thereafter.
(Data from Horlocker TT: Anesthesia and pain management, in Berry DJ, Trousdale RT, Dennis D, Paprosky W (eds): Revision Hip and Knee Arthroplasty. Philadelphia, PA, Lippincott Williams and Wilkins, 2008.)

**Table 2 | Oral Opioid Analgesics**

| Analgesic | Dose | Dosing Interval | Maximum Daily Dosage | Comments |
|---|---|---|---|---|
| Extended-release oxycodone | 10-20 mg | 12 h | | Limited to total of four doses to avoid accumulation and opioid-related adverse effects. |
| Extended-release morphine | 15-30 mg | 8-12 h | | Limited to total of four doses to avoid accumulation and opioid-related adverse effects. |
| Oxycodone | 5-10 mg | 4-6 h | | Oxycodone-acetaminophen and oxycodone-aspirin combination products also available.* |
| Hydromorphone | 2-4 mg | 4-6 h | | Also available as suppository (3 mg), with 6-8 h effect. |
| Hydrocodone | 5-10 mg | 4-6 h | | All preparations contain acetaminophen.* |
| Codeine | 30-60 mg | 4 h | | Codeine-acetaminophen and codeine-aspirin combination products also available.* |
| Propoxyphene | 50-100 mg | 4-6 h | 600 mg | Propoxyphene-acetaminophen and propoxyphene-aspirin combination products also available.* |
| Tramadol | 50-100 mg | 6 h | 400 mg (lower for patient with renal or hepatic disease) | Tramadol-acetaminophen combination also available.* |

*Dosage of combination products is limited by maximum acetaminophen or aspirin dosage.*

*(Data from Lennon RL, Horlocker TT (eds): Mayo Clinic Analgesic Pathway: Peripheral Nerve Blockade for Major Orthopedic Surgery. Florence, KY, Mayo Clinic Scientific Press, Taylor and Francis Group, 2005.)*

48 hours after surgery, with subsequent oral administration. The PCA device can be programmed for several variables, including bolus dose, lockout interval, and background infusion (Table 1). The optimal bolus dose is determined by the relative potency of the opioid. An insufficient dose results in inadequate analgesia, and an excessive dose increases the potential for adverse effects, including respiratory depression. The lockout interval is determined based on the onset of analgesic effects. A too-short lockout interval allows the patient to self-administer an additional dose before achieving the full analgesic effect and may result in overdosing, but a too-long lockout interval prevents adequate analgesia. The optimal bolus dose and lockout interval are not known, although ranges have been determined. Varying the settings within these ranges appears to have little effect on analgesia or adverse effects. Most PCA devices allow a background infusion to be added. Although routine use of this feature in opioid-naïve adult patients is not recommended, a background opioid infusion may have a role for opioid-tolerant patients. Individual patient pain tolerance may require the PCA regimen to be adjusted to maximize the benefits and minimize the incidence of adverse effects.

Despite their ease of administration and titration, parenteral opioids may not provide adequate analgesia after major upper extremity surgery, particularly with movement (as demonstrated by patient pain scores in the moderate to severe range during the first 2 days after surgery).[6,10]

The adverse effects of opioid administration can be severe in patients who have undergone a major orthopaedic procedure. A systematic review of patients receiving opioid PCA reported gastrointestinal adverse effects (nausea, vomiting, ileus) in 37%, cognitive effects (somnolence and dizziness) in 34%, pruritus in 15%, urinary retention in 16%, and respiratory depression in 2%.[12]

### Oral Opioids

Oral opioids are available in immediate-release and controlled-release formulations (Table 2). Although immediate-release oral opioids are effective in relieving moderate or severe pain, they must be administered as often as every 4 hours. Interruption of the dosing schedule, particularly during the night, may lead to an increase in pain. Administration on an as-needed basis may lead to delays and a subsequent increase in pain. The US Agency for Healthcare Policy and Research guidelines for acute pain management recommend that a fixed dosing schedule be used for postsurgical opioid medication extending more than 48 hours.[13] The adverse effects of oral opioids are considerably fewer and less severe than those of intravenous opioids and are primarily gastrointestinal.[12]

A controlled-release formulation of oxycodone (OxyContin; Purdue Pharma, Norwalk, CT) provides a therapeutic opioid concentration and sustained pain relief over an extended period. Administration of controlled-release oxycodone for a period of 72 hours

### Table 3 | Nonopioid Analgesics

| Analgesic | Dose | Dosing Interval | Maximum Daily Dosage | Comments |
|---|---|---|---|---|
| Acetaminophen | 500-1,000 mg PO | 4-6 h | 4,000 mg | As effective as aspirin. Dosage of 1,000 mg is more effective than 650 mg in some patients. |
| Celecoxib | 400 mg initially, then 200 mg PO | 12 h | 800 mg | The only COX-2 inhibitor available in North America. |
| Aspirin | 325-1,000 mg PO | 4-6 h | 4,000 mg | The most potent antiplatelet effect. |
| Ibuprofen | 200-400 mg PO | 4-6 h | 3,200 mg | Dose of 200 mg is equal to 650 mg of aspirin or acetaminophen. |
| Naproxen | 500 mg PO | 12 h | 1,000 mg | Dose of 250 mg is equal to 650 mg of aspirin, with longer duration. |
| Ketorolac | 15-30 mg PO, IM, IV | 4-6 h | 60 mg (> 65 years); 120 mg (≤ 65 years) | Dose of 15 mg is comparable to 10 mg morphine. Dose should be reduced in patients < 50 kg or with renal impairment. Duration of administration should not exceed 5 days. |
| Tramadol | 50-100 mg PO | 6 h | 400 mg; lower for patient with renal or hepatic disease | A combination of tramadol and acetaminophen is available. |

*PO = orally, IM = intramuscularly, IV = intravenously.*

*(Data from Lennon RL and Horlocker TT (eds): Mayo Clinic Analgesic Pathway: Peripheral Blockade for Major Orthopaedic Surgery. Florence, KY, Mayo Clinic Scientific Press, Taylor and Francis Group, 2006.)*

after surgery improves analgesia and is associated with less sedation, vomiting, and sleep disturbance than oxycodone administered on a fixed-dose or as-needed basis.[14] Therefore, a multimodal analgesic approach may include scheduled administration of controlled-release oxycodone combined with as-needed administration of immediate-release oxycodone to relieve breakthrough pain. This regimen maximizes analgesic effect and decreases adverse effects.

## Nonopioid Analgesia

The addition of nonopioid analgesics to the postsurgical analgesic regimen reduces opioid use, improves analgesia, and decreases opioid-related adverse effects (Table 3). The multimodal effect is maximized by selecting analgesics that have complementary sites of action. For example, acetaminophen primarily acts centrally, and other nonsteroidal anti-inflammatory drugs (NSAIDs) have a peripheral effect.

### Acetaminophen

The mechanism of the analgesic action of acetaminophen has not been fully determined. It may act primarily by inhibiting prostaglandin synthesis in the central nervous system. Acetaminophen has very few adverse effects and is an important addition to the multimodal postsurgical pain regimen, although the total daily dosage must be limited to 4,000 mg. Acetaminophen should be administered on a schedule, rather than on an as-needed basis, to maximize its pharmacologic effects. Many oral analgesics consist of an opioid-acetaminophen combination (Table 2). In these preparations, the opioid dosage is restricted by the acetaminophen dosage.

### Nonsteroidal Anti-Inflammatory Drugs

NSAIDs act through the cyclooxygenase (COX) enzymatic pathway and ultimately block individual prostaglandin pathways. In general, NSAIDs block both the COX-1 and COX-2 pathways. The COX-1 pathway is involved in prostaglandin $E_2$–mediated gastric mucosal protection, as well as the thromboxane effect on coagulation. The inducible COX-2 pathway is primarily involved in generating the prostaglandins that modulate pain and fever and has no effect on platelet function or coagulation. Therefore, COX-2 inhibitors have the advantages of a lack of platelet inhibition and a decreased incidence of gastrointestinal effects.

The introduction of selective COX-2 inhibitors represented a breakthrough in perisurgical pain management. Because they do not interfere with the coagulation system, COX-2 inhibitors can be used presurgically until the time of surgery and can be resumed during the immediate postsurgical period. Perisurgical administration of rofecoxib has been shown to have a significant opioid-sparing effect after major orthopaedic surgery,

**Table 4 | Brachial Plexus Regional Anesthesia and Analgesia for Shoulder and Elbow Surgery***

| Technique | Level of Blockade | Peripheral Nerves Blocked | Surgical Applications | Comments |
|---|---|---|---|---|
| Axillary | Peripheral nerve | Radial, ulnar, median (musculocutaneous unreliably blocked) | Forearm and hand (less frequently used for elbow) | Unsuitable for proximal humerus or shoulder surgery. Patient must be able to abduct the arm. |
| Infraclavicular | Cords | Radial, ulnar, median, musculocutaneous, axillary | Elbow, forearm, hand | Catheter site (near coracoid process) is easy to maintain. No risk of hemothorax, pneumothorax. |
| Supraclavicular | Distal trunk-proximal cord | Radial, ulnar, median, musculocutaneous, axillary | Midhumerus, elbow, forearm, hand | Phrenic nerve paresis in 30%. Risk of pneumothorax. Unsuitable for outpatient procedure. |
| Interscalene | Upper and middle trunk | Entire brachial plexus (inferior trunk [ulnar nerve] not blocked in 15% to 20%) | Shoulder, proximal humerus, midhumerus | Phrenic nerve paresis in 100% (for block duration). Unsuitable for patients unable to tolerate 25% reduction in pulmonary function. |

*Duration of block: when performed with long-acting local anesthetic (bupivacaine, ropivacaine), 12 to 20 h; when performed with intermediate-acting local anesthetic (lidocaine, mepivacaine), 4 to 6 h.*

with no significant increase in bleeding.[15,16] Despite their efficacy, two of the three types of COX-2 inhibitors (rofecoxib [Vioxx; Merck, Whitehouse Station, NJ] and valdecoxib [Bextra; Searle, Skokie, IL]) have been voluntarily removed from general use because of an associated increase in the relative risk of cardiovascular events, including heart attack and stroke, after 18 months of treatment.

The most important adverse effects limiting the use of NSAIDs for postsurgical pain control include platelet dysfunction, gastric ulcers or bleeding, and renal failure.[17] Platelet inhibition can be avoided and gastrointestinal effects can be minimized by using COX-2 rather than COX-1 inhibitors. However, all NSAIDs have the potential to cause serious renal impairment. Inhibition of the COX enzyme may have only a minor effect in a patient with healthy kidneys but can lead to a serious adverse effect in an elderly patient or a patient with a low-volume condition such as blood loss, dehydration, cirrhosis, or heart failure. Therefore, NSAIDs should be used cautiously in patients with underlying renal dysfunction, especially when volume depletion is a concern because of blood loss.[17] The effect of NSAIDs on bone formation and healing is a consideration in orthopaedic patients. Although there are conflicting data, evidence from animal studies suggests that COX-2 inhibitors inhibit bone healing;[18] there is currently no evidence that COX-2 inhibitors have a clinically important effect on human bone ingrowth. Thus, the adverse effects of COX-2 inhibitors must be weighed against the benefits. Until definitive clinical studies are performed, it is reasonable to be cautious in using NSAIDs, especially COX-2 inhibitors, if bone healing is critical.

### Tramadol
Tramadol (Ultram; Ortho McNeil Pharmaceutical, Raritan, NJ) is a centrally acting analgesic that is structurally related to morphine and codeine. Its analgesic effect occurs through binding to the opioid receptors and blocking norepinephrine and serotonin reuptake. Tramadol has gained popularity because the incidence of adverse effects is low. These adverse effects include respiratory depression and constipation, as well as the potential for addiction. Tramadol has been shown to provide analgesia for acute pain comparable to that of opioid and other nonopioid analgesics and superior to that of placebo. Thus, tramadol may be used as an alternative to opioids in a multimodal approach to postsurgical pain, especially in patients who cannot tolerate opioid analgesics.

### Brachial Plexus Regional Analgesia
Four distinct approaches can be used to block the brachial plexus (Table 4). Continuous brachial plexus block is more often used to provide postsurgical analgesia than intrasurgical anesthesia. Although the block produces analgesia in all nerve distributions, it may not provide satisfactory surgical anesthesia, even with administration of more potent local anesthetic solutions. Recent applications of peripheral nerve blocks have allowed prolonged postsurgical analgesia using an indwelling catheter.[10,19,20] A brachial plexus catheter may be inserted using an interscalene, infraclavicular, or axillary approach. A postsurgical indwelling catheter can be left in place 4 to 7 days without causing adverse effects.[21] A continuous infusion of a local anesthetic solution, such as bupivacaine 0.125%, prevents vasospasm and increases circulation after limb or digit replantation or vascular repair. More concentrated solutions provide

## Table 5 | Patient Instructions for At-Home Use of a Brachial Plexus Catheter

You are receiving local anesthetic through a small catheter near your nerves to help with your pain after surgery. This anesthetic may not take away all of your pain, but it should help greatly. You may take your pain medicines as prescribed by your doctor. The nurse will review your pain medicines with you.

The local anesthetic will initially make your arm very numb. Over time, the degree of numbness will decrease, but your arm probably will not feel normal until the catheter is removed. Because your arm or leg will not function normally, *you should not drive.*

The doctors and nurses will review the pump instructions with you. If you have any problems with the pump, call the technical support telephone number or the number the doctor has given you.

You should keep your arm in a sling unless you are undergoing physical therapy.

The following complications sometimes occur:

- The catheter can fall out. If this happens, take some of your pain medicine and turn the pump off.
- Fluid can leak around the catheter. You can change or reinforce the dressing, if necessary. Fluid leaking is usually not a problem.
- The catheter can migrate into a blood vessel and cause a high level of local anesthetic to be released. If this happens, you may experience any of the following symptoms:
  - drowsiness
  - dizziness
  - blurred vision
  - slurred speech
  - poor balance
  - tingling around your lips and mouth.

Call your physician for medical assistance if you experience any of these symptoms:

- unusual drowsiness
- uncontrollable pain
- uncontrollable vomiting.

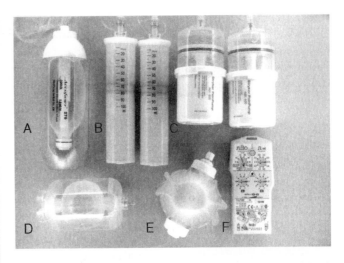

**Figure 4** Disposable portable infusion pumps for intra-articular and neural sheath infusion at home. **A,** Accufuser (McKinley Medical, Wheat Ridge, CO). **B,** Sgarlato (Sgarlato Laboratories, Los Gatos, CA). **C,** Stryker PainPump (Stryker Instruments, Kalamazoo, MI). **D,** MedFlo II (MPS Acacia, Brea, CA). **E,** C-Bloc (I-Flow, Lake Forest, CO). **F,** Microject PCA (Sorenson Medical, West Jordan, UT). *(Reproduced with permission from Ilfeld BM, Morey TE, Enneking FK: The delivery rate accuracy of portable infusion pumps used for continuous regional analgesia. Anesth Analg 2002;95:1331-1336.)*

complete sensory block and allow early joint mobilization after a painful surgical procedure at the elbow.[22]

Although persistent upper extremity block is not a contraindication to discharge from the hospital, the patient should be informed during the postsurgical visit of the anticipated duration of the block and instructed to protect the blocked extremity until resolution. Applications for ambulatory, at-home use provide superior analgesia with fewer adverse effects than conventional systemic analgesia[10] (Table 5). The selection of local anesthetic for ambulatory analgesia is based on the desired duration and degree of sensory or motor block.[22,23]

Neurologic dysfunction and intravascular injection are the most important issues associated with peripheral blockade. In a study of more than 50,000 peripheral blocks, six seizures occurred, and 12 patients reported postsurgical nerve injury. Most neurologic complications were transient.[24] In 521 patients who underwent single-injection interscalene block for major shoulder surgery,

the frequency of nerve dysfunction at 1 and 9 months was 0.9% and 0.2%, respectively.[25] Paresthesia during needle insertion and surgery performed in the sitting position were identified as predictors of neurologic sequelae related to interscalene block.[26] Neurologic complications are uncommon following the use of an indwelling brachial plexus catheter, despite prolonged catheter placement and extended exposure to local anesthesia.[27]

### Intra-Articular Catheters

Intra-articular injection of local anesthetics is a well-established method of providing short-term analgesia for an ambulatory procedure. Near-complete pain relief is often achieved for 4 to 6 hours, after which the local anesthetic effect resolves and systemic analgesics are required. The introduction of disposable elastomeric and programmable pumps has allowed extended infusion (2 to 4 days) of local anesthetics (Figure 4).[28] Intra-articular infusion pumps do not provide a complete blockade of the brachial plexus, compared with neural sheath catheters, and analgesia is often incomplete. The addition of oral opioids may be required, although at a comparatively low dosage.[7,19] All patients provided with infusion of local anesthetic solutions must be educated on the signs and symptoms of local anesthesia toxicity and instructed on contacting their physician for assistance (Table 5).

### Summary

Surgery involving the shoulder or elbow may be performed under general or regional anesthesia with equal safety and efficacy. However, the methods used to provide postsurgical analgesia in patients undergoing elbow or shoulder surgery can substantially improve outcomes, including joint range of motion and length of hospital stay. Recent studies found that a combination of brachial plexus block and oral analgesics, when administered on a schedule, provides a quality of analgesia and functional outcome superior to that of systemic intravenous opioid analgesia, with fewer adverse effects. Continued collaboration between orthopaedic surgeons and anesthesiologists is necessary to further advance the perisurgical treatment of patients undergoing shoulder or elbow surgery.

## Annotated References

1. Neal JM, Hebl JR, Gerancher JC, Hogan QH: Brachial plexus anesthesia: Essentials of our current understanding. *Reg Anesth Pain Med* 2002;27:402-428.

   Techniques used for brachial plexus blockade, including approaches to the plexus, methods of neural localization, complications, and perisurgical outcomes, are presented in this evidence-based review.

2. Urmey WF, Talts KH, Sharrock NE: One hundred percent incidence of hemidiaphragmatic paresis associated with interscalene brachial plexus anesthesia as diagnosed by ultrasonography. *Anesth Analg* 1991; 72:498-503.

3. Urmey WF, McDonald M: Hemidiaphragmatic paresis during interscalene brachial plexus block: Effects on pulmonary function and chest wall mechanics. *Anesth Analg* 1992;74:352-357.

4. Sardesai AM, Chakrabarti AJ, Denny NM: Lower lobe collapse during continuous interscalene brachial plexus local anesthesia at home. *Reg Anesth Pain Med* 2004;29:65-68.

   This case report describes a lower lobe collapse secondary to phrenic nerve paresis following interscalene block in a single patient.

5. Wu CL, Rouse LM, Chen JM, Miller RJ: Comparison of postoperative pain in patients receiving interscalene block or general anesthesia for shoulder surgery. *Orthopedics* 2002;25:45-48.

   In a retrospective review of patients undergoing shoulder surgery, general anesthesia and single-injection interscalene block analgesia were compared for adverse effects, recovery room stay, and time to hospital discharge.

6. Wilson AT, Nicholson E, Burton L, Wild C: Analgesia for day-case shoulder surgery. *Br J Anaesth* 2004;92: 414-415.

   A prospective observational study evaluated the efficacy and duration of analgesia in patients who received a single-injection interscalene block for moderately severe ambulatory shoulder surgery.

7. Chao D, Young S, Cawley P: Postoperative pain management for arthroscopic shoulder surgery: Interscalene block versus patient-controlled infusion of 0.25% bupivacaine. *Am J Orthop* 2006;35:231-234.

   A prospective, randomized study compared the analgesic efficacy of a single-injection interscalene block with that of a continuous intra-articular infusion following subacromial decompression.

8. Boardman ND, Cofield RH: Neurologic complications of shoulder surgery. *Clin Orthop Relat Res* 1999; 368:44-53.

9. Ekatodramis G, Borgeat A, Huledal G, Jeppsson L, Westman L, Sjovall J: Continuous interscalene analgesia with ropivacaine 2 mg/ml after major shoulder surgery. *Anesthesiology* 2003;98:143-150.

   A prospective, randomized study compared continuous and single-injection interscalene analgesia after major shoulder surgery.

10. Boezaart AP: Continuous interscalene block for ambulatory shoulder surgery. *Best Pract Res Clin Anaesthesiol* 2002;16:295-310.

    This best-practice review described alternative approaches and management of continuous interscalene block.

11. Myles PS, Williams DL, Hendrata M, Anderson H, Weeks AM: Patient satisfaction after anaesthesia and surgery: Results of a prospective survey of 10,811 patients. *Br J Anaesth* 2000;84:6-10.

12. Wheeler M, Oderda GM, Ashburn MA, Lipman AG: Adverse events associated with postoperative opioid analgesia: A systematic review. *J Pain* 2002;3:159-180.

    The frequency of opioid-related adverse effects was compared after epidural, parenteral, and oral administration.

13. Acute Pain Management Guideline Panel: *Acute Pain Management: Operative or Medical Procedures and Trauma-Clinical Practice Guideline.* Rockville, MD, US Department of Health and Human Services, AHCPR Publication No. 92-0032, 1992.

14. Reuben SS, Connelly NR, Maciolek H: Postoperative analgesia with controlled-release oxycodone for outpatient anterior cruciate ligament surgery. *Anesth Analg* 1999;88:1286-1291.

15. Reuben SS, Connelly NR: Postoperative analgesic effects of celecoxib or rofecoxib after spinal fusion surgery. *Anesth Analg* 2000;91:1221-1225.

16. Reuben SS, Fingeroth R, Krushell R, Maciolek H: Evaluation of the safety and efficacy of the perioperative administration of rofecoxib for total knee arthroplasty. *J Arthroplasty* 2002;17:26-31.

A prospective, randomized clinical trial of rofecoxib found improved pain scores and no increase in bleeding with perisurgical rofecoxib administration, compared with placebo.

17. Stephens JM, Pashos CL, Haider S, Wong JM: Making progress in the management of postoperative pain: A review of the cyclooxygenase 2-specific inhibitors. *Pharmacotherapy* 2004;24:1714-1731.

   The role of COX-2–specific inhibitors as a component of multimodal analgesia in postsurgical patients is discussed.

18. Gajraj NM: Cyclooxygenase-2 inhibitors. *Anesth Analg* 2003;96:1720-1738.

   The pharmacology and role of COX-2 inhibitors in postsurgical pain management are examined in this comprehensive review.

19. Delaunay L, Souron V, Lafosse L, Marret E, Toussaint B: Analgesia after arthroscopic rotator cuff repair: Subacromial versus interscalene continuous infusion of ropivacaine. *Reg Anesth Pain Med* 2005;30:117-122.

   A prospective, randomized study compared pain at rest and motion in patients receiving a continuous interscalene or subacromial local anesthetic infusion after rotator cuff repair.

20. Klein SM, Nielsen KC, Martin A, et al: Interscalene brachial plexus block with continuous intraarticular infusion of ropivacaine. *Anesth Analg* 2001;93:601-605.

   In a prospective, randomized study, the use of single-injection interscalene block alone and combined with continuous intra-articular infusion was compared in patients undergoing shoulder arthroscopy.

21. Ilfeld BM, Enneking FK: A portable mechanical pump providing over four days of patient-controlled analgesia by perineural infusion at home. *Reg Anesth Pain Med* 2002;27:100-104.

   After discharge following an open rotator cuff repair, a patient successfully used an interscalene perineural catheter and a mechanical infusion pump to provide a variable rate of continuous infusion, as well as patient-controlled boluses of local anesthetic, for more than 4 days.

22. O'Driscoll SW, Giori NJ: Continuous passive motion (CPM): Theory and principles of clinical application. *J Rehabil Res Dev* 2000;37:179-188.

23. Borgeat A, Kalberer F, Jacob H, Ruetsch YA, Gerber C: Patient-controlled interscalene analgesia with ropivacaine 0.2% versus bupivacaine 0.15% after major open shoulder surgery: The effects on hand motor function. *Anesth Analg* 2001;92:218-223.

   Analgesic efficacy and block characteristics of 0.2% ropivacaine and 0.15% bupivacaine administered through an interscalene catheter were compared in a prospective, randomized study of patients after major shoulder surgery.

24. Auroy Y, Benhamou D, Bargues L, et al: Major complications of regional anesthesia in France: The SOS regional anesthesia hotline service. *Anesthesiology* 2002;97:1274-1280.

   The frequency and severity of serious complications (including death, cardiac arrest, and nerve injury), as well as their prognosis, were prospectively evaluated after 158,083 regional anesthesia procedures.

25. Borgeat A, Ekatodramis G, Kalberer F, Benz C: Acute and nonacute complications associated with interscalene block and shoulder surgery: A prospective study. *Anesthesiology* 2001;95:875-880.

   The incidence, etiology, and evolution of complications after interscalene brachial plexus block were prospectively studied in 521 patients who underwent major shoulder surgery.

26. Candido KD, Sukhani R, Doty R Jr, et al: Neurologic sequelae after interscalene brachial plexus block for shoulder/upper arm surgery: The association of patient, anesthetic, and surgical factors to the incidence and clinical course. *Anesth Analg* 2005;100:1489-1495.

   This observational study evaluated frequency, severity, and prognosis related to neurologic complications after use of single-injection interscalene block in 693 consecutive patients.

27. Bergman BD, Hebl JR, Kent J, Horlocker TT: Neurologic complications of 405 continuous axillary catheters. *Anesth Analg* 2003;96:247-252.

   Infectious, hemorrhagic, and neurologic complications associated with 405 consecutive axillary catheters were retrospectively reviewed.

28. Yamaguchi K, Sethi N, Bauer GS: Postoperative pain control following arthroscopic release of adhesive capsulitis: A short term retrospective review study of the use of an intra-articular pain catheter. *Arthroscopy* 2002;18:359-365.

   In a retrospective clinical review, analgesia provided by intermittent injection of local anesthetic through an indwelling intra-articular catheter was evaluated in patients undergoing arthroscopic release of adhesive capsulitis.

# Chapter 55

# Magnetic Resonance Arthrography of the Shoulder

Kimberly K. Amrami, MD

## Introduction

Magnetic resonance arthrography (MRA) is increasingly important in the diagnosis of complex shoulder conditions. It has become the standard imaging modality for suspected glenohumeral instability and labral tears. The technique for direct MRA of the shoulder, the indications for its use, and its disease-specific clinical applications continue to evolve.

## Technical Considerations

MRA of the shoulder combines MRI and joint distension to show intra-articular structures such as the labrum and glenohumeral ligaments, which may be well seen only with the separation gained by adding fluid to the joint. A variety of techniques and contrast agents can be used. Indirect MRA of the shoulder involves intravenous injection of a contrast agent, followed by exercise of the joint and delayed imaging.[1] In indirect MRA, the joint fluid is mixed with a gadolinium contrast agent, but the joint may not be consistently distended. Direct MRA relies on direct injection into the joint, usually under fluoroscopic guidance. Early in the history of MRI, saline was injected to distend the joint before imaging, but this method has largely been replaced by injection of dilute gadolinium, which allows the radiologist to distinguish between the fluid in the joint and the fluid around the joint.[2-4]

The patient's shoulder is prepared and draped for MRA as for conventional radiography, and the skin is anesthetized using 1% lidocaine. The shoulder is placed in neutral to slightly external rotation to avoid contact with the biceps tendon during needle placement. A 22-gauge spinal needle is advanced into the shoulder joint, using one of two methods. The needle can be advanced to the inferior third of the lateral cortical margin of the humeral head at the glenohumeral joint and then into the joint, after slight internal rotation. Alternatively, the needle can be advanced under fluoroscopic guidance into the rotator cuff interval by placement just inferior to the coracoid process, with the final needle position against the humeral head. In rare instances, usually when cellulitis or another skin condition is present over the anterior chest wall and shoulder, the needle is placed using a posterior approach.[5]

The needle's intra-articular location can be confirmed by injecting a small amount of iodinated contrast material into the joint. If necessary, the needle position can then be adjusted before the gadolinium injection to prevent gadolinium instillation outside the joint, which could confound interpretation. Alternatively, the iodinated contrast can be administered as part of the dilute gadolinium mixture. The use of this method requires confidence that the initial needle placement was correct. The choice of method depends solely on operator experience and preference.

The gadolinium is diluted to a 1:200 concentration, which is optimal for bright contrast on T1-weighted imaging at 1.5 and 3.0 Tesla (T), which are the magnetic field strengths most commonly used in clinical imaging.[6] This concentration can be achieved by combining 0.1 mL of gadolinium with either 20 mL of saline or a combination of saline and a few milliliters of iodinated contrast. At the surgeon's request, bupivacaine, with or without a steroid, can safely be added. The initial injection is watched under fluoroscopy to ensure that the injectate reaches the joint. In general, a minimum of 12 mL is injected into the joint. The injection ideally continues until the patient feels some discomfort, which in some patients requires as much as 20 mL. Distension of the joint is critical for optimal imaging.

The patient is immediately brought into the MRI suite, which should be in reasonable proximity to the room in which the injection was performed. A dedicated shoulder radiofrequency coil should always be used to achieve the highest possible image quality and detect subtle abnormalities. Most shoulder imaging is performed with the patient's arm at the side and in neutral or slight external rotation of the shoulder. The standard postinjection imaging series consists of studies in three planes: axial to the shoulder, sagittal parallel to the bony glenoid and perpendicular to the belly of the supraspinatus muscle, and coronal parallel to the supraspinatus muscle. The field of view should be no greater than 14 cm, and the in-plane resolution should be at least 0.5 × 0.5 mm, with a slice thickness no greater than 3 to 4 mm, a matrix minimum of 256 × 256, and 2 excitations.

The brightness of the gadolinium contrast on T1-weighted images results from its paramagnetic effect. Marrow and subcutaneous fat also have a bright appearance, so fat suppression is used to make the images less difficult to interpret. Most contrast imaging is therefore performed using T1-weighted sequences with short repetition and echo times and with chemical fat suppression. T1-weighted images with fat suppression are obtained in all three planes. Imaging without fat suppression as well as fluid-sensitive imaging (T2 or proton density weighted) with fat suppression can be helpful in assessing abnormalities such as bone marrow edema, fluid outside the joint, and abnormalities of articular cartilage.

The abduction–external rotation (ABER) position can be used for additional imaging if there are questions regarding the joint capsule itself or the inferior glenohumeral ligament complex (IGHLC).[2,3,7] This position is used only as an adjunct to standard imaging. The patient elevates the arm overhead and rests the dorsum of the hand on the forehead. The ABER position puts tension on the capsule and capsular ligaments and reveals partial tears better than conventional positioning.[1,8] The presence of subtle cartilaginous Bankart lesions of the anterior glenoid, as suggested on other images, can sometimes be confirmed by using the ABER position.

Some researchers have proposed creating an arthroscopic-like view of the joint by obtaining images with isotropic resolution (using a voxel of equal dimensions in all planes), then performing image reconstruction. This technique has not been used extensively in clinical practice because of the substantial time and work required for image acquisition and processing.

## Indications

MRA of the shoulder usually is performed in relatively young patients who may have glenohumeral instability, a labral tear, or, rarely, pathology affecting the rotator interval. These conditions are difficult to diagnose using unenhanced MRI of the shoulder.[2,3,7,9] MRA is not usually required to confirm a diagnosis of rotator cuff pathology, although it is occasionally used for that purpose.

MRA has a dual advantage. It distends the joint to separate structures that are otherwise difficult to differentiate from one another (for example, the redundant joint capsule and the glenohumeral ligaments). MRA also highlights and outlines structures such as the anterior labrum. If a tear or avulsion is present, the contrast will be seen within or deep to the structure of interest, thereby facilitating a diagnosis such as periosteal sleeve avulsion or labral tear.[2,3,10,11] Unenhanced shoulder MRI is an excellent tool for evaluating the rotator cuff and moderate or advanced arthritis of the glenohumeral joint, as well as masses and other lesions about the shoulder.[12,13] Conventional MRI is insensitive for diagnosing labral pathology or determining the etiology of unidirectional shoulder instability; MRA is the preferred imaging study for these conditions. MRA usually should be performed after plain radiography in patients with specific indications who are able to undergo MRI.

## The Labroligamentous Complex
### Anatomic Considerations
#### Glenohumeral Ligaments

The glenohumeral ligaments are condensations of the joint capsule and are somewhat variable in appearance on MRI. The IGHLC originates at the anatomic neck of the humerus and inserts on the anterior, inferior, and posterior glenoid labrum. On sagittal images, it is seen to form the axillary pouch with neutral positioning. The anterior and posterior bands usually can be identified with adequate joint distention on MRA (Figure 1). Visualization of the anterior band at its insertion and as a continuous structure is important because the insertion is the place at which the IGHLC is most often damaged after anterior joint dislocation. The anterior band of the IGHLC is best seen using ABER positioning, which should be added to conventional positioning if there is a question of subtle signal abnormality (Figure 2). The anterior band should appear as dark gray or black on all sequences, as it is composed primarily of organized collagen.

Artifact resulting from the so-called magic angle effect may alter the signal of highly organized structures such as the tendons and ligaments of the glenolabral complex.[7] In the magic angle effect, highly organized structures are oriented at 55° to the static magnetic field (the long axis of the magnet for 1.5-T and 3-T magnets) on MRI. This phenomenon is commonly seen with the short and intermediate echo times (< 50 ms) used in shoulder imaging. The magic angle effect is manifested by local increased signal, which may mimic a tear or tendinopathy. It is commonly seen in the supraspinatus and infraspinatus tendons at their attachments on the greater tuberosity and also is common in the IGHLC because of its curved orientation in the inferior joint recess. Using the ABER position effectively eliminates the magic angle effect by altering the angle of the IGHLC relative to the magnet.

The middle glenohumeral ligament (MGHL) functions as an anterior stabilizer, most effectively when the humerus is in approximately 45° of abduction. An isolated MGHL injury is rare. The MGHL has a much more variable imaging appearance than the IGHLC or superior glenohumeral ligament (SGL).[2,12] The size of

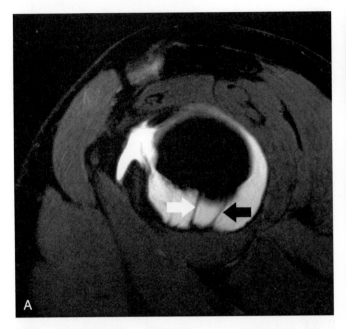 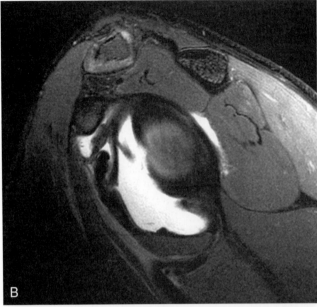

**Figure 1** **A,** Parasagittal T1-weighted MRA study with fat suppression, showing the normal anterior (*light arrow*) and posterior (*dark arrow*) bands of the IGHLC. **B,** Parasagittal T2-weighted MRA study with fat suppression, showing the normal bicipitolabral complex, including the adjacent MGHL.

the MGHL ranges from large and bulky to relatively slender and sheetlike, and it is absent in as many as 30% of patients. When the MGHL has a linear or sheetlike appearance, it inserts on either the scapula or the anterosuperior glenoid (Figure 3). A more cordlike, rounded MGHL typically inserts with the SGL at the base of the biceps on the superior glenoid rim. The MGHL has this cordlike appearance when the anterosuperior labrum is small or absent (as in the Buford complex). When present, the MGHL consistently appears between the glenoid and the humerus, anterior to the edge of the glenoid, as a low-signal structure similar in signal intensity to the nearby glenoid labrum. The radiologist can follow its course by scrolling through the serial axial images and can view the ligament in its entirety on coronal images. Like the IGHLC, the MGHL has low signal intensity on all sequences. Unlike the IGHLC, it is rarely affected by the magic angle effect.

The SGL can be seen on axial images of the shoulder if joint fluid or intra-articular gadolinium is used to distend the joint and separate it from the superior labrum and biceps anchor (Figure 4). The SGL is not considered as important as the IGHLC and MGHL for anterior stabilization and appears to primarily function to limit external rotation when the arm is adducted.[7]

### Glenoid Labrum

The glenoid labrum is extremely important in shoulder joint stability. The labrum acts to deepen the shallow bony glenoid, increasing the area of contact with the humeral head. In addition to its primary role as a static stabilizer, it acts as a buffer, improving stability through

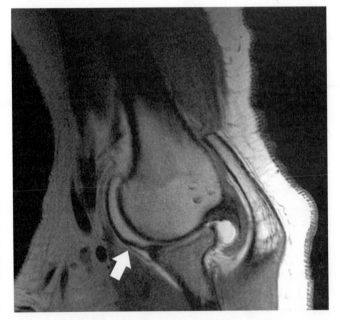

**Figure 2** Parasagittal proton density–weighted MRA study with ABER positioning, showing the taut anterior band of the IGHLC (*arrow*).

the midrange of motion. Thus, the labrum is to some extent a dynamic stabilizer.

Before the development of high-resolution MRA of the shoulder, diagnostic arthroscopy was required to evaluate the labrum. Unenhanced MRI of the shoulder sometimes reveals a labral abnormality when a large tear is present, with or without a paralabral cyst. However, more subtle abnormalities are best seen after a contrast agent is administered to achieve joint

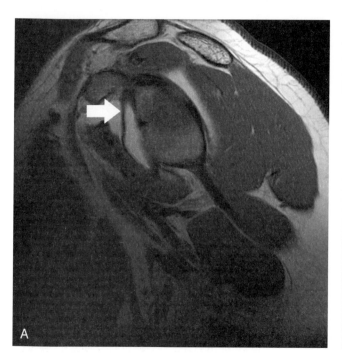

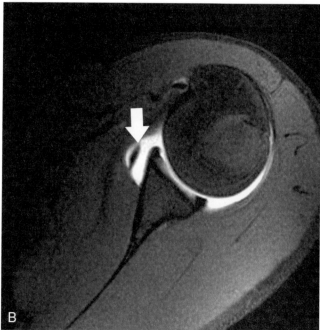

**Figure 3** **A,** Paracoronal proton density-weighted MRA study, showing an MGHL with a sheetlike configuration (*arrow*). **B,** Axial T1-weighted MRA study showing a cordlike MGHL just anterior and lateral to the anterior labrum (*arrow*).

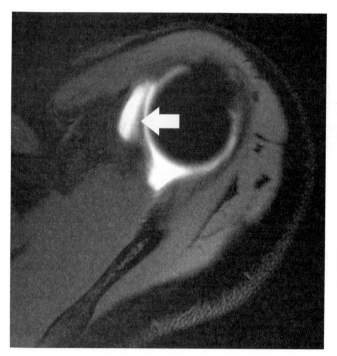

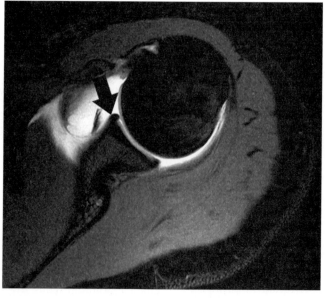

**Figure 5** Axial T1-weighted MRA study with fat suppression, showing a normal, rounded anterior labrum (*arrow*).

**Figure 4** Axial T1-weighted MRA study with fat suppression, showing a normal SGL (*arrow*).

distention. When labral pathology is suspected, MRA is the preferred method of imaging.[2,9,14-17]

Because the labrum is composed of fibrocartilage, in its normal state it has low signal intensity on all MRI sequences. Irregularities and tears of the labrum can be brightly outlined using gadolinium on T1-weighted images with fat suppression (Figure 5). It is also possible on MRA to distinguish mucoid degenerative changes from tears; a tear will imbibe the contrast agent, but a degenerated labrum will not. The wide range of normal variation in labral shape and size, especially in the anterosuperior labrum, can cause difficulty in evaluating images of the anterior labrum.

The role of capsular anatomy in glenohumeral instability is controversial, partly because surgeons use different definitions of joint laxity. Capsular anatomy is extremely variable, and even an experienced radiologist who is interpreting good-quality images may have difficulty categorizing capsular insertions and identifying capsular pathology such as capsular stripping.[18] Shoulder MRI is usually performed with the patient's arm in the neutral position. Optimal patient comfort may require some internal rotation, which exaggerates the appearance of redundancy because of relaxation of the anterior band of the IGHLC and can mimic capsular stripping (if fluid is seen between the folds of the capsule). Arthroscopy is often performed with the arm in partial abduction; this position elevates the anterior band of the IGHLC and greatly alters its appearance. The presence of fluid or contrast agent in the normal joint recesses between the IGHLC and other glenohumeral ligaments may cause the joint to appear exceptionally large. In addition, the normal interligamentous joint recesses may appear as capsular stripping from the humerus or glenoid.[7,19] The normal medial attachment of the MGHL also may mimic pathology. The arthrographic procedure itself can lead to rents in the capsule and extra-articular leakage of contrast agent, especially if the joint is overdistended. Each of these factors can cause difficulty in the interpretation of images. Often, the only truly consistent sign of joint laxity is subluxation of the humeral head, as seen on MRI, but this condition may be secondary to degenerative changes rather than capsular laxity or labral injury.

### Normal Variation in the Labroligamentous Complex
Although the most common configuration of the labrum is triangular, the wide range of normal variation includes a blunted or rounded appearance that can mimic posttraumatic change, especially in the anterosuperior labrum. The anterosuperior labrum is located between the biceps insertion superiorly and the glenoid notch inferiorly.[19] It can be small or even absent. Detachment of the anterior labrum from the glenoid is a common variant that can be mistaken for a tear. Most commonly, the entire anterosuperior labrum is detached; a recess between the labrum and glenoid can be seen on MRA when contrast or fluid is present.[10,11,20] The presence of this sublabral foramen or sublabral hole can cause confusion in interpreting images.[19] A focal traumatic detachment of the labrum can be difficult to distinguish from a small sublabral hole, especially in a throwing athlete with an isolated anterosuperior labral injury. If a tear is present, there is usually residual labral tissue on the glenoid rim, an extension of the tear beyond the sublabral foramen, or fraying of the labrum (compared with the smooth margin of the sublabral foramen or hole). Sometimes the radiologist is able to offer the surgeon only a list of conditions and normal variants possibly represented by the images.

Depending on the plane of section, the cordlike MGHL may appear more angular as it obliquely traverses the joint to insert on the biceps anchor than it appears in direct cross section. The combination of this angular appearance and an absent anterosuperior labrum, called the Buford complex, can be mistaken for a detached and torn labrum.[7] To avoid misdiagnosis, the radiologist should scroll through serial images to follow the entire length of the structure and should correlate images in different planes, especially the oblique coronal view. This process usually allows definitive identification of the Buford complex as a prominent MGHL.

Only three structures are present in the anterosuperior quadrant of the shoulder joint: the labrum, the MGHL, and the subscapularis muscle. During MRA, contrast fluid helps keep these structures separate from one another. To resolve any ambiguity, each structure should be followed throughout its length, from origin to insertion. Following this simple rule can improve the radiologist's accuracy in assessing the complex variations present in the shoulder joint, especially in the anterosuperior quadrant.

### Anatomic Lesions
#### Labral Tears
Isolated tears of the labrum can be caused by trauma that is acute or repetitive, as occurs in throwing athletes. The anterosuperior labrum is most commonly affected, although tears of the posterior labrum are seen in posterior impingement syndromes, usually associated with repeated overhead throwing or trauma.[21]

Tears of the anteroposterior labrum usually are best seen using a combination of axial and oblique coronal imaging. On MRA, tears can be distinguished from intrasubstance degeneration because the contrast agent in the tear is very bright on T1-weighted, fat-suppressed sequences (Figure 6). If labral disruption from the bony glenoid is present, the contrast agent will be insinuated beneath the labrum, making the detachment more conspicuous than it is on an unenhanced image (in which the displaced labrum may appear flush against the bone).

A superior labrum anterior and posterior (SLAP) tear is common and usually is best seen on MRA with contrast in the joint. A very large SLAP tear or a tear with an associated paralabral cyst is more conspicuous on conventional MRI studies.[2,3,10,11,17,19,22-24] A SLAP tear differs from a localized tear of the anterior or posterior labrum in extending anterior and posterior to the biceps anchor. SLAP tears are classified into four types, which recently have been expanded by the addition of three types representing more complex lesions. Type I involves only fraying of the labrum, with an intact biceps anchor; it is notoriously hard to see, even on high-quality MRA. In type II, the labrum is frayed and

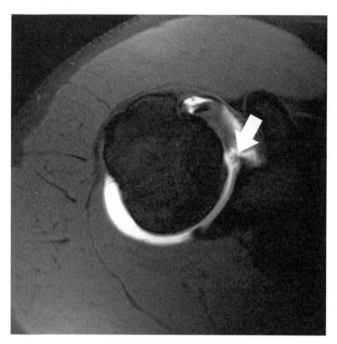

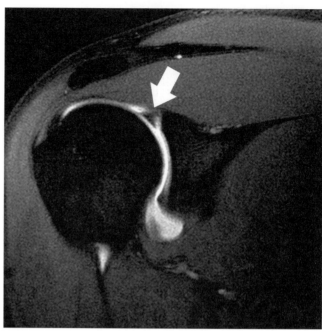

**Figure 6** Axial T1-weighted MRA study with fat suppression, showing an isolated anterior labral tear with fraying (*arrow*).

**Figure 7** Coronal T1-weighted MRA study with fat suppression, showing a type II SLAP tear. The area shown is just posterior to the bicipitolabral complex (*arrow*).

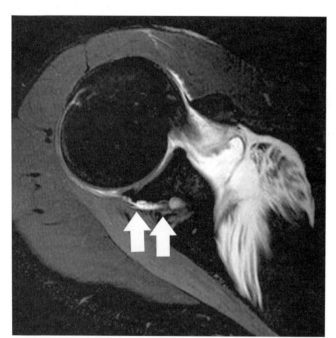

**Figure 8** Axial T1-weighted MRA study with fat suppression, showing a type II SLAP tear with a posterior paralabral cyst (*arrows*). Contrast within the cyst is compatible with communication between the cyst and the joint via the labral tear.

chor; splitting and contrast are seen within the fibers of the biceps tendon itself.

A paralabral cyst is pathognomonic of a labral tear and is most frequently seen with a type II SLAP tear. Although paralabral cysts usually can be identified on unenhanced T2-weighted MRI sequences with fat suppression, they can be better seen on MRA. The cyst should fill with contrast agent as evidence of the connection to the labral tear and the joint (Figure 8). Identification of the connection prevents a possible resection of the cyst without repair of the tear, which almost inevitably leads to a recurrence of the cyst and its symptoms.

The radiographic classification of SLAP tears is not highly correlated with arthroscopic findings. MRI and arthroscopy require different positioning of the shoulder, and the structures therefore may have a very different appearance.[7,10,25,26] There is wide variation in surgeons' classification of SLAP tears, and both radiologists and surgeons may mistake normal variations in labral anatomy for pathology.[24,27] The radiologist usually should describe the tear, rather than attempting to classify the tear by type. The description should be limited to the extent of the tear, any displacement of the labrum, and biceps anchor involvement.

### Glenoid Labrum Articular Disruption Lesions
In a glenoid labrum articular disruption lesion, a complete or partial labral tear extends to the adjacent articular cartilage.[7,28] The extent of the cartilage injury can be seen on conventional MRI using cartilage-sensitive sequences such as proton density–weighted imaging,

detached from the glenoid rim and biceps anchor; the characteristic MRA finding is a tear with contrast between the detached labrum and the rim, with the biceps anchor still attached to the displaced labrum (Figure 7). Type III is a bucket-handle tear of the labrum. Type IV is a type III tear with an extension into the biceps an-

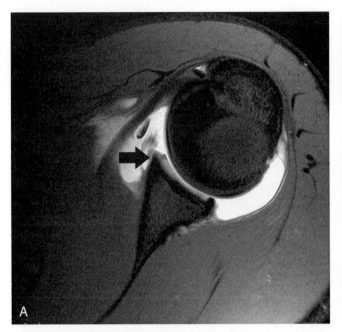 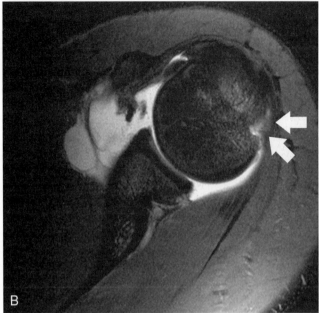

**Figure 9**  **A,** Axial T1-weighted MRA study with fat suppression, showing a cartilaginous Bankart lesion on the anteroinferior labrum (*arrow*). **B,** In the same patient, an axial T2-weighted MRA study with fat suppression, showing a Hill-Sachs deformity and bone marrow edema associated with anterior shoulder dislocation (*arrows*).

with or without fat suppression; these images should be included as an adjunct to MRA. A defect involving the full thickness of the cartilage can be seen on MRA. However, the signal intensity of the cartilage in a partial tear may be similar to the gadolinium contrast in the joint and therefore difficult to detect.

### Bankart and Bankart Variant Lesions

A Bankart lesion is an avulsion of the labroligamentous complex from its attachment on the anteroinferior glenoid, usually involving the anteroinferior quadrant.[7,22,29] The anteroinferior labrum is almost invariably torn. The Bankart lesion is the most common anatomic lesion resulting from anterior shoulder dislocation. A Bankart lesion may be restricted to the labrum or associated with a fracture of the rim of the glenoid (Figure 9). The fracture is best seen on axial T2-weighted images with fat suppression; it is not visible on the T1-weighted sequences with fat suppression typically used for MRA. A Bankart lesion can be difficult to see in the absence of a fracture or labral displacement. In an occult Bankart lesion, ABER positioning often can reveal the bony or labral fragment. A Bankart lesion is often associated with a Hill-Sachs deformity, which is an impaction fracture on the posterior humeral head caused by contact with the anterior glenoid rim during dislocation. The anterior band of the IGHLC may be avulsed as part of this injury, and it should be examined closely for continuity.

MRI, including MRA, should not be performed immediately after acute injury because the presence of significant soft-tissue edema and hemorrhage can confound image interpretation. MRI is usually obtained

when recurrent dislocation occurs or symptoms persist after resolution of the acute injury.

The scapular periosteal attachment to the labroligamentous complex is avulsed in a bony Bankart lesion. The periosteum remains attached in a Bankart variant lesion. If the labrum is displaced medially and inferiorly, it can roll up on itself, stripping the periosteum along the medial border of the scapula. This anterior labroligamentous periosteal sleeve avulsion (ALPSA) lesion is best seen on axial images with intra-articular contrast, which will show both the bare rim of the glenoid and the coiled-up labrum and periosteum.[7] The radiologist must take care to distinguish this finding from an absent labrum. Periosteal stripping occasionally will appear anteriorly as a thickened joint capsule, especially if it is chronic and fibrosis is present. A subtle ALPSA lesion is best seen using ABER positioning, which puts tension on the joint capsule and pulls it away from the anterior margin of the scapula (Figure 10).

In both an ALPSA lesion and a Perthes lesion, the periosteum is stripped along the medial border of the scapula. In a Perthes lesion, the periosteum is not rolled up on itself with the labrum but instead is separated from the bone. A Perthes lesion can be extremely difficult to detect on imaging. The anatomic positions of the labrum and periosteum may be normal in the absence of joint distention and in the neutral position, particularly if the injury is chronic and resynovialization has occurred along the labrum. On MRA, careful attention must be paid to subtle offsets in the labrum relative to the glenoid, as well as to any thickening or irregularity of the labrum. ABER positioning with tension applied

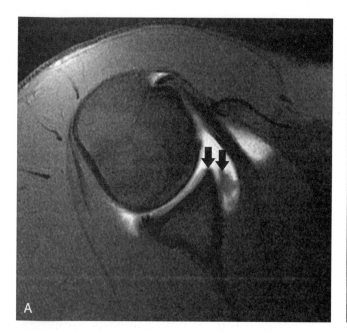
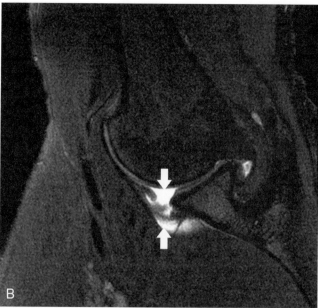

**Figure 10** **A,** Axial T1-weighted MRA study with fat suppression, showing a torn anterior labrum with periosteal striping and displacement of the labrum posteriorly consistent with an ALPSA lesion (*arrows*). **B,** In the same patient, axial T1-weighted MRA study with ABER positioning, showing the displacement of the labrum away from the glenoid and rolling up of the redundant periosteum (*arrows*).

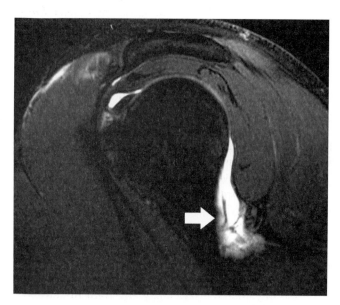

**Figure 11** Sagittal T2-weighted image with fat suppression, showing an avulsion of the posterior band of the IGHLC from the neck of the humerus (*arrow*).

to the capsule can reveal the adherent labrum and the contrast-filled gap between the avulsed labrum and bony glenoid.[7,19]

Posterior shoulder dislocations are uncommon, but they can occur after a fall with the arm in adduction and internal rotation. This position puts tension on the labrum and posterior joint capsule. A force causing posterior subluxation or dislocation of the anterior humerus can result in injury to the structures already under tension. The resulting disruption of the posterior labroliga-

mentous complex is called a reverse Bankart lesion.[7,21,25,26,29] Like the classic Bankart lesion, a reverse Bankart lesion can involve bone, cartilage, or the labrum, separately or in combination. A fracture or contusion of the anterior humeral head may result from impaction on the posterior rim of the glenoid; this condition is called a reverse Hill-Sachs deformity. MRA can best show these changes, and ABER positioning generally is not required. A reverse Bankart lesion is commonly associated with a complete or partial undersurface tear of the subscapularis muscle, which can be seen on conventional or enhanced MRI.

The glenohumeral ligaments may be injured at their capsular attachments without an associated labral injury. Although an isolated injury to the MGHL is rare, the IGHLC is commonly injured during anterior shoulder dislocation or extreme subluxation. A humeral avulsion of the glenohumeral ligaments lesion occurs when the IGHLC is avulsed from its humeral attachment while the glenoid attachment on the labrum remains intact.[30,31] Clinical and radiographic diagnosis is difficult unless MRA is used. The injury is often best seen on sagittal images showing the anterior and posterior bands of the IGHLC. An avulsion injury from the humeral shaft may cause cortical irregularity. Routine radiographs are usually normal, and these lesions are commonly diagnosed some time after the initial injury. The anterior band is most commonly affected, although the posterior band can also be affected (Figure 11). There may be associated rotator cuff or chondral injuries, but the labrum is usually intact.

## *Other Lesions Associated With Instability*

Imaging usually is not helpful in diagnosing multidirectional instability. Imaging reveals only subluxation of the humeral head, which is a nonspecific finding that is also seen with degenerative change or rotator cuff incompetence.

MRI is extremely sensitive for the chondral injuries and abnormalities that commonly occur with labroligamentous pathology. Hyaline articular cartilage has distinctive imaging features when it is compared with the fibrocartilage of structures such as the labrum. Normal hyaline cartilage appears gray on proton density–weighted sequences, becoming brighter in signal intensity as the cartilage degenerates and more free water enters the cartilage. As a result, unenhanced MRI is adequate for showing signal changes in cartilage. However, high-resolution imaging with joint distention and proton density–weighted imaging, both of which are features of a routine MRA examination, show both focal defects and subtle changes of chondromalacia with great accuracy and correlation with arthroscopy.

## Summary

High-resolution MRA is useful in assessing unidirectional instability and all types of labroligamentous pathology. Knowledge of normal anatomic variations such as the sublabral foramen is essential to avoid overdiagnosis of labral pathology. Examination tailored to specific clinical indications, including special positioning such as ABER, can lead to imaging that will assist the surgeon in diagnosis and surgical planning. Communication between the radiologist and surgeon ensures an optimal radiographic examination.

## Annotated References

1. Wintzell G, Larsson H, Larsson S: Indirect MR arthrography of anterior shoulder instability in the ABER and the apprehension test positions: A prospective comparative study of two different shoulder positions during MRI using intravenous gadodiamide contrast for enhancement of the joint fluid. *Skeletal Radiol* 1998;27:488-494.

2. Chung CB, Corrente L, Resnick D: MR arthrography of the shoulder. *Magn Reson Imaging Clin N Am* 2004;12:25-38.

   The indications and techniques for MRA of the shoulder are discussed in this excellent review.

3. Jbara M, Chen Q, Marten P, Morcos M, Beltran J: Shoulder MR arthrography: How, why, when. *Radiol Clin North Am* 2005;43:683-692.

   The sensitivity, specificity, and accuracy of MRA of the shoulder and unenhanced shoulder MRI are compared. Techniques, applications, interpretation of images, and potential pitfalls are included.

4. Stoller DW: MR arthrography of the glenohumeral joint. *Radiol Clin North Am* 1997;35:97-116.

5. Catalano OA, Manfredi R, Vanzulli A, et al: MR arthrography of the glenohumeral joint: Modified posterior approach without imaging guidance. *Radiology* 2007;242:550-554.

   A posterior approach to glenohumeral joint injection for MRA used bony landmarks without fluoroscopic guidance. Of 147 patients, 85% had successful injection on the first attempt, showing that this is an acceptable alternative technique.

6. Stecco A, Brambilla M, Puppi AM, Lovisolo M, Boldorini R, Carriero A: Shoulder MR arthrography: In vitro determination of optimal gadolinium dilution as a function of field strength. *J Magn Reson Imaging* 2007;25:200-207.

   This phantom study looked at the appearance of different concentrations of gadolinium at a range of magnetic field strengths (0.5 to 3.0 T). Although the optimal dilution varied slightly between high and low fields, the standard dosage of 1.5 T is clinically adequate for all systems.

7. Tirman PFJ: Glenohumeral instability, in Steinbach LS (ed): *Shoulder Magnetic Resonance Imaging*. Philadelphia, PA, Lippincott-Raven, 1998, pp 135-167.

8. Choi JA, Suh SI, Kim BH, et al: Comparison between conventional MR arthrography and abduction and external rotation MR arthrography in revealing tears of the antero-inferior glenoid labrum. *Korean J Radiol* 2001;2:216-221.

   Conventional axial and ABER positioning were compared for visualizing tears of the anteroinferior labrum in 30 patients. Seventy percent of tears were visible with both techniques, and 27% were better visualized using ABER positioning ($P < 0.05$). The utility of ABER positioning in these patients was confirmed.

9. Rowan KR, Andrews G, Spielmann A, Leith J: MR shoulder arthrography in patients younger than 40 years of age: Frequency of rotator cuff tear versus labroligamentous pathology. *Australas Radiol* 2007; 51:257-259.

   Of 332 patients referred for MRA, 89 had a history that did not suggest labral pathology; 19% had a labral tear, indicating a significant risk of unsuspected labral pathology. The conclusion is that MRA should be the study of choice for detecting shoulder pathology in young patients.

10. Jee WH, McCauley TR, Katz LD, Matheny JM, Ruwe PA, Daigneault JP: Superior labral anterior posterior (SLAP) lesions of the glenoid labrum: Reliability and accuracy of MR arthrography for diagnosis. *Radiology* 2001;218:127-132.

    In 80 patients who underwent MRA and arthroscopy, high interobserver reliability ($K = 0.77$) confirmed that

MRA is an accurate and reliable method of diagnosing SLAP tears.

11. Mohana-Borges AV, Chung CB, Resnick D: Superior labral anteroposterior tear: Classification and diagnosis on MRI and MR arthrography. *AJR Am J Roentgenol* 2003;181:1449-1462.

    The anatomy of the labroligamentous complex and its normal variants are reviewed, with radiographic and arthroscopic classification of SLAP tears.

12. Farber A, Fayad L, Johnson T, et al: Magnetic resonance imaging of the shoulder: Current techniques and spectrum of disease. *J Bone Joint Surg Am* 2006; 88(suppl 4):64-79.

    This comprehensive review describes the technique and application of unenhanced MRI of the shoulder from an orthopaedic perspective.

13. Morag Y, Jacobson JA, Miller B, De Maeseneer M, Girish G, Jamadar D: MR imaging of rotator cuff injury: What the clinician needs to know. *Radiographics* 2006;26:1045-1065.

    The anatomy and biomechanics of the rotator cuff are reviewed for radiologists who perform and interpret MRI of the shoulder.

14. Woertler K, Waldt S: MR imaging in sports-related glenohumeral instability. *Eur Radiol* 2006;16:2622-2636.

    MRA was found to be superior to unenhanced MRI in the evaluation of glenohumeral instability.

15. Applegate GR, Hewitt M, Snyder SJ, Watson E, Kwak S, Resnick D: Chronic labral tears: Value of magnetic resonance arthrography in evaluating the glenoid labrum and labral-bicipital complex. *Arthroscopy* 2004;20:959-963.

    MRA and arthroscopy for chronic shoulder pathology were compared in 36 patients who underwent both procedures. The accuracy of MRA was found to be 92% and 86% in detecting SLAP tears and labral tears, respectively.

16. Chandnani VP, Yeager TD, DeBerardino T, et al: Glenoid labral tears: Prospective evaluation with MRI imaging, MR arthrography, and CT arthrography. *AJR Am J Roentgenol* 1993;161:1229-1235.

17. Dinauer PA, Flemming DJ, Murphy KP, Doukas WC: Diagnosis of superior labral lesions: Comparison of noncontrast MRI with indirect MR arthrography in unexercised shoulders. *Skeletal Radiol* 2007;36: 195-202.

    In 104 patients, indirect MRA and noncontrast MRI of the shoulder without exercise were compared with arthroscopic results. Although indirect MRA was found to be preferable to unenhanced studies, its low specificity (58% to 71%) makes it less valuable than direct MRA for diagnosis.

18. Volpi D, Olivetti L, Budassi P, Genovese E: Capsulo-labro-ligamentous lesions of the shoulder: Evaluation with MR arthrography. *Radiol Med (Torino)* 2003;105:162-170.

    MRA and arthroscopic evaluation were compared in 58 patients with glenohumeral instability. The surgical findings confirmed MRA results in 25 of 27 patients, and MRA was more accurate than unenhanced MRI in these patients.

19. Robinson G, Ho Y, Finlay K, Friedman L, Harish S: Normal anatomy and common labral lesions at MR arthrography of the shoulder. *Clin Radiol* 2006;61: 805-821.

    The normal anatomy of the labroligamentous complex and its normal variants are well illustrated using MRA. Common labroligamentous pathologies also are described and illustrated.

20. Maffet MW, Gartsman GM, Moseley B: Superior labrum-biceps tendon complex lesions of the shoulder. *Am J Sports Med* 1995;23:93-98.

21. Tuite MJ, Petersen BD, Wise SM, Fine JP, Kaplan LD, Orwin JF: Shoulder MR arthrography of the posterior labrocapsular complex in overhead throwers with pathologic internal impingement and internal rotation deficit. *Skeletal Radiol* 2007;36:495-502.

    MRA of the shoulder was reviewed in 26 athletes and 26 control subjects. Athletes with posterior impingement had a thicker labrum and shallower capsular recess. If these signs are present, the posterior cuff and labrum should be closely inspected for tears.

22. Waldt S, Burkart A, Imhoff AB, Bruegel M, Rummeny EJ, Woertler K: Anterior shoulder instability: Accuracy of MR arthrography in the classification of anteroinferior labroligamentous injuries. *Radiology* 2005;237:578-583.

    MRA of the shoulder was reviewed in 104 patients with anterior shoulder instability, with arthroscopic correlation. Accuracy in detecting a Bankart, ALPSA, Perthes, or glenoid labrum articular disruption lesion was 80%, 77%, 50%, or 100%, respectively. Overall accuracy in detecting labroligamentous pathology was 89%.

23. Nam EK, Snyder SJ: The diagnosis and treatment of superior labrum, anterior and posterior (SLAP) lesions. *Am J Sports Med* 2003;31:798-810.

    This review supports the use of MRA as the primary diagnostic imaging test for suspected SLAP lesions.

24. Snyder SJ, Karzel RP, Del Pizzo W, Ferkel RD, Friedman MJ: SLAP lesions of the shoulder. *Arthroscopy* 1990;6:274-279.

25. Tung GA, Hou DD: MR arthrography of the posterior labrocapsular complex: Relationship with glenohumeral joint alignment and clinical posterior instability. *AJR Am J Roentgenol* 2003;180:369-375.

The relationship of posterior alignment of the glenohumeral joint and posterior labrocapsular tears as seen on MRA was reviewed in 24 patients and 70 control subjects. Increased posterior translation was found to be associated with longer and more severe posterior labrocapsular lesions.

26. Hall FM: Comment: MR arthrography of the posterior labrocapsular complex. *AJR Am J Roentgenol* 2003;181:595.

The role of a dynamic evaluation of glenohumeral instability under fluoroscopy as an adjunct to the arthrographic procedure is discussed.

27. Gobezie R, Warner JJ: SLAP lesion: What is it . . . really? *Skeletal Radiol* 2007;36:379.

The extreme variability of both radiographic and arthroscopic interpretation and classification of SLAP lesions is discussed.

28. Amrami KK, Savcenko V, Dahm DL, Sundaram M: Radiologic case study: Reverse Bankart lesion with posterior labral tear. *Orthopedics* 2002;25:779-780.

This case report confirms the utility of MRA in diagnosing and classifying posterior labral tears with a cartilaginous Bankart lesion.

29. Takase K, Yamamoto K: Intraarticular lesions in traumatic anterior shoulder instability: A study based on the results of diagnostic imaging. *Acta Orthop* 2005;76:854-857.

Thirty patients underwent CT or MR arthrography after shoulder dislocation and before surgery. Bankart lesions were detected in all patients. However, the anteroinferior glenohumeral ligament could not be seen on MRA in 14 patients; that it may be difficult to visualize with MRA after severe detachment of the joint capsule.

30. Chhabra A, Diduch DR, Anderson M: Arthroscopic repair of a posterior humeral avulsion of the inferior glenohumeral ligament (HAGL) lesion. *Arthroscopy* 2004;20(suppl 2):73-76.

Posterior HAGL lesions are uncommon but may be a source of posterior joint instability. This case report reviews the mechanism of injury and diagnostic imaging with MRA.

31. Chung CB, Sorenson S, Dwek JR, Resnick D: Humeral avulsion of the posterior band of the inferior glenohumeral ligament: MR arthrography and clinical correlation in 17 patients. *AJR Am J Roentgenol* 2004;183:355-359.

MRA was used in 17 patients with a posterior HAGL lesion, with arthroscopic correlation in 8 patients. This lesion may be present in a subgroup of patients with multidirectional instability, and MRA is the imaging study of choice.

# Index